AEW 5502 010843
02
745.592075
T756 a3 1994
4.95
T5-CCM-241
7.95
FRAYSER
JUN 1994
DISCARDED BY
MEMPHIS PUBLIC LIBRARY

1994 TOYS & PRICES

Edited by Roger Case & Tom Hammel

© 1993 by
Krause Publications

All rights reserved. No portion of this book
may be reproduced in any form without permission.

Published by

700 E. State Street • Iola, WI 54990-0001
Telephone: 715/445-2214

Library of Congress Number 93-77554
ISBN: 0-87341-264-8
Printed in the United States of America

Acknowledgements

Books like this are never written unaided, especially first editions. This book is the result of an exhaustive process of compiling data, sifting through thousands of entries, correcting errors, verifying values and weeding out duplications, and then arranging it all in a form that is, we hope, attractive, accurate, and easy to use. It took the labors and long hours of many people to produce what you now hold and all of them deserve a big round of applause. Some of them deserve standing ovations, and some much more than that.

First, the editors wish to thank the staff of Krause Publications, particularly Linda Maurer and Brenda Mazemke for data entry and Book Editor Mary Sieber for coordinating production. We also wish to thank the production department staff.

If the editors personally owned all the toys illustrated in this book and knew everything there was to know about every toy listed, we would be walking encyclopedias and rich enough not to need to learn another thing for the rest of our lives. As it is, we are neither, and we owe a large debt to all those people who generously lent us photographs and the benefit of their great knowledge of their special subjects.

The dealers and collectors who lent us photos include Wayne Mitchell, Gary Sohmers of Wex Rex, Paul Deion of The Wayback Machine, Bruce Whitehill, Peter Fritz of Toy A Day, James Koval, Barry Goodman of Toy Sensations, George Newcomb of Plymouth Rock Toy Co., Allan Shrem of The Walls of Fame, Mike Stannard of Toys 'N Stuf, Al Kasishke, Wade Johnson of Carolina Hobby Expo, Vincent Santelmo, The Ertl Company, Apple Patch Toys, R.H. Bruce, Gene Harris Auction Center, Bob Peirce, Marcie Melillo, Pam Bilger, Dale Womer of Hobby Lobby, Mark Huckabone, Anthony Balasco of Figures, Ed and Laura Hock, Sue Sternfeld, Larry Aikins, Jon Shapiro, Dan Casey, and Hill Design.

We owe a particular debt of thanks to those expert contributors who assisted us the pricing of the various sections. They include Wayne Mitchell, Paul Fink, Marcie Melillo, Pam Bilger, Fremont Brown, Bob Peirce, Anthony Balasco, Wade Johnson, Dan Harris, Steve Butler, Dan Casey, Al Kasishke, David Payne, Ed Hock, James Crane, Audree Anderson, Jon Shapiro, Dale Womer, Sue Sternfeld, Vincent Santelmo, and George Newcomb.

We wish to express our sincere gratitude to all who have helped create this first edition of Toys & Prices. We look forward to bringing you bigger and better editions in the years to come.

Contents

Welcome to the Ground Floor

You hold in your hands the first edition of *Toys & Prices*, the guide to collectible toy values. If you are an active toy collector, then you may need no more introduction than the fact that this book is produced by the editorial staff of *Toy Shop* and *Toy Collector And Price Guide* magazines. Both are products of Krause Publications of Iola, Wisconsin, the world's leading hobby publisher.

Krause Publications has been producing periodicals and magazines for various segments of the collecting hobby since 1952, notably in the fields of coins, sports cards, music, comics and automobiles among others. In the process we have produced numerous books which, over time, have come to be recognized as the "Standard Catalogs" of their respective fields. It is our goal to achieve that accolade for the book you now hold, *Toys & Prices*.

If you are a newcomer to toy collecting or are simply interested in what the toys of your youth are now worth, this is a fascinating and valuable reference. You might find it shocking as well, as many toys of vintages as recent as the 1970s and 1980s are now valued in the hundreds of dollars. Toys from the 1960s and on back can reach the thousands of dollars, including, quite possibly, some of yours. Browse through this guide and see for yourself.

The appeal of toys is universal and timeless, and recapturing lost youth is the prime attraction of toy collecting. The toys we played with as children have over time become powerfully invested with memories. Not all of us were ever inspired to collect stamps, coins, or sports cards, but we all had toys. Think back for a moment, to the birthdays and holidays of your youth. One special event will likely come to mind. When was it? Who was there? What was that favorite toy you received? Where is it now?

Look in this book and you just might find it.

Barbie, Buddy L, Matchbox, Arcade, Marx and many others are names filled with magic, and their mere utterance can at times conjure volumes of long forgotten recollection. Whether we unearth them from deep closets or buy them at shows or through the mail, the artifacts of our childhoods, once more turning over in our hands, rolling across our floors or sitting on our desks can act like crystal balls into those long passed times of excitement and innocence. Each of us has a personal mythology of our own youth, a quiet reverence for a special time in our lives. Our toys are the keys to the vaults of memory, opening the doors and lifting the shades of time. They speak to us across distances measured in years and decades, telling us tales of long ago, of our long ago. They reconnect us with our most important ancestors, the children we ourselves once were, and warm us in the soft glow of bottled afternoon suns, the rat-a-tat-tat of epic backyard battles, lilac breezes across sun-dappled Alice in Wonderland tea sets on the porch, and the hundred sounds of children playing just beyond our hearing. The sights, sounds, smells and textures of time are in our toys just waiting for us to pick them up, call them back, and come out and play.

Toys as Hot Collectibles

The universal appeal and emotional rewards of toy collecting are primary reasons why thousands of new collectors join the worldwide community of hobbyists each month. A not insignificant secondary reward is the financial one, as can be seen on any page of this book. A toy that sold new in 1966 for $1 might be worth $10, $100 or even $1,000 today. In 10 years it might be worth $10,000. While certainly not guaranteed, this scenario is possible, and this potential is undoubtedly a driving factor in the explosive growth of the hobby.

Toy collecting has been called the hottest collectible field of the 1990s, and it has everything in its favor. Plentiful and often affordable items to collect, the thrill of the hunt, the display potential of colorful items, intellectual and emotional rewards, an unlimited pool of potential collectors, a tremendous just-plain-fun factor, and the prospect of financial gain all combine perfectly in toy collecting. And even though the number of collectors grows daily and prices for many toys are now in the hundreds of dollars, the hobby is young enough that a collector starting today can still have the feeling of "getting in on the ground floor."

And it's exciting, folks. Toy auctions are setting records on a monthly basis. "New" fields such as board games, PEZ dispensers and fast food collectibles are being recognized and developed. Toy shows are popping up all over the country--and all over the world--like mechanical rabbits.Toy magazines like *Toy Shop* and *Toy Collector And Price Guide* are enjoying record growth, and new titles hoping to share in the wealth appear on the national newsstands every month. It is no longer irrational to consider financing part of your children's college educations by shopping at Toys R Us. World and national economies notwithstanding, right now is boom time in toy collecting. Come on in, the water's just swell.

Representative Sampling of Toys

A time honored cliché of collecting is that there are as many reasons for collecting as there are collectors. Its equally true that in toy collecting there are as many ways to collect as there are collectors. The potential collecting specialties are so numerous, and the volume of information in each field is so encyclopedic, that any attempt to create an all-knowing, all-telling guide to the entire hobby would be simply impossible. Areas as diverse as Disneyana, Barbie, GI Joe, mechanical banks and Star Wars have all fostered specialized shows, magazines and collector's clubs. Each of these areas and many more has engendered comprehensive reference books that seek to present the totality of information on their respective subjects. Many are well written and invaluable to specialized and advanced collectors.

If we tried to do that here, you would need a truck to load the book and a mortgage to pay for it. Our goal is to provide you with a representative sampling of toys and their accurate current retail values across a number of popular fields, so that you may browse and learn from a range of areas with ease.

The interrelation of toys across many areas is another reason why we chose to present you a sampling of fields as opposed to an in-depth study of one or two. If you are interested space toys, you can find examples listed not just in our chapter on science fiction toys, but also in vehicles, toy guns, games, action figures, Marx toys, character toys and model kits. The vast expanse of Disney-related toys is represented in virtually every chapter. We have attempted to organize the material in a logical and easy-to-use manner, but how you use this book is up to you. We encourage you to read the chapter introductions and then browse as you see fit.

We have also attempted to make this book a comfortable size to carry to garage sales and shows. So now when you see a complete Disneyland Give-A-Show Projector in the box at $25, you can check right away to see if it's a good deal or not. You can have the information where and when you need it most, when the chance to buy is before you, not hours later at home. (By the way, it is a good deal. We list it at $175 Mint In The Box.)

Pricing & Grading

As most of this book is comprised of toy descriptions and pricing, a few words are called for about how and where we got them. Our primary sources of pricing data comes from print retail ads in magazines such as *Toy Shop* and *Toy Collector And Price Guide*, dealer price lists, observed prices at toy shows, and auction prices realized from auction houses across the country. Information is compiled by category (for example, action figures or banks) and entered into databases. These databases are reviewed, averaged and edited by the staff of *Toy Collector And Price Guide*. Before it is printed, each database is then sent out for a final accuracy review by a recognized authority in the subject field. These contributing experts are some of the leading dealers and collectors in America, and they are named on our acknowledgements page.

The final results you see in this book are what we feel are accurate and current average retail prices across a range of grades for each item. If you take exception to any of the prices presented in this book, we ask you to discuss them with us, as the editors made the final decisions on pricing in *Toys & Prices*, not our contributors. We must also stress the prices listed are not offers to buy or sell--*they are merely guidelines to what you could expect to pay for an item at a show or by mail.*

If you are a student of price guides, you can find numerous situations in which values for identical items will vary widely from source to source. A number of factors can cause this. Geographical areas of the country can play a part, as prices on some items are higher in some parts of the country than others. Farm toys may be nonexistent at a show in Boston but be the primary focus of a show in the Midwest. Economics can also impact dealer prices. A retail shop dealer based in an industrially depressed area will probably sell an item for less than a dealer in a boom region because of the pressures of lower local traffic and the constant need for cash flow. Grading itself is highly subjective, and even slight perceived differences in quality and condition of an item can greatly affect the asking price. One person's Mint-In-The-Box might be another person's Very Good, particularly if the one is selling and the other one is buying.

If you are buying this book to estimate the value of your collection before you sell, please bear this subjectivity of grading in mind. Read our definitions of various grades on the page titled "How to Use *Toys & Prices*," and try to grade your toys as conservatively as possible. Please also bear in mind that grading criteria change from category to category, and that grading a cast iron bank requires different standards than grading an action figure. Additionally, you should not expect to receive retail prices from dealers when you sell, as they obviously must make a profit on their purchases in order to stay in business.

Finally, if you see a price in this book or any other guide that seems completely out of line, don't accept it simply because it's in print. It may be an error of data entry, or it may be based on incomplete information. If you do notice what seems to be a glaring error, please let us know about it, so we can research it for the next edition. Likewise, if you own an item not listed here, we would appreciate the chance to add it to our database, particularly if you can provide us with data on the size, year and manufacturer. Photos are most welcome, but please send a duplicate as we regret we cannot return them.

In collecting as in life, knowledge is power. Our introductory chapters in this book are just that, introductory. If you are genuinely interested in building a collection in any of the fields covered in this book, we recommend you seek specialized guides for your chosen field and learn as much as you can. Ask your local bookstore what books are available, or check the pages of *Toy Shop* or *Toy Collector And Price Guide* for ads by book dealers who specialize in hobby titles. We will be happy to send you a free copy of either magazine. Just write us and ask.

Ultimately, all prices are set at the point of sale between the buyer and seller. The collectible field is an area in which the phrase "Let the buyer beware" is particularly true. It is also a field which places great value on the wisdom of "Forewarned is forearmed." Arming you is what this book is all about. We hope that you will enjoy it and use it to enhance your appreciation of the artistry, history and sheer pleasure offered you in the wonderful world of toys.

Happy Collecting,

Tom Hammel

Metal Banks

The riddle of the chicken and the egg might just as well be applied to banks and money. While a bank is defined as a place where you put money, money can also be defined as what you put into a bank. One calls to mind images of cave dwellers scratching around for a secure crevice into which to stuff a precious flint, or an islander searching out a safe hiding place for his precious periwinkle shells. Is the currency intrinsically valuable, or does it take the act of depositing it to give the medium its value? Is the bank perhaps more valuable than the money it holds?

Sometimes, yes.

This section will briefly discuss the development of the two major forms of classic cast-iron banks -- mechanical banks and still banks -- and their modern offspring, die cast vehicle banks.

Mechanical Banks

Mechanical banks are viewed by many as the royalty of American toys. They are among the oldest extant American toys, and they have been collected longer as well. The age of mechanical banks began with the end of the Civil War and the dawning of the industrial age, and for collecting purposes ended with the beginning of World War II.

The rise of factories during the Civil War laid the groundwork for the coming industrial revolution, and its weapon would be iron. Prior to the Civil War, most toys were made of wood, tin or sheet metal. The new process of casting iron, with its durability and lower cost, made it the metal of choice for a wide range of manufacturers, including toy makers. The new process allowed design innovations not previously possible, and toy makers were quick to creatively exploit its potential.

The toys of the day reflected their time, the attitudes, activities, personalities and morals of the day. Americans believed in frugality both as a morally dictated behavior and as a means toward a secured future, and parents of the day strove to instill the virtue in their children. Many of the nursery rhymes and ditties of the time espoused thrift as their moral, and children were encouraged to save their pennies at every turn. Toy makers saw to it that those parents had clever and colorful allies in the forms of the banks themselves.

In 1869, the first patent was issued for a cast-iron mechanical bank, Hall's Excelsior Bank. It was also the first of many banks designed as buildings, a concept which by imitation and variation grew into the largest category in the still bank field. Other main categories of mechanical banks can be roughly categorized into animal banks, depicting elephants, birds, and all manner of other creatures; human banks featuring people in various activities such as football players in the Calamity Bank or the excessively rare Girl Skipping Rope; coin-shooting banks such as the Creedmore Bank and the William Tell;

and darkie banks including the numerous variations of Jolly Nigger banks and the Bad Accident bank.

Mechanical banks are loosely defined as a children's toy designed to promote saving in which the coin, when deposited, sets in motion some mechanism or action. Still banks are receptacles only; depositing coins in them causes no action. In short, if you drop in the coin and something happens, the bank is most likely mechanical. If nothing happens, the bank is still.

There is a difference in the definitions of mechanical in the hobby itself. Some banks once considered mechanical are now grouped under the heading of semi-mechanical. For example, in some banks the coin, while falling into the bank, strikes and rings a bell. Other banks require actions by the depositor to achieve the deposit itself, again, not qualifying the bank for mechanical status.

The degree of action varies from the simple closing of a mouth or nod of a head to complex multiple figure actions involving music, acrobatics, pratfalls and sporting events. Along with rarity, complexity and subject matter of design, complexity of action is a primary factor in determining value in mechanical banks. Intricacy of design and action made for more expensive banks, production costs were higher, retail prices were higher, and, subsequently, fewer were sold.

Speaking Dog Bank, 1885, Shephard Hardward Co.

Some banks never made it into commercial production at all. Bank designers were required to submit working pattern samples with their patent applications, and sometimes these patterns are all that remain of a failed patent bid. Other banks were never intended for commercial production, but were instead made for personal reasons. As literal one-of-a-kind examples, surviving banks of this type are obviously very rare and command prices in accordance with their rarity. Some banks were produced by manufacturers in an attempt to fool collectors into believing they were legitimate older banks. These are now nearly as old as the originals they cleverly imitated, and have come to be accepted in many collections for what they are, just as ancient counterfeit coins have come to be accepted alongside their contemporary but genuine counterparts. Fakes, yes, but historical fakes.

One other category requires mention here: modern reproductions. From great paintings to banks to tin toys and model kits, the greater the value of an item, the greater its renown and influence, the greater also is its potential for reproduction. Whether intended as outright forgeries or as honest replicas and marked as such, these items can and do find their way from time to time into dealer stock, priced as the genuine article. Reproduction labels and imprints can be filed away, the banks can be artificially aged, screws replaced and other telltale areas changed in order to raise the price of a bank from $50 to $5,000.

Interestingly, originals and reproductions are sometimes marketed side by side. One national mail-order catalog offers customers the choice of original banks at $4,000, or reproductions at $50.

Collectors entering this field are well advised to confine their initial dealings to reputable dealers and auction houses with qualified and impartial expert staffs. Reproductions also exist in the area of cast-iron still banks, so caution should be the watchword here as well.

Still Banks

The same companies that made mechanical banks also frequently made still banks as less expensive alternatives to their mechanical cousins. Several banks can be found in both still and mechanical versions. The names Arcade, Ives, Kenton and Stevens, among others, are familiar to still and mechanical bank collectors alike. Again, building banks are perhaps the largest single type of still banks, with other main categories being animals, people and busts, and appliances like safes, clocks, mailboxes, globes and so on. The range of still banks is much broader than mechanical banks, with over 200 building banks alone available to collectors. The variety of objects depicted is wonderfully vast, ranging from comic personality caricatures to historical busts to houses, lighthouses, refrigerators, radios, beehives, purses, fruit, miniature cash registers, loaves of bread, ships, taxicabs and almost every conceivable object known to Americans between the Civil War and World War II.

Columbian Magic Savings Bank, 1892, Magic Introduction Co.

Building banks span a range from Lincoln's Cabin in pottery to cottages, Victorian houses and mansions to skyscrapers. Commemorative banks were particularly popular with banks being made resembling the Washington Monument, the National Bank of Los Angeles, the Century of Progress building, the Eiffel Tower and numerous other actual locations. Other building banks offered variations on general themes such as Home Savings Banks, State Banks, and churches.

One notable class of still bank is the registering bank. Often in the shape of a safe or cash register, these banks typically accept only certain coins, such as dimes or nickels. They keep a running tally of deposits and pop open once the bank is filled at $5 or $10. While their delayed reaction mechanism has earned them places in some mechanical collections, they are generally classed as still banks.

Another type of still bank bearing mention is the conversion. These fall into three main types: commercial factory conversions, individual factory conversions, and home conversions. Many factories engaged in casting iron produced a variety of products, of which banks were just a line. A popular sideline was iron doorstops in various shapes. At times factory operators would convert these doorstops into banks and release them for sale to the public. These were commercial factory conversions. Sometimes factory employees would take it upon themselves to convert such objects into banks to take home as gifts for their children or friends. These were converted in the factory of origin, but were not officially authorized and so are considered individual factory conversions. The third type is the home conversion. These were typically also made by fathers as gifts for their children, and generally exhibit care in craftsmanship. Bear in mind that fraudulently intended conversions have also been created, with the sole purpose of ripping off the collecting public.

A note on restoration: As in many other areas of collecting, restoration of banks is strongly discouraged in the marketplace. Unless undertaken by an experienced professional, the restoration of a bank can result in irreparable damage to the value of the piece.

While most collectible still banks were made of cast iron, other materials were frequently employed as well, including glass, pottery and other ceramics, brass, lead, tin, wood, composition materials and even plastic. The still bank section of this book concentrates on cast-iron banks. Modern ceramic and plastic banks can also be found under their respective character headings in the "Character Toys" section of this book.

Modern Die Cast Vehicle Banks

Still banks of taxicabs and touring cars are the direct ancestors of today's die cast vehicle banks. The modern market was pioneered by the Ertl Company of Dyersville, Iowa. Compared to the life-spans of cast-iron banks, die cast banks were almost literally born yesterday. The first bank, a replica 1913 Model T Parcel Post Mail Service bank, rolled off the assembly line in 1981. Since then, thousands of banks have followed, creating in the process a rapidly growing, ravenous market. Prices on early and low production models have risen annually, with a few rarities selling for over $2,000 each today.

The Ertl Company's success has spawned both spin-offs and competitors. Currently, the farm town of Dyersville is home to three die cast vehicle companies, all thriving in a booming national market.

Ertl banks represent one major diversion from classic banks of old in that most are different models only from the skin on out. These banks are collected not by variety of model styles but by variety of corporate sponsors. At present, Ertl offers roughly three dozen body styles in scales of 1/25, 1/30 and 1/43, but these can bear thousands of different corporate imprints. Numerous companies such as Amoco, the American Red Cross, Hershey's Chocolate and Texaco have adopted a plan of releasing a new model annually.

Model #0531 John Deere Bank, 1984, Ertl.

With several hundred models annually released directly into the collector market, collectors are now faced with such variety that they are forced to develop their own collecting specialties. Some collectors confine their efforts to collecting the various banks of Iowa, Iowa State, Nebraska, and other universities. Others collect oil company banks or beverage company banks like Anheuser-Busch or RC Cola and Clearly Canadian. Harley-Davidson is a particularly popular imprint. Here as in other collecting fields, there are as many ways to collect as there are collectors.

Identification of Ertl banks is fairly easy, but confusing. All banks are numbered, but the numbers on the banks are not model numbers. Model numbers are printed only on boxes. The numbers on the banks represent the day and year the bank was built. For example, if your bank is numbered 1255, your bank was made on the 125th day of 1985. The first three digits are the days and the last is the year. Most collectors and all dealers identify their banks by the number printed on the box, but banks are also easily identifiable by make of vehicle, color scheme and corporate sponsor.

Many Ertl banks are also serial numbered by the corporate sponsor after they have left the Ertl factory. This practice is common and reinforces the limited edition aspect of the banks. Most sponsors will order only one run of banks, again with an eye toward collectibility, but the sizes of individual orders vary by company from as low as 504 banks to a couple hundred thousand.

Bank collecting, like other hobbies, is a matter ultimately of discretionary income. The prices of many cast-iron mechanical banks have put them in the realm of the wealthy and major investors only. Still banks are also frequently priced beyond the means of casual collectors, but their values are in general a fraction of mechanicals, making them perhaps better investment vehicles for collectors of moderate means. Die cast banks are the last metal banks still affordable by average and beginning collectors, and that alone is part key to their explosive success. All three types offer the collector a piece of history and beauty, and each field has its unique attractions and benefits. Whichever field you choose, you will find ample challenge, camaraderie, and reward.

MECHANICAL BANKS

A.C Williams

BANK	TYPE	YEAR	DESCRIPTION	GOOD	VG	EX
Elephant Moves Trunk (Large)	Cast Iron	1905	The trunk of the elephant moves when coin is inserted, trunk automatically closes the slot as soon as coin is deposited, 6 3/4" long	150	250	400

Bankers Thrift Corp.

BANK	TYPE	YEAR	DESCRIPTION	GOOD	VG	EX
Feed the Goose	White Metal	1927	Press the tail feathers lever and the goose opens his mouth; toss in a coin and release, the mouth closes, coin is swallowed and his wings rotate	250	400	600

Banks & Sons

BANK	TYPE	YEAR	DESCRIPTION	GOOD	VG	EX
Punch and Judy	Iron/Tin	1929	Pressing lever makes figures rise, put coin in slot; releasing lever makes figures fall back into bank as coin drops	2700	5000	7000

Beverly Novelty Corp.

BANK	TYPE	YEAR	DESCRIPTION	GOOD	VG	EX
Sweet Thrift	Tin	1928	Candy dispenser; drop coin in slot and open drawer to receive candy; 5 3/4" tall; red, green or yellow	100	150	250

Buddy "L" Co.

BANK	TYPE	YEAR	DESCRIPTION	GOOD	VG	EX
Thrifty Animal Bank	Tin	1940	A registering bank with two coin slots, one takes dimes which become visible as acorns on the tree and the second slot is a still bank; the top of bank pops off when full	175	350	450

Calumet Baking Powder Co

BANK	TYPE	YEAR	DESCRIPTION	GOOD	VG	EX
Calumet, Large	Cardboard	1924	Put coin in slot, making box sway back and forth in 'thanks'	175	300	450
Calumet, Small	Tin	1924	Put coin in slot, making box sway back and forth in 'thanks'	150	250	350

Chamberlain & Hill

BANK	TYPE	YEAR	DESCRIPTION	GOOD	VG	EX
Clown Bust	Cast Iron	1880s	English bank; put coin in hand; pressing lever makes arm lift coin and clown swallows it	1700	2500	4000
Little Moe	Cast Iron	1931	Place coin in Moe's hand, press the lever on his left shoulder, he raises his right arm, his tongue flips in and he swallows the coin as he lowers his arm, tipping his hat	250	400	600

Charles Bailey

BANK	TYPE	YEAR	DESCRIPTION	GOOD	VG	EX
Springing Cat	Lead/Wood	1882	Lock cat in place, put coin in slot; pulling lever makes cat move toward coin as a mouse appears, knocks coin into bank, and escapes back into bank, leaving cat with open jaws	3500	6000	8000

Chein

BANK	TYPE	YEAR	DESCRIPTION	GOOD	VG	EX
Clown, Chein	Tin	1939	Press the lever and the clown sticks out his tongue, place coin on tongue release the lever and he retracts his tongue pulling coin into bank	35	50	95
Monkey Tips Hat	Tin	1940s	Drop a coin into bank, making monkey tip his hat	45	75	100

Edward J. Colby

BANK	TYPE	YEAR	DESCRIPTION	GOOD	VG	EX
Safety Locomotive	Cast Iron	1887	The weight of the money as it's dropped on the cab will (when it's full), loosen the smokestack, then it can be lifted out and the money poured from the opening	650	1000	1400

Enterprise Mfg. Co.

BANK	TYPE	YEAR	DESCRIPTION	GOOD	VG	EX
Elephant, Man Pops Out	Cast Iron and Wood	1884	Push man into howdah or lift trunk to cock mechanism, close howdah lid, put coin in elephant's mouth; pressing lever drops trunk into mouth, dropping coin and man pops up from howdah; 5 3/8" tall	400	600	900
Independence Hall	Cast Iron	1875	Semi-mechanical bronze finish bank; drop coin in tower and pull lever to make bell ring	200	300	450
Memorial Money Bank	Cast Iron	1876	Slide the lever forwards to expose the coin slot, deposit coin, release the lever and it snaps back to ring the Liberty Bell	300	600	900

F. W. Smith

BANK	TYPE	YEAR	DESCRIPTION	GOOD	VG	EX
Give Me A Penny	Wood	1870	Bureau with drawer; open drawer and picture rises at back, saying 'Give Me A Penny"; putting coin in drawer and closing it makes coin drop and picture fall back into cabinet	1100	2000	3000

Faith Mfg. Co.

BANK	TYPE	YEAR	DESCRIPTION	GOOD	VG	EX
Treasure Chest Musical Bank	White Metal	1930	Bronze or silver finish domed chest; wind mechanism, dropping coin in slot makes music play	300	500	700

Ferdinand Strauss Corp.

BANK	TYPE	YEAR	DESCRIPTION	GOOD	VG	EX
Little Jocko	Steel/White Metal	1912	Drop penny into cup, turn the crank, the monkeys dance and music plays	250	400	650

Ferdinand Strauss Corp.

BANK	TYPE	YEAR	DESCRIPTION	GOOD	VG	EX
Thrifty Tom's Jigger Bank	Tin Litho	1910	Drop coin into the slot and Thrifty Tom does a dance that lasts until the spring winds down	200	450	850

German

BANK	TYPE	YEAR	DESCRIPTION	GOOD	VG	EX
Monkey With Tray	Tin	1900s	Unclothed monkey squats on square base with zoo scenes; put coin on tray; pressing tail makes monkey raise tray, head tilt back and swallow coin	150	300	450
Monkey With Tray, Uniformed	Tin	1900s	Uniformed monkey squats on square base with animal scenes; put coin on tray; pressing tail makes monkey raise tray, head tilt back and swallow coin	250	350	550

Haji

BANK	TYPE	YEAR	DESCRIPTION	GOOD	VG	EX
Juke Box Bank	Tin Litho	1950s	Marked "100 Select-O-Matic" on both sides; insert coin, wind up, turntable turns, music plays	65	110	165

Henry C. Hart Mfg. Co.

BANK	TYPE	YEAR	DESCRIPTION	GOOD	VG	EX
Smyth X-Ray Bank	Cast Iron	1898	Set coin in the path of the scope slot and look into the eyepiece; you will see through the coin and out the other end of the bank; press lever and the coin is deposited in the bank	550	1000	1500

Hubley

BANK	TYPE	YEAR	DESCRIPTION	GOOD	VG	EX
Elephant Howdah Bank, Pull Tail	Cast Iron	1934	Put coin in elephant's trunk; pulling tail makes animal lift coin over head, dropping coin in howdah	300	450	600
Monkey Bank	Cast Iron	1920s	9" long, painted dark green base, put coin in monkey's mouth; pressing lever makes monkey spring forward, dropping coin into organ	300	600	1000
Trick Dog Bank (6 Part Base)	Cast Iron	1888	Deposit coin in dog's mouth; pressing lever makes dog jump through clown's hoop and coin is deposited in his barrel	300	600	800
Trick Dog Bank, Solid Base	Cast Iron	1920s	Deposit coin in dog's mouth; pressing lever makes dog jump through clown's hoop and coin is deposited in his barrel	200	450	650

Hugo Mfg. Co.

BANK	TYPE	YEAR	DESCRIPTION	GOOD	VG	EX
Wireless Bank	Iron/Tin/ Wood	1926	Battery operated; putting coin on roof of bank and clapping hands makes cover swing over, dropping coin into bank	200	350	450

Top to Bottom: Milking Cow, 1885, J & E Stevens; Initiating Bank--First Degree, 1880, Mechanical Novelty Works; Speaking Dog Bank, 1885, Shepard Hardward Co.; Clown on Globe, 1890, J & E Stevens.

Introduction Co.

BANK	TYPE	YEAR	DESCRIPTION	GOOD	VG	EX
Columbian Magic	Cast Iron	1892	Swing open the shelf and place a coin on it, close the shelf and the coin is deposited in bank	85	150	200

Ives

BANK	TYPE	YEAR	DESCRIPTION	GOOD	VG	EX
Bulldog Savings Bank	Cast Iron	1878	8 1/2" long; put coin in man's hand, press lever, making dog jump, bite coin, and fall back, dropping coin into bank	1000	2000	3000
Registering Dime Savings Bank	Cast Iron	1890	Deposit dime in chute and pull lever to right, then left and the dime will be deposited and door locked, amount registered on dial; when $10 is deposited door will unlock and pop out	200	400	600

J & E Stevens Co.

BANK	TYPE	YEAR	DESCRIPTION	GOOD	VG	EX
Acrobat	Cast Iron	1883	Deposit coin in opening, press lever which causes the gymnast to kick the clown causing the clown to stand on his head while coin is deposited in bank	2000	3000	4000
Artillery Bank	Cast Iron	1900s	#24668, 8" long, 6" tall; put coin in barrel, press lever, making soldier drop arm to signal firing, hammer snaps and fires coin through building window	550	900	1400
Bad Accident Mule	Cast Iron	1890s	10" long, painted; deposit coin under the feet of the driver, press lever, boy jumps into the road, frightening the mule; he rears, the cart and driver are thrown backwards and coin falls in cart	850	1500	2000
Billy Goat Bank	Cast Iron	1910	Deposit coin in slot and pull wire loop forward, goat jumps forward and coin falls in bank	600	1000	1800
Bird on Roof	Cast Iron	1878	Deposit coin in slot on bird's head, pull the wire lever on left side of house, the bird tilts forward, coin rolls into the chimney	650	1000	1500
Bismark Pig	Lead	1883	Lock mechanism, put coin in slot over tail, press the pig's tail, Bismark figure pops up and coin drops	1800	3500	6000
Boy Robbing Bird's Nest	Cast Iron	1906	8" tall; deposit coin in slot and press the lever on the tree; as the boy falls, the coin disappears in the tree	1000	1800	2500
Boy Scout Camp	Cast Iron	1912	9 1/2" long; drop coin into tent; pressing lever makes Scout raise flag as coin drops	1500	2500	4000
Breadwinners	Cast Iron	1886	Put coin in end of club, cock hammer; pressing button makes 'Labor' hit 'Monopoly', "sending the rascals up" and dropping coin into loaf of bread	3500	7000	12000
Bull and Bear, Single Pendulum	Iron/Lead	1930s	Put coin in pendulum on tree stump; pressing lever releases pendulum to swing, dropping coin into either bull or bear	800	1200	1800
Bulldog Bank	Cast Iron	1880s	Put coin on dog's nose, pull his tail, the dog opens his mouth and swallows the coin.	175	300	650

J & E Stevens Co.

BANK	TYPE	YEAR	DESCRIPTION	GOOD	VG	EX
Cabin Bank	Cast Iron	1885	3 1/2" tall, shows darkie in front of cabin; put coin on roof, flip lever to make figure flip and push coin into bank with his feet	300	600	850
Calamity	Cast Iron	1905	Cock tackles into position, put coin in slot in front of fullback; pressing lever activates tackles and coin drops in the collision	3000	5000	7000
Called Out Bank	Cast Iron	1900	9" tall; push soldier into bank, drop coin into slot, making soldier pop up and drop coin into bank	850	1400	2000
Cat and Mouse, Cat Balancing	Cast Iron	1891	8 1/2" tall; put coin in slot and lock mouse into position; pressing lever makes mouse disappear and kitten appears holding mouse on a ball	1000	1700	2500
Chief Big Moon	Cast Iron	1899	10" long; put coin in slot in fish tail, push lever, making frog spring up from pond, dropping coin	900	1400	2700
Clown on Globe	Cast Iron	1890	Clown straddles globe on footed base; pressing lever makes globe and clown move and change positions, leaving clown standing on head; 9" tall	650	1000	1500
Creedmore Bank	Cast Iron	1877	9 3/4" long, painted; pull back lever on gun, put coin in slot; pressing man's foot shoots coin into tree	400	625	850
Cupola Circular Building	Cast Iron	1874	Push the doorbell lever and the top pops up exposing the cashier, who pivots back and returns to his forward position	2000	3000	4500
Darktown Battery Bank	Cast Iron		#24670, 10" long, 7 1/4" tall, painted; three lads play ball, red, blue and yellow pitcher's uniform; put coin in pitcher's hand; pressing lever to pitch coin, batter swings and misses, catcher drops	800	1500	2700
Dentist	Cast Iron	1880s	9 1/2" long; coin drops into dentist's pocket; press lever at figure's feet, making dentist pull patient's tooth, patient falls backward, dropping coin into gas bag	2000	3500	5000
Eagle and Eaglets	Cast Iron	1883	#24671, 7 3/4" long, 6" tall, painted; put coin in eagle's beak; pressing lever makes eaglets rise, eagle tilts forward and drops coin into nest	600	950	1600
Elephant and Three Clowns	Cast Iron	1883	6" tall, painted; place coin between the rings held by acrobat, move the ball on the feet of the other acrobat and the elephant hits coin with his trunk and coin falls into bank	600	1000	1500
Frog on Round Base	Cast Iron	1872	Press frog's right foot and put coin in his mouth; release lever and he swallows coin and winks	350	450	700
Gem Registering Bank	Cast Iron	1893	Floral embossed rectangular bank with dials at one end; turn thumb piece to top, insert coin, turn thumb piece to bottom, dropping coin into bank	300	500	750
General Butler	Cast Iron	1880s	Figure of Butler holds dollar bills in one hand, mouth is coin slot, inscribed "Bullion and yachts for myself and my friends, dry bread and greenbacks for the people."	1000	1800	2500

J & E Stevens Co.

BANK	TYPE	YEAR	DESCRIPTION	GOOD	VG	EX
Germania Exchange	Cast Iron/ Lead	1880s	Goat on a keg; put coin on goat's tail; turning faucet makes goat drop coin and lifts up a glass of beer	3500	7000	12000
Girl Skipping Rope	Cast Iron	1890	Blonde girl in light blue dress jumps rope by means of an ornately housed mechanism	10000	15000	18000
Hall's Excelsior Bank	Cast Iron & Wood	1869	Value varies according to color of bank; 5" tall, yellow version, monkey sits atop building; put coin on tray in monkey's lap, pull string and monkey disappears inside	300	600	850
Hall's Liliput	Cast Iron	1877	Coin laid on plate is carried around by the cashier and placed in the bank; cashier returns to its place and cycle can begin again	350	500	650
Hall's Liliput, No Tray	Cast Iron/ Brass Figure	1877	Coin laid on plate is carried around by the cashier and placed in the bank, cashier returns to its place and cycle can begin again	400	550	700
Harlequinn	Cast Iron	1907	Bring figure's hand halfway around to position and place coin in slot and press lever	2000	3000	5000
Hen and Chick	Cast Iron	1901	Place coin in front of hen in slot, raise the lever and as the hen calls, the chicken springs from under her for the coin and disappears	1100	1700	2200
Home Bank with Dormers	Cast Iron	1872	Pull knob, place penny on its edge in front of the cashier, push the knob to the right, and the coin is deposited in the rear of the bank in vault	650	1000	1500
Horse Race, Straight Base	Cast Iron	1870	Pull cord to start spring, place the horses' heads opposite the star, deposit the coin in the opening and the race will begin	3500	5500	8000
I Always Did 'Spise a Mule--Jockey	Cast Iron	1879	#24672, 10 1/2" long, 8" tall; put coin in jockey's mouth; pressing lever makes mule kick, throwing jockey which drops coin into bank	400	800	1200
I Always Did 'Spise a Mule-Bench	Cast Iron	1897	Put the mule and boy into position; when the knob is touched, the base causes the mule to kick the boy over, throwing the coin from the bench into the receptacle below	850	1350	1800
Indian Shooting Bear	Cast Iron	1883	10 3/8" long; put coin on rifle barrel; pressing level makes Indian shoot coin into bear	450	800	1200
Jonah and the Whale, Jonah Emerges	Cast Iron	1880s	Deposit coin in side of whale; pull Jonah into position by pulling tail backwards; press the lever, the coin is deposited and Jonah will appear	12000	20000	27000
Lion Hunter	Cast Iron	1911	Hunter figure shoots coin into lion's mouth	2000	3000	4000
Magic Bank	Cast Iron	1873	6" tall; open door to find cashier, put coin on his tray; pressing lever makes cashier disappear and drop coin in building	400	600	1000
Magician Bank	Cast Iron	1901	8" tall; put coin on table; pressing lever makes magician lower hat over coin, dropping coin into bank while magicican nods head	2500	3500	5000
Milking Cow	Cast Iron	1885	Deposit coin in cow's back, the lever under the cow's throat is pressed, the cow will kick up its hind leg, upset the boy and the milk pail and deposit coin	3000	5000	7000

Top to Bottom: Organ Bank, Miniature, 1890s, Kyser & Rex; Organ Bank with Cat and Dog, 1882, Kyser & Rex; Circus Bank, 1888, Shepard Hardware Co.; Jolly Nigger, 1880s, England; Cabin Bank, 1885, J & E Stevens; Jonah and the Whale, 1890s, Shepard Hardware Co.

J & E Stevens Co.

BANK	TYPE	YEAR	DESCRIPTION	GOOD	VG	EX
Monkey and Coconut	Cast Iron	1886	8 1/2" tall; put coin in monkey's hand; pressing lever makes monkey drop coin into coconut	350	900	1500
National Bank	Cast Iron	1873	Place coin on door ledge and push doorbell; the door revolves, slinging the coin into the bank, the man behind the window of the door quickly moves to the right to get out of the way	2000	3500	5000
New Creedmore Bank	Cast Iron	1891	Place coin on barrel of rifle, press right foot and coin is shot into the bull's eye of the target; as coin enters it strikes gong bell	350	750	1200
Novelty Bank	Cast Iron	1873	Open door and put coin on tray, release door which closes by a spring and teller turns and drops coin into vault	300	500	700
Organ Grinder and Dancing Bear	Tin	1890s	6 7/8" long, 5 1/2" tall, 4 3/4" wide, painted windup; put coin in slot; pushing button makes grinder deposit coin , play organ, and bear dance	2300	3500	5000
Owl, Turns Head	Cast Iron	1880	7 1/2" tall, brown bird with yellow highlights, glass eyes; insert coin in branch; pressing lever makes owl turn head as coin drops	250	400	550
Paddy and the Pig	Cast Iron	1882	8 1/2" tall; put coin in pig's nose; pressing lever makes pig kick coin into Paddy's mouth	900	1700	2500
Panorama Bank	Cast Iron	1876	Place coin in slot on roof and next picture appears in the window	2500	4500	6500
Patronize the Blind Man	Cast Iron	1878	Place coin in the blind man's hand, the dog takes the coin and deposits it in the bank and returns to his position	2000	3000	4500
Pelican Bank, Baseball Player	Cast Iron	1878	8" tall; close bird's beak, put coin into top of head which makes beak open revealing a baseball player's head	1000	1500	2000
Pig in a High Chair	Cast Iron	1897	5 1/4" tall; put coin on tray; pressing lever makes tray bring coin to pig's mouth	250	400	575
Professor Pug Frog's Great Bicycle Feat	Cast Iron	1886	place coin on rear wheel; turning crank Makes frog spin, dropping coin into bank	1500	3500	5000
Reclining Chinaman	Cast Iron	1882	8 1/4" long; put coin in slot on log, press lever to make figure raise hand, showing hand of cards and saluting the depositor; as coin falls, rat runs out of the end of the log	1500	2200	3500
Sportsman (Fowler)	Cast Iron	1892	Place a coin in slot, set the trap, place the bird on the trap and push the lever; bird rises in the air and the sportsman fires, downing bird; bank can use paper caps	7500	12000	18000
Tammany Bank	Cast Iron	1873	6" tall; fat politician sits in chair, yellow vest, brown jacket, blue pants; put coin in his hand and he drops it into his pocket	400	600	850
Teddy and the Bear	Cast Iron	1907	10" long, painted; cock gun and put coin in it, push bear into tree and close cover; pressing lever makes Teddy lower head in aim, gun fires coin into tree and bear pops up	650	1150	1550
Toad on Stump	Cast Iron	1886	Press lever to open toad's mouth, put coin on mouth and release lever, dropping coin into bank	275	575	700

J & E Stevens Co.

BANK	TYPE	YEAR	DESCRIPTION	GOOD	VG	EX
United States and Spain	Cast Iron	1898	U.S. cannon faces Spanish ship; cock cannon and insert paper cap; pressing lever fires cap and shot which strikes ship's mast while coin drops	2000	4500	6500
United States Safe Bank	Cast Iron	1880	Drop coin in slot, making top flip up showing a small bank book in which to write entry of deposit.	400	850	1250
Watch Dog Safe	Cast Iron	1890s	Drop coin in top of bank, lift lever, coin falls into the bank as the dog opens his mouth and barks; release and mouth closes	175	350	450
William Tell	Cast Iron	1896	10 1/2" long; lock lever on gun, lower head to aim; lowering boy's arm reveals apple, put coin on gun, press shooter's foot to fire coin into castle, knocking down apple, ringing a gong	350	600	800
World's Fair Bank, with Lettering	Cast Iron	1893	Deposit coin on Columbus' feet; pressing lever makes the Indian Chief popup from log, offering peace pipe as Columbus salutes him	350	600	850

J. Barton & Smith Co.

BANK	TYPE	YEAR	DESCRIPTION	GOOD	VG	EX
Boy on Trapeze	Cast Iron	1891	9 1/2" tall, painted; place a coin in the slot on the boy's head and he revolves	600	1200	1800

J. Harper & Co.

BANK	TYPE	YEAR	DESCRIPTION	GOOD	VG	EX
Dinah	Cast Iron	1911	Deposit coin in Dinah's hand and press the lever; she raises her hand, her eyes roll back and her tongue flips in as she swallows the coin	350	500	650
Football	Cast Iron	1895	Place a coin on the platform in front of the player's foot, press the lever and he kicks the coin into the goal net	800	1600	2400
Giant in Tower	Cast Iron	1892	Put coin in slot and giant leans forward	6000	10000	15000
Grenadier Bank	Cast Iron	1890s	Soldier shoots coin into tree stump	350	650	1100
Hoop-La Bank	Cast Iron	1895	Place coin in dog's mouth and press the lever, the dog jumps thru the hoop and deposits the coin in the barrel	450	750	1000
Jolly Nigger in High Hat	Cast Iron	1880s	Put coin in hand; pressing lever makes arm raise, dropping coin into mouth, eyes roll and tongue moves back into mouth as coin drops	250	400	650
Kiltie	Cast Iron	1931	Deposit coin in Scotchman's hand and press the lever; he raises his arm, lowers his eyes and deposits coin in his shirt pocket	750	1200	1700
Little Joe (Darkie Bank)	Cast Iron	1910	Put coin in Joe's hand; pressing lever makes him lift and swallow coin	150	250	375
Queen Victoria Bust	Cast Iron	1887	Drop coin into slot in crown, making eyes roll. Note: This bank was also made in brass.	3000	5000	7500
Tommy Bank	Cast Iron	1914	Cock the rifle, lay a coin in front of the launcher and press the lever on top of soldier's left side; the coin is shot into the tree as his head rises	1500	2500	3500
Volunteer Bank	Cast Iron	1885	Length 10"; cock rifle and put coin in slot; pressing lever makes man fire rifle, shooting coin into tree stump	350	500	750

J. Harper & Co.

BANK	TYPE	YEAR	DESCRIPTION	GOOD	VG	EX
Wimbledon Bank	Cast Iron	1885	Cock rifle in reclining redcoat's hands, put coin on barrel; pressing lever shoots coin into tree as soldier's head rises	3500	5500	8000

Jacob & Co.

BANK	TYPE	YEAR	DESCRIPTION	GOOD	VG	EX
Lucky Wheel Money Box	Tin	1929	Deposit coin in top of bank; the wheel spins and stops at one of twelve fortune messages	300	500	700

James A. Serrill

BANK	TYPE	YEAR	DESCRIPTION	GOOD	VG	EX
Bureau, Five Knob	Wood	1869	Place coin in open drawer; closing drawer makes coin drop	200	350	500
Bureau, Three Knob	Wood	1869	Place coin in open drawer; closing drawer makes coin drop	300	400	550

Judd Mfg. Co.

BANK	TYPE	YEAR	DESCRIPTION	GOOD	VG	EX
Bear and Tree Stump	Cast Iron	1880s	5" tall; put coin on bear's tongue; pressing lever makes tongue lift coin and drop it into bank	300	400	550
Bill E. Grin Bank	Cast Iron	1887	4 1/2" tall; dropping coin on top of head makes tongue jut and eyes blink	450	750	1000
Boy and Bulldog	Cast Iron	1870s	Deposit coin between the boy and the dog; pulling lever makes boy lean forward and 'push' coin into bank, the dog moves backwards at the same time and coin falls	400	650	1000
Bucking Mule, Miniature	Cast Iron	1870s	Put coin in slot; releasing donkey makes him throw man, knocking coin into bank	450	750	1000
Bulldog Standing	Cast Iron	1870s	Coin is placed on dog's tongue and tail is lifted; when tail is released the coin is deposited	350	500	650
Butting Goat	Cast Iron	1870s	Deposit coin on holder on tree trunk; lifting the tail causes the goat to spring forward depositing coin in bank. Base length 4 3/4"	550	900	1200
Circus Ticket Collector	Cast Iron	1830	Deposit coin on top of barrel and the man's head nods his thanks.	350	650	900
Dog on Turntable	Cast Iron	1870s	5 1/4" long, 5" tall; turn the handle and dog goes in and deposits penny, coming out of the other door for more	250	400	500
Gem Bank	Cast Iron	1878	Pull dog back from bank, put coin on tray, lift dog's tail making dog move and drop coin into building	200	350	450
Mosque Bank	Cast Iron	1880s	9" tall, electroplated; put coin on tray on gorilla's head, turning lever makes gorilla turn, dropping coin into bank	300	650	1000
Peg-Leg Begger	Cast Iron	1875s	Insert coin in slot on hat and the begger nods his thanks	750	1200	1700

Keim & Co. (Germany)

BANK	TYPE	YEAR	DESCRIPTION	GOOD	VG	EX
Crowing Rooster	Tin	1937	Push coin through slot into bank; makes a crowing sound	300	500	800

Top to Bottom: Darktown Battery, 1888, J & E Stevens; Mason Bank, 1887, Shepard Hardward Co.; Monkey Bank, 1920s, Hubley; Trick Dog Bank, 1920s, Hubley; Hen and Chick, 1901, J & E Stevens; Eagle and Eaglets, 1883, J & E Stevens; Chief Big Moon, 1889, J & E Stevens.

Kenton Mfg. Co.

BANK	TYPE	YEAR	DESCRIPTION	GOOD	VG	EX
Bear, Slot in Chest	Cast Iron	1870s	Deposit coin in the bear's chest and his mouth opens and closes	750	1000	1500
Mama Katzenjammer	Cast Iron	1908	Deposit coin in Mama's back in slot; her eyes roll up and return to their original position	3000	5000	7500
Frog on Rock	Cast Iron	1920s	Press small lever under frog's mouth and he opens to deposit coin	200	350	475
Owl, Slot in Book	Cast Iron	1926	Height 5 3/4"; deposit a coin in the slot and Blinkey's eyes will roll down and back	150	275	500
Owl, Slot in Head	Cast Iron	1926	Deposit coin in slot, eyes roll forward; height 5 5/8"	150	300	650
Rabbit in Cabbage	Cast Iron	1925	Length 4 1/2", white with a green base; press coin into the slot and ears will rise and then flop back down	200	350	500
Turtle Bank	Cast Iron	1920s	Press a coin in the slot and Pokey's neck extends and then returns	7500	12000	17000

Kingsbury Mfg. Co.

BANK	TYPE	YEAR	DESCRIPTION	GOOD	VG	EX
Keene Savings Bank	Tin Litho	1902	Drop coin in bank, press lever to show amount	200	300	450

Kyser & Rex Co.

BANK	TYPE	YEAR	DESCRIPTION	GOOD	VG	EX
Boys Stealing Watermelon	Cast Iron	1880s	6 1/2" long; put coin in slot on top of dog house; pressing lever makes boy move toward watermelon, dog comes out of house, and coin drops	600	1200	2000
Butting Buffalo	Cast Iron	1888	Place coin into tree trunk; pressing lever makes buffalo 'butt' boy up trunk while raccoon flees into tree	1200	2000	3000
Chimpanzee	Cast Iron	1880	Green version; push coin slide toward monkey with log book, making monkey lower head and arm to 'log in' deposit, ringing a bell	1200	2000	2700
Chimpanzee Bank	Cast Iron	1880	Red variant; push coin slide toward monkey with log book, making monkey lower head and arm to 'log in' deposit, ringing a bell	1400	2200	3000
Coin Registering Bank	Cast Iron	1890s	When the last nickel or dime is deposited totaling $5 the door will pop off and the money can be taken out	1200	2000	3000
Confectionery Bank	Cast Iron	1881	8 1/2" tall; depicts lady at candy counter; coin dropped into slot, button pushed, making figure slide to receive candy; bell rings as coin drops	2000	4000	7000
Dog with Tray	Cast Iron	1880	Place coin on plate; the dog faithfully deposits it in the vault	1500	2200	3500
Hindu	Cast Iron	1882	Deposit coin in mouth and press the lever on the back of the head, his eyes roll down and his tongue swings down, causing the coin to fall into the bank	800	1300	1800
Lion and Two Monkeys	Cast Iron	1883	9" long; put coin in monkey's hand; pressing lever makes monkey lower hand and drop coin into lion's mouth	350	650	1000
Mammy and Child	Cast Iron	1884	Put coin on apron; pressing lever makes Mammy lower spoon to baby, Mammy's head lowers and baby's leg lifts as coin drops	3000	4500	6000

Kyser & Rex Co.

BANK	TYPE	YEAR	DESCRIPTION	GOOD	VG	EX
Merry-Go-Round	Cast Iron	1888	Put coin in slot, turn the handle and chimes will ring, the figures will revolve and the attendant turns, raises stick, and coin drops	7500	11000	15000
Mikado	Cast Iron	1886	Put coin under right hat and turn crank, making coin mysteriously move to left hat, which is lifted to show you this.	15000	25000	35000
Motor Bank	Cast Iron	1889	Wind the rod with key, drop a coin in slot and the trolley car is set in motion	10000	15000	20000
Mule Entering Barn	Cast Iron	1880	8 1/2" long, gray barn version; put coin between mule's hind legs; pushing lever makes mule kick coin into barn and dog appears.	600	1000	1500
Organ Bank	Cast Iron	1881	6" tall, brown organ, monkey in blue pants and coat, yellow hat; turn handle and a chime of bells will ring while monkey deposits coins placed in tambourine, tipping his hat in thanks	250	500	750
Organ Bank with Boy and Girl	Cast Iron	1882	7 1/2" tall; put coin on tray; turning crank makes monkey lower tray, dropping coin into bank while boy and girl turn.	300	600	950
Organ Bank with Cat and Dog	Cast Iron	1882	#24663, 8 1/2" tall; put coin on tray; turning crank makes monkey lower tray dropping coin into bank while cat and dog rotate	300	550	800
Organ Bank, Miniature	Cast Iron	1890s	Put coin in slot; turning crank makes bells ring, monkey turn, and coin drop	275	500	650
Presto Bank	Cast Iron	1894	Pull drawer open and deposit coin, release drawer and coin is deposited in bank	150	250	375
Rabbit Standin (small)	Cast Iron		Put coin in rabbit's paws; pressing tail moves ears and drops coin	250	400	650
Rollerskating Bank	Cast Iron	1880s	Place coin in roof slot, press lever, the skaters glide to the rear of the rink as the coin is deposited in bank, the man turns to give a little girl a wreath	12000	18000	25000
Rooster Bank	Cast Iron	1900s	Put coin on rooster's tail; pressing lever causes the rooster to move his head in a crowing position, money is deposited, 6 1/4"	200	300	400
Uncle Remus	Cast Iron	1891	5 3/4" long, painted; deposit coin on roof and press the chicken's head, the policeman moves toward Uncle Remus who slams the door to prevent getting caught	1700	2300	3500
Uncle Tom, No Star, Lapels	Cast Iron	1882	Put coin on tongue; pressing lever makes Tom swallow coin and move eyes	175	300	450
Uncle Tom, With Lapels and Star	Cast Iron	1882	Put coin on tongue; pressing lever makes Tom swallow coin and move eyes	175	300	450
Zoo Bank	Cast Iron	1890s	Building bank; put coin in slot; pressing monkey's face makes coin drop and shutters open on lower windows, and faces of lion and tiger appear through windows	450	750	1000

Louis Marx & Co.

BANK	TYPE	YEAR	DESCRIPTION	GOOD	VG	EX
Dapper Dan	Tin	1910	Deposit coin into the slot and Dapper Dan dances until the spring winds down; to reset wind the key clockwise	250	375	500

Louis Mfg. Co.

BANK	TYPE	YEAR	DESCRIPTION	GOOD	VG	EX
Electric Safe	Sheet Metal	1904	Twist the center knob in a clockwise direction until it stops, coin slot becomes operational, rotate dial counterclockwise and the coin falls into the bank	175	300	400

McLoughlin Brothers

BANK	TYPE	YEAR	DESCRIPTION	GOOD	VG	EX
Guessing Bank, Man's Figure	Cast Iron	1877	Man sits atop a clock with numbers from 1 to 6 repeated around dial; dropping coin makes dial spin and land on a number; bank reads, "Pays Five For One If You Call the Number"	1200	2000	3000

Mechanical Novelty Works

BANK	TYPE	YEAR	DESCRIPTION	GOOD	VG	EX
Initiating Bank, First Degree	Cast Iron	1880	10 1/2" long, Eddy's patent on base; place coin on boy's tray, push lever, the goat butts boy forward and the frog moves upward as the coin slides from the tray into the frog's mouth	5000	7000	9000
Initiating Bank, Second Degree	Cast Iron	1880	Goat is pressed down to lock mechanism; put coin on man's tray; pressing lever makes goat butt man, dropping coin into frog's mouth	3000	5000	8000
Squirrel and Tree Stump	Cast Iron	1881	Pressing lever makes squirrel move and drop coin into stump	450	850	1300

Melvisto Novelty Co.

BANK	TYPE	YEAR	DESCRIPTION	GOOD	VG	EX
Kick Inn	Wood	1921	Place coin on the ledge and push the lever on edge of base, the donkey kicks the ledge with his hind feet; ledge moves upward and tosses the coin into the side of the inn	200	300	450

National Brass Works

BANK	TYPE	YEAR	DESCRIPTION	GOOD	VG	EX
Chandlers Bank	Cast Iron	1900s	Open the drawer, put in coin, closing drawer drops coin into bank	200	350	450
Fortune Teller Savings Bank	Cast Iron	1901	Drop a nickel in the slot of the lever give a sharp jerk backwards, the wheel will spin; when it stops pull lever forward and your fortune will appear in window	350	600	800

Ole Storle

BANK	TYPE	YEAR	DESCRIPTION	GOOD	VG	EX
Butting Ram	Cast Iron	1895	Put coin on tree limb; pressing lever makes ram butt coin into bank while boy thumbs his nose	2000	4000	6000

Regina Music Box Corp.

BANK	TYPE	YEAR	DESCRIPTION	GOOD	VG	EX
Musical Savings Bank, Regina	Wood/Metal	1894	Bank is styled like a mantle clock; wind up mechanism, drop in coin, music plays	2500	4000	6000

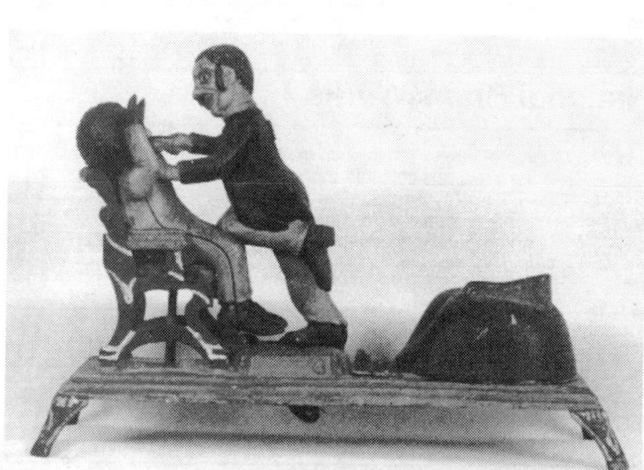

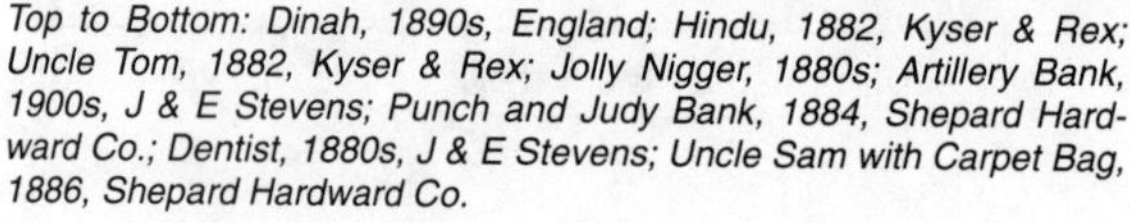

Top to Bottom: Dinah, 1890s, England; Hindu, 1882, Kyser & Rex; Uncle Tom, 1882, Kyser & Rex; Jolly Nigger, 1880s; Artillery Bank, 1900s, J & E Stevens; Punch and Judy Bank, 1884, Shepard Hardward Co.; Dentist, 1880s, J & E Stevens; Uncle Sam with Carpet Bag, 1886, Shepard Hardward Co.

Richard Elliot Co.

BANK	TYPE	YEAR	DESCRIPTION	GOOD	VG	EX
Pistol Bank	Cast Iron	1909	5 1/2" long; pull trigger halfway back, a hook appears from end of the barrel, place a dime on hook and pull trigger; coin is snatched and pistol fires when deposited	450	750	1000

S & E

BANK	TYPE	YEAR	DESCRIPTION	GOOD	VG	EX
Santa at the Desk	Tin Litho, Cloth, Vinyl		Deposit coin in large phone and dial Santa's number, the phone rings and he will pick it up and nod his head, as he's writing Merry Xmas on a lighted piece of paper. Desk 6X8"	250	450	675

Saalheimer & Strauss

BANK	TYPE	YEAR	DESCRIPTION	GOOD	VG	EX
Clever Dick	Tin	1920s	German bank; put coin on dog's nose; pressing lever makes him toss coin and swallow it	300	600	850
Jolly Joe Clown, with Verse	Tin	1030s	Push lever down, making tongue jut and eyes close; put coin on tongue; lifting lever makes tongue recede into mouth , dropping coin, and eyes open	350	600	850
Minstrel Bank	Tin Litho	1928	7 1/2" tall; press lever making tongue stick out, put coin on tongue, lift lever to make coin retract on tongue into bank	350	600	900
Monkey and Parrot	Tin	1925	Put coin into monkey's hands; pressing lever makes monkey toss coin into parrot's mouth	250	350	450
Scotchman	Tin	1930s	German bank; lifting lever makes eyes blink and tongue jut; put coin on tongue and lower lever to make tongue recede and drop coin into bank	200	300	400
Humpty Dumpty Bank	Cast Iron	1882	8 1/2" tall; put coin in Humpty's hand, press lever, making him drop coin into bank	225	450	750
Jonah and the Whale	Cast Iron	1890s	Put coin on Jonah's back; pressing lever makes Jonah turn toward whale's mouth, dropping coin into mouth	900	2000	3500
Leap Frog Bank	Cast Iron	1891	7 1/2" long; put standing boy behind stooping one, put coin in slot; pressing lever makes standing boy leap over other one, who pushes lever on tree, dropping coin into bank	750	1500	2200
Mason Bank	Cast Iron	1887	7 1/4" long; drop coin onto hod, press lever, making hod move and drop coin into brick wall	2000	4000	6000
Punch and Judy, Large Letters	Cast Iron	1884	7 1/2" tall; put coin on Judy's tray, press lever and Judy deposits coin while Punch tries to hit her with stick	600	1000	1500
Punch and Judy, Small Letters	Cast Iron	1884	7 1/2" tall; put coin on Judy's tray, press lever and Judy deposits coin while Punch tries to hit her with stick	600	1000	1500
Santa at the Chimney	Cast Iron	1889	6" tall, painted; put coin in his hand; pressing lever makes him drop coin into chimney	800	1300	1850
Stump Speaker Bank	Cast Iron	1886	9 3/4" tall, painted; place coin in hand, press the small knob on top of the box, which lowers the arm and opens the satchel to deposit the coin; release lever and mouth moves up and down	650	1000	1500

Saalheimer & Strauss

BANK	TYPE	YEAR	DESCRIPTION	GOOD	VG	EX
Trick Pony	Cast Iron	1885	7" long, 8" tall; put coin in horse's mouth, pulling lever makes pony drop coin in trough	600	950	1200
Uncle Sam with Carpet Bag	Cast Iron	1886	11 1/2" tall; put coin in Sam's hand; pressing lever lowers coin into his carpet bag	1000	1700	2500

Shephard Hardware Co.

BANK	TYPE	YEAR	DESCRIPTION	GOOD	VG	EX
Artillery Bank	Cast Iron	1892	Nickel plate version, coin is placed in the cannon, the hammer is pushed back; pressing the thumb piece fires the coin into the fort	550	900	1400
Circus Bank	Cast Iron	1888	Place coin on money receptacle, turn the crank and pony goes around the ring and the clown deposits coin	3000	5000	8000
Picture Gallery Bank	Cast Iron	1885	Place coin in hand of center figure and he deposits coin; all the letters of the alphabet and numbers 1 to 26 are shown in rotation; also 26 animals or objects with short word for each letter	4500	7500	9000
Speaking Dog	Cast Iron	1885	Deposit coin on girl's plate; when thumb piece is pressed the girl's arm moves, depositing coin through trap door on bench and dog wags his tail and moves his mouth	850	1300	1700

Starkie (England)

BANK	TYPE	YEAR	DESCRIPTION	GOOD	VG	EX
Jolly Nigger in High Hat	Aluminum	1920	Put coin in hand; pressing lever makes figure swallow coin while eyes roll and ears wiggle	250	400	650
Starkie's Aeroplane	Aluminum	1919	Move plane up pole and lock in place, put coin in slot on plane; pressing lever makes plane coast down pole, dropping coin in bank base	900	1500	2000
Tank and Cannon	Cast Iron or Aluminum	1919	Cannon fires coin into tank bank	400	650	850

Stollwerck (Germany)

BANK	TYPE	YEAR	DESCRIPTION	GOOD	VG	EX
Stollwerck Hand Shadows	Tin	1880s	Candy dispenser; deposit coin in slot on top, pull drawer handle to dispense candy; decorated with art of a woman's arm making shadow animal	100	250	400
Stollwerck Postman	Tin	1900s	Candy vending machine decorated with images on a postal theme; drop coin in slot, pull handle to receive candy	200	350	500
Stollwerck Red Riding Hood	Tin	1900s	Candy vending machine decorated with images of Red Riding Hood; drop coin in slot, pull handle to receive candy	175	300	450

Straits Mfg. Co.

BANK	TYPE	YEAR	DESCRIPTION	GOOD	VG	EX
Joe Socko Novelty Bank	Tin	1930s	Joe Palooka is turned clockwise as coin is deposited into slot making him turn quickly, swinging his right arm and knocking down his opponent. Base length 3 1/2"	250	400	650

Straits Mfg. Co.

BANK	TYPE	YEAR	DESCRIPTION	GOOD	VG	EX
Popeye Knockout Bank with Box	Tin	1929	Turn Popeye to the right, lift his opponent to his feet and when the coin is deposited Popeye will deliver knockout punch	250	450	650

Unknown

BANK	TYPE	YEAR	DESCRIPTION	GOOD	VG	EX
Atlas Bank	Iron & Wood		Iron base with white metal figure holding wooden globe with paper litho map; put coin in slot, pulling lever makes coin fall into bank, making globe spin	1000	1500	2000
Bull Tosses Boy In Well	Brass		7" long; put coin in boy's hands; pressing lever makes bull spring and boy jumps back, dropping coin in well	750	1200	1700
Darky in the Chimney	Wood		Pull the drawer out and the darkey emerges; front door knob when turned counterclockwise allows the trap door in base of bank to be removed	550	1000	1400
Elephant Three Stars	Cast Iron	1884	Place coin in the elephant's trunk, touch his tail and the coin will be thrown into his head	200	300	450
Haley's Elephant	Cast Iron		8" long, painted gray with red and gold blanket	350	500	650
Hold the Fort, Seven Hole	Cast Iron	1877	Pull back the ring until rod is in position, tip the bank, place the coin on target and drop the shot in the cannon; shot follows the coin into the bank and escapes out of the bottom	2000	3500	5000
Lighthouse	Cast Iron	1891	Two slots, one is a still bank, other on top of tower takes nickels; the button on top of tower will permit the bank to open only after 100 nickels are deposited	400	650	900
Little Miss Muffet	Tin Litho	1930s	Drop coin into bank and spider appears in window	150	225	275
National, Your Savings	Cast Iron	1900s	Replica cash register, with one slot and key each for pennies, nickels, dimes and quarters; dropping coin and pressing key rings a bell	275	450	600
Octagonal Fort Bank	Cast Iron	1890	Also called Fort Sumter, cock mechanism, put coin in barrel end; pressing lever makes coin fire into tower; 10 3/4" long	1200	2200	3500
Schley Bottling Up Cervera	Cast Iron	1899	Bottle neck shows two portraits, Schley and Cervera; coins can only be dropped when Cervera is visible; shake bank to pull up Cervera picture, dropping coin will make Schley's picture return	4500	8000	12000
Tabby Bank	Cast Iron	1887	Cat sits atop large egg, waiting for chick to hatch; drop coin in slot in cat's back and the chick moves its head	250	450	650
Trick Savings Bank	Wood		Deposit coin, coin disappears with drawer closed; height 5 1/2"	55	125	200

Unknown (England)

BANK	TYPE	YEAR	DESCRIPTION	GOOD	VG	EX
Clown Bank, Arched Top	Tin	1930s	Press lever to make tongue jut out, put coin on tongue; lifting lever makes tongue recede, dropping coin	70	100	150

Unknown (England)

BANK	TYPE	YEAR	DESCRIPTION	GOOD	VG	EX
Clown, Black Face	Tin	1930s	Press lever to jut out tongue, put coin on tongue and release lever to drop coin into bank	150	300	450
Jolly Nigger, String Tie	Aluminum	1890s	Put coin in his hand; pressing level makes him lift coin and swallow it, tongue pulling back and eyes rolling	175	300	500
Victorian Money Box	Wood		Dropping coin into box makes girl in doorway curtsy	800	1300	1800

Unknown (France)

BANK	TYPE	YEAR	DESCRIPTION	GOOD	VG	EX
Cigarette Vending	Tin	1920s	Dispenses real candy cigarettes, illustrated with scenes of children smoking	75	150	250

Unknown (Germany)

BANK	TYPE	YEAR	DESCRIPTION	GOOD	VG	EX
Cross Legged Minstrel	Tin	1909	Put coin in slot; pressing lever makes man tip his hat to you	250	450	550
Saluting Sailor	Tin		Pressing lever makes sailor lift left arm, exposing coin slot while saluting with right arm; dropping coin and releasing lever completes cycle	300	600	900

W.S. Reed

BANK	TYPE	YEAR	DESCRIPTION	GOOD	VG	EX
Girl in Victorian Chair	Cast Iron	1880	Girl in blue dress sits with dog in her lap in a highback wicker chair; put coin in chair top and press lever, making coin drop and dog lean forward	2000	3000	4500
Red Riding Hood	Cast Iron	1880s	Put coin in slot in pillow; moving lever makes Grandma's mask shift, revealing the wolf; Red turns her head in 'fear' and coin drops	8500	14000	18000

Weeden Mfg. Co.

BANK	TYPE	YEAR	DESCRIPTION	GOOD	VG	EX
Japanese Ball Tosser Safe	Tin	1888	Tin windup; put coin in slot, wind mechanism, making figure move arms, appearing to juggle balls	125	250	500
Weeden's Plantation Darkie Bank	Tin	1888	5 1/2" tall, windup bank; putting coin in slot at side of house makes banjo player play and other figure dance	750	1250	1850

Wm. Morrison

BANK	TYPE	YEAR	DESCRIPTION	GOOD	VG	EX
Home Bank with Tickets, Morrison's	Tin	1900s	Place 50 tickets in bank, deposit coin in slot and pull desk in front of cashier as far as it will go and coin is deposited in the vault; don't release until you receive your ticket	300	400	550
Home Bank, No Dormers	Tin Litho	1872	6" tall, 5" wide, no dormers, bank teller in cage; put coin in side of building, pull tray in front of teller to get a receipt	650	1000	1500

Wrightsville Hrdw. Co.

BANK	TYPE	YEAR	DESCRIPTION	GOOD	VG	EX
Camera	Cast Iron	1888	Rotating lever makes picture pop up	800	1500	2200

CAST IRON BANKS

Abendroth Bros.

BANK	DESCRIPTION	YEAR	GOOD	EX
Gem Stove	4 3/4", brown finish		75	175
York Stove	4" tall, unpainted, "York Stove"		225	475

Alamo Iron Works

BANK	DESCRIPTION	YEAR	GOOD	EX
Alamo	1 7/8"tall, 3 3/8" wide, unpainted bronze finish	1930s	200	450

Allen Mfg. Co.

BANK	DESCRIPTION	YEAR	GOOD	EX
A.A.O.S.M.S. Shriner's Fez	2 3/8" red fez with tassle and gold lettering	1920s	250	650

Arcade

BANK	DESCRIPTION	YEAR	GOOD	EX
Andy Gump	4 3/8" tall, Andy sits reading a paper, painted	1928	500	950
Bank of Columbia	4 7/8", unpainted, "Bank of Columbia"	1800s	150	375
Bird Cage Bank, (Crystal Bank)	3 7/8" tall, similar to Crystal Bank #926, but glass is replaced by open mesh	1900s	50	125
Bulldog, Standing	2 1/4", painted	1900s	250	450
Cash Register with Mesh	3 3/4" tall, red finish with gold-bronze mesh	1900s	50	125
Cat with Soft Hair, Seated	4 1/4" x 2 7/8"	1900s	85	225
Century of Progress Building	4 1/2" x 7", white, "A Century Of Progress" building from Chicago World's Fair	1933	800	1500
Donkey "I Made St. Louis Famous"	4 11/16" tall, gray finish	1903	800	1500
Donkey (small)	4 1/2" tall, blue, gold or gray finish	1910s	85	175
Eggman (Wm. Howard Taft)	4 1/8" tall	1910	850	1850
Elephant with Tucked Trunk	2 3/4" x 4 5/8", red or green	1900s	65	125
G. E. Radio Bank	3 3/4" tall, brown cabinet radio on 4 legs	1930s	125	275
General Sheridan on Base	6" tall, General seated on rearing horse	1910s	250	650
Globe on Wire Arc	4 5/8"tall, painted spinning globe, red continents	1900s	65	135
Good Luck Horseshoe	4 1/4" tall, Buster Brown & Tige with horse inside horseshoe	1908	150	300
Goose Bank	3 3/4", unpainted	1920s	85	175
Hall Clock	5 5/8" tall, dark finish with gold highlights	1923	300	650
Holstein Cow	2 1/2" tall, 4 5/8" long, black finish	1910s	125	350
Horse, "Beauty"	4 1/8" x 4 3/4", black with raised "Beauty" on side	1900s	85	150
Horse, Prancing	4 1/4" tall, black with gray hooves	1910s	55	125
Hot Point Electric Stove	6", white, on legs	1925	85	150
Kelvinator Bank	#832, 4 1/2" tall, white with grey trim replica refrigerator	1930s	150	350
Liberty Bell with Yoke	3 1/2"	1920s	25	65
Limousine	8 1/16" long, black with white rubber tires	1920s		
Limousine	same as # 1478, but with steel wheels	1921	1200	2400
Limousine Yellow Cab	repaint of version #1478	1921	1400	2600
Lion, Tail Right	4" tall	1900s	55	100
Majestic Radio Bank	4 1/2" tall, mahogany finish replica of a floor standing radio on 4 legs, coin slot in back, with key	1930s	125	200
Majestic Refrigerator Bank	4 1/2" tall, in red, green or blue with gold trim, replica of single door fridge on 4 legs, coin slot in back, with key lock	1930s	375	600
Model T Ford	4" tall, black	1920s	650	1250
Newfoundland Dog	3 5/8" x 5 3/8", blue or green finish	1930s	100	225
Peters Weatherbird	4 1/4" tall		750	2500

Arcade

BANK	DESCRIPTION	YEAR	GOOD	EX
Polar Bear, Begging	5 1/4", white variant of # 715	1900s	275	450
Policeman Bank	5 5/8" tall, blue with aluminum finish on gloves and star, gold buttons, black shoes, flesh face and hands	1930s	250	1000
Possum	2 3/8" tall, 4 3/8" long, silver finish	1910s	125	450
Rabbit, Small, Seated	3 5/8" tall	1910s	125	325
Red Goose Shoes on Base	5 1/2", on pedestal w/base	1920s	300	750
Red Goose Shoes, Squatty	4" tall, red body, yellow feet	1920s	275	475
Rhino	2 5/8" tall, 5" long, gold	1910s	225	525
Rooster	4 5/8", black with red comb	1910s	125	350
Save for Ice, Ice Box	4 1/4" tall, white, "Save For Ice"		175	450
Seal on Rock	3 1/2", black	1900s	175	475
Squatty "Red Goose Shoes"	3 7/8"	1920s	225	575
State Bank	4 1/8" tall, bronze finish	1910s	85	175
Sun Dial	4 5/16" tall	1900s	650	1750
Teddy Bear	2 1/2" x 3 7/8"	1900	125	275
Templetone Radio	4 1/2", red	1930s	275	575
Work Horse with Flynet	4" tall	1910s	300	550
Yellow Cab	7 7/8" long, orange and black, rubber tires	1921	1500	2200

Bartlett Mayward Co.

BANK	DESCRIPTION	YEAR	GOOD	EX
Grenade with Pin	4 1/4"		85	175

Barton Smith Co.

BANK	DESCRIPTION	YEAR	GOOD	EX
Fidelity Trust Vault, Lord Fauntleroy	6 1/2" x 5 7/8"	1890	300	650

Blevins, Charlotte

BANK	DESCRIPTION	YEAR	GOOD	EX
Edison Bust	5 5/16"	1972	35	65
Nixon Bust	5 5/16"	1972	25	55

Braun, Chas. A.

BANK	DESCRIPTION	YEAR	GOOD	EX
Basket Registering Bank, Woven	2 7/8" x 3 3/4"	1902	50	125

Chamberlain & Hill

BANK	DESCRIPTION	YEAR	GOOD	EX
Space Heater with Bird	English, 6 1/2" tall	1890s	175	375

Dent

BANK	DESCRIPTION	YEAR	GOOD	EX
Air Mail Bank on Base	6 3/8" tall, red	1920	40	95
Stop Sign	5 5/8" tall, green with red and gold highlights	1920	325	800

Enterprise Mfg. Co.

BANK	DESCRIPTION	YEAR	GOOD	EX
Globe Bank With Eagle	5 3/4", painted red with eagle atop globe	1875	100	300
Independence Hall	10" tall, deep red/brown finish	1875	450	1150
Independence Hall Tower	9 1/2"	1876	225	475

Ferrosteel

BANK	DESCRIPTION	YEAR	GOOD	EX
Tank Savings Bank	9 1/2" long, "Tank Savings Bank"	1919	150	375

Filler, Lou

BANK	DESCRIPTION	YEAR	GOOD	EX
Buckeye (SBCCA)	3 1/2", painted "Ohio The Buckeye State", "SBCC 1973"	1973	25	150

Fish, O.B.

BANK	DESCRIPTION	YEAR	GOOD	EX
U.S. Mail Bank with Combination lock	6 7/8" tall, silver gray with red lettering	1903	225	475

Gobeille, W.M.

BANK	DESCRIPTION	YEAR	GOOD	EX
Beehive with Brass Top	5 1/2" tall on base, unpainted		350	750

Grey Iron Casting Co.

BANK	DESCRIPTION	YEAR	GOOD	EX
1 Pounder Shell Bank	8" artillery shell, "1 Pounder Bank"	1918	20	65
1926 Sesquicentenial Bell	3 3/4" x 3 7/8" diam.	1926	75	200
Battleship Maine	5 1/4" tall, 6 5/8" long, "Maine"	1800s	650	2500
Bungalow Bank	3 3/4" x 3", white cottage with green roof	1900s	225	425
Cat with Bow, Seated	4 3/8" tall, brown finish	1922	225	475
Cat with Long Tail	4 3/8" tall, 6 3/4" long	1910s	375	875
Columbia Tower	6 7/8", unpainted 3 story tower	1897	400	900
Dolphin Boat Bank	4 1/2" tall, sailor boy in boat holds anchor	1900s	500	850
Domed Mosque Bank	3 1/8"tall, bronze finish	1900s	65	145
Domed Mosque Bank	4 1/4" tall, gold/bronze finish	1900s	85	175
Doughboy	7" tall, painted World War I soldier	1919	350	850
Dutch Boy	6 3/4" tall		600	850
Dutch Girl	6 1/2" tall, bronze finish		600	850
Foreman	4 1/2", painted	1951	175	350
General Pershing Bust	7 3/4" tall, bronze finish	1918	75	150
Globe on Arc	5 1/4" tall, red	1900s	100	300
Husky	5"	1910s	200	550
Mermaid Boat	4 1/2" tall, companion piece to Dolphin, girl in boat holds fish	1900s	350	850
Merry-Go-Round	4 5/8" tall, unpainted	1920s	175	450
North Pole Bank	4 1/4", unpainted, "Save Your Money And Freeze It"	1920s	375	775
One Story House	3" tall	1900s	65	175
Roof Bank	5 1/4"	1900s	125	300
Saddle Horse	4 3/8" tall	1928	375	650
Spitz	4 1/4", bronze finish	1928	225	575
Street Car	4 1/2" long, painted	1891	250	650
U.S. Treasury Bank	3 1/4", painted	1920s	250	475
Washington Bell with Yoke	2 3/4", red	1932	125	250
Washington, George, Bust	8" tall, bronze finish	1920s	850	1450

Harper, J.M.

BANK	DESCRIPTION	YEAR	GOOD	EX
Billy Possum ("Possum & Taters")	3" x 4 3/4", on base "Billy Possum"	1909	1200	2500
Carpenter Safe	4 3/8"	1907	2500	5000
George Washington Bust on Safe	5 7/8" tall	1903	1000	2500

Harper, J.M.

BANK	DESCRIPTION	YEAR	GOOD	EX
I Made Chicago Famous, Large Pig	2 5/8" x 5 5/16"	1902	250	450
I Made Chicago Famous, Small Pig	2 1/8" x 4 1/8"	1902	200	350
Indian Family	3 5/8" X 5 1/8", unpainted	1905	850	1750
Liberty Bell	3 3/4"	1905	275	550
Little Red Riding Hood Safe	5 1/16" tall, painted	1907	2000	4000
Mother Hubbard Safe	4 1/2" tall	1907	1500	5000
Nesting Doves Safe	5 1/4", bronze finish	1907	1500	3500
Policeman Safe	5 1/4"	1907	1250	4500
Stork Safe	5 1/2"	1907	850	1750
Taft-Sherman Bust	4" tall, one side Smiling Jim, other side Peaceful Bill	1908	1000	1750
Tower Bank	9 1/4" tall, unpainted, brown finish	1900s	175	375
Two Goats Butting	4 1/2", two goats on tree stump, "Two Kids" on base		950	2000
Ulysses S. Grant Bust on Safe	5 5/8" tall	1903	1750	3000

Hubley

BANK	DESCRIPTION	YEAR	GOOD	EX
Baseball on Three Bats	5 1/4"	1914	200	850
Bear with Honey Pot	6 1/2" tall, painted		75	150
Billy Bounce	4 11/16" tall, silver painted body	1900s	375	850
Boxer Bulldog	4 1/2", seated, bronze finish	1900s	125	175
Boy with Large Football	5 1/8" tall, brown	1914	2000	3000
Bulldog, Seated	3 7/8"	1928	200	400
Cadet	5 3/4" tall, blue uniform with gold trim	1905	300	650
Camel, Small	4 3/4" x 3 7/8"	1920s	100	225
Cannon	3" tall, 6 7/8" long, black cannon on red wheels	1914	2500	5000
Cash Register Savings Bank	4 3/4", unpainted, "Cash Register Savings Bank"	1906	500	750
Cat with Bow	4 1/8"	1930s	275	575
Cutie Dog	3 7/8", painted	1914	65	150
Dog Smoking Cigar	4 1/4", painted, white body, red bow tie.		450	850
Duck	4 3/4", white painted body	1930s	150	275
Duck on Tub "Save for a Rainy Day"	5 3/8"	1930s	95	325
Dutch Boy on Barrel	5 5/8"	1930s	75	150
Dutch Girl Holding Flowers	5 1/2" tall, painted, iron trap in base	1930s	100	175
Elephant with Chariot (large)	4 3/4" tall, also produced without chariot	1900s	2000	3000
Elephant with Chariot, Small	7" long, gray elephant, red chariot, yellow wheels	1906	1400	2200
Elephant with Howdah, Short Trunk	3 3/4" tall, painted gray with red belt	1910	125	275
Elephant, "GOP 1936"	3 1/2" tall, "GOP 1936"	1936	750	1200
Elephant, Circus	3 7/8", painted, with lavender pants and red dotted white shirt	1930s	150	350
Fido	5", painted, white body, black eyes and ears, red collar	1914	60	115
Fido on Pillow	7 3/8"long , painted	1920s	100	200
Foxy Grandpa	5 1/2" tall, painted	1920s	150	375
GE Refrigerator, Small	3 3/4", blue	1930s	75	200
Give Me A Penny	5 1/2" tall black figure in hat, painted	1900s	200	450
Hall Clock	5 1/4" tall, brown finish, paper face	1900s	275	400
Hall Clock with Cast Face	5 3/26" tall	1920s	275	375
Hoover/Curtis Elephant "GOP"	3 3/8", ivory finish	1928	675	1450
Indian with Tomahawk	5 7/8"	1900s	175	425
King Midas	4 1/2" tall, painted	1930s	1250	2500

Top to Bottom: Minuteman, 1905, Hubley; Columbia Tower, 1897, Grey Iron Casting Co.; Mammy, 1970s; Multiplying Bank, 1883, J & E Stevens; Bear Seated On Log; The Capitalist, 1913, Ober Manufacturing Co.

Hubley

BANK	DESCRIPTION	YEAR	GOOD	EX
Kitty Bank	4 3/4" tall, painted, white body with blue bow	1930s	65	125
Laughing Pig	2 1/2", painted		125	275
Lion, Tail Left	3 3/4" tall, bronze finish	1910s	100	175
Mailbox on Legs, Large	5 1/2" tall, green street corner box replica	1920s	85	225
Mailbox on Legs, Small	3 3/4" tall, green replica street corner mailbox	1928	35	100
Mammy with Hands on Hips	5 1/4" tall, red dress, white apron	1900s		
Mascot	5 3/4" tall, boy stands on baseball	1914	850	1500
Mean Standing Bear	5 1/2"		100	225
Minuteman	6" tall, painted	1905	175	450
Organ Grinder	6 3/16" x 2 1/8", painted		125	350
Oriental Boy on Pillow	5 1/2" tall, painted	1920s	85	200
Ornate Hall Clock	5 7/8" tall, tan finish, paper face	1900s	125	375
Pelican	4 3/4", painted white	1930s	350	1000
Puppo	4 7/8" tall, painted bee on body	1920s	125	225
Puppo on Pillow	5 5/8" x 6", painted brown, cream, black, pink	1920s	150	275
Rabbit, Large, Seated	4 5/8" tall, painted white with pink highlights	1900s	125	375
Radio Bank	3 5/16" tall, metallic blue	1928	100	375
Rooster	4 3/4" by Hubley and A.C. Williams, brown finish with red comb and wattle	1910s	125	300
Sailor, Medium	5 1/4" tall	1910s	225	475
Santa Claus	5 3/4", painted with arms folded in front	1900s	450	950
Santa Claus With Tree	5 3/4" tall with arms folded in front, tree at back, painted	1910s	450	950
Scottie, seated	4 7/8" x 6, black finish, red collar	1930s	125	300
Thoroughbred	5 1/4", bronze finish	1946	75	150
Triangular Building	6" tall, "Bank"	1914	325	675
U.S. Mail with Eagle	4" x 4"	1906	175	325
Wirehaired Terrier	4 5/8", painted	1920s	125	275
Wise Pig, The	6 5/8" tall, painted off white pig holding plaque	1930s	85	225

Iron Art

BANK	DESCRIPTION	YEAR	GOOD	EX
Frog	4 1/8", deep green finish	1973	75	125

Ives

BANK	DESCRIPTION	YEAR	GOOD	EX
Palace	7 1/2" tall, 8" wide	1885	850	3000
Santa with (Removable) Wire Tree	7 1/4" tall, with removable ornate tree	1890s	875	1500

Judd, H.L.

BANK	DESCRIPTION	YEAR	GOOD	EX
1876 Bank, Large	3 3/8" tall, building bank with bronze/copper finish	1895	75	175
Barrel	2 3/4" tall	1873	100	225
City Bank with Teller	5 1/2", bronze finish		400	700
Home Bank	4" x 3 1/2", dark finish	1890s	150	375
Lost Dog	5 3/8", unpainted	1890s	275	850

Kenton

BANK	DESCRIPTION	YEAR	GOOD	EX
Building with Belfry	8" tall, in browns		550	2000
Columbia	4 1/2" tall, silver finish building bank		600	900
Columbia Bank	8 3/4" tall, bronze finish	1890s	600	1000
Columbia Bank	5 3/4" tall, unpainted silver finish	1890s	300	700
Crosley Radio, Large	5 1/8" tall, green with gold highlights	1930s	650	1250

Kenton

BANK	DESCRIPTION	YEAR	GOOD	EX
Crosley Radio, Small	4 5/16" tall, green	1930s	150	350
Donkey with Blanket	3 7/8" tall, painted, gray with red blanket	1930s	450	850
Duck, Round	4"tall, painted, yellow body, red beak and top of head	1930s	225	450
Elephant with Bent Knee	3 1/2", tan finish	1904	200	375
Flat Iron Building Bank	5 1/2" tall, silver	1900s	85	225
Globe on Claw Feet	6"		175	375
Globe Safe with Hinged Door	5"	1900s	100	225
Gunboat	8 1/2" long, blue hull, white top, twin masts		650	1200
High Rise Building	7" tall		200	550
High Rise, Tiered	5 3/4"		125	350
New Heatrola Bank	4 1/2" tall, green finish with red trim	1920s	85	275
Oregon Gunboat	11" long, blue hull, gray guns, black and red stacks, "Oregon"		850	1800
Ox	4 3/8", painted		85	150
Radio Bank with 3 Dials	3" tall, 4 5/8" long, red	1920s	100	350
Radio with Combination Door	4 1/2" red, metal sides and back	1930s	125	375
State Bank	8" x 7"	1900	550	1000
State Bank	3" tall, unpainted building bank	1890s	95	200
Statue of Liberty	6 1/16" tall, also made by A.C. Williams, #1165, 6 3/8" tall	1900s	85	125
Statue of Liberty	6 3/8" tall, silver finish with gold highlights	1900s	100	175
Statue of Liberty, Large	9 1/2" tall, silver gray finish, gold highlights	1900s	350	850
Steamboat with Small Wheels	7 7/16" long, silver finish		175	425
Tower	4 1/8", unpainted, "Tower"	1915	175	375
Trolley Car	5 1/4" long, painted silver	1900s	225	650
U.S. Mail	4 3/4" tall, silver gray with red lettering	1900s	100	
275				
U.S. Mail with Eagle	4 1/8" x 3 1/2"	1930s	85	175
U.S. Mail, Small	3 5/8" x 2 3/4", silver or green mail box with red lettering	1900s	75	150
Woolworth Building	7 7/8" tall, bronze finish	1915	100	185
Woolworth Building	5 3/4" x 1 1/4"	1915	85	150

Keyless Lock Co.

BANK	DESCRIPTION	YEAR	GOOD	EX
Tabernacle Savings	2 1/4" x 5", unpainted		850	1250

Knerr, George

BANK	DESCRIPTION	YEAR	GOOD	EX
Buffalo Nickel	3 7/8"	1970s	5	20
Chicken Feed Bag	4 5/8", "Chicken Feed"	1973	35	250
Clown Bust	4 7/8", painted	1973	100	350
Hard Hat	1 15/16" tall, white with red lettering	1970s	100	250
Indian Head Penny	3 1/4" diam.	1972	10	35
Pot Bellied Stove	5 3/4" tall, flat black finish	1968	5	15
Rabbit with Carrot	3 3/8", painted white, orange and green carrot	1972	85	175
Rocking Horse (SBCCA)	5 5/8", white with red saddle, "SBCC"	1975	350	550
Uncle Sam Hat	2" x 3", red, white and blue		125	250
Whale of a Bank	2 3/4" x 5 3/16", "A Whale of a Bank"	1975	85	175
White Horse on Base	9 1/2" tall	1973	125	225

Kyser & Rex

BANK	DESCRIPTION	YEAR	GOOD	EX
Apple	5 1/4" tall, painted apple on twig with leaves	1882	600	1200
Arabian Safe	4 9/16" x 4 1/4"	1882	100	300
Bank of England Safe	identical to Egyptian Safe except front is embossed Bank of England	1882	350	550
Beehive Bank	2 3/8"	1882	250	500
Camel, Kneeling	2 1/2" tall, 4 3/4" long	1889	350	750
Castle Bank, Small	3" x 2 13/16"	1882	200	375
Coin Registering Bank	6 3/4" with red doors and dome, "Coin Registering Bank"	1890	2500	6500
Dime Registering Coin Barrel	4" x 2 1/2", unpainted	1889	125	225
Egyptian Tomb	6 1/4 " tall, Square safe on base, decorated with Sphinx and obelisk on front, sides show, pyramid, walled ruins and urn with flowers, gold	1882	450	750
Fidelity Safe, Large	3 5/8" tall, green with gold trim, "Fidelity Safe"	1880	150	300
Finial Bank	5 3/4" tall, 4 3/8" wide, building bank with single finial on roof	1887	275	550
Globe Savings Fund Bank	7 1/8", painted "Globe Savings Fund 1888"	1889	1800	3000
Ironmaster's House	4 1/2", unpainted	1884	600	850
Japanese Safe	5 3/8" tall	1882	100	300
Japanese Safe	5 1/2" tall, painted	1883	125	375
Log Cabin	2 1/2" x 3 1/4", painted	1882	175	400
Pavillion	3 1/8" x 3"	1880	225	450
Penny Register Pail	2 3/4", unpainted	1889	125	250
Presto Trick Bank	4 1/2" tall, red doors and roof	1892	250	750
Pugdog, seated	3 1/2", painted	1889	250	475
Roller Safe	3 11/16" x 2 7/8"4"	1882	125	245
Star Safe	2 5/8" tall	1882	150	450
State Bank	5 1/2" tall, bronze building bank	1890s	125	250
Tower Bank	6 7/8" building with tower rising from roof, "Tower Bank 1890"	1890	1200	2200
Town Hall Bank	4 5/8", red, "Town Hall Bank"	1882	375	750
Villa	5 9/16" unpainted except for red finial	1894	375	700
Villa Bank	3 7/8" x 3 3/8", "1882"	1882	375	700
Young America	4 3/8" x 3 1/8" safe	1882	125	275

Lane Art

BANK	DESCRIPTION	YEAR	GOOD	EX
Lighthouse	9 1/2" tall, "Light of the World"	1950s	125	250

Lane Chair Co.

BANK	DESCRIPTION	YEAR	GOOD	EX
Show Horse	5 7/8" tall	1973	75	150

Liberty Toy Co.

BANK	DESCRIPTION	YEAR	GOOD	EX
Mellow Furnace	3 9/16" x 3 1/8", brown finish		125	225

Littlestown Hdw & Found.

BANK	DESCRIPTION	YEAR	GOOD	EX
Flags Bank (SBCCA)	3 1/4" tall, 6" square white pyramid with color US flags	1976	75	125

Magic Introduction Co.

BANK	DESCRIPTION	YEAR	GOOD	EX
Administration Building	5", unpainted	1893	250	650

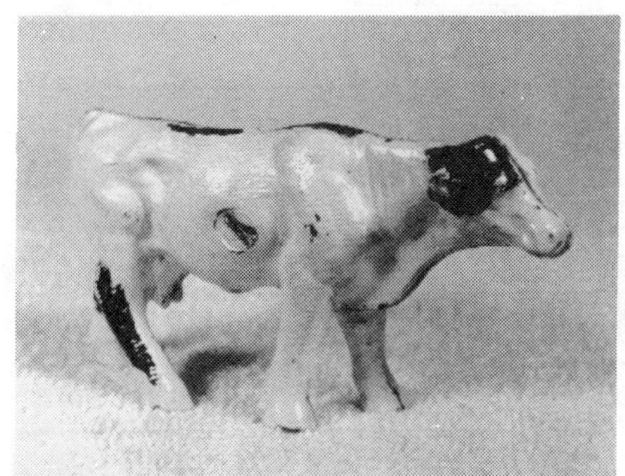

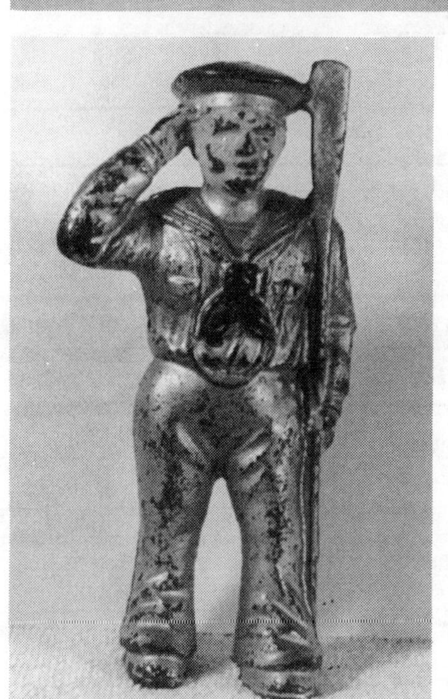

Top to Bottom: Holstein Cow, 1910s, Arcade; Pavillion, 1880, Kyser & Rex; Yellow Cab, 1921, Arcade; Palace, 1885, Ives; Sailor, 1910s, Hubley; Newfoundland Dog, 1930s, Arcade.

Magic Introduction Co.

BANK	DESCRIPTION	YEAR	GOOD	EX
Columbia Magic Savings Bank	5", unpainted, "Columbia Magic Savings Bank"	1892	300	700
Hub	5" x 5 1/4" x 1 5/8"	1892		

Manning, C.J.

BANK	DESCRIPTION	YEAR	GOOD	EX
Rocking Chair	6 3/4" tall, brown finish	1898	1500	2750

Martin, Mary A.

BANK	DESCRIPTION	YEAR	GOOD	EX
Potato	5 1/4" long, "Bank"	1897	850	1250

Nicol

BANK	DESCRIPTION	YEAR	GOOD	EX
Basket Puzzle Bank	2 3/4" tall, 3 1/2" wide, unpainted	1894	300	550
Postal Savings Mailbox	6 3/4"	1920s	85	275
White City Barrel #1 on Cart	5" long, unpainted, "White City Puzzle Savings Bank, A Barrel of Money"	1894	275	475
White City Barrel, Large	5 1/8" tall, silver finish barrel	1893	175	275
White City Pail	2 5/8" tall, silver finish pail with handle	1893	125	200
White City Puzzle Safe #10	4 5/8", unpainted	1893	125	225
White City Puzzle Safe #12	4 7/8", unpainted	1893	150	325

Ober Mfg. Co.

BANK	DESCRIPTION	YEAR	GOOD	EX
Bear Stealing Pig	Ober #1011, 5 1/2" tall, painted	1913	400	950
Capitalist, The (Everett True)	5" tall, painted	1913	1000	1500

Ohio Foundry Co.

BANK	DESCRIPTION	YEAR	GOOD	EX
Four Tower	5 3/8", painted white building with red roof	1949	25	55
House with Basement	4 5/8" square, painted	1893	850	1600

Ouve, A.

BANK	DESCRIPTION	YEAR	GOOD	EX
Indian Seated on Log	3 5/8" tall, unpainted	1970s	85	150

Penncraft

BANK	DESCRIPTION	YEAR	GOOD	EX
Liberty Bell, Miniature	3 1/2" x 1 3/4"		20	35

Piaget

BANK	DESCRIPTION	YEAR	GOOD	EX
Phoenix Dime Register Trunk	3 3/4" x 5" steamer trunk	1890	125	250
Trunk on Dolly	2 5/8" x 3 9/16"	1890	175	350

Riverside Foundry

BANK	DESCRIPTION	YEAR	GOOD	EX
Capitol Bank	5 1/8"	1981	50	100

Roche, E.M. Co.

BANK	DESCRIPTION	YEAR	GOOD	EX
Time Safe	7" tall, 3 3/4" wide, unpainted		375	750

Russell, Edward K.

BANK	DESCRIPTION	YEAR	GOOD	EX
Humpty Dumpty, Seated	5 3/8" tall, painted	1974	75	125

Schneider & Trenkramp Co.

BANK	DESCRIPTION	YEAR	GOOD	EX
Reliable Parlor Stove	6 1/4"		425	750

Service Foundry

BANK	DESCRIPTION	YEAR	GOOD	EX
Bethel College Administration Building	2 7/8" x 5 1/4"	1935	175	350

Shimer Toy Co.

BANK	DESCRIPTION	YEAR	GOOD	EX
Church Window Safe	3 1/16"	1890s	50	125
Daisy	2 1/8" tall, red safe bank	1899	50	150
Dime Savings	2 1/2" safe, "Dime Savings"	1899	200	425
Electric Railroad	8 1/4"long	1893	2500	5000
Home Savings Bank	5 7/8", painted	1899	125	475
Oak Stove	2 3/8" tall, unpainted	1899	125	475
Safe Deposit	3 5/8", "Safe Deposit"	1899	85	150

Smith & Egge

BANK	DESCRIPTION	YEAR	GOOD	EX
Boston State House	6 3/4" tall, painted	1800s	3000	4500
Moody & Sankey	5" painted, 2 oval portraits on front	1870	800	1500
Nest Egg, "Horace"	3 3/8" tall on base, bronze finish egg on side	1873	450	850

Somerville, W.J.

BANK	DESCRIPTION	YEAR	GOOD	EX
Key	5 1/2" long, silver finish skeleton key	1905	250	600

Stevens, J. & E.

BANK	DESCRIPTION	YEAR	GOOD	EX
Battleship Maine	6" tall, 10 1/4" long ,white	1901	500	1500
Battleship Oregon	4 7/8" long, silver finish	1890s	200	350
Cupola Bank	3 1/4" tall, black	1870s	75	150
Cupola Bank	4 1/4" x 3 3/8" red and gray	1872	100	175
Floral Safe (National Safe)	4 5/8" x 4 1/8"	1898	125	275
Four Tower	5 3/4", unpainted with gold highlights		125	375
General Butler	6 1/2" tall, painted head on frog body	1884	1200	3500
Home Bank with Crown	5 1/4", painted, "Home Bank"	1872	475	1200
Home Savings Bank with Dog Finial	5 3/4" tall	1891	125	450
Home Savings Bank with Finial	3 1/2" tall, mustard finish	1891	125	375
Jarmulowsky Building	7 3/4"tall, bronze finish building bank		1200	2000
Jewel Safe	5 3/8", unpainted	1907	125	250
Junior Cash Register, Small	5 1/4" x 4 5/8" elaborate cast with slot at top	1920s	175	375
Kodak Bank	4 1/4" tall, 5" wide, "Kodak Bank"	1905	200	450
Man in Barrel	3 3/4" tall, painted	1890s	175	300
Metropolitan Bank	5 7/8", "Metropolitan Bank"	1872	125	275

Stevens, J. & E.

BANK	DESCRIPTION	YEAR	GOOD	EX
Multiplying Bank	6 1/2" painted building	1883	700	1750
National Safe	3 3/8" tall, unpainted	1800s	65	125
Pay Phone Bank	7 3/16", unpainted	1926	350	1500
Roof Bank	5 1/4" x 3 3/4"	1887	125	325
Shell Out	4 3/4" long, conch shell on base, off white	1882	225	650
Trust Bank	7 1/4"	1800s	875	2500
Victorian House	4 1/2", unpainted deep gray finish	1892	175	375

Unicast Foundry

BANK	DESCRIPTION	YEAR	GOOD	EX
Harleysville Bank	2 5/8" tall, 5 1/4" long, white with gray roof	1959	75	225

US Hdwre. Co.

BANK	DESCRIPTION	YEAR	GOOD	EX
Man on Cotton Bale	4 7/8" tall, painted darkie sits on hay bale, red scarf, yellow pants	1898	1400	2500

Various

BANK	DESCRIPTION	YEAR	GOOD	EX
Quadrafoil House	3 1/8" tall, made by numerous companies	1900s	125	225

Vermong Novelty Works

BANK	DESCRIPTION	YEAR	GOOD	EX
Cupola Bank	5 1/2" tall, painted building with center roof cupola	1869	300	550
Owl	4 1/4", painted	1930	75	325
Vindex Bulldog	5 1/4" tall, painted, "Vindex Toys"	1931	125	275

Watkins, Bob

BANK	DESCRIPTION	YEAR	GOOD	EX
L'il Tot	5 7/8"	1982	125	175

Williams, A.C.

BANK	DESCRIPTION	YEAR	GOOD	EX
Armoured Car	3 3/4" tall, 6 3/4" long, red car on gold wheels	1900s	600	1800
Aunt Jemima	5 7/8", also called Mammy with Spoon	1900s	125	300
Auto	5 3/4" long, black , red wheels, 4 passengers	1910?	500	1200
Baseball Player	5 3/4 inches, gold	1909	100	300
Baseball Player	5 3/4" tall, in various paint colors	1910s	200	450
Be Wise Owl	4 7/8" x 2 1/2"	1900s	150	375
Bear, Begging	5 3/8", bronze finish	1900s	75	150
Billiken	4 1/4" tall, on square base, bronze finish, red cap	1909	55	125
Billiken on Throne	6 1/2" tall	1909	65	175
Boy Scout	5 7/8" tall, brown finish	1910s	50	125
Buffalo Bank	3 1/8" x 4 3/8", gold	1900s	50	175
Buster Brown & Tige	5 1/2"	1900s	100	250
Camel, Large	7 1/4" x 6 1/4"	1900s	200	375
Campbell Kids	3 5/16" x 4 1/8"	1900s	150	350
Cat on Tub	4 1/8" tall, bronze finish	1920s	100	175
Cat with Ball	2 1/2" tall	1900s	200	375
Clown	6 1/4", gold and red with tall curved hat	1908	125	250
Colonial House with Porch, Large	4" tall, white	1900s	100	225
Colonial House with Porch, Small	3 " tall, brown finish with red, green or gold roof	1910s	75	175

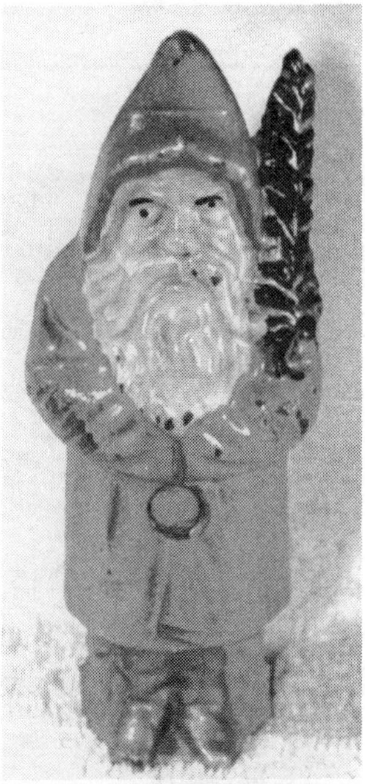

Top to Bottom: Baseball Player, 1909, A.C. Williams; Woolworth Building, 1915, Kenton; Santa with Tree, 1910s, Hubley; Guessing Bank, 1882; Fido on Pillow, 1920s, Hubley; Jewel Safe, 1907, J & E Stevens; World's Fair Administration Building, 1893.

Williams, A.C.

BANK	DESCRIPTION	YEAR	GOOD	EX
Cow	3 3/8" x 5 1/4", brown or red finish	1920	75	125
Darkey Sharecropper	5 1/2" tall, toes visible on one foot	1900s	75	350
Dog on Tub	4 1/16" x 2" diam., bronze finish	1920s	125	200
Domed Bank	3" tall	1899	20	55
Donkey, Large	6 13/16" tall, painted	1920s	150	225
Double Door	5 7/16" building with 2 doors, painted white with gold highlights	1900s	200	375
Duck Bank	4 7/8", unpainted	1900s	150	275
Elephant on Bench on Tub	3 7/8"	1920s	125	225
Elephant on Tub	5 3/8", in bronze finish	1920s	100	185
Elephant on Tub, Decorated	5 3/8", painted version of #483	1920s	125	200
Elephant on Wheels	4" tall, unpainted	1920s	150	250
Elephant with Howdah, Large	4 7/8" x 6 3/8"	1900s	65	125
Elephant with Howdah, Large	6 3/4", gold	1900s	85	150
Elephant with Howdah, Small	3 1/2" x 5"	1900s	65	125
Football Player	5 7/8" tall, bronze finish	1910s	250	425
Graf Zeppelin	6 5/8" long, silver gray finish	1920s	85	225
Graf Zeppelin on Wheels	7 3/4" long silver pulltoy bank	1934	150	425
Hanging Mailbox	5 1/8" tall, green, wall mount mailbox replica, gold lettering	1920s	45	95
Horse on Tub, Decorated	5 5/6"	1920s	135	300
Horse on Wheels	4 1/4", deep red finish	1920	150	450
Horse, Prancing, Large	7 3/16" tall, bronze finish	1910s	75	145
Horse, Rearing on Oval Base	5 1/8" x 4 7/8"	1920s	95	250
Horseshoe with Mesh	Horse head inside horseshoe that forms end of mesh coin cage , bronze finish		65	125
Lion on Tub, Decorated	5 1/2" tall	1920s	125	225
Lion on Tub, Plain	7 1/2" tall, bronze finish	1920s	100	200
Lion on Tub, small	4 1/8" tall, brown or green finish	1920s	85	175
Lion on Wheels	4 1/2" x 5 1/2", gold	1920s	145	225
Lion, Ears Up	3 5/8" x 4 1/2"	1930s	75	125
Lion, Small	2 1/2" x 3 5/8"	1934	85	150
Lion, Tail Right	3 1/2" x 4 15/16"	1920s	55	100
Lion, Tail Right	5 1/4" tall, bronze finish	1900s	55	150
Main Street Trolley with People	3" x 6 3/4" bronze finish	1920s	175	475
Main Street Trolley Without People	6 3/4" long, no people	1920s	175	400
Mosque, Large, (3 Story)	3 1/2" tall, 3 story building	1920s	45	125
Mulligan Policeman (Keystone Cop)	5 3/4", painted	1900s	175	350
Mutt & Jeff	4 1/4" x 3 1/2", gold	1900s	75	275
One Car Garage	2 1/2", painted	1920s	125	250
Penthouse Building	5 7/8" tall, silver finish	\	350	650
Pig, Seated	3" x 4 9/16"	1900s	35	85
Presto "Bank"	3 5/8" tall, silver finish with gold dome	1900s	85	175
Professor Pug Frog Bank	3 1/4"	1900s	275	550
Rabbit Standing, Large	6 1/4" tall, brown metal finish	1908	125	325
Rabbit, Begging	5 1/8"	1900s	85	275
Reindeer, Large	9 1/2" tall, bronze finish	1900s	125	250
Reindeer, Small	6 1/4" tall, bronze finish		75	135
Skyscraper Bank	5 1/2" tall, silver building bank with 4 gold posts	1900s	85	150
Skyscraper Bank	4 3/8" tall, silver building bank with 4 gold posts	1900s	85	125
Skyscraper with Six Posts	6 1/2" tall, silver building bank with gold posts	1900s	125	450

Williams, A.C.

BANK	DESCRIPTION	YEAR	GOOD	EX
Songbird on Stump	4 3/4", bronze finish	1900s	300	750
St. Bernard with Pack, Large	5 1/2" x 7 3/4"	1900s	125	225
St. Bernard with Pack, Small	3 3/4" x 5 1/2"	1900s	85	175
Steamboat	7 5/8" long, brown finish	190s	125	375
Tank Bank 1918, Small	2 3/8"long, gold finish	1920s	65	150
Tank Bank USA 1918, Large	3" tall x 3 11/16" long, gold finish	1920s	100	200
Teddy Roosevelt Bust	5" tall	1919	175	450
Three Wise Monkeys	3 1/4" tall, 3 1/2" wide	1900s	225	475
Time Is Money Clock Bank	3 1/2" tall, alarm clock shaped, gold finish, "Time Is Money"	1910s	125	200
Turkey, Large	4 1/4" x 4", painted wattle	1900s	250	475
Turkey, Small	3 3/8" tall, red head and wattle	1900s	150	275
Two Car Garage	2 1/2", painted	1920s	125	275
Two Faced Black Boy, Large	4 1/8" tall	1900s	125	350
Two Faced Black Boy, Small	3 1/8" x 2 3/4", negro toy bank, painted	1900s	85	300
Two Faced Devil	4 1/4" tall, deep red	1004	550	950
Two Story House	3 1/16" tall, brown finish with red roof	1930s	75	150
Two-Faced Indian	4 5/16" tall, bronze finish with painted highlights	1900s	1500	2750
U.S. Navy Akron Zeppelin	6 5/8" long, silver finish, "US Navy Akron"	1930	175	450
United Banking and Trust, Building Bank	3" tall, bronze finish		225	450
Washington Monument	6" tall	1900s	150	325

Wilton Products Co.

BANK	DESCRIPTION	YEAR	GOOD	EX
Covered Wagon	6 5/8" long, unpainted		10	25
Gettysburg Bank	4 3/4" x 7 1/4" gray monument with reclining soldier	1960	75	200
Republic Pig	7" tall, painted pig in business suit	1970s	35	85

Wing

BANK	DESCRIPTION	YEAR	GOOD	EX
Elephant with Tin Chariot	8" long, red chariot	1900s	1000	1600

Worley, Laverne A.

BANK	DESCRIPTION	YEAR	GOOD	EX
Toy Soldier	7 1/2" tall, painted, "SBCCA"	1982	15	65

Wright, John

BANK	DESCRIPTION	YEAR	GOOD	EX
Amish Boy	5" tall, painted	1970	10	65
Amish Boy in White Shirt	5" tall, blue coveralls, black hat	1971	10	65
Amish Girl	5" tall, painted	1970	10	65
Apollo (plain)	4 1/4", unpainted	1968	20	65
Apollo 8	4 1/4", red, white and blue	1968	20	75
Bulldog, Large	6", painted	1960s	25	65
Cat with Bow, Seated	4 3/8" x 2 7/8", painted, white body, red bow		25	50
Covered Bridge	2 1/2" tall, 6 1/8" long, white with red roof	1960s	35	75
Dry Sink	3" x 2 3/4", dark finish	1970	25	45
Elephant Trumpeting	7 1/4" tall, black finish	1971	15	35
English Setter	8 1/2" tall, black	1970	125	275
Gold Eagle	5 3/4"	1970	5	20
Lamb	3 1/4" tall, painted white with black highlights	1970	35	75
Lucky Cabin	4 1/8" tall, painted with horseshoe over door	1970	35	65
Mickey Mouse	5 x 3 3/4" bookend bank, painted	1970s	85	125
Queen Stove	3 3/4" to cook top, "Queen" on oven door	1975	25	65

Wright, John

BANK	DESCRIPTION	YEAR	GOOD	EX
Reindeer on Base	10" x 8"	1973	75	125
Spaniel, Large	10 1/2" long, painted	1960s	65	125
Treasure Chest	2 3/4" x 4", smaller version is #928	1970	60	35

Wrightsville Hdw. Co.

BANK	DESCRIPTION	YEAR	GOOD	EX
Camera Bank	4 5/16" tall, bronze finish bellows camera on tripod	1800s	2500	5000

Unknown Maker

BANK	DESCRIPTION	YEAR	GOOD	EX
$100,000 Money Bag	3 5/8" tall, silver gray finish		300	600
Alphabet Bank	3 1/2 ", octagonal.		700	1800
Amherst Buffalo	5 1/4" tall, 8" long	1930s	150	350
Art Deco Elephant	4 3/8" tall, red		100	225
Baby in Cradle	3 1/4" tall, rocking cradle	1890s	500	1200
Basset Hound	3 1/8", bronze finish		550	1100
Bean Pot	3", red cooking pot, nickel registering		150	375
Bear Seated on Log	7"		400	950
Beehive Registering Savings Bank	5 3/8" x 6 1/2"	1891	200	425
Bicentennial Bell	4" x 4" diam.	1976	25	45
Bird Bank Building	5 7/8" unpainted cupola building with bird on top, "Bank New York""		450	1250
Bismark Bank,(Pig)	3 3/8", "Bismark Bank"	1883	100	300
Bismark Pig with Rider	7 1/4" tall, 6 1/2" long, bronze finish	1880s	1000	3500
Boss Tweed	3 7/8" tall	1870s	1200	3500
Bull on Base	4" tall, unpainted		200	450
Bull with Long Horns	3 11/16" tall, painted		50	125
Bust of Man	5"		100	350
Captain Kidd	5 5/8" tall, Kidd stands by tree trunk with shovel, base reads "Captain Kidd"	1900s	275	450
Cash Register Savings Bank	5 5/8" tall, round face on 3 claw foot feet, "Cash Register Savings Bank"	1880s	350	750
Champion Heater	4 1/8" green and black, "Champion"		125	375
Chantecleer (Rooster)	4 5/8", bronze finish, painted face and comb	1911	100	350
Chipmunk with Nut	4 1/16", black		300	950
Church Towers	6 3/4"		850	1800
City Bank with Chimney	6 3/4" tall, painted	1870s	500	1200
City Bank with Crown	5 1/2" tall, painted with red "crown" on roof	1870s	500	1000
Coca Cola	3 3/8" tall, red and green with logo		600	1500
Cross	9 1/4" tall, dark finish, "God Is Love" on base		500	850
Crown Bank on Legs, Small	4 5/8", painted		600	850
Decker's Iowana, (Pig)	2 5/16", unpainted		75	200
Derby, "Pass Around the Hat"	1 5/8" tall, 3 1/8" long		100	225
Donkey	3 1/4" tall, black with red yoke			
Donkey on Base	6 9/16" tall		250	650
Dormer Bank	4 3/4" tall, painted building bank with red roof		3500	6000
Dutch Boy	8 1/4" tall, doorstop conversion		150	275
Eagle Bank Building	9 3/4" tall, painted building with gold eagle on roof		450	650
Eagle with Ball, Building	10 3/4" tall, building with eagle and ball on roof		850	1400
Elephant with Raised Slot	4 1/2"tall, gray body, gold blanket		150	350
Elephant with Swivel Trunk	2 1/2", black finish with gold swivel trunk		125	250
Elephant with Turned Trunk, Seated	4 1/4", unpainted		450	850
Elf	10" tall, painted, converted doorstop		150	450

Unknown Maker

BANK	DESCRIPTION	YEAR	GOOD	EX
Fort	4 1/8", unpainted bronze finish "Fort"	1910s	125	275
Fort Mt. Hope	2 7/8" tall		85	385
Frowning Face	5 5/8" tall, hanging bank, chin drops below surface level		850	1400
Gas Pump	5 3/4" tall, red		275	550
Globe on Hand	4", bronze finish	1893	375	1275
Grandpa's Hat	2 1/4" tall, 3 7/8" wide, top hat		225	450
Hanging Mailbox on Platform	7 1/4" tall, red box hangs on post in platform base	1800s	650	1500
Hen on Nest	3", bronze finish with red highlights	1900s	100	1750
Hippo	2"tall, 5 3/16" long, bronze with red highlights		3500	6000
Home Savings	10 1/2" painted, "Property of Peoples Savings Bank, Grand Rapids, Mich."		175	450
Home Savings Bank	9 5/8" tall, painted		175	450
Honey Bear	2 1/2", silver finish unpainted bear sits eating honey		675	1200
Horse, Prancing with Belly Band	4 1/2", light bronze finish		175	375
Horse, Rearing on Pebbled Base	7 1/4" x 6 1/2", gold finish		85	165
House with Bay Window	5 5/8" tall, painted	1874	900	1800
House with Chimney Slot	2 7/8" x 2 13/16", painted		275	475
House with Knight	7 1/4" unpainted "Savings Bank" with knight figure on roof peak		375	850
Humphrey-Muskie Donkey	4 1/2" tall, pale silver finish, "Humphrey Muskie 68"	1968	10	35
Humpty Dumpty	5 1/2" tall, painted, white egg, red brick wall	1930s	375	850
Independence Hall	8 1/8" tall, 15 1/2" long, mustard building on base with bell tower	1875		
Indian Chief Bust	4 7/8", unpainted	1978	35	85
Indiana Paddle Wheeler	7 1/8" long, black with red trim	1896	4000	8000
International Eagle on Globe	8" x 8", unpainted		1200	2500
John Brown Fort	3" tall, red with white cupola		85	135
Key, St. Louis World's Fair	5 3/4" long, dark finish	1904	275	700
Klondyke	3 1/4" cube		650	1200
Labrador Retriever	4 1/2" black finish with gold collar		125	375
Lamb, Small	3 3/16", painted white		200	375
Lighthouse	10 1/4" tall, red tower rises from unpainted base	1891	1200	2800
Lincoln High Hat ("Pass Around the Hat")	2 3/8" tall, black finish	1880s	125	200
Lion, Tail Between Legs	3" x 5 1/4"		85	145
Mammy	8 1/4" tall, doorstop conversion, red dress, white apron	1970s	10	25
Marietta Silo	5 1/2" gray finish		275	500
Marshall Stove	3 7/8", red		125	225
Mary & Little Lamb	4 3/8" tall, painted white with red trim	1901	350	850
McKinley/Teddy Elephant	2 1/2" tall, bronze finish	1900	350	650
Mickey Mouse, Hands on Hips	9" tall, painted		125	450
Middy with Clapper	5 1/4" brown finish	1887	150	275
Mosque, Small, (2 Story)	2 7/8" tall, 2 story building		35	115
Newfoundland Dog with Pack	4 11/16" tall		85	175
Nixe	4 1/2" tall, silver boy in boat, "Nixe"		350	1250
Nixon/Agnew Elephant	2 5/8"	1968	15	35
Old Abe with Shield, Eagle	3 7/8", unpainted	1880	375	975
Old South Church	10" tall, bronze finish		2000	4500
Oriental Camel	3 3/4" tall, on rockers		85	325
Osborn Pig	2" x 4", "You can bank on the Osborn..."		100	350
Oscar the Goat	7 3/4" tall, black with silver hooves and horns		75	175

Unknown Maker

BANK	DESCRIPTION	YEAR	GOOD	EX
Owl on Stump	3 5/8", red		65	125
Park Bank Building	4 3/8" painted building, "Park Bank"		450	1450
Parlor Stove	6 7/8", gray and black		275	425
Parrot on Stump	6 1/4", painted		125	450
Pearl Street Bank	4 1/4", unpainted, silver finish, "Pearl Street Bank"		350	750
Peg Legged Pirate	5 1/4", unpainted		25	85
Pig, A Christmas Roast	3 1/4" x 7 1/8"		85	250
Plymouth Rock 1620	3 7/8" long, "1620"		650	1800
Polish Rooster	5 1/2"		850	2200
Polish Rooster	5 1/2" tall, painted		850	2200
Pooh Bank	5" x 4 7/8"		5	15
Presto Bank	4 1/4" tall building, silver with gold dome		85	175
Presto Bank	3 1/4" tall, silver finish, "Bank"		65	150
Put Money in Thy Purse	2 3/4" tall change purse, black, "Put Money in Thy Purse"	1886	625	950
Puzzle Try Me	2 11/16" tall, safe, "Puzzle Try Me"	1868	475	975
Quilted Lion	3 3/4" tall, 4 3/4" long, bronze finish		185	425
Rabbit Lying Down	2 1/8" x 5 1/8", unpainted		175	575
Reclining Cow	2 1/8" tall, 4" long, black		100	400
Recording Bank	6 5/8" x 4 1/4"		125	450
Red Ball Safe	3", red ball on base		175	425
Red Goose Shoes on Pedestal	4 7/16" red goose on bronze base		175	350
Rhesus Monkey	8 1/2" converted doorstop, painted		35	125
Rochester Clock	5" tall with working clock		225	650
Rooster, Large	6 3/4", unpainted except for red comb and wattle	1913	550	1250
Rumplestiltskin	6 x 2 1/4"	1910s	200	450
Safety Locomotive	3 1/4" tall, gray	1887	1250	2200
San Gabriel Mission	4 5/8" x 3 3/4", painted, musical building		2000	7500
Scrollwork Safe	2 3/4" tall	1900s	85	225
Security Safe	4 1/2" tall, red door	1894	125	275
Security Safe Deposit	3 7/8" tall	1881	95	150
Six Sided Building, Two Story	3 3/8" tall		100	275
Six-Sided Building	2 3/8" tall, unpainted		225	575
Space Heater with Flowers	English, 6 1/2" tall, oriental motif, red finish	1890s	175	375
Squirrel with Nut	4 1/8"		425	1250
Sunbonnet Sue	7 1/2", painted	1970	65	165
Tank Bank 1919	3" x 5 1/2", silver finish, "1919"		125	225
Trick Buffalo	5 1/2" tall, black		750	1500
Tug Boat	5 1/2" long, red, pulltoy		4500	7500
Turtle Bank	1" tall, 3 7/16" long		2000	3500
U.S. Bank, Eagle Finial	9 1/4" tall, green with gold trim	1890s	850	1400
Ulysses S. Grant Bust	5 1/2" tall	1976	125	250
Victorian House	3 1/4" tall, gray metallic finish		150	275
Watch Dog Safe	5 1/8", with brass handle, dog stands guard on front		1850	4000
Water Spaniel with Pack (I Hear A Call)	5 3/8" x 7 7/8"	1900	225	450
Weaver Hen	6", white with red comb and wattle, "Weaver"	1970s	20	50
Westside Presbyterian Church	3 3/4" x 3 5/8", silver finish	1916	350	750
Whippet on Base	3 1/2" tall, gold finish		75	125
Wisconsin Beggar Boy	6 7/8" tall, "Help the Crippled Children of Wisconsin"		525	900
Wisconsin War Eagle	2 7/8"	1880	675	1500
Work Horse on Base	9" tall, painted white		75	125
World's Fair Adminstration Building	6" x 6", painted	1893	1400	2250

ERTL BANKS

NO.	BANK	MODEL	YEAR	MIB
9452UA	A&W Root Beer #1	1917 Model T Van, White Body, White Trim	1991	35
9827UP	A&W Root Beer #2	1905 Ford Delivery Van, White	1991	35
1323	A.J. Seibert Co.	1913 Model T Van, White Body, Red Trim	1987	125
	Abington, MD. Fire Department	1926 Seagrave Pumper White Body, Red Trim	1991	30
9746	AC Rochester #1 United Auto Workers	1950 Chevy Panel, Red Body, Black Trim	1989	110
7551	AC Rochester #2 United Auto Workers	Step Van	1991	25
9019	ACE Hardware	1918 Runabout, Red Body, Black Trim	1989	75
9038	ACE Hardware #1	1918 Runabout, Red/White Body, Black Trim	1989	25
7697EO	ACE Hardware #2	1926 Mack W/Crates, Red Body, Black/ Brown Trim	1990	30
9459	ACE Hardware #3 Marked "3rd Edition"	1932 Ford Panel, Red Body, White Trim	1989	20
9690	ACE Hardware #4	1918 Runabout	1991	25
9643	Achenbach's Pastry Shop	Step Van, White Body, White Trim	1989	30
	Adamstown, MD. Carroll Manor VFD Co. 14	1926 Seagrave Pumper, White Body, Green Trim	1991	30
9444	Agway #1	1913 Model T Van, White Body, Red Trim	1986	215
9195	Agway #2	1918 Runabout, Black Body, Black Trim	1987	30
9743	Agway #3	1905 Ford Delivery Van, Black Body, Black Trim	1988	30
9687	Agway #4 Ltd. Ed	1932 Ford Panel, Black Body, Silver Trim	1989	25
7514	Agway #5 Ltd. Ed W/Spare	1917 Model T Van, Blue Body, Blue Trim	1990	25
9375	Agway #6 Ltd. Ed	1923 Chevy Truck, White Body, Gold Trim	1991	20
9705EO	Agway #7	1918 Barrel Runabout, Gray Body, Black Trim	1991	20
9218	Alberta	1913 Model T Van 1 Of 10 Canadian Provinces, White Body, Brown Trim	1985	30
9201	Alex Cooper Auctioneers	1913 Model T Van, White Body, Red Trim	1984	55
9155	Alka-Seltzer #1	1918 Runabout, Blue Body, Beige/Blue Trim	1987	135
9791	Alka-Seltzer #2	1917 Model T Van, White Body, Blue Trim	1988	35
9737	Alka-Seltzer #3	1932 Ford Panel, Light Blue Body, Dark Blue Trim	1991	25
9892	Allen Organ	1931 Hawkeye Truck, White Body, Black Trim	1991	30
9460	Allerton, Illinois Centennial	1913 Model T Van, White Body, Red Trim	1986	30
1369	Allied Van Lines #1	1913 Model T Van, Orange Body, Black Trim	1983	75
2136	Allied Van Lines #2	Horse & Carriage, Orange Body, Black Trim	1984	60
2119	Allied Van Lines #3	1917 Model T Van, Orange Body, Black Trim	1985	60
9776	Allied Van Lines #4	1937 Ford Tractor/Trailer, Orange Body, Black Trim	1988	60
7517UO	Allied Van Lines #5	1947 IH Tractor/Trailer, Orange Body, Trim	1990	30
9723	Allied Van Lines #6	1923 Chevy Truck, Black Body, Gold Trim	1991	30
1201	Allis-Chalmers "A-C"	1926 Mack Truck, Tan Body, Black Trim	1984	35
2226EO	Allis-Chalmers "A-C"	1918 Runabout, Orange Body, Black Trim	1989	25
9735UP	Alzheimer's Association	1918 Barrel Runabout, White Body, Purple Trim	1991	25
9680	Alzheimer's Association Ltd. Ed	1913 Model T Van, White Body, Purple Trim	1989	55
9594UO	Alzheimer's Association #2 Ltd. Ed	1905 Ford Delivery Van, White Body, Purple Trim	1990	30
9672EO	American Quincentennial	1913 Model T Van, White Body, Red/Blue Trim	1991	30
9294	American Red Cross #1	1913 Model T Van, Black Body, White Trim	1987	35
9294	American Red Cross #2	1913 Model T Van, Black Body, White Trim	1988	40
9294	American Red Cross #3 W/ Spare Tire	1913 Model T Van, White Body, Red Trim	1989	45
9294	American Red Cross #4 Gold Spokes L.E.	1913 Model T Van, White Body, Red Trim	1989	25

Ertl Banks

NO.	BANK	MODEL	YEAR	MIB
9685	American Red Cross #5 Ltd. Ed.	1905 Ford Delivery Van, Black Body, Trim	1989	30
2984UO	American Red Cross #6 Ltd. Ed.	1950 Chevy Panel, Red Body, Black Trim	1990	40
7616	American Red Cross #7 Ltd. Ed.	1926 Mack W/Crates, Red Body, Brown Trim	1990	35
9529	American Red Cross #8	1913 Model T Van, White Body, Red Trim	1991	30
1340	American Toy Trucker	1913 Model T Van	1991	25
9150	Amoco	1913 Model T Van, White Body, Red Trim	1987	150
1333	Amoco	1905 Ford Delivery Van, White Body, Red Trim	1988	70
9777	Amoco "Customer First"	1923 Chevy Truck	1991	25
9373	Amoco #1	1926 Mack Tanker, Silver Body, Red Trim	1986	150
9173	Amoco #2	1926 Mack Tanker, White Body, Red Trim	1987	330
9447	Amoco #3	1926 Mack Tanker, Silver Body, Black Trim	1987	125
9151	Amoco (Certicare)	1913 Model T Van, White Body, Red Trim	1987	45
7668UA	Amoco (Certicare)	1932 Ford Panel, White Body, Black Trim	1990	45
9496	Amoco - Atlas Auto Products	1905 Ford Delivery Van, White Body, Red Trim	1988	40
9563UA	Amoco-Red Crown Gas-Stand. Oil Ltd. Ed.	Horse Team & Tanker, Black Body, Red Trim	1990	25
9660	Amoco 100th Anniversary Ltd. Ed.	1918 Runabout, White Body, Black/Blue Trim	1989	40
9745	Amoco 100th Anniversary Ltd. Ed.	1917 Model T Van, White Body, Blue Trim	1989	30
9288	Amoco Food Shop	1918 Barrel Runabout, White Body, Black/Tan Trim	1991	20
9673	Amoco Stanolind #1 Polarine Oil & Grease	1917 Model T Van, Orange Body And Trim	1989	155
9060	Amoco Stanolind #2 Polarine Ltd. Ed.	1926 Mack Tanker, Orange Body, Black Trim	1989	160
9383	Amoco Stanolind #3 Polarine Lubricants	1926 Mack Tanker, Orange Body, Black Trim	1989	125
7657UA	Amoco Stanolind #4 Ltd. Ed.	1932 Ford Panel, Dark Green Body, Black Trim	1990	155
7658	Amoco Stanolind #5 Polarine Ltd. Ed.	1931 Hawkeye W/Crates, Green Body, Black Trim	1991	125
7659UA	Amoco Stanolind #6 Polarine	Horse Team & Tanker, Green Body, Red Trim	1991	50
9287	Amoco Stanolind #8 Polarine	1918 Barrel Runabout, Green Body, Black Trim	1991	60
1320UA	Amoco-Red Crown Gasoline-Standard Oil	1923 Chevy Truck, Green Body, Black Trim	1991	25
9454	Amsouth	1913 Model T Van, White Body, Blue Trim	1986	40
9358	Amstel Light Beer	1931 Hawkeye Truck, Red Body, White/Black Trim	1991	25
1322UA	Andrews Toy Shop Ltd. Ed.	1913 Model T Van, White Body, Blue Trim	1990	25
9498EO	Anheuser Busch #4	1932 Ford Panel, Red Body, Black Trim	1991	20
9047	Anheuser-Busch #2	1926 Mack W/Crates, Red Body, Black Trim	1989	20
7574EO	Anheuser-Busch #3	1931 Hawkeye Truck, Red Body, Black Trim	1990	20
9766	Anheuser-Busch (Chrome) 1st Issue	1918 Barrel Runabout, Red Body, Black Trim	1988	90
9766	Anheuser-Busch (Chrome) 2nd Re-Issue	1918 Barrel Runabout, Red Body, Black Trim	1990	30
9264	Anthracite Battery	1905 Ford Delivery Van, White Body, Red Trim	1987	45
9282UO	Antique Power Magazine	1923 Chevy Truck, Red Body, Black Trim	1991	30
9367	Arkansas 150th Anniversary	1913 Model T Van, White Body, Red Trim	1986	504
9353	Arkansas Razorbacks	1913 Model T Van, White Body, Red Trim	1985	40
9938UO	Arm & Hammer	1932 Ford Panel, Yellow Body, Red Trim	1989	40

Ertl Banks

NO.	BANK	MODEL	YEAR	MIB
9229UO	Arm & Hammer-Church & Dwight Co. Inc.	1931 Hawkeye W/Crates, Yellow Body, Red Trim	1991	25
7553UO	Arm & Hammer W/Spare	1932 Ford Panel, Yellow Body, Red Trim	1990	70
9486	Arm And Hammer	1913 Model T Van, Yellow Body, Red Trim	1987	75
9828	Arm And Hammer	1905 Ford Delivery Van, Yellow Body, Red Trim	1988	45
9828	Arm And Hammer (Decal)	1905 Ford Delivery Van, Yellow Body, Red Trim	1989	30
9738UP	Armor-All	1905 Ford Delivery Van, White Body, Black Trim	1991	40
9891	Armour Food	1913 Model T Van, White Body, Red Trim	1988	60
9975	Armstrong/Pirelli Tire Co.	1913 Model T Van	1991	35
9270	Arrow Distributing #1 Ltd. Ed.	1932 Ford Panel, White Body, Blue Trim	1987	80
9725	Arrow Distributing #2	1950 Chevy Panel, Silver Body And Trim	1988	65
9328	Arrow Distributing #3	1918 Runabout, Blue Body, White Trim	1989	30
7542UO	Arrow Distributing #4	1905 Ford Delivery Van, White Body, Red Trim	1990	30
9609	Arrow Distributing #5	1923 Chevy Truck	1991	30
7550UO	Artworks (Donneckers)	1905 Ford Delivery Van, White Body, Red Trim	1990	30
9118UP	Asheville Office Supply-1st In Series	1931 Hawkeye Truck, White Body, Black Trim	1991	25
9212	Associated Grocers Of Colorado	1913 Model T Van, White Body, Trim	1984	35
1248	Atlanta Falcons	1913 Model T Van, Silver Body, Red Trim	1984	40
9666	Atlantic Refining And Marketing	1930 Diamond T Tanker, Blue Body, White Trim	1991	25
9514	Atlas Van Lines #1	1926 Mack Truck, White Body, Blue Trim	1987	95
9771	Atlas Van Lines #2 Ltd. Ed.	1932 Ford Panel, White Body, Red Trim	1988	35
9577	Atlas Van Lines #3 W/ Spare Ltd. Ed.	1913 Model T Van, White Body, Blue Trim	1989	35
7612UA	Atlas Van Lines #4 Ltd. Ed.	1937 Ford Tractor/Trailer, White Body, Blue Trim	1990	35
9428	Baby Boy Congratulations	1905 Ford Delivery Van, Pink Body, Blue Trim	1991	15
9427	Baby Girl Congratulations	1905 Ford Delivery Van, Pink Body, Blue Trim	1991	15
9210UP	Baker Oil Tools	1926 Mack Truck, Yellow Body, Blue Trim	1990	35
9262UO	Baltimore Fire Dept. #1	1926 Seagrave Pumper, Red Body And Trim	1991	45
9153	Baltimore Gas And Electric	1932 Ford Panel, Black Body, Light Brown Trim	1987	130
9870	Baltimore Gas And Electric #2	1918 Runabout, Black Body, Trim	1988	30
9752	Baltimore Gas And Electric #3	1950 Chevy Panel, Gold Body, Black Trim	1989	35
2102UO	Baltimore Gas And Electric #4	Step Van, Beige Body, Blue Trim	1990	30
9651UA	Baltimore, MD Fire Dept. #2	1926 Seagrave Pumper, Red Body, White Trim	1991	30
9630	Barnsdall #1 Sample	1930 Diamond T Tanker	1991	75
9826	Barq's Root Beer #1	1913 Model T Van, Met. Silver Body And Trim	1988	45
9072	Barq's Root Beer #2	1932 Ford Panel W/Spare Tire, Met. Silver Body And Trim	1989	35
9054UO	Barq's Root Beer #3	1918 Barrel Runabout, Silver Body, Black Trim	1990	35
9361UP	Barrett Jackson Car Auction	1950 Chevy Panel, Black Body, White Trim	1990	40
9271	Barrick's Farm Sales	1913 Model T Van, White Body, Red Trim	1987	25
9007	Basehor, Kansas	1905 Ford Delivery Van, White Body, Red Trim	1989	25

Ertl Banks

NO.	BANK	MODEL	YEAR	MIB
9311	Beckman High School #1	1905 Ford Delivery Van, Green Body, Gold Trim	1989	30
1656UO	Beckman High School #2	1913 Model T Van, Green Body, Yellow Trim	1990	25
9801	Bell System	Horse & Carriage, Dark Brown Body, Light Brown Trim	1988	30
9803	Bell System	1932 Ford Panel, Black Body And Trim	1988	35
2141	Bell Telephone #1	Horse & Carriage, Dark Blue Body, Black Trim	1984	75
9203	Bell Telephone #1	1950 Chevy Panel, Olive Body And Trim	1984	55
9298	Bell Telephone #1	1918 Runabout W/O Ladder, Olive Body, Black Trim	1987	35
9203	Bell Telephone #2	1950 Chevy Panel, Olive Body And Trim	1985	40
9800	Bell Telephone #2	1918 Runabout W/Ladder, Dark Green Body, Black Trim	1988	35
9203	Bell Telephone #3	1950 Chevy Panel Wide Tires, Black Body, Gold/Black Trim	1991	35
7610IU	Bell Telephone AT&T	1905 Ford Delivery Van, Black Body And Trim	1990	25
7609UO	Bell Telephone Canada	1905 Ford Delivery Van, Black Body And Trim	1990	30
2142	Bell Telephone Yellow Pages	1926 Mack Truck, Yellow Body, Black Trim	1984	55
9695	Bell Telephone 70th Anniversary	1913 Model T Van, Grey Body, Black Trim	1981	95
1327	Bell Telephone Of Canada	1913 Model T Van, Black Body And Trim	1981	30
2117	Bell Telephone Pioneers Of America	1913 Model T Van, Black Body And Trim	1985	25
9802	Bell Telephone Of America	1937 Ford Tractor/Trailer, White Body, Blue Trim	1988	40
9646	Bell Telephone System	1913 Model T Van, Black Body And Trim	1981	40
1319	Ben Franklin	1918 Runabout, Grey Body, Red Trim	1989	25
9688	Ben Franklin	1905 Ford Delivery Van, Grey Body, Red Trim	1989	25
9157	Ben Franklin Ltd. Ed.	1932 Ford Panel, Grey Body, Red Trim	1991	20
9386	Big "A"	1923 Chevy Truck	1991	20
1366UA	Big "A" Wagner Brake	1918 Runabout, Black Body, Red Trim	1990	25
9482	Big "A" Auto Parts	1905 Ford Delivery Van, White Body, Red Trim	1987	50
9094	Big "A" Auto Parts	1926 Mack Truck, Black Body, Red Trim	1989	25
9772	Big "A" Auto Parts Ltd. Ed.	1917 Model T Van, Black Body And Trim	1988	30
1324UA	Big "A" Auto Parts Ltd. Ed.	1918 Runabout, White Body, Black Trim	1991	25
9981	Big Bear Family Center	1918 Runabout, White/Black Body, Brown Trim	1988	25
9006	Big Bear Family Center	1905 Ford Delivery Van, White Body, Red Trim	1989	30
9760	Biglerville Hose Co.	1913 Model T Van, White Body, Red Trim	1988	30
9626	Binkley-Hurst Bros. 50th Anniversary	1913 Model T Van, White Body, Red Trim	1989	30
9500	BJR Auto Radiator Service	1913 Model T Van, Silver Body, Blue Trim	1986	70
9059	BJR Auto Radiator Service	1932 Ford Panel, Black Body, Silver Trim	1989	75
7614UO	BJR Auto Radiator Service	1950 Chevy Panel, Red Body, Black Trim	1990	55
1339UO	Blank Bank	1913 Model T Van, White Body, Red Trim		15
1340UA	Blank Bank	1913 Model T Van, White Body, Blue Trim		15
1341UO	Blank Bank	1917 Model T Van, White Body, Blue Trim		15
2127UO	Blank Bank	1926 Mack Truck, Black Body, White Trim		15
2132UO	Blank Bank	1932 Ford Panel, White Body, Red Trim		15
9061UO	Blank Bank	1937 Ford Tractor/Trailer, Dark Blue Body, Silver Trim		15
9066UO	Blank Bank	1937 Ford Tanker Trailer, Red Body, White Trim		15
9099UO	Blank Bank	1918 Runabout, Green Body, White Trim		15

Ertl Banks

NO.	BANK	MODEL	YEAR	MIB
9113UO	Blank Bank	1905 Ford Delivery Van, White Body, Dark Blue Trim		15
9231UA	Blank Bank	1913 Model T Van, White Body, Black Trim		15
9274UO	Blank Bank	1913 Model T Van, Yellow Body, Blue Trim		15
9295UO	Blank Bank	1932 Ford Panel, White Body, Blue Trim		15
9297UO	Blank Bank	1917 Model T Van, White Body, Trim		15
9319UO	Blank Bank	1913 Model T Van, White Body, Green Trim		15
9320UO	Blank Bank	Step Van, White Body, Trim		15
9380UO	Blank Bank	1918 Runabout, White Body, Black Trim		15
9425UO	Blank Bank	1926 Mack Tanker, Red Body, White Trim		15
9480UO	Blank Bank	1937 Ford Tractor/Trailer, White Body, Trim		15
9611UO	Blank Bank	1926 Mack Truck, Red Body, White Trim		15
9650UO	Blank Bank	1918 Barrel Runabout, Green/Black Body, White Trim		15
9735UO	BLank Bank	1905 Ford Delivery Van, Yellow Body, Red Trim		15
9820UO	Blank Bank	1905 Ford Delivery Van, Orange Body, White Trim		15
9829UO	Blank Bank	1918 Runabout, Dark Blue Body, White Trim		15
9831UO	Blank Bank	1918 Runabout, Red Body, Trim		15
9832UO	Blank Bank	1918 Runabout, Brown Body, White Trim		15
9836UA	Blank Bank	1913 Model T Van, White Body, Brown Trim		15
9838UA	Blank Bank	1913 Model T Van, White Body, Red Trim		15
9839UO	Blank Bank	1913 Model T Van, Red Body, Black Trim		15
9860UO	Blank Bank	1905 Ford Delivery Van, Dark Blue Body		15
9837UA	Blank Bank W/Gold Spokes	1905 Ford Delivery Van, White Body, Red Trim		15
9400UO	Blank Bank W/Red Spokes	1905 Ford Delivery Van, White Body, Red Trim		15
9029	Blue Ball National Bank	1913 Model T Van, White Body, Dark Blue Trim	1991	50
9257	Bookmobile (Coos Bay)	1913 Model T Van, White Body, Red Trim	1985	40
9716	Boone Co. Fair	1905 Ford Delivery Van, White Body, Blue Trim	1988	35
9372	Boone County Fair	1918 Runabout	1991	35
9346	Borg Warner #1 Ltd. Ed.	1913 Model T Van, White Body, Red Trim	1985	70
9390	Borg Warner #2 Ltd. Ed.	1913 Model T Van, White Body, Red Trim	1986	50
9029	Bost Bakery	1917 Model T Van, White Body, Trim	1988	30
9235	Bost Bakery #1 (Gold Spokes)	1913 Model T Van, White Body, Red Trim	1985	200
9235	Bost Bakery #1 (Red Spokes) Ltd. Ed.	1913 Model T Van, White Body, Red Trim	1985	35
9437	Bost Bakery #2	1913 Model T Van, White Body, Red Trim	1986	40
9170	Bost Bakery Ltd. Ed.	1926 Mack Tanker, White Body, Red Trim	1987	30
9143	Boumi Temple Circus #1	1926 Mack Truck	1991	40
9986	Boumi Temple Circus #2 Ltd. Ed.	1931 Hawkeye Truck, Red Body, Yellow Trim	1991	35
9823	Brendle's (Gold Spokes)	1917 Model T Van, White Body, Blue Trim	1988	35
9823	Brendle's (Red Spokes)	1917 Model T Van, White Body, Blue Trim	1988	115
9028	Breyer's Ice Cream	1905 Ford Delivery Van, Black Body, Trim	1988	70
9986	Briggs & Stratton	1918 Runabout, White Body, Black Trim	1988	135
9509	Briggs & Stratton	1937 Ford Tractor/Trailer, White Body, Trim	1989	35
9221	British Columbia (1 Of 10 Canadian Prov)	1913 Model T Van, White Body, Pink Trim	1985	30
9880	Broadlands Centennial	1905 Ford Delivery Van, White Body, Blue Trim	1988	25
9441	Brownberry Bakeries	1913 Model T Van, White Body, Trim	1986	55
9287	Buckeye, Arizona	1905 Ford Delivery Van, White Body, Blue Trim	1987	55
1315	Budweiser	1913 Model T Van, White Body, Red Trim	1983	150
9877	Bumper To Bumper	1950 Chevy Panel, White Body	1991	35

Ertl Banks

NO.	BANK	MODEL	YEAR	MIB
1357	Bush's Pork & Beans	1905 Ford Delivery Van, White Body, Red Trim	1990	30
9333	Bussmann Fuses 75th Anniversary	1918 Runabout, White Body, Black Trim	1989	65
9699UO	C.R.'s Friendly Market	1917 Model T Van, White Body, Orange Trim	1989	30
9888UP	California Department Of Forestry	1926 Seagrave Pumper, Red Body	1991	30
9394	Campbell's Pork & Beans	1905 Ford Delivery Van, Red Body, Black Trim	1986	70
9184	Campbell's Pork & Beans	1918 Runabout, White Body, Red Trim	1987	70
9226	Canada	1913 Model T Van, White Body, Red Trim	1985	25
2133	Canada Dry Ginger Ale	1913 Model T Van, Green Body, Trim	1985	125
7680UO	Canada Dry Ginger Ale	1918 Barrel Runabout, Green/White Body, Black Trim	1990	35
2139	Cardinal Foods	1913 Model T Van, White Body, Red Trim	1984	90
2106	Carl Buddig Meats	1913 Model T Van, Red Body, Trim	1984	75
9089	Carl's Chicken Barbeque	Step Van, White Body, Trim	1989	25
9314UA	Carlisle - "The Flea Marketeers"	1931 Hawkeye W/Crates, Red Body, Black Trim	1991	30
9315UP	Carlisle - Antiques At Carlisle	1905 Ford Delivery Van, Blue Body, Yellow Trim	1991	30
9340UP	Carlisle - Spring 1991 Coll. Car Events	1926 Mack Tanker, Red Body, White Trim	1991	35
9875	Carlisle Fall '91	1931 Hawkeye W/Crates, Red Body, Black Trim	1991	30
9470	Carlisle Good Guy's East Coast Nat'l	1932 Ford Panel, Yellow Body	1991	30
9682	Carlisle H.S. Thundering Herd	1913 Model T Van, White Body, Green Trim	1989	25
9937UA	Carlisle H.S. Thundering Herd	1918 Runabout, Green Body	1989	25
2140UP	Carlisle H.S. Thundering Herd	1937 Ford Tractor/Trailer, White Body, Trim	1990	35
7570UO	Carlisle Productions - Fall Carlisle	1950 Chevy Panel, Red Body	1990	70
9662UP	Carlisle, PA. Union Fire Co.	1926 Seagrave Pumper	1991	30
9178	Carnation	1913 Model T Van, White Body, Red Trim	1987	40
9179	Carnation	1926 Mack Tanker, White Body, Red Trim	1987	50
9281	Carretta Trucking	1931 Hawkeye Trucker	1991	25
9464	Castrol #1 - Blk Tire/Wht Spokes	1926 Mack Tanker, White Body, Green Trim	1986	130
9464UP	Castrol #2 - Wht Tire/Grn Spokes L.E.	1926 Mack Tanker, White Body, Green Trim	1987	50
9701	Castrol GTX	1913 Model T Van	1991	25
9463	Castrol Motor Oil #1 -Blk Tire/Wht Spokes	1913 Model T Van, White Body, Green Trim	1986	50
9463	Castrol Oil #2 - Wht Tire/ Gld Spokes L.E.	1913 Model T Van, White Body, Green Trim	1987	45
9271UP	Cedarburg WI. F.D. 125th Anniversary	1926 Seagrave Pumper, Red Body	1991	35
9317	Celotex	1926 Mack Truck, Red Body, Black Trim	1987	550
9475	Celotex	1913 Model T Van, White Body, Red Trim	1987	90
9196	Central Hawkeye Gas Engine	1905 Ford Delivery Van, White Body, Red Trim	1987	30
9762UP	Chambersburg PA Junior Hose & Truck Co.	1926 Seagrave Pumper, Yellow Body	1991	95
9068UO	Champion Spark Plug	1918 Runabout, White Body, Black Trim	1990	35
9031	Charter Oak Centennial	1918 Runabout, White Body, Black Trim	1989	20
7548UP	Check The Oil - IPCA #1	1937 Ford Tanker Trailer, White Body, Red Trim	1991	55

Top to Bottom: All Ertl Banks; Model #9434 Lion Coffee 125th Anniversary; #9056 Daily Press; #9575 Sun-maid Raisins; #9001 Publix Dari-Fresh; #9311 Beckman High School #1; #9013 Winn-Dixie #11; #9633 Frito-Lay; #9064 Ertl Collector's Club; #9746 AC Rochester #1; The set of ten Canadian Provinces Banks, 1985, plus Canada Bank, in center, 1985.

Ertl Banks

NO.	BANK	MODEL	YEAR	MIB
9111UO	Check The Oil - IPCA #2	1930 Diamond T Tanker, Yellow Body, Black Trim	1991	30
9023UO	Chee-Tos Cheese Snacks	Step Van, Blue Body, White/Red Trim		25
1662UP	Chemical Bank	1905 Ford Delivery Van, White Body, Blue Trim	1990	30
9252	Cherry Mash- Chase Candy Co.	1905 Ford Delivery Van, Red Body, Gold Trim	1991	35
9873	Chevrolet #1 Heartbeat Of America	1950 Chevy Panel, White Body, Black Trim	1989	55
9561UO	Chevrolet #1 Today's Truck	1950 Chevy Panel, Black Body, Trim	1989	35
9561UP	Chevrolet #2 Today's Truck	1950 Chevy Panel, White Body, Black Trim	1990	25
9561	Chevrolet #3 Today's Truck Wide Tires	1950 Chevy Panel, Black Body, Trim	1991	25
9873UP	Chevrolet #2 Today's Truck	1950 Chevy Panel, White Body, Black Trim	1990	25
9317UP	OK Chevrolet	1923 Chevy Truck, Blue Body, 5 Color Trim	1991	25
9317 UO	Super Service, AR-JAY #9111	1923 Chevy Truck, Blue Body, Yellow Trim	1991	25
9799UO	AR-JAY Sales Co.	1923 Chevy Truck, Burgundy Body, Silver Trim	1991	25
9931	Chevrolet Barrel 1/43 Dime Bank	1930 Chevy Stake Truck, Blue Body, Graphic Trim	1990	10
9048	Chevrolet Heartbeat Of America	1950 Chevy Tractor Trailer, White On White	1989	25
9408	Chevrolet Today's Truck	1950 Chevy Panel, Wide Tires, Red On Red	1991	25
9761	Chevrolet Today's Truck	1950 Chevy Panel, Wide Tires, Blue On Blue	1991	25
9471	Chevrolet 1/43 Dime Bank	1930 Chevy Delivery Van, Blue Body, Yellow Trim	1991	10
9823UP	Chevrolet Fire Department	1926 Seagrave Pumper, Red Body, Gold Trim	1991	20
9111	Chevrolet Super Service	1923 Chevy Truck, Black Body, Blue And Yellow Trim	1991	25
9245UA	Chevrolet Vintage Chevy Club	1923 Chevy Truck, Cream Body, Green Trim	1991	25
7653UP	Chevron Supreme Gasoline	1937 Ford Tanker Trailer, Red Body, Grey Trim	1991	35
7545	Chicago Cubs	1926 Mack Truck, White Body, Blue Trim	1990	30
9386	Chicago Tribune	Step Van, White On White	1987	105
9102	Chicago Tribune	1917 Model T Van, Black On Black	1988	65
9017	Chicago Tribune	Horse & Carriage, Black On Black	1989	50
2150	Chicago Tribune	1917 Model T Van, Spare Tire, Black On Black	1989	40
9882	Chipco	1905 Ford Delivery Van, Black Body, Green Trim	1988	35
9662	Chiquita Bananas	1913 Model T Van, Yellow Body, Blue Trim	1989	65
9290	Christmas 1991	1918 Runabout, Green Body, Red Trim	1991	15
9584	Christmas-Happy Holidays 1989	1913 Model T Van, White Body, Red Trim	1989	35
7575DO	Christmas-Happy Holidays 1990	1905 Ford Delivery Van, Red Body, Green Trim	1990	20
9825	Chrome King-American Bumper	1913 Model T Van, Silver On Silver	1988	30
9474OU	Churchill Truck Lines	1926 Mack Truck, Black Tires, Red Body, White Trim	1991	30
9698OU	Churchill Truck Lines	1926 Mack Truck, White Tires, Red Body, White Trim	1991	50
1249	Cincinnati Bengals	1913 Model T Van, White Body, Orange Trim	1984	40
7666UP	Cintas	Step Van, White	1990	60
9820	Citgo	1931 Hawkeye Truck	1991	40
9307	Citgo #1 Lubricants	1926 Mack Tanker, White Body, Black Trim	1988	300
9456EA	Citgo #2 Lubricants	1918 Barrel Runabout, Black Body, White Trim		100

Ertl Banks

NO.	BANK	MODEL	YEAR	MIB
7537	Citgo #3 Lubricants	1913 Model T Van, Spare Tire, White Body, Red Trim	1989	60
9854	Citgo #4 Lubricants	1905 Ford Delivery Van, White Body, Green Trim	1991	25
7567UO	Classic Motorbooks 25th Anniversary	1950 Chevy Panel, Blue Body, Silver Trim	1990	35
9741UP	Clayton Auto Parts	1950 Chevy Panel, Blue Body, Gold Trim	1991	25
9236UA	Clearly Canadian Sparkling Water #1	1913 Model T Van, White Body, Blue Trim	1991	35
9238UP	Clearly Canadian Sparkling Water #2	1926 Mack Truck, White Body, Black Trim	1991	40
9523	Clemson University	1918 Runabout, White Body, Orange And Black Trim	1989	50
9775	Clemson University Limited Edition	1913 Model T Van, White Body, Orange Trim	1988	50
9374UP	Clyde Beatty Brothers Circus	1950 Chevy Tractor Trailer, Red On Red	1991	30
9391UP	Clyde Beatty Brothers Circus	1937 Ford Tractor Trailer, Red On Red	1991	30
9245	CO-OP, The Farm Store	1913 Model T Van, Tan Body, Green Trim	1985	40
9188	Coast To Coast	1913 Model T Van, White Body, Black Trim	1987	40
9742	Coast To Coast	1905 Ford Delivery Van, White Body, Black Trim	1988	25
9049	Coast To Coast	1926 Mack Truck With Crates, White Body, Black And Brown Trim	1989	25
9115EP	Coast To Coast Hardware Store	1923 Chevy Truck, White Body, Black Trim	1991	20
2105EO	Coast To Coast Hardware Store	1918 Runabout, White Body, Black Trim	1990	25
9339	Cohen & Sons, William	1926 Mack Truck, Red Body, Tan Trim	1989	60
9240UP	Coles Express	1937 Ford Tractor Trailer, Orange Body, Silver Trim	1991	30
9284UP	Colorado Springs Rod & Custom Car Club	1932 Ford Panel, Black Body, White Trim	1991	30
9619UP	Columbia, Missouri, Fire Department	1926 Seagrave Pumper	1991	30
7507UO	Comet Cleanser	1905 Ford Delivery Van, Metallic Green Body, Gold Trim	1990	30
9750	Conoco #1	1926 Mack Truck, Silver Body, Green Trim	1989	230
7523UA	Conoco #2	Horse Team And Tanker, Black Body, White Trim	1990	40
9500UA	Conoco #3	1937 Ford Tanker Trailer, Green Body, Silver Trim	1991	25
9146	Coors Beer	1918 Barrel Runabout	1991	35
9256	Corona Beer #3	1926 Mack Truck	1991	40
9296	Corona Beer	1931 Hawkeye Tanker, Red Spokes, Yellow Body, Blue Trim	1991	30
9254	Corona Extra Beer #1	1918 Barrel Runabout, Blue Body, Black Trim	1991	30
9255	Corona 'Extra Beer #2	1931 Hawkeye Truck, Blue Body, White Trim	1991	35
925	Country Fresh Milk	1913 Model T Van, White Body, Blue Trim	1991	20
1345UO	Country General	1918 Runabout, White Body, Red Trim	1990	25
9307UO	Country Store	Horse Team And Wagon, Red Body, White Trim	1991	25
7564UO	Country Store-Reiman First Edition	1926 Mack Truck, Yellow Body, Black Trim	1990	30
1640	Country Time Lemonade (Not A Bank)	1913 Model T Van, Yellow Body, Green Trim	1981	35
9401UO	Covington Savings & Loan, 105th Anniversary	1905 Ford Delivery Van, White Body, Blue Trim	1991	35
9981UP	Covongton, Kentucky, Fire Department	1926 Seagrave Pumper, Red	1991	30
9008	Crescent Electric Supply	1913 Model T Van, White Body, Blue Trim	1989	75

Ertl Banks

NO.	BANK	MODEL	YEAR	MIB
	Creswell, Oregon	1926 Seagrave Pumper, White	1991	30
9042	Cub Foods	1931 Hawkeye Truck, White Body, Black Trim	1991	30
1324	Cumberland Valley Tractor Pullers 1988	1926 Mack Tanker, Silver Body, Red Trim	1988	35
9657	Cumberland Valley Tractor Pullers 1989	1932 Ford Panel, Silver Body, Black Trim	1989	40
9761UO	Cumberland Valley Tractor Pullers 1990	1937 Ford Tractor Trailer, Silver Body, Blue Trim	1990	35
9393UP	Cumberland Valley Tractor Pullers 1991	1926 Mack Truck, Red Body, White Trim	1991	30
9013UP	Cumberland Valley Volunteer Firemen's Assn.	1926 Seagrave Pumper, White Body, Red Trim	1991	30
7529UO	Currie's	1905 Ford Delivery Van, White Body, Red Trim	1990	30
9204	Cycle-AM Motocross	1913 Model T Van, White Body, Red Trim	1984	90
9056	Daily Press	1905 Ford Delivery Van, White Body, Red Trim	1989	60
9521	Daily Press, Newport News, Virginia	1913 Model T Van, White Body, Red Trim	1987	150
9525	Dairy Farm	1913 Model T Van, Black On Black	1987	250
9525	Dairy Farm, (Not A Bank)	1913 Model T Van, Black On Black	1987	475
9144	Dairy Queen	1913 Model T Van, White Body, Red Trim	1987	120
9284	Dairy Queen	1937 Ford Tractor Trailer, White On White	1988	90
9033	Dairy Queen	1918 Runabout, Red Body, Black Trim	1989	50
9034	Dairy Queen	1932 Ford Panel, White Body, Blue Trim	1989	45
9178UA	Dairy Queen	1950 Chevy Panel, Red Body, White Trim	1991	150
9681UA	Dairy Queen	1926 Seagrave Pumper, Red	1991	30
9448UA	Dairy Queen, 50 Years	1913 Model T Van, Metallic Gold Body, Black Trim	1989	80
9285	Dairy Queen Limited Edition	1917 Model T Van, White On White	1988	80
1247	Dallas Cowboys	1913 Model T Van, Silver Body, Blue Trim	1984	50
9424	Decorah, Iowa	1905 Ford Delivery Van, White Body, Red Trim	1986	30
9143	Decorah, Iowa	1918 Runabout, Blue Body, Beige Trim	1987	30
9762	Decorah, Iowa	1932 Ford Panel, White Body, Blue Trim	1988	30
9255	Decorah, Iowa, Chamber Of Commerce	1913 Model T Van, White Body, Red Trim	1985	45
9677	Decorah, Iowa, Chamber Of Commerce	1926 Mack Truck, White Body, Red Trim	1989	30
9681	Delaval	Step Van, White On White	1989	105
9522	Delaware Valley Old Time Power & Equip.	1905 Ford Delivery Van, White Body, Red Trim	1986	30
9492	Delaware Valley Old Time Power & Equip.	1918 Runabout, White Body, Black Trim	1987	30
9806	Democratic Party, Election '88	1905 Ford Delivery Van, White Body, Blue Trim	1988	105
1667	Detroit News	1913 Model T Van, Red Body, Blue Trim	1983	75
2209	Deutz-Allis	1913 Model T Van, White Body, Blue Trim	1987	25
2217	Deutz-Allis	1905 Ford Delivery Van, White Body, Black Trim	1989	20
9438	Diamond Crystal Salt	1926 Mack Truck, Red Body, Black Trim	1986	250
9414	Diamond Crystal Salt	1913 Model T Van, White Body, Red Trim	1987	75
9881	Diamond Walnut Growers	1931 Hawkeye With Crates	1991	20
9073	Dixie Brewing	1918 Barrel Runabout, Green Body, Black And White Trim	1989	35
9728	Dixie Brewing	1937 Ford Tractor Trailer, Both Doors Labeled, White On White	1988	200
9728	Dixie Brewing Limited Edition	1937 Ford Tractor Trailer, White On White	1988	75

Ertl Banks

NO.	BANK	MODEL	YEAR	MIB
7516UO	Dobyns-Bennett High School, Kingsport, Tennessee	1950 Chevy Panel, Maroon Body, White Trim	1990	75
9206UP	Dolly Madison	Step Van, White	1990	55
9458UA	Domino's Pizza	1913 Model T Van, White Body, Blue Trim	1991	45
9460UP	Domino's Pizza	1950 Chevy Panel, White Body, Black Trim	1991	45
9824	Domtar Gypsum	1913 Model T Van, White Body, Blue Trim	1989	25
9215	Double "J" Limited Edition	1913 Model T Van, White Body, Red Trim	1985	25
7572	Dr. Pepper	1926 Mack Truck, Red Body, White Trim	1990	55
7573UO	Dr. Pepper	1918 Runabout, White Body, Red Trim	1990	55
9234UO	Dr. Pepper	1913 Model T Van, White Body, Red Trim	1991	50
9235UP	Dr. Pepper	1926 Mack Truck, White Body, Red Trim	1991	55
9841	Dr. Pepper	1918 Barrel Runabout	1991	35
9739	Dr. Pepper Special Edition	1905 Ford Delivery Van, White Body, Red Trim	1988	45
7572	Dr. Pepper Museum, Waco Texas	1926 Mack Truck, Red Body, White Trim	1991	
7573	Dr. Pepper Museum, Waco Texas	1918 Runabout, White Body, Red Trim	1991	25
7672UO	Drake, The (Hilton Hotels)	1932 Ford Panel, White Body, Blue Trim	1990	45
2113	Drake Hotel	1913 Model T Van, White Body, Red Trim	1984	95
9617	Dreyer's Ice Cream	1905 Ford Delivery Van, Cream Body, Black Trim	1989	30
9497UP	Dubuque Fire Department	1926 Seagrave Pumper, Red On Red	1991	30
1657	Dubuque G&CC Invitational Golf #1	1917 Model T Van, White Body, Blue Trim	1990	135
9726	Dubuque G&CC Invitational Golf #2	1913 Model T Van, White Body, Red Trim	1991	75
9503	Dubuque, Iowa	1905 Ford Delivery Van, White Body, Red Trim	1986	30
1321	Durona Productions	1913 Model T Van, Cream On Cream	1982	700
9313	Durona Productions	1932 Ford Panel, White Body, Blue Trim	1986	325
9529	Dyersville Historical Society	1905 Ford Delivery Van, White Body, Red Trim	1986	35
9490	Dyersville Historical Society	1913 Model T Van, White Body, Red Trim	1987	35
9883	Dyersville Historical Society	1918 Runabout, Red Body, Black Trim	1988	35
9037	Dyersville Historical Society	1932 Ford Panel, White Body, Red Trim	1989	30
7571UO	Dyersville Historical Society	1918 Barrel Runabout, Red And Black Body, White Trim	1990	25
9360	East Buchanan, Iowa	1913 Model T Van, White Body, Red Trim	1985	30
7627	East Tennessee University	1913 Model T Van, White Body, Blue Trim	1990	30
9366UA	Eastern Iowa Brass Band, Mt. Vernon, Iowa	1913 Model T Van, White Body, Red Trim	1991	25
1317UP	Eastview Pharmacy	1950 Chevy Panel, Blue Body, Silver Trim	1990	95
9671	Eastview Pharmacy, Limited Edition	1913 Model T Van, White Body, Blue Trim	1989	105
9896UP	Eastview Pharmacy	1913 Model T Van With Spare Tire, White Body, Red Trim	1991	25
9325	Eastwood Company #1, 1989	1950 Chevy Panel, Blue On Blue	1989	200
9325	Eastwood Company #1, 1990	1950 Chevy Panel, Blue On Blue	1989	300
9562UO	Eastwood Company #2	1932 Ford Panel With Spare Tire, Tan Body, Maroon Trim	1990	75
2985UO	Eastwood Company #3	1931 Hawkeye Truck, Green Body, Black Trim	1990	50
7664UO	Eastwood Company #4	1937 Ford Tractor Trailer, Red Body, Green Trim	1990	165
2141UP	Eastwood Company #5	1930 Diamond T Tanker, Blue On Blue	1990	75

Ertl Banks

NO.	BANK	MODEL	YEAR	MIB
1666	Eastwood Company #6	1926 Seagrave Pumper, Red On Red	1991	65
9122	Eastwood Company #7, 2nd Christmas	1947 IH Tractor Trailer, Blue Body, White Trim	1991	30
9027UP	Edelbrock	1932 Ford Panel, White Body, Red Trim, Only 96 Units Sold To Public	1991	300
9644	Edy's Ice Cream	1905 Ford Delivery Van, Cream Body, Black Trim	1989	30
9696UP	Eldon Iowa Fire Department	1926 Seagrave Pumper, White	1991	30
9399	Elma, Iowa	1913 Model T Van, White Body, Blue Trim	1986	225
9759UA	Elmira Maple Festival Ltd. Ed.	1905 Ford Delivery Van,White Body, Red Trim	1990	30
9454UP	Elmira Maple Festival, Ontario, Canada	1926 Mack Truck, White Body, Black Trim	1991	30
9656	Elmira Syrup Festival	1913 Model T Van, White Body, Blue Trim	1989	25
9455	Entenmann's	1913 Model T Van, White Body, Blue Trim	1986	75
1317	Entenmann's	Step Van, White Body, Trim	1987	85
9780	Entenmann's	Step Van, White Body, Trim	1988	95
9141	Ephrata Fair 1989	1913 Model T Van, Black Body, Blue Trim	1989	30
7541UO	Ephrata Fair 1990	1950 Chevy Panel, Red Body, Black Trim	1990	30
9794PO	Ertl Collector's Club	1918 Runabout, Red Body, White Trim	1991	35
1660PA	Ertl Collector's Club Ltd. Ed.	Step Van, Black Body	1990	45
1668	Ertl Collectors Club	1913 Model T Van, White Body, Red Trim	1983	95
9064	Ertl Collectors Club	1950 Chevy Panel, Gold Body, White Trim	1989	80
9737	Ertl N.Y. Premium Incentive Show Ltd. Ed.	1905 Ford Delivery Van, Silver Body, Black Trim	1988	50
7554UA	Ertl Safety Award	1913 Model T Van, White Body, Blue Trim	1990	100
9898UA	Ethyl Gasoline Company #1	1932 Ford Panel, Black Body, Yellow Trim	1991	35
9566UO	Evers Toy Store	Horse Team & Tanker, White Body, Black Trim	1990	20
9378	F-D-R Associates Ltd. Ed.	1905 Ford Delivery Van, Silver Body, Black Trim	1987	45
9064UA	Fallston, Md. Vol. Fire Dept. Co. 13	1926 Seagrave Pumper, Yellow Body	1991	30
9035UA	Fannettsburg,Pa. Metal Twnshp Co. 21	1926 Seagrave Pumper, Red Body, White Trim	1991	30
2104	Fanny Farmer	1913 Model T Van, White Body, Brown Trim	1983	35
7622	Farm Bureau Co-Op	1913 Model T Van, White Body, Red Trim	1990	25
9233	Farm Toy Capital Of The World #1 L.E.	1913 Model T Van, White Body, Green Trim	1986	90
9510	Farm Toy Capital Of The World #2 L.E.	1918 Runabout, Blue Body, Blue/Beige Trim	1986	80
9189	Farm Toy Capital Of The World #3 L.E.	1926 Mack Tanker, Silver Body, Red Trim	1987	70
9779	Farm Toy Capital Of The World #4 L.E.	1932 Ford Panel, Black Body, Silver Trim	1988	50
9107	Farm Toy Capital Of The World #5 L.E.	1905 Ford Delivery Van, Green Body, Black Trim	1989	30
1664UP	Farm Toy Capital Of The World #6 L.E.	1931 Hawkeye Truck, Red Body, Black Trim	1990	35
9424	Father's Day 1991	1905 Ford Delivery Van, Beige Body, Green Trim	1991	15
9334	Federal Express	Step Van, White Body, Trim	1989	45
6125	Felix Grundy Days Ltd. Ed.	1913 Model T Van, White Body, Red Trim	1989	25
7617UA	Field Of Dreams-Universal Studios Ltd. Ed.	1905 Ford Delivery Van, White Body, Blue Trim	1990	45
9186	Fina	1926 Mack Tanker, White Body, Blue Trim	1987	75
9043	Fina	1905 Ford Delivery Van, White Body, Blue Trim	1989	35

Top to Bottom: All Ertl Banks; Model #9474 Mrs. Baird's; #9879 Gulf Oil & Refining; #9801 Bell System; #9898 Trucklite; #9802 Bell Telephone of America; #1311, 1351 and 1355 Iowa Hawkeyes #1, #2 and #3; #9461 Lennox #1; #9455 Entemann's; #9463 Castrol Motor Oil #1; #9505 Fina--Employee Issue; #9460 Allerton Illinois Centennial; #9500 BJR Auto Radiator Service; #9462 Saia Trucking; #9426 Graduation Class of 1991; #9459 Ace Hardware #3.

Ertl Banks

NO.	BANK	MODEL	YEAR	MIB
9285	Fina	1932 Ford Panel	1991	20
9505	Fina - Employee Issue	1918 Runabout, Blue Body, White Trim	1991	25
9502	Fina - For Employee Issue Only	1918 Runabout, White Body, Blue Trim	1991	60
9407	Fina - Ltd. Ed.	1913 Model T Van, White Body, Blue Trim	1987	45
9456	Fina - Ltd. Ed.	1917 Model T Van, White Body, Trim	1989	105
9502UA	Fina - Ltd. Ed.	1918 Runabout, White Body, Blue Trim	1991	25
9369	Firehouse Films (Durona)	1950 Chevy Panel, Red Body, Black Trim	1990	160
9465UP	Firehouse Films - John Sturner Chief	1926 Seagrave Pumper, Red Body	1991	90
2988UO	First National Bank (Oklahoma) Ltd. Ed.	1918 Runabout, White Body, Gold Trim	1990	50
9208	First National Bank (Texas) Ltd. Ed.	1932 Ford Panel, White Body, Blue Trim	1991	35
1318	First Tennessee Bank #1 Ltd. Ed.	1917 Model T Van, White Body, Blue Trim	1988	160
9331	First Tennessee Bank #2 Ltd. Ed.	1918 Runabout, White Body, Black/Blue Trim	1989	30
9044	Flav-O-Rich Ltd. Ed.	1913 Model T Van, White Body, Red Trim	1989	30
7551UO	Flint Piston Service - U.A.W. #2	Step Van, White Body	1990	65
9857	Food City - Ltd. Ed.	1905 Ford Delivery Van, Silver Body, Black Trim	1988	30
9279	Food Lion - Ltd. Ed.	1913 Model T Van, Gold Body, Blue Trim	1987	30
9978	Forbes Magazine	1950 Chevy Panel	1991	35
2118	Ford	1932 Ford Panel		30
0865	Ford	1905 Ford Delivery Van, White Body, Blue Trim	1986	25
0837EO	Ford	1918 Runabout, White Body, Blue Trim	1987	25
1334	Ford #1	1913 Model T Van, White Body, Blue Trim	1981	35
1322	Ford #2 (Nat'l Truck Dlrs) Ltd. Ed.	1913 Model T Van, White Body, Blue Trim	1983	105
9871	Ford Motorsports #1	1905 Ford Delivery Van, White Body, Blue Trim	1988	30
2151	Ford Motorsports #2	1918 Runabout, White Body, Blue Trim	1989	30
1658	Ford Motorsports #3	1913 Model T Van, White Body, Blue Trim	1990	35
0374	Ford New Holland #5	1917 Model T Van, White Body, Blue Trim	1990	20
9379	Four-H Clubs Of America	1913 Model T Van, White Body, Blue Trim	1987	35
9701	Four-H Clubs Of America	1917 Model T Van, White Body, Trim	1988	30
9848	Four-H Clubs Of America	1905 Ford Delivery Van, White Body, Green Trim	1988	35
9302	Franco-American	1926 Mack Truck, Red Body, Green Trim	1986	60
9710	Freihofer Baking Co.	Step Van, Red Body, Trim	1988	35
9632	Frito-Lay	1913 Model T Van, White Body, Red Trim	1989	30
9633	Frito-Lay	1950 Chevy Panel, Orange Body, Trim	1989	40
9634	Frito-Lay	Step Van, White Body, Tan Trim	1989	45
9085	Fuller Brush Co.	1905 Ford Delivery Van, White Body, Red Trim	1989	30
9043	Future Farmers Of America	1905 Ford Delivery Van		25
9456	Future Farmers Of America	1917 Model T Van		35
9531	Future Farmers Of America	1913 Model T Van, White Body, Blue Trim	1987	35
9763	FWD/Seagrave - "Pride Of Seagrave"	1926 Seagrave Pumper 2nd Run 2561, Red Body	1991	35
9763	FWD/Seagrave - "Pride Of Seagrave"	1926 Seagrave Pumper 1st Run 1721, Red Body	1991	35
9598UO	Gateway Toy Show #1 9th Anniversary	1950 Chevy Tractor/Trailer, White Body, Trim	1989	55
9259UO	Gateway Toy Show #2 10th Anniversary	1931 Hawkeye Truck, White Body, Black Trim	1991	55

Ertl Banks

NO.	BANK	MODEL	YEAR	MIB
9358	Genstar (Gypsum Products Co.)	1913 Model T Van, White Body, Blue Trim	1985	25
9251	Georgia Tech - Not A Bank	1932 Ford Roadster, Met. Gold Body, White Trim	1985	120
9368	Gilbertville, Iowa	1932 Ford Panel, White Body, Red Trim	1986	65
9246	Gilbertville, Iowa 3rd Annual Commty Day	1913 Model T Van, White Body, Red Trim	1985	50
9890UP	Gilmore Oil #1	1931 Hawkeye Tanker, Red Body, Beige Trim	1991	40
9891UP	Gilmore Oil #1	1931 Hawkeye Pumper	1991	60
9891UP	Gilmore Oil - Sampler	1931 Hawkeye Tanker, Beige Body, Red Trim	1991	40
1353UO	Glaxo	1932 Ford Panel, White Body, Blue Trim	1990	30
9266	Glendale Medical Center	1913 Model T Van, White Body, Blue Trim	1987	60
1655	Global Van Lines	1913 Model T Van, Light Blue Body, Black Trim	1983	45
1655UO	Global Van Lines	1913 Model T Van, Light Blue Body, Black Trim	1990	25
9118	Golden Flake	Step Van, White Body, Trim	1987	70
9678UO	Goldsboro Fire Dept.	1926 Seagrave Pumper	1991	30
9524	Good (J.F. Good Co.)	1913 Model T Van, White Body, Trim	1986	120
9603	Good (J.F. Good Co.)	1918 Runabout, White Body, Brown Trim	1988	40
9332	Good (J.F. Good Co.	1926 Mack Truck, White Body, Red Trim	1989	20
9146	Goshen, H. & W. Dairy	Horse & Carriage, White Body, Orange Trim	1987	70
	Goshen, Oregon Fire District	1926 Seagrave Pumper, Light Green Body, Dark Green Trim	1991	30
9426	Graduation Class Of 1991 Congratulations	1913 Model T Van, Yellow Body, Black Trim	1991	15
9885UP	Grapette Soda #1	1932 Ford Panel, Purple Body, Black Trim	1991	35
2139UO	Grauer's Paint	1932 Ford Panel, White Body, Red Trim	1990	30
9475	Greencastle PA Rescue Hose Co. #1	1926 Seagrave Pumper, Red Body	1991	75
7652UO	Gulf - That Good Gulf Gasoline	1926 Mack Tanker, Orange Body, Blue Trim	1990	90
7652UO	Gulf - That Good Gulf Gasoline (Reissue)	1926 Mack Tanker, Orange Body, Blue Trim	1990	45
9443	Gulf Ohio Gas Marketing	1932 Ford Panel, White Body, Red Trim	1984	400
9443	Gulf Ohio Pipeline	1932 Ford Panel, White Body, Red Trim	1984	450
9156UP	Gulf Oil & Refining - "1991"	1950 Chevy Panel, Orange Body, Black Trim	1991	165
9880	Gulf Oil & Refining Co.	1931 Hawkeye Tanker	1991	50
9879	Gulf Oil & Refining Co. W/ Spare	1932 Ford Panel	1991	50
9878	Gulf Oil & Refining W/O Spare	1932 Ford Panel	1991	50
9211	Gulf Refining	1950 Chevy Panel, Orange Body, Black Trim	1984	2500
9158UO	Gulf Refining	1926 Mack Tanker, Orange Body, White Trim	1991	75
9157UA	Gulf Refining #1	1931 Hawkeye Tanker, Orange Body, White Trim	1991	60
1365	H.E. Butts	1913 Model T Van, White Body, Red Trim	1983	25
2145	Hamm's Beer	1913 Model T Van, White Body, Blue Trim	1984	75
7619UO	Hamm's Beer	1926 Mack Truck, White Body, Red Trim	1990	35
7635EO	Hardware Hank	1917 Model T Van, Red Body, Black Trim	1990	20
9784	Harley-Davidson #1	1918 Runabout, Olive Body, Black Trim	1988	135
9135UO	Harley-Davidson #2	1926 Mack W/Crates, Red Body, Brown Trim	1989	325
7525UA	Harley-Davidson #3	1932 Ford Panel, Black Body, Trim	1990	225
9362	Harley-Davidson #4	Horse Team & Wagon, Black Body, Cream Trim	1991	100
	Harpers Ferry, W. VA	1926 Seagrave Pumper	1991	30
2108	Hartford Provisions	1913 Model T Van, White Body, Red Trim	1983	250
9533	Hawkeye Tech	1913 Model T Van, White Body, Red Trim	1986	30
9373UP	HCH Research High Reach Aerial Platforms	Step Van, White Body, Trim	1991	30

Ertl Banks

NO.	BANK	MODEL	YEAR	MIB
9250	Heartland Popcorn	1905 Ford Delivery Van, Red Body	1991	30
9379	Heatcraft	1923 Chevy Truck	1991	25
7562UA	Heatcraft - Lennox Ltd. Ed.	1926 Mack Truck, White Body, Red Trim	1990	30
1312	Heating Alternatives Ltd.	1913 Model T Van, White Body, Red Trim	1987	30
9749	Heilig Meyers	1926 Mack Truck, Green Body, Trim	1989	25
9700	Heilig Meyers 75th Ann. (1913-1988)	1913 Model T Van, Green Body, Trim	1988	30
9570UO	Heineken Beer #1	1918 Barrel Runabout, Green/White Body, Black Trim	1989	160
9356	Heineken Beer #2	1950 Chevy Panel, Green Body, White Trim	1991	35
9357	Heineken Beer #3	1931 Hawkeye Truck, Green Body, White Trim	1991	35
1345	Heinz "57"	1913 Model T Van, White Body, Trim	1981	75
9669	Hemmings Motor News #1 (Irish Green)	1932 Ford Panel, Light Green Body, Black Trim	1989	75
9669	Hemmings Motor News #2 (British Green)	1932 Ford Panel, Green Body, Black Trim	1989	45
9669	Hemmings Motor News #2 (British Green)	1932 Ford Panel, Green Body, Black Trim	1990	25
9461UP	Hemmings Motor News #3	1950 Chevy Panel, Green Body, Trim	1991	25
9462UP	Hemmings Motor News #4	1923 Chevy Truck, Green Body, Trim	1991	25
9370	Henderson Centennial	1913 Model T Van, White Body, Blue Trim	1986	30
9889	Henny Penny	1913 Model T Van, White Body, Red Trim	1988	30
9890	Henny Penny	1905 Ford Delivery Van, White Body, Red Trim	1988	40
9945UO	Henny Penny	1918 Runabout, White Body, Black Trim	1989	25
9946UO	Henny Penny	1932 Ford Panel, White Body, Red Trim	1989	25
9368	Herr's Snack Foods - Potato Chips	Step Van, White Body, Blue Trim	1991	30
9799	Hershey Auto Club	1917 Model T Van, White Body, Trim	1988	90
9084	Hershey Auto Club	1918 Barrel Runabout, Tan Body, Brown Trim	1989	75
7640UO	Hershey Auto Club	1926 Mack Truck, White Body, Black Trim	1990	35
9779	Hershey Auto Club	1926 Seagrave Pumper, Red Body	1991	35
7639UO	Hershey Auto Club (Regional)	1905 Ford Delivery Van, White Body, Maroon Trim	1990	40
9198	Hershey Auto Club (Regional)	1950 Chevy Panel, White Body, Pink Trim	1991	75
9511	Hershey Chocolate Syrup	Horse Team & Tanker, Brown Body, Trim	1991	25
1349UO	Hershey's Chocolate Milk	1926 Mack Tanker, Brown Body, Trim	1990	45
9665	Hershey's Cocoa	1905 Ford Delivery Van, White Body, Brown Trim	1989	65
2129	Hershey's Golden Almond	1913 Model T Van 1000+, Gold Plt Body, Metalize Trim	1990	65
2126UO	Hershey's Kisses	1950 Chevy Panel 1000+, Chrome Body, Metalize Trim	1990	65
1350UO	Hershey's Milk Chocolate	1913 Model T Van, Brown Body, Trim	1990	25
1351UO	Hershey's Milk Chocolate With Almonds	1913 Model T Van, Brown Body, Trim	1990	25
9349	Hershey's Sweet Milk Chocolate	1931 Hawkeye Truck, Brown Body, Trim	1991	25
9348	Hershey's Sweet Milk Chocolate W/Almonds	1931 Hawkeye Truck, Brown Body, Trim	1991	25
9768	Hills Department Stores	1913 Model T Van, White Body, Red Trim	1988	25
9427	Hinckley & Schmitt	1913 Model T Van, White Body, Blue Trim	1986	25
9435	Hires Root Beer	1918 Ford Barrel Runabout, Red Body, Tan Trim	1991	30
9179	Hobo Days 1991		1991	25
9601	Hoffman Laroche	1913 Model T Van, White Body, Red Trim	1988	150
9974	Hoffman Laroche	1905 Ford Delivery Van, White Body, Blue Trim	1988	135
9470	Holiday Wholesale	Step Van, White Body, Blue Trim	1987	30

Ertl Banks

NO.	BANK	MODEL	YEAR	MIB
9477	Holly Cliff Farms #1	1926 Mack Tanker, Silver Body, Red Trim	1987	30
9972	Holly Cliff Farms #2	1926 Mack Truck, White Body, Black Trim	1989	35
9849UP	Holly Cliff Farms #3	1926 Mack Tanker, Red Body, White Trim	1991	35
7709DO	Holt Mfg. #1 (Caterpillar)	1905 Ford Delivery Van, Black On Black	1989	20
2434	Holt Mfg. #2 (Caterpillar)	1926 Mack Truck, Red Body, Grey Trim	1991	20
9784	Protivin, Iowa, Holy Trinity	1918 Ford Runabout, White Body, Black Trim	1988	35
2149	Home Federal Savings	1926 Mack Truck, White Body, Black Trim	1984	35
1356	Home Hardware #1	1913 Model T Van, Yellow Body, Black Trim	1982	175
2109	Home Hardware #2	1926 Mack Truck, Yellow Body, Black Trim	1984	100
9250	Home Hardware #3	1932 Ford Panel, Yellow Body, Black Trim	1985	55
9401	Home Hardware #4	1905 Ford Delivery Van, Yellow Body, Black Trim	1986	45
9145	Home Hardware #5	1918 Ford Runabout, Yellow Body, Black Trim	1987	45
9819	Home Hardware #6	1950 Chevy Panel, Yellow Body, Black Trim	1988	35
9012	Home Hardware #7	1926 Mack Truck With Crates, Yellow Body, Black Trim	1989	35
9011	Home Hardware #8	1917 Model T Van, Yellow Body, Black And Tan Trim	1989	30
9200EP	Home Hardware #9	1931 Hawkeye Truck, Yellow Body, Black Trim	1991	25
9154	Home Hardware #10	1937 Ford Tractor Trailer	1991	25
9844	Home Savings & Loan	1905 Ford Delivery Van, White Body, Blue Trim	1988	20
9845	Home Savings & Loan	1913 Model T Van, White Body, Red Trim	1988	30
9846	Home Savings & Loan	1918 Ford Runabout, White Body, Black Trim	1988	25
9292	Home Savings & Loan	1926 Mack Truck, White Body, Red Trim	1989	40
9309	Home Savings & Loan	1921 Ford Panel, White Body, Blue Trim	1989	40
9651	Homestead Collectibles	1905 Ford Delivery Van, White Body, Red Trim	1989	35
9451	Hormel Meats	1917 Model T Van, White On White	1991	65
9306UA	Horseless Carriage Carriers, Inc.	1937 Ford Tractor Trailer, White Body, Green Trim	1991	30
1661	Hostess Cakes #1	1913 Model T Van, White Body, Black Trim	1982	50
9422	Hostess Cakes #2	1913 Model T Van, White Body, Blue Trim	1986	30
9388UP	Hot Rod Magazine	1931 Hawkeye Truck, Red Body, Black Trim	1991	30
9256	Coos Bay, House Of Books	1013 Model T Van, White Body, Red Trim	1985	30
1366	Howard Brand Discounts	1913 Model T Van, White Body, Red Trim	1983	30
9781	Hudson Bay Company	1913 Model T Van, Black On Black	1988	35
9627	Hummelstown, PA, Fire Department (Toy Show)	1926 Seagrave Pumper, Red	1991	30
1346UO	Husker Harvest Days	1918 Ford Runabout, White Body, Red Trim	1990	25
9610	I.B.C.	Step Van, White On White	1988	55
9139	Idaho Centennial 1890-1990	1913 Model T Van, White Body, Red Trim	1989	30
2963UO	Ideal Trucking	1937 Ford Tractor Trailer, White	1990	35
9851	IDED	1918 Ford Runabout, White Body, Black Trim	1988	80
9849	IDED (Ertl Logo)	1918 Ford Runabout, White Body, Black Trim	1988	110
1651	IGA #1	1913 Model T Van, White Body, Red Trim	1983	55
2138	IGA #2	1926 Mack Truck, White Body, Red Trim	1984	45
2126	IGA #3	1913 Model T Van, White Body, Red Trim	1984	45
9350	IGA #4 (60th Anniversary)	1932 Ford Panel, White Body, Red Trim	1985	50
9120	IGA #5	1905 Ford Delivery Van, White Body, Red Trim	1987	25
9023	IGA #6	1918 Ford Runabout, Red Body, Black Trim	1988	25
9015	IGA #7	1950 Chevy Panel, Red Body, White Trim	1989	25
7696EO	IGA #8	1931 Hawkeye Truck, White Body, Red Trim	1990	25
9375EO	IGA #9	1923 Chevy Truck, White Body, Gold Trim	1991	20
9212	IGA #10 (65th Anniversary)	1926 Mack Truck, White Body, Red Trim	1991	25

Ertl Banks

NO.	BANK	MODEL	YEAR	MIB
9794	IGA Credit Union	1905 Ford Delivery Van, White Body, Blue Trim	1988	25
9455UP	Imperial Oil, Canada	1931 Hawkeye Tanker, Black Body, Red Trim	1991	60
2107	Imperial Palace #1	1913 Model T Van, Grey Body, Black Trim	1983	40
9943UO	Imperial Palace #2	1926 Mack Truck, White Body, Blue Trim	1989	40
9236	Independence, Iowa (Chamber Of Commerce)	1913 Model T Van, White Body, Red Trim	1984	35
9359	Independence, Iowa (Christmas)	1913 Model T Van, White Body, Red Trim	1985	35
9359	Independence, Iowa (Christmas)	1913 Model T Van, White Body, Red Trim	1985	650
9303	Independence, Iowa (Christmas)	1905 Ford Delivery Van, White Body, Red Trim	1986	30
9499	Independence, Iowa (Christmas)	1905 Ford Delivery Van, White Body, Blue Trim	1987	35
9888	Independence, Iowa (Christmas)	1918 Ford Runabout, Red On Red	1988	30
9253	Independence, Iowa (4th Of July, 1985)	1913 Model T Van, White Body, Red Trim	1985	30
9248	Independence, Iowa (4th Of July, 1986)	1913 Model T Van, White Body, Blue Trim	1986	30
9194	Independence, Iowa (4th Of July, 1987)	1918 Ford Runabout, White Body, Black Trim	1987	25
9507	Independence, Iowa (Lion's Club)	1913 Model T Van, Grey Body, Blue Trim	1986	70
9288	Independence, Iowa (Lion's Club)	1917 Model T Van, White Body, Blue Trim	1987	35
9813	Indianapolis 500	1918 Ford Runabout, White Body, Black Trim	1988	45
1311	Iowa Hawkeyes #1	1913 Model T Van, Yellow Body, Black Trim	1983	55
1351	Iowa Hawkeyes #2	1913 Model T Van, Yellow Body, Black Trim	1982	30
1311	Iowa Hawkeyes #3	1913 Model T Van, Black Body, Yellow Trim	1983	55
1663	Iowa Hawkeyes #4	1926 Mack Truck, Yellow Body, Black Trim	1983	60
2148	Iowa Hawkeyes #5	1950 Chevy Panel, White On White	1984	55
2135	Iowa Hawkeyes #6	1926 Mack Truck, Yellow Body, Black Trim	1984	35
9180	Iowa Hawkeyes #7	1918 Ford Runabout, Yellow Body, Black Trim	1987	35
9810	Iowa Hawkeyes #8	1905 Ford Delivery Van, Black Body, Yellow Trim	1988	35
9748	Iowa Hawkeyes #9	1932 Ford Panel, Yellow Body, Black Trim	1989	40
9804EO	Iowa Hawkeyes 1/43 Dime Bank	1930 Chevy Delivery Truck, Yellow Body, Black Trim	1991	15
1665UO	Iowa Hawkeyes #10 (10th Anniversary Edition)	1931 Hawkeye With Crates, Yellow Body, Black Trim	1990	30
9805UP	Iowa Hawkeyes #11	1931 Hawkeye Truck, Yellow Body, Black Trim	1991	25
1346	Iowa Fireman's Assn. 105th	1913 Model T Van, White Body, Red Trim	1983	185
2137	Iowa Fireman's Assn. 106th	1913 Model T Van, White Body, Red Trim	1984	
9237	Iowa Fireman's Assn. 107th	1913 Model T Van, White Body, Red Trim	1985	60
9165	Iowa Fireman's Assn. 109th	1005 Ford Delivery Van, White Body, Red Trim	1987	55
9201UA	Iowa Fireman's Assn. 113th, Dyersville	1926 Seagrave Pumper, Red On Red	1991	165
9701	Iowa Jaycee Express	1913 Model T Van, Grey Body, Black Trim	1990	80
9457UO	Iowa Jaycee Express Limited Edition	1918 Ford Runabout, Beige Body, Blue Trim	1990	25
9259	Iowa State Cyclones #1	1913 Model T Van, Yellow Body, Red Trim	1985	30
9834	Iowa State Cyclones #2	1905 Ford Delivery Van, Yellow Body, Red Trim	1988	35

Top to Bottom: All Ertl Banks; Model #1664 Toy Farmer #1; #1349 Tractor Supply Co. #1; #1660 Wonder Bread; #1359 Otasco #1; #1661 Hostess Cakes #1; #1321 Durona Productions; #1657 Dubuque G & CC Invitational Golf #1; #1330 Sunbeam Bread; #9843 US Mail #2; #9023 IGA #6; #9723 Allied Van Lines #6; #9785 Watkin's Inc.; #9777 Otasco #7; #9793 Lennox #3; #9740 Texaco #5; #9800 Bell Telephone #2; #9888 Independence Iowa Christmas; #9399United Hardware; #9445 Schneider's Meats; #1092 Massey-Harris; #2209 Deutz-Allis; #9431 Publix; #0379 New Holland.

Ertl Banks

NO.	BANK	MODEL	YEAR	MIB
9127	Iowa State Cyclones #3	1950 Chevy Panel, Red Body, Yellow Trim	1989	40
1312UP	Iowa State Cyclones #4	1918 Ford Runabout, Red Body, Yellow Trim	1990	30
9422UP	Iskenderian Cams #2	1932 Ford Panel, White Body, Red And Blue Trim	1991	35
9422UP	Iskenderian Cams	1932 Ford Panel, White Body, Red And Blue Trim, Error Bank, Company Name Is Misspelled	1991	110
9232	J.C. Penney	Horse And Carriage, Tan Body, Black Trim	1985	65
9234	J.C. Penney	1932 Ford Panel, Beige Body, Black Trim	1985	75
1328	J.C. Penney	1918 Ford Runabout, White Body, Blue Trim	1988	35
9640	J.C. Penney	1950 Chevy Panel, Yellow On Yellow	1989	30
9641	J.C. Penney	1926 Mack Truck, White Body, Blue Trim	1989	30
2976UO	J.C. Penney	1918 Ford Barrel Runabout, Red Body, Tan Trim	1990	25
2977UO	J.C. Penney	1926 Mack Truck With Crates, Yellow Body, Black Trim	1990	20
9444UP	J.C. Penney	1931 Hawkeye Truck, Green Body, Black Trim	1991	25
9447UP	J.C. Penney	1923 Chevy Truck, White Body, Black Trim	1991	25
9445UP	J.C. Penney	Horse Team And Wagon, Red Body, Beige Trim	1991	25
1354	J.C. Penney #1	1913 Model T Van, White Body, Red Trim	1983	145
1354	J.C. Penney #2	1913 Model T Van, Grey Body, Black Trim	1983	95
1354	J.C. Penney #3	1913 Model T Van, Yellow Body, Black Trim	1985	40
1326	J.C. Penney (Golden Rule)	1905 Ford Delivery Van, Orange Body, Black Trim	1988	35
9639	J.C. Penney (Golden Rule)	1917 Model T Van, Green Body, Black Trim	1989	25
2975UO	J.C. Penney	1932 Ford Panel With Spare Tire, Beige Body, Red Trim	1990	35
0216	J.I. Case	1926 Mack Truck, Tan Body, Black Trim	1984	35
0699	J.I. Case	1905 Ford Delivery Van, Tan Body, Grey Trim	1987	20
0668	J.I. Case	1913 Model T Van, Red On Red	1988	20
0401	J.I. Case	1905 Ford Delivery Van, Red Body, Black Trim	1989	25
0286	J.I. Case	1913 Model T Van	1990	25
2147	J.L. Kraft	1913 Model T Van, Yellow Body, Black Trim	1985	90
1321	J.T. General Store	1913 Model T Van, Beige On Beige	1982	35
9674	J.T. General Store (90th Anniversary)	1905 Ford Delivery Van, Beige Body, Brown Trim	1989	25
9852	Jack Daniels	1905 Ford Delivery Van, Black On Black	1988	65
9077	Jack Daniels	1918 Ford Runabout With Barrels, Black On Black	1989	50
9342	Jack Daniels	1931 Hawkeye Truck With Crates, Black Body, Red Trim	1991	35
9050	Jackson Brewery	1905 Ford Delivery Van, White Body, Red Trim	1989	35
9344	Janesville, Iowa	1913 Model T Van, White Body, Red Trim	1985	25
9258	Jesup, Iowa, Chamber Of Commerce	1913 Model T Van, White Body, Red Trim	1985	30
7661UO	Jim Beam #116 (Northern Ohio)	1932 Ford Panel, White Body, Blue Trim	1990	55
1313UO	Jim Beam (District #1)	1905 Ford Delivery Van, White Body, Blue Trim	1990	45
9412	Jim Beam (District #5) #1	1913 Model T Van, White Body, Red Trim	1986	245
9387	Jim Beam (District #5) #2	1932 Ford Panel, White Body, Blue Trim	1987	95
9729	Jim Beam (District #5) #3	1918 Ford Runabout, White Body, Black Trim	1988	85
9676	Jim Beam (District #5) #4	1905 Ford Delivery Van, Yellow Body, Red Trim	1989	85
2964UO	Jim Beam (District #5) #5	1918 Ford Runabout With Barrels, Red Body, Beige Trim	1990	75
7442	Jim Beam (District #6)	1932 Ford Panel	1990	30

Ertl Banks

NO.	BANK	MODEL	YEAR	MIB
9683	Jim Beam (District #8)	1913 Model T Van, White Body, Red Trim	1989	35
9647	Jim Beam (District #9)	1917 Model T Van, White Body, Blue Trim	1989	35
1316	Jim Beam (District #9) Susquehanna	1950 Chevy Panel, Blue Body, Silver Trim	1990	75
2125UO	Jim Beam, Sugar River Beamers	1905 Ford Delivery Van, White Body, Red Trim	1990	30
9989	Jim Beam (District #10)	1926 Mack Truck, White Body, Black Trim	1988	35
9440UO	Jim Beam, Ohio #257 Lakeshore	1932 Ford Panel, White Body, Blue Trim	1991	35
9464	Jim Beam, Northwest	1918 Ford Runabout	1991	30
9818	Jim's Auto Sales	1913 Model T Van, White Body, Red Trim	1988	25
0531	John Deere #1	1926 Mack Truck, Green Body, Yellow Trim	1984	75
5534	John Deere #2	1926 Mack Truck, Green Body, Yellow Trim	1986	50
5564EO	John Deere #3	1926 Mack Truck, Yellow Body, Green Trim	1989	25
5621	John Deere I	1950 Chevy Panel, Green Body, Yellow Trim	1989	35
5621	John Deere II	1950 Chevy Panel, Wide Tire Version, Green Body, Yellow Trim	1989	25
9459	Johnson Wax	1913 Model T Van, White Body, Red Trim	1987	185
9232UA	Jolt Cola	1913 Model T Van, Red Body, Black Trim	1991	35
9253	Kaminsky Barrel	1918 Ford Runabout With Barrels	1991	25
9272	Kansas State Fair	1913 Model T Van, White Body, Blue Trim	1987	225
9272	Kansas State Fair	1913 Model T Van, White Body, Red Trim	1987	75
7560UO	Kauffman's Orchard Apple Farm	1918 Ford Runabout, White Body, Black Trim	1990	30
7662UA	Kerr McGee Oil Co.	1932 Ford Panel With Spare Tire, Grey Body, Black Trim	1990	35
9773	Kerr McGee Oil Co.	1926 Mack Tanker, Grey Body, Black Trim	1988	50
9130	Kerr McGee Oil Co. Limited Edition	1913 Model T Van, Grey Body, Black Trim	1989	45
9702	Key Federal Bank	1918 Ford Runabout, White Body, Black Trim	1988	35
9703	Key Federal Bank	1932 Ford Panel, White Body, Blue Trim	1988	35
9175	Key-Aid	1913 Model T Van, White Body, Red Trim	1987	40
9485	Key-Aid	1905 Ford Delivery Van,White Body, Red Trim	1988	25
1332UA	Key-Aid Limited Edition	1931 Hawkeye With Crates, Green Body, Black Trim	1990	25
9944	Key-Aid	1932 Ford Panel, Black Body, Silver Trim	1989	20
9030UP	Keystone Soil & Water	1950 Chevy Panel, White	1991	25
9110UO	Keystone Wood Specialties	1950 Chevy Panel, White	1991	35
9351	Kidde	1913 Model T Van, White Body, Red Trim	1985	40
9854	King Edward Cigars	1913 Model T Van, Red Body, Black Trim	1988	40
9174	Kingsport, Tennessee #1	1918 Ford Runabout, White Body, Black Trim	1987	100
7682UA	Kingsport, Tennessee (Citivan)	1932 Ford Panel, Black Body, Silver Trim	1990	40
9394UP	Kingsport, Tennessee #2	1917 Model T Van, White On White	1991	25
9884UP	Kiwanis International	1905 Ford Delivery Van, White Body, Blue Trim	1991	25
9590UO	Kodak	1932 Ford Panel, Yellow Body, Red Trim	1991	80
9985	Kodak #1	1905 Ford Delivery Van, Gold Spokes, Yellow Body, Red Trim	1987	200
9985	Kodak #2	1905 Ford Delivery Van, Red Spokes, Yellow Body, Red Trim	1987	100
9985UP	Kodak	1905 Ford Delivery Van, Red Spokes, Yellow Body, Red Trim	1991	45
9675	Kraft Dairy Group	1917 Model T Van, White On White	1989	35
9511	Kroger Foods	1013 Model T Van, White Body, Blue Trim	1986	55
9362	Kuiken Brothers	1913 Model T Van, White Body, Red Trim	1985	30
9874UP	Los Angeles County Fire Department	1926 Seagrave Pumper, Red	1991	35
9352UP	Los Angeles Dodgers	1905 Ford Delivery Van, White Body, Blue Trim	1991	55

Ertl Banks

NO.	BANK	MODEL	YEAR	MIB
7667UA	Los Angeles Times	1917 Model T Van, Blue On Blue	1990	45
9437UP	Lake City, Colorado, Area Medical Center	1913 Model T Van, White Body, Red Trim	1991	25
9519	Lake Odessa, Michigan, Centennial	1913 Model T Van, White Body, Blue Trim	1986	30
9159UP	Lawry's Seasoning Salt	1959 Chevy Panel, Orange Body, Black Trim	1991	45
9117	Lawson Products	1950 Chevy Panel, Brown Body, Yellow Trim	1991	55
2123UO	Light Commercial Vehicle Assn.	1913 Model T Van, White Body, Green Trim	1990	35
9170UP	Lea & Perrins	1913 Model T Van	1991	35
9477UP	Lehman Hardware	1926 Mack Truck, Red Body, White Trim	1991	25
9578UO	Leidy's	1937 Ford Tractor Trailer, White	1989	30
7569UO	Leinenkugel's	1918 Ford Runabout With Barrels, Red And Black Body, White Trim	1990	75
9703UP	Leinenkugel's	1926 Mack Truck With Crates, Red Body, White Trim	1991	45
9461	Lennox #1	1913 Model T Van, White Body, Red Trim	1986	125
9192	Lennox #2	1932 Ford Panel, White Body, Red Trim	1987	55
9793	Lennox #3	1918 Ford Runabout, Red Body, White Trim	1988	30
9323	Lennox #4 Limited Edition	1905 Ford Delivery Van, White Body, Red Trim	1989	25
7561UA	Lennox #5 Limited Edition	1926 Mack Truck, White Body, Red Trim	1990	30
9378	Lennox #6	1923 Chevy Truck	1991	25
2120	LePage Glue	1913 Model T Van, Yellow Body, Red Trim	1984	35
	Libertyville, Kansas, Creamery	1912 Ford T Open Van, White Body, Black Trim	1991	25
2107UP	Link-Belt	1918 Ford Runabout, Red Body, Black Trim	1990	35
9306	Lion Coffee #1	1913 Model T Van, Red On Red	1988	55
9434	Lion Coffee #2 (125th Anniversary)	1905 Ford Delivery Van, White Body, Green Trim	1989	35
9344	Lion Coffee #3	1931 Hawkeye Truck, Black Body, Red Trim	1991	25
7505	Lipton Tea #1	1913 Model T Van, White Body, Red Trim	1989	165
9377	Little Debbie #1	Step Van, White On White	1987	100
9377UO	Little Debbie #2	Step Van, White On White	1990	65
2146	Lolli Pups	1913 Model T Van, Yellow Body, Brown Trim	1984	40
9648	London Fog	1937 Ford Tractor Trailer		30
9166UO	Lone Star Beer	1918 Ford Runabout With Barrels, Red Body, Black And White Trim	1991	40
9167UP	Lone Star Beer	1926 Mack Truck	1991	50
9168	Lone Star Beer	1926 Mack Truck With Crates	1991	40
9165UP	Lone Star Beer	1913 Model T Van, White Body, Red Trim	1991	50
9653UP	Long Island, New York, Vol. Fire Department	1926 Seagrave Pumper, White Body, Black Trim	1991	35
9704	Longview, Illinois	1917 Model T Van, White Body, Blue Trim	1988	20
9679	Loras College, Limited Edition	1913 Model T Van, White Body, Purple Trim	1989	35
9858UA	Loras College, National Catholic Basketball	1913 Model T Van, White Body, Red Trim	1991	15
9516	Louisiana State University	1913 Model T Van, White Body, Purple Trim	1986	40
9165	Lyons Coffee	1931 Hawkeye Truck	1991	30
9308UO	Minnesota Industrial Tools	Step Van, Silver	1990	35
9608	MAC Tools	1950 Chevy Panel, Grey On Grey	1988	290
9391	Mace Brothers	1913 Model T Van, White Body, Red Trim	1986	55
9589UA	Madison Electric, Limited Edition	1913 Model T Van, Blue Body, White Trim	1990	100
9412UP	Malatesta Moving	1931 Hawkeye Truck, Green Body, Black Trim	1991	35
9220	Manitoba, Canada	1913 Model T Van, White Body, Green Trim	1985	30
9783	Marathon Oil	1926 Mack Truck, Silver Body, Red Trim	1988	275
1650	Marshall Fields	1913 Model T Van, White Body, Green Trim	1983	65
1650	Marshall Fields	1913 Model T Van, White Body, Green Trim, Boxed With Candy	1983	125

Ertl Banks

NO.	BANK	MODEL	YEAR	MIB
9658	Marshfield, Wisconsin, Chamber Of Commerce	1926 Mack Truck, White Body, Green Trim	1989	25
9856	Martin's Potato Chips	Step Van, White On White	1988	35
1348	Massey Ferguson	1913 Model T Van	1990	15
1122	Massey Ferguson	1926 Mack Truck, Tan Body, Black Trim	1984	35
1089	Massey Ferguson	1918 Ford Runabout, Red Body, Black And Yellow Trim	1989	25
1092	Massey-Harris	1913 Model T Van, Gold Body, Red Trim	1987	25
9659	Matco	Step Van	1989	55
9476	Maurice's	1932 Ford Panel, Grey Body, Maroon Trim	1987	35
9267	Mayer's Well Drilling	1913 Model T Van, White Body, Blue Trim	1987	35
	McAdoo, Pennsylvania	1926 Seagrave Pumper, Burgundy	1991	30
9043UA	McConnellsburg, PA Vol. Fire Co. #1	1926 Seageave Pumper, Red	1991	30
9161UP	McGee's Plumbing	Step Van	1991	35
9495	McGlynn Bakery	Step Van, White On White	1987	85
2112	McGlynn Bakery #1	1913 Model T Van, Red Spokes, White Body, Black Trim	1984	45
2112	McGlynn Bakery #2	1913 Model T Van, Black Spokes, White Body, Black Trim	1986	35
9299UO	Medicine Shoppe	1905 Ford Delivery Van, White Body, Blue Trim	1991	25
9352	Meijer Foods	1913 Model T Van, Red Body, White Trim	1985	35
9318	Mellon Bank	1913 Model T Van, White Body, Green Trim	1987	25
1358UO	Mellon Bank	1950 Ford Delivery Van, White Body, Green Trim	1990	25
9980	Merit Oil	1926 Mack Tanker, White Body, Red Trim	1988	105
9316	Merita Bread (American Bakeries)	1913 Model T Van, White Body, Red Trim	1987	35
1316	Merita Bread (American Bakeries)	1917 Model T Van, White On White	1987	35
9568UA	Meyer's Funeral Home	1932 Ford Panel, Black Body, Silver Trim	1990	40
1325	Michigan Milk Producers Assn.	1913 Model T Van, White Body, Red Trim	1983	95
9388	Michigan Milk Producers Assn.	1905 Ford Delivery Van, White Body, Blue Trim	1991	25
9172	Michigan Sesquicentennial	1913 Model T Van, White Body, Blue Trim	1987	35
9604	Michigan State University #2	1950 Chevy Panel	1991	25
9026	Michigan State University, Rose Bowl	1917 Model T Van, White On White	1988	35
9410UO	Mid-Missouri 10th Anniversary Toy Show	1950 Chevy Tractor Trailer, White Body, Red Trim	1991	25
9850	Mike's Trainland #1	1937 Ford Tractor Trailer, White On White	1988	60
9411	Mike's Trainland #2	1913 Model T Van, White Body, Red Trim	1989	30
9221UO	Mike's Trainland #3	1905 Ford Delivery Van, Blue On Blue	1990	30
9112UA	Miller Beer "Sharps"	1913 Model T Van	1991	35
2116UO	Miller Beer #1	1905 Ford Delivery Van, White Body, Red Trim	1991	45
9276UP	Miller Beer #2	1905 Ford Delivery Van, White Body, Red Trim	1991	40
9277UP	Miller Beer #3	1913 Model T Van, White Body, Red Trim	1991	40
9269	Miller High Life Beer	1950 Chevy Panel, Metallic Gold	1991	25
9270UP	Miller High Life Beer	1950 Chevy Tractor Trailer, Red Body, Gold Trim	1991	25
9268UP	Miller High Life Fire Truck	1926 Seagrave Pumper, Red Body, Gold And Black Trim	1991	30
9740	Miller Lite Beer	1950 Chevy Panel, Blue	1991	25
1246	Minnesota Vikings	1913 Model T Van, White Body, Purple Trim	1984	35
9119UP	Mission Industries	Step Van, White Body, Red Trim	1991	25

Ertl Banks

NO.	BANK	MODEL	YEAR	MIB
2143Uo	Missouri Tourism, "Wake Up To Missouri"	1905 Ford Delivery Van, Blue	1990	25
9308	MMPA (75th Anniversary)	1905 Ford Delivery Van	1991	25
9742UO	Mobil Oil	1931 Hawkeye Tanker	1991	60
9716UP	Mobil Oil #1 (Gargoyle)	1931 Hawkeye Tanker, Grey Body, Black Trim	1991	35
9717	Mobil Oil #2	1931 Hawkeye Truck, Grey	1991	35
9743UO	Mobil Oil #2	1913 Model T Van, White Body, Red Trim	1991	45
9760UP	Mobil Oil #3	1926 Mack Tanker, Red Body, White Trim	1991	60
9719UO	Monghan Township, PA, Vol. Fire Department	1926 Seagrave Pumper, Red On Red	1991	25
7511UR	Monroe Shocks, "America Rides Monroe"	1913 Model T Van, Yellow Body, Blue Trim	1990	35
7511UO	Monroe Shocks, "Monroe"	1913 Model T Van, Yellow Body, Blue Trim	1990	35
7511UP	Monroe Shocks, "The World Rides Monroe"	1913 Model T Van, Yellow Body, Blue Trim	1990	35
9350	Monroe Shocks #4	1931 Hawkeye Truck, Blue Body, Yellow Trim	1991	30
9747	Montana Centennial	1913 Model T Van, White Body, Red Trim	1989	25
9542	Montgomery Ward #1	1913 Model T Van, Green Body, Black Trim	1981	200
9052	Montgomery Ward #2	1917 Model T Van, Brown On Brown	1982	95
1363	Montgomery Ward #3	1926 Mack Truck, Yellow Body, Black Trim	1983	60
1367	Montgomery Ward #4	Horse And Carriage, Blue Body, Black Trim	1983	60
2110	Montgomery Ward #5	1932 Ford Panel, Yellow Body, Green Trim	1984	65
9230	Montgomery Ward #6	1905 Ford Delivery Van, Red Body, Black Trim	1985	40
9364	Monticello, Iowa	1913 Model T Van, White Body, Red Trim	1986	40
9585UO	Moorman Mfg. Co.	1905 Ford Delivery Van, White Body, Red Trim	1990	30
9472	Moorman Mfg. Co.	1913 Model T Van	1991	35
9787	Morton Salt	1905 Ford Delivery Van, Blue On Blue	1988	55
9811UP	Mount Horeb, Wisconsin, Fire Department	1926 Seagrave Pumper, Red	1991	25
7670UO	Mountain Dew	1950 Chevy Panel, Green Body, White Trim	1990	35
9474	Mrs. Baird's	Horse And Carriage, White Body, Blue Trim	1987	125
9894UP	Muffler Wagon	1950 Chevy Panel, Black Body, Blue Trim	1991	25
9732UO	Mustang Club	1932 Ford Panel, Red Body, White Trim	1991	25
9187	Mutual Savings & Loan	1905 Ford Delivery Van, White Body, Blue Trim	1987	25
9851UA	Myers Food Rite	1913 Model T Van, White Body, Blue Trim	1991	25
9479	N.E.W. Hobby	Step Van, White On White	1987	25
9104UO	N.E.W. Hobby	1950 Chevy Panel, Blue On Blue	1991	25
1653	Nabisco Almost Home Cookies	1913 Model T Van, Tan Body, Red Trim	1984	65
9699	Nabisco Premium Saltine Crackers	1913 Model T Van, Yellow Body, Maroon Trim	1981	325
9467	NASA	Step Van, White On White	1989	40
9347	Nash Finch	1913 Model T Van, White Body, Red Trim	1985	120
9481UO	National Street Rod Association #2	1937 Ford Tractor Trailer, Red Body, White Trim	1991	25
7504	National Street Rod Association	1937 Ford Tractor Trailer, White On White	1990	75
9505	National Van Lines #1	1913 Model T Van, White Body, Blue Trim	1986	65
9119	National Van Lines #2	1932 Ford Panel, White Body, Blue Trim	1987	95
1342	National Van Lines #3	1905 Ford Delivery Van, White Body, Blue Trim	1988	60
2117UA	National Van Lines, Limited Edition	1913 Model T Van, Blue And Black Body, Silver Trim	1991	40
2131	Neilson's Ice Cream	1913 Model T Van, White On White	1984	30
9347	Nestles Quik	1913 Model T Van, Yellow Body, Blue Trim	1991	35
9223	New Brunswick, Canada	1913 Model T Van, White Body, Purple Trim	1985	25

Top to Bottom: All Ertl Banks; Model #9044 Flavo-Rich; #7551 Flint Piston Service; #9771 Atlas Van Lines #2; #9354 Sasco Aloe Vera; #9325 Eastwood #1; #9122 Unique Gardens; #2101 Salvation Army.

Ertl Banks

NO.	BANK	MODEL	YEAR	MIB
9053UA	New Franklin, PA, Vol. Fire Department	1926 Seagrave Pumper, White	1991	25
0379	New Holland	1905 Ford Delivery Van, Yellow Body, Red Trim	1987	15
9415	New Holland	1913 Model T Van, Yellow Body, Red Trim	1986	175
9397	New Holland, Limited Edition	1913 Model T Van, Yellow Body, Red Trim	1986	125
9397	New Holland Tractors	1913 Model T Van, Yellow Body, Red Trim	1986	30
9640LU	New York Fire Department	1926 Seagrave Pumper, Red	1991	35
9224	Newfoundland, Canada	1913 Model T Van, White Body, Purple Trim	1985	25
2111Uo	Nintendo, Super Mario Brothers	Step Van, White On White	1991	75
2113UP	Nintendo, Super Mario Brothers	1913 Model T Van, White Body, Red Trim	1991	85
9642	Nittany Machinery Association	1913 Model T Van, White Body, Red Trim	1989	30
9207UO	Norand Data Systems	1926 Mack Truck With Crates, White Body, Black Trim	1990	25
9030	North American Van Lines	1937 Ford Tractor Trailer, Red And Tan Body, Red Trim	1988	65
9045	North Dakota Centennial	Horse And Carriage, Tan Body, Black Trim	1989	30
9690	North Dakota Centennial	1913 Model T Van, White Body, Brown Trim	1989	25
9517	Northern Electric	1905 Ford Delivery Van, Black On Black	1986	40
9222	Nova Scotia, Canada	1913 Model T Van, White Body, Red Trim	1985	25
9228UA	Oakwood Food Markets (43rd Anniversary)	1913 Model T Van, White Body, Brown Trim	1991	25
9822	Oakwood Mobile Homes	1917 Model T Van, White Body, Blue Trim	1988	30
9505	Obsolete Iron Street Rods, Reno, Nevada	1932 Ford Panel, White Body, Blue Trim	1991	25
9978	Ocean Spray	1918 Ford Runabout With Barrels	1991	40
9361	Oelwein, Iowa, Chamber Of Commerce	1913 Model T Van, White Body, Red Trim	1985	25
9733UO	Ohio Dept. Of Transportation (Spina Bifida)	1926 Mack Truck, Yellow Body, Black Trim	1991	25
9872UP	Oilzum (Petroleum Pioneer Series #1)	1931 Hawkeye Tanker, Black Body, Orange Trim	1991	45
9478	Old Country	Step Van, White On White	1987	95
7636UO	Old El Paso	1905 Ford Delivery Van, Yellow Body, Red Trim	1990	45
1359UO	Old Farmers Almanac (200th Anniversary)	1913 Model T Van, Beige	1991	35
9173	Old Milwaukee Beer #1	1918 Ford Runabout With Barrels, Red Body, White Trim	1991	35
9174	Old Milwaukee Light #2	1918 Ford Runabout With Barrels, Red Body, White Trim	1991	25
9175	Old Milwaukee Beer #3	1950 Chevy Panel, Red On Red	1991	30
2115UP	Olivet Union, Nazarine University	1905 Ford Delivery Van, Yellow Body, Purple Trim	1990	25
9790	Omro, Ohio, Fire Department	1926 Seagrave Pumper	1991	30
9217	Ontario, Canada	1913 Model T Van, White Body, Green Trim	1985	25
9389	Orkin #1	1913 Model T Van, White Body, Red Trim	1987	35
9842	Orkin #2	1905 Ford Delivery Van, White Body, Red Trim	1988	30
9286	Oroweat	Step Van, White On White	1987	60
9807UP	Oshawa Fire Department #5, Ontario, Canada	1926 Seagrave Pumper, Red On Red	1991	35
1359	Otasco #1	1913 Model T Van, Yellow Body, Black Trim	1982	95
1368	Otasco #2 (65th Anniversary)	1913 Model T Van, Yellow Body, Black Trim	1983	45
2134	Otasco #3	1926 Mack Truck, Yellow Body, Black Trim	1984	50

Ertl Banks

NO.	BANK	MODEL	YEAR	MIB
9342	Otasco #4	1950 Chevy Panel, Yellow On Yellow	1985	110
9371	Otasco #5	1932 Ford Panel, Yellow Body, Black Trim	1986	100
9168	Otasco #6	1918 Ford Runabout, Yellow Body, Black Trim	1987	50
9777	Otasco #7 (70th Anniversary)	1918 Ford Runabout, White Body, Blue And Black Trim	1988	45
9767	Our Own Hardware	1913 Model T Van, White Body, Red Trim	1988	25
9142	Overnite Trucking	1913 Model T Van, Silver Body, Blue Trim	1987	235
9068	Overnite Trucking	1937 Ford Tractor Trailer, Blue Cab, Silver Trailer	1989	90
7519Uo	P.J. Valves	1905 Ford Delivery Van, White Body, Blue Trim	1990	30
9244	Pacific Coast Oil Co.	Horse Team And Tanker, Black	1991	35
9467	Parcel Post Mail Service	1913 Model T Van, Black On Black	1981	150
9402	Partytime Ice Co.	1913 Model T Van, White Body, Blue Trim	1991	25
1357	Peavey	1913 Model T Van, White Body, Red Trim	1982	25
9263	Penn State	1917 Model T Van, White Body, Blue Trim	1987	75
9512	Penn State	1918 Ford Runabout, White Body, Blue Trim	1989	35
9258UP	Pennsylvania State Farm Show #1	1917 Model T Van, Blue Body, White Trim	1991	25
9615	Pennzoil	1931 Hawkeye Tanker, Yellow Body, Black Trim	1991	45
9877	People's National Bank	1913 Model T Van, White Body, Green Trim	1988	145
9581UO	People's National Bank	1918 Ford Runabout, Blue Body, White Trim	1990	45
9364	People's National Bank, Limited Edition	1905 Ford Delivery Van, White Body, Red Trim	1991	25
9341	Pepsi Cola	1931 Hawkeye With Crates, White Body, Blue And Red Trim	1991	35
9438	Pepsi Cola	1926 Mack Truck	1991	125
1314	Pepsi Cola	1917 Model T Van, White Body, Blue Trim	1987	110
9736	Pepsi Cola	1905 Ford Delivery Van, White Body, Blue Trim	1988	60
6936	Pepsi Cola	1918 Ford Runabout, Blue Body, Black And White Trim	1989	55
9635	Pepsi Cola	1950 Chevy Panel, Narrow Tires, Blue Body, White Trim	1989	55
9637	Pepsi Cola I	1932 Ford Panel, White Body, Blue Trim	1989	55
9637	Pepsi Cola II	1932 Ford Panel, New Style, White Body, Blue Trim	1991	35
9635	Pepsi Cola II	1950 Chevy Panel With Wide Tires, Blue Body, White Trim	1991	25
1652	Pet Milk	1913 Model T Van, Orange Spokes, White Body, Black Trim	1983	85
1652	Pet Milk	1913 Model T Van, Red Spokes, White Body, Black Trim	1984	60
9573UO	Petty Enterprises #1	1913 Model T Van, Blue Body, Red Trim	1989	75
9682	Petty Enterprises #1	1905 Ford Delivery Van, Blue Body, Red Trim	1991	45
9683	Petty Enterprises #1	1905 Ford Delivery Van, Blue On Blue	1991	100
9574UO	Petty Enterprises #2	1913 Model T Van, Blue On Blue	1989	85
9835	Philadelphia Cream Cheese	1913 Model T Van, Silver On Silver	1988	45
9787	Phillips 66	1926 Mack Tanker, Black Body, White Trim	1991	50
9230UA	Phillips 66 #1 (New Logo)	1913 Model T Van, White Body, Black Trim	1991	325
9407UP	Phillips 66 #1 (Old Logo)	1931 Hawkeye Tanker, Orange Body, Black Trim	1990	120
9121	Phillips 66 #2 "Explosives"	1932 Ford Panel	1991	35
9231UO	Phillips 66 #2 (New Logo, 1st Run)	1926 Mack Tanker, Red Body, White Trim	1991	250
9231UO	Phillips 66 #2 (New Logo, 2nd Run)	1926 Mack Tanker, Red Body, White Trim	1991	225
9728	Phillips 66 (Sampler)	1932 Ford Panel	1991	65

Ertl Banks

NO.	BANK	MODEL	YEAR	MIB
1298	Pittsburgh Steelers	1913 Model T Van, White Body, Black Trim	1984	45
9933UO	Pizza Today Magazine	1932 Ford Panel, Yellow Body, Black Trim	1990	35
2917	Pocono Antique Bazaar	1913 Model T Van, White Body, Brown Trim	1990	25
9211	Potelco	1918 Ford Runabout With Barrels, Yellow On Yellow	1991	25
9273	Poynors Home & Auto	1932 Ford Panel, White Body, Blue Trim	1987	30
9240UA	Preferred Hotels	1917 Model T Van, White	1991	35
9579UO	Preston Trucking Co.	1937 Ford Tractor Trailer, Orange	1990	40
9219	Prince Edward Island, Canada	1913 Model T Van, White Body, Orange Trim	1985	25
9431	Publix	1950 Chevy Panel, White Body, Green Trim	1986	95
9436	Publix	1905 Ford Delivery Van, White Body, Green Trim	1986	35
9718	Publix	1937 Ford Tractor Trailer, White Body, Green Trim	1988	40
9693	Publix	1926 Mack Truck With Crates, Green Body, Brown Trim	1989	30
9185DO	Publix Danish Bakery	1918 Ford Runabout	1991	20
9183DO	Publix Dari-Fresh	1931 Hawkeye Truck	1991	20
9184DO	Publix Deli	1950 Chevy Panel	1991	20
9182DO	Publix Floral	1923 Chevy Truck	1991	20
9186DO	Publix Produce	1931 Hawkeye Truck	1991	20
9187DO	Publix Transportation	1930 Diamond T Tanker, Green Body	1991	20
1337	Publix #1	1913 Model T Van, White Body, Green Trim	1981	45
9248	Publix #1	1932 Ford Panel, White Body, Green Trim	1985	45
2115	Publix #1	1926 Mack Truck, Black Tires, Red Spokes, White Body, Green Trim	1984	125
9149	Publix #1	1918 Ford Runabout, White Body, Green Trim	1987	55
9147	Publix #2 Food & Pharmacy	1932 Ford Panel, White Body, Green Trim	1987	35
1337	Publix #2	1913 Model T Van, Red Wheels, White Body, Green Trim	1984	35
9719	Publix #2	1926 Mack Tanker, White Cab And Body, Green Trim	1988	35
2115	Publix #2	1926 Mack Truck, White Tires, Green Spokes, White Body	1985	90
9723	Publix #2 (Pleasure)	1918 Ford Runabout, White Body, Green Trim	1988	25
9694	Publix #3 (The Deli)	1918 Ford Runabout, White Body, Brown Trim	1989	25
1337	Publix #3 Limited Edition	1913 Model T Van, White Body, Green Trim	1985	95
9430	Publix Dari-Fresh	1926 Mack Tanker, White Body, Green Cab And Trim	1986	45
9001	Publix Dari-Fresh	1905 Ford Delivery Van, White Body, Green Trim	1989	25
9695	Publix Dari-Fresh	1937 Ford Tanker Trailer, White Body, Green Trim	1989	35
7686DO	Publix Dari-Fresh	1931 Hawkeye Tanker, White Body, Green Trim	1990	25
7689DO	Publix Deli	1905 Ford Delivery Van, Orange Body, Brown Trim	1990	20
7687DO	Publix Floral	1918 Ford Runabout, White Body, Green Trim	1990	20
9721	Publix Food & Pharmacy	1905 Ford Delivery Van, White Body, Black Trim	1988	25
7688DO	Publix Food & Pharmacy	1913 Model T Van, Green Body, White Trim	1990	20
9720	Publix Produce	1926 Mack Truck, White Body, Green Trim	1988	30
9696	Publix Produce	1932 Ford Panel, Green Body, White Trim	1989	40
7685DO	Publix Produce	1931 Hawkeye Truck, White Body, Green Trim	1990	20
9249	Publix Danish Bakery	1913 Model T Van, White Body, Brown Trim	1985	35

Ertl Banks

NO.	BANK	MODEL	YEAR	MIB
9435	Publix Danish Bakery	1932 Ford Panel, White Body, Brown Trim	1986	30
9152	Publix Danish Bakery	1905 Ford Delivery Van, White Body, Brown Trim	1987	30
9722	Publix Danish Bakery	1950 Chevy Panel, Brown Body, White Trim	1988	35
9697	Publix Danish Bakery	1917 Model T Van, White Body, Brown Trim	1989	25
7690DO	Publix Danish Bakery #2	1932 Ford Panel, With Spare Tire, White Body, Orange Trim	1990	35
9692	Publix Food & Pharmacy	1950 Chevy Panel, Green Body, White Trim	1989	35
9148	Publix Produce Limited Edition	1917 Model T Van, White Body, Green Trim	1987	35
9698	Publix	1950 Chevy Tractor Trailer With Reefer, White Body, Green Trim	1989	35
9103UO	Purina	1913 Model T Van, White Body, Red Trim	1991	25
9515	Quakertown National Bank #1	1913 Model T Van, White Body, Blue Trim	1986	60
9291	Quakertown National Bank #2	1932 Ford Panel, White Body, Blue Trim	1987	50
9979	Quakertown National Bank #3	1905 Ford Delivery Van, White Body, Blue Trim	1988	50
9417	Quakertown National Bank #4	1918 Ford Runabout, Blue Body, White Trim	1989	35
1370UP	Quakertown National Bank #5	1917 Model T Van, White Body, Blue Trim	1990	25
9195UU	Quaker State Motor Oil	1913 Model T Van, White Body, Green Trim	1991	85
9196UP	Quaker State Motor Oil	1926 Mack Tanker, Green Body, White Trim	1991	60
9491	Quality Farm & Fleet #1	1913 Model T Van, White Body, Red Trim	1987	30
9609	Quality Farm & Fleet #2	1905 Ford Delivery Van	1988	30
9609	Quality Farm & Fleet #3	1918 Ford Runabout, White Body, Red Trim	1989	25
9958	Quality Farm & Fleet #4	1937 Ford Tractor Trailer	1991	30
9216	Quebec, Canada	1913 Model T Van, White Body, Blue Trim	1985	25
9827	R.C. Cola	1917 Model T Van, White Body, Blue Trim	1988	40
9108	Ragrai XVII	1905 Ford Delivery Van, White Body, Blue Trim	1989	25
9314	RCA #1	1913 Model T Van, White Body, Black Trim	1987	50
9315	RCA #2	1905 Ford Delivery Van, White Body, Red Trim	1987	55
9275	RCA #3	1926 Mack Truck, White Body, Red Trim	1987	40
1344	RCA #4	1918 Ford Runabout, Black Body, White Trim	1988	35
1343	RCA #5	1917 Model T Van, White Body, Red Trim	1988	35
9621	RCA #6	1932 Ford Panel, White Body, Black Trim	1989	35
7654UO	Red Crown Gasoline #1 (1st Run)	1931 Hawkeye Tanker, Red On Red	1990	50
7654UO	Red Crown Gasoline #1 (2nd Run)	1931 Hawkeye Tanker, Red On Red	1990	40
7654UO	Red Crown Gasoline #1 (3rd Run)	1931 Hawkeye Tanker, Red On Red	1991	40
2130	Red Rose Tea	1913 Model T Van, Red On Red	1984	40
9808	Reese's Peanut Butter Cups	1923 Chevy Truck, Orange Body, Brown Trim	1991	25
9809	Reese's Pieces	1950 Chevy Panel, Orange Body	1991	25
	Regina, Saskatchewan, Canada	1926 Seagrave Pumper, Burgundy	1991	25
9712	Renninger's Antique Market, Adamstown, PA	1905 Ford Delivery Van, White Body, Red Trim	1988	35
9894	Renninger's Antique Market, Adamstown, PA	1918 Ford Runabout With Barrels, White Body, Red Trim	1989	35
7556UO	Renninger's Antique Market, Adamstown, PA	1932 Ford Panel, White Body, Red Trim	1990	30

Ertl Banks

NO.	BANK	MODEL	YEAR	MIB
9714	Renninger's Antique Market, Kutztown, PA	1905 Ford Delivery Van, Black Body, Red Trim	1988	35
9895	Renninger's Antique Market, Kutztown, PA	1918 Ford Runabout With Barrels, Black Body, Red Trim	1989	35
7555	Renninger's Antique Market, Kutztown, PA	1932 Ford Panel, Black Body, Red Trim	1990	30
9713	Renninger's Antique Market, Mt. Dora, FL	1905 Ford Delivery Van, Brown On Brown	1988	35
9896	Renninger's Antique Market, Mt. Dora, FL	1918 Ford Runabout With Barrels, Tan Body, Brown Trim	1989	35
7557UO	Renninger's Antique Market, Mt. Dora, FL	1932 Ford Panel, Beige Body, Brown Trim	1990	30
9369	Republican Central Comm., Douglas County	1913 Model T Van, White Body, Red Trim	1986	75
9805	Republican Party, Election 1988	1905 Ford Delivery Van, White Body, Red Trim	1988	165
9731	Reynolds Aluminum	1917 Model T Van, White On White	1988	55
9162	Reynolds Wrap	1913 Model T Van, Silver Body, Blue Trim	1987	250
9290	Richlandtown	1926 Mack Tanker, White Body, Red Trim	1987	50
2969UO	Richlandtown	1905 Ford Delivery Van, White Body, Red Trim	1990	30
9027	Ringling Brothers Circus	1913 Model T Van, Red On Red	1988	175
9726	Ringling Brothers Circus	1937 Ford Tractor Trailer, White Body, Yellow Trim	1988	145
9121	Riverview Nursery	1926 Mack Tanker, White Body, Red Trim	1987	65
9804	Riverview Nursery (Purina)	1937 Ford Tractor Trailer, White On White	1988	35
9082	Rogersville, Tennessee	1932 Ford Panel With Spare Tire, Black Body, Silver Trim	1989	75
2108UP	Rogersville, Tennessee, Heritage Days	1918 Ford Runabout, Red Body, Black Trim	1990	30
9418	Round Top Arms	1918 Ford Runabout, White Body, Black Trim	1989	25
9275UA	Route 66	1918 Ford Runabout, Black On Black	1991	65
9162/A	Route 66, Arizona	1918 Ford Runabout	1991	45
9162/C	Route 66, California	1918 Ford Runabout	1991	45
9162/I	Route 66, Illinois	1918 Ford Runabout	1991	45
9162/K	Route 66, Kansas	1918 Ford Runabout	1991	45
9116UA	Route 66, Main Street USA	1932 Ford Panel With Spare Tire, White Body, Black Trim	1991	65
9116UA	Route 66, Main Street USA	1932 Ford Panel Without Spare Tire, White Body, Black Trim	1991	225
9162/M	Route 66, Missouri	1918 Ford Runabout	1991	45
9162/N	Route 66, New Mexico	1918 Ford Runabout	1991	45
9162/O	Route 66, Oklahoma	1918 Ford Runabout	1991	45
9162/T	Route 66, Texas	1918 Ford Runabout	1991	45
9446	Rubschlager Bakery	1913 Model T Van, White Body, Red Trim	1986	40
1356	Ryder Trucking	1937 Ford Tractor Trailer, White Body, Black And Red Trim	1991	35
9205	S&F Toys #1	1913 Model T Van, Grey Body, Maroon Trim	1984	20
9205	S&F Toys #2	1913 Model T Van, Grey Body, Maroon Trim	1989	20
9217	Sachs, Finley	1913 Model T Van, White Body, Red Trim	1991	20
9340	Sacred Heart Church	1913 Model T Van, White Body, Red Trim	1985	30
7508UO	Safeguard Soap	1950 Chevy Panel, Beige	1991	30
9289	Safety Kleen	Step Van, Yellow On Yellow	1987	45
9506	Safety Kleen (Drycleaner Service)	1913 Model T Van, Yellow Body, Black Trim	1986	45
9506	Safety Kleen (Parts Cleaner Service)	1913 Model T Van, Yellow Body, Black Trim	1986	45
9462	Saia Trucking	1913 Model T Van, White Body, Red Trim	1986	395
2101	Salvation Army	Step Van, White On White	1987	100
9109	Salvation Army	1913 Model T Van, White Body, Red Trim	1987	100
1297	San Francisco 49ers	1913 Model T Van, Gold Body, Red Trim	1984	80

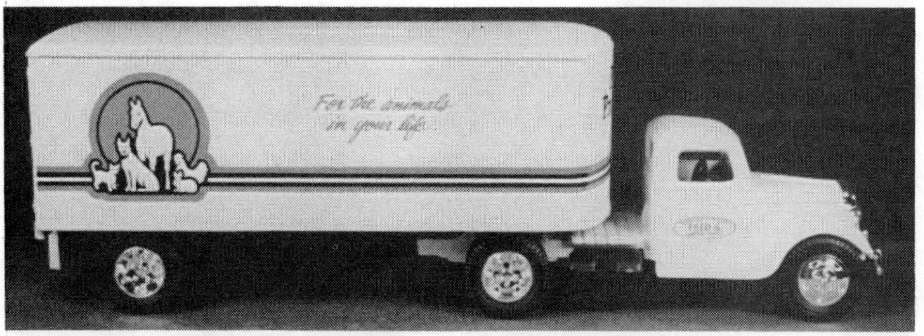

Top to Bottom: All Ertl Banks; Model 9111UO Check the Oil #2; #9766 Anheuser-Busch; #9804 Riverview Nursery; #9978 Ocean Spray; #0531 John Deere #1; #0379 New Holland; #2917 Pocono Antique Bazaar.

Ertl Banks

NO.	BANK	MODEL	YEAR	MIB
9941	Sara Lee	1950 Chevy Panel, Maroon Body, Black Trim	1989	50
9354	Sasco Aloe Vera	1917 Model T Van, Grey Body, Maroon Trim	1985	25
9225	Saskatchewan, Canada	1913 Model T Van, White Body, Orange Trim	1985	20
9228	Schneider Meats	1926 Mack Truck, Orange Body, Blue Trim	1985	125
9229	Schneider Meats	1932 Ford Panel, Orange Body, Blue Trim	1985	115
9445	Schneider Meats	1950 Chevy Panel, Orange Body, Black Trim	1986	150
1332	Schneider Meats	1913 Model T Van, Orange Body, Blue Trim	1984	40
2120	Schneiders	1913 Model T Van	1991	25
9210	Schwan's Ice Cream	1950 Chevy Panel, Brown On Brown	1984	125
9652	Scott Tissue #1	1917 Model T Van, Gold Spokes, White Body, Blue Trim	1989	85
9652UP	Scott Tissue #2	1917 Model T Van, Silver Spokes, White Body, Blue Trim	1990	45
2121UO	Sealed Power Piston Rings	1905 Ford Delivery Van, White Body, Red Trim	1990	25
9834UA	Sealed Power Piston Rings	1918 Ford Runabout, White Body, Red Trim	1991	25
1663UP	Sealed Power Speed-Pro	1905 Ford Delivery Van, Black Body, Red Trim	1990	25
2129	Sears	1913 Model T Van, Black Body, White Trim	1984	30
7510UA	Servistar	1918 Ford Runabout, Grey Body, Black And Red Trim	1990	20
9817	Servistar	1905 Ford Delivery Van, Grey Body, Red Trim	1988	35
9036	Servistar	1913 Model T Van, Grey Body, Blue Trim	1989	25
9155	Seven Eleven	1926 Mack Truck, White Body, Green Trim	1991	35
9153UP	Seven Eleven	1913 Model T Van	1991	35
1662	Seven-Up	1913 Model T Van,White Body, Green Trim	1988	185
9676UP	Shamrock #1	1931 Hawkeye Tanker, Green Body, White Trim	1991	35
1347	Shelby Life Insurance	1905 Ford Delivery Van, White Body, Blue Trim	1988	85
9097UP	Shepherdstown, West Virginia, Fire Department	1926 Seagrave Pumper	1991	30
9036UA	Shippensburg, PA, Vigilant Hose Co.	1926 Seagrave Pumper, Red	1991	25
9039	Shopko	1913 Model T Van, White Body, Blue Trim	1989	30
9426	Shoprite	1913 Model T Van, Yellow Body, Red Trim	1986	35
9163	Shoprite	1918 Ford Runabout, Yellow Body, Red Trim	1987	30
9711	Shoprite	1905 Ford Delivery Van, Yellow Body, Red Trim	1988	15
9666	Shoprite	1926 Mack Truck With Crates, Yellw Body, Red Trim	1989	25
9143	Shrine Circus	1926 Mack Truck, Red Body	1991	45
9204UP	Sico Independent Oil Co.	Horse Team And Tanker, Yellow Body, Black Trim	1991	45
1335	Sidney Fire	1913 Model T Van, White Body, Red Trim	1988	20
9871UA	Sidney, Illinois, Fire Dpeartment	1926 Seagrave Pumper	1991	25
9619	Silver Springs Flea Market	1918 Ford Runabout, White Body, Black Trim	1988	30
2972UO	Silver Springs Speedway	1932 Ford Panel, White Body, Red Trim	1990	55
2119UP	Sinclair	1926 Mack Tanker, White Body, Green Trim	1990	65
2120UO	Sinclair	1926 Mack Tanker, White Body, Green Trim	1990	55
2119UP	Sinclair	1926 Mack Tanker, White Body, Green Trim	1991	85
9483	Sinclair #3	1918 Ford Runabout	1991	30
9709UO	Slice	Step Van, White Body, Green Trim	1991	30
9493	Smoke Craft	1918 Ford Runabout, White Body, Black Trim	1987	30
9494	Smoke Craft	1905 Ford Delivery Van, White Body, Red Trim	1987	30
9164	Smoke Craft #1	1913 Model T Van, White Body, Blue Trim	1987	55
9653	Smoke Craft Meats	Step Van, White On White	1989	40

Ertl Banks

NO.	BANK	MODEL	YEAR	MIB
9654	Smoke Craft Meats	1932 Ford Panel, White Body, Blue Trim	1989	35
9124	Smokey The Bear #1	1913 Model T Van, White Body, Green Trim	1989	40
9123	Smokey The Bear #2	1918 Ford Runabout, Green And White Body, Black Trim	1989	45
2147	Smokey The Bear #3	1937 Ford Tractor Trailer, White	1991	30
2146	Smokey The Bear #4	1931 Hawkeye Truck, Green Body, White Trim	1991	30
2147	Smokey The Bear #5	1937 Ford Tractor Trailer	1991	30
9269	Sohio Gas	1926 Mack Tanker, White Body, Red Trim	1987	335
9879	South Dakota Centennial	Horse And Carriage, Blue Body, Black Trim	1988	35
9199	Southern States Oil	1926 Mack Tanker, Silver Body, Red Trim	1987	250
9797	Southern States Oil	1926 Mack Truck, Grey Body, Red Trim	1988	40
9322	Southern States Oil	1918 Ford Runabout, Red Body, Black Trim	1989	45
7628UO	Southern States Oil	1937 Ford Tractor Trailer, Red Body, Black Trim	1990	35
1991	Southwest Airlines	1950 Chevy Panel		30
9741	Sparklettes Water	1926 Mack Truck, Green On Green	1988	30
9247	Spartan Food Stores	1913 Model T Van, Green On Green	1985	30
9654UP	Springfield, Oregon, Fire Department	1926 Seagrave Pumper, Orange Body, Black Trim	1991	30
9304	St. Columbkille	1913 Model T Van, White Body, Blue Trim	1986	35
9476	State Line Auto Auction	1950 Chevy Panel, White	1991	30
9688UO	Stayton, Oregon, Fire District	1926 Seagrave Pumper, Yellow	1991	30
9167	Steamtown, USA	1926 Mack Tanker, White Body, Red Trim	1987	100
9604	Steelcase	1905 Ford Delivery Van, Blue Body, Silver Trim	1988	30
9041	Steelcase	1926 Mack Truck With Crates, Black Body, Brown Trim	1989	40
7502UO	Steelcase	1937 Ford Tractor Trailer, White Body, Black Trim	1990	45
7503UO	Steelcase	1932 Ford Panel, Blue Body, Silver Trim	1990	30
1657	Steelcase #1	1913 Model T Van, Red Spokes With Gold Trim, Blue Body, Silver Trim	1982	95
9265	Steelcase #2	1918 Ford Runabout, Blue Body, Black Trim	1987	45
1657	Steelcase #2	1913 Model T Van, Chrome Spokes, Blue Body, Silver Trim	1989	45
1657	Steelcase #3	1913 Model T Van, Red Spokes With Chrome Trim, Blue Body, Silver Trim	1989	100
9841	Stevens Brothers Cartage (Bekins)	1926 Mack Truck, White Body, Black Trim	1988	35
9224	Still Transfer Company	1937 Ford Tractor Trailer, White Body, Red Trim	1990	25
9006	Storey	1931 Hawkeye Wrecker, Red Body, Black Trim	1991	75
9353	Strawberry Point, Iowa	1913 Model T Van, White Body, Red Trim	1990	35
7679UO	Stroh's Beer	1918 Ford Runabout With Barrels, Red And Black Body, Red Trim	1990	35
9618	Sunholidays Travel	1918 Ford Runabout, White Body, Black Trim	1988	30
9169UP	Sun Records	1950 Chevy Panel, Yellow Body, Black Trim	1991	35
9518	Sunbeam Bread	1913 Model T Van, White Body, Red Trim	1986	100
9631	Sunbeam Bread	1913 Model T Van, White Body, Red Trim	1989	45
1329UO	Sunbeam Bread	1950 Chevy Panel, Yellow Body, Blue Trim	1991	30
9638	Sunbeam Bread Step Van #1	Step Van, Yellow Body, Blue Trim	1989	35
9638	Sunbeam Bread Step Van #2	Step Van, Yellow Body, Blue Trim	1991	25
1330	Sunbeam Bread	1932 Ford Panel With Spare Tire, Blue Body, Yellow Trim	1990	35
9575	Sunmaid Raisins	1905 Ford Delivery Van, Red On Red	1989	30
9576	Sunmaid Raisins	Step Van, Red On Red	1990	40
9796UO	Sunoco #1	1926 Mack Tanker, Blue Body, Yellow Trim	1991	50

Ertl Banks

NO.	BANK	MODEL	YEAR	MIB
9796UO	Sunoco #1 Sampler	1926 Mack Tanker, Blue Body, Silver Trim	1991	85
9026UP	Sunsweet	1950 Chevy Panel	1991	35
9663EO	Super Valu #1	1932 Ford Panel With Spare Tire, White Body, Red Trim	1990	25
9721EP	Super Valu #2	1923 Chevy Truck, White Body, Red Trim	1991	25
9466UO	Support The U.S. Armed Forces	1950 Chevy Panel, Blue Body, White Trim	1991	25
7613UO	Support Your Local Fire Department	1950 Chevy Panel, Red On Red	1990	25
7506UO	Support Your Local Police	1950 Chevy Panel, Black On Black	1990	25
7540UO	Support Your Local Sheriff	1950 Chevy Panel, Black On Black	1990	30
9294UA	Sussex County Farm & Horse Show	1931 Hawkeye Truck	1991	45
9146UP	Sussex County Farm & Horse Show (Coors)	1918 Ford Runabout, Silver Body, White And Blue Trim	1991	35
7632UO	Sussex County Farm & Horse Show (Coors)	1905 Ford Delivery Van, White Body, Red Trim	1990	50
7631UP	Sweet 'n Low	1950 Chevy Panel, Pink Body, Black Trim	1991	55
2140	Swiss Valley #1	1913 Model T Van, White Body, Red Trim	1984	75
9343	Swiss Valley #2	1913 Model T Van, White Body, Red Trim	1885	55
9847	Swiss Valley #3	1905 Ford Delivery Van, White Body, Orange Trim	1988	35
9345	Tabasco	1931 Hawkeye Truck With Crates, Red Body, Green Trim	1991	30
9878	Tabasco (McIlhenny)	1905 Ford Delivery Van, White Body, Orange Trim	1988	25
9078	Tabasco (McIlhenny)	1918 Ford Runabout With Barrels, Orange Body, Black Anf White Trim	1989	30
9420	Tennessee Homecoming 1986	1913 Model T Van, White Body, Red Trim	1986	175
9465	Terminix International #1	1913 Model T Van, White Body, Orange Trim	1986	45
9840	Terminix International #2	1917 Model T Van, White On White	1988	25
9086	Terminix International #3	1905 Ford Delivery Van, White Body, Orange Trim	1989	30
9346	Terminix International #4	1932 Ford Panel, White Body, Orange Trim	1991	25
2128	Texaco #1 Sampler	1913 Model T Van, Applied Label, White Body, Red Trim	1984	1450
2128	Texaco #1	1913 Model T Van, Silk Screened, White Body, Red Trim	1984	650
2128	Texaco #1	1913 Model T Van, Silk Screened, White Body, Red Trim	1986	650
9238	Texaco #2	1926 Mack Tanker, White Body, Red Trim	1985	400
9238	Texaco #2 Sampler	1926 Mack Tanker, White Body, Red Trim	1985	500
9396	Texaco #3	1932 Ford Panel, White Body, Red Trim	1986	300
9396	Texaco #3 Sampler	1932 Ford Panel, White Body, Red Trim	1986	325
9321	Texaco #4	1905 Ford Delivery Van, Black Body, Red Trim	1987	75
9376	Texaco #4 Sampler	1905 Ford Delivery Van, White Body, Red Trim	1987	195
9740	Texaco #5	1918 Ford Runabout, Black Body, Red Trim	1988	50
9740	Texaco #5 Sampler	1918 Ford Runabout, Gold Spokes, Black Body, Red Trim	1988	125
9040VO	Texaco #6	1926 Mack Truck, Marker 1925 Mack, Red Body, Black Trim	1989	65
9330	Texaco #7 Sampler	1930 Diamond T Tanker, Missing #7 Mark On Bottom, Red Body, Black Trim	1990	135
9330VO	Texaco #7	1930 Diamond T Tanker, Embossed, Red Body, Black Trim	1990	45
9613	Thompson Trucking	1937 Ford Tractor Trailer, White Body, Yellow Trim	1989	30
9268	Thunderhills #1	1913 Model T Van, White Body, Blue Trim	1987	325

Ertl Banks

NO.	BANK	MODEL	YEAR	MIB
9792	Thunderhills #2	1905 Ford Delivery Van, White Body, Red Trim	1988	250
9326	Thunderhills #3	1926 Mack Truck, White Body, Black Trim	1989	200
7566UO	Thunderhills #4	1918 Ford Runabout, White Body, Black Trim	1990	25
9736	Thunderhills #5	1923 Chevy Truck, Green Body, White Trim	1991	175
7509	Tide Soap	1913 Model T Van, Orange	1990	30
1321	Tioga County, NY, Bicentennial	1913 Model T Van, White Body, Blue Trim	1990	30
9948UO	Tisco	1926 Mack Truck, White Body, Green Trim	1989	150
9949UO	Tisco	1918 Ford Runabout, White Body, Black Trim	1989	30
9649UO	Tisco	Step Van, White Body, Red Trim	1990	45
9983UA	Tisco	1905 Ford Delivery Van, White Body, Red Trim	1990	150
9983UO	Tisco	1917 Model T Van, White Body, Black Trim	1990	25
9489	Titleist Golf Balls	1913 Model T Van, White Body, Red Trim	1987	50
1338UPO	Tom's Snack Foods	Step Van, New Logo, Tan Body	1990	30
1337UO	Tom's Snack Foods	Step Van, Old Logo, Tan Body, Red Trim	1990	30
9739UP	Tonka Toys	1913 Model T Van, White Body, Red Trim	1991	35
9142	Tower City Ambulance	1917 Model T Van	1991	20
1664	Toy Farmer #1	1913 Model T Van, White Body, Blue Trim	1983	20
9483	Toy Farmer #2 (10th Anniversary)	1913 Model T Van, Red Body, Blue Trim	1987	25
9442	Toy Shop #1	1926 Mack Truck, White Body, Red Trim	1989	30
2118	Toy Shop #2	1913 Model T Van, White Body, Red Trim	1990	20
9480	Toy Tractor Times #1	1937 Ford Tractor Trailer, White On White	1988	30
9480	Toy Tractor Times #2	1937 Ford Tractor/Trailer, White Body, Trim	1988	30
2105	Toymaster	1913 Model T Van, Yellow Body, Trim	1984	35
9208	Tractor Supply Company	1932 Ford Panel, White Body, Red Trim	1984	60
9207	Tractor Supply Company	1950 Chevy Panel, White Body, Trim	1985	65
9356	Tractor Supply Company	1917 Model T Van, Red Body, White Trim	1986	30
9356	Tractor Supply Company	1917 Model T Van, White Body, Red Trim	1986	25
9530	Tractor Supply Company	1918 Runabout, White Body, Red Trim	1986	30
9133	Tractor Supply Company	1926 Mack W/Crates, Red Body, Black Trim	1989	35
1349	Tractor Supply Company #1	1913 Model T Van, White Body, Red Trim	1982	40
2121	Tractor Supply Company #1	1926 Mack Truck, Red Body, White Trim	1984	55
9355	Tractor Supply Company #1	1905 Ford Delivery Van, Red Body, White Trim	1986	25
1349	Tractor Supply Company #2	1913 Model T Van, Red Body, White Trim	1983	40
9357	Tractor Supply Company	1905 Ford Delivery Van, White Body, Red Trim	1986	25
2100	Tractor Supply Company #2-50th Anniversary	1926 Mack Truck, White Body, Red Trim	1987	40
9416	Traer, Iowa Lions Club	1913 Model T Van, White Body, Purple Trim	1986	45
1311	Trappey "Bull Brand" Hot Sauce	1905 Ford Delivery Van, Cream Body, Red Trim	1990	35
9754	Tremont Area Ambulance Association	1913 Model T Van, White Body, Blue Trim	1989	30
7665UO	Tremont Area Ambulance Association	1932 Ford Panel, White Body, Blue Trim	1990	40
7637UO	Tropicana Orange Juice	1905 Ford Delivery Van, White Body, Orange Trim	1990	75
9798	Tropicana Orange Juice	1932 Ford Panel, Orange Body, Green Trim	1991	25
9898	Trucklite	1937 Ford Tractor/Trailer, White Body, Trim	1988	30
1348	True Value #1	1913 Model T Van, White Body, Blue Trim	1982	175
9501	True Value #10 - 10th Anniversary	1931 Hawkeye Truck, White Body, Blue Trim	1991	20
1362	True Value #2	1926 Mack Truck, Red Body, Black Trim	1983	80
1296	True Value #3	1950 Chevy Panel (Marked 1948 Chevy Panel), Light Brown Body, Trim	1984	75

Ertl Banks

NO.	BANK	MODEL	YEAR	MIB
9232	True Value #4	1932 Ford Panel, White Body, Blue Trim	1985	55
9366	True Value #5	1918 Runabout, White Body, Blue Trim	1986	40
9301	True Value #6	1905 Ford Delivery Van, White Body, Red Trim	1987	35
9105	True Value #7	1926 Mack W/Crates, Brown Body, Red Trim	1988	25
9623	True Value #8	1918 Barrel Runabout, Red Body, Black Trim	1989	25
7625EO	True Value #9	Horse Team & Tanker, Red Body, Black Trim	1990	25
9260	Trustworthy Hardware #1 Ltd. Ed.	1917 Model T Van, White Body, Brown Trim	1985	60
9395	Trustworthy Hardware #2	1905 Ford Delivery Van, White Body, Brown Trim	1986	30
9375	Trustworthy Hardware #3 Ltd. Ed.	1926 Mack Truck, White Body, Brown Trim	1987	30
9774	Trustworthy Hardware #4 Ltd. Ed.	1918 Runabout, Brown Body, Black Trim	1988	30
9744	Trustworthy Hardware #5 W/Spare	1913 Model T Van, White Body, Brown Trim	1989	25
9100YA	Trustworthy Hardware #6 Ltd. Ed. Sample	1932 Ford Panel, Brown Body, Silver Trim	1990	65
9100UA	Trustworthy Hardware #6 W/Spare Ltd. Ed.	1932 Ford Panel, White Body, Brown Trim	1990	35
9377UA	Trustworthy Hardware Stores #7	1918 Barrel Runabout, Black Body, Brown Trim	1991	20
9302	Trustworthy Hardware Stores Ltd. Ed.	1918 Barrel Runabout, Black Body, Brown Trim - Hardware Show	1991	35
9846	Tulsa, OK Fire Department	1926 Seagrave Pumper	1991	30
2106UP	Turner Hydraulics	1931 Hawkeye Truck, White Body, Black Trim	1990	30
1659	U.S. Mail	1905 Ford Delivery Van, White Body, Blue Trim	1988	95
9727	U.S. Mail	1937 Ford Tractor/Trailer, White Body, Trim	1988	40
9730	U.S. Mail	1917 Model T Van, White Body, Trim	1988	40
9532	U.S. Mail	1913 Model T Van, White Body, Trim	1989	25
9209UO	U.S. Mail	Step Van, White Body, Red/White/Black Trim	1990	70
9532	U.S. Mail #1 (Limited Edition)	1913 Model T Van, White Body, Trim	1987	35
9843	U.S. Mail #2 Ltd. Ed. W/ Spare	1918 Runabout, White Body, Trim	1988	25
9052	U.S. Mail #3 Ltd. Ed. W/ Spare	1932 Ford Panel, White Body, Blue Trim	1989	25
7641UA	U.S. Mail #4 Ltd. Ed.	1905 Ford Delivery Van, Blue Body, Red Trim	1990	30
9169	U.S. Mail (Express Mail)	1926 Mack Truck, White Body, Black Trim	1987	115
9893	U.S. Mail (Express Mail)	1937 Ford Tractor/Trailer. White Body, Trim	1988	85
9532	U.S. Mail (With Reversed Eagle)	1913 Model T Van, White Body, Trim	1986	275
2136	U.S. Mail - 1/43 Dime Bank	1932 Ford Panel, White Body, Red/White/ Black Trim	1990	10
9296	U.S. Mail - W/O Spare	1918 Runabout, White Body, Black Trim	1987	65
9051	U.S. Mail	1932 Ford Panel, White Body, Dark Blue Trim	1989	65
1352	U.S. Mail W/Spare Ltd. Ed.	1923 Chevy Truck, Green Body, Black Trim	1991	25
9795	U.S.A. Baseball Team	1905 Ford Delivery Van, White Body, Navy Blue Trim	1988	60
9202	Unique Gardens	1913 Model T Van, White Body, Red Trim	1984	35
9122	Unique Gardens	1926 Mack Tanker, White Body, Red Trim	1987	65
9233UA	United Airlines #1	1913 Model T Van, White Body, Blue/Red Trim	1991	40
9152UP	United Airlines Cargo	1926 Mack Truck	1991	40
9299	United Hardware	1950 Chevy Panel, Red Body, White Trim	1987	50
2100	United Van Lines #1	1913 Model T Van, White Body, Black Trim	1984	55
9227	United Van Lines #2	Horse & Carriage, White Body, Black Trim	1985	40

Ertl Banks

NO.	BANK	MODEL	YEAR	MIB
9393	United Van Lines #3	1905 Ford Delivery Van, White Body, Black Trim	1986	25
9715	United Van Lines #4 Ltd. Ed.	1917 Model T Van, White Body, Black Trim	1988	30
9096	United Van Lines #5 Ltd. Ed.	1918 Runabout, White Body, Black Trim	1989	25
9821	University Of Florida "Gators"	1905 Ford Delivery Van, White Body, Orange Trim	1988	55
9497	University Of Indiana	1913 Model T Van, White Body, Red Trim	1987	30
9605	University Of Kansas (Jayhawks)	1913 Model T Van, White Body, Red Trim	1988	25
9816	University Of Kansas - '88 Nat'l Champs	1905 Ford Delivery Van, White Body, Blue Trim	1988	40
9513	University Of Michigan "Wolverines"	1913 Model T Van, Yellow Body, Blue Trim	1989	40
1330	University Of Nebraska (Go Big Red)	1913 Model T Van, White Body, Red Trim	1982	50
9300	University Of North Iowa	1913 Model T Van, White Body, Trim	1986	400
9655	University Of Wisconsin	1913 Model T Van, White Body, Red Trim	1989	30
9622	V & S Variety Stores #1	1905 Ford Delivery Van, White Body, Orange Trim	1989	35
7625EO	V & S Variety Stores #2	1918 Runabout, Black Body, Orange Trim	1990	25
9522EO	V & S Variety Stores #3	1913 Model T Van, Grey Body, Black Trim	1991	15
9616	Valley Forge	1926 Mack Truck, White Body, Red Trim	1989	75
9345	Vintage Chevrolet Club	1923 Chevy Truck	1991	35
	Virginville, PA. Community Fire Dept. 33	1926 Seagrave Pumper, Lime Green Body	1991	30
2968	W.R. Meadows Inc.	1916 Model T Van, Green Body, White Trim	1990	90
2142UP	W.W. Irwin Gasoline Maintenance Company	1905 Ford Delivery Van, Light Blue Body	1990	30
9531UP	Walgreen Co.	1913 Model T Van, Beige Body, Red Trim	1991	35
9137	Washington State Centennial	1913 Model T Van, White Body, Red Trim	1989	25
7522UO	Washington Suburban Sanitary Commission	1926 Mack Tanker, Black Body, Red Trim	1990	30
9700UP	Washington D.C. Fire Dept. Eng. Co. #16	1926 Seagrave Pumper. Red Body	1991	35
9786	Watkin's Inc.	1905 Ford Delivery Van, Black Body, Red Trim	1988	55
9276	Weber's Supermarket	1913 Model T Van, White Body, Red Trim	1987	30
2122RO	Weil-McLain Boiler - 1 Of 3 Piece Set	1926 Mack Truck, Red Body, Black Trim	1990	30
21122RO	Weil-McLain Boiler - 1 Of 3 Piece Set	1905 Ford Delivery Van, White Body, Red Trim	1990	30
2122RO	Weil-MCLain Boiler - 1 Of 3 Piece Set	1917 Model T Van, White Body, Blue Trim	1990	30
9724UO	Wellsville, PA. Fire Dept. 50th Anniversary	1926 Seagrave Pumper. Red Body, Trim	1991	30
9237UP	West Bend Ltd. Ed.	1913 Model T Van, White Body, Black Trim	1991	40
1329	Western Auto	1913 Model T Van, Red Body, Black Trim	1981	110
1353	Western Auto - Not A Bank	1932 Ford Roadster, Red Body, Black Trim	1982	130
9481	Wheatbelt Stores - Five Point	1913 Model T Van, Tan Body, Brown Trim	1987	25
1358	Wheelers	1913 Model T Van, White Body, Red Trim	1982	30
9004	White House (National Fruit Products)	1913 Model T Van, Yellow Body, Green Trim	1989	175
9005	White House (National Fruit Products)	1913 Model T Van, Yellow Body, Green Trim	1989	200
7882	White Idea Farm Equipment	Dime Bank	1991	10
9897	Wilson Foods	1918 Runabout, Red Body, Black Trim	1988	35
9144EO	Winn-Dixie	1923 Chevy Truck, White Body, Green Trim	1991	20

Ertl Banks

NO.	BANK	MODEL	YEAR	MIB
1364	Winn-Dixie #1 (Red Spokes)	1913 Model T Van, White Body, Green Trim	1983	55
1364	Winn-Dixie #1 (White Spokes)	1913 Model T Van, White Body, Green Trim	1984	45
9014	Winn-Dixie #10 - Ltd. Ed.	1926 Mack W/ Crates, White Body, Green/ Brown Trim	1989	30
9013	Winn-Dixie #11 - Ltd. Ed.	1950 Chevy Panel, White Body, Green Trim	1989	35
7694	Winn-Dixie #12 W/Spare Ltd. Ed.	1913 Model T Van, White Body, Green Trim	1990	25
7693	Winn-Dixie #13 Ltd. Ed.	1931 Hawkeye Truck, White Body, Green Trim	1990	25
2125	Winn-Dixie #2	1926 Mack Truck, Green Body, White Trim	1984	60
9341	Winn-Dixie #3	1932 Ford Panel, White Body, Green Trim	1985	55
9423	Winn-Dixie #4	1932 Ford Panel, Green Body, White Trim	1986	45
9392	Winn-Dixie #5	1905 Ford Delivery Van, White Body, Green Trim	1986	55
9116	Winn-Dixie #6	1918 Runabout, Green Body, White Trim	1987	30
9117	Winn-Dixie #7	1905 Ford Delivery Van, Green Body, White Trim	1987	30
9706	Winn-Dixie #8 - Ltd. Ed.	1937 Ford Tractor/Trailer, White Body, Green Trim	1988	30
9707	Winn-Dixie #9 (W/Spare Tire)	1932 Ford Panel, White Body, Green Trim	1988	35
9821	Wireless-Minnesota Public Radio	1932 Ford Panel, Green Body, Black Trim	1991	35
9810TO	Wix Oil Filters	1932 Ford Panel, White Body, Red Trim	1991	15
1660	Wonder Bread #1	1913 Model T Van, White Body, Black Trim	1982	75
9421	Wonder Bread #2	1913 Model T Van, White Body, Black Trim	1986	40
9161	Wonder Bread #3	1913 Model T Van, White Body, Black Trim	1987	25
9498	Wood Heat	1905 Ford Delivery Van, White Body, Blue Trim	1987	35
9978	Wood Heat	1937 Ford Tractor/Trailer, White Body, Trim	1989	35
9266UP	Woody's Automotive	1950 Chevy Panel, Orange Body	1991	30
9114	Worldwide Products	Step Van, Blue/White Body	1987	75
7539UO	Worthington Firehouse	1905 Ford Delivery Truck, White Body, Red Trim	1990	40
9171	Wrangler Jeans	1913 Model T Van	1991	35
9402	Yelton Trucking	1913 Model T Van, White Body, Red Trim	1986	30
9171	Yelton Trucking - Limited Edition	1926 Mack Tanker, White Body, Red Trim	1987	40
9627	Yoder Popcorn	Step Van, White Body, Trim	1989	55
9071UO	York Peppermint Patties	1937 Ford Tractor/Trailer, Blue Body, Silver Trailer	1990	105
9069	York Peppermint Patties #1 W/ Spare	1932 Ford Panel, Silver Body, Trim	1990	105
9069UO	York Peppermint Patties #2	1932 Ford Panel, Silver Body, Trim	1991	35
9263	York, PA. - 250 Years Ltd. Ed.	1917 Model T Van	1991	30
9429	Yuengling Beer	1913 Model T Van, White Body, Red Trim	1986	125
9176	Yuengling Beer	1905 Ford Delivery Van, White Body, Red Trim	1987	120
9770	Yuengling Beer	1937 Ford Tractor/Trailer	1988	125
9216	Zinc Corp.	1913 Model T Van, White Body, Blue Trim	1991	30

Mechanical Tin Toys

Metal toys produced before World War I could be considered works of art as such. If a toy had a multicolored scheme, it was painted by hand.

But the advent of chromolithography changed the way most toys were produced. Chromolithography was actually developed late in the 19th century. The technique allowed multicolor illustrations to be printed on tinplate. The flat tin sheets were subsequently molded into toys.

Starting in the 1920s, lithographed tin toys began to dramatically change toy production. American manufacturers began to mass produce these colorful toys and offer them to the buying public at far better prices than those demanded for the classic European toys that had dominated until this time.

With mass production came mass appeal. New tin mechanical toys were based on the characters and celebrities that were popular at the time. The newspaper comic strips and Walt Disney movies provided already popular subject matter for toy marketers.

Among the most well-known makers of mechanical tin toys were Marx, Chein, Lehmann and Straus. Others included Courtland, Girard, Ohio Art, Schuco, Unique Art and Wolverine.

Many of these manufacturers had business relationships with each other. Over the years, some would be found working together, producing toys for others, distributing others' toys or being absorbed by other companies. There appeared to be even some flat-out copying of others' ideas.

One of the advantages of lithography was that it allowed old toys to be recycled in many ways. When a character's public appeal began to wane, a new image could be printed on the same old toy and, presto, a new toy. Or when a toy company was absorbed by another, its tired old models could be dusted off and dressed up with new lithography to produce new toys.

Many of the mechanical tin wind-up toys show up in surprisingly similar versions with another manufacturer's name on them.

Of the companies listed here, Marx was no doubt the most prolific. The company's founder, Louis Marx, at one time was employed by another leading toy maker, Ferdinand Strauss. He left Strauss in 1918 to start his own company. Some of his first successes were new versions of old Strauss toys, the Climbing Monkey and Alabama Coon Jigger.

Many of the popular Marx tin wind-ups were based on popular characters. One of the most sought-after is the Merrymakers Band, which was a group of Mickey Mouse-type musicians. Some of the other highly valued character toys are the Amos 'n Andy Fresh Air Taxi, the Donald Duck Duet, Popeye the Champ and Superman Rollover Airplane.

While Marx went on to produce many, many kinds of toys, other companies, such as Chein, specialized only in inexpensive lithographed tin. And like Marx, Chein also capitalized on popular cartoon characters, producing several Popeye toys, among others. J. Chein and Company, which was founded

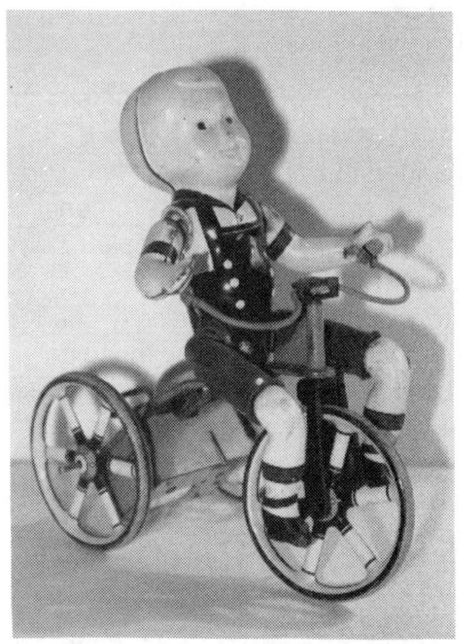

Top: Kiddie Cyclist by Unique Art; Right: Clown in Barrel, 1930s, by Chein.

in 1903, was best know for its carnival-themed mechanical toys. Its Ferris wheel is fairly well known among toy collectors, and was made in several lithographed versions, including one with a Disneyland theme. It also produced a number of affordable tin banks.

Girard was founded shortly after Chein, but didn't start producing toys until 1918. It subcontracted toys for Marx and Straus in the 1920s. In fact, several Girard and Marx toys are identical, having been produced in the same plant with different names on them. Marx later took over the company in the 1930s.

New Jersey-based Unique Art isn't known for an extensive line of toys, but it produced some that are favorites among tin toy collectors. It, too, reportedly was acquired by Marx at some point.

There are many other companies that produced lithographed tin toys not included in this section, particularly German and Japanese companies. Lehmann and Schuco, both German firms, are the only non-American toy makers listed in here. More lithographed tin toys can be found in the vehicles section of this book.

Prices shown here are for toys in Mint, Excellent and Good conditions. Toys will usually command a premium over the listed price if they are in their original boxes.

TIN TOYS

Chein

NAME	DESCRIPTION	GOOD	EX	MINT
Banks				
Cash Box	1930's, 2" high	35	45	60
Cash Box	1930, 2" high, round trap	25	35	50
Child's Safe Bank	1900's, 5 1/2" high	45	65	90
Child's Safe Bank	1910, 4" high, sailboat on front of door	25	55	80
Child's Safe Bank	1910, 3" high, dog on front of door	30	50	70
Church	1930's, 4" high	25	55	80
Drum	1930's, 2 1/2" high	25	35	50
God Bless America	1930's, 2 1/2" high, drum shaped	35	45	60
Happy Days Cash Register	1930's, 4" high	60	85	120
Humpty Dumpty	1934, 5 1/4" high	75	100	150
Log Cabin	1930's, 3" high	120	175	200
Mascot Safe	1914, 5" high, large	25	50	75
Mascot Safe	1914, 4" high, small	30	45	65
New Deal	1930's, 3 1/4" high	60	90	125
Prosperity Bank, with band	1930's, 2 1/4" high, pail shaped	35	45	65
Prosperity Bank, without band	1930's, 2 1/4" high, pail shaped	25	35	50
Roly Poly	1940's, 6" high	125	250	350
Scout	1931, 3 1/4" high, cylinder	125	175	250
Three Little Pigs	1930's, 3" high	70	100	150
Treasure Chest	1930's, 2" high	25	35	50
Uncle Sam	1934, 4" high, hat shaped	35	45	60
Mechanical Banks				
Church	1954, 3 1/2" high	85	135	175
Clown	1931, 5" high	95	135	175
Clown	1949, 5" high, says bank on front	50	70	95
Elephant	1950's, 5" high	85	100	135
Monkey	1950's, 5 1/4" high, tin litho	75	95	125
National Duck	1954, 3 1/2" high	95	150	225
National Duck, Disney characters	6 1/2" high, Donald's tongue receives money	85	145	185
Register	Dime bank	25	35	55
Uncle Wiggly	1950's, 5" high	40	60	90
Miscellaneous Toys				
Army Drummer	1930's, 7" high, plunger-activated	85	125	175
Drum		25	35	50
Easter Basket, nursery rhyme figures		25	35	50
Easter Egg with chicken on top	1938, 5 1/2", tin, opens to hold candy	20	30	50
Helicopter, Toy Town Airways	1950's, 13" long, friction drive	50	75	100
Indian in Headdress	1930's, 5 1/2" high	80	125	175
Marine	Hand on belt	75	100	150
Melody Organ Player	1 roll	55	85	120
Musical Top Clown	1950's, 7" high, clown head handle	50	75	110
Player Piano	8 rolls	200	300	450
Sand Toy Set	Duck mold, sifter, frog on card	25	35	55
Sand Toy, monkey bends and twists	7" high	20	30	55
Scuba Diver	10" long	85	145	185
See-Saw Sand Toy, bright colors	1930's, boy and girl on see-saw move	35	45	60
See-Saw Sand Toy, pastel colors	1930's, boy and girl on see-saw move	100	165	210

Chein

NAME	DESCRIPTION	GOOD	EX	MINT
Snoopy Bus	1962	175	250	350
Space Ride, lever action with music	tin litho, boxed	100	200	300
Sparkler Toy	5", on original card	15	25	50
Teeter-Totter	11", to work pour water or sand onto board	25	35	50

Tin Windups

NAME	DESCRIPTION	GOOD	EX	MINT
"Hercules" Ferris Wheel		175	275	375
Airplane, square-winged	Early tin, 7" wingspan	75	100	140
Alligator with Native on Its Back		100	150	200
Army Cargo Truck	1920's, 8" long	175	250	350
Army Plane	11" wingspan	100	150	200
Army Sergeant		75	115	150
Army Truck, cannon on back	8 1/2" long	20	30	50
Army Truck, open bed	8 1/2" long	20	30	50
Barnacle Bill	1930's, looks like Popeye, waddles	225	400	550
Barnacle Bill in barrel	1930's, 7" high	225	400	550
Bear with hat, pants, shirt, bow tie	1938	35	60	75
Bunny, bright colors	1940's, tin litho	20	30	50
Cabin Cruiser	1940's, 9" long	20	30	50
Cat	With wood wheels	40	55	75
Chick, brightly colored clothes, polka dot bow-tie	4" high	20	35	50
Chicken pushing wheelbarrow	1930's	26	40	55
China Clipper	10" long	125	175	250
Clown Balancing	1930's, 5" tall	20	45	65
Clown Boxing	8" tall, tin	275	435	600
Clown in Barrel	1930's, 8" high, waddles	200	300	400
Clown with Parasol	1920's, 8" tall, springs parasol on nose	100	140	175
Dan-Dee Dump Truck		150	225	300
Disneyland Ferris Wheel	1940's	490	625	850
Disneyland Roller Coaster		425	650	875
Doughboy, WWI soldier with rifle	1920's, 6" high, tin litho	125	185	250
Drummer Boy	1930's, 9" high, with shako	70	100	130
Duck	1930, 4" high, waddles	30	40	55
Duck, long-beaked in orange sailor suit	1930, 6" high, waddles	50	75	100
Ferris Wheel, 6 compartments	1930's, 16 1/2" high, ringing bell	295	350	525
Ferris Wheel, The Giant Rides	16" high	45	70	90
Greyhound Bus	6" long, wood tires	100	150	220
Handstand Clown		100	160	195
Happy Hooligan	1932, 6" high, tin litho	250	275	350
Hercules Ferris Wheel		175	275	375
Indian	4" high, red with headdress	60	90	125
Jumping Rabbit	1925	125	175	250
Junior Bus	9" long, yellow	85	125	175
Mack "Hercules" Motor Express	19 1/2" long, tin litho	125	175	250
Mack "Hercules" Truck	7 1/2" long	100	150	175
Mark 1 Cabin Cruiser	1957, 9" long	20	30	55
Mechanical Aquaplane, No. 39	1932, 8 1/2" long, boat-like pontoons	125	175	250
Mechanical Fish	1940's, 11" long	20	35	55

Chein

NAME	DESCRIPTION	GOOD	EX	MINT
Merry-Go-Round with swan chairs	11"	450	600	750
Motorboat	1950's, 9" long	15	25	50
Motorboat, crank action	1950's, 7" long	15	25	50
Musical Aero Swing	1940's, 10" high	225	350	450
Musical Merry-Go-Round	Small version	100	175	225
Musical Toy Church	1937, crank music box	50	70	90
Peggy Jane Speedboat		40	60	85
Pelican		120	175	250
Penguin in tuxedo	1940, tin litho	30	40	50
Pig		30	40	55
Playland Merry-Go-Round	1930's, 9 1/2" high	300	600	750
Playland Whip, No. 340	4 bump cars, driver's head wobbles	400	600	800
Popeye in barrel		375	550	750
Popeye the heavy hitter	Bell and mallet	900	1200	1800
Popeye with punching bag		1000	1250	1400
Rabbit in shirt and pants	1938	15	25	35
Ride-A-Rocket, carnival ride	1950's, 19" high, 4 rockets	350	500	750
Roadster	1925, 8 1/2" long, tin litho	15	20	65
Roller Coaster	1938, includes 2 cars	225	350	525
Roller Coaster	1950's, includes 2 cars	225	350	525
Royal Blue Line Coast to Coast Service		300	450	600
Sandmill	Beach scene on side	125	175	225
Santa's Elf	1925, 6" high, boxed	225	325	450
Sea Plane	1930's, silver, red, and blue	10	175	250
Seal	Balancing barbells	60	90	125
Ski-Boy	1930's, 8" long, tin	125	225	300
Ski-Boy	1930's, 6" long, tin	125	225	300
Speedboat	14" long	125	165	195
Touring Car	7" long, tin litho	40	60	75
Turtle with Native on Its Back	1940's, tin litho	100	175	225
Walk on Hands Clown	Striped pants	110	130	175
Walk on Hands Clown	Polka dot pants	120	150	195
Woody Car	1940's, 5" long, red	75	190	250
Yellow Cab	7" long	190	210	250
Yellow Taxi	Early tin, 6" long, orange and black	100	175	250

Courtland

NAME	DESCRIPTION	GOOD	EX	MINT
Bakery Delivery Truck	"Pies, Cakes, Rolls, Fresh Bread," 7" long, 1950s	110	150	190
Bakery Panel Truck #4000	"Hot Buns & Hot Donuts," 7" long	110	150	185
Black Diamond Coal Truck	13" long	110	150	185
Caterpillar Tractor	5 1/2" long	70	90	110
Checker Cab #4000		130	170	210
Circus Elephant and Lions Cart	11 1/2" long, 1940s	100	130	160
City Meat Panel Truck #4000	7" long	115	150	185
Express & Hauling Stake Truck	9" long, 1940s	100	130	160
Farm Tractor	9" long	85	110	135
Fire Patrol No. 2 Truck	9" long, 1940s	110	150	185
Ice Cream Scooter	With ringing bell, 6 1/2" long, 1940s	210	285	360
State Police Car	7" long	70	90	110

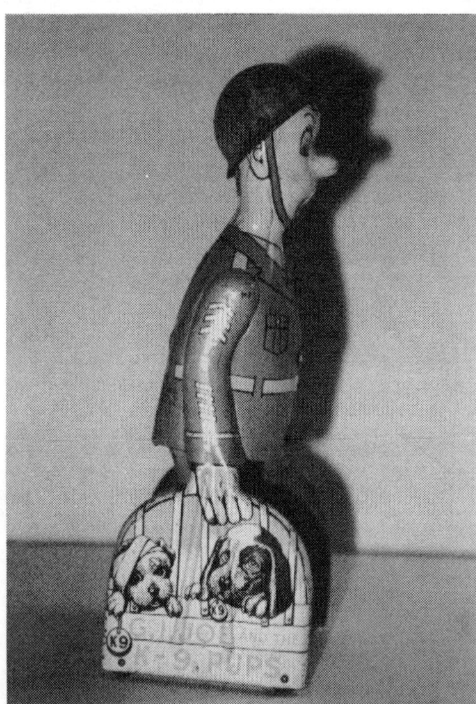

Top to Bottom: Lincoln Tunnel, 1935, by Unique Art; GI Joe and the K-9 Pups, 1941, by Unique Art; Motorcyclist by Marx; Rodeo Joe Crazy Car, 1950s, by Unique Art; Li'l Abner and the Dogpatch Band by Unique Art.

Girard

NAME	DESCRIPTION	GOOD	EX	MINT
Airplane with Twirling Propellor		200	300	500
Airways Express Air Mail Tri Motor Airplane	13" long	250	400	650
Cabriolet Coupe	14" long	250	400	650
Coupe	Windup with electric lights	250	500	750
Fire Chief Car	10" long	140	200	275
Fire Fighter Steam Boiler	Early 1900s	300	400	500
Flasho The Mechanical Grinder	1920s	100	140	175
Gobbling Goose		120	160	200
Railroad Handcar		190	225	300
Whiz Sky Fighter	9" long	270	360	450

Lehmann

NAME	DESCRIPTION	GOOD	EX	MINT
"Aha" Truck		675	925	1200
"Auton" Boy & Cart		275	375	495
"Galop" Race Car	1920s	350	475	600
"Ito" Sedan and Driver		700	1100	1350
"Wild West" Bucking Bronco		600	825	1075
Ajax Acrobat	Does somersaults, 10" tall	650	900	1200
Alabama Jigger	Windup tap dancer on square base, 1920s	600	825	1075
Captain of Kopenick	Early 1900s	800	1050	1450
Crocodile	Walks, mouth opens	400	550	725
Dancing Sailor		575	750	1000
Dancing Sailor		800	1050	1450
Delivery Van	"Huntley & Palmers Biscuits"	650	950	1350
Express Man & Cart		350	475	625
Flying Bird	Flapping tin litho	220	275	395
Gustav The Climbing Miller		500	725	900
KADI	Chinese men carrying box	825	1050	1500
Lehmann's Autobus		1200	1700	2500
Li-La Car	Driver in rear, women passengers	1000	1400	1850
Masuyama		1200	1700	2500
Mikado Family		2000	2800	3900
Minstrel Man	Early 1900s	400	600	850
New Century Cycle	Driver and black man with umbrella	750	1100	1800
Ostrich Cart		475	650	875
Paddy Riding Pig		600	825	1100
Quack Quack	Duck pulling babies	275	385	500
Rooster and Rabbit	Rooster pulls rabbit on cart	525	725	975
Sea Lion		175	275	375
Sedan and Garage		275	375	550
Shenandoah Zeppelin		150	195	275
Skier	Windup skier, 1920s	725	950	1300
Taxi	10" long, 1920s	0	0	0
Tut-Tut Car	Driver has horn	175	1500	2000
Zebra Cart "Dare Devil"	1920s	350	475	650
Zig-Zag	Handcar-type vehicle on oversized wheels	1050	1450	2000

Marx

Battery Operated Toys

NAME	DESCRIPTION	GOOD	EX	MINT
Benjali Prowling Tiger	Growls, 12" long	75	100	175
Brewster the Rooster	Stop and go action, 10" tall	100	150	200
Disneyland Haunted House Bank	Battery operated, 1950's	50	90	150

Marx

NAME	DESCRIPTION	GOOD	EX	MINT
Drummer Boy	Moving eyes, 1930's	100	150	200
Fishing Kitty	Tin and cloth, battery operated, 9" tall	125	165	250
Frankenstein	1950's	600	900	1200
Fred Flintstone on Dino		250	350	550
Hootin' Hollow Haunted House	1960's	500	800	1200
Mighty King Kong		150	250	350
Mighty Long Gorilla	Remote controlled, tin, plush	80	125	200
Mister Mercury Robot	Remote controlled, 13" tall	300	500	750
Mounted Leopard Head	Head moves, roars, eyes light, tin and plastic, 1960's	75	125	150
NASA Moon Helicopter	Remote controlled, 7" long	75	100	150
Nutty Mad Indian	12" tall, 1960's	50	80	125
Pete the Parrot	Talking parrot perched on litho tin branch, 16 1/2" tall	100	200	300
Snappy the Dragon	1960's	1000	2000	3000
Whistling Spook Tree	Bump and go, 14" tall	450	650	895
Za-Zoom Bike Engine	1960's	50	75	100

Buildings and Rooms

NAME	DESCRIPTION	GOOD	EX	MINT
Airport	1930's	60	90	125
Automatic Car Wash	Garage, car, tin windup	125	200	250
Automatic Firehouse with Fire Chief Car	Friction car, tin firehouse with plastic doors, 1940's	100	150	200
Automatic Garage	Family car, tin windup	50	90	125
Blue Bird Garage	Tin, 1937	125	200	250
Brightlite Filling Station	Pump with round top says "Fresh Air," 1930's	200	300	400
Brightlite Filling Station	Rectangular shaped pumps, battery operated, late 1930's	175	250	350
Brightlite Filling Station	Bottle shaped gas pumps, battery operated, tin, 1930's	200	300	400
Bus Terminal	1937	100	200	300
Busy Airport Garage	Tin litho, 1936	150	250	350
Busy Parking Lot	Five heavy gauge streamline autos, 1937	225	325	425
Busy Street	Six vehicles waiting to get gas, 1935	175	250	350
City Airport	With two metal planes, 1938	75	100	175
Crossing Gate House		90	130	175
Crossover Speedway	150", 1941	100	150	200
Crossover Speedway	Litho buildings on bridge, 2 cars litho drivers, 144", 1938	100	150	200
Dick Tracy Automatic Police Station	Station and car	300	450	650
Gas Pump Island		100	150	200
General Alarm Fire House	Windup alarm bell, steel chief car and patrol truck, 1938	175	250	350
Greyhound Bus Terminal	Tin, 1938	125	200	250
Gull Service Station	Tin litho, 1940's	180	280	375
Hollywood Bungalow House	Garage, awnings, tin, celluloid, 1935	150	250	350
Home Town Drug Store	Tin litho, 1930's	100	195	225
Home Town Favorite Store	Tin litho, 1930's	100	195	245
Home Town Fire House	Tin litho, 1930's	115	195	245
Home Town Grocery Store	Tin litho, 1930's	100	195	225
Home Town Meat Market	Tin litho, 1930's	105	195	225
Home Town Movie Theatre	Tin litho, 1930's	145	215	275
Home Town Police Station	Tin litho, 1930's	105	195	225
Home Town Savings Bank	Tin litho, 1930's	105	195	225
Honeymoon Garage	Heavy gauge litho steel, 1935	175	250	350
Lincoln Highway Set	Pumps, oil-grease rack, traffic light and car, 1933	350	525	700
Loop-the-Loop Auto Racer	1 3/4" long car, 1931	100	150	250
Magic Garage	Litho garage, friction town car, 1934	75	125	175

Marx

NAME	DESCRIPTION	GOOD	EX	MINT
Magic Garage	Litho garage, windup car, 1934	75	125	175
Main Street Station	Litho garage, 4" windup steel vehicles	150	250	350
Metal Service Station	Litho, 1949-50	225	325	550
Military Airport		100	150	200
Model School House	1960's	35	50	70
Mot-O-Run 4 Lane Hi-Way	Cars, trucks, buses move on electric track, 27" track, 1949	125	200	250
New York World's Fair Speedway	Litho track, two red cars, 1939	275	400	550
Newlywed's Bathroom	Tin litho, 1920's	95	110	145
Newlywed's Bedroom	Tin litho, 1920's	95	110	145
Newlywed's Dining Room	Tin litho, 1920's	95	110	145
Newlywed's Kitchen	Tin litho, 1920's	95	110	145
Newlywed's Library	Tin litho, 1920's	95	110	145
Roadside Rest Service Station	Laurel and Hardy at counter with stools in front, 1935	550	850	1200
Roadside Rest Service Station	Laurel and Hardy at counter no stool in front, 1938	400	600	850
Service Station	2 pumps, 2 friction vehicles, 1929	275	350	550
Service Station Gas Pumps	Tin litho, windup, 9" tall	50	80	125
Sky Hawk Flyer	Tin-plated, windup, two planes, tower 7 1/2" tall	150	225	150
Stunt Auto Racer	Two blue racers, 1931	175	250	350
Sunnyside Garage	Litho cardboard garage, ten vehicles, 1935	325	500	650
Sunnyside Service Station	Oil cart, two pumps, litho garage, tin windup, 1934	125	200	250
TV and Radio Station		100	200	300
Universal Motor Repair Shop	Tin, 1938	225	350	550
Used Car Market	Base, several vehicles and signs, 1939	225	350	550
Whee-Whiz Auto Racer	Four 2" multicolored racers with litho driver, 1925	275	450	600

Miscellaneous Toys

NAME	DESCRIPTION	GOOD	EX	MINT
Army Code Sender	Pressed steel	10	15	20
Baby Grand Piano	Tin, with piano-shaped music books	40	60	80
Big Shot		65	100	130
Cat Pushing Ball	Lever action, wood ball, tin, 1938	60	80	125
Cat with Ball	Cable-operated, tin litho	35	50	75
Champion Skater	Ballet dancer	60	90	120
Flashy Flickers Magic Picture Gun	1960's	25	50	50
Hopalong Cassidy on his Horse	1950's wind-up	175	250	375
Hopping Rabbit	Metal and plastic, 4" tall, 1950's	20	30	50
Jack in the Music Box	1950's	30	45	60
Jumping Frog	Tin	20	30	50
Jungle Man Spear	Tin	100	145	175
King Kong	On wheels, with spring-loaded arms, 6 1/2" tall	35	50	70
Mysterious Woodpecker	Tin	35	55	75
Pathe Movie Camera	Tin litho, 6" tall, 1930's	50	75	100
Rooster	Large	40	65	85
Roy Rogers and Trigger	1950's	150	200	275
Searchlight	Tin litho, 3 1/2" tall	35	55	75
Toto the Acrobat		100	150	250
Warriors of the World Historic Trader Cards	1963, boxed complete set	60	100	125

Trains

NAME	DESCRIPTION	GOOD	EX	MINT
Commodore Vanderbilt Train	Track, windup	80	120	190
Crazy Express Train	Plastic and litho, windup, 12" long, 1960's	150	225	300

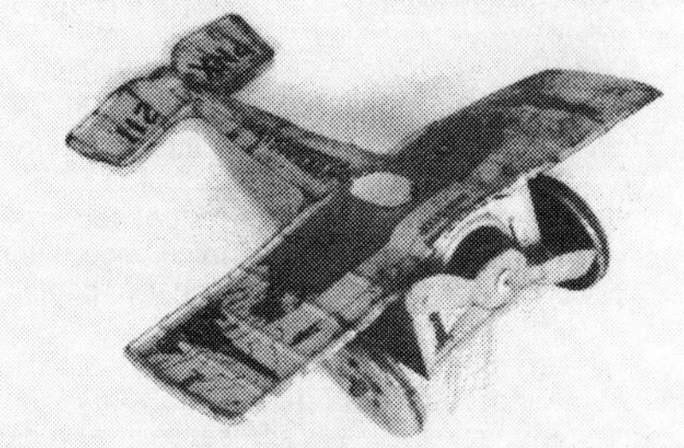

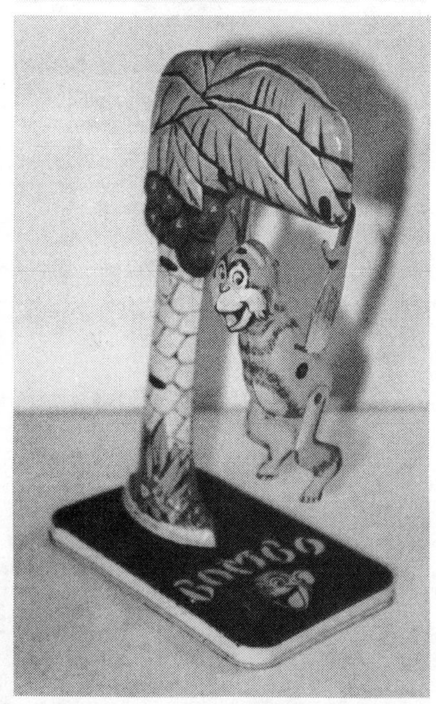

Top to Bottom: Jazzbo Jim, 1920s, by Unique Art; GI Joe and His Jouncing Jeep, 1940s, by Unique Art; Spirit of America, 1930s, by Chein; Howdy Doody and Buffalo Bob at the Piano, by Unique Art; Bombo the Monk, 1930s, By Unique Art.

Marx

NAME	DESCRIPTION	GOOD	EX	MINT
Disneyland Express	Locomotive and 3 tin cars, tin windup, 21 1/2" long, 1950's	300	500	650
Disneyland Express, Casey Jr. Circus Train	Tin windup, 12" long	175	275	350
Disneyland Train	Goofy drives locomotive with 3 tin cars, windup, 1950	75	130	175
Engine Train	Ten cars, no track, HO, 1960's	85	125	170
Flintstones Choo Choo Train "Bedrock Express"	Tin windup, 13" long, 1950's	300	450	600
Glendale Depot Railroad Station Train	Accessories, tin, 1930's	100	175	225
Mickey Mouse Express Train Set	Tin litho, plastic, 1952	300	450	600
Mickey Mouse Meteor Train	Four cars/engine, windup, 1950's	300	500	650
Musical Choo-Choo	1966	45	60	90
Mystery Tunnel	Tin windup	75	125	150
New York Central Engine Train	Four cars, tin litho	250	375	500
New York Circular with Train, with airplane	Tin windup, 1928	425	650	900
New York Circular with Train, without airplane	Tin windup, 1928	400	600	850
Popeye Express, with airplane	1936	900	1250	1800
Railroad Watch Tower	Electric light, 9" tall	45	60	90
Roy Rogers Stagecoach Train	Hard plastic and tin litho, windup, 14" long, 1950's	150	250	350
Scenic Express Train Set	Tin windup, 1950's	80	120	160
Subway Express	With plastic tunnel, 1954	225	350	450
Train Set	Plastic locomotive, tin cars, windup, 6" long, 1950's	75	100	150
Trolley No. 200	Headlight, bell, tin windup, 9" long, 1920's	250	375	500
Tunnel	Depicts farm scene, rolling hills, houses, tin litho	125	200	250
Walt Disney Train Set	Ranger-sized train set, tin litho, windup, 21 1/2" long, 1950	225	350	450

Wagons and Carts

NAME	DESCRIPTION	GOOD	EX	MINT
Bluto, Brutus, Horse and Cart	Celluloid figure, metal, 1938	450	650	900
Busy Delivery	Open three-wheel cart, windup, 9" long, 1939	300	450	600
Farm Wagon	Horse pulling wagon, 10" long, 1940's	75	100	150
Horse and Cart	With driver, 9 1/2" long, 1950's	50	80	100
Horse and Cart	Windup, 7" long, 1934	100	150	200
Horse and Cart with Clown Driver	Windup, 7 5/8" long, 1923	150	250	350
Pinocchio Busy Delivery	On unicycle facing 2-wheel cart, windup, 7 3/4" long, 1939	300	450	600
Popeye Horse and Cart	Tin windup	300	450	600
Rooster Pulling Wagon	Tin litho, 1930's	150	250	350
Toylands Farm Products Milk Wagon	Tin windup, 10 1/2" long, 1930's	80	125	175
Toylands Milk and Cream Wagon	Balloon tires, tin litho, windup 10" long, 1931	125	200	250
Toytown Dairy Horsedrawn Cart	Tin windup, 10 1/2" long, 1930's	100	175	225
Two Donkeys Pulling Cart	With driver, tin litho, windup, 10 1/4" long, 1940's	90	125	175

Marx

NAME	DESCRIPTION	GOOD	EX	MINT
Wagon with Two-Horse Team	Late 1940's, tin windup	50	90	125
Wagon with Two-Horse Team	1950, tin windup	40	65	85

Windup Toys

NAME	DESCRIPTION	GOOD	EX	MINT
Acrobatic Marvel Monkey	Balances on two chairs, tin, 1930's	80	125	175
Acrobatic Marvel Rocking Monkey	Tin litho, 13 1/4" tall, 1930's	200	325	425
Acrobatic Pinocchio	Tin	125	200	250
Amos and Andy Walkers	Walker, tin litho, 11" tall, 1930	900	1350	1600
Andy "Andrew Brown" of Amos 'n Andy	Walker, tin, 12" tall, 1930's	450	675	900
B.O. Plenty Holding Sparkle Plenty	Tin litho, 8 1/2" tall, 1940's	190	275	350
Balky Mule	Tin litho, 8 3/4" long, 1948	75	130	175
Ballerina	6" tall	50	75	100
Barney Rubble Riding Dino	Tin, 8" long, 1960's	175	295	375
Bear Cyclist	Lever action, metal, litho, 5 3/4" tall, 1934	75	125	175
Bear Waddler	Tin, 4" tall, 1960's	40	65	85
Beat!! The Komikal Kop	Tin, 1930's	80	150	200
Big Parade	Tin litho, moving vehicles, soldiers, etc., 1928	400	650	850
Big Three Aerial Acrobats	Tin, 1920	300	450	600
Black Man with Bananas	Tin, 1920's	440	660	880
Boy on Trapeze	Tin	80	125	175
Busy Bridge	Vehicles on bridge, tin litho, 24" long, 1937	300	450	600
Busy Miners	Tin litho miners car, 16 1/2" long, 1930's	125	200	300
Butter and Egg Man	Walker, tin litho, windup	900	1350	1800
Cake Nodders, Donald Duck, Mickey, Goofy, Pluto		50	100	125
Captain America	5" tall, 1968	70	125	140
Cat and Ball	Tin, 5 1/2"	40	60	75
Cat with Ball	Tin, 4" long	30	50	65
Charleston Trio	One adult, two child dancers, 9" tall, 1921	625	900	1150
Charlie McCarthy Bass Drummer	Walks fast beating drum that he pushes along, tin litho, 1939	450	675	900
Charlie McCarthy Walker	1930's	225	350	450
Chicken Snatcher	Tin, 1927	800	1000	1800
Chipmunk	Tin	60	90	125
Chompy the Beetle	Tin, with action and sound, 6" tall, 1960's	75	125	150
Clancy	Walker, tin windup, 11" tall, 1931	250	375	500
Climbing Fireman	Tin and plastic, 1950's	100	150	200
Coast Defense Revolving Airplane	Circular with 3 cannons, tin windup, 1929	100	150	200
Cowboy on Horse	Tin, 6" tall, 1925	80	125	175
Cowboy Rider	Black horse version, tin, 7", 1930's	200	350	425
Cowboy Rider	With lariat on black horse, tin, 1941	150	200	300
Cowboy Riding a Horse	With lasso, 1940's	90	150	175
Crazy Dora		220	290	350
Dapper Dan Coon Jigger	Tin litho, 10" tall, 1922	475	725	950
Dapper Dan Jigger Bank	Tin litho, windup, 10" tall, 1923	400	650	850
Dapper Dan the Jigger Porter	Tin litho, 9 1/2" tall, 1924	350	525	700
Daschshund	Walker, hard plastic, 3" long, 1950's	30	45	60
Dippy Dumper	Tin	75	125	150
Disney Cash Register Bank	Tin litho, 1950's	50	75	100
Donald Duck	Plastic, 6 1/2" tall, 1960's	50	75	100
Donald Duck and Scooter	1960's	80	140	175
Donald Duck Bank	Lever action, tin litho, 1940	65	95	125
Donald Duck Duet	Donald and Goofy, tin, 10 1/2" tall, 1946	325	475	650

Marx

NAME	DESCRIPTION	GOOD	EX	MINT
Donald Duck Toy	Tail spins, plastic, 7" tall, 1950's	75	125	150
Donald Duck Toy Walker	With 3 nephews	100	125	250
Donald the Drummer	Tin, 10" tall, 1940's	150	250	350
Donald the Skier	Plastic, wears metal skis, 10 1/2" tall, 1940's	150	250	350
Dopey	Walker, tin, 8" tall, 1938	150	250	350
Doughboy Walker		250	325	400
Drummer Boy "Let the Drummer Boy Play While You Swing & Sway	Walker, tin litho, windup, 1939	300	450	600
Dumbo	Rollover action, tin, 4" tall, 1941	150	225	300
Easter Rabbit	Holds litho Easter basket, tin, 5" tall	50	75	100
Ferdinand the Bull	Tail spins, tin litho, 4" tall, 1938	150	250	350
Ferdinand the Bull and the Matador	Tin litho, 5 1/2" tall, 1938	225	425	550
Figaro, from Pinocchio	Rollover action, tin, 5" long, 1940	65	100	145
Fireman On Ladder	Tin, 24" tall	100	175	250
Flipping Monkey		60	90	120
Flippo the Jumping Dog, See Me Jump	Tin litho, 3" tall, 1940	65	100	130
Flutterfly	Tin litho, 3" long, 1929	125	175	225
Fred Flintstone on Dino	8" long, 1962	200	350	450
George the Drummer Boy	Moving eyes, tin, 9" tall, 1930's	150	225	300
George the Drummer Boy	Stationary eyes, tin, 9" tall, 1930's	100	175	225
Gobbling Goose	Lays golden eggs, tin, 1940's	120	200	275
Golden Pecking Goose	Tin litho, 9 1/2" long, 1924	175	250	350
Goofy	Tail spins, plastic, 9" tall, 1950's	50	75	100
Goofy the Walking Gardener	Holds a wheelbarrow, tin, 9" tall, 1960	200	350	450
Hap/Hop Ramp Walker	Hard plastic, 2 1/2" tall , 1950's	50	75	100
Harold Lloyd Funny Face	Walker, tin windup, 11" tall, 1928	250	375	500
Hey Hey the Chicken Snatcher	Black man with dog hanging behind, tin, 8 1/2" tall, 1926	900	1200	1800
Honeymoon Cottage, Honeymoon Express 7	Tin, square base	150	225	300
Honeymoon Express	1940's, circular train and plane	220	335	400
Honeymoon Express	1927, old-fashioned train on circular track, tin	200	300	350
Honeymoon Express	1947, streamlined train on circular track, tin	180	200	275
Honeymoon Express	1920's, tin litho lettering on base	175	230	290
Honeymoon Express	1935, M10000 streamline train, tin windup	150	245	300
Honeymoon Express, with airplane	1940, M10000 train w/ black windows, yellow sides, red bridge	100	150	200
Honeymoon Express, with airplane	1946, red, yellow, black # 6 great northern streamline train	90	135	175
Honeymoon Express, with airplane	1948-52, freight train with No. 4127 Lumar Line caboose	125	185	245
Honeymoon Express, with airplane	1936, M10000 train w/red roof, Wimpy & Sappo lithos on tunnel	120	210	275
Honeymoon Express, with airplane	1937, M10000 train w/red roof, two green tinted tunnels	120	185	250
Honeymoon Express, with airplane	1938, M10000 train w/red roof, green tunnels, copper bridge	120	185	245
Honeymoon Express, with airplane	1939, M10000 train w/red roof, green tunnels, silver bridge	150	245	300
Honeymoon Express, with flagman	1930, British steamer passenger express train	120	175	250
Honeymoon Express, with flagman	1926	240	350	475
Honeymoon Express, without airplane	1940, M10000 train w/ black windows, yellow sides, red bridge	90	150	185
Honeymoon Express, without airplane	1946, red, yellow, black # 6 great northern streamline train	90	150	185

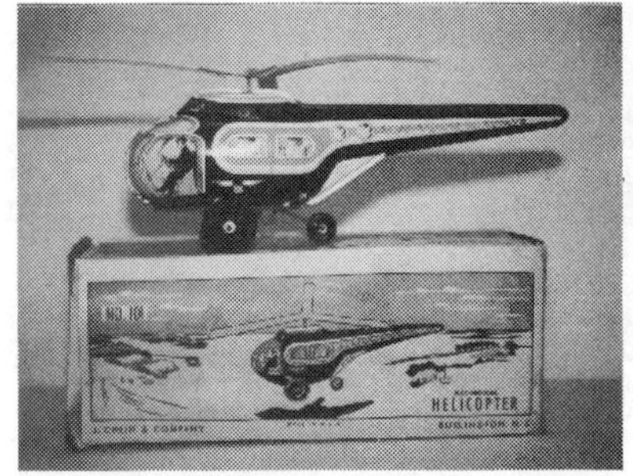

Top to Bottom: Monkey Mechanical Bank, 1950s, by Chein; Ferris Wheel--The Giant Ride, by Chein; Mechanical Helicopter, Toy Town Airways, 1950s, by Chein; Wee Scottie, 1952, by Marx; Roll Over Airplane, by Marx .

NAME	DESCRIPTION	GOOD	EX	MINT
Honeymoon Express, without airplane	1948-52, freight train with No. 4127 Lumar Line caboose	65	90	125
Honeymoon Express, without airplane	1936, M10000 train w/red roof, Wimpy & Sappo lithos on tunnel	90	155	210
Honeymoon Express, without airplane	1937, M10000 train w/red roof, two green tinted tunnels	90	150	185
Honeymoon Express, without airplane	1938, M10000 train w/red roof, green tunnels, copper bridge	90	150	185
Honeymoon Express, without airplane	1939, M10000 train w/red roof, green tunnels, silver bridge	90	135	175
Honeymoon Express, without flagman	1930, British steamer passenger express train	85	120	175
Honeymoon Express, without flagman	1933	90	150	185
Honeymoon Express, without flagman	1926	175	300	425
Hopalong Cassidy Rocking Horse Cowboy	Tin, 11 1/4" tall, 1946	275	500	750
Hoppo the Monkey	Plays cymbals, tin, 8" tall, 1925	125	200	250
Howdy Doody	Plays banjo and moves head, tin 5" tall, 1950	300	425	650
Howdy Doody	Does jig and Clarabell sits at piano, tin, 5 1/2" tall, 1950	525	700	850
Jazzbo Jim Roof Dancer	9" tall, 1920's	375	550	750
Jetsons Figure	4" tall, 1960's	100	165	200
Jiminy Cricket Pushing Bass Fiddle	Walker	110	150	220
Jiving Jigger	Tin, 1950	175	250	350
Jocko Climbing Monkey	1930's	90	140	175
Jocko Monkey	On string, tin litho, 9 1/2" long, 1950's	40	60	80
Joe Penner and His Duck Goo-Goo	Tin, 7 1/2" tall, 1934	300	450	650
Jumbo The Climbing Monkey	Litho, 9 3/4" tall, 1923	175	250	350
Jungle Book Dancing Bear	Plastic	50	75	100
Knockout Champs Boxing Toy	Tin litho, 1930's	225	350	450
Leopard	Growls and walks, 1950	80	125	165
Let the Drummer Boy Play	Tin, 1930's	175	275	375
Little King Walking Toy	Walkers, plastic, 3" tall, 1963	60	100	125
Little Orphan Annie and Sandy	Tin, 1930's	200	300	400
Little Orphan Annie Skipping Rope	Tin	150	225	300
Little Orphan Annie's Dog Sandy	Tin litho	50	75	100
Lone Ranger and Silver	Tin, 8" tall, 1938	200	300	400
Mad Russian Drummer	7" tall	325	400	575
Main Street	Street scene with moving cars, traffic cop, tin litho, 1927	325	500	650
Mammy's Boy	Walker, eyes move, tin litho, windup, 11"tall, 1929	175	250	350
Merry Makers Minstrel Bank	Four mice and piano, tin windup, 1930's	750	900	1400
Merrymakers Band	With marquee, mouse band, tin-plated litho, 1931	750	1100	1550
Merrymakers Band	Without marquee, mouse band, tin-plated litho, 1931	500	750	1000
Mickey and Donald Handcar	Plastic, 1948	75	130	175
Mickey Mouse	Tail spins, 7" tall	70	100	200
Mickey Mouse Express	Train and plane action, tin	300	450	550
Minnie	Tin, 7" tall	225	350	500
Minnie Mouse In Rocker	Tin, 1950's	250	350	500
Minstrel Figure	Tin, 11" tall	75	125	150
Monkey Cyclist	Litho, 9 3/4" tall, 1923	125	200	275

Marx

NAME	DESCRIPTION	GOOD	EX	MINT
Moon Creature	5 1/2" tall	90	140	200
Moon Mullins and Kayo on Handcar	Tin, 6" long, 1930's	300	450	600
Mortimer Snerd Band "Hometown Band"	1935	750	1100	1500
Mortimer Snerd Bass Drummer	Walks fast beating drum that he pushes along, tin litho, 1939	450	675	900
Mortimer Snerd Walker Toy	Walker, tin litho, windup, 1939	175	250	350
Mother Goose	7 1/2" tall, 1920's	100	200	300
Mother Penguin with Baby Penguin on Sled	Walker, hard plastic, 3" long, 1950's	40	60	85
Musical Circus Horse	Pull toy, metal drum rolls with chimes, 10 1/2" long, 1939	100	150	200
Mystery Cat	Tin litho, 8 1/2" long, 1931	125	200	250
Mystery Pluto	Sniffs ground, 8" tall, 1948	100	150	250
Mystery Sandy Dog	Little Orphan Annie's Dog Sandy, tin, 8 1/2" long, 1938	175	280	375
Nodding Goose		35	50	75
Nutty Indian Drummer		75	100	150
Pecos Bill	Twirls rope, plastic, 10" tall, 1950's	100	150	200
Pikes Peak Mountain Climber	Vehicle on track	400	600	800
Pinched	Square based, open circular track, 1927	325	520	695
Pinocchio	5" tall, 1950's	150	250	350
Pinocchio	Standing erect, eyes skyward, tin, 9" tall, 1938	150	225	300
Pinocchio the Acrobat	Tin, rocking, 16" tall, 1939	125	200	250
Pinocchio Walker	Stationary eyes, tin, 1930's	225	300	450
Pinocchio Walker	Animated eyes, tin, 8 1/2" tall, 1939	200	275	400
Pluto Drum Major	Tin	225	355	475
Pluto Toy	Mechanical, plastic, 1950's	65	95	145
Pluto Watch Me Roll-Over	8" long, 1939	125	180	275
Poor Fish	Tin litho, 8 1/2" long, 1936	75	130	175
Popeye Acrobat	Tin	350	500	750
Popeye and Olive Oyl Jiggers	On cabin roof, tin litho, 10" tall, 1936	850	1200	1500
Popeye Express	Carrying parrots in cages, tin ltho, 8 1/4" tall, 1932	425	600	850
Popeye Handcar	Popeye and Olive Oyl rubber, metal handcar, 1935	1000	1500	1800
Popeye Jigger	On cabin roof, tin, 10" tall, 1936	400	650	900
Popeye the Champ Big Fight Boxing Toy	Tin and celluloid, 7" long, 1936	1500	2500	3200
Porky Pig Cowboy with Lariat	Tin, 8" tall, 1949	125	200	250
Porky Pig Rotating Umbrella, with top hat	Tin, 8" tall, 1939	195	250	375
Porky Pig Rotating Umbrella, without top hat	Tin, 8" tall, 1939	195	250	475
Red Cap Porter	Tin	200	375	595
Red the Iceman	Tin with wood ice cube	1000	1500	2000
Ride 'Em Cowboy	Tin	95	145	185
Ring-A-Ling Circus	Tin litho, 7 1/2" diameter base, 1925	500	250	1000
Rodeo Joe	Tin, 1933	125	200	250
Roll Over Cat	Black cat pushing ball, tin litho, 8 1/2" long, 1931	75	100	150
Roll Over Pluto		150	225	300
Running Scottie	Metal, 12 1/2" long, 1938	75	130	175
Smitty Riding A Scooter	8" tall, 1932	450	675	900
Smokey Joe The Climbing Fireman	21" tall	150	250	350

Marx

NAME	DESCRIPTION	GOOD	EX	MINT
Smokey Joe the Climbing Fireman	1930s, 7 1/2" tall	125	200	275
Smokey Sam the World Fireman	7" tall, 1950's	100	150	200
Snappy the Miracle Dog	Came with dog house, tin litho, 3 1/2" long, 1931	90	150	200
Snoopy Bus		625	950	1250
Somstepa Jigger	8" tall	200	300	400
Spic and Span Drummer and Dancer	Tin litho, 10" tall, 1924	600	900	1200
Spic Coon Drummer	Tin, 8 1/2" tall, 1924	500	750	1000
Stop, Look and Listen	1927	300	400	600
Streamline Speedway	Two racers on track	100	150	200
Subway Express	Tin, 1950's	85	125	170
Superman Holding Airplane	Tin, 6" wingspan on airplane, 1940	600	900	1250
The Carter Climbing Monkey	8 1/2" tall, 1921	145	225	290
Tidy Tim Streetcleaner	Pushes wagon, tin litho, 8" tall, 1933	225	350	450
Tiger	Plush with vinyl head, walks, growls	50	75	100
Tom Tom Jungle Boy	Tin, 7" tall	50	75	100
Tony the Tiger	Plastic, whirling tail action, 7" tall, 1960's	75	100	150
Tumbling Monkey	4 1/2" tall, 1942	95	150	190
Tumbling Monkey and Trapeze	5 3/4" tall, 1932	150	250	350
Walking Popeye	1930's	300	450	650
Walking Popeye Carrying Parrot Cages	Tin litho, windup, 8 1/4" tall, 1932	250	400	650
Walking Porter	Carries two suitcases covered w/labels, tin, 8" tall, 1930's	150	200	300
Wee Running Scottie	Tin litho, 5 1/2" long, 1930's	80	125	165
Wee Running Scottie	Tin litho, 5 1/2" long, 1952	35	50	75
Wise Pluto	Tin	125	200	250
WWI Soldier	Prone position with rifle	60	100	125
Xylophonist	Tin, 5" long	25	35	50
Zippo Monkey	Tin litho, 9 1/2", 1938	80	100	175

Ohio Art

NAME	DESCRIPTION	GOOD	EX	MINT
Automatic Airport	Two planes circle tower	300	400	500
Coney Island Roller Coaster	1950s	165	185	250

Schuco

NAME	DESCRIPTION	GOOD	EX	MINT
"Combinato" Convertible	7 1/2" long, 1950s	150	200	250
"Curvo" Motorcycle	5" long, 1950s	150	200	250
"Mauswagen"	Tin & cloth mice and wagon	300	400	500
"Schuco Turn" Monkey on Suitcase	Tin and cloth, 1950s	180	240	300
1917 Ford		60	80	100
Airplane and Pilot	Friction toy, oversized pilot, 1930s	180	240	300
Bavarian Boy	Tin and cloth boy with beer mug, 5" tall, 1950s	120	160	200
Bavarian Dancing Couple	Tin & cloth, 5" high	120	160	200
Black Man	Tin & cloth, 5" high	300	400	500
Clown Playing Violin	Tin and cloth, 4 1/2" tall, 1950s	150	200	250
Dancing Boy and Girl	Tin and cloth, 1930s	180	240	300
Dancing Mice	Large and small mouse, tin and cloth, 1950s	135	180	225
Dancing Monkey With Mouse	Tin and cloth, 1950s	135	180	225
Drummer	Tin and cloth, 5" tall, 1930s	120	160	200
Examico 4001 Convertible	Maroon tin windup, 5 1/2"	175	250	375

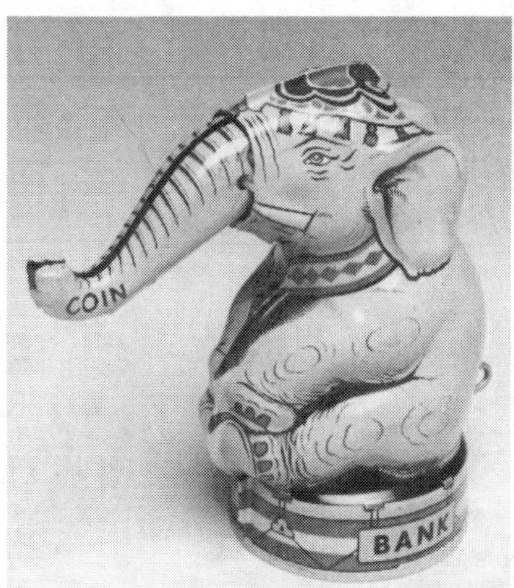

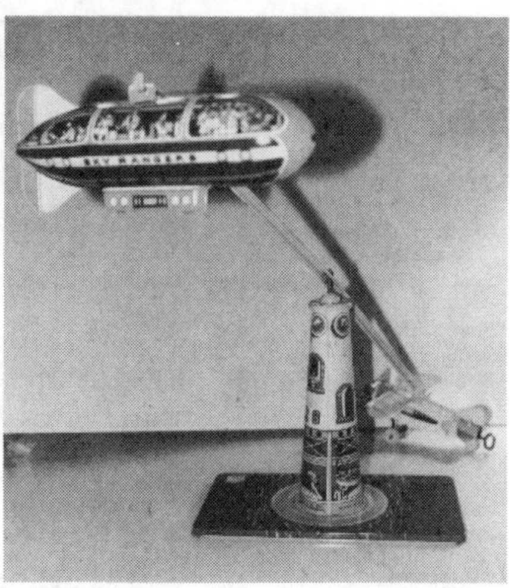

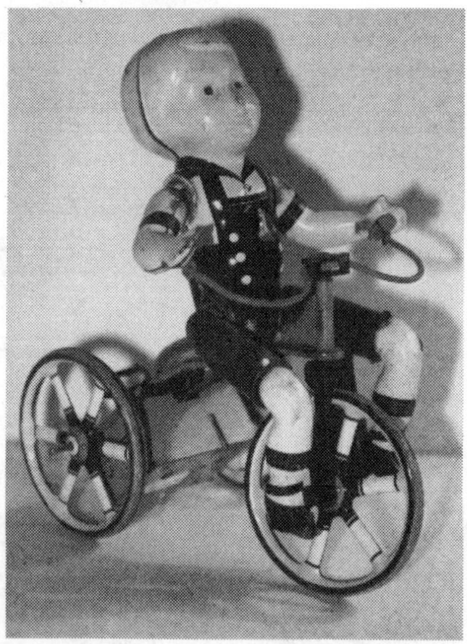

Top to Bottom: Mechanical Elephant Bank, 1950s, by Chein; Sky Rangers, 1933, by Unique Art; Capitol Hill Racer, 1930s, by Unique Art; Milton Berle Crazy Car, 1950s, by Marx; Kiddie Cyclist, 1930s, by Unique Art.

Schuco

NAME	DESCRIPTION	GOOD	EX	MINT
Flic 4520	Traffic cop type figure	150	200	250
Fox And Goose	Tin and cloth, fox holding goose in cage, 1950s	150	200	250
Juggling Clown	Tin and cloth, 4 1/2" tall	210	280	350
Mercer Car #1225		0	0	
Mickey & Minnie Dancing	Tin & cloth	900	1200	1500
Monk Drinking Beer	Tin & cloth, 5" high	105	140	175
Monkey Drummer	Tin and cloth, 1950s	150	200	250
Monkey in Car	1930s	450	600	750
Monkey on Scooter	Tin and cloth, 1930s	150	200	250
Monkey Playing Violin	Tin and cloth, 1950s	150	200	250
Studio #1050 Race Car		100	160	225
Tumbling Boy	Tin and cloth, 1950s	150	200	250
Yes-No Monkey		210	280	350

Strauss

NAME	DESCRIPTION	GOOD	EX	MINT
Boston Confectionery Co. Truck	Yellow, 9" long	500	675	825
Bus De Lux	Blue, 1920s	525	700	900
Circus Wagon	8 1/2" long	675	900	1150
Clown Crazy Car	1920s	350	500	750
Dandy Jim Clown Dancer	10" tall	425	575	725
Dizzie Lizzie		475	620	800
Flying Air Ship Los Angeles	Aluminum, 10" long, 1920s	475	625	800
Ham and Sam	6"x6 1/2" multicolored	1000	1350	1700
Interstate Double Decker Bus	Green and yellow, 10 1/2" long	600	800	1000
Interstate Double Decker Bus	Brown and yellow, 11" long	400	535	695
Jazzbo Jim	Dancer on rooftop	535	700	900
Jenny The Balking Mule	Farmer and reluctant mule, 9" long	250	375	450
Jitney Bus	Green and yellow, 9 1/2" long	325	450	575
Knockout Prize Fighters	Windup boxers, 1920s	275	250	450
Leaping Lena	9" long	325	450	575
Miami Sea Sled	Yellow and red, 15" long	325	450	575
Play Golf	12" long	400	525	695
Pool Player		200	300	425
Red Cap Porter	With wagon and trunk	400	525	685
Rollo Chair	Windup cart pushed by figure, 7" long	675	900	1175
Santee Clause	Santa in sleigh, two reindeer, clockwork, 11" long	800	1200	1600
Timber King Tractor Trailer		100	135	170
Tip Top Wheelbarrow		325	450	575
Tombo Alabama Coon Jigger	11" high	400	600	800
Travel Chicks	Chickens on railroad car, windup	265	350	450
Trik Auto	7" long, says "Trik Auto"	325	450	575
Trik Auto	Red and yellow windup, 6 1/2" long	325	450	575
What's It? Car	Multicolored litho, 9 1/2" long	800	1075	1375
Yell-O-Taxi	7 1/2" long	495	675	850

Unique Art

NAME	DESCRIPTION	GOOD	EX	MINT
Artie the Clown in his Crazy Car		265	350	450
Bombo the Monk		170	225	275
Butter and Egg Man		350	450	595
Capitol Hill Race		120	170	220
Casey The Cop		500	675	895

Unique Art

NAME	DESCRIPTION	GOOD	EX	MINT
Dandy Jim		400	535	685
Daredevil Motor Cop		235	315	400
Finnegan the Porter		150	200	255
Flying Circus		675	900	1250
G.I. Joe and His Jouncing Jeep		100	150	200
G.I. Joe and His K-9 Pups		100	150	200
Gertie the Galloping Goose		165	225	295
Hee Haw	Donkey pulling milk cart	165	225	295
Hillbilly Express		200	275	350
Hobo Train		225	350	450
Hott and Trott		1225	1750	2300
Howdy Doody & Buffalo Bob at Piano		950	1250	1800
Jazzbo Jim		200	300	400
Kid-Go-Round		235	310	400
Kiddy Go-Round		235	300	400
Krazy Kar		300	400	515
Li'l Abner and His Dogpatch Band		400	500	650
Lincoln Tunnel		375	400	550
Motorcycle Cop		115	165	195
Musical Sail-Way Carousel		200	275	350
Pecking Goose, Witch and Cat		275	350	450
Rodeo Joe Crazy Car		200	275	350
Rollover Motorcycle Cop		200	275	350
Sky Rangers		350	475	575

Wolverine

NAME	DESCRIPTION	GOOD	EX	MINT
"Sandy Andy" Fullback	Kicking fullback, 8" tall	270	360	450
Battleship	14" long, 1930s	90	145	185
Crane	Red and blue, 18" high	60	80	100
Drum Major	Round base, 13"	150	200	250
Express Bus		195	260	325
Jet Roller Coaster	21" long	95	150	200
Merry-Go-Round		180	240	300
Mystery Car		150	200	250
Submarine	13" long	150	200	250
Sunny and Tank	Yellow and green, 14 1/2" long	120	160	200
Yellow Taxi	13" long, 1940s	210	280	350
Zilotone	Clown on xylophone, with musical discs, 1920s	650	800	950

Top to Bottom: Toytown Dairy Horse Cart, 1930s, by Marx; Popeye Express, 1932, by Marx; Fred Flintstone Riding Dino Wind-Up, 1962, by Marx; Dapper Dan Coon Jigger, 1922, by Marx; See-Saw Sand Toy, 1930s, by Chein.

Action Figures

Specialists in different collecting fields often feel their particular area is the greatest thing since sliced bread. Action figure collectors are no exception to this, but they do have one argument in their favor -- they may be right this time. Action figure collecting is one of the fastest growing and potentially largest collectible areas since the baseball card boom of the 1980s. *Toy Shop* magazine, the monthly bible of the toy collecting hobby, presents a plethora of action figures for sale in each issue. In fact, so many figures are for sale that you might conclude that toys in general and action figures in particular are common items. And strangely enough, in a way, you would be right. In some places, namely toy stores, action figures are literally climbing the walls.

So why collect them if you can buy them right off the shelves at the store? The answer to this is that for many collectors, that's exactly how it's done.

The Beginning of Time

Some action figure collectors act as if time began in the 1960s. The 20th century is broken into two great periods, BAF (Before Action Figures) and AAF (After Action Figures.) This has a lot to do with the definition of action figures entailing an articulated, poseable body. Of course, boys played with toy soldiers even before the turn of the century. But these were solid, immobile figures that had no realistically movable parts. The same held true for the plastic soldiers of the 1950s. If you are a stickler for semantics, then action figures were created in the 1960s and the story does begin there. The reality is not quite as epochal as all that, but the 1960s did see the convergence of several cultural influences and technologies that changed American life in many ways, including how toys would be sold.

Television had replaced the dinner table and parlor radio as the family hearth. The sturdy cabinet in the corner of the living room glowed with a captivating power only hinted at by radio, and which has never been challenged since. It was a working window not only onto a wide world of people and places, but also of neat things to buy. While Mom sat on the couch and Dad sat in his chair, the youngsters clustered on the floor, bathing in the new light, soaking up the names and attributes of their new friends and heroes: Barbie, Superman, Batman, GI Joe. And watching lots of commercials. Toy commercials.

From 1961 to 1963, toy makers watched with envy and despair as Mattel's Barbie, aided by TV, took the world of girl's toys by storm. If only boys could be induced to play with dolls, but no, that could never be. Not as long as dolls were dolls. The solution to this dilemma ranks as one of the great examples of marketing spin of all time. If boys won't play with dolls, then call them something else. How about "action figures?"

Hasbro's first test of GI Joe, the male answer to Barbie, debuted at the New York International Toy Fair in early 1964. Toy Fair is the annual new products bash for the entire toy industry, where toy makers meet toy retailers and determine what children will ask for on their wish lists for the coming year.

Countless toys ideas have died without ever seeing production, all due to lack of buyer interest at Toy Fair.

The Toy Fair buyers met the 12-inch GI Joe with hopes and reservations. They wanted to believe that a successful Barbie for boys had been created, but as much as Hasbro people touted Joe as America's Movable Fighting Man, the buyers still heard doll. Make that doll for boys. They wished Hasbro all the best and retreated in droves.

Virtually no orders were generated at Toy Fair, so in June, with no fanfare or ad support at all, Hasbro released the new toy directly into a New York test market. All the test stores sold out within a week, and the invasion of America was on. By year's end, Joe had earned Hasbro some $17 million in spite of sales lost due to product shortages.

GI Joe was the first true fully articulated action figure for boys, but he would not be alone long. 1965 saw Gilbert's James Bond figures attempt unsuccessfully to capitalize on the new wave of boy's figures. Marx also entered the ring with their Best of the West series, but Joe had a seemingly limitless arsenal of battle-geared appeal.

The first successful challenge to GI Joe came from Ideal's Captain Action. While Joe had established his one identity with record speed, Captain Action was a man of many faces. Ideal designed Captain Action to establish not only his own identity, but also to capitalize on those of many popular super heroes. Joe was just Joe, but Captain Action was Spider-Man, Batman, Superman, the Lone Ranger and a host of others. Today Captain Action figures and sets command the second highest prices in the action figure market, second only to the classic GI Joes.

Ideal's brief foray into the world of super hero action figures paved the way for many more to come. While GI Joe was forced to temper his image and soften it from the quintessentially military Green Beret Joe of 1967 into the Adventure Team Joe of 1970, super heroes were largely immune to the Vietnam protests that forced Joe's change of mission. By 1969, Ideal tired of Captain Action's complex licensing agreements and discontinued the series, but another company was waiting in the wings.

It was Mego. In 1972 Mego released its first super hero series, the six-figure set of World's Greatest Super Heroes. These eight-inch-tall cloth and plastic figures were joined by 28 others by the time the series ended 10 years later. Mego supplemented this super hero line with licensed film and TV characters, notably Planet of the Apes, Star Trek and the Dukes of Hazzard, as well as with historic figures representing the Old West and the World's Greatest Super Knights of the apparently super Round Table.

1977 saw another milestone in action figure history, one that everybody on the block ironically missed at the time. An outer space movie called "Star Wars" had, from nowhere, become a smash hit, and nobody had made any toys to support it at all. Just one company -- Kenner -- held the rights to merchandise toys, and it had done nothing with them. When Kenner realized the magnitude of "Star Wars" potential, it rushed toys through production, but it didn't have time to get action figures on the shelves by Christmas. Kenner in-

Right: Captain America by Mego; Captain Action by Ideal.

Left: Hordak figure from Masters of the Universe by Mattel; The Original GI Joe Action Soldier by Hasbro.

stead essentially pre-sold the figures, using a promotion they called the Early Bird Certificate Package, which entitled the owner to mail delivery of the first four figures as soon as they were available. By Christmas 1978, the line had swelled to 17 figures accompanied by the first of a deluge of accessories. The "Star Wars" figures also established the third standardization of size for action figures. GI Joe and Captain Action were 12-inch figures. Mego figures were eight inches tall. Kenner's Star Wars line set figures at 3-3/4 inches tall, and their tremendous popularity cemented that size as a new standard that holds to this day.

The next size to be established was the six-inch figure set by Mattel's highly successful and lucrative 1981 "Masters of the Universe" series. What in no small part accounted for the series' profitability was the fact that the "Masters of the Universe" series was created first as a toy line, and licensing was then sold by Mattel to television and film, not the other way around. Mattel also upped the manufacturing ante by endowing the figures with action features such as punching and grabbing movements, thus enhancing their play value and setting another standard in the process.

Hasbro then scored again with the 1985 introduction of the next evolutionary level of action figures, the transforming figure. The aptly named "Transformers" did just that -- change from innocuous looking vehicles into menacing robots with a few deft twists, and then back again. Hasbro's little mutating robots also transformed the toy industry, spawning numerous competitors and introducing the element of interchangeability of elements into toy design. It should be noted here that Hasbro did not invent the transforming robot. That credit goes to a Japanese line called GoDaiKins. But Hasbro perfected the mass merchandising of the concept like no company before it.

Today's present generation of micro chip-powered talking and sound effect-laden toys are now the standard of the industry, but this standard too will undoubtedly be made obsolete by future evolutions of control and interaction. We are most likely just a few holiday wish lists away from fully remote-controlled robotic warriors that will meet in tabletop combat while we control their every move from easy chairs.

Action figures are big business, and hot series like "Star Trek" and "Teenage Mutant Ninja Turtles" are now regularly ranked in the top 20 best-selling lines by industry trade papers. A casual stroll through the toy aisles of any department store provides ample firsthand evidence. Hardware and housewares may be slow, but there are always shoppers in the toy aisles. New lines quickly replace slow sellers, many of which soon find new life in the collector market. If it was on the store shelves last week but is gone this week, then it will probably show up in a collector magazine next month -- at a suitably higher price. Again, an enduring character identity is a key to continued demand and future appreciation. "Star Trek: The Next Generation" and those Turtles have proven themselves worthy long-term franchises, and are joining the ranks of "Star Wars" and "Masters of the Universe" as blue chip stocks of the action figure market.

The action figure aisles are now attracting more adults, and they are not always buying for their kids. More and more adults are buying action figures as collectibles and investments. And those investments will, in years hence, feed the needs of tomorrow's collectors, the ones who are, right now, sitting on the floor playing with Riker, Picard, Donatello and Fester.

ACTION FIGURES

A-Team

NAME	MNP	MIP
*3-3/4" figures & accessories (unless noted) by Galoob		
A-Team Four Figure Set	12	30
Amy Allen Figure, 6-1/2"	10	25
Armored Attack Adventure with B.A. Figure	8	20
B.A. Baracus Figure, 6-1/2"	8	20
Bad Guys Four-Figure Set: Viper, Rattle, Cobra, Python	10	25
Cobra Figure, 6-1/2"	6	15
Combat Attack Gyrocopter	10	25
Command Center Playset	14	35
Corvette with Face Figure	8	20
Face Figure, 6-1/2"	6	15
Hannibal Figure, 6-1/2"	6	15
Interceptor Jet Bomber with Murdock	10	25
Murdock Figure, 6-1/2"	8	20
Off Road Attack Cycle	8	20
Python Figure, 6-1/2"	6	15
Rattler Figure, 6-1/2"	6	15
Tactical Van Playset	6	15
Viper Figure, 6-1/2"	6	15

Captain Action

12" Posable Figures

NAME	MNP	MIP
*Figures and accessories made by Ideal, 1966-67		
Captain Action, box photo Captain Action	200	375
Captain Action, parachute offer on box	275	600
Captain Action, photo box	200	675
Captain Action, with Lone Ranger on box, red shirt	200	300
Captain Action, with Lone Ranger on box, blue shirt	200	325
Dr. Evil	300	600

9" Figures

NAME	MNP	MIP
Action Boy	275	650
Action Boy, with space suit	350	825

Accessories

NAME	MNP	MIP
Action Cave Carrying Case, vinyl	400	0
Directional Communicator Set	110	300
Dr. Evil Sanctuary	600	0
Jet Mortar	110	225
Parachute Pack	100	225
Power Pack	125	250
Quick Change Chamber, Cardboard, Sears Exclusive	325	750
Silver Streak Amphibian	500	950
Silver Streak Garage, cardboard, w/ Silver Streak Vehicle, Sears Exclusive	400	500

Captain Action

NAME	MNP	MIP
Survival Kit, 20 pieces	125	275
Vinyl Headquarters Carrying Case, Sears Exclusive	85	200
Weapons Arsenal, ten pieces	110	225

Action Boy Costumes

NAME	MNP	MIP
Aqualad	300	525
Robin	300	625
Superboy	300	625

Captain Action Costumes

NAME	MNP	MIP
Aquaman	160	350
Aquaman, with videomatic ring	180	400
Batman	225	450
Batman, with videomatic ring	250	500
Buck Rogers, with videomatic ring	450	895
Captain America	220	425
Captain America, with videomatic ring	225	465
Flash Gordon	200	425
Flash Gordon, with videomatic ring	225	475
Green Hornet, with videomatic ring	1000	3200
Lone Ranger, blue shirt, with videomatic ring	300	800
Lone Ranger, red shirt	170	465
Phantom	150	400
Phantom, with videomatic ring	175	475
Sergeant Fury	200	475
Spider-Man, with videomatic ring	550	1500
Steve Canyon	150	350
Steve Canyon, with videomatic ring	175	475
Superman	200	425
Superman, with videomatic ring	225	525
Tonto, with videomatic ring	375	925
*5-1/4" figures & accessories (unless noted) by Kenner		
Bad to the Bone Ghost Figure	4	10
Banshee Bomber Gooper Ghost with Ecto-Plazm	3	8
Brain Blaster Ghost Haunted Human Figure	3	8
Bug-Eye Ghost	3	7
Dracula	3	7
Ecto Bomber with Bomber Ghost Figure	4	10
Ecto-1	10	25
Ecto-1A with Ambulance Ghost	8	20
Ecto-2 Helicopter	5	12
Ecto-3	4	10
Ecto-Glow Egon Figure	4	10
Ecto-Glow Louis Tully Figure	6	15
Ecto-Glow Peter Figure	4	10
Ecto-Glow Ray Figure	4	10
Ecto-Glow Winston Zeddmore Figure	6	15
Egon Spengler & Gulper Ghost Figure	6	15
Fearsome Flush Figure	2	5
Firehouse Headquarters	10	25

Captain Action

NAME	MNP	MIP
Frankenstein	3	7
Fright Feature Egon Figure	4	10
Fright Feature Janine Melnitz Figure	4	10
Fright Feature Peter Figure	4	10
Fright Feature Ray Figure	4	10
Fright Feature Winston Figure	4	10

Ghostbusters

NAME	MNP	MIP
Ghost Pooper	3	7
Ghost Sweeper	4	10
Ghost Zapper	5	12
Gobblin' Goblin Nasty Neck	6	15
Gobblin' Goblin Terrible Teeth	6	15
Gobblin' Goblin Terror Tongue	6	15
Gooper Ghost Slimer Figure	6	15
Gooper Ghost Sludge Bucket	2	6
Gooper Ghost Squisher with Ecto-Plazm	2	6
Granny Gross Haunted Human Figure	3	8
H2 Ghost Figure	2	6
Hard Hat Horror Haunted Human Figure	4	10
Highway Haunter	3	8
Hunchback	3	7
Mail Fraud Haunted Human Figure	3	7
Mini Ghost Mini-Gooper Figure	3	7
Mini Ghost Mini-Shooter Figure	3	7
Mini Ghost Mini-Trap Figure	3	7
Mummy	3	7
Peter Venkman & Grabber Ghost Figure	6	15
Proton Pack	10	25
Pull Speed Ahead Ghost	3	7
Ray Stantz & Wrapper Ghost Figure	6	15
Screaming Hero Egon Figure	4	10
Screaming Hero Janine Melnitz Figure	4	10
Screaming Hero Peter Figure	4	10
Screaming Hero Ray Figure	4	10
Screaming Hero Winston Figure	4	10
Slimed Hero Egon Figure	4	10
Slimed Hero Louis Tully & Four Eyed Ghost	4	10
Slimed Hero Peter Venkman & Tooth Ghost	4	10

Ghostbusters

NAME	MNP	MIP
Slimed Hero Ray Stantz & Vapor Ghost	4	10
Slimed Hero Winston Figure	4	10
Slimer Figure with Food	12	30
Slimer Plush Figure, 13"	10	25
Slimer with Proton Pack, red or blue	14	35
Stay-Puft Marshmallow Man Figure, 13-3/4"	10	25
Stay-Puft Marshmallow Man Plush Figure	8	20
Super Fright Feature Egon Spengler with Slimy Spider	4	10
Super Fright Feature Janine with Boo Fish Ghost	6	15
Super Fright Feature Peter Venkman & Snake Head	4	10
Super Fright Feature Ray Figure	4	10
Super Fright Feature Winston Zeddmore & Meanie Wienie	4	10
Terror Trash Haunted Human Figure	4	10
Tombstone Tackle Haunted Human Figure	3	7
Winston Zeddmore & Chomper Ghost Figure	7	18
Wolfman	3	7
X-Cop Haunted Human Figure	3	7
Zombie	3	7

Ghostbusters, Filmation

*Produced in 1986 by Schaper

NAME	MNP	MIP
Belfry and Brat-A-Rat Figures	6	15
Bone Troller	8	20
Eddie Figure	6	15
Fangster Figure	6	15
Fib Face Figure	6	15
Futura Figure	6	15
Ghost Popper Ghost Buggy	14	35
Haunter Figure	6	15
Jake Figure	6	15
Jessica Figure	6	15
Mysteria Figure	6	15
Prime Evil Figure	6	15
Scare Scooter Vehicle	8	20
Scared Stiff Figure	6	15
Time Hopper Vehicle	6	15
Tracy Figure	6	15

Top to Bottom: All GI Joe: Sea Adventurer, Land Adventurer, and Air Adventurer Figure boxes, 1970; Combat Field Pack Set, 1964; Combat Field Jacket Set, 1964.

GI JOE

Accessories

NO.	NAME	DESCRIPTION	YEAR	EX	MNP	MIP
7319-5	Equipment Tester Set		1972	12	20	30

Action Marine Series

NO.	NAME	DESCRIPTION	YEAR	EX	MNP	MIP
7711	Beachhead Assault Tent Set	Tent, flamethrower, pistol belt, first-aid pouch, mess kit with utensils and manual	1964	100	180	275
7715	Beachhead Fatigue Pants		1964	75	130	200
7714	Beachhead Fatigue Shirt	Adventure Pack	1964	85	145	225
7712	Beachhead Field Pack Set	Cartridge belt, rifle, grenades, field pack, entrenching tool, canteen and manual	1964	150	250	375
7713	Beachhead Field Pack	M-1 rifle, bayonet, entrenching shovel and cover, canteen w/cover, belt, mess kit w/cover, field pack, flamethrower, first aid pouch, tent, pegs and poles (complete), tent camo and camo	1964	50	100	375
7718	Beachhead Flamethrower Set	Reissued Adventure Pack	1967	60	100	155
7718	Beachhead Flamethrower Set	Adventure Pack	1964	50	85	130
7716	Beachhead Mess Kit Set	Adventure Pack	1964	45	75	110
7717	Beachhead Rifle Set	Bayonet, cartridge belt, hand grenades and M-1 rifle	1964	60	100	150
7717	Beachhead Rifle Set	Reissued Adventure Pack	1967	70	115	175
7703	Communications Field Radio/ Telephone Set	Reissued Adventure Pack	1967	65	115	175
7703	Communications Field Set	Adventure Pack	1964	50	80	125
7704	Communications Flag Set	Flags for Army, Navy, Air Corps, Marines and United States	1964	150	250	400
7702	Communications Poncho	Poncho, field radio and telephone, map and case, binoculars and wire roll	1964	50	85	130
7701	Communications Post Poncho Set	Field radio and telephone, wire roll, carbine, binoculars, map, case, manual	1964	115	195	300
7710	Dress Parade Set	Reissued Adventure Pack	1968	300	500	775
7732	Jungle Fighter Set	Reissued Adventure Pack	1968	625	1050	1650
7732	Jungle Fighter Set	Bush hat, jacket w/emblems, pants, flamethrower, field telephone, knife and sheath, pistol belt, pistol, holster, canteen w/cover and knuckle knife	1967	600	975	1500
7726	Marine Automatic Machine Gun Set	Adventure Pack	1967	125	200	325
7722	Marine Basics Set	Adventure Pack	1966	60	105	160
7723	Marine Bunk Bed Set	Adventure Pack	1966	135	225	350
7723	Marine Bunk Bed Set	Reissued Adventure Pack	1967	150	250	375
7710	Marine Deluxe Dress Parade Set	Marine jacket, trousers, pistol belt, shoes, hat, M-1 rifle and manual	1964	100	175	275
7730	Marine Demolition Set	Includes figure with camo shirt and pants, cap, boots, mine detector and harness, land mine	1966	115	195	300
7730	Marine Demolition Set	Reissued Adventure Pack	1968	185	310	475
7721	Marine First Aid Set	First-aid pouch, arm band and helmet	1964	40	70	110

Accessories

NO.	NAME	DESCRIPTION	YEAR	EX	MNP	MIP
7721	Marine First Aid Set	Adventure Pack	1965	45	75	115
7720	Marine Medic Set	Reissued Adventure Pack	1967	75	130	200
7710	Marine Medic Set	Adventure Pack	1965	70	115	175
7719	Marine Medic Set w/stretcher	First-aid shoulder pouch, stretcher, bandages, arm bands, plasma bottle, stethoscope, Red Cross Flag and manual	1964	150	275	425
7719	Marine Medic Set w/stretcher	Adventure Pack	1965	165	275	450
7725	Marine Mortar Set	Adventure Pack	1967	115	195	300
7727	Marine Weapons Rack Set	Adventure Pack	1967	150	200	350
7708	Paratrooper Camouflage Set	Netting and foliage	1964	30	50	75
7707	Paratrooper Helmet Set	Adventure Pack	1964	30	50	75
7709	Paratrooper Parachute Pack	Adventure Pack	1964	45	75	120
7706	Paratrooper Small Arms Set	Reissued Adventure Pack	1967	70	120	185
7731	Tank Commander Set	Includes figure, "leather" jacket, helmet and visor, insignia, radio with tripod, machine gun, ammo box	1967	275	450	700
7731	Tank Commander Set	Reissued Adventure Pack	1968	325	550	850

Action Pilot Series

NO.	NAME	DESCRIPTION	YEAR	EX	MNP	MIP
7822	Air Academy Cadet Set	Deluxe set with figure, dress jacket, shoes, and pants, garrison cap, saber and scabbard, white M-1 rifle, chest sash and belt sash	1967	250	350	850
7822	Air Academy Cadet Set	Reissued Adventure Pack	1968	400	650	1000
7814	Air Force Basics Set	Adventure Pack	1966	65	110	170
7814	Air Force Basics Set	Reissued Adventure Pack	1967	75	125	195
7816	Air Force Mae West Air Vest & Equipment Set	Adventure Pack	1967	115	195	300
7813	Air Force Police Set	Adventure Pack	1965	90	150	250
7813	Air Force Police Set	Reissued Adventure Pack	1967	100	175	275
7815	Air Force Security Set	Air Security radio and helmet, cartidge belt, pistol and holster	1967	400	650	1000
7825	Air/Sea Rescue Set	Includes figure with black air tanks, rescue ring, buoy, depth gauge, face mask, fins, orange scuba outfit	1967	350	850	1200
7825	Air/Sea Rescue Set	Reissued Adventure Pack	1968	400	850	1200
7824	Astronaut Set	Helmet w/visor, foil space suit, booties, gloves, space camera, propellant gun, tether cord, oxygen chest pack, silver boots, white jumpsuit and cloth cap	1967	475	775	1200
7824	Astronaut Set	Reissued Adventure Pack	1968	400	650	1000
7812	Communications Set		1964	75	125	200
7820	Crash Crew Set	Fire proof jacket, hood, pants and gloves, silver boots, belt, flash light, axe, pliers, fire extinguisher, stretcher, strap cutter	1966	175	295	450
7804	Dress Uniform Jacket Set	Adventure Pack	1964	100	175	275
7805	Dress Uniform Pants	Adventure Pack	1964	90	150	225
7803	Dress Uniform Set	Air Force jacket, trousers, shirt, tie, cap and manual	1964	550	975	1500
7806	Dress Uniform Shirt & Equipment Set	Adventure Pack	1964	100	165	250

Accessories

NO.	NAME	DESCRIPTION	YEAR	EX	MNP	MIP
7823	Fighter Pilot Set	Working parachute and pack, gold helmet, Mae West vest, green pants, flash light, orange jump suit, black boots	1967	400	650	1000
7823	Fighter Pilot Set	Reissued Adventure Pack	1968	475	775	1200
7812	Scramble Communications Set	Reissued Adventure Pack	1967	100	165	250
7812	Scramble Communications Set	Poncho, field telephone and radio, map w/case, binoculars and wire roll	1965	90	150	225
7810	Scramble Crash Helmet	Helmet, face mask, hose, tinted visor	1964	75	130	200
7810	Scramble Crash Helmet	Reissued Adventure Pack	1967	90	150	225
7808	Scramble Flight Suit	Gray flight suit, air vest, green parachute pack, helmet with visor, oxygen mask, flare gun, knife and scabbard, clipboard with pencil, .45 pistol and holster, belt, boots	1964	115	195	300
7808	Scramble Flight Suit	Reissued Adventure Pack	1967	125	225	350
7811	Scramble Parachute Pack	Adventure Pack	1964	50	85	135
7807	Scramble Parachute Set	Deluxe set, gray flight suit, orange air vest, white crash helmet, pistol belt w/.45 pistol, holster, clipboard, flare gun and parachute w/insert	1964	150	250	400
7809	Scramble Parachute Set	Reissued Adventure Pack	1967	75	125	200
7802	Survival Life Raft Set	Raft with oars and sea anchor	1964	90	150	225
7801	Survival Life Raft Set	Raft with oars, flare gun, knife, air vest, first-aid kit, sea anchor and manual	1964	125	225	350
		Action Sailor Series				
7624	Annapolis Cadet	Reissued Adventure Pack	1968	450	750	1150
7624	Annapolis Cadet	Garrison cap, dress jacket, pants, shoes, sword, scabbard, belt and white M-1 rifle, (add $300 for photo box)	1967	300	525	825
7625	Breeches Buoy	Yellow jacket and pants, chair and pulley, flare gun, blinker light	1967	225	475	850
7625	Breeches Buoy	Reissued Adventure Pack	1968	250	475	850
7623	Deep Freeze	Reissued Adventure Pack	1968	250	350	900
7623	Deep Freeze	White boots, fur parka, pants, snow shoes, ice axe, snow sled w/rope and flare gun	1967	300	500	775
7620	Deep Sea Diver Equipment Set	Diving suit, helmet with breast plates, weighted belts and shoes, air pump, hose, tools, signal floats	1964	250	425	650
7620	Deep Sea Diver Set	Underwater uniform, helmet, upper and lower plate, sledge hammer, buoy w/rope, gloves, compass, hoses, lead boots and weight belt	1965	200	275	900
7620	Deep Sea Diver Set	Reissued Adventure Pack	1968	200	275	900
7604	Frogman Scuba Bottom Set	Adventure Pack	1964	20	35	50
7605	Frogman Scuba Equipment Set	Adventure Pack	1964	45	75	115
7606	Frogman Scuba Tank Set	Adventure Pack	1964	20	35	50
7603	Frogman Scuba Top Set	Adventure Pack	1964	45	80	125

Top to Bottom: All GI Joe: Action Soldier Figure, 1964; Man of Action Figure, 1970; Adventure Team Headquarters ad panel, 1972.

Accessories

NO.	NAME	DESCRIPTION	YEAR	EX	MNP	MIP
7602	Frogman Underwater Demolition Set	Headpiece, face mask, swim fins, rubber suit, scuba tank, depth gauge, knife, dynamite and manual	1964	175	295	450
7621	Landing Signal Officer	Jumpsuit, signal paddles, goggles, cloth head gear, headphones, clipbaord (complete), binoculars and flare gun	1966	165	275	425
7610	Navy Attack Helmet Set	Shirt and pants, boots, yellow life vest, blue helmet, flare gun, binoculars, signal flags	1964	45	75	125
7611	Navy Attack Life Jacket	Adventure Pack	1964	45	75	115
7607	Navy Attack Set	Life jacket, field glasses, blinker light, signal flags, manual	1964	75	130	200
7609	Navy Attack Work Pants Set	Adventure Pack	1964	40	65	100
7608	Navy Attack Work Shirt Set	Adventure Pack	1964	45	75	110
7628	Navy Basics Set	Adventure Pack	1966	50	80	125
7619	Navy Dress Parade Set	Billy club, cartridge belt, bayonet and white dress rifle	1964	30	55	85
7619	Navy Dress Parade Rifle Set	Adventure Pack	1965	55	90	135
7602	Navy Frogman	Reissued Adventure Pack	1968	250	400	600
7626	Navy L.S.O. Equipment Set	Helmet, headphones, signal paddles, flare gun	1966	40	65	100
7627	Navy Life Ring Set	U.S.N. life ring, helmet sticker, blue ammo box	1966	30	50	75
7618	Navy Machine Gun Set	Adventure Pack	1965	45	75	120
7601	Sea Rescue	Life raft, oar, anchor, flare gun, first-aid kit, knife, scabbard, manual	1964	100	175	275
7622	Sea Rescue Set	Reissued with life preserver	1966	115	195	300
7612	Shore Patrol	Dress shirt, tie and pants, helmet, white belt, .45 and holster, billy club, boots, arm band, sea bag	1964	225	375	600
7612	Shore Patrol	Adventure Pack	1967	600	975	1500
7613	Shore Patrol Dress Jumper Set	Adventure Pack	1964	60	100	150
7614	Shore Patrol Dress Pant Set	Adventure Pack	1964	45	75	125
7616	Shore Patrol Helmet and Small Arms Set	White belt, billy stick, white helmet, .45 pistol	1964	40	65	100
7615	Shore Patrol Sea Bag Set	Adventure Pack	1964	18	30	45

Action Soldier Series

NO.	NAME	DESCRIPTION	YEAR	EX	MNP	MIP
8007.83	Adventure Pack with 16 items	Adventure Pack	1968	90	150	225
8006.83	Adventure Pack with 12 items	Adventure Pack	1968	80	140	215
8008.83	Adventure Pack with 14 pieces	Adventure Pack	1968	80	140	215
8005.83	Adventure Pack with 12 items	Adventure Pack	1968	75	125	200
7549-83	Adventure Pack, Army Bivouac Series		1968	450	775	1200
7813	Air Police Equipment	Gray field phone, carbine, white helmet and bayonet	1964	60	105	160
8000	Basic Footlocker	Wood tray	1964	40	65	100

Accessories

NO.	NAME	DESCRIPTION	YEAR	EX	MNP	MIP
7513	Bivouac Deluxe Pup Tent Set	M-1 rifle and bayonet, shovel and cover, canteen and cover, mess kit, cartridge belt, machine gun, tent, pegs, poles, camoflage, sleeping bag, netting, ammo box	1964	90	150	225
7514	Bivouac Machine Gun Set	Reissue	1967	50	80	125
7514	Bivouac Machine Gun Set	Machine gun set and ammo box	1964	35	60	95
7512	Bivouac Sleeping Bag Set	Mess kit, canteen, bayonet, cartridge belt, M-1 rifle, manual	1964	90	150	250
7515	Bivouac Sleeping Bag	Zippered bag	1964	20	35	50
7511	Combat Camoflaged Netting Set	Foliage and posts	1964	15	25	35
7572	Combat Construction Set	Orange safety helmet, work gloves, jack hammer	1967	150	250	375
7573	Combat Demolition Set		1967	115	195	295
7571	Combat Engineer Set	Helmet, machine gun, tripod and transit	1967	150	250	375
7504	Combat Fatigue Pants Set		1964	70	115	175
7503	Combat Fatigue Shirt Set		1964	75	130	200
7505	Combat Field Jacket		1964	90	150	250
7501	Combat Field Jacket Set	Jacket, bayonet, cartridge belt, hand grenades, M-1 rifle and manual	1964	150	250	400
7506	Combat Field Pack & Entrenching Tool		1964	30	50	75
7502	Combat Field Pack Deluxe Set	Field jacket, pack, entrenching shovel w/cover, mess kit, first-aid pouch, canteen w/cover	1964	125	225	350
7507	Combat Helmet Set	With netting and foliage leaves	1964	30	55	85
7509	Combat Mess Kit	Plate, fork, knife, spoon, canteen	1964	30	50	75
7705	Combat Paratrooper Parachute Pack Set	First-aid pouch, pistol, belt, carbine, 6 grenades, knife, scabbard, canteen, manual	1964	135	225	350
7510	Combat Rifle and Helmet Set	Bayonet, M-1 rifle, belt and grenades	1967	90	150	225
7508	Combat Sandbags Set		1964	18	30	45
7520	Command Post Field Radio and Telephone Set	Field radio, telephone with wire roll and map	1964	40	65	100
7520	Command Post Field Radio and Telephone Set	Reissue	1967	60	100	150
7517	Command Post Poncho Set	Poncho, field radio and telephone, wire roll, pistol, belt and holster, map and case and manual	1964	90	150	225
7519	Command Post Poncho		1964	20	35	50
7518	Command Post Small Arms Set	Holster and .45 pistol, belt, grenades	1964	75	80	125
8009.83	Dress Parade Adventure Pack with 37 pieces	Adventure Pack	1968	550	975	1500
7533	Green Beret and Small Arms Set	Reissue	1967	100	165	250
7533	Green Beret and Small Arms Set		1966	90	150	250
5978	Green Beret Machine Gun Outpost Set	Sear exclusive	1966	450	775	1200
7538	Heavy Weapons Set	mortar launcher and shells, M-60 machine gun, grenades, flak jacket, shirt and pants	1967	175	295	450
7538	Heavy Weapons Set	Reissue	1968	225	375	575

Accessories

NO.	NAME	DESCRIPTION	YEAR	EX	MNP	MIP
7720	Medic Set	Stretcher, medic bag, Red Cross flag and arm band, helmet, first-aid pouch, stethoscope, plasma bottle, crutches, bandages, splints	1964	35	60	95
7523	Military Police Duffle Bag Set		1964	20	35	50
7526	Military Police Helmet and Small Arms Set		1964	45	75	110
7526	Military Police Helmet and Small Arms Set	Reissue	1967	48	80	125
7524	Military Police Ike Jacket	Jacket with red scarf and arm band	1964	45	75	115
7525	Military Police Ike Pants	Matches Ike Jacket	1964	35	60	95
7521	Military Police Uniform Set	Includes figure, with Ike jacket and pants, scarf, boots, helmet, belt with ammo pouches, .45 pistol and holster, billy club, armband, duffle bag	1964	200	325	500
7539	Military Police Uniform Set	Includes figure in green or tan uniform, black and gold MP Helmet, billy club, belt, pistol and holster, MP armband and red tunic	1967	700	1150	1800
7539	Military Police Uniform Set	Reissue	1968	900	1500	2300
7530	Mountain Troops Set	Snow shoes, ice axe, ropes, grenades, camoflage pack, web belt, manual	1964	70	120	185
7516	Sabotage Set	Dingy and oar, blinker light, detonator w/strap, TNT, wool stocking cap, gas mask, binoculars, green radio and .45 pistol and holster	1967	165	275	425
7516	Sabotage Set	Reissue in photo box	1968	475	775	1200
7531	Ski Patrol Deluxe Set	White parka, boots, goggles, mittens, skis, poles and manual	1964	250	425	650
7527	Ski Patrol Helmet and Small Arms Set		1965	45	75	120
7527	Ski Patrol Helmet and Small Arms Set	Reissue	1967	55	90	135
7527	Ski Patrol Set	Helmet, grenades and white belt	1964	40	65	100
7529	Snow Troops Set	Reissue	1967	50	90	135
7529	Snow Troops Set	Parka, pants, boots, 'bear' helmet, pack, snow shoes, white M-1 rifle, belt with ammo pouches, gloves, skis and ski poles, grenades, goggles	1966	40	65	100
7528	Special Forces Bazooka Set		1966	60	100	150
7528	Special Forces Bazooka Set	Reissue	1967	60	100	150
7532	Special Forces Uniform Set		1966	250	425	650
7537	West Point Cadet Uniform Set	Dress jacket, pants, shoes, chest and bolt sash, parade hat w/plume, saber, scabbard and white M-1 rifle	1967	250	425	675
7537	West Point Cadet Uniform Set	Reissue	1968	350	585	900

Action Soldiers of the World

NO.	NAME	DESCRIPTION	YEAR	EX	MNP	MIP
8305	Australian Jungle Fighter Set		1966	150	250	400

Top to Bottom: All GI Joe: Adventures of GI Joe Adventure Packs, Eight Ropes of Danger, 1970, and Fantastic Freefall, 1970, Action Sailor Figure and Action Marine Figure, both 1964; Adventure of GI Joe Spacewalk Mystery Set with Astronaut, 1969; Adventure Team Demolition Set, 1971.

Accessories

NO.	NAME	DESCRIPTION	YEAR	EX	MNP	MIP
8304	British Commando Set	Sten submachine gun, gas mask and carrier, canteen and cover, cartridge belt, rifle, "Victoria Cross" medal, manual	1966	125	225	350
8303	French Resistance Fighter Set	Shoulder holster, Lebel pistol, knife, grenades, radio, 7.65 submachine gun, "Croix de Guerra" medal, counter-intelligence manual	1966	115	195	300
8300	German Storm Trooper		1966	150	250	400
8301	Japanese Imperial Soldier Set	Field pack, Nambu pistol and holster, Arisaka rifle with bayonet, cartridge belt, "Order of the Kite" medal, counter-intelligence manual	1966	175	295	450
8302	Russian Infantry Man Set	DP light machine gun, bipod, field glasses and case, anti-tank grenades, ammo box, "Order of Lenin" medal, counter-intelligence medal	1966	150	250	375

Adventure Team

NO.	NAME	DESCRIPTION	YEAR	EX	MNP	MIP
7490	Adventure Team Headquarters Set	Adventure Team playset	1972	70	115	175
7495	Adventure Team Training Center Set	Rifle rack, logs, barrel, barber wire, rope ladder, 3 tires, 2 targets, escape slide, tent and poles, first aid kit, respirator and mask, snake, instructions	1973	55	90	140
7345	Aerial Reconnaissance Set	Jumpsuit, helmet, aerial recon vehicle with built-in camera	1971	25	40	60
7420	Attack at Vulture Falls	Super Deluxe Set	1975	25	40	65
7414	Black Widow Rendezvous	Super Deluxe Set	1975	30	50	75
7328-5	Buried Bounty	Deluxe Set	1975	15	25	35
7437	Capture of the Pygmy Gorilla Set	Adventure Pack	1970	85	145	225
8032	Challenge of Savage River	Deluxe Set	1975	18	30	45
7313	Chest Winch Set	Reissued Adventure Pack	1974	15	25	35
7313	Chest Winch Set	Adventure Pack	1972	12	20	30
8033	Command Para Drop	Deluxe Set	1975	20	35	50
7308-3	Copter Rescue Set	Blue jumpsuit, red binoculars	1973	12	20	30
7412	Danger of the Depths Set	Adventure Pack	1970	55	90	135
7338-1	Danger Ray Detection	Magnetic ray detector, solar communicator with headphones, 2-piece uniform, instructions and comic	1975	30	50	80
7309-2	Dangerous Climb Set	Adventure Pack	1973	12	20	30
7608-5	Dangerous Mission Set	Green shirt, pants, hunting rifle	1973	12	20	30
7371	Demolition Set	Adventure Pack with land mines, mine detector and carrying case	1971	25	40	60
7370	Demolition Set	Armored suit, face shield, bomb, bomb disposal box, extension grips	1971	18	30	45
7309-5	Desert Explorer Set	Adventure Pack	1973	12	20	30
7308-6	Desert Survival Set	Adventure Pack	1973	12	20	30
8031	Dive to Danger	Mike Powers set, orange scuba suit, fins, mask, spear gun, shark, buoy, knife and scabbard, mini sled, air tanks, comic	1975	75	130	200
7328-6	Diver's Distress	Deluxe Set	1975	15	25	35

Accessories

NO.	NAME	DESCRIPTION	YEAR	EX	MNP	MIP
7364	Drag Bike Set	3-wheel motorcycle brakes down to backpack size	1971	15	25	40
7422	Eight Ropes of Danger Set	Adventure Pack	1970	60	100	160
7374	Emergency Rescue Set	Shirt, pants, rope ladder and hook, walkie talkie, safety belt, flashlight, oxygen tank, axe, first aid kit	1971	25	40	60
7360	Escape Car Set	Adventure Pack	1971	15	25	40
7319-1	Escape Slide Set	Adventure Pack	1972	12	20	30
8028-2	Fangs of the Cobra	Deluxe Set	1975	12	20	30
7423	Fantastic Freefall Set	Adventure Pack	1970	65	115	175
7982	Fight for Survival Set w/ Polar Explorer	Adventure Pack	1969	225	375	575
7308-2	Fight for Survival Set	Brown shirt and pants, machete	1973	12	20	30
7351	Fire Fighter Set	Adventure Pack	1971	18	30	45
7431	Flight For Survival Set	Adventure Pack	1970	150	250	375
7361	Flying Rescue Set	Adventure Pack	1971	18	30	45
7425	Flying Space Adventure Set	Adventure Pack	1970	150	260	400
8000	Footlocker	Adventure Pack	1974	25	45	65
7328-4	Green Danger		1975	15	25	35
7415	Hidden Missile Discovery Set	Adventure Pack	1970	55	90	135
7308-1	Hidden Treasure Set	Shirt, pants, pick axe, shovel	1973	10	20	30
7342	High Voltage Escape Set	Net, jumpsuit, hat, wrist meter, wire cutters, wire, warning sign	1971	30	50	75
7343	Hurricane Spotter Set	Slicker suit, rain measure, portable radar, map and case, binoculars	1971	25	40	65
7421	Jaws of Death	Super Deluxe Set	1975	25	40	65
7339-2	Jettison to Safety	Infrared terrain scanner, mobile rocket pack, 2-piece flight suit, instructions and comic	1975	30	50	80
7309-3	Jungle Ordeal Set	Adventure Pack	1973	12	20	30
7373	Jungle Survival Set	Adventure Pack	1971	25	40	65
7372	Karate Set	Adventure Pack	1971	25	40	65
7311	Laser Rescue Set	Reissued Adventure Pack	1974	15	25	35
7311	Laser Rescue Set	Hand-held laser with backpack generator	1972	12	20	30
7353	Life-Line Catapult Set	Adventure Pack	1971	15	25	40
7328-3	Long Range Recon	Deluxe Set	1975	15	25	35
7319-2	Magnetic Flaw Detector Set	Adventure Pack	1972	12	20	30
7339-3	Mine Shaft Breakout	Sonic rock blaster, chest winch, 2-piece uniform, netting, instructions, comic	1975	15	25	40
7340	Missile Recovery Set	Adventure Pack	1971	20	35	55
	Mystery of the Boiling Lagoon	Sears, pontoon boat, diver's suit, diver's helmet, weighted belt and boots, depth gauge, air hose, buoy, nose cone, pincer arm, instructions	1973	100	165	250
7338-2	Night Surveillance	Deluxe Set	1975	15	30	45
7416	Peril of the Raging Inferno	Fire proof suit, hood and boots, breathing apparatus, camera, fire extinguisher, detection meter, gaskets	1975	85	145	225
7309-4	Photo Reconnaissance Set	Adventure Pack	1973	12	20	30
8028-1	Race for Recovery		1975	12	20	30
7341	Radiation Detection Set	Jumpsuit with belt, "uranium ore", goggles, container, pincer arm	1971	25	45	65

Accessories

NO.	NAME	DESCRIPTION	YEAR	EX	MNP	MIP
7339-1	Raging River Dam Up		1975	15	25	40
7350	Rescue Raft Set	Adventure Pack	1971	15	25	40
7413	Revenge of the Spy Shark	Super Deluxe Set	1975	30	50	75
7312	Rock Blaster	Sonic blaster with tripod, backpack generator, face shield	1972	9	15	25
7315	Rocket Pack Set	Adventure Pack	1972	12	20	30
7315	Rocket Pack Set	Reissued Adventure Pack	1974	15	25	35
7319-3	Sample Analyzer Set	Adventure Pack	1972	12	20	30
7439.16	Search for the Abominable Snowman Set	Sears, white suit, belt, goggles, gloves, rifle, skis and poles, show shoes, sled, rope, net, supply chest, binoculars, Abominable Snowman, comic book	1973	125	210	325
7375	Secret Agent Set	Adventure Pack	1971	25	40	65
7328-1	Secret Courier	Deluxe Set	1975	15	25	35
7309-1	Secret Mission Set	Adventure Pack	1973	10	20	30
8030	Secret Mission Set	Deluxe Set	1975	20	35	50
7411	Secret Mission to Spy Island Set	Comic , inflatable raft with oar, binoculars, signal light, flare gun, TNT and detonator, wire roll, boots, pants, sweater, black cap, camera, radio with earphones, .45 submachine gun	1970	60	100	150
7308-4	Secret Rendezvous Set	Parka, pants, flare gun	1973	12	20	30
7319-6	Seismograph Set	Adventure Pack	1972	12	20	30
7338-3	Shocking Escape	Escape slide, chest pack climber, jumpsuit with gloves and belt, high voltage sign, instructions and comic	1975	18	30	45
7362	Signal Flasher Set	Large back pack type signal flash unit	1971	20	35	50
7440	Sky Dive to Danger	Super Deluxe Set	1975	30	50	75
7314	Solar Communicator Set	Reissue	1974	15	25	35
7314	Solar Communicator Set	Adventure Pack	1972	15	25	35
7312	Sonic Rock Blaster Set	Adventure Pack	1972	12	20	30
7312	Sonic Rock Blaster Set	Reissued Adventure Pack	1974	15	25	35
8028-3	Special Assignment	Deluxe Set	1975	9	15	25
7319-4	Thermal Terrain Scanner Set	Adventure Pack	1972	12	20	30
7480	Three in One Super Adventure Set	Cold of the Arctic, Heat of the Desert and Danger of the Jungle Adventure Pack	1971	200	325	500
7480	Three in One Super Adventure Set	Danger of the Depths, Secret Mission to Spy Island and Flying Space Adventure Packs	1971	200	325	500
7328-2	Thrust into Danger	Deluxe Set	1975	15	25	35
59289	Trouble at Vulture Pass	Sears exclusive, Super Deluxe Set	1975	30	50	75
7363	Turbo Copter Set	Strap-on one man helicopter	1971	18	30	45
7309-6	Undercover Agent Set	Trenchcoat and belt, walkie-talkie	1973	12	20	30
7310	Underwater Demolition Set	Reissued Adventure Pack	1974	15	25	35
7310	Underwater Demolition Set	Hand-held propulsion device, breathing apparatus, dynamite	1972	12	20	30
7354	Underwater Explorer Set	Self propelled underwater device	1971	20	35	50
7344	Volcano Jumper Set	Jumpsuit with hood, belt, nylon rope, chest pack, TNT pack	1971	20	35	55
7436	White Tiger Hunt Set	Hunter's jacket and pants, hat, rifle, tent, cage, chain, campfire, white tiger, comic	1970	75	130	200
7353	Windboat Set	Back pack, sled with wheels, sail	1971	15	25	40
7309-4	Winter Rescue Set	Replaced Photo Reconnaissance Set - Adventure Pack	1973	15	25	40

Top to Bottom: All GI Joe: Action Soldier of the World Figures, Australian Jungle Fighter, 1966, and Japanese Imperial Soldier, 1966; Black Adventurer Figure box, 1976; Official Jeep Combat Set, 1965.

Accessories

NO.	NAME	DESCRIPTION	YEAR	EX	MNP	MIP
		Adventures of GI Joe				
7940	Adventure Locker	Footlocker	1969	75	150	275
7941	Aqua Locker	Footlocker	1969	100	200	300
7942	Astro Locker	Footlocker	1969	100	200	300
7920	Danger of the Depths Underwater Diver Set	Basic Adventure Pack	1969	125	225	350
7950	Eight Ropes of Danger Set	Deluxe Adventure Pack, diving suit, treasure chest, octopus	1969	150	250	375
7951	Fantastic Freefall Set	Includes figure with parachute and pack, blinker light, air vest, flash light, crash helmet with visor and oxygen mask, dog tags, orange jump suit, black boots	1969	150	255	390
7982.83	Flight for Survival Set w/o Polar Explorer	Reissued Adventure Pack	1969	200	350	525
7952	Hidden Missile Discovery Set	Deluxe Adventure Pack	1969	150	250	385
7953	Mouth of Doom Set	Deluxe Adventure Pack	1969	125	210	325
7921	Mysterious Explosion Set	Basic Adventure Pack	1969	115	195	300
7923	Perilous Rescue Set	Basic Adventure Pack	1969	150	250	400
7922	Secret Mission to Spy Island Set	Basic Adventure Pack	1969	150	245	375
		G.I. Joe Action Series, Army, Navy, Marine and Air Force				
8000	Basic Footlocker	Adventure Pack	1965	40	65	100
8002.83	Footlocker Adventure Pack with 22 items	Adventure Pack	1968	90	155	240
8001.83	Footlocker Adventure Pack with 15 pieces	Adventure Pack	1968	90	150	225
8002.83	Footlocker Adventure Pack with 15 pieces	Adventure Pack	1968	85	145	225
8000.83	Footlocker Adventure Pack with 16 pieces	Adventure Pack	1968	85	145	225

Figure Sets

NO.	NAME	DESCRIPTION	YEAR	EX	MNP	MIP
		Action Girl Series				
8060	G.I. Nurse	Red Cross hat and arm band, white dress, stockings, shoes, crutches, medic bag, stethescope, plasma bottle, bandages and splints	1967	1175	1950	3000
		Action Marine Series				
7700	Action Marine	Fatigues, green cap, boots, dog tags, insignias and manual	1964	150	250	375
90711	Marine Medic Series	Camo shirt and pants, boots, Red Cross helmet, flag and arm bands, crutch, bandages, splints, first aid pouch, stethoscope, plasma bottle, stretcher, medic bag, belt with ammo pouches	1967	525	875	1350
7790	Talking Action Marine		1967	270	450	700
7790	Talking Action Marine	Figure with camo shirt and pants, cap, boots, dog tags	1968	250	425	650
90712	Talking Adventure Pack and Field Pack Equip.	Talking Adventure Pack	1968	300	450	1200

Top to Bottom: Super Powers Action Figures, Samurai, Tyr, Shazam (Captain Marvel) and Darkseid, Kenner, 1984-86; Indiana Jones Action Figure, Kenner.

Figure Sets

NO.	NAME	DESCRIPTION	YEAR	EX	MNP	MIP
90711	Talking Adventure Pack and Tent Set	Talking Adventure Pack	1968	300	450	1200

Action Pilot Series

NO.	NAME	DESCRIPTION	YEAR	EX	MNP	MIP
7800	Action Pilot	Orange jumpsuit, blue cap, black boots, dog tags, insignias, manual, catalog and club application	1964	150	275	450
7890	Talking Action Pilot	Talking Adventure Pack	1967	575	975	1500

Action Sailor Series

NO.	NAME	DESCRIPTION	YEAR	EX	MNP	MIP
7600	Action Sailor	White cap, denim shirt and pants, boots, dog tags, navy manual and insignias	1964	125	225	350
7643-83	Navy Scuba Set	Adventure Pack	1968	550	900	1400
7690	Talking Action Sailor		1967	450	750	1200
90621	Talking Landing Signal Officer	Talking Adventure Pack	1968	950	1600	2500
90612	Talking Shore Patrol Equipment Set	Talking Adventure Pack	1968	950	1600	2500

Action Soldier Series

NO.	NAME	DESCRIPTION	YEAR	EX	MNP	MIP
7500	Action Soldier	Fatique cap, shirt, pants, boots, dog tags, army manual and insignias, helmet, belt with pouches, M-1 rifle	1964	115	195	300
7900	Black Action Soldier		1965	600	1000	1600
5904	Canadian Mountie Set	Sears exclusive	1967	575	975	1500
8030	Desert Patrol Attack Jeep Set	G.I. Joe Desert Fighter figure, jeep with steering wheel, spare tire, tan tripod, gun and gun mount and ring, black antenna, tan jacket and shorts, socks, goggles	1967	900	1500	2500
5969	Forward Observer Set	Sears exclusive	1966	275	475	750
7536	Green Beret	Field radio, bazooka rocket, bazooka, green beret, jacket, pants, M-16 rifle, grenades, camo scarf, belt pistol and holster	1966	950	1600	2500
7522	Jungle Fighter		1966	55	95	145
7522	Jungle Fighter	Reissue	1967	60	100	150
7531	Machine Gun Emplacement Set	Sears exclusive	1965	300	525	800
7590	Talking Action Soldier		1967	350	575	900
7590	Talking Action Soldier		1968	225	375	575
90517	Talking Adventure Pack, Command Post Equip.		1968	300	450	1200
7557-83	Talking Adventure Pack, Mountain Troop Series		1968	300	450	1200
90532	Talking Adventure Pack, Special Forces Equip.		1968	300	450	1200
90513	Talking Aventure Pack, Bivouac Equipment		1968	750	1300	2000

Action Soldiers of the World

NO.	NAME	DESCRIPTION	YEAR	EX	MNP	MIP
8205	Australian Jungle Fighter	Standard set with action figure and equipment	1966	275	350	1400

Top to Bottom: Indiana Jones and the Temple of Doom Action Figures, Mola Ram, Indy, Giant Thuggee, LJN; Super Powers Action Figures, Lex Luthor and Flash, Kenner 1984-86.

Figure Sets

NO.	NAME	DESCRIPTION	YEAR	EX	MNP	MIP
8105	Australian Jungle Fighter	Jacket, shorts, socks, boots, bush hat, belt, "Victoria Cross" medal, knuckle knife, flamethrower, entrenching tool, bush knife and sheath	1966	275	350	1750
8204	British Commando	Standard set with action figure and equipment	1966	275	375	1400
8104	British Commando	Deluxe set with helmet, night raidfgreen jacket, pants, boots, canteen and cover, gas mask and cover, belt, Sten sub machine gun, gun clip and "Victoria Cross" medal	1966	275	375	1750
8111-83	Foreign Soldiers of the World	Talking Adventure Pack, Sears exclusive	1968	1150	1950	3000
8203	French Resistance Fighter	Standard set with action figure and equipment	1966	200	350	1400
8103	French Resistance Fighter	Deluxe set with figure, beret, short black boots, black sweater, denim pants, "Croix de Guerre" medal, knife, shoulder holster, pistol, radio, sub machine gun and grenades	1966	200	300	1750
8100	German Storm Trooper	Deluxe set with figure, helmet, jacket, pants, boots, Luger pistol, holster, cartridge belt, cartridges, "Iron Cross" medal, stick grenades, 9MM Schmeisser, field pack	1966	250	400	1750
8200	German Storm Trooper	Standard set with action figure and equipment	1966	250	400	1400
8201	Japanese Imperial Soldier	Standard set with action figure and equipment	1966	400	600	1400
8101	Japanese Imperial Soldier	Deluxe set with figure, Arisaka rifle, belt, cartridges, field pack, Nambu pistol, holster, bayonet, "Order of the Kite" medal, helmet, jacket, pants, short brown boots	1966	400	600	1750
8202	Russian Infantry Man	Standard set with action figure and equipment	1966	250	375	1400
8102	Russian Infantry Man	Deluxe set with action figure, fur cap, tunic, pants, boots, ammo box, ammo rounds, anti-tank grenades, belt, bipod, DP light machine gun, "Order of Lenin" medal, field glasses and case	1966	250	375	1750
5038	Uniforms of Six Nations		1967	575	950	1450

Adventure Team

NO.	NAME	DESCRIPTION	YEAR	EX	MNP	MIP
7272	Air Adventurer	Adventure Pack with "New" Life-Like action figure, uniform and equipment	1976	45	75	115
7282	Air Adventurer	Adventure Pack action figure with Life-Like Body and Kung Fu Grip	1974	90	150	225
7282	Air Adventurer	Adventure Pack with "New" action figure, uniform and equipment	1976	50	85	135
7403	Air Adventurer	includes figure with kung fu grip, orange flight suit, boots, insignia, dog tags, rifle, boots, warranty, club insert	1970	70	115	175
7273	Black Adventurer	Adventure Pack	1976	45	75	120
7283	Black Adventurer	Adventure Pack	1976	50	85	130

Top to Bottom: Masters of the Universe, Monstroid vehicle, Evil-Lyn and Flying Fists He-Man Action Figures, Mattel, 1980s.

Figure Sets

NO.	NAME	DESCRIPTION	YEAR	EX	MNP	MIP
7283	Black Adventurer	Adventure Pack figure with Life-Like Body and Kung Fu Grip	1974	90	150	240
7404	Black Adventurer	Includes figure, shirt with insignia, pants, boots, dog tags, shoulder holster with pistol	1970	75	125	190
8026	Bulletman	Adventure Pack	1976	35	55	85
7278	Eagle Eye Black Commando	Adventure Pack	1976	50	80	125
7276	Eagle Eye Land Commander	Adventure Pack	1976	45	75	115
7277	Eagle Eye Man of Action	Adventure Pack	1976	45	80	125
8050	Intruder Commander	"New" Life-Like action figure and equipment	1976	30	50	80
8051	Intruder Warrior	"New" Life-Like action figure with equipment	1976	40	65	100
7270	Land Adventurer	Adventure Pack	1976	30	50	80
7280	Land Adventurer	Action figure with Life-Like Body and Kung Fu Grip	1974	75	130	200
7280	Land Adventurer	Adventure Pack	1976	40	65	100
7401	Land Adventurer	Includes figure, camo shirt and pants, boots, insignia, shoulder holster and pistol, dog tags and team inserts	1970	60	100	150
7284	Man of Action	Adventure Pack figure with Life-Like Body and Kung Fu Grip	1974	90	150	230
7284	Man of Action	Adventure Pack	1976	50	85	130
7274	Man of Action	Adventure Pack	1976	40	70	110
7500	Man of Action	Includes figure, shirt and pants, boots, insignia, dog tags, team inserts	1970	70	115	180
8025	Mike Powers/Atomic Man	Figure with "atomic" flashing eye, arm that spins hand-held helicopter	1975	30	50	75
7271	Sea Adventurer	Adventure Pack	1976	35	60	90
7281	Sea Adventurer	Adventure Pack figure with Life-Like Body and Kung Fu Grip	1974	80	135	210
7281	Sea Adventurer	Adventure Pack	1976	40	70	110
7402	Sea Adventurer	Includes figure, shirt, dungarees, insignia, boots, shoulder holster and pistol	1970	60	100	160
8040	Secret Mountain Outpost		1975	35	55	85
7290	Talking Adventure Team Commander	Talking Adventure Pack figure with Life-Like Body and Kung Fu Grip	1974	115	195	300
7291	Talking Adventure Team Black Commander	Talking Adventure Pack figure with Life-Like Body and Kung Fu Grip	1974	250	450	600
7400	Talking Adventure Team Commander	Includes figure, 2-pocket green shirt, pants, boots, insignia, instructions, dog tag, shoulder holster and pistol	1970	100	165	250
7406	Talking Adventure Team Black Commander	Talking Adventure Pack	1973	175	295	450
7590	Talking Astronaut	Talking Adventure Pack	1970	125	225	350
7291	Talking Black Commander	Adventure Pack	1976	85	145	225
7290	Talking Commander	Adventure Pack	1976	75	125	195
7292	Talking Man of Action	Adventure Pack	1976	85	145	225
7590	Talking Man of Action	Talking figure, shirt, pants, boots, dog tags, rifle, insignia, instructions	1970	120	195	300
7292	Talking Man of Action	Talking Adventure Pack figure with Life-Like Body and Kung Fu Grip	1974	125	225	350

Top to Bottom: Marvel Super Heroes Secret Wars, Doom Roller vehicle, Hobgoblin on European card, and Captain America Action figures, Mattel, 1984-85.

Figure Sets

NO.	NAME	DESCRIPTION	YEAR	EX	MNP	MIP
		Adventures of GI Joe				
7910	Aquanaut	Adventure Pack	1969	775	1300	2000
7905	Negro Adventurer	Sears exclusive, includes painted hair figure, blue jeans, pullover sweater, shoulder holster and pistol, plus product letter from Sears	1969	500	900	1400
7980	Sharks Surprise Set w/ Frogman	With figure, orange scuba suit, blue sea sled, air tanks, harpoon, face mask, treasure chest, shark, instructions and comic	1969	200	325	500
7615	Talking Astronaut	Hard-hand figure with white coveralls with insignias, white boots, dog tags	1969	300	525	800

Vehicle Sets

NO.	NAME	DESCRIPTION	YEAR	EX	MNP	MIP
		Action Pilot Series				
8040	Crash Crew Fire Truck Set	Adventure Pack	1967	1300	2200	3500
8020	Official Space Capsule Set	Space capsule, record, space suit, cloth space boots, space gloves, helmet with visor	1966	200	275	475
5979	Official Space Capsule Set w/ flotation	Sears exclusive with collar, life raft and oars	1966	250	425	650
		Action Sailor Series				
8050	Official Sea Sled and Frogman Set	Adventure Pack, without cave	1966	225	400	600
5979	Official Sea Sled and Frogman Set	Sears, with figure and underwater cave, orange scuba suit, fins, mask, tanks, sea sled in orange and black	1966	275	475	750
		Action Soldier Series				
5693	Amphibious Duck	Irwin, 26 inches long	1967	250	450	700
5397	Armored Car	Irwin, friction powered, 20 inches long	1967	250	425	650
5395	Helicopter	Irwin, friction powered, 28 inches long	1967	275	475	750
5396	Jet Fighter Plane	Irwin, friction powered, 30 inches long	1967	300	525	800
5652	Military Staff Car	Irwin, friction powered, 24 inches long	1967	250	425	650
5651	Motorcycle and Sidecar	Irwin, 14 inches long, khaki, with decals	1967	135	225	350
7000	Official Combat Jeep Set	Trailer, steering wheel, spare tire, windshield, cannon, search light, shell, flag, guard rails, tripod, tailgate and hood, without Moto-Rev Sound	1965	200	300	500
7000	Official Jeep Combat Set	With Moto-Rev Sound	1965	250	425	650
5694	Personnel Carrier/ Mine Sweeper	Irwin, 26 inches long	1967	275	475	750
		Adventure Team				
	Action Sea Sled	J.C. Penney, 13", Adventure Pack	1973	18	30	45

Top to Bottom: Archie and Jughead figures from The Archies series, 1975; Dwight D. Eisenhower figure; Johnny West figure from Best of the West series, 1960s, all from Marx.

Vehicle Sets

NO.	NAME	DESCRIPTION	YEAR	EX	MNP	MIP
7005	Adventure Team Vehicle Set	Adventure Pack	1970	110	195	300
23528	All Terrain Vehicle	14", Adventure Pack	1973	20	35	50
59158	Amphicat	By Irwin, scaled to fit 2 figures	1973	35	60	90
	Avenger Pursuit Craft	Sears exclusive	1976	100	165	250
7498	Big Trapper	Adventure set without action figure	1976	70	115	175
7494	Big Trapper Adventure with Intruder	Adventure set with action figure	1976	85	145	225
7480	Capture Copter	Vehicle set, no action figure included	1976	65	110	165
7481	Capture Copter Adventure with Intruder	Vehicle set with action figure included	1976	85	145	225
59114	Chopper Cycle	15", Adventure Pack	1973	18	30	45
59751	Combat Action Jeep	18", Adventure Pack	1973	40	65	100
7000	Combat Jeep and Trailer		1976	90	150	225
7439	Devil of the Deep	Adventure Pack	1974	45	80	125
7460	Fantastic Sea Wolf Submarine		1975	45	80	125
7450	Fate of the Troubleshooter	Adventure Pack	1974	45	75	110
59189	Giant Air-Sea Helicopter	28", Adventure Pack	1973	30	50	75
7380	Helicopter	J.C. Penney, 14" helicopter in yellow with working winch	1973	50	80	125
7380	Helicopter		1976	60	100	150
7499	Mobile Support Vehicle Set	Adventure Pack	1972	125	225	350
	Recovery of the Lost Mummy Adventurer Set	Sears exclusive Adventure Pack	1971	125	210	325
7493	Sandstorm Survival Adventure		1974	75	130	200
7418	Search for the Stolen Idol Set	Adventure Pack	1971	100	175	275
7441	Secret of the Mummys Tomb Set	With Land Adventurer figure, shirt, pants, boots, insignia, pith helmet, pick, shovel, Mummy's tomb, net, gems, vehicle with winch, comic	1970	125	210	325
7442	Sharks Surprise Set w/ Sea Adventurer	Adventure Pack	1970	135	225	350
	Signal All Terrain Vehicle	J.C. Penney, 12", Adventure Pack	1973	18	30	45
7470	Sky Hawk	5 and 3/4 foot wingspan	1975	40	65	100
7010	Space-A-Matic Set	Adventure Pack	1970	200	350	550
7445	Spacewalk Mystery Set w/Astronaut	Adventure Pack	1970	150	260	400
79-59301	Trapped in the Coils of Doom	Adventure Pack	1974	55	95	145

Adventures of GI Joe

NO.	NAME	DESCRIPTION	YEAR	EX	MNP	MIP
7980.83	Sharks Surprise Set without Frogman	Adventure Pack	1969	175	295	450
7981	Sharks Surprise Set without Frogman	Adventure Pack	1969	225	390	600
7981.83	Spacewalk Mystery Set without Spaceman	Reissued Adventure Pack	1969	200	350	550

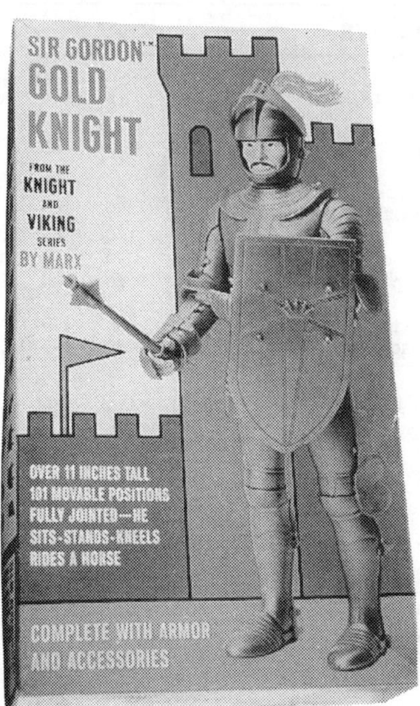

Top to Bottom: Sir Gordon The Gold Knight from Knight and Viking series, 1968; Stony Smith Battling Soldier figure, 1960s; Geronimo figure from Fort Apache Fighters series, 1960s; Mike Hazard Double Agent figure, all from Marx.

Indiana Jones, Adventures of

NAME	MNP	MIP
Belloq in Ceremonial Robe, in mailer box	6	15
Belloq in Ceremonial Robe, on card	200	500
Cairo Swordsman doll	4	10
Convoy Truck	14	35
German Mechanic Figure	14	35
Indiana Jones Action Figure	40	100
Indiana Jones Action Figure, 12" tall	100	250
Indiana Jones in German Uniform	18	45
Map Room Set	20	50
Marion Ravenwood Figure	70	175
Sallah Figure	18	45
Streets of Cairo Set	18	45
Toht	4	10
Well of Souls	30	75

Kenner Super Powers

5" Figures

*Figures and accessories made by Kenner, 1984-86

NAME	MNP	MIP
Aquaman	15	35
Batman	20	50
Braniac	15	30
Clark Kent, mail-in figure	60	0
Cyborg	50	135
Cyclotron	25	50
Darkseid	5	15
Desaad	10	30
Doctor Fate	15	40
Firestorm	10	25
Flash	5	15
Golden Pharoah	25	50
Green Arrow	20	50
Green Lantern	20	45
Hawkman	20	50
Joker	10	25
Kalibak	5	15
Lex Luthor	5	15
Mantis	10	30
Martian Manhunter	10	30
Mr. Freeze	15	35
Mr. Miracle	50	150
Orion	15	30
Parademon	15	35
Penguin	20	40
Plastic Man	25	60
Red Tornado	25	50
Robin	15	40
Samurai	25	50
Shazam (Captain Marvel)	15	30
Steppenwolf, on card	10	50
Steppenwolf,in mail-in bag	10	0
Superman	15	30
Tyr	15	40
Wonder Woman	10	20

Kenner Super Powers

NAME	MNP	MIP

Accessories

NAME	MNP	MIP
Collector's Case	10	20

Playsets

NAME	MNP	MIP
Hall of Justice	30	100

Vehicles

NAME	MNP	MIP
Batcopter	40	75
Batmobile	40	75
Darkseid Destroyer	25	50
Delta Probe One	15	30
Justice Jogger Wind-Up	10	20
Kalibak Boulder Bomber	10	20
Lex-Soar 7	10	20
Supermobile	15	30

M.A.S.H.

*3-3/4" figures & accessories, unless noted.

NAME	MNP	MIP
Ambulance with Hawkeye Figure	14	35
B.J. Figure	4	10
B.J. Large Figure, 8"	10	25
Col. Potter Figure	4	10
Father Mulcahy Figure	4	10
Hawkeye Figure	4	10
Hawkeye Large Figure, 8"	10	25
Helicopter with Hawkeye Figure	8	20
Hot Lips Figure	6	15
Hot Lips Large Figure, 8"	12	30
Jeep with Hawkeye Figure	10	25
Klinger Figure	4	10
Klinger in Drag Figure	14	35
Mash Figures Collectors Set	26	65
Winchester Figure	4	10

Marvel Secret Wars

4" Action Figures

*Figures and accessories made by Mattel, 1984-85

NAME	MNP	MIP
Baron Zemo	15	35
Captain America	10	25
Constrictor (foreign release)	30	60
Daredevil	15	35
Doctor Doom	10	20
Doctor Octopus	10	20
Electro (foreign release)	30	60
Falcon	20	40
Hobgoblin	30	60
Ice Man (foreign release)	30	60
Iron Man	20	35
Kang	10	20
Magneto	10	20
Spider-Man, black outfit	25	50
Spider-Man, red and blue outfit	20	40
Three Figure Set	55	90

Top to Bottom: CHiPs Free Wheeling Motorcycle, 1979: Planet of the Apes card back showing character line, 1975: Jaclyn Smith Doll, 1977; Flash Gordon Playset, 1977, all from Mego.

Marvel Secret Wars

NAME	MNP	MIP
Two Figure Set	0	50
Wolverine, black claws	25	60
Wolverine, silver claws	25	50

Accessories

NAME	MNP	MIP
Secret Messages Pack	1	5

Playsets

NAME	MNP	MIP
Tower of Doom	10	25

Vehicles

NAME	MNP	MIP
Doom Copter	10	35
Doom Copter with Doctor Doom	15	55
Doom Cycle	6	20
Doom Cycle with Doctor Doom	10	40
Doom Roller	10	20
Doom Star Glider with Kang	15	30
Freedom Fighter	10	30
Star Dart with Spider-Man (black outfit)	25	50
Turbo Copter	10	40
Turbo Cycle	5	20

Marx Action Figures

Archies, 1975

NAME	MNP	MIP
Archie	20	40
Betty	23	45
Jughead	20	40
Veronica	20	40

Astronauts, 1969

NAME	MNP	MIP
Jane Apollo Astronaut	35	75
Johnny Apollo Astronaut	35	75
Kennedy Space Center Astronaut	35	75

Best of the West Series, 1960s

NAME	MNP	MIP
Bill Buck	100	200
Brave Eagle	45	90
Buckboard with Horse and Harness	35	75
Chief Cherokee	45	90
Daniel Boone	100	200
Davy Crockett	100	200
Fighting Eagle	45	90
General Custer	40	80
Geronimo	45	90
Geronimo and Pinto	40	80
Jamie West	32	65
Jane West	40	80
Janice West	32	65
Jay West	32	65
Johnny West	40	80
Johnny West Covered Wagon, with horse and harness	35	75
Johnny West with Comanche	65	125
Josie West	32	65
Pancho Horse, for 9" figures	20	40
Princess Wild Flower	50	100
Sam Cobra	45	90

Marx Action Figures

NAME	MNP	MIP
Sheriff Garrett	40	80
Thunderbolt Horse	35	75
Zeb Zachary	40	80

Fort Apache Fighters, 1960s

NAME	MNP	MIP
Captain Maddox	35	70
Fighting Eagle	35	70
Fighting Eagle and Comanche	50	100
General Custer	35	70
Geronimo	35	70

Johnny West Adventure Series, 1975

NAME	MNP	MIP
Jeb Gibson	125	275
Johnny West with Quick Draw	35	70
Sam Cobra with Quick Draw	40	80
Sheriff Garrett	35	70
Thunderbolt, Western ranch horse	25	50

Miscellaneous

NAME	MNP	MIP
Johnny Kolt Cowboy	150	300
Mike Hazard	150	275

Noble Knight Series, 1968

NAME	MNP	MIP
Bravo Armor Horse	100	130
The Black Knight	75	190
The Gold Knight	60	120
The Silver Knight	60	120
Valiant Armor Horse	100	130
Valor Armor Horse	100	130
Victor Armor Horse	100	130

Soldiers

NAME	MNP	MIP
Dwight D. Eisenhower	125	250
Stony Smith, battling soldier	125	250
Stony Smith, paratrooper	115	225
Stony Smith, trooper	125	250

Vikings, 1960s

NAME	MNP	MIP
Eric the Viking	35	65
Mighty Viking Horse	30	60
Odin the Viking Chieftan	35	65

Masters of the Universe

5 3/4" Action Figures

*Figures and accessories made by Mattel, early 1980s

NAME	MNP	MIP
Battle Armor He-Man	10	20
Battle Armor Skeletor	5	20
Beast Man	5	15
Blade	10	20
Blast-Attak	5	15
Buzz-Off	5	15
Buzz-Saw Hordak	5	15
Clamp Champ	5	15
Clawful	10	20
Dragstor	5	15

Top to Bottom: The Walton's Truck, 1975; Chopper figure from Starsky & Hutch series, 1976; The Amazing Spider-Man, 1977; Ralph figure from Happy Days series, 1976, all from Mego.

Masters of the Universe

NAME	MNP	MIP
Evil-Lyn	5	15
Extendar	5	15
Faker	15	40
Faker (re-issue)	5	15
Fisto	5	15
Grizzlor	5	15
Gwildor	5	15
He-Man, original version	10	25
Hordak	5	15
Horde Trooper	5	15
Jitsu	10	20
King Hiss	5	15
King Randor	10	25
Kobra Khan	5	15
Leech	5	15
Man-At-Arms	10	20
Man-E-Faces	10	20
Mantenna	5	15
Mekaneck	5	15
Mer-Man	5	20
Modulok	5	20
Mosquitor	5	15
Moss Man	5	15
Multi-Bot	5	20
Ninjor	5	20
Orko	5	15
Prince Adam	5	20
Ram Man	15	35
Rattlor	5	15
Rio Blast	5	15
Roboto	5	15
Rokkon	5	15
Rotar	5	15
Saurod	5	20
Scare Glow	10	25
Skeletor, original version	10	25
Snake Face	5	20
Snout Spout	5	15
Sorceress	10	25
Spikor	10	20
SSSqueeze	5	15
Stinkor	5	15
Stonedar	5	15
Stratos, blue wings	10	20
Stratos, red wings	10	20
Sy-Klone	5	15
Teela	5	15
Trap Jaw	10	20
Tri-Klops	10	20
Tung Lashor	5	15
Twistoid	5	15
Two-Bad	5	15
Webstor	5	15
Whiplash	5	15
Zodac	10	20

Accessories

NAME	MNP	MIP
Battle Bones Carrying Case	5	10
Battle Cat	10	25
Battle Cat with He-Man (original version)	20	40
Beam-Blaster and Artilleray	15	30
Jet Sled	5	15
Mantisaur	8	15
Megalaser	5	15
Monstroid Creature	15	30
Night Stalker	5	15
Night Stalker with Jitsu	10	25
Panthor (evil cat)	10	25
Panthor with Skeletor (original version)	15	40
Screech	5	15
Screech with Skeletor (original version)	10	25
Stilt Stalkers	5	15
Stridor Armored Horse	5	15
Stridor with Fisto	10	25
Weapons Pak	2	5
Zoar	5	15
Zoar with Teela	15	30

Deluxe Action Figures

NAME	MNP	MIP
Dragon Blaster Skeletor	10	25
Flying Fists He-Man	10	25
Hurricane Hordak	10	25
Terror Claws Skeletor	10	25
Thunder Punch He-Man	10	25

GraySkull Dinosaur Series

NAME	MNP	MIP
Bionatops	10	25
Turbodaltyl	10	25
Tyrantisaurus Rex	10	25

Meteorbs

NAME	MNP	MIP
Astro Lion	5	10
Comet Cat	5	10
Cometroid	5	10
Crocobite	5	10
Dinosorb	5	10
Gore-illa	5	10
Orbear	5	10
Rhinorb	5	10
Tuskor	5	10
Ty-Gyr	5	10

Playsets

NAME	MNP	MIP
Castle GraySkull	25	75
Eternia	100	200
Fright Zone	25	50
Slime Pit	10	20
Snake Mountain	25	50

Vehicles

NAME	MNP	MIP
Attak Trak	10	20
Bashasaurus	10	20
Battle Ram	10	30
Blasterhawk	15	30
Dragon Walker	10	20
Fright Fighter	10	25
Land Shark	10	20
Laser Bolt	10	20
Point Dread	10	40
Road Ripper	10	20
Roton	10	20
Spydor	15	35
Wind Raider	10	20

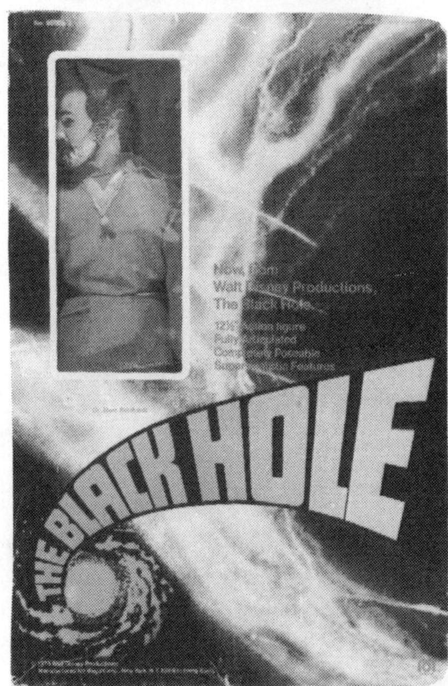

Top to Bottom: Ivanhoe figure from World's Greatest Super Knights series 1974; Buck Rogers figure, 1979; Dr. Hans Reinhardt figure from The Black Hole series, 1979; Boss Hogg figure from The Dukes of Hazzard series, 1981, all from Mego.

MEGO

Mego Super Heroes

Comic Action Heroes

3 3/4" Figures

NAME	MNP	MIP
Aquaman, 1975	30	60
Batman, 1975	20	50
Captain America, 1975	20	50
Green Goblin, 1975	22	55
Hulk, 1975	20	50
Joker, 1975	20	50
Penguin, 1975	20	50
Robin, 1975	20	50
Shazam, 1975	20	50
Spider-Man, 1975	20	50
Superman, 1975	20	45
Wonder Woman, 1975	20	40

Accessories

NAME	MNP	MIP
Collapsing Tower, 1975, w/ Invisible Plane & Wonder Woman	50	100
Exploding Bridge with Batmobile, 1975	75	150
Fortress of Solitude with Superman, 1975	100	200
The Mangler, 1975	55	110

Die-Cast Series

6" Figures

NAME	MNP	MIP
Batman, 1979	35	90
Hulk, 1979	25	65
Spider-Man, 1979	30	75
Superman, 1979	30	70

Large Figures

12 1/2" Figures

NAME	MNP	MIP
Amazing Spider-Man, 1978, boxed	30	60
Batman, 1978, boxed	50	100
Captain America, 1978, boxed	75	150
Hulk, 1978, boxed	25	50

Superman

NAME	MNP	MIP
General Zod, 1978	50	100
Jor-El, 1978	50	100
Lex Luthor, 1978	50	100
Superman Playset, 1978	75	150
Superman, 1978	50	125

Wonder Woman

NAME	MNP	MIP
Major Steve Trevor, 1978	26	65
Queen Hippolyte, 1978	40	100
Queen Nubia, 1978	40	100
Wonder Woman with Diana Prince outfit, 1978	55	80
Wonder Woman Playset, 1978	50	100

Official World's Greatest Super Heroes

8" Figures

NAME	MNP	MIP
Aquaman, 1972, boxed	75	150
Aquaman, 1972, carded	75	150
Batgirl, 1973, boxed	125	300
Batgirl, 1973, carded	125	200
Batman, fist fighting, 1975, boxed	150	350
Batman, painted mask, 1972, carded	50	100
Batman, painted mask, 1972, boxed	50	150
Batman, removable mask, 1972, Kresge card only	200	450
Batman, removable mask, 1972, boxed	200	350
Bruce Wayne, 1974, boxed, Montgomery Ward exclusive	400	500
Captain America, 1972, boxed	60	200
Captain America, 1972, carded	60	150
Catwoman, 1973, boxed	100	200
Catwoman, 1973, carded	100	200
Clark Kent, 1974, boxed, Montgomery Ward exclusive	400	500
Conan, 1975, boxed	120	300
Conan, 1975, carded	120	300
Dick Grayson, 1974, boxed, Montgomery Ward exclusive	400	500
Falcon, 1974, boxed	60	150
Falcon, 1974, carded	600	200
Green Arrow, 1973, boxed	100	250
Green Arrow, 1973, carded	100	400
Green Goblin, 1974, boxed	90	225
Green Goblin, 1974, carded	90	300
Human Torch, Fantastic Four, 1975, boxed	25	90
Human Torch, Fantastic Four, 1975, card	25	40
Incredible Hulk, 1974, boxed	20	100
Incredible Hulk, 1974, carded	20	45
Invisible Girl, Fantastic Four, 1975, boxed	30	150
Invisible Girl, Fantastic Four, 1975, card	30	60
Iron Man, 1974, boxed	75	125
Iron Man, 1974, carded	75	250
Isis, 1076, boxed	75	250
Isis, 1976, carded	75	125
Joker, 1973, boxed	60	150
Joker, 1973, carded	60	150
Joker, fist fighting, 1975, boxed	150	400
Lizard, 1974, boxed	75	200
Lizard, 1974, carded	75	250
Mr. Fantastic, Fantastic Four, 1975, boxed	30	140
Mr. Fantastic, Fantastic Four, 1975, card	30	60

Mego Super Heroes

NAME	MNP	MIP
Mr. Mxyzptlk, open mouth, 1973, boxed	50	75
Mr. Mxyzptlk, open mouth, 1973, carded	50	150
Mr. Mxyzptlk, smirk, 1973, boxed	60	150
Penguin, 1973, carded	60	125
Penguin, 1973, boxed	60	125
Peter Parker, 1974, boxed, Montgomery Ward exclusive	400	500
Riddler, 1973, boxed	100	250
Riddler, 1973, carded	100	400
Riddler, fist fighting, 1975, boxed	125	400
Robin, fist fighting, 1975, boxed	125	350
Robin, painted mask, 1972, boxed	60	150
Robin, painted mask, 1972, carded	60	90
Robin, removable mask, 1972, boxed	250	400
Shazam, 1972, boxed	75	200
Shazam, 1972, carded	75	150
Spider-Man, 1972, boxed	15	90
Spider-Man, 1972, carded	15	40
Supergirl, 1973, boxed	150	400
Supergirl, 1973, carded	150	400
Superman, 1972, boxed	50	125
Superman, 1972, carded	50	100
Tarzan, 1972, boxed	50	150
Tarzan, 1976, Kresge card only	60	225
Thing, Fantastic Four, 1975, boxed	40	150
Thing, Fantastic Four, 1975, carded	40	60
Thor, 1975, boxed	150	300
Thor, 1975, carded	150	300
Wonder Woman, 1973, boxed	100	250
Wonder Woman, 1973, Kresge card only	100	350

Accessories

NAME	MNP	MIP
Super Hero Carry Case, 1973	40	65
Supervator, 1974	60	120

Playsets

NAME	MNP	MIP
Aquaman vs. the Great White Shark, 1978	200	500
Batcave Playset, 1974, vinyl	125	250
Batman's Wayne Foundation Penthouse, 1977, fiberboard	600	1200
Hall of Justice, 1976, vinyl	125	250

Vehicles

NAME	MNP	MIP
Batcopter, 1974, boxed	75	150
Batcopter, 1974, carded	55	110
Batcycle, black, 1975, carded	60	150
Batcycle, black, 1975, boxed	75	185
Batcycle, blue, 1974, carded	75	135
Batcycle, blue, 1974, boxed	75	170
Batmobile and Batman	40	100
Batmobile, 1974, boxed	50	100
Batmobile, 1974, carded	50	120
Captain Americar, 1976	100	200
Green Arrowcar, 1976	175	350
Jokermobile, 1976	150	300
Mobile Bat Lab, 1975	125	250
Spidercar, 1976	50	100

Pocket Super Heroes

3 3/4" Figures

NAME	MNP	MIP
Aquaman, 1976, white card	50	100
Batman, 1976, red card	20	40
Batman, 1976, white card	20	40
Captain America, 1976, white card	50	100
Captain Marvel, 1979, red card	20	40
General Zod, 1979, red card	5	10
Green Goblin, 1976, white card	50	100
Hulk, 1976, white card	15	40
Hulk, 1979, red card	15	30
Joker, 1979, red card	20	40
Jor-El (Superman), 1979, red card	7	15
Lex Luthor (Superman), 1979, red card	7	15
Penguin, 1979, red card	20	40
Robin, 1979, red card	20	40
Robin, 1976, white card	20	40
Spider-Man, 1976, white card	15	40
Spider-Man, 1979, red card	15	30
Superman, 1979, red card	15	30
Superman, 1976, white card	15	30
Wonder Woman, 1979, white card	20	40

Accessories

NAME	MNP	MIP
Batcave, 1981	120	300

Vehicles

NAME	MNP	MIP
Batmachine, 1979	40	100
Batmobile, 1979, with Batman and Robin	80	200
Invisible Jet, 1979	50	125
Spider-Car, 1979, with Spider-Man	30	75
Spider-Machine, 1979	40	100

Super Hero Bendables

5" Figures

NAME	MNP	MIP
Aquaman, 1972	48	120
Batgirl, 1972	48	120
Batman, 1972	36	90
Captain America, 1972	36	90
Catwoman, 1972	70	175
Joker, 1972	60	150
Mr. Mxyzptlk, 1972	50	125
Penguin, 1972	60	150
Riddler, 1972	60	150
Robin, 1972	30	75
Shazam, 1972	50	125
Supergirl, 1972	70	175
Superman, 1972	30	75
Tarzan, 1972	24	60
Wonder Woman, 1972	40	100

Mego Super Heroes

NAME	MNP	MIP

Teen Titans

6 1/2" Figures

NAME	MNP	MIP
Aqualad, 1976, carded	175	350
Kid Flash, 1976, carded	175	300
Speedy, 1976, carded	300	500
Wondergirl, 1976, carded	200	400

Miscellaneous Mego Figures

Action Jackson

8" Figures

NAME	MNP	MIP
Action Jackson, blonde hair, 1974	15	30
Action Jackson, black hair, 1974	15	30
Action Jackson, brown hair, 1974	15	30
Action Jackson, blonde bearded, 1974	15	30
Action Jackson, black bearded, 1974	15	30
Action Jackson, brown bearded, 1974	15	30
Action Jackson, black version, 1974	25	60

Accessories

NAME	MNP	MIP
Parachute Plunge, 1974	5	15
Strap-On Helicopter, 1974	5	15
Water Scooter, 1974	5	15

Outfits

NAME	MNP	MIP
Air Force Pilot, 1974	6	12
Army Outfit, 1974	6	12
Aussie Marine, 1974	6	12
Baseball, 1974	6	12
Fisherman, 1974	6	12
Football, 1974	6	12
Frog Man, 1974	6	12
Hockey, 1974	6	12
Jungle Safari, 1974	6	12
Karate, 1974	6	12
Navy Sailor, 1974	6	12
Rescue Squad, 1974	6	12
Scramble Cyclist, 1974	6	12
Secret Agent, 1974	6	12
Ski Patrol, 1974	6	12
Snowmobile Outfit, 1974	6	12
Surf and Scuba Outfit, 1974	6	12
Western Cowboy, 1974	6	12

Playsets

NAME	MNP	MIP
Jungle House, 1974	40	85
Lost Continent Playset, 1974	40	85

Vehicles

NAME	MNP	MIP
Adventure Set, 1974	40	85
Campmobile, 1974	40	85

Misc. Mego Figures

NAME	MNP	MIP
Dune Buggy, 1974	30	60
Formula Racer, 1974	30	60
Mustang, 1974	30	60
Rescue Helicopter, 1974	40	85
Safari Jeep, 1974	40	85
Scramble Cycle, 1974	20	40
Snow Mobile, 1974	10	20

American West Series

8" Figures

NAME	MNP	MIP
Buffalo Bill Cody, 1973, boxed	40	75
Buffalo Bill Cody, 1973, carded	40	100
Cochise, 1973, boxed	40	75
Cochise, 1973, carded	40	100
Davy Crockett, 1973, boxed	70	110
Davy Crockett, 1973, carded	70	140
Shadow (Horse), 1973, carded	70	140
Sitting Bull, 1973, boxed	45	90
Sitting Bull, 1973, carded	45	125
Wild Bill Hickok, 1973, boxed	40	75
Wild Bill Hickok, 1973, carded	40	125
Wyatt Earp, 1973, boxed	40	75
Wyatt Earp, 1973, carded	40	125

Playsets

NAME	MNP	MIP
Dodge City Playset, 1973, vinyl	100	200

Black Hole

12" Figures

NAME	MNP	MIP
Captain Holland, 1979	25	50
Dr. Alan Durant, 1979	25	50
Dr. Hans Reinhardt, 1979	25	50
Harry Booth, 1979	30	60
Kate McCrae, 1979	35	80
Pizer, 1979	25	50

3 3/4" Figures

NAME	MNP	MIP
Captain Holland, 1979	10	20
Dr. Alan Durant, 1979	10	20
Dr. Hans Reinhardt, 1979	10	25
Harry Booth, 1979	10	25
Humanoid, 1980	70	135
Kate McCrae, 1979	10	25
Maximillian, 1979	17	40
Old B.O.B., 1980	60	120
Pizer, 1979	10	20
S.T.A.R., 1980	60	120
Sentry Robot, 1980	25	60
V.I.N.cent., 1979	30	60

Buck Rogers

12" Figures

NAME	MNP	MIP
Buck Rogers, 1979	25	50
Doctor Huer, 1979	25	50
Draco, 1979	25	50
Droconian Guard, 1979	25	50
Killer Kane, 1979	25	50
Tiger Man, 1979	25	50
Walking Twiki, 1979	25	50

Miscellaneous Mego Figures

NAME	MNP	MIP
3 3/4" Figures		
Ardella, 1979	5	15
Buck Rogers, 1979	15	30
Doctor Huer, 1979	5	10
Draco, 1979	5	10
Draconian Guard, 1979	10	20
Killer Kane, 1979	5	10
Tiger Man, 1979	5	15
Twiki, 1979	10	20
Wilma Deering, 1979	12	25
3 3/4" Playsets		
Star Fighter Command Center, 1979	17	50
3 3/4" Vehicles		
Draconian Marauder, 1979	25	50
Land Rover, 1979	20	40
Laserscope Fighter, 1979	20	40
Star Fighter, 1979	25	50
Starseeker, 1979	30	60

C.H.I.P.S. Figures

NAME	MNP	MIP
3 3/4" Figures		
Jimmy Squeaks, 1979, carded	5	15
Jon, 1979, carded	5	15
Launcher with Motorcycle, 1979, carded	25	50
Motorcycle, 1979, carded	5	15
Ponch, 1979, carded	5	15
Sarge, 1979, carded	10	20
Wheels Willie, 1979, carded	5	15
8" Figures		
Jon, 1979, carded	20	40
Motorcycle, 1979, carded	30	60
Ponch, 1979, carded	15	30
Sarge, 1979, carded	25	50

Commander Power

NAME	MNP	MIP
Figure with Vehicle		
Commander Power with Lightning Cycle, 1975, packaged	20	40

Dukes of Hazzard

NAME	MNP	MIP
3 3/4" Figures		
Bo Duke, 1981, carded	8	15
Boss Hogg, 1981, carded	8	15
Cletus, 1981, carded	15	30
Cooter, 1981, carded	15	30
Coy Duke, 1981, carded	15	30
Daisy Duke, 1981, carded	12	25
Luke Duke, 1981, carded	8	15
Rosco Coltrane, 1981, carded	15	30
Uncle Jesse, 1981, carded	15	30
Vance Duke, 1981, carded	15	30
3 3/4" Figures Vehicles		
Dasiy Jeep with Daisy, 1981, boxed	25	50
General Lee Car with Bo and Luke, 1981, boxed	25	50
8" Figures		
Bo Duke, 1981, carded	15	30
Boss Hogg, 1981, carded	15	30
Coy Duke (card says Bo), 1982, carded	25	50
Daisy Duke, 1981, carded	25	50
Luke Duke, 1981, carded	15	30
Vance Duke (card says Luke), 1982, carded	25	50

Flash Gordon

NAME	MNP	MIP
9" Figures		
Dale Arden, 1976	35	70
Dr. Zarkow, 1976	55	110
Flash, 1976	55	110
Ming, 1976	30	60
Playsets		
Flash Gordon Playset, 1976	55	110

Happy Days

NAME	MNP	MIP
Fonzie, 1978, boxed	25	50
Fonzie, 1978, carded	25	50
Potsy, 1978, carded	25	50
Ralph, 1978, carded	25	50
Richie, 1978, carded	25	50
Playsets		
Fonzie's Garage Playsets, 1978	60	125
Vehicles		
Fonzie's Jalopy, 1978	40	80
Fonzie's Motorcycle, 1978	40	80

James Bond: Moonraker

NAME	MNP	MIP
12" Figures		
Drax, 1979	60	120
Holly, 1979	60	120
James Bond, 1979	25	60
James Bond, deluxe version, 1979	150	300
Jaws, 1979	215	415

Laverne and Shirley

NAME	MNP	MIP
12" Figures		
Laverne and Shirley, 1978, boxed	50	100
Lenny and Squiggy, 1978, boxed	75	150

Miscellaneous Mego Figures

NAME	MNP	MIP
Love Boat		
4" Figures		
Captain Stubing, 1981, carded	5	15
Doc, 1981, carded	5	15
Gopher, 1981, carded	5	15
Isaac, 1981, carded	5	15
Julie, 1981, carded	5	15
Vicki, 1981, carded	5	15
Mad Monster Series		
8" Figures		
Mad Monster Castle, 1974, vinyl	300	600
The Dreadful Dracula, 1974	80	160
The Horrible Mummy, 1974	45	90
The Human Wolfman, 1974	75	150
The Monster Frankenstein, 1974	45	90
Micronauts		
Alien Invaders Accessories		
Karrio, 1979	10	20
Alien Invaders Carded		
Antron, 1979	15	30
Centaurus, 1980	35	70
Kronos, 1980	35	70
Lobros, 1980	35	70
Membros, 1979	15	30
Repto, 1979	13	25
Alien Invaders Playsets		
Deluxe Rocket Tubes,	20	40
Rocket Tubes, 1978	23	50
Alien Invaders Vehicles		
Alphatron	5	10
Aquatron, 1977	10	20
Betatron	5	10
Gammatron	5	10
Hornetroid, 1979	20	40
Hydra, 1976	7	15
Mobile Exploration Lab, 1976	17	35
Solarion, 1978	15	30
Star Searcher, 1978	15	40
Taurion, 1978	11	22
Terraphant, 1979	20	40
Boxed Figures		
Andromeda, 1977	10	25
Baron Karza, 1977	15	30
Biotron, 1976	10	25
Force Commander, 1977	10	25
Giant Acroyear, 1977	10	25
Megas, 1981	10	25
Microtron, 1976	5	20
Nemesis Robot, 1978	7	15
Oberon, 1977	10	25
Phobos Robot, 1978	12	25

NAME	MNP	MIP
Carded Figures		
Acroyear II, 1977; red, blue, orange	7	15
Acroyear, 1976; red, blue, orange	10	20
Galactic Defender, 1978; white, yellow,	7	15
Galactic Warriors, 1976; red, blue, orange	4	10
Pharoid, with Time Chamber, 1977; blue, orange,	10	20
Space Glider, 1976; blue, green, orange	5	10
Time Traveler, clear plastic, 1976; yellow, orange	3	10
Time Traveler, solid plastic, 1976; yellow, orange	5	15
Micropolis Playsets		
Galactic Command Center, 1978	20	40
Interplanetary Headquarters, 1978	20	40
Mega City, 1978	20	30
Microrail City, 1978	20	40
Playsets		
Astro Station, 1976	10	20
Stratstation, 1976	15	30
Vehicle		
Battle Cruiser, 1977	30	60
Vehicles		
Crater Cruncher with figure, 1976	5	15
Galactic Cruiser, 1976	7	17
Hydro Copter, 1976	10	25
Neon Orbiter, 1977	6	20
Photon Sled with figure, 1976	5	15
Rhodium Orbiter, 1977	6	20
Thorium Orbiter, 1977	6	20
Ultronic Scooter with figure, 1976	5	15
Warp Racer with figure, 1976	5	15
One Million BC		
Dimetrodon, 1976, boxed	75	150
Grok, 1976, carded	25	50
Hairy Rino, 1976, boxed	75	150
Mada, 1976, carded	25	50
Orm, 1976, carded	25	50
Trag, 1976, carded	25	50
Tribal Lair Gift Set, 1976, with 5 figures	0	180
Tribal Lair, 1976	60	120
Tyrannosaur, 1976, boxed	75	150
Zon, 1976, carded	25	50
Planet of the Apes		
8" Figures		
Astronaut Burke, 1975, carded	50	100
Astronaut Burke, 1975, boxed	50	130
Astronaut Verdon, 1975, carded	50	90

Miscellaneous Mego Figures

NAME	MNP	MIP
Astronaut Verdon, 1975, boxed	50	140
Astronaut, 1975, carded	50	100
Astronaut, 1973, boxed	50	150
Cornelius, 1975, carded	40	75
Cornelius, 1973, boxed	40	140
Dr. Zaius, 1975, carded	40	60
Dr. Zaius, 1973, boxed	40	150
Galen, 1975, carded	40	90
Galen, 1975, boxed	40	140
General Urko, 1975, carded	50	100
General Urko, 1975, boxed	50	130
General Ursus, 1975, carded	50	100
General Ursus, 1975, boxed	50	120
Soldier Ape, 1975, carded	30	60
Soldier Ape, 1973, boxed	30	140
Zira, 1973, boxed	30	150
Zira, 1975, carded	30	60

Accessories

NAME	MNP	MIP
Action Stallion, brown motorized, 1975, boxed	50	100
Battering Ram, 1975, boxed	20	40
Dr. Zaius' Throne, 1975, boxed	20	40
Jail, 1975, boxed	20	40

Playsets

NAME	MNP	MIP
Forbidden Zone Trap, 1975	65	125
Fortress, 1975	60	120
Treehouse, 1975	50	100
Village, 1975	60	130

Vehicles

NAME	MNP	MIP
Catapult and Wagon, 1975, boxed	25	50

Robin Hood and His Merry Men

8" Figures

NAME	MNP	MIP
Friar Tuck, 1974	25	50
Little John, 1974	45	80
Robin Hood, 1974	75	150
Will Scarlet, 1974	75	150

Star Trek

12" Figures

NAME	MNP	MIP
Arcturian, 1979, boxed	30	60
Captain Kirk, 1979, boxed	25	55
Decker, 1979, boxed	45	115
Ilia, 1979, boxed	25	50
Klingon, 1979, boxed	40	85
Mr. Spock, 1979, boxed	30	60

3 3/4" Alien Figures

NAME	MNP	MIP
Acturian, 1980, carded	75	150
Betelgeusian, 1980, carded	75	150
Klingon, 1980, carded	75	150
Megarite, 1980, carded	75	150
Rigellian, 1980, carded	75	150
Zatanite, 1980, carded	75	150

3 3/4" Figures

NAME	MNP	MIP
Captain Kirk, 1979, carded	10	25
Decker, 1979, carded	10	25
Dr. McCoy, 1979, carded	10	25
Ilia, 1979, carded	8	15
Mr. Spock, 1979, carded	10	25
Scotty, 1979, carded	10	25

8" Alien Figures

NAME	MNP	MIP
Andorian, 1976, carded	200	400
Cheron, 1975, carded	75	150
Gorn, 1975, carded	80	180
Mugato, 1976, carded	150	300
Neptunian, 1975, carded	100	225
Romulan, 1976, carded	300	600
Talos, 1976, carded	165	300
The Keeper, 1975, carded	75	175

8" Figures

NAME	MNP	MIP
Captain Kirk, 1974, carded	25	50
Dr. McCoy, 1974, carded	35	75
Gift set: Enterprise bridge with figures, 1976	0	250
Klingon, 1974, carded	25	50
Lt. Uhura, 1974, carded	50	100
Mr. Spock, 1974, carded	25	50
Scotty, 1974, carded	35	80

Playsets

NAME	MNP	MIP
Command Bridge (for 3 3/4" figures), 1980	45	105
Enterprise Bridge (for 8" figures), 1976	60	150
Mission to Gamma VI (for 8" figures), 1976	200	500

Starsky and Hutch

8" Figures

NAME	MNP	MIP
Captain Dobey, 1976	25	50
Car, 1976	65	125
Chopper, 1976	25	40
Huggy Bear, 1976	25	40
Hutch, 1976	15	40
Starsky, 1976	15	40

Waltons

8" Figures

NAME	MNP	MIP
Grandma and Grandpa, 1975	25	50
John Boy and Ellen, 1975	25	50
Mom and Pop, 1975	25	50

Accessories

NAME	MNP	MIP
Barn, 1975	50	100
Country Store, 1975	50	100
Truck, 1975	40	80

Playsets

NAME	MNP	MIP
Farm House, 1975	50	100
Farm House with the 6 figures, 1975	0	200

Miscellaneous Mego Figures

Wizard of Oz

4" Munchkin Figures

NAME	MNP	MIP
Dancer, 1974, boxed	75	150
Flower Girl, 1974, boxed	75	150
General, 1974, boxed	75	150
Lolly Pop Kid, 1974, boxed	75	150
Mayor, 1974, boxed	75	150

8" Figures

NAME	MNP	MIP
Cowardly Lion, 1974, boxed	20	40
Dorothy with Toto, 1974, boxed	20	40
Glinda the Good Witch, 1974, boxed	20	40
Scarecrow, 1974, boxed	25	50
Tin Woodsman, 1974, boxed	20	40
Wicked Witch, 1974, boxed	50	100
Witch's Monkey, 1974, boxed	75	150
Wizard of Oz, 1974, loose	35	0

Playsets

NAME	MNP	MIP
Emerald City with eight 8" figures, 1974	125	350
Emerald City with Wizard of Oz, 1974	43	100
Munchkin Land, 1974	150	300
Witch's Castle, 1974, Sears Exclusive	250	400

World's Greatest Super Knights

8" Figures

NAME	MNP	MIP
Castle Playset, 1975	80	160
Ivanhoe, 1975, boxed	60	120
Jousting Horse, 1975, battery operated	40	70
King Arthur, 1975, boxed	60	120
Sir Galahad, 1975, boxed	75	150
Sir Lancelot, 1975, boxed	75	150
The Black Knight, 1975, boxed	80	160

World's Greatest Super Pirates

8" Figures

NAME	MNP	MIP
Black Beard, 1974, boxed	70	150
Captain Patch, 1974, boxed	70	150
Jean LaFitte, 1974, boxed	80	160
Long John Silver, 1974, boxed	80	160

Teenage Mutant Ninja Turtles

*4-1/2" figures & accessories (unless noted), Playmates

NAME	MNP	MIP
Ace Duck Action Figure	3	7
April O'Neil, Blue Stripe	12	30
April O'Neil, No Stripe	60	150
April O'Neil, Red Stripe	22	55
Baxter Stockman Action Figure	10	25
Bebop Action Figure	3	8
Bebop Giant Turtle Figure, 13"	14	35
Breakfightin' Raphael (Wacky Action)	3	7
Casey Jones Action Figure	2	6
Cheapskate Skateboard	4	11
Chrome Dome	3	7
Creepy Crawlin' Splinter Wacky Action Figure	3	8
Dirt Bag	3	7
Don The Undercover Turtle	3	7
Donatello Action Figure	8	20
Donatello Giant Turtle Figure, 13"	8	20
Flushomatic	4	10
Foot Cruiser	14	35
Foot Ski	4	10
Foot Soldier Action Figure	8	20
Fugitoid	3	7
General Traag Action Figure	3	8
Genghis Frog Action Figure	3	8
Grand Slam Raph	3	7
Ground Chuck	3	7
Headspinnin' Bebop Wacky Action Figure	2	6
Hose'em Down Don	3	7
Knucklehead	4	11
Krang Action Figure	5	13
Leatherhead Action Figure	10	25
Leo the Sewer Samurai	3	7
Leonardo Action Figure	8	20
Leonardo Giant Turtle Figure, 13"	8	20
Lieutenant Leo	3	7
Machine Gunnin' Rocksteady Wacky Action Figure	3	8
Make My Day Leo	3	7
Mega Mutant Killer Bee	3	8
Mega Mutant Needlenose	8	20
Metalhead Action Figure	3	7
Michelangelo Action Figure	8	20
Michelangelo Giant Turtle Figure, 13"	8	20
Midshipman Mike	3	7
Mike the Sewer Surfer	3	7
Mike's Pizza Chopper Backpack	4	10
Mondo Gecko Action Figure	3	7
Movie Don	3	7
Movie Leo	3	7
Movie Mike	3	7
Movie Raph	3	7
Muckman and Joe Eyeball Action Figure	3	7
Mutagen Man	3	7
Mutant Sewer Cycle with Sidecar	4	10
Napoleon Bonafrog	3	7
New April with Press Pass	10	25
New April without Press Pass	40	100
Ninja Newscycle	5	12

Teenage Mutant Ninja Turtles

NAME	MNP	MIP
Oozey	4	10
Panda Khan	3	7
Pizza Face	4	9
Pizza Powered Sewer Dragster	5	12
Pizza Thrower	14	35
Pro Pilot Don	3	7
Psycho Cycle	10	25
Rahzer	3	7
Raph the Green Teen Beret	3	7
Raph The Space Cadet	3	7
Raph's Sewer Dragster	6	16
Raph's Sewer Speedboat	5	12
Raphael Action Figure	8	20
Raphael Giant Turtle Figure, 13"	8	20
Rat King Action Figure	3	7
Ray Fillet Action Figure, purple torso	14	35
Ray Fillet Action Figure, yellow torso	6	15
Ray Fillet Action Figure, red torso	4	10
Retrocatapult	4	10
Retromutagen Ooze	2	4
Rock & Roll Michaelangelo (Wacky Action)	3	7
Rocksteady Action Figure	8	20
Rocksteady Giant Turtle Figure, 13"	14	35
Scumbag Action Figure	3	7
Sewer Seltzer Cannon	4	10
Sewer Swimmin' Don (Wacky Action)	3	7
Shredder Action Figure	8	20
Slam Dunkin' Don	3	7
Slapshot Leo	3	7
Slash Action Figure	6	15
Slice 'n Dice Shredder Wacky Action Figure	3	8
Sludgemobile	7	18
Splinter Action Figure	8	20
Storage Shell Don	3	7
Storage Shell Leo	3	7
Storage Shell Michaelangelo	3	7
Storage Shell Raphael	3	7
Super Shredder	4	9

Toy Vehicles

Modern man has always had a love affair with his machines that move. Partial evidence of this is the amazing number of toy vehicles that have been produced in the 20th century. In fact, it could be reasonably argued that toy vehicles are collected more than any other type of toy.

With the dawning of the modern industrial age, the mass production of real-life automobiles and their toy counterparts seemed to go hand-in-hand. As cars were rolling off assembly lines, their miniature replicas were not far behind.

It wasn't just cars and trucks that were among the favorite subjects of toy makers. Any sort of vehicle that moved people or things from one place to another was a natural for miniaturization. Boats, airplanes and wagons all fall into this category.

And the types and manufacturers of toy vehicles were as varied as the real things. Toy makers built them out of everything from cast iron and tin to paper and plastic.

The earliest toy automobiles came along soon after their big daddy originals in the late 19th century and were produced in cast iron. But it wasn't until after World War I that toy automobile production really began to hit its stride.

Firms such as Arcade and Hubley are among the most well-known and sought-after manufacturers of early cast iron vehicles.

Cars, trucks and buses produced by Arcade Manufacturing of Freeport, Ill., are highly valued among toy vehicle collectors. Arcade actually began producing toys in the late 1800s, but it wasn't until around 1920 when the company reportedly issued its first toy vehicle, a replica of a Chicago Yellow Cab. After that came more realistic models of actual cars, trucks and buses. "They Look Real" was the company's slogan.

Hubley is another name associated with quality toy vehicles. This Pennsylvania company began manufacturing cast iron toys in the 1890s, mostly horse-drawn wagons, trains and guns. By the 1930s, Hubley was producing the cast iron cars that became their most well-known products. Many were patterned from actual automobiles of the day, while others were apparently looser interpretations of reality. Some of the Hubley vehicles also included company names, and some of the most interesting pieces had separate nickel-plated grilles.

As the toy manufacturing world changed, the toy makers either kept pace or became dinosaurs. Hubley began phasing out cast metal in the 1940s, and after a toy-making hiatus during World War II, came back with authentic die cast white metal replicas of real cars. Hubley began producing plastic products, as well, in the 1950s, and many collectors find the firm's plastic vehicles to be a cut above the typical offerings of the period.

One of the best makers of smaller scale cast iron vehicles was the A.C. Williams Company. The Ohio company began producing toys in the late

1800s, but its toy vehicles sought by today's collectors were generally produced in the 1920s-30s. The smaller cars and airplanes produced by A.C. Williams were intended for the five-and-dime market of the time. Williams' toys are difficult for the novice collector to identify, as there are no company markings on the toys.

While heavy cast iron toys had been the rule at the turn of the century, lithographed tinplate toys began stealing a large part of the market in the 1920s. One of the world's leading producers of these toys was Louis Marx. Over the years, Marx produced an extensive line of toy cars, trucks, airplanes and farm equipment, not only in tin, but also in steel and later in plastic.

Marx capitalized on the popularity of certain celebrities and comic strip characters, incorporating them into its toy vehicles. With lithography, it was easy to put a new character into a car and thus have a brand new toy ready for market. Characters such as Mickey Mouse, Donald Duck, Dick Tracy, Blondie and Dagwood, Charlie McCarthy, Amos 'n Andy and Milton Berle show up in Marx cars.

One of the most famous manufacturers of toy cars and (especially) trucks was Buddy L. These large-scale pressed steel toys were not the kind of toys bought for display or quiet play on the living room floor. These were those BIG trucks approaching two feet in length that all boys loved to get down on their knees in the dirt with.

Buddy L toys grew out of the Moline Pressed Steel Company of Moline, Illinois. The name, Buddy L, was for the son of the company's owner, reportedly for whom the first toys were produced. The Buddy L toys most sought by collectors were produced in the 1920s and '30s and were of very heavy-duty construction. Starting in the early 1930s, the company began to use lighter weight materials.

The Buddy L name has remained, but its post-World War II toys are not considered at all in the same league as its early issues, which command high collector prices today.

Buddy L is best remembered for its heavy-duty trucks, but another name that was synonymous with trucks was Smith-Miller. Founded by Bob Smith and Matt Miller, the company specialized in "Famous Trucks In Miniature." Smith-Miller was also known as Miller-Ironson Corp. later in its life, but it is more commonly referred to as Smitty Toys. It produced large cast metal and aluminum trucks.

Because of their outstanding quality, some of the Mack trucks made by Smith-Miller are very highly regarded among toy collectors. The Smith-Miller name continues today, with new limited edition trucks produced for collectors.

Wyandotte is another company associated with pressed steel vehicles. Known as both Wyandotte Toys or All Metal Products, this Michigan company produced several large steel vehicles with baked enamel finishes in the 1930s. Not all Wyandotte toys are marked, which tends to cause some confusion among collectors, but the vehicles can often be identified by their art

Top: Chrysler Airflow by Hubley; Right: Milton Berle Crazy Car by Marx.

deco-type styling and wooden wheels. Marx is reported to have bought some of the Wyandotte products before the company went out of business in the 1950s.

And yet another company that produced large steel toys was Structo. The company originally produced metal construction sets, but developed a line of vehicles in the 1920s.

While major toy companies were producing vehicles in cast iron, tin and steel, others began making toys in rubber. Probably the best-known manufacturer of rubber toys is the Auburn Rubber Company of Auburn, Indiana. From the mid-1930s into the 1950s, Auburn produced rubber cars, trucks, tractors, motorcycles, airplanes, trains and boats. The company is known for producing replicas of actual vehicles as well as race cars of its own design. And there probably isn't anyone who has spent much time looking at toys who hasn't seen an Auburn rubber tractor. You could find replicas of most of the major tractor models and even get the accompanying implements.

In the 1950s, Auburn began to abandon rubber as its material of choice, and soon it was producing vehicles made only of vinyl. It wasn't many years later before Auburn was out of business.

Another popularly collected type of toy vehicle is the smaller die cast models, generally in the range of three to six inches in length. Probably the leading producer of this type of vehicle was Tootsietoys.

The company dates back to before the turn of the century to Samuel Dowst of Chicago. The trade name for the toy products, which would eventually become the firm's mainstay, came from Dowst's daughter, Tootsie. Although a few toy cars were produced by the firm before 1920, it was during the Roaring Twenties when the name Tootsietoys began to regularly appear. By the 1930s, the company was producing a wide line of toys, many of which are highly prized by collectors today. Tootsietoys' Federal vans from the 1920s are among the most sought-after toys, particularly those with company logos.

The company also produced several boxed toy sets, which were assortments of various vehicles, including cars, boats and airplanes. These sets in their original boxes are highly valued.

Being mass produced and economically priced, Tootsietoys were widely available in the five-and-dime arena. The success of these products no doubt led to several competitors.

One of those competitors was Barclay, which also manufactured die cast vehicles, although most were generally considered of lower quality than Toosietoys. The first Barclay vehicles had metal tires, but in the mid-1930s, white rubber tires on wooden axles were introduced. Metal axles soon replaced the wood, and black tires replaced white after World War II.

Another competitor emerged from Europe. Dinky Toys were manufactured from 1933 through the 1970s in England and France. Their vehicles were high quality die cast, at least until the mid-1960s, generally in 1/43 scale. Identifying them is easy, as the name Dinky appears on the bottom.

Yet another competitor in this classification of small die cast vehicles would be Corgi, which came on the scene in the late 1950s. Corgi was the trade name for the die cast toys which were produced by England's Mettoy Company.

One of the best known series of toy cars today is Matchbox. These die cast beauties are roughly three inches in length. However, Lesney, the company that produced them, did produce several larger cars before it began the Matchbox line. Some of these early Lesney vehicles are valued at up to $2,000 each.

The Lesney company originated in England after World War II. The name came from the combination of parts of the two founders' first names, LESlie and RodNEY Smith. After tinkering with several products, including a few larger vehicles, the company hit paydirt with small cars that would eventually be dubbed Matchbox after a packaging concept. Soon the company adopted a plan of issuing 75 models each year, called the 1-75 Series. Lesney also issued a larger series of four- to six-inch cars called Models of Yesteryear.

Matchbox vehicles were immensely popular, so much so that in the United States, Mattel decided to introduce a similar line called Hot Wheels. The California-based company gave its cars a California-type appeal, focusing on colorful hot rods that appealed to youngsters.

In the head-to-head battle that followed, Lesney at one time was producing 5.5 million toys a week. Eventually, Lesney lost the battle and went into receivership. Matchbox was restructured and sold twice, eventually landing with the U.S. toy maker Tyco.

There are many other toy cars collected today than are listed in this book. For example, a wide variety of tin toy cars came out of Japan after World War II. While many Japanese toy companies emerged during that period, only Bandai is listed here.

VEHICLES

Arcade

NAME	DESCRIPTION	GOOD	EX	MINT
	Airplanes			
Airplane	Cast iron, 6" long	90	135	180
Boeing United Airplane	White rubber wheels, two propellors, cast iron, 5" wingspan, 1936	95	145	200
	Boats and Ships			
Battleship New York	Cast iron, 20" long, 1912	800	1200	1600
Showboat	Cast iron, 10 3/4" long, 1934	475	715	950
	Buses			
ACF Coach	Dual rear wheels, front door opens and closes, cast iron, 11 1/2" long, 1925	1200	1600	2200
Bus	Cast iron, 8" long	400	600	800
Century of Progress Bus	Cast iron, 7 5/8" long, 1933	125	165	265
Century of Progress Bus	Cast iron, 10 1/2" long, 1933	145	215	300
Century of Progress Bus	Cast iron, 14 1/2" long, 1933	175	250	500
Century of Progress Bus	Cast iron, 12" long, 1933	165	235	350
Century of Progress Bus	Cast iron, 6" long, 1933	40	60	90
Double Deck Bus	Cast iron, 8" long, 1938	350	525	700
Double Deck Bus	Green, white rubber wheels with red centers, 'Chicago Motor Coach' on side, cast iron, 8 1/4" long, 1936	425	650	850
Double Deck Bus	Rubber wheels, cast iron, 8" long, 1936	100	150	200
Double Deck Yellow Coach Bus	Nickel-plated driver, rubber balloon tires, cast iron, 13 1/2" long, 1926	800	1200	1500
Fageol Bus	Cast iron, 13" long	335	500	675
Fageol Safety Bus	Bright enamel colors, cast iron, 12" long, 1925	350	525	700
Fageol Safety Bus	Nickel-plated wheels, with or without driver, cast iron, 7 3/4" long, 1926	180	275	350
Great Lakes Expo Bus	Large, white rubber wheels with blue centers, cast iron, 11 1/4" long, 1936	300	575	1000
Great Lakes Expo Bus	Small, white rubber wheels, cast iron, 7 1/4" long, 1936	225	385	695
Greyhound Cross Country Bus	"Greyhound Lines GMC" on top, white rubber wheels, cast iron, 7 3/4" long, 1936	125	215	300
Greyhound Trailer Bus	White with blue cab, 'GMC Greyhound Lines' on top, blue centered rubber wheels, cast iron, 10 1/2" long	125	175	265
Sightseeing Bus	1933	125	200	300
	Cars			
Andy Gump and Old 348	Bright red car, green trim, green disc wheels with red hubcaps, cast iron, 7 1/4" long, 1923	800	1350	1800
Auto Racer	Cast iron, 7 3/4" long, 1926	200	295	375
Boattail Racer	Nickel plated wheels, cast iron, 5" long	75	115	150
Buick Coupe	Green body, cast iron, 8 1/2" long, 1927	1300	3500	5500
Buick Sedan	Green body, cast iron, 8 1/2" long, 1927	1200	3200	5000
Checker Cab	Deep green, cast iron, 9" long	500	750	1200
Checker Cab	Plain two row checker, cast iron, 8" long			
Checker Cab	Yellow body with black roof, cast iron, 9 1/4" long, 1932			
Chevrolet	White tires, 8" long, 1928	125	185	250
Chevrolet Cab	Metal tires, cast iron, 8" long, 1920's	400	600	800

Arcade

NAME	DESCRIPTION	GOOD	EX	MINT
Chevrolet Coupe	Arizona gray body, spare wheel and tire on rear of car, with or without rubber balloon tires, cast iron, 8 1/4" long, 1927	110	1800	3200
Chevrolet Sedan	Algerian blue body, spare wheel and tire on rear of car, with or without rubber balloon tires, cast iron, 8 1/4" long, 1927	1000	1700	2900
Chevrolet Superior Roadster	Cast iron, 7" long, 1924	800	1250	1700
Chevrolet Superior Sedan	Cast iron, 7" long, 1924			
Chevrolet Superior Touring Car	Cast iron, 7" long, 1923	850	1300	2000
Chevrolet Utility Coupe	Cast iron, 7" long, 1924	650	1000	1300
Chevy Coupe	Cast iron, 8" long, 1929	400	600	800
Coupe	Red painted cast iron, 5" long, 1928	90	135	180
Coupe	Two-toned, metal wheels, 5" long, 1920's	80	125	165
Coupe	Solid wheels, 6 1/2" long, 1920's	425	650	850
Coupe	Solid wheels, no spokes, cast iron, 6 3/4" long, 1920's	125	185	250
Coupe	With or without rubber tires, removable driver, cast iron, 9" long, 1922	375	575	750
DeSoto Sedan	White rubber wheels, cast iron, 4" long, 1936	75	100	175
Ford Coupe	Nickel-plated wheels, no driver, cast iron, 5" long, 1926	150	225	325
Ford Coupe	With or without rubber tires, cast iron, 6 1/2" long, 1927	225	350	450
Ford Fordor Sedan	With or without rubber tires, removable driver, 6 1/2" long, 1920's	850	1275	1700
Ford Fordor Sedan	Nickel-plated wheels, no driver, cast iron, 5" long, 1926	650	950	1200
Ford Sedan and Covered Wagon Trailer	Cast iron, sedan 5 1/2" long, trailer 6 1/2" long, 1937	850	1200	1800
Ford Touring Car	With or without rubber tires, removable driver, cast iron, 6 1/2" long, 1926	450	650	900
Ford Tudor Sedan	With or without rubber tires, removable driver, cast iron, 6 1/2" long, 1920's	400	600	850
Ford Tudor Sedan	Visor over front windshield, with or without rubber tires, driver, cast iron, 6 1/2" long, 1926	450	600	865
Ford With Rumble Seat In Back		40	60	80
Ford Yellow Cab	Special edition for Chicago World's Fair, cast iron, 6 7/8" long, 1933	700	1000	1450
Limousine Yellow Cab	Yellow with black body stripe, nickel-plated driver, spare tire at rear, cast iron, 8 1/2" long, 1930	650	850	1300
Model A	Cast iron, 8 1/2" long	225	325	450
Model A	Cast iron, 6 3/4" long, 1928	175	225	300
Model A Coupe		425	650	850
Model A Ford	White rubber tires, cast iron, 1929	225	350	450
Model A Sedan	Orange, cast iron, 6 3/4" long, 1928	700	1050	1400
Model T	Rubber tires, 6" long	125	185	250
Model T Sedan, center door	Cast iron, 6 1/2" long, 1923	100	150	200
Pierce Arrow Coupe	'Silver Arrow' on sides, cast iron, 7 1/4" long, 1936	150	225	425
Plymouth Sedan	Cast iron, 4 3/4" long, 1933	100	185	275
Pontiac Sedan	White rubber wheels, cast iron, 4 1/4" long, 1936	85	145	185
Racer	Driver's head and number highlighted with gold bronze, cast iron, 8" long, 1936			
Racer	White rubber tires, cast iron, 5 3/4" long, 1936	50	75	100

Arcade

NAME	DESCRIPTION	GOOD	EX	MINT
Red Top Cab	Cast iron, 8" long, 1924	700	1200	2500
Reo Coupe	Cast iron, 9 3/8" long, 1931	850	1500	3750
Runabout Auto	Wood, pressed steel, steel, cast iron, 8 1/2" long, 1908			
Sedan	Cast iron, 5" long, 1920's	100	150	200
Sedan	Cast iron, 8" long, late 1930's	125	185	250
Sedan with Red Cap Trailer	Cast iron, sedan 5 7/8" long, trailer 2 1/2" long, 1939	165	225	375
Yellow Cab	Rubber tires, cast iron, 8" long, 1924	500	750	1000
Yellow Cab	Rubber tires, cast iron, 9" long, 1925	600	825	1200
Yellow Cab	Rubber tires, cast iron, 5 1/4" long, 1925	475	650	850
Yellow Cab	Bright yellow body, black top, white rubber wheels with black centers, cast iron, 8 1/4" long, 1936	1250	2000	3000
Yellow Cab	Yellow with 'Yellow Cab' in black on top, cast iron, 4 1/4" long, 1936	650	900	1250

Emergency Vehicles

NAME	DESCRIPTION	GOOD	EX	MINT
Ambulance	Cast iron, 6" long, 1932	150	225	300
Ambulance	Cast iron, 8" long, 1932			
Fire Engine	Red enamel with gold striping, cast iron, 7 1/2" long, 1926	400	600	800
Fire Engine	Red, white rubber tires with green centers, cast iron, 4 1/2" long, 1936	125	175	250
Fire Engine	Red trimmed in gold bronze, white rubber wheels with blue centers, cast iron, 6 1/4" long, 1936	150	225	300
Fire Engine	Red trimmed in gold bronze, white rubber wheels with blue centers, cast iron, 9" long, 1936	300	450	750
Fire Ladder Truck	Red trimmed in gold bronze, white rubber wheels with blue centers, cast iron, 7" long, 1936	400	600	800
Fire Ladder Truck	Red trimmed in gold bronze, ladders yellow, white rubber wheels blue centers, cast iron, 12 1/2" long with ladders, 1936	475	750	950
Fire Pumper	With six firemen, cast iron, 13 1/4" long, 1938	500	800	1000
Fire Trailer Truck	Red trimmed in gold bronze, two-piece fire engine, cast iron, truck 16 1/4" long, with ladders 20" long, 1936	500	775	1000
Fire Truck	Cast iron, 15" long	175	265	350
Hook and Ladder Fire Truck	Cast iron, 16" long	275	415	550
Mack Fire Apparatus Truck	Bright red truck, hose reel, removable extention ladders, bell that rings, cast iron, 21" long, 1925	400	600	850
Mack Fire Apparatus Truck	Red trimmed in gold, yellow extension ladders, imitation hose, nickeled driver, nickeled bell that rings, 21" long, 1936	650	900	1200
Pontiac Boiler Fire Truck	Cast iron	200	315	400
Pontiac Ladder Fire Truck	Cast iron, 7" long	210	325	425

Farm and Construction Equipment

NAME	DESCRIPTION	GOOD	EX	MINT
'Ten' Caterpillar Tractor	Cast iron, 7 1/2" long, 1929	550	850	1200
Allis-Chalmers Tractor	Cast iron, 3" long, 1934	65	95	130
Allis-Chalmers Tractor	Cast iron, 6" long, 1940	125	220	265
Allis-Chalmers Tractor	Cast iron, cast in driver, 7" long, 1940	135	225	270
Allis-Chalmers Tractor	Cast iron, separate plated driver, 7" long, 1940	185	275	370
Allis-Chalmers Tractor Trailer	Red tractor, trimmed gold bronze, green trailer, cast iron, 13" long, 1936	100	150	200

Arcade

NAME	DESCRIPTION	GOOD	EX	MINT
Allis-Chalmers Tractor with Earth Mover	Cast iron, 5" long, 1934	95	145	190
Avery Tractor	Gray frame with gold striping, red wheels, flat radiator, cast iron, 4 1/2" long, 1929	100	150	200
Caterpillar Tractor	Yellow trimmed in black, black wheels, nickeled steel track and driver, cast iron, 7 3/4" long, 1936	500	850	1000
Caterpillar, No. 270	Steel, 8 1/2" long, 1920's	500	750	1000
Crawler	Driver, chain tracks, cast iron, 3" long, 1930			
Crawler	Driver, chain tracks, cast iron, 3 7/8" long, 1930	160	245	325
Crawler	Driver, chain tracks, cast iron, 5 5/8" long, 1930	325	450	650
Crawler	Nickel-plated driver and tracks, cast iron, 6 5/8" long, 1930	425	625	850
Crawler	Nickel-plated driver and tracks, cast iron, 7 1/2" long, 1930	625	950	1250
Fairbanks-Moorse	Small portable Z-engine, no wheels, cast iron, 3 1/2" long, 1930			
Ford Tractor	Cast iron, 1/12 scale, 1941	100	150	200
Ford Tractor	Cast iron, 3 1/4" long, 1926	100	150	200
Ford Tractor	Cast iron, cast in driver, 1/25 scale, 1940	100	150	200
Ford Tractor	Cast iron, cast in driver, with plow, 1/25 scale, 1940	200	300	400
Fordson F/Loader Tractor	Rear crank operated loader, cast iron, 1/16 scale	200	275	350
Fordson Tractor	Disk rubber wheels, cast iron, 3 1/2" long, 1936	75	100	150
Fordson Tractor	Cast iron, 4 3/4" long, 1926	75	100	150
Fordson Tractor	Cast iron, 5 3/4" long, 1932	100	150	200
Fordson Tractor	With or without lugs on rear wheels, cast iron, 6" long, 1926	275	400	575
International-Harvester A Tractor	Cast iron, 1/12 scale, 1941	500	750	900
International-Harvester Crawler	Cast iron, 1/16 scale	375	565	750
International-Harvester Crawler	Cast iron, plated driver, 1/16 scale, 1941	275	415	550
International-Harvester Crawler	Cast iron, plated driver, 1/16 scale, 1936	275	415	550
International-Harvester M Tractor	Rubber wheels, cast iron, 5 1/4" long, 1941	300	400	550
International-Harvester M Tractor	Rubber wheels, cast iron, 7" long, 1940	350	475	650
John Deere Open Flywheel Tractor	Cast iron, 1/16 scale, 1941	175	265	350
John Deere Wagon	Wooden box, iron running gear, cast iron, 1/16 scale, 1940	150	225	300
McCormick-Deering Farmall Tractor	Gray body trimmed in gold, red wheels, driver, cast iron, 6 1/4" long, 1936	300	450	600
McCormick-Deering M Tractor	Wood wheels, cast iron, 4 1/4" long, 1942	175	250	400
McCormick-Deering Plow	Red frame, yellow wheels, aluminum bronze plow, shares and disks, cast iron, 7 3/4" long, 1926	250	400	600
McCormick-Deering Plow	Red frame, cream wheels, aluminum plow, shares and disks, cast iron, 7 3/4" long, 1936	175	250	325
McCormick-Deering Thresher	Assorted colors with gold striping, red grain pipe, 9 1/2" long, 1936	100	175	250
McCormick-Deering Thresher	Gray, red trim, cream colored wheels, cast iron, 12" long, 1929	150	225	300

NAME	DESCRIPTION	GOOD	EX	MINT
McCormick-Deering Tractor	Belt pulley, cast iron, 1/16 scale, 1925	450	650	850
McCormick-Deering Tractor	Assorted colors trimmed in gold, nickeled driver, cast iron, 7 1/2" long, 1936	300	400	500
Oliver Planter	Red or green, 1/25 scale, cast iron, 1950	35	50	75
Oliver Plow	Red with nickel-plated wheels, aluminum bronze plow shares, 6 3/4" long, 1926	225	350	475
Oliver Plow	Red enamal finish, blades striped with aluminum bronze, 6 1/2" long, 1926	225	350	475
Oliver Plow	Red cast iron, 1/16 scale, 1940	75	115	150
Oliver Plow	Red or green cast iron, 1/25 scale, 1940	25	35	50
Oliver Spreader	Yellow, cast iron, 1/16 scale, 1940	185	280	375
Oliver Tractor	Red or green with rubber tires, cast iron, 5 1/4" long, 1946	40	65	85
Oliver Tractor	Red or green, cast iron, 7 1/2" long, 1940	175	265	350
Threshing Machine	Gray and white, red trim, cast iron, 10" long	160	245	325

Tanks

NAME	DESCRIPTION	GOOD	EX	MINT
Army Tank with Gun	Shoots steel balls, cast iron, 8" long, 1940	85	130	175

Trucks

NAME	DESCRIPTION	GOOD	EX	MINT
'Yellow Baby' Dump Truck	Cast iron, 10 3/4" long, 1935	2000	3500	5500
Auto Express 548 Truck	Flatbed, cast iron, 9" long	225	350	450
Borden's Milk Bottle Truck	'Borden's' cast on side, cast iron, 6 1/4" long, 1936	1500	2750	8000
Carry-Car Truck and Trailer Set	Red truck, green trailer, with three 3 3/4" Austin vehicles, cast iron, 14 1/4" long, 1936	650	1150	1700
Carry-Car Truck and Trailer Set	Red truck, green trailer, with four vehicles, cast iron, 28" long, 1936	700	1400	2200
Carry-Car Truck Trailer	Cast iron, 24 1/2" long, 1928	750	1300	1900
Century of Progress Truck	Cast iron, 10" long, 1933	60	95	125
Chevrolet Panel Delivery Van	White rubber tires with colored centers, cast iron, 4" long, 1936	90	165	225
Chevrolet Stake Truck		90	165	225
Chevrolet Utility Express Truck	Cast iron, 9 1/4" long, 1923	450	675	900
Chevrolet Wrecker		90	165	225
Chrome Wheeled Truck	Cast iron, 7" long	225	350	450
Delivery Truck	Yellow, cast iron, 8 1/4" long, 1926	800	1200	1500
Dump Truck	Spoked wheels, low bed, cast iron, 6" long	75	115	150
Dump Truck	Cast iron, 6 1/2" long, 1941	75	115	150
Dump Truck	Red chassis, green dump body, white rubber tires with green centers, cast iron, 4 1/2" long, 1936	50	65	85
Ford Anthony Dump Truck	Nickel-plated spoked wheels, black enamel finish with gray dump body, cast iron, 8 1/2" long, 1926	1250	2000	2500
Ford Weaver Wrecker	Cast iron, 8 1/4" long, 1928	700	950	1400
Ford Weaver Wrecker, Model A	Cast iron, 11" long, 1926	550	800	1200
Ford Weaver Wrecker, Model T	Cast iron, 11" long, 1926	600	875	1300
Ford Wrecker	White rubber wheels, cast iron, 7" long, 1936	125	200	300
Gasoline Truck	Cast iron, 13" long, 1920's	600	900	1200
Ice Truck	Red, cast iron, 7" long, 1930's	175	225	350
International Delivery Truck	Cast iron, 9 1/2" long, 1936	1250	1875	2500
International Dump Truck	Cast iron, 10 3/4" long, 1930	200	300	400
International Dump Truck	White rubber wheels with red centers, cast iron, 10 1/2" long, 1935	275	415	550
International Dump Truck	Red cab, green dump, cast iron, 9 1/2" long, 1940	600	950	1250

Arcade

NAME	DESCRIPTION	GOOD	EX	MINT
International Harvester Dump Truck	Cast iron, 11" long, 1941	300	465	675
International Harvester Pickup	Cast iron, 9 1/2" long, 1941	200	325	500
International Stake Truck	White rubber wheels with red centers, cast iron, 12" long, 1935	500	750	900
International Stake Truck	Yellow, cast iron, 9 1/2" long, 1940	600	750	1250
International Wrecker Truck	Cast iron, 11" long	1250	1875	2500
Mack Dump Truck	Assorted colors trimmed in gold bronze, 'Mack' decals on doors, dual rear wheels, cast iron, 12 1/4" long, 1936	750	1125	1500
Mack Dump Truck	Cast iron, 13" long	375	565	750
Mack Dump Truck	Light grey or blue, gold trim, white tires, cast iron, 12" long, 1925	700	1050	1400
Mack Gasoline Truck	Cast iron, 13 1/4" long, 1925	325	485	650
Mack High Dump	Nickel-plated levers mechanically raise the dump bed, cast iron, 8 1/2" long, 1930	750	1100	1400
Mack High Dump	Cast iron, 12 3/8" long, 1931	750	1075	1400
Mack Ice Truck	Ice blocks and tongs, cast iron, 8 1/2" long, 1931	350	525	700
Mack Ice Truck	Ice blocks and tongs, cast iron, 10 3/4" long, 1931	550	750	950
Mack Lubrite Tank Truck	Cast iron, 13 1/4" long, 1925	1200	2000	3000
Mack Oil Truck	Cast iron, 10" long, 1920's	350	525	700
Mack Tank Truck	Cast iron with tin tank, 12 3/4" long, 1929	1200	1800	2900
Mack Tank Truck	Assorted colors with gold trim, nickeled driver, dual rear wheels, tank holds water, cast iron, 13" long, 1936	1100	1800	2500
Mack Tank Truck	Nickel-plated driver, cast iron, 13 1/4" long, 1926	1000	1500	2000
Mack Wrecker Truck	White rubber tires, cast iron, 11" long	250	375	500
Model-A Stakebody Truck	Iron wheels, cast iron, 7 1/2" long, 1920's	150	225	300
Plymouth Wrecker		100	185	275
Pontiac Stake Truck	White rubber tires, cast iron, 6 1/4" long, 1936	225	350	500
Pontiac Stake Truck	White rubber tires, cast iron, 4 1/4" long, 1936	65	95	165
Pontiac Stake Truck		85	145	185
Pontiac Wrecker	White rubber tires, cast iron, 4 1/4" long, 1936	70	100	175
Pontiac Wrecker		85	145	185
Red Baby Dump Truck	Bright red truck, white enameled tires, crank dump, cast iron, 10 3/4" long, 1924	1200	1800	2400
Red Baby Truck	Bright red truck, white enameled tires, cast iron, 10 1/4" long, 1924	600	850	1350
Semi Truck	Cast iron, 1920's	50	75	100
Stake Truck	Cast iron, 7" long	110	175	225
Tow Truck	Cast iron, 4" long	55	85	110
Transport	Double-deck semi-trailer with four sedans, cast iron and pressed steel, 18 1/2" long, sedans 4 3/4" long, 1938	500	800	1000
White Delivery Truck	Cast iron, 8 1/2" long, 1931	1250	2100	3300
White Moving Van	Cast iron, 13 1/2" long, 1928	6000	8500	13500

Vehicle Banks

NAME	DESCRIPTION	GOOD	EX	MINT
Ford Touring Car Bank	Removable driver, cast iron, 6 1/2" long, 1925	650	975	1300
Mack Dump Truck Bank	Cast iron, 13" long	375	565	750
Yellow Cab Bank	Cast iron, 8" long, 1924	475	775	1000
Yellow Cab Bank	With or without rubber tires, cast iron, 9" long, 1926	600	900	1200
Yellow Cab Bank	Cast iron, 8 1/2" long, 1930	650	1400	2000

Arcade

NAME	DESCRIPTION	GOOD	EX	MINT
	Wagons, Carts and Trailers			
Auto Dump Wagon	Red and gold, cast iron, 7" long, 1920	80	120	160
Circus Wagon	Circus wagon with driver and two horses, 'Big Six Circus & Wild West' on side of wagon, 14 1/2" long, 1936	300	450	600
Ice Wagon	With black horses trimmed in gold, cast iron, 11 3/4" long, 1926	575	875	1300
McCormick-Deering Weber Wagon	Removable wagon seat and box, with two horses, cast iron, overall length 12 1/8" long, 1925	50	75	100
Panama Dump Wagon	Gray, nickeled pick and shovel, cast iron, 12 3/4" long, 1926	150	225	300
Panama Dump Wagon	Gray, with two horses, cast iron, nickeled pick and shovel, 14 1/4" long, 1926	175	225	300
Whitehead & Kales Truck Trailer	Sides and end gates removable by sections, cast iron, 8 1/2" long, 1926	100	150	200

Auburn

NAME	DESCRIPTION	GOOD	EX	MINT
	Airplanes			
Clipper Plane	Rubber, 7" wingspan, 1941	10	20	25
Dive Bomber	Rubber, 4" wingspan, 1937	10	20	25
Pursuit Ship Plane	4" wingspan, 1941	10	20	25
Two-Engine Transport Plane	1937	10	20	27
	Boats and Ships			
Battleship	Rubber, 8 1/4" long, 1941	15	25	30
Cruiser	Rubber	15	25	30
Freighter	Rubber, 8" long, 1941	15	25	30
Submarine	Rubber, 6 1/2" long, 1941	10	20	27
	Cars			
1947 Buick Coupe	#100 on license plate, 7" long	75	115	150
Airport Limousine	Rubber, 8" long	25	40	50
Fire Chief's Car	Red, yellow wheels	7	10	15
Ford	Rubber, 1930's	10	20	25
Race Car	Rubber, 6" long, 1930's	15	25	30
Race Car	Red, rubber, 6" long	40	65	85
Race Car With Goggled Driver	Rubber, 10" long	50	75	100
Racer	Rubber	20	30	40
Racer	Red vinyl with white plastic tires	25	40	50
Sedan	Green, rubber, license #500R	15	25	30
Sedan	Cast iron driver	25	40	50
	Emergency Vehicles			
Fire Engine	Red, rubber, 8" long	15	25	30
Fire Truck	Black rubber wheels	7	10	15
Rescue Truck	Dark army green	15	25	30
	Farm and Construction Equipment			
Allis-Chalmers Tractor	Red and silver plastic, 1/16 scale, 1950	25	40	50
Earthmover	Red front, yellow back, plastic wheels	15	25	30
Giant Tractor	Red tractor, silver motor, black tires, 7" long, 1950's	30	45	60
John Deere Tractor	Plastic, 1/20 scale	25	40	50
Minneapolis Moline Tractor	Red, large rubber tires, rubber 1/16 scale, 1950	25	40	50

Auburn

NAME	DESCRIPTION	GOOD	EX	MINT
Tractor and Wagon	Orange tractor, silver motor, black tires, red spreader wagon, yellow spoke tires	75	115	150

Motorcycles

NAME	DESCRIPTION	GOOD	EX	MINT
Motorcycle		20	30	40
Police Cycle	Red rubber, drive chain, 6" long, 1950's	50	75	100

Trucks

NAME	DESCRIPTION	GOOD	EX	MINT
2 1/2 Ton Truck		20	30	40
Army Jeep	Olive drab	5	7	10
Army Recon Half Truck	Bright green	10	15	20
Stake Truck	Rubber	15	25	30
Telephone Truck	6 1/2" long	35	55	75

Bandai

Buses

NAME	DESCRIPTION	GOOD	EX	MINT
Volkswagen Bus	Red and white, battery operated, 9 1/2" long, 1960's	65	150	275

Cars

NAME	DESCRIPTION	GOOD	EX	MINT
1915 Ford Touring Car	7" long	90	135	180
1960 Rolls Royce Silver Cloud	Blue body, white top, electric lights, 12" long	350	525	700
Cadillac	Gold fins, black top, tin, 11 1/2" long, 1959	150	225	300
Cadillac	8" long	100	175	275
Cadillac	White, hardtop, friction powered, 11" long, 1959	100	175	275
Cadillac	Copper, hardtop, friction powered, 11" long, 1960	75	125	175
Cadillac	Gold, hardtop, friction powered, 17" long, 1960's	195	350	550
Cadillac Convertible	Red, green interior, friction powered, 11" long, 1959	175	300	400
Cadillac Convertible	Black, friction powered, 11" long, 1960	180	275	380
Cadillac Convertible	White, red interior, friction powered, 17" long, 1963	200	400	600
Chevrolet Corvette	White and black, battery operated, 8" long, 1962	75	125	175
Chevrolet Corvette	Red, friction powered, 8" long, 1963	75	125	175
Chevrolet Impala Convertible	White, friction powered, 11" long, 1961	250	400	550
Chevrolet Impala Sedan	Cream, friction powered, 11" long, 1961	225	350	500
Citroen	Blue and white, friction powered, 12" long, 1958	300	650	1000
Corvair Bertone	White, battery operated, tin, 12" long, 1963	70	120	175
Cougar	White, battery operated, tin	100	150	200
Excalibur Roadster	White body, red fenders, black top, battery operated, rubber wheels, motor sparks, 11" long	135	200	275
Ferrari	Silver with red interior, battery operated, tin, gearshift n floor, working lights, horn, and engine noise, 11" long, 1958	300	550	850
Ford Convertible	Green, friction powered, 12" long, 1955	350	650	900
Ford Convertible	Red and black or two tone green, friction powered, 12" long, 1957	150	275	375
Ford Country Sedan	Blue and white, friction powered, 10 1/2" long, 1961	65	100	140

NAME	DESCRIPTION	GOOD	EX	MINT
Ford F.B.I. Mustang	Black and white, friction powered, 11" long, 1965	75	100	140
Ford Flower Delivery Wagon	Blue, friction powered, 12" long, 1955	275	400	650
Ford G T	Red battery operated, 10" long, 1960's	100	150	200
Ford Mustang	Red, battery operated, 11" long, 1965	125	200	275
Ford Mustang	Red, battery operated, 13" long, 1967	80	125	175
Ford Mustang	Silver and black, battery operated, 11" long, 1965	65	100	145
Ford Ranchero	Two tone blue, friction powered, 12"long, 1955	175	250	350
Ford Ranchero	Black and red, friction powered, 12" long, 1957	175	250	350
Ford Standard Fresh Coffee Wagon	Black and orange, friction powered, 12" long, 1955	350	625	975
Ford Station Wagon	Cream and black, two tone green, or red and black, friction powered, 12" long, 1955	75	125	200
Ford Thunderbird	Red or red and black, friction powered, 8" long, 1962	65	100	150
Ford Thunderbird	Red and black, friction powered, 10 3/4" long, 1965	100	175	225
Ford Wagon	Green body, black top, 12" long	300	450	600
Ford Wagon	Blue and white, friction powered, 12" long, 1957	90	150	200
GT-40	Blue, hood and trunk open, rubber tires, tin, battery operated, 11" long	100	150	200
Isetta	White and two tone green, 3 wheels, friction powered, 6 1/2" long, 1950's	200	300	400
Jaguar XK 140 Convertible	Various colors, 9 1/2" long, 1950s	125	200	275
Jaguar XK-E	Red, battery operated, 10" long, 1960's	100	150	250
Lincoln Continental	Turquoise and white, matching interior, 1958	150	250	375
Lincoln Continental Convertible	White, red interior, 1958	200	300	425
Lincoln Mark III	Turquoise and whote, friction powered, 11" long, 1958	150	275	375
Lotus	Blue, battery operated, 9 1/2" long	110	175	225
Lotus Elite	Red and black, friction powered, 8 1/2" long, 1950's	75	100	150
Mazda 360 Coupe	Blue, friction powered, 7" long, 1960	65	100	125
Mercedes Benz 300 SL Coupe	Silver and black, friction powered, 8" long, 1950's	160	245	325
Mercedes-Benz Taxi	Black, battery operated, 10" long, 1960's	125	250	350
MG 1600 Mark II	Red, friction powered, 8 1/2" long, 1950's	75	125	175
MG TF	Green, friction powered, 8" long, 1955	75	125	175
Old Timer Police Car	Battery operated, 8" long	60	95	125
Olds Toronado	Gold, battery operated, 11" long, 1966	30	50	65
Oldsmobile	Surrey top, friction, 1900's	75	115	150
Plymouth Valiant	Blue, windup, 8" long	50	75	100
Pontiac Firebird	Red, battery operated, 9 1/2" long, 1967	75	125	175
Porsche 911	White, battery operated, 10" long, 1960's	90	150	200
Racer with Hand Control		85	130	175
Rolls-Royce Convertible	Several colors available, 12" long, friction, 1950's	200	300	450
Rolls-Royce Hardtop Sedan	Blue, black, white, rare version with working headlights, battery operated, 12" long, 1950's	275	400	600
Subaru 360	Red, friction powered, 8" long, 1959	75	125	175
Taxi	Friction, 1950's	75	115	150
Volkswagen	Red, battery operated, 8" long, 1960's	35	75	100
Volkswagen	Blue, battery operated, 10 1/2" long, 1960's	75	125	175

Bandai

NAME	DESCRIPTION	GOOD	EX	MINT
Volkswagen	Red, battery operated, 15" long, 1960's	95	150	225
Volkswagen	Red, with sun roof, battery operated, 15" long, 1960's	90	150	225
Volkswagen Convertible	White, battery operated, 7 1/2" long, 1960's	50	95	125

Emergency Vehicles

NAME	DESCRIPTION	GOOD	EX	MINT
Plymouth Ambulance	White, red cross on doors, friction powered, 12" long, 1961	35	50	75
Rambler Ambulance	White, friction powered, 11" long, 1962	40	75	100

Motorcycles

NAME	DESCRIPTION	GOOD	EX	MINT
Police Auto Cycle	Battery operated, hard plastic, 10" long, 1970's	100	150	200

Sets

NAME	DESCRIPTION	GOOD	EX	MINT
Ferrari and Speed Boat	White car, red and white speed boat with white trailer, tin, overall 23" long, 1958	350	650	900
Lincoln Continental and Cabin Cruiser	Turquoise and white car and cruiser, red car interior and cruiser trailer, overall 23" long, 1958	300	550	800
Rambler Wagon and Cabin Cruiser	Green and white Rambler wagon, red trailer, friction powered rambler, electric boat motor, overall 23" long, 1959	200	400	600
Rambler Wagon and Shasta Trailer	Green and white Rambler wagon, yellow and white trailer, 11" long wagon, 12" long trailer, 1959	200	400	600
Rambler, Trailer and Cabin Cruiser	Turquoise and white Rambler, red trailer, cruiser color varies, overall 35" long, 1959	350	650	1000

Trucks

NAME	DESCRIPTION	GOOD	EX	MINT
1958 Ford Ranchero Pickup Truck	8" long	110	175	225
Land Rover	Maroon, 8" long	125	185	250
Land Rover	Red, friction powered, 7 1/2" long, 1960	75	100	150
Volkswagen Truck	Blue, open flatbed cargo section, battery operated, 8" long, 1960's	90	150	200

Barclay

Airplanes

NAME	DESCRIPTION	GOOD	EX	MINT
Dirigible Plane	4 3/8" long, 1930's	7	10	15
Lindy-Type Plane	4" wingspan, 1930's	7	10	15
Monoplane	Single engine plane	15	28	35
Monoplane	Single engine plane, red propeller, red metal wheels	15	30	40
U.S. Army Single Engine Transport Plane	White rubber wheels, 1940	10	15	20
U.S. Army Small Pursuit Plane	Lead, rubber wheels, 1941	10	15	20

Buses

NAME	DESCRIPTION	GOOD	EX	MINT
Double-Decker Bus	4" long	20	30	40

Cannons

NAME	DESCRIPTION	GOOD	EX	MINT
Cannon	Barrel elevated, 2 1/2" long	15	25	35
Cannon	1931	20	30	40
Cannon	Very large wheels, 4" long	15	20	25

Barclay

NAME	DESCRIPTION	GOOD	EX	MINT
Cannon	Silver with black rubber wheels, 7 3/4" long	20	30	40
Cannon	Spoked wheels, 3" long	10	15	20
Coast Defense Rifle Cannon	4 1/2" long	25	40	50
Howitzer Cannon	Horizontal loop hitch, 4 wheels, 3" long	15	25	35
Howitzer Cannon	Vertical loop hitch, 4 wheels, 3" long	15	25	35
Mortar Cannon	Swivels on base, 3" long	20	30	40
Spring-Firing Cannon	Spoked wheels, 4" long	20	25	35

Cars

NAME	DESCRIPTION	GOOD	EX	MINT
Armoured Car	1937	15	25	35
Car Carrier	With two cars	25	40	55
Coupe	1930's	20	30	40
Coupe	3" long, 1930's	15	25	35
Race Car	White tires, 4" long	25	40	55

Trucks

NAME	DESCRIPTION	GOOD	EX	MINT
Beer Truck	Slush metal, 4" long	15	25	35
Mack Pickup Truck	3 1/2" long	25	40	55
Milk Truck #377	With milk cans	25	40	55
Open Truck	3 1/2" long	10	20	25
Stake Truck	Slush metal, 5" long	15	25	35

VEHICLES

Brooklin

Cars

NAME	DESCRIPTION	GOOD	EX	MINT
1932 Packard Light 8 Coupe		35	50	70
1933 Pierce Arrow	Silver	35	50	70
1934 Chrysler Airflow Sedan	Four door	35	50	70
1935 Dodge "City Ice Delivery" Van		40	60	80
1935 Dodge "Dr.Pepper" Van		45	70	90
1935 Dodge "Sears Roebuck" Van		40	60	80
1940 Ford Sedan Delivery "Ford Service"		40	60	80
1941 Packard Clipper" Van		40	60	80
1948 Tucker Torpedo		35	50	70
1949 Buick Roadmaster		35	55	75
1949 Mercury Coupe	Two door	30	45	65
1952 Hudson Hornet Convertible	1/43 scale	30	45	65
1952 Studebaker Champion Starlight Coupe		40	60	80
1953 Buick Skylark		35	50	70
1953 Pontiac Sedan Delivery Gulf Oil Truck	1/43 scale	30	45	60
1953 Pontiac Sedan Delivery Mobil Oil Truck	1/43 scale	30	45	60
1953 Studebaker Commander	1/43 scale	30	45	60
1953 Studebaker Indiana State Police	1/43 scale	50	75	100
1954 Dodge 500 Indy Pace Car	1/43 scale	50	75	100
1955 Chrysler 300		30	45	60
1956 Ford Fairline Victoria	Two door	25	40	55
1956 Ford Thunderbird 500	Hardtop	30	45	65
1956 Lincoln Continental		30	45	60
1956 Lincoln Continental Mark II Coupe		30	45	65

Brooklin

NAME	DESCRIPTION	GOOD	EX	MINT
1956 Lincoln Continental MKII		30	45	65
1957 Ford Fairlane Skyliner Police	1/43 scale	30	45	60
1958 Edsel Citation	Two door hardtop	30	45	30
1958 Pontiac Bonneville		30	45	65
1960 Ford Sunliner Convertible	1/43 scale	30	45	60
1963 Chevrolet Corvette Stingray Coupe		35	55	75
1968 Shelby Mustang GT 500		35	55	75
Lincoln Mark	1/43 scale	30	45	60
Mini Marquee Packard Convertible	1/43 scale	50	75	100
Tucker	1/43 scale	30	45	60

Buddy L

Airplanes

NAME	DESCRIPTION	GOOD	EX	MINT
5000 Monocoupe "The Lone Eagle"	Orange wing, black fuselage and tail with tailskid, all steel high wind cabin monoplane, 9 7/8" wingspan, 1929	250	450	550
Army Tank Transport Plane	Low-wing monoplane, two small four-wheel tanks that clip beneath wings, 27" wingspan, 1941	250	375	500
Catapult Airplane and Hangar	5000 Monocoupe with tailwheel, 9 7/8" wingspan, olive-gray hangar, black twin-spring catapult, 1930	1000	1500	2000
Four Motor Air Cruiser	White, red engine cowlings, yellow fuselage and twin tails, four engine monoplane, 27" wingspan, 1952	200	300	400
Four-Engine Transport	Green wings, white engine cowlings, yellow fuselage and twin tails, four engine monoplane, 27" wingspan, 1949	200	300	400
Hangar and Three 5000 Monocoupes	Olive-gray hangar, windows outlined in red or orange, planes 9 7/8" wingspan, all steel high wing cabin monoplanes, 1930	1500	2250	3000
Transport Airplane	White wings and engine cowlings, red fuselage and twin tails, four engine monoplane, 27" wingspan, 1946	200	300	400

Boats and Ships

NAME	DESCRIPTION	GOOD	EX	MINT
LST Landing Ship	Navy gray flat-bottomed steel hull, ship 12 3/4" long, with 4 1/4" long tank and 5" long troop transport, 1976	125	185	250
Tug Boat	Medium bluish-gray-green hull, keel and rudder, gray pilot house, cabin and deck, 28" long, 1928	5000	7500	10000

Buses

NAME	DESCRIPTION	GOOD	EX	MINT
Coach	Bluish gray-green, opening front doors, interior has 22 chairs plus 2 benches over back wheels, 29 1/4" long, 1927	3000	6000	9000
Greyhound Bus	White roof, blue and white sides, blue front has yellow headlights, 16 1/2" long, 1938	275	415	550
Greyhound Bus	White roof and back, blue and white sides and front, 16 3/4" long, 1949	200	300	400

NAME	DESCRIPTION	GOOD	EX	MINT
	Cars			
Army Staff Car	Olive drab body, 15 3/4" long, 1964	100	150	200
Bloomin' Bus	Chartreuse body, white roof and supports, similar to VW minibus, 10 3/4" long, 1969	90	135	180
Buddywagen	Red body with white roof, 10 3/4" long, 1966	100	150	200
Buddywagen	Red body with white roof, no chrome v on front, 10 3/4" long, 1967	95	145	190
Chrysler Six Passenger Airflow Sedan	Pressed steel, 17 1/4" long, 1934	0	0	0
Colt Sportsliner	Red open body, white hardtop, off-white seats and interior, 10 1/4" long, 1967	35	50	70
Colt Sportsliner	Light blue-green open body, white hardtop, pale tan seats and interior, 10 1/4" long, 1968	30	45	65
Colt Utility Car	Red open body, white plstic seats, floor and luggage space, 10 1/4" long, 1967	35	50	70
Colt Utility Car	Light orange body, beige-tan interior, 10 1/4" long, 1968	30	45	65
Country Squire Wagon	Off-white hood fenders, endgate and roof, brown wood-grain side panels, 15 1/2" long, 1963	85	130	175
Country Squire Wagon	Red hood fenders, endgate and roof, brown wood-grain side panels, 15" long, 1965	75	115	150
Deluxe Convertible Coupe	Metallic blue enamel front, sides and deck, cream top retracts into rumble seat, 19" long, 1949	300	450	600
Desert Rats Command Car	Light tan open body, light beige interior, black .50-caliber machine gun swivels, tits, on post between seats, 10 1/4" long, 1967	50	75	100
Desert Rats Command Car	Light tan open body, light beige interior, black .50-caliber machine gun swivels, tits, on post between seats, 10 1/4" long, blackwall tires, 1968	45	65	90
DeSoto Airflow Sedan	Pressed steel, 17" long, 1934	0	0	0
Flivver Coupe	Black except for red 8-spoke wheels, black hubs, aluminum tires, flat, hard-top roof on enclosed glass-window-style body, 11" long, 1924	775	1100	1550
Flivver Roadster	Black except for red 8-spoke wheels, black hubs, aluminum tires, simulated soft, folding top, 11" long, 1924	1000	1500	2000
Jr. Camaro	Metallic blue body, white racing stripes across hood nose, 9" long, 1968	50	75	100
Jr. Flower Power Sportster	Purple hood, fenders and body, white roof and supports, white plastic seats, lavender and orange five-petal blossom decals on hood top, roof, and sides, 6" long, 1969	35	55	75
Jr. Sportster	Blue hood and open body, white hardtop and upper sides, 6" long, 1968	35	55	75
Mechanical Scarab Automobile	Red radically streamlined body, bright metal front and rear bumpers, 10 1/2" long, 1936	200	300	500
Police Colt	Deep blue open body, white hardtop, "POLICE" across top of hood, "POLICE 1" on sides, 10 1/4" long, 1968	50	75	100

NAME	DESCRIPTION	GOOD	EX	MINT
Ski Bus	White body and roof, similar to VW minibus, 10 3/4" long, 1967	75	115	150
Station Wagon	Light blue-green body and roof, 15 1/2" long, 1963	75	115	150
Streamline Scarab	Red, radically streamlined body, non-mechanical, 10 1/2" long, 1941	145	225	290
Suburban Wagon	Powder blue or white body and roof, 15 1/2" long, 1963	75	115	150
Suburban Wagon	Gray-green body and roof, 15 3/4" long, 1964	70	100	140
Town and Country Convertible	Maroon front, hood, rear deck and fenders, gray top retracts into rumble seat, 19" long, 1947	300	450	600
Travel Trailer and Station Wagon	Red station wagon, 2-wheel trailer with red lower body and white steel camper-style upper body, 27 1/4" long, 1965	150	225	300
Yellow Taxi with Skyview	Yellow hood, roof and body, red radiator front and fenders, 18 1/2" long, 1948	325	500	675

Emergency Vehicles

NAME	DESCRIPTION	GOOD	EX	MINT
Aerial Ladder and Emergency Truck	Red except for white ladders, bumper and steel disc wheels, three 8-rung steel ladders, 22 1/4" long, 1952	200	300	400
Aerial Ladder and Emergency Truck	Red except for white ladders, bumper and steel disc wheels, three 8-rung steel ladders, no rear step, no siren or SIREN decal, 22 1/4" long, 1953	225	345	450
Aerial Ladder Fire Engine	Red tractor, wraparound bumper and semi-trailer, 2 aluminum 13-rung extension ladders on sides, swivel-base aluminum central ladder, 26 1/2" long, 1960	125	185	250
Aerial Ladder Fire Engine	Red tractor and semi-trailer, white plastic bumper with integral grill guard, 2 aluminum 13-rung extension ladders on sides, swivel-base aluminum central ladder, 26 1/2" long, 1961	125	185	250
Aerial Ladder Fire Engine	Red tractor and semi-trailer, chrome one-piece wraparound bumper, slotted grille, 2 aluminum 13-rung extension ladders on sides, swivel-base aluminum central ladder, 26 1/2" long, 1966	125	185	250
Aerial Ladder Fire Engine	Red cab-over-engine tractor and semi-trailer units, two 13-rung white sectional ladders and swivel-mounted aerial ladder with side rails, 25 1/2" long, 1968	100	150	200
Aerial Ladder Fire Engine	Snub-nose red tractor and semi-trailer, white swivel-mounted aerial ladder with side rails, 2 white 13-rung sectional ladders, 27 1/2" long, 1970	100	150	200
Aerial Truck	Red except for nickel ladders, black hand wheel, brass bell, and black hubs, 39" long with ladder down, 1925	850	1300	1700
Ameican LaFrance Aero-Chief Pumper	Red cab-over-engine and body, white underbody, rear step and simulated hose reels, black extension ladders on right side, 25 1/2" long, 1972	125	185	250
Brute Fire Pumper	Red cab-over-engine body and frame, 2 yellow 5-rung sectional ladders on sides of open body, 5 1/4" long, 1969	50	75	100

Top to Bottom: All from Buddy L; Coca Cola Delivery Trucks, 1971; Texaco Tanker; Tow Truck; IHC "Red Baby" Express Truck, 1928; Army Supply Truck, 1956; 49 LST, 1950; Hydraulic Dump Truck, 1965.

Buddy L

NAME	DESCRIPTION	GOOD	EX	MINT
Brute Hook-n-Ladder	Red cab-over-engine tractor and detachable semi-trailer, white elevating, swveling aerial ladder with side rails, 10" long, 1969	30	40	55
Extension Ladder Fire Truck	All red except for silver -painted ladders and yellow removable rider seat, enclosed cab, 35" long, 1945	200	300	400
Extension Ladder Rider Fire Truck	Duo-tone slant design, tractor has white front, lower hood sides and lower doors, red hood top, cab and frame, red semi-trailer, white 10-rung and 8-rung ladders, 32 1/2" long, 1949	150	225	300
Extension Ladder Trailer Fire Truck	Red tractor with enclosed cab, boxy fenders, red semi-trailer with fenders, two white 8-rung side ladders, 10-rung central extension ladder, 29 1/2" long, 1955	200	300	400
Extension Ladder Trailer Fire Truck	Red tractor unit and semi-trailer, enclosed cab, two white 13-rung side extension ladders on sides, white central ladder on swivel base, 29 1/2" long, 1956	125	185	250
Fire and Chemical Truck	Duo-tone slant design, white front, lower hood sides and lower doors, rest is red, bright-metal or white 8-rung ladder on sides, 25" long, 1949	125	185	250
Fire Department Emergency Truck	Red streamlined body, enclosed cab, chrome one-piece grille, bumper, and headlights, 12 3/4" long, 1953	100	150	200
Fire Engine	Red except for nickel-plated upright broiler, nickel rims and flywheels on dummy water pump, brass bell, 23 1/4" long, 1925-29	3000	4000	5000
Fire Engine	Red except for nickel rim flywheels on dummy pump, brass bell, dim-or-bright electric headlights, 25 1/2" long, 1933	1500	2000	2500
Fire Hose and Water Pumper	Red except for 2 white 5-rung ladders and 2 removable fire extinguishers, enclosed cab, 12 1/2" long, 1950	100	150	200
Fire Hose and Water Pumper	Red except for 2 white 5-rung ladders and 1 red and white removable fire extinguisher, enclosed cab, 12 1/2" long, 1952	100	150	200
Fire Pumper	Red cab-over-engine and open body, 11-rung white 10" ladder on each side, 16 1/4" long, 1968	100	150	200
Fire Pumper with Action Hydrant	Red wraparound bumper, hood cab and cargo section, aluminum 9-rung ladders, white hose reel, 15" long, 1960	75	115	150
Fire Truck	All red except for white ladders, black rubber wheels, enclosed cab, 12" long, 1945	75	115	150
Fire Truck	Duo-tone slant design, tractor has white front, lower hood sides and lower doors, red hood top, cab and frame, red semi-trailer, rubber wheels with black tires, 32 1/2" long, 1953	200	300	400
Fire Truck	Bright red, except for black inverted L-shaped crane mounted in socket on seat back, open driver's seat, 26" long, 1924	1500	2500	3500

NAME	DESCRIPTION	GOOD	EX	MINT
Fire Truck	Bright "fire engine" red, except for black inverted L-shaped crane mounted in socket on seat back, red floor, open driver's seat, 26" long, 1925	1800	3000	4500
Fire Truck	Bright "fire engine" red, red floor, open driver's seat, 26" long, 1928	550	900	1100
Fire Truck	Red except for black solid-rubber firestone tires on red 7-spoke embossed metal wheels, two 18 1/2" red steel sectional ladders, 26" long, 1930	950	1500	1900
Fire Truck	Red except for nickel or white ladders, bright-metal radiator grille and black removable rider saddle, 25 1/2" long, 1935	250	375	500
Fire Truck	Duo-tone slant design, yellow front, single-bar bumper, hood sides and removable rider seat, rest is red, 25 1/2" long, 1936	250	375	500
Fire Truck	Duo-tone slant design, yellow front, bumper, hood sides and skirted fenders, rest is red, nickel ladders, 28 1/2" long, 1939	550	850	1100
Fire Truck	Red except for 2 white ladders, enclosed cab, bright metal grille and headlights, 25" long, 1948	125	200	250
GMC Deluxe Aerial Ladder Fire Engine	White tractor and semi-trailer units, golden 13-rung extension ladder on sides, golden central aerial ladder, black and white DANGER battery case with 2 flashing lights, 28" long, 1959	225	345	450
GMC Extension Ladder Trailer Fire Engine	Red tractor with chrome GMC bar grille, red semi-trailer, white 13-rung extension ladders on sides, white swiveling central ladder with side rails, 27 1/4" long, 1957	100	150	200
GMC Fire Pumper with Horn	Red except for aluminum-finish 11-rung side ladders and white reel of black plastic hose in open cargo section, chrome GMC bar grille, 15" long, 1958	100	150	200
GMC Hydraulic Aerial Ladder Fire Engine	Red tractor unit with chrome GMC bar grille, red semi-trailer, white 13-rung extension ladders on sides, white swiveling central ladder, 26 1/2" long, 1958	125	185	250
GMC Red Cross Ambulance	All white, removable fabric canopy with a red cross and "Ambulance" in red capitals, 14 1/2" long, 1960	85	130	175
Hook & Ladder Fire Truck	Medium-dark red, except for black inverted L-shaped crane mounted in socket on seat back, open driver's seat, 26" long, 1923	1200	1800	2400
Hose Truck	All red except for 2 white hose pipes, white cord hose on reeland brass nozzle, electric headlights with red bulbs, 21 3/4" long, 1933	225	350	450
Hydraulic Aerial Truck	Duo-tone slant design, yellow bumper, radiator front, fenders, lower hood sides and removable rider saddle, rest is red, nickel extension ladders, 41" long with ladders, 1939	1500	2500	3500
Hydraulic Aerial Truck	Red except for black removable rider saddle and twisted-wire removable pull-n-ride handle, nickel extension ladders, 40" long, 1933	1000	2000	3000

NAME	DESCRIPTION	GOOD	EX	MINT
Hydraulic Aerial Truck	Duo-tone slant design, yellow front, single-bar bumper, chassis, radiator, front fender, lower sides and removable rider saddle, rest is red, 40" long with ladders down, 1936	550	825	1100
Hydraulic Aerial Truck	Red except for brass bell on cowl, nickel ladders mounted on 5 1/2" turntable rotated by black hand wheel, 39" long, 1927	850	1300	1700
Hydraulic Aerial Truck	Red except for brass bell on cowl, nickel ladders mounted on 5 1/2" turntable rotated by black hand wheel, 2-bar nickel front bumper, 39" long, 1930	1000	1500	2500
Hydraulic Aerial Truck	Red except for brass bell on cowl, nickel ladders mounted on 5 1/2" turntable rotated by black hand wheel, 2-bar nickel front bumper, nickel-rim headlights in red shells, 39" long, 1931	1200	1750	2500
Hydraulic Aerial Truck	Duo-tone slant design, red hood and body, yellow rider seat, nickel extension ladders, 41" long with ladders, 1941	650	975	1300
Hydraulic Snorkel Fire Pumper	Red cab-over-engine and open rear body, white 11-rung 10" ladder on each side, snorkel pod with solid sides, 21 " long, 1969	100	150	200
Hydraulic Water Tower Truck	Red except nickel water tower, dim-or-bright electric headlights, brass bell, 44 7/8" long with tower down, 1933	1200	2000	3000
Hydraulic Water Tower Truck	Red except nickel water tower, dim-or-bright electric headlights, brass bell, added-on bright-metal grille, 44 7/8" long with tower down, 1935	2000	4000	6000
Hydraulic Water Tower Truck	Duo-tone slant design, yellow bumper, hood sides, front fenders, rest is red, electric headlights, added-on bright-metal grille, 44 7/8" long with tower down, 1936	1200	2000	3000
Hydraulic Water Tower Truck	Duo-tone slant design, yellow front, single-bar bumper and hood sides, red hood top, enclosed cab and water tank, brass bell, nickel water tower, 46" long with tower down, 1939	1200	2000	3000
Jr. Fire Emergency Truck	Red cab-over-engine and body, one-piece chrome wraparound narrow bumper and 24-hole grille with plastic vertical-pair headlights, 6 3/4" long, 1968	50	75	100
Jr. Fire Emergency Truck	Red cab-over-engine and body, wider one-piece chrome wraparound narrow bumper and 4-slot grille with 2 square plastic headlights, 6 3/4" long, 1969	50	75	100
Jr. Fire Snorkel Truck	Red cab-over-engine and body, chrome one-piece narrow wraparound bumper and 24-hole grille with plastic vertical-pair headlights, 11 1/2" long, 1968	100	150	200
Jr. Fire Snorkel Truck	Red cab-over-engine and body, full-width chrome one-piece bumper and 4-slot grille with 2 square plastic headlights, 11" long, 1969	60	150	200
Jr. Hook-n-Ladder Aerial Truck	Red cab-over-engine tractor and semi-trailer, white high-sides ladder, chrome one-piece wraparound bumper and 24-hole grille, plastic veritcal-pair headlights, 17" long, 1967	100	150	200

NAME	DESCRIPTION	GOOD	EX	MINT
Jr. Hook-n-Ladder Aerial Truck	Red cab-over-engine tractor with one-piece 4-slot grille and 2 square plastic headlights, red semi-trailer, white high-sides ladder, plastic vertical-pair headlights, 17" long, 1969	75	115	150
Ladder Fire Truck	Red except for bright-metal V-nose radiator, headlights and ladder, black wooden wheels, 12" long, 1941	125	200	250
Ladder Truck	Red except for 2 yellow sectional ladders, enclosed square cab, 22 3/4" long, 1933	300	450	600
Ladder Truck	Red except for 2 yellow ladders, enclosed square cab with sharply protruding visor, 22 3/4" long, 1934	200	300	400
Ladder Truck	Red except for 2 yellow ladders, enclosed square cab with sharply protruding visor, bright-metal radiator front, 22 3/4" long, 1935	250	375	500
Ladder Truck	Duo-tone slant design, white front, hood sides, fenders and 2 ladders, rest is red, square enclosed cab with sharply protruding visor, 22 3/4" long, 1936	150	225	300
Ladder Truck	Duo-tone slant design, white front, hood sides, fenders and 2 ladders, rest is red, square enclosed cab with sharply protruding visor, no headlights, 22 3/4" long, 1937	135	200	275
Ladder Truck	Duo-tone slant design, white front, fenders, hood sides and 2 ladders, rest is red, enclosed cab, 24" long, 1939	200	300	400
Ladder Truck	All red except for bright-metal grille and headlights, 2 white ladders, 24" long, 1939	200	300	400
Ladder Truck	All red except for yellow severely streamlined, skirted fenders and lower doors, white ladders, bright-metal grille, no bumper, 17 1/2" long, 1940	200	300	400
Ladder Truck	Modified duo-tone slant design, white front, front fenders and lower doors, white ladders, bright-metal grille, no bumper, 17 1/2" long, 1941	200	300	400
Ladder Truck	Red except for 2 white ladders, bright-metal radiator grille and headlights, 24" long, 1941	125	200	250
Police Squad Truck	Yellow front and front fenders, dark blue-green body, yellow fire extinguisher, 21 1/2" long over ladders, 1947	275	500	750
Pumping Fire Engine	Red except for nickel stack on boiler, nickel rims on pump flywheels, nickel-rim headlights and searchlight, 23 1/2" long, 1929	3000	3500	4000
Rear Steer Trailer Fire Truck	Red except for 2 white 10-rung ladders, chrome one-piece grille, headlights and bumper, 20" long, 1952	125	200	250
Red Cross Ambulance	All white, removable fabric canopy with a red cross and "Ambulance" in red capitals, 14 1/2" long, 1958	60	95	125
Suburban Pumper	Red station-wagon body, white plastic wraparound bumpers, one-piece grille and double headlights, 15" long, 1964	100	150	200

NAME	DESCRIPTION	GOOD	EX	MINT
Texaco Fire Chief American LaFrance Pumper	Promotional piece, red rounded-front enclosed cab and body, white one-piece underbody, running boards and rear step, 25" long, 1962	200	300	400
Trailer Ladder Truck	Duo-tone slant design, tractor unit has yellow front, lower hood sides and lower doors, red hood top, enclosed cab and semi-trailer, nickel 10-rung ladders, 30" long with ladders, 1940	200	300	400
Trailer Ladder Truck	All red except for cream removable rider saddle, 3 bright-metal 10-rung ladders, 20" long over ladders, 1941	150	225	300
Water Tower Truck	Red except nickel 2-bar front bumper, red nickel-rim headlights plus searchllight on cowl, nickel latticework water tower, 45 1/2" long with tower down, 1929	3000	4500	6000
Jr. Hook-n-Ladder Aerial Truck	Red cab-over-engine tractor and semi-trailer, white high-sides ladder, one-piece chrome 4-slot grille, 2 square plastic headlights, 17" long, 1969	75	115	150

Farm and Construction Equipment

NAME	DESCRIPTION	GOOD	EX	MINT
Aerial Tower Tramway	Two tapering dark green 33 1/2" tall towers and 12" square bases, black hand crank, 1928	3000	4000	5000
Big Derrick	Red mast and 20" boom, black base, 24" tall, 1921	600	900	1200
Brute Articulated Scooper	Yellow front-loading scoop, cab, articulated frame and rear power unit, black radiator, exhaust, steering wheel and driver's seat, 5 1/2" long, 1970	50	75	100
Brute Double Dump Train	Yellow hood, fenders and back on tractor unit, yellow coupled bottom-dumping earth carriers, 9 1/2" long, 1969	50	75	100
Brute Dumping Scraper	Yellow hood, fenders and back on 2-wheel tractor unit, yellow scraper-dump unit, 7" long, 1970	50	75	100
Brute Farm Tractor-n-Cart	Bright blue tractor body and rear fenders, green plastic radiator, engine, exhaust and driver's seat, bright blue detachable, square, 2-wheel open cart, 6 1/4" long, 1969	30	40	55
Brute Road Grader	Yellow hood, cab, frame and adjustable blade, black radiator, driver's seat and steering wheel, 6 1/2" long, 1970	50	75	100
Cement Mixer on Treads	Medium gray except for black treads and water tank, 16" tall, 1929-31	2500	3500	4500
Cement Mixer on Wheels	Medium gray except for black cast steel wheels and water tank, 14 1/2" tall, 1926-29	700	900	1500
Concrete Mixer	Medium gray except for black cast-steel wheels, black water tank, with wood-handle, steel-blade scoop shovel, 17 3/4" long with tow bar up, 1926	475	715	950
Concrete Mixer	Green except for black cast-steel wheels, crank, gears, and band mixing drum, 10 1/2" long, 1930	175	265	350
Concrete Mixer	Yellow-orange frame and base, red hopper and drum, black crank handle, 10 1/2" long, 1936	110	175	225
Concrete Mixer	Red frame and base, cream-yellow hopper, drum and crank handle, 10 1/2" long, 1941	125	185	250

NAME	DESCRIPTION	GOOD	EX	MINT
Concrete Mixer	Green frame, base, crank, crank handle and bottom of mixing drum, gray hopper and top of drum, 9 5/8" long, 1949	100	150	200
Concrete Mixer on Tread	Gray except for black water tank, with wood-handle, steel-blade scoop shovel, 15 3/4" long, 1929	1500	2500	4000
Concrete Mixer with Motor Sound	Green frame, base, crank, crank handle and bottom of mixing drum, gray hopper and top of drum, with rat-rat-tat motor-noise sound when crank rotates drum, 9 5/8" long, 1950	75	115	150
Dandy Digger	Yellow seat lower control lever and main boom, black underframe, skids, shovel and arm, 38 1/2" long with shovel arm extended, 1953	75	115	150
Dandy Digger	Red main frame, operators, seat and boom, black shovel, arm, under frame and twin skids, 27" long, 1931	100	160	215
Dandy Digger	Yellow main frame, operators, seat and boom, green shovel, arm, under frame and twin skids, 27" long, 1936	85	130	175
Dandy Digger	Yellow main frame, operators, seat and boom, brown shovel, arm, under frame and twin skids, 27" long, 1941	95	145	195
Dandy Digger	Yellow seat, lower control lever and main boom, black underframe, skids, shovel, arm and control lever, 38 1/2" long with shovel arm extended, 1953	75	115	150
Digger	Red main frame, operators, seat and boom, black shovel, arm, lower frame and twin skids, curved connecting rod, boom tilts down for digging, 11 1/2" long with shovel arm extended, 1935	100	150	200
Dredge	Red corrugated roof and base with 4 wide black wheels, red hubs, black boiler, floor, frame boom and clamshell bucket, 19" long, 1924	750	1000	1500
Dredge on Tread	Red corrugated roof and base with crawler treads with red side frames, red hubs, black boiler, floor, frame boom and clamshell bucket, 21" long, 1929	5000	7000	9000
Giant Digger	Red main frame, operators, seat and boom, black shovel, arm, lower frame and twin skids, boom tilts down for digging, 42" long with shovel arm extended, 1931	275	415	550
Giant Digger	Red main frame, operators, seat and boom, black shovel, arm, lower frame and twin skids, curved connecting rod, boom tilts down for digging, 31" long with shovel arm extended, 1933	265	395	525
Giant Digger	Yellow main frame, operators, seat and boom, green shovel, arm, lower frame and twin skids, boom tilts down for digging, 11 1/2" long with shovel arm extended, 1936	85	130	175
Giant Digger	Yellow main frame, operators, seat and boom, brown shovel, arm, lower frame and twin skids, boom tilts down for digging, 11 1/2" long with shovel arm extended, 1941	75	115	155

Buddy L

NAME	DESCRIPTION	GOOD	EX	MINT
Gradall	Bright yellow truck and superstructure, black plastic bumper and radiator, 32" long with digging arm extended, 1965	250	500	750
Hauling Rig with Construction Derrick	Duo-tone slant design tractor, yellow bumper, lower hood and cab sides, white upper hood and cab, white trailer except for yellow loading ramp, overall 38 1/2" long, 1953	175	250	400
Hauling Rig with Construction Derrick	Yellow tractor unit, green semi-trailer, winch on front of trailer make rat-tat motor sound, 36 3/4" long, 1954	110	175	225
Hoisting Tower	Dark green, hoist tower and three distribution chutes, 29" tall, 1928-31	1500	2000	2500
Husky Tractor	Bright yellow body and large rear fenders, black engine block, exhaust, steering wheel and driver's seat, 13" long, 1966	50	75	100
Husky Tractor	Bright blue body and large rear fenders, black engine block, exhaust, steering wheel and driver's seat, 13" long, 1969	40	60	80
Husky Tractor	Bright yellow body, red large rear fenders and wheels, black engine block, exhaust, steering wheel and driver's seat, 13" long, 1970	30	45	65
Improved Steam Shovel	Black except for red roof and base, 14" tall, 1927-29	1000	1500	2000
Improved Steam Shovel on Treads	Black except for red roof and tread frames, 17" tall, 1929-30	5000	7000	9000
Junior Excavator	Red shovel, arm, underframe, control lever and twin skids, yellow boom, rear lever, frame and seat, 28" long, 1945	75	115	150
Junior Line Steam Shovel on Treads	Black except for red roof and tread frames, 14" tall, 1930-32	1000	1500	2000
Mechanical Crane	Orange removable roof, boom and wheels in black cleated rubber crawler treads, olive-green enclosed cab and base, hand crank with rat-tat motor noise, 20" tall, 1950	175	265	350
Mechanical Crane	Orange removable roof, boom, yellow wheels in white rubber crawler treads, olive-green enclosed cab and base, hand crank with rat-tat motor noise, 20" tall, 1952	150	225	300
Mobile Construction Derrick	Orange laticework main mast, swiveling base, yellow latticework boom, green clamshell bucket and main platform base, 25 1/2" long with boom lowered, 1953	150	250	350
Mobile Construction Derrick	Orange laticework main mast, swiveling base, yellow latticework boom, gray clamshell bucket, green main platform base, 25 1/2" long with boom lowered, 1955	150	250	350
Mobile Construction Derrick	Orange laticework main mast, swiveling base, yellow latticework boom, gray clamshell bucket, orange main platform base, 25 1/2" long with boom lowered, 1956	150	250	350
Mobile Power Digger Unit	Clamshell dredge mounted on 10-wheel truck, orange truck, yellow dredge cab on swivel base, 31 3/4" long with boom lowered, 1955	125	185	250

NAME	DESCRIPTION	GOOD	EX	MINT
Mobile Power Digger Unit	Clamshell dredge mounted on 6-wheel truck, orange truck, yellow dredge cab on swivel base, 31 3/4" long with boom lowered, 1956	115	175	230
Overhead Crane	Black folding end frames and legs, braces, red crossbeams and platform, 45" long, 1924	2000	2500	3000
Pile Driver on Treads	Black except for red roof and tread frames, 22 1/2" tall, 1929	5000	7500	10000
Pile Driver on Wheels	Black except for red roof and base, 22 1/2" tall, 1924-27	800	1500	3000
Polysteel Farm Tractor	Orange molded plastic 4-wheel tractor, silver radiator front, headlights, and motor parts, 12" long, 1961	75	115	150
Pull-n-Ride Horse-Drawn Farm Wagon	Red 4-wheel steel hopper-body wagon, detailed litho horse, 22 3/4" long, 1952	150	225	300
Road Roller	Dark green except for red roof and rollers, nickel plated steam cylinders, 20" long, 1929-31	3000	4000	5000
Ruff-n-Tuff Tractor	Yellow grille, hood and frame, black plastic engine block and driver's seat, 10 1/2" long, 1971	50	75	100
Sand Loader	Warm gray except for 12 black buckets, 21" long, 18" high, 1924	300	500	700
Sand Loader	Warm gray except for 12 black buckets, chain-tension adjusting device at bottom of elevator side frames, 21" long, 1929	225	335	450
Sand Loader	Yellow except for 12 black buckets, chain-tension adjusting device at bottom of elevator side frames, 21" long, 1931	175	265	350
Scoop-n-Load Conveyor	Cream body frame, green loading scoop, black circular crank operates black rubber cleated conveyor belt, 18" long, 1953	75	115	150
Scoop-n-Load Conveyor	Cream body frame, green loading scoop, black circular crank operates black rubber cleated conveyor belt, "PORTABLE" decal in red, 18" long, 1954	65	100	135
Scoop-n-Load Conveyor	Cream body frame, red loading scoop and chute, bright-plated circular crank operates black rubber cleated conveyor belt, "PORTABLE" decal in white, 18" long, 1955	60	95	125
Scoop-n-Load Conveyor	Cream body frame, red loading scoop and chute, bright-plated circular crank operates black rubber cleated conveyor belt, "PORTABLE" decal in yellow, 18" long, 1956	55	85	115
Side Conveyor Load-n-Dump	Yellow plastic front end including cab, yellow steel bumper, green frame and dump body, red conveyor frame with chute, 20 1/2" long, 1953	70	125	145
Side Conveyor Load-n-Dump	All steel yellow cab, hood, bumper and frame, white dump body and tailgate, red conveyor frame with chute, 21 1/4" long, 1954	65	100	135
Side Conveyor Load-n-Dump	All steel yellow cab, hood, bumper and frame, deep blue dump body, white tailgate, red conveyor frame with chute, 21 1/4" long, 1955	60	95	125

NAME	DESCRIPTION	GOOD	EX	MINT
Sit-n-Ride Dandy Digger	Yellow seat, lower control lever and main boom, green underframe, skids, shovel, arm and control lever, 38 1/2" long with shovel arm extended, 1955	75	115	150
Small Derrick	Red 20" movable boom and 3 angle-iron braces, black base and vertical mast, 21 1/2" tall, 1921	500	750	1000
Steam Shovel	Black except for red roof and base, 25 1/2" tall, 1921-22	150	200	250
Traveling Crane	Red crane, carriage, and long cross beams, hand wheel rotates crane boom, 46" long, 1928	1275	1900	2550
Trench Digger	Yellow main frame, base, and motor housing, red elevator and conveyor frame and track frames, 20" tall, 1928-31	3500	5000	7500

Sets

NAME	DESCRIPTION	GOOD	EX	MINT
Army Combination Set	Searchlight repair-it truck, transport truck and howitzer, ammunition conveyor, stake delivery truck, ammo, soldiers, 1956	300	400	500
Army Commando Set	14 1/2" truck, searchlight unit, two-wheel howitzer, soldiers, 1957	125	185	250
Big Brute 3-Piece Hi-Way Set	Bulldozer, dump truck, yellow 4-wheel trailer, 1971	100	150	200
Big Brute 3-Piece Road Set	Cement mixer truck, scooper, dump truck, 1971	125	185	250
Big Brute 4-Piece Freeway Set	Scraper, grader, scooper and dump truck, 1971	125	185	250
Brute 5-Piece Hi-Way Set	Bulldozer, grader, scraper, dumping scraper and double dump train, 1970	50	75	100
Brute Fire Department Set	Semi-trailer aerial ladder truck, fire pumper, fire wrecker, brute tow truck, 1970	75	115	150
Brute Fleet Set	Car carrier with 2 plastic coupes, dump truck, pickup truck, cement mixer truck, tow truck, 1969	85	130	175
Delivery Set Combination	16 1/2" long wrigley express truck, 15" long sand and stone dump truck, 14 1/4" long freight conveyor and 14 1/4" long stake delivery truck, 1955	175	265	350
Family Camping Set	Camper-n-cruiser truck, 15 1/2" long maroon suburban wagon, and brown/light gray-beige folding teepee camping trailer, 1963	60	95	125
Family Camping Set	Blue camping trailer and suburban wagon, blue camper-n-cruiser, 1964	50	75	100
Farm Combination Set	Cattle transport stake truck with 6 plastic steers, hydraulic farm supplies trailer dump truck, trailer and 3 farm machines and farm machinery trailer hauler truck, 1956	100	150	200
Fire Department Set	Aerial ladder fire engine, fire pumper with action hydrant that squirts water, 2 plastic hoses, 2 plastic firemen, fire chief's badge, 1960	250	375	500
Freight Conveyor and Stake Delivery Truck	Blue frame 14 1/4" long conveyor, red, white and yellow body 14 3/4" long truck, 1955	125	185	250
GMC Air Defense Set	15" long, GMC army searchlight truck, 15" long, GMC signal corps truck, two 4-wheel trailers, plastic soliders, 1957	250	400	500

NAME	DESCRIPTION	GOOD	EX	MINT
GMC Brinks Bank Set	Silvery gray, barred windows on sides and in double doors, coin slot and hole in roof, brass padlock with 2 keys, pouch, paper play money, 2 gray plastic guard figures, 16" long, 1959	250	300	400
GMC Fire Department Set	Red GMC extension ladder trailer and GMC pumper with ladders and hose reel, 4-wheel red electric searchlight trailer, warning barrier, red plastic helmet, 4 firemen, policeman, 1958	275	415	550
GMC Hi-Way Maintenance Fleet	All orange, maintenance truck with trailer, sand & stone dump truck, scoop-n-load conveyor, sand hopper, steel scoop shovel, 4 white steel road barriers, 1957	200	300	400
GMC Livestock Set	Red fenders, hood, cab and frame, white flatbed cargo section , 6 section of brown plastic rail fencing, 5 black plastic steers, 14 1/2" long, 1958	200	300	400
GMC Western Roundup Set	Blue fenders, hood, cab and frame, white flatbed cargo section, plastic 6 sections of rail fencing with swinging gate, rearing and standing horse, 2 cowboys, calf, steer, 1959	200	300	400
Hi-Way Maintenance Mechanical Truck & Concrete Mixer	20" truck plus movable ramp, with duo-tone slant design, blue lower hood sides, yellow hood top and cab, 10 3/4" blue and yellow mixer, overall 36" long, 1949	160	245	325
Highway Construction Set	Orange and black bulldozer and driver, truck with orange pickup body, orange dump truck, 1962	200	300	400
Interstate Highway Set	All orange, parks department dumper, landscape truck, telephone truck, 3 lichen trees, 2 sawhorse barriers, steel scoop shovel, 2 metal drums, 4 orange traffic cones, 4 workmen, 1959	250	400	500
Interstate Highway Set	All orange, husky dumper, contractor's truck and ladder, utility truck, plastic pickaxe, spade, shovel, nail keg, 1960	250	350	500
Jr. Animal Farm Set	6 1/2" long Jr. Giraffe Truck, 6 1/4" long Jr. Kitty Kennel, 11 1/4" long Jr. Pony Trailer with Sportster, 1968	125	185	250
Jr. Fire Department	17" long Jr. hook-n-ladder aerial truck, 11 1/2" long Jr. fire snorkel, 6 3/4" long Jr. fire emergency truck, all have 24-hole chrome grilles, 1968	125	185	250
Jr. Fire Department	17" long Jr. hook-n-ladder aerial truck, 11 1/2" long Jr. fire snorkel, 6 3/4" long Jr. fire emergency truck, all have 4-slot grilles and 2 square plastic headlights, 1969	125	185	250
Jr. Hi-Way Set	Yellow and black Jr. scooper tractor, yellow and white Jr. cement mixer truck, yellow Jr. dump truck, 1969	200	300	400
Jr. Sportsman Set	Jr. camper pickup with red cab and body and yellow camper, towing 6" plastic runabout on yellow 2-wheel boat trailer, 1971	50	75	100
Loader, Dump Truck, and Shovel Set	Conveyor, green body sand and gravel dump truck, 8 3/4" long green-enameled steel scoop shovel, 1954	100	150	200

Buddy L

NAME	DESCRIPTION	GOOD	EX	MINT
Loader, Dump Truck, and Shovel Set	Conveyor, blue body sand and gravel dump truck, 8 3/4" long blue-enameled steel scoop shovel, 1955	85	130	175
Mechanical Hauling Truck and Concrete Mixer	Truck with duo-tone slant design, red-orange lower hood sides, dark green upper hood, cab, trailer and ramp, 9 5/8" green mixer, gray hopper, 38" long with ramps, 1950	160	245	325
Mechanical Hauling Truck and Concrete Mixer	Truck with duo-tone slant design, red-orange lower hood sides, dark green upper hood, cab, ramp, yellow trailer, 9 5/8" green mixer, gray hopper, 38" long with ramps, 1951	150	225	300
Polysteel Farm Set	Blue milkman truck with rack and 9 milk bottles, red and gray milk tanker, orange farm tractor, 1961	75	115	150
Road Builder Set	Green and white cement mixer truck, yellow and black bulldozer, red dump truck, husky dumper, 1963	200	300	400
Truck with Concrete Mixer Trailer	22" truck with duo-tone slant design,green fenders and lower sides, yellow squarish cab and body, 10" mixer with yellow frame and red hopper, overall 34 1/2" long, 1937	175	265	350
Truck with Concrete Mixer Trailer	22" truck with duo-tone slant design,green front and lower hood sides, yellow upper hood, cab and body, 10" mixer with yellow frame and red hopper, overall 32 1/2" long, 1938	165	250	330
Warehouse Set	Coca-cola truck, 2 hand trucks, 8 cases coke bottles, store-door delivery truck, lumber, sign, 2 barrels, forklift, 1958	175	265	350
Warehouse Set	Coca-cola truck, 2 hand trucks, 8 cases coke bottles, store-door delivery truck, sign, 2 barrels, forklift, 1959	150	225	300
Western Roundup Set	Turquoise fenders, hood, cab and frame, white flatbed cargo section, plastic 6 sections of rail fencing with swinging gate, rearing and standing horse, 2 cowboys, calf, steer, 1960	100	150	200

Trucks

NAME	DESCRIPTION	GOOD	EX	MINT
"Big Fella" Hydraulic Rider Dumper	Duo-tone slant design, yellow front and lower hood, red upper cab, dump body and upper hood, rider seat has large yellow sunburst-style decal, 26 1/2" long, 1950	110	175	225
"Standard Oil" Tank Truck	Duo-tone slant design, white upper cab and hood, red lower cab, grill, fenders and tank, rubber wheels, electric headlights, 26" long, 1936-37	2000	3500	5000
Air Force Supply Transport	Blue, blue removable fabric canopy, rubber wheels, decals on cab doors, 14 1/2" long, 1957	125	250	350
Air Mail Truck	Black front, hood fenders, enclosed cab and opening doors, red enclosed body and chassis, 24" long, 1930	675	1000	1400
Allied Moving Van	Tractor and semi-trailer van, duo-tone slant design, black front and lower sides, orange hood top, cab and van body, 29 1/2" long, 1941	600	900	1200

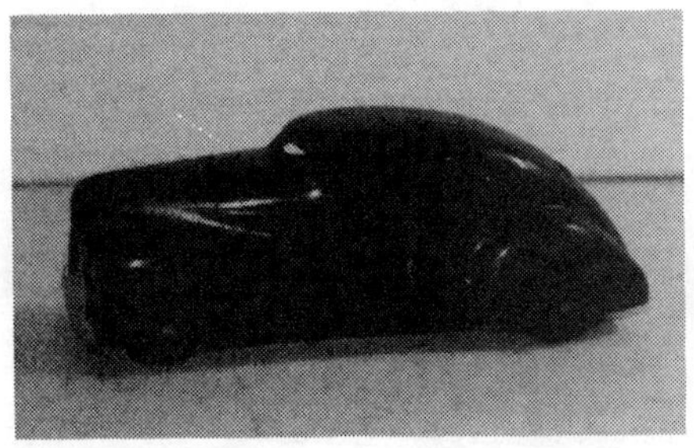

Top to Bottom: Sedan, Wyandotte; Stake Bed Truck, 1930s, Wyandotte; L Tanker, 1930, Wyandotte; 1913 Mercer, Schuco; Road Tug Service Truck, 1966, Structo; GT-40, Bandai; Steam Shovel, Structo; Excalibur, Bandai.

Buddy L

NAME	DESCRIPTION	GOOD	EX	MINT
Army Electric Searchlight Unit	Shiny olive drab flatbed truck, battery operated searchlight, 14 3/4" long, 1957	125	225	325
Army Half-Track and Howitzer	Olive drab with olive drab carriage, 12 1/2" truck, 9 3/4" gun, overall 22 1/2" long, 1953	85	130	175
Army Half-Track with Howitzer	Olive drab steel, red firing knob on gun, 17" truck, 9 3/4" gun, overall 27" long, 1955	100	150	200
Army Medical Corps Truck	White, black rubber tires on white steel disc wheels, 29 1/2" long, 1941	125	185	250
Army Searchlight Repair-It Truck	Shiny olive drab truck and flatbed cargo section, 15" long, 1956	70	100	145
Army Suppy Truck	Shiny olive drab truck and removable fabric cover, 14 1/2" long, 1956	65	100	135
Army Transport Truck and Trailer	Olive drab truck, 20 1/2" long, trailer 34 1/2" long, 1940	250	350	450
Army Transport with Howitzer	Olive drab, 12" truck, 9 3/4" gun, overall 28" long, 1953	100	150	200
Army Transport with Howitzer	Olive drab steel, 17" truck, 9 3/4" gun, overall 27" long, 1955	150	250	350
Army Transport with Howitzer	Olive drab steel, re-firing knob on gun, 17" truck, 9 3/4" gun, overall 27" long, 1954	115	175	230
Army Transport with Tank	Olive drab, 15 1/2" long truck, 11 1/2" long detachable 2-wheel trailer, overall 26 1/2" long, 7 1/2" long tank, 1959	100	150	200
Army Troop Transport with Howitzer	Dark forest green truck and gun, canopy mixture of greens, 14" long truck, 12" long, gun, overall 25 3/4" long, 1965	100	150	200
Army Truck	Olive drab, 20 1/2" long, 1939	110	175	225
Army Truck	Olive drab, 17" long, 1940	150	200	250
Atlas Van Lines	Green tractor unit, chrome one-piece toothed grille and headlights, green lower half of semi-trailer van body, cream upper half, silvery roof, 29" long, 1956	200	300	400
Auto Hauler	Yellow cab-over-engine tractor unit and double-deck semi-trailer, three 8" long vehicles, 25 1/2" long, 1968	75	115	150
Auto Hauler	Snub-nose medium blue tractor unit and double-deck semi-truck trailer, 3 plastic coupes, overall 27 1/2" long, 1970	65	95	130
Baggage Rider	Duo-tone horizontal design, green bumper, fenders and lower half of truck, white upper half, 28" long, 1950	250	175	500
Baggage Truck	Black front, hood, and fenders, doorless cab, yellow four-post stake sides, 2 chains across back, 26 1/2" long, 1927	2000	3000	4000
Baggage Truck	Black front, hood, and fenders, open door cab, yellow four-post stake sides, 2 chains across back, 26 1/2" long, 1930	950	1425	1900
Baggage Truck	Green front, hood, and fenders, non-open doors, yellow cargo section slat sides, 26 1/2" long, 1933-34	1000	2000	3000
Baggage Truck	Green front, hood, and fenders, non-open doors, yellow cargo section solid sides, 26 1/2" long, 1933	1000	2000	3000
Baggage Truck	Green front, hood, and fenders, non-open doors, yellow cargo section slat or solid sides, metal grille, 26 1/2" long, 1935	1000	2000	3000

NAME	DESCRIPTION	GOOD	EX	MINT
Baggage Truck	Duo-tone slant design, yellow fenders, green hood top, cab, and removable rider seat, 26 1/2" long, 1936	1200	2400	3600
Baggage Truck	Duo-tone slant design, yellow skirted fenders and cargo section, green hood top, enclosed cab, 27 3/4" long, 1938	1000	2000	3000
Baggage Truck	Green hood, fenders, and cab, yellow cargo section, no bumper, 17 1/2" long, 1945	175	265	350
Baggage Truck	Black front, hood, and fenders, enclosed cab with opening doors, nickel-rim, red-shell headlights, yellow stake body, 26 1/2" long, 1930-32	6000	9000	12000
Big Brute Dumper	Yellow cab-over-engine, frame and tiltback dump section with cab shield, striped black and yellow bumper, black grille, 8" long, 1971	50	75	100
Big Brute Mixer Truck	Yellow cab-over-engine, body and frame, white plastic mixing drum, white plastic seats, 7" long, 1971	35	50	70
Big Mack Dumper	Off-white front, hood cab and chassis, blue-green tiltback dump section, white plastic bumper, 20 1/2" long, 1964	75	115	150
Big Mack Dumper	Yellow front, hood cab, chassis and tiltback dump section, black plastic bumper, 20 1/2" long, 1967	70	100	140
Big Mack Dumper	Yellow front, hood cab, chassis and tiltback dump section, black plastic bumper, single rear wheels, 20 1/2" long, 1968	65	95	130
Big Mack Dumper	Yellow front, hood cab, chassis and tiltback dump section, black plastic bumper, heavy-duty black ballon tires on yellow plastic 5-spoke wheels, 20 1/2" long, 1971	60	90	120
Big Mack Hydraulic Dumper	Red hood, cab and tiltback dump section with cab shield, white plastic bumper, short step ladder on each side, 20 1/2" long, 1968	50	75	100
Big Mack Hydraulic Dumper	White hood, cab and tiltback dump section with cab shield, white plastic bumper, short step ladder on each side, 20 1/2" long, 1969	45	65	90
Big Mack Hydraulic Dumper	Red hood, cab and tiltback dump section with cab shield, dump body sides have a large circular back, white plastic bumper, short step ladder on each side, 20 1/2" long, 1970	40	60	80
Boat Transport	Blue flatbed truck carrying 8" litho metal boat, boat deck white, hull red, truck 15" long, 1959	100	200	300
Borden's Milk Delivery Van	White upper cab-over-engine van body and sliding side doors, yellow lower body, metal-handle yellow plastic tray and 6 white milk bottle with yellow caps, 11 1/2" long, 1965	125	200	275
Brute Car Carrier	Bright blue cab-over-engine tractor unit and detachable double-deck semi-trailer, 2 plastic cars, 10" long, 1969	60	95	125
Brute Cement Mixer Truck	Sand-beige cab-over-engine body and frame, white plastic mixing drum, white plastic seats, 5 1/4" long, 1968	35	55	75

NAME	DESCRIPTION	GOOD	EX	MINT
Brute Cement Mixer Truck	Blue cab-over-engine body and frame, white plastic mixing drum, white plastic seats, white-handled crank rotates drum, 5 1/4" long, 1969	30	45	65
Brute Dumper	Red cab-over-engine body and cab shield on tiltback dump section, wide chrome wraparound bumper, 5" long, 1968	35	55	75
Brute Monkey House	Yellow cab-over-engine body, striped orange and white awning roof, cage on back, 2 plastic monkeys, 5" long, 1968	50	75	100
Brute Monkey House	Yellow cab-over-engine body, red and white awning roof, cage on back, 2 plastic monkeys, 5" long, 1969	40	60	80
Brute Sanitation Truck	Lime green cab-over-engine and frame, white open-top body, wide chrome wraparound bumper, 5 1/4" long, 1969	50	75	100
Buddy "L" Milk Farms Truck	White body, black roof, short hood with black wooden headlights, 13 1/2" long, 1945	175	350	525
Buddy "L" Milk Farms Truck	Light cream body, red roof, nickel glide headlights, sliding doors, 13" long, 1949	200	400	600
Camper	Bright medium blue steel truck and camper body, 14 1/2" long, 1964	60	95	125
Camper	Medium blue truck and back door, white camper body, 14 1/2" long, 1965	50	75	100
Camper-n-Cruiser	Powder blue pickup truck and trailer, pale blue camper body, 24 1/2" long, 1963	60	95	125
Camper-n-Cruiser	Bright medium blue camper with matching boat trailer and 8 1/2" long plastic sport cruiser, ovreall 27" long, 1964	50	75	100
Campers Truck	Turquoise pickup truck, pale turquoise plastic camper, 14 1/2" long, 1961	55	85	110
Campers Truck with Boat	Green-turquoise pickup truck, lime green camper body, red plastic runabout boat on camper roof, 14 1/2" long, 1962	50	100	150
Campers Truck with Boat	Green-tuquoise pickup, no side mirror, lime green camper body with red plastic runabout boat on top, 14 1/2" long, 1963	50	100	150
Camping Trailer and Wagon	Bright medium blue suburban wagon, matching teepee trailer, overall 24 1/2" long, 1964	60	95	125
Cattle Transport Truck	Red with yellow stake sides, 15" long, 1956	75	115	150
Cattle Transport Truck	Green and white with white stake sides, 15" long, 1957	75	115	150
Cement Mixer Truck	Turquoise body, tank ends, and chute, white side ladder, water tank, mixing drum and loading hopper, 16 1/2" long, 1964	60	95	125
Cement Mixer Truck	Red body, tank ends, and chute, white side ladder, water tank, mixing drum and loading hopper, 15 1/2" long, 1965	75	115	150
Cement Mixer Truck	Red body, tank ends, and chute, white water tank, mixing drum and loading hopper, black wall tires, 15 1/2" long, 1967	60	95	125
Cement Mixer Truck	Red body, tank ends, and chute, white water tank, mixing drum and loading hopper, whitewall tires, 15 1/2" long, 1968	50	75	100

Buddy L

NAME	DESCRIPTION	GOOD	EX	MINT
Cement Mixer Truck	Snub-nosed yellow body, cab, frame and chute, white plastic mixing drum, loading hopper and water tank with yellow ends, 16" long, 1970	35	50	70
Charles Chip Delivery Truck Van	Tan-beige body, decal on sides has brown irregular center resembling a large potato chip, 1966	125	200	275
City Baggage Dray	Green front, hood, and fenders, non-open doors, yellow stake-side cargo section, 19" long, 1934	200	400	600
City Baggage Dray	Green front, hood, and fenders, non-open doors, yellow stake-side cargo section, bright metal grille, 19" long, 1935	200	400	600
City Baggage Dray	Duo-tone slant design, green front and fenders, yellow hood top and cargo section, 19" long, 1936	200	400	600
City Baggage Dray	Duo-tone slant design, green front and fenders, yellow hood top and cargo section, dummy headlights, 19" long, 1937	200	400	600
City Baggage Dray	Duo-tone slant design, green front and skirted fenders, yellow hood top, enclosed cab and cargo section, 20 3/4" long, 1938	175	350	500
City Baggage Dray	Light green except for aluminum-finish grille, no bumper, black rubber wheels, 20 3/4" long, 1939	175	350	500
City Baggage Dray	Cream except for aluminum-finish grille, no bumper, black rubber wheels, 20 3/4" long, 1940	175	350	500
Coal Truck	Black hopper body and fully enclosed cab with opening doors, red wheels, 25" long, 1930	3000	4500	6000
Coal Truck	Black front, hood, fenders, doorless cab, red chassis and disc wheels, 25" long, 1926	1500	2500	3500
Coal Truck	Black front, hood, fenders, sliding discharge door on each side of hopper body, red chassis and disc wheels, 25" long, 1927	1200	2400	3200
Coca-Cola Bottling Route Truck	Bright yellow, with small metal hand truck, 8 or 6 yellow cases of miniature green Coke bottles, 14 3/4" long, 1955	75	115	150
Coca-Cola Delivery Truck	Orange-yellow cab and double-deck, open-side cargo, 2 small hand trucks, 4 red and 4 green cases of bottles, 15" long, 1960	60	95	125
Coca-Cola Delivery Truck	Orange-yellow cab and double-deck, open-side cargo, 2 small hand trucks, 4 red and 4 green cases of bottles, 15" long, 1963	45	65	90
Coca-Cola Delivery Truck	Orange-yellow cab and double-deck, open-side cargo, 2 small hand trucks, 4 red and 4 green cases of bottles, 15" long, 1964	60	95	125
Coca-Cola Delivery Truck	Red lowercab-over-engine and van body, white upper cab, left side of van lifts to reveal 10 miniature bottle cases, 9 1/2" long, 1971	25	40	55
Coca-Cola Route Truck	Bright yellow, with 2 small metal hand trucks and 8 yellow cases of miniature green Coke bottles, 14 3/4" long, 1957	110	175	225

Buddy L

NAME	DESCRIPTION	GOOD	EX	MINT
Coke Coffee Co. Delivery Truck Van	Black lower half of body, orange upper half, roof and sliding side doors, 1966	85	130	175
Colt Vacationer	Blue/white colt sportsliner with trailer carrying 8 1/2" long red/white plastic sport cruiser, overall 22 1/2" long, 1967	60	95	125
Curtiss Candy Trailer Van	Blue tractor and bumper, white semi-trailer van, blue roof, chrome one-piece toothed grille and headlights, white drop-down rear door, 32 3/4" long with tailgate/ramp lowered, 1955	250	400	500
Dairy Transport Truck	Duo-tone slant design, red front and lower hood sides, white hood top, cab and semi-trailer tank body, tank opens in back, 26" long, 1939	150	225	300
Deluxe Auto Carrier	Turquoise tractor unit, aluminum loading ramps, 3 plastic cars, overall 34" long including, 1962	70	125	145
Deluxe Camping Outfit	Turquoise pickup truck and camper, and 8 1/2" long plastic boat on pale turquoise boat trailer, overall 24" long, 1961	60	95	125
Deluxe Hydraulic Rider Dump Truck	Duo-tone slant design, red front and lower hood sides, white upper cab, dump body and chassis, red or black removable rider saddle, 26" long, 1948	175	265	350
Deluxe Motor Market	Duo-tone slant design, red front, curved bumper, lower hood and cab sides, white hood top, body and cab, 22 1/4" long, 1950	250	350	500
Deluxe Rider Delivery Truck	Duo-tone horizontal design, deep blue lower half, gray upper half, red rubber disc wheels, black barrel skid, 22 3/4" long, 1945	135	200	270
Deluxe Rider Delivery Truck	Duo-tone horizontal design, gray lower half, blue upper half, red rubber disc wheels, black barrel skid, 22 3/4" long, 1945	135	200	270
Deluxe Rider Dump Truck	Various colors, dual rear wheels, no bumper, 25 1/2" long, 1945	75	115	150
Double Hydraulic Self-Loader-n-Dump	Green front loading scoop with yellow arms attached to cab sides, yellow hood and enclosed cab, orange fram and wide dump body, 29" long with scoop lowered, 1956	85	130	175
Double Tandem Hydraulic Dump and Trailer	Truck has red bumper, hood, cab and frame, 4-wheel trailer with red tow and frame, both with white tiltback dump bodies, 38" long, 1957	85	130	175
Double-Deck Boat Transport	Light blue steel flatbed truck carrying three 8" white plastic boats with red decks, truck 15" long, 1960	100	200	300
Dr. Pepper Delivery Truck Van	White, red, and blue, 1966	85	130	175
Dump Body Truck	Black front, hood, open driver's seat and dump section, red chassis, crank windlass with ratchet raises dump bed, 25" long, 1921	800	1400	2000
Dump Body Truck	Black front, hood, open driver's seat and dump section, red chassis, chain drive dump mechanism, 25" long, 1923	1200	1800	2500
Dump Truck	Black enclosed cab and opening doors, front and hood, red dump body and chassis, crank handle lifts dump bed, 24" long, 1931	750	1125	1500

NAME	DESCRIPTION	GOOD	EX	MINT
Dump Truck	Yellow upper hood and enclosed cab, red wide-skirt fenders and open-frame chassis, blue dump body, no bumper, 17 1/4" long, 1940	85	130	175
Dump Truck	Black enclosed cab and opening doors, front and hood, red dump body and chassis, simple lever arrangement lifts dump bed, 24" long, 1930	650	975	1300
Dump Truck	Yellow enclosed cab, front and hood, red dump section, no bumper, 20" long, 1934	275	415	550
Dump Truck	Yellow enclosed cab, front and hood, red dump section, no bumper, bright-metal radiator, 20" long, 1935	325	485	650
Dump Truck	Duo-tone slant design, yellow enclosed cab and hood, red front and dump body, no bumper, bright-metal headlights, 20" long, 1936	250	375	500
Dump Truck	Duo-tone slant design, yellow enclosed cab and hood, red front and dump body, no bumper, dummy headlights, 20" long, 1937	250	375	500
Dump Truck	Duo-tone slant design, red lower cab, lower hood, front and dump body, yellow upper hood, upper cab and chassis, no bumper, 22 1/4" long, 1939	250	375	500
Dump Truck	Duo-tone slant design, red front, fenders and lower doors, white upper, bright radiator grille and headlights, no bumper, 22 1/4" long, 1939	250	375	500
Dump Truck	Green except for cream hood top and upper enclosed cab, no bumper, bright-metal headlights and grille, 22 1/4" long, 1941	85	130	175
Dump Truck	White upper hood, enclosed cab, wide-skirt fenders and open-frame chassis, orange dump body, bright-metal grille, no bumper, 17 3/8" long, 1941	85	130	175
Dump Truck	Red hood top and cab, white or cream dump body and frame, no bumper, 17 1/2" long, 1945	75	115	150
Dump Truck	Various colors, black rubber wheels, 12" long, 1945	50	75	100
Dump Truck	Duo-tone slant design, red front, fenders and dump body, yellow hood top, upper sides, upper cab and chassis, no bumper, 22 1/2" long, 1948	125	185	250
Dump Truck-Economy Line	Dark blue dump body, remainder is yellow, bright-metal grille and headlights, no bumper or running boards, 12" long, 1941	75	115	150
Dump-n-Dozer	Orange husky dumper truck and orange flatbed 4-wheel trailer carrying orange bulldozer, 23" long including trailer, 1962	75	115	150
Dumper with Shovel	Turquoise body, frame and dump section, white one-piece bumper and grille guard, large white steel scoop shovel, 15" long, 1962	75	115	150
Dumper with Shovel	Medium green body, frame and dump section, white one-piece bumper and grille guard, no side mirror, large white steel scoop shovel, 15" long, 1963	75	115	150

Buddy L

NAME	DESCRIPTION	GOOD	EX	MINT
Dumper with Shovel	Medium green body, frame and dump section, white one-piece bumper and grille guard, no side mirror, large white steel scoop shovel, spring suspension on front axle only, 15" long, 1964	75	115	150
Dumper with Shovel	Orange body, frame and dump section, chrome one-piece grille, no bumper guard, no side mirror, large white steel scoop shovel, no spring suspension, 15 3/4" long, 1965	75	115	150
Express Trailer Truck	Red tractor unit, hood, fenders and enclosed cab, green semi-trailer van with removable roof and drop-down rear door, 23 3/4" long, 1933	350	525	700
Express Trailer Truck	Red tractor unit, hood, fenders and enclosed cab, green semi-trailer van with removable roof and drop-down rear door, bright-metal dummy headlights, 23 3/4" long, 1934	350	525	700
Express Truck	All black except red frame, enclosed cab with opening doors, nickel-rim, red-shell headlights, 6 rubber tires, double bar front bumper, 24 1/2" long, 1930-32	3000	4500	6000
Farm Machinery Hauler Trailer Truck	Blue tractor unit, yellow flatbed semi-trailer, 31 1/2" long, 1956	125	185	250
Farm Suppies Automatic Dump	Duo-tone slant design, blue curved bumper, front, lower hood sides and cab, yellow upper hood, cab and rest of body, 22 1/2" long, 1950	125	185	250
Farm Supplies Dump Truck	Duo-tone slant design, red front, fenders and lower hood sides, yellow upper hood, cab and body, 22 3/4" long, 1949	125	185	250
Farm Supplies Hydraulic Dump Trailer	Green tractor unit, long cream bocy on semi-trailer, 14 rubber wheels, 26 1/2" long, 1956	100	150	200
Fast Delivery Pickup	Yellow hood and cab, red open cargo body, removable chain across open back, 13 1/2" long, 1949	100	150	200
Finger-Tip Steering Hydraulic Dumper	Powder blue bumper, fenders, hood, cab and frame, white tiltback dump body, 22" long, 1959	75	115	150
Fisherman	Light tan pickup truck with tan steel trailer carrying plastic 8 1/2" long sport crusier, overall 24 1/4" long, 1962	80	120	160
Fisherman	Pale blue-green station wagon with 4-wheel boat trailer carrying plastic 8 1/2" long boat, overall 27 1/2" long, 1963	75	115	150
Fisherman	Metallic sage green pickup truck with boat trailer carrying plastic 8 1/2" long sport cruiser, overall 25" long, 1964	70	100	140
Fisherman	Sage gray-green and white pickup truck with steel trailer carrying plastic 8 1/2" long sport cruiser, overall 25" long, 1965	65	95	130
Flivver Dump Truck	Black except for red 8-spoke wheels, black hubs, aluminum tires, flat, open dump section with squared-off back with latching, drop-down endgate, 11" long, 1926	1500	2500	3500

Buddy L

NAME	DESCRIPTION	GOOD	EX	MINT
Flivver Huckster Truck	Black except for red 8-spoke wheels, black hubs, aluminum tires, flat, continous hard top canopy extending from enclosed cab over cargo section, 14" long, 1927	2500	4000	5500
Flivver One-Ton Express Truck	Black except for red 8-spoke wheels, black hubs, aluminum tires, flat, enclosed cab, operating steering wheel, open cargo section, 14 1/4" long, 1927	3500	5000	6500
Flivver Scoop Dump Truck	Black except for red 8-spoke wheels, 12 1/2" long, 1926-27, 1929-30	1500	2500	3500
Flivver Truck	Black except for red 8-spoke wheels with aluminum tires, black hubs, 12" long, 1924	1000	1500	2000
Ford Flivver Dump Cart	Black except for red 8-spoke wheels, black hubs, aluminum tires, flat, short open dump section tapers to point on each side, 12 1/2" long, 1926	1500	2500	3500
Frederick & Nelson Delivery Truck Van	Medium green body, roof and sliding side doors, 1966	125	200	275
Freight Delivery Stake Truck	Red hood, bumper, cab and frame, white cargo section, yellow 3-post, 3-slat removable stake sides, 14 3/4" long, 1955	75	125	150
Front Loader Hi-Lift Dump Truck	Red scoop and arms attached to white truck at rear fenders, green dump body, 17 3/4" long with scoop down and dump body raised, 1955	85	130	175
Giant Hydraulic Dumper	Red bumper, frame, hood and cab, light tan tiltback dump body and cab shield 23 3/4" long, 1960	125	185	250
Giant Hydraulic Dumper	Overall color turquoise, dump lever has a red plastic tip, 22 3/4" long, 1961	135	200	275
Giraffe Truck	Powder blue hood, white cab roof, high-sided open-top cargo section, 2 orange and yellow plastic giraffes, 13 1/4" long,1968	60	95	125
GMC Air Force Electric Searchlight Unit	All blue flatbed, off white battery operated searchlight swivel mount, decals on cab doors, 14 3/4" long, 1958	125	250	350
GMC Airway Express Van	Green hood,cab and van body, latching double rear doors, shiny metal drum coin bank and metal hand truck, 17 1/2" long with rear doors open, 1957	200	300	350
GMC Anti-Aircraft Unit with Searchlight	15" truck with four-wheel trailer, battery operated, over 25 1/4" long, 1957	200	300	400
GMC Army Hauler with Jeep	Shiny olive drab tractor unit and flatbed trailer, 10" long jeep, overall 31 1/2" long, 1958	175	275	375
GMC Army Transport with Howitzer	Shiny olive drab, 14 1/2" long, truck, overall with gun 22 1/2" long, 1957	200	300	400
GMC Brinks Armored Truck Van	Silvery gray, barred windows on sides and in double doors, coin slot and hole in roof, brass padlock with 2 keys, pouch, paper play money, 3 gray plastic guard figures, 16" long, 1958	250	300	400
GMC Coca-Cola Route Truck	Lime-yellow, with small metal hand truck and 8 cases of miniature green Coke bottles, 14 1/8" long, 1957	150	250	350
GMC Coca-Cola Route Truck	Orange-yellow, with 2 small metal hand truck and 8 cases of miniature green Coke bottles, 14 1/8" long, 1958	150	250	350

NAME	DESCRIPTION	GOOD	EX	MINT
GMC Construction Company Dumper	Pastel blue including control lever onleft and dump section with cab shield, hinged tailgate, chrome GMC bar grille, six wheels, 16" long, 1958	150	250	350
GMC Construction Company Dumper	Pastel blue including control lever onleft and dump section with cab shield, hinged tailgate, chrome GMC bar grille, four wheels, 16" long, 1959	150	250	350
GMC Deluxe Hydraulic Dumper	Pastel blue, chrome GMC bar grille, attached headlights, yellow steel scoop shovel on left side, 19" long over scraper blade, 1959	175	275	375
GMC Hi-Way Giant Trailer	Blue tractor, blue and white van, chrome GMC bar grille and headlights, blue roof on semi-trailer, white tailgate doubles as loading ramp, 18-wheeler, 31 1/4" long, 1957	200	300	400
GMC Hi-Way Giant Trailer Truck	Blue tractor, blue and white van, chrome GMC bar grille and headlights, blue roof on semi-trailer, white tailgate doubles as loading ramp, 14-wheeler, 30 3/4" long, 1958	175	275	375
GMC Husky Dumper	Red hood, bumper, cab and chassis, chrome GMC bar grille and nose emblem, white oversize dump body, red control lever on right side, 17 1/2" long, 1957	150	250	350
GMC Self-Loading Auto Carrier	Yellow tractor and double-deck semi trailer, 3 plastic cars, overall 33 1/4" long, 1959	200	300	400
GMC Signal Corps Unit	Both olive drab, 14 1/4" long truck with removable fabric canopy, 8" long four-wheel trailer, 1957	70	125	145
Grocery Motor Market Truck	Duo-tone slant design, yellow front, lower hood sides, fenders and lower doors, white hood top, enclosed cab and body, no bumper, 20 1/2" long, 1937	275	415	550
Grocery Motor Market Truck	Duo-tone slant design, yellow front, lower hood sides, skirted fenders and lower doors, white hood top, cab and body, no bumper, 21 1/2" long, 1938	275	415	550
Heavy Hauling Dumper	Red hood, bumper, cab and frame, cream tiltback dump body, 20 1/2" long, 1955	75	125	150
Heavy Hauling Dumper	Red hood, bumper, cab and frame, cream oversize dump body, hinged tailgate, 21 1/2" long, 1956	70	125	140
Heavy Hauling Hydraulic Dumper	Green hood, cab and frame, cream tiltback dump body, and cab shield, raising dump body almost to vertical, 23" long, 1956	70	105	140
Hertz Auto Hauler	Bright yellow tractor and double-deck semi- trailer, 3 plastic vehicles, 27" long, 1965	100	150	200
Hi-Lift Farm Supplies Dump	Red plastic front end including hood and enclosed cab, yellow dump body, cab shield and hinged tailgate, 21 1/2" long, 1953	100	175	225
Hi-Lift Farm Supplies Dump	All steel, red front end including hood and enclosed cab, yellow dump body, cab shield and hinged tailgate, 23 1/2" long, 1954	100	175	225

NAME	DESCRIPTION	GOOD	EX	MINT
Hi-Lift Scoop-n-Dump Truck	Orange truck with deeply fluted sides, dark green scoop on front rises to empty load into hi-lift cream-yellow dump body, 16" long, 1952	85	130	175
Hi-Lift Scoop-n-Dump Truck	Orange truck with deeply fluted sides, dark green scoop on front rises to empty load into hi-lift light cream dump body, 16" long, 1953	80	125	165
Hi-Lift Scoop-n-Dump Truck	Orange truck with deeply fluted sides, dark green scoop on front rises to empty load into deep hi-lift slightly orange dump body, 16" long, 1955	75	115	155
Hi-Lift Scoop-n-Dump Truck	Orange hood, fenders and cab, yellow front loading scoop and arms attached to fenders, white frame, dump body and cab shield, 17 3/4" long, 1956	70	125	145
Hi-Lift Scoop-n-Dump Truck	Blue hood, fenders and cab, yellow front loading scoop and arms attached to fenders, white frame, dump body, cab shield, and running boards, 17 3/4" long, 1957	65	100	135
Hi-Tip Hydraulic Dumper	Orange hood, cab and frame, cream tiltback dump body, and cab shield, raising dump body almost to vertical, 23" long, 1957	75	115	150
Hi-Way Maintenance Truck with Trailer	All orange except for black rack of 4 simulated floodlights behind cab, 19 1/2" long including small 2-wheel trailer, 1957	100	150	200
Highway Hawk Trailer Van	Bronze cab tractor, chrome metallized plastic bumper, grille, air cleaner and exhaust, 19 3/4" long, 1985	50	75	100
Husky Dumper	Orange wraparound bumper, body, frame and dump section, hinged tailgate, plated dump lever on left side, 15 1/4" long, 1960	75	115	150
Husky Dumper	White plastic wraparound bumper, tan body, frame and dump section, hinged tailgate, plated dump lever on left side, 15 1/4" long, 1961	70	125	140
Husky Dumper	Bright yellow, chrome one piece bumper, slotted rectangular grill and double headlights, 14 1/2" long, 1966,	75	115	150
Husky Dumper	Red hood, cab, chassis and dump section, chrome one-piece bumper and slotted grille with double headlights, 14 1/2" long, 1968	60	95	125
Husky Dumper	Yellow hood, cab, fram and tiltback dump section with cab shield, crome one-piece wraparound bumper, 14 1/2" long, 1969	50	75	100
Husky Dumper	Snub-nose red body, tiltback dump section snda cab shield, full-width crome bumperless grille, deep-tread whitewall tires, 14 1/2" long, 1970	45	70	90
Husky Dumper	Snub-nose red body, tiltback dump section snda cab shield, full-width crome bumperless grille, white-tipped dump-control lever on left, deep-tread whitewall tires, 14 1/2" long, 1971	40	60	80
Hydraulic Auto Hauler with Four GMC Cars	Powder blue GMC tractor, 7" long plastic cars, overall 33 1/2" long including loading ramp, 1958	200	300	400

NAME	DESCRIPTION	GOOD	EX	MINT
Hydraulic Construction Dumper	Red front, cab and chassis, large green dump section with cab shield, 15 1/4" long, 1962	65	100	135
Hydraulic Construction Dumper	Tan-beige front, cab and chassis, large green dump section with cab shield, 15 1/4" long, 1963	60	95	125
Hydraulic Construction Dumper	Bright blue front, cab and chassis, large green dump section with cab shield, 15 1/2" long, 1964	50	75	100
Hydraulic Construction Dumper	Bright green front, cab and chassis, large green dump section with cab shield, 14" long, 1965	50	75	100
Hydraulic Construction Dumper	Medium blue front, cab and chassis, large green dump section with cab shield, 15 1/4" long, 1967	50	75	100
Hydraulic Dump Truck	Black front, hood, fenders, open seat, and dump body, red chassis and disc hweels with aluminum tires, 25" long, 1926	1000	1500	2000
Hydraulic Dump Truck	Black front, hood, fenders, dark reddish maroon dump body, red chassis and disc wheels with 7 embossed, simulated spokes, black hubs, 25" long, 1931	1500	2500	3500
Hydraulic Dump Truck	Black front, hood, fenders and enclosed cab, red dump body, chassis and wheels with 6 embossed, simulated spokes, bright hubs, 24 3/4" long, 1933	325	485	650
Hydraulic Dump Truck	Duo-tone slant design, red hood sides, dump body and chassis, white upper hood, cab and removable rider seat, electric headlights, 24 3/4" long, 1936	1000	2000	3000
Hydraulic Dump Truck	Duo-tone slant design, red front, lower hood sides, dump body and chassis, white upper hood and cab, 26 1/2" long, 1939	1500	2500	3500
Hydraulic Dumper	Green, plated dump lever on left side, large hooks on left side hold yellow or off-white steel scoop shovel, white plastic side mirro and grille guard, 17" long, 1961	125	185	250
Hydraulic Dumper with Shovel	Green, plated dump lever on left side, large hooks on left side hold yellow or off-white steel scoop shovel, 17" long, 1960	125	185	250
Hydraulic Hi-Lift Dumper	Duo-tone slant design, green hood nose and lower cab sides, remainder white except for chrome grille, enclosed cab, 24" long, 1953	75	115	150
Hydraulic Hi-Lift Dumper	Green hood, fenders, cab, and dump-body supports, white dump body with cab shield, 22 1/2" long, 1954	85	130	175
Hydraulic Hi-Lift Dumper	Blue hood, fenders, cab, and dump-body supports, white dump body with cab shield, 22 1/2" long, 1955	75	115	150
Hydraulic Hi-Way Dumper with Scraper Blade	Orange except for row of black square across scraper edges, one-piece chrome 8-hole grille and double headlights, 17 3/4" long over blade and raised dump body, 1958	75	115	150

Buddy L

NAME	DESCRIPTION	GOOD	EX	MINT
Hydraulic Highway Dumper	Orange except for row of black square across scraper edges, one-piece chrome 8-hole grille and double headlights, no scraper blade, 17 3/4" long over blade and raised dump body, 1959	50	75	100
Hydraulic Husky Dumper	Red body, frame, dump section and cab shield, 15 1/4" long, 1962	65	100	135
Hydraulic Husky Dumper	Red body, white one-piece bumper and grille guard, heavy side braces on dump section, 14" long, 1963	50	75	100
Hydraulic Rider Dumper	Duo-tone slant design, yellow front and lower hood, red upper cab, dump body and upper hood, 26 1/2" long, 1949	175	265	350
Hydraulic Sturdy Dumper	Lime green hood, cab, fram and tiltback dump section, green lever on left side controls hydraulic dumping, 14 1/2" long, 1969	50	75	100
Hydraulic Sturdy Dumper	Yellow hood, cab, fram and tiltback dump section, green lever on left side controls hydraulic dumping, 14 1/2" long, 1969	50	75	100
Hydraulic Sturdy Dumper	Snub-nose greenish-yellow body, cab and tiltback dump section, white plastic seats, 14 1/2" long, 1970	45	70	90
Ice Truck	Black front, hood, fenders and doorless cab, yellow open cargo section, canvas sliding cover, 26 1/2" long, 1926	2000	3000	4000
Ice Truck	Black front, hood, fenders and enclosed cab, yellow open cargo section, canvas, ice cakes, miniature tongs, 26 1/2" long, 1930	3000	4500	6000
Ice Truck	Black front, hood, fenders and enclosed cab, yellow ice compartment, canvas, ice cakes, miniature tongs, 26 1/2" long, 1933-34	2000	3000	4000
Ice Truck	Black front, hood, fenders and enclosed cab, yellow ice compartment, 26 1/2" long, 1933	2000	3000	4000
IHC "Red Baby" Express Truck	Red doorless roofed cab, open pickup body, chassis and fenders, 24 1/4" long, 1928	1000	1500	2000
IHC "Red Baby" Express Truck	Red except for black hubs and aluminum tires, 24 1/4" long, 1929	3000	4500	6000
Insurance Patrol	Red including open driver's seat and body, brass bell on cowl and full-length handrails, 27" long, 1925	650	1000	1300
Insurance Patrol	Red including open driver's seat and body, brass bell on cowl and full-length handrails, no CFD decal, 27" long, 1928	625	950	1250
International Delivery Truck	Red except for removable black rider saddle, black-edged yellow horizontal strip on cargo body, 24 1/2" long, 1935	225	350	450
International Delivery Truck	Duo-tone slant design, red front, bumper and lower hood sides, yellow hood top, upper sides, cab and open cargo body, 24 1/2" long, 1936	200	300	400

Top to Bottom: GMC Mobil Tanker, Smith Miller; Ford Hi-Way Dump Truck, Tonka; Ford Suburban Pumper, 1960, Tonka; Ford Minute Maid Truck, 1955, Tonka; Wrecker and Coupe, 1930s, Barclay; GMC Bank of America Armored Truck, 1949, Smith Miller; Chevy U-Haul Truck, Nylint.

NAME	DESCRIPTION	GOOD	EX	MINT
International Delivery Truck	Duo-tone slant design, red front, bumper and lower hood sides, yellow hood top, upper sides, cab and open cargo body, bright metal dummy headlights, 24 1/2" long, 1938	150	225	300
International Dump Truck	Red except for bright-metal radiator grille, and black removable rider saddle, 25 3/4" long, 1935	325	485	650
International Dump Truck	Duo-tone slant design, yellow radiator, fenders, lower hood and detachable rider seat, rest of truck is red, 25 3/4" long, 1936	315	475	630
International Dump Truck	Red, with red headlights on radiator, black removable rider saddle, 25 3/4" long, 1938	125	185	250
International Railway Express Truck	Duo-tone slant design, yellow front, lower hood sides and removable vab top, green hood top, enclosed cab and van body, electric headlights, 25" long, 1937	350	525	700
International Railway Express Truck	Duo-tone slant design, yellow front, lower hood sides and removable vab top, green hood top, enclosed cab and van body, dummy headlights, 25" long, 1938	345	525	690
International Wrecker Truck	Duo-tone slant design, yellow upper cab, hood, and boom, red lower cab, fenders, grill and body, rubber tires, removable rider seat, 32" long, 1938	1500	2500	3500
Jewel Home Service Truck Van	Dark brown body and sliding side doors, 1967	125	200	275
Jewel Home Shopping Truck Van	Pale mint green upper body and roof, darker mint green lower half, no sliding doors, 1968	125	200	275
Jolly Joe Ice Cream Truck	White except for black roof, black tires and wooden wheels, 17 1/2" long, 1947	225	350	450
Jolly Joe's Popsicle Truck	White except for black roof, black tires and wooden wheels, 17 1/2" long, 1948	275	425	550
Jr. Animal Ark	Fushcia lapstrake hull, four black tires, 10 pairs of plastic animals, 5" long, 1970	40	60	80
Jr. Auto Carrier	Yellow cab-over-engine tractor unit and double-deck semi-trailer, 2 red plastic cars, 15 1/2" long, 1967	50	75	100
Jr. Auto Carrier	Bright blue cab-over-engine tractor unit and double-deck semi-trailer, 2 plastic cars, 17 1/4" long, 1969	60	95	125
Jr. Beach Buggy	Yellow hood, fenders and topless jeep body, red plastic seats, white plastic surfboard that clips to roll bar and windshield, truck 6" long, 1969	45	65	90
Jr. Beach Buggy	Lime green hood, fenders and topless jeep body, red plastic seats, lime green plastic surfboard that clips to roll bar and windshield, truck 6" long, 1971	35	50	70
Jr. Buggy Hauler	Fuschia jeep body with orange seats, orange 2-wheel trailer tilts to unload sandpiper beach buggy, 12" long including jeep and trailer, 1970	35	55	75
Jr. Camper	Red cab and pickup body wih yellow camper body, 7" long, 1971	50	75	100

Buddy L

NAME	DESCRIPTION	GOOD	EX	MINT
Jr. Canada Dry Delivery Truck	Two-tone green and pale lime green cab-over-engine body, hand truck, 10 cases of green bottles, 9 1/2" long, 1968	100	150	200
Jr. Canada Dry Delivery Truck	Two-tone green and pale lime green cab-over-engine body, hand truck, 10 cases of green bottles, 9 1/2" long, 1969	85	130	170
Jr. Cement Mixer Truck	Blue cab-over-engine body, frame and hopper, white plastic mixing drum, white plastic seats, 7 1/2" long, 1968	50	75	100
Jr. Cement Mixer Truck	Blue cab-over-engine body, frame and hopper, white plastic mixing drum, white plastic seats, wide one-piece chrome bumper, 7 1/2" long, 1969	35	50	70
Jr. Dump Truck	Red cab-over-engine, frame and tiltback dump section, plastic vertical headlights, 7 1/2" long, 1967	50	75	100
Jr. Dumper	Avocado cab-over-engine, frame and tiltback dump section with cab shield, one-piece chrome bumper and 4-slot grille, 7 1/2" long, 1969	335	55	75
Jr. Giraffe Truck	Turquoise cab-over-engine body, white cab roof, plastic giraffe, 6 1/2" long, 1968	50	75	100
Jr. Giraffe Truck	Turquoise cab-over-engine body, white cab roof, plastic giraffe, 6 1/4" long, 1969	40	60	80
Jr. Kitty Kennel	Pink cab-over-engine body, white cab roof, 4 white plastic cats, 6 1/4" long, 1969	55	85	115
Jr. Kitty Kennel	Pink cab-over-engine body, white cab roof, 4 colored plastic cats, 6 1/4" long, 1968	60	95	125
Jr. Sanitation Truck	Blue cab-over-engine, white frame, refuse body and loading hopper, 10" long, 1968	75	115	150
Jr. Sanitation Truck	Yellow cab-over-engine and underframe, refuse body and loading hopper, full width bumper and grille, 10" long, 1969	75	115	150
Junior Line Air Mail Truck	Black enclosed cab, red chassis and body, headlights and double bar bumper, 6 rubber tires, 24" long, 1930-32	3000	4000	5000
Junior Line City Dray	Black, front, hood and fenders, 5-digit decal license plate, 24" long, 1930	400	5500	7000
Junior Line Dairy Truck	Stake-bed style truck, black front, hood, and enclosed cab with opening doors, blue-green stake body, red chassis, 6 miniature milk cans with removable lids, 24" long, 1930	1500	2500	3500
Junior Line Dump Truck	Black enclosed cab, front, hood and chassis, red dump body front and back are higher than sides, 21" long, 1933	1500	2500	3500
Kennel Trucks	Medium blue pickup body and cab, clear plastic 12 section kennel with 12 plastic dogs fits in cargo box, 13 1/2" long, 1964	60	90	120
Kennel Trucks	Turquoise pickup body and cab, clear plastic 12 section kennel with 12 plastic dogs fits in cargo box, 13 1/2" long, 1965	60	95	125

NAME	DESCRIPTION	GOOD	EX	MINT
Kennel Trucks	Bright blue pickup body and cab, clear plastic 12 section kennel with 12 plastic dogs fits in cargo box, 13 1/4" long, 1966	95	145	190
Kennel Trucks	Bright blue pickup body and cab, clear plastic 12 section kennel with 12 plastic dogs fits in cargo box, 13 1/4" long, 1967	85	130	175
Kennel Trucks	Cream yellow pickup body and cab, clear plastic 12 section kennel with 12 plastic dogs fits in cargo box, 13 1/4" long, 1968	80	120	160
Kennel Trucks	Red-orange pickup body and cab, yellow roof 6 section kennel with 6 plastic dogs fits in cargo box, 13 1/4" long, 1969	65	100	135
Kennel Trucks	Snub-nosed red orange body and cab, plastic kennel section in back, 6 kennels with 6 plastic dogs, 13 1/4" long, 1970	60	95	125
Lumber Truck	Black front, hood, fenders, cabless open seat and low-sides cargo bed, red bumper, chassis and a pair of removable solid stake sides, load of lumber pieces, 24" long, 1924	1200	2400	3600
Lumber Truck	Black front, hood, fenders, doorless cab and low-sides cargo bed, red bumper, chassis and a pair of removable solid stake sides, load of 12 to 16 lumber pieces, 25 1/2" long, 1926	2000	3000	4000
Mack Hydraulic Dumper	Red front, hood, cab, chassis and tiltback dump section with cab shield, white plastic bumper, 20 1/2" long, 1965	60	95	125
Mack Hydraulic Dumper	Red front, hood, cab, chassis and tiltback dump section with cab shield, white plastic bumper, short step ladder on each side, 20 1/2" long, 1967	50	75	100
Mack Quarry Dumper	Orange front, hood cab and chassis, blue-green tiltback dump section, white plastic bumper, 20 1/2" long, 1965	75	115	150
Mammoth Hydraulic Quarry Dumper	Deep green hood, cab and chassis, red heavily braced tiltback dump section, black plastic bumper, 23" long, 1962	65	100	135
Mammoth Hydraulic Quarry Dumper	Deep green hood, red cab, chassis and heavily braced tiltback dump section, black plastic bumper, 22 1/2" long, 1963	60	90	125
Marshall Field Delivery Truck Van	Hunter's green body, sliding doors and roof, 1966	125	200	275
Milkman Truck	Medium blue hood, cab and flatbed body, white side rails, eight 3" white plastic milk bottles with red or green caps, 14 1/4" long, 1961	110	175	225
Milkman Truck	Deep cream hood, cab and flatbed body, white side rails, fourteen 3" white plastic milk bottles with red caps, 14 1/4" long, 1962	100	150	200
Milkman Truck	Light blue hood, cab and flatbed body, white side rails, fourteen 3" white plastic milk bottles with red and green caps, 14 1/4" long, 1963	85	130	175

Buddy L

NAME	DESCRIPTION	GOOD	EX	MINT
Milkman Truck	Light yellow hood, cab and flatbed body, white side rails, fourteen 3" white plastic milk bottles with red and green caps, 14 1/4" long, 1964	75	115	150
Milkman Truck	Medium blue hood, cab and flatbed body, white side rails, eight 3" white plastic milk bottles with red or green caps, 14 1/4" long, 1961	110	175	225
Milkman Truck	Deep cream hood, cab and flatbed body, white side rails, fourteen 3" white plastic milk bottles with red caps, 14 1/4" long, 1962	100	150	200
Milkman Truck	Light blue hood, cab and flatbed body, white side rails, fourteen 3" white plastic milk bottles with red and green caps, 14 1/4" long, 1963	85	130	175
Milkman Truck	Lime yellow hood, cab and flatbed body, white side rails, fourteen 3" white plastic milk bottles with red and green caps, 14 1/4" long, 1964	75	115	150
Mister Buddy Ice Cream Truck	White cab-over-engine van body, pale blue or off-white plastic underbody and floor, 11 1/2" long, 1964	75	115	150
Mister Buddy Ice Cream Truck	White cab-over-engine van body, red plastic underbody and floor, 11 1/2" long, 1966	65	100	135
Mister Buddy Ice Cream Truck	White cab-over-engine van body, red plastic underbody and floor, red bell knob, 11 1/2" long, 1967	55	85	115
Model T Flivver Truck	Black except for red 8-spoke wheels with aluminum tires, black hubs, 12" long, 1924	1000	1500	2000
Motor Market Truck	Duo-tone horizontal design, white hood top, upper cab and high partition in cargo section, yellow-orange grille, fenders, lower hood and cab sides, 21 1/2" long, 1941	200	350	550
Moving Van	Black front, hood and seat, red chassis and disc wheels with black hubs, green van body, roof extends forward above open driver's seat, 25" long, 1924	1200	2000	3000
Overland Trailer Truck	Yellow tractor unit with encllosed cab, red semi-trailer and 4-wheel full trailer with removable roofs, length of 3 units 39 3/4" long, 1935	350	525	700
Overland Trailer Truck	Duo-tone slant design, green and yellow tractor unit with yellow cab, red semi-trailer and 4-wheel full trailer with yellow removable roofs, length of 3 units 39 3/4" long, 1936	325	485	650
Overland Trailer Truck	Duo-tone slant design, green and yellow semi-streamlined tractor and green hood sides, yellow hood, chassis, enclosed cab, 40" long over three units, 1939	350	550	700
Overland Trailer Truck	Duo-tone horizontal design, red and white tractor has red front, lower half chassis, chassis, enclosed cab, 40" long over three units, 1939	350	550	700

Buddy L

NAME	DESCRIPTION	GOOD	EX	MINT
Pepsi Delivery Truck	Powder blue hood and lower cab, white upper cab and double-deck cargo section, 2 hand trucks, 4 blue cases of red bottles, 4 red cases of blue bottles, 15" long, 1970	60	95	125
Polysteel Boat Transport	Medium blue soft plastic body, steel flatbed carrying 8" white plastic runabout boat with red deck, truck 12 1/2" long, 1960	75	115	150
Polysteel Coca-Cola Delivery Truck	Yellow plastic truck, slanted bottle racks, 8 red coke cases with green bottles, small metal hand truck, 12 1/2" long, 1961	50	75	100
Polysteel Coca-Cola Delivery Truck	Yellow plastic truck, slanted bottle racks, 8 green coke cases with red bottles, small metal hand truck, 12 1/4" long, 1962	60	90	120
Polysteel Dumper	Green soft molded plastic front, cab and frame, yellow steel dump body with sides rounded at back, hinged tailgate, 13" long, 1959	100	150	200
Polysteel Dumper	Medium blue soft molded plastic front, cab and frame, off-white steel dump body with sides rounded at back, hinged tailgate, 13" long, 1960	87	130	175
Polysteel Dumper	Orange plastic body and tiltback dump section with cab shield, "Come-Back Motor" if truck is pulled backward it rolls ahead when released, 13" long, 1961	75	115	150
Polysteel Dumper	Orange plastic body and tiltback dump section with cab shield, no "Come-Back Motor", no door decals, 13 1/2" long, 1962	60	95	125
Polysteel Highway Transport	Red soft plastic tractor, cab roof lights, double horn, radio antenna and side fuel tanks, white steel semi-trailer van, 20 1/2" long, 1960	100	150	200
Polysteel Hydraulic Dumper	Beige soft molded-plastic front, cab and frame, off-white steel dump section with sides rounded at rear, 13" long, 1959	60	95	125
Polysteel Hydraulic Dumper	Red soft molded-plastic front, cab and frame, light green steel dump section with sides rounded at rear, 13" long, 1960	80	120	160
Polysteel Hydraulic Dumper	Yellow soft plastic body, frame and tiltback ribbed dump section with cab shield, 13" long, 1961	75	115	150
Polysteel Hydraulic Dumper	Red soft plastic body, frame and tiltback ribbed dump section with cab shield, 13" long, 1962	65	100	130
Polysteel Milk Tanker	Red soft plastic tractor unit, light bluish-gray semi-trailer tank with red ladders and five dooms, 22" long, 1961	60	95	125
Polysteel Milk Tanker	Turquoise soft plastic tractor unit, light bluish-gray semi-trailer tank with red ladders and five dooms, 22" long, 1961	60	95	125
Polysteel Milkman Truck	Light blue soft plastic front, cab and frame, light yellow steel open cargo section with 9 oversized white plastic milk bottles, 11 3/4" long, 1960	65	100	130

VEHICLES

Buddy L

NAME	DESCRIPTION	GOOD	EX	MINT
Polysteel Milkman Truck	Light blue soft plastic front, cab and frame, light blue steel open cargo section with 9 oversized white plastic milk bottles, 11 3/4" long, 1961	60	95	125
Polysteel Milkman Truck	Turquoise soft plastic front, cab and frame, light blue steel open cargo section with 9 oversized white plastic milk bottles with red caps, 11 3/4" long, 1962	35	50	70
Polysteel Supermarket Delivery	Medium blue soft molded-plastic front, hood, cab and frame, steel off-white open cargo section, 13" long, 1959	75	115	150
Pull-N-Ride Baggage Truck	Duo-tone horizontal design, light cream upper half, off-white lower half and bumper, 24 1/4" long, 1953	150	225	300
R E A Express Truck	Dark green cab-over-engine van body, sliding side doors, double rear doors, white plastic one-piece bumper, 11 1/2" long, 1964	200	300	400
R E A Express Truck	Dark green cab-over-engine van body, sliding side doors, double rear doors, white plastic one-piece bumper, no spring suspension, 11 1/2" long, 1965	130	195	260
R E A Express Truck	Dark green cab-over-engine van body, sliding side doors, double rear doors, white plastic one-piece bumper, no spring suspension, side doors are embossed "BUDDY L", 11 1/2" long, 1966	125	185	250
Railroad Transfer Rider Delivery Truck	Duo-tone horizontal design, yellow upper half, hood top, cab and slatted caro sides, green lower half, small hand truck, 2 milk cans with removable lids, 23 1/4" long, 1949	70	100	140
Railroad Transfer Store Door Delivery	Duo-tone horizontal design, yellow hood top, cab and upper body, red lower half of hood and body, small hand truck, 2 metal drums with coin slots, 23 1/4" long, 1950	90	135	180
Railway Express Truck	Red tractor unit, enclosed square cab, green 12 1/4" long 2-wheel semi-trailer van with removable roof, "Wrigley's Spearmint Gum" poster on trailer sides, 23" long, 1935	375	565	750
Railway Express Truck	Duo-tone slant design, tractor unit has white skirted fenders and hood sides, green hood top, enclosed cab and chassis, green semi-trailer with white removable roof, 25" long, 1939	350	475	700
Railway Express Truck	Duo-tone slant design, tractor has silvery and hood sides, green hood top, enclosed cab, green semi-trailer, "Wrigley's Spearmint Gum" poster on trailer sides, 23" long, 1935	400	600	800
Railway Express Truck	Black front hood, fenders, seat and low body sides, dark green van body, red chassis, 25" long, 1926	2200	3500	4500
Railway Express Truck	Dark green or light green screen body, double-bar nickel front bumper, brass radiator knob, red wheels, 25" long, 1930	1500	2500	3500

Buddy L

NAME	DESCRIPTION	GOOD	EX	MINT
Railway Express Truck	Yellow and green tractor unit has white skirted fenders and hood sides, green hood top, enclosed cab and chassis, green semi-trailer with yellow removable roof, 25" long, 1940	330	495	660
Railway Express Truck	Duo-tone horizontal design, tractor unit has yellow front, lower door and chassis, green hood top and enclosed upper cab, semi-trailer has yellow lower sides, 25" long, 1941	325	485	650
Railway Express Truck	Deep green plastic "Diamond T" hood and cab, deep green steel frame and van body with removable silvery roof, small 2-wheel hand truck, steel 4-rung barrel skid, 21" long, 1952	200	300	400
Railway Express Truck	Green plastic hood and cab, green steel high-sides open body, frame and bumper, small 2-wheel hand truck, steel 4-rung barrel skid, 20 3/4" long, 1953	125	185	250
Railway Express Truck	Green all-steel hood, cab, frame and high-sides open bady, sides have 3 horizontal slots in upper back corners, 22" long, 1954	75	115	150
Ranchero Stake Truck	Medium green, white plastic one-piece bumper and grille guard, 4-post, 4-slat fixed stake sides and cargo section, 14" long, 1963	50	75	100
Rider City Special Delivery Truck Van	Duo-tone horizontal design, yellow upper half including hood top and cab, brown removable van roof, warm brown front and lower half of van body, 24 1/2" long, 1949	150	225	300
Rider Dump Truck	Duo-tone horizontal design, yellow hood top, upper cab and upper dump body, red front, hood sides, lower doors and lower dump body, no bumper, 21 1/2" long, 1945	160	245	325
Rider Dump Truck	Duo-tone horizontal design, yellow hood top, upper cab and upper dump body, red front, hood sides, lower doors and lower dump body, no bumper, 23" long, 1947	75	115	150
Rider Van Lines Trailer	Duo-tone slant design, black front and lower hood sides and doors, deep red hood top, enclosed cab and chassis, 35 1/2" long, 1949	350	525	700
Rival Dog Food Delivery Van	Cream front, cab and boxy van body, metal drum coin bank with "RIVAL DOG FOOD" label in blue, red, white and yellow, 16 1/2" long, 1956	160	245	325
Robotoy	Black fenders and chassis, red hood and enclosed cab with small visor, green dump body's front and back are higher than sides, 21 5/8" long, 1932	750	1000	1500
Rockin' Giraffe Truck	Powder blue hood, cab, and high-sided open-top cargo section, 2 orange and yellow plastic giraffes, 13 1/4" long, 1967	75	115	150
Ruff-n-Tuff Cement Mixer Truck	Yellow snub-nosed cab-over-engine body, frame and water-tank ends, white plastic water tank and mixing drum, white seats, 16" long, 1971	35	55	75

Buddy L

NAME	DESCRIPTION	GOOD	EX	MINT
Ruff-n-Tuff Log Truck	Yellow snub-nose cab-over-engine, frame and shallow truck bed, black full-width grille, 16" long, 1971	50	75	100
Saddle Dump Truck	Duo-tone slant design, yellow front, fenders and removable rider seat, red enclosed square cab and dump body, no bumper, 19 1/2" long, 1937	200	300	400
Saddle Dump Truck	Duo-tone slant design, yellow front, fenders, lower hood and cab, and removable rider seat, rest of body red, no bumper, 21 1/2" long, 1939	125	185	250
Saddle Dump Truck	Duo-tone horizontal design, deep blue hood top, upper cab and upper dump body, orange fenders radiator front lower two-thirds of cab and lower half of dump body, 21 1/2" long, 1941	85	130	175
Sand and Gravel Rider Dump	Duo-tone horizontal design, blue lower half, yellow upper half including hoop top and enclosed cab, 24" long, 1950	350	525	700
Sand and Gravel Truck	Black body, doorless roofed cab and steering wheel, red chassis and disc wheels with black hubs, 25 1/2" long, 1926	1500	2500	3500
Sand and Gravel Truck	Dark or medium green hood, cab, roof lights and skirted body, white or cream dump section, 13 1/2" long, 1949	100	150	200
Sand and Gravel Truck	Duo-tone horizontal design, red front, bumper, lower hood, cab sides, chassis and lower dump body sides, white hood top, enclosed cab and upper dump body, 23 3/4" long, 1949	350	525	700
Sand and Gravel Truck	Black except for red chassis and wheels, nickel-rim, red-shell headlights, enclosed cab with opening doors, 25 1/2" long, 1930-32	2000	3000	5000
Sand Loader and Dump Truck	Duo-tone horizontal design, yellow hood top and upper dump blue cab sides, frame and lower dump body, red loader on dump with black rubber conveyor belt, 24 1/2" long, 1950	175	265	350
Sand Loader and Dump Truck	Duo-tone horizontal design, yellow hood top and upper dump blue cab sides, frame and lower dump body, red loader on dump with black rubber conveyor belt, 24 1/2" long, 1952	60	95	125
Sanitation Service Truck	Blue front fenders, hood, cab and chassis, white encllosed dump section and hinged loading hopper, one-piece chrome bumper, plastic windows in garbage section, 16 1/2" long, 1967	100	150	200
Sanitation Service Truck	Blue front fenders, hood, cab and chassis, white encllosed dump section and hinged loading hopper, one-piece chrome bumper, no plastic windows in garbage section, 16 1/2" long, 1968	75	115	150
Sanitation Service Truck	Blue snub-nose hood, cab and frame, whote cargo dump body and rear loading unit, 2 round plastic headlights, 17" long, 1972	75	115	150
Sears, Roebuck Delivery Truck Van	Gray-green and off-white, no side doors, 1967	125	200	275
Self-Loading Auto Carrier	Medium tan tractor unit, 3 plastic cars, overall 34" long including loading ramp, 1960	85	130	175

NAME	DESCRIPTION	GOOD	EX	MINT
Self-Loading Boat Hauler	Pastel blue tractor and semi-trailer with three 8 1/2" long boats, overall 26 1/2" long, 1962	100	200	300
Self-Loading Boat Hauler	Pastel blue tractor and semi-trailer with three 8 1/2" long boats, no side mirror on truck, overall 26 1/2" long, 1963	125	225	350
Self-Loading Car Carrier	Lime green tractor unit, 3 plastic cars, overall 33 1/2" long including, 1963	75	115	150
Self-Loading Car Carrier	Beige-yellow tractor unit, 3 plastic cars, overall 33 1/2" long including, 1964	60	95	125
Shell Pickup and Delivery	Reddish-orange hood and body, open cargo section with solid sides, chain across back, red coin-slot oil drum with Shell emblem and lettering, 13 1/4" long, 1950	135	200	275
Shell Pickup and Delivery	Yellow-orange hood and body, open cargo section, 3-curved slots toward rear in sides, chains across back, red coin-slot oil drum with Shell emblem and lettering, 13 1/4" long, 1952	125	185	250
Shell Pickup and Delivery	Yellow-orange hood and body, open cargo section with 3-curved slots toward rear in sides, red coin-slot oil drum with Shell emblem and lettering, 13 1/4" long, 1953	110	175	225
Smoke Patrol	Lemon-yellow body, six wheels, garden hose attaches and water squirts through large chrome swivel-mount water cannon on rear deck, 7" long, 1970	50	75	100
Sprinkler Truck	Black front, hood, fenders and cabless open driver's seat, red bumper and chassis, bluish-gray-green water tank, 25" long, 1929	2500	3500	4500
Stake Body Truck	Black cabless open driver's seat, hood, front fenders and flatbed body, red chassis and 5 removable stake sections, 25" long, 1921	825	1300	1875
Stake Body Truck	Black cabless open driver's seat, hood, front fenders and flatbed body, red chassis and 5 removable stake sections, cargo bed with low sidesboards, drop-down tailgate, 25" long, 1924	725	1200	1675
Standard Coffee Co. Delivery Truck Van	1966	125	200	275
Stor-Dor Delivery	Red hood and body, open cargo body with 4 long horizontal slots in sides, plated chains across open back, 14 1/2" long, 1955	125	185	250
Street Sprinkler Truck	Black front, hood, front fenders and cabless open driver's seat, red bumper and chassis, bluish-gray-green water tank, 25" long, 1929	1000	1800	2600
Street Sprinkler Truck	Black front, hood, and fenders, open cab, nickel-rim, red-shell headlights, double bar front bumper, bluish-gray-green water tank, 6 rubber tires, 25" long, 1930-32	3000	3500	4000
Sunshine Delivery Truck Van	Bright, yellow cb-over-engine van body and opening double rear doors, off-white plastic bumper and under body, 11 1/2" long, 1967	125	200	275

NAME	DESCRIPTION	GOOD	EX	MINT
Super Motor Market	Duo-tone horizontal design, white hood top, upper cab and high partition in cargo section, yellow-orange lower hood and cab sides, semi-trailer carrying supplies, 21 1/2" long, 1942	300	500	700
Supermarket Delivery	All white except for rubber wheels, enclosed cab, pointed nose, bright-metal one-piece grille, 13 3/4" long, 1950	125	185	250
Supermarket Delivery	Blue bumper, front, hood, cab and frame, one-piece chrome 4-hole grille and headlights, 14 1/2" long, 1956	75	115	150
Tank and Sprinkler Truck	Black front, hood, fenders, doorless cab and seat, dark green tank and side racks, black or dark green sprinkler attachment, 26 1/4" long with sprinkler attachment, 1924	4000	5500	7000
Teepee Camping Trailer and Wagon	Maroon suburban wagon, 2-wheel teepee trailer and its beige plastic folding tent, overall 24 1/2" long, 1963	150	225	300
Texaco Tank Truck	Red steel GMC 550-series blunt-nose tractor and semi-trailer tank, 25" long, 1959	175	250	400
Tom's Toasted Peanuts Delivery Truck Van	Light tan-beige body, no seat or sliding doors, blue bumpers, floor and underbody, 11 1/2" long, 1973	125	200	275
Trail Boss	Red, square-corner body with sloping sides, open cockpit, white plastic seat, 7" long, 1970	40	60	80
Trail Boss	Lime green, square-corner body with sloping sides, open cockpit, yellow plastic seat, 7" long, 1971	35	55	75
Trailer Dump Truck	Cream tractor unit with enclosed cab, dark blue semi-trailer dump body with high sides and top-hinged opening endgate, no bumper, 20 3/4" long, 1941	75	115	155
Trailer Van Truck	Red tractor and van roof, blue bumper, white semi-trailer van, chrome one-piece toothed grille and headlights, white drop-down rear door, 29" long with tailgate/ramp lowered, 1956	150	225	300
Trailer Van with Tailgate Loader	Green high-impacted styrene plastic tractor on steel frame, cream steel detachable semi-trailer van with green roof and crank operated tailgate, 33" long with tailgate lowered, 1953	125	185	250
Trailer Van with Tailgate Loader	Green steel tractor, bumper, chrome one-piece toothed grille and headlights, cream van with green roof and tailgate loader, 31 3/4" long, with tailgate down, 1954lgate lowered, 1953	125	185	250
Traveling Zoo	Red high side pickup with yellow plastic triple-cage unit, 6 campartments with plastic animals, 13 1/4" long, 1965	85	130	175
Traveling Zoo	Red high side pickup with yellow plastic triple-cage unit, 6 campartments with plastic animals, 13 1/4" long, 1967	75	115	150
Traveling Zoo	Yellow high side pickup with red plastic triple-cage unit, 6 campartments with plastic animals, 13 1/4" long, 1969	65	95	130
Traveling Zoo	Snub-nosed yellow body and cab, 6 red plastic cages with 6 plastic zoo animals, 13 1/4" long, 1970	60	95	125

Buddy L

NAME	DESCRIPTION	GOOD	EX	MINT
U.S. Army Half-Track and Howitzer	Olive drab, 12 1/2" truck, 9 3/4" gun, overall 22 1/2" long, 1952	75	115	150
U.S. Mail Delivery Truck	Blue cab, hood, bumper, frame and removable roof on white van body, 23 1/4" long, 1956	225	400	575
U.S. Mail Delivery Truck	White upper cab-over-engine, sliding side doors and double rear doors, red belt-line stripe on sides and front, blue lower body, 11 1/2" long, 1964	125	200	275
U.S. Mail Truck	Shiny olive green body and bumper, yellow-cream removable van roof, enclosed cab, 22 1/2" long, 1953	225	400	575
United Parcel Delivery Van	Duo-tone horizontal design, deep cream upper half except for brown removable roof, chocolate brown front and lower half, 25" long, 1941	250	450	650
Utility Delivery Truck	Duo-tone slant design, blue front and lower hood sides, gray hood top, cab and open body with red and yellow horizontal stripe, 22 3/4" long, 1940	250	450	650
Utility Delivery Truck	Duo-tone horizontal design, green upper half including hood top, dark cream lower half, green wheels, red and yellow horizontal stripe, 22 3/4" long, 1941	125	185	250
Utility Dump Truck	Duo-tone slant design, red front, lower doord and fenders, gray chassis and enclosed upper cab, royal blue dump body, yellow removable rider seat, 25 1/2" long, 1940	125	185	250
Utility Dump Truck	Duo-tone slant design, red front, lower door and fenders, gray chassis, red upper hood, upper enclosed cab and removable rider seat, yellow body, 25 1/2" long, 1941	85	130	175
Van Freight Carriers Trailer	Bright blue streanlined tractor and enclosed cab, cream-yellow semi-trailer van, removable silvery roof, 22" long, 1949	65	100	135
Van Freight Carriers Trailer	Red streamlined tractor, bright blue enclosed cab, cream-yellow semi-trailer van, white removable van roof, 22" long, 1952	55	85	115
Van Freight Carriers Trailer	Red streamlined tractor, bright blue enclosed cab, light cream-white semi-trailer van with removable white roof, 22" long, 1953	125	185	250
Wild Animal Circus	Red tractor unit and semi-trailer, three cages with plastic elephant, lion, tiger, 26" long, 1966	150	225	300
Wild Animal Circus	Red tractor unit and semi-trailer, three cages with 6 plastic animals (adult and baby), 26" long, 1967	110	175	225
Wild Animal Circus	Red tractor unit and semi-trailer, trailer cage doors lighter red than body, 26" long, 1970	100	150	200
Wrecker Truck	Black front, hood, and fenders, open cab, 4 rubber tires, red wrecker body, 26 1/2" long, 1930	5000	7000	9000
Wrecker Truck	Duo-tone slant design, red upper cab, hood, and boom, white lower cab, grill, fenders, body, rubber wheels, electric headlights, removable rider seat, 31" long, 1936	1000	2000	3000

Buddy L

NAME	DESCRIPTION	GOOD	EX	MINT
Wrecker Truck	Black open cab, red chassis and bed, disc wheels, 26 1/2" long, 1928-29	2000	4000	6000
Wrigley Express Truck	Forest green except for chrome one-piece, three-bar grille and headlights, "Wrigley's Spearmint" poster on sides, 16 1/2" long, 1955	135	200	275
Zoo-A-Rama	Lime green Colt Sportsliner with four-wheel trailer cage, cage contains plastic tree, monkeys and bears, 20 3/4" long, 1967	100	150	200
Zoo-A-Rama	Sand yellow four-wheel trailer cage, matching Colt Sportsliner with white top, 3 plastic animals, 20 3/4" long, 1968	100	150	200
Zoo-A-Rama	Greenish-yellow four-wheel trailer cage, matching Colt Sportsliner with white top, 3 plastic animals, 20 3/4" long, 1969	85	130	175

Corgi

Airplanes

NAME	DESCRIPTION	GOOD	EX	MINT
Daily Planet Jet-Copter, No. 929		35	55	75
Spidercopter, No. 928		50	75	100

Boats and Ships

NAME	DESCRIPTION	GOOD	EX	MINT
Beatle's Yellow Submarine, No. 803		75	200	500

Cars

NAME	DESCRIPTION	GOOD	EX	MINT
Arnold Sundquist's Jet Car, No. 169		25	40	55
Batmobile, No. 267		85	130	175
Black Beauty Green Hornet, No. 268		250	375	500
Camaro Convertible	1968	35	55	75
Can-Am Porsche 917-10, No. 397		25	40	50
Dick Dastardly Car, No. 809		50	75	100
Elf Tyrrell Ford F-1, No. 158		20	35	45
Ferrari 312 B2 Formula 1, No. 152		20	30	40
Firebird, No. 343		50	75	100
Hesketh 308 Formula 1 Car, No. 160		20	35	45
James Bond Aston Martin, No. 261	Gold	125	185	250
James Bond Lotus Esprit, No. 269		75	115	150
Kojak's Buick, No. 290		40	60	80
Lotus, No. 154		45	65	90
Metropolis Buick, No. 260		37	55	75
Monkeemobile, No. 277		200	300	400
Patrick Eagle Indy Car, No. 159		25	40	50
Penguinmobile, No. 259		35	55	75
Saint's Volvo, No. 257		75	115	150
Starsky & Hutch Ford Torino, No. 292		50	75	100

Corgi

NAME	DESCRIPTION	GOOD	EX	MINT
State Landau-Queen's Jubilee, No. 41		20	30	40
The Professional's Ford Capri, No. 342		50	75	100
Thunderbird	1958	35	55	75
Thunderbird, No. 215		110	165	225
Vegas Thunderbird, No. 348		75	115	150

Motorcycles

NAME	DESCRIPTION	GOOD	EX	MINT
Spiderbike, No. 266	White tires	110	175	225

Sets

NAME	DESCRIPTION	GOOD	EX	MINT
Batman Triple Pack Gift Set, No. GS-40		225	335	450
Batmobile and Batboat, No. GS-3		200	300	400
Giant Daktari, No. 14		200	300	400
Land Rover-Pony Trailer, No. 2		75	115	150
Police Cortina, No. 18	Helicopter, ambulance	65	95	130
Tarzan Gift Set, No. GS-36		225	335	450

Space Vehicles

NAME	DESCRIPTION	GOOD	EX	MINT
Buck Rogers Starfighter, No. 647		45	70	90
James Bond Moon Buggy, No. 811		100	150	200
OO7 Space Shuttle, No. 649		45	70	90

Trucks

NAME	DESCRIPTION	GOOD	EX	MINT
Berliet Wrecker Truck, No. 1144		25	40	50
Canteen Truck, No. 471		25	40	50
Decca Radar Van, No. 1106		125	185	250
Holmes Wrecker, No. 1142		85	130	175
Human Cannonball Truck, No. 1163		35	55	75
Ice Cream Truck, No. 428		25	40	50
Jeep Tower Van, No. 65-14		125	185	250
Land Rover and Elephant, No. GS-19		50	75	100
Spider-Man Van, No. 436		25	40	50
Super Van, No. 435		25	40	50
Toy Van, No. 422		175	265	350
Vanwall, No. 150		75	115	150

Dinky

Accessories

NO.	NAME	GOOD	EX	MINT
13	"Halls Distemper" sign	150	300	600
47A	4 face traffic light	10	15	25
766	British Road Signs	70	115	175
F49D/592	Esso Gas Pumps	40	60	85
12A	G.P.O. Pillar Box	20	35	65
45	Garage	75	150	300
752	Goods Yard Crane	50	75	100
994	Loading ramp (for 582/982)	20	35	65
1003	Passengers	55	80	125

NAME	DESCRIPTION	GOOD	EX	MINT
42D	Point Duty Policeman	20	35	65
778	Road Repair Boards	10	20	30
786	Tyre rack with tyres "Dunlop"	10	20	30
	Aircraft			
749/992	Avro Vulcan Delta Wing Bomber	100	2000	5000
70A/704	Avro York	60	85	130
710	Beechcraft Bonanza 535	50	75	100
62B	Bristol Blenheim	60	85	130
998	Bristol Britannia	135	200	350
F60Z	Cierva Autogiro	75	100	150
702/999	DH Comet Airline	75	100	150
70E	Gloster Meteor	25	40	70
722	Hawker Harrier	75	100	150
66A	Heavy Bomber	145	225	450
60A	Imperial Airways Liner	135	200	350
F804	Nord 2501 Noratlas	120	175	275
60H	Singapore Flying Boat	115	170	250
F60C/892	Super G Constellation	120	175	275
734	Supermarine Swift	45	65	85
	Buses & Taxis			
40H/254	Austin Taxi	60	95	135
F29D	Autobus Parisien	80	135	200
F29F/571	Autocar Chausson	70	120	175
283	B.O.A.C. Coach	55	80	115
953	Continental Touring Coach	135	200	350
F24XT	Ford Vedette Taxi	60	95	135
284	London Taxi	25	35	50
29F/280	Observation Coach	50	75	100
F1400	Peugeot 404 Taxi	50	75	100
266	Plymouth Canadian Taxi	60	95	135
289	Routemaster Bus "Tern Shirts"	75	100	150
297	Silver Jubilee Bus	25	35	50
	Cars			
36A	Armstrong Siddeley, blue or brown	85	130	200
106/140A	Austin Atlantic Convertible, blue	60	95	150
342	Austin Mini-Moke	20	30	45
131	Cadillac Eldorado	60	95	135
32/30A	Chrysler Airflow	130	250	450
F550	Chrysler Saratoga	70	120	190
F535/24T	Citroen 2 cv	50	70	90
F522/24C	Citroen DS-19	60	80	115
F545	DeSoto Diplomat, green	80	135	215
F545	DeSoto Diplomat, orange	60	85	125
191	Dodge Royal	75	115	150
27D/344	Estate Car	45	70	115
212	Ford Cortina Rally Car	35	55	75
148	Ford Fairlane	150	300	700
148	Ford Fairlane, pale green	30	55	80
57/005	Ford Thunderbird (Hong Kong)	50	70	100
F565	Ford Thunderbird, S. African Issue, blue	80	135	215
238	Jaguar D-Type	60	86	125
157	Jaguar XK 120, green, yellow, red	50	75	100
157	Jaguar XK 120, turquoise, cerise	80	125	200
157	Jaguar XK 120, white	120	200	400
157	Jaguar XK 120, yellow/grey	80	125	200
241	Lotus Racing Car	20	30	50
231	Maserati Race Car	45	75	110

Top to Bottom: All from Dinky Toys; Model 986 Mighty Antar; Model 576 Panhard Esso Tanker; Model 965 Euclid Dumper; Model 152b Reconnaissance Car; Model 579 Simca Glass Truck; Model 514 Slumberland Guy Van; Model 553 Leyland Cement Truck; Model 899 Delahaye Fire Truck; Model 501 Foden Truck; Model 661 Recovery Tractor.

Dinky

NO.	NAME	GOOD	EX	MINT
161	Mustang Fastback	35	55	75
F545	Panhard PL17	45	70	90
F521/24B	Peugeot 403	50	75	100
115	Plymouth Fury Sports	35	55	80
F524/24E	Renault Dauphine	50	75	100
30B	Rolls Royce (1940's Version)	65	100	125
198	Rolls Royce Phantom V	50	75	100
145	Singer Vogue	40	55	80
153	Standard Vanguard	60	85	120
F24Y/540	Studebaker Commander	65	90	130
24C	Town Sedan	85	130	200
105	Triumph TR-2, grey	60	85	120
105	Triumph TR-2, yellow	75	110	175
129	Volkswagen 1300 Sedan	20	35	60
187	VW Karman Ghia	50	75	100

Emergency Vehicles

NO.	NAME	GOOD	EX	MINT
30F	Ambulance	100	160	275
F501	Citroen DS19 Police	75	95	160
F25D/562	Citroen Fire Van	60	85	135
555/955	Commer Fire Engine	60	85	135
F32D/899	Delahaye Fire Truck	100	160	275
195	Fire Chief Land Rover	35	50	85
F551	Ford Taunus Police	50	75	100
255	Mersey Tunnel Police	60	85	135
244	Plymouth Police Car	25	35	50
268	Range Rover Ambulance	25	35	50
25H/25	Streamlined Fire Engine (Post-War)	75	100	175
263	Superior Criterion Ambulance	50	75	100
956	Turntable Fire Escape (Bedford)	75	110	175
251	USA Police Car (Pontiac)	35	50	85
278	Vauxhall Victor Ambulance	55	85	115

Farm & Construction

NO.	NAME	GOOD	EX	MINT
305	"David Brown" Tractor	35	50	75
984	Atlas Digger	30	45	70
561	Blaw Knox Bulldozer	45	75	115
965	Euclid Dump Truck	45	75	115
37N/301	Field Marshall Tractor	60	85	135
105A	Garden Roller	15	25	35
324	Hayrake	30	40	60
27A/300	Massey-Harris Tractor	50	75	100
27G/342	Moto-cart	35	50	75
437	Muir Hill 2wl Loader	30	40	60
F830	Richier Road Roller	75	100	150
963	Road Grader	30	45	70
F595	Salev Crane	65	100	135

Military

NO.	NAME	GOOD	EX	MINT
622	10 Ton Army Wagon	50	85	125
621	3 Ton Army Wagon	50	85	125
692	5.5 Medium Gun	25	40	65
618	AEC with Helicopter	50	85	125
F883	AMX Bridge Layer	75	100	175
F80C/817	AMX Tank	50	75	100
677	Armoured Command Vehicle	50	85	125
30SM/625	Austin Covered Truck	85	135	275
601	Austin Paramoke	25	35	50
25WM/60	Bedford Military Truck	80	125	250
620	Berliet Missile Loader	75	100	175

Dinky

NO.	NAME	GOOD	EX	MINT
F806	Berliet Wrecker	60	90	140
651	Centurian Tank	40	60	85
612	Commando Jeep	25	35	50
30HM/624	Daimlet Ambulance	80	125	250
F810	Dodge Command Car	40	60	85
630	Ferret Armoured Car	25	35	50
F823	GMC Tanker	125	250	500
F816	Jeep	40	60	85
F80F/820	Military Ambulance	50	75	100
626	Military Ambulance	50	75	100
667	Missile Servicing Platform	75	100	175
152B	Reconnaisance Car	50	85	125
661	Recovery Tractor	60	90	140
161A	Searchlight (Pre-War)	100	175	350
660	Tank Transporter	75	100	175
	Motorcycles & Caravans			
240/44B	A.A. motorcycle patrol (Post-War)	30	45	60
190	Caravan	30	45	60
30G	Caravan (Post-War)	40	60	85
30G	Caravan (Pre-War)	50	75	100
F564	Caravane Caravelair	65	100	150
42B	Police motorcycle patrol (Post-War)	30	45	60
42B	Police motorcycle patrol (Pre-War)	50	75	100
37B	Police motorcyclist (Post-War)	30	45	60
37B	Police motorcyclist (Pre-War)	50	75	100
271	TS motorcycle patrol (Swiss Version)	65	100	150
	Space			
F281	"Pathe News" Camera Car	65	100	150
102	"The Prisoner" Mini-Moke	115	200	340
361	Galactic War Chariot	30	45	70
102	Joe's Car	60	90	140
357	Klingon Battle Cruiser	30	45	70
100	Lady Penelope's Fab 1, pink version	80	135	220
100	Lady Penelope's Fab 1, shocking pink version	115	200	340
F1406	Renault Sinpar	80	135	220
485	Santa Special Model T Ford	65	100	150
350	Tiny's Mini-Moke	60	85	120
371/803	U.S.S. Enterprise	30	45	70
	Trucks			
974	A.E.C. Hoyner Transporter	60	90	130
471	Austin Van "Nestles"	60	100	150
472	Austin Van "Raleigh"	60	100	150
470	Austin Van "Shell/BP"	60	100	150
14A/400	B.E.V. Truck	30	45	90
482	Bedford Van "Dinky Toys"	80	135	200
F898	Berliet Transformer Carrier	135	300	550
923	Big Bedford "Heinz" (Baked Beans)	100	165	275
408/922	Big Bedford (blue/yellow)	90	135	210
408/922	Big Bedford (maroon/fawn)	80	120	185
449	Chevrolet El Camino	35	65	100
F561	Citroen "Cibie" Delivery Van	65	95	140
F586	Citroen Milk Truck	145	275	600
F35A/582	Citroen Wrecker	75	120	225
571/971	Coles Mobile Crane	40	70	100
25B	Covered Wagon ("Carter Paterson")	150	300	500
25B	Covered Wagon (green, grey)	65	115	160

Dinky

NO.	NAME	GOOD	EX	MINT
28N	Delivery Van ("Atco", type 2)	200	375	600
28N	Delivery Van ("Atco", type 3)	135	200	350
28E	Delivery Van ("Ensign", type 1)	300	500	1000
28B	Delivery Van ("Pickfords", type 1)	300	500	1000
28B	Delivery Van ("Pickfords", type 2)	200	375	600
30W/421	Electric Articulated Vehicle	60	85	120
941	Foden "Mobilgas" Tanker	145	300	600
942	Foden "Regent" Tanker	135	250	500
503/903	Foden Flat Truck w/ Tailboard 1, grey/blue	140	210	450
503/903	Foden Flat Truck w/ Tailboard 1, red/black	140	210	450
503/903	Foden Flat Truck w/ Tailboard 2, blue/ yellow	90	125	210
503/903	Foden Flat Truck w/ Tailboard 2, green/ green	100	150	230
417	Ford Transit Van	15	20	30
25R	Forward Control Wagon	45	65	90
431	Guy 4 Ton Truck	70	110	185
514	Guy Van "Lyons"	275	550	1600
514	Guy Van "Slumberland"	135	300	575
431	Guy Warrior 4 Ton	150	270	450
449/451	Johnston Road Sweeper	25	50	75
419/533	Leland Comet Cement Truck	85	140	210
944	Leland Tanker "Shell/BP"	125	215	400
	Leyland Tanker "Corn Products"	700	1200	3000
25F	Market Gardeners Wagon (yellow)	65	115	160
280	Midland Bank	60	85	120
986	Mighty Antar with Propeller	125	215	400
273	Mini Mino Van ("R.A.C.")	65	115	150
274	Mini Minor Van (Joseph Mason Paints)	150	300	500
260	Morris Royal Mail	65	115	150
22C	Motor Truck (red, green, blue)	80	120	200
22C	Motor Truck (red/blue)	150	350	650
F32C/576	Panhard ("Esso")	75	120	170
F32AJ	Panhard ("Kodak")	140	250	450
F32AB/55	Panhard ("SNCF")	100	165	280
25D	Petrol Wagon ("Power")	150	300	500
982/582	Pullmore Car Transporter	75	125	175
F561	Renault Estafette	50	75	110
F571	Saviem Race Horse Van	125	225	400
F33C/579	Simca Glass Truck (grey/green)	75	120	170
F33C/579	Simca Glass Truck (yellow/green)	100	150	250
30P/440	Studebaker Tanker ("Mobilgas")	70	100	140
422/30R	Thames Flat Truck	45	75	110
31B/451	Trojan ("Dunlop")	70	110	160
F38A/895	Unic Bucket Truck	75	120	170
F36A/897	Willeme Log Truck	75	120	200
F36B/896	Willeme Semi	85	130	225

Hotwheels

Buses

S'Cool Bus	1971	37	55	75

Cars

1931 Woody	1969	8	14	24
1932 Vicky	1969	8	16	30
1936 Coupe	1969	8	16	28
1957 T-Bird	1969	12	18	30
AMX/2	1971	12	18	35

Hotwheels

NAME	DESCRIPTION	GOOD	EX	MINT
Baja Bruiser	1974	10	15	20
Beach Bomb	1969	25	37	50
Beatnik Bandit	1968	10	15	20
Boss Hoss	1971	12	25	55
Boss Hoss	With black roof, 1971	12	30	55
Boss Hoss, Chrome	1970	15	22	30
Brabham Repco	1969	6	8	10
Bugeye	1971	12	20	40
Bugeye	Shell promo pack, 1973	22	33	45
Chapparal 2G	1969	6	12	20
Classic 1931 Ford Woody		8	14	24
Classic Nomad	1970	15	30	45
Custom AMX	1969	15	22	45
Custom Barracuda	1968	15	30	50
Custom Camaro	1968	20	30	40
Custom Charger	Large rear wheels, 1969	15	35	55
Custom Charger	1969	15	35	55
Custom Corvette	1968	12	20	45
Custom Cougar	1968	18	35	65
Custom Eldorado	1968	12	18	28
Custom Firebird	1968	12	25	35
Custom Fleetside	1968	12	28	45
Custom Mustang	1968	15	30	50
Custom T-Bird	1968	12	18	30
Custom VW	1968	6	12	18
Deora	1968	15	35	55
Evil Weevil	1971	8	22	30
Ford J Car	1968	7	10	15
Ford MK IV	1969	5	8	12
Grasshopper	1971	10	18	28
Heavy Chevy	1970	16	30	40
Hot Heap	1968	7	10	15
Indy Eagle	1969	7	10	12
Jack Rabbit Special	1970	5	7	10
Jet Threat	1971	10	15	20
King Kuda	1970	12	25	35
Light My Firebird	1970	12	25	35
Lincoln Continental	1969	12	18	25
Lola GT	1969	4	8	12
Lotus Turbine	1969	5	7	10
Mantis	1970	8	12	16
McLaren	1969	5	7	10
Mercedes 280	1969	8	12	16
Mercedes C111	1971	18	35	60
Mighty Maverick	1970	20	30	40
Mod Quad	1970	12	18	25
Mongoose	1970	20	30	55
Mongoose	1971	20	30	55
Mongoose Drag	1971	15	30	50
Moving Van	1970	12	20	28
Nitty Gritty Kitty	1970	12	20	35
Olds 442	1971	50	125	225
Peepin Bomb	Shell promo pack, 1973	10	20	30
Porsch 917	1970	8	12	15
Power Pad	1970	15	25	35
Python	1968	8	12	17
Red Baron	1970	8	10	12
Red Baron	1973	17	25	35
Revvers	1973	8	15	25
Rolls Royce	Black roof, 1969	8	18	30
Rolls Royce	1969	8	12	15

Hot Wheels

NAME	DESCRIPTION	GOOD	EX	MINT
Rrrumblers	Cab and trailer, 1971	30	50	100
Rrrumblers	1972	10	15	20
Sand Crab	1970	7	10	15
Seasider with Boat	1970	25	45	65
Shelby Turbine	1969	7	10	12
Silhouette	1968	6	9	12
Sizzlers Boss 302	1970	17	25	35
Sizzlers Firebird Trans Am	1970	12	18	25
Snake	1970	20	30	55
Snake Drag	1971	15	30	50
Snorkel	1971	25	37	50
Special Delivery	1971	10	18	25
Splittin Image	1969	10	15	20
Strip Teaser	1971	12	24	35
Sugar Caddy	1971	22	33	45
Sweet Sixteen	1973	45	75	115
Swingin Wing	1970	12	18	25
T24	1971	22	33	45
The Demon	1970	10	15	20
TNT Bird	1970	12	18	25
Torero	1969	5	8	12
Tow Truck	1970	7	18	28
Tri Baby	1970	8	16	24
Turbofire	No engine hatch, 1969	5	7	10
Turbofire	1969	5	7	10
Twinmill	1969	7	10	15
What 4	1971	12	18	35
Whip Creamer	1970	10	15	20

Emergency Vehicles

NAME	DESCRIPTION	GOOD	EX	MINT
Ambulance	1970	10	15	30
Fire Chief Cruiser	1970	8	12	16
Fire Engine	1970	15	22	36

Farm and Construction Equipment

NAME	DESCRIPTION	GOOD	EX	MINT
Scooper	1971	20	35	65

Trucks

NAME	DESCRIPTION	GOOD	EX	MINT
Dump Truck	1970	12	18	25
Paddy Wagon	1970	7	10	12
Peepin Bomb	1970	5	7	12
Racer Rig	Cab and trailer, 1971	30	45	75
Waste Wagon	1971	25	45	75

Hubley

Airplanes

NAME	DESCRIPTION	GOOD	EX	MINT
American Eagle Airplane	WWII Fighter, 11" wingspan	150	225	300
American Eagle Carrier Plane	Cast metal, 11" wingspan, 1971	60	95	125
American Plane	Trimotor, open cockpit, co-pilot, pilot, cast iron	950	1425	1900
B-17 Bomber	15" wingspan	125	185	250
Bremen Junkers Monoplane		185	245	375
Corsair-Type Fighter Plane		30	45	65
Delta Wing Jet		60	95	125
DO-X Plane	Six engines, 5 7/8" wingspan, 1935	165	200	285
Flying Circus	12" wingspan	45	70	90
Lindy Plane	Cast iron, 13 1/4" long	425	645	850

Hubley

NAME	DESCRIPTION	GOOD	EX	MINT
Lindy Plane	Cast iron, 10" wingspan	325	500	650
Navy WWII Fighter	Folding wings and wheels	30	45	65
P-38 Fighter	Camouflage paint, 12 1/2" wingspan	75	100	185
P-38 Plane	Black rubber tires	70	95	165
Piper Cub Plane	Pot metal	50	75	115
Sea Plane	Orange and blue, 2 engines	35	55	75
Single Engine Fighter	3 1/2"	60	90	120
U.S. Air Force	12" wingspan	25	45	75
U.S. Army Monoplane	7 5/8" wingspan, 1941	50	75	100
U.S. Army Single Engine Fighter Plane	Black rubber tires	20	35	50

Boats and Ships

NAME	DESCRIPTION	GOOD	EX	MINT
Penn Yan Motorboat	15" long	1700	2600	3500

Buses

NAME	DESCRIPTION	GOOD	EX	MINT
School Bus	Metal, wooden wheels	60	85	125
Service Coach	Cast iron, 5" long	675	900	1500

Cars

NAME	DESCRIPTION	GOOD	EX	MINT
Auto and Trailer	Cast iron, 6 3/4" long, 1939	175	235	295
Auto and Trailer	Cast iron, sedan 7 1/4" long, trailer 7 1/8" long, 1936	185	245	315
Buick Convertible	Opening top, 6 1/2" long	50	65	90
Buick Convertible	Top down, 6 1/2" long	45	60	80
Cadillac	Black rubber tires, die cast with tin bottom plate	25	40	70
Car Carrier With Four Cars	Cast iron, 10" long	300	475	675
Chrysler Airflow	6" long	145	200	350
Chrysler Airflow	Battery operated lights, cast iron, 1934	1250	1900	2750
Chrysler Airflow Car	Cast iron, 4 1/2" long	110	195	325
Coupe	Cast iron, 9 1/2" long, 1928	900	1400	1800
Coupe	Cast iron, 8 1/2" long, 1928	600	1100	1500
Coupe	Cast iron, 7" long, 1928	400	650	800
Ford Convertible	Cast iron, V/8, 1930's	65	100	185
Ford Coupe	Cast iron, V/8, 1930's	65	100	185
Ford Model-T	Movable parts	100	150	200
Ford Sedan	Cast iron, V/8, 1930s	65	100	185
Ford Town Car	Cast iron, V/8, 1930s	65	100	185
Limousine	Cast iron, 7" long, 1918	250	325	400
Lincoln Zephyr	1937	125	165	225
Mr. Magoo Car	Old timer car, battery operated, 9" long, 1961	75	115	150
Open Touring Car	Cast iron, 7 1/2" long, 1911	675	900	1250
Packard Roadster	9 1/2" long, 1930	90	145	250
Packard Straight 8	Hood raises, detailed cast motor, cast iron, 11" long, 1927	7500	12750	18000
Race Car #22	Cast iron, 7 1/2" long	40	55	85
Race Car #2241	7" long, 1930's	50	75	100
Racer	White rubber wheels, cast iron, 7" long	200	300	400
Racer	Cast iron, 10 3/4" long, 1931	75	150	250
Racer	Nickel-plated driver, cast iron, 4 3/4" long, 1960's	75	115	150
Racer	Red with black wheels, silver grille and driver, 7 1/2" long	35	55	75
Racer #12	Die cast, prewar	60	95	125
Racer #629	7" long, 1939	50	75	135
Roadster	Cast iron, 7 1/2" long, 1920	75	150	225
Sedan	Cast iron, 7" long, 1920's	175	265	350
Service Car	5" long, 1930's	75	115	150
Speedster	Cast iron, 7" long, 1911	5000	7500	9500

Hubley

NAME	DESCRIPTION	GOOD	EX	MINT
Station Wagon	Die cast	50	75	100
Streamlined Racer	Cast iron, 5" long	70	125	140
Studebaker	Take-apart, 5" long	225	335	450
Tinytown Station Wagon and Boat Trailer		45	70	90
Touring Car	Lady and her dog seated in back, driver in front, 10" long, 1920	650	1000	1450
Yellow Cab	With luggage rack, cast iron, 8" long, 1940	325	500	700

Cycles

NAME	DESCRIPTION	GOOD	EX	MINT
Marathon Rider	Bicycle, cast iron	200	300	400

Emergency Vehicles

NAME	DESCRIPTION	GOOD	EX	MINT
Ahrens-Fox Fire Engine	Cast iron, 11 1/2" long, 1932	5000	6500	8000
Auto Fire Engine	Cast iron, 15" long, 1912	4200	5500	7000
Fire Engine	Blue and green, large rear wheels with smaller front wheels, cast iron, 10 3/4" long, 1920's	4500	5750	7500
Fire Engine	Cast iron, 14 1/2" long, 1932	1575	2250	3000
Fire Truck	5" long, 1930's	50	75	100
Fire Truck No. 468		60	95	125
Hook and Ladder Fire Truck	Rubber wheels, die cast, 18" long	150	250	500
Hook and Ladder Truck	Cast iron, 8" long	75	100	165
Hook and Ladder Truck	Cast iron, 23" long, 1912	1850	3000	4500
Hook and Ladder Truck	Cast iron, 16 1/2" long, 1926	850	1200	1700
Ladder Fire Truck	Cast iron, 5 1/2" long	40	60	80
Ladder Truck	14" long, 1940's	150	275	500
Police Patrol	With three policemen, cast iron, 11" long, 1919	900	1450	2500
Pumper Fire Truck	Plastic, 1950's	25	45	65
Seven Man Fire Patrol	Cast iron, 15" long, 1912	3575	5700	7500
Special Ladder Truck	Cast iron, 13" long, 1938	465	575	975

Farm and Construction Equipment

NAME	DESCRIPTION	GOOD	EX	MINT
Avery	Round radiator, cast iron, 4 1/2" long, 1920	175	300	450
Diesel Road Roller	Plastic, 1950's	15	25	40
Elgin Street Sweeper	Brush sweeps dirt into a bin in the body, uniformed driver, cast iron, 8 1/2" long, 1930	4000	8000	11500
Farm Trailer	With gate, 8" long	30	45	60
Ford 4000	Blue and gray, die cast, 1/12 scale	75	125	175
Ford 6000	Blue and gray, die cast, 1/12 scale, 1963	75	125	175
Ford 961 Powermaster	Red and gray, die cast, 1/12 scale, 1961	75	125	200
Ford 961 Powermaster	Red and gray, row crop, die cast, 1/12 scale, 1961	75	125	200
Ford 961 Select-O-Speed	Red and gray, die cast, 1/12 scale, 1962	65	125	175
Ford Commander 6000	Blue and gray, die cast, 1/12 scale, 1963	75	135	195
Fordson	With loader, cast iron, 8 1/2" long, 1938	750	1250	1700
Fordson	Cast iron, 5 1/2" long	150	225	300
Fordson F	With crank and driver, cast iron, 5 1/2" long	150	225	300
Huber Road Roller	Large, with standing driver, cast iron, 15" long, 1927	1675	2250	3750
Huber Steam Roller	Cast iron, 1/25 scale, 1929	365	450	600
Huber Steam Roller	Cast iron, 3 1/4" long, 1929	100	150	215
Junior Tractor		60	95	125
Oliver 70 Orchard	Fenders over rear wheels, cast iron, 5" long, 1938	175	300	575
Road Scraper	Plastic, 1950's	30	45	60
Steam Shovel	Red, nickel-plated boom, cast iron, 4 3/4" long	75	115	150
Tractor	Yellow, 5 1/4" long	35	55	75

NAME	DESCRIPTION	GOOD	EX	MINT
Tractor and Farmer	Plastic	25	35	55
Tractor Shovel	Cast iron, 8 1/2" long, 1933	1250	1650	2000

Motorcycles

NAME	DESCRIPTION	GOOD	EX	MINT
Crash Car	Motorcycle with cart on back, cast iron, 9" long, 1930's	1000	1650	2000
Harley-Davidson Parcel Post	Cast iron, 10" long, 1928	2500	3500	4750
Harley-Davidson Sidecar Motorcycle	Cast iron, 9" long, 1930	900	1625	1900
Hill Climber	Cast iron, 6 3/4" long, 1935	375	500	900
Indian 4-cylinder Motocycle	Cast iron, 9" long, 1929	1700	2425	3000
Indian Air Mail	Cast iron, 9 1/4" long, 1929	1575	2650	3500
Indian Armored Car	Motorcyle police, cast iron, 8 1/2" long, 1928	1750	3500	6000
Indian Motorcycle	Cast iron, 9" long	600	850	1500
Motorcycle	Harley-Davidson, cast iron, 7 1/2" long, 1932	300	450	800
Motorcycle	Three wheels, cast iron	400	600	800
Motorcycle Cop With Sidecar	Harley-Davidson, cast iron	700	1000	1500
Motorcycle Crash Car	With cart on back, cast iron, 5" long, 1930"s	85	135	195
Motorized Sidecar Motorcycle	Clockwork motor, cast iron, 8 1/2" long, 1932	4000	6250	10000
P.D. Motorcycle Cop	Red cycle, black cop, plastic	35	65	95
Patrol Motorcycle	Green, 6 1/2" long	275	350	475
Popeye Patrol	Cast iron, 9" long, 1938	425	600	950
Popeye Spinach Delivery	Red motorcycle, cast iron, 6" long, 1938	375	500	750
Traffic Car	Three-wheel transport vehicle, cast iron, 12" long, 1930	600	950	1500

Trucks

NAME	DESCRIPTION	GOOD	EX	MINT
Auto Dump Coal Wagon	Cast iron, 16 1/4" long, 1920	800	1200	1500
Auto Express with Roof	Cast iron, 9 1/2" long, 1910	500	875	1200
Auto Truck	Spoke wheels, cast iron, 10" long, 1918	600	1200	1650
Auto Truck	Five-ton truck, cast iron, 17 1/2" long, 1920	1000	1650	2250
Bell Telephone Truck	12" long, 1940	50	75	100
Bell Telephone Truck	Spoke wheels, cast iron, 5 1/2" long, 1930	225	335	450
Bell Telephone Truck	White tires, winch works, cast iron, 10" long, 1930	375	565	850
Bell Telephone Truck	No driver, solid white tires, cast iron, 3 3/4" long, 1930	150	225	300
Bell Telephone Truck	Solid white tires, cast iron, 7" long, 1930	165	235	350
Borden's Milk Truck	Cast iron, 7 1/2" long, 1930	1650	2850	4250
Compressor Truck	1953 Ford	60	90	120
Delivery Van	Cast iron, 4 1/2" long, 1932	365	475	675
Dump Truck	Cast iron, 7 1/2" long	225	335	450
Dump Truck	White rubber tires, 4 1/2" long, 1930's	100	150	200
Dump Truck	Plastic, 1950's	25	35	55
Gas Tanker	5 1/2" long	115	225	295
General Shovel Truck	Dual rear wheels, cast iron, 10" long, 1931	400	600	975
Ingersoll-Rand Compressor	Cast iron, 8 1/4" long, 1933	3250	6500	10000
Lifesaver Truck	Cast iron, 4 1/4" long	350	475	700
Long Bed Dump Truck	Series 510, Ford, cast iron	110	175	300
Mack Dump Truck	Cast iron, 11" long, 1928	600	800	1450
Merchants Delivery Truck	Cast iron, 6 1/4" long, 1925	400	600	850
Milk Truck	Cast iron, 3 3/4" long, 1930	115	200	295
Model A Cab with Side Dump Trailer	Cast iron, 12 7/8" long, 1931	0	0	0
Nucar Transport	With four vehicles, cast iron, 16" long, 1932	675	1200	1500
Open Bed Auto Express	Cast iron, 9 1/2" long, 1910	725	1200	1700

Hubley

NAME	DESCRIPTION	GOOD	EX	MINT
Panama Shovel Truck	Mack truck, cast iron, 13" long, 1934	625	1000	1350
Railway Express Truck	Cast iron	135	225	275
Shovel Truck	Metal, 10" long	250	375	500
Stake Bed Truck	Cast iron, 3" long	75	115	150
Stake Truck	Die cast, 7" long, 1950's	75	115	150
Stake Truck	Cast metal, 7" long	60	95	125
Stake Truck	White rubber tires, 7" long, 1930's	85	130	175
Stake Truck	White cab, blue stake bed, 12" long	100	150	200
Stockyard Truck #851	With three pigs	60	95	165
Tanker	Cast iron, 7" long, 1940's	85	130	175
Tow Truck	Cast iron	50	75	100
Tow Truck	Ford, cast metal, 7" long, 1950's	50	65	165
Tow Truck	9" long	135	225	275
Truckmixer	Ford, mixer cylinder rotates when truck moves, cast iron, 8" long, 1932	50	85	185
Wrecker	Whitewall tires, green and white, 11 1/2" long	25	50	75
Wrecker	Cast iron, 5" long	60	95	125
Wrecker	6" long	70	125	145
Wrecker	Ford, die cast	30	55	125
Wrecker	Red, die cast, 9 1/2" long, 1940's	60	95	165

Wagons and Carts

NAME	DESCRIPTION	GOOD	EX	MINT
Alphonse in Mule Pulled Wagon	6 1/2" long	225	335	450
Alphonse in Wagon with Two Goats Pulling	13 3/4" long, 1900's	100	150	210

Marx

Airplanes

NAME	DESCRIPTION	GOOD	EX	MINT
727 Riding Jet	Jet engine sound	150	225	300
Air-Sea Power Bombing Set	12" wingspan, 1940's	325	450	650
Airmail Biplane	4 engines, tin windup, 18" wingspan, 1936	225	325	450
Airmail Monoplane	2 engines, tin windup, 1930	100	150	225
Airplane	Light fuselage, tin windup	125	175	250
Airplane	Medium fuselage, tin windup	125	150	250
Airplane	Monoplane, adjustable rudder, tin windup, 9 1/4" wingspan	150	225	300
Airplane	Adjustable rudder, tin windup, 10" wingspan, 1926	150	225	300
Airplane	Tin windup, 9 1/4" wingspan, 1926	150	225	300
Airplane	Mail biplane, tin windup, 9 3/4" wingspan, 1926	150	225	300
Airplane	Two propellers, tin windup, 9 7/8" wingspan, 1927	200	300	400
Airplane	Twin engine, tin windup, 9 1/2" wingspan	100	150	200
Airplane	No engines, tin windup, 9 1/2" wingspan	135	200	275
Airplane	Monoplane, pressed steel, 9" wingspan, 1942	110	165	225
Airplane #90	Tin windup, 5" wingspan, 1930	240	360	480
Airplane with Parachute	Monoplane, tin windup, 13" wingspan, 1929	115	170	225
Airways Express Plane	Tin windup, 13" wingspan, 1929	200	300	400
American Airlines Airplane	Passenger plane, tin windup, 27" wingspan, 1940	130	190	250
American Airlines Flagship	Pressed steel, wood wheels, 27" wingspan, 1940	200	300	400
Army Airplane	Tin, mechanical fighter, 7" wingspan	125	170	230

NAME	DESCRIPTION	GOOD	EX	MINT
Army Airplane	2 engines, tin windup, 18" wingspan, 1938	125	190	250
Army Airplane	Biplane, tin windup, 25 3/4" wingspan, 1930	225	340	450
Army Airplane	18" wingspan, 1951	150	225	300
Army Bomber	Tri-motor, 25 1/2" wingspan, 1935	250	375	500
Army Bomber	2 engines, tin windup, 18" wingspan, 1940's	250	375	500
Army Bomber	Monoplane, litho machine gun & pilot, 25 1/2" wingspan, 1935	300	450	600
Army Bomber with Bombs	Camouflage pattern, metal, windup, 12" wingspan, 1930's	100	150	200
Army Fighter Plane	Tin windup, 5" wingspan, 1940's	100	150	200
Autogyro	Tin windup, 27" wingspan, 1940's	150	225	300
Blue and Silver Bomber	2 engines, tin windup, 18" wingspan, 1940	190	280	375
Bomber	Four propellers, metal, windup, 14 1/2" wingspan	100	150	200
Bomber with Tricycle Landing Gear	Four engine, tin windup, 18" wingspan, 1940	225	325	425
Camouflage Airplane	Four engines, 18" wingspan, 1942	125	200	275
China Clipper	4-engines, tin windup, 18 1/4" wingspan, 1938	100	150	200
City Airport	Extra tower and planes, 1930's	125	190	250
Crash-Proof Airplane	Monoplane, tin windup, 11 3/4" wingspan, 1933	100	150	200
Cross Country Flyer	19" tall, 1929	375	550	725
Dagwood's Solo Flight Airplane	Windup, 9" wingspan, 1935	200	300	400
Dare Devil Flyer	Tin windup, 1929	115	170	225
Dare Devil Flyer	Zeppelin shaped, 1928	225	350	450
DC-3 Airplane	Aluminum, windup, 9 1/2" wingspan, 1930's	125	190	250
Eagle Air Scout	Monoplane, tin windup, 26 1/2" wingspan, 1929	200	300	400
Fighter Jet, USAF	Battery operated, 7" wingspan	90	135	180
Fighter Plane	Battery operated, remote controlled, 1950's	90	135	180
Fix All Helicopter		275	400	550
Flip-Over Airplane	Tin windup	200	300	400
Floor Zeppelin	9 1/2" long, 1931	225	340	450
Floor Zeppelin	16 1/2" long, 1931	350	525	700
Flying Fortress 2095	Sparkling, 4 engines, 1940	150	245	325
Flying Zeppelin	Windup, 9" long, 1930	225	340	450
Flying Zeppelin	Windup, 17" long, 1930	350	525	700
Flying Zeppelin	Windup, 10" long	275	400	550
Four-Motor Transport Plane	Friction, tin litho	120	180	250
Golden Tricky Airplane		75	115	150
Hangar with One Plane	1940's	150	225	300
International Airline Express	Monoplane, tin windup, 17 1/2" wingspan, 1931	200	300	400
Jet Plane	Friction, 6" wingspan, 1950's	65	90	120
Little Lindy Airplane	Friction, 2 1/4" wingspan, 1930	200	300	400
Looping Plane	Silver version, tin windup, 7" wingspan, 1941	225	325	425
Lucky Stunt Flyer	Tin windup, 6" long, 1928	150	225	300
Mammoth Zeppelin, 1st mammoth	Pull toy, 28" long, 1930	400	600	800
Mammoth Zeppelin, 2nd mammoth	Pull toy, 28" long, 1930	375	575	750
Municipal Airport Hangar	1929	100	150	200
Overseas Biplane	Three propellers, tin windup, 9 7/8" wingspan, 1928	150	275	300
PAA Clipper Plane	Pressed steel, 27" wingspan, 1952	125	175	225

Marx

NAME	DESCRIPTION	GOOD	EX	MINT
PAA Passenger Plane	Tin litho, 14" wingspan, 1950's	120	175	225
Pan American	Pressed steel, 4 motor, 27" wingspan, 1940	90	150	300
Piggy Back Plane	Tin windup, 9" wingspan, 1939	100	150	200
Pioneer Air Express Monoplane	Tin litho, pull toy, 25 1/2" wingspan	125	190	250
Popeye Flyer	Popeye and Olive Oyl in plane, tin litho tower, windup, 1936	475	700	950
Popeye Flyer	Wimpy and Swee'Pea litho on tower, 1936	600	900	1200
Popeye the Pilot	Number 47 on side of plane, 8 1/2" wingspan, 1936	300	450	600
Pursuit Planes	One propeller, 8" wingspan, 1930's	125	200	250
Rollover Airplane	Tin windup, forward and reverse, 6" wingspan, 1947	200	300	400
Rollover Airplane	Tin windup, 1920's	200	300	425
Rookie Pilot	Tin litho, windup, 7" long, 1930's	225	340	550
Seversky P-35	Single-engine plane, 16" wingspan, 1940's	125	200	275
Sky Bird Flyer	Two planes, 9 1/2" tower, 1947	275	400	550
Sky Cruiser Two-Motored Transport Plane	18" wingspan, 1940's	125	175	250
Sky Flyer	Biplane and Zeppelin, 8 1/2" tall tower, 1927	225	340	450
Sky Flyer	9" tall tower, 1937	150	225	300
Spirit of America	Monoplane, tin windup, 17 1/2" wingspan, 1930	325	500	650
Spirit of St. Louis	Tin windup, 9 1/4" wingspan, 1929	150	225	300
Stunt Pilot	Tin windup	175	250	350
Superman Rollover Airplane	Tin windup, 1940's	1400	2100	2800
Tower Flyers	1926	175	250	350
Trans-Atlantic Zeppelin	Windup, 10" long, 1930	225	350	450
TWA Biplane	4 engine, 18" wingspan	225	350	450
U.S. Marines Plane	Monoplane, tin windup, 17 7/8" wingspan, 1930	200	300	400
Zeppelin	Friction pull toy, steel, 6" long	100	200	250
Zeppelin	Flies in circles, windup, 17" long, 1930	350	525	700
Zeppelin	Friction, pull toy, 28" long	375	550	750
Zeppelin	All metal, pull toy, 28" long, 1929	400	600	800
Zeppelin	Pull toy, 28" long	375	550	750

Boats and Ships

NAME	DESCRIPTION	GOOD	EX	MINT
Battleship USS Washington	Friction, 14" long, 1950's	50	75	100
Caribbean Luxury Liner	Sparkling, friction, 15" long	50	75	100
Luxury Liner Boat	Tin, friction	100	150	200
Mosquito Fleet Putt Putt Boat		40	55	75
River Queen Paddle Wheel Station	Plastic	50	75	100
Sparkling Warship	Tin windup, 14" long	50	75	100
Tugboat	Plastic, battery operated, 6" long, 1966	50	75	100

Buses

NAME	DESCRIPTION	GOOD	EX	MINT
American Van Lines Bus	Cream and red, tin windup, 13 1/2" long	65	100	130
Blue Line Tours Bus	Tin litho, windup, 9 1/2" long, 1930's	150	225	300
Bus	Red bus, 4" long, 1940	35	50	70
Coast to Coast Bus	Tin litho, windup, 10" long, 1930's	125	200	250
Greyhound Bus	Tin litho, windup, 6" long, 1930's	100	150	200
Liberty Bus	Tin litho, windup, 5" long, 1931	75	125	150
Mystery Speedway Bus	Tin litho, windup, 14" long, 1938	200	300	400
Royal Bus Lines Bus	Tin litho, windup, 10 1/4" long, 1930's	135	200	270
Royal Van Co. Truck "We Haul Anywhere"	Tin windup, 9" long, 1920's-30's	140	225	280

NAME	DESCRIPTION	GOOD	EX	MINT
School Bus	Steel body, wooden wheels, pull toy, 11 1/2" long	125	200	250

Cars

NAME	DESCRIPTION	GOOD	EX	MINT
Amos 'n' Andy Fresh Air Taxicab	Tin litho, windup, 8" long, 1930	650	875	1400
Anti-Aircraft Gun on Car	5 1/4" long	50	75	100
Army Car	Battery operated	65	100	130
Army Staff Car	Litho steel, tin windup, 1930's	125	200	275
Army Staff Car	With flasher and siren, tin windup, 11" long, 1940's	75	125	150
Big Lizzie Car	Tin windup, 7 1/4" long, 1930's	75	125	150
Blondie's Jalopy	Tin litho, 16" long, 1941	325	500	650
Boat Tail Racer #3	Tin windup, 5" long, 1930's	40	55	75
Bouncing Benny Car	Pull toy, 7" long, 1939	325	500	650
Bumper Auto	Large bumpers front and rear, tin windup, 1939	60	100	135
Cadillac Coupe	8 1/2" long, 1931	175	275	350
Cadillac Coupe	Trunk w/ tools on luggage carrier, tin windup, 11" long, 1931	200	300	400
Camera Car	Heavy guage steel car, 9 1/2" long, 1939	850	1300	1700
Careful Johnnie	Plastic driver, 6 1/2" long, 1950's	100	150	200
Charlie McCarthy "Benzine Buggy" Car	With white wheels, tin windup, 7" long, 1938	450	625	895
Charlie McCarthy "Benzine Buggy" Car	With red wheels, tin windup, 7" long, 1938	600	900	1200
Charlie McCarthy and Mortimer Snerd Private Car	Tin windup, 16" long, 1939	600	900	1200
Charlie McCarthy Private Car	Windup, 1935	1450	2200	2900
College Boy Car	Blue car with yellow trim, tin windup, 8" long, 1930's	300	450	600
Convertible Roadster	Nickel-plated tin, 11" long, 1930's	175	275	350
Coo Coo Car	8" long, tin windup, 1931	375	575	750
Crazy Dan Car	Tin windup, 6" long, 1930's	140	225	285
Dagwood the Driver	Tin litho, windup	475	650	725
Dagwood the Driver	8" long, tin windup, 1941	200	300	400
Dan Dipsy Car	Nodder, tin windup, 5 3/4" long, 1950's	250	375	450
Dick Tracy Police Car	9" long	150	225	300
Dick Tracy Police Station Riot Car	Friction, sparkling, 7 1/2" long, 1946	130	200	260
Dick Tracy Squad Car	Yellow flashing light, tin litho, windup, 11" long, 1940's	250	375	500
Dick Tracy Squad Car	Battery operated, tin litho, 11 1/4" long, 1949	170	275	350
Dick Tracy Squad Car	Friction, 20" long, 1948	125	170	225
Dippy Dumper	Brutus or Popeye, celluloid figure, tin windup, 9", 1930's	350	525	700
Disney Parade Roadster	Tin litho, windup, 1950's	100	150	200
Donald Duck Disney Dipsy Car	Plastic Donald, tin windup, 5 3/4" long, 1953	425	650	850
Donald Duck Go-Kart	Plastic and metal, friction, rubber tires, 1960's	75	130	175
Donald the Driver	Plastic Donald, tin car, windup, 6 1/2" long, 1950's	200	300	400
Dora Dipsy Car	Nodder, tin windup, 5 3/4" long, 1953	400	600	800
Dottie the Driver	Nodder, tin windup, 6 1/2" long, 1950's	150	225	300
Drive-Up Self Car	Turns left, right or straight, 1940	100	150	200
Driver Training Car	Tin windup, 1930's	80	120	160
Electric Convertible	Tin and plastic, 20" long	65	100	130
Falcon	Plastic bubble top, black rubber tires	50	75	100
Funny Fire Fighters	7" long, tin windup, 1941	800	1200	1600

Top to Bottom: Harley Davidson Motorcycle with Sidecar, 1930s, Hubley; Buick Convertible, Hubley; Chrysler Airflow, 1930s, Hubley; Hubley Van, Hubley; Racer, Auburn; Tractor and Wagon, Auburn; Austin Transport Set, 1930, A. C. Williams.

NAME	DESCRIPTION	GOOD	EX	MINT
Funny Fire Fighters	7" long, tin windup, 1941	800	1200	1600
Funny Flivver Car	Tin litho, windup, 7" long, 1926	275	425	550
G-Man Pursuit Car	Sparks, 14 1/2" long, 1935	190	285	380
Gang Buster Car	Tin windup, 14 1/2" long, 1938	200	300	400
Giant King Racer	Dark blue, tin windup, 12 1/4" long, 1928	250	375	500
Hot Rod #23	Friction motor, tin, 8" long, 1967	45	75	90
Huckleberry Hound Car	Friction	125	200	250
International Agent Car	Tin windup	30	55	75
International Agent Car	Friction, tin litho, 1966	60	100	125
Jaguar	Battery operated, 13" long	225	325	450
Jalopy	Tin driver, friction, 1950's	125	200	250
Jalopy Car	Tin driver, motor sparks, crank, windup	140	225	280
Jolly Joe Jeep	Tin litho, 5 3/4" long, 1950's	150	225	300
Joy Riders Crazy Car	Tin litho, windup, 8" long, 1928	340	500	675
Jumping Jeep	Tin litho, 5 3/4" long, 1947	210	325	425
King Racer	Yellow body, red trim, tin windup, 8 1/2" long, 1925	375	575	750
King Racer	Yellow with black outlines, 8 1/2" long, 1925	250	430	575
Komical Kop	Black car, tin litho, windup, 7 1/2" long, 1930's	450	675	900
Leaping Lizzie Car	Tin windup, 7" long, 1927	250	375	500
Learn To Drive Car	Windup	110	165	220
Lonesome Pine Trailer and Convertible Sedan	22" long, 1936	375	600	795
Machine Gun on Car	Hand crank activation on gun, 3" long	75	130	175
Magic George and Car	Litho, 1940's	170	250	350
Mechanical Speed Racer	Tin windup, 12" long, 1948	125	200	275
Mickey Mouse Disney Dipsy Car	Plastic Mickey, tin windup, 5 3/4" long, 1953	425	655	875
Mickey the Driver	Plastic Mickey, tin car, windup, 6 1/2" long, 1950's	170	250	350
Midget Racer "Midget Special" #2	Miniature car, clockwork-powered, 5" long, 1930's	125	200	250
Midget Racer "Midget Special" #7	Miniature car, tin windup, 5" long, 1930's	125	200	250
Milton Berle Crazy Car	Tin litho, windup, 6" long, 1950's	250	375	500
Mortimer Snerd's Tricky Auto	Tin litho, windup, 7 1/2" long, 1939	400	600	800
Mystery Car	Press down activation, 9" long, 1936	125	200	250
Mystery Taxi	Press down activation, steel, 9" long, 1938	160	250	325
Nutty Mad Car	Blue car with goggled driver, friction, hard plastic, 1960's	75	130	175
Nutty Mad Car	Red tin car, vinyl driver, friction, 4" long, 1960's	100	150	210
Nutty Mad Car	With driver, battery operated, 1960's	100	150	200
Old Jalopy	Tin windup, driver, "Old Jalopy" on hood, 7" long, 1950	225	325	425
Parade Roadster	With Disney characters, tin litho, windup, 11" long, 1950	225	325	450
Peter Rabbit Eccentric Car	Tin windup, 5 1/2" long, 1950's	250	375	500
Queen of the Campus	With four college students heads, 1950	250	400	525
Race 'N Road Speedway	HO scale racing set, 1950's	60	100	125
Racer #12	Tin litho, windup, 16" long, 1942	225	325	450
Racer #3	Miniature car, tin windup, 5" long	75	125	150
Racer #4	Miniature car, tin windup, 5" long	75	125	150
Racer #5	Miniature car, tin windup, 5" long, 1948	75	125	150
Racer #61	Miniature car, tin windup, 4 3/4" long, 1930	75	125	150
Racer #7	Miniature car, tin windup, 5" long, 1948	75	125	150
Racing Car	Two man team, tin litho, windup, 12" long, 1940	125	200	250
Racing Car	Plastic driver, tin windup, 27" long, 1950	100	175	225

Marx

NAME	DESCRIPTION	GOOD	EX	MINT
Roadster	11 1/2" long, 1949	100	150	200
Roadster and Cannon Ball Keeper	Windup, 9" long	175	250	350
Roadster Convertible with Trailer and Racer	Mechanical, 1950	125	200	275
Rocket Racer	Tin litho, 1935	275	425	550
Rolls Royce	Black plastic, friction, 6" long, 1955	40	60	80
Royal Coupe	Tin litho, windup, 9" long, 1930	175	275	350
Secret Sam Agent 012 Car	Tin litho, friction, 5" long, 1960's	40	65	85
Sedan	Battery operated, plastic, 9 1/2" long	175	275	350
Sheriff Sam and His Whoppee Car	Plastic, tin windup, 5 3/4" long, 1949	200	300	400
Siren Police Car	15" long, 1930's	75	125	150
Smokey Sam the Wild Fireman Car	6 1/2" long, 1950	125	200	250
Smokey Stover Whoopee Car	1940's	175	275	350
Snoopy Gus Wild Fireman	7" long, 1926	500	750	1000
Speed Cop	Two 4" all tin windup cars, track, 1930's	175	275	350
Speed King Racer	Tin litho, windup, 16" long, 1929	325	500	650
Speed Racer	13" long, 1937	250	375	500
Speedway Coupe	Tin windup, battery operated headlights, 8" long, 1938	200	300	400
Speedway Set	Two windup sedans, figure eight track, 1937	250	375	500
Sports Coupe	Tin, 15" long, 1930's	125	200	250
Station Wagon	Green with wood-grained pattern, windup, 7" long, 1950	50	75	100
Station Wagon	Litho family of four with dogs on back windows, 6 3/4" long	60	100	125
Station Wagon	Light purple with wood-grained pattern, windup, 7 1/2" long	60	100	125
Station Wagon	Friction, 11" long, 1950	125	200	250
Streamline Speedway	Two tin windup racing cars, 1936	175	275	350
Stutz Roadster	Driver, 15" long, windup, 1928	325	500	650
Super Hot Rod	"777" on rear door, 11" long, 1940's	200	300	400
Super Streamlined Racer	Tin windup, 17" long, 1950's	125	200	275
The Marvel Car, Reversible Coupe	Tin windup, 1938	125	200	250
Tricky Safety Car	6 1/2" long, 1950	100	150	200
Tricky Taxi	Black and white version, tin windup, 4 1/2" long, 1935	160	250	325
Tricky Taxi	Red, black and white, tin windup, 4 1/2" long, 1940's	175	275	350
Uncle Wiggly, He Goes A Ridin' Car	Rabbit driving, tin windup, 7 1/2" long, 1935	425	650	850
Walt Disney Television Car	Friction, 7 1/2" long, 1950's	125	200	250
Western Auto Track	Steel, 24" long	75	125	150
Whoopee Car	Witty slogans, tin litho, windup, 7 1/2" long, 1930's	375	580	775
Whoopee Cowboy Car	Bucking car, cowboy driver, tin windup, 7 1/2" long, 1930's	400	600	800
Woody Sedan	Tin friction, 7 1/2" long	60	100	125
Yellow Taxi	Windup, 7" long, 1927	275	425	575
Yogi Bear Car	Friction, 1962	50	85	115

Emergency Vehicles

NAME	DESCRIPTION	GOOD	EX	MINT
Ambulance	Tin litho, 11" long	125	175	250
Ambulance	13 1/2" long, 1937	225	350	450
Ambulance with Siren	Tin windup	100	150	200
Army Ambulance	13 1/2" long, 1930's	250	375	500
Boat Tail Racer # 2	Litho, 13" long, 1948	125	200	250

Marx

NAME	DESCRIPTION	GOOD	EX	MINT
Chief-Fire Department No. 1 Truck	Friction, 1948	60	90	120
Chrome Racer	Miniature racer, 5" long, 1937	85	125	170
City Hospital Mack Ambulance	Tin litho, windup, 10" long, 1927	190	280	375
Electric Car	Runs on electric power, license # A7132, 1933	225	325	450
Electric Car	Windup, 1933	175	250	350
Fire Chief Car	Working lights, 16" long	125	200	250
Fire Chief Car	Windup, 6 1/2" long, 1949	75	125	150
Fire Chief Car	Battery operated headlights, windup, 11" long, 1950	100	150	200
Fire Chief Car	Friction, loud fire siren, 8" long, 1936	150	250	325
Fire Chief Car with Bell	10 1/2" long, 1940	175	250	350
Fire Engine	Sheet iron, 9" long, 1920's	100	175	235
Fire Truck	Battery operated, two celluloid firemen, 12" long	50	75	100
Fire Truck	Friction, all metal, 14" long, 1945	90	135	180
Giant King Racer	Pale yellow, tin windup, 12 1/2" long, 1928	225	325	450
Giant King Racer	Red, 13" long, 1941	200	300	400
Giant Mechanical Racer	Tin Litho, 12 3/4" long, 1948	100	175	225
H.Q-Staff Car	14 1/2" long, 1930's	325	500	650
Hook and Ladder Fire Truck	3 tin litho firemen, 13 1/2" long	90	135	180
Hook and Ladder Fire Truck	Plastic ladder on top, 24" long, 1950	90	135	180
Plastic Racer	6" long, 1948	50	75	100
Racer with Plastic Driver	Tin litho car, 16" long, 1950	150	225	300
Rocket-Shaped Racer #12	1930's	275	425	550
Siren Fire Chief Car	Red car with siren, 1934	225	325	450
Siren Fire Chief Truck	Battery operated, 15" long, 1930's	100	175	225
Tricky Fire Chief Car	4 1/2" long, 1930's	250	375	500
V.F.D. Emergency Squad	With ladder, metal, electrically powered, 14" long, 1940's	70	125	140
V.F.D. Fire Engine	With hoses and siren, 14" long, 1940's	120	180	240
V.F.D. Hook and Ladder Fire Truck	33" long, 1950	140	225	280
War Department Ambulance	1930's	100	150	200

Farm and Construction Equipment

NAME	DESCRIPTION	GOOD	EX	MINT
Aluminum Bulldog Tractor Set	Tin windup, 9 1/2" long tractor, 1940	250	375	500
American Tractor	With accessories, tin windup, 8" long, 1926	150	225	300
Army Design Climbing Tractor	Tin windup, 7 1/2" long, 1932	80	120	160
Automatic Steel Barn and Mechanical Plastic Tractor	Tin windup, 7" long red tractor, 1950	85	125	170
Bulldozer Climbing Tractor	Caterpillar type, tin windup, 10 1/2" long, 1950's	45	75	90
Bulldozer Climbing Tractor	Bumper auto, large bumpers, tin windup, 1939	50	75	100
Caterpillar Climbing Tractor	Yellow tractor, tin windup, 9 1/2" long, 1942	75	125	150
Caterpillar Climbing Tractor	Orange tractor, tin windup, 9 1/2" long, 1942	100	175	225
Caterpillar Tractor and Hydraulic Lift	Tin windup, 1948	50	75	100
Climbing Tractor	With driver, tin windup, 1920's	50	100	125
Climbing Tractor	Tin windup, 8 1/4" long, 1930	100	150	200
Climbing Tractor with Chain Pull	Tin windup, 7 1/2" long, 1929	150	225	300
Co-Op Combine	Tin friction, 6"	30	45	60
Construction Tractor	Reversing, tin windup, 14" long, 1950's	100	150	200
Copper-Colored Tractor with Scraper	Tin windup, 8 1/2" long, 1942	90	135	180
Covered Wagon	Friction, tin litho, 9" long	20	30	40

VEHICLES

Marx

NAME	DESCRIPTION	GOOD	EX	MINT
Crawler	With or without blades and drivers, litho, 1/25 scale, 1950	75	125	150
Crawler with Stake Bed	Litho, 1/25 scale, 1950	75	130	175
Farm Tractor	Tin driver	50	75	100
Farm Tractor and Implement Set	Tin windup, tractor mower, hayrake, three-gang plow, 1948	200	300	400
Farm Tractor Set	40 pieces, tin windup, 1939	325	500	650
Farm Tractor Set	40 pieces, 8 1/2" long copper colored tractor, windup, 1940	300	450	600
Farm Tractor Set and Power Plant	32 pieces, tin windup, 1938	200	300	400
Hill Climbing Dump Truck	Tin windup, 13 1/2" long, 1932	140	210	280
Industrial Tractor Set	Orange and red heavy gauge plate tractor, 7 1/2" long, 1930	145	225	290
International Harvester Tractor	Diesel, driver and set of tools, 1/12 scale, 1954	75	125	150
Magic Barn and Tractor	Plastic tractor, tin litho barn, 1950's	70	100	140
Mechanical Tractor	Tin windup, 5 1/2" long, 1942	125	200	275
Midget Climbing Tractor	Tin windup, 5 1/4" long, 1935	125	200	250
Midget Road Building Set	Tin windup, 5 1/2" long tractor, 1939	200	300	400
Midget Tractor	Copper-colored all metal, tin windup, 5 1/4" long, 1940	40	60	80
Midget Tractor	Red all metal, tin windup, 5 1/4" long, 1940	30	45	60
Midget Tractor and Plow	Tin windup, 1937	70	100	140
Midget Tractor with Driver	Red all metal, tin windup, 5 1/4" long, 1940	40	60	80
No. 2 Tractor	Red with black wheels, tin windup, 8 1/2" long, 1940	95	150	190
Plastic Sparkling Tractor Set	Tin windup, 6 1/2" long tractor with 10 1/2" long wagon, 1950	40	60	80
Plastic Tractor with Scraper	Tin windup, 8" long with road scraper, 1949	50	75	100
Power Grader	Black or white wheels, 17 1/2" long	50	100	125
Power Shovel		50	75	100
Reversible Six-Wheel Farm Tractor-Truck	Tin windup, 13 3/4" steel tractor, 7 1/2" stake truck, 1950	80	125	160
Reversible Six-Wheel Tractor	Red steel tractor, tin windup, 11 3/4" long, 1940	200	300	400
Self-Reversing Tractor	Tin windup, 10" long, 1936	125	200	275
Sparkling Climbing Tractor	Tin windup, 8 1/2" long, 1950's	100	150	200
Sparkling Climbing Tractor	Tin windup, 10" long, 1940's	175	275	350
Sparkling Heavy Duty Bulldog Tractor	With road scraper, tin windup, 11" long, 1950's	40	60	80
Sparkling Hi-Boy Climbing Tractor	10 1/2" long, 1950's	25	40	50
Sparkling Tractor	With driver and trailer, tin windup, 16" long, 1950's	60	90	120
Sparkling Tractor	With plow blade, tin windup, 1939	50	75	100
Sparkling Tractor and Trailer Set "Marborook Farms"	Tin windup, 21" long, 1950's	55	75	110
Steel Farm Tractor and Implements	Tin windup, 15" long steel bulldozer tractor, 1947	160	240	320
Super Power Reversing Tractor	Tin windup, 12" long, 1931	100	150	210
Super Power Tractor and Trailer Set	Tin windup, 8 1/2" tractor, 1937	125	200	250
Super-Power Bulldog Tractor with V-Shaped Plow	Aluminum finish, tin windup, 1938	75	130	175
Super-Power Climbing Tractor and Nine Piece Set	Tin windup, 9 1/2" long tractor, 1942	160	240	320
Super-Power Giant Climbing Tractor	Tin windup, 13" long, 1939	180	270	360
Tractor	Tin windup, 8 1/2" long, 1941	100	175	225

NAME	DESCRIPTION	GOOD	EX	MINT
Tractor	Red tractor, tin windup, 8 1/2" long, 1941	100	175	225
Tractor and Equipment Set	Five pieces, tin windup, 16" long tractor, 1949	160	240	320
Tractor and Mower	Tin windup, 5" long litho steel tractor, 1948	50	75	100
Tractor and Six Implement Set	Tin windup, 8 1/2" long aluminum tractor, 1948	160	240	320
Tractor and Trailer	Tin windup, 16 1/2" long, 1950's	40	60	80
Tractor Road Construction Set	36 pieces, tin windup, 8 1/2" long tractor, 1938	200	325	425
Tractor Set	Seven pieces, tin windup, 8 1/2" long tractor, 1932	125	200	275
Tractor Set	Five pieces, tin windup, 8 1/2" long tractor, 1935	70	100	140
Tractor Set	Four pieces, tin windup, 8 1/2" long, 1936	100	150	200
Tractor Set	32 pieces, tin windup, 1937	180	270	360
Tractor Set	Five pieces, tin windup, 8 1/2" tractor, 1938	90	135	180
Tractor Set	40 pieces, tin windup, 8 1/2" long, 1942	300	450	600
Tractor Set	Two pieces, tin windup, 19" long steel tractor, 1950	65	100	130
Tractor Trailer and Scraper	Tin windup, 8 1/2" long tractor, 1946	80	120	160
Tractor Train with Tractor Shed	Tin windup, 8 1/2" long, 1936	100	150	200
Tractor with Airplane	Windup, 5 1/2" long tractor, 27" wingspan on airplane, 1941	250	375	500
Tractor with Driver	Windup, 1940's	100	150	200
Tractor with Earth Grader	Tin windup, mechanical, 21 1/2" long, 1950's	40	60	85
Tractor with Plow and Scraper	Aluminum tractor, tin windup, 1938	70	125	140
Tractor with Plow and Wagon	Tin windup, 1934	70	125	140
Tractor with Road Scraper	Tin windup, 8 1/2" long climbing tractor, 1937	90	125	180
Tractor with Scraper	Tin windup, 8 1/2" long, 1933	70	125	140
Tractor with Trailer and Plow	Tin windup, 8 1/2" long, 1940	80	120	160
Tractor, Trailer, and V-Shaped Plow	Tin windup, 8 1/2" steel tractor, 1939	85	125	170
Tractor-Trailer Set	Tin windup, 8 1/2" long copper-colored tractor, 1939	70	125	140
Yellow and Green Tractor	Tin windup, 8 1/2" long, 1930	90	135	180

Motorcycles

NAME	DESCRIPTION	GOOD	EX	MINT
Motorcycle Cop	Tin litho, mechanical, siren, 8 1/4" long	75	125	150
Motorcycle Police	Red uniform on cop, tin windup, 8" long, 1930's	125	200	250
Motorcycle Police #3	Tin windup, 8 1/2" long	100	150	200
Motorcycle Policeman	Orange and blue, tin windup, 8" long, 1920's	100	150	250
Motorcycle Trooper	Tin litho, windup, 1935	80	120	160
Motorcyle Delivery Toy	"Speedy Boy Delivery Toy" on rear of cart, tin windup, 1932	175	275	350
Motorcyle Delivery Toy	"Speedy Boy Delivery Toy" on side of cart, tin windup, 1930's	175	280	375
Mystery Police Cycle	Yellow, tin windup, 4 1/2" long, 1930's	75	125	150
Mystic Motorcycle	Tin litho, windup, 4 1/4" long, 1936	75	130	175
Mystic Motorcycle	Tin litho, windup, 4 1/4" long, 1936	225	350	450
P.D. Motorcyclist	Tin windup, 4" long	40	60	80
Pinched Roadster Motorcycle Cop	In circular track, tin windup, 1927	125	200	275
Pluto Motorcycle with Siren	1930's	150	225	300
Police Motorcycle with Sidecar	Tin windup, 8" long, 1930's	425	650	850
Police Motorcycle with Sidecar	Tin windup, 3 1/2" long, 1930's	300	450	600
Police Motorcycle with Sidecar	Tin litho, windup, 8" long, 1950	175	280	375
Police Patrol Motorcycle with Sidecar	Tin windup, 1935	110	165	220

VEHICLES

NAME	DESCRIPTION	GOOD	EX	MINT
Police Siren Motorcycle	Tin litho, windup, 8" long, 1938	150	225	300
Police Squad Motorcycle Sidecar	Tin litho, windup, 1950	175	275	350
Police Squad Motorcycle Sidecar	Tin litho, windup, 8" long, 1950	100	150	200
Police Tipover Motorcycle	Tin litho, windup, 8" long, 1933	200	300	400
Rookie Cop	Yellow with driver, tin litho, windup, 8" long, 1940	175	275	350
Sparkling Soldier Motorcycle	Tin litho, windup, 8" long, 1940	175	275	350
Speeding Car and Motorcycle Policeman	Tin litho, windup, 1939	90	150	180
Tricky Motorcycle	Tin windup, 4 1/2" long, 1930's	100	150	200

Tanks

NAME	DESCRIPTION	GOOD	EX	MINT
Anti-aircraft Tank Outfit	4 flat metal soldiers, tank, anti-aircraft gun, etc, 1941	90	135	180
Anti-aircraft Tank Outfit	3 tanks made of cardboard	150	225	300
Army Tank	Sparking climbing tank, tin windup, 1940's	150	225	300
Climbing Fighting Tank	Tin windup	90	135	180
Climbing Tank	Tin windup, 9 1/2" long, 1930	125	200	250
Doughboy Tank	Doughboy pops out, tin litho, windup, 9 1/2" long, 1930	150	225	300
Doughboy Tank	Sparking tank, tin windup, 10" long, 1937	125	200	250
Doughboy Tank	Tin windup, 10" long, 1942	150	225	300
E12 Tank	Makes rat-a-tat-tat or rumbling noise, tin windup, 1942	100	150	200
E12 Tank	Green tank, 9 1/2" long, tin windup, 1942	150	225	300
M48T Tank	Battery operated, 1960's	50	100	125
Midget Climbing Fighting Tank	Tin litho, windup, 5 1/4" long, 1931	90	135	180
Midget Climbing Fighting Tank	Wide plastic wheels, supergrid tread, 5 1/4" long, 1951	100	150	200
Midget Climbing Fighting Tank	5 1/2" long, 1937	100	175	225
Refrew Tank	Tin windup	75	125	150
Rex Mars Planet Patrol Tank	Tin windup, 10" long, 1950's	150	225	300
Sparkling Army Tank	Tan or khaki hull, tin litho, windup, 1938	95	150	190
Sparkling Army Tank	Yellow hull, E12 Tank, tin litho, windup, 1942,	100	150	200
Sparkling Army Tank	Camouflage hull, 2 olive guns, tin windup, 5 1/2" long	100	150	200
Sparkling Army Tank	Camouflage hull, 2 khaki guns, tin windup, 5 1/2" long	125	200	250
Sparkling Climbing Tank	Tin windup, 10" long, 1939	110	165	210
Sparkling Space Tank	Tin windup, 1950's	250	375	500
Sparkling Super Power Tank	Tin windup, 9 1/2" long, 1950's	75	125	150
Sparkling Tank	Tin windup, 4" long, 1948	75	130	175
Superman Turnover Tank	Superman lifts tank, 4" long, tin windup, 1940	250	375	500
Tank	Pop up army man shooting	150	225	300
Turnover Army Tank	Camouflage, tan or khaki hull, tin windup, 1938	175	275	350
Turnover Army Tank	Tin windup, 9" long, 1930	150	225	300
Turnover Tank	Tin litho, windup, 4" long, 1942	100	150	200

Trucks

NAME	DESCRIPTION	GOOD	EX	MINT
"Run Right To Read's" Truck	14" long, 1940	125	200	250
A&P Super Market Truck	Pressed steel, rubber tires, litho, 19" long	50	100	135
Aero Oil Co. Mack Truck	Tin litho, friction, 5 1/2" long, 1930	125	200	275
Air Force Truck	32" long	75	125	150
American Railroad Express Agency Inc. Truck	Open cab, 7" long, 1930's	100	150	225

Marx vehicles, top to bottom: Uncle Wiggly, He Goes A Ridin' Car, 1935; Donald Duck Disney Dipsy Car, 1953; Looping Plane, silver finish, 1941; Doughboy Tank, 1930; Dick Tracy Squad Car, 1940s.

NAME	DESCRIPTION	GOOD	EX	MINT
American Truck Co. Mack Truck	Friction, 5" long	100	150	200
Armored Trucking Co. Mack Truck	Black cab, yellow printing, windup, 9 3/4" long	200	300	400
Armored Trucking Co. Truck	Tin litho, windup, 10" long, 1927	100	150	200
Army Truck	Tin, 12" long, 1950	60	90	120
Army Truck	20" long	50	75	100
Army Truck	Canvas top, 20" long, 1940's	150	225	300
Army Truck	Olive drab truck, 4 1/2" long, 1930's	125	200	250
Army Truck with Rear Benches and Canopy	Olive drab paint, 10" long	75	125	150
Artillery Set	3 piece set, 1930	100	150	200
Auto Carrier	2 yellow plastic cars, 2 ramp tracks. 14" long, 1950	125	200	250
Auto Mac Truck	Yellow and red, 12" long, 1950	50	75	100
Auto Transport Mack Truck and Trailer	Dark blue cab, dark green trailer, windup, 11 1/2" long, 1932	150	225	300
Auto Transport Mack Truck and Trailer	Medium blue cab, friction, 11 1/2" long, 1932	150	225	325
Auto Transport Mack Truck and Trailer	Dark blue cab, windup, 11 1/2" long, 1932	150	225	300
Auto Transport Truck	Pressed steel, with two plastic cars, 14" long, 1940	75	125	150
Auto Transport Truck	With 2 tin litho cars, 34" long, 1950's	60	90	120
Auto Transport Truck	With 3 windup cars, 22 3/4" long, 1931	250	375	500
Auto Transport Truck	With 3 racing coupes, 22" long, 1933	250	375	500
Auto Transport Truck	Double decker transport truck, 24 1/2" long, 1935	275	425	550
Auto Transport Truck	With dump truck, roadster and coupe, 30 1/2" long, 1938	275	425	550
Auto Transport Truck	With 3 cars, 21" long, 1940	250	375	500
Auto Transport Truck	21" long, 1947	175	250	350
Auto Transport Truck	With 2 plastic sedans, wooden wheels, 13 3/4" long, 1950	75	130	175
Auto Transwalk Truck	With 3 cars, 1930's	175	250	350
Bamberger Mack Truck	Dark green, windup, 5" long, 1920's	200	300	400
Big Load Van Co. Hauler and Trailer	With little cartons of products, 12 3/4" long, 1927	200	300	400
Big Load Van Co. Mack Truck	Windup, 13" long, 1928	225	350	450
Big Shot Cannon Truck	Battery operated, 23" long, 1960's	150	250	325
Cannon Army Mack Truck	9" long, 1930's	175	250	350
Carpenter's Truck	Stake bed truck, pressed steel, 14" long, 1940's	175	250	350
Carrier with Three Racers	Tin litho, windup, 22 3/4" long, 1930	150	225	325
Cement Mixer Truck	Red cab, tin finish mixing barrel, 6" long, 1930's	100	150	200
City Coal Co. Mack Dump Truck	14" long, 1934	225	350	475
City Delivery Van	Yellow steel truck, 11" long	140	210	280
City Sanitation Dept. "Help Keep Your City Clean" Truck	12 3/4" long, 1940	60	90	120
Coal Truck	Battery operated, automatic dump, forward and reverse, tin	75	125	150
Coal Truck	1st version, red cab, litho blue and yellow dumper, 12" long	140	225	280
Coal Truck	2nd version, light blue truck, 12" long	140	225	280
Coal Truck	3rd version, Lumar Co. truck, 10" long, 1939	150	250	310
Coca-Cola Truck	Tin, 17" long, 1940's	125	200	250
Coca-Cola Truck	Yellow, 20" long, 1950	150	225	300
Coca-Cola Truck	Stamped steel, 20" long, 1940's	175	250	350

NAME	DESCRIPTION	GOOD	EX	MINT
Coke Truck	Red steel, 11 1/2" long, 1940's	100	175	225
Contractors and Builders Truck	10" long	125	200	250
Curtiss Candy Truck	Red plastic truck, 10" long, 1950	125	200	250
Dairy Farm Pickup Truck	22" long	60	100	125
Delivery Truck	Blue truck, 4" long, 1940	100	175	225
Deluxe Delivery Truck	With six delivery boxes, stamped steel, 13 1/4" long, 1948	100	150	200
Deluxe Trailer Truck	Tin and plastic, 14" long, 1950's	70	100	145
Dodge Salerno Engineering Department Truck		600	900	1200
Dump Truck	4 1/2" long, 1930's	100	175	225
Dump Truck	Motor, tin friction, 12" long, 1950's	50	75	100
Dump Truck	Red cab, gray bumper, yellow bed, 18" long, 1950	100	150	200
Dump Truck	6" long, 1930's	100	150	200
Dump Truck	Red cab, green body, 6 1/4" long	50	75	100
Dump Truck	Yellow cab, blue bumper, red bed, 18" long, 1950	100	150	200
Emergency Service Truck	Friction, tin	125	200	275
Emergency Service Truck	Friction, tin, searchlight behind car and siren	150	225	300
Firestone Truck	Metal, 14" long, 1950's	50	75	100
Ford Heavy Duty Express Truck	Cab with canopy, 1950's	60	100	125
Gas Truck	Green truck, 4" long, 1940	60	90	120
Giant Reversing Tractor Truck	With tools, tin windup, 14" long, 1950's	75	130	175
Gravel Truck	1st version, pressed steel cab, red tin dumper, 10" long, 1930	100	150	200
Gravel Truck	2nd version, metal, 8 1/2" long, 1940's	75	125	150
Gravel Truck	3rd version, metal with "Gravel Mixer" drum, 10" long, 1930's	100	150	200
Grocery Truck	Cardboard boxes, tinplate and plastic, 14 1/2" long	90	150	180
Guided Missile Truck	Blue, red and yellow body, friction, 16" long, 1958	75	125	150
Hi-Way Express Truck	Pressed steel	95	150	190
Hi-Way Express Truck	Tin, tin tires, 16" long, 1940's	50	75	100
Hi-Way Express Truck	"Nationwide Delivery," 1950's	100	150	200
Hi-Way Express Van Truck	Metal, 15 1/2" long, 1940's	100	150	200
Jalopy Pickup Truck	Tin windup, 7" long	60	90	120
Jeep	11" long, 1946-50	75	130	175
Jeepster	Mechanical, plastic	110	165	220
Lazy Day Dairy Farm Pickup Truck and Trailer	22" long	45	75	90
Lincoln Transfer and Storage Co. Mack Truck	Wheels have cut out spokes, tin litho, windup, 13" long, 1928	350	525	700
Lone Eagle Oil Co. Mack Truck	Bright blue cab, green tank, windup, 12" long, 1930	225	350	450
Lumar Contractors Scoop/ Dump Truck	17 1/2" long, 1940's	75	125	150
Lumar Lines and Gasoline Set	1948	250	375	500
Lumar Lines Truck	Red cab, aluminum finished trailer, 14" long	125	200	250
Lumar Motor Transport Truck	Litho, 13" long, 1942	75	130	175
Machinery Moving Truck		60	90	120
Mack Army Truck	Pressed steel, windup, 7 1/2" long	70	100	140
Mack Army Truck	Friction, 5" long, 1930	125	200	250
Mack Army Truck	Khaki brown body, windup, 10 1/2" long	125	225	275
Mack Army Truck	13 1/2" long, 1929	225	350	450
Mack Dump Truck	Dark red cab, medium blue bed, windup, 10" long, 1928	150	225	300
Mack Dump Truck	Medium blue truck, windup, 13" long, 1934	200	300	400

NAME	DESCRIPTION	GOOD	EX	MINT
Mack Dump Truck	Silver cab, medium blue dump, windup, 12 3/4" long, 1936	225	355	475
Mack Dump Truck	No driver, 19" long, 1930	300	450	600
Mack Dump Truck	Tin litho, windup, 13 1/2" long, 1926	225	350	550
Mack Railroad Express Truck #7	Tin, 1930's	75	125	150
Mack Towing Truck	Dark green cab, windup, 8" long, 1926	175	275	350
Mack U.S. Mail Truck	Black body, windup, 9 1/2" long	250	375	500
Magnetic Crane and Truck	1950	175	275	350
Mammouth Truck Train	Truck with 5 trailers, 1930's	150	250	325
Marcrest Dairy Truck	White truck with 3 glass bottles, 14" long	150	275	350
Meadowbrook Dairy Truck	14" long, 1940	150	275	350
Mechanical Sand Dump Truck	Steel, 1940's	100	150	200
Medical Corps Ambulance Truck	Olive drab paint, 1940's	100	150	200
Merchants Transfer Mack Truck	Red open-stake truck, 10" long	225	350	450
Merchants Transfer Mack Truck	13 1/3" long, 1928	250	375	500
Military Cannon Truck	Olive drab paint, cannon shoots marbles, 10" long, 1939	125	200	250
Milk Truck	White truck, 4" long, 1940	60	90	120
Miniature Mayflower Moving Van	Operating lights	60	90	125
Motor Market Truck	10" long, 1939	100	175	225
Navy Jeep	Windup	50	75	100
North American Van Lines Tractor Trailer	Windup, 13" long, 1940's	100	175	225
Panel Wagon Truck		30	55	75
Pet Shop Truck	Plastic, 6 compartments with 6 different vinyl dogs, 11" long	125	200	250
Pickup Truck	Blue and yellow with wood tires, 9" long, 1940's	50	75	100
Polar Ice Co. Ice Truck	13" long, 1940's	100	175	225
Police Patrol Mack Truck	Windup, 10" long	200	300	400
Popeye Dippy Dumper Truck	Popeye figure is celluloid, tin windup	325	500	650
Pure Milk Dairy Truck	Glass bottles, pressed steel, 1940	55	80	110
R.C.A. Television Service Truck	Plastic Ford panel truck, 8 1/2" long, 1948-50	150	225	300
Railway Express Agency Truck	Green closed van truck, 1940's	90	135	180
Range Rider	Tin windup, 1930's	250	375	500
Reversing Road Roller	Tin windup	60	100	125
Road Builder Tank	1950	125	200	250
Rocker Dump Truck	17 1/2" long	60	90	120
Roy Rogers and Trigger Cattle Truck	Metal, 15" long, 1950's	60	100	135
Royal Oil Co. Mack Truck	Dark red cab, medium green tank, windup, 8 1/4" long, 1927	200	300	400
Royal Van Co. Mack Truck	1927	250	375	500
Royal Van Co. Mack Truck	Red cab, tin litho and paint, windup, 9" long, 1928	210	315	420
Sand and Gravel Truck "Builders Supply Co."	Tin windup, 1920	150	225	300
Sand Truck	Tin litho, 12 1/2" long, 1940's	125	200	275
Sand Truck	9" long, 1948	100	150	200
Sand-Gravel Dump Truck	Tin litho, 12" long, 1950	150	225	300
Sand-Gravel Dump Truck	Blue cab, yellow dump with "Gravel" on side, tin, 1930's	140	225	285
Sanitation Truck	1940's	135	200	270
Searchlight Truck	Pressed steel, 9 3/4" long, 1930's	160	250	325
Side Dump Truck	1940	90	130	175
Side Dump Truck	10" long, 1930's	140	225	280

NAME	DESCRIPTION	GOOD	EX	MINT
Side Dump Truck and Trailer	15" long, 1935	150	225	300
Sinclair Tanker	Tin, 14" long, 1940's	150	225	300
Stake Bed Truck	Rubber stamped chicken on one side of truck bunny on other	100	150	200
Stake Bed Truck	Pressed steel, wooden wheels, 7" long, 1936	60	90	120
Stake Bed Truck	Red cab, green stake bed, 20" long, 1947	100	150	200
Stake Bed Truck	Medium blue cab, red stake bed, 10" long, 1940	75	130	175
Stake Bed Truck	Red cab, yellow and red trailer, 14" long	100	150	200
Stake Bed Truck	Red cab, blue stake bed, 6" long, 1930's	75	125	150
Stake Bed Truck and Trailer	Red truck, silver stake bed	125	200	250
Streamline Mechanical Hauler, Van, and Tank Truck Combi	Heavy guage steel, 10 3/8" long, 1936	170	275	350
Sunshine Fruit Growers Truck	Red cab, yellow and white trailer with blue roof, 14" long	100	150	200
Tipper Dump Truck	Windup, 9 3/4" long, 1950	75	130	175
Tow Truck	Aluminum finish, tin litho windup, 6 1/4" long	75	125	150
Tow Truck	Aluminum finish, windup, 6 1/4" long	95	150	190
Tow Truck	10" long, 1935	125	200	250
Tow Truck	Red cab, yellow towing unit, 6" long, 1930's	137	200	275
Toyland Dairy Truck	10" long	140	210	280
Toyland's Farm Products Mack Milk Truck	With 12 wooden milk bottles, 10 1/4" long, 1931	200	300	400
Toytown Express Truck	Plastic cab	45	70	95
Tractor Trailer with Dumpster	Blue and yellow hauler, tan dumpster	125	200	250
Truck	Prewar, pressed steel, windup	100	175	225
Truck Train	Stake hauler and five trailers, 41" long, 1933	250	400	525
Truck Train	Stake hauler and four trailers, 41" long, 1938	350	550	725
Truck with Electric Lights	15" long, 1930's	110	165	220
Truck with Electric Lights	Battery operated lights, 10" long, 1935	125	200	250
Truck with Searchlight	Toolbox behind cab, 10" long, 1930's	150	225	300
U.S. Air Force Willys Jeep	Tin body, plastic figures	70	100	140
U.S. Army Jeep with Trailer		100	150	200
U.S. Mail Truck	Metal, 14" long, 1950's	225	350	450
U.S. Trucking Co. Mack Truck	Dark maroon cab, friction, 5 1/2" long, 1930	100	150	200
Van Truck	Plastic, 10" long, 1950's	40	60	80
Western Auto Truck	Steel, 25" long	60	90	125
Willys Jeep	Steel, 12" long, 1938	125	200	250
Willys Jeep and Trailer	1940's	100	160	215
Wrecker Truck	1930's	145	225	290

Wagons and Carts

NAME	DESCRIPTION	GOOD	EX	MINT
Bluto, Brutus' Horse and Cart	Celluloid figure, metal, 1938	325	500	650
Busy Delivery	Open three-wheel cart, windup, 9" long, 1939	175	275	350
Farm Wagon	Horse pulling wagon, 10" long, 1940's	55	80	110
Horse and Cart	With driver, 9 1/2" long, 1950's	45	75	90
Horse and Cart	Windup, 7" long, 1934	100	150	200
Horse and Cart with Clown Driver	Windup, 7 5/8" long, 1923	75	125	150
Pinocchio Busy Delivery	On unicycle facing 2-wheel cart, windup, 7 3/4" long, 1939	125	200	250
Popeye Horse and Cart	Tin windup	200	300	400
Rooster Pulling Wagon	Tin litho, 1930's	100	150	200

Marx

NAME	DESCRIPTION	GOOD	EX	MINT
Toylands Farm Products Milk Wagon	Tin windup, 10 1/2" long, 1930's	65	100	130
Toylands Milk and Cream Wagon	Balloon tires, tin litho, windup 10" long, 1931	125	200	250
Toytown Dairy Horsedrawn Cart	Tin windup, 10 1/2" long, 1930's	100	175	225
Two Donkeys Pulling Cart	With driver, tin litho, windup, 10 1/4" long, 1940's	50	75	100
Wagon with Two-Horse Team	Late 1940's, tin windup	35	55	75
Wagon with Two-Horse Team	1950, tin windup	30	50	65

NO.	NAME	DESCRIPTION	GOOD	EX	MINT
43-F	0-4-0 Steam Loco	Red cab, bin and tanks, black boiler, coal, and base, 3" long, 1978	4	5	7
47-A	1 Ton Trojan Van	Red body, no windows, 2 1/4" long, 1958	25	35	45
73-A	10 Ton Pressure Refueller	Bluish gray body, six gray plastic wheels, 2 5/8" long, 1959	20	25	35
4-H	1957 Chevy	Metallic rose body, chrome interior, large 5 arch rear wheels, 2 15/16"long, 1979	2	8	12
42-G	1957 Ford T-Bird	Red convertible, white interior, silver grill and trunk mounted spare, 1982	3	5	6
30-B	6-Wheel Crane Truck	Silver body, orange crane, metal or plastic hook, gray wheels, 2 5/8" long, 1961	20	30	40
30-C	8 Wheel Crane Truck	Green body, orange crane, red or yellow hook, 8 black wheels on 4 axles, 3" long, 1965	15	20	25
30-D	8-Wheel Crane Truck	Red body, yellow plastic hook, five spoke thin wheels, 3" long, 1970	5	7	10
51-C	8-Wheel Tipper	Blue tinted windows, eight black plastic wheels, 3" long, 1969	7	10	15
51-D	8-Wheel Tipper	Yellow cab, silver/gray tipper, blue windows, five spoke thin wheels, 3" long, 1970	4	6	8
65-E	Airport Coach	White top and roof, metallic blue bottom, amber windows, yellow interior, comes with varying airline logo decals, 3" long, 1977	5	10	15
51-A	Albion Chieftan	Yellow body, tan and light tan bags, small round decal on doors, 2 1/2" long, 1958	10	20	25
75-D	Alfa Carabo	Pink body, ivory interior, black trunk, five spoke wide wheels, 3" long, 1971	3	4	5
61-B	Alvis Stalwart	White body, yellow plastic removable canopy, green windows, six plastic wheels, 2 5/8" long, 1966	20	30	50
69-E	Armored Truck	Red body, white plastic roof, silver/gray base and grill, "Wells Fargo" on sides, 2 13/16" long, 1978	3	5	8
50-E	Articulated Truck	Purple tinted windows, small wide wheels, five spoke wide wheels, 2 3/4" long, 1973	6	8	12
30-G	Articulated Truck	Blue cab, white grill, silver/gray dumper, 5 spoke accent wheels, 3" long, 1981	3	5	6
53-A	Aston Martin DB2 Saloon	Metallic light green, 2 1/2" long, 1958	20	30	40
19-C	Aston Martin Racing Car	Metallic green, metal steering wheel and wire wheels, black plastic tires, 2 1/2" long, 1961	20	30	45
15-B	Atlantic Tractor Super	Orange body, tow hook, spare wheel behind cab on body, 2 5/8" long, 1959	20	30	40
16-A	Atlantic Trailer	Tan body, six metal wheels, tan tow bar, 3 1/8" long, 1956	15	25	35
16-B	Atlantic Trailer	Orange body, eight gray plastic wheels with knobby treads, 3 1/4" long, 1957	25	50	80
32-G	Atlas Extractor	Red/orange body, gray platform, turret and treads, black wheels, 3" long 1981	2	4	6
23-E	Atlas Truck	Metallic blue cab, silver interior, orange dumper, red and yellow labels on doors , 3" long, 1975	6	8	10
23-G	Audi Quatro	White body, red and black print sides, clear windows, "Audi Sport" on doors, 1982	2	3	5
71-A	Austin 200 Gallon Water Truck	Olive green body, four black plastic wheels, 2 3/8" long, 1959	15	25	30
36-A	Austin A50	Silver grill, with or without silver rear bumper, no windows, 2 3/8" long, 1957	15	20	30
29-B	Austin A55 Cambridge Sedan	Two-tone green, light green roof and rear top half of body, dark metallic green hood and lower body, 2 3/4" long, 1961	10	20	25
68-A	Austin MK II Radio Truck	Olive green body, four black plastic wheels, 2 3/8" long, 1959	20	25	30
17-B	Austin Taxi Cab	Maroon body, 2 1/4" long, 1960	35	50	70
1-D	Aveling Barford Road Roller	Green body, canopy, tow hook, 2 5/8" long, 1962	7	10	15

NO.	NAME	DESCRIPTION	GOOD	EX	MINT
43-B	Aveling Barford Tractor Shovel	Yellow body, yellow or red driver, four large plastic wheels, 2 5/8" long, 1962	10	15	25
16-E	Badger Exploration Truck	Metallic red body, silver grill, 2 1/4" long, 1974	3	4	6
13-F	Baja Dune Buggy	Metallic green, orange interior, silver motor, 2 5/8" long, 1971	3	4	6
58-A	BEA Coach	Blue body, four wheels with small knobby treads, 2 1/2" long, 1958	20	25	35
30-E	Beach Buggy	Pink, yellow paint splatters, clear windows, 2 1/2" long, 1970	3	4	6
47-E	Beach Hopper	Dark metallic blue body, hot pink splattered over body, bright orange interior, tan driver, 2 5/8" long, 1974	3	4	5
14-C	Bedford Ambulance	White body, silver trim, two rear doors open, 2 5/8" long, 1962	40	60	80
28-A	Bedford Compressor Truck	Silver front and rear grills, metal wheels, 1 3/4" long, 1956	25	35	45
42-A	Bedford Evening News Van	Yellow/orange body, silver grill, 2 1/4" long, 1957	25	35	45
27-A	Bedford Low Loader	Light blue cab, dark blue trailer, silver grill and side gas tanks, four metal wheels on cab, two metal wheels on trailer, 3 1/8" long, 1956	225	350	450
27-B	Bedford Low Loader	Green cab, tan trailer, silver grill, four gray wheels on cab, two wheels on trailer, 3 3/4" long, 1959	35	55	75
29-A	Bedford Milk Delivery Van	Tan body, white bottle load, 2 1/4" long, 1956	15	25	30
17-A	Bedford Removals Van	Maroon body, peaked roof, gold grill, 2 1/8" long, 1956	65	115	150
40-A	Bedford Tipper Truck	Red cab, silver grill, two front wheels, four dual rear wheels, 2 1/8" long, 1957	25	40	50
3-B	Bedford Ton Tipper	Gray cab, gray wheels, dual rear wheels, 2 1/2" long, 1961	10	15	20
13-A	Bedford Wreck Truck	Tan body, red metal crane and hook, 2" long, 1955	30	40	55
13-B	Bedford Wreck Truck	Tan body, red metal crane and hook, crane attached to rear axle, 2 1/8" long, 1958	30	45	60
23-A	Berkeley Cavalier Trailer	Decal on lower right rear of trailer, metal wheels, flat tow hook, 2 1/2" long, 1956	20	30	40
26-E	Big Banger	Red body, blue windows, small front wheels, large rear wheels, 3" long, 1972	4	6	8
12-F	Big Bull	Orange body, green plow blade, base and sides, chrome seat and engine, orange rollers, 2 1/2" long, 1975	4	6	8
22-F	Blaze Buster	Red body, silver interior, yellow label, 5 spoke slicks, 3" long, 1975	4	6	8
61-C	Blue Shark	Metallic dark blue, white driver, clear glass, four spoke wide wheels, 3" long, 1971	3	4	6
23-B	Bluebird Dauphine Trailer	Green with gray plastic wheels, decal on lower right rear of trailer, door on left rear side opens, 2 1/2" long, 1960	75	135	200
56-C	BMC 1800 Pininfarina	Clear windows, ivory interior, five spoke wheels, 2 3/4" long, 1970	7	10	15
45-D	BMW 3.0 CSL	Orange body, yellow interior, 2 7/8" long, 1976	3	5	7
53-B	BMW M1	Silver gray metallic body with plastic hood, red interior, black stripes and "52" on sides, 2 15/16" long, 1981	2	4	5
9-C	Boat and Trailer	White, hull, blue deck, clear windows, five spoke wheels on trailer, 3 1/4" long, 1966	4	6	9
9-D	Boat and Trailer	White, hull, blue deck, clear windows, five spoke wheels on trailer, 3 1/4" long, 1970	3	5	6
72-E	Bomag Road Roller	Yellow body, base and wheel hubs, black plastic roller, 2 15/16" long, 1979	2	4	6

NO.	NAME	DESCRIPTION	GOOD	EX	MINT
44-E	Boss Mustang	Yellow body, amber windows, silver interior, clover leaf wide wheels, 2 7/8" long, 1972	3	4	6
25-C	BP Petrol Tanker	Yellow hinged cab, white tanker body, six black plastic wheels, 3" long, 1964	8	15	20
52-B	BRM Racing Car	Blue or red body, white plastic driver, yellow wheels, 2 5/8" long, 1965	10	20	25
54-C	Cadillac Ambulance	White body, blue tinted windows, white interior, red cross labels on sides, 2 3/8" long, 1970	5	7	10
27-C	Cadillac Sedan	With or without silver grill, clear windows, white roof, silver wheels, 2 3/4" long, 1960	20	30	40
38-G	Camper	Red body, off white camper, unpainted base, 3" long 1980	3	5	7
16-D	Case Tractor Bulldozer	Red body, yellow base, motor and blade, black plastic rollers, 2 1/2" long, 1969	5	9	12
18-C	Caterpillar Bulldozer	Yellow body with driver, green rubber treads, 2 1/4" long, 1961	10	15	25
18-B	Caterpillar Bulldozer	Yellow body and driver, yellow blade, No. 18 cast on back of blade, metal rollers, 2" long, 1958	30	45	65
18-D	Caterpillar Crawler Bulldozer	Yellow body, no driver, green rubber treads, 2 3/8" long, 1964	30	45	60
18-A	Caterpillar D8 Bulldozer	Yellow body and driver, red blade and side supports, 1 7/8" long, 1956	25	35	45
8-A	Caterpillar Tractor	Driver has same color hat as body, metal rollers, rubber treads, crimped axles, 1 1/2" long, 1955	40	60	80
8-B	Caterpillar Tractor	Yellow body and driver, large smoke stack, metal rollers, rubber treads, crimped axles, 1 5/8" long, 1959	20	35	45
8-C	Caterpillar Tractor	Yellow body and driver, large smoke stack, metal rollers, rubber treads, rounded axles, 1 7/8" long, 1961	10	15	25
8-D	Caterpillar Tractor	Yellow body, no driver, plastic rollers, rubber treads, rounded axles, 2" long, 1964	10	15	20
37-D	Cattle Truck	Yellow body, gray plastic box with fold down rear door, black plastic wheels, green tinted windows, 2 1/4" long, 1966	7	10	15
37-E	Cattle Truck	Gray plastic box, white plastic cattle inside, five spoke thin wheels, green tinted windows, 2 1/2" long, 1970	5	7	10
71-F	Cattle Truck	Metallic brown body, yellow/orange cattle carrier, 3" long, 1976	4	6	7
25-H	Celica GT	Blue body, black base, white racing stripes and "78" on roof and doors, 2 15/16" long, 1978	3	7	12
25-J	Celica GT	Yellow body, blue interior, red "Yellow Fever" on hood, side racing stripes, clear windows, large rear wheels, 1982	2	4	6
3-A	Cement Mixer	Blue body and rotating barrel, orange metal wheels, 1 5/8" long, 1953	25	35	45
19-G	Cement Truck	Red body, yellow plastic barrel with red stripes, large wide arch wheels, 3" long, 1976	4	5	7
41-F	Chevrolet Ambulance	White body, blue windows and dome light, gray interior, 2 15/16" long, 1978	4	7	10
57-B	Chevrolet Impala	Pale blue roof, metallic blue body, green tinted windows, 2 3/4" long, 1961	20	25	35
20-C	Chevrolet Impala Taxi Cab	Orange/yellow or bright yellow body, ivory or red interior and driver, 3" long, 1965	10	15	20
44-G	Chevy 4x4 Van	Green body and windows, white "Ridin High" with horse and fence on sides, 1982	2	3	5
34-G	Chevy Pro Stocker	White body, red interior, clear front and side windows, frosted rear window, 3" long, 1981	2	3	5
68-E	Chevy Van	Orange body, unpainted base and grill, large rear wheels, 3" long, 1979	3	5	7
49-D	Chop Suey Motorcycle	Metallic dark red body, yellow bull's head on front handle bars, 2 3/4" long, 1973	5	7	10

NO.	NAME	DESCRIPTION	GOOD	EX	MINT
12-G	Citroen CX	Metallic body, silver base and lights, blue plastic hatch door, 3" long, 1979	4	8	12
66-A	Citroen DS 19	Light or dark yellow body, with or without silver grill, four plastic wheels, 2 1/2" long, 1959	20	30	40
51-E	Citroen SM	Clear windows, frosted rear windows, five spoke wheels, 3" long, 1972	3	4	6
65-C	Claas Combine Harvester	Red body, yellow plastic rotating blades and front wheels, black plastic front tires, solid rear wheels, 3" long, 1967	7	10	15
39-D	Clipper	Metallic dark pink, amber windows, bright yellow interior, 3" long, 1973	3	4	5
11-H	Cobra Mustang	Orange body, "The Boss" on doors, 1982	2	3	5
37-B	Coca Cola Lorry	Orange/yellow body, uneven case load, open base, metal rear fenders, 2 1/4" long, 1957	35	75	100
37-C	Coca Cola Lorry	Yellow body of various shades, even case load, silver wheels, black base, 2 1/4" long, 1960	35	55	75
51-F	Combine Harvester	Red body, black painted base, yellow plastic grain chute, 2 3/4" long, 1978	3	5	8
69-A	Commer 30 CWT Van	Silver grill, sliding left side door, four plastic wheels, yellow "NESTLE'S" decal on upper rear panel, 2 1/4" long, 1959	20	30	40
47-B	Commer Ice Cream Canteen	Metallic blue body, cream or white plastic interior with man holding ice cream cone, black plastic wheels, 1963	60	95	125
21-C	Commer Milk Truck	Pale green body, clear or green tinted windows, ivory or cream bottle load, 2 1/4" long, 1961	20	30	40
50-A	Commer Pickup Truck	With or without silver grill and bumpers, four wheels, 2 1/2" long, 1958	35	55	75
62-G	Corvette	Metallic red body, unpainted base, gray interior, 1979	2	4	6
40-F	Corvette T Roof	White body and interior, black "09" on door, red and black racing stripes, 1982	2	3	5
26-G	Cosmic Blues	White body, blue "COSMIC BLUES" and stars on sides, 2 7/8" long, 1970	2	3	4
74-E	Cougar Village	Metallic green body, yellow interior, unpainted base, 3 1/16" long, 1978	3	4	6
41-A	D-Type Jaguar	Dark green body, tan driver, open air scoop, 2 13/16" long, 1957	20	30	45
41-B	D-Type Jaguar	Dark green body, tan driver, silver wheels, open and closed air scoop, 2 7/16" long, 1960	70	100	145
58-C	D.A.F. Girder Truck	Cream body shades, green tinted windows, six black wheels, red plastic girders, 3" long, 1968	7	10	15
58-D	D.A.F. Girder Truck	Green windows, five spoke thin wheels, red plastic girders, 2 7/8" long, 1970	5	7	10
47-C	DAF Tipper Container Truck	Aqua or silver cab, yellow tipper box with light gray or dark gray plastic roof, 3" long, 1968	6	8	12
47-D	DAF Tipper Container Truck	Silver cab, yellow tipper box, five spoke thin wheels, 3" long, 1970	4	6	8
14-A	Daimler Ambulance	Cream body, silver trim, no number cast on body, "AMBULANCE" cast on sides, 1 7/8" long, 1956	20	35	45
14-B	Daimler Ambulance	Silver trim, "AMBULANCE" cast on sides, red cross on roof, 2 5/8" long, 1958	40	65	85
74-B	Daimler Bus	Double deck, white plastic interior, four black plastic wheels, 3" long, 1966	10	15	20
74-C	Daimler Bus	Double deck, white plastic interior, five spoke thin wheels, 3" long, 1970	7	10	15
67-E	Datsun 260Z 2+2	Metallic burgundy body, black base and grill, yellow interior, 3" long, 1978	3	4	6
24-G	Datsun 280ZX	Black body and base, clear windows, 5 spoke wheels, 2 7/8" long, 1979	2	3	5
33-E	Datsun or 126X	Yellow body, amber windows, silver interior, 3" long, 1973	5	8	10

NO.	NAME	DESCRIPTION	GOOD	EX	MINT
9-A	Dennis Fire Escape Engine	Red body, metal wheels, no front bumper, 2 1/4" long, 1955	15	20	30
20-F	Desert Dawg Jeep 4x4	White body, red top and stripes, white "Jeep" and yellow, red and green, "Desert Dawg" decal, 1982	2	3	5
1-A	Diesel Road Roller	Dark green body, flat canopy, tow hook, driver, 1 7/8" long, 1953	15	25	35
1-H	Dodge Challenger	Red body, white plastic top, silver interior, wide five spoke wheels, 2 15/16" long, 1976	3	5	8
63-G	Dodge Challenger	Green body, black base, bumpers and grill, clear windows, 2 7/8" long, 1980	3	5	7
52-C	Dodge Charger	Clear windows, black interior, five spoke wide wheels, 2 7/8" long, 1970	4	6	8
63-C	Dodge Crane Truck	Yellow body, green windows, six black plastic wheels, rotating crane cab, 3"long, 1968	7	10	15
63-D	Dodge Crane Truck	Yellow body, green windows, four spoke wide wheels, yellow plastic hook, 2 3/4" long, 1970	5	7	10
70-D	Dodge Dragster	Pink body, clear windows, silver interior, five spoke wide front wheels, 3" long, 1971	7	10	15
13-D	Dodge Wreck Truck	Green cab and crane, yellow body, green windows, 3" long, 1965	300	500	700
13-E	Dodge Wreck Truck	Yellow cab, rear body, red plastic hook, green windows, 3" long, 1970	10	15	20
43-E	Dragon Wheels Volkswagen	Light green body, amber windows, silver interior, orange on black "Dragon Wheels" on sides, large rear wheels, 2 13/16" long, 1972	5	7	9
58-B	Drott Excavator	Red or orange body, movable front shovel, green rubber treads, 2 5/8" long, 1962	35	50	70
2-A	Dumper	Green body, red dumper, gold trim, thin driver, green painted wheels, 1 5/8" long, 1953	35	50	70
2-B	Dumper	Green body, red dumper, no trim color, fat driver, 1 7/8" long, 1957	20	30	40
48-C	Dumper Truck	Red body, green tinted windows, 3" long, 1966	10	20	25
48-D	Dumper Truck	Bright blue cab, yellow body, green windows, 3" long, 1970	5	7	10
25-A	Dunlop Truck	Dark blue body, silver grill, 2 1/8" long, 1956	10	20	25
57-E	Eccles Trailer Caravan	Orange roof, green plastic interior, five spoke thin wheels, 3" long, 1970	5	7	10
20-B	ERF 686 Truck	Dark blue body, silver radiator, eight plastic silver wheels, No. 20 cast on black base, 2 5/8" long, 1959	25	45	60
6-C	Euclid Quarry Truck	Yellow body, 3 round axles, 2 front black plastic wheels, 2 solid rear dual wheels, 2 5/8" long, 1964	15	25	30
6-B	Euclid Quarry Truck	Yellow body, four ribs on dumper sides, plastic wheels, 2 1/2" long, 1957	10	20	25
35-D	Fandango	White body, red interior, chrome rear engine, large 5 spoke rear wheels, 3" long, 1975	3	5	8
58-F	Faun Dump Truck	Yellow cab and dumper, black base, 2 7/8" long, 1976	5	10	15
70-F	Ferrari 308 GTB	Red body and base, black plastic interior, side stripe, 2 15/16" long, 1981	2	3	5
75-B	Ferrari Berinetta	Metallic green body of various shades, ivory interior and tow hook, four wire or silver plastic wheels, 3" long, 1965	10	20	25
75-C	Ferrari Berinetta	Ivory interior, five spoke thin wheels, 2 3/4" long, 1970	5	7	10
73-B	Ferrari F1 Racing Car	Light and dark red body, plastic driver, white and yellow "73" decal on sides, 2 5/8" long, 1962	15	25	30
61-A	Ferret Scout Car	Olive green, tan driver faces front or back, four black plastic wheels, 2 1/4" long, 1959	10	20	25
56-B	Fiat 1500	Silver grill, red interior and tow hook, brown or tan luggage on roof, 2 1/2" long, 1965	10	15	20

NO.	NAME	DESCRIPTION	GOOD	EX	MINT
9-G	Fiat Abarth	White body, red interior, 1982	2	3	5
18-E	Field Car	Yellow body, tan plastic roof, ivory interior and tow hook, green plastic tires, 2 5/8" long, 1969	75	145	200
18-F	Field Car	Yellow body, tan roof, red wheels, ivory interior and tow hook, 2 5/8" long, 1970	5	7	10
29-C	Fire Pumper Truck	Red body, metal grill, white plastic hose and ladders, 3" long, 1966	3	7	10
29-D	Fire Pumper Truck	Red body, metal grill, white plastic hose and ladders, 3" long, 1970	2	5	8
53-G	Flareside Pick-up	Blue body, white interior, grill and pipes, clear windshield, lettered with "326", "Baja Bouncer" and "B.F. Goodrich", 1982	2	4	5
11-F	Flying Bug	Metallic red, gray windows, small five spoke front wheels, large five spoke rear wheels, 2 7/8" long, 1972	5	7	10
63-B	Foamite Fire Fighting Crash Tender	Red body, six black plastic wheels, white plastic hose and ladder on roof, 2 1/4" long, 1964	10	15	20
21-D	Foden Concrete Truck	Orange/yellow body and rotating barrel, green tinted windows, eight plastic wheels, 3" long, 1968	3	5	7
21-E	Foden Concrete Truck	Red body, orange barrel, green base and windows 5 spoke wheels, 2 7/8" long, 1970	2	3	5
26-A	Foden Ready Mix Concrete Truck	Orange body and rotating barrel, silver or gold grill, four silver plastic wheels, 1 3/4" long, 1956	65	100	130
26-B	Foden Ready Mix Concrete Truck	Orange body, gray plastic rotating barrel, with or without silver grill, six gray wheels, 2 124" long, 1961	85	130	175
7-B	Ford Anglia	Blue body, green tinted windows, 2 5/8" long, 1961	10	15	20
54-D	Ford Capri	Ivory interior and tow hook, clear windows, five spoke wide wheels, 3" long, 1971	3	4	6
45-B	Ford Corsair with Boat	Pale yellow body, red interior and tow hook, green roof rack with green plastic boat, 2 3/8" long, 1965	10	15	20
25-E	Ford Cortina	Clear windows, ivory interior and tow hook, thin five spoke wheels, 2 3/4" long, 1970	3	6	8
55-H	Ford Cortina	Metallic gold/green body, unpainted base and grill, wide multispoke wheels, 3 1/16" long, 1979	3	4	5
55-I	Ford Cortina	Metallic tan body, yellow interior, blue racing stripes, 1982	2	4	6
25-D	Ford Cortina G.T.	Light brown body in various shade, ivory interior and tow hook, 2 7/8" long, 1968	4	7	10
31-A	Ford Customline Station Wagon	Yellow body, no windows, with or without red painted tail lights, 2 5/8" long, 1957	20	30	40
9-F	Ford Escort RS2000	White body, black base and grill, tan interior, wide multispoke wheels, 3" long, 1978	3	5	7
59-B	Ford Fairlane Fire Chief's Car	Red body, ivory interior, clear windows, four plastic wheels, 2 5/8" long, 1963	50	75	100
55-B	Ford Fairlane Police Car	Silver grill, ivory interior, clear windows, four plastic wheels, 2 5/8" long, 1963	35	55	75
31-B	Ford Fairlane Station Wagon	Green or clear windows, with or without red painted tail lights, 2 3/4" long, 1960	20	30	35
59-C	Ford Galaxie Fire Chief's Car	Red body, ivory interior, driver and tow hook, clear windows, four black plastic wheels, 2 7/8" long, 1966	7	10	15
59-D	Ford Galaxie Fire Chief's Car	Red body, ivory interior and tow hook, clear windows, four spoke thin wheels, 2 7/8" long, 1970	5	7	10
55-C	Ford Galaxie Police Car	White body, ivory interior, driver and tow hook, clear windows, 2 7/8" long, 1966	10	15	20
45-C	Ford Group 6	Metallic green body, ivory interior, clear windows, five spoke wide wheels, 3" long, 1970	5	7	10
41-C	Ford GT	White or yellow body, red interior, clear windows, yellow or red plastic wheels, 2 5/8" long, 1965	20	30	40

Top to Bottom: Model 15-C Refuse Truck; Model 40-B1 1961 Leyland Royal Tiger Coach; Model 26-A Foden Ready Mix Concrete Truck; Model 44-B Rolly Royce Phantom V; Model 44-D Refrigerator Truck'; Model 37-C Coca Cola Lorry; Model 43-B Aveling Barford Tractor Shovel.

Matchbox

NO.	NAME	DESCRIPTION	GOOD	EX	MINT
41-D	Ford GT	White body, red interior, clear windows, five spoke wheels, 2 5/8" long, 1970	5	7	10
71-C	Ford Heavy Wreck Truck	Red cab, white bumper, amber or green windows, 3" long, 1968	50	75	100
71-D	Ford Heavy Wreck Truck	Red cab, white body, green windows and dome light, four spoke wide wheels, 3" long, 1970	15	25	30
8-F	Ford Mustang	Wide five spoke wheels, interior and tow hook same color, 2 7/8" long, 1970	7	10	15
8-E	Ford Mustang Fastback	White body, red interior, clear windows, 2 7/8" long, 1966	7	10	15
6-E	Ford Pick-up	Red body, white removable canopy, five spoke wheels, 2 3/4" long, 1970	5	7	10
6-D	Ford Pick-up	Red body, white removable plastic canopy, four black plastic wheels, 2 3/4" long, 1968	10	15	20
30-A	Ford Prefect	Blue body, metal wheels, silver grill, black tow hook, 2 1/4" long, 1956	40	60	80
7-C	Ford Refuse Truck	Orange cab, gray plastic dumper, silver metal loader, 3" long, 1966	7	10	15
7-D	Ford Refuse Truck	Gray plastic body, silver metal dumper, 3" long, 1970	6	8	12
63-A	Ford Service Ambulance	Olive green body, four plastic wheels, round white circle on sides with red cross, 2 1/2" long, 1959	15	20	30
70-A	Ford Thames Estate Car	Yellow upper, bluish/green lower, four plastic wheels, 2 1/8" long, 1959	10	15	20
59-A	Ford Thames Van	Silver grill, four plastic knobby wheels, 2 1/8" long, 1958	50	75	100
75-A	Ford Thunderbird	Cream top half, pink bottom half, green tinted windows, 2 5/8" long, 1960	25	35	45
39-C	Ford Tractor	Blue body, black plastic steering wheel and tires, with or without yellow hood, 2 1/8" long, 1967	4	8	12
46-F	Ford Tractor	Blue body, black base, large black plastic rear wheels, 2 3/16" long, 1987	3	5	8
66-F	Ford Transit	Orange body, unpainted base, yellow interior, green windows, 2 3/4" long, 1977	2	3	4
61-D	Ford Wreck Truck	Red body, black base and grill, frosted amber windows, 3" long, 1978	3	5	7
33-B	Ford Zephyr 6MKIII	Blue/green body shades, clear windows, ivory interior, 2 5/8" long, 1963	15	20	30
53-D	Ford Zodiac	Clear windows, ivory interior, five spoke wheels, 2 3/4" long, 1970	5	7	10
39-A	Ford Zodiac Convertible	Peach/pink body shades, tan driver, metal wheels, silver grill, 2 5/8" long, 1957	35	65	90
53-C	Ford Zodiac MK IV	Metallic silver blue body, clear windows, ivory interior, four black plastic wheels, 2 3/4" long, 1968	7	10	15
33-A	Ford Zodiac MKII Sedan	With or without silver grill, with or without red painted tail lights, 2 5/8" long, 1957	20	30	45
72-A	Fordson Tractor	Blue body with tow hook, 2" long, 1959	10	20	25
15-F	Fork Lift Truck	Red body, yellow hoist, 2 1/2" long, 1972	3	4	6
34-E	Formula 1 Racing Car	Metallic pink, white driver, clear glass, wide four spoke wheels, 2 7/8" long, 1971	7	10	15
36-F	Formula 5000	Orange body, silver rear engine, large clover leaf rear slicks, 3" long, 1975	5	7	10
28-H	Formula Racing Car	Gold body, silver engine and pipes, white driver and "Champion", black "8" on front and sides, large clover leaf rear wheels, 1982	2	3	5
22-E	Freeman Inter-City Commuter	Clear windows, ivory interior, five spoke wide wheels, 3" long, 1970	5	7	10
63-E	Freeway Gas Truck	Red cab, purple tinted windows, small wide wheels on front, clover leaf design, 3" long, 1973	10	15	20
62-A	General Service Lorry	Olive green body, six black wheels, 2 5/8" long, 1959	15	25	30
44-D	GMC Refrigerator Truck	Red ribbed roof cab, turquoise box with gray plastic rear door that opens, green windows, 1967	7	10	15

NO.	NAME	DESCRIPTION	GOOD	EX	MINT
44-D	GMC Refrigerator Truck	Green windows, four spoke wheels, gray plastic rear door, 2 13/16" long, 1970	5	7	10
26-C	GMC Tipper Truck	Red tipping cab, silver tipper body with swinging door, four wheels, 2 5/8" long, 1968	5	7	10
26-D	GMC Tipper Truck	Red cab, silver/gray tipper body, four spoke wide wheels, 2 1/2" long, 1970	10	15	20
66-C	Greyhound Bus	Silver body, white plastic interior, clear or dark amber windows, six black plastic wheels, 3" long, 1967	25	35	45
66-D	Greyhound Bus	Silver body, white interior, amber windows, five spoke thin wheels, 3" long, 1970	5	7	10
70-B	Grit Spreader Truck	Dark red cab, four black plastic wheels, 2 5/8" long, 1966	5	7	10
70-C	Grit Spreader Truck	Red cab, yellow body, green windows, gray plastic rear pull, 2 5/8" long, 1970	6	8	12
4-F	Gruesome Twosome	Metallic gold body, wide five spoke wheels, 2 7/8" long, 1971	5	7	10
23-F	GT 350	White body, blue stripes on hood, roof and rear deck, 2 7/8" long, 1970	3	4	5
7-E	Hairy Hustler	Metallic bronze, silver interior, five spoke front wheels, clover leaf rear wheels, 2 7/8" long, 1971	5	7	10
50-G	Harley Davidson Motorcycle	Silver/brown metallic frame and tank, chrome engine and pipes, brown rider, 2 11/16" long, 1980	2	3	5
66-B	Harley Davidson Motorcycle/ Sidecar	Metallic bronze body, three wire wheels, 2 5/8" long, 1962	30	45	65
69-B	Hatra Tractor Shovel	Orange or yellow movable shovel arms, four plastic tires, 3" long, 1965	20	30	40
40-C	Hay Trailer	Blue body with tow bar, yellow plastic racks, yellow plastic wheels, 3 3/4" long, 1967	3	5	8
55-G	Hellraiser	White body, unpainted base and grill, silver rear engine, 3" long, 1975	3	5	7
15-G	Hi Ho Silver	Metallic pearl gray body, 2 1/2" long, 1971	7	10	15
56-D	Hi-Tailer	White body, silver engine and windshield, wide five spoke front wheels, wide clover leaf rear wheels, 3" long, 1974	4	6	8
43-A	Hillman Minx	With or without silver grill, with or without red painted tail lights, 2 5/8" long, 1958	15	20	30
38-C	Honda Motorcycle and Trailer	Metallic blue/green cycle with wire wheels, black plastic tires, orange trailer, 2 7/8" long, 1967	10	15	20
38-D	Honda Motorcycle and Trailer	Yellow trailer with five spoke thin wheels, 2 7/8" long, 1970	4	7	10
18-G	Hondarora Motorcycle	Red frame and fenders chrome bars, fork, engine, black seat, 2 3/8" long, 1975	5	15	25
17-E	Horse Box	Blue tinted windows, five spoke thin wheels, white plastic horses inside box, 2 3/4" long, 1970	4	6	8
40-E	Horse Box	Orange cab, off white van with tan plastic door, small wheels, 2 13/16" long, 1977	4	5	7
17-D	Horse Box, Ergomatic Cab	Red cab, green plastic box, gray side door, 1969	10	15	20
7-A	Horse Drawn Milk Float	Orange body, white driver and bottle load, brown horse with white mane and hoofs, 2 1/4" long, 1954	35	55	75
46-G	Hot Chocolate	Metallic brown front lid and sides, black roof, 2 13/16" long, 1972	3	4	5
67-D	Hot Rocker	Metallic lime/green body, white interior and tow hook, five spoke wide wheels, 3" long, 1973	3	5	7
36-E	Hot Rod Draguar	Metallic red body, clear canopy, wide five spoke wheels, 2 13/16" long, 1970	4	6	8
2-G	Hovercraft	Metallic green top, tan base, silver engine, yellow windows, 3 1/8" long, 1976	4	8	12
72-D	Hovercraft	White body, black bottom and base, red props, 3" long, 1972	4	7	10

NO.	NAME	DESCRIPTION	GOOD	EX	MINT
17-C	Hoveringham Tipper	Red body, orange dumper, 2 7/8" long, 1963	7	10	15
42-C	Iron Fairy Crane	Red body, yellow/orange crane, black plastic wheels, yellow plastic single cable hook, 3" long, 1969	7	10	15
42-D	Iron Fairy Crane	Four spoke wheels, yellow plastic hook, 3" long, 1970	25	35	45
14-D	Iso Grifo	Blue body, light blue interior and tow hook, clear windows, 3" long, 1968	5	7	10
14-E	Iso Grifo	Five spoke wheels, clear windows, 3" long, 1969	3	4	5
65-A	Jaguar 3.4 Litre Saloon	Silver grill, silver or black bumpers, four gray plastic wheels, 2 1/2" long, 1959	7	10	15
65-B	Jaguar 3.8 Litre Sedan	Red body shades, green tinted windows, four plastic wheels, 2 5/8" long, 1962	5	7	10
28-C	Jaguar Mark 10	Light brown body, off white interior, working hood, gray motor and wheels, 2 3/4" long, 1964	35	65	90
32-A	Jaguar XK 140 Coupe	With or without silver grill, with or without red painted tail lights, 2 3/8" long, 1957	20	30	40
32-B	Jaguar XKE	Metallic red body, ivory interior, clear or tinted windows, 2 5/8" long, 1962	15	20	35
38-F	Jeep	Olive green body, black base and interior, wide 5 spoke reverse accent wheels, no hubs, 2 3/8" long, 1976	5	8	12
5-H	Jeep 4x4 Golden Eagle	Brown body, wide 4 spoke wheels, eagle decal on hood, 1982	2	5	8
72-B	Jeep CJ5	Yellow body, red plastic interior/tow hook, four yellow wheels, black plastic tires, 2 3/8", 1966	10	15	20
72-C	Jeep CJ5	Red interior and tow hook, eight spoke wheels 2 3/8" long, 1970	5	7	10
53-F	Jeep CJ6	Red body, unpainted base, bumper and winch, 5 spoke rear accent wheels, 2 15/16" long, 1977	2	3	5
71-B	Jeep Gladiator Pickup Truck	Red body, clear windows, green or white interior, four black plastic wheels, fine treads, 2 5/8" long, 1964	18	25	30
2-F	Jeep Hot Rod	Cream seats and tow hook, large wide four spoke wheels, 2 5/16" long, 1971	7	10	15
50-B	John Deere Tractor	Green body and tow hook, yellow plastic wheels, 2 1/8" long, 1964	10	20	25
51-B	John Deere Trailer	Green tipping body with tow bar, two small yellow wheels, three plastic barrels, 2 5/8" long, 1964	25	35	45
11-C	Jumbo Crane	Yellow body, black plastic wheels, 3" long, 1965	5	10	15
71-E	Jumbo Jet Motorcycle	Dark metallic blue body, red elephant head on handle bars, wide wheels, 2 3/4" long, 1973	4	6	8
38-A	Karrier Refuse Collector	Silver grill headlights and bumper, 2 3/8" long, 1957	15	25	30
50-C	Kennel Truck	Metallic green body, clear or blue tinted canopy, four plastic dogs, 2 3/4" long, 1969	7	10	15
50-D	Kennel Truck	Green windows, light blue tinted canopy, four plastic dogs, 2 3/4" long, 1970	5	7	10
45-E	Kenworth Caboner Aerodyne	White body with blue and brown side stripes, silver grill, tanks and pipes, 1982	2	3	5
41-G	Kenworth Conventional Aerodyne	Red cab and chassis, silver tanks and pipes, black and white stripes on cab, 1982	2	3	5
27-F	Lamborghini Countach	Yellow body, silver interior and motor, five spoke wheels, 2 7/8" long, 1973	5	7	10
20-D	Lamborghini Marzel	Amber windows, ivory interior, 2 3/4" long, 1969	15	20	35
33-C	Lamborghini Miura	Metal grill, silver plastic wheels, red or white interior, clear or frosted back window, 2 3/4" long, 1969	10	15	20
33-D	Lamborghini Miura	Clear windows, frosted rear window, five spoke wheels, 2 3/4" long, 1970	25	40	50

NO.	NAME	DESCRIPTION	GOOD	EX	MINT
36-B	Lambretta TV 175 Motor Scooter and Sidecar	Metallic green, three whells, 2" long, 1961	25	35	45
12-A	Land Rover	Olive green body, tan driver, metal wheels, 1 3/4" long, 1955	20	25	35
12-B	Land Rover	Olive green body, no driver, tow hook, 2 1/4" long, 1959	35	55	75
57-C	Land Rover Fire Truck	Red body, blue tinted windows, white plastic ladder on roof, 2 1/2" long, 1966	10	15	20
57-D	Land Rover Fire Truck	Red body, blue tinted windows, white plastic removable ladder, 2 1/2" long, 1970	5	7	10
32-C	Leyland Petrol Tanker	Green cab, white tank body, blue tinted windows, eight plastic wheels, 3" long, 1968	25	40	50
32-D	Leyland Petrol Tanker	Green cab, white tank body, blue tinted windows, five spoke thin wheels, 3" long, 1970	10	20	25
40-B	Leyland Royal Tiger Coach	Silver/gray body, green tinted windows four plastic wheels, 3" long, 1961	10	15	20
31-C	Lincoln Continental	Clear windows, ivory interior, black plastic wheels, 2 7/8" long, 1964	10	15	20
31-D	Lincoln Continental	Clear windows, ivory interior, five spoke wheels, 2 3/4" long, 1970	5	7	10
28-G	Lincoln Continental MK-V	Red body, tan interior, 3" long, 1979	10	15	20
5-C	London Bus	Red body, silver grill and headlights, 2 9/16" long, 1961	10	20	25
5-A	London Bus	Red body, gold grill, metal wheels, 2" long, 1954	30	45	60
5-D	London Bus	Red body, white plastic seats, black plastic wheels, 2 3/4" long, 1965	7	10	15
5-B	London Bus	Red body, 2 1/4" long, 1957	30	45	60
56-A	London Trolley Bus	Red body, two trolley poles on top of roof, six wheels, 2 5/8" long, 1958	45	70	90
17-F	Londoner Bus	Red body, white interior, five spoke wide wheels, 3" long, 1972	10	15	20
21-A	Long Distance Coach	Light green body, black base, "London to Glasgow" orange decal on sides, 2 1/4" long, 1956	10	20	25
21-B	Long Distance Coach	Green body, black base, No. 21 cast on baseplate, "London to Glasgow" orange decal on sides, 2 5/8" long, 1958	20	60	45
5-E	Lotus Europa	Metallic blue body, clear windows, ivory interior and tow hook, 2 7/8" long, 1969	5	7	10
19-D	Lotus Racing Car	White driver, large rear wheels, 2 3/4" long, 1966	10	15	20
19-E	Lotus Racing Car	Metallic purple, white driver, five spoke wide wheels with clover leaf design, 2 3/4" long, 1970	5	10	15
60-D	Lotus Super Seven	Butterscotch, clear windshield, black interior and trunk, four spoke wide wheels, 2 7/8" long,1971	5	7	10
49-A	M3 Army Personnel Carrier	Olive green body, gray rubber treads, 2 1/2" long, 1958	15	25	30
28-D	Mack Dump Truck	Orange body, green windows, four large plastic wheels, 2 5/8" long, 1968	4	7	10
28-E	Mack Dump Truck	Pea green body, green windows, large ballon wheels with clover leaf design, 2 5/8" long, 1970	2	4	6
35-A	Marshall Horse Box	Red cab, brown horse box, silver grill, three rear windows in box, 2" long, 1957	20	25	35
52-A	Maserati 4 Cl. T/ 1948	Red or yellow body, cream or white driver with or without circle on left shoulder, 2 3/8" long, 1958	10	17	25
32-E	Maserati Bora	Metallic burgundy, clear windows, bright yellow interior, wide five spoke wheels, 3" long, 1972	5	7	10
4-A	Massey Harris Tractor	Red body with rear fenders, tan driver, four spoke metal front wheels, 1954	30	40	55
4-B	Massey Harris Tractor	Red body, no fenders, tan driver, solid metal front wheels, hollow inside rear wheels, 1 5/8" long, 1957	25	40	50

NO.	NAME	DESCRIPTION	GOOD	EX	MINT
72-F	Maxi Taxi	Yellow body, black "MAXI TAXI" on roof, five spoke wheels, 3" long, 1973	2	3	4
66-E	Mazda RX 500	Orange body, purple windows, silver rear engine, five spoke wide wheels, 3" long, 1971	3	4	5
31-G	Mazda RX-7	White body, black base, burgundy stripe, black "RX-7", 3" long, 1979	3	4	5
31-H	Mazda RX-7	Gray body with sunroof, black interior, 1982	15	25	35
10-A	Mechanical Horse and Trailer	Red cab with three metal wheels, gray trailer with two metal wheels, 2 3/8" long, 1955	15	25	35
10-B	Mechanical Horse and Trailer	Red cab, ribbed bed in trailer, metal front wheels on cab, 2 15/16" long, 1958	25	35	45
6-F	Mercedes 350 SL	Orange body, black plastic convertible top, light yellow interior, 3" long, 1973	5	7	10
56-E	Mercedes 450 SEL	Metallic blue body, unpainted base and grill, 3" long, 1979	3	4	5
3-D	Mercedes Ambulance	Ivory interior, red cross label on side doors, 2 7/8" long, 1970	2	5	8
53-B	Mercedes Benz 220 SE	Silver grill, clear windows, ivory interior, four wheels, 2 3/4" long, 1963	15	25	30
27-D	Mercedes Benz 230 SL	Unpainted metal grill, red plastic interior and tow hook, black plastic wheels, 3" long, 1966	3	6	8
27-E	Mercedes Benz 230 SL	Metal grill, blue tinted windshield, five spoke wheels, 2 7/8" long, 1970	7	10	15
46-C	Mercedes Benz 300 SE	Clear windows, ivory interior, black plastic wheels, 2 7/8" long, 1968	4	7	10
46-D	Mercedes Benz 300 SE	Clear windows, ivory interior, five spoke thin wheels, 2 7/8" long, 1970	5	10	15
3-C	Mercedes Benz Ambulance	Varying body colors, white interior and stretcher, blue windows and dome light, metal grill, black plastic wheels, 2 7/8" long, 1968	4	7	10
1-F	Mercedes Benz Lorry	Metallic gold, removable orange or yellow canopy, 3" long, 1970	4	6	8
1-E	Mercedes Benz Lorry	Pale green body, removable orange plastic canopy, 3" long, 1967	5	7	10
68-B	Mercedes Coach	White plastic top half, white plastic interior, clear windows, four black plastic wheels, 2 7/8" long, 1965	30	40	55
42-F	Mercedes Container Truck	Red body, black base and grill, removable ivory container with red top and back door, six wheels, 3" long, 1977	4	5	7
56-F	Mercedes Taxi	Tan plastic interior, unpainted base, clear plastic windows, red "Taxi" sign on roof, 3" long, 1980	3	4	5
2-D	Mercedes Trailer	Pale green body, removable orange canopy, tow hook, black plastic wheels, 3 1/2" long, 1968	5	7	10
2-E	Mercedes Trailer	Metallic gold body, removable canopy, rotating tow bar, 3 1/4" long, 1970	3	4	5
49-B	Mercedes Umimog	Silver grill, four black plastic tires, 2 1/2" long, 1967	10	15	20
62-C	Mercury Cougar	Metallic lime green body shades, red plastic interior and tow hook, silver wheels, 3" long, 1968	7	10	15
62-D	Mercury Cougar	Red interior and tow hook, five spoke thin wheels, 3" long, 1970	3	4	6
62-E	Mercury Cougar "Rat Rod"	Red interior and tow hook, small five spoke front wheels, larger five spoke wide rear windows, 3" long, 1970	4	6	8
59-E	Mercury Fire Chief's Car	Red body, ivory interior, two occupants, clear windows, five spoke wide wheels, 3" long, 1971	5	7	10
55-D	Mercury Police Car	White body, ivory interior with two figures, clear windows, four silver wheels with black plastic tires, 3" long, 1968	10	15	20
55-E	Mercury Police Car	White body, ivory interior, two occupants, five spoke thin wheels, 3" long, 1970	5	7	10
55-F	Mercury Police Station Wagon	White body, ivory interior, no occupants, five spoke wide wheels, 3" long, 1971	5	7	10

Top to Bottom: Model 32-B Jaguar XKE; Model 34-B Volkswagen Caravette Camper Van; Model 56-C BMC 1800 Pinafarina; Model 59-B Ford Fairlane Fire Chief's Car; Model 10-D Pipe Truck; Model 53-B Snowtrac Tractor; Model 70-D Dodge Dragster; Model 58-C D.A.F. Girder Truck.

NO.	NAME	DESCRIPTION	GOOD	EX	MINT
73-C	Mercury Station Wagon	Metallic lime green body shades, ivory interior with dogs in rear, 3 1/8" long, 1968	7	10	15
73-D	Mercury Station Wagon	Red body, ribbed rear roof, ivory interior with two dogs, 3" long, 1970	4	6	8
73-E	Mercury Station Wagon	Red body, ribbed rear roof, ivory interior with two dogs, 3" long, 1972	3	5	7
35-C	Merryweather Fire Engine	Metallic red body, blue windows, white removable ladder on roof, five spoke thin wheels, 3" long, 1969	5	7	10
48-A	Meteor Sports Boat and Trailer	Metal boat with tan deck and blue hull, black metal trailer with tow bar, 2 3/8" long, 1958	30	45	60
19-A	MG Midget	White body, tan driver, red seats, spare tire on trunk,2" long, 1956	50	60	75
19-A	MG Sports Car	Silver grill and headlights, tan driver, red painted seats, 2" long, 1956	35	50	70
19-B	MG Sports Car	Silver or gold grills, tan driver, 2 1/4" long, 1958	30	45	65
64-B	MG-1100	Green body, ivory interior, driver, dog and tow hook, clear windows, four black plastic wheels, 2 5/8" long, 1966	5	7	10
64-C	MG-1100	Ivory interior and tow hook, one occupant and dog, clear windows, 2 5/8" long, 1970	7	10	15
19-B	MGA Sports Car	White body variation, silver wheels, tan driver, silver or gold grills, 2 1/4" long, 1958	50	95	125
51-G	Midnight Magic	Black body, silver stripes on hood, five spoke front wheels, clover leaf rear windows, 1972	2	3	4
14-F	Mini Haha	Red body, pink driver, silver engine, large spoke rear slicks, 2 3/8" long, 1975	5	9	12
74-A	Mobile Refreshment Canteen	Cream, white, or silver body, upper side door opens with interior utensils, "Refreshment" on front side, 2 5/8" long, 1959	20	40	60
1-G	Mod Rod	Yellow body, tinted windows, red or black wheels, 2 7/8" long, 1971	10	15	20
25-F	Mod Tractor	Metallic purple, orange/yellow seat and tow hook, 2 1/8" long, 1972	10	15	20
73-G	Model A Ford	Off white body, black base, green fenders and running boards, 1979	2	3	5
3-E	Monteverdi Hai	Dark orange body, blue tinted windows, ivory interior, 2 7/8" long, 1973	3	6	8
60-A	Morris J2 Pickup	Blue body, open windshield and side door windows, four plastic wheels, 2 1/4" long, 1958	15	25	30
46-A	Morris Minor 1000	Dark green body, metal wheels, no windows, 2" long, 1958	20	30	45
2-C	Muirhill Dumper	Red cab, green dumper, black plastic wheels, 2 1/6" long, 1961	10	20	25
54-G	NASA Tracking Vehicle	White body, silver radar screen, red windows, blue "Space Shuttle Command Center", red "NASA" on roof, 1982	2	3	5
36-C	Opel Diplomat	Metallic light gold body, white interior and tow hook, clear windows, black plastic wheels, 2 3/5" long, 1966	10	15	20
36-D	Opel Diplomat	Ivory interior and tow hook, clear windows, five spoke thin wheels, 2 7/8" long, 1970	5	7	10
74-F	Orange Peel	White body, wide orange and black stripe and black "ORANGE PEEL" on each side, 3" long, 1971	3	4	5
47-F	Pannier Tank Loco	Green body, black base and insert, 6 large plastic wheels, 3" long, 1979	3	5	7
8-H	Pantera	White body, blue base, red/brown interior, five spoke rear slicks, 3" long, 1975	35	45	60
54-E	Personnel Carrier	Olive green body, green windows, black base and grill, tan men and benches, 3" long, 1976	4	5	7
43-G	Perterbilt Conventional	Black cab and chassis, silver grill, fenders and tanks, red and white side stripes, 6 wheels, 3" long, 1982	2	3	5

NO.	NAME	DESCRIPTION	GOOD	EX	MINT
19-H	Peterbilt Cement Truck	Green body, orange barrel, "Big Pete" decal on hood, 1982	2	3	5
30-H	Peterbilt Quarry Truck	Yellow body, gray dumper, silver tanks, "Dirty Dumper" on sides, 6 wheels, 1982	2	4	6
56-G	Peterbilt Tanker	Blue cab, white tank with red "Milks's the One", silver tanks, grill, and pipes, 1982	15	25	40
48-E	Pi-Eyed Piper	Metallic blue body, amber windows, small front wheels, large rear wheels, 2 7/8" long, 1972	5	7	10
46-B	Pickford Removal Van	Green body, with or without silver grills, 2 5/8" long, 1960	15	30	50
10-D	Pipe Truck	Red body, gray pipes, "Leyland" or "Ergomatic" on front base, eight black plastic wheels, 2 7/8", 1966	7	10	15
10-E	Pipe Truck	Black pipe racks, eight five spoke thin wheels, 2 7/8" long, 1970	4	6	8
10-F	Piston Popper	Metallic blue body, white interior, 2 7/8" long, 1973	4	6	8
60-F	Piston Popper	Yellow body, red windows, silver engine, labels top and sides, large rear wheels, 1982	2	3	5
59-F	Planet Scout	Metallic green top, green bottom and base, silver interior, grill and roof panels, large multispoke rear wheels, 2 3/4" long 1975	4	5	7
10-G	Plymouth Gran Fury Police Car	White body w/black detailing, "Police" on doors, white interior, 3" long, 1979	3	4	5
52-D	Police Launch	White deck, blue hull and men, 3" long, 1976	2	4	6
33-F	Police Motorcyclist	White frame, seat and bags, silver engine and pipes, wire wheels, 2 1/2" long, 1977	5	7	10
20-E	Police Patrol	White body, "Police" on orange side stripe, orange interior, 2 7/8" long, 1975	6	8	12
39-B	Pontiac Convertible	Purple body, with or without silver grill, cream or ivory interior, silver wheels, 2 3/4" long, 1962	30	50	75
4-G	Pontiac Firebird	Metallic blue body, silver interior, slick tires, 2 7/8" long, 1975	2	7	12
22-C	Pontiac Gran Prix Sports Coupe	Light gray interior and tow hook, clear windows, four black plastic wheels, 3" long, 1964	6	9	12
22-D	Pontiac Gran Prix Sports Coupe	Light gray interior, clear windows, five spoke thin wheels, 3" long, 1970	2	4	6
16-G	Pontiac Trans Am	White body, red interior, clear windows, blue eagle decal, 1982	2	3	4
35-F	Pontiac Trans Am T Roof	Black body, red interior, yellow "Turbo" on doors, yellow eagle on hood, 1982	2	3	5
43-C	Pony Trailer	Yellow body, clear windows, gray plastic rear fold-down door, four plastic wheels, 2 5/8" long, 1968	7	10	15
43-D	Pony Trailer	Yellow body, clear windows, gray rear door, five spoke thin wheels, 2 5/8" long, 1970	3	5	7
68-C	Porsche 910	Amber windows, ivory interior, five spoke wheels, 2 7/8" long, 1970	7	10	15
3-F	Porsche Turbo	Metallic brown body, black base, yellow interior, wide five arch wheels, 3" long, 1978	4	7	10
15-A	Prime Mover	Silver trim on grill and tank, tow hook same color as body, 2 1/8" long, 1956	25	35	45
59-G	Prosche 928	Metallic brown body, black base, wide 5 spoke wheels, 3" long, 1980	3	5	6
6-A	Quarry Truck	Orange cab, gray dumper with six vertical ribs, metal wheels, 2 1/8" long, 1954	20	30	40
29-E	Racing Mini	Clear windows, five spoke wide wheels, 2 1/4" long, 1970	5	7	10
44-F	Railway Passenger Car	Cream plastic upper and roof, red metal lower, black base, 3 1/16" long, 1978	3	5	7
14-G	Rallye Royal	Metallic pearl gray body, black plastic interior, five spoke wide wheels, 2 7/8" long, 1973	3	4	5
48-G	Red Rider	Red body, white "Red Rider" and flames on sides, 2 7/8" long, 1972	2	3	4

NO.	NAME	DESCRIPTION	GOOD	EX	MINT
15-C	Refuse Truck	Blue body, gray dumper with opening door, 2 1/2" long, 1963	10	15	20
36-G	Refuse Truck	Red metallic body, silver/gray base, orange plastic container, 3" long, 1980	2	3	4
62-F	Renault 17TL	White interior, green tinted windows, green "9" in yellow and black circle, 3" long, 1974	5	7	10
21-G	Renault 5TL	Yellow body and removable rear hatch, tan interior, silver base and grill, 2 11/16" long, 1978	4	9	15
1-I	Revin' Rebel	Orange body, blue top, black interior, large five spoke rear wheels, 1982	2	3	5
19-F	Road Dragster	Ivory interior, silver plastic motor, 2 7/8" long, 1970	3	4	6
1-B	Road Roller	Pale green body, canopy, tow hook, dark tan or light tan driver, 2 1/4" long, 1953	25	45	65
1-C	Road Roller	Light green or dark green body, canopy, metal rollers, tow bar, driver, 2 3/8" long, 1958	20	25	35
21-F	Road Roller	Yellow body, red seat, black plastic rollers, 2 5/8" long, 1973	7	10	15
11-A	Road Tanker	Green body, flat base between cab and body, gold trim on front grill, gas tanks, metal wheels, no number cast, 2" long, 1955	175	265	350
11-B	Road Tanker	Red body, gas tanks, "11" on baseplate, black plastic wheels, 2 1/2" long, 1958	30	55	75
44-B	Rolls Royce Phantom V	Clear windows, ivory interior, black plastic wheels, 2 7/8" long, 1964	15	20	30
44-A	Rolls Royce Silver Cloud	Metallic blue body, no windows, with or without silver grill, 2 5/8" long, 1958	15	20	25
24-C	Rolls Royce Silver Shadow	Metallic red body, ivory interior, clear windows, silver hub caps or solid silver wheels, 3" long, 1967	10	15	20
24-D	Rolls Royce Silver Shadow	Ivory interior, clear windows, five spoke wheels, 3" long, 1970	5	7	10
69-C	Rolls Royce Silver Shadow Coupe	Amber windshield, five spoke wheels, 3" long, 1969	5	7	10
39-E	Rolls Royce Silver Shadow II	Metallic silver gray body, red interior, clear windshield, 3 1/16" long, 1979	3	5	7
7-G	Rompin' Rabbit	White body, red windows, yellow lettered "Rompin Rabbit" on side, 1982	2	3	5
54-B	S & S Cadillac Ambulance	White body, blue tinted windows, white interior, red cross decal on front doors, 2 7/8" long, 1965	10	15	20
65-D	Saab Sonnet	Metallic blue body, amber windows, light orange interior and hood, five spoke wide wheels, 2 3/4" long, 1973	5	7	10
12-C	Safari Land Rover	Clear windows, white plastic interior and tow hook, black plastic wheels, 2 1/3" long, 1965	7	10	15
12-D	Safari Land Rover	Metallic gold, clear windows, tan luggage, five spoke thin wheels, 2 13/16" long, 1970	30	45	65
67-A	Saladin Armoured Car	Olive green body, rotating gun turret, six black plastic wheels, 2 1/2" long, 1959	15	20	25
48-F	Sambron Jacklift	Yellow body, black base and insert, no window, orange and yellow fork and boom combinations, 3 1/16" long, 1977	4	7	10
54-A	Saracen Personnel Carrier	Olive green body, six black plastic wheels, 2 1/4" long, 1958	10	17	25
11-D	Scaffolding Truck	Silver body, green tinted windows, black plastic wheels, 2 1/2" long, 1969	4	7	10
11-E	Scaffolding Truck	Silver/gray body, green tinted windows, yellow pipes, 2 7/8" long, 1969	4	6	8
64-A	Scammel Breakdown Truck	Olive green, double cable hook, six black plastic wheels, 2 1/2" long, 1959	15	25	30
16-C	Scammel Mountaineer Dump Truck/ Snow Plow	Gray cab, orange dumper body, six plastic wheels, 3" long, 1964	10	20	25

Matchbox

NO.	NAME	DESCRIPTION	GOOD	EX	MINT
5-F	Seafire Boat	White deck, blue hull, silver engine, red pipes, 2 15/16" long, 1975	6	8	10
75-F	Seasprite Helicopter	White body, red base, black blades, 1977	3	5	7
12-E	Setra Coach	Clear windows, ivory interior, five spoke thin wheels, 3" long, 1970	5	7	10
29-F	Shovel Nose Tractor	Yellow body and base, red plastic shovel, silver engine, 2 7/8" long, 1976	8	15	20
24-F	Shunter	Metallic green body, red base, tan instruments, no window, 3" long, 1978	3	5	7
26-F	Site Dumper	Yellow body and dumper, black base, 2 5/8" long, 1976	2	3	5
60-B	Site Hut Truck	Blue body, blue windows, four black plastic wheels, 2 1/2" long, 1966	7	10	15
60-C	Site Hut Truck	Blue cab, blue windows, five spoke thin wheels, 2 1/2" long, 1970	5	7	10
41-E	Siva Spider	Metallic red body, cream interior, clear windows, wide five spoke wheels, 3" long, 1972	5	7	10
37-G	Skip Truck	Red body, yellow plastic bucket, light amber windows, silver interior, 2 11/16" long, 1976	3	5	7
64-D	Slingshot Dragster	Pink body, white driver, five spoke thin front wheels, eight spoke wide rear wheels, 3" long, 1971	7	10	15
13-G	Snorkel Fire Engine	Red body, yellow plastic snorkel and fireman, 3" long, 1977	3	5	7
35-B	Snowtrac Tractor	Red body, silver painted grill, green windows, white rubber treads, 2 3/8" long, 1964	10	15	20
37-F	Soopa Coopa	Metallic blue, amber windows, yellow interior, 2 7/8" long, 1972	3	4	5
48-B	Sports Boat and Trailer	Plastic boat, red or white deck, hulls in red, white or cream, gold or silver motors, blue metal 2 wheel trailers, boat 2 3/8" long, trailer 2 5/8" long, 1961	35	65	80
4-E	Stake Truck	Cab colors vary, 2 7/8" long, 1970	5	7	10
4-D	Stake Truck	Yellow cab, green tinted windows, 2 7/8" long, 1967	6	8	12
20-A	Stake Truck	Gold trim on front grill and side gas tanks, ribbed bed, metal wheels, 2 3/8" long, 1956	50	75	100
38-E	Stingeroo Cycle	Metallic purple body, ivory horse head at rear of seat, five spoke wide rear wheels, 3" long, 1973	4	6	8
46-E	Stretcha Fetcha	White body, blue windows, pale yellow interior, 2" long, 1972	6	8	12
28-F	Stroat Armored Truck	Metallic gold body, brown plastic observer coming out of turret, five spoke wide wheels, 2 5/8" long, 1974	8	15	25
42-B	Studebaker Lark Wagonaire	Blue body, sliding rear roof panel, white plastic interior and tow hook, 3" long, 1965	10	15	20
10-C	Sugar Container Truck	Blue body, eight gray plastic wheels, "Tate & Lyle" decals on sides and rear, 2 5/8" long, 1961	30	55	75
37-H	Sun Burner	Black body, red and yellow flames on hood and sides, 3" long, 1972	2	3	4
30-F	Swamp Rat	Green deck, yellow plastic hull, tan soldier, black engine and prop, 3" long, 1976	2	4	6
27-G	Swing Wing Jet	Red top and fins, white belly and retractable wings, 3" long, 1981	2	3	5
62-B	T.V. Service Van	Cream body, green tinted windows with roof window, four plastic wheels, 2 1/2" long, 1963	25	40	50
53-E	Tanzara	Orange body, silver interior, small front wheels, larger rear wheels, 3" long, 1972	3	4	5
24-E	Team Matchbox	White driver, silver motor, wide clover leaf wheels, 2 7/8" long, 1973	15	20	25
28-B	Thames Trader Compressor Truck	Yellow body, black wheels, 2 3/4" long, 1959	20	25	35
13-C	Thames Wreck Truck	Red body, bumper and parking lights, 2 1/2" long, 1961	15	25	30

NO.	NAME	DESCRIPTION	GOOD	EX	MINT
74-D	Toe Joe	Metallic lime green body, yellow interior, five spoke wide wheels, 2 3/4" long, 1972	3	4	6
23-C	Trailer Caravan	Yellow or pink body with white roof, blue removable interior, 2 7/8" long, 1965	4	7	10
4-C	Triumph Motorcycle and Sidecar	Silver/blue body, wire wheels, 2 1/8" long, 1960	25	40	60
42-E	Tyre Fryer	Metallic red body, cream interior, clear windows, wide five spoke wheels, 3" long, 1972	3	4	6
5-G	US Mail Jeep	Blue body, white base and bumpers, black plastic seat, white canopy, wide 5 arch rear wheels, 2 3/8" long, 1978	5	10	15
34-F	Vantastic	Orange body, white base and interior, silver engine, large rear slicks, 2 7/8" long, 1975	4	7	9
22-B	Vauxhall Cresta	With or without silver grill, tow hook, plastic wheels, 2 5/8" long, 1958	25	40	50
40-D	Vauxhall Guildsman	Pink body, light green windows, light cream interior and tow hook, wide five spoke wheels, 3" long, 1971	3	4	5
22-A	Vauxhall Sedan	Dark red body, cream or off white roof, tow hook, 2 1/2" long, 1956	20	30	35
38-B	Vauxhall Victor Estate Car	Yellow body, red or green interior, clear windows, 2 5/8" long, 1963	10	18	25
45-A	Vauxhall Victor Saloon	Yellow body, with or without green tinted windows, with or without silver grill, 2 3/8" long, 1958	10	15	20
31-E	Volks Dragon	Red body, purple tinted windows, 2 1/2" long, 1971	3	4	5
25-B	Volkswagen 1200 Sedan	Silver-blue body, clear or tinted windows, 2 1/2" long, 1960	25	40	50
15-D	Volkswagen 1500 Saloon	Off white body and interior, clear windows, "137" on doors, 2 7/8" long, 1968	10	20	30
15-E	Volkswagen 1500 Saloon	Clear windows, "137" on doors, red decal on front, 2 7/8" long, 1968	7	15	20
67-B	Volkswagen 1600 TL	Ivory interior, four black plastic tires, 2 3/4" long, 1967	10	15	20
67-C	Volkswagen 1600 TL	Ivory interior, clear windows, five spoke wheels, 2 5/8" long, 1970	5	7	10
34-C	Volkswagen Camper Car	Silver body, orange interior, black plastic wheels, raised roof, six windows, 2 5/8" long, 1967	15	20	30
34-D	Volkswagen Camper Car	Silver body, orange interior, black plastic wheels, short raised sun roof, 2 5/8" long, 1968	10	20	25
7-F	Volkswagen Golf	Green body, black base and grill, 2 7/8" long, 1976	4	8	12
34-B	Volkswagen Microvan	Light green body, dark green interior, flat roof window tinted green, 2 3/5" long, 1962	20	30	35
34-A	Volkswagen Microvan	Blue body, gray wheels, "Matchbox International Express" on sides, 2 1/4" long, 1957	30	40	50
23-D	Volkswagon Camper	Orange top, clear windows, 5 spoke wheels, 2 1/8" long, 1970	5	7	10
73-F	Weasel	Metallic green body, large five spoke slicks, 2 7/8" long, 1974	3	4	6
24-A	Weatherhill Hydraulic Excavator	Metal wheels, "Weatherhill Hydraulic" decal on rear, 2 3/8" long, 1956	20	25	35
24-B	Weatherhill Hydraulic Excavator	Yellow body, small and medium front wheels, large rear wheels, 2 5/8" long, 1959	10	15	20
57-F	Wild Life Truck	Yellow body, red windows, light tinted blue canopy, 2 3/4" long, 1973	3	4	6
57-A	Wolseley 1500	With or without grills, four wheels, 2 1/8" long, 1958	20	30	35
58-E	Woosh-n-Push	Yellow body, red interior, large rear wheels, 2 7/8" long, 1972	3	4	5
35-E	Zoo Truck	1981	4	7	10

Nylint

NAME	DESCRIPTION	GOOD	EX	MINT
	Cars			
Howdy Doody Pump Mobile	8 1/2" long	250	450	650
	Emergency Vehicles			
Ladder Truck	Postwar, 30" long	100	175	250
Farm and Construction Equipment				
Michigan Shovel	Bright yellow, bucket tips automatically when raised to boom, boom raises and lowers, 10 wheels, steerable front wheels, 31 1/2" long	125	200	275
Payloader	Bright red, 3 3/4" rubber tires, 18" long, 1955	125	187	250
Road Grader	Sturdy blade can be raised, lowered, or tilted, tandem-pivoted rear wheels, 3 3/4 steel wheels, 19 1/4" long, 1955	100	175	225
Speed Swing Pettibone	Orange, raise or lower bucket and tip to dump, steerable wheels, 3 3/4" rubber tires, "Pettibone" decal on sides, 19" long	200	300	400
Street Sweep	Windup, 8 1/4" long	175	262	350
Tournahopper Dozer	Huge hopper, pull lever at rear opens wide clamshell jaws for bottom dumping, 3 3/4" rubber-tired steel wheels, 22 1/2" long	100	150	200
Tournarocker Dozer	Oversized hopper, crank action hoist, 3 3/4" rubber-tired steel wheels, 18" long, 1955	75	125	175
Tournatractor Dozer	Yellow, big powerful adjustable blade on front, pivoted tow-bar on rear, 14 3/4" long, 1955	100	150	200
Traveloader	Orange, synchronized feeders, buckets, and rubber conveyor belt, hand crank, steel wheels with 3 3/4" rubber tires, 30" long	200	300	400
	Trucks			
Guided Missile Launder	1957	75	125	175
Tournahauler	Dark green, tractor with enclosed cab, platform trailer, slide-out ramps, 41 1/2" long with ramp extended, 1955	125	150	250
U-Haul Ford Truck and Trailer	With trin I-Beam suspension	125	187	250

Schuco

NAME	DESCRIPTION	GOOD	EX	MINT
	Cars			
1902 Mercedes Simplex 32PS	Windup, 8 1/2" long	125	187	250
1913 Mercer	Windup, 7 1/2" long	87	130	175
Renault 6CV Model 1911	Open two-seater, 7" long	125	1897	250
Sedan	Blue, tin litho, windup, 4 1/2" long, 1950's	200	300	400
	Sets			
Highway Patrol Official Squad Car Road Set	1958	100	150	200
	Tanks			
Military Miniature Tank	Keywind	37	55	75
	Trucks			
Van	Battery operated, 4" long	75	112	150

NAME	DESCRIPTION	GOOD	EX	MINT
	Emergency Vehicles			
'L' Mack Aerial Ladder	All red with gold lettering and polished aluminum surface, 'S-M-F-D' decals on hood and trailer sides, 6 wheeler, 1950	375	475	795
	Trucks			
'B' Mack Associated Truck Lines	Red cab, polished aluminum trailer, decals on trailer sides, 6 wheel tractor, 8 wheel trailer, 1954	500	850	1200
'B' Mack Blue Diamond Dump	All white truck with blue decals, hydraulic piston, 10 wheeler, 1954	600	950	1300
'B' Mack Lumber Truck	Yellow cab and timber deck, 3 rollers, loading bar and 2 chains, 6 wheeler, load of 9 timbers, 1954	450	650	1000
'B' Mack Orange Dump Truck	Construction orange all over, no decals, hydraulic piston, 10 wheeler, 1954	650	1150	1650
'B' Mack P.I.E.	Red cab, polished trailer, 6 wheel tractor, 8 wheel trailer, 1954	375	600	850
'B' Mack Searchlight	Dark red paint schemes, fully rotating and elevating searchlight, battery operated, 1954	500	775	1100
'B' Mack Silver Streak	Yellow cab, unpainted, unpolished trailer sides, 'Silver Streak' decal on both sides, 6 wheel tractor, 8 wheel trailer, 1954	450	775	1050
'B' Mack Watson Bros.	Yellow cab, polished aluminum trailer, decals on trailer sides and cab doors, 10 wheel tractor, 8 wheel trailer, 1954	650	1100	1500
'L' Mack Army Materials Truck	All Army green, flatbed with dark green canvas, 10 wheeler, load of 3 wood barrels, 2 boards, large and small crate, 1952	375	500	750
'L' Mack Army Personnel Carrier	All Army green, wood sides, Army seal on door panels, military star on roof, 10 wheeler, 1952	375	500	750
'L' Mack Bekins Van	All white, covered with 'Bekins' decals of all descriptions, 6 wheel tractor, 4 wheel trailer, 1953	1000	1650	2000
'L' Mack Blue Diamond Dump	White cab, white dump bed, blue fenders and chassis, hydraulically operated, 10 wheeler, 1952	425	750	1050
'L' Mack International Paper Co.	White tractor cab, 'International Paper Co' decals on sides, 6 wheel tractor, 4 wheel trailer, 1952	375	650	900
'L' Mack Lyon Van	Silver gray cab, dark blue fenders and frame, silver-gray van box with 'Lyon' decal in blue lettering, 6 wheeler, 1950	425	800	1100
'L' Mack Material Truck	Light metallic green cab, dark green fenders and frame, wood flatbed, 6 wheeler, load of 2 barrels and 6 timbers, 1950	400	600	875
'L' Mack Merchandise Van	Red cab, black fenders and frame, 'Smith-Miller' decals on both sides of van box, double rear doors, 6 wheeler, 1951	425	695	1000
'L' Mack Mobil Tandem Tanker	All red cab, 'Mobilgas' and 'Mobiloil' decals on tank sides, 6 wheel tractor, 6 wheel trailer, 1952	450	725	1000
'L' Mack Orange Hydraulic Dump	Orange cab, orange dump bed, hydraulically operated, 10 wheeler, may or may not have 'Blue Diamond' decals, 1952	850	1500	1950

NAME	DESCRIPTION	GOOD	EX	MINT
'L' Mack Orange Materials Truck	All orange, flatbed with canvas, 10 wheeler, load of 3 barrels, 2 boards, large and small crate, 1952	400	650	900
'L' Mack P.I.E.	All red tractor, polished aluminum trailer, 'P.I.E.' decals on sides and front, 6 wheel tractor, 8 wheel trailer, 1950	395	550	850
'L' Mack Sibley Van	Dark green cab, black fenders and frame, dark green van box with 'Sibley's' decal in yellow on both sides, 6 wheeler, 1950	850	1375	1850
'L' Mack Tandem Timber	Red and black cab, 6 wheeler, load of 6 wood lumber rollers, 2 loading bars, 4 chains and 18 or 24 boards, 1950	400	550	725
'L' Mack Tandem Timber	Two-tone green cab, 6 wheeler, load of 6 wood lumber rollers, 2 loading bars, 4 chains, and 18 timbers, 1953	400	550	725
'L' Mack Telephone Truck	All dark or two-tone green truck, 'Bell Telephone System' decals on truck sides, 6 wheeler, 1952	475	750	975
'L' Mack West Coast Fast Freight	Silver with red and black or silver cab and chassis, 'West Coast-Fast Freight' decals on sides of box, 6 wheeler, 1952	475	775	1000
Chevy Arden Milk Truck	Red cab, white wood body, 4 wheeler, 1945	275	465	800
Chevy Bekins Van	Blue die cast cab, all white trailer, 14 wheeler, 1945	275	350	750
Chevy Coca-Cola Truck	Red cab, wood body painted red, 4 wheeler, 1945	300	600	850
Chevy Flatbed Tractor-Trailer	Unpainted wood trailer, unpainted polished cab, 14 wheeler, 1945	250	300	500
Chevy Heinz Grocery Truck	Yellow cab, load of 4 waxed cases, 1946	225	325	475
Chevy Livestock Truck	Polished, unpainted tractor cab and trailer, 1946	175	275	375
Chevy Lumber	Green cab, load of 60 polished boards and 2 chains, 1946	150	195	275
Chevy Lyon Van	Blue cab, silver trailer, 1946	165	325	500
Chevy Material Truck	Green cab, no side rails, load of 3 barrels, 2 cases and 18 boards, 1946	135	185	225
Chevy Stake	Yellow tractor cab	185	250	425
Chevy Tampa Anmature Works	Royal blue cab, white wood body, 4 wheeler, 1945	300	500	850
Chevy Transcontinental Vanliner	Blue tractor cab, white trailer, 'Bekins' logos and decals on trailer sides, 1946	200	350	495
Chevy Union Ice Truck	Blue cab, white body, load of 8 waxed blocks of ice, 1946	300	495	800
Ford Bekins Van	Red sand-cast tractor, gray sheet metal trailer, 14 wheeler, 1944	275	500	750
Ford Coca-Cola Truck	Red sandcast cab, wood body painted red, 4 wheeler, 1944	400	650	900
GMC 'Be Mac' Tractor-Trailer	Red cab, plain aluminum frame, 'Be Mac Transport Co.' in white letters on door panels, 14 wheeler, 1949	250	350	700
GMC 'Drive-O'	Red cab, red dump body, runs forward and backward with handturned control at end of 5 1/2 ft. cable, 6 wheeler, 1949	175	300	450
GMC Arden Milk Truck	Red cab, white painted wood body with red stakes, 4 wheeler, 1947	200	425	650
GMC Bank of America Truck	Dark brownish green cab and box, 'Bank of America' decal on box sides, 4 wheeler, 1949	115	165	275
GMC Bekins Van-Liner	Blue cab, metal trailer painted white, 14 wheeler, 1947	175	275	425

Smith-Miller

NAME	DESCRIPTION	GOOD	EX	MINT
GMC Coca-Cola Truck	Red cab, yellow wood body, 4 wheeler, load of 16 Coca-Cola cases, 1947	400	675	895
GMC Coca-Cola Truck	All yellow truck, red Coca-Cola decals, five spoke hubs, 4 wheeler, load of 6 cases each with 24 plastic bottles, 1954	275	450	750
GMC Dump Truck	All red truck, 6 wheeler, 1950	150	200	285
GMC Emergency Tow Truck	White cab, red body and boom, 'Emergency Towing Service' on body side panels, 4 wheeler, 1953	185	250	400
GMC Furniture Mart	Blue cab, off-white body, "Furniture Mart", Complete Home Furnishings' markings on body sides, 4 wheeler, 1953	135	275	295
GMC Heinz Grocery Truck	Yellow cab, wood body, 6 wheeler, 1947	250	325	450
GMC Hi-Way Freighter Tractor-Trailer	Red tractor cab, hardwood bed on trailer with full length wood fences, 'Fruehauf' decal on trailer, 14 wheeler, 1948	150	210	325
GMC Kraft Foods	Yellow cab, yellow steel box, large 'Kraft' decal on both sides, 4 wheeler, 1948	200	300	450
GMC Lumber Tractor-Trailer	Metallic blue cab and trailer, 3 rollers and 2 chains, 14 wheeler, 1949	185	250	350
GMC Lumber Truck	Green cab, 6 wheeler, 1947	165	215	300
GMC Lyon Van Tractor-Trailer	Blue tractor cab, 'Lyons Van' decals on both sides, fold down rear door, 14 wheeler, 1948 (add 20% for drop-side trailer)	165	250	400
GMC Machinery Hauler	Construction orange cab and lowboy trailer, 'Fruehauf' decal on gooseneck, 13 wheeler, 1949	150	225	335
GMC Machinery Hauler	All construction orange, 2 loading ramps, 10 wheeler, 1953	200	295	425
GMC Marshall Field & Company Tractor-Trailer	Dark green cab and trailer, double rear doors, never had Smith-Miller decals, 10 wheeler, 1949	295	395	500
GMC Material Truck	Green cab, wood body, 6 wheeler, load of 3 barrels, 3 cases and 18 boards, 1947	115	150	250
GMC Material Truck	Yellow cab, natural finish hardwood bed and sides, 4 wheeler, load of 4 barrels and 2 timbers, 1949	125	175	265
GMC Mobilgas Tanker	Red cab and tanker trailer, large "Mobilgas", "Mobiloil" emblems on sides and rear panel of tanker, 14 wheeler, 1949	135	225	400
GMC Oil Truck	Orange cab, rear body unpainted, 6 wheeler, load of three barrels, 1947	115	185	265
GMC P.I.E.	Red cab, polished aluminum box trailer, double rear doors, 'P.I.E.' decals on sides and front panels, 14 wheeler, 1949	150	265	350
GMC People's First National Bank and Trust Company	Dark brownish green cab and box, 'People's First National Bank & Trust Co.' decals on box sides, 1951	165	250	385
GMC Rack Truck	Red or yellow cab, natural finish wood deck, red stake sides, 6 wheeler, 1948	135	200	325
GMC Redwood Logger Tractor-Trailer	Green or maroon cab, unpainted aluminum trailer with 4 hardwood stakes, load of 3 cardboard logs, 1948	365	585	700
GMC Rexall Drug Truck	Orange cab and closed steel box body, 'Rexall' logo on both sides and on front panel of box, 4 wheeler, 1948	500	750	1000
GMC Scoop Dump	Rack and pinion dump with a scoop, five spoke wheels, 6 wheeler, 1954	275	350	575

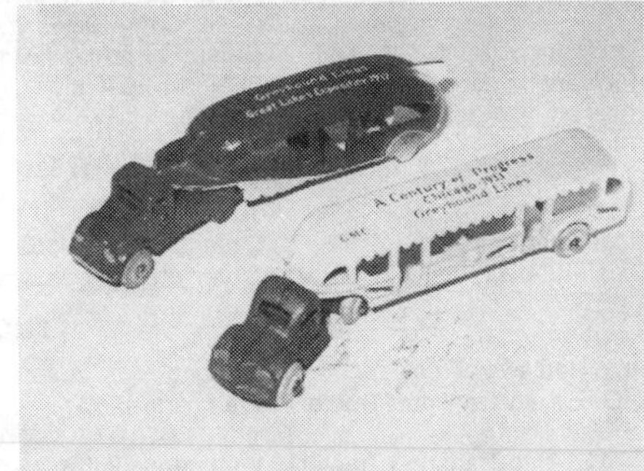

Top to Bottom: Chrysler Convertibles, Tootsietoy; LaSalle Coupe, Tootsietoy; Ford Coupes, 1935 and 1934, Tootsietoy; Lincoln Touring Cars, 1920s, A. C. Williams; Ford Stake Bed Truck, 1926, Arcade; Chevy Panel Delivery Van, 1936, Arcade; Greyhound Buses, 1937 and 1933, Arcade.

VEHICLES

Smith-Miller

NAME	DESCRIPTION	GOOD	EX	MINT
GMC Searchlight Truck	Four wheel truck pulling four wheel trailer, color schemes vary, 'Hollywood Film Ad' on truck body side panels, 1953	300	415	695
GMC Silver Streak	Unpainted polished cab and trailer, wrap around sides and shield, some had tail gate, 1950	140	200	300
GMC Sunkist Special Tractor-Trailer	Cherry-maroon tractor cab, natural mahogany trailer bed, 14 wheeler, 1947	165	275	475
GMC Super Cargo Tractor-Trailer	Silver-gray tractor cab, hardwood bed on trailer with red wraparound side rails, 14 wheeler, load of 10 barrels, 1948	150	225	395
GMC Timber Giant	Green or maroon cab, unpainted aluminum trailer with 4 hardwood stakes, load of 3 cardboard logs, 1948	175	285	495
GMC Tow Truck	White cab, red body and boom, five spoke cast hubs, 'Emergency Towing Service' on body side panels, 4 wheeler, 1954	95	135	200
GMC Transcontinental Tractor-Trailer	Red tractor cab, hardwood bed on trailer with full length wood fences, 'Fruehauf' decal on trailer, 14 wheeler, 1948	150	210	325
GMC Triton Oil Truck	Blue cab, mahogany body unpainted, 6 wheeler, load of 3 Triton Oil drum (banks) and side chains, 1947	115	185	265
GMC U.S. Treasury Truck	Gray cab and box, 'U.S. Treasury' insignia and markings on box sides, 4 wheeler, 1952	235	325	475

Structo

Cars

NAME	DESCRIPTION	GOOD	EX	MINT
DeLuxe Auto	Solid disc wheels, rounded fenders, pressed steel, 16" long, 1921	350	550	750
Roadster	Pressed steel, 10 1/2" long, 1919	200	295	450

Emergency Vehicles

NAME	DESCRIPTION	GOOD	EX	MINT
Fire Engine	Pressed steel, 18" long truck with 18" long ladders, 1927	200	300	400
Fire Pumper Truck	Steel, 21" long, 1920's	225	350	450
Hook and Ladder Fire Truck	36" long, 1940's	62	93	125
Hook and Ladder Fire Truck	32" long	62	93	125

Farm and Construction Equipment

NAME	DESCRIPTION	GOOD	EX	MINT
Crawler	10" long, 1928	175	250	400
Road Grader	Orange, single-blade, 18 1/2" long, 1960's	20	35	55
Steam Shovel	Green steel, wood wheels	40	55	75

Trucks

NAME	DESCRIPTION	GOOD	EX	MINT
Auto Haulaway Truck	20" long	100	150	200
C.O.E. Auto Transport Tractor-Trailer	With cars, 1950's	30	40	55
C.O.E. Auto Transport Tractor-Trailer	With cars, 1960's	20	25	35
Camper Truck	11" long, 1960's	50	75	100
Cattle Farms Inc. Trailer	Orange trailer, green cab	87	130	175
Cement Mixer	Steel, 22" long	150	225	300
Cement Truck	20" long, 1950's	95	150	200
Communications Truck	Blue, 21" long	50	85	165
Dispatch Truck	Green and gray	87	130	175

Structo

NAME	DESCRIPTION	GOOD	EX	MINT
Dump Truck	15" long, 1960's	15	20	30
Dump Truck	13" long, 1960's	15	20	28
Excavation Truck		175	262	350
Flat Bed Tractor Truck	27" long, 1950's	125	200	275
Flat Bed Truck	20 1/2" long, 1940's	75	125	150
Flat Bed Truck	20 1/2" long, 1950's	50	75	125
Garage Truck	1940's	60	90	150
Hi-Lift Dump Truck	12" long	50	85	135
Highway Maintenance Platform Truck	12" long	50	75	125
Hydraulic Dump Truck	Red, pressed steel, 12 1/2" long, 1950's	75	100	175
Hydraulic Sanitation Truck	1960's	50	75	100
Overland Freight Lines Truck	21" long, 1950s	125	200	275
Pickup Truck	17" long, 1950's	40	55	85
Police Patrol Truck	17" long	137	205	275
Power & Light Turbine Utility Truck	17 1/2" long	75	112	150
Road Tug Service Truck	1966	87	130	175
Scoop/Dump Truck	20" long, 1950's	125	185	275
Steel Dump Truck	1940's	100	150	200
Tractor-Trailer Truck	1960's	75	125	175
Transport Truck	Red trailer, blue cab	137	205	275
U.S. Mail Truck	17" long, 1930's	250	350	550
Wrecker Truck	21" long, 1930's	100	150	200

Tonka

Cars

NAME	DESCRIPTION	GOOD	EX	MINT
Dune Buggy	1970	15	20	35
Volkswagen Bug	Blue with white interior, 1960s	25	35	60
Volkswagen Bug	Black, 1968	15	20	35

Construction Vehicles

NAME	DESCRIPTION	GOOD	EX	MINT
Clark Melroe 1399 Hydrostatic Bobcat	Black, 1/24 scale, 1979	15	20	30

Emergency Vehicles

NAME	DESCRIPTION	GOOD	EX	MINT
Aerial Ladder Fire Truck	1960	100	150	250
Fire Truck	32" long, 1950	250	375	500
Ford Aerial Ladder Truck	Red, cast siren on right fender, 1955	150	225	300
Ford Hydraulic Aerial Ladder Truck	Red, 1958	90	135	180
Ford Hydraulic Aerial Ladder Truck	White, 1959	125	185	250
Ford Rescue Squad	White, 1959	95	145	190
Ford Suburban Pumper	White, blackwalls, 1959	120	180	240
Ford Suburban Pumper	Red, blackwheels, 1958	90	135	180
Ford Suburban Pumper	Red, whitewalls, 1960	95	145	190
Ford Suburban Pumper	Red, with thread fittings, 1956	135	225	275
Ford Suburban Pumper	Red, without thread fittings, 1957	115	175	230
Ford T.F.D. Aerial Ladder Truck	Red, "T.F.D." decals on tractor, 1956	160	250	325
Ford T.F.D. Tanker	White, 1958	200	300	400
Ford Tonka Tanker	Red, hard plastic tank trailer with hoses, 1960	100	150	225
International Rescue Squad Metro Van	White, red "Rescue Squad" and large red cross on side of body, 1956	85	150	250
Pumper Truck	c1950	175	265	350

NAME	DESCRIPTION	GOOD	EX	MINT
Farm and Construction Equipment				
Aerial Sand Loader	Red	375	565	750
Ford Aerial Sand Loader	Overhead travelling crane with clam bucket and loading hopper	80	120	160
Ford Crane and Clam	Yellow and black, heavy steel, 26" long, 1947	165	250	350
Ford Giant Dozer and Trailer	Orange, 1961	95	145	190
Ford Road Grader	Orange	40	55	95
Ford Steam Shovel	Orange and black, heavy steel, 16" long, 1947	145	200	275
Tractor	1963	75	140	220
Sets				
Construction Set	Mobile clam, state hi-way dept. hydraulic dump, giant bulldozer, 1961	150	250	375
Fire Department	Hydraulic aerial ladder in white, suburban pumper in white, fire chiefs badge, 1959	500	750	1100
Fire Department	Hydraulic aerial ladder in red, suburban pumper in red, rescue squad, fire chief's badge, 1959	425	700	1000
Hi-Way Construction Set	Road grader, dragline and trailer, state hi-way dump, 1959	325	475	700
Road Builder Set	Road grader, state hi-way dump, shovel and carry-all trailer, Big Mike with plow, 6 highway signs, 2 road barrels, 1958	500	700	1000
State Hi-Way Department	Road grader, state hi-way dump, state hi-way pickup, hi-way service, 6 highway signs, 2 road barriers, 1959	300	575	800
State Highway Department	Road grader, state hi-way pickup, state hi-way dump, hi-way service truck, 6 highway signs, 2 road barrels, 1956	500	700	1000
State Turnpike	Small bulldozer, state hi-way pickup, mobile dragline, state hi-way dump, 2 highway signs, 1 barrier, 1960	275	4500	7000
Tonka Fire Department	Hydraulic aerial ladder, suburban pumper, rescue squad, fire chief's badge, 1957	400	650	900
Tonka Fire Department	Hydraulic aerial ladder, suburban pumper, T.F.D. tanker, fire chief's badge, 1958	300	550	700
Trucks				
Allied Moving Van	1958	100	165	215
Boat Transport	1960	75	125	175
Camper	1973	20	35	50
Camper Pickup Truck	1962	60	95	125
Camper Truck G	c1950	50	75	100
Carnation Milk Truck		225	335	450
Dump Truck	1970	20	35	50
Federal Allied Van In Storage	c1950	275	425	550
Ford Ace Tractor and Trailer	All red, with "Ace Hardware" decals	110	175	225
Ford Air Express Truck	Midnight blue, steel box, 1959	95	145	190
Ford Allied Van	Orange, 1959	80	120	160
Ford Allied Van	Orange, 1954	120	180	240
Ford Allied Van	Orange, with duck decal, 1957	100	150	200
Ford Allied Van	Orange, 1951	150	225	300
Ford American Wrecker	Red	75	115	150
Ford Big Mike	Orange, extra long dump bed with plow, 1958	225	335	450
Ford Big Mike	Orange, extra long dump bed without plow, 1958	200	300	400
Ford Big Mike	Orange, long dump bed, with plow, 1957	225	335	450

Tonka

NAME	DESCRIPTION	GOOD	EX	MINT
Ford Big Mike	Orange, long dump bed, without plow, 1957	200	300	400
Ford Boat Transport Truck	Metallic blue, 4 plastic boats and 2 outboard motors, 1959	135	225	275
Ford Boat Transport Truck	Metallic blue, 4 plastic boats and 2 outboard motors, white walls, 1961	125	185	250
Ford Car Carrier	Cream, 3 plastic autos on carrier, 1959	120	180	240
Ford Car Carrier	Yellow, 3 plastic autos on carrier, whitewalls, 1961	60	90	120
Ford Cement Mixer	Red truck, white mixing barrel and water tank, 1960	100	200	300
Ford Coast to Coast Utility Truck	Red cab, yellow utility body	75	115	150
Ford Cross Country Freight Semi-Truck	White	150	200	250
Ford Dragline and Trailer	Lime green and black, 1959	130	195	260
Ford Dump Truck	Red cab, green dump body, 1949	60	95	130
Ford Dump Truck	Red cab and frame, green body, 1958	50	75	100
Ford Dump Truck	Red cab, green dump body, 1954	60	95	125
Ford Express Truck	Green cab, red box, fold down end gate, 1950	115	175	230
Ford Farm Stake Truck	Six separate side stake assemblies, 1958	70	125	140
Ford Fisherman Truck	Blue and white, steel cap, 1960	60	90	120
Ford Flatbed Semi	Red tractor, plywood trailer with four metal posts, 1953	85	135	170
Ford Gambles Pickup Truck	White	85	165	225
Ford Gambles Semi Truck	White	150	275	350
Ford Gasoline Truck	Red, 1958	200	300	400
Ford Grain Hauler	Red tractor, aluminum trailer, 1954	100	150	200
Ford Grain Hauler	Red tractor, aluminum trailer, plywood floor in trailer, 1952	100	150	200
Ford Green Giant Transport	All white, Green Giant decals are everywhere, with refrigeration unit, 1954	110	165	275
Ford Green Giant Transport	All white, the giant is holding a pea pod and yellow ear of corn, mounted with refrigeration unit, 1953	120	180	285
Ford Green Giant Utility Truck	White, solid rubber wheels, "Green Giant Co." on truck doors, 1954	75	115	150
Ford Hardware Hank Van		150	225	300
Ford Hi-Way Service Truck	Orange, sides fold down on dump bed, with plow, 1956	125	185	250
Ford Hi-Way Service Truck	Orange, sides fold down on dump bed, without plow, 1956	200	300	400
Ford Hi-Way Service Truck'n	Orange, without plow, 1958	80	120	160
Ford Hi-Way Service Truck'n	Orange, with plow, 1958	110	165	220
Ford Hydraulic Dump Truck	Bronze, 1958	55	85	110
Ford Hydraulic Dump Truck	Bronze, 1957	65	95	130
Ford Hydraulic Land Rover	Orange, 1959	200	300	400
Ford J. & R. Fox Express Truck	All blue	125	185	250
Ford Janney Semple Hill & Co. Tractor and Trailer	Red tractor, red and white trailer	125	185	250
Ford Jewel Tea Semi	Dark brown tractor and trailer, wood trailer floor, 1955	150	225	300
Ford Livestock Van	Red, 1958	100	150	200
Ford Livestock Van	All red, drop down door back of trailer, 1954	110	165	220
Ford Livestock Van	All red, with steer head decal, 1956	100	150	200
Ford Livestock Van	All red, "Livestock" decal on trailer's front panel, 1952	100	150	200

NAME	DESCRIPTION	GOOD	EX	MINT
Ford Logger Truck	Red cab, aluminum trailer, load of 4 logs, 4 semi-finished timbers and 2 chains, 1959	100	150	200
Ford Logger Truck	Red tractor, aluminum trailer, load of 9 logs and 2 chains, 1954	120	180	240
Ford Logger Truck	Red cab, aluminum trailer, load of 9 logs and 2 chains, 1953	110	165	220
Ford Lumber Truck	Red cab and frame, load of 36 finished boards and 2 chains to secure load, 1955	90	125	225
Ford Lumber Truck	Red cab and frame, load of 36 finished boards and 1 chain to secure load, 1957	90	125	225
Ford Marshall Field & Co. Semi	Forest green	175	225	400
Ford Marshall Field & Co. Tractor and Trailer	One color greenish-brown	150	200	375
Ford Meier and Frank Co. Tractor and Trailer	Two-toned tractor; blue-green upper half and black bottom	125	200	300
Ford Minute Maid Semi		200	350	450
Ford Minute Maid Truck	All white, 1955	300	400	650
Ford Mobile Clam	Orange, 1961	80	120	160
Ford Mobile Dragline	Orange, 1960	85	130	170
Ford Nationwide Moving Van	White, 1958	150	225	300
Ford Our Own Hardware Tractor and Trailer	Two-tone trailer	165	235	400
Ford Our Own Hardware Utility Truck	Orange	75	115	150
Ford Pickup Truck	Tailgate secured with chains and hooks, 1958	50	75	115
Ford Pickup Truck	Snap-shut tailgate, whitewalls and solid wheel discs, 1959	35	55	100
Ford Pickup Truck	Red, flare side rear fenders, 1955	60	90	145
Ford Pickup Truck	Midnight blue, flare side rear fenders, 1956	50	75	135
Ford Pickup Truck with Tow Hitch	Midnight blue, 1957	60	90	120
Ford Platform Stake Truck	White walls, 1959	90	175	250
Ford Power Boom Loader	1960	95	145	190
Ford Republic Van Lines Semi		150	225	300
Ford Sanitary Service Truck	Rectangular body, white with black loading apparatus, 2 black refuse bins, black loading scoop, 1959	125	185	250
Ford Sanitary Service Truck	Rectangular body, 1959	100	150	200
Ford Sanitary Truck	Curved body, white with black loading apparatur, black refuse bin, 1960	150	175	350
Ford Sanitary Truck	Curved body, 1960	100	150	200
Ford Service Truck	Metallic blue, steel box and aluminum ladder, white walls, 1959	75	115	150
Ford Shovel and Carry-All Trailer	Orange, 1957	135	225	270
Ford Shovel and Carry-All Truck	Orange or lime green, 1958	135	225	275
Ford Shovel and Carry-All Truck	1954	125	185	250
Ford Sportsman Truck	Steel cap, blackwalls, no boat, 1958	95	150	225
Ford Sportsman Truck	Steel cap, whitewalls, with boat, 1959	75	125	195
Ford Stake Truck	Red cab, frame and flatbed, green stakes, 1955	110	165	220
Ford Star-Kist Utility Truck	Green cab and frame, white body, with can decals on body side panels	90	135	180
Ford Star-Kist Utility Truck	Green cab and frame, white body, no decals	75	115	150

NAME	DESCRIPTION	GOOD	EX	MINT
Ford Star-Kist Van	Red cab, blue box, 1954	225	345	450
Ford State Hi-Way Dept. Dump Truck	Orange, "975" decal on door panel, 1956	65	95	130
Ford State Hi-Way Dept. Dump Truck	Black pumper, no number on decal, 1957	55	85	110
Ford State Hi-Way Dept. Hydraulic Dump Truck	Orange, 1960	75	115	150
Ford State Hi-Way Dept. Pickup Truck	Orange, 1956	70	125	250
Ford State Hi-Way Dump Truck	Orange or lime green, 1958	60	90	120
Ford State Hi-Way Pickup Truck	Orange, 1958	45	67	90
Ford Steel Carrier	Orange tractor, green trailer, 1954	110	165	220
Ford Steel Carrier	Orange tractor, green trailer, 1950	75	112	150
Ford Stock Rack Truck	White cab and frame, red livestock rack, 1958	85	125	170
Ford Stock Rack Truck	Midnight blue cab and frame, 1957	100	150	200
Ford Tandem Air Express Truck	Midnight blue, 1959	120	180	240
Ford Tandem Platform Stake Truck	Bronze, 1959	110	165	220
Ford Terminix Service Truck	Orange	80	120	160
Ford Thunderbird Express	White truck, decal wraps around front of trailer, 1958	110	165	220
Ford Thunderbird Express	Red and white truck, decal only on side of trailer, 1960	110	165	220
Ford Thunderbird Express	White truck, single axle trailer, 1957	110	195	275
Ford Tonka Cargo King	Red tractor, aluminum trailer, 1956	110	165	220
Ford Tonka Freighter	Orange and red tractor, green trailer	110	165	220
Ford Tonka Gasoline Truck	Red, 1957	200	300	400
Ford Tonka Tanker Standard Oil Semi		125	185	250
Ford Tonka Toy Transport	1949	110	165	220
Ford Tractor-Carry-All Trailer with Crane and Clam	Green trailer, yellow tractor, 1949	200	325	450
Ford Tractor-Carry-All Trailer with Steam Shovel	Blue trailer, red tractor, 1949	185	250	350
Ford United Van Lines Semi		125	185	250
Ford Utility Truck	1958	60	95	125
Ford Utility Truck	Orange cab and frame, green body, 1954	75	115	150
Ford Utility Truck	With end chain, 1950	85	130	175
Ford Wheaton Semi Truck	White	100	150	200
Ford Wheaton Van Lines Semi		110	175	225
Ford Wrecker	White with black boom, 1958	50	75	100
Ford Wrecker	White with black boom, whitewalls, 1960	50	75	100
Ford Wrecker	Red cab, frame and boom, white body, 1954	75	115	150
Ford Wrecker	White body, red boom, 1955	75	115	150
Ford Wrecker	Blue truck, red boom, "Official Service Truck" on side, 1949	60	95	125
Ford Yonkers Truck and Trailer Truck	All black, yellow decal with red outline	75	115	150
Hydraulic Dump Truck	"Mighty Tonka" Series, 1976	20	35	50
International Carnation Milk Truck Metro Van	White, 1955	75	115	150
International Frederick & Nelson Metro Van	Forest green	85	130	175
International Midwest Milk Truck Metro Van	White, c1950	100	150	200
International Parcel Delivery Metro Van	Dark brown, 1954	65	100	135

Tonka

NAME	DESCRIPTION	GOOD	EX	MINT
International Parcel Delivery Metro Van	Dark brown, with aluminum step, 1957	75	115	150
Jeep	Blue	20	30	40
Pickup Truck	Steel, 12" long, c1950	20	25	35
Pickup Truck	1958	200	300	400
State Highway Crane Truck		75	115	150
Winnebago Camper	"Mighty Tonka" Series, 1973	45	75	100
Wrecker	1973	35	65	95

Tootsietoys

Airplanes

NAME	DESCRIPTION	GOOD	EX	MINT
Aero-Dawn	1928	15	30	40
Atlantic Clipper	2" long	5	7	10
Autogyro	1934	25	35	50
Autogyro Plane	Helicopter type propellor on top, front propellor	30	40	65
B-Wing Seaplane	1926	15	20	30
Beechcraft Bonanza	Orange, front propellor	6	10	15
Bleriot Plane	1910	25	35	50
Crusader		50	85	100
Curtis P-40	Light green	85	135	185
Dirigible U.S.N. Los Angeles		25	35	45
Douglas D-C 2 TWA Airliner	1935	15	30	40
F-94 Starfire	Green, 4 engines, 1970's	5	7	10
F9F-2 Panther Shooting Star		10	15	20
Fly-N-Gyro	1938	30	40	65
KOP-1 USN		15	20	30
Low Wing Plane	Miniature	15	25	35
Navion	Red, front propellor	6	10	12
Navy Jet	Red, 1970's	5	7	10
Navy Jet Cutlass	Red with silver wings	7	15	20
P-38 Plane	9 3/4" wingspan	40	60	85
Piper Cub	Blue, front propellor	7	15	25
S-58 Sikorsky Helicopter	1970's	15	30	45
Snow Skids Airplane	Rotating prop, 4' wingspan	40	60	80
Supermainliner		25	35	55
Top Wing Plane	Miniature	15	25	35
Transport Plane	1941	20	30	40
Tri-Motor Plane	Three propellors	50	85	115
TWA Electra		20	35	45
Twin Engine Airliner	10 windows	20	30	40
U.S. Army Plane	1936	20	25	35
UX214 Monoplane	4', 1930's	45	70	95
Waco Bomber	Blue bottom half and silver upper half or silver bottom half and red upper half	50	85	100

Boats and Ships

NAME	DESCRIPTION	GOOD	EX	MINT
Battleship	Silver with a little red on top, 6" long, 1939	15	20	25
Carrier	Silver with a little red on top	15	20	25
Cruiser	Silver with a little red on top, 6" long, 1939	15	20	25
Destroyer	4" long, 1939	7	10	15
Freighter	6" long, 1940	15	20	25
Submarine	4" long, 1939	7	10	15
Tanker	All black, 6" long, 1940	15	20	25
Tender	4" long, 1940	7	10	15
Transport	6" long, 1939	15	20	25
Yacht	4" long, 1940	7	10	15

Tootsietoys

NAME	DESCRIPTION	GOOD	EX	MINT
	Buses			
Fageol Bus	1927-33	30	40	55
GMC Greyhound Bus	Blue and silver, 1948	25	40	55
GMC Scenicruiser Bus	Blue and silver, raised passenger roof with windows, 6" long, 1957	25	45	60
Greyhound Bus	Blue, 1937-41	30	60	85
Overland Bus	1929-33	35	45	65
Twin Coach Bus	Red with solid black tires, 3" long, 1950	20	25	35
	Cannons and Tanks			
Army Tank	1931-41	35	50	65
Army Tank		7	10	15
Four Wheel Cannon	4" long, 1950's	7	10	15
Long Range Cannon		7	10	15
Six Wheel Army Cannon	1950's	10	15	20
	Cars			
Andy Gump 348 Car	Pot metal, 3" long	225	325	400
Armored Car	'U.S. Army' on sides, camouflage, solid black tires, 1938-41	20	30	40
Auburn Roadster		15	20	25
Austin-Healy	Light brown open top, 6" long, 1956	20	25	35
Baggage Car		10	15	20
Bluebird Daytona Race Car		25	35	45
Boat Tail Roadster	Red, open top, 6" long	25	35	55
Brougham		65	100	130
Buick Brougham		20	35	45
Buick Coupe	Blue with solid white wheels, 1924	20	35	45
Buick Coupe		20	35	45
Buick Estate Wagon	Yellow and maroon with solid black wheels, 6" long, 1948	35	55	65
Buick Experimental Car	Blue with solid black wheels, detailed tin bottom, 6" long, 1954	25	40	50
Buick LaSabre	Red open top, solid black wheels, 6" long, 1951	25	45	55
Buick Roadmaster	Blue with solid black wheels, 4-door, 1949	25	40	50
Buick Roadster		20	35	45
Buick Roadster	Yellow open top, solid black wheels, 4" long, 1938	20	35	45
Buick Sedan	6" long	25	35	45
Buick Special	4" long, 1947	15	25	35
Buick Station Wagon	Green with yellow top, solid black wheels, 6" long, 1954	20	35	45
Buick Tourer	Red with solid white wheels, 1925	20	35	45
Buick Touring		20	35	45
Cadillac	HO series, blue car with white top, 2" long, 1960	15	20	25
Cadillac 60	Reddish-orange with solid black wheels, 4-door, 1948	20	35	45
Cadillac 62	Reddish-orange with white top, solid black wheels, 4-door, 6" long, 1954	20	35	45
Cadillac Brougham		25	35	45
Cadillac Coupe	Blue and tan, solid black wheels	25	35	45
Cadillac Sedan		25	35	45
Cadillac Touring Car	1926	25	35	45
Chevrolet Brougham		20	35	45
Chevrolet Coupe		20	35	45
Chevrolet Roadster		20	35	45
Chevrolet Sedan		20	35	45
Chevrolet Touring		100	150	200

NAME	DESCRIPTION	GOOD	EX	MINT
Chevy Bel Air	Yellow with solid black wheels, 3" long, 1955	10	15	20
Chevy Coupe	Green with solid black wheels	25	35	45
Chevy Fastback	Blue with solid black wheels, 3" long, 1950	15	20	25
Chrysler Convertible	Bluish-green with solid black wheels, 4" long, 1960	15	25	30
Chrysler Experimental Roadster	Orange open top, solid black wheels	25	40	50
Chrysler New Yorker	Blue with solid black wheels, 4-door, 6" long, 1953	25	35	45
Chrysler Windsor Convertible	Green open top, solid black wheels, 4" long, 1941	25	35	45
Chrysler Windsor Convertible	Open top, solid black wheels, 6" long, 1950	60	90	110
Classic Series 1906 Cadillac or Studebaker	Green and black, spoke wheels	15	20	25
Classic Series 1907 Stanley Steamer	Yellow and black, spoke wheels, 1960-65	15	20	25
Classic Series 1912 Ford Model T	Black with red seats, spoke wheels	15	20	25
Classic Series 1919 Stutz Bearcat	Black and red, solid wheels	15	20	25
Classic Series 1929 Ford Model A	Blue and black, solid black tread wheels, 1960-65	15	20	25
Corvair	Red, 4" long, 1960's	35	55	75
Corvette Roadster	Blue open top, solid black wheels, 4" long, 1954-55	20	25	35
Coupe	Metal, 1921	35	45	60
Coupe	Miniature	20	25	35
DeSoto Airflow	Green with solid white wheels	20	35	45
Doodlebug	Same as Buick Special	60	75	100
Ferrari Racer	Red with gold driver, solid black wheels, 6" long, 1956	10	15	20
Ford	Red with open top, solid black wheels, 6" long, 1940	20	25	35
Ford and Trailer	Powder blue car with solid white wheels, 2-wheel white trailer with 3 windows on each side	25	35	50
Ford B Hotrod	1931	7	10	15
Ford Convertible Coupe	1934	35	50	70
Ford Convertible Sedan	Red with solid black wheels, 3" long, 1949	10	18	22
Ford Coupe	Powder blue with tan top, solid white wheels, 1934	35	50	70
Ford Coupe	Blue or red with solid white wheels, 1935	25	35	40
Ford Customline	Blue with solid black wheels, 1955	12	16	20
Ford Fairlane 500 Convertible	Red with solid black wheels, 3" long, 1957	10	12	15
Ford Falcon	Red with solid black wheels, 3" long, 1960	7	10	15
Ford LTD	Blue with solid black wheels, 4" long, 1969	15	20	25
Ford Mainliner	Red with solid black wheels, 4-door, 3" long, 1952	12	18	22
Ford Model A Coupe	Blue with solid white wheels	25	35	45
Ford Model A Sedan	Green with solid black wheels	25	35	45
Ford Ranch Wagon	Green with yellow top, 4-door, 4" long, 1954	15	25	30
Ford Ranch Wagon	Red with yellow top, 4-door, 3" long, 1954	12	18	22
Ford Roadster	Powder blue with open top, solid white wheels	30	40	55
Ford Sedan	1934	35	50	70
Ford Sedan	Powder blue with white solid wheels, 1935	25	35	45
Ford Sedan	Lime green with solid black wheels, 4-door, 3" long, 1949	12	18	22

NAME	DESCRIPTION	GOOD	EX	MINT
Ford Station Wagon	Powder blue with white top, solid black wheels, 6" long, 1959	15	20	25
Ford Station Wagon	Blue with solid black wheels, 3" long, 1960	10	15	20
Ford Station Wagon	Red with white top, solid black wheels, 4-door, 6" long, 1962	25	40	50
Ford Tourer	Open top, red with silver spoke wheels	20	30	40
Ford V-8 Hotrod	Red with open top, solid black wheels, open silver motor, 6" long, 1960	15	20	25
Graham Convertible Coupe	Rear spare tire, 1933-35	60	115	135
Graham Convertible Coupe	Side spare tire, 1933-35	60	115	135
Graham Convertible Sedan	Rear spare tire, 1933-35	60	115	135
Graham Convertible Sedan	Side spare tire, 1933-35	60	115	135
Graham Coupe	Rear spare tire, 1933-35	60	115	135
Graham Coupe	Side spare tire, 1933-35	60	115	135
Graham Roadster	Rear spare tire, 1933-35	60	115	135
Graham Roadster	Side spare tire, 1933-35	60	115	135
Graham Sedan	Rear spare tire, 1933-35	60	115	135
Graham Sedan	Side spare tire, 1933-35	60	115	135
Graham Towncar	Rear spare tire, 1933-35	60	115	135
Graham Towncar	Side spare tire, 1933-35	60	115	135
Insurance Patrol	Miniature	20	25	35
International Station Wagon	4" long, 1940's	30	45	50
International Station Wagon	Red and yellow, solid white wheels, 1939-41	20	25	40
International Station Wagon	Red and yellow, 3" long	20	25	40
International Station Wagon	Orange with solid black wheels, postwar	15	20	25
Jaguar Type D	Green with solid black wheels, 3" long, 1957	7	10	15
Jaguar XK 120 Roadster	Green open top, solid black wheels, 3" long	7	10	15
Jaguar XK 140 Coupe	Blue with solid black wheels, 6" long	20	30	40
Kaiser Sedan	Blue with solid black wheels, 6" long, 1947	30	40	50
Kayo Ice		250	325	400
La Salle Coupe		125	170	225
La Salle Sedan	Red with solid black wheels, 3" long	15	20	25
Lancia Racer	Dark green with solid black wheels, 6" long, 1956	7	10	15
Large Bluebird Racer	Green with yellow solid wheels	25	35	45
LaSalle Convertible		135	195	250
LaSalle Convertible Sedan		135	195	250
LaSalle Sedan		125	170	225
Limousine	Blue with silver spoke wheels	25	40	55
Lincoln Capri	Red with yellow top, solid black wheels, 2-door, 6" long	20	35	45
Mercedes 190 SL Coupe	Powder blue with solid black wheels, 6" long, 1956	25	40	50
Mercury	Red with black wheels, 4-door, 4" long, 1952	20	30	35
Mercury Custom	Blue with solid black wheels, 4-door, 4" long, 1949	20	30	35
Mercury Fire Chief Car	Red with solid black wheels, 4" long, 1949	25	35	45
MG TF Roadster	Red open top, solid black wheels, 6" long, 1954	20	25	35
MG TF Roadster	Blue open top, solid black wheels, 3" long, 1954	16	20	25
Moon Mullins Police Car	1930's	250	300	375
Nash Metropolitan Convertible	Red with solid black tires, 1954	30	35	45
Observation Car		10	15	20
Offenhauser Racer	Dark blue with solid black wheels, 4" long, 1947	15	20	25
Oldsmobile 88 Convertible	Yellow with solid black wheels, 4" long, 1949	15	25	35

Tootsietoys

NAME	DESCRIPTION	GOOD	EX	MINT
Oldsmobile 88 Convertible	Bright green with solid black wheels, 6" long, 1959	20	25	35
Oldsmobile 98	White body with blue top, skirted fenders, solid black wheels, 4" long, 1955	20	25	35
Oldsmobile 98	Red body with yellow top, open fenders, solid black wheels, 4" long, 1955	20	25	35
Oldsmobile 98 Staff Car		20	25	35
Oldsmobile Brougham		25	35	45
Oldsmobile Coupe		25	35	45
Oldsmobile Roadster	Orange and black, solid white wheels	25	35	45
Oldsmobile Sedan		25	35	45
Oldsmobile Touring		25	35	45
Open Touring	Green with open top, solid white wheels	25	35	45
Packard	White body with blue top, solid black wheels, 4-door, 6" long, 1956	25	35	45
Plymouth	Dark blue with solid black wheels, 2-door, 3" long, 1957	10	15	20
Plymouth Sedan	Blue with solid black wheels, 4-door, 3" long, 1950	12	18	22
Pontiac Fire Chief	Red with solid black wheels, 4" long, 1950	20	35	45
Pontiac Sedan	Green with solid black wheels, 2-door, 4" long, 1950	15	25	35
Pontiac Star Chief	Red with solid black wheels, 4-door, 4" long, 1959	15	25	30
Porsche Roadster	Red with open top, solid black wheels, 2-door, 6" long, 1956	18	25	35
Pullman Car		10	15	20
Racer	Miniature	25	40	50
Racer	Orange with solid black wheels, 3" long, 1950's	10	15	20
Rambler Wagon	Dark green with yellow top, black wheels with yellow insides, 1960's	16	22	30
Rambler Wagon	Blue with solid black wheels, 4" long, 1960	16	22	30
Roadster		65	100	130
Roadster	Miniature	20	25	35
Sedan		65	100	130
Sedan	Miniature	20	25	35
Small Racer	Blue with driver, solid white wheels, 1927	60	95	125
Smitty		250	375	500
Studebaker Coupe	Green with solid black wheels, 3" long, 1947	25	35	45
Studebaker Lark Convertible	Lime green with solid black wheels, 3" long, 1960	7	10	15
Tank Car	Miniature	20	25	35
Thunderbird Coupe	Powder blue with solid black wheels, 4" long, 1955	15	30	35
Thunderbird Coupe	Blue with solid black wheels, 3" long, 1955	15	20	25
Torpedo Coupe		15	20	25
Triumph TR 3 Roadster	Solid black wheels, 3" long, 1956	7	10	15
Uncle Walt in a Roadster	1932	275	325	400
Uncle Willie		275	325	400
VW Bug	Metallic gold with solid black tread wheels, 6" long, 1960	15	25	30
VW Bug	Lime green with solid black tread wheels, 3" long, 1960	5	7	10
Yellow Cab Sedan	Green with solid white wheels, 1921	10	20	25

Emergency Vehicles

NAME	DESCRIPTION	GOOD	EX	MINT
American LaFrance Pumper	All red, 3" long, 1954	15	20	25
Chevy Ambulance	Army green, red cross on roof top, army star on top of hood, 4" long, 1950	15	25	35
Chevy Ambulance	Yellow, red cross on top, 4" long, 1950	15	25	35

Tootsietoys

NAME	DESCRIPTION	GOOD	EX	MINT
Fire Hook and Ladder	Red and blue with side ladders	25	40	50
Fire Water Tower Truck	Blue and orange, red water tower	40	60	80
Graham Ambulance	White with red cross on sides	65	95	125
Graham Army Ambulance		65	95	125
Hook and Ladder	With driver, 1937-41	30	45	60
Hook and Ladder	Red and silver	25	40	50
Hook and Ladder		20	25	35
Hose Car	With figure driving and figure standing in back by water gun, 1937-41	30	40	55
Hose Wagon	All red except silver hose, solid white rubber wheels, 3" long, pre-war	20	25	35
Hose Wagon	All red, solid black rubber wheels, postwar	20	25	35
Insurance Patrol	All red, solid white wheels, prewar	20	25	35
Insurance Patrol	All red, solid black rubber wheels, postwar	20	25	35
Insurane Patrol	With driver	30	40	55
Mack L-Line Fire Pumper	Red with ladders on sides	35	65	75
Mack L-Line Hook and Ladder	Red with silver ladder	35	65	75

Farm and Construction Equipment

NAME	DESCRIPTION	GOOD	EX	MINT
Cat Bulldozer	Yellow, 6" long	25	45	55
Cat Scraper	Yellow with solid black wheels, silver blade, 6" long, 1956	15	25	35
Caterpillar Tractor	Miniature	15	25	30
Caterpillar Tractor	1931	10	15	20
D7 Crawler with Blade	1/50 scale, die cast, 1956	25	35	50
D8 Crawler with Blade	1/87 scale, die cast	20	30	40
Farm Tractor	With driver	70	100	145
Ford Tractor	Red with loader, die cast, 1/32 scale	30	40	60
Grader	1/50 scale, die cast, 1956	20	30	45
International Tractor		7	10	15
Steamroller	1931-34	100	150	200

Sets

NAME	DESCRIPTION	GOOD	EX	MINT
Box Trailer and Road Scraper Set	With driver on road scraper	125	200	255
Contractor Set	Pickup truck with three wagons	65	100	130
Four Car Transport Set	Tractor-trailer, flatbed trailer carries cars	60	90	135
Freight Train	Five piece set	40	60	80
Grand Prix #1687 Set	Seven vehicles, 1969	60	95	125
Midget Series	Yellow stake truck, red limo, green doodlebug, yellow railcar, blue racer, red fire truck, 1" long, 1936-41	5	7	10
Midget Series	Green cannon, blue tank, green armored car, green tow truck, green camelback van, 1" long, 1936-41	5	7	10
Midget Series	Assorted ships, 1" long, 1936-41	5	7	10
Midget Series	Single engine plane, St. Louis, bomber, Atlantic Clipper, 1" long, 1936-41	5	7	10
Milk Trailer Set	Tractor with three milk tankers	100	150	200
Passenger Train	Five piece set	40	60	80
Playtime Set	6 cars, 2 trucks, 2 planes	400	500	850
Tractor with Scoop Shovel and Wagon	Red tractor with silver scoop shovel, flatbed trailer, 1946-52	125	185	250

Space Vehicles

NAME	DESCRIPTION	GOOD	EX	MINT
Buck Rogers Attack Cruiser	Cast metal, 5" long, 1930's	90	140	185
Buck Rogers Battle Cruiser	1937	50	75	100
Buck Rogers Blast Attack Ship	Cast metal, 4 1/2" long, 1937	75	100	150
Buck Rogers Rocket Ships	Set of four with two figures, 1937	350	800	1100
Buck Rogers Venus Duo Destroyer	Cast metal, 5" long, 1937	50	75	100
Rocket Launcher		40	60	80

Tootsietoys

NAME	DESCRIPTION	GOOD	EX	MINT
Trailers				
Boat Trailer	2-wheel	7	10	15
Horse Trailer	Red with white top, 2-wheel, solid black tread wheels	7	10	15
House Trailer	Powder blue with solid black wheels, 2-wheel, door opens	10	15	20
Restaurant Trailer	Yellow with solid black tread wheels, 2-wheel, open sides	20	30	40
Small House Trailer	2-wheel, three side windows, 1935	25	40	50
U-Haul Trailer	Red with solid black tread wheels, 2-wheel, U-Haul logo on sides	10	15	20
Trains				
Borden's Milk Tank Car	White embossed metal painted	10	15	25
Box Car		10	15	20
Caboose	All red	7	10	15
Coal Car		10	15	20
Cracker Jack Tootsietoy Railroad Car	Embossed white metal, painted orange, black rubber tires, 3" long, 1930's	85	130	175
Fast Freight Set	Five piece set, 1940	40	60	80
Log Car	Silver body, red wheels, load of logs chained on flatbed car	10	15	20
Milk Tank Car	Yellowish top with narrow red strip along bottom	10	15	20
Oil Tank Car	Silver top with narrow red strip along bottom, 'Sinclair' on sides	10	15	20
Passenger Train Set	Four-piece set, 1925	65	100	130
Pennsylvania Engine		20	30	45
Refrigerator Car	Yellowish sides with narrow red strip along bottom, black roof	10	15	20
Santa Fe Engine		15	20	25
Stock Car	All red	10	15	20
Stock Car		10	15	20
Tootsietoy Flyer	Three piece set, 1937	30	45	60
Wrecking Crane	Green crane on silver flatbed car with red wheels	10	15	20
Zephyr Railcar	Dark green, 4' long, 1935	35	50	70
Trucks				
Army Half Truck	1941	35	55	75
Army Jeep	Windshield up, 6" long, 1950's	15	25	30
Army Jeep CJ3	Extended back, windshield down, 4" long, 1950	7	10	15
Army Jeep CJ3	No windshield, 3" long, 1950	10	15	20
Army Supply Truck	With driver	25	40	50
Box Truck	Red with solid white wheels, 3" long	10	15	20
Buick Delivery Van		25	35	45
Cadillac Delivery Van		25	35	45
Chevrolet Delivery Van		25	35	45
Chevy Cameo Pickup	Green with solid black wheels, 4" long, 1956	15	25	35
Chevy El Camino	Red	20	25	35
Chevy El Camino Camper and Boat	Blue vehicle with red camper, black and white boat on top of camper	25	35	45
Chevy Panel Truck	Light green with solid black wheels, 4" long, 1950	25	30	35
Chevy Panel Truck	Green, 3" long, 1950	12	18	22
Chevy Panel Truck	Green, front fenders opened, 3" long, 1950's	12	18	22

Tootsietoys

NAME	DESCRIPTION	GOOD	EX	MINT
Civilian Jeep	Burnt orange, open top, solid black wheels, 3" long, 1950	7	10	15
Civilian Jeep	Red, open top, solid black wheels, 4" long, 1950	15	20	25
Civilian Jeep	Blue with solid black tread wheels, 6" long, 1960	15	20	25
CJ3 Army Jeep	Open top, no steering wheel cast on dashboard, 3" long, 1950	10	15	20
CJ5 Jeep	Red with solid black tread wheels, windshield up, 6" long, 1960's	15	20	25
CJ5 Jeep	Red with solid black tread wheels, windshield up, 6" long, 1950's	15	25	30
Coast to Coast Van	9" long	50	75	100
Commercial Tire Van	'Commercial Tire & Supply Co.' on sides	100	150	200
Diamond T K5 Dump Truck	Yellow cab and chassis, green dump body, 6" long	25	35	45
Diamond T K5 Grain Semi	Red tractor and green trailer	30	45	55
Diamond T K5 Stake Truck	Orange, open sides, 6" long, 1940	25	35	45
Diamond T K5 Stake Truck	Orange, closed sides, 6" long, 1940	25	35	45
Diamond T K5 Tootsietoy Semi	Red tractor and light green closed trailer	25	45	55
Diamond T Metro Van	Powder blue, 6" long	65	75	100
Diamond T Tow Truck	Red with silver tow bar	25	35	45
Dodge D100 Panel	Green and yellow, 6" long	30	40	55
Dodge Pickup	Lime green, 4" long	20	30	35
Federal Bakery Van	Black with solid cream wheels, 1924	55	85	110
Federal Florist Van	Black with solid cream wheels, 1924	115	165	200
Federal Grocery Van	Black with solid cream wheels, 1924	45	70	90
Federal Laundry Van	Black with solid cream wheels, 1924	55	85	110
Federal Market Van	Black with solid cream wheels, 1924	55	85	110
Federal Milk Van	Black with solid cream wheels, 1924	55	85	110
Ford C600 Oil Tanker	Bright yellow, 3" long	7	10	15
Ford C600 Oil Tanker	Red, 4" long, 1962	15	29	25
Ford Econoline Pickup	Red 1962	15	29	25
Ford F1 Pickup	Orange, closed tailgate, 3" long, 1949	12	18	22
Ford F1 Pickup	Orange, open tailgate, 3" long, 1949	12	18	22
Ford F6 Oil	Orange, 4" long, 1949	10	15	20
Ford F6 Oil Tanker	Red with Texaco, Sinclair, Shell or Standard on sides, 6" long, 1949	30	45	55
Ford F6 Pickup	Red, 4" long, 1949	15	25	30
Ford F600 Army Anti-Aircraft Gun	Tractor-trailer flatbed, guns on flatbed	20	25	35
Ford F600 Army Radar	Tractor-trailer flatbed, yellow radar unit on flatbed, 6" long, 1955	20	25	35
Ford F600 Army Stake Truck	Tractor-trailer box, army star on top of trailer box roof and 'U.S. Army' on sides, 6" long, 1955	25	40	50
Ford F600 Stake Truck	Light green, 6" long, 1955	15	25	30
Ford Pickup	3" long, 1935	25	40	50
Ford Shell Oil Truck		35	50	65
Ford Styleside Pickup	Orange, 3" long, 1957	10	15	20
Ford Texaco Oil Truck		35	50	65
Ford Wrecker	3" long, 1935	30	40	45
Graham Wrecker	Red and black	65	95	125
Hudson Pickup	Red, 4" long, 1947	25	40	50
International Bottle Truck	Lime green	30	45	55
International Car Transport Truck	Red tractor orange double-deck trailer with cars	35	50	65
International Gooseneck Trailer	Orange tractor and flatbed trailer	30	40	50
International K1 Panel Truck	Blue, 4" long	20	30	35
International K11 Oil Truck	Green, comes with oil brands on sides, 6" long	30	45	55

Tootsietoys

NAME	DESCRIPTION	GOOD	EX	MINT
International RC180 Grain Semi	Green tractor and red trailer	15	25	30
International Sinclair Oil Truck	6" long	35	50	65
International Standard Oil Truck	6" long	35	50	65
Jeepster	Bright yellow with open top, solid black wheels, 3" long, 1947	20	30	35
Jumbo Pickup	6" long, 1936-41	25	35	45
Jumbo Wrecker	6" long, 1941	30	40	55
Mack Antiaircraft Gun		25	40	50
Mack B-Line Cement Truck	Red truck with yellow cement mixer, 1955	20	35	45
Mack B-Line Oil Tanker	Red tractor and trailer, 'Mobil' decal on side of trailer	20	35	45
Mack B-Line Stake Trailer	Red tractor, orange closed trailer, 1955	20	35	45
Mack Coal Truck	'City Fuel Company' on sides of box	60	100	135
Mack Coal Truck	Orange cab with blue bed, 1925	25	40	50
Mack Coal Truck	Red cab with black bed, 1928	30	40	55
Mack Dairy Tanker	1930's	75	100	150
Mack L-Line Dump Truck	Yellow cab and chassis, light green dump body, 6" long, 1947	20	35	45
Mack L-Line Semi and Stake Trailer	Red tractor and trailer	75	95	125
Mack L-Line Semi-Trailer	Red tractor cab, silver semi-trailer, 'Gerard Motor Express' on sides	85	115	145
Mack L-Line Stake Truck	Red with silver bed inside	25	35	45
Mack L-Line Tow Truck	Red with silver tow bar	25	35	45
Mack Log Hauler	Red cab, trailer with load of logs, 1940's	75	95	135
Mack Long Distance Hauling Truck	1930's	75	115	150
Mack Mail Truck	Red cab with light brown box, 'U.S. Mail Airmail Service' on sides, 3" long, 1920's	45	55	85
Mack Milk Truck	Enclosed cab, 'Tootsietoy Dairy' on side of milk tanker	60	95	125
Mack Oil Tanker	'DOMACO' on side of tanker	60	95	125
Mack Oil Truck	Red cab with orange tanker, 1925	25	40	50
Mack Searchlight Truck	1931-41	25	40	50
Mack Stake Trailer-Truck	Enclosed cab, open stake trailer, 'Express' on sides of trailer	55	90	115
Mack Stake Truck	Orange cab with red stake bed, 1925	30	40	55
Mack Trailer-Truck		55	85	110
Mack Transport	Enclosed cab with flatbed trailer	100	150	200
Mack Transport	Yellow, 1941, with cars at angle	250	375	500
Mack Van Trailer-Truck	Enclosed cab and box trailer	75	100	135
Mack Wrigley's Spearmint Gum Truck	4" long	90	125	200
Model T Pickup	3" long, 1914	25	40	50
Oil Tanker	Green with solid white wheels	15	25	30
Oil Tanker	Blue and silver, two caps on top of tanker, 3" long	18	20	25
Oil Tanker	All orange, four caps on top of tanker, 3" long, postwar	18	20	25
Oil Tanker	Blue, three caps on top, 2" long, 1932	20	25	35
Oldsmobile Delivery Van		25	35	45
Sinclair Oil Truck	6" long	35	50	65
Special Delivery	1936	20	25	35
Stake Truck	Miniature	25	40	50
Tootsietoy Dairy	Enclosed cab with attached milk tanker plus tanker trailer	60	95	125
Tootsietoy Oil Tanker	Red cab, silver tanker, "Tootsietoy Line" on side, 1950's	60	95	125
Wrecker		30	50	70
Wrigley's Box Van	With or without decal, 1940's	45	60	75

Williams, A.C.

NAME	DESCRIPTION	GOOD	EX	MINT
Cars				
Dream Car	Cast iron, 4 7/8" long, 1930	75	150	250
Ford Roadster	1936	450	550	650
Lincoln Touring Cars	Spoked wheels, cast iron, 8 3/4" long, 1924	200	375	500
Racer	Yellow, cast iron, 8 1/2" long, 1932	300	450	600
Taxi	Cast iron, 5 1/4" long, 1920	200	350	500
Touring Cars	Disc wheels, cast iron, 9 1/8" long, 1922	500	850	1250
Touring Cars	Solid wheels, cast iron, 11 3/4" long, 1917	500	750	1200
Trucks				
Austin Transport Set	With three vehicles, cast iron, 12 1/2" long, 1930	500	850	1250
Interchangeable Delivery Truck	Cast iron, 7 1/4" long, 1932	175	250	350
Moving Van	Cast iron, 4 3/4" long 1930	150	225	300
Pickup Truck	Cast iron, 4 3/4" long, 1926	75	100	125

VEHICLES

Wyandotte

NAME	DESCRIPTION	GOOD	EX	MINT
Airplanes				
Airliner Plane	Metal, two engines, wooden wheels	35	55	75
American Airlines Flagship Plane	28" wingspan	70	125	140
Army Bomber	Pressed steel, two engines	35	55	75
China Clipper	13" wingspan	55	85	115
High Wing Passenger Monoplane	18" wingspan	70	125	145
Military Air Transport Plane	13" wingspan	60	95	125
P-38 Plane	9 3/4" wingspan	25	40	50
Twin Engine Airliner	4 3/4" wingspan	20	30	40
Boats and Ships				
Pocket Battleship	Tin litho, 7" long	25	40	55
S.S. America	7" long, 1930's	35	55	75
Sand O' Land	Tin litho, sand toy, 10" long, 1940's	25	40	50
Buses				
Era Tractor-Trailer Wyandotte Truck Lines	Red and green, 25" long	150	200	300
Cannons				
Cannon	Shoots marbles, 14" long	35	55	75
Cars				
Cadillac Station Wagon	Steel, 1941	250	400	500
Cord Coupe Model 810	Pressed steel, 13" long, 1936	200	300	400
Humphrey Mobile (Joe Palooka)	Tin litho, windup, 1940's	200	300	400
Sedan	Blue, rubber wheels, pressed steel, 6" long	35	55	75
Woody Station Wagon	Steel	250	400	500
Emergency Vehicles				
Ambulance	Steel, wood tires, 11" long, 1930's	60	95	125

Wyandotte

NAME	DESCRIPTION	GOOD	EX	MINT
Farm and Construction Equipment				
Sturdy Construction Co. Steam Shovel	Litho, 20" long	75	115	150
Space Vehicles				
Flash Gordon Strat-O-Wagon	9" long	60	95	125
Trucks				
Auto Service Truck	Red plastic cab, blue and white bed, 15" long, 1950's	50	75	110
Car Hauler	Yellow and red metal tractor, 22" long	100	150	200
Car Hauler	Red plastic tractor, 22" long	50	75	100
Circus Truck and Trailer	Embossed wooden wheels, litho steel, 19" long, 1936	250	400	500
Construction Truck	Red and yellow cab, blue trailer, wood wheels, 24" long	85	130	175
Dump Truck	Red and white cab, blue bed, 13" long, 1950's	75	115	150
Dump Truck	Pressed steel, 6" long, 1930's	75	115	150
Era Express Open Truck	Blue and white bed, 22" long, 1940's	75	150	225
Flatbed with Steam Shovel	24" long	125	175	300
Highway Freight Truck	Blue tractor, red trailer, 17" long	100	150	200
L Tanker	Orange, pressed steel, 11" long, 1930	90	130	180
Military Amphibian	21" long	95	150	225
Motor W Fleet Side Dump Truck	Yellow cab, blue dump bed, 18" long	85	130	175
Nationwide Air Rail Service Truck	Red and white, 12" long	100	150	200
Scoop Dump Truck	Red and yellow cab, red bed, 16" long	65	85	125
Service Car Truck	Red cab, white bed, 12" long, 1950's	50	75	125
Side Dump	Red and white cab, green bed, wood wheels, 20" long	100	150	200
Stake Truck	10" long, 1930's	90	140	185
Stake Truck	Green, battery operated lights, 10" long	70	125	145
Stake Truck	All red, black wood wheels, pressed steel, 1930's	50	75	100
Stake Truck	Red cab, turquoise stake bed, black spoke wheels, 10" long	90	140	185
Woody Convertible	Steel, with retractable hard top ,1941	125	200	250
Wrecker	Red cab, yellow bed sides, 22" long	100	150	200
Wrecker	Red cab and bed, orange boom, 13" long, 1940's	50	100	145
Wrecker	Blue cab, red bed, 12" long, 1950's	35	65	90
Wyandotte Truck Lines	Cab-tractor-trailer, red and yellow, litho, 23" long	125	185	250

Games

By Bruce Whitehill (The Big Game Hunter)

The earliest known board game manufactured in the United States was a game called The Travellers Tour Through the United States manufactured by F & R. Lockwood in 1822. Over 150 years later, the existence of that game was known only to a handful of people. By the 1970s, few people were collecting early American games, and even fewer were bothering to research or write about the field. Old games were relegated to a box lot status -- the undervalued, left-over items discovered with the wonderful toys in someone's attic; it was not unusual to find a dozen games thrown in a box with "make me an offer" scribbled on the side.

This changed radically during the 1980s. People started taking an interest in the colorful game boards as well as in the beautifully lithographed game boxes, and in the unusual implements which could sometimes be found therein. Collectors began to realize that many games told a story about American culture, not only in terms of leisure but with regard to events, themes and trends of the time that Americans held to be important. By 1984, there were enough collectors bumping into one another at East Coast flea markets and antique shows to prompt the formation of a club. The American Game Collectors Association was established, consisting mostly of collectors concentrated in the game company corridor (the area where most games were manufactured), from Pittsburgh to Boston. This was the first national group of people who viewed games as works of art, and collected games to admire rather than play.

Until the end of the '80s, the price of most games made the hobby as attractive as the box covers. Beautifully illustrated games from the 19th century could be purchased for under $50, and historic pieces, such as Milton Bradley's first game, The Checkered Game of Life, could be found for as little as $25. Most games fell into the $10-$20 range with games for a starter set (Anagrams, Pit, Rook, Flinch, Authors, Tiddly Winks, Bingo and Lotto) selling for around $5.

With the recognition given this under-appreciated area of Americana came the expected rise in prices, helped by the hoopla created with well-publicized auctions offering historic pieces, such as an original (pre-Parker Brothers) Monopoly set. The newsmaker at the end of 1992 was an astronomical $65,000 that the Forbes Gallery paid at auction for an original, hand-drawn, circular Monopoly board on oilcloth, 1933, by Charles Darrow, the man who sold Parker Brothers the now world-classic game based on Elizabeth Magie's patented 1904 The Landlords Game.

Also in 1992, at an auction of early games and toys, a McLoughlin Company Little Fireman Game (1897) sold for over $6,000, an 1891 Bliss Game of Shopping went for $1,500, and Parker Brother's The Wonderful Game of Oz (1921) with pewter playing pieces reached $1,800. A.J.H. Singers Game

The Captive Princess, Milton Bradley.

of Goosey Gander (1890) sold for $1,150, and a Milton Bradley To the North Pole by Airship attained a price of $700. These were beautiful games made by the most prominent companies. However, a 1902 game called Wedding Bells by a virtually unknown company (Walter Hart) reached a gavel price of $800, suggesting an emerging trend in which the manufacturer's name will be of less importance, and the value of an item will be attributed more to the quality (and possible social significance) of the piece.

American games have clearly come into their own as collectibles. Games are no longer listed as a subsection of toys. There have been over three outstanding game auctions in the past few years, numerous game exhibits, and regional meetings and annual conventions of the international American Game Collectors Association. With a membership now approaching 300, the club brings together people from across North America, Europe, and Australia (write AGCA, 49 Brooks Ave., Lewiston, ME 04240). Values of early games have skyrocketed, and games have shown great investment potential.

But the field is still a new one, and the market continues to offer interesting games within the reach of any collector's budget. Antique shops are beginning to stock games (co-ops are a good place to look), and some flea markets are ripe with dealers who have games among their toys and playthings. And the growing network of collectors supports a lot of buying and selling of games by mail (*Toy Shop* is an excellent source for locating games from the 1950s and later, and the AGCA is the best connection for collectors looking for games both old and new.)

There are many areas to focus on within the field of American games. Some historians are interested primarily in only the earliest games -- anything from the 1840s (or earlier) when W. & S.B. Ives produced numerous card games and the famed Mansion of Happiness (1843), up to Bradley's The Checkered Game of Life in 1860. By this date, with the advent of new technology in lithography, the era of hand-colored game boxes and cards was at an end, and games were being mass produced.

Many collectors specialize in the games of the later 19th century -- the golden age when game boxes and game boards were adorned with incredibly beautiful, detailed color illustrations. McLoughlin Brothers, after the success of John McLoughlin's hand-colored games in the 1850s, produced magnificent pieces of game art, especially during the 1880s and '90s, earning its place in history as the premiere company for collectors of antique games. McLoughlin Bros. continued manufacturing wonderful items until it was bought by Milton Bradley Company in 1920.

Parker Brothers, the same company that today manufactures games at the Milton Bradley plant in Springfield, Massachusetts, under the ownership of Hasbro, began in 1883 with mostly small card games invented by its founder, George S. Parker. Within a decade of its modest beginnings, Parker Bros. was producing superb adult strategy games and intricately detailed covers nearly comparable to McLoughlin's.

Milton Bradley Company, though the oldest name in games still in use today, took more of an educational bent. Its less sophisticated illustrations aimed at children have made 19th century Bradley games less valued to collectors, compared with the products of McLoughlin, Parker, and some of the other prominent game publishers (many of them originally lithographic businesses) of the 1800s: R. Bliss, Chaffee & Selchow, Clark & Sowdon, and J.H. Singer. Also, Bradley was so prolific that it is easier to locate more early Bradley games than those by his rivals.

Another noteworthy company, Selchow & Righter, was started in 1867 as E.G. Selchow & Company. The company introduced Parcheesi around that time (the game was patented in 1874), but Selchow & Righter were jobbers (that is, they sold other companies' games) until they began manufacturing their own games in 1927. Early S&R games are prizes, and many of the company's products from the mid-1930s into the 1950s are sought after. However, the company began to concentrate on less collectible word games after the success of Scrabble.

Games from the 19th century are usually collected for their graphics or historic value. However, 20th century games, especially the more current items, are desired primarily for their themes or characters (the real or fictional personalities on whom the games are based). Sports games, especially

Winnie Winkle Glider Race Game, Milton Bradley.

baseball and most notably games that indicate specific teams or players, are highly valued.

Games from both World Wars are of great interest. So are games that reflect a noteworthy event in American history, such as Lindbergh's flight across the Atlantic. This country's fascination with transportation and travel, especially our love affair with the automobile, the allure of air travel and space travel, and our interest in the destinations of domestic and international journeys, have all been translated into many styles of games.

Items and themes that appeal to collectors in other fields (i.e., whatever collectibles are hot and trendy) are the clue to what is prized in the game arena. The area of cross-collectibles has helped make games so popular as collectibles -- a battle game from World War I may be valued considerably higher to a collector of military memorabilia than to a game collector; collectors of black ephemera often outbid game collectors for games depicting black characters and caricatures.

Television games have become a collectible field of their own. Most major shows (and many obscure ones) after the mid-'50s generated games based on the stars or their adventures. The key companies were Ideal, Lowell, and Transogram in addition to the ever-present Milton Bradley. The little-known Bettye-B company secured some early TV licenses and was a pioneer in the three-dimensional (vacuum-form) game board.

The value of a TV game depends on the relative value of other memorabilia from the TV show, as well as the rarity of the game. (Minor roles are played by company name and quality of illustrations.) At present, games based on Hanna-Barbera cartoon shows, monster shows, westerns, sci-fi series, and some mystery/adventure shows have the highest value; games taken from quiz shows are worth the least, with the notable exception of Masquerade Party (which contains famous personalities) and quiz shows hosted by famous personalities (such as Groucho Marx).

Though the quality of manufactured games generally declined after the 1950s, licensing became a major marketing tool, and games sold (and still sell) in part because they portrayed the likenesses of everything from cartoon characters to famous people. Character games, other than those from television, include radio and film stars, political figures, entertainers, and especially sports personalities (Red Barber's Baseball is one of the most asked-for games).

Collectible character games of the future may include Simpsons Mystery of Life (Cardinal, 1990), Trump, The Game (Milton Bradley, 1989), Duran Duran (Milton Bradley, 1985), or any of the games from the current flock of hit TV shows, such as Beverly Hills 90201, and Cheers. (There are two Cheers games, both of which should increase in value now that the series has ended.)

Since there is so much for a new collector to choose from, what should the novice avoid? Everything is fair game, and there are collectors who even specialize in some of the more common items. For example, games of Authors (manufactured by dozens of companies from the mid-1800s to the present) may be commonplace, but they are very playable games and collectively offer a nearly complete history of American and world literature.

The games that are least expensive and easiest to find (hence, the lowest resale value) are those in the starters set mentioned earlier, and Old Maid, Peter Coddles, Touring, Fish Pond, Snap, and Jack Straws or Pick-Up Sticks. Parcheesi may be old, but sets are plentiful. And Monopoly games, despite the hundreds or thousands spent for the earliest pre-Parker Brothers' sets, are bountiful and worth very little even if the board reads 1935. (This date appears on sets until 1946; look for 1935 editions with one or no patent numbers, but even these are valued well under $100.)

There are a number of factors to consider, in addition to the theme or the quality of illustration or graphic design, in determining the value of games. Generally, board games warrant a higher price than card games, and larger games are more expensive than smaller ones. Company name is important, with major companies (such as those mentioned earlier) still demanding a steeper price than lesser-known companies. For instance, a game from the late teens with the McLoughlin name on it may be worth four times the value of the identical game from the early 1920s with the Milton Bradley name replacing McLoughlin's. Rarity, then, is important primarily within the framework of a major company or theme. Age is influential only within periods; for 19th and early 20th century games, with all else being equal, the older the game the more valuable. However, some television games are worth much more than games from a century before; generally, TV games from the 1960s and

'70s have a higher value than those from the '50s (reflecting the age and corresponding nostalgia period of the main body of current collectors).

Though what is shown on the box is more important than what's in it, components of a game can contribute greatly to its value. As might be expected, a removable folded game board is of more interest than a boxbottom board; ivoroid, celluloid, Bakelite, and metal implements are valued more than wooden ones, which in turn are better than paper (cardboard) or plastic pieces. Newer games may be valued for their gizmos and gadgets, or their special components, such as glow-in-the-dark pieces, for example. Materials and style of construction of both components and box affect value. Unusual contents, including promotional sheets, special spinners or teetotums (early top-like spinners), or other devices can add appreciably to a game's value.

As with any collectible, condition is paramount. Games assure a higher price if they are complete and in excellent, unscathed condition. A reduction in value for missing common pieces (such as pawns) or tears to the box cover depends primarily on the type of game and the other value indicators. When looking to buy, remember that games can be cleaned, repaired, restored, used for parts, or displayed effectively in parts.

Other factors that may influence value include the region of the country where the game is found (prices in the Northeast and California tend to be higher), whether it is interesting to play, its current social or cultural significance, and whether another copy of the game has sold recently and at what price. At a 1992 auction, Bulls and Bears, The Great Wall Street Game, an 1883 McLoughlin treasure, was bid to an unbelievable $28,000 (when only one copy of the game was known). A few months later a second, more worn copy sold at auction for a mere $13,000. There is supposed to be another copy or two floating around (and I'm sure more that we haven't heard about), and once the hype dies down, the game should settle in at a mid-four-figure range.

Game collecting is now one of the fastest-growing, most interesting, and most profitable collectible interests in the country. There are many reasons to collect games: their nostalgic appeal, their cultural significance, the aesthetic value (including the exceptional illustrations on game boxes, boards, and cards), the implements (from carved wood to molded pewter pieces, from marble to ivory), and the investment value. And, yes, some people even collect old games because at least some of them will always be fun to play.

Bruce Whitehill, known as The Big Game Hunter, is the world's foremost authority on American games and author of *Games; American Games and Their Makers, 1822-1992, with Values*. For an autographed copy send $23 ($19.95 + $3.05 p&h) to 620 Park Ave. #202, Rochester, NY 14607-2994.

GAMES

Board Games

NAME	COMPANY	DATE	GOOD	EX	MINT
$25,000 Pyramid	Cardinal Industries	c1980	10	15	25
$64,000 Question Quiz Game	Lowell	1955	30	60	90
1-2-3 Game Hot Spot!	Parker Brothers	1961	5	10	15
12 O'clock High Game	Ideal	1965	30	45	70
2 For The Money	Hasbro	1955	20	30	45
25 Ghosts	Lakeside	1969	15	25	40
300 Mile Race	Warren	c1955	30	50	80
4-5-6 Pick Up Sticks	Doremus Schoen & Co.		10	15	25
400 Game, The	J.H. Singer	c1890	100	150	250
4000 A.D. Interstellar Conflict Game	House Of Games	1972	10	15	25
77 Sunset Strip	Lowell	1960	40	65	100
A Day With Ziggy Game	Milton Bradley	1977	15	20	30
A Merry Game of Posting	J.H. Singer	c1890	180	300	480
A-Team	Parker Brothers	1984	5	10	15
A.A. Milne's Winnie-The-Pooh Game	Kerk Guild	1931	50	85	135
A.D.T. Messenger Boy (Small Version)	Milton Bradley	1915	40	70	110
Abbott & Costello Who's On First?	Selchow & Righter	1978	5	10	15
ABC, Game of		1914	60	100	160
Abcdarian, The	Chaffee & Selchow	1899	40	65	100
Acquire	Avalon Hill	1961	15	25	40
Across The Channel	Wolverine Supply & Mfg. Co.	1926	50	85	135
Across The Continent	Parker Brothers	1892	100	175	250
Across The Continent	Parker Brothers	1952	40	80	120
Across The Continent	Parker Brothers	c1910	60	100	150
Across The Continent	Parker Brothers	1922	150	250	500
Across The Sea Game		1914	60	100	160
Across The Yalu	Milton Bradley	1905	65	110	175
Adam Ant			30	50	80
Add-Too	All-Fair	1940	15	20	35
Addams Family	Milton Bradley	1973	40	65	95
Addams Family Game	Ideal	1965	65	100	175
Admiral Byrd's South Pole Game	Parker Brothers	c1930	175	275	450
Admirals	Parker Brothers	c1960	120	1756	225
Admirals, The Naval War Game	Merchandisers, Inc.	1939	75	120	190
ADT Delivery Boy	Milton Bradley	1890	120	200	320
Advance And Retreat, Game of	Milton Bradley	c1900	95	175	250
Advance To Boardwalk	Parker Brothers	1985	5	10	15
Adventure In Science, An	Jacmar Mfg. Co.	1950	20	30	50
Adventures of Popeye Game	Transogram	1957	50	75	125
Adventures of Robin Hood	Bettye-B Co.	1956	45	75	120
Adventures of Sir Lancelot	Lisbeth Whiting	1975	40	70	110
Adventures of Superman Game	Milton Bradley	c1952	25	40	65
Adventures of The Nebs	Milton Bradley	1925	45	75	120
Adventures of Tom Sawyer And Huck Finn	Stoll & Edwards	1925	70	120	185
Aero-Chute	American Toy Works	1940	50	75	150
Aeroplane Race	Wolverine Supply & Mfg. Co.	c1922	60	95	150
After Dinner	Frederick H. Beach (Beachcraft)	1937	10	20	30
Agent Zero-M Spy Detector	Mattel	1964	30	50	80
Aggravation	Lakeside	1970	5	10	15
Air Assault On Crete	Avalon Hill	1977	10	20	30
Air Base Checkers	Einson-Freeman Publishing Corp.	1942	20	30	50

Board Games

NAME	COMPANY	DATE	GOOD	EX	MINT
Air Empire	Avalon Hill	1961	15	25	40
Air Mail, The	Archer Toy Co.	1930	75	125	200
Air Mail, The Game of	Milton Bradley	c1927	100	200	300
Air Race Around The World	Lido Toy	c1950	25	45	70
Air Ship Game, The	McLoughlin Brothers	1904	300	500	700
Air Ship Game, The	McLoughlin Brothers	1912	145	240	375
Airplane Speedway Game	Samuel Lowe Co.	1941	20	30	50
Aldjemma	Corey Games	1944	30	45	70
Alee-Oop	Royal Toy Co.	1937	30	50	70
Alfred Hitchcock 'Why?'	Milton Bradley	1965	10	15	25
Alfred Hitchcock Presents Mystery Game	Milton Bradley	1958	20	35	55
Ali Baba	Selchow & Righter		50	100	150
Alice in Wonderland	Parker Brothers	c1930	60	100	200
Alice In Wonderland, Game of	Stoll & Edwards	1923	50	85	135
Alien	Kenner	1979	30	45	70
All American Football		c1935	35	55	90
All In The Family	Milton Bradley	1972	10	20	30
All My Children		1985	5	10	20
All Star Baseball	Cadeco Ellis	1960	30	45	70
All The King's Men	Parker Brothers	1979	6	10	15
All-Star Baseball Fame	Cadaco-Ellis	1962	15	25	40
Alley Oop, Game of	Royal Toy Co.		15	30	50
Ally Sloper	Milton Bradley		50	85	135
Ambuscade, Constellations And Bounce	McLoughlin Brothers	1877	195	325	520
America's Yacht Race	McLoughlin Brothers	1904	450	750	1200
American Boy Game	Milton Bradley	c1920	75	125	200
American Revolution, The New Game of The	Lorenzo Burge	1844	960	1600	2400
Amusing Game of Innocence Abroad, The	Parker Brothers	1888	135	225	350
Amusing Game of the Corner Grocery		c1890	100	200	325
Anagrams	Cutler & Saleeby Co.		15	25	40
Ancient Game of The Mandarins, The	Parker Brothers	1923	45	75	120
Andy Gump, His Game	Milton Bradley	1924	60	120	200
Anex-A-Gram	The Embossing Co.	1938	15	25	40
Animal & Bird Lotto	All-Fair	1926	15	20	35
Animal Crackers	Milton Bradley	c1970	4	7	11
Annette's Secret Passage	Parker Brothers	1958	25	40	65
Annie Oakley	Milton Bradley	1950	45	75	120
Annie Oakley	Milton Bradley	1955	30	45	70
Annie-The Movie Game	Parker Brothers	1981	4	6	10
Anti-Monopoly	Anti-Monopoly, Inc.	c1970	20	35	55
Anti-Monopoly	Anti-Monopoly, Inc.	1973	25	45	70
Apple's Way	Milton Bradley	1974	15	25	40
Arabian Nights, Game of	National Games, Inc.		30	45	70
Archies, The	Whitman	1969	25	45	65
Arena	R. Bliss Mfg. Co.	1896	120	200	320
Arnold Palmer Game			20	30	50
Around The World In 80 Days Game	Transogram	1957	25	40	65
Arrest & Trial	Transogram		20	35	55
Art Linkletter's House Party		1968	10	20	30
As The World Turns	Parker Brothers	1966	25	40	65
Assembly Line	Selchow & Righter	1953	35	60	95
Atom Ant Game	Transogram	1966	45	70	110
Attack, Game of	R. Bliss Mfg. Co.	1889	300	500	800
Aurora Pursuit! Game	Aurora	1973	5	10	15
Authors	J.H. Singer	c1890	25	50	75
Authors	Whipple & Smith	1861	50	100	150
Auto Game, The	Milton Bradley	1906	60	100	160

Board Games

NAME	COMPANY	DATE	GOOD	EX	MINT
Auto Race	All-Fair	1922	65	110	175
Auto Race Game	Milton Bradley	1925	85	145	225
Auto Race Game	Milton Bradley	1930	40	80	120
Auto Race Jr.	All-Fair	1925	75	125	200
Automobile Race, Game of The	McLoughlin Brothers	1904	725	1200	1900
B-17 Queen of The Skies	Avalon Hill	1983	6	10	15
B.T.O. (Big Time Operator)	Bettye-B Co.	1956	30	45	70
Babe Ruth's Baseball Game	Milton Bradley	1926	200	500	1000
Baby Barn Yard	B.L. Fry Products Co.	c1940	15	25	40
Bagatelle, Game of	McLoughlin Brothers	1898	200	350	550
Bagdad, The Game of The East	Clover Games	1940	25	40	65
Balloonio	Frederick H. Beach (Beachcraft)	1937	20	40	50
Bamboozle	Milton Bradley	1962	15	25	40
Bamboozle, Or The Enchanted Isle	Milton Bradley	1876	100	200	350
Banana Tree	Marx	1977	10	15	25
Bang, Game of	McLoughlin Brothers	1903	100	165	250
Bango! Bango!	Schaper		10	20	30
Banner Lye Checkerboard	Geo E. Schweig & Son	c1930	15	20	35
Barage	Corey Games	1941	20	30	50
Barbapapa Takes A Trip	Selchow & Righter	1977	3	5	8
Barbie's Keys To Fame	Mattel		35	65	100
Barbie's Little Sister Skipper Game	Mattel	1964	15	25	35
Barbie, Queen of The Prom		c1960	25	40	65
Baretta	Milton Bradley	1976	15	25	40
Barnabas Collins Game	Milton Bradley	1969	35	60	95
Barney Google And Spark Plug Game	Milton Bradley	1923	100	200	300
Barney Miller	Parker Brothers	1977	10	15	25
Barnstormer	Marx	c1970	20	35	55
Base Ball, Game of	J.H. Singer	c1890	150	250	400
Base-Ball, Game of	McLoughlin Brothers	1886	750	1300	2000
Baseball	Samuel Lowe Co.	1942	15	25	40
Baseball Game	All-Fair	1930	100	250	500
Basilinda	E.I. Horsman	1890	105	175	275
Basketball	Samuel Lowe Co.	1942	15	25	40
Basketball Strategy	Avalon Hill	1974	10	15	25
Bat Masterson	Lowell	1958	45	75	120
Batman	Hasbro	1978	10	15	25
Batman And Robin Game	Hasbro	1965	45	75	120
Batman Game	Milton Bradley	1966	40	65	100
Battle Checkers	Pen Man	1925	15	30	45
Battle Cry	Milton Bradley	1962	25	40	65
Battle Game, The	Parker Brothers	c1890	120	200	300
Battle of Ballots	All-Fair	1931	50	80	150
Battle of Manila	Parker Brothers	1899	300	550	750
Battle of The Planets			15	25	35
Battleship	Milton Bradley	1965	10	15	25
Battlestar Galactica	Parker Brothers	1978	10	15	25
Beany & Cecil Jumpin' DJ Game			25	55	100
Beany & Cecil Match It			30	50	80
Beany & Cecil Talk To Cecil	Mattel		45	75	120
Bear Hunt, Game of	Milton Bradley	1923	45	70	110
Beat Inflation	Avalon Hill	1961	15	25	40
Beat The Buzz	Kenner	1958	10	15	25
Beat The Clock	Milton Bradley	c1960	6	10	16
Beat The Clock	Lowell	1954	35	60	95
Beatles Flip Your Wig Game	Milton Bradley	1964	60	90	150
Beauty And The Beast, Game of	Milton Bradley	1905	45	75	120
Beetle Bailey	Milton Bradley	1963	20	30	50
Behind The '8' Ball Game	Selchow & Righter	1969	25	40	65

Games, top to bottom: Skirmish, American Heritage Series, 1975, Milton Bradley; Beatles Flip Your Wig Game, 1964, Milton Bradley; Wanted Dead Or Alive, 1959, Lowell; Star Wars Escape From Death Star Game, c1980, Kenner.

Board Games

NAME	COMPANY	DATE	GOOD	EX	MINT
Bell Boy Game, The	Chaffee & Selchow	1898	425	700	1100
Ben Casey MD Game	Transogram	1961	15	20	35
Bengalee	Advance Games	c1940	20	35	55
Benny Goodman Swings	Toy Creations	c1930	50	95	150
Bermuda Triangle	Milton Bradley	1976	10	15	25
Betsy Ross And The Flag	Transogram	c1950	20	30	50
Beverly Hillbillies	Standard Toycraft, Inc.	1963	40	65	100
Bewitched	T. Cohn Inc.	1965	40	60	90
Bible Boys	Zondervan Publishing House	1901	10	15	25
Bible Characters	F.G. Decker & O.F. Decker	c1890	20	35	55
Bible Characters	Zondervan Publishing House	1939	10	15	25
Bible Lotto	Goodenough And Woglom Co.	1933	10	15	25
Bible Quotto	Goodenough And Woglom Co.	1932	6	10	15
Bible Rhymes	Goodenough And Woglom Co.	1933	10	15	25
Bicycle Game, The New	Parker Brothers	1894	400	700	1000
Bicycle Race, Game of	McLoughlin Brothers	1891	325	550	850
Bicycle Race, The	Chaffee & Selchow	1898	325	550	850
Big Apple	Rosebud Art Co., Inc.	1938	30	50	80
Big Bad Wolf Game	Parker Brothers	c1930	20	35	55
Big Business	Parker Brothers	1936	75	125	200
Big Business	Transogram	1937	20	35	55
Big Foot	Milton Bradley	1977	10	15	25
Big League Baseball Game	3M	1966	15	25	40
Big Six; Christy Mathewson Indoor Baseball Game	Piroxloid Prod. Corp.	1922	150	250	400
Big Town	Lowell	1954	50	80	125
Bike Race, The	Master Toy Co.	c1940	25	50	75
Bild-A-Word	Educational Card & Game Co.	1929	20	35	55
Billionaire	Parker Brothers	1973	10	20	30
Billy Bumps Visit To Boston Game		c1890	60	100	175
Billy Whiskers	Saalfield Pub. Co.	1923	45	75	120
Bing Crosby Call Me Lucky	Parker Brothers	1954	40	75	110
Bingo	Rosebud Art Co., Inc.	c1925	15	25	40
Bingo Or Beano	Parker Brothers	c1940	10	15	20
Bingo-Matic	Transogram	1954	5	10	20
Bionic Crisis	Parker Brothers	1975	6	10	15
Bionic Man			10	15	25
Bionic Woman	Parker Brothers	1976	3	5	10
Bird Brain	Milton Bradley	1966	10	15	25
Bird Lotto	Sam'l Gabriel Sons & Co.	c1940	20	35	55
Bird Watcher	Parker Brothers	1958	75	110	150
Black Beauty	Stoll & Edwards	1921	40	65	110
Black Beauty	Transogram	1957	25	50	65
Black Box	Parker Brothers	1978	5	10	15
Black Falcon of The Flying G-Men, The	Ruckelshaus Game Corp.	1939	175	300	475
Black Hole Space Alert	Whitman		5	10	15
Black Sambo, Game of	Sam'l Gabriel Sons & Co.	1939	90	145	225
Blackout	Milton Bradley	1939	50	75	100
Blade Runner		1982	40	65	100
Blast Off	Selchow & Righter	1953	50	90	125
Blitzkrieg	Avalon Hill	1965	15	25	40

Board Games

NAME	COMPANY	DATE	GOOD	EX	MINT
Blockade	Milton Bradley	1898	25	40	75
Blockade	Corey Games	1941	35	60	95
Blockhead	Russell Mfg. Co.	1954	10	15	25
Blondie	Parker Brothers	c1970	6	10	15
Blondie And Dagwood's Race For The Office	Jaymar	1950	30	45	70
Blondie Goes To Leisureland	Westinghouse	1935	30	45	70
Blow Football Game		1912	30	50	80
Blox-O	Lubbers & Bell	1923	10	15	25
Bluff	Games Of Fame	1944	15	25	40
Bo Bang & Hong Kong	Parker Brothers	1890	275	450	700
Bo Peep Game	McLoughlin Brothers	1895	195	325	520
Bo Peep, The Game of	J.H. Singer	1890	90	150	240
Boake Carter's Star Reporter	Parker Brothers	1937	105	175	285
Bobbsey Twins	Milton Bradley	1957	30	45	70
Body Language	Milton Bradley	1975	15	25	40
Boggle	Parker Brothers	1976	5	19	15
Bomb The Navy	J. Pressman & Co.	c1940	20	30	50
Bombardier Game	Maco		30	50	80
Bombardment, Game of	McLoughlin Brothers	1898	100	150	300
Bombs Away	Toy Creations	c1944	30	50	80
Bonanza Michigan Rummy Game	Parker Brothers	1964	30	45	70
Bonkers	Parker Brothers		10	20	30
Boom Or Bust	Parker Brothers	1951	100	200	300
Boris KarlOff's Monster Game	Gems	1965	50	85	135
Boston-New York Motor Tour	American Toy Mfg.	c1920	90	150	240
Bottle-Quoits	Parker Brothers	1897	50	85	140
Bottoms Up		c1970	3	5	8
Bottoms Up	Bettye-B Co.	1956	15	25	40
Bottoms Up	The Embossing Co.	1934	20	35	55
Bowl And Score	Lowe	1962	6	10	15
Bowl Bound	Sports Illustrated Games		35	45	70
Bowling	Parker Brothers	1896	80	135	215
Boy Scout Progress Game	Parker Brothers	1926	75	150	300
Boy Scouts	Mcloughlin Brothers	c1910	125	200	325
Boy Scouts (Untitled)	McLoughlin Brothers	1914	110	185	295
Boy Scouts, The Game of	Parker Brothers	1926	200	350	500
Boys Own Football Game	McLoughlin Brothers	c1900	325	575	900
Bradley's Circus Game	Milton Bradley	1882	60	100	160
Bradley's Telegraph Game	Milton Bradley	c1900	85	145	225
Bradley's Toy Town Post Office	Milton Bradley	c1910	90	150	240
Brain Waves	Milton Bradley	1977	15	20	30
Branded	Milton Bradley	1966	30	45	70
Brass Monkey Game, The	U.S. Game Systems	1973	30	50	80
Break The Bank	Bettye-B Co.	1955	35	60	95
Breaker 1-9	Milton Bradley	1976	5	10	15
Brett Ball	9th Inning	1981	30	45	70
Bride Bingo	Leister Game Co.	1957	20	35	55
Bringing Up Father Game	Embee Distributing Co.	1920	45	75	120
Broadcast Baseball	J. Pressman & Co.		30	45	70
Broadside	Milton Bradley	1962	15	25	40
Broadside Gangway	Transogram		20	40	75
Broadway	Parker Brothers	1917	75	125	250
Brownie Character Ten Pins Game		c1890	125	200	300
Brownie Horseshoe Game	M.H. Miller Co.	c1900	30	50	80
Brownie Ring Toss	M.H. Miller Co.	c1920	30	50	80
Brownies, The Game of	Clark & Sowdon		175	300	475
Bruce Jenner Decathlon Game	Parker Brothers	1979	4	7	11
Buck Rogers And His Cosmic Rocket Wars Game		1934	30	50	80

Board Games

NAME	COMPANY	DATE	GOOD	EX	MINT
Buck Rogers Seige of Gigantica Game		1934	60	100	160
Buckaroo		1947	20	35	55
Bucket Ball	Marx	1972	10	15	25
Bucking Bronco	Transogram	c1930	30	50	80
Buffalo Bill, The Game of	Parker Brothers	1898	100	165	250
Buffalo Hunt	Parker Brothers	1898	20	35	55
Buffalo Hunt Game		1914	60	100	160
Bug-A-Boo	Whitman	1968	10	15	20
Bugaloos		1971	10	20	30
Bugle Horn Or Robin Hood, Game of	McLoughlin Brothers	1895	350	650	975
Bugs Bunny	Milton Bradley		30	45	70
Bugs Bunny Under The Cawit Game	Whitman	1972	15	25	40
Bugville Games	Animate Toy Co.	1915	45	75	120
Building Boom	Kohner	c1950	6	10	15
Built-Rite Frisky Flippers Slide Bar Game		c1950	5	10	15
Built-Rite Swish Basketball Game		c1950	7	15	25
Bulls And Bears	McLoughlin Brothers	1896	13000	20000	
Bulls And Bears	Parker Brothers	1936	75	125	200
Bullwinkle Hide & Seek Game	Milton Bradley	1961	25	40	65
Bullwinkle's Super Market Game	Whitman	c1970	27	45	72
Bunny Rabbit, Or Cottontail & Peter, The Game of	Parker Brothers	1928	85	145	225
Buried Treasure, The Game of	Russell Mfg. Co.	c1930	35	60	95
Burke's Law	Transogram		20	30	50
Buster Brown At Coney Island	J. Ottmann Lith. Co.	c1890	225	350	550
Buster Brown Hurdle Race	J. Ottmann Lith. Co.	c1890	330	550	880
Buying And Selling Game		1903	20	35	55
Cabbage Patch Kids	Parker Brothers	1984	5	10	15
Cabby	Selchow & Righter	1940	40	65	100
Cabin Boy	Milton Bradley	1910	60	100	160
Cadet Game, The	Milton Bradley	1905	50	80	125
Cake Walk Game, The	Parker Brothers	c1900	450	750	1200
Call My Bluff	Milton Bradley	1965	15	20	30
Calling All Cars	Parker Brothers	c1938	45	75	90
Calvin & The Colonel High Spirits	Milton Bradley	1962	10	20	30
Camelot	Parker Brothers	1955	20	30	50
Camelot	Parker Brothers	1930	30	45	70
Camp Granada Game, Allan Sherman's	Milton Bradley	1968	10	15	25
Camp Runamuck	Ideal	1965	30	45	70
Can You Catch It Charlie Brown?	Ideal	1976	10	15	20
Candyland	Milton Bradley	1949	25	50	90
Cannonball Run			5	10	15
Caper	Parker Brothers	1970	20	30	50
Capital Cities Air Derby, The	All-Fair	1929	150	250	400
Capital Punishment	Hammerhead	1981	40	70	125
Captain America	Milton Bradley	1977	10	15	25
Captain America Game	Milton Bradley	1966	40	65	105
Captain Caveman And The Teen Angels	Milton Bradley	1981	6	10	15
Captain Crunch Island Adventure Game	Warren		7	15	20
Captain Gallant Desert Fort Game	Transogram	1956	10	20	30
Captain Hop Across Junior	All-Fair	1928	100	200	300
Captain Kangaroo		1956	25	40	65
Captain Kidd	Parker Brothers	1896	135	225	360
Captain Kidd Junior	Parker Brothers	1926	35	55	90
Captain Video Game	Milton Bradley	1952	75	125	200
Captive Princess	McLoughlin Brothers	1899	55	95	150

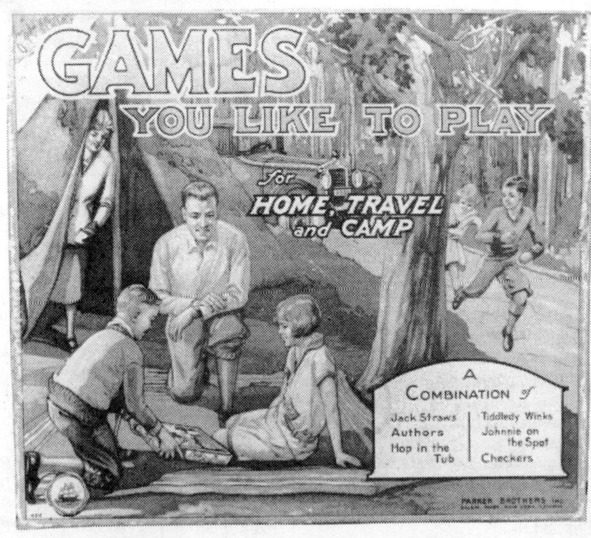

Games, top to bottom: Wild Bill Hickok, 1955, Built-Rite; King Zor, c1964, Ideal; Gunsmoke, c1950, Lowell; Games You Like To Play, c1920, Parker Brothers.

NAME	COMPANY	DATE	GOOD	EX	MINT
Captive Princess	McLoughlin Brothers	1880	135	225	360
Captive Princess Tournament And Pathfinders, Games of	McLoughlin Brothers	1888	100	200	300
Capture The Fort	Valley Novelty Works	c1914	45	75	120
Car 54... Where Are You?	Allison		75	125	175
Cardino	Milton Bradley	1970	10	15	25
Careers	Parker Brothers	1957	30	50	80
Careers	Parker Brothers	1965	10	20	30
Cargo For Victory	All-Fair	1943	50	75	125
Cargoes	Selchow & Righter	1934	50	75	150
Carrier Strike	Milton Bradley	1977	15	25	45
Case of The Elusive Assassin, The	Ideal	1967	40	65	105
Casey Jones	Saalfield	1959	30	45	70
Casper the Friendly Ghost Game	The Cottie Co.	1974	15	20	30
Casper The Friendly Ghost Game	Milton Bradley	1959	10	20	30
Casper The Friendly Ghost Game	Schaper	1974	7	15	20
Cat	Carl F. Doerr	1915	15	25	40
Cat & Mouse	Parker Brothers	1964	7	15	20
Cat And Witch	Whitman	c1940	25	45	70
Cat, Game of	Chaffee & Selchow	1900	270	450	725
Catching Mice, Game of	McLoughlin Brothers	1888	150	250	400
Cats & Mice, Cantaloupe, Lost Diamond Games	McLoughlin Brothers		210	350	560
Cats And Dogs	Parker Brothers	1929	100	200	300
Cattlemen, The	Selchow & Righter	1977	10	15	25
Centipede	Milton Bradley	1983	6	10	15
Centurions			5	10	15
Century Run Bicycle Game, The	Parker Brothers	1897	210	350	550
Challenge Yahtzee	Milton Bradley	1974	7	15	20
Champion Game of Baseball, The	Proctor Amusement Co.	c1890	60	100	160
Champion Spark Plug Road Race			15	25	40
Championship Base Ball Parlor Game	Grebnelle Novelty Co.	1914	150	250	400
Championship Baseball	Championship Games Inc.	1966	10	20	30
Championship Basketball	Championship Games Inc.	1966	10	20	30
Championship Golf	Championship Games Inc.	1966	10	20	30
Champs, The Land of Brawno	Selchow & Righter	1940	30	50	80
Characteristics	W. & S.B.Ives	1845	180	300	480
Charge, The	E.O. Clark	c1898	180	300	480
Charlie Chan Game	Whitman	1939	30	50	80
Charlie Chan, The Great Charlie Chan Detective Game	Milton Bradley	1937	75	125	250
Charlie McCarthy Game of Topper	Whitman	1938	20	35	55
Charlie McCarthy Put And Take Bingo Game	Whitman	1938	30	45	70
Charlie McCarthy's Flying Hats	Whitman	1938	25	40	65
Charlie's Angels	Milton Bradley	1977	6	10	15
Charlie's Angels, (Farrah Fawcett box)	Milton Bradley	1977	10	20	45
Chasing Villa	Smith, Kline & French	1920	65	110	175
Checkered Game of Life	Milton Bradley	1860	600	1000	1600
Checkered Game of Life	Milton Bradley	1866	240	400	640
Checkered Game of Life	Milton Bradley	1911	95	160	250
Checkers & Avion	American Toy Works	1925	30	50	75
Chee Chow	Sam'l Gabriel Sons & Co.	1939	15	25	40
Cheerios Hook The Fish	General Mills	c1930	15	25	40
Chem-Action	Borg-Warner Chemicals		6	10	15

Board Games

NAME	COMPANY	DATE	GOOD	EX	MINT
Cherrios Bird Hunt	General Mills	c1930	15	25	40
Chess	Milton Bradley	1977	3	5	8
Chessindia	Clark & Sowdon	c1895	55	95	155
Chester Gump		1938	30	45	75
Chevy Chase	Hamilton-Myers	1890	75	125	200
Cheyenne	Milton Bradley	1958	50	85	140
Chicken In Every Plot, A	Animal Town Game Co.	c1980	20	30	50
Chin-Chow And Sum Flu	Novitas Sales Co.	c1925	6	10	15
China	Wilkens Thompson Co.	1905	50	85	135
Ching Gong	Samuel Gabriel & Sons	1937	30	65	100
CHIPS	Ideal	1981	7	10	20
CHIPS Game	Milton Bradley	1977	4	7	10
Chiromagica, Or The Hand of Fate	McLoughlin Brothers	1901	225	375	600
Chistmas Goose	McLoughlin Brothers	1890	500	850	1300
Chit Chat Game	Milton Bradley	1963	6	10	15
Chitty Chitty Bang Bang			20	30	50
Chivalrie Lawn Game		1875	60	100	160
Chivalry	Parker Brothers	c1925	30	50	80
Chocolate Splash	Willis G. Young	1916	51	85	135
Chopper Strike	Milton Bradley	1976	10	15	25
Christmas Jewel, Game of The	McLoughlin Brothers	1899	360	600	950
Christmas Mail	J. Ottmann Lith. Co.	c1890	390	650	1000
Chute-5	Lowe	1973	3	5	8
Chutes & Ladders	Milton Bradley	1956	10	15	25
Chutes And Ladders	Milton Bradley	1943	25	40	60
Chutes And Ladders	Milton Bradley	1974	7	15	20
Chutzpah	Middle Earth	1967	25	50	75
Chutzpah	Cadaco	1967	10	15	25
Cimarron Strip	Ideal	1967	50	85	135
Cinderella	Stoll & Edwards	1923	30	45	75
Circus Game		1914	75	125	200
Circus Game		1947	15	25	40
Citadel	Parker Brothers	1940	65	110	175
Cities	All-Fair	1932	25	40	56
City of Gold	Zulu Toy Mfg. Co.	1926	50	85	135
Civil War Game	Parker Brothers	1961	35	55	90
Civilization	Avalon Hill	1982	7	10	20
Classic Derby	Doremus Schoen & Co.	c1930	30	50	80
Clean Sweep	Schaper	c1960	20	30	50
Clipper Race	Sam'l Gabriel Sons & Co.	c1930	45	75	120
Close Encounters	Parker Brothers	1977	7	15	20
Clown Tenpins Game		1912	60	100	160
Clue	Parker Brothers	1972	4	7	11
Clue	Parker Brothers	1979	5	10	15
Clue	Parker Brothers	1949	25	40	65
Coast To Coast	Master Toy Co.	c1940	15	25	40
Coastal Defense Game	Baldwin Mfg. Co.		50	85	135
Cock-A-Doodle-Doo Game		1914	60	100	160
Cocked Hat, Game of	J.H. Singer	1892	150	250	400
College Basketball	Cadaco-Ellis	1954	20	30	55
College Football	Sports Illustrated Games		20	30	50
Columbo	Milton Bradley	1973	6	10	15
Combat	Ideal	1963	35	60	100
Combat At Anzio Beachhead	Ideal	1963	35	60	95
Combination Board Games	Wilder Mfg. Co.	1922	40	65	100
Comin' Round The Mountain	Einson-Freeman Publishing Corp.	1954	30	50	80
Concentration 25th Anniversary Edition	Milton Bradley	1982	6	10	16
Concentration 3rd Edition	Milton Bradley	1960	12	20	32

Board Games

NAME	COMPANY	DATE	GOOD	EX	MINT
Coney Island Playland Park	Vitaplay Toy Co.	c1940	54	90	144
Conflict	Parker Brothers	1942	50	100	150
Conspiracy	Milton Bradley	1982	4	7	11
Construction Game	Wilder Mfg. Co.	1925	75	100	200
Contack	Volume Sprayer Mfg. Co.	1939	21	35	56
Coon Hunt Game, The	Parker Brothers	1903	450	750	1200
Cootie	Schaper	1949	20	35	50
Corn & Beans	E.G. Selchow	1875	51	85	136
Corner The Market	Whitman	1938	24	40	64
Cortella	Atkins & Co., Publishers	1915	21	35	56
Cottontail And Peter, The Game of	Parker Brothers	1922	72	120	192
Count Down Space	Transogram		30	50	80
Countdown	E. S. Lowe	1967	25	45	75
Country Club Golf	Hustler Toy Corp.	c1920	75	125	200
Country Store, The	J.H. Singer	c1890	75	125	200
County Farm Game	Parker Brothers		45	75	120
Covered Wagon	Zulu Toy Mfg. Co.	1927	51	85	136
Cowboy Game, The	Chaffee & Selchow	1898	210	350	560
Cowboy Roundup	Parker Brothers	1952	15	25	40
Cows In Corn	Stirn & Lyon	1889	7	11	18
Crash, The New Airplane Game	Nucraft Toys	1928	30	50	80
Crazy Traveler Game		1892	60	100	160
Crazy Traveller	Parker Brothers	1908	36	60	96
Creature Features	Athol	1975	15	25	50
Creature From The Black Lagoon	Hasbro	1963	105	175	280
Crime & Mystery	Frederick H. Beach (Beachcraft)	c1940	15	25	40
Criss Cross Words	Alfred Butts	1938	90	150	240
Crokinole	E.I. Horsman		39	65	104
Crooked Man Game		1914	45	75	120
Crosby Derby	Fishlove Industries	1947	39	65	104
Cross Country	Samuel Lowe Co.	1941	20	30	50
Cross Country Marathon	Milton Bradley	c1920	50	75	100
Cross Country Racer	Automatic Toy Co.	1940	45	75	120
Cross Country, The Three Chipmunks			27	45	72
Cross Up	Milton Bradley	1974	15	25	40
Crossing The Ocean	Parker Brothers	1893	87	145	232
Crossword Anagrams	The Embossing Co.		9	15	24
Crosswords	National Games, Inc.	1954	12	20	32
Crow Hunt	Parker Brothers	c1904	40	60	90
Crusade	Sam'l Gabriel Sons & Co.	c1930	27	45	72
Cuckoo, A Society Game	J.H. Singer	1891	45	75	120
Curious George Game, The	Parker Brothers	1977	4	6	10
Curly Locks Game		1910	60	100	160
Curse of The Cobras Game	Ideal	1982	12	20	32
Cut Up Shopping Spree Game	Milton Bradley	1968	6	10	16
Daisy Clown Ring Game	Schacht Rubber Mfg. Co.	1927	9	15	24
Daisy Horseshoe Game	Schacht Rubber Mfg. Co.	1927	9	15	24
Dallas (Television Role Playing)	SPI	1980	4	7	11
Daniel Boone Trail Blazer		1964	45	75	120
Dark Shadows Game	Whitman	1968	39	65	104
Darrow Monopoly	Charles Darrow	1934	1500	2500	4000
Dastardly & Muttley	Milton Bradley	1969	25	45	65
Dating Game, The	Hasbro	1967	15	25	40
Davy Crocket Rescue Race Game	Gabriel	c1950	57	95	152
Davy Crockett Adventure Game	Gardner	1956	45	75	120
Davy Crockett Frontierland Game	Parker Brothers	1955	45	75	120
Davy Crockett Radar Action Game	Ewing Mfg. & Sales Co.	1955	51	85	136
Dawn of The Dead		1978	21	35	56
Day At The Circus, Game of	McLoughlin Brothers	1898	300	400	600

Games, top to bottom: The Deputy, 1960, Milton Bradley; The Flintstones Stone Age Game, 1961, Transogram; Jackie Gleason's Story Stage Game, 1955, Utopia Enterprises; Captain Video, 1952, Milton Bradley.

Board Games

NAME	COMPANY	DATE	GOOD	EX	MINT
Dealer's Choice	Parker Brothers	1972	13	22	35
Deck Derby	Wolverine Supply & Mfg. Co.	c1920	36	60	96
Decoy	Selchow & Righter	1940	45	75	120
Defenders of The Flag Game		c1920	24	40	64
Deluxe Wheel of Fortune	Pressman	1986	5	8	13
Democracy	Toy Creations	1940	15	25	40
Dennis The Menace Baseball Game		1960	6	10	16
Department Store, Game of Playing	McLoughlin Brothers	1898	510	850	1360
Deputy Dawg TV Lotto		1961	21	35	56
Deputy Game, The	Milton Bradley	1960	30	50	80
Derby Day	Parker Brothers	1930	45	75	120
Derby Day		1959	21	35	56
Derby Steeple Chase, The	Mcloughlin Brothers	1890	90	150	240
Detective, The Game of	R. Bliss Mfg. Co.	1889	1200	2000	3200
Detectives Game, The	Transogram	1961	30	50	80
Dewey's Victory	Parker Brothers	c1900	120	200	320
Diamond Heart	McLoughlin Brothers	1902	111	185	296
Dick Tracy Crime Stopper	Ideal	1963	57	95	152
Dick Tracy Detective Game	Einson-Freeman Publishing Corp.	1933	45	75	120
Dick Tracy Detective Game	Whitman	1937	39	65	104
Dick Tracy Master Detective Game	Selchow & Righter	1961	12	20	32
Dick Tracy The Master Detective Game	Selchow & Righter	1961	30	50	80
Dick Van Dyke Board Game	Standard Toycraft, Inc.	1964	45	75	120
Dip Flip			5	9	14
Diplomacy	Avalon Hill	1976	15	25	40
Diplomacy	Games Research	1961	21	35	56
Direct Hit	Northwestern Products	c1950	40	70	110
Dirty Water-The Water Polution Game	Urban Systems	1970	8	15	20
Discretion	Volume Sprayer Mfg. Co.	1942	30	45	75
Disney Mouseketeer	Parker Brothers	1964	40	65	100
Disney Queen of Hearts	Golden		7	15	20
Disney Return To Oz Game	Western Publishing	1985	10	15	25
Disney's Pinocchio Board Game	Parker Brothers	c1960	10	15	25
Disneyland Game	Transogram		10	15	25
Dispatcher	Avalon Hill	1958	20	35	55
District Messenger Boy, Game of	McLoughlin Brothers	1886	250	400	550
District Messenger Boy, Game of	McLoughlin Brothers	1904	90	150	240
Diver Dan	Milton Bradley		9	15	25
Doc Holiday	Transogram		30	50	80
Doctor Doolittle's Magic Answer Machine	Bar-Zim		7	15	20
Doctor Kildare Game		1967	10	15	25
Dog Race	Transogram	1937	50	75	100
Dog Show, The	J.H. Singer	c1890	45	70	110
Dog Sweepstakes	Stoll & Eisen	1935	45	75	120
Dogfight	Milton Bradley	1962	30	45	70
Dollar A Second	Lowell	1955	20	30	50
Dollars & Sense	Sidney Rogers gitten	1946	100	150	200
Domain	Parker Brothers	1983	2	3	5
Donald Duck Big Game Box	Whitman	1979	10	15	20
Donald Duck Party Game	Parker Brothers	1938	50	75	150
Donald Duck Tiddley Winks Game		c1950	6	10	15
Donald Duck's Own Game	Walt Disney	c1930	25	40	65
Donald Duck's Party Game	Parker Brothers	c1950	10	20	35
Dondi Potato Race Game	Hasbro	c1950	35	55	90
Donkey Kong	Milton Bradley		3	5	8
Donkey Party Game	Saalfield Publishing	1950	15	25	40
Double Trouble	Milton Bradley	1987	3	5	8

Board Games

NAME	COMPANY	DATE	GOOD	EX	MINT
Dr. Busby	J.H. Singer	c1890	40	80	100
Dr. Kildare	Ideal	1962	10	20	30
Dr. Kildare's Perilous Night	Ideal	1962	25	40	65
Dracula Mystery Game	Hasbro	c1960	45	75	120
Dracula's 'I Vant To Bite Your Finger' Game	Hasbro	1981	10	20	30
Dragnet	Parker Brothers	1955	70	115	185
Dragnet	Transogram	1955	35	60	95
Dragnet Radar Action Game		c1950	10	15	25
Dragnet Triple Fire Target Game		1955	15	25	40
Dragon's Lair	Milton Bradley	1983	7	10	20
Dreamland Wonder Resort Game	Parker Brothers	1914	150	250	400
Drew Pearson's Predict-A-Word			6	10	20
Driver Ed	Cadaco	1973	6	10	20
Drummer Boy Game		1914	60	100	160
Drummer Boy Game, The	Parker Brothers	c1890	100	150	250
Dubble Up	Sam'l Gabriel Sons & Co.	c1940	15	25	40
Dudes, Game of The	R. Bliss Mfg. Co.	1890	225	375	600
Dukes of Hazzard	Ideal	1981	6	10	15
Dune	Parker Brothers	1984	6	10	15
Dungeon Dice	Parker Brothers	1977	5	8	15
Dungeons & Dragons	Mattel	1980	6	10	15
Duplicate Ad-Lib	Lowe	1976	5	10	15
Duran Duran Game	Milton Bradley	1985	15	25	40
Dynomutt		1977	10	15	25
E.T. The Extra Terrestrial	Parker Brothers	1982	6	10	15
Eagle Bombsight	Toy Creations	c1940	25	40	65
East Is East And West Is West	Parker Brothers	c1920	75	150	250
Easy Money	Milton Bradley	1936	35	55	90
Eckha	Milton Bradley		45	75	120
Ed Wynn The Fire Chief	Selchow & Righter	1937	45	75	120
Eddie Cantor's Tell It To The Judge	Parker Brothers	c1930	40	65	104
Edgar Bergen's Charlie McCarthy Game of Topper	Whitman	1938	15	20	32
Edgar Bergen's Charlie McCarthy Put And Take Bingo Game		1938	20	35	56
Election	Fireside Game Co.	1896	20	35	55
Electra Woman And Dyna Girl	Ideal	1977	10	15	25
Electric Baseball	Einson-Freeman Publishing Corp.	1935	35	60	95
Electric Questioner	Knapp Electric & Novelty Co.	1920	20	35	55
Electric Speed Classic	J. Pressman & Co.	1930	390	650	1000
Electro Gameset	Knapp Electric & Novelty Co.	1930	30	45	70
Electronic Radar Search	Ideal	1967	10	15	25
Elementaire Musical Game	Theodore Presser	1896	20	35	55
Ella Cinders	Milton Bradley	1944	40	80	100
Ellsworth Elephant Game	Selchow & Righter	1960	30	45	70
Elmer Layden's Scientific Football Game	Cadaco Ltd.	1936	50	100	150
Elsie (The Cow) Game, The	Selchow & Righter	1941	50	100	200
Elvis Presley Game 'King of Rock'			6	10	15
Emenee Chocolate Factory		1966	6	10	15
Emergency	Milton Bradley	1971	10	15	25
Emily Post Popularity Game	Selchow & Righter	1970	15	20	35
Empire Auto Races	Empire Plastics	c1950	20	30	50
Enchanted Forest Game		1914	120	200	320
Endurance Run	Milton Bradley	1930	75	125	200
Enemy Agent	Milton Bradley	1976	15	20	30

Board Games

NAME	COMPANY	DATE	GOOD	EX	MINT
Entertainment Trivia Game	Lakeside	1984	5	10	15
Entre's Fun & Games In Accounting	Entrepreneurial Games	1988	4	7	12
Errand Boy, The	McLoughlin Brothers	1891	150	250	350
Escape From New York	TSR	1980	10	15	25
Escape From The Death Star	Parker Brothers	1977	20	35	55
Ethan Allen's All-Star Baseball	Cadaco Ltd.	1941	30	50	80
Evening Parties, Game of	Parker Brothers	c1910	180	300	480
Eye Guess 2nd Edition	Milton Bradley	1966	15	20	30
F-Troop	Ideal	1965	45	75	120
F.B.I.	Transogram	1958	35	55	90
Fact Finder Fun	Milton Bradley	1963	10	15	25
Fairyland Game	Milton Bradley	c1880	60	95	150
Fall Guy, The	Milton Bradley	1981	10	15	25
Family Affair	Whitman	1967	25	40	65
Family Feud	Milton Bradley	1985	6	10	15
Family Feud	Milton Bradley	1977	10	15	25
Family Ties Game, The	Apple Street	1986	10	15	25
Famous Paintings	Parker Brothers		30	45	70
Fan-Tel	O. Schoenhut, Inc.	1937	20	40	60
Fang Bang	Milton Bradley	1966	10	15	25
Fangface	Parker Brothers	1979	5	8	13
Fantastic Four	Milton Bradley		10	20	35
Fantastic Voyage Game	Milton Bradley	1968	15	25	40
Farmer Jones' Pigs	McLoughlin Brothers	1890	165	275	440
Fashionable English Sorry Game, The	Parker Brothers	1934	115	190	300
Fast Mail Game	Milton Bradley	1910	105	175	275
Fat Albert	Milton Bradley	1973	15	25	40
Favorite Steeple Chase	J.H. Singer	c1895	60	100	160
Felix The Cat Dandy Candy Game		1957	10	15	25
Felix The Cat Game	Milton Bradley	1960	25	40	65
Felix The Cat Game	Milton Bradley	1968	15	25	40
Ferdinand The Bull Chinese Checkers Game		c1930	60	100	160
Fibber McGee	Milton Bradley	1936	25	40	65
Fibber McGee And The Wistful Vista Mystery	Milton Bradley	1940	30	45	70
Fig Mill	Willis G. Young	1916	25	40	65
Fighter Bomber	Cadaco	1977	15	25	40
Fighting With The Boers	Parker Brothers		150	250	400
Finance	Parker Brothers	1962	10	20	35
Finance	Parker Brothers	1937	25	40	65
Finance And Fortune	Parker Brothers	1936	35	50	75
Fire Alarm Game	Parker Brothers	1899	1300	2300	3600
Fire Department	Milton Bradley	c1930	50	80	125
Fire Fighters Game	Milton Bradley	1909	120	200	325
Fire Fighters!	Russell Mfg. Co.	1957	15	25	40
Fireball XL-5	Milton Bradley	1963	75	125	200
Firefighters	Hasbro		50	85	135
Fish Pond	National Games, Inc.	c1950	45	75	125
Fish Pond	E.O. Clark	c1890	50	100	150
Fish Pond	Wilder Mfg. Co.	c1920	20	30	50
Fishbait	Ideal	1965	40	60	80
Flag Travelette	Archarena Co.	1895	45	75	120
Flagship Airfreight The Airplane Cargo Game	Milton Bradley	1946	40	70	115
Flapper Fortunes	The Embossing Co.	1929	20	30	50
Flash	J. Pressman & Co.	c1940	30	40	60
Flash Gordon	House Of Games	c1970	15	20	35
Fling-A-Ring	Wolverine Supply & Mfg. Co.	c1930	20	35	55

Games, top to bottom: The Beverly Hillbillies Card Game, 1963, Milton Bradley; The Fugitive Game, 1966, Ideal; Howdy Doody's TV Game, c1950, Milton Bradley; The Twilight Zone, c1960, Ideal.

Board Games

NAME	COMPANY	DATE	GOOD	EX	MINT
Flintstone's Dino The Dinosaur Game	Transogram	1961	45	75	120
Flintstone's Hoppy The Hopperoo Game	Transogram	1964	45	75	120
Flintstones	Milton Bradley	1980	15	20	35
Flintstones	Milton Bradley	1971	15	25	40
Flintstones Big Game Hunt			15	20	30
Flintstones Mitt-Full Game	Whitman	1962	40	65	100
Flintstones Stone Age Game	Transogram	1961	20	35	55
Flip 'N Skip	litlle Kennys	1971	5	10	15
Flip Flop Go	Mattel	1962	6	10	15
Flip It	American Toy Works	1925	40	60	80
Flip It	Deluxe Game Corp.	1940	20	30	50
Flipper	Mattel		30	50	80
Flivver Game	Milton Bradley	1927	75	150	300
Floating Satellite Target Game			15	25	40
Flowers, Game of	Cincinnati Game Co.	1899	45	75	120
Flying Aces	Selchow & Righter	c1940	50	75	100
Flying Nun Game, The	Milton Bradley	1968	20	30	50
Flying The Beam	Parker Brothers	1941	75	125	250
Flying The United States Airmail	Parker Brothers	1929	80	135	215
Fonz Game, The	Milton Bradley	1976	15	25	40
Fooinstein	Coleco		15	25	40
Foot Race, The	Parker Brothers	c1900	60	100	160
Football	Wilder Mfg. Co.	c1930	50	80	125
Football, Game of	Parker Brothers	c1890	60	100	160
Football, The Game of	George A. Childs	1895	75	125	200
Formula One Car Race Game	Parker Brothers	1968	35	65	100
Fortress America	Milton Bradley	1986	25	40	65
Fortune	Parker Brothers	c1938	40	70	110
Fortune Teller, The	Milton Bradley	1905	60	100	160
Fortune Telling & Baseball Game		1889	85	140	225
Fortune Telling Game	Whitman	1934	100	200	300
Forty-Niners Gold Mining Game	National Games, Inc.	c1930	25	40	65
Foto World	Cadaco Ltd.	1935	90	150	240
Foto-Electric Football	Cadaco Ltd.	c1930	45	75	120
Foto-Finish Horse Race	J. Pressman & Co.	c1940	30	45	70
Foto-Football			20	35	55
Fox And Geese	McLoughlin Brothers	1903	210	350	550
Fox And Hounds	Parker Brothers	1948	35	60	95
Fox And Hounds Game		1912	60	100	160
Fox Hunt	Milton Bradley	1905	40	65	100
Fox Hunt	E.S. Lowe, Inc.	c1930	20	35	50
Foxy Grandpa Hat Party	Selchow & Righter	c1906	55	90	145
Frankenstein Game	Hasbro	1962	60	100	160
Freddy Krueger			10	15	25
Frenzy			20	35	55
Frisko	The Embossing Co.	1937	20	30	50
Frog He Would A Wooing Go, The	McLoughlin Brothers	1898	450	750	1200
Frog School Game		1914	45	75	120
Frog Who Would A Wooing Go, The	United Game Co.	c1920	45	75	120
Fu Manchu's Hidden Hoard	Ideal	1967	35	55	90
Fuedel	3M	1967	15	25	40
Fugitive	Ideal	1966	90	150	240
Fun At The Circus	McLoughlin Brothers	1897	360	600	950
Fun At The Zoo; A Game	Parker Brothers	1902	120	200	325
Fun Kit	Frederick H. Beach (Beachcraft)	1939	15	20	35
Funky Phantom Game	Milton Bradley	1971	10	15	25
G-Men Clue Games	Whitman	c1935	30	50	80
G.I. Joe	International Games	1982	15	25	40
G.I. Joe Adventure	Hasbro	1982	20	30	50

Board Games

NAME	COMPANY	DATE	GOOD	EX	MINT
G.I. Joe Card Game	Whitman	1965	10	15	25
G.I. Joe Marine Paratrooper	Milton Bradley	1965	30	45	70
Gang Busters Game	Whitman	1939	50	80	130
Gang Busters Game	Lynco	1938	150	250	400
Gang Way For Fun	Transogram	1964	25	40	65
Garfield	Parker Brothers	1981	4	6	10
Garfield Kitty Letters	Parker Brothers		10	15	25
Garrison's Gorillas	Ideal	1967	45	75	120
Gay Puree		1962	25	40	65
Gene Autry Dude Ranch			55	95	150
General Headquarters	All-Fair	c1940	50	75	100
General Hospital	Cardinal Industries	c1980	15	20	30
General Hospital	Parker Brothers	1974	10	15	25
Gentle Ben Animal Hunt Game	Mattel	1967	15	25	40
Geographical Lotto Game		1921	20	30	50
Geography Game	A. Flanagan Co.	c1910	15	25	40
George of the Jungle Game	Parker Brothers	1968	40	65	125
Ges It Game	Knapp Electric & Novelty Co.	1936	20	35	55
Get Beep Beep The Road Runner Game	Whitman	1975	15	25	35
Get The Balls Baseball Game		1930	20	30	50
Get The Picture	Worlds Of Wonder	1987	6	10	15
Gettysburg	Avalon Hill	1960	20	30	50
Ghosts	Milton Bradley	1985	4	6	10
Giant Wheel Horse Race Game	Remco	c1950	50	85	135
Gil Hodges Pennant Fever			45	75	120
Gilligan's Island	T. Cohn Inc.	1965	120	200	325
Gly-Dor	All-Fair	1931	60	100	200
Go Bang	J.H. Singer	c1898	40	60	90
Go For Broke	Selchow & Righter	1965	10	15	25
Go To The Head of The Class	Milton Bradley	1938	20	50	75
Godfather	Family Games	1971	6	10	15
Godzilla Game	Mattel	1963	30	50	80
Going To Sunday School	McLoughlin Brothers		135	225	360
Going To The Fire Game		1914	90	150	240
Going, Going, Gone!	Milton Bradley	1975	9	15	25
Gold Hunters, The	Parker Brothers	c1900	105	175	280
Goldenlocks & The Three Bears	McLoughlin Brothers	1890	390	650	1000
Golf, The Game of	J.H. Singer	c1898	100	150	250
Golf, The Game of	Clark & Sowdon	1905	325	550	850
Gomer Pyle Game	Transogram	c1960	35	60	95
Gong Show	Milton Bradley	1975	15	25	40
Good Ol'Charlie Brown Game	Milton Bradley	1971	15	20	30
Good Old Aunt, The	McLoughlin Brothers	1892	150	250	400
Good Old Game of Innocence Abroad, The	Parker Brothers	1888	180	300	475
Good Things To Eat Lotto	Sam'l Gabriel Sons & Co.	c1940	15	25	40
Goodbye Mr. Chips	Parker Brothers		10	15	25
Goofy's Mad Maze	Whitman	c1970	6	10	15
Goonies	Milton Bradley	c1980	10	15	20
Goosey Gander, Or Who Finds The Golden Egg, Game of	J.H. Singer	1890	675	1150	1800
Goosy Goosy Gander	McLoughlin Brothers	1896	300	500	800
Grande Auto Race	Atkins & Co., Publishers	c1920	50	85	135
Great American Flag Game, The	Parker Brothers	1940	35	60	100
Great American Game, Baseball, The	Hustler Toy Corp.	1923	105	175	275
Great American War Game	J.H. Hunter	1899	600	1000	1600
Great Charlie Chan Detective Mystery Game, The	Milton Bradley	1937	80	130	210

Board Games

NAME	COMPANY	DATE	GOOD	EX	MINT
Great Family Amusement Game, The	Einson-Freeman Publishing Corp.	c1889	20	35	55
Great Grape Ape Game, The	Milton Bradley	1975	15	25	40
Green Ghost Game	Transogram	1965	65	95	150
Gremlins	International Games	1984	10	15	25
Greyhound Racing Game	Rex Manufacturing Co.	1938	15	25	40
Grizzly Adams Game	House Of Games	1978	15	25	40
Groucho's TV Quiz Game	Pressman	1954	50	75	150
Groucho's You Bet Your Life	Lowell	1955	75	125	250
Guinness Book of World Records Game, The	Parker Brothers	1979	5	9	15
Gulf Strike		1983	15	25	40
Gumby			8	15	25
Gunsmoke Game	Lowell	c1950	40	65	100
Gusher	Carrom Industries	1946	45	75	120
Gym Horseshoes	Wolverine Supply & Mfg. Co.	1930	30	45	70
Gypsy Fortune Telling Game, The	Milton Bradley	c1895	135	220	350
Hair Bear Bunch	Milton Bradley		6	10	15
Half-Time Football	Lakeside	1979	5	9	15
Halma	Milton Bradley	1885	30	45	70
Halma	E.I. Horsman	1885	35	60	75
Hand of Fate	McLoughlin Brothers	1901	1200	2000	3200
Handicap Golf	Sports Illustrated Games		35	55	90
Hang On Harvey	Ideal	1969	15	20	30
Hangman	Milton Bradley	1976	5	8	15
Happiness	Milton Bradley	1972	7	11	20
Happy Days	Parker Brothers	1976	15	25	45
Happy Family, The	Milton Bradley	c1910	15	25	40
Happy Hooligan Bowling Type Game		1925	60	100	160
Hardwood Ten Pins Wooden Game		1889	60	100	160
Hardy Boys Mystery game, The	Milton Bradley	1968	15	25	40
Hardy Boys Treasure	Parker Brothers	1960	20	30	50
Hare And Hounds	Selchow & Righter	1890	150	250	450
Harlequin, The Game of The	McLoughlin Brothers	1895	150	200	300
Hashimoto	Transogram	1963	30	45	70
Haunted House Game	Ideal	1963	65	100	175
Haunted Mansion	Lakeside	c1970	30	50	80
Have Gun Will Travel Game	Parker Brothers	1959	50	85	135
Hawaii Five-O	Remco		15	25	40
Hawaiian Eye	Transogram	1960	95	160	250
Hawaiian Punch Game	Milton Bradley		20	30	50
Hector Heathcote	Transogram	1963	50	85	135
Heedless Tommy	McLoughlin Brothers	1893	240	400	640
Hel-Lo Telephone Game	J.C. Singer	1898	95	150	250
Helps To History	A. Flanagan Co.	1885	20	35	55
Hen That Laid The Golden Egg, The	Parker Brothers	1900	105	175	275
Hendrik Van Loon's Wide World Game	Parker Brothers	1935	35	65	100
Heroes of America	Educational Card & Game Co.	c1920	20	35	55
Hi-Ho! Cherry-O	Whitman	1975	6	10	15
Hi-Q			5	10	15
Hi-Way Henry	All-Fair	1928	400	800	1500
Hialeah Horse Racing Game	Milton Bradley	c1940	40	65	100
Hickety Pickety	Parker Brothers	1924	45	75	120
Hidden Authors	Clark & Sowdon		10	20	30
Hide And Seek, Game of	McLoughlin Brothers	1895	175	300	475
Hide N Seek	Ideal	1967	10	15	25
Hip Flip	Parker Brothers	1968	6	10	15
Hippety Hop	Corey Games	c1947	25	40	65

Games, top to bottom: Get Smart Card Game, 1966, Ideal; Pop the Hat, c1920, Milton Bradley; Peg Base Ball Game, 1924, Parker Brothers; Flipper Flips, c1960, Mattel; Hopalong Cassidy Game, c1950, Milton Bradley.

Board Games

NAME	COMPANY	DATE	GOOD	EX	MINT
Hippodrome Circus Game	Milton Bradley	1895	75	150	200
Hippodrome, The	E.O. Clark	c1900	150	200	400
Hit The Beach	Milton Bradley	1965	40	60	90
Hit The Spot			20	35	55
Hock Shop			10	20	30
Hockey	1942	1942	15	25	40
Hocus Pocus	Transogram	c1960	30	45	70
Hogan's Heroes Game	Transogram	1966	45	75	120
Hold That Tiger	J. Pressman & Co.		50	85	135
Hold The Fort	Parker Brothers	1895	75	150	200
Hold Your Horses	Klauber Novelty	c1930	10	20	30
Holiday	Replogie Globes Inc.	1958	40	65	100
Hollywood Go	Parker Brothers	1954	30	45	75
Hollywood Squares	Ideal	1974	6	10	15
Hollywood Squares	Milton Bradley	1980	4	6	10
Home Baseball Game	McLoughlin Brothers	1900	900	1700	2300
Home Defenders	Saalfield	1941	15	25	50
Home Game	Pressman	c1950	30	50	80
Home Games	The Martin Co.	c1900	105	175	275
Honey Bee Game	Milton Bradley	1913	50	85	135
Honey West	Ideal	1965	50	85	135
Honeymooners Game	TSR	1986	7	12	20
Hood's Spelling School	C.I. Hood	1897	20	35	55
Hoodoo	Tryne	c1950	7	12	20
Hoop-O-Loop	Wolverine Supply & Mfg. Co.	1930	20	30	50
Hopalong Cassidy Chinese Checkers Game		c1950	15	25	40
Hopalong Cassidy Game	Milton Bradley	c1950	30	45	70
Hornet	Samuel Lowe Co.	1941	30	45	70
Horse Race	E.S. Lowe, Inc.	1943	10	20	30
Horses	Modern Makers	1927	45	75	125
Hot Spot	Parker Brothers	1961	10	20	30
Hot Wheels Wipe-Out Board Game	Mattel	1968	30	50	80
Houndcats Game	Milton Bradley	c1970	8	15	25
House Party	Whitman	1968	10	15	25
How Good Are You	Whitman	1937	10	15	25
How To Succeed In Business Without Really Trying	Milton Bradley	1963	10	15	25
Howdy Doody Electric Carnival Game	Harret-Gilmar, Inc.	c1950	35	50	75
Howdy Doody TV Studio			40	65	100
Howdy Doody's 3 Ring Circus	Harett-Gilmar, Inc.	1950	45	75	120
Howdy Doody's Own Game	Parker Brothers	1949	75	125	200
Huckleberry Hound	Milton Bradley	1981	10	20	35
Huckleberry Hound Bumps	Transogram	1960	20	35	55
Huckleberry Hound Pinball			20	35	55
Huckleberry Hound Spin-O-Game		1959	45	75	120
Huckleberry Hound Western Game	Milton Bradley	1959	25	40	65
Hullabaloo	Remco	1965	50	85	135
Humor Rumor		c1969	10	20	30
Humpty Dumpty Game	Lowell	c1950	6	10	15
Hunt For Red October	TSR	1988	5	15	25
Hunting The Rabbit	Clark & Sowdon	c1895	70	115	185
Hurdle Race	Milton Bradley	1905	75	125	200
Hymn Quartets	Goodenough And Woglom Co.	1933	10	15	25
I Dream of Genie Game	Milton Bradley	1965	35	55	90
I Spy	Ideal	1965	50	95	150
I'm George Gobel, And Here's The Game	Schaper	1955	40	60	80

Board Games

NAME	COMPANY	DATE	GOOD	EX	MINT
Improved Geographical Game, The	Parker Brothers	1890s	60	100	160
Improved Steeple Chase Game, The	McLoughlin Brothers	1892	120	200	320
In And Out The Window	Sam'l Gabriel Sons & Co.	c1940	20	35	55
Incredible Hulk	Milton Bradley	1978	6	10	15
Incredible Hulk Smash Up Action Game	Ideal		10	15	25
India	Parker Brothers	1940	15	20	30
India Bombay	Cutler & Saleeby Co.	c1910	25	40	65
India, An Oriental Game	McLoughlin Brothers	c1890	100	165	265
India, Game of	Milton Bradley	c1910	20	30	50
Indian Scout, Game of			15	25	40
Indiana Jones Raiders of The Lost Ark	Kenner	1981	20	35	55
Indians And Cowboys	Sam'l Gabriel Sons & Co.	c1940	40	65	100
Indoor Horseshoes	Milton Bradley		20	35	55
Input	Milton Bradley	1984	4	7	15
Inspector Gadget	Milton Bradley	1983	15	25	40
Intercollegiate Football	Hustler Toy Corp.	1923	50	85	135
International Spy, Game of	All-Fair	1943	50	85	135
International Yacht Race	McLoughlin Brothers		100	175	250
Interpretation of Dreams	Hasbro	1969	10	15	25
Intrigue	Milton Bradley	1954	35	60	95
Inventors, The	Parker Brothers	1974	7	12	20
Ipcress File	Milton Bradley	1966	40	70	110
Ironside	Ideal	1976	55	95	150
J. Fred Muggs 'Round The World Game	Sam'l Gabriel Sons & Co.		45	75	120
Jace Pearson's Tales of The Texas Rangers	E.E. Fairchild	1955	50	75	125
Jack And Jill	Milton Bradley	1909	60	100	160
Jack And Jill	Parker Brothers	c1890	55	95	150
Jack And The Bean Stalk	Parker Brothers	1895	45	70	115
Jack And The Bean Stalk, The Game of	McLoughlin Brothers	1898	550	900	1450
Jack And The Beanstalk	National Games, Inc.	1946	30	45	75
Jack And The Beanstalk Adventure Game	Transogram	1957	25	50	75
Jack Barry's Twenty One	Lowe	1956	20	30	50
Jack Spratt Game		1914	45	75	120
Jack The Ripper			30	45	70
Jack-Be-Nimble	The Embossing Co.	c1940	20	35	55
Jackie Gleason's And AW-A-A-A-Y We Go!	Transogram	1956	75	125	200
Jackie Gleason's Story Stage Game	Utopia Enterprises, Inc.	1955	100	200	300
Jackpot	Milton Bradley	1975	7	11	20
Jackpot	B.L. Fry Products Co.	1943	15	25	40
James Bond 007 Goldfinger Game	Milton Bradley	1966	50	85	135
James Bond 007 Thunderball Game	Milton Bradley	1965	50	85	135
James Bond Secret Agent 007 Game	Milton Bradley	1964	15	25	40
James Bond You Only Live Twice	Victory Games	1984	5	8	13
Jan Murray's Charge Account			25	40	65
Jan Murray's Treasure Hunt		c1950	10	15	25
Japan, The Game of	J. Ottmann Lith. Co.	1903	180	300	480
Japanese Games of Cash And Akambo	McLoughlin Brothers	1881	150	250	400
Jeane Dixon's Game of Destiny	Milton Bradley	1968	7	12	20
Jeep Board, The	E.S. Lowe, Inc.	1944	15	25	40
Jeepers	Games Of Fame	1945	15	25	40
Jeopardy	Milton Bradley	1964	10	15	25

Board Games

NAME	COMPANY	DATE	GOOD	EX	MINT
Jeopardy 10th Edition	Milton Bradley	1972	4	7	12
Jerome Park Steeple Chase	McLoughlin Brothers		105	175	280
Jetson's	Transogram	1963	85	140	225
Jetsons Fun Pad Game	Milton Bradley	1963	50	75	125
Jetsons Race Through Space Game	Milton Bradley	1985	5	10	15
JFK Game			20	30	50
Jockey	Carrom Industries	c1920	35	60	95
John Drake Secret Agent	Milton Bradley	1966	30	45	70
John Gilpin, Rainbow Backgammon And Bewildered Travelers	McLoughlin Brothers	1875	150	250	400
Johnny Get Your Gun	Parker Brothers	1928	45	75	120
Johnny Ringo	Transogram	c1959	75	125	200
Joker's Wild	Milton Bradley	1973	5	10	15
Jolly Game of Goose, The	J.P. Beach	1851	750	1250	2000
Jolly Pirates	Russell Mfg. Co.	1938	20	35	55
Jonathan Livingston Seagull	Mattel	1973	6	10	15
Jonny Quest Game	Transogram	1964	60	100	160
Journey To Bethlehem, The	Parker Brothers	1923	95	160	250
Jubilee	Cadaco	c1950	6	10	15
Jumbo Jet	Jumbo	1963	6	10	15
Jumpy Tinker	Toy Creations	c1920	20	30	50
Jungle Hunt	Rosebud Art Co.,Inc.	c1940	30	50	75
Junior Auto Race Game		1925	30	50	80
Junior Bingo-Matic	Transogram	1968	6	10	15
Junior Combination Board	McLoughlin Brothers	1905	105	175	280
Junior Executive	Whitman	1963	7	15	20
Junior Football	Deluxe Game Corp.	1944	30	45	70
Junior Motor Race	Wolverine Supply & Mfg. Co.	1925	40	70	110
Justice	Lowell	1954	30	45	75
Justice League of America	Hasbro	1967	105	175	275
Ka Bala	Transogram	1965	65	100	150
Kan-Oo-Win-It	McLoughlin Brothers	1893	345	575	925
Kar-Zoom	Whitman	1964	15	20	35
Kate Smith's Own Game America	Toy Creations	c1940	40	65	100
Keeping Up With The Jone's	Parker Brothers	1921	50	85	135
Keeping Up With The Jone's, The Game of	H.J. Phillips Co.	1921	75	100	200
Kennedys, The	Transogram	1962	35	55	90
Kentucky Derby	Whitman	1960	15	25	40
Kentucky Derby Racing Game	Whitman	1938	20	30	50
Kentucky Jones	T. Cohn Inc.	1964	25	40	65
Keyword	Parker Brothers	1954	5	10	15
Kilkenny Cats, The Amusing Game of	Parker Brothers	1890	60	100	160
King Kong Game	Ideal	1966	10	15	30
King Kong Game	Milton Bradley	1966	10	15	25
King Leonardo And His Subjects Game	Milton Bradley	1960	30	50	80
King Zor, The Dinosaur Game	Ideal	c1964	20	35	55
King's Quoits, New Game of	McLoughlin Brothers	1893	210	350	550
Kings	Akro Agate Co.	1931	55	95	150
Kings, The Game of	Josiah Adams	1845	70	115	185
Kismet	Lakeside	1971	3	5	8
KISS On Tour Game	Aucoin	1978	20	30	50
Kitty Kat Cup Ball	Rosebud Art Co., Inc.	c1930	40	60	100
Klondike Game	Parker Brothers	c1890	345	575	900
Klondike Nugget Game		c1890	195	325	550
Knight Rider	Parker Brothers	1983	7	12	20
Ko-Ko The Clown	All-Fair	1940	20	30	50
Kojack	Milton Bradley	1975	7	12	20
Komikal Konversation Kards	Selchow & Righter	1893	20	30	50

Games, top to bottom: The Jolly Game of Goose, 1851, J.P. Beach; Comic Action Heroes Game, Milton Bradley; Ironside Game, 1976, Ideal; The MAD Magazine Game, 1979, Parker Brothers.

Board Games

NAME	COMPANY	DATE	GOOD	EX	MINT
Kommisar	Selchow & Righter	c1960	10	15	25
Korg 70,000 BC	Milton Bradley	1974	10	15	25
Kreskin's ESP	Milton Bradley	1966	10	20	30
Kriegspiel	Avalon Hill		6	10	15
Kriegspiel Junior	Parker Brothers	1915	50	80	125
Krull	Parker Brothers	1983	6	10	15
Kukla & Ollie	Parker Brothers	1962	30	45	70
La Haza	Supply Sales Corp.	1923	10	20	30
Lame Duck, The	Parker Brothers	1928	60	100	160
Lancer	Remco	1968	70	120	190
Land And Sea War Games	Samuel Lowe Co.	1941	40	65	100
Land of The Giants	Ideal	1968	60	100	160
Land of The Lost	Milton Bradley	1975	35	60	95
Laramie	Lowell	1960	45	75	120
Lasso The Jumping Ring		1912	60	100	160
Last Straw	Schaper	1966	5	10	15
Laugh-In's Squeeze Your Bippy Game	Hasbro	1968	60	100	160
Laverne & Shirley Game	Parker Brothers	1977	9	15	25
Le Choc	Milton Bradley	c1919	50	85	135
League Parlor Base Ball	R. Bliss Mfg. Co.	1889	600	1000	1600
Leap Frog Game	McLoughlin Brothers	1900	165	275	440
Leap Frog, Game of	McLoughlin Brothers	1910	45	75	120
Leave It To Beaver Ambush Game		1959	40	65	100
Leave It To Beaver Money Maker	Hasbro	1959	40	65	100
Leave It To Beaver Rocket To The Moon	Hasbro	1959	40	65	100
Lee At Havana	Chaffee & Selchow	1899	55	90	145
Lee Vs. Meade: Battle of Gettysburg	Gamut of Games	1974	15	25	50
Legend of Jessie James Game, The	Milton Bradley	1965	75	125	200
Legend of The Lone Ranger			5	10	15
Let's Go To College	Einson-Freeman Publishing Corp.	1944	30	45	70
Let's Make A Deal Game	Ideal	c1970	10	15	25
Letter Carrier, The	McLoughlin Brothers	1890	80	135	215
Letters	E.I. Horsman	1878	30	45	70
Letters Or Anagrams	Parker Brothers	c1890	30	50	80
Leverage	Milton Bradley	1982	4	6	10
Library of Games	American Toy Works	1938	15	25	40
Lie Detector Game	Mattel	1961	30	50	75
Lieutenant	Transogram	1963	85	140	225
Life Boat Game	Parker Brothers		300	500	800
Life In The Wild West	R. Bliss Mfg. Co.	1894	300	500	800
Life of The Party	Rosebud Art Co., Inc.	c1940	35	50	75
Life's Mishaps & Bobbing 'Round The Circle, The Games of	McLoughlin Brothers	1891	330	550	875
Life, The Game of	Milton Bradley	1960	10	15	25
Limited Mail & Express Game, The	Parker Brothers	1894	90	150	240
Lindy Hop-Off	Parker Brothers	1927	200	400	800
Linus the Lionhearted Uproarious Game	Transogram	1965	50	85	135
Lippy the Lion Game	Transogram	1963	25	45	70
Literature Game	L.J. Colby & Co.	1897	15	25	40
Little America Antarctic Game	Whitman		100	165	265
Little Black Sambo	Cadaco Ltd.	1952	80	150	250
Little Black Sambo, Game of	Einson-Freeman Publishing Corp.	1934	75	150	250
Little Bo-Beep Game		1914	60	100	160
Little Boy Blue	Milton Bradley	c1910	50	85	135
Little Colonel	Selchow & Righter	c1936	75	100	175
Little Cowboy Game, The	Parker Brothers	c1895	105	175	275

Board Games

NAME	COMPANY	DATE	GOOD	EX	MINT
Little Creepies Monster Game	The Toy Factory	1974	6	10	15
Little Drummer, The	J. Ottmann Lith. Co.		60	100	160
Little Goldenlocks And The Three Bears	McLoughlin Brothers	1890	330	550	875
Little House On The Prairie	Parker Brothers	1978	15	25	40
Little Jack Horner, A Game	Milton Bradley	c1910	45	75	120
Little League Baseball Game	Standard Toycraft, Inc.	c1950	25	45	70
Little Nemo Game		1914	60	100	160
Little Orphan Annie	Parker Brothers	1981	10	20	30
Little Orphan Annie Game	Milton Bradley	1927	125	250	300
Little Orphan Annie Travel Game	Milton Bradley		25	45	70
Little Orphan Annie Treasure Hunt Game	Wander Co.		20	35	55
Little Red Riding Hood Game		1914	90	150	240
Little Red Schoolhouse		1952	20	35	55
Little Shoppers	Gibson Game Co.	1915	150	250	400
Little Soldier Game		1914	60	100	160
Little Soldier, The	United Game Co.	c1900	95	160	250
Logomachy Or War of Words Game		1903	25	40	65
London Bridge	J.C. Singer	c1899	100	150	250
London Game, The	Parker Brothers	1898	165	275	440
Lone Ranger Game, The	Parker Brothers	1938	40	60	90
Long Shot	Parker Brothers	1962	45	75	125
Looney Tunes Game	Milton Bradley	1968	50	75	100
Looping The Loop	Advance Games	c1940	25	40	65
Los Angeles Dodgers Baseball Game	Ed-U-Cards Mfg. Co.	1964	30	50	80
Lost In Space Game	Milton Bradley	1965	45	75	120
Lost In The Woods	McLoughlin Brothers	1895	660	1100	1700
Lotto	Milton Bradley	1932	6	10	15
Love Boat World Cruise		1980	5	10	15
Loving Game, The	R.J.E. Enterprises	1987	4	6	10
Lowell Thomas' World Cruise	Parker Brothers	1937	50	75	125
Lucan, The Wolf Boy	Milton Bradley	1977	5	10	15
Luck, The Game of	Parker Brothers	1892	60	100	160
Lucky Break	Gabriel	1975	10	20	30
Lucky Strike	International Toy Co.	1972	5	10	15
Lucy Show Game, The	Transogram	1962	60	100	160
Lucy's Tea Party (Peanuts)	1971		20	35	55
Ludwig Von Drake Ball Toss Game		c1960	6	10	15
Luftwaffe	Avalon Hill	1971	15	25	40
M*A*S*H Game	Milton Bradley	1981	15	25	40
MacDonald's Game, The	Milton Bradley	1975	15	20	30
Macy's Pirate Treasure Hunt	Einson-Freeman Publishing Corp.	1942	20	35	55
Mad Magazine Game, The	Parker Brothers	1979	15	25	40
Mad, What Me Worry?	Milton Bradley	1987	6	10	15
Magilla Gorilla	Ideal	1964	40	65	100
Magnetic Fish Pond Game	McLoughlin Brothers	1891	175	300	500
Magnetic Flying Saucers	Pressman	c1950	21	35	55
Magnetic Jack Straws	E.I. Horsman	1891	27	45	70
Magnetic Treasure Hunt	American Toy Works	c1930	15	25	40
Magnificent Race	Parker Brothers	1975	10	25	40
Mail, Express Or Accommodation, Game of	Milton Bradley	c1920	135	225	360
Mail, Express Or Accommodation, Game of	McLoughlin Brothers	1895	450	750	1200
Major League Base Ball Game	Philadelphia Game Mfg. Co.	1912	1500	2500	4000
Major League Baseball	Cadaco	1965	10	20	30
Man from U.N.C.L.E. Thrush Ray Gun Affair Game	Ideal	1966	50	85	135

Board Games

NAME	COMPANY	DATE	GOOD	EX	MINT
Man Hunt	Parker Brothers	1937	75	125	250
Man In The Moon	McLoughlin Brothers	1901	2100	3500	5600
Mandrake The Magician	Milton Bradley		10	15	25
Maniac	Ideal	1979	7	15	20
Mansion of Happiness	W. & S.B. Ives	1843	300	500	1000
Mansion of Happiness	D.P. Ives & Co.	1864	180	300	475
Mansion of Happiness, The	McLoughlin Brothers	1895	510	850	1350
Marathon Game, The	Rosebud Art Co., Inc.	c1930	75	100	150
Marble Head	Milton Bradley		6	10	15
Margie, The Game of Whoopie	Milton Bradley	1961	25	50	75
Marlin Perkin's Zoo Parade	Cadaco-Ellis	1965	35	60	95
Marriage, The Game of	J.C. Singer	c1899	75	125	200
Martin Luther King Jr.	Cadaco	1980	6	10	15
Mary Hartman Mary Hartman	Reiss Games	c1976	20	35	55
Mary Poppins	Parker Brothers	1964	20	35	55
Mary Poppins Carousel Game	Parker Brothers	1964	15	25	40
Masquerade Party	Bettye-B Co.	1955	45	75	120
Mastermind	Invicta	c1970	5	10	15
Masterpiece, The Art Auction Game	Parker Brothers	1971	10	15	25
Match 'em	All-Fair	1926	12	20	30
Match Game 3rd Edition, The	Milton Bradley	1963	15	25	40
Matchbox Traffic Game		c1960	25	45	70
McDonald's Farm	Selchow & Righter	1948	12	20	30
McDonaldland Pop-Up	Parker Brothers		10	15	25
McHale's Navy Game	Transogram	1962	30	50	80
Meet The Missus	Fitzpatrick Bros.	1937	45	75	115
Meet The Presidents	Selchow & Righter	1953	15	25	40
Melvin The Moon Man	Remco	c1960	50	85	135
Men Into Space	Milton Bradley	1960	50	100	150
Mental Whoopee	Simon & Schuster	1936	10	15	25
Merry Game of Old Maid, The	McLoughlin Brothers	1898	180	300	475
Merry Milkman, The	Hasbro	1955	60	120	200
Merry-Go-Round	Chaffee & Selchow	1898	1500	2000	3000
Merv Griffin's Word For Word	Mattel	1963	5	10	15
Messenger Boy Game	J.H. Singer	1910	45	75	120
Messenger, The	McLoughlin Brothers	1890	75	125	200
Mexican Pete- I Got It	Parker Brothers	c1940	20	40	60
Miami Vice: The Game	Pepperlane	1984	6	10	15
Mickey Mantle's Big League Baseball	Gardner	c1955	45	75	120
Mickey Mouse	Parker Brothers	1976	6	10	15
Mickey Mouse	Jacmar Mfg. Co.	1950	35	55	90
Mickey Mouse Big Box of Games & Things To Color		c1930	45	75	120
Mickey Mouse Circus Game	Marks Brothers	c1930	180	300	475
Mickey Mouse Coming Home Game	Marks Brothers	c1930	100	165	265
Mickey Mouse Lotto Game	Jaymar	c1950	10	15	25
Mickey Mouse Pop Up Game	Whitman	c1970	7	15	20
Mickey Mouse Roll'em Game	Marks Brothers	c1930	90	150	240
Mickey Mouse Skill Roll Puzzle Game			20	30	50
Mickey Mouse Slugaroo		c1950	20	30	50
Mickey Mouse Treasure Hunt	1960		20	35	55
Mid Life Crisis	Gameworks Inc.	1982	4	7	12
Midget Auto Race	The Cracker Jack Co.	c1930	10	15	25
Midget Auto Race Game	Wolverine Supply & Mfg. Co.		40	65	105
Mighty Hercules Game	Hasbro	1963	60	100	160
Mighty Mouse	Milton Bradley	1978	15	20	30
Miles At Porto Rico	Chaffee & Selchow	1899	50	80	130
Million Dollar Man			10	15	25
Milton The Monster	Milton Bradley	1966	25	45	70
Mind Over Matter	Transogram	1968	10	15	25

Games, top to bottom: Wolfman Mystery Game, 1963, Hasbro; Shazam, Captain Marvel's Own Game, c1950, Reed & Associates; Groucho's You Bet Your Life Game, 1955, Lowell; Rich Uncle, 1946, Parker Brothers.

NAME	COMPANY	DATE	GOOD	EX	MINT
Miss America Pageant Game			15	25	40
Miss Muffet Game		1914	60	100	160
Miss Popularity Game	Milton Bradley	1961	20	35	55
Mission Impossible	Ideal	1967	50	85	135
Mission Impossible	Berwick	1975	10	15	25
Mister Ed Game	Parker Brothers	1962	25	50	100
Mistress Mary, Quite Contrary	Parker Brothers	c1905	60	105	165
Modern Game Assortment	J. Pressman & Co.	c1930	25	40	65
Moneta: 'Money Makes Money', Game of	F.A. Wright Publishers	1889	90	150	240
Monkees Game	Transogram	1968	30	50	80
Monkey Shines	All-Fair	1940	20	30	50
Monkeys And Coconuts	Schaper	1965	10	15	20
Monopolist, Mariner's Compass And Ten Up	McLoughlin Brothers	1878	500	1000	2000
Monopoly	Parker Brothers	1935	50	75	150
Monopoly Jr. Edition	Parker Brothers	1936	15	30	45
Monopoly Library Edition	Parker Brothers	c1960	7	12	20
Monopoly, 1935 Commemorative Edition	Parker Brothers	1985	35	55	90
Monster Game	Ideal	1977	45	75	120
Monster Game, The	Milton Bradley	1965	15	25	40
Monster Mansion	Milton Bradley	1981	7	12	20
Monster Squad	Milton Bradley	1977	35	65	95
Moon Blast Off	Schaper		20	30	50
Moon Mullins	Milton Bradley	1927	40	65	100
Moon Shot	Cadaco	c1960	35	55	90
Moon Tag, Game of	Parker Brothers	1957	75	125	200
Mork And Mindy	Milton Bradley	1978	5	10	15
Mostly Ghostly	Cadaco	1975	15	20	30
Mother Goose Bowling Game	Charles M. Crandall Co.	1884	510	850	1300
Mother Goose, Game of		1914	75	125	200
Mother Goose, Game of	Stoll & Edwards	1921	30	50	80
Mother Hubbard Game		1914	60	100	160
Motor Cycle Game	Milton Bradley	1905	100	165	265
Motor Race, The	Wolverine Supply & Mfg. Co.	c1922	75	125	200
Movie Inn	Willis G. Young	1917	45	75	120
Movie Millions	Transogram	1938	100	200	300
Movie Moguls	RGI	1970	6	10	15
Movie-Land Lotto	Milton Bradley	c1920	45	75	120
Moving Picture Game	Milton Bradley	c1920	70	120	190
Moving Picture Game, The	Milton Bradley	c1920	70	120	190
Mr. Bug Goes To Town	Milton Bradley	1955	50	125	175
Mr. Doodle's Dog	Selchow & Righter	c1940	30	50	80
Mr. Ed Board Game	Parker Brothers	1962	6	10	15
Mr. Machine Game	Ideal	1961	40	65	100
Mr. Magoo Visits The Zoo	Lowell	1961	25	45	70
Mr. Novak	Transogram		15	25	40
Mr. Potato Head			20	35	55
Mr. Ree	Selchow & Righter	1957	25	45	70
Mr. Ree	Selchow & Righter	1937	60	100	200
Mt. Everest	Sam'l Gabriel Sons & Co.	1955	15	25	40
Mug Shots	Cadaco	1975	7	12	20
Munsters Game	Milton Bradley	1966	65	95	150
Muppet Show	Parker Brothers	1977	10	15	25
Murder She Wrote	Warren	1985	4	6	10
Mushmouse & Punkin Puss	Ideal	1964	45	75	120
Mutuels	Mutuels, Inc.	1938	85	150	295
My Fair Lady	Standard Toycraft, Inc.	c1960	15	20	30

Board Games

NAME	COMPANY	DATE	GOOD	EX	MINT
My Favorite Martian	Transogram	1963	50	90	125
Mystery Checkers	Creative Designs	c1950	15	20	30
Mystery Date	Milton Bradley	1966	40	60	100
Mystery Mansion	Milton Bradley	1984	7	12	20
Mystic Skull The Game of Voodoo	Ideal	1965	30	50	80
Mystic Wheel of Knowledge	Novel Toy	c1950	15	25	40
Mythology, Game of	Peter G. Thompson	1884	25	45	70
Name That Tune	Milton Bradley	1959	20	30	50
Napoleon Solo Man From U.N.C.L.E. Game	Ideal	1965	25	45	70
Napoleon, Game of	Parker Brothers	1895	775	1300	2000
National Derby Horse Race	Whitman	1938	20	35	55
National Game of The American Eagle, The	W. & S.B. Ives	1844	2000	4000	5000
National Inquirer	Tyco	1991	10	15	20
National Lampoon's Sellout	Cardinal Industries	c1970	4	7	12
National Pro Football Hall of Fame Game	Cadaco	1965	15	25	40
National Velvet Game	Transogram	c1950	20	30	50
Naval Maneuvers	McLoughlin Brothers	1920	120	200	320
Navigator	Whitman	1938	45	75	120
NBC Peacock	Selchow & Righter	1966	12	20	30
NBC TV News	Dadan	1960	15	25	40
Nearsighted Mister Magoo Maddening Misadventures Game, The	Transogram	1970	45	75	120
Nebbs, Game of The	Milton Bradley	c1930	20	30	50
Nebula	Nebula Inc.	1976	4	6	10
Neck And Neck	The Embossing Co.	1929	25	40	65
Neck And Neck	Wolverine Supply & Mfg. Co.	1930	50	80	130
Nellie Bly	J.H. Singer	c1898	55	90	145
New Adventure of Gilligan, The	Milton Bradley	1974	12	20	30
New Adventures of Pinocchio, The	Lowell	1961	25	45	70
New And Improved Fish Pond Game	McLoughlin Brothers	c1890	75	125	200
New Avengers Shooting Game	Denys Fisher	1976	165	275	440
New Bicycle Game, The	Parker Brothers	1894	345	575	920
New Frontier	Colorful Products, Inc.	1962	30	50	80
New Game of Hunting, The	McLoughlin Brothers	1904	360	600	960
New Game of Madrap, The		1914	45	75	120
New Game Piggies, The	Selchow & Righter	1894	330	550	880
New York World's Fair	Milton Bradley	1964	45	75	120
Newlywed Game 1st Edition	Hasbro	1967	10	14	20
Newport Yacht Race	McLoughlin Brothers		135	225	360
Newsboy, Game of The	R. Bliss Mfg. Co.	1890	1200	2000	3200
Nightmare On Elm Street	Cardinal Industries	1989	7	12	20
Nine Men Morris	Milton Bradley	c1930	25	45	70
No Respect, The Rodney Dangerfield Game	Milton Bradley	1985	15	25	40
No Time For Sergeants	Lowell		30	50	80
No-Joke	Volume Sprayer Mfg. Co.	1941	12	20	30
Nok-Hockey	Carrom Industries	c1947	20	35	55
Noma Party Quiz	Noma Electric Corp.	1947	20	35	50
North Pole Game, The	Milton Bradley	1907	45	75	120
Northwest Passage		1969	12	20	30
Nuclear Escalation			12	20	30
Number Please TV Quiz	Parker Brothers	1961	15	25	40
Numble	Selchow & Righter	1968	12	20	30
Nurses, The	Ideal		10	15	25
Oak Leaves	Fireside Game Co.		20	30	50

Board Games

NAME	COMPANY	DATE	GOOD	EX	MINT
Object Lotto	Sam'l Gabriel Sons & Co.	c1940	15	25	40
Obsession	Mego	1978	5	10	15
Ocean To Ocean Flight Game	Wilder Mfg. Co.	1927	55	95	150
Off To See The Wizard		1968	10	15	25
Office Boy, The	Parker Brothers	1889	150	250	500
Official Hockey	Toy Creations	c1940	20	30	50
Official Radio Basketball Game	Toy Creations	1939	45	75	120
Official Radio Football Game	Toy Creations	1940	45	75	120
Oh Magoo Game			12	20	30
Oh, Nuts! Game	Ideal	1968	10	15	25
Oh-Wah-Ree	Avalon Hill	1966	4	7	12
Old Maid	Chaffee & Selchow	1898	25	45	70
Old Maid As Played By Mother Goose, Game of	Clark & Sowdon	1892	20	30	50
Old Maid Or Matrimony, Game of	McLoughlin Brothers	1890	150	250	500
Old Mother Goose	Chaffee & Selchow	c1898	105	175	275
Old Mother Hubbard, Game of	Milton Bradley	c1890	60	100	160
Old Mrs. Goose, Game of	Milton Bradley	c1910	50	85	135
Oldtimers	Frederick H. Beach (Beachcraft)	1940	15	20	30
Ollo	Games Of Fame	1944	15	25	40
On Guard	Parker Brothers	1967	6	10	15
On The Mid-Way	Milton Bradley	c1925	45	75	120
One Two Button Your Shoe	Master Toy Co.	c1940	15	25	40
Open Championship Golf Game	Beacon Hudson Co.	c1930	45	75	120
Operation	Milton Bradley	1965	10	15	25
Opportunity Hour	American Toy Works	1940	20	35	55
Orbit	Parker Brothers	1959	25	55	100
Original Game of Zoom	All-Fair	c1940	45	75	120
Ouija	William Fuld	1920	15	25	40
Our Defenders	Master Toy Co.	1944	40	65	100
Our Gang Bingo		1958	50	85	135
Our Gang Tipple-Topple Game	All-Fair	1930	300	600	1000
Our Union	Fireside Game Co.	1896	25	40	65
Outboard Motor Race, The	Milton Bradley	c1930	35	55	90
Outdoor Survival	Avalon Hill	1972	6	10	15
Outer Limits	Milton Bradley	1964	110	180	275
Outwit	Parker Brothers	1978	5	10	15
Overland Limited, The	Milton Bradley	c1920	45	75	120
Owl And The Pussy Cat, The	E.O. Clark	c1900	210	350	550
P.T. Boat 109 Game	Ideal	1963	30	50	90
Pac-Man	Milton Bradley	1980	4	6	10
Pan-Cake Tiddly Winks	Russell Mfg. Co.	c1920	55	90	145
Pana Kanal, The Great Panama Canal Game	Chaffee & Selchow	1913	65	110	175
Panama Canal Game	Parker Brothers	c1910	135	225	350
Panic Button	Mego	1978	7	15	20
Panzer Blitz	Avalon Hill	1970	12	20	30
Panzer Leader	Avalon Hill	1974	10	15	25
Parcheesi	H.B. Chaffee	c1880	90	150	240
Parcheesi (Gold Seal Edition)	Selchow & Righter	1964	7	12	20
Park & Shop	Traffic Game Co.	c1952	40	70	110
Park And Shop Game	Milton Bradley	1960	20	35	55
Parker Brothers Post Office Game	Parker Brothers	c1910	105	175	275
Parlor Base Ball		1878	1750	2900	4500
Parlor Golf	Chaffee & Selchow	c1897	55	90	145
Partridge Family	Milton Bradley	1974	7	15	20
Partridge Family			6	10	15
Password	Milton Bradley	1963	10	16	25
Password 25th Anniversary Edition	Milton Bradley	1986	3	5	8

Games, top to bottom: James Bond, Secret Agent Game, 1964, Milton Bradley; Mary Poppins Carousel Game, 1964, Parker Brothers; Battle Line Game, c1960, Ideal; Foto-Electric Football, c1970, Cadaco; Mighty Heroes on the Scene Game, c1960, Transogram.

NAME	COMPANY	DATE	GOOD	EX	MINT
Pathfinder	Milton Bradley	1977	5	10	10
Patty Duke Game	Milton Bradley	1963	25	40	75
Paydirt	Avalon Hill	1979	10	18	30
Pe-Ling	Cookson & Sullivan	1923	25	45	70
Peanuts The Game of Charlie Brown And His Pals	Selchow & Righter	1959	20	30	50
Pebbles Flintstone Game	Transogram	1962	20	35	55
Peg At My Heart	Willis G. Young	1914	20	35	55
Peg Base Ball	Parker Brothers	1924	105	175	275
Peg'ity	Parker Brothers	c1925	25	45	70
Peggy	Parker Brothers	1923	35	55	90
Pegpin, Game of	Stoll & Edwards	1929	25	45	70
Pennant Chasers Baseball Game	Craig Hopkins	1946	25	45	70
Penny Post	Parker Brothers	1892	150	250	400
People Trivia Game	Parker Brothers	1984	7	11	20
Perquackey	Lakeside	1970	3	5	8
Perry Mason Case of The Missing Suspect Game	Transogram	1959	20	30	50
Personalysis	Lowell	1957	15	25	40
Peter Coddle's Trip To New York	Parker Brothers	1934	10	15	25
Peter Gunn Dectective Game		1960	20	40	60
Peter Pan	Transogram	1953	40	65	105
Peter Pan	Selchow & Righter	1927	100	200	400
Peter Peter Pumpkin Eater	Parker Brothers	1914	60	100	160
Peter Potamus Game	Ideal	1964	30	50	80
Peter Rabbit Game	Sam'l Gabriel Sons & Co.	c1940	45	75	120
Peter Rabbit Game	Milton Bradley	1910	55	95	150
Petticoat Junction	Standard Toycraft, Inc.	1963	35	55	90
Phalanx	Whitman	1964	35	55	90
Phantom	Transogram	1965	95	160	255
Phil Silvers' You'll Never Get Rich Game	Gardner	1955	60	100	160
Philip Marlowe	Transogram	1960	25	40	65
Philippines, A Family Game	J.C. Singer	c1898	55	95	150
Philo Vance	Parker Brothers	1937	75	125	250
Phoebe Snow, Game of	McLoughlin Brothers	1899	150	250	350
Pigskin Vegas	Jokari/US	1980	6	10	15
Pilgrim's Progress, Going To Sunday School, Tower of Babel	McLoughlin Brothers	1875	240	400	640
Pimlico	Metro	c1940	25	45	70
Pinafore	Fuller, Upham & Co.	1879	45	75	120
Pink Panther	Cadaco	1981	4	7	12
Pink Panther	Milton Bradley		10	15	25
Pink Panther Game	Warren Paper Products Co.	1977	30	50	80
Pinocchio	Parker Brothers	1977	5	8	15
Pinocchio	Milton Bradley	1939	55	95	150
Pinocchio Pitfalls Marble Game		1940	30	50	80
Pinocchio Ring The Nose Game		1940	20	30	50
Pioneers of The Santa Fe Trail	Einson-Freeman Publishing Corp.	1935	25	40	65
Pirate & Traveller	Milton Bradley	1936	30	50	75
Pirate And Traveller	Milton Bradley	1953	20	35	55
Pirate Ship	Samuel Lowe Co.	1940	15	25	40
Pirate's Island	Corey Games	1942	105	175	275
Pirates Gold	All-Fair	c1940	15	25	40
Pirates Raid	Stoll & Einson	1934	50	80	130
Pitfalls	Milton Bradley		80	135	215
Pizza Party	Parker Brothers	1987	4	6	10
Planet of The Apes Game	Milton Bradley	1974	7	12	20

Board Games

NAME	COMPANY	DATE	GOOD	EX	MINT
Play Radio Game	Rudolph Toy & Novelty	c1930	25	40	65
Play Your Hunch			20	35	55
Plotz!	Parker Brothers	1971	20	35	55
Plymouth Drag Race Game	Day	1967	20	35	55
Poche--The New Parisian Game	McLoughlin Brothers	1890	1000	1700	2500
Point of Law	3M	1972	6	10	15
Poker-Keeno	Cadaco	1977	4	7	12
Politics Game, The	Oswald B. Lord	1935	45	75	120
Politics, Or The Race For The Presidency, Game of	W.S. Reed Toy Co.	1887	180	300	480
Politics, Oswald B. Lord's Game of	Parker Brothers	c1940	40	65	105
Polly Pickles, Queen of The Movies	Parker Brothers	1921	75	125	200
Pollyanna	Parker Brothers	1940	14	30	50
Pollyanna; The Glad Game	Parker Brothers	c1915	40	70	110
Pon-E-Run	All-Fair	1929	20	30	50
Pony Express	Stoll & Edwards	1926	35	55	90
Pool, Game of	Chaffee & Selchow	1898	450	750	1200
Poor Jenny, The Game of	All-Fair	1927	100	200	300
Pop Yer Top!	Milton Bradley	1968	15	20	30
Pop-O-Matic Yipes!	Ideal	1983	4	7	11
Pope Or Pagan, The Game of	W. & S.B. Ives	1844	3000	4000	5000
Popeye	Parker Brothers	1983	7	12	20
Popeye Movie Game	Milton Bradley	1983	7	12	20
Popeye Party Game	Whitman	1937	45	75	120
Popeye Pipe Toss Game	Rosebud Art Co., Inc.	1935	50	75	125
Popeye Ring Toss	Transogram		35	55	90
Popeye Ring Toss Game	Rosebud Art Co., Inc.	1933	50	85	135
Popeye The Sailor Shipwreck Game	Einson-Freeman Publishing Corp.	1933	75	150	300
Popeye's Nail-It Game		c1950	25	45	70
Popeye's Sliding Boards And Ladders Game	Warren	1958	25	40	65
Popeye's Treasure Map Game	Whitman	1977	6	10	15
Popeye's Where's Me Pipe Game		1937	20	35	55
Poppin' Hoppies Game	Ideal	1968	7	12	20
Postal Telegraph Boy	E.O. Clark	c1900	90	150	240
Poucho Checkers	Gabriel	1977	15	25	40
Price Is Right Game		1958	20	30	50
Prince And Princess, The Game of	McLoughlin Brothers	1905	135	225	360
Prince Valiant Game	Transogram	c1950	10	15	25
Princess In The Tower	Parker Brothers	1890s	90	150	240
Prisoner's Base	Parker Brothers	1896	105	175	275
Pro Golf	Avalon Hill	1984	3	5	10
Pro Quarterback	Championship Games Inc.	1966	12	20	30
Probe	Parker Brothers	1974	5	10	15
Probe	Parker Brothers	1964	8	15	20
Professor Quiz Radio Game	Mind Building Games Institute	1939	55	95	150
Progressive Queries		1900	20	35	55
Psyche Paths	Funtastics	1969	10	15	25
Psychology of The Hand	Baker & Bennett Co.	1919	20	30	50
Public Assistance			45	75	120
Pull The Rug Out	Schaper	1970	6	10	15
Pung Chow	Pung Chow Co. Inc.	1923	30	50	80
Puss In Boots	McLoughlin Brothers	1897	700	1200	1900
Puss In The Corner	Parker Brothers	1895	60	100	160
Puss, Game of	Milton Bradley	c1911	75	125	200
Puss-In-Boots Game		1910	15	25	40
Pussy And The Three Mice, Game of	McLoughlin Brothers	1890	330	550	880

NAME	COMPANY	DATE	GOOD	EX	MINT
Put-N-Take Spin Game	James L. Decker Products Co.	c1947	25	40	65
Pyramids	Knapp Electric & Novelty Co.	c1930	10	20	30
Qubic	Parker Brothers	1965	5	7	12
Questo	Corey Games	1939	10	15	25
Quick Draw McGraw	Milton Bradley	1960	20	30	50
Quiz Kids Electric Quizzer	Rapaport Brothers, Inc.	c1940	30	50	80
Quiz Kids Own Game Box	Parker Brothers	c1940	30	55	95
Quizzical Questions By Dr. Quiz	Jaymar	c1940	15	25	40
Rabbit Hunt, Game of	McLoughlin Brothers	1870	120	200	320
Race For The Cup Game		1914	60	100	160
Race For The North Pole	Milton Bradley	c1909	15	25	40
Race To Saturn		1935	40	65	105
Raceway	B&B Toy Mfg. Co.	c1950	20	30	50
Rack-O	Milton Bradley	1966	5	10	15
Radar Search Game	Ideal	1969	10	20	30
Radio Amateur Hour Game	Milton Bradley	c1930	75	125	200
Radio Game	Milton Bradley	c1920	25	45	70
Radio Game	Wilder Mfg. Co.	c1927	25	45	70
Radio Game For Little Folks	All-Fair	1926	75	125	200
Radio Questionaire	Radio Questionaire Corp.	1928	30	50	75
Radio Ramble	Selchow & Righter	1927	100	200	300
Raffles	Corey Games	1939	30	50	75
Raggedy Ann Game	Milton Bradley	1974	10	15	25
Raggedy Ann's Magic Pebble Game	Milton Bradley	1941	30	50	80
Rainy Day Golf	Selchow & Righter	c1920	60	100	160
Ralph Edwards This Is Your Life		c1950	6	10	15
Ramar of The Jungle	Dexter Wayne	c1952	75	125	200
Rambles	American Publishing	1881	195	275	400
Rat Patrol Game	Transogram	1966	45	75	120
Rawhide	Lowe	1959	50	85	135
Raymar of The Jungle New Jungle Game	Dexter Wayne	1953	30	50	80
React-Or		1979	15	25	40
Ready-Clown 3-Ring Circus Game	Parker Brothers	1952	25	40	65
Rebel, The	Ideal	1961	50	85	135
Red Riding Hood, Game of	Chaffee & Selchow	1898	50	85	135
Red Ryder Target Game	Whitman	1939	55	95	150
Reddy Clown 3-Ring Circus Game	Parker Brothers	1952	15	25	55
Reese's Pieces Game	Ideal	1983	5	8	15
Restless Gun	Milton Bradley	c1950	15	25	40
Rex And The Kilkenny Cats Game	Parker Brothers	1892	45	75	120
Rich Uncle	Parker Brothers	1946	35	50	80
Rich Uncle The Stock Market Game	Parker Brothers	c1955	30	50	80
Richie Rich	Milton Bradley	1982	3	5	10
Ricochet Rabbit Game	Ideal	1965	45	75	120
Rifleman Game		1959	50	75	150
Rin-Tin-Tin Game	Transogram	c1950	10	15	25
Ring-A-Peg	E.I. Horsman	1885	25	45	70
Rip Van Winkle	Clark & Sowdon	c1890	75	125	200
Ripley's Believe It Or Not	Whitman	1979	6	10	15
Risk	Parker Brothers	1975	12	20	30
Risk	Parker Brothers	1959	25	50	75
Rival Policemen	McLoughlin Brothers	1896	1000	1500	3000
Riverboat Game	Parker Brothers (Disney)	c1950	20	35	55
Road Runner Game	Milton Bradley	1968	35	60	85
Road Runner Pop Up Game	Whitman	1982	20	30	50
Robert Schuller's Possibility Thinkers Game	Selchow & Righter	1977	3	5	10

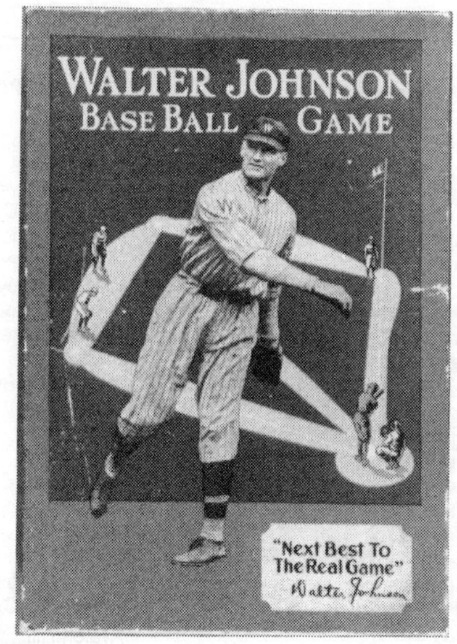

Games, top to bottom: Tiddledy Winks, c1910, Parker Brothers; Walter Johnson Base Ball Game; Jan Murray's Charge Account TV Word Game, c1950; Wagon Train, 1960, Milton Bradley.

Board Games

NAME	COMPANY	DATE	GOOD	EX	MINT
Robin Hood	Harett-Gilmar, Inc.	1955	30	50	80
Robin Hood Game	Parker Brothers	c1970	7	15	20
Robinson Crusoe, Game of	Milton Bradley	1909	75	100	200
Robo Cop-The Ultra Police Game	Parker Brothers		25	45	70
Robot Sam The Answer Man	Jacmar Mfg. Co.	1950	25	45	70
Rock Trivia	Pressman	1984	5	10	15
Rocket Race	Stone Craft	1958	100	165	250
Rocket Race To Saturn	Lido Toy	c1950	15	20	35
Rol-A-Lite	Durable Toy & Novelty	c1947	45	75	120
Roll And Score Poker	Lowe	1977	4	7	12
Roly Poly Game		1910	30	50	80
Rough Riders, The Game of	Clark & Sowdon	c1898	450	700	1000
Round The World Game	Milton Bradley	1914	60	100	160
Round The World With Nellie Bly	McLoughlin Brothers	1890	210	350	560
Round Up	Milton Bradley		45	75	120
Route 66 Game	Transogram	1960	75	125	200
Roy Rogers Game		c1950	20	35	55
Roy Rogers Horseshoe Game	Ohio Art		10	20	30
Royal Game of Kings And Queens	McLoughlin Brothers	1892	375	650	1000
Runaway Sheep	R. Bliss Mfg. Co.	1892	165	275	450
Russian Campaign, The	Avalon Hill	1976	3	5	10
S.O.S.	Durable Toy & Novelty	c1947	40	70	110
S.W.A.T. Game	Milton Bradley	c1970	10	15	25
Sailor Boy Game		1910	60	100	160
Salvo	Ideal	1961	15	25	40
Scavenger Hunt	Milton Bradley	1983	3	5	10
Scooby-Doo And Scrappy Doo	Milton Bradley	1983	20	30	50
Scoop	Parker Brothers	1956	20	35	75
Scout, The	E.O. Clark	c1900	105	175	280
Scouting, Game of	Milton Bradley	c1930	55	90	145
Scrabble	Selchow & Righter	1953	5	12	20
Scrambles	Frederick H. Beach (Beachcraft)	1941	15	20	30
Screwball The Mad Mad Mad Game	Transogram	1960	30	50	80
Screwball, A Mad Mad Game	Transogram	1960	75	125	200
Scruples	Milton Bradley	1986	5	10	15
Sealab 2020 Game	Milton Bradley	1973	6	10	15
Secret Agent Man	Milton Bradley	1966	25	40	65
Secret of NIMH	Whitman	1982	6	10	15
Seduction	Createk	1966	20	30	45
Sergeant Preston Game	Milton Bradley	c1950	10	15	25
Seven Seas	Cadaco-Ellis	1960	30	50	80
Seven Up	Transogram	c1960	7	12	20
Shazam, Captian Marvel's Own Game	Reed & Associates	c1950	30	50	80
Shopping, Game of	R. Bliss Mfg. Co.	1891	900	1500	2400
Show-Biz	Lowell		40	65	105
Shufflebug, Game of		1921	20	30	50
Siege of Havana, The	Parker Brothers	1898	180	300	480
Silly Carnival	Whitman	1969	7	12	20
Silly Safari	Topper	1966	40	65	105
Simpsons Mystery of Life, The	Cardinal Industries	1990	5	7	10
Sinbad	Cadaco	1978	20	30	50
Sinking of The Titanic, The	Ideal	1976	25	45	70
Sippa Fish	Frederick H. Beach (Beachcraft)	1936	20	30	50
Six Million Dollar Man	Parker Brothers	1975	5	7	10
Skatterbug, Game of	Parker Brothers	1951	30	50	80
Ski-Hi New York To Paris	Cutler & Saleeby Co.	1927	100	200	300
Skillful Bowling	Hoffman Lion Co.		25	45	70
Skip-A-Cross	Cadaco Ltd.	1953	10	15	25

NAME	COMPANY	DATE	GOOD	EX	MINT
Skippy, Game of	Milton Bradley	1932	45	75	120
Skirmish	Milton Bradley	1975	20	35	55
Skirmish At Harper's Ferry	McLoughlin Brothers	1891	330	550	875
Skully	Ideal	1961	3	5	10
Skunk	Schaper	c1950	7	12	20
Sky Hawks	All-Fair	1931	120	200	320
Sky's The Limit, The	Kohner	1955	15	25	40
Skyscraper	Parker Brothers	1937	75	100	200
Smog	Urban Systems	1970	9	15	25
Smokey: The Forest Fire Prevention Bear	Ideal	1961	40	65	105
Smurf Game	Milton Bradley	1984	4	7	12
Snagglepuss Fun At The Picnic Game	Transogram	1961	40	60	100
Snake Eyes	Selchow & Righter		30	50	80
Snake Game	McLoughlin Brothers	c1890	50	85	135
Snakes In The Grass	Kohner	c1960	10	15	25
Snap Dragon	H.B. Chaffee	1903	135	225	360
Sniff	The Embossing Co.	c1940	20	30	50
Snoopy & The Red Baron	Milton Bradley	1970	10	15	25
Snoopy Game (Peanuts)	Selchow & Righter	1960	25	45	70
Snow White And The Seven Dwarfs Game	Parker Brothers	1938	30	50	80
Snow White And The Seven Dwarfs The Game of	Milton Bradley	1938	45	75	120
Snow White Boardgame		c1970	6	10	15
Snuffy Smith Game	Milton Bradley	c1970	12	20	30
Snug Harbor	Milton Bradley	c1930	50	85	135
Socko The Monk, The Game of	Einson-Freeman Publishing Corp.	1935	15	25	40
Solarquest	Western Publishing	1986	6	10	15
Soldier Boy Game		1914	60	100	160
Solid Gold Music Trivia	Ideal	1984	6	10	15
Solitaire (Lucille Ball)	Milton Bradley	1973	4	7	12
Sons of Hercules	Milton Bradley		20	35	55
Soupy Sales Sez Go-Go-Go Game	Milton Bradley	c1960	55	95	150
Space 1999 Game	Milton Bradley	1975	10	15	25
Space Age Game	Parker Brothers	1953	45	75	120
Space Angel Game	Transogram	1966	20	35	55
Space Shuttle 101	Media-Ungame	1978	15	25	40
Spaceship Journey to Jupiter	All-Fair		100	250	325
Spe-Dem Auto Race	All-Fair	1922	80	135	215
Speculation	Geo S. Parker Brothers	c1885	40	65	105
Speedorama	Jacmar Mfg. Co.	c1950	30	50	80
Spider And Fly Game	Milton Bradley	c1925	30	50	80
Spider And The Fly	Marx	1981	12	20	30
Spider's Web	McLoughlin Brothers	1898	50	85	135
Spider's Web Game, The	Multiple Plastics	1969	7	12	20
Spider-Man With The Fantastic Four	Milton Bradley	1977	10	15	25
Spin It	Milton Bradley	c1910	15	25	40
Spin The Bottle	Hasbro	1968	6	10	15
Spin Welder	Mattel	c1960	7	12	20
Spiro T. Agnew American History Challenge Game	Sam'l Gabriel Sons & Co.	1971	20	35	55
Spot Cash	Milton Bradley	1959	7	15	20
Spot-A-Plane Game	Toy Creations		25	45	70
Spy Vs Spy	Milton Bradley	1986	10	15	25
Squails	Adams & Co.	c1870	40	65	105
Squails	Milton Bradley	1877	35	60	95
Squatter: The Australian Wool Game	John Sands, Australia	c1960	15	25	45
Stadium Checkers	Schaper	c1954	7	12	20

Board Games

NAME	COMPANY	DATE	GOOD	EX	MINT
Stagecoach West Game	Transogram	1961	60	100	160
Stanley In Africa	R. Bliss Mfg. Co.	1891	420	700	1120
Star Reporter	Parker Brothers	c1937	30	50	80
Star Ride	Einson-Freeman Publishing Corp.	1934	15	25	40
Star Team Battling Spaceships	Ideal	1968	10	15	25
Star Trek Adventure Game	West End Games	1985	45	75	120
Star Trek Game	Ideal	c1960	45	75	120
Star Wars Adventures of R2D2 Game	Kenner	1977	12	20	30
Star Wars Battle At Sarlacc's Pit	Parker Brothers	1983	10	15	25
Star Wars ESB Yoda The Jedi Master Game			10	15	25
Star Wars Escape From Death Star Game			6	10	15
Star Wars ROTJ Ewoks Save The Trees	Parker Brothers	1984	10	15	25
Star Wars Wicket the Ewok	Parker Brothers	1983	7	12	20
Star Wars X-Wing Aces Target Game		1978	20	30	50
State Capitals, Game of	Parker Brothers	1952	12	20	30
States, Game of The	Milton Bradley	1975	4	6	10
Stay Alive	Milton Bradley	1971	4	6	10
Steeple Chase, Game of	E. O. Clark	c1900	60	100	160
Steeple Chase, Game of	Milton Bradley	c1910	40	65	105
Steps of Toyland	Parker Brothers	1954	20	35	55
Steps To Health Coke Game	CDN	1938	40	70	110
Steve Canyon	Lowell	1959	35	65	100
Steve Scott Space Scout Game	Transogram	1952	10	15	25
Sting, The	Ideal	1976	25	45	70
Sto-Quoit	T.H.Stough Co.	c1920	10	15	25
Stock Exchange	Parker Brothers	1936	30	50	80
Stock Exchange, The Game of	Stox, Inc.	c1940	40	65	105
Stock Market	Avalon Hill	1970	7	12	20
Stock Market Game	Sam'l Gabriel Sons & Co.	1955	20	30	50
Stoney Burk	Transogram	1963	15	25	40
Stop & Go	Einson-Freeman Publishing Corp.	1936	25	50	75
Stop And Go	All-Fair	1928	75	150	250
Stop And Shop	All-Fair	1930	100	150	300
Stop Thief	Einson-Freeman Publishing Corp.		25	45	70
Stop, Look, And Listen, Game of	Milton Bradley	1926	35	50	75
Straight Arrow	Selchow & Righter	1950	25	45	70
Strat: The Great War Game	Strat Game Co., Inc.	1915	25	45	70
Strategic Command	Transogram	c1950	25	45	70
Stratego	Milton Bradley	1961	15	25	40
Strategy, Game of	McLoughlin Brothers	1891	240	400	650
Strategy, Game of Armies	Corey Games	1938	40	50	80
Strato-Matic Baseball		1969	10	15	25
Stratosphere	Parker Brothers	c1930	35	60	95
Stratosphere	Whitman	1936	100	200	300
Street Car Game, The	Parker Brothers	c1890	120	200	320
Stunt Box	Frederick H. Beach (Beachcraft)	1941	12	20	30
Submarine Drag	Willis G. Young	1917	50	85	135
Substitute Golf	John Wanamaker	1906	120	200	325
Sugar Bowl	Transogram	c1950	20	35	55
Summit	Milton Bradley	1961	25	35	50
Sunken Treasure	Milton Bradley	1976	7	12	20
Sunken Treasure	Parker Brothers	1948	15	25	45
Super Powers	Parker Brothers	1984	15	25	40

Games, top to bottom: Bullwinkle Hide 'N Seek Game, 1961, Milton Bradley; Jetsons Out of This World Game, 1963, Transogram; The New Adventures of Gilligan, 1974, Milton Bradley; The Man from U.N.C.L.E., 1966, Ideal.

Board Games

NAME	COMPANY	DATE	GOOD	EX	MINT
Super Spy	Milton Bradley	1971	15	25	40
Supercar Road Race	Standard Toycraft, Inc.	1962	40	65	105
Supercar To The Rescue Game	Milton Bradley	1962	35	60	95
Supercoach TV Football	Coleco		15	25	40
Superman & Superboy	Milton Bradley	1967	40	65	105
Superman Game	Merry Manufacturing Co.	1966	35	55	90
Superman Game	Hasbro	1965	45	75	120
Superman II	Milton Bradley	1981	10	20	35
Superman III	Parker Brothers	1982	20	30	50
Superman Match Game	Ideal		10	15	25
Superman Speed Game	Milton Bradley		30	50	80
Superman, Adventures of	Milton Bradley	1942	145	240	375
Superman, Calling	Transogram	1954	120	200	325
Superstar Baseball!	Avalon Hill		15	20	30
Superstition	Milton Bradley	1977	10	15	25
Surfside 6	Lowe	1961	60	120	200
Surprise Package	Ideal	1961	12	20	30
Susceptibles, The	McLoughlin Brothers	1891	325	550	875
Swahili Game	Milton Bradley	1968	15	20	30
Swayze	Milton Bradley	1954	20	35	55
Sweep	Selchow & Righter	1929	25	40	65
Swing A Peg	Milton Bradley	c1890	30	50	80
Swoop	Whitman	1969	7	12	20
Sword In The Stone Game	Parker Brothers	c1960	10	15	25
T.G.O. Klondyke	J.C. Singer	c1899	150	250	400
T.H.E. Cat	Ideal		50	85	135
T.V. Bingo	Selchow & Richter	1970	3	5	10
Tabit	John Norton Co.	1954	25	35	75
Tactics II	Avalon Hill	1984	6	10	15
Taffy's Party Game	Transogram	c1960	10	15	25
Take It And Double	Frederick H. Beach (Beachcraft)	1943	20	35	55
Take It Or Leave It	Zondine Game Co.	1942	25	45	70
Tales of Wells Fargo	Milton Bradley	1959	40	65	105
Tank Battle	Milton Bradley	1975	10	20	35
Tantalizer	Northern Signal Co.	1958	25	50	85
Tarzan	Milton Bradley	1984	5	10	15
Tarzan To The Rescue	Milton Bradley	1976	10	15	25
Taxi Cabby	Selchow & Righter		30	50	80
Teddy's Bear Hunt	Bowers & Hard	1907	375	650	1040
Teed Off!	Milton Bradley	1966	15	25	40
Teeko	John Scarne Games, Inc.	c1948	20	30	50
Telegrams	Whitman	1941	40	70	110
Telegraph Boy, Game of The	McLoughlin Brothers	1888	250	350	450
Telepathy	Cadaco-Ellis	1939	65	110	175
Tell Bell, The	Knapp Electric & Novelty Co.	1928	50	75	150
Tell It To The Judge	Parker Brothers	1959	50	75	100
Temple of Fu Manchu Game, The	Pressman	1967	20	30	50
Ten-Four, Good Buddy	Parker Brothers	1976	5	7	12
Tennessee Tuxedo	Transogram	1963	75	125	200
Tension	Kohnes	1970	7	12	20
Terrytoons Hide N' Seek Game	Transogram	1960	20	35	55
Tete-A-Tete	Clark & Sowdon	1892	45	75	120
Texas Millionaire	Texantics	1955	45	75	120
The Egg And I	Capex Co. Inc.	1947	30	50	80
The Flight To Paris	Milton Bradley	1927	150	250	400
The Kennedy's	Transogram	1962	40	65	105
The Love Boat Game	The Ungame Company		10	15	25
The My Fair Lady Game	Standard Toycraft, Inc.	c1962	25	40	65

Board Games

NAME	COMPANY	DATE	GOOD	EX	MINT
The Pines	Fireside Game Co.	1896	15	25	40
The Space Shuttle	The Ungame Company	1981	15	25	40
The Ungame	The Ungame Company		6	10	15
Them Bones Game	Mego		20	30	50
They're Off, Race Horse Game	Parker Brothers	c1930	15	20	35
Thing Ding Robot Game	Schaper	1961	115	195	310
Thinking Man's Football	3M	1969	15	20	30
Third Reich	Avalon Hill	1974	7	12	20
This Is Your Life	Lowell	1954	15	25	35
Thorton W. Burgess Animal Game	Saalfield Publishing Co.	1925	70	115	175
Three Bears	Milton Bradley	c1910	20	35	55
Three Blind Mice, Game of	Milton Bradley	c1930	25	45	70
Three Guardsmen, The	Milton Bradley		25	40	65
Three Little Kittens	Milton Bradley	c1910	60	100	160
Three Little Pigs Game	Einson-Freeman Publishing Corp.	1933	55	95	150
Three Little Pigs, The Game of The	Kenilworth Press	1933	100	165	265
Three Men In A Tub	Milton Bradley	1935	40	65	105
Three Men On A Horse	Milton Bradley	1936	40	65	105
Three Musketeers	Milton Bradley	1958	35	55	90
Three Point Landing	Advance Games	1942	35	55	90
Through The Clouds	Milton Bradley	1931	75	125	200
Through The Locks To The Golden Gate	Milton Bradley	c1905	75	125	200
Tic-Tac Dough	Transogram	1957	20	30	45
Ticker	Glow Products Co.	1929	45	75	120
Tiddle Winks	Doremus Schoen & Co.		15	25	40
Tiddley Winks Game	Wilder Mfg. Co.	c1920	40	65	104
Tiger Hunt, Game of	Chaffee & Selchow	1899	270	450	720
Tiger Tom, Game of	Milton Bradley	c1920	40	65	104
Time Machine	American Toy Mfg.	1961	70	115	184
Time Tunnel Game, The	Ideal	1966	90	150	240
Ting-A-Ling, The Game of	Stoll & Edwards	1920	25	45	70
Tinkerpins	Toy Creations	1916	55	90	145
Tiny-Tim Game of Beautiful Things, The	Parker Brothers	1970	25	45	70
Tip-It Game	Ideal		10	15	25
Tipit	Wolverine Supply & Mfg. Co.	1929	15	20	30
Tit-Tat-Toe	The Embossing Co.	1929	15	25	40
Tit-Tat-Toe, Three In A Row	Austin & Craw	1896	45	75	120
To The Aid of Your Party	Leister Game Co.	1942	15	25	40
Tobaggan Slide	Hamilton-Myers	c1890	225	385	600
Tobagganing At Christmas, Game of	McLoughlin Brothers	1899	400	600	800
Toboggan Slide	J.H. Singer	c1890	50	85	135
Toll Gate, Game of	McLoughlin Brothers	c1890	105	175	275
Tom & Jerry	Milton Bradley	1977	10	15	25
Tom & Jerry	Selchow & Righter		20	30	50
Tom & Jerry Adventure In Blunderland	Transogram	1965	25	45	70
Tom Sawyer On The Mississippi	Einson-Freeman Publishing Corp.	1935	50	80	125
Tom Sawyer, The Game of	Milton Bradley	1937	45	75	120
Tom Seaver Baseball			15	20	30
Tomorrowland Rocket To Moon		1956	50	80	130
Toonerville Trolley Game	Milton Bradley	1927	100	200	400
Toonin Radio Game	All-Fair	1925	150	300	500
Tootsie Roll Train Game	Hasbro	1969	20	30	50
Top Cat Game	Transogram	1962	25	45	70
Top Cop	Cadaco-Ellis	1961	40	65	105
Top-Ography	Cadaco Ltd.	1941	35	60	80

Board Games

NAME	COMPANY	DATE	GOOD	EX	MINT
Topsy Turvey, Game of	McLoughlin Brothers	1899	150	250	400
Tortoise And The Hare	Russell Mfg. Co.	1922	45	85	175
Touchdown	Cadaco Ltd.	1937	65	110	175
Touche Turtle Game	Ideal	1964	75	100	175
Tourist, The, A Railroad Game	Milton Bradley	c1900	50	85	135
Tournament	Mayhew & Baker	1858	180	300	480
Town & Country Traffic Game	Ranger Steel Products Corp.	c1950	75	125	200
Town Hall	Milton Bradley	1939	20	30	50
Toy Town Bank	Milton Bradley	1910	90	150	240
Toy Town Conductors Game	Milton Bradley	1910	105	175	280
Toy Town Telegraph Office	Parker Brothers	c1910	120	200	320
Trade Winds: The Caribbean Sea Pirate Treasure Hunt	Parker Brothers	1959	20	30	50
Traffic Game	Matchbox	1968	35	55	90
Traffic Hazards	Trojan Games	1939	20	35	55
Traffic Jam	Harett-Gilmar, Inc.	1954	40	60	80
Traffic, Game of	Milton Bradley		60	100	200
Trailer Trails	Offset Gravure Corp.	1937	35	60	95
Train For Boston	Parker Brothers	1900	400	600	800
Transatlantic Flight, Game of The	Milton Bradley	1925	125	250	500
Transport Pilot	Cadaco Ltd.	1938	25	40	65
Trap-A-Tank	Wolverine Supply & Mfg. Co.	c1920	40	70	115
Trapped	Bettye-B Co.	1956	50	75	100
Travel America	Jacmar Mfg. Co.	1950	15	25	40
Travel, The Game of	Parker Brothers	1894	225	375	900
Travel-Lite	Saxon Toy Corp.	1946	45	75	120
Treasure Hunt	All-Fair	1940	20	30	50
Treasure Island	Harett-Gilmar, Inc.	1954	30	50	80
Treasure Island	Stoll & Edwards	1923	25	45	70
Treasure Island	Stoll & Einson	1934	25	45	70
Treasure Island, Game of	Gem Publishing Co.	1923	40	65	105
Tri Ominoes, Deluxe	Pressman	1978	3	5	10
Triangular Dominos	Frank H. Richards	1885	35	60	95
Trick Trak Game	Transogram		30	50	80
Trilby	E.I. Horsman	1894	270	450	720
Trip Around The World, A	Parker Brothers	c1920	25	45	70
Trip Round The World, Game of	McLoughlin Brothers	1897	300	500	800
Trip To Washington	Milton Bradley	1884	45	75	120
Triple Play	Milton Bradley	1978	5	10	15
Triple Play	National Games, Inc.	c1930	12	20	30
Triple Yahtzee	Lowe	1972	4	6	10
Tripples	Aladdin		7	12	20
Trolley Ride, The Game of The	Hamilton-Myers	c1890	210	350	560
Trunk Box Lotto Game	McLoughlin Brothers	1890s	25	40	65
Trust Me	Parker Brothers	1981	5	8	13
Truth Or Consequences			20	35	55
Tumblin Five Acrobats	Doremus Schoen & Co.	c1925	12	20	30
Turn Over	Milton Bradley	1908	75	100	175
Turnover	Chaffee & Selchow	1898	50	85	135
Tutoom, Journey To The Treasures of Pharoah	All-Fair	1923	120	200	320
TV Guide Game		1984	8	13	20
Twentieth Century Limited	Parker Brothers	c1900	90	150	240
Twiggy, Game of	Milton Bradley	1967	20	30	50
Twilight Zone Game	Ideal	c1960	45	75	120
Twinkles Trip to the Star Factory	Milton Bradley	1960	45	75	120
Twister	Milton Bradley	1966	10	15	25
Twixt	Avalon Hill		12	20	30
Two For The Money	Lowell	c1950	7	12	20

Games, top to bottom: Snagglepuss Fun at the Picnic Game, 1916, Transogram; 77 Sunset Strip, 1960, Lowell; Pebbles Flintstone Game, 1962, Transogram; Leave It To Beaver Rocket to the Moon Game, 1959, Hasbro.

NAME	COMPANY	DATE	GOOD	EX	MINT
U.N. Game of Flags		1961	12	20	30
U.S. Air Force, Game of	Transogram	c1950	25	45	70
U.S. Postman Game		1914	60	100	160
Uncle Jim's Question Bee	Kress	1938	20	30	50
Uncle Sam At War With Spain, Great Game of	Rhode Island Game Co.	1898	325	550	900
Uncle Sam's Mail	McLoughlin Brothers	1893	210	350	550
Uncle Wiggily's New Airplane Game	Milton Bradley	c1920	25	45	70
Uncle Wiggily's Woodland Games		1936	6	10	15
Uncle Wiggly	Parker Brothers	1979	4	7	12
Undercover: The Game of Secret Agents	Cadaco-Ellis	1960	20	35	55
Underdog	Milton Bradley	1964	90	150	225
Underdog Save Sweet Polly	Whitman	1972	25	45	70
Undersea World of Jacques Cousteau	Parker Brothers	1968	20	35	50
Ungame, The	The Ungame Company	1975	4	6	10
Untouchables, The	Transogram		45	75	120
Van Loon Story of Mankind Game, The	Kerk Guild	1931	50	85	135
Vanderbilt Cup Race	Bowers & Hard	1906	200	400	600
Vassar Boat Race, The	Chaffee & Selchow	1899	420	700	1100
Vest Pocket Checker Set	The Embossing Co.	1929	15	25	40
Vest Pocket Quoits	Colorful Creations	1944	25	45	70
Victo	Spare Time	1943	15	25	40
Victory	Klak Co., New Haven, Ct.	c1920	105	175	275
Video Village	Milton Bradley	1960	25	50	75
Vietnam	Victory Games	1984	10	15	25
Vignette Author	E.G. Selchow	1874	35	60	95
Vince Lombardi			40	65	105
Virginian, The	Transogram	1962	50	90	150
Visit of Santa Claus, Game of The	McLoughlin Brothers	1899	300	500	800
Visit To The Farm	R. Bliss Mfg. Co.	1893	300	500	800
Visit To Walt Disney World Game	Milton Bradley	c1970	15	20	35
Voice of The Mummy	Milton Bradley	c1960	20	35	55
Voodoo Doll Game	Schaper	1967	20	35	55
Vox-Pop	Milton Bradley	1938	25	45	60
Voyage Around The World, Game of	Milton Bradley	c1930	105	175	275
Voyage To The Bottom of The Sea			25	40	65
Wackiest Ship In The Army	Ideal	1964	40	65	105
Wacky Races Game	Milton Bradley	c1970	15	25	40
Wagon Train	Milton Bradley	1960	25	40	65
Wahoo	Zondine Game Co.	c1947	15	20	30
Walking The Tightrope	Milton Bradley	c1920	40	70	110
Walking The Tightrope	McLoughlin Brothers	1897	125	250	400
Wally Gator Game	Transogram	1963	40	65	100
Walt Disney 101 Dalmatians	Whitman	1960	20	35	55
Walt Disney Character-My First Game	Sam'l Gabriel Sons & Co.	1955	10	15	25
Walt Disney Ski Jump Target Game	American Toy Works	c1930	35	60	95
Walt Disney's 20,000 Leagues Under The Sea	Jacmar Mfg. Co.	1954	45	75	120
Walt Disney's Game Parade		c1930	30	50	80
Walt Disney's Jungle Book	Parker Brothers	1967	15	25	45
Walt Disney's Official Frontier Land	Parker Brothers	c1950	25	45	70
Walt Disney's Sleeping Beauty Game	Whitman	1958	30	50	80
Walt Disney's Swamp Fox Game	Parker Brothers	1960	30	50	80
Walt Disney's Uncle Remus Game	Parker Brothers	c1930	50	85	135
Walt Disney's Zorro Game	Parker Brothers	1966	45	75	120
Waltons	Milton Bradley	1974	10	20	35

Board Games

NAME	COMPANY	DATE	GOOD	EX	MINT
Wang, Game of	Clark & Sowdon	1892	25	45	70
Wanted Dead or Alive	Lowell	1959	50	75	125
War At Sea	Avalon Hill	1976	10	20	30
War of Nations	Milton Bradley	1915	40	65	105
Ward Cuff's Football Game	Continental Sales Co.	1938	125	200	300
Watch On De Rind	All-Fair	1931	150	250	400
Watergate Scandal, The	American Symbolic Corp.	1973	15	20	30
Waterloo	Avalon Hill	1962	30	50	80
Waterloo	Parker Brothers	1895	325	550	900
Watermelon Frolic	E.I. Horsman	1900	135	225	360
Watermelon Patch	Craig Hopkins	c1940	25	45	70
Waterworks	Parker Brothers	1972	6	10	15
Way To The White House, The	All-Fair	1927	75	125	250
We, The Magnetic Flying Game	Parker Brothers	1928	100	200	300
Weird-Ohs Game, The	Ideal	1964	85	145	230
Welcone Back Kotter	Ideal	1977	15	25	35
Wendy, The Good Little Witch	Milton Bradley	1966	85	145	230
West Point		1902	90	150	240
What Shall I Be	Selchow & Righter	1966	10	15	25
What's My Line Game	Lowell	c1950	25	45	65
What's My Name?	Jaymar	c1920	15	25	40
Wheel of Fortune	Pressman	1985	5	8	13
Where's The Beef? (Wendy's)	Milton Bradley	1984	6	10	15
Which Witch?	Milton Bradley	1970	15	25	35
Whippet Race	J. Pressman & Co.	c1940	20	35	55
Whirl-A-Ball	Pressman	1978	10	15	25
Whirlpool Game	McLoughlin Brothers	c1890	20	35	55
White Shadow Basketball Game,The	Cadaco	1980	10	15	25
Who Am I? (Pinky Lee)	Pressman	c1950	60	100	160
Who Framed Roger Rabbit?	Milton Bradley	1987	20	35	55
Who What Or Where?	Milton Bradley	1970	5	8	13
Who's On First (Abbott & Costello)	Selchow & Righter		15	25	85
Who, Game of	Parker Brothers	1951	30	50	80
Whodunit	Selchow & Righter	1972	10	15	25
Whosit?	Parker Brothers	1976	6	10	15
Wide Awake, Game of	McLoughlin Brothers	1899	150	250	400
Wide World	Parker Brothers	1962	15	25	40
Wide World And A Journey Round It	Parker Brothers	1896	165	275	450
Wild Bill Hickock	Built-Rite	1955	45	75	125
Wild Kingdom Game	Teaching Concepts	1977	20	35	50
Wild West Cardboard Game		1914	90	150	250
Wild West, Game of The	R. Bliss Mfg. Co.	1889	390	650	1000
Wildlife	E.S. Lowe, Inc.	1971	30	50	80
Willow	Parker Brothers	1988	6	10	15
Winky Dink Official TV Game Kit		c1950	20	30	50
Winnie The Pooh	Parker Brothers	1979	5	8	13
Winnie The Pooh Game	Parker Brothers	1959	30	50	80
Winnie-The-Pooh Game	Parker Brothers	1933	75	125	200
Witch Pitch Game	Parker Brothers	1970	15	25	40
Witzi-Wits	All-Fair	1926	25	50	75
Wizard of Oz Game	Lowe	1962	20	30	50
Wizard of Oz Game, The	Cadaco	1974	10	15	25
Wizard, The	Fulton Specialty Co.	1921	15	25	40
Wolfman Mystery Game	Hasbro	1963	120	200	320
Wonderbug Game	Ideal	1977	6	10	15
Wonderful Game of Oz (pewter pieces)	Parker Brothers	1921	500	1000	2000
Wonderful Game of Oz (wooden pieces)	Parker Brothers	1921	165	275	450

Board Games

NAME	COMPANY	DATE	GOOD	EX	MINT
Woody Woodpecker's Crazy Mixed Up Color Factory	Whitman	1972	12	20	30
Woody Woodpecker's Moon Dash Game	Whitman	1976	12	20	30
Wordy	J. Pressman & Co.	1938	25	45	70
World Flyers, Game of The	All-Fair	1926	150	300	500
World of Micronauts	Milton Bradley	1978	10	15	25
World Series Parlor Baseball	Cliffton E. Hooper	1916	150	250	400
World Wide Travel	Parker Brothers	1957	25	45	70
World's Columbian Exposition, Game of The	R. Bliss Mfg. Co.	1893	450	750	1200
World's Educator Game		1889	45	75	120
World's Fair Game	Parker Brothers	1890s	120	200	325
World's Fair Game		1939	60	90	150
World's Fair Game, The	Parker Brothers	1892	800	1400	2200
WPA, Work, Progress, Action	All-Fair	1935	100	200	300
Wyatt Earp Game	Transogram	1958	20	30	50
X-Plor-US	All-Fair	1922	60	100	150
Yacht Race	J. Pressman & Co.	c1930	150	250	400
Yacht Race	Parker Brothers	1961	60	100	160
Yacht Race	Clark & Sowdon	c1890	135	225	350
Yachting, Game of	J.H. Singer	c1898	25	45	70
Yahtzee	E. S. Lowe	1956	6	10	15
Yale-Princeton Foot Ball Game	McLoughlin Brothers	1895	575	950	1500
Yankee Doodle!	Cadaco-Ellis	1940	30	50	75
Yankee Doodle, A Game of American History	Parker Brothers	1895	285	475	750
Yankee Trader	Corey Games	1941	35	60	80
Yertle, The Game of	Revell	1960	55	95	150
Yogi Bear	Milton Bradley	1971	20	35	65
Yogi Bear Break A Plate Game	Transogram	c1960	50	80	130
Yogi Bear Cartoon Game		c1950	3	5	10
Yogi Bear Game	Milton Bradley	1971	7	12	20
Yogi Bear Go Fly A Kite		1961	40	65	105
You Don't Say!	Milton Bradley		10	15	25
Young America Target Game	Parker Brothers		45	75	120
Young Athlete, The	Chaffee & Selchow	1898	425	700	1150
Yours For A Song	Lowell	1962	20	35	55
Yuneek Game	McLoughlin Brothers	1889	450	750	1200
Zaxxon	Milton Bradley	1982	6	10	15
Zig Zag Zoom	Ideal	1970	10	20	30
Zingo	Empire Plastics	c1950	15	20	30
Zip Code Game	Lowell	1964	35	55	90
Zip-Top	Deluxe Game Corp.	1940	35	55	90
Zippy Zepps	All-Fair	c1930	275	450	725
Zok, The Jumbo Fun Sized Game	Hasbro		7	15	25
Zoo Hoo	Lubbers & Bell	1924	50	75	100
Zorro Target Game W/Dart Gun	Knickerbocker Plastic Co.	c1950	20	30	50
Zulu Blowing Game	Zulu Toy Mfg. Co.	1927	50	85	135

Card Games

NAME	COMPANY	DATE	GOOD	EX	MINT
12 O'Clock High	Milton Bradley	1966	30	45	70
ABC	Parker Brothers	c1902	25	40	65
Addams Family	Milton Bradley	1965	30	45	75
Airship Game, The.	Parker Brothers	1916	30	50	80
Allegrando	Theodore Presser	1884	20	35	55
Allie-Patriot Game	McDowell And Mellor	1917	30	50	80
American History, The Game of	Parker Brothers	c1890	30	50	80

Games, top to bottom: "Pitch Em," c1929, Wolverine; Weird Ohs Game, 1964, Ideal; Star Trek, Milton Bradley; The Detectives, 1961, Transogram.

Card Games

NAME	COMPANY	DATE	GOOD	EX	MINT
Amusing Game of Conundrums	John Mcloughlin	1853	750	1300	2000
Anagrams	Peter G. Thompson	c1885	20	35	55
Apple Pie	Parker Brothers	1895	20	35	55
Archie Bunker		1972	10	15	20
Astronomy	Cincinnati Game Co.	1905	15	25	40
At Ease	Leister Game Co.	1945	25	40	65
Auction Letters	Parker Brothers	1900	20	35	55
Authors	E.E. Fairchild	1945	15	20	35
Authors Illustrated	Clark & Sowdon	1893	35	45	75
Authors, Game of	Milton Bradley	c1890	20	35	65
Authors, Game of Standard	McLoughlin Brothers	c1890	25	50	75
Authors, The Game of	Parker Brothers	c1890	15	25	40
Authors, The New Game of Pictorial	McLoughlin Brothers	1888	20	30	50
Autographs	Leister Game Co.	1945	30	45	75
Avilude	West & Lee Co.	1873	50	85	135
Balance The Budget	Elten Game Corp.	1938	30	45	70
Bali	I-S Ultd.	1954	15	25	40
Bally Hoo	Sam'l Gabriel Sons & Co.	1931	30	50	80
Betty Boop Bridge		c1930	50	75	100
Beverly Hillbillies Game, The	Milton Bradley	1963	25	35	50
Beverly Hills Game		1963	15	20	35
Bewitched Stymie Game		c1960	20	30	50
Bible ABC's And Promises	Judson Press	c1940	5	10	15
Bible Authors	Evangelical Pub. Co.	1895	10	15	25
Bible Cities	Nellie T. Magee	c1920	10	15	25
Bible Quiz Lotto	Jack Levitz	1949	20	30	50
Billy Bump's Visit To Boston	Geo S.Parker Brothers	1888	20	35	55
Bird Center Etiquette	Home Game Co.	1904	30	45	70
Birds, Game of	Cincinnati Game Co.	1899	30	50	80
Black Cat Fortune Telling Game, The	Parker Brothers	1897	65	110	175
Block	Parker Brothers	1905	15	20	35
Blondie Playing Game	Whitman	1941	25	40	65
Botany	G.H. Dunston	c1900	20	35	55
Bourse, Or Stock Exchange	Flinch Card Co.	1903	20	30	50
Boy Scouts, The Game of	Parker Brothers	1912	50	85	135
Bozo The Clown	Ed-U-Cards Mfg. Co.		6	10	15
Buck Rogers In The 25th Century	All-Fair	1936	175	300	475
Bugle Horn Or Robin Hood	McLoughlin Brothers	c1850	300	495	775
Bullwinkle Card Game	Ed-U-Cards Mfg. Co.	1962	15	25	40
Bunco	Home Game Co.	1904	20	35	55
Buster Brown At The Circus	Selchow & Righter	c1900	195	325	520
Camouflage, The Game of	Parker Brothers	1918	25	40	65
Captain Jinks	Parker Brothers	c1900	20	30	50
Challenge	John Scarne Games, Inc.	c1947	15	25	40
Characters, A Game of	F.G. Decker & O.F. Decker	1889	25	40	65
Characters, Game of	L.J. Colby & Co.	c1889	15	25	40
Charlie Chan Game	Whitman	1939	30	50	80
Charlie McCarthy Question And Answer Game	Whitman	1938	30	45	70
Charlie McCarthy Rummy Game	Whitman	1938	20	35	55
Chestnut Burrs	Fireside Game Co.	1896	15	25	40
Cinderella	Milton Bradley	1921	15	25	40
Cinderella	Milton Bradley	1905	30	45	70
Cinderella	Parker Brothers	1895	35	55	90
Cinderella Or Hunt The Slipper	McLoughlin Brothers	1887	50	85	135
Cities	All-Fair	1945	20	35	55
City Life, Or The Boys of New York, The Game of	McLoughlin Brothers	1889	50	80	130

Card Games

NAME	COMPANY	DATE	GOOD	EX	MINT
Cock Robin	Parker Brothers	1895	25	40	65
Cock Robin And His Tragical Death, Game of	McLoughlin Brothers	1885	40	65	100
Colliwogg	Milton Bradley	1907	125	200	300
Columbia's Presidents And Our Country, Game of	McLoughlin Brothers	1886	195	325	520
Combat	Milton Bradley	1964	20	30	50
Comic Card Game	Milton Bradley		15	25	40
Comic Conversation Cards	J. Ottmann Lith. Co.	c1890	55	90	145
Comic Leaves of Fortune-The Sibyl's Prophecy	Charles Magnus	c1850	345	575	900
Comical Game of 'Who', The	Parker Brothers	c1910	35	50	75
Comical Game of Whip, The	Russell Mfg. Co.	c1920	20	35	55
Comical History of America	Parker Brothers	1924	30	50	75
Comical Snap, Game of	McLoughlin Brothers	1903	35	55	90
Commanders of Our Forces, The	E.C. Eastman	1863	87	145	232
Commerce	J. Ottmann Lith. Co.	c1900	39	65	104
Competition, Or Department Store	Flinch Card Co.	1904	21	35	56
Conquest of Nations, Or Old Games With New Faces, The	Willis P. Hazard	1853	54	90	144
Costumes And Fashions, Game of	Milton Bradley	1881	15	25	40
County Fair, The	Parker Brothers	1891	45	75	120
Cousin Peter's Trip To New York, Game of	McLoughlin Brothers	1898	36	60	96
Cowboys & Indians	Ed-U-Cards Mfg. Co.	1949	15	25	40
Crow Cards, 12 Great Games In 1	Milton Bradley	1910	9	15	24
Dallas Game	Mego	1980	5	8	13
Daniel Boone Wilderness Trail	Transogram	1964	24	40	64
Defenders of The Flag	Noble & Noble, Publishers	1922	27	45	72
Defenders of The Flag	Stoll & Edwards	1922	27	45	72
Derby Day	Parker Brothers	c1900	21	35	56
Dewey At Manila	Chaffee & Selchow	1899	39	65	104
Dick Tracy Playing Card Game	Whitman	1934	39	65	104
Dick Tracy Super Detective Mystery Card Game	Whitman	1937	24	40	64
Din	E.I. Horsman	1905	15	25	40
Dixie Land, Game of	The Fireside Game Co.	1897	30	45	70
Doctor Busby Card Game		1910	25	40	60
Doctor Quack, Game of	Russell Mfg. Cc.	c1922	25	40	65
Doctors And The Quack	Parker Brothers	c1890	35	60	95
Donald Duck Game	Whitman	c1930	10	20	30
Donald Duck Game	Whitman	1941	20	30	50
Donald Duck Playing Game	Whitman	1941	25	40	65
Double Eagle Anagrams	McLoughlin Brothers	1890	35	55	90
Double Flag Game, The	McLoughlin Brothers	1904	45	75	120
Down The Pike With Mrs. Wiggs At The St. Louis Exposition	Milton Bradley	1904	30	50	80
Dr. Busby	Milton Bradley	1937	45	60	80
Dr. Busby	J. Ottmann Lith. Co.	c1900	40	60	100
Dr. Fusby, Game of	McLoughlin Brothers	c1890	40	80	125
Elite Conversation Cards	McLoughlin Brothers	1887	20	35	55
Excursion To Coney Island	Milton Bradley	c1880	35	55	90
Excuse Me!	Parker Brothers	1923	10	15	25
Famous Authors	Parker Brothers	1943	10	15	25
Famous Authors	Parker Brothers	1910	40	65	100
Favorite Art, Game of	Parker Brothers	1897	30	50	80
Five Hundred, Game of	Home Game Co.	c1900	20	35	55
Five Little Pigs	J.H. Singer	c1890	25	40	65
Flags	Cincinnati Game Co.	1896	15	25	40
Flags	Cincinnati Game Co.	1899	15	25	40

Card Games

NAME	COMPANY	DATE	GOOD	EX	MINT
Flinch	Flinch Card Co.	1902	6	10	15
Flinch	Parker Brothers	1902	5	7	10
Flintstone's Cut Ups Game	Whitman	1963	20	30	50
Flintstones Animal Rummy	Ed-U-Cards Mfg. Co.	1960	6	10	15
Foolish Questions	Wallie Dorr Co.	c1920	30	45	70
Fortune Telling	All-Fair	1945	25	50	75
Fortune Telling Game	Stoll & Edwards	c1930	25	40	65
Fortune Telling Game, The	Parker Brothers	c1890	40	65	100
Fortunes, Game of	Cincinnati Game Co.	1902	45	75	120
Fox And Geese, The New	McLoughlin Brothers	1888	45	75	120
Foxy Grandpa At The World's Fair	J. Ottmann Lith. Co.	c1904	150	250	400
Fractions	Cincinnati Game Co.	1902	10	15	25
Frank Buck's Bring 'em Back Alive Game	All-Fair	1937	55	95	150
Funny Bones Game	Parker Brothers	1968	5	7	11
G-Men	Milton Bradley	1936	20	30	50
Gamevelope	Morris Systems Publishing Co.	c1944	20	35	55
Gavitt's Stock Exchange	W.W. Gavitt	1903	20	30	50
Geographical Cards	Peter G. Thompson	1883	20	30	50
Geography Up To Date	Parker Brothers	c1890	30	50	75
George Washington's Dream	Parker Brothers	c1900	20	35	55
Get Smart Game	Ideal	1966	30	50	80
Gidget	Milton Bradley	1966	15	25	40
Go Go Go	Arrco Playing Card Co.	c1950	6	10	15
Goat, Game of	Milton Bradley	1916	15	25	40
Gold Rush, The	The Cracker Jack Co.	c1930	10	15	25
Golden Egg	McLoughlin Brothers	c1850	285	475	750
Gong Hee Fot Choy	Zondine Game Co.	1948	15	20	30
Good Old Game of Corner Grocery, The	Parker Brothers	c1900	40	60	90
Good Old Game of Dr. Busby	Parker Brothers	c1900	40	60	80
Good Old Game of Dr. Busby, The	United Game Co.	c1920	25	50	75
Grandma's Game of Useful Knowledge	Milton Bradley	c1910	20	30	50
Grandmama's (Improved) Arithmetical Game	McLoughlin Brothers	1887	30	45	70
Grandmama's (Improved) Game of Useful Knowledge	McLoughlin Brothers	1887	30	45	70
Grandmama's Sunday Game: Bible Questions, Old Testament	McLoughlin Brothers	1887	50	85	135
Great Battlefields	Geo S. Parker Brothers	1886	70	120	195
Great Composer, The	Theodore Presser	c1901	25	40	65
Group Sounding	Garrard Press	1945	10	15	25
Guess Again, The Game of	McLoughlin Brothers	c1890	40	65	100
Gypsy Fortune Telling Game	McLoughlin Brothers	1909	50	75	150
H.M.S. Pinafore	McLoughlin Brothers	1880	75	125	200
Have-U It?	Selchow & Righter	1924	15	25	40
Heads And Tails	Parker Brothers	c1900	20	30	50
Hens And Chickens, Game of	McLoughlin Brothers	1875	105	175	275
Hey What?	Parker Brothers	1907	10	20	30
Hidden Titles	Parker Brothers	1908	10	15	25
Historical Cards	Peter G. Thompson	1884	20	30	50
History Up To Date	Parker Brothers	c1900	35	50	75
Hokum	Parker Brothers	1927	15	25	40
Hollywood Movie Bingo	Whitman	1937	40	70	110
Home History Game	Milton Bradley	c1910	35	50	65
Hood's War Game	C.I. Hood	1899	30	50	80
Hoot	Russell Mfg. Co.	c1930	40	65	100
Hoot	Saalfield Publishing Co.	c1926	30	50	80
Hopalong Cassidy Canasta Game			10	20	30

Games, top to bottom: Surfside 6, 1961, Lowe; Disney's Fantasyland Game, Parker Brothers; The Monkees Game, 1968, Transogram; Battle of the Planets, Milton Bradley.

Card Games

NAME	COMPANY	DATE	GOOD	EX	MINT
Hoppy Get-Well Game			30	50	80
House That Jack Built	Parker Brothers	c1900	35	60	85
House That Jack Built, The	McLoughlin Brothers	1887	35	55	90
Household Words, Game of	Household Words Game Co.	1916	50	85	135
How Silas Popped The Question	Parker Brothers	1915	30	40	60
Howdy Doody Game	Russell Mfg. Co.	1954	20	30	50
I Doubt It	Parker Brothers	c1910	20	35	55
I Survived New York!	City Enterprises	1981	4	7	12
Illustrated Mythology	Cincinnati Game Co.	1896	15	25	40
Illya Kuryakin Card Game	Milton Bradley	1966	20	30	40
Improved Game of Peter Coddle	McLoughlin Brothers	1900	25	40	65
Improved Historical Cards	McLoughlin Brothers	1900	20	35	55
Industries, Game of	A.W. Mumford Co.	c1897	15	25	40
Ivanhoe	Geo S. Parker Brothers	1886	30	50	80
James Bond (Live and Let Die) Tarot Game	US Games Systems	1973	15	35	50
Japanese Oracle, Game of	McLoughlin Brothers	1875	60	100	160
Johnny's Historical Game	Geo S. Parker Brothers	c1890	35	50	80
Jumping Frog, Game of	J.H. Singer	c1890	45	75	100
Just Like Me, Game of	McLoughlin Brothers	1899	40	65	105
Know Your States	Garrard Press	1955	10	15	25
Komical Konversation Kards	Parker Brothers	1893	30	50	75
Let's Play Basketball	The D.M.R. Co.	1965	10	15	25
Letters Improved For The Logomachist	Noyes & Snow	1878	20	35	55
Li'l Abner's Spoof Game	Milton Bradley	1950	40	65	100
Library of Games	Russell Mfg. Co.	1939	15	25	40
Lindy Flying Game	Parker Brothers	1927	50	80	130
Lindy Flying Game, The New	Nucraft Toys	1927	30	45	70
Little Orphan Annie Rummy Cards	Whitman	1937	25	40	65
Lost Heir, The Game of	McLoughlin Brothers	1893	45	75	120
Make A Million	Rook Card Co.	1934	10	15	25
Man from U.N.C.L.E.	Milton Bradley	1965	15	30	45
Match	Garrard Press	1953	10	15	25
Mayflower, The	Fireside Game Co.	1897	15	25	40
Mickey Mouse Bridge Game	Whitman	1935	25	40	65
Mickey Mouse Canasta Jr.	Russell Mfg. Co.	1950	20	45	75
Mickey Mouse Jr. Royal Rummy	Whitman	c1970	4	7	15
Mickey Mouse Library of Games	Russell Mfg. Co.	1946	25	45	70
Mickey Mouse Old Maid Game	Whitman	c1930	25	45	75
Mille Bornes			10	15	25
Mother Hubbard	McLoughlin Brothers	1875	40	65	100
Movie-Land Keeno	Wilder Mfg. Co.	1929	100	200	300
Mr. President USA	Decor		10	15	20
Mr. T Game	Milton Bradley	1983	2	4	6
Munsters Game	Milton Bradley	1966	25	45	70
Musical Lotto	Tudor Metal Products Corp.	1936	25	40	65
Mythology	Cincinnati Game Co.	1900	15	25	40
Nations Or Quaker Whist, Game of	McLoughlin Brothers	1898	50	80	130
Nations, Game of	Milton Bradley	1908	15	25	40
Naughty Molly	McLoughlin Brothers	1905	45	75	120
Nerds Boxed Game	Milton Bradley	c1930	12	20	30
New Lindy Flying Game, The	Nucraft Toys	1927	25	45	70
New York World's Fair Children's Game	Ed-U-Cards Mfg. Co.	1964	15	25	40
Nosey, The Game of	McLoughlin Brothers	1905	225	300	550
Nuclear War	Douglas Malewicki	1965	20	30	50
Old Curiosity Shop	Novelty Game Co.	1869	135	225	360
Old Maid	J.H. Singer	c1890	12	20	30

Card Games

NAME	COMPANY	DATE	GOOD	EX	MINT
Old Maid Card Game		1889	20	30	50
Old Maid Fun Full Thrift Game	Russell Mfg. Co.	c1940	20	30	50
Old Maid, Game of	McLoughlin Brothers	1870	50	80	125
Old Maid, With Characters From Famous Nursery Rhymes	All-Fair	c1920	30	50	75
Oliver Twist, The Good Old Game of	Geo S. Parker	c1888	90	153	245
Oops!! Travel Game	Warren		10	15	25
Our Bird Friends	Sarah H. Dudley	1901	20	30	50
Our National Life	Cincinnati Game Co.	1903	15	20	30
Patch Word	All-Fair	1938	10	15	25
Paws & Claws	Clark & Sowdon	c1895	35	60	95
Pepper	Parker Brothers	1906	10	15	25
Peter Coddle And His Trip To New York	J.H. Singer	c1890	20	30	50
Peter Coddle Tells of His Trip To Chicago	Parker Brothers	c1890	25	45	70
Peter Coddle's Dinner Party	Clark & Sowdon		20	35	55
Peter Coddle's Trip To New York	Milton Bradley	1925	15	25	40
Peter Coddle's Trip To New York, The Game of	Parker Brothers	1888	25	45	70
Peter Coddle's Trip to the World's Fair	Parker Brothers	1939	50	75	100
Peter Coddles	J. Ottmann Lith. Co.	c1890	25	45	70
Picture Reading Game	Parker Brothers	c1910	15	20	35
Pinky Lee's Who Am I Game	Ed-U-Cards Mfg. Co.	c1950	20	30	50
Pinocchio Playing Card Game	Whitman	1939	35	60	95
Pit	Parker Brothers	1919	20	30	40
Popeye Playing Card Game	Whitman	1934	35	60	90
Portrait Authors	West & Lee Co.	1873	25	40	65
Ports And Commerce, The Game of	Parker Brothers	1899	20	30	50
Pucks Portfolio	Degen, Estes & Co.	1866	60	100	160
Quick Wit	Parker Brothers	1938	20	30	50
Quien Sabe Cowboy	Parker Brothers	1906	35	55	90
Quit	Parker Brothers	1905	15	20	30
Quiz	Parker Brothers	c1920	15	20	30
Quiz Me, Game of Geography	Milton Bradley	1940	10	15	25
Radio Game	Parker Brothers	1923	45	75	120
Red Riding Hood And The Wolf, The New Game	McLoughlin Brothers	1887	50	85	135
Rex	J. Ottmann Lith. Co.	c1920	25	40	65
Robinson Crusoe For Little Folks, Game of	E.O. Clark	c1900	25	45	70
Roodles	Flinch Card Co.	1912	20	30	40
Rook	Parker Brothers	1906	5	8	12
Rook	Rook Card Co.	1906	5	10	15
Roosevelt At San Juan	Chaffee & Selchow	1899	50	85	135
Sabotage	Games Of Fame	1943	25	45	70
Skeeter	Arrco Playing Card Co.	c1950	6	10	15
Skippy	All-Fair	1936	45	75	120
Skit Scat	McLoughlin Brothers	1905	40	70	110
Snap	E.I. Horsman	1883	55	95	150
Snap, Game of	Milton Bradley	c1910	20	35	55
Snap, Game of	McLoughlin Brothers	1892	40	65	105
Snap, The Game of	Parker Brothers	c1905	25	40	65
Snoopy Card Game			10	15	25
Stage	C.M. Clark Publishing Co., Inc.	1904	40	60	80
Strategy Poker Fine Edition	Milton Bradley	1967	5	7	12
Superheroes Card Game	Milton Bradley	1978	5	10	15
Superman Game	Whitman	1966	30	50	80
Syllable	Garrard Press	1948	10	15	25
Take-Off	Russell Mfg. Co.	c1930	15	20	30

Card Games

NAME	COMPANY	DATE	GOOD	EX	MINT
Telegraph Messinger Boy, Game of The	McLoughlin Brothers	1886	35	60	95
The Golden Egg	R.H. Pease	c1845	165	275	440
The Lion & The Eagle, Or The Days of '76	E.H. Snow	1883	50	80	130
The Lost Heir, Game of	Milton Bradley	c1910	20	35	55
Three Bears, The	Stoll & Edwards	1922	20	35	55
Three Merry Men	Amsdan & Co.	1865	40	65	105
Toot	Parker Brothers	1905	25	45	70
Totem	West & Lee Co.	1873	45	75	120
Touring	Wallie Dorr Co.	1906	25	40	65
Touring	Parker Brothers	1926	25	40	65
Trail Drive	Arrco Playing Card Co.	c1950	10	15	25
Traits, The Game of	Goodenough And Woglom Co.	1933	15	25	40
Trip Through Our National Parks: Game of Yellowstone, A	Cincinnati Game Co.	c1910	15	25	40
Trips of Japhet Jenkens & Sam Slick	Milton Bradley	1871	20	35	55
Trolley	Snyder Bros.	1904	25	40	65
Trolley Came Off, The	Parker Brothers	c1900	45	75	120
Twenty Five, Game of	Milton Bradley	1925	6	10	15
United States History, The Game of	Parker Brothers	1903	15	25	40
Uno	International Games	1972	15	25	40
Venetian Fortune Teller, Game of	Parker Brothers	1898	75	125	175
Verborum	Peter G. Thompson	1883	20	30	50
Walt And Skeezix Gasoline Alley Game	Milton Bradley	1927	75	150	200
War And Diplomacy	Chaffee & Selchow	1899	50	85	135
War of Words	McLoughlin Brothers	1910	35	60	95
Welcome Back Kotter Game	Milton Bradley	1976	15	25	40
What Would You Do?	Geo E. Schweig & Son	1933	10	15	25
When My Ship Comes In	Geo S. Parker	1888	25	45	70
Where Do You Live	J.H. Singer	c1890	30	50	80
Where's Johnny	McLoughlin Brothers	1885	45	75	120
Which Is It? Speak Quick Or Pay	McLoughlin Brothers	1889	45	75	120
Whip, The Comical Game of	Russell Mfg. Co.	1930	25	50	75
Who Is The Thief	Whitman	1937	25	40	65
Whyoo!	Milton Bradley	1906	30	50	75
Wise Old Owl	Novel Toy	c1950	20	35	55
Wogglebug Game of Conumdrums, The	Parker Brothers	1905	100	200	300
Worth While	Geo B. Doan & Co.	1907	25	40	65
Yankee Pedlar, Or What Do You Buy	John Mcloughlin	c1850	725	1200	1900
Young Folks Historical Game	McLoughlin Brothers	c1890	25	35	50
Young Peddlers, Game of The	Mayhew & Baker	1859	55	95	150
Young People's Geographical Game	Parker Brothers	c1900	15	20	30
Zoom	Whitman	1941	35	55	90

Skill/Action Games

NAME	COMPANY	DATE	GOOD	EX	MINT
400, Aristrocrat of Games, The	Morris Systems Publishing Co.	1933	15	25	40
Aero Ball	Game Makers, Inc.	c1940	30	50	75
Airways	Lindstrom Tool & Toy Co.	c1950	30	50	75
Angry Donald Duck Game	Mexico	c1970	40	65	100
Aurora Monday Night Football With Roger Staubach	Aurora	1972	15	25	40
Bag of Fun	Rosebud Art Co., Inc.	1932	15	20	35
Bambino	Bambino Products Co.	1934	75	125	200
Bang Bird	Doremus Schoen & Co.	1924	20	30	50

Games, top to Bottom: Milton The Monster, 1966, Milton Bradley; Star Trek Game, 1966, Ideal; Captain Gallant, 1956, Transogram; The Family Affair Game, 1967, Whitman.

Skill/Action Games

NAME	COMPANY	DATE	GOOD	EX	MINT
Barber Pole	Parker Brothers	1908	35	55	85
Barn Yard Tiddledy Winks	Parker Brothers	c1910	50	85	135
Baron Munchausen Game, The	Parker Brothers	1933	35	55	90
Baseball	Tudor	c1960	25	40	60
Bash!	Ideal	1967	10	15	25
Basket Ball	Russell Mfg. Co.	1929	100	200	300
Batman Batarang Toss	Pressman	1966	150	250	400
Batman Pin Ball	Marx	1966	55	95	150
Bats in the Belfry	Mattel	1964	30	45	70
Battles, Or Fun For Boys, Game of	McLoughlin Brothers	1889	425	700	1100
Bazooka Bagatelle	Marx		35	60	95
Bean-Em	All-Fair	1931	150	250	500
Big Game Hunt, The	Carrom Industries	c1947	15	25	40
Big Sneeze Game, The	Ideal	1968	10	15	20
Bingo	All-Fair	1929	15	25	40
Bobb, Game of	McLoughlin Brothers	1898	300	500	800
Bomber Ball	Game Makers, Inc.	c1940	40	60	80
Booby Trap	Parker Brothers	1965	10	15	25
Bop The Beetle	Ideal	1963	20	35	55
Bottle Imps, Game of	Milton Bradley	1907	300	500	800
Bow-O-Winks	All-Fair	1932	60	120	200
Bowl-A-Matic	Eldon	1963	45	75	120
Bowling Alley	N.D. Cass	c1921	20	35	55
Boy Hunter, The	Parker Brothers	1925	60	100	160
Brownie Auto Race Game	Jeannetee Toy & Novelty Co.	c1920	45	70	110
Brownie Kick-In Top	M.H. Miller Co.	c1910	35	60	95
Bugs Bunny Game	Ideal	1975	15	25	40
Bula	Games Of Fame	1943	30	45	70
Bull In The China Shop	Milton Bradley	1937	20	30	50
Buster Brown, Pin The Tail On The Tiger Game		c1900	60	100	160
Busto	All-Fair	1931	20	35	55
Buzzing Around	Parker Brothers	1924	40	65	100
Candid Camera Target Shot	Lindstrom Tool & Toy Co.	c1950	20	30	50
Careful The Toppling Tower	Ideal	1967	10	15	25
Cavalcade Derby Game	Wyandotte	c1930	50	85	135
Chinaman Party	Selchow & Righter	1896	75	130	210
Chinese Laundry Man Bean Bag Toss	Price Klein Co.		600	1000	1600
Chivalry, The Game of	Geo S. Parker	1888	90	150	240
Click	Akro Agate Co.	c1930	50	85	135
Clown Winks	Sam'l Gabriel Sons & Co.	c1930	15	25	40
Combination Tiddledy Winks	Milton Bradley	1910	40	65	100
Cones & Corns	Parker Brothers	1924	39	65	104
Conette	Milton Bradley	1890	45	75	120
Coney Island Penny Pitch	Novel Toy	c1950	33	55	88
Contack	Parker Brothers	c1939	12	20	32
Crazy Clock Game	Ideal	1964	40	60	90
Crazy Traveller	Parker Brothers	c1920	36	60	96
Crickets In The Grass	Madmar Quality Co.	c1920	35	50	75
Crow Hunt	Parker Brothers	1930	50	85	150
Crows In The Corn	Parker Brothers	1930	45	75	120
Deck Ring Toss Game		1910	30	50	80
Dee Vs Meade: Battle of Gettysburg	Gamut Of Games	1974	60	100	160
Deputy Dawg Hoss Toss		1973	15	25	40
Dig	Parker Brothers	1940	15	25	40
Dim Those Lights	All-Fair	1932	200	400	800
Disk	Madmar Quality Co.	c1900	35	55	90
Diving Fish	C.E. Bradley Corp.	c1920	20	30	50
Dodging Donkey, The	Parker Brothers	c1920	45	75	120

Skill/Action Games

NAME	COMPANY	DATE	GOOD	EX	MINT
Donkey Party	Selchow & Righter	1887	15	25	40
Down And Out	Milton Bradley	1928	50	100	250
Duck On The Rock	Milton Bradley		20	30	50
Dynamite Shack Game	Milton Bradley	1968	6	10	15
Faba Baga Or Parlor Quiots	Morton E. Converse Co.	1883	40	65	100
Facts In Five	3M	1967	15	25	40
Fairies' Cauldron Tiddledy Winks Game, The	Parker Brothers	1925	35	50	75
Fascination	Remco	1962	10	20	35
Fascination	Selchow & Righter	1890	35	50	75
Feeley Meeley Game	Milton Bradley	1967	7	15	20
Felix The Bead Game Under Glass			10	20	35
Fiddlestix	Plaza Mfg. Co.	c1937	10	15	25
Fireball XL-5 Magnetic Dart Game	Magic Wand	1963	75	125	200
Fish Pond, Game of	Wescott Brothers	c1910	30	50	80
Fish Pond, The Game of	McLoughlin Brothers	1890	150	250	400
Fishing Game	Martin Co.	1899	30	45	70
Five Wise Birds, The	Parker Brothers	1923	30	45	70
Flap Jacks	All-Fair	1931	75	150	300
Flea Circus Magnetic Action Game	Mattel	1968	15	25	40
Flintstones Bowling Game			15	25	40
Flintstones Brake Ball	Whitman	1962	45	75	120
Flintstones Mechanical Shooting Gallery	Marx	1962	75	125	200
Flintstones Pin Ball			15	25	40
Flitters	The Martin Co.	1899	45	75	120
Floor Croquet Game		1912	60	100	160
Flying Nun Marble Maze Game, The	Hasbro	1967	45	75	120
Four And Twenty Blackbirds		c1890	650	1100	1700
Four Dare Devils, The	Marx, Hess & Lee, Inc.	1933	40	65	100
Friendly Folk of Gruesome Mansion, The			20	30	50
Gee-Wiz Horse Race	Wolverine Supply & Mfg. Co.	1928	50	85	135
Genuine Steamer Quoits	Milton Bradley	1924	15	25	40
Grab A Loop	Milton Bradley	1968	7	12	20
Green Hornet Quick Switch Game	Milton Bradley	1966	180	300	475
Hands Down	Ideal	1965	10	15	25
Happitime Bagatelle	Northwestern Products	1933	30	45	70
Happy Landing	Transogram	1938	30	45	70
Hi Pop	Advance Games	1946	20	35	55
Hop-Over Puzzle	J. Pressman & Co.	c1930	20	35	55
Hopalong Cassidy Bean Bag Toss Game		c1950	10	20	30
Hopalong Cassidy Lasso Game			120	200	325
Howdy Doody Dominoes Game	Ed-U-Cards Mfg. Co.	1951	60	100	160
Huggin The Rail	Selchow & Righter	1948	45	65	100
Hungry Willie	Transogram	c1930	40	70	110
Hunting In The Jungle	A. Gropper	c1920	30	45	70
I-Qubes	Arl-Hi Co.	1948	10	15	25
I-Qubes	Capex Co. Inc.	1948	10	15	25
Jack Straws, The Game of	Parker Brothers	c1901	25	35	60
Jamboree	Selchow & Righter	c1937	60	100	150
James Bond Message From M Game	Ideal	1966	165	275	440
Japanola	Parker Brothers	1928	35	60	95
Jaunty Butler	All-Fair	1932	75	150	250
Jav-Lin	All-Fair	1931	105	175	280
Jim Prentice Electric Baseball			15	30	45
Jim Prentice Electric Football			7	11	20
Jolly Clown Spinette	Milton Bradley	1932	30	45	70
Jolly Robbers	Wilder Mfg. Co.	1929	50	75	125
Jumping Jupiter	Sam'l Gabriel Sons & Co.	c1940	30	50	80

Skill/Action Games

NAME	COMPANY	DATE	GOOD	EX	MINT
Jungle Hunt	Gotham Pressed Steel Corp.	1940	30	45	70
Jungle Jump-Up Game	Judson Press	c1940	30	45	70
KaBoom!	Ideal	1965	10	15	25
Katzenjammer Kids Hockey	Jaymar	c1940	40	65	100
Katzy Party	Selchow & Righter	c1900	70	120	195
Ker-Plunk	Ideal	1967	5	10	15
Kimbo	Parker Brothers	c1950	10	15	25
Kindergarten Lotto	Strauss Mfg. Co.	1904	50	80	130
King Arthur	Northwestern Products	c1950	25	40	65
King Pin Deluxe Bowling Alley	Baldwin Mfg. Co.	1947	10	20	30
Knockout Andy	Parker Brothers	1926	30	45	70
Knockout, Electronic Boxing Game	Northwestern Products	c1950	90	150	240
Krokay	Transogram	1955	30	50	75
Kuit-Kuts	The Regensteiner Corp.	1922	20	30	50
Land of The Lost Pinball	Larami	1975	10	20	30
Leaping Lena	Parker Brothers	c1920	60	90	125
Little Orphan Annie Bead Game		c1930	20	35	55
Little Orphan Annie Shooting Game	Milton Bradley	c1930	30	50	80
Lone Ranger And Tonto Spin Game, The	Pressman	c1967	15	25	40
Lone Ranger Target Game	Marx	1939	70	115	185
Magnetic Fish Pond	Milton Bradley	1948	15	25	65
Mammoth Conette	Milton Bradley	1898	90	150	240
Man From U.N.C.L.E. Pinball Game		1966	80	135	215
Mar-Juck	The Regensteiner Corp.	1923	20	30	50
Marathon Game	Sports Games Co.	1978	10	20	35
Marble Muggins	American Toy Mfg.	c1920	60	100	160
Marx-O-Matic Tin Basketball Game	Marx	c1950	150	250	400
Meteor Game	A.C. Gilbert	1916	25	45	70
Mickey Mouse Funny Facts Electric Game	Einson-Freeman Publishing Corp.		35	60	95
Mickey Mouse Haunted House			210	350	550
Mickey Mouse Miniature Pinball Game	Marks Brothers	c1930	20	35	55
Mickey Mouse Shooting Game	Marks Brothers	c1930	120	200	320
Mickey Mouse Skittle Ball Game	Marks Brothers	c1930	60	100	160
Mickey Mouse Soldier Target Set	Marks Brothers	c1930	60	100	160
Mouse Trap	Ideal	1963	25	45	70
Mumbly Peg	All-Fair	c1920	25	50	75
NFL All-Pro Football Game	Ideal	1967	15	25	40
Nixon Ring Toss		c1970	20	30	50
Official NFL Football Game	Ideal	1968	20	30	50
Old Time Shooting Gallery	Warren	1940	15	25	40
Par-A-Shoot Game	Baldwin Mfg. Co.	1947	15	25	40
Peeza	Toy Creations	1935	25	45	70
Pickie	Games Of Fame	1945	25	40	65
Ping Pong	Parker Brothers	1902	50	75	150
Pinky Lee & The Runaway Frankfurter Game			25	45	70
Pinocchio Target Game	American Toy Works	1938	90	150	240
Pinocchio The Merry Puppet Game	Milton Bradley	1939	25	40	65
Pitch'em, The Game of Indoor Horse Shoes	Wolverine Supply & Mfg. Co.	c1929	15	25	40
Pitch, Game of	Parker Brothers	1914	30	50	70
Pitch-A-Ring	Milton Bradley	1905	15	25	40
Plus One	Milton Bradley	1980	5	10	15
Poker Ball Pin Game	Lindstrom Tool & Toy Co.	c1950	12	20	30
Polly Put The Kettle On	Parker Brothers	1923	40	65	105
Pop And Plop Shooting Game	All-Fair	1928	75	150	200
Poppin-Ball	Parker Brothers	1910	40	65	105
Potato Race	Parker Brothers	1902	55	95	150

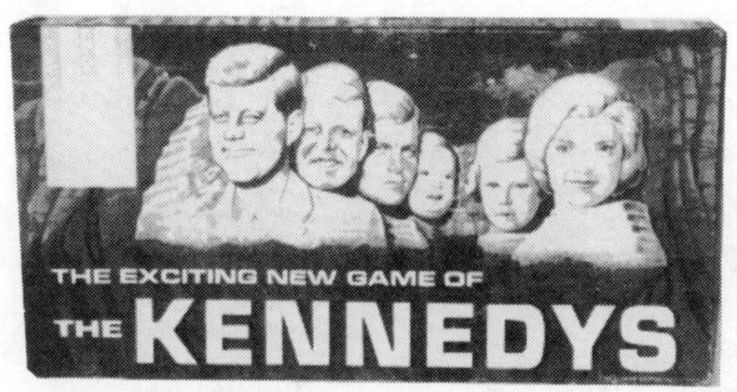

Games, top to bottom: Hawaii Five-O, c1960, Remco; Bat Masterson, 1958, Lowell; Stingray Game, c1960, Transogram; The Kennedys, 1962, Transogram.

Skill/Action Games

NAME	COMPANY	DATE	GOOD	EX	MINT
Pretzel Jetzel Machine Game	Transogram		35	55	90
Pursuit	Aurora	1973	25	45	70
Put It In The Bank	Sam'l Gabriel Sons & Co.	c1940	20	35	55
Quiz Kids Radio Question Bee	Whitman	1945	15	25	40
Race-A-Car Speedway Game	Transogram		35	55	90
Ranger Commandos	Parker Brothers	1942	35	60	125
Rat Patrol Spin Game	Pressman	c1967	40	65	105
Red Ryder 'Whirli-Crow' Target Game	Daisy	c1940	150	250	400
Ride 'em Cowboy	Gotham Pressed Steel Corp.	1939	25	45	70
Ring My Nose	Milton Bradley	1926	60	100	160
Ring Scaling	Martin Co.	c1900	25	45	70
Rocket Patrol Magnetic Target Game	American Toy Products Co.	c1950	45	75	120
Rollin' Checkers			35	55	90
Saratoga: 1777	Gamut Of Games	1974	30	50	80
Shuffle-Board, The New Game of	Sam'l Gabriel Sons & Co.	1920	50	85	135
Simba	All-Fair	1932	75	150	200
Smitty Game	Milton Bradley	c1930	40	65	105
Snap-Jacks	Sam'l Gabriel Sons & Co.	c1940	15	25	40
Snow White And The Seven Dwarfs	American Toy Works	1938	150	250	400
Speed Circuit	3 M	1971	15	30	45
Spin 'em Target Game	All Metal Product Co.	c1930	25	40	65
Stak, International Game of	Marks Brothers	1937	30	60	90
Star Wars Return of The Jedi			20	30	50
Stax	Marks Brothers	c1930	12	20	30
Superman Action Game	American Toy Works	1940	60	100	160
Superman Spln Game	Pressman	c1967	40	65	105
Suspense	Northwestern Products	c1950	15	20	30
Table Croquet	Milton Bradley	c1890	60	100	160
Tactics	Northwestern Products	1940	25	45	70
Tickle Bee	Schaper	1956	15	20	35
Tiddledy Wink Tennis	E.I. Horsman	1890	45	75	120
Tiddledy Winks, Game of	Parker Brothers	c1910	35	55	90
Time Bomb	Milton Bradley	1965	35	50	75
Time Tunnel Spin Game, The	Pressman	c1967	60	100	160
Tinker Toss	Toy Creations	c1920	25	40	65
Tip The Bellboy	All-Fair	1929	120	200	325
Tip Top Fish Pond	Milton Bradley	c1930	20	35	55
Tipp Kick	Top Set	c1970	15	25	40
Toss-O	Lubbers & Bell	1924	10	15	25
Touchdown	Milton Bradley	c1930	150	250	400
Tournament Labyrinth	Pressman	c1980	10	15	25
Toy Town Target With Repeating Pistol	Milton Bradley	1911	55	95	150
Trap Shot	Parker Brothers		100	165	265
Traps And Bunkers, A Game of Golf	Milton Bradley	c1930	25	40	65
Tru-Action Electric Harness Race Game	Tudor	c1950	20	35	55
Try-It Maze Puzzle Game	Milton Bradley	1965	7	12	20
United States Air Mail Game, The	Parker Brothers	c1930	50	85	135
Untouchables, The	Marx	c1950	95	160	250
Wa-Hoo Pick-Em Up Sticks	Doremus Schoen & Co.	c1936	15	25	40
Washington's Birthday Party	Russell Mfg. Co.	1911	55	95	150
Watermelon Patch Game	McLoughlin Brothers	1896	600	1200	2000
Wonder Tiddley Winks	Martin Co.	1899	20	35	55
Wow! Pillow Fight For Girls Game	Milton Bradley	1964	10	20	30
Zowie Horseshoe Game	James L. Decker Products Co.	c1947	20	35	55

Games, top to bottom: Shotgun Slade, c1960, Milton Bradley; Dick Tracy Playing Card Game, 1934, Whitman; Dragnet, 1955, Transogram; Mighty Mouse Rescue Game, 1978, Milton Bradley; Melvin The Moon Man, c1960, Remco.

Food-Related Collectibles

Nothing fascinates humanity like itself. Our museums, libraries, car dealerships and shopping malls are so filled with products of intellectual and material pursuits that we can have no hope of ever sampling them all. As the information society shrinks the world to the width of a fiber optic strand, our cultural possibilities seem to expand in inverse proportion. American culture has reshaped the world in its own self-image-of-the-week, and our collective interest never wavers. American auto-archaeology progresses with each turn of the page, press of the button and click of the mouse.

This fascination takes myriad forms, some grand and some modest, but to the true collector nothing is without value. Cast iron banks may hold no interest for a PEZ collector, and a bank collector may have no interest in PEZ, but this is a matter of personal preference, not a reflection on the collectible validity of an entire field. Most collectors seek the toys of their youth, and the toys of choice change from generation to generation. The universe of toys is a big place and all fields from Marklin to Mattel have their place in it.

In this section we look at several collectible fields that can be grouped together by the common denominator of food. Additionally, they are all relatively new fields, with beginnings traceable to 1935, 1952, and 1979, respectively. As recent entries to the time line of toys, these fields hold much promise in terms of the high numbers of potential collectors they can attract. Young fields are also more easily manipulated, and collectors must be on guard against being misled by manufactured market booms. For these reasons alone they warrant close watching. The next decade in particular will tell which, if any, of these fields will grow into a major constellation in the toy firmament.

Lunch Boxes

In 1935, the firm of Geuder, Paeschke and Frey produced a small oval lunch tin with a lid and wire handle, which they called the Mickey Mouse Lunch Kit. Decorated with an early long-nosed Mickey on the lid and other Disney characters on the side band, this is considered the first true American character lunch box. Lunch kits had been in manufacture since the 1920s, but this was the first kit to use an established children's character as a selling point. It took the star power of television to launch the lunch box industry out of the domed steel domain of workmen into the colorful art boxes generations of children carried to school each day.

As World War II ended, Aladdin Industries returned to providing millions of workmen with sturdy if uninspired lunch kits designed to take the beating of the workplace. The great change came in 1950 when Aladdin released a pair of rectangular steel boxes, one red and one blue, sporting scalloped color decals of the TV western hero of the day, Hopalong Cassidy. In short order, 600,000 boxes were sold and carried to school by proud young owners. The youth market had been found and it would never be ignored again.

The envious classmates of those first Hoppy boxers would not be denied. For 1952 the scallop decal gave way to a rectangular one, shaped more like a TV screen. American Thermos, Aladdin's chief competitor, would not be denied either. It went one up on Aladdin by introducing the 1953 Roy Rogers box in full color lithography. Aladdin responded by issuing a new 1954 Hoppy box in full color litho, and the lunch box era officially began.

Throughout the latter 1950s, the box wars were fought in earnest between Aladdin and American Thermos, with occasional challenges by ADCO Liberty, Ohio Art, and Okay Industries. The smaller firms produced some classic boxes, notably Mickey Mouse and Donald Duck (1954), Howdy Doody (1954) and Davy Crockett (1955) from ADCO Liberty; and Captain Astro (1966), Bond XX (1967), Snow White (1980) and Pit Stop (1968) from Ohio Art. Okay Industries weighed in briefly later on with the now highly prized Wake Up America (1973) and Underdog (1974) boxes, but from the beginning it had always been a two-horse race.

Porky's Lunch Wagon Dome, 1959, King Seeley Thermos.

The popular boxes of each year mirrored the stars, heroes and interests of the times. From the westerns and space explorations of the late 1950s through the 1960s, Americans enjoyed a golden age of cartoon and film heroes such as the Flintstones (1962), Dudley Doright (1962), Bullwinkle and Rocky (1962) and Mary Poppins (1965). As the decade progressed, America grew more aggressive, turning towards such violent heroes as the Man From U.N.C.L.E. (1966), Rat Patrol (1967), and GI Joe (1967) before Vietnam changed the national consciousness.

The early 1970s brought us such innocuous role models as H.R. Pufnstuf (1970), The Partridge Family (1971) and Bobby Sherman (1972), and by decade's end we were greeting new promises and threats from beyond in Close Encounters (1978) and Star Wars (1978).

The metal box reigned supreme through the mid-1980s when parental groups began calling for a ban on metal boxes as deadly weapons. The industry capitulated, and by 1986 both Aladdin and American Thermos were producing all their boxes in plastic. Both firms continue production today.

The switch to plastic was not nearly as abrupt as might be expected. Aladdin and Thermos had been making plastic and vinyl boxes since the late 1950s. These included many character boxes that had no counterparts in metal, which increased their desirability and helped the plastic and vinyl box fields gain recognition and acceptance as collectibles.

Vinyl boxes were made of lower cost materials, consisting basically of cardboard sheathed in shower curtain grade vinyl. They were not as popular as metal boxes, and their poor construction combined with lower unit sales have resulted in a field with higher rarity factors than the metal box arena. Vinyl was more affordable to small companies, which produced numerous limited-run boxes for sale or use as premiums.

Vinyl box collecting is an emerging field with few firmly established prices compared to the relative maturity of the metal box market, so any price guide such as this will be more open to debate. As the field matures, the pricing precedents of sales will build into a stronger body of knowledge.

For the reader's benefit, this book will list lunch kits alphabetically in three categories according to box composition: plastic, steel and vinyl.

PEZ

1952 saw the inauspicious introduction to American shores of an Austrian mint in a handy dispenser. Long popular in the homeland, the pocket candy lost something in the translation from German to English. The marketing cure for this was successful beyond all expectations.

PEZ was created in 1927 as a peppermint candy and breath mint sold in a clever package, which dispensed the candies one at a time. Highly successful in Europe, it became the fashionable adult candy of its time. But its launch in America found a disinterested public. It was quickly decided that PEZ would be reinvented as a children's candy for the American market with fruit-flavored candies replacing the staid pfefferminz of old. The dispensers were redesigned and given colorful heads in the shapes of popular cartoon characters, and American children quickly claimed the new candy as their own.

Today PEZ is available everywhere from your local K Mart to the corner store, and few Americans can handle a dispenser without evoking a few childhood memories in the process. This ability to reconnect us, either with our own childhoods or with our national past, is central to collectibility in any field, and a PEZ dispenser holds a rich postwar legacy in its little plastic container.

PEZ collectors nationwide have formed clubs, published newsletters, and now hold national conventions each year. The once lowly candy holder has grown in popularity and respect to the point that rare dispensers are now highly prized collectibles and have been recently sold by firms such as Christies Auction House in New York.

The PEZ market has developed some noteworthy variations on standard collecting procedures. In many fields a toy still in the original package commands a premium over the same toy with no package. This is not usually the case in PEZ collecting. Pre-blister card era PEZ dispensers were packaged in boxes or cellophane bags, which did not allow for either display or handling of the toys themselves. Experts hold that condition of the dispenser itself is paramount, and that a dispenser in original packaging commands no premium over a loose one, with some exceptions. These exceptions apply to certain multiple piece dispensers or sets, such as "Make A Face," which consists of several detachable parts, and dispensers on unusual display cards such as the "Space Gun." Another notable exception is the "Stand By Me" dispenser, which was packaged with a pack of candy and a miniature poster from the movie of the same name.

Since dispenser stems are easily interchangeable, PEZ authorities hold that only variations in head configuration or coloring affect value. There is no difference in value between dispensers with different colored stems but the same head.

Finally there is the matter of feet and no feet. This refers to the presence or absence of a flattened rounded base on the stem resembling flat shoes. PEZ dispensers released in America before 1987 were all of the no-feet variety, so a dispenser with feet was made after that year. However, certain older molds continued to be produced with no feet after 1987 as well, but these are common dispensers with little variance in value between feet and no-feet varieties. The major difference in value here applies to older no-feet dispensers that were discontinued and reissued after 1987 with feet.

Bugs Bunny PEZ Dispenser.

The field continues to grow, and PEZ continues to produce a limited number of new dispensers each year, but the total universe of PEZ still numbers less than 350 dispensers. The serious collector can find common dispensers in abundance, scarce ones with persistence, and can still hope to amass a complete collection. Additionally, many dispensers are easily affordable, as the following price guide will show.

One last note is called for here. The Pez market is currently experiencing a period of rapid growth. Market volatility is a factor that must be considered when making purchases, particularly when a collectible item or category is in a hot period. Even a modest influx of collectors into a small market can cause prices to rocket, as can a run of national attention or simple speculation by dealers and investors. Only time can tell if these periods of frenetic activity will establish new market levels or dissipate as the market returns to prior levels, leaving some lucky sellers with large profits and some unlucky buyers with overvalued goods.

McDonald's Happy Meal Toys and Other Fast Food Premiums

Collecting McDonald's Happy Meal and other fast food toys is a recent but already highly developed area. There are numerous branches of a national

McDonald's Collector's Club, and a convention is held in Chicago each year. Several books have been written on the subject in spite of the fact that the first national-campaign Happy Meal was not issued until 1979.

The typical Happy Meal customer is under 12 years old, an age range not renowned for gentle play habits. Thus, condition of toys is the critical factor. Only very rare toys hold any value at all if found in less than excellent condition. This price guide will classify condition in only two grades: Mint In Package, and Excellent Loose. MIP toys have never been removed from their packages and are valued on average at 200 percent of Excellent Loose toys. Excellent Loose toys have no packages and exhibit minor evidence of play, but they remain clean and intact.

Rarity is also a primary factor in determining value. The age of a toy plays a role in this, as does popularity. Modern Disney movie tie-in toys are frequently worth more than older toys because of the strong Disneyana collector market. The same holds true for popular cartoon or comic character items.

Another factor affecting rarity is distribution. Some McDonald's and other fast-food company campaigns were run only in certain regions of the country. The toys of these campaigns are known as regionals, and command higher than average prices due to their limited release areas.

Several years back some toys had to be recalled, resulting in the design of special one-piece toys for younger children, commonly called "Under 3" toys. Under 3s are not produced for each campaign, and are not normally advertised in the in-store displays. Lower numbers of these toys are released, again resulting in premiums typically 20 percent higher than the regular toys of the same campaign.

One more factor deserves mention -- the international toy. Major film and comic character toy campaigns sometimes run worldwide with little or no changes from country to country. Sometimes only the package printing is changed. But occasionally foreign market toys are never released in America. These toys are highly valued by some collectors simply due to their foreign status. Other collectors also consider aspects such as popular character affiliation when calculating the value of these toys. Again, as the market matures, these values and item inventories will establish themselves.

Like PEZ, the market for fast-food toys is new and experiencing rapid growth.

While the universe of collectible PEZ items is much smaller than the fast-food sector, PEZ has the advantage of nearly 30 more years of exposure to the American public, falling into the period of greatest nostalgia for the majority of baby boom collectors. The 10-year-old McDonald's customer of 1979 will not turn 30 years old until 1999, but it seems likely that nostalgia will accompany following generations into their middle years, as it has for baby boomers. As McDonald's is the first global restaurant, and popular film and TV tie-ins are now the rule of the day, the future of this field looks secure.

LUNCH BOXES

Plastic

Aladdin

NAME	DESCRIPTION	YEAR	BOX NM	BOTTLE NM
101 Dalmations	Plastic box with matching bottle	1990	6	3
18 Wheeler	Matching plastic bottle	1978	30	10
Atari Missile Command Dome	Plastic box with matching bottle	1983	20	5
Back to School	Plastic box with matching bottle	1980	10	4
Beach Bronto	Plastic box, no bottle	1984	25	0
Beauty & the Beast	Plastic box with matching bottle	1991	6	3
Care Bears	Plastic box with matching bottle	1986	5	2
Cinderella	Plastic box with matching bottle	1992	5	2
Dick Tracy	Plastic with matching bottle	1989	10	5
Dino Riders	Plastic with matching bottle	1988	10	4
Disney on Parade	Plastic bottle, glass liner	1970	30	15
Duck Tales (4X4/Game)	Plastic with matching bottle	1986	10	4
Dukes of Hazzard	Plastic with matching bottle	1981	15	5
Dukes of Hazzard Dome	Plastic with matching bottle	1981	20	5
Dune	Plastic with matching bottle	1984	20	8
Ed Grimley	Plastic with matching bottle	1988	20	5
Fievel Goes West	Plastic with matching bottle	1991	10	4
Flash Gordon Dome	Plastic with matching bottle	1979	40	10
Food Fighters	Plastic with matching bottle	1988	10	5
G.I. Joe, (Space Mission)	Plastic with matching bottle	1989	20	5
G.I. Joe, Live the Adventure	Plastic with matching bottle	1986	20	5
Geoffrey	Plastic with matching bottle	1981	30	10
Get Along Gang	Plastic with matching bottle	1983	8	2
Goonies	Plastic box with matching bottle	1985	15	5
Incredible Hulk Dome	Plastic with matching bottle	1980	30	10
It's Not Just the Bus - Grayhound	Plastic with matching bottle	1980	40	10
Jetsons, The Movie	Plastic with matching bottle	1990	10	5
Los Angeles Olympics	Plastic with matching bottle	1984	20	5
Mad Balls	Plastic with matching bottle	1986	10	3
Max Headroom (Coke)	Plastic with matching bottle	1985	20	5
Mickey & Minnie Mouse in Pink Car	Plastic box with matching bottle	1988	10	3
Mickey Mouse & Donald Duck	Plastic box with matching bottle	1984	10	3
Mickey Mouse & Donald Duck See-Saw	Plastic box with matching bottle	1986	10	3
Mickey Mouse at City Zoo	Plastic box with matching bottle	1985	10	3
Mickey Mouse Head	Plastic box with matching bottle	1989	20	5
Mickey on Swinging Bridge	Plastic box with matching bottle	1987	10	2
Mickey Skate Boarding	Plastic box with matching bottle	1980	18	5
Monster in My Pocket	Plastic box with matching bottle	1990	8	3
Mr. T	Plastic box with matching bottle	1984	12	3
Nosy Bears	Plastic box with matching bottle	1988	8	2
Popeye Dome	Plastic box with matching bottle	1979	20	5
Raggedy Ann & Andy	Plastic red box with matching bottle	1988	12	5
Rocketeer	Plastic box with matching bottle	1990	5	2
Scooby Doo	Plastic blue box with matching bottle	1984	25	8
Scooby-Doo, A Pup Named	Plastic box with matching bottle	1988	10	5
Snow White	Plastic red box with matching bottle	1980	20	5
Spare Parts	Plastic box with generic plastic bottle	1982	20	5
Sport Goofy	Plastic red box with matching bottle	1986	30	5
Strawberry Shortcake	Plastic box with matching bottle	1980	5	2
Superman II Dome	Plastic red box with matching bottle	1986	30	5
Superman, This is a Job For	Plastic box, red, no bottle	1980	20	0

Plastic

NAME	DESCRIPTION	YEAR	BOX NM	BOTTLE NM
Talespin	Plastic box with matching bottle	1986	5	2
Thundarr the Barbarian Dome	Plastic dome box with matching bottle	1981	20	5
Timeless Tales	Plastic box with matching bottle	1989	5	2
Tom & Jerry	Plastic box with matching bottle	1989	15	5
Transformers	Plastic red box, matching bottle	1985	12	3
V (TV Series)	Box, plastic bottle	1984	140	40
Wayne Gretzky	Plastic box, blue or orange rim, with matching bottle	1980	40	10
Wayne Gretzky Dome	Plastic box with matching bottle	1980	55	10
Wild Fire	Plastic lavender box with matching bottle	1986	5	2
Wizard of Oz, 50th Anniversary	Plastic box with matching bottle	1989	10	5
Woody Woodpecker	Plastic yellow box, red plastic bottle	1972	50	40
Wuzzles	Plastic box with matching bottle	1985	8	3

Aladdin, Canada

NAME	DESCRIPTION	YEAR	BOX NM	BOTTLE NM
Sesame Street	Plastic box, yellow, matching plastic bottle	1985	10	5
Transformers Dome	Plastic dome box, generic plastic bottle	1986	15	5

D.A.S.

NAME	DESCRIPTION	YEAR	BOX NM	BOTTLE NM
Fire Engine Co. 7	Plastic with generic plastic bottle	1985	15	2

Deka

NAME	DESCRIPTION	YEAR	BOX NM	BOTTLE NM
Beach Party (blue/pink)	Plastic box with generic plastic bottle	1988	15	5
Bozostuffs	Plastic box with matching bottle	1988	20	5
Deka 4X4	Plastic box with generic plastic bottle	1988	25	5
Ghostbusters	Plastic with matching bottle	1986	10	3
Punky Brewster	Plastic box with matching bottle	1984	15	4

Fesco

NAME	DESCRIPTION	YEAR	BOX NM	BOTTLE NM
Pickle	Plastic pickle box, no bottle made	1972	100	0

Fisher Price

NAME	DESCRIPTION	YEAR	BOX NM	BOTTLE NM
Fisher Price Mini Lunch Box	Plastic box, red w/barnyard scenes, matching bottle	1962	10	2
McDonald's Happy Meal	Plastic	1986	15	0

Fun Design

NAME	DESCRIPTION	YEAR	BOX NM	BOTTLE NM
Lunch Man with Radio	Plastic box, with built-in radio, no bottle	1986	18	0
Lunch'n Tunes Safari	Plastic box with built-in radio, no bottle	1986	25	0
Lunch'n Tunes Singing Sandwich	Plastic box with built-in radio, no bottle	1986	25	0
Munchie Tunes Bear with Radio	Plastic box with built-in radio	1986	25	5
Munchie Tunes Punchie Pup w/Radio	Plastic box with built-in radio	1986	25	5
Munchie Tunes Robot with Radio	Plastic box with built-in radio	1986	25	5

Fundes

NAME	DESCRIPTION	YEAR	BOX NM	BOTTLE NM
Dinorocker with Radio & Headset	Plastic	1986	30	0

Top to Bottom: Plastic Scooby Doo, Thermos, 1973; Canadian Plastic Incredible Hulk, Aladdin, 1976; Canadian Plastic Star Trek, Aladdin, 1974; Vinyl Barbie and Midge Brunch Bag; Vinyl Peanuts, KST, 1967; Canadian Plastic Star Wars kit; Canadian Plastic Rice Crispies, Aladdin, 1975; Canadian Plastic Fred's Menu kit.

Plastic

NAME	DESCRIPTION	YEAR	BOX NM	BOTTLE NM
	Hummer			
Snak Shot Camera	Plastic camera shaped box, blue or green, with generic plastic bottle	1987	20	2
	King Seeley Thermos			
Popeye, Truant Officer	Plastic red box, matching metal bottle (Canada)	1964	250	35
	Moldmark Industries			
Colonial Bread Van	Plastic box and bottle	1984	50	10
Rainbow Bread Van	Plastic box and bottle	1984	50	10
	Servo			
Bear with Heart (3-D)	Plastic	1987	12	0
Jetsons (paper picture)	Plastic with matching bottle	1987	40	5
Jetsons 3-D	Plastic box, blue or purple, matching bottle	1987	25	5
Popeye & Son	Plastic red box, flat paper label, with matching bottle	1987	10	4
Popeye & Son 3-D	Plastic box, red or yellow, with matching bottle	1987	25	5
Race Cars	Plastic	1987	20	0
Yogi's Treasure Hunt	Plastic box, flat paper label, with matching bottle	1987	25	5
Yogi's Treasure Hunt 3-D	Plastic 3-D box, green or pink, with matching bottle	1987	20	5
	Superseal			
Kermit's Frog Scout Van	Plastic box, no bottle	1989	15	0
Miss Piggy's Safari Van	Plastic box, pink, no bottle	1989	15	0
	Taiwan			
Crestman Tubular!	Plastic box, matching plastic bottle	1980	20	3
Peter Pan Peanut Butter	Plastic yellow box, red imprinting, matching bottle	1984	30	10
	Thermos			
Animalympics Dome	Plastic box with matching bottle	1979	20	5
Astronauts	Plastic box, matching bottle	1986	8	3
Back to the Future	Plastic box with matching bottle	1989	15	6
Bang Bang	Plastic box with matching bottle	1982	15	5
Barbie with Hologram Mirror	Plastic box with matching bottle	1990	10	4
Batman (dark blue)	Plastic box with matching bottle	1989	10	4
Batman (light blue)	Plastic box with matching bottle	1989	20	4
Batman Returns	Plastic box with matching bottle	1991	10	3
Bee Gees	Plastic yellow box with matching bottle	1978	30	10
Beetlejuice	Plastic box with matching bottle	1980	10	4
Big Jim	Plastic box with matching bottle	1976	40	20
C.B. Bears	Plastic	1977	20	5
Centurions	Plastic box with matching bottle	1986	10	3
Chiclets	Plastic box, no bottle	1987	20	0
Chipmunks, (Alvin and the)	Plastic box with matching bottle	1983	15	5
Chips	Plastic box with matching bottle	1977	30	5
Days of Thunder	Plastic with matching bottle	1988	10	5
Dinobeasties	Plastic	1988	5	0

Plastic

NAME	DESCRIPTION	YEAR	BOX NM	BOTTLE NM
Disney's Little Mermaid	Plastic with generic plastic bottle	1989	8	3
Dunkin Munchkins	Plastic with matching bottle	1972	25	8
Ecology Dome	Plastic with matching bottle	1980	20	5
Entenmann's	Plastic	1989	10	0
Ewoks	Plastic with matching bottle	1983	20	5
Fame	Plastic with matching bottle	1972	20	5
Flintstone Kids	Plastic box with matching bottle	1987	10	5
Fraggle Rock	Plastic with matching bottle	1987	12	3
Frito Lay's	Plastic box, no bottle	1982	25	0
Garfield (food fight)	Plastic with matching bottle	1979	15	5
Garfield (lunch)	Plastic with matching bottle	1977	15	5
Go Bots	Plastic box with matching bottle	1984	8	2
Golden Girls	Plastic with matching bottle	1984	10	3
Gumby	Plastic box with matching bottle	1986	15	5
Hot Wheels	Plastic box, matching bottle	1984	8	3
Howdy Dowdy Dome	Plastic dome box, matching plastic bottle	1977	25	5
Inspector Gadget	Plastic with matching bottle	1983	20	8
Jabber Jaw	Plastic with matching bottle	1977	50	10
Kermit the Frog, Lunch With	Plastic, yellow, with matching bottle	1988	18	5
Kool-Aid Man	Plastic with matching bottle	1986	15	5
Lisa Frank	Plastic with matching bottle	1980	10	3
Little Orphan Annie	Plastic with matching bottle	1973	40	10
Looney Tunes Birthday Party	Plastic with matching bottle blue or red	1989	10	5
Looney Tunes Dancing	Plastic box, matching bottle	1977	20	5
Looney Tunes Playing Drums	Plastic with matching bottle	1978	20	5
Looney Tunes Tasmanian Devil	Plastic with generic plastic bottle	1988	12	5
Lucy's Luncheonette	Plastic box, Peanuts characters,with matching bottle	1981	15	5
Lunch Time with Snoopy Dome	Plastic with matching bottle	1981	15	5
Marvel Super Heroes	Plastic with matching bottle	1990	15	5
Menudo	Plastic with matching bottle	1984	12	5
Mighty Mouse	Plastic box with matching bottle	1979	35	10
Muppets (blue)	Plastic box with matching bottle	1982	12	4
Muppets Dome	Plastic red box with matching bottle	1981	20	5
New Kids on the Block (pink/ orange)	Plastic box with matching bottle	1990	5	2
Peanuts, Weinie Roast	Plastic box with matching bottle	1985	10	4
Pee Wee's Playhouse	Plastic box with generic plastic bottle	1987	10	5
Q-Bert	Plastic box with matching bottle	1983	10	2
Rainbow Bright	Plastic box with matching bottle	1983	5	2
Robot Man and Friends	Plastic box with matching bottle	1984	10	4
Rocky Roughneck	Plastic box with matching bottle	1977	20	5
Roller Games	Plastic box with matching bottle	1989	15	3
S.W.A.T. Dome	Plastic box with matching bottle	1975	30	8
Scooby Doo	Plastic green box with matching bottle	1973	35	10
Shirt Tales	Plastic box with matching bottle	1981	10	2
Sky Commanders	Plastic box with generic plastic bottle	1987	10	5
Smurfette	Plastic box with matching bottle	1984	10	5
Smurfs	Plastic blue box with matching bottle	1984	10	5
Smurfs Dome	Plastic box with matching bottle	1981	20	5
Smurfs Fishing	Plastic box with matching bottle	1984	10	5
Snoopy Dome	Plastic blue box with matching bottle	1978	20	5
Snorks	Plastic box with matching bottle	1984	8	3
Sport Billy	Plastic blue box with matching bottle	1982	15	5
Star Com. U.S. Space Force	Plastic box with matching bottle	1987	10	5
Star Trek Next Generation	Plastic blue box, group picture, matching bottle	1988	10	5

Plastic

NAME	DESCRIPTION	YEAR	BOX NM	BOTTLE NM
Star Trek Next Generation	Plastic red box, Picard, Data, Wesley, matching bottle	1989	20	5
Star Wars, Droids	Plastic with matching bottle	1985	20	5
Tang Trio	Plastic red or yellow box with generic plastic bottle	1988	10	2
Teenage Mutant Ninja Turtles	Plastic box with generic plastic bottle	1990	6	3
Tiny Toon Adventures	Plastic box with matching bottle	1990	5	2
Tweety & Sylvester	Plastic box with matching bottle	1986	15	5
Where's Waldo	Plastic box with matching bottle	1990	5	1
Who Framed Roger Rabbit	Plastic box, red or yellow, with matching bottle	1987	15	5
World Wrestling Federation	Plastic box with matching bottle	1986	10	5
Wrinkles	Plastic box with matching bottle	1984	8	3

Universal

NAME	DESCRIPTION	YEAR	BOX NM	BOTTLE NM
Civil War, The	Plastic box, generic "Thermax" bottle	1961	250	10
Movie Monsters	Plastic box, matching bottle	1979	35	12

unknown

NAME	DESCRIPTION	YEAR	BOX NM	BOTTLE NM
ALF	Red plastic		18	0
Flintstones	Plastic box, premium, Denny's Restaurants		15	0
Official Lunch Football	Plastic football shaped box, red or brown	1974	100	0

Steel

Adco Liberty

NAME	DESCRIPTION	YEAR	BOX NM	BOTTLE NM
Davy Crockett/Kit Carson	Steel box	1955	200	0
Howdy Doody	Steel box	1954	225	0
Lone Ranger	Steel box, red rim, blue band, no bottle	1955	450	0
Luggage Plaid	Steel box, no bottle	1955	75	0
Mickey Mouse & Donald Duck	Steel box with matching steel bottle	1954	240	100
Mickey Mouse/Donald Duck	Steel box, steel/glass bottle	1954	75	75

Aladdin

NAME	DESCRIPTION	YEAR	BOX NM	BOTTLE NM
240 Robert	Steel lunch box with plastic bottle	1978	2000	750
Adam-12	Steel box with matching plastic thermos	1973	50	15
America on Parade	Steel box with matching plastic bottle	1976	30	10
Annie Oakley & Tagg	Steel box with matching steel thermos	1955	175	50
Annie, The Movie	Steel box, plastic bottle	1982	25	5
Archies	Steel box with matching plastic bottle	1969	70	20
Astronauts	Steel box with matching plastic bottle	1969	65	20
Back in '76	Steel box and plastic bottle	1975	30	5
Batman	Steel box with matching steel thermos	1966	145	55
Battlestar Galactica	Steel box with matching plastic bottle	1978	40	10
Beatles	Steel box, blue, with matching bottle	1966	300	100
Bedknobs & Broomsticks	Steel box with plastic bottle	1972	50	40
Beverly Hillbillies	Steel box with matching steel bottle	1963	130	35
Bionic Woman, with Car	Steel box and plastic bottle	1977	35	10
Bionic Woman, with Dog	Steel box with matching plastic bottle	1978	35	10
Black Hole	Steel box with matching plastic bottle	1979	40	10
Bonanza	Steel black rim box, steel thermos	1968	120	50
Bonanza	Steel brown rim box with matching steel bottle	1963	95	45
Bonanza	Steel green rim box with steel thermos	1963	80	40
Bozo the Clown Dome	Steel dome box and plastic bottle		175	70

LUNCH BOXES

Top to Bottom: Peanuts steel bottle from 1966 KST kit; Beverly Hillbillies, Aladdin, 1963; Roy Rogers & Dale Evans Double R Bar Ranch kit, American Thermos, 1957; Space: 1999, KST, 1976; H.R. Pufnstuf, Aladdin, 1970; Porky's Lunch Wagon Dome, American Thermos, 1959; Hopalong Cassidy kit, Aladdin, 1952.

Steel

NAME	DESCRIPTION	YEAR	BOX NM	BOTTLE NM
Bread Box Dome	Steel dome with Campbell's Soup bottle	1968	250	100
Buccaneer Dome	Steel dome box, matching bottle	1957	200	60
Buck Rogers	Steel box with matching plastic bottle	1979	20	5
Bugaloos	Steel box with matching plastic bottle	1971	70	10
Cable Car Dome	Steel dome box and steel/glass bottle	1962	175	60
Care Bear Cousins	Steel box with matching plastic thermos	1985	10	2
Care Bears	Steel box and plastic bottle	1984	7	3
Charlie's Angels	Steel box with matching plastic bottle	1978	35	10
Chavo	Steel box with matching plastic bottle	1979	90	10
Chuck Wagon Dome	Steel dome box, matching bottle	1958	140	55
Cracker Jack	Steel box with matching plastic bottle	1969	55	10
Cyclist, The: Dirt Bike	Steel box and plastic bottle	1979	45	10
Daniel Boone	Steel box with matching steel bottle	1955	350	50
Daniel Boone	Steel box with matching steel bottle	1965	120	40
Debutante	Steel box with matching steel bottle	1958	90	20
Denim Diner Dome	Steel dome, matching plastic bottle	1975	20	5
Dick Tracy	Steel box with matching steel bottle	1967	120	55
Disco	Steel box with matching plastic bottle	1979	30	5
Disco Fever	Steel box with matching plastic bottle	1980	30	5
Disney Express	Steel box with matching plastic bottle	1979	20	5
Disney Fire Fighters Dome	Steel dome box, matching plastic bottle	1974	80	20
Disney School Bus Dome	Steel dome box, steel/glass bottle	1968	35	20
Disney School Bus Dome	Steel dome box, yellow, matching plastic bottle	1968	0	20
Disney World	Steel box with matching plastic	1972	20	10
Disney's Magic Kingdom	Steel box, plastic bottle	1980	12	5
Disney's Rescuers, The	Steel box, plastic bottle	1977	18	5
Disney's Robin Hood	Steel box, plastic bottle	1974	55	20
Disney, Wonderful World of	Steel box, plastic bottle	1982	12	5
Disneyland (Castle)	Steel box with matching steel bottle	1957	125	35
Disneyland (Monorail)	Steel box with matching steel bottle	1968	150	35
Doctor Dolittle	Steel box with matching steel bottle	1968	80	35
Double Decker	Steel box with matching plastic bottle	1970	60	25
Dr. Doolittle	Steel box, steel/glass bottle		90	40
Dr. Seuss	Steel box with matching plastic bottle	1970	70	20
Drag Strip	Steel box with matching plastic bottle	1975	35	10
Dragon's Lair	Steel box with matching plastic bottle	1983	20	4
Duchess	Steel box, steel/glass bottle	1960	60	45
Dukes of Hazzard	Steel box with matching plastic bottle	1983	20	5
E.T., The Extra Terrestrial	Steel box, matching plastic bottle	1982	30	8
Emergency!	Steel box, plastic bottle	1973	45	10
Emergency!	Steel dome box, plastic bottle	1977	80	12
Evel Knievel	Steel box, plastic bottle	1974	40	12
Fall Guy	Steel box with matching plastic bottle	1981	15	5
Flintstones	Steel box, matching plastic bottle	1973	45	15
Flintstones	Steel box, orange, 1st issue, matching bottle	1962	75	30
Flintstones	Steel box, yellow, 2nd issue, matching bottle	1963	95	35
Flying Nun	Steel box with matching steel bottle	1968	110	40
Fox and the Hound	Steel box and plastic bottle	1981	30	5
Gentle Ben	Steel box, plastic bottle, glass liner	1968	75	20
Globe-Trotter Dome	Steel dome box, matching steel/glass bottle	1959	120	40
Gomer Pyle	Steel box with matching steel bottle	1966	100	35
Gremlins	Steel box with matching plastic bottle	1984	20	8
Grizzly Adams Dome	Steel box, plastic bottle	1977	60	10
Gunsmoke	Steel 'mule splashing' box with matching bottle	1972	55	15
Gunsmoke	Steel 'stagecoach' box, matching bottle	1973	100	15
Gunsmoke	Steel box, plastic bottle	1959	120	35
Gunsmoke, Double L Version	Steel box, double L error version, matching bottle	1959	375	40

Steel

NAME	DESCRIPTION	YEAR	BOX NM	BOTTLE NM
Gunsmoke, Marshal Matt Dillon	Steel box with matching steel bottle	1962	160	55
H.R. Pufnstuf	Steel box with matching plastic bottle	1970	90	20
Have Gun, Will Travel	Steel	1960	250	0
He-Man & Masters of the Universe	Steel box with matching plastic bottle	1984	5	5
Heathcliff	Steel box with matching plastic bottle	1982	20	4
Hector Heathcote	Steel box with matching steel bottle	1964	170	55
Hogan's Heroes Dome	Steel dome box, steel/glass bottle	1966	175	70
Hollie Hobby	Steel box, red rim, matching plastic bottle	1968	10	5
Holly Hobbie	Steel box with matching plastic bottle	1973	5	1
Holly Hobbie	Steel box with matching plastic bottle	1979	5	1
Hopalong Cassidy	Steel box, black rim, steel/glass bottle	1954	175	50
Hopalong Cassidy	Steel box, full litho, matching steel bottle	1952	210	70
Hopalong Cassidy	Steel box, red or blue, steel/glass bottle	1950	95	35
Huckleberry Hound	Steel box, steel/glass bottle	1961	60	30
Incredible Hulk, The	Steel box, plastic bottle	1978	30	10
It's About Time Dome	Steel dome box, matching bottle	1967	200	50
It's About Time Dome	Steel dome box, steel/glass bottle	1967	140	50
James Bond 007	Steel box with matching steel bottle	1966	130	35
Jet Patrol	Steel box with matching steel bottle	1957	250	55
Jetsons	Steel dome, steel/glass bottle	1968	850	160
Jetsons Dome	Steel dome box, matching bottle	1963	675	175
Johnny Lightning	Steel box, plastic bottle	1970	45	5
Jonathan Livingston Seagull	Steel box with matching plastic bottle	1973	50	20
Jungle Book	Steel box with matching steel bottle	1968	55	30
Junior Miss	Steel box with matching plastic bottle	1978	30	10
Kellogg's Breakfast	Steel box, plastic bottle	1969	75	20
Krofft Supershow	Steel box with matching plastic bottle	1976	30	8
Land of the Giants	Steel box and plastic bottle	1968	75	20
Land of the Lost	Steel box with matching plastic bottle	1975	50	8
Laugh-In (Helmet)	Steel box, Helmet on back, matching plastic bottle	1969	90	25
Laugh-In (Tricycle)	Steel box, trike on back, matching plastic bottle	1969	100	15
Legend of the Lone Ranger	Steel box, plastic bottle	1980	35	8
Lidsville	Steel box with matching plastic bottle	1971	90	25
Little Friends	Steel box with matching plastic bottle	1982	750	150
Ludwig Von Drake	Steel box, steel/glass bottle	1962	175	50
Marvel Super Heroes	Steel box, black rim, matching plastic bottle	1976	35	5
Mary Poppins	Steel box, steel/glass bottle	1965	70	25
Masters of the Universe	Steel box with matching plastic bottle	1983	10	2
Mickey Mouse Club	Steel box, red rim, sky boat, matching bottle	1977	30	3
Mickey Mouse Club	Steel box, white, matching steel bottle	1976	40	20
Mickey Mouse Club	Steel box, yellow, steel/glass bottle	1963	45	20
Miss America	Steel box with matching plastic bottle	1972	30	10
Monroes	Steel box with matching steel bottle	1967	125	35
NFL Quarterback	Steel box with matching steel bottle	1964	70	35
Osmonds, The	Steel box with matching plastic bottle	1973	50	15
Our Friends	Steel box with matching plastic bottle	1982	500	175
Pac-Man	Steel box with matching plastic bottle	1980	10	4
Paladin	Steel box with matching steel bottle	1960	240	160
Pebbles & Bamm Bamm	Steel box with matching plastic bottle	1971	55	20
Pete's Dragon	Steel box with matching plastic bottle	1978	35	10
Peter Pan	Steel box with matching plastic bottle, Disney	1969	80	30
Pinocchio	Steel box, plastic bottle	1971	60	20
Planet of the Apes	Steel box with matching plastic bottle	1974	65	15
Police Patrol	Steel box, plastic bottle	1978	140	10
Popeye	Steel 'arm wrestling' box, plastic bottle	1980	25	5

Steel

NAME	DESCRIPTION	YEAR	BOX NM	BOTTLE NM
Popples	Steel box, plastic bottle	1986	10	1
Psychedelic Dome	Steel dome box, plastic bottle	1969	210	30
Raggedy Ann & Andy	Steel box, plastic bottle	1973	25	5
Rat Patrol	Steel box, steel/glass bottle	1967	80	40
Rifleman, The	Steel box, steel/glass bottle	1961	200	50
Robin Hood	Steel box, matching bottle	1956	100	40
Ronald McDonald, Sheriff	Steel box, plastic bottle	1982	30	5
Rose Petal Place	Steel box, plastic bottle	1983	20	3
Rough Rider	Steel box, plastic bottle	1973	30	5
Secret of NIMH	Steel box, plastic bottle	1982	45	5
Secret Wars	Steel box, plastic bottle	1984	45	10
Sesame Street	Steel box, yellow rim, plastic bottle	1983	10	7
Sigmund and the Sea Monsters	Steel box, plastic bottle	1974	35	15
Six Million Dollar Man	Steel box, plastic bottle	1974	35	5
Six Million Dollar Man	Steel box, plastic bottle	1978	35	5
Skateboarder	Steel box, plastic bottle	1977	35	5
Snow White, Disney	Steel box, orange rim, plastic bottle	1975	35	5
Space Explorer Ed McCauley	Steel box with matching steel thermos	1960	385	85
Spider-Man & Hulk	Steel box, Captain America on back, plastic bottle	1980	30	5
Sport Goofy	Steel box, yellow rim, plastic bottle	1983	25	9
Star Trek Dome	Steel dome box, matchin bottle	1968	575	175
Steve Canyon	Steel box, steel/glass bottle	1959	10	40
Strawberry Shortcake	Steel box, plastic bottle	1980	10	4
Strawberry Shortcake	Steel box, plastic bottle	1981	10	4
Street Hawk	Steel box, plastic bottle	1985	125	40
Super Friends	Steel box, matching plastic bottle	1976	40	10
Super Powers	Steel box, plastic bottle	1983	30	5
Superman	Steel box, red rim 'Daily Planet Office' on back, matching bottle	1978	25	10
Tarzan	Steel box, steel/glass bottle	1966	70	35
Thundercats	Steel box, plastic bottle	1985	20	3
Tom Corbett Space Cadet	Steel blue or red paper decal box, steel/glass bottle	1952	200	70
Tom Corbett Space Cadet	Steel box, full litho, matching bottle	1954	475	75
Transformers	Steel red box, matching plastic bottle	1986	10	5
U.S. Mail Dome	Steel dome box, plastic bottle	1969	40	10
Universal's Movie Monsters	Steel box, plastic bottle	1980	40	5
Voyage to the Bottom of the Sea	Steel box, steel/glass bottle	1967	300	50
Waltons, The	Steel box, plastic bottle	1973	30	5
Welcome Back Kotter	Steel box, flat or embossed face, red rim, matching plastic bottle	1977	40	5
Wild Bill Hickock	Steel box, steel/glass bottle	1955	100	45
Wild, Wild West	Steel box, plastic bottle	1969	150	20
Winnie the Pooh	Steel box, blue rim, plastic bottle	1976	150	35
Yogi Bear & Friends	Steel box, black rim, matching steel bottle	1961	95	30
Zorro	Steel box, black band, steel/glass bottle	1958	90	40
Zorro	Steel box, red band, steel/glass bottle	1966	90	40

American Thermos

NAME	DESCRIPTION	YEAR	BOX NM	BOTTLE NM
Berenstein Bears	Steel box with matching plastic thermos	1983	25	5
Boating	Steel box with matching steel bottle	1959	400	125
Brave Eagle	Steel box with red, blue, gray or green band, matching steel bottle	1957	200	10
Corsage	Steel box with matching steel thermos	1958	50	20
Firehouse Dome	Steel dome box, steel/glass bottle	1959	300	100
Happy Days	Steel box with matching plastic bottle	1977	20	4
Mork & Mindy	Steel box with matching plastic bottle	1979	25	5

Steel

NAME	DESCRIPTION	YEAR	BOX NM	BOTTLE NM
Roy Rogers & Dale Dbl R Bar Ranch	Steel box, blue or red band, woodgrain tall bottle	1954	90	40
Roy Rogers & Dale Dbl R Bar Ranch	Steel eight scene box, red or blue band, matching bottle	1955	60	40
Roy Rogers & Dale Evans	Steel cowhide back box, red or blue band, matching bottle	1955	80	40
Roy Rogers & Dale on Rail	Steel box, red or blue band, matching bottle	1957	90	40
Satellite	Steel box, matching bottle	1958	75	25
Toppie Elephant	Steel box, yellow, matching bottle	1957	1550	750
Wee Pals Kid Power	Steel box with matching plastic bottle	1974	20	5

Cheinco

NAME	DESCRIPTION	YEAR	BOX NM	BOTTLE NM
Donald Duck	Steel box, no bottle made	1980	15	0

Continental Can

NAME	DESCRIPTION	YEAR	BOX NM	BOTTLE NM
Joe Palooka	Steel box, no bottle	1949	30	0

General Steel Ware, Canada

NAME	DESCRIPTION	YEAR	BOX NM	BOTTLE NM
Sleeping Beauty	Steel box, generic steel bottle	1960	450	55

Holtemp

NAME	DESCRIPTION	YEAR	BOX NM	BOTTLE NM
Davy Crockett	Steel with matching steel bottle	1955	100	40

King Seeley Thermos

NAME	DESCRIPTION	YEAR	BOX NM	BOTTLE NM
A-Team, The	Steel box, plastic bottle	1985	10	3
Addams Family	Steel box with matching plastic bottle	1974	80	10
Americana	Steel box, steel/glass bottle	1958	325	125
Apple's Way	Steel box, plastic bottle	1975	75	5
Astronaut Dome	Steel dome box, steel/glass bottle	1960	125	35
Atom Ant/Secret Squirrel	Steel box with matching steel bottle	1966	200	50
Auto Race	Steel box with matching steel bottle	1967	50	25
Barbie Lunch Kit	Tall steel/glass bottle, vinyl lunch box	1962	150	40
Battle Kit	Steel box with matching steel thermos	1965	75	30
Battle of the Planets	Steel box with matching plastic bottle	1979	40	10
Bee Gees	Steel Barry back box, matching plastic bottle	1978	30	10
Bee Gees	Steel Maurice back box with matching plastic bottle	1978	40	5
Bee Gees	Steel Robin back box, matching plastic bottle	1978	40	5
Blondie	Steel box with matching steel bottle	1969	100	35
Bobby Sherman	Steel box with matching steel bottle	1972	55	25
Brady Brunch	Steel box with matching steel bottle	1970	150	60
Cabbage Patch Kids	Steel box with matching plastic thermos	1984	12	2
Campus Queen	Steel box with matching steel thermos	1967	35	15
Chan Clan, The	Steel box, plastic bottle	1973	85	15
Chitty Chitty Bang Bang	Steel box with matching steel bottle	1969	45	25
Circus Wagon	Steel dome box, steel/glass bottle	1958	300	110
Clash of the Titans	Steel box with matching plastic bottle	1981	30	8
Close Encounters of the Third Kind	Steel box, plastic bottle	1978	80	5
Cowboy in Africa, Chuck Connors	Steel box with matching steel thermos	1968	190	35
Curiosity Shop	Steel box with matching steel bottle	1972	45	20
Dark Crystal	Steel box with matching plastic bottle	1982	10	3
Dutch Cottage	Steel dome box, steel/glass bottle	1958	650	150
Dyno Mutt	Steel box, plastic bottle	1977	45	7
Exciting World of Metrics, The	Steel box, plastic bottle	1976	25	5
Family Affair	Steel box with matching steel bottle	1969	60	30

LUNCH BOXES

Steel

NAME	DESCRIPTION	YEAR	BOX NM	BOTTLE NM
Fat Albert and the Cosby Kids	Steel box, plastic bottle	1973	25	6
Fess Parker	Steel box with matching steel bottle	1965	140	35
Fireball XL5	Steel box, steel/glass bottle	1964	140	45
Flipper	Steel box with matching steel bottle	1966	125	50
Fonz, The	Steel box, plastic bottle	1978	25	4
Fraggle Rock	Steel box with matching plastic bottle	1984	15	5
Fritos	Steel box, generic bottle	1975	85	3
Funtastic World of Hanna Barbera	Steel box, Flintstones & Yogi, plastic bottle	1978	25	5
Funtastic World of Hanna Barbera	Steel box, Huck Hound, plastic bottle	1977	25	5
G.I. Joe	Steel box, plastic bottle	1982	12	3
G.I. Joe	Steel box, steel/glass bottle	1967	75	40
Get Smart!	Steel box, steel/glass bottle	1966	165	40
Goober and the Ghostchasers	Steel box with matching plastic bottle	1974	35	8
Green Hornet	Steel box with matching steel bottle	1967	275	95
Guns of Will Sonnett, The	Steel box, steel/glass bottle	1968	85	40
Hair Bear Bunch, The	Steel box, plastic bottle	1972	35	10
Hardy Boys Mysteries	Steel box with matching plastic bottle	1977	30	5
Harlem Globetrotters	Steel box with matching steel bottle in either blue or purple uniforms	1971	45	35
Hee Haw	Steel box with matching steel bottle	1971	65	20
Home Town Airport Dome	Steel dome box, steel/glass bottle	1960	1100	150
Hong Kong Phooey	Steel box, steel/glass bottle	1975	25	15
Hot Wheels	Steel box with matching steel bottle	1969	60	20
How the West Was Won	Steel box with matching plastic bottle	1979	35	5
Indiana Jones	Steel box with matching plastic bottle	1984	15	5
Indiana Jones Temple of Doom	Steel box with matching plastic bottle	1984	15	5
Julia	Steel box with matching steel bottle	1969	65	30
King Kong	Steel box, plastic bottle	1977	29	6
KISS	Steel box, plastic bottle	1977	65	8
Knight Rider	Steel box with matching plastic bottle	1984	20	5
Korg	Steel box, matching plastic bottle	1975	30	5
Kung Fu	Steel box with matching plastic bottle	1974	50	8
Lance Link, Secret Chimp	Steel box with matching steel bottle	1971	75	30
Lawman	Steel box, generic bottle	1961	80	25
Little House on the Prairie	Steel box with matching plastic bottle	1978	50	10
Looney Tunes TV Set	Steel box, steel/glass bottle	1959	135	60
Lost in Space Dome	Steel dome box, steel/glass bottle	1967	550	40
Magic of Lassie	Steel box with matching plastic bottle	1978	35	10
Major League Baseball	Steel box, matching bottle	1968	60	20
Man from U.N.C.L.E.	Steel box with matching steel bottle	1966	140	35
Mr. Merlin	Steel box with matching plastic bottle	1982	20	5
Munsters	Steel box with matching steel bottle	1965	160	60
Muppet Babies	Steel box with matching plastic bottle	1985	12	5
Muppet Movie	Steel box, plastic bottle	1979	30	6
Muppet Show	Steel box, plastic bottle	1978	16	6
Muppets	Steel box, back shows Animal, Fozzie or Kermit, matching plastic bottle	1979	20	5
Nancy Drew	Steel box, plastic bottle	1978	20	5
NFL	Steel box , blue rim, matching plastic bottle	1978	20	5
NFL	Steel box , red rim, matching plastic bottle	1976	20	5
NFL	Steel box, yellow rim, plastic bottle	1975	20	10
Orbit	Steel box with matching steel bottle	1963	150	35
Partridge Family	Steel box, plastic or steel bottle	1971	45	30
Peanuts	Red steel 'pitching' box, plastic bottle	1976	25	5
Peanuts	Steel 'pitching' box, yellow face, green band, matching bottle	1980	20	5
Peanuts	Steel box, orange rim, matching steel bottle	1966	35	15
Peanuts	Steel red rim 'psychiatric' box, plastic bottle	1973	35	5

Steel

NAME	DESCRIPTION	YEAR	BOX NM	BOTTLE NM
Pele	Steel box with matching plastic bottle	1975	40	8
Pets'n Pals	Steel box with matching steel bottle	1961	55	20
Pigs In Space	Steel box with matching plastic bottle	1977	20	5
Pink Gingham	Steel box with matching plastic bottle	1976	25	4
Pink Panther & Sons	Steel box with matching plastic bottle	1984	20	4
Play Ball	Steel box, game on back, steel bottle	1969	60	25
Polly Pal	Steel box with matching plastic bottle	1975	10	4
Popeye	Steel 'Popeye in boat' box with matching steel bottle	1964	100	30
Porky's Lunch Wagon	Steel dome box, steel/glass bottle	1959	350	65
Racing Wheels	Steel box, plastic bottle	1977	50	5
Rambo	Steel box with matching plastic bottle	1985	8	3
Red Barn Dome	Steel dome box, closed door version, plain Holtemp bottle	1957	50	20
Red Barn Dome	Steel dome box, open open door version, matching steel bottle	1958	35	20
Road Runner	Steel box, lavender or purple rim, steel or plastic bottle	1970	50	25
Roy Rogers & Dale Dbl R Bar Ranch	Steel box, steel/glass bottle	1953	80	40
Roy Rogers Chow Wagon Dome	Steel dome box, steel/glass bottle	1958	165	45
Saddlebag	Steel box, generic plastic bottle	1977	60	5
Satellite	Steel bottle	1960	110	35
Scooby Doo	Steel box, yellow or orange rim, plastic bottle	1973	30	5
Secret Agent T	Steel box, matching bottle	1968	70	30
Smurfs	Steel blue box, plastic bottle	1983	110	5
Snoopy Dome	Steel dome, yellow, "Have Lunch With Snoopy", matching bottle	1968	35	5
Space Shuttle Orbiter Enterprise	Steel box, plastic bottle	1977	45	10
Space: 1999	Steel box, plastic bottle	1976	45	10
Speed Buggy	Steel box, red rim, plastic bottle	1974	100	35
Star Trek, The Motion Picture	Steel box, matching bottle	1980	50	10
Star Wars	Steel box, cast or stars on band, matching plastic bottle	1978	40	5
Star Wars Return of the Jedi	Steel box, plastic bottle	1983	40	10
Star Wars, Empire Strikes Back	Steel box, plastic bottle	1980	40	10
Stars and Stripes Dome	Steel dome box, matching plastic bottle	1970	50	11
Submarine	Steel box, steel/glass bottle	1960	75	30
Superman	Steel box, red rim, 'under fire' art on back, matching steel/glass bottle	1967	75	50
Teenager	Steel box, generic bottle	1957	70	25
Teenager Dome	Steel dome box, generic bottle	1957	120	10
Trigger	Steel box, no bottle	1956	130	
UFO	Steel box, plastic bottle	1973	90	10
Wagon Train	Steel box, generic bottle	1964	100	30
Wags 'n Whiskers	Steel box, matching plastic bottle	1978	18	4
Western	Steel box, tan or red rim, steel/glass bottle	1963	80	45
Yankee Doodles	Steel box, plastic bottle	1975	15	2
Yellow Submarine	Steel box, steel/glass bottle	1968	250	150

Kruger

NAME	DESCRIPTION	YEAR	BOX NM	BOTTLE NM
Davy Crockett	Steel box, no bottle made	1955	350	0

Ohio Art

NAME	DESCRIPTION	YEAR	BOX NM	BOTTLE NM
Airline	Steel box, no bottle made	1969	60	0

Steel

NAME	DESCRIPTION	YEAR	BOX NM	BOTTLE NM
Animal Friends	Steel, either yellow or red background behind name	1978	25	0
Basketweave	Steel box, no bottle made	1968	45	0
Bond XX	Steel box, no bottle	1967	150	0
Bond-XX Secret Agent	Steel box, no bottle made	1966	200	0
Canadian Pacific Railroad	Steel box, no bottle	1970	12	0
Captain Astro	Steel box, no bottle made	1966	210	0
Children's	Steel box, no bottle made	1984	10	0
Color Me Happy	Steel box, no bottle made	1984	90	0
Early West Oregon	Steel box, no bottle	1982	25	0
Early West Pony Express	Steel box, no bottle	1982	25	0
Floral	Steel box, no bottle made	1970	12	0
Frontier Days	Steel box, no bottle	1957	210	0
Frost Flowers	Steel box, no bottle	1962	60	0
Fruit Basket	Steel box, no bottle made	1975	15	0
Ghostland	Steel box with spinner game, no bottle	1977	35	0
Hansel and Gretel	Steel box, no bottle	1982	55	0
Highway Signs	Steel box, no bottle	1972	50	0
Indian Territory	Steel box, plastic bottle	1982	20	
Jack and Jill	Steel box	1982	400	0
Little Red Riding Hood	Steel box, no bottle made	1982	25	0
Luggage Plaid	Steel box, no bottle	1957	75	22
My Lunch	Steel box, no bottle	1976	30	
Oregon Trail	Steel box, plastic bottle	1982	20	5
Para-Medic	Steel box, no bottle	1978	45	0
Patriotic	Steel box, no bottle made	1974	45	0
Pennant	Steel basket type box, no bottle	1950	30	0
Pit Stop	Steel box, generic bottle	1968	225	25
Pony Express	Steel box	1982	19	
Pro Sports	Steel box, no bottle made	1974	50	0
School Days, Disney Characters	Steel box, no bottle made	1960	115	0
See America	Steel box, no bottle made	1972	35	0
Snow White, with Game	Steel box, no bottle	1980	35	0
Sport Skwirts	All four sports box	1982	35	0
Sport Skwirts, Jimmy Blooper	Steel box, no bottle	1982	25	0
Sport Skwirts-Freddie Face Off	Steel box, no bottle	1982	25	0
Sport Skwirts-Willie Dribble	Steel box, no bottle	1982	25	0
Sports Afield	Steel box, no bottle made	1957	130	0
Tapestry	Steel box, no bottle	1963	60	0
Three Little Pigs	Steel box, red rim, generic/plastic bottle	1982	45	0
Train	Steel box, no bottle made	1971	25	0
Traveler	Steel box, no bottle made	1962	40	0
Wild Frontier	Steel box, spinner game on back, no bottle	1977	30	0

Okay

NAME	DESCRIPTION	YEAR	BOX NM	BOTTLE NM
Campbell Kids	Steel box matching steel thermos	1973	120	140
NFL	Steel box, black rim, steel/glass bottle	1972	110	125

Okay Industries

NAME	DESCRIPTION	YEAR	BOX NM	BOTTLE NM
Action Jackson	Steel box, matching steel bottle	1973	600	200
Boston Bruins	Steel box, steel/glass bottle	1973	350	125
Children, Blue	Steel box with matching steel bottle	1974	160	30
Children, Yellow	Steel box with matching steel bottle	1974	210	30
Mod Floral	Steel box with matching steel bottle	1975	225	150
NHL	Steel box, plastic bottle	1970	525	225
Smokey Bear	Steel box, plastic bottle	1975	225	200
Track King	Matching steel bottle	1975	225	125

Steel

NAME	DESCRIPTION	YEAR	BOX NM	BOTTLE NM
Underdog	Steel box, plastic bottle	1974	800	300
Wake Up America	Steel box, matching steel bottle	1973	600	250
Washington Redskins	Steel box, steel bottle	1970	200	120

Omni Graphics

NAME	DESCRIPTION	YEAR	BOX NM	BOTTLE NM
VW Bus Dome	Steel dome box, plastic bottle	1960	450	80

Thermos

NAME	DESCRIPTION	YEAR	BOX NM	BOTTLE NM
Red Barn Dome, Cutie	Steel box with matching steel/glass bottle	1972	25	15

Universal

NAME	DESCRIPTION	YEAR	BOX NM	BOTTLE NM
All American	Steel box, steel/glass bottle	1954	350	65
Bullwinkle & Rocky	Steel blue box with matching steel bottle	1962	450	220
Carnival	Steel box with matching steel bottle	1959	425	210
Cartoon Zoo Lunch Chest	Steel box, steel/glass bottle	1962	300	125
Casey Jones	Steel dome box, steel/glass bottle	1960	650	150
Dudley Do-Right	Steel box with matching steel bottle	1962	550	225
Flag-O-Rama	Steel box, steel/glass bottle	1954	400	80
Gene Autry	Steel box, steel/glass bottle	1954	325	150
Great Wild West	Steel box with matching steel bottle	1959	350	130
Knight in Armor	Steel box with matching steel bottle	1959	425	150
Little Dutch Miss	Steel box with matching steel bottle	1959	110	60
Pathfinder	Steel box with matching steel bottle	1959	375	125
Popeye	Steel 'Popeye socks Bluto' box, matching bottle	1962	450	200
Supercar	Steel box, steel/glass bottle	1962	250	125
Superman	Steel box, blue rim	1954	800	
U.S. Space Corps	Steel box, plastic bottle	1961	350	95

Unknown

NAME	DESCRIPTION	YEAR	BOX NM	BOTTLE NM
Pinocchio	Square	1938	150	0
Pinocchio	Steel round tin with handle	1938	200	0
Space Ship	Decoware, dark blue square	1950	250	0

Vinyl

Abeama Industries

NAME	DESCRIPTION	YEAR	BOX NM	BOTTLE NM
Boy on the Swing	Vinyl, brown		100	0

Adco Liberty

NAME	DESCRIPTION	YEAR	BOX NM	BOTTLE NM
Barnum's Animals	Vinyl box, no bottle	1978	50	0

Air Flite

NAME	DESCRIPTION	YEAR	BOX NM	BOTTLE NM
Beatles, The	Vinyl box, no bottle made	1965	500	0

Aladdin

NAME	DESCRIPTION	YEAR	BOX NM	BOTTLE NM
Alice in Wonderland	Vinyl with matching plastic bottle	1972	160	15
All Star	Vinyl	1960	500	30
Annie 1	Vinyl box with matching plastic bottle	1981	50	15
Ballerina	Vinyl box, pink, steel/glass bottle	1962	110	40
Barbarino Brunch Bag	Zippered vinyl bag, plastic bottle	1977	70	8
Beatles Brunch Bag	Vinyl zipper bag, matching bottle	1966	400	100

Vinyl

NAME	DESCRIPTION	YEAR	BOX NM	BOTTLE NM
Blue Gingham Brunch Bag	Zippered vinyl box and plastic bottle	1975	25	5
Bobby Soxer	Vinyl	1959	400	0
Calico Brunch Bag	Zippered vinyl bag, plastic bottle	1980	25	5
Carousel	Vinyl box, matching steel/glass bottle	1962	500	30
Charlie's Angels Brunch Bag	Vinyl zipper bag, plastic bottle	1978	70	10
Coca-Cola	Vinyl box, styrofoam bottle	1947	135	10
Combo Brunch Bag	Zippered vinyl bag, steel/glass bottle	1967	825	55
Dawn	Vinyl box with matching plastic bottle	1972	125	15
Dawn	Vinyl with matching plastic bottle	1971	125	15
Dawn Brunch Bag	Vinyl zippered bag, plastic bottle	1971	60	10
Denim Brunch Bag	Zippered vinyl bag, plastic bottle	1980	30	5
Donny & Marie	Vinyl box, long hair version, matching plastic bottle	1977	75	10
Donny & Marie	Vinyl box, short hair version, with matching plastic bottle	1978	95	20
Donny & Marie Brunch Bag	Vinyl zipper bag, plastic bottle	1977	60	10
Dr. Seuss	Vinyl box, plastic bottle	1970	350	15
Fess Parker Kaboodle Kit	Vinyl box, matching steel bottle	1960s	450	35
Frog Flutist	Vinyl box with matching plastic bottle	1975	65	10
Gigi	Vinyl box with matching steel/glass bottle	1962	175	35
Glamour Gal	Vinyl box, steel/glass bottle	1960	220	35
Go-Go Brunch Bag	Vinyl box, plastic bottle	1966	130	10
Holly Hobbie	Vinyl white bag, matching plastic bottle	1972	40	5
Ice Cream Cone	Vinyl with matching plastic bottle	1975	50	10
It's a Small World	Vinyl with matching steel/glass bottle	1968	175	40
Jonathan Livingston Seagull	Vinyl with matching plastic bottle	1974	135	10
Junior Deb	Vinyl box, steel/glass bottle	1960	170	35
Kaboodle Kit	Vinyl box, pink or white, no bottle	1960s	200	0
Kewtie Pie	Vinyl box, steel/glass bottle		75	30
Kodak Gold	Vinyl	1970s	35	15
Kodak II	Vinyl	1970s	35	15
Linus the Lion-Hearted	Vinyl box, steel/glass bottle	1965	400	80
Love	Vinyl with matching plastic bottle	1972	125	15
Mam'zelle	Vinyl box, plastic bottle	1971	150	10
Mardi-gras	Vinyl box with matching plastic bottle	1971	55	10
Mary Ann	Vinyl box with matching steel/glass bottle	1960	70	20
Mary Poppins	Vinyl box with matching plastic bottle	1973	135	25
Mary Poppins Brunch Bag	Vinyl bag, steel/glass bottle	1966	150	50
Mod Miss Brunch Bag	Vinyl box, plastic bottle	1969	50	10
Mushrooms	Vinyl box with matching plastic bottle	1972	70	20
New Zoo Review	Vinyl box, plastic bottle	1975	300	30
Pac-Man (Puffy)	Vinyl	1985	20	0
Peter Pan	Vinyl white box, matching plastic bottle	1969	175	25
Pink Panther	Vinyl box with matching plastic bottle	1980	65	10
Princess	Vinyl box, steel/glass bottle	1963	135	50
Psychedelic (yellow)	Vinyl box with matching steel/glass bottle	1969	125	45
Pussycats, The	Vinyl box, plastic bottle	1968	150	10
Sabrina	Vinyl yellow box with matching plastic bottle	1972	190	15
Sesame Street	Vinyl box, orange, matching plastic bottle	1979	35	10
Sesame Street	Vinyl box, yellow, matching plastic bottle	1981	35	5
Shari Lewis	Vinyl box with matching steel/glass bottle	1963	300	50
Sleeping Beauty, Disney	Vinyl white box, matching plastic bottle	1970	175	25
Snow White	Vinyl white box with matching plastic bottle	1975	170	15
Stewardess	Vinyl box, steel/glass bottle	1962	495	35
Strawberry Shortcake	Vinyl box with matching plastic bottle	1980	35	5
Tammy	Vinyl box with matching steel/glass bottle	1964	190	35
Tammy & Pepper	Vinyl box with matching steel/glass bottle	1965	190	35
Tinkerbell, Disney	Vinyl box, plastic bottle	1969	255	35
Twiggy	Vinyl box with matching steel/glass bottle	1967	200	45
U.S. Mail Brunch Bag	Zippered vinyl bag, plastic bottle	1971	200	10

Vinyl

NAME	DESCRIPTION	YEAR	BOX NM	BOTTLE NM
Winnie the Pooh	Vinyl box, steel/glass bottle		500	45
Wonder Woman (blue)	Vinyl box with matching plastic bottle	1977	100	10
Wonder Woman (yellow)	Vinyl box with matching plastic bottle	1978	100	10
Wrangler	Vinyl box, steel/glass bottle	1982	50	40
Ziggy's Munch Box	Vinyl box, plastic bottle	1979	90	10

American Thermos

NAME	DESCRIPTION	YEAR	BOX NM	BOTTLE NM
Lunch 'n Munch	Vinyl box with corsage bottle	1959	500	35

Ardee

NAME	DESCRIPTION	YEAR	BOX NM	BOTTLE NM
Ballerina	Vinyl box, black, Thermax bottle	1960s	700	20
Boston Red Sox	Vinyl box	1960s	50	0
Cars	Vinyl	1960	135	0
Cowboy	Vinyl box, plain "syro" plastic bottle	1960	170	10
Fishing	Vinyl box with styrofoam bottle	1970	120	10
Girl & Poodle	Vinyl box with styrofoam bottle	1960	120	10
Goat Butt Mountain	Vinyl box, plain "styro" plastic bottle	1960	150	10
I Love a Parade	Vinyl box, plain "styro" plastic bottle	1970	50	10
Lassie	Vinyl box with styrofoam bottle	1960s	120	10
Moon Landing	Vinyl box, styro bottle	1960	140	10

Avon

NAME	DESCRIPTION	YEAR	BOX NM	BOTTLE NM
Highway Signs Snap Pack	Vinyl	1988	40	0

Babcock

NAME	DESCRIPTION	YEAR	BOX NM	BOTTLE NM
Challenger, Space Shuttle	Vinyl puffy box, no bottle	1986	245	0
L'il Jodie (Puffy)	Vinyl	1985	45	0

Bayville

NAME	DESCRIPTION	YEAR	BOX NM	BOTTLE NM
All American	Vinyl box with styrofoam bottle	1976	115	10
All Dressed Up	Vinyl lunch box with styrofoam bottle	1970s	90	10
Buick 1910	Vinyl box with styrofoam bottle	1974	135	10
Happy Powwow	Vinyl box, red or blue, with styrofoam bottle	1970s	60	10
Little Ballerina	Vinyl box with styrofoam bottle	1975	70	10

Dart

NAME	DESCRIPTION	YEAR	BOX NM	BOTTLE NM
Little Old Schoolhouse	Vinyl	1974	45	0
Mr. Peanut Snap Pack	Vinyl snap close bag, no bottle	1979	55	0

Feldco

NAME	DESCRIPTION	YEAR	BOX NM	BOTTLE NM
Dream Boat	Vinyl box with styrofoam bottle	1960	400	10

Gary

NAME	DESCRIPTION	YEAR	BOX NM	BOTTLE NM
Coco the Clown	Vinyl box with styrofoam bottle	1970s	95	10
Pebbles & Bamm-Bamm	Vinyl box with matching plastic bottle	1973	175	20
Penelope & Penny	Vinyl yellow box with styrofoam btl.	1970s	70	10

Hasbro

NAME	DESCRIPTION	YEAR	BOX NM	BOTTLE NM
Dateline Lunch Kit	Vinyl box in blue/pink, no bottle made	1960	240	0

King Seeley Thermos

NAME	DESCRIPTION	YEAR	BOX NM	BOTTLE NM
Alvin & Chipmunks	Vinyl lunch box/matching plastic bottle	1963	325	90

Vinyl

NAME	DESCRIPTION	YEAR	BOX NM	BOTTLE NM
Banana Splits	Vinyl with matching steel/glass bottle	1969	330	50
Barbie & Francie	Black vinyl, matching steel/glass bottle	1965	90	35
Barbie & Midge	Vinyl, black, with matching steel/glass bottle	1965	95	35
Barbie & Midge Dome	Vinyl with matching glass/steel bottle	1964	250	40
Barbie Softy	Vinyl, pink, plastic bottle is unmatched	1988	6	2
Barbie, World of	Vinyl, blue box, matching steel/glass bottle	1971	45	5
Barbie, World of	Vinyl, pink box, matching steel/glass bottle	1971	45	5
Beany & Cecil	Vinyl box, steel/glass bottle	1963	375	75
Betsey Clark Munchies Bag	Vinyl zipper bag, plastic bottle	1977	25	7
Betsy Clark	Vinyl yellow box with matching plastic bottle	1977	25	5
Bullwinkle	Blue vinyl box, steel/glass bottle	1963	525	100
Bullwinkle	Vinyl box, yellow, generic steel bottle	1963	450	40
Captain Kangaroo	Vinyl box, steel/glass bottle		290	45
Casper the Friendly Ghost	Vinyl blue box, orange steel thermos	1966	350	55
Corsage	Vinyl box, steel/glass bottle	1970	130	20
Cottage	Vinyl	1974	70	0
Deputy Dawg	Vinyl box, steel/glass bottle		125	45
Eats 'n Treats	Blue vinyl box, steel/glass bottle		300	20
G.I. Joe	Vinyl with generic plastic bottle	1989	12	2
Junior Nurse	Vinyl box, steel/glass bottle	1963	220	50
Liddle Kiddles	Vinyl box with matching steel/glass bottle	1969	180	45
Lunch'n Munch	Vinyl box, steel/glass bottle	1959	55	25
Monkees	Vinyl box with matching steel/glass bottle	1967	325	65
Peanuts	Vinyl green 'baseball' box, steel bottle	1971	80	20
Peanuts	Vinyl red 'baseball' box, steel bottle	1969	80	20
Peanuts	Vinyl red 'kite' box, steel/glass bottle	1967	80	20
Peanuts	Vinyl white 'piano' box, steel bottle	1973	60	20
Pony Tail	Vinyl white box, fold over lid, steel/glass bottle	1965	240	35
Pony Tail Tid-Bit-Kit	Vinyl box with steel/glass satellite bottle	1962	255	40
Ponytails Poodle Kit	Vinyl box, steel/glass bottle	1960	200	20
Ringling Bros. Circus	Vinyl orange box with matching steel/glass bottle	1970	325	45
Ringling Bros. Circus	Vinyl puffy blue box, steel/glass bottle	1971	95	40
Roy Rogers Saddlebag, Brown	Vinyl box with steel/glass bottle	1960	200	45
Roy Rogers Saddlebag, Cream	Vinyl box, steel/glass bottle	1960	400	40
Sizzlers, Hotwheels	Vinyl box with matching steel/glass bottle	1971	175	35
Skipper	Vinyl box, steel/glass bottle	1965	175	35
Smokey the Bear	Vinyl box, steel/glass bottle	1965	325	45
Snoopy Munchies Bag	Vinyl box, plastic bottle	1977	70	8
Snoopy, Softy	Vinyl with matching plastic bottle	1988	12	2
Soupy Sales	Vinyl blue box, no bottle made	1966	600	0
Twiggy	Vinyl box, steel/glass bottle	1967	125	65
Yosemite Sam	Vinyl box with matching steel/glass bottle	1971	350	55

Prepac

NAME	DESCRIPTION	YEAR	BOX NM	BOTTLE NM
Junior Miss Safari	Vinyl box, no bottle	1962	135	0

Standard Plastic Products

NAME	DESCRIPTION	YEAR	BOX NM	BOTTLE NM
Beatles Kaboodles Kit, The	Vinyl box, no bottle made	1965	600	0

Thermos

NAME	DESCRIPTION	YEAR	BOX NM	BOTTLE NM
Deputy Dawg	Vinyl box, no bottle	1964	500	0
Pony Tail with Gray Border	Vinyl white box, original art with gray border added,no bottle	1960s	200	0

Vinyl

NAME	DESCRIPTION	YEAR	BOX NM	BOTTLE NM
Universal				
Ballet	Vinyl box, red, plastic generic bottle	1961	1000	20
Mary Ann Lunch 'N Bag	Vinyl bag, no bottle made	1960	100	0
Sports Kit	Vinyl box	1960	700	20
Unknown				
Fun to See'n Keep Tiger	Vinyl box, no bottle made	1960	250	0
Little Kiddles	Vinyl		70	0
Robo Warriors	Vinyl box, no bottle made	1970	35	0
Snow White, Disney	Vinyl fold over lid tapered box, no bottle	1967	250	0
Spirit of '76	Vinyl, red		100	0
Volkwein Bros., Inc.				
Bach's Lunch	Vinyl box, red, with styrofoam bottle	1975	145	10

PEZ

Christmas

NAME	DESCRIPTION	NM	MINT
Angel A*	No feet, hair and halo	15	35
Rudolph	No feet, brown deer head, red nose	15	35
Santa Claus A	No feet, ivory head with painted hat	80	150
Santa Claus B	No feet, small head with flesh painted face, black eyes, red hat	85	195
Santa Claus C	No feet, large head with white beard, flesh face, red open mouth and hat	1	10
Santa Claus C	With feet, removable red hat, white beard	1	3
Snowman	No feet, black hat, white face, removable black facial features	3	15
Snowman A	No feet, black hat, white head, removable facial features	5	25

Circus

NAME	DESCRIPTION	NM	MINT
Big Top Elephant With Hair*	No feet, yellow head and red hair	125	225
Big Top Elephant, Flat Hat*	No feet, gray-green head, red flat hat	35	60
Big Top Elephant, Pointed Hat*	No feet, orange head with blue pointed hat	35	75
Clown with Chin*	No feet, long chin clown face with hat and hair	25	45
Clown with Collar	No feet, yellow collar, red hair, clown face and green hat	15	40
Giraffe	No feet, orange head with horns, black eyes	40	75
Gorilla	No feet, black head with red eyes and white teeth	15	40
Lion with Crown	No feet, black mane, green head with yellow cheeks and red crown	40	70
Little Lion	No feet, yellow head with brown mane	15	35
Monkey Sailor	No feet, cream face, brown hair, white sailor cap	20	45
Monkey with Baseball Cap*	No feet, monkey head and ball cap, white eyes	35	75
Pony-Go-Round	No feet, orange head, white harness, blue hair	25	60

FOOD-RELATED

Crazy Fruit

NAME	DESCRIPTION	NM	MINT
Orange	No feet, orange head with face and leaves on top	65	145
Pear	No feet, yellow pear face, green visor	500	800
Pineapple	No feet, pineapple head with greenery and sunglasses	600	900

Die Cuts

NAME	DESCRIPTION	NM	MINT
Bozo the Clown	Die cut Bozo and Butch on stem, no feet, white face, red hair and nose	75	125
Casper The Friendly Ghost		100	145
Donald Duck		100	175
Easter Bunny Die Cut	No feet, die cut	400	550
Mickey Mouse Die Cut	No feet, die-cut stem with Minnie, die cut face mask	75	120

Disney

NAME	DESCRIPTION	NM	MINT
Baloo*	With feet, blue head	10	35
Baloo*	No feet, blue head	15	30
Bambi	With feet,	5	25
Bouncer Beagle		5	25

Disney

NAME	DESCRIPTION	NM	MINT
Captain Hook	No feet, black hair, flesh face winking with right eye open	20	45
Chip (Chip & Dale)*	No feet, black top hat, tan head with white cheeks, brown nose, foreign issue	15	65
Dalmation Pup	With feet, white head with left ear cocked, foreign issue	15	35
Dewey	No feet, blue hat, white head, yellow beak, small black eyes	5	25
Donald Duck A	No feet, blue hat, one-piece head and bill, open mouth	5	15
Donald Duck B	With feet, blue hat, white head and hair with large eyes, removable beak	1	3
Dopey	No feet, flesh colored die cut face with wide ears, orange cap	100	200
Duck Child	No feet, blue or green hat, yellow beak, small eyes	10	25
Dumbo*	With feet, blue head with large ears, yellow hat	15	60
Dumbo*	No feet, gray head with large ears, red hat	35	65
Goofy A*	No feet, red hat, painted nose, removable white teeth	5	50
Goofy B*	Same as version A except teeth are part of head	25	50
Goofy D	With feet, beige snout, green hat	1	3
Gyro Gearloose		5	25
Huey	No feet, red hat, white head, yellow beak, small black eyes	5	25
Huey, Dewey or Louie Duck	With feet, red, blue, or green stem and matching cap, white head and orange beak	10	20
Jiminy Cricket	No feet, green hatband and collar, flesh face, black top hat	30	65
King Louie	No feet, brown hair and 'sideburns' over light brown head	15	35
King Louie	With feet, brown hair and 'sideburns' over light brown head	10	25
Li'l Bad Wolf	No feet, black ears, white face, red tongue	15	25
Li'l Bad Wolf	With feet, black ears, white face, red tongue	12	25
Louie	No feet, green hat, white head, yellow beak, small black eyes	5	25
Mary Poppins	No feet, flesh face, reddish hair, lavender hat	350	500
Mickey Mouse A	No feet, black head and ears, pink face, mask with cut out eyes and mouth, nose pokes through mask	40	60
Mickey Mouse B	No feet, painted face, non-painted black eyes and mouth	50	100
Mickey Mouse C	No feet, flesh face, removable nose, painted eyes	5	15
Mickey Mouse D	No feet, flesh face mask embossed white and black eyes	3	15
Mickey Mouse E	With feet, flesh face, bulging black and white eyes, oval nose	1	3
Mowgli	No feet, black hair over amber-brown head	15	35
Mowgli	With feet, black hair over amber-brown head	2	25
Peter Pan	No feet, green hat, flesh face, orange hair	80	160
Pinocchio A*	No feet, red or yellow cap, pink face, black painted hair	75	125
Pinocchio B	No feet, black hair, red hat	45	85
Pluto A	No feet, yellow head, long black ears, small painted eyes	5	20
Pluto C	With feet, yellow head, long painted black ears, large white and black decal eyes	1	5
Practical Pig A	No feet, blue hat, pointed up ears, small cheeks, round nose	10	35
Practical Pig B	No feet, blue hat, large cheeks, half nose	10	35
Practical Pig C	With feet, blue hat, large cheeks, half round nose	5	15
Scrooge McDuck A	No feet, white head, yellow beak, black top hat and glasses, white sideburns	10	25
Scrooge McDuck B	With feet, white head, removable yellow beak, tall black top hat and glasses, large eyes	5	20

Disney

NAME	DESCRIPTION	NM	MINT
Snow White*	No feet, flesh face, black hair with ribbon and matching collar	75	125
Thumper	No feet, orange face	40	75
Tinkerbell	No feet, pale pink stem, white hair, flesh face with blue and white eyes	75	150
Winnie the Pooh	With feet, yellow head	10	45
Zorro	No feet, flesh face, black mask and hat	20	50

Easter

NAME	DESCRIPTION	NM	MINT
Bunny 1990	With feet, long ears, white face	1	3
Bunny Original A	No feet, narrow head and tall ears	300	425
Bunny Original B	No feet, tall ears and full face, smiling buck teeth	300	425
Bunny W/Fat Ears	No feet, wide ear version	1	15
Chick in Egg, No Hat*	No feet, yellow chick in egg shell, no hat	75	150
Chick in Egg, With Hat*	No feet, yellow chick in egg shell, red hat	5	20
Duckie with Flower*	No feet, flower, duck head with beak	25	55
Lamb	No feet, white head with a pink bow	3	10
Rooster*	No feet, head, comb, and wattle	15	40

Eerie Spectres

NAME	DESCRIPTION	NM	MINT
Air Spirit	No feet, reddish triangular fish face	25	45
Diabolic	No feet, soft orange monster head with black and red tints	25	45
Scarewolf	No feet, soft head with orange painted hair, and ears	25	55
Vamp	No feet, light gray head on black collar, green tinted hair and face, red teeth	35	55
Zombie	No feet, burgundy and black soft head	25	55

Full Bodied

NAME	DESCRIPTION	NM	MINT
Santa, Full Bodied	Full body stem with painted Santa suit and hat	110	150
Space Trooper*	Robotic figure with backpack	150	225

Halloween

NAME	DESCRIPTION	NM	MINT
Dr. Skull A	No feet, black cowl, white head	5	15
Dr. Skull B	With feet, black collar	1	5
Jack O Lantern*	No feet, orange stem, carved face	3	15
Mr. Ugly*	No feet, black hair, green head, red eyes and buck teeth	15	60
Mr. Ugly*	No feet, black hair, yellow face, red eyes and buck teeth	45	125
Octopus*	No feet, black, orange or red head	25	60
One-Eyed Monster*	No feet, gorilla head with one eye missing	25	80
Witch 1 Piece*	No feet, black stem with witch embossed on stem, orange 1 piece head	100	165
Witch 3 Piece A	With feet, red head and hair, green mask, black hat	1	5
Witch 3 Piece B*	No feet, chartruse face, black hair, orange hat	35	80

Humans

NAME	DESCRIPTION	NM	MINT
Astronaut A*	No feet, helmet, yellow visor, small head	135	250
Astronaut B	No feet, green stem, white helmet, yellow visor, large head	60	100

Humans

NAME	DESCRIPTION	NM	MINT
Betsy Ross	No feet, dark hair and white hat, Bicentennial issue	40	80
Captain (Paul Revere)	No feet, blue hat, Bicentennial issue	45	85
Cowboy	No feet, human head, brown hat	200	400
Daniel Boone	No feet, light brown hair under dark brown hat, Bicentennial issue	85	150
Football Player	No feet, white stem, red helmet with white stripe	45	125
Indian Brave*	No feet, small human head, indian headband with one feather, Bicentennial issue	100	200
Indian Chief*	No feet, warbonnet, Bicentennial issue	50	85
Indian Squaw	No feet, black hair in braids with headband	45	85
Pilgrim	No feet, pilgrim hat, blond hair, hat band	85	125
Pilot	No feet, blue hat, grey headphones	45	95
Spaceman	No feet, clear helmet over flesh-color head	75	125
Stewardess	No feet, light blue flight cap, blond hair	45	100
Uncle Sam	No feet, stars and stripes on hat band, white hair and beard, Bicentennial issue	50	100
Wounded Soldier	Bicentennial Series, no feet, white bandage, brown hair	80	150

Kooky Zoo

NAME	DESCRIPTION	NM	MINT
Cockatoo*	No feet, yellow beak and green head, red head feathers	25	60
Cow A*	No feet, cow head, separate nose	20	45
Cow B	No feet, blue head, separate snout, horns, ears and eyes	65	125
Crocodile	No feet, green head with red eyes	45	100
Panda A*	No feet, yellow head with black eyes and ears	125	200
Panda A*	No feet, white head with black eyes and ears	5	15
Panda B*	With feet, white head with black eyes and ears	1	3
Panther	No feet, blue head with pink nose	45	65
Puzzy Cat*	No feet, cat head with hat	25	50
Raven*	No feet, black head, beak, and glasses	20	35
Yappy Dog*	No feet, black floppy ears and nose, green or orange head	35	85

Licenced Characters

NAME	DESCRIPTION	NM	MINT
Garfield With Teeth	With feet, orange head, wide painted toothy grin	5-25	18
Arlene	With feet, pink head, Garfield's 'girlfriend'	5	15
Asterix	No feet, blue hat with wings, yellow mustache, European	250	350
Brutus	No feet, black beard and hair	85	150
Bullwinkle	No feet, brown head, yellow antlers	150	200
Casper The Friendly Ghost	No feet, white face	50	80
Fozzie Bear	With feet, brown head, bow tie, small brown hat	1	5
Garfield	With feet, orange head	1	3
Garfield With Visor	With feet, orange face, green visor	1	8
Gonzo	With feet, blue head, yellow eyelids bow tie	1	3
Green Hornet	No feet, green mask and hat	150	300
Kermit	With feet, green head	1	5
Little Orphan Annie	No feet, light brown hair, flesh face with black painted features	40	65
Miss Piggy	With feet, pink face, yellow hair	1	5

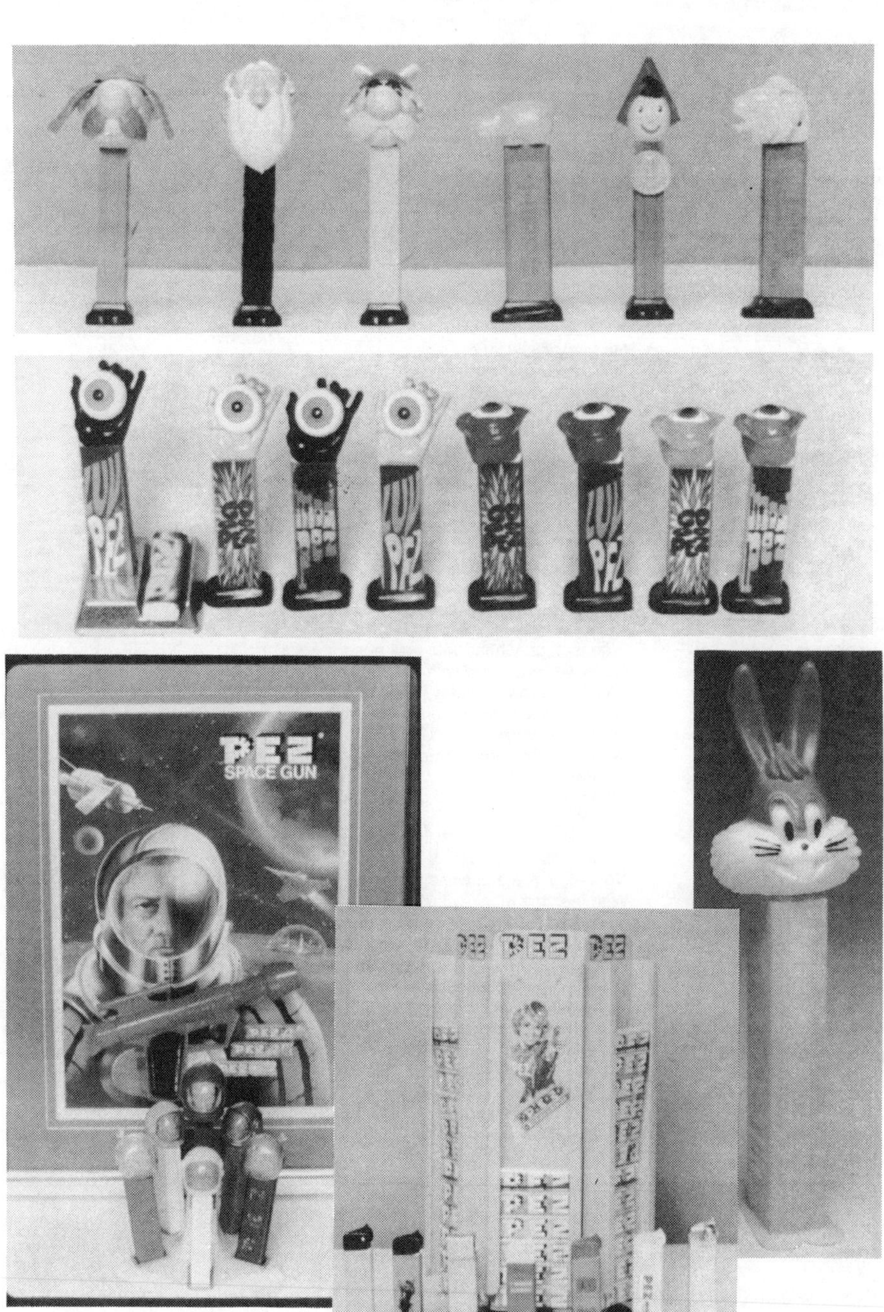

Top to Bottom: PEZ dispensers; Obelix, Mueslix, Asterix, Hippo, Sparefroh, 1962 Lions Club; Psychedelic Eye and Psychedelic Flower variations; Space Gun and display and Astronaut variations; Bugs Bunny with feet; PEZ store display with various Regular dispensers including Witch Regular (2nd from left) and Arithmetic (4th from left).

Licensed Characters

NAME	DESCRIPTION	NM	MINT
Mueslix	No feet, white beard, moustache and eyebrows,European	850	1200
Nermal	With feet, gray stem and head	5	20
Obelix	No feet, red mustache and hair, blue hat, European	250	400
Olive Oyl	No feet, black hair and flesh painted face	95	150
Papa Smurf	With feet, red hat, white beard, blue face	3	15
Peter PEZ	No feet, blue top hat that says PEZ, white face, yellow hair	65	100
Popeye A	No feet, yellow face, painted hat	45	95
Popeye B	No feet, removable white sailor cap	20	35
Popeye C	No feet, one eye painted, removeable pipe and cap	35	75
Smurf	No feet, blue face, white hat	3	15
Smurf	With feet, red hat	25	60
Smurfette	With feet, blue face, yellow hair, white hat	3	15

Merry Music Makers

NAME	DESCRIPTION	NM	MINT
Camel	With feet, brown face with red fez hat	15	25
Clown	With feet, green hat, with a clown face, foreign issue	5	20
Dog	No feet, orange dog face with black ears, foreign issue	10	25
Donkey	With feet, gray head with pink nose	10	25
Duck	No feet, brown head with yellow beak	10	25
Duck	With feet, brown head with yellow beak	10	18
Frog	No feet, yellow and green head with black eyes, foreign issue	25	40
Frog	With feet, yellow and green head with black eyes, foreign issue	12	25
Indian	With feet, black hair and green headband with feather, foreign issue	5	15
Koala	With feet, brown head with a black nose, foreign issue	15	40
Lamb	No feet, pink stem, white head	10	25
Monkey	With feet, tan monkey face in brown head, foreign issue	10	25
Panda	With feet, white head, foreign issue	6	15
Parrot	With feet, red hair, yellow beak and green eyes	5	25
Penguin	With feet, penguin head with yellow beak and red hat, foreign issue	5	25
Pig	With feet, pink pig head	20	40
Rhino	With feet, green head, red horn, foreign issue	15	35
Rooster	No feet, head, comb	10	25
Rooster	With feet, head, comb	5	20
Tiger	With feet, tiger head with white snout	5	15

MGM

NAME	DESCRIPTION	NM	MINT
Barney Bear	No feet, brown head, white cheeks and snout, black nose	15	35
Barney Bear	With feet, brown head, white chheks and snout, black nose	15	35
Droopy Dog	No feet, white face, flesh snout, black ears and red hair	5	25
Jerry (Tom & Jerry)	No feet, brown face, pink lining in ears	20	40
Jerry (Tom & Jerry)	With feet, brown face, pink lining in ears	10	25
Spike	With feet, brown face, pink snout	5	25
Tike	With feet, brown head	10	25
Tom A (Tom & Jerry)	No feet, gray cat head with painted black features	20	35
Tom B (Tom & Jerry)	With feet, gray cat head with removable facial features	5	20
Tyke	With feet, brown face	5	15

Miscellaneous

NAME	DESCRIPTION	NM	MINT
Arithmetic*	No feet, headless dispenser with white top, side of body has openings with columns of numbers	150	400
Baseball Dispenser Set	No feet, baseball glove with ball, white homeplate marked "PEZ" and bat	300	325
Baseball Glove	No feet, brown baseball glove with white ball	150	250
Candy Shooter	Black PEZ Gun with PEZ monogram on stock	100	200
Candy Shooter	Red body, white grip, with German license and Doppel (Double) PEZ candy	100	150
Make-A-Face	No feet, oversized head with 18 different facial parts	750	1500
Personalized (Regular)	No feet, no head, stem with label for monograming, and top	150	225
Psychedelic Eye*	No feet, decal design on stem, beige hand with green eye	250	450
Psychedelic Flower*	No feet, stem with decal on side, green eye in flower center	300	500
Regular*	No feet, no head, stem with top only	100	225
Space Gun 1950s*	Various color bodies in red, dark blue, black, maroon, green, yellow, silver or light blue, with white triggers, butts	150	225
Space Gun 1980s*	Red space gun with black handgrips, on blister pack	50	125
Whistles*	Stems with police whistles on top	1	25
Zorro with Logo	No feet, zorro mask and black hat, says Zorro on stem	75	125

Olympics

NAME	DESCRIPTION	NM	MINT
Alpine	No feet, green hat with beige plume, black mustache	350	600
Vucko Wolf with Bobsled Hat*	1984 Yugoslavia Olympics issue, with feet, gray or brown face with bobsled helmet	200	500
Vucko Wolf with Ski Hat*	1984 Yugoslavia Olympics issue, with feet, grtay or brown face with ski hat	200	500
Vucko Wolf*	1984 Yugoslavia Olympics issue, with feet, gray or brown face	200	500
Winter Olympics Snowman	1976 Innsbruck, red nose and hat, white head with arms extended, black eyes, blue smile	250	400

Peanuts

NAME	DESCRIPTION	NM	MINT
Snoopy	With feet, with white head and black ears	1	3
Charlie Brown	With feet, crooked smile, blue cap	1	5
Charlie Brown W/Tongue	With feet, blue cap, smile with red tongue at corner	15	25
Charlie Brown, Eyes Closed	With feet, blue cap	20	50
Lucy	With feet, black hair,	1	5
Woodstock	With feet, yellow head	1	3

PEZ Pals

NAME	DESCRIPTION	NM	MINT
Boy with Cap*	No feet, white hair, blue cap	15	40
Boy*	No feet, brown hair	3	15
Bride*	No feet, white veil, light brown, blond or red hair	450	800
Doctor	No feet, white hair and mustache, gray reflector on white band, black stethoscope	35	55
Engineer	No feet, blue hat	30	50
Fireman	No feet, black mustache, red hat with gray #1 insignia	25	35
Girl*	No feet, blond pigtails	5	20
Girl*	With feet, pigtails	1	15
Groom	No feet, black top hat, white bow tie	100	300
Knight*	No feet, gray helmet with plume	80	145
Maharajah	No feet, green turban with red inset	25	40

PEZ Pals

NAME	DESCRIPTION	NM	MINT
Mexican	No feet, yellow sombrero, black beard and mustache combination	20	45
Nurse*	No feet, girl's hair, white nurse's cap	40	65
Pirate	No feet, red cap, patch over right eye	30	45
Policeman	No feet, blue hat with gray badge	15	40
Ringmaster	No feet, white bow tie, white hat with red hatband, and black handlebar moustache	65	130
Sailor	No feet, blue hat, white beard	75	100
Sheik*	No feet, white head drape, headband	25	55
Sheriff	No feet, brown hat with badge	50	95
Cocoa Marsh Spaceman	No feet, clear helmet on small male head, with Cocoa Marsh embossed on side	85	150
Donkey Kong Jr.	No feet, blond monkey face, dark hair, white cap with J on it	275	500
Golden Glow	No feet, no head, gold stem and top	125	250
Hippo	No feet, green stem with" Hippo" inprinted on side, hippo on top, foreign issue	400	500
Lions Club Lion	No feet, stem imprinted Lions Club Inter'l Convention writing, yellow roaring lion head	400	900
Sparefroh (foreign issue)	No feet, green stem, red triangle hat, coin glued on stem	175	300
Stand By Me	dispenser packed with mini poster of film	125	275

Superheroes

NAME	DESCRIPTION	NM	MINT
Batgirl	Soft Head Superhero, no feet,blue mask, black hair	45	115
Batman	Soft head Superhero, no feet, blue mask	65	115
Batman	With feet	1	5
Batman with Cape	No feet, blue cape, mask and hat	65	150
Batman*	No feet, blue hat and black face mask	1	15
Captain America*	No feet, blue cowl, black mask with white letter A	30	70
Hulk A	No feet, dark green head, black hair	15	35
Hulk B	No feet, light green head, dark green hair	5	15
Hulk B	With feet, light green head, tall dark green hair	1	5
Joker	Soft Head Superhero, no feet, green painted hair	60	100
Penguin	Soft Head Superhero, no feet, yellow top hat, black painted monocle	45	100
Spider-Man A	No feet, red head with black eyes	5	15
Spider-Man B	With feet, bigger red head	1	5
Thor	No feet, yellow hair, gray winged helmet	75	150
Wonder Woman	Soft Head Superhero, no feet, black hair and yellow band with star	40	80
Wonder Woman	With feet, red stem	1	5
Wonder Woman*	No feet, black hair and yellow band with red star	1	5

Trucks

NAME	DESCRIPTION	NM	MINT
Truck A*	Cab, stem body, single rear axle	35	100
Truck B*	Cab, stem body, dual rear axle and dual arch fenders	25	65
Truck C*	Cab, stem body, dual rear wheels with single arch fender, movable wheels	1	15
Truck D*	Cab, stem body, dual rear wheels, single arch fender, nonmovable wheels	1	5

Universal Monsters

NAME	DESCRIPTION	NM	MINT
Creature From Black Lagoon	No feet, green head and matching stem	150	250

Universal Monsters

NAME	DESCRIPTION	NM	MINT
Frankenstein	No feet, black hair, gray head	150	250
Wolfman	No feet, black stem, gray head	150	250

Warner Brothers

NAME	DESCRIPTION	NM	MINT
Foghorn Leghorn	No feet, brown head, yellow beak, red wattle	25	45
Bugs Bunny*	No feet, dark gray head with white cheeks	1	20
Bugs Bunny*	With feet, gray head with white cheeks	1	5
Cool Cat	With feet, orange head, blue snout, black ears	10	30
Daffy Duck A	No feet, black head, yellow beak, removable white eyes	1	15
Daffy Duck B	With feet, black head, yellow beak	1	5
Foghorn Leghorn	With feet, brown head, yellow beak, red wattle	10	15
Henry Hawk	No feet, light brown head, yellow beak	15	35
Merlin Mouse	No feet, gray head with flesh cheeks, green hat	10	35
Merlin Mouse	With feet, gray head with flesh cheeks, green hat	10	35
Petunia Pig	No feet, black hair in pig tails	30	60
Roadrunner A	No feet, purple head, yellow beak	15	30
Roadrunner B	With feet, purple head, yellow beak	10	25
Speedy Gonzales	No feet, brown head, yellow sombrero	5	25
Speedy Gonzales	With feet, greenish head, yellow sombrero	5	25
Sylvester	No feet, black head, white whiskers, red nose	5	10
Sylvester	With feet, black head, white whiskers, red nose	1	5
Tweety Bird	No feet, yellow head	1	15
Tweety Bird	With feet, yellow head	1	3
Wile E. Coyote	No feet, brown head	5	25
Wile E. Coyote	With feet, brown head	5	25

FAST FOOD

Kids' Meals Premiums

NAME	DESCRIPTION	YEAR	EX (loose)	MIP
	Arby's			
Babar at the Beach Summer Sippers	Set of three squeezie bottles; orange, yellow or purple top	1991	2@	Didn't come packaged
Babar Figures	Set of four; Babar with sunglasses, elephant with binoculars, Babar with monkey, and with camera	1990	1@	2@
Babar License Plates	Set of four: Paris, Brazil, USA, North Pole	1990	1@	2@
Babar Puzzles	Set of four; Cousin Arthur's New Camera, Babar's Gondola Ride, Babar and the Haunted Castle, Babar's Trip to Greece	1990	2.50@	4@
Babar Stampers	Set of three; Babar, Flora, Arthur	1990	1@	2@
Babar Storybooks	Set of three; Read Get Ready, Set, Go, Calendar-Read and Have Fun-Read and Grow and Grow	1991	1.50@	2.75@
Babar World Tour Vehicles	Set of three vehicles; Babar in helicopter, Arthur on trike, Zephyr in car	1990	2@	3@
Little Miss Figures	Set of seven; Giggles, Shy, Splendid, Late, Naughty, Star, Sunshine	1981	2@	4.25@
Looney Tunes Car-Tunes	Set of six, Sylvester's Cat-illac, Daffy's Dragster, Yosemite Sam's Rackin Frackin Wagon, Taz' Slush Musher, Bugs' Buggy, Roadrunner's Racer	1990	2@	3@
Looney Tunes Characters	Set of three, Tazmanian Devil as pilot, Daffy as student, Sylvester as fireman	1991	2@	3.50@
Looney Tunes Christmas Ornament	Bugs, Porky Pig		3@	6@
Looney Tunes Figures	Bugs, Daffy, Taz, Elmer, Roadrunner, and Wile E. Coyote	1988	2@	4@
Looney Tunes Figures	Stiff legged figures; Elmer, Roadrunner, Bugs, Daffy, Coyote, Taz	1988	2@	4@
Looney Tunes Figures	Figures on oval base, Tasmanian Devil, Tweetie, Porky, Bugs, Yosemite Sam, Sylvester, Pepe Le Pew	1987	2.50@	4@
Looney Tunes Pencil Toppers	Sylvester, Yosemite, Porky, Bugs, Taz, Daffy, Tweety	1988	1@	3@
Mr. Men Figures	Set of 12; Bump, Clever, Daydream, Funny, Greedy, Grumpy, Happy, Lazy, Noisy, Rush, Strong, Tickle	1981	2@	4.25@
	Big Boy			
Helicopters	Set of plastic vehicles; Ambulance, Police, Fire Department	1991		4@
Monster In My Pocket	Various secret monster packs	1991	2@	4@
	Burger King			
Adventure Kits	Set of four activity kits with crayons; Passport, African Adventure, European Escapades, Worldwide Treasure Hunt	1991	1.35@	2.50@
Aladdin	Set of five figures; Jafar and Iago, Genie in Lamp, Jasmine and Rajah, Abu, Aladdin and the Magic Carpet	1992	2@	4@
Alf	Joke & riddle disc, door knob card, sand mold, refrigerator magnet	1987	1@	2@
Alf Puppets	Puppets with records; Sporting with Alf, Cooking with Alf, Born to Rock, Surfing with Alf	1987	2.50@	5@ No package but w/tags

Kids' Meals Premiums

NAME	DESCRIPTION	YEAR	EX (loose)	MIP
Alvin and the Chipmunks	Set of three toys; super ball, stickers, pencil topper	1987	1@	2@
Animal Boxes	Set of four activity booklets; bear, hippo, lion, one more	1986	1@	2@
Aquaman Tub Toy	Green		2.50	5
Archie Cars	Set of four, Archie in red car, Betty in aqua car, Jughead in green car, Veronica in purple car	1991	2@	4@
Barnyard Commandos	Set of four; Major Legger Mutton in boat, Sgt. Shoat & Sweet in plane, Sgt. Wooley Pullover in sub, Pvt. Side O'Bacon in truck	1991	1@	2@
Batman Toothbrush Holder			2	4
Beauty & the Beast PVC Figures	Set of four PVC figures; Belle, Beast, Chip, Cogsworth	1991	2@	4@
Beetlejuice	Set of six figures; Uneasy Chair, Head Over Heels, Ghost to Ghost TV, Charmer, Ghost Post, Peek A Boo Doo	1990	1@	2@
Bicycle License Plate			1	3
Bicycle Safety Fun Booklet			2	4
BK Kids Action Figures	Set of four; Boomer, I.Q., Jaws, Kid Vid	1991	2@	4@
Bone Age Skeleton Kit	Set of four dinos; T-Rex, Dimetron, Mastadon, Similodon	1989	2@	4@
Bone Age Skeleton Kit Boxes	The Past is a Blast, The Greatest Mystery in History	1989	1@	2@
Burger King Clubhouse	Full size for kids to play in		15	35
Burger King Socks	Rhinestone accents		2	5
Calendar "20 Magical Years" Walt Disney World		1992	2	4
Capitol Critters	Set of four; Hemmet for Prez in White House, Max at Jefferson Memorial, Muggle at Lincoln Memorial, Presidential Cat	1992	2@	3@
Capitol Critters Cartons	Punch out masks; dog, chicken, duck, panda, rabbit, tiger, turtle	1992	1@	2@
Captain Planet	Set of 4 flip over vehicles; Captain Planet & Hoggish Greedily, Linka, Ma-Ti & Dr. Blight ecomobile, Verminous Skumm & Kwane helicopter, Wheeler and Duke Nukem snowmobile	1991	1@	2@
Captain Planet Cartons	Containers; Powerbase Spaceship, Biodread Patroller Spaceship, Powerjet XT-7	1991	1.50@	3@
Christmas Cassette Tapes	Set of three Christmas sing-a-long tapes; Joy to the World/ Silent Night, We Three Kings/ O Holy Night, Deck the Halls/ Night Before Christmas	1989	1@	2@
Christmas Crayola Bear Plush Toys	Red, yellow, blue or purple	1986	2@	4@
Coloring Book	Keep Your World Beautiful		2	4
Crayola Coloring Books	Set of six books; Boomer's Color Chase, I.Q.'s Computer Code, Kids Club Poster, Jaws' Colorful Clue, Snaps' Photo Power, Kid Vid's Video Vision	1990	1.75@	3.50@
Dino Meals	Punch-out sheets; Stegosaurus, Woolly Mammoth, T-Rex, Triceratops	1987	3@	6@
Disney 20th Anniversary Figures	Set of four wind up vehicles with connecting track; Minnie, Donald, Roger Rabbit, Mickey	1992	2.50@	6@
Fairy Tale Cassette Tapes	Set of four fairy tale cassettes; Goldilocks, Jack in the Beanstalk, Three Little Pigs, Hansel and Gretel	1989	1.25@	2.50@
Freaky Fellas	Set of four, blue, green, red, yellow, each with a roll of Life Savers candy	1992	1@	3@

Top to Bottom: Beauty and the Beast, 1991, Burger King; The Land Before Time, 1988, Pizza Hut; Teenage Mutant Ninja Turtles bicycle horn, Burger King; Noids, 1987, Domino's Pizza; Definitely Dinosaurs bead game, 1989, Wendy's; BK Kids Water Club Mates, 1991, Burger King; Babar World Tour Vehicles, Arby's, 1990.

Kids' Meals Premiums

NAME	DESCRIPTION	YEAR	EX (loose)	MIP
Go-Go Gadget Gizmos	Set of four Inspector Gadget toys; gray copter, black inflatable, orange scuba, green surfer	1991	2@	4@
Golden Junior Classic Books	Set of four; Roundabout Train, The Circus Train, Train to Timbucktoo, My Little Book of Trains		1@	2@
Goof Troop Bowlers	Set of four; Goofy, Max, Pete, P.J.	1992	1@	2@
It's Magic	Set of four; Magic Trunk, Disappearing Food, Magic Frame, Remote Control	1992	1@	2@
Kid Transformers	Set of six; Bloomer w/Super Show, Kid Vid w/ SEGA Gamestar, I.Q. w/World Book Mobile, Snaps w/Camera Car, Jaws w/ Burger Racer and Wheels w/Turbo Wheelchair	1990	2@	4@
Lickety Splits	Plastic wheeled food items, Apple Pie Man, Flame Broiler Buggy, Drink Man, French Fry Man, Croissant Man, Chicken Tenders, French Toast Man	1990	1@	2@
Masters of the Universe Cups	Thunder Punch He-Man Saves the Day, He-Man and Roboto to the Rescue, He-Man Takes on the Evil Horde, Skeletor	1985	1@	2@
Matchbox Boxes (Buildings)	Punch-out buildings; apartment, fire station, engine and firemen, restaurant, barn horse whirl and wheel game	1989	1.50@	3@
Matchbox Cars	Set of four vehicles; blue Mountain Man 4X4, yellow Corvette, red Ferrari, Black & white police car	1989	3@	6@
Mealbots	Paper masks with 3-D lenses, red Broil Master, blue Winter Wizard, gray Beta Burger, yellow Galactic Guardians	1986	3.75@	7.50@
Nerfuls	Rubber characters, interchangeable, set of four, Bitsy Ball, Fetch, Officer Bob, Scratch	1985	2@	4@
Pilot Paks	Set of four styrofoam airplanes; two seater, sunburst, lightning, one more	1988	4@	8@
Pinocchio	Set of five toys, pail and following inflatables, Beach ball, Figaro, Jiminy Cricket, Monstro	1992	1@	2@
Purrtenders	Set of four plush toys; Hop-purr, Flop-purr, Scamp-purr, Romp-purr	1988	2@	4@
Purrtenders	Set of four; Free Wheeling Cheese Rider, Flip-Top Car, Radio Bank, Storybook	1988	1.50@	3@
Record Breakers	Set of six cars; Aero, Indy, Dominator, Accelerator, Fastland, Shockwave	1989	3@	6@
Rodney & Friends, Reindeer	Plush toys with holiday fun booklets; Ramona Holiday Sweets and Treats, Rodney Holiday Fun and Games Box, Rhonda Holiday decorating box	1987	4@	8@
Sea Creatures	Terrycloth wash mitts; Stella Starfish, Dolly Dolphin, Sammy Seahorse, Ozzie Octopus	1989	1.50@	3@
Simpsons	Set of five figures, Bart with backpack, Homer with skunk, Lisa with sax, Maggie with turtle, Marge with birds	1991	1@	2@
Simpsons Cups	Set of four	1991	1@	2@
Simpsons Dolls	Set of five soft plastic dolls; Bart, Homer, Lisa, Marge, Maggie	1991	2@	4@
Spacebase Racers	Set of five plastic vehicles; Moon Man Rover, Skylab Cruiser, Starship Viking, Super Shuttle, Cosmic Copter	1989	2@	4@

Top to Bottom: Flintstones Fun Squirters, 1991, Denny's; Barnyard Commandos, 1991, Burger King; The Simpsons Dolls, 1991, Burger King; Fender Bender 500 Racers, 1990, Hardee's; Water Blasters, 1990, Long John Silver's; California Raisins, 1988, Hardee's.

NAME	DESCRIPTION	YEAR	EX (loose)	MIP
Super Heroes Cups	Set of five cups with figural handles; Batman, Robin, Wonder Woman, Darkseid, Superman	1984	2.50@	5@
Teenage Mutant Ninja Turtles Badges	Six different, Michaelanglo, Leonardo, Raphael, Donatello, Heroes In a Half Shell, Shredder	1990	1@	2@
Thundercats	Set of four toys; cup/bank, Snarf strawholder, light switch plate, secret message ring	1986	3@	6@
Top Kids	Set of four spinning tops with figural heads; Wheels , Kid Vid, two more	1992	2@	3@
Tricky Treaters Boxes	Monster Manor, Creepy Castle, Haunted House	1989	1.25@	2.50@
Tricky Treaters PVC Figures	Set of three; Frankie Steen, Gourdy Goblin, Zelda Zoom Broom	1989	3@	6@
Water Club Mates	Set of four; Lingo's Jet Ski, Snaps in Boat, Wheels on raft, I.Q. on dolphin	1991	2@	4@
Chucky E Cheese Pizza				
Chucky E Cheese PVC Figures		1980s	3@	5@
Dairy Queen				
Suction Cup Throwers	Set of four		2@	3.75@
Denny's				
Dino-Makers	Set of six, including blue dino, purple elephant, orange bird	1991	2@	3@
Flintstones Dino Racers	Set of six: Fred, Bam-Bam, Dino, Pebbles, Barney, Wilma	1991	2@	4@
Flintstones Fun Squirters	Set of six; Fred w/telephone, Wilma w/ camera, Dino w/flowers, Bam Bam w/ soda, Barney, Pebbles	1991	1@	2@
Flintstones Glacier Gliders	Set of six; Bam Bam, Barney, Fred, Dino, Hoppy, Pebbles	1990	1@	2@
Flintstones Mini Plush	In packages of 2: Fred/Wilma, Betty/Barney, Dino/Hoppy, Pebbles/Bamm Bamm, each 4" tall	1989	2@	4@
Flintstones Rock & Rollers	Set of six: Fred w/guitar, Barney w/sax, Bam Bam, Dino w/piano, Elephant, Pebbles	1990	2@	4@
Flintstones Stone-Age Cruisers	Set of six: Fred in green car, Wilma in red car, Dino in blue car, Pebbles in purple bird, Bam Bam in orange car, Barney in yellow car w/sidecar	1991	2@	4@
Flintstones Vehicles	Set of eight: Fred, Barney, Pebbles, Wilma, Betty, Bamm Bamm, Dino	1990	2@	4@
Jetsons Game Packs	Set of six: George, Elroy, Judy, Astro, Rosie, Jane	1992	1@	2@
Jetsons Go Back to School	Set of six school tools: mini dictionary, folder, message board, pencil & topper, pencil box, triangle & curve	1992	1@	2@
Jetsons Puzzle Ornaments	Set of twelve: six shapes in two colors each green/clear or purple/clear	1992	.50@	1@
Jetsons Space Balls (Planets)	Set of six: Jupiter, Neptune, Earth, Saturn, Mars, glow-in-the-dark Moon	1992	3@	4@
Jetsons Space Cards	Set of five: Spacecraft, Phenomenon, Astronomers, Constellations, Planets	1992	1@	2@
Jetsons Space Travel Coloring Books	Set of six books: each with four crayons	1992	.75@	1.50@

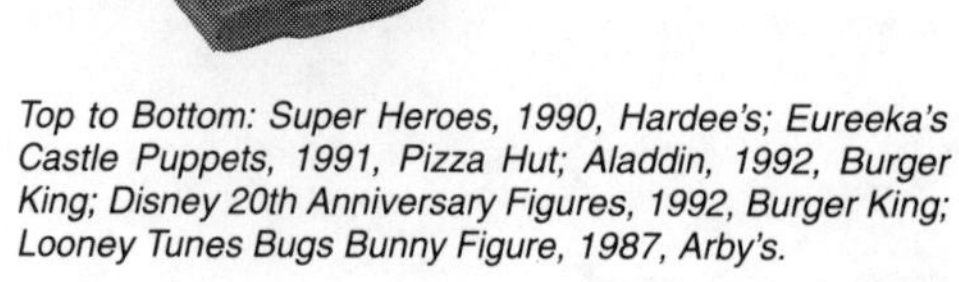

Top to Bottom: Super Heroes, 1990, Hardee's; Eureeka's Castle Puppets, 1991, Pizza Hut; Aladdin, 1992, Burger King; Disney 20th Anniversary Figures, 1992, Burger King; Looney Tunes Bugs Bunny Figure, 1987, Arby's.

NAME	DESCRIPTION	YEAR	EX (loose)	MIP
Domino's Pizza				
Noids	Set of seven figures: Boxer, Clown, He Man, Holding Bomb, Holding Jack Hammer, Hunchback, Magician	1987	1@	2@
Quarterback Challenge Cards	Pack of four cards	1991	.50@	1@
Hardee's				
California Raisins	Third set, of four; Alotta Stile in pink boots, Anita Break w/package under her arm, Benny bowling, Buster w/skateboard	1991	2@	3@
California Raisins	First set, of four; dancer w/blue & white shoes, singer w/mike, sax player, fourth with sunglasses	1987	3@	6@
California Raisins	Second set, of six; w/guitar in orange sneakers, on rollerskates w/yellow sneakers, with radio w/ yellow sneakers, surfer w/red sneakers, trumpet player w/ blue sneakers	1988	3@	5@
California Raisins Plush	Set of four, each 6" tall; lady in yellow shoes, dancer in yellow hat, with mike in white shoes, in sunglasses w/orange hat	1988	3@	6@
Days of Thunder Racers	Set of four cars: Mello Yellow #51, Hardee's #18 orange, City Chevy #46, Superflo in pink/white	1990	2@	4@
Disney's Animated Classics Plush Toys	Pinocchio, Bambi		2.50@	5@
Ertl Camaro	Marked Hardee's Roadrunner	1990	3	6
Fender Bender 500 Racers	Set of five: Quickdraw/Babalouie's Covered Wagon, Huckleberry/Snagglepuss's truck, Wally Gator/Magilla's Toilet, Dick Dastardly/Mutley's rocket racer, Yogi/ Booboo's basket	1990	2@	4@
Finger Crayons	Set of four: not marked Hardee's		1.50@	3@
Flintstones First 30 Years	Set of five: Fred w/TV, Barney w/grill, Pebbles w/phone, Dino w/jukebox, Bam Bam w/ pinball	1991	1.25@	2.50@
Food Squirters	Set of four: chesseburger, hot dog, shake, fries	1990	1@	2@
Gremlin Adventures	Set of five book and record sets: Gift of the Mogwai, Gismo & the Gremlins, Escape from the Gremlins, Gremlins Trapped, The Late Gremlin	1989	2@	4@
Halloween Hideaways	Set of four: Goblin in blue caldron, ghost in yellow bag, cat in pumpkin, bat in stump	1989	2@	4@
Home Alone 2	Set of four	1992	1@	2@
Kazoo Crew Sailors	Set of four: brown bear, monkey, rabbit, rhino	1991	1@	2@
Little Golden Books	Set of four: The Little Red Caboose, The Three Bears, Old MacDonald Had a Farm, Three Little Kittens		1@	2@
Pound Puppies	Set of six: white w/black spots, black, brown, gray w/brown spots, gray w/black ears, tan w/black ears	1991	1.50@	3@
Shirt Tales Plush Dolls	Set of five, each 7" tall: Bogey, Pammy, Tyg, Digger, Rick		2@	4@
Smurfin' Smurfs	Set of four surfers: Papa w/red board, boy w/ orange board, girl w/purple board, dog w/ blue board	1990	1.50@	3@
Smurfs Box	Smurf Solution, Smurf Angle, Smurf Surprise, Stop & Smurf the Flowers	1990	1@	2@

NAME	DESCRIPTION	YEAR	EX (loose)	MIP
Super Heroes	Marvel figures in vehicles; She Hulk, Hulk, Captain America, Spider-Man	1990	3@	6@
Tang Mouth Figures	Set of four: Lance, Tag, Flap, Annie	1989	2@	4@
Waldo's Straw Buddies	Set of four: Waldo, Girl, Wizard	1990	1.50@	3@
Waldo's Travel Adventure	Complete set of four		1.50@	3@
International House of Pancakes				
Pancake Kid Refrigerator Magnets	Chocolate Chip Charlie and Bonnie Blueberry		3@	6@
Pancake Kids	Set of six		2@	4@
Pancake Kids	Set of eight	1992	2@	4@
Pancake Kids Stuffed Figures	Chocolate Chip Charlie and Bonnie Blueberry			5@
Jack-In-The-Box				
Jack Pack Puzzle Books	Set of three		3@	6@
Magnets	Set of three		1.50@	3@
Scratch and Sniff	Pineapple/lilac			3
Kentucky Fried Chicken				
Alvin and the Chipmunks	Canadian issues; Alvin and Theodore	1991	2.50@	5@
Alvin and the Chipmunks	Canadian issues; Alvin and Simon	1992	2@	4@
Long John Silver's				
Adventure on Volcano Island	Paint with water activity book	1991	2	4
Fish Cars	Red and yellow cars shaped like fish, w/ stickers	1989	1.50@	3@
Sea Walkers	Set of four packaged with string; Parrot, Penguin, Turtle and Sylvia	1990	2.50@	5@
Sea Walkers	Set of four packaged w/o string; Parrot, Penguin, Turtle and Sylvia	1990	2.50@	5@
Sea Watchers Kaleidoscopes	Set of three: orange, yellow, pink	1991	2.50@	5@
Treasure Trolls		1992		3@
Water Blasters	Set of three: Billy Bones, Captain Flint, Ophelia Octopus	1990	2.50@	5@
Pizza Hut				
Beauty & the Beast Puppets	Set of four: Belle, Beast, Chip, Cogsworth	1992	3@	5@
Eureeka's Castle Puppets	Set of three: Batly, Eureeka, Magellan	1991	2@	4@
Land Before Time Puppets	Set of six: Spike, Sharptooth, Petri, Little Foot, Cera, Ducky	1988	2@	4@
Rax				
Optic Top	Spinning optic top		3	6
Sipper	Yellow		2	4
Roy Rogers				
Critters	Set of eight: blue eyes-yellow, blue eyes-orange, blue eyes-purple, blue eyes-red, yellow eyes-orange, yellow eyes-yellow, pink eyes, orange, pink eyes-purple		1@	2@
Gator Tales	Set of four		1@	2@
Gumby	Gumby, blue girl		4	8
Ickky Stickky Bugs	Set of sixteen		1.50@	3@
Skateboard Kids (figurines)	Yellow knee pads, orange knee pads, purple knee pads, red knee pads		2.50@	5@

NAME	DESCRIPTION	YEAR	EX (loose)	MIP
Star Searchers	Saucer w/green top and orange pilot, sled w/ orange top and purple bottom, sled w/ purple top and orange bottom, sled w/ green top and orange bottom, robot w/ orange head, green front		1.50@	3@
Sonic Drive In				
Paper Bag Man	Set of two (?); Marbles, Bookworm	1989	2@	4@
Taco Bell				
Happy Talk Sprites	Yellow Spark, white Twink		2@	4@
Hugga Bunch Plush Dolls				4@
Wendy's				
Alf Tales	Set of six: Sleeping Alf, Alf Hood, Little Red Riding Alf, Alf of Arabia, Three Little Pigs, Sir Gordon of Melmac	1990	2@	5@
Alien Mix-Ups	Set of six: red Crimsonoid, blue Blueziod, green Limetoid, orange Spotasoid, yellow Yellowboid, Purple Purpapoid	1990	2@	4@
All Dogs Go To Heaven	Set of six: Anne Marie, Car Face, Charlie, Flo, Itchy, King Gator	1989	2@	4@
Definitely Dinosaurs	Set of four: blue Apatosaurus, gray T-Rex, yellow Anatosaurus, green Triceratops	1988	2@	4@
Definitely Dinosaurs	Set of five: green Ankylosaurus, blue Parasaurolophus, green Ceratosaurus, yellow Stegosaurus, pink Apatosaurus	1989	2@	4@
Fast Food Racers	Set of five: hamburger, fries, shake, salad, kid's meal	1990	3@	5@
Furskins Plush dolls	Set of three, 7" tall: Boone in plaid shirt and red pants, Farrell in plaid shirt and blue jeans, Hattie in pink and white dress	1988	2@	4@
Glass Hangers	Yellow turtle, yellow frog, yellow penguin and purple gator		2.50@	5@
Glo Friends	Set of 12 (?); Book Bug, Bop Bug, Butterfly, Clutter Bug, Cricket, Doodle Bug, Globug, Granny Bug, Skunk Bug, Snail Bug, Snug Bug	1988	1@	2@
Good Stuff Gang	Cool Stuff, Cat, Hot Stuff, Overstuffed, Bear, Penguin	1985	4@	8@
Jetsons	Set of six figures in spaceships: George, Judy, Jane, Elroy, Astro, Spacely	1989	3.50@	6@
Jetsons, The Movie, Space Gliders	Set of six PVC figures on wheeled bases; Astro, Elroy, Judy, Fergie, Grunchee, George	1990	2@	4@
Micro Machines Super Sky Carriers	Set of six kits that connect to form Super Sky Carrier	1990		5@
Mighty Mouse	Set of six: Bat Bat, Cow, Mighty Mouse, Pearl Pureheart, Petey, Scrappy	1989	2.50@	5@
Play-Doh Fingles	Set of three finger puppet molding kits: green dough with black mold, blue dough with green mold, yellow dough with white mold	1989	3@	6@
Potato Head Kids	Set of six: Captain Kid, Daisy, Nurse, Policeman, Slugger, Sparky	1987	2@	5@
Speed Writers	Set of six car shaped pens: black, blue, fucshia, green, orange red	1991	2@	4@
Summer Fun	Float pouch, sky saucer	1991	2@	4@
Teddy Ruxpin	Set of five: Professor Newton Gimmick, Teddy, Wolly Wahts- It, Fob, Grubby Worm	1987	2@	4@
Too Kool for School	Set of five		2@	4@
Tricky Tints	Set of four		2@	4@

Kids' Meals Premiums

NAME	DESCRIPTION	YEAR	EX (loose)	MIP
Wacky Wind-Ups	Set of five: Milk Shake, Biggie French Fry, Stuff Potato, Hamburger, Hamburger in box	1991	2.50@	5@
World Wildlife Foundation	Set of four plush toys: panda, snow leopard, koala, tiger	1988	4@	8@
World Wildlife Foundation	Set of four books: All About Koalas, All About Tigers, All About Snow Leopards, All About Pandas	1988	1@	2@
Yogi Bear & Friends	Set of six: Ranger Smith in kayak, Boo Boo on skateboard, Yogi on skates, Cindy on red scooter, Huckleberry in inner tube, Snagglepuss with surf board	1990	2@	4@
	Whataburger			
Posable Animals	Horse, camel, giraffe, dog, cat, rabbit and monkey		1.50@	3@
	White Castle			
Camp White Castle			3	6
Camp White Castle Bowls	Bowls, heavy orange plastic		3@	6@
Castle Creatures				5@
Castle Friends Bubble Makers	Set of four		1.50@	3@
Castle Meal Friends	Set of six	1991	2@	4@
Castle Meal Friends	Set of five	1992	2@	4@
Castleburger Dudes Wind Up Toys	Set of four		2@	4@
Cosby Kids	Set of four		1.50@	3@
Easter Pals	Rabbit with carrot, rabbit with purse		2@	4@
Glow in the Dark Pull Apart Monsters	Set of three		1@	2@
Godzilla Squirter			3	6
Holiday Huggables	Candy Canine, Kitty Lights, Holly Hog			4.50@
Nestle's Quik Plush Bunny				7
Push 'N GO GO GO!	Set of three		2@	4@
Silly Putty	Set of three		2@	4@
Stunt Grip Geckos	Set of four		2@	4@
Tiara	Ballerina's Tiara		3	6
Tootsie Roll Express	Set of four		2@	4@
Totally U Back To School	Pencil, pencil case		2@	4@
Willis the Dragon	Christmas giveaway		3	6
Willis the Dragon Sunglasses			2	4

McDonald's Happy Meal Premiums

NAME	DESCRIPTION	YEAR	EX (loose)	MIP
101 Dalmatians	Set of four PVC figures, Lucky, Pongo, Sergeant Tibbs, Cruella.	1991	2@	4@
3-D Happy Meal (regional)	Set of four cartons with 3-D designs with 3-D glasses inside; Bugsville, High Jinx, Loco Motion, Space Follies	1981	8@	12@
Adventures of Ronald McDonald	Set of seven rubber figures, Ronald, Birdie, Big Mac, Captain Crook, Mayor McCheese, Hamburglar, Grimace	1981	3@	5@
Airport	Birdie Bentwing Blazer, Fry Guy Flyer, Grimace Bi-Plane, Big Mac Helicopter (green), Ronald Sea Plane	1986	4@	8@
Alvin & The Chipmunks (regional)	Set of four figures; Simon, Theodore, Brittany and Alvin	1991	3.50@	6@

McDonald's Happy Meal Premiums

NAME	DESCRIPTION	YEAR	EX (loose)	MIP
American Tail	Set of four books; Fievel and Tiger, Fievel's Friends, Fievel's Boat Trip, Tony and Fievel	1986	2@	3@
Animal Riddles	Eight different rubber figures 2-2 1/2" tall, condor, snail, turtle, mouse, anteater, alligator, pelican, dragon, in various colors	1979	2@	3@
Astronauts	Four different	1991	2.50@	5@
Astrosnicks 1	Eight different 3" rubber space creatures, Scout, Thirsty, Robo, Laser, Snickapotomus, Sport, Ice Skater, Astralia	1983	5@	10@
Astrosnicks 2	Six different rubber space creatures, Copter, Drill, Ski, Racing, Perfido, Commander	1984	5@	10@
Astrosnicks 3	Total of 14 figures, many same as 1984 series, but without "M" logo; Commander, Robo, Perfido, Galaxo, Laser, Copter, Scout, Snikapotamus, boy, Pyramido, Racer, Astrosnick rocket	1985	7@	14@
Back to the Future	4 different figures, Marty, Einstein, Verne, Doc	1992	2@	4@
Bambi	Set of four, Owl, Flower, Thumper, Bambi	1988	2@	4@
Barbie	8 different plastic dolls, Ice Capades, All American, Lights & Lace, Hawaiian Fun, Happy Birthday, Costume Ball, Wedding Day Midge, My First Barbie	1991	4@	8@
Barbie	Set of eight dolls, Sparkle Eyes, Roller Blade, Rappin Rockin, My First Ballerina, Snap-On, Sun Sensation, Birthday Surprises, Rose Bride	1992	3@	5@
Batman Returns Press & Go Vehicles	Set of four, Catwoman, Batman, Penguin in vehicles and Batmobile	1992	3@	6@
Beach Ball	Set of three balls tied to Olympics; Grimace in kayak, Ronald, Birdie on sailboat	1984	4@	6.50@
Beach Ball	Set of three inflatables; red Ronald, blue Birdie, yellow Grimace	1986	3@	5@
Beach Toys	Set of eight, four inflatables; Fry Kid Super Sailer, Birdie Seaside Submarine, Grimace Bouncin' Beach ball, Ronald Fun Flyer, four sand toys; 2 buckets, shovel and rack	1989	2@	4@
Beachcomber	White pail with blue lid, and shovel	1986	5@	10@
Bedtime	Set of four items with boxed tube of Crest toothpaste, Ronald toothbrush, Ronald bath mitt, Ronald glow-in-the-dark star figure, Ronald cup	1989	4@	6@
Berenstain Bear Story Books	Set of four, Attic Treasure, Substitute Teacher, Eager Beavers, Life With Papa	1990	2@	4@
Berenstain Bears II	Set of four figures, Papa with wheelbarrow, Mama with shopping cart, Brother with scooter, Sister with wagon	1987	2.50@	5@
Berenstain Bear Test Market Set	Set of four Christmas figures, Papa with wheelbarrow, Mama with shopping cart, Brother on scooter, Sister on sled	1986	10@	20@
Bigfoot	Set of four Ford trucks with two wheel sizes, Bigfoot, Ms. Bigfoot, Shuttle, Bronco	1987	2.50@	5@
Black History	Set of two coloring books	1988	2.50@	5@
Boats'n Floats	Set of four plastic container boats, Chicken McNugget lifeboat, Birdie float, Fry Kids raft, Grimace power boat	1987	10@	20@
Cabbage Patch	Set of five Christmas dolls, Tiny Dancer, Holiday Pageant, Holiday Dreamer, Fun On Ice, All Dressed Up	1992	2@	4@

Top to Bottom: All from McDonald's; Looney Tunes Wacky Quack-Up Cars, 1993; Rescuers Down Under Viewer, 1990; 101 Dalmatians in-store display, 1991; Tonka Loader, 1992; Tiny Toons Flip Car, 1991; Bambi figures, 1988; Bedtime bath mitt, 1989.

McDonald's Happy Meal Premiums

NAME	DESCRIPTION	YEAR	EX (loose)	MIP
Camp McDonaldland	Set of four, utensils, Birdie camper mess kit, collapsible cup, canteen	1990	2@	4@
Castle Maker/Sand Castle	Set of four molds: Dome, square, cylindrical and rectangle	1987	2@	4@
Changeables	Set of six different figures that change into robots, Big Mac, Shake, Egg McMuffin, Quarter Pounder, French Fries, Chicken McNuggets	1987	2.50@	5@
Changeables	Set of eight different figures that turn into robots, Large Fries, Quarter Pounder, Hot Cakes, Big Mac, Chesseburger, Shake, Soft Serve Cone, Small Fries	1989	2@	4@
Chip 'N Dale's Rescue Rangers	Set of four figures in fanciful vehicles; Monterey Jack in Propelaphone, Gadget in Rescue Racer, Chip in Whirlicupter, Dale in Rotoroadster	1989	3@	6@
Circus	Set of eight; 1. Fun house mirror, 2. Acrobat Ronald, 3.French Fry Faller, 4. Strong Gong, 5 & 6. Punchout sheets, 7 & 8. Fun house and puppet show background	1983	5@	8@
Circus Parade	Set of four; Ringmaster Donald, Birdie Rider, Grimace Calliope, Fry Guy and elephant	1991	3@	5@
Circus Wagon	Set of four rubber toys; poodle, chimp, clown, horse	1979	5@	10@
Commandrons	Set of four robots on blister cards; Solardyn, Magna, Motron, Velocitor	1985	6.50@	15@
CosMc Crayola	Set of five coloring kits, Crayolas, two with markers, chalk sticks, paint set	1988	2@	5@
Crayola Magic	Set of three stencil kits with crayons or markers; triangles with marker, rectangles with crayons, circles with crayons	1986	3.50@	7@
Crazy Vehicles	Set of four; Ronald's dune buggy, Hamburglar's train, Birdie's airplane, Grimace's car	1991	3@	5@
Design-O-Saurs	Set of four plastic interchangeable parts: Ronald on Tyrannosaurus, Grimace-Pterodactyl, Fry Guy-Brontosaurus, Hamburglar-Triceratops	1987	4@	7.50@
Dink the Dinosaur	Set of six dino finger puppets, each packed with diorama and description; Dink, Flapper, Amber, Crusty, Scat, Shyler	1990	4@	6@
Dinosaur Days	Set of six rubber dinos in different colors; Pteranodon, Triceratops, Stegosaurus, Dimetrodon, T-Rex, Ankylosaurus	1981	2@	4@
Discover the Rain Forest	Set of four activity books with punch out figures, Sticker Safari, Wonders in the Wild, Paint It Wild, Ronald and the Jewel of the Amazon Kingdom	1991	2.50@	5@
Disney Favorites	Set of four activity books; Lady and the Tramp, Dumbo, Cinderella, The Sword in the Stone	1987	3@	5@
Duck Tales I	Set of four toys; telescope, duck code quacker, magnifying glass, wrist decoder	1988	3@	6@
Duck Tales II	Set of four toys; Uncle Scrooge in red car, Launchpad in plane, Huey, Dewey and Louie on jet ski, Webby on blue trike	1988	4@	8@
Dukes of Hazzard	Set of five container vehicles, regional; white Caddy, Jeep, cop car and pickup, orange General Lee Charger	1982	10@	20@
Dukes of Hazzard	Set of six white plastic cups, national; Luke, Boss Hogg, Bo, Sheriff Roscoe, Daisy, Uncle Jesse	1982	10@	15@

McDonald's Happy Meal Premiums

NAME	DESCRIPTION	YEAR	EX (loose)	MIP
Fast Macs	Set of four pull-back action cars; white Big Mac police car, yellow Ronald jeep, red Hamburglar racer, pink Birdie convertible	1984	2.50@	5@
Feeling Good	Set of five grooming toys; A. Grimace soap dish, B. Fry Guy sponge, C. Birdie mirror, D. Ronald or Hamburglar toothbrush, E. Captain Crook comb	1985	2.50@	5@
Fitness Fun	Set of eight toys	1992	1@	2@
Flintstone Kids (regional)	Set of four figures in animal vehicles, Betty, Barney, Fred, Wilma	1987	3@	5@
Fraggle Rock	Set of four; Gobo in carrot car, Red in raddish car, Mokey in eggplant car, Wembly and Boober in pickle car	1988	1@	3@
Fraggle Rock Doozers (regional)	Set of two; Cotterpin in forklift and Bulldoozer in bulldozer	1988	5@	10@
Fry Benders	Set of four bendable fry figures with accessories; Grand Slam, Froggy, Roadie, Freestyle	1990	3@	6@
Fun To Go	Set of seven cartons with games and activities;	1977	3.50@	6@
Fun with Food	Set of four multi-piece toys with faces; hamburger, fries, soft drink, McNuggets	1989	3@	6@
Funny Fry Friends	Set of eight toys; Too Tall, Tracker, Rollin' Rocker, Sweet Cuddles, ZZZ's, Gadzooks, Matey, Hoops	1990	3@	6@
Garfield	Set of four figures; on scooter, on skateboard, in jeep, with Odie on motorscooter	1989	2.50@	5@
Good Morning	Set of four grooming items; Ronald toothbrush, McDonaldland comb, Ronald play clock, white plastic cup	1991	2@	4@
Gravedale High (regional)	Set of four mechanical Halloween figures; Cleofatra, Frankentyke, Vinnie Stoker, Sid the Invisible Kid	1991	4@	8@
Halloween Boo Bags	Set of three glow-in-the-dark vinyl bags; Witch, Ghost and Frankie	1991	2.50@	5@
Halloween Buckets	Set of three pumpkin-shaped buckets; McGoblin, McPumpkin, McBoo	1986	2@	4@
Halloween Buckets	Set of three lidded pails with black plastic strap handles, with safety stickers attached; orange pumpkin, white glow-in-dark ghost, Green witch	1990	2@	4@
Halloween Buckets	Ghost, witch, pumpkin	1992	2@	3@
Happy Pails, Olympics	Set of four with shovels; swimming, cycling, track, Olympic Games	1984	5@	10@
Hook	Set of four figures, Peter Pan, Mermaid, Rufio, Hook	1991	2@	4@
Hot Wheels	Set of eight cars per coast of USA	1983	3.25@	6.50@
Hot Wheels	Split promo with Barbie, set of 8 cars; purple or orange Z28 Camaro, white or yellow '55 Chevy, green or black '63 Corvette, turquoise or red '57 T-Bird	1991	3.50@	6@
I Like Bikes	Set of four bike accessories; Ronald Basket, Grimace mirror, Birdie spinner, Fry Guy horn	1990	4@	8@
Jordan Fitness	Set of four; water bottle, disc, football, baseball	1992	1@	2@
Jungle Book	Set of four wind-up figures; Baloo the bear, Shere Kahn the tiger, King Louie the orangutan, Kaa the snake	1990	2@	4@
Kissy Fur	Set of eight rubber figures, some furry surfaced; Toot, Gus, Floyd, Jolene, Lennie, Beehonie, Duane, Kissy Fur	1987	5@	10@

McDonald's Happy Meal Premiums

NAME	DESCRIPTION	YEAR	EX (loose)	MIP
Lego Building Sets	Set of four Duplo kits; airplane, ship, truck, helicopter	1984	3.75@	7.50@
Lego Building Sets	Under 3 Duplo toys; animal or building	1984	5@	10@
Lego Building Sets	Under 3 toys by Duplo; bird or boat	1986	7.50@	15@
Lego Little Travelers Building Sets	Four different sets; blue tanker boat, green airplane, red roadster, yellow helicopter	1986	5@	10@
Lego Motion	Eight different kits; Gyro Bird, Lightning Striker, Land Laser, Sea Eagle, Wind Whirler, Sea Skimmer, Turbo Force, Swamp Stinger	1989	4@	6@
Lion Circus	Set of four rubber figures, bear, elephant, hippo, lion	1979	3@	5@
Little Engineer	Set of five train engines; Birdie Bright Lite, Fry Girl's Express, Fry Guy's Flyer, Grimace Streak, Ronald Rider	1987	3@	6@
Little Gardener	Set of four tools and seed packets; Ronald Water Can, Birdie Shovel, Grimace Rake, Fry Guy Pail	1989	2@	4@
Little Golden Books	Set of five books; Country Mouse and City Mouse, Tom & Jerry, Pokey Little Puppy, Benji, Monster at the End of This Block	1982	4@	7@
Little Mermaid	Set of four figures; Flounder, Ursula, Prince Eric, Ariel with Sebastian	1989	2@	4@
Lost Arches	Pericope, Flashlight, phone, camera	1991	2@	3@
Mac Tonight	Set of six figures in vehicles; sports car, off-roader, motorcycle, scooter, jet ski, airplane	1990	5.50@	7@
Magic Show	Set of four tricks; string pull, disappearing hamburger patch, magic tablet, magic picture	1985	3@	6@
Matchbox Mini-Flexies	Eight different rubber cars; Cosmobile, Hairy Hustler, Planet Scout, Hi-Tailer, Datsun, Beach Hopper, Baja Buggy	1979	3@	5@
McBunny Pails	Set of three different Easter pails; Pinky, Fluffy, Whiskers	1989	7@	12@
McDino Changeables	Set of 8 dinosaurs; Happy Mealodon, Quarter Pounder Cheesosaur, Big Macosaurus Rex, McNuggetosaurus, Hotcakesodactyl, Large Fryosaur, Trishakatops, McDino cone	1991	2@	4@
McDonaldland Band	Set of eight music toys; Grimace saxophone, Fry Guy trumpet and whistle, Ronald harmonica, whistle and pan pipes, kazoo, Hamburglar whistle	1987	2.50@	5@
McDonaldland Carnival	Set of four toys; Birdie on swing, Grimace in turn-around, Hamburglar on ferris wheel, Ronald on carousel	1990	3@	6@
McDonaldland Connectables	Set of four toys that can be connected to form a train of vehicles; Grimace in wagon, Birdie on a trike, Hamburglar in airplane, Ronald in a race car	1991	4@	8@
McDonaldland Express	Set of four train car containers; Ronald engine, caboose, freight car, coach car	1982	19@	38@
McDonaldland Junction	Train set of four snap together cars; yellow Birdie's Parlor car, red or blue Ronald Engine, purple Grimace caboose, green or white Hamburglar flat car	1983	4@	7@
McDonaldland Play-Doh	Set of eight colors, orange, purple, red, yellow, blue, green, white, pink	1986	3@	5@

Top to Bottom: All from McDonald's; Changeables, 1987; Muppet Babies, 1987; Peanuts, 1990; Barbie, 1992.

McDonald's Happy Meal Premiums

NAME	DESCRIPTION	YEAR	EX (loose)	MIP
McDrive thru Crew	Set of four vehicle toys; fries in potato roadster, shake in milk cartion, McNugget in egg roadster, hamburger in ketchup bottle	1990	4@	6@
McNugget Buddies	Set of ten rubber figures and accessories; Sparky, Volley, Corny, Drummer, Cowpoke, Sarge, Snorkel, First Class, Rocker, Boomerang	1989	3@	6@
Michael Jordon Fitness	Set of eight toys	1992	1@	1@
Mickey's Birthdayland	Set of five characters in vehicles, Minnie's convertible, Donald's train, Goofy's Jalopy, Mickey's roadster, Pluto's rumbler	1989	3@	6@
Mighty Mini 4 X 4s	Set of four big wheel vehicles; Cargo Climber, Dune Buster, L'il Classic, Pocket Pickup	1991	3@	6@
Mix'em Up Monsters	Set of four monsters with interchangeable parts; Corkle, Thugger, Gropple, Blibble	1990	4@	8@
Moveables (hard to find)	Set of six vinyl bendies; Birdie, Captain Crook, Fry Girl, Hamburglar, Professor, Ronald	1988	5@	8@
Muppet Babies	Four different; Kermit on red skateboard, Fozzie on hobby horse with wheels, Gonzo on tricycle with red wheels, Piggy in pink convertible	1987	2.50@	5@
Muppet Babies	Four different; Piggy on trike, Gonzo in airplane, Fozzie in wagon, Kermit on soapbox car	1991	2@	4@
Music (Records in Sleeves)	Set of four 45 RPM records in sleeves with different songs and colored labels; labels were green, yellow, purple, blue	1985	5@	10@
My Little Pony	Split promo with Transformers, set of six; Minty, Snuzzle, Blossom, Cotton Candy, Blue Belle, Butterscotch	1985	6@	12@
Mystery of the Lost Arches	4 different	1991	1@	3@
Mystery of the Lost Arches	Set of four; Mini-cassette, Phone, Telescope, Camera	1992	1.50@	3@
Nature's Helpers	Four different	1990	1@	2@
Nature's Helpers	Set of five garden tools with seeds; 1. hinged trowel, 2. rake, 3. water can, 4. terrarium, 5. bird feeder	1991	1.50@	3@
New Archies (regional)	Set of six figures in bumper cars, Moose, Reggie, Archie, Veronica, Betty, Jughead	1988	4.50@	9@
New Food Changeables	Set of eight; Krypto Cup, Fry Bot, Turbo Cone, Macro Mac, Gallacta Burger, Robo Cakes, C-2 Cheeseburger, Fry Force	1989	3@	5@
Old McDonald's Farm	Set of six figures: Farmer, Wife, rooster, pig, sheep, cow	1986	5@	10@
Old West	Set of six rubber figures; cowboy, frontiersman, lady, Indian, Indian woman, Sheriff	1981	4@	6@
Oliver and Company	Set of four figures; Oliver, Georgette, Francis and Dodger	1988	2.50@	5@
On the Go	Set of five games; stop light bead game, Ronald slate board lift pad, Hamburglar lift pad, stop and go bead game, decal transfer	1985	3@	5@
Peanuts	Set of four characters in vehicles; Charlie, Snoopy, Lucy, Linus	1990	2@	4@
Pencil Puppets	Six different pencil toppers in shapes of McDonaldland characters	1978	5@	7@

McDonald's Happy Meal Premiums

NAME	DESCRIPTION	YEAR	EX (loose)	MIP
Piggsburg Pigs (regional)	Set of four figures on vehicles; Rembrandt in hotrod, Huff & Puff wolves on catapult, Piggy & Crackers on crate car, Portly & Pighead on motorcycle	1991	4@	6@
Playmobile	Set of five toys and accesories; Farmer, Sheriff, Indian, Umbrella Girl, Horse and saddle	1982	10@	15@
Popoids	Set of four interconnecting constructor kits; cylinder, triangle, sphere, cube	1985	7@	15@
Potato Head Kids	Set of eight toys;	1992	2.50@	5@
Raggedy Ann & Andy	Set of four toys; Andy on slide, Grouchy on carousel, Ann with swing, camel on seesaw	1990	6@	12@
Rescuers Down Under	Set of four slide viewing movie camera toys; Jake, Wilbur, Bernard and Bianca, Cody	1990	3@	5@
Runaway Robots	Set of six, dark blue Skull, green Coil, red Flame, purple Bolt, blue Beak and yellow Jab	1988	7@	14@
Safari Adventure	Six different rubber animals; alligator, monkey, gorilla, tiger, hippo, rhino	1980	3@	5@
Sailors	Set of four floating toys: Hamburglar Sailboat, Ronald Airboat, Grimace Sub and Fry Kids Ferry	1987	5@	10@
School Days	Set of five school tools; 1. Pencils, Ronald, Grimace, Hamburglar, 2. Erasers, Ronald, Grimace, Hamburglar, Captain Crook, Birdie, 3. Pencil sharpener, 4. Ruler, 5. Pencil case	1984	3@	5@
Ship Shape 1	Set of four boat containers with stickers; Hamburglar, Ronald, Grimace, Captain Crook	1983	20@	30@
Ship Shape 2	Set of four boat containers with stickers, same as issued in 1983	1985	20@	30@
Sky-Busters	Set of six rubber airplanes; Skyhawk AAf, Phantom f$E, Mirage F1, United DC-10, MIG-21, Tornado	1982	3@	5@
Smart Duck	Set of six rubber figures; Duck, Cat, Donkey, Chipmunk, two rabbits	1979	3@	5@
Snow White	Prince, Snow White, Doc, Bashful, Sleepy, Queen Witch, U3		3	5.50
Space Aliens	Set of eight rubber monsters; lizard man, vampire bat, gill face, tree monster, winged fish, cyclops, veined brain, insectman	1979	3@	5@
Space Raiders	Set of eight rubber aliens; Drak, Dard, flying saucer, Rocket Kryoo-5, Horta, Zama, Rocket Ceti-3, Rocket Altair-2	1979	3@	5@
Sport Ball	Four different: Basketball, Baseball, Football and Tennis Ball	1988	2@	4@
Sportsball	Set of four balls; Baseball, Football, Basketball, Soccer	1990	2@	4@
Star Trek	Set of five toys; 1. Rings, Kirk, Spock, Starfleet insignia, Enterprise	1979	10@	15@
Star Trek	Set of five toys; 2. Starfleet game	1979	10	15
Star Trek	Set of five toys; 3. Set of five video viewers, each with a different story	1979	10@	15@
Star Trek	Set of five toys; 4. Set of four glitter iron-ons of characters, Kirk, Spock, McCoy, Ilia, packaged in pairs	1979	10@	15@
Star Trek	Set of five toys; 5. Navigation bracelet with decals	1979	15	30

McDonald's Happy Meal Premiums

NAME	DESCRIPTION	YEAR	EX (loose)	MIP
Stomper Mini 4X4	Set of eight big wheel cars; Tercel, AMC Eagle, Chevy S-10 Pickup, Chevy Van, Chevy Blazer, Ford Ranger, Jeep Renegade, Dodge Ram,	1986	5@	10@
Super Looney Tunes	Set of four figures with costumes; Super Bugs, Bat Duck, Taz Flash, Wonder Pig	1991	3@	5@
Super Mario Brothers	Set of four action figures; Mario, Luigi, Little Gooma, Koopa	1990	2@	4@
Super Summer	Sand Castle Pail with shovel, Sand Pail with rake, Fish Sand Mold, Sailboat, Beach Ball	1988	2@	4@
Tail Spin	Under 3 toys; Baloo's seaplane or Wildcat's jet	1990	5@	6@
Tail Spin	Set of four characters in airplanes; Molly, Balloo, Kit, Wildcat	1990	2@	4@
Tinosaurs	Set of eight figures; Link the Elf, Baby Jad, Merry Bones, Dinah, Time Traveller Fern, Tiny, Grumpy Spell, Kave Kolt Kobby	1986	5@	10@
Tiny Toons Flip Cars	Set of four cars, each with two characters depending on which side is up; Montana Max/Gobo Dodo, Babs/Plucky Duck, Hampton/Devil, Elmyra/Buster Bunny	1991	2@	4@
Tom & Jerry Band	Set of four characters with instruments; Tom at keyboard, Jerry on drums, Spike on bass, Droopy at the mike	1990	4@	7@
Tonka	Set of five; Fire Truck, Loader, Cement Mixer, Dump Truck, Backhoe	1992	2@	4@
Turbo Macs	Set of four pull back action cars with characters driving and large "M" on hood; Ronald, Grimace, Birdie, Hamburglar	1990	3@	5@
Under Sea	Set of six cartons with undersea art, alligator, dolphin, hammerhead shark, sea turtle, seal, walrus	1980	1@	2@
United Airlines Friendly Skies	Set of 2 airplanes with United markings, either Ronald or Grimace flying	1991	5@	10@
What is it	Set of six rubber animals; skunk, squirrel, bear, owl, baboon, snake	1979	1.25@	2.50@
Wild Animal Toy Books	Complete set of four plus under three	1991	2.50@	5@
Winter World	Set of five flat vinyl tree ornaments; Ronald, Hamburglar, Grimace, Mayor McCheese, Birdie	1983	5@	8@
Yo Yogi (regional)	Set of four characters	1991	4@	6@
Young Astronauts	Set of four snap together models; Apollo Command Module, Argo Land Shuttle, Space Shuttle, Cirrus Vtol	1986	5@	10@
Young Astronauts (regional)	Set of four vehicles	1992	3@	5@
Zoo Face	Set of four rubber noses and makeup kits; alligator, monkey, tiger, toucan	1988	3@	5@

Miscellaneous Restaurant Toys

Arby's

Megaphone, Minnesota Twins 25th Anniversary		1986	1	2

Arthur Treachers

Flintstone, Pebbles Cup	Yabba Dabba Dew plastic cup	1974	10	20

Top to Bottom: All from McDonald's; Berenstain Bears, 1987; Tiny Toons Flip Car (flipped view of same car pictured in this section), 1991; Super Mario Brothers in-store display, 1990; Cabbage Patch Kids Holiday figures, 1992.

Miscellaneous Restaurant Toys

NAME	DESCRIPTION	YEAR	EX (loose)	MIP
	Big Boy			
Action Figures	Complete set of four; skater, pitcher, surfer, race driver	1990	4@	6@
Big Boy Bank, Large	Produced from 1966-1976, 18" tall, full color	1960s	175	400
Big Boy Bank, Medium	Produced from 1966-1976, 9" tall, brown	1960s	75	150
Big Boy Bank, Small	Produced from 1966-1976, 7" tall, painted red/white	1960s	65	150
Big Boy Board Game		1960s	75	150
Big Boy Kite	Kite with image of Bog Boy	1960s	10	25
Big Boy Nodder		1960s	100	200
Big Boy Playing Cards	Produced in four designs	1960s	20	50
Big Boy Stuffed Dolls	Set of three, Big Boy, girl friend Dolly, both 12" tall, and dog Nuggets, appx. 7" tall (Note:all are currently being reproduced)	1960s	30@	65@
	Burger King			
Doll Cloth Cartoon King Doll	16" tall	1972	20	35
Frisbee	Small yellow or orange, embossed Burger King		2	4
Lunch Box	Blue plastic box embossed with Bk logo		2	5
Sports Watches	In white or yellow		2@	5@
Super Bowl Poster		1992	2	4
Teenage Mutant Ninja Turtles Poster		1991	2	4
	Chesty Boy			
Chesty Boy Squeek Toy	8" tall	1950	35	75
	Chucky E Cheese			
Chucky E Cheese Bank	pPastic	1980	15	25
	Dairy Queen			
Radio Flyer Replica			4	8
	Goodhumor Ice Cream			
Ice Cream Bar Doll		1975	20	30
	Hardee's			
Backpack	Orange		2	4
Beach Bunnies	Set of four; girl with ball, boy with skateboard, girl with skates and boy with frisbee	1989	2@	4@
Frisbee	4 3/4" wide, white with yellow imprinting		1	3.50
Ghostbusters Headquarters Posters			1	3
Super Bowl Cloisonne Pins	Set of 25 officially licensed NFL Super Bowl pins, plus one error pin.	1991	1.50@	3@
Waldo and Friends Holiday Ornaments	Set A and B		5@	10@
	International House of Pancakes			
Pancake Kids Lunch Box		1992	2	5
	Kentucky Fried Chicken			
Colonel Sanders Figure	9" tall	1960s	35	60
Colonel Sanders Nodder	7" tall	1960s	35	75
WWF Stampers	Set of four, Canadian issues		2@	4@
	Little Caesar's			
Stuffed Pizza Pizza Man			2	5

Miscellaneous Restaurant Toys

McDonald's

NAME	DESCRIPTION	YEAR	EX (loose)	MIP
Astrosnicks Rocket	9 1/2" rocketship coupon with Happy Meal	1984	15	30
Baseball Cards (Donruss '92)	Set of 32 cards with checklist	1992	12	24
Baseball Cards (Hoops '92)	Set of 62 cards	1992	12	24
Baseball Cards (Hoops '92)	Set of 70 cards, including eight extra Chicago Bulls cards	1992	18	36
Baseball Cards (Topps '91)	Set of 44 cards	1991	18	36
Batman Cups w/flying lids	Set of six, Batman, Penguin for Mayor, Catwoman, Batmobile, Ballroom Scene,	1992	2@	Not packaged
Birdie Bike Horn - Japan	Made for kid's bike		4	9
Birdie Magic Trick	Green or orange			5 @
Captain Crook Bike Reflector - Canada	Blue plastic	1988	2	Not packaged
Christmas Ornaments	Fry Guy and Fry Girl cloth hanging ornaments, 3 1/2" tall	1987	2@	5@
Colorful Puzzles - Japan	Dumbo, Mickey & Minnie, Dumbo & Train		5@	10@
Coloring Stand-Ups	Characters and backgrounds to color, punch out and stand	1978	4@	8@
Combs	Capt. Crook-red, Grimace-yellow, Ronald-yellow, blue or purple, Grimace Groomer-green	1988	2@	Not packaged
Construx	Set of four pieces used to make a spaceship; axle, wing, body cylinder, canopy	1986	7@	15@
Crayola Squeeze Bottle, Kay Bee	Regional set of four with coupon			10@
Double Bell Alarm Clock	Wind up alarm clock with silver bells, hammer ringer, silver feet, image of Ronald on face with head tilted over folded hands, as if asleep			40
E.T. Posters	Set of four posters, 17"x24"; A.Boy and ET on bike	1985	5	11
E.T. Posters	B. Boy and ET finger touch, C. ET and radio	1985	5@	8@
E.T. Posters	D. ET waving	1985	5	10
Favorite Friends	Set of seven character punch-out cards	1978	2@	5@
French Fry Radio	Large red fry container with fries AM/FM radio	1977		40
Friendship Spaceship Ring		1985	3	4
Frisbee - Canada	3" around, blue, early Ronald image		1	2
Ghostbusters	Set of five school tools; Slimer pencil, Stay Puft pad and eraser, containment chamber pencil case, Stay Puft pencil sharpener, Ghostbusters ruler	1987	3@	7@
Glow in the Dark Yo-Yo	No markings or dates	1978	2	5
Golf Ball	McDonald's logo		1	3
Good Times Great Taste Record			2	4
Grimace Bank	Ceramic bank, purple, 9" tall	1985	10	20
Grimace Enamel Pin	Enamel pin		6	12
Grimace Miniature Golf		1986	3	5
Grimace Sponge	Grimace, Grimace Car Wash		2@	4@
Grimace Ring		1970	8	15
Halloween Certificate Book w/Roger Rabbit Puffy Sticker		1988	3	5
Halloween Pumpkin Ring	Orange pumpkin face ring		1	3
Hamburglar Doll	7" stuffed doll, by Remco, part of set of seven, sold on blister card	1976	25	35
Hamburglar Hockey		1979	2	4

Miscellaneous Restaurant Toys

NAME	DESCRIPTION	YEAR	EX (loose)	MIP
High Flying	Set of three kites: Ronald, Birdie and Hamburglar	1987	3@	8@
Honey, I Shrunk the Kids Cups	Set of three white 20 oz. plastic cups; Giant bee, on the dog's nose, riding the ant	1988	1.50@	3.50@
Looney Tunes Christmas Dolls - Canada	Set of four, Sylvester in nightgown & cap, Tasmanian Devil in Santa hat, Bugs in winter scarf and Tweetie dressed as elf		3@	6@
Luggage Tags	Set of four; Birdie, Grimace, Ronald, Hamburglar		2@	4@
Mac Tonight	Fingertronic foam puppet	1988	6	15
Mac Tonight Enamel Pin	Moonface and slogan enamel pin	1988	2	4
Mac Tonight Sunglasses	Adult	1988	2	5
McDonald's All-Star Race Team (MAXX) '91	Complete set of cards	1991	5	15
McDonald's All-Star Race Team (MAXX) '92	Complete set of 36 cards	1992	5	15
McDonald's Playing Cards	Two decks to a set		2	5
McDonald's Spinner Top - Holland			2	4
Mickey's Birthdayland	Set of four Under 3 vehicles, Mickey's convertible, Goofy's car, Minnie's convertible, Donald's Jeep	1989	2@	4@
Minnesota Twins Baseball Glove	Twins logo on side, Coca-Cola inside glove, McDonald's satin logo on back, given to the first 100 kids at the 1984 game	1984	40	75
Minute Maid Juice Bottles	Mini squeeze bottles	1991	1@	1.50@
Norman Rockwell Brass Ornament	Clear acrylic, "Christmas Trio" gift boxed	1978	3	7
Norman Rockwell Brass Ornament	50th Annivesary Norman Rockwell design, gift packaged with McDonald & Coca-Cola logos	1983	3	7
On The Go Lunch Box	Three colors: Green, red or blue with arches on handles, stickers and embossed McDonaldland Characters going to schools	1988	2@	4@
Paint with Water	Paintless coloring board with self contained frame and easel	1978	5	10
Pin, Ronald in Christmas Wreath	Enamel pin		6	12
Punkin' Makins	Cutouts in character faces to attach to Halloween pumpkins; Ronald, Goblin, Grimace	1977	7@	15@
Rescuers Down Under Xmas Ornament	Miss Bianca, Bernard	1990	2@	4@
Rings	Set of five rings with character heads; Big Mac, Captain Crook, Grimace, Hamburglar, Ronald	1977	5@	10@
Roger Rabbit Scarf - Japan	McDonald's logo, Japanese writing on scrarf	1988	10	20
Ronald "Shoe Wallet" - Canada	Ronald yellow shoe wallet, attach to shoes with laces	1987	1	2
Ronald Bank	Ronald sitting with legs crossed, 7 1/2" tall		5	12
Ronald Bike Seat Pad - Japan			4	9
Ronald Cookie Cutter	Green with balloons	1987	2	3
Ronald Foldable LCD Clock - Japan			4	9
Ronald Inflatable 12"	Weighted base	1990	2	5
Ronald Magic Tablet			1	3
Ronald McDonald Doll	14" vinyl head with a soft body by Dakin		15	35
Ronald McDonald Doll	7" doll, by Remco		12	25
Ronald McDonald Maze	Lift up mystery game	1979	4	10

Miscellaneous Restaurant Toys

NAME	DESCRIPTION	YEAR	EX (loose)	MIP
Ronald Plastic Flyers	Ronald with legs and arms extended red or yellow		1@	3@
Ronald Popsicle Maker - Canada	Green or yellow	1984	1@	3@
Ronald Shoe & Sock Game - Japan	Plastic with ball and string - in Japanese writing		5	10
Ronald Tote Bag - Japan	Writing in Japanese		5	10
Santa Claus the Movie Reindeer Xmas Ornament		1985	4	5
Sindy Doll	Dressed in older McDonald's uniform	1970	4	8
Singing Wastebasket Bank	5 1/8" white plastic basket with coin slot in top		6	Not packaged
Speedie "Touch of Service" Pin	Enamel pin		6	12
Spinner Baseball Game	Green plastic with four characters	1983	5	
Sticker Club	Set of five different sticker sheets; reflectors, scratch and sniff, color designs, action stickers, puffy designs	1985	1@	3@
Stocking, Merry Christmas To my Pal	Plastic stocking	1981	3	5
Sunglasses	Hamburglar, Ronald w/yellow lenses or Ronald McDonald on stem		2@	4@
Tic Tac Mac Game	Yellow base, Grimace is X, Ronald is O	1981	2	5
Tootler Harmonica		1985	1	3
Tops	Set of three finger tops in red, blue and green	1978		7@
Trays, Serving	Set of six white plastic wedge shaped trays with pictures of characters; Ronald, Big Mac, Mayor McCheese, Hamburglar, Grimace, Captain Crook		3@	7@
Walt Disney Video Viewer - Cinderella - Japan			5	10
Who Framed Roger Rabbit Cups	Roger Rabbit-Hollywood, Benny the Cab, Roger Being Chased	1988		Not packaged
Wrist Wallets	Set of four watch-type bands with coin holding dial with character faces; Ronald, Captain Crook, Big Mac, Hamburglar	1977	5@	10@
Yo Yo	Half red, half yellow	1979	2	5

Pizza Hut

NAME	DESCRIPTION	YEAR	EX (loose)	MIP
Universal Monster Cups/ Holograms	Set of three		2@	5@

Roy Rogers

NAME	DESCRIPTION	YEAR	EX (loose)	MIP
Skateboard Kids Figures			2@	5@

Tastee Freeze

NAME	DESCRIPTION	YEAR	EX (loose)	MIP
Roy Campanella Figure			20	35

Wendy's

NAME	DESCRIPTION	YEAR	EX (loose)	MIP
Fun Flyers	3 1/2" wide in red, yellow or blue		1@	2.50@
Where's the Beef Stickers	Set of six	1984	1	3

Science Fiction and Space Toys

Some would trace the modern age of science fiction to 1956 and "Forbidden Planet." By any reckoning it is a classic film, and the toy world would certainly be poorer for the lack of Robby the Robot. But through one medium or another, science fiction has enthralled millions through the years, arguably as many as 230 years, back to Swift's "Gulliver's Travels."

The first universally acclaimed work of science fiction was Mary Shelley's "Frankenstein" or "The Modern Prometheus," and her vision gave way to those of Verne, Wells, Burroughs, Lovecraft, Heinlein, Asimov, Clarke and Bradbury, who led us into the modern day's vast variety of writers and their memorable characters. Frankenstein, while often considered more a movie monster than a science fiction character, has nonetheless become one of the most enduring and widely embraced characters in all fiction. Like many classic examples of the genre, Frankenstein has become symbolic of both the hopes and perils of the age of science, and his spiritual offspring are legion, including dear Robby the Robot.

Even with its classical pedigree, science fiction is almost exclusively a product of the 20th century, as the scientific "foundation" had to exist before the fiction community could extrapolate upon it. In particular, science fiction is a phenomenon of the atomic age. It was World War II more than any event in the century that opened our eyes to the equally wondrous and horrific potential of applied science. "Forbidden Planet" juxtaposed with "The Day the Earth Stood Still." The hope of "Close Encounters" was tempered by the pessimism of "Blade Runner." We had "Weird Science" and "Neuromancer" and a thousand other visions of our future simultaneously enticing us forward and warning us away.

Just as the fiction of science captivated readers of all ages, so did the toys of science fiction. Buck Rogers and Flash Gordon may have told us that the heavens could be treacherous places, but they also promised some really cool tools to get there. Spaceships and rockets and ray guns indeed!

Buck Rogers made his first appearance in 1928, the same year that Mickey Mouse was introduced in "Steamboat Willie." In 1929, Buck went from pulp to newsprint, becoming the first science fiction comic strip. Flash followed Buck into print in 1934 and was an immediate success. Within two years Flash was on the silver screen, played by Buster Crabbe. Buck finally made it to the screen in 1939, played by -- you guessed it -- Buster Crabbe.

During this period, Marx produced numerous toys in support of each character, including two ships that have become classics of the space toy field. Opinions vary as to which wind-up is better executed, Buck Rogers' 25th Century Rocket Ship or Flash Gordon's Rocket Fighter. Both were made by Marx and both are considered superb examples of tin character space toys.

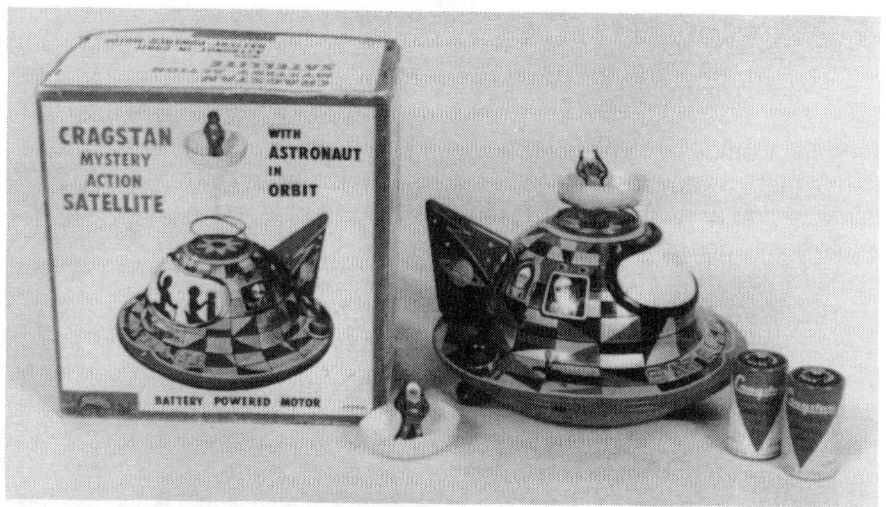

Top: Mystery Action Satellite by Cragstan; Left: The original Robert the Robot, 1955, by Ideal; Above: Star Wars Land of the Jawas Playset, 1978, by Kenner.

The 1935 Buck Rogers' ship is 12 inches long and beautifully lithographed in the style of the comic strip art with vivid art deco designs. The 1939 Flash Gordon Rocket Fighter shows Flash manning the guns of a brilliantly colored red and yellow open cockpit rocketship. Both are worthy of centerpiece status in many collections.

No discussion of space toys would be complete without mention of ray guns. Here again Marx is a major player, producing numerous generic space guns as well as character items such as the Flash Gordon Signal Pistol and Flash Gordon Water Pistol. Daisy Manufacturing also produced several classics, including the Buck Rogers Rocket Pistol, the 1936 XZ-44 Liquid Helium Water Pistol, and the 1936 XZ-38 Disintegrator Pistol. Other companies, such as Hubley and Wyandotte, made memorable contributions to the art as well.

Space toys run in an uninterrupted stream through most of the 20th century. The 1930s and 1940s saw Buck and Flash. The 1950s saw fiction become reality with the growth of a new medium, television. "Captain Video" was the first space series on TV, appearing in the summer of 1949. Buzz Correy and his Space Patrol and Tom Corbett -- Space Cadet would feed the appetite for adventure until 1956 when the heavens took on a visual scale and grandeur never seen before in "Forbidden Planet."

In 1966, when a low budget outer space western called "Star Trek" went on the air, few dreamed that life for millions would never be the same. Even though the original show ran only three seasons, its impact and legacy are undeniable. The phenomenon of "Star Trek" has grown far beyond cult status, and the extraordinary success of "Star Trek: The Next Generation" has only broadened its reach. Star Trek toys and memorabilia of all types are eagerly traded at shows and Star Trek conventions nationwide, and in light of this, many Trek toys would seem undervalued.

Finally, if you are going to talk about space toys, sooner or later you must talk about "Star Wars." The array of books, models, figures, playsets and other toys, clothing and sundry items released since the 1977 opening of "Star Wars" continued unabated until nearly 1988. The license gained a new lease in 1987 with the opening of Star Tours at Disneyland and Disney World, generating still more new merchandise. In terms of diversity of toys, the universe of "Star Wars" is easily the most fully realized and diversely populated in all science fiction. Star Wars figures, vehicles and playsets are the most widely traded science fiction toys on the market today, and the rumors of new films in the series to be released by 1995 or 1997 have fueled the market. The high international recognition of the "Star Wars" films and license is excellent assurance of the continuing popularity of its toys.

In general, the field of science fiction toys is one with particular growth potential, given the prevalence of science fiction in today's culture and the exceptional strength of franchises like "Star Trek" and "Star Wars." With recent generations having been weaned on the likes of Luke Skywalker, Han Solo, Spock, Picard and now Benjamin Cisco, it is a foregone conclusion that as they enter the collector market, many of them will choose science fiction and space toys as the basis of their collections.

SPACE TOYS

Aliens

TOY	MANUFACTURER	YEAR	GOOD	EX	MIB
Alien Figure (18" tall)	Kenner	1979	90	130	195
Alien Warrior (base and egg)	Halcyon		20	30	45
Aliens Commodore Computer Game	Commodore	1985	15	25	35
Colorforms Aliens Set			10	15	25

Buck Rogers

TOY	MANUFACTURER	YEAR	GOOD	EX	MIB
25th Century Scientific Laboratory (complete with three manuals)	Porter Chem. Co.	1934	700	1025	1575
Atomic Pistol U-235	Daisy	1945	100	145	225
Atomic Pistol U-238	Daisy	1946	100	145	225
Atomic Pistol U-238 Leather Holster (holster only)	Daisy	1946	30	40	65
Battle Fleet of Rocket Ships	Nat'l Fireworks Co.	1937	35	50	80
Buck Rogers & His Atomic Bomber Jigsaw Puzzle	Puzzle Craft	1945	125	180	275
Buck Rogers 25th Century Police Rocket Ship (tin wind-up, 12" long, 1935)	Marx		225	350	450
Buck Rogers 25th Century Rocket Ship (Buck and Wilma in window, tin windup)	Marx		350	575	775
Buck Rogers Chemistry Set (Advanced, complete with manual)	Grooper Co.	1937	330	470	725
Buck Rogers Chemistry Set (Beginners, complete with manual)	Grooper Co.	1937	275	390	600
Buck Rogers Figure (1 3/4" tall, cast figure, gray)	Tootsietoy	1937	100	145	225
Buck Rogers Films (set of six)	Irwin	1936	125	180	275
Buck Rogers Jupiter Film (16mm film)		1936	20	30	45
Buck Rogers Lead Figure Set (2 1/2" tall, Buck, Wilma & Killer Kane)	Cocomalt	1934	75	105	160
Buck Rogers Puzzle	Milton Bradley	1950	25	35	50
Chase of Killer Kane	Nat'l Fireworks Co.	1937	70	100	150
Chief Explorer Badge		1936	100	145	225
Chief Explorer Folder		1936	80	115	175
Clock	Huckleberry Time	1970s	35	50	75
Combat Set (gun & holster XZ-32)	Daisy	1934	295	425	650
Combat Set (gun & holster XZ-37)	Daisy	1935	230	325	500
Combat Set XZ-40	Daisy	1935	195	275	425
Combat Set XZ-42	Daisy	1935	195	275	425
Comic Book of Buck Rogers	Marvel	1979	2	3	5
Communicator Set (with silver Twiki figure)			10	15	25
Confidential Rocket Ranger Bulletins			35	50	75
Disintegrator Pistol XZ-38	Daisy	1935	100	145	225
Doctor Huer's Invisible Ink Crystals		1936	90	130	200
Electric Caster Rocket Ship	Marx	1930s	150	210	325
Fighting Fleet Poster (17" x 11" backside of Interplanetary Fleet kit)			55	80	125
Fireless Rocket Ships	Nat'l Fireworks Co.	1937	35	50	80
Flying Space Ship	Spotswood	1936	195	275	425
Game of the 25th Century		1934	170	245	375
Hearing Aide "Acousticon" Jr. (large pinback)	Dictograph Products	1937	230	325	500
Holster XZ-33	Daisy	1934	70	100	150
Holster XZ-39	Daisy	1935	70	100	150
Inlaid Jigsaw Puzzle (space station scene, 14" x 10")	Milton Bradley	1952	10	15	25
Interplanetary Games (set of three boards)		1934	285	400	625
Interplanetary Space Fleet Construction Kits (seven different)		1934	150	210	325

SPACE

Buck Rogers

TOY	MANUFACTURER	YEAR	GOOD	EX	MIB
Lead Figure Set (Buck, Wilma, Kane, Ardella, Doctor Huer & Robot)	Britains		1125	1625	2500
Leather Helmet XZ-34	Daisy	1935	330	470	725
Leather Holster XZ-36	Daisy	1935	70	100	150
Liquid Helium Water Pistol XZ-44 (copper finish)	Daisy	1936	180	260	400
Liquid Helium Water Pistol XZ-44 (red & yellow finish)	Daisy	1936	195	275	425
Lite-blaster Flashlight		1936	180	260	400
Paddle Ball "Comet Socker"	Lee-Tex	1935	35	50	75
Pencil Boxes	American Pencil	1930s	80	115	175
Pendant Watch	Huckleberry Time	1970s	125	180	275
Pocket Knife	Adolph Kastor	1934	285	400	625
Pocket Watch	E. Ingraham Co.	1935	425	600	925
Pocket Watch	Huckleberry Time	1970s	100	145	225
Police Patrol Ship (wind-up)	Marx	1939	330	475	725
Popsicle Pete's Radio Gift News (15" x 10")			35	50	75
Punch-out Bag (balloon with characters)	Morton Salt	1942	45	65	100
Repeller Ray Ring (brass with inset green stone)			425	600	925
Ring of Saturn (red stone, glow-in-the-dark white plastic, crocodile base)	Post Corn Toasties	1944	150	210	325
Rocket Football (silver)	Edward K. Tryon	1935	150	210	325
Rocket Pistol XZ-31 (9 1/2")	Daisy	1934	125	180	275
Rocket Pistol XZ-35 (7 3/4")	Daisy	1935	100	145	225
Rocket Rangers Flying Needle Rocket Ship Plan (red or white)		1941	35	50	75
Rocket Rangers Iron-on Transfers (set of three)			35	50	75
Rocket Rangers Membership Card			55	80	120
Rocket Roller Skates	Marx	1935	1400	2000	3100
Rocket Ship (12" tall, wind-up)	Marx	1934	275	400	625
Rubber Balls	Lee-Tex	1935	45	65	100
Rubber Banks Gun Punch-out Card (5" x 10")	Onward School Supply	1940	35	50	75
Satellite Pioneers Cadet Commission (with autographed postcard)		1958	23	35	50
Satellite Pioneers Map of the Solar System		1958	23	35	50
Satellite Pioneers Membership Card	Greenduck	1958	35	50	75
Satellite Pioneers Pinback (green or blue)	Greenduck	1958	23	35	50
Satellite Pioneers Secret Order #1		1958	18	26	40
Satellite Pioneers Starfinder		1958	23	35	50
School Crayons Ship Box & Pencils	American Pencil	1935	100	145	225
School Kit Bag			70	100	150
Solar Scouts Member Badge (gold)		1935	35	50	75
Solar Scouts Radio Club Manual		1936	100	145	225
Sonic Ray Gun (yellow plastic with code folder)	Norton-Honer	1950s	45	65	100
Space Glasses	Norton-Honer	1955	45	65	100
Space Ranger Halolight Ring	Sylvania	1952	55	80	125
Space Ranger Kit (11" x 15" envelope with six punch-out sheets)	Sylvania	1952	35	50	75
Spaceship Commander Banner		1936	100	145	225
Spaceship Commander Folder with Chief Explorer Appl.		1936	55	80	125
Spaceship Commander Stationery		1936	55	80	125
Spaceship Commander Whistle Badge		1936	45	65	100
Strato-Kite	Aero-Kite Co.	1946	23	30	45
Super Foto Camera	Norton-Honer	1955	45	65	100
Super Scope Telescope (9" plastic telescope)	Norton-Honer	1955	45	65	100
Super Sonic Glasses		1953	55	80	125
Superdreadnought Model SD51X Construction Kit (6 /12" balsa wood)		1936	235	340	525
Sweater Emblem (three colors)			160	225	350
Telescoper	Popsicle		55	80	125
The Battle of Mars	Nat'l Fireworks Co.	1937	35	50	80

Buck Rogers

TOY	MANUFACTURER	YEAR	GOOD	EX	MIB
The Sun Gun of Saturn	Nat'l Fireworks Co.	1937	35	50	80
Tootsie Toy Rocket Ships (Buck Rogers Battle Cruiser, runs on a string)	Dowst Mfg.	1937	125	180	275
Tootsie Toy Rocket Ships (Flash Blast Attack Ship 4 1/2" runs on a string)	Dowst Mfg.	1937	100	145	225
Toy Wrist Watch	GLJ Toys	1978	11	16	25
Two Way Trans-Ceiver	DA Myco	1948	45	65	100
U.S.N. Los Angeles Dirigible Figure (5" tall, cast figure, gold)	Tootsietoy	1937	100	145	225
Uniform	Sackman Bros.	1934	950	1350	2100
Walkie Talkies	Remco	1950s	70	100	150
Whistling Rocket Ship	Muffets	1939	55	80	125
Wilma Figure (1 3/4" tall, cast figure, gold)	Tootsietoy	1937	80	115	175
Wilma Handkerchief		1936	100	145	225
Wilma Pendant (brass with chain)			135	195	300
Wrist Watch	Huckleberry Time	1970s	70	100	150

Doctor Who

TOY	MANUFACTURER	YEAR	GOOD	EX	MIB
Ace Figure	Denys Fisher	1976	11	16	25
Anniversary Set (Dr. Who, Melanie, K-9, Tardis, base, five-side console)	Denys Fisher	1976	275	390	600
Cyberman	Denys Fisher	1976	11	16	25
Cyberman Robot Doll (10" tall)	Denys Fisher	1970s	250	350	550
Dalek	Denys Fisher	1976	14	20	30
Dalek	Marx	1960s	9	13	20
Dalek Army Gift Set	Denys Fisher	1976	46	60	95
Dalek Bagatelle	Denys Fisher	1976	70	100	150
Dalek Shooting Game (8" x 20" litho board with Daleks in action)	Marx	1965	225	325	500
Davros (villain with left arm)	Denys Fisher	1976	11	16	25
Doctor Who Card Set (set of twelve 2 x 3" color octagon cards)		1970s	14	20	30
Doctor Who Character Card Set (24 cards)	Denys Fisher	1976	18	26	40
Doctor Who Daleks Oracle Question & Answer Board Game		1965	115	165	250
Doctor Who Doll (10" tall with scarf & screwdriver)	Denys Fisher	1976	90	130	200
Doctor Who Tardis Playset	Denys Fisher	1970s	205	295	450
Doctor Who Trump Card Game		1970s	9	13	20
Doctor Who...Dodge the Daleks Board Game (robots firing at the sci-fi guy)		1965	115	165	250
Ice Warrior (villain)	Denys Fisher	1976	9	13	20
K-9 (the Doctor's dog)	Denys Fisher	1976	7	10	15
Mel (pink or blue jacket)	Denys Fisher	1976	9	13	20
Seventh Doctor, The (grey or brown jacket)	Denys Fisher	1976	9	13	20
Tardis (the Doctor's transporter)	Denys Fisher	1976	225	325	500

Flash Gordon

TOY	MANUFACTURER	YEAR	GOOD	EX	MIB
Adventure on the Moons of Mongo Game	House of Games	1977	16	23	35
Flash Gordon Arresting Ray (picture of Flash on handle, 12" long)	Marx	1939	225	350	450
Flash Gordon Featured Funnies Jigsaw Puzzle (9 1/2" X 14 puzzle)		1930s	65	95	145
Flash Gordon Figure (wood composition figure of Flash 5" tall)		1944	135	195	300
Flash Gordon Hand Puppet (rubber head)		1950s	100	145	225
Flash Gordon Kite (21" x 17", paper)		1950s	60	90	135
Flash Gordon Pencil Box		1951	85	120	185

Flash Gordon

TOY	MANUFACTURER	YEAR	GOOD	EX	MIB
Flash Gordon Rocket Fighter (tin wind-up, 12" long)	Marx	1939	200	300	400
Flash Gordon Ship (3" die cast metal)		1975	11	16	25
Flash Gordon Space Outfit	Esquire Novelty	1951	105	155	235
Flash Gordon Three Puzzle Boxed Set	Milton Bradley	1951	125	180	275
Flash Gordon Tray Puzzle	Milton Bradley	1951	55	80	120
Flash Gordon Two-Way Telephone (1940's)	Marx		75	125	150
Flash Gordon Wallet (with zipper)		1949	80	115	175
Flash Gordon Water Pistol (7 1/2" plastic)	Marx	1950s	185	260	400
Flash Gordon Wrist Watch (medium chrome case, Flash in front of city)	Bradley	1979	80	115	175
Rocket Fighter (12", wind-up)	Marx	1940	205	295	450
Solar Commando Set	Premier Products	1950s	75	110	165
Three Color Ray Gun	Nasta	1976	9	13	20

Land of the Giants

TOY	MANUFACTURER	YEAR	GOOD	EX	MIB
Land of the Giants Board Game	Ideal	1968	75	105	160
Land of the Giants Coloring Book (photos on cover)		1970s	40	60	90
Land of the Giants Space Sled (battery op.)		1970s	275	390	600
Space Sled	Remco		285	400	625
View-Master Reels (reel set with booklet)	View-Master	1970s	25	35	55
Wrist Flashlight	Bantamlite	1970s	35	65	100
Wrist Flashlight	Bantamlite		45	65	100

Lost in Space

TOY	MANUFACTURER	YEAR	GOOD	EX	MIB
Lost in Space Robot	Remco	1965	175	325	500
Lost in Space Robot (10" tall, stop & go action, blinking lights)	AHI	1977	23	35	50
Robot (talking 16" tall)	Matsudaya		45	80	125
Robot (wind-up)	Matsudaya		10	15	25

Miscellaneous

TOY	MANUFACTURER	YEAR	GOOD	EX	MIB
Astro Base (22" tall, red & white astronaut base)	Ideal	1960	225	325	500
Astro Boy Mask (blue hair with boy smiling)		1960s	20	45	65
Astro Boy Mask/Glasses (blue glasses with Astro boy hair on top)		1960s	20	45	65
Astro-ray Space Gun (10")			20	30	45
Astronaut Halloween Costume	Collegeville	1960	18	25	40
Astronaut Halloween Costume	Ben Cooper	1962	18	25	40
Astronaut Space Commander Play Suit (green outfit & cap)	Yankeeboy	1950s	35	50	80
Atomic Disintegrator (cap gun)	Hubley	1940s	50	70	110
Cherilea Space Gun (miniature scale, die cast)	Marx		27	40	60
Dan Dare & the Aliens Ray Gun (21" color tin litho gun)		1950s	105	155	235
Martian Bobbing Head (7" tall, blue vinyl plastic)		1960s	23	35	50
Men into Space Astronaut Space Helmet (plastic helmet with visor)	Ideal	1960s	35	50	75
Moon Map Jigsaw Puzzle (10 x 14" picture of the moon's surface)	Selchow & Righter	1970	14	20	30
Rex Mars Atomix Pistol Flashlight (plastic, 1950's)	Marx		50	75	100
Rocket Gun (7" hard yellow/green plastic with spring loaded plunger)	Jak-Pak	1958	9	13	20
Rocky Jones Space Ranger (14 x 16" colorbook)	Whitman	1951	25	39	60

Miscellaneous

TOY	MANUFACTURER	YEAR	GOOD	EX	MIB
Space Hopper Child's Rubbers (5 x 6" black rubber overshoes)		1950s	23	29	45
Space Safari Planetary Playset (with vehicles, astronauts, aliens)		1969	45	65	95
Space Water Pistol	Nasta	1976	7	10	15
Sparkling Ray Gun	Nasta	1976	7	10	15
TV Space Riders Coloring Book (14 X 15")	Abbott	1952	7	10	15
V-Enemy Visitor Doll (12" tall)	LJN	1984	16	23	35

Planet of the Apes

TOY	MANUFACTURER	YEAR	GOOD	EX	MIB
Planet of Apes "Galen" Bank			25	35	55
Planet of the Apes Color-Vue Set	Hasbro	1970s	30	45	65
Planet of the Apes Fun-Doh Modeling Molds (molds of Zir)	Chemtoy	1974	20	30	45
Planet of the Apes Photo Puzzles (96 pc. puzzles in can)	H.G. Toys		7	10	15
Planet of the Apes Trash Can (oval can)	Chein	1967	25	35	55
Planet of the Apes View-Master Reels (set of three reels with booklet)	View-Master	1970s	15	25	35
Planet of the Apes Wagon (friction powered prison wagon)	AHI		20	45	65

Robots

TOY	MANUFACTURER	YEAR	GOOD	EX	MIB
Answer Game Machine (battery operated robot performs math tricks)			300	650	900
Attacking Martian (10")	S.H.	1960s	45	65	100
B.O. Robot (7-1/2", electric remote control)		1950s	325	450	700
Big Max & his Electronic Conveyor (9")	Remco		50	70	110
Captain Astro (6", wind-up)		1970	40	55	85
Chief Robotman (12")	KO	1965	400	850	1200
Countdown-Y (9")	Cragstan	1960s	100	145	225
Electric Robot (plastic, 15" tall)	Marx		125	200	275
Forbidden Planet Robby Figure (16" tall, talking)	Matsudaya		80	115	175
Forbidden Planet Robby Figure (5" tall, wind-up)	Matsudaya		16	23	35
Frankenstein Robot (tin and plastic battery operated)			550	900	1400
Laughing Robot	Marx		50	70	110
Launching Robot (10")	S.H.	1975	25	35	55
Lunar Robot (wind-up, companion to Thunder Robot)			225	450	650
Lunar Spaceman (12", battery operated)		1978	20	30	45
Magnor (9")	Cragstan	1975	23	35	50
Mechanical Interplanetary Explorer (8", wind-up)		1950s	180	260	400
Mechanical Moon Creature (6", wind-up)	Marx	1960	90	130	200
Mechanical Spaceman (6", wind-up)		1960s	40	60	90
Mechanical Television Spaceman (7", wind-up)	ALPS	1965	45	60	95
Mechanized Robot (13", battery operated)		1960s	425	600	925
Mekanda Robo (6 1/2")	Zncron	1981	12	26	40
Mini Robot (2 1/2" tall, blue plastic wind-up robot)			14	20	30
Moon Creature (mechanical, wind-up, 5 1/2" tall)	Marx	1960s	115	170	260
Myrobo (9", battery operated)		1970s	25	35	55
Outer Space Ape Man Robot	Ilco	1970s	14	20	30
Outer Space Robot (10", battery operated)		1979	20	30	45
Plastic Spaceman (wind-up)	Irwin	1950	45	65	100
Radio Control Robot	Bilko	1970s	25	35	55
Red, Blue & Silver Robot (plastic with antenna, metal key)		1970s	11	16	25

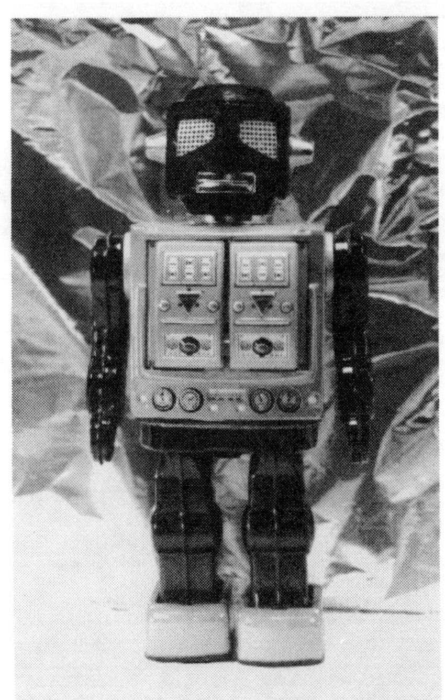

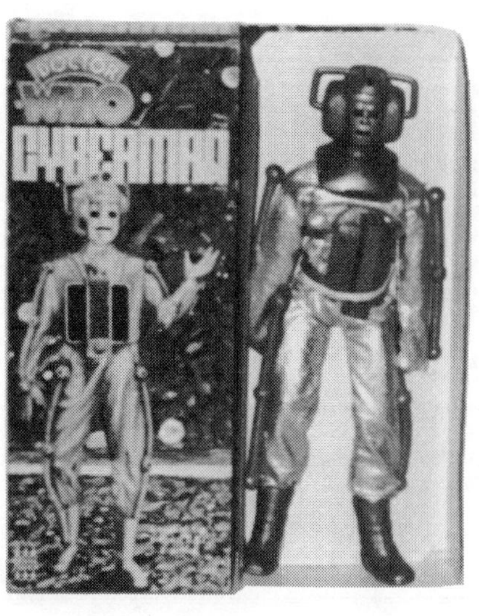

Top to Bottom: Attacking Martian Robot, 1960s, by S.H. (Japan); Dr. Who Cyberman, 1976, Denys Fisher; Space:1999 Action Figures of Professor Bergman, Commander Koenig, and Dr. Russel, 1976, by Mattel.

Robots

TOY	MANUFACTURER	YEAR	GOOD	EX	MIB
Rendezvous 7.8 (15")	Yanoman		170	245	375
Ro-Gun "It's A Robot" (Sho-gun type robot that changes into rifle)	Arco	1984	11	16	25
Robert the Wonder Toy (14")	Ideal	1960	90	130	200
Robot (plastic and metal, 12" tall, 1967)	Marx		115	165	250
Robot 2500	Durham Industries	1979	14	20	30
Robot Commando (19")	Ideal	1960s	60	85	130
Robot Tank II (10", battery operated)		1965	150	210	325
Robot YM-3 (5" tall)	Matsudaya	1985	14	20	30
Sky Robot (8")	S.H.	1970s	20	30	45
Space Guard Pilot (8")	Asak	1975	20	30	45
Sparky Robot (7")	KO	1960	45	65	100
Star Robot (black robot)	CDO	1970s	10	15	20
Super Astronaut	S.J.M.	1981	11	16	25
TR-2 Robotank (5", battery operated)		1975	35	50	75
TV Spaceman (battery operated)		1965	90	130	200
Zerak the Blue Destroyer Zeroid (6" metal blue plastic with motor)	Ideal	1968	45	65	100

Space Ships

TOY	MANUFACTURER	YEAR	GOOD	EX	MIB
Eagle Lunar Module (9")		1960s	80	115	175
Friendship 7 (9 1/2", friction)			35	50	75
Inter-Planet Toy Rocketank Patrol (10")	Macrey	1950	30	45	70
Jupiter Space Station (8")	TN (Japan)	1960s	90	125	195
Moon-Rider Space Ship (tin wind-up, 1930's)	Marx		125	200	250
Mystery Space Ship (35mm astronauts and moonmen, rocket, launchers)	Marx	1960s	50	75	100
Rocket Fighter (with tail fin and sparking action, tin wind-up)	Marx	1950s	250	375	500
Rocket Fighter Spaceship (celluloid window, tin wind-up, 12" long)	Marx	1930s	125	200	250
Satellite X-107 (9")	Cragstan	1965	90	130	200
Sky Patrol Jet (5x13x5" bump and go battery op. gunner)	TN (Japan)	1960s	295	425	650
Solar-X Space Rocket (15")	TN (Japan)		45	65	100
Space Bus (tin helicopter, battery operated with wired remote)			350	500	750
Space Pacer (7", battery operated)		1978	23	29	45
Space Ship (bronze, hard plastic)	Marx		40	60	90
Space Survey X-09 (battery operated tin and plastic flying saucer)			175	350	525
Space Train (9" long, engine & three metallic cars)		1950s	18	26	40
Super Space Capsule (9 1/2")		1960s	70	100	150
X-3 Rocket Gyro		1950s	25	35	50

Star Trek

TOY	MANUFACTURER	YEAR	GOOD	EX	MIB
"Passage to Moauv" Book/Record Set			5	8	11
20th Anniversary Vulcan Ears	Ballantine		4	5	7
Action Toy Book	Random House	1976	7	10	15
Antican Alien Figure, ST:TNG (3 3/4", fully poseable)	Galoob	1988	14	20	30
Attemped Hijacking of the U.S.S. Enterprise & Officers	H.G. Toys	1974	6	8	12
Battle on the Planet Klingon Puzzle (150 pieces)	H.G. Toys	1974	5	7	10
Battle on the Planet Romulon Puzzle (150 pieces)	H.G. Toys	1974	5	7	10
Beanbag Chair, ST:TMP (group drawing)			25	35	55

Star Trek

TOY	MANUFACTURER	YEAR	GOOD	EX	MIB
Bop Bag (plastic, inflatable Spock)		1975	55	80	125
Bowl, ST:TMP (plastic)	Deka	1979	3	4	6
Bridge Punch-out Book, ST:TMP	Wanderer	1979	7	10	15
Bridge Scene Frame Tray Puzzle (8 1/2" x 11" tray)	Whitman	1978	2	3	5
Bulletin Board, ST:TMP (die cut board with four pens)	Milton Bradley	1979	6	8	12
Cartoon Puzzle	Whitman	1978	4	5	7
Clock (Enterprise orbiting planet, rectangular)		1989	23	33	50
Clock (white wall clock, 20th Anniversary logo, Star Trek Fan Club)		1986	14	20	30
Collegeville Halloween Costume (Spock, Kirk, Ilia or Klingon)		1979	11	16	25
Colorforms Adventure Set (plastic stick-ons)	Colorforms	1975	14	20	30
Comb & Brush Set (6" x 3", blue, oval brush)		1977	14	20	30
Communicators (black plastic walkie talkies with flip-up grid)	McNerney	1989	35	50	75
Communicators (walkie talkies, blue plastic with flip-up grid)	Mego	1976	70	100	150
Communicators, ST:TMP (plastic wrist band walkie talkie)	Mego	1980	90	130	200
Controlled Space Flight (plastic Enterprise, battery operated)	Remco	1976	80	115	175
Data Figure, ST:TNG (3 3/4", fully poseable)	Galoob	1988	7	10	15
Digital Travel Alarm	Lincoln Enterprises		14	20	30
Enterprise Jigsaw Puzzle, ST:TMP (551 pieces)	Aviva	1979	9	13	20
Enterprise Make A Model, ST:TNG	Chatham River Press	1990	4	5	8
Enterprise Punch-out Book, ST:TMP	Wanderer	1979	9	13	20
Enterprise Puzzle, ST:IV (551 pieces "The Voyage Home")	Mind's Eye Press	1986	14	20	30
Enterprise Puzzle, ST:TMP (100 pieces)	Arrow		4	6	9
Enterprise Puzzle, ST:TMP (15 piece sliding puzzle)	Larami	1979	5	7	10
Enterprise Puzzle, ST:TMP (250 piece color photo)	Milton Bradley	1979	5	7	10
Enterprise Watch, ST:TMP	Bradley		20	30	45
Enterprise Watch, ST:TMP (gold plated silver men & women styles)	Rarities Mint	1989	55	80	125
Enterprise, ST:III (4" long, die cast with black plastic stand)	Ertl	1984	7	10	15
Enterprise, ST:IV (24", silver plastic, inflatable)	Sterling	1986	20	30	45
Enterprise, ST:TMP (20" long, white plastic, lights & sound)	South Bend	1979	80	115	175
Enterprise, ST:TNG (6" long, die cast with detachable saucer section)	Galoob	1988	9	13	20
Excelsior, ST:III (4" long, die cast with black plastic stand)	Ertl	1984	7	10	15
Ferengi Alien Figure, ST:TNG (3 3/4", fully poseable)	Galoob	1988	25	35	50
Ferengi Fighter, ST:TNG (orange plastic with moveable canopy & guns)	Galoob	1989	20	30	45
Ferengi Halloween Costume, ST:TNG	Ben Cooper	1988	7	10	15
Figurine Painting (plastic figurine, brush & five paints)	Milton Bradley	1979	14	20	30
Flashlight (battery operated, small phaser shape)		1976	6	8	12
Flashlight, ST:TMP (hand flashlight)	Larami	1979	6	8	12
Force Field Capture Puzzle (150 pieces)	H.G. Toys	1976	4	6	9
Giant in the Universe Pop-up Book	Random House	1977	14	20	30
Golden Trivia Game (trivia cards, game board & dice)	Western Publishing	1985	20	30	45

Star Trek

TOY	MANUFACTURER	YEAR	GOOD	EX	MIB
Helmet (plastic, electronic sound, flashing red light on top)	Remco	1976	55	80	125
Kirk & Officers Beaming Down Puzzle (150 pieces)	H.G. Toys	1974	5	7	10
Kirk & Spock or Spock Mirror (two sizes available)		1977	11	16	25
Kirk & Spock Watch, ST:TMP (LCD rectangular)	Bradley		25	35	55
Kirk Bank (12" plastic)	Play Pal	1975	25	35	55
Kirk Figure, ST:III (3 3/4" tall with communicator, poseable)	Ertl	1984	9	13	20
Kirk Figure, ST:TMP (13" tall, soft body with plastic head)	Knickerbocker	1979	16	23	35
Kirk Figure, ST:V (7" tall, posed statuette)	Galoob	1989	25	35	55
Kirk Halloween Costume (plastic mask, one piece jumpsuit)	Ben Cooper	1975	9	13	20
Kirk Needlepoint Kit (number 10 mesh canvas with white background)	Arista	1980	16	23	35
Kirk or Spock Halloween Costumes (lightweight, tie-on jumpsuit)	Ben Cooper	1967	11	16	25
Kirk Puzzle, ST:TMP (15 piece sliding puzzle)	Larami	1979	5	7	10
Kirk, Mr. Spock, Dr. McCoy Puzzle (150 pieces)	H.G. Toys	1976	4	6	9
Kite (TV Enterprise or Spock)	Hi-Flyer	1975	14	20	30
Kite, ST:III (pictures Enterprise)	Lever Bros.	1984	14	20	30
Kite, ST:TMP (picture of Spock)	Aviva	1976	11	16	25
Klaa Figure, ST:V (7" tall, posed statuette)	Galoob	1989	25	35	55
Klingon Bird of Prey, ST:III (3 1/2", die cast with black plastic stand)	Ertl	1984	7	10	15
Klingon Figure, ST:III (3 3/4" tall with pet, fully poseable)	Ertl	1984	7	10	15
Klingon Halloween Costume (plastic mask, one piece jumpsuit)	Ben Cooper	1975	9	13	20
Klingon Halloween Costume, ST:TNG	Ben Cooper	1988	7	10	15
LaForge Figure, ST:TNG (3 3/4", fully poseable)	Galoob	1988	3	4	6
Light Switch Cover, ST:TMP	American Tack & Hdw.	1985	6	8	12
Magic Slates (four different designs)	Whitman	1979	7	10	15
Make-a-Game Book	Wanderer	1979	7	10	15
McCoy Figure, ST:V (7" tall, posed statuette)	Galoob	1989	25	35	55
Metal Detector (metal detector with U.S.S. Enterprise decal)	Jetco	1976	100	145	225
Mirror (2" x 3" metal, with black & white photo of crew)		1966	1	2	3
Mission to Gamma VI (18" high plastic cave creature)	Mego	1976	350	475	750
Mix 'n Mold (three separate kits: Kirk, Spock or McCoy)		1975	35	50	75
Movie Viewer (3" red & black plastic)	Chemtoy	1967	11	16	25
Paint by Numbers (large) (canvas paint, Kirk, Spock & Enterprise)	Hasbro	1972	35	50	75
Paint by Numbers (small) (canvas paint, Kirk, Spock & Enterprise)	Hasbro	1972	23	35	50
Pen & Poster Kit (line posters & felt tipped pens)	Open Door	1976	11	16	25
Pen & Poster Kit, ST:III (3-D poster "Search for Spock")	Placo	1984	9	13	20
Pennant "Paramount Pictures Adventure" (9" x 21-1/2")	Universal Studios	1988	5	7	10
Pennant, "Spock in Vulcan Robes", ST:II (12" x 30" "Spock Lives")	Image Products	1982	6	8	12
Pennant, "The Wrath of Khan", ST:II (12" x 30" black w/ Enterprise)	Image Products	1982	6	8	12
Phaser (Astro Buzz-Ray Gun with three color flash beam)	Remco	1967	80	115	175

Star Trek

TOY	MANUFACTURER	YEAR	GOOD	EX	MIB
Phaser (black plastic, electronic sound, flashlight projects target)	Remco	1975	35	50	75
Phaser Battle Game (black plastic, 13" high battery op. target game)	Mego	1976	195	275	425
Phaser, ST:III (white & blue plastic gun with light & sound effects)	Daisy	1984	35	50	75
Phaser, ST:TNG (gray plastic light & sound hand phaser)	Galoob	1988	14	20	30
Picard Figure, ST:TNG (3 3/4", fully poseable)	Galoob	1988	3	4	6
Pinball Game, ST:TMP (12", plastic, two styles Kirk or Spock)	Azrak-Hamway		23	35	50
Pinball Game, ST:TMP (electronic pinball game)	Bally	1979	200	295	450
Pocket Flix (battery operated movie viewer & film cartridge)	Ideal	1978	18	25	40
Pop-up Book, ST:TMP	Wanderer	1980	11	16	25
Q Alien Figure, ST:TNG (3 3/4", fully poseable, black outfit)	Galoob	1988	23	35	50
Riker Figure, ST:TNG (3 3/4", fully poseable)	Galoob	1988	2	3	5
Role Playing Game, 2001 Deluxe Edition	FASA		20	30	45
Scottie Figure, ST:III (3 3/4" tall with phaser, fully poseable)	Ertl	1984	7	10	15
Selay Alien Figure, ST:TNG (3 3/4", fully poseable, green reptile)	Galoob	1988	16	23	35
Shuttlecraft Galileo, ST:TNG	Galoob	1989	16	23	35
Space Design Center, ST:TMP	Avalon	1979	70	100	150
Spock & Enterprise 20th Anniversary Digital Watch, ST:TMP	Lewco	1986	9	13	20
Spock & Enterprise Halloween Costume	Ben Cooper	1973	11	16	25
Spock Bank (12" plastic)	Play Pal	1975	25	35	55
Spock Chair, ST:TMP (inflatable)		1979	16	23	35
Spock Ears, ST:TMP	Aviva	1979	7	10	15
Spock Figure, ST:III (3 3/4" tall with phaser, fully poseable)	Ertl	1984	9	13	20
Spock Figure, ST:TMP (13" tall, soft body with plastic head)	Knickerbocker	1979	16	23	35
Spock Figure, ST:V (7" tall, posed statuette)	Galoob	1989	25	35	55
Spock Halloween Costume (plastic mask, one piece jumpsuit)	Ben Cooper	1975	9	13	20
Spock in Space Suit Frame Tray Puzzle (8 1/2" x 11" tray)	Whitman	1978	2	3	5
Spock Needlepoint Kit (14" x 18" number 10 mesh canvas)	Arista	1980	16	23	35
Spock Puzzle, ST:TMP (15 piece sliding puzzle)	Larami	1979	5	7	10
Spock Puzzle, ST:TMP (551 pieces)	Aviva	1979	9	13	20
Spock Tray (17 1/2" metal lap tray with legs "Mr. Spock")	Aviva	1979	9	13	20
Spock Watch, ST:TMP	Bradley		20	30	45
Star Trek Cartoon Puzzle	Whitman	1978	4	5	7
Star Trek Color & Activity Book	Whitman	1979	2	3	5
Star Trek Coloring Book	Saalfield	1979	7	10	15
Star Trek II USS Enterprise Ship (3" metal die cast)	Corgi	1982	9	13	20
Star Trek Paint by Number Set	Hasbro	1974	11	16	25
Star Trek Puzzle	Marvel	1976	5	7	10
Star Trek Puzzle "The Alien"		1975	7	10	15
Star Trek TMP Dinnerware Set	Deka	1979	16	23	35
Star Trek TMP Poster Pen Set (14x20")	Aviva	1979	9	13	20
Star Trek Watch (Spock on dial with revolving Enterprise)	Bradley	1979	45	65	100
Star Trek Writing Tablet (8 x 10")		1967	11	16	25
Starship U.S.S. Enterprise & Its Officers Puzzle (300 pieces)	H.G. Toys	1974	9	13	20

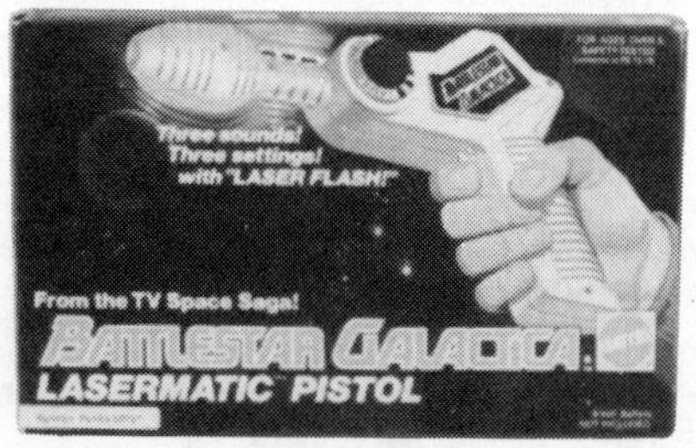

Space Explorer TV Robot, 1965, battery operated, by S.H. (Japan); Star Trek Oil Paint By Number Coloring Set, Hasbro; Rocket Fighter, 1950, by Marx; Battlestar Galactica Lasermatic Pistol, 1976, by Mattel.

Star Trek

TOY	MANUFACTURER	YEAR	GOOD	EX	MIB
Sybok Figure, ST:V (7" tall, posed statuette)	Galoob	1989	25	35	55
Telescreen (plastic, battery operated target game with light & sound)	Mego	1976	70	100	150
The Role Playing Game, 2004 Basic Set (three reading books)	FASA		7	10	15
The Role Playing Game, Second Deluxe Edition	FASA		14	20	30
Tracer Gun (plastic pistol with colored plastic discs)	Rayline	1966	45	65	100
Tracer Scope (rifle with discs)	Rayline	1968	55	80	125
Transporter Frame Tray Puzzle (8 1/2" x 11" tray)	Whitman	1978	2	3	5
Tricorder (blue plastic tape recorder, battery operated)	Mego	1976	70	100	150
Trillions of Trilligs Pop-up Book	Random House	1977	16	23	35
U.S.S. Enterprise Action Playset (8" dolls, stools, console)	Mego	1975	125	180	275
U.S.S. Enterprise Bridge, ST:TMP (white plastic)	Mego	1980	70	100	150
Utility Belt	Remco	1975	45	65	100
View-Master (16 page story booklet with three viewer reels)	GAF	1968	7	10	15
View-Master (16 page story booklet with three viewer reels)	GAF	1974	7	10	15
View-Master (talking) (three viewer reels "Mr. Spock's Time Trek")	GAF	1974	11	16	25
View-Master Double-Vue, ST:TMP (double plastic cassette)	GAF	1981	11	16	25
View-Master Gift Pak, ST:TMP (viewer, three reels, 3-D posters)	GAF	1979	35	50	75
View-Master, ST:II (with three reels)	View-Master	1982	7	10	15
View-Master, ST:TMP (story booklet with three reels)	GAF	1979	7	10	15
Wastebasket, ST:TMP (13" high, metal rainbow painting)	Chein	1979	11	16	25
Wastepaper Basket (black metal)	Chein	1977	35	50	75
Water Pistol (white plastic, shaped like U.S.S. Enterprise)	Azrak-Hamway	1976	20	30	45
Water Pistol, ST:TMP (gray plastic, early phaser)	Aviva	1979	11	16	25
Worf Figure, ST:TNG (3 3/4", fully poseable)	Galoob	1988	3	4	6
Yar Figure, ST:TNG (3 3/4", fully poseable)	Galoob	1988	7	10	15
Yo-Yo, ST:TMP (blue sparkle plastic)	Aviva	1979	7	10	15

Star Wars

TOY	MANUFACTURER	YEAR	GOOD	EX	MIB
"Assault on Death Star" Movie Cartridge			14	20	30
"Battle in Hyperspace" Movie Cartridge			14	20	30
"Danger at the Cantina" Movie Cartridge			14	20	30
"Destroy Death Star" Movie Cartridge			14	20	30
"May the Force be with You" Movie Cartridge			9	13	20
"Planet of the Hoojibs" Book/Record Set			4	5	7
"The Maverick Moon" Book	Random House		2	3	5
"The Mystery of the Rebellious Robot" Book	Random House		2	3	5
3-D Electronic Quartz Sceni-Clock	Bradley	1982	16	23	35
3-D Ewok Perk-Up Sticker Sets			5	7	10
ABC Fun	Random House	1985	6	8	12
Aboard the Millennium Falcon Jigsaw Puzzle (1000 pieces)			7	10	15
Admiral Ackbar Figurine Paint Set	Craftmaster		9	13	20
Attack of the Sand People Jigsaw Puzzle (140 pieces)	Kenner		5	7	10
Backpack, ROTJ			11	16	25
Bantha Jigsaw Puzzle, The (140 pieces)	Kenner		6	8	12

SPACE

Star Wars

TOY	MANUFACTURER	YEAR	GOOD	EX	MIB
Battle on Hoth Paint Set			11	16	25
Ben Kenobi & Darth Vader Poster	Proctor & Gamble	1978	9	13	20
Blanket			14	20	30
Boba Fett Cake Pan			11	16	25
Boba Fett Figure (bisque)	Towle/Sigma	1983	45	65	100
Boba Fett Poster			7	10	15
Bubble Bath (four different, each)			6	8	12
Burger Chef Fun Book	Kenner	1978	6	8	12
C-3PO & R2-D2 Alarm Clock	Bradley	1980	16	23	35
C-3PO & R2-D2 Digital Watch	Bradley	1970s	55	80	125
C-3PO & R2-D2 Watch (digital, rectangular)	Bradley	1970s	30	45	65
C-3PO & R2-D2 Watch (digital, round face)	Bradley	1970s	45	65	95
C-3PO & R2-D2 Watch (digital, round, musical)	Bradley	1970s	70	100	150
C-3PO & R2-D2 Watch (vinyl band, drawing)	Bradley	1970s	45	60	95
C-3PO & R2-D2 Watch (vinyl band, photo)	Bradley	1970s	30	45	65
C-3PO & R2-D2 Watch (white border, photo)	Bradley	1970s	45	65	95
C-3PO Bank (ceramic)	Roman Ceramics	1977	25	35	55
C-3PO Bust Case			20	30	45
C-3PO Cake Pan			11	16	25
C-3PO Cookie Jar	Roman Ceramics	1977	80	115	175
C-3PO Earrings			7	10	15
C-3PO Figurine Paint Set	Craftmaster		9	13	20
C-3PO Mug (ceramic)	Sigma		16	23	35
C-3PO Pencil Tray	Sigma		23	35	50
C-3PO Pendant			9	13	20
C-3PO Picture Frame	Sigma		20	30	45
C-3PO Ring			10	14	22
C-3PO Stickpin			6	8	12
C-3PO Tape Dispenser	Sigma		23	35	50
Cantina Band Jigsaw Puzzle (500 pieces)	Kenner		6	8	12
Cast Coloring Book	Kenner		5	7	10
Charm Bracelet			7	10	15
Chewbacca & C-3PO Coloring Book	Kenner		5	7	10
Chewbacca & Leia Coloring Book	Kenner		5	7	10
Chewbacca Bandolier Strap Case			11	16	25
Chewbacca Bank	Sigma	1983	25	35	55
Chewbacca Medal	W. Berrie	1980	6	8	12
Chewbacca Mug (ceramic)	Sigma		18	25	40
Chewbacca Pendant			9	13	20
Chewbacca Poster	Burger King	1978	5	7	10
Chewbacca Punching Bag (50")	Kenner	1977	45	65	100
Chewbacca's Activity Book	Random House		2	3	5
Chewbacca, Han, Leia & Lando Coloring Book	Kenner		5	7	10
Chewbacca/Darth Vader Bookends	Sigma		25	35	55
Chewbecca Birthday Candle	Wilton		6	8	12
Darth Vader & Ben Kenobi Duel Jigsaw Puzzle	Kenner		5	7	10
Darth Vader & Imperial Guard Roller Skates			16	23	35
Darth Vader & Stormtroopers Coloring Book	Kenner		5	7	10
Darth Vader & Stromtroopers Poster			7	10	15
Darth Vader Bank	Adam Joseph	1983	9	13	20
Darth Vader Bank (anodized silver plated)	Leonard Silver	1981	45	65	95
Darth Vader Bank (ceramic)	Roman Ceramics	1977	25	35	55
Darth Vader Beach Towel			6	8	12
Darth Vader Belt Buckle	Leather Shop	1977	14	20	30
Darth Vader Birthday Candle	Wilton		6	8	12
Darth Vader Cookie Jar	Roman Ceramics	1977	80	115	175
Darth Vader Digital Watch	Bradley	1970s	30	45	65
Darth Vader Duty Roster (school supplies)			5	7	10
Darth Vader Earrings			7	10	15
Darth Vader Figure (bisque)	Towle/Sigma	1983	30	45	65
Darth Vader Glow-in-the-Dark Paint Set			9	13	20

Star Wars

TOY	MANUFACTURER	YEAR	GOOD	EX	MIB
Darth Vader Mug (ceramic)	Sigma		16	23	35
Darth Vader Pendant			9	13	20
Darth Vader Picture Frame	Sigma		30	45	65
Darth Vader Pillow		1983	9	13	20
Darth Vader Poster	Burger King	1978	5	7	10
Darth Vader Poster	Nestea	1980	9	13	20
Darth Vader Poster (life size)			9	13	20
Darth Vader Premium Poster	Proctor & Gamble	1980	4	5	8
Darth Vader Punching Bag (50")	Kenner	1977	25	40	60
Darth Vader Ring	W. Berrie	1980	6	8	12
Darth Vader Speaker Phone	ATC	1983	55	80	125
Darth Vader SSP Van (black)	Kenner	1978	18	25	40
Darth Vader Stickpin			6	8	12
Darth Vader Watch (star & planet on face)	Bradley	1970s	45	65	95
Darth Vader Watch (vinyl band)	Bradley	1970s	30	45	65
Darth Vader's Activity Book	Random House		2	3	5
Darth Vader, R2-D2 & C-3PO Cookie Jar (hexagon)	Sigma		55	80	125
Death Star Poster	Proctor & Gamble	1978	9	13	20
Degobah Play-Doh Set			16	23	35
Degobah Premium Poster	Burger King	1980	5	7	10
Droid Dilemma, The (book)	Random House	1979	4	5	8
Droid Wall Clock	Bradley		20	30	45
Droids Digital Watch	Bradley	1970s	30	45	65
Droids Dinnerware Set			11	16	25
Duel Racing Set	Lionel	1978	60	85	135
Electric Toothbrush	Kenner	1980	16	23	35
Electric Toothbrush	Kenner	1978	16	23	35
Emperor's Royal Guard Bank	Adam Joseph	1983	9	13	20
Empire Strikes Back Dinnerware Set			16	23	35
Empire Strikes Back Panorama Book, The	Random House		14	20	30
Empire Strikes Back Pop-up Book, The	Random House	1980	11	16	25
Empire Strikes Back Poster Album Vol. 1			11	16	25
Empire Strikes Back Radio Program Poster			14	20	30
Empire Strikes Back Sketchbook, The	Ballantine	1980	14	20	30
Empire Strikes Back Storybook, The	Random House	1980	9	13	20
Empire Strikes Back Wall Clock	Bradley		20	30	45
Escape from the Monster Ship (book)	Random House	1985	6	8	12
Ewok Music Box Radio			18	25	40
Ewok Teaching Clock			20	30	45
Ewoks Coloring Books (each)	Kenner	1983	7	10	15
Ewoks Digital Watch	Bradley	1970s	30	45	65
Ewoks Give-A-Show Projector with Strips	Kenner	1984	18	25	40
Ewoks Play-Doh Set			11	16	25
Ewoks Watch (vinyl band)	Bradley	1970s	30	45	65
Fan Club Kit			16	23	35
Flying R2-D2 Rocket Kit	Estes	1978	9	13	20
Fuzzy as an Ewok (book)	Random House	1985	6	8	12
Galactic Emperor Figure (bisque)	Towle/Sigma	1983	35	50	75
Gamorrean Guard Figure (bisque)	Towle/Sigma	1983	25	35	55
Gamorrean Guard Mug (ceramic)	Sigma		10	20	30
Gamorrean Guard Bank	Adam Joseph	1983	7	10	15
Give-A-Show Projector with Strips	Kenner	1979	23	35	50
Han & Chewbacca Jigsaw Puzzle (140 pieces)	Kenner		6	8	12
Han Solo Figure (bisque)	Towle/Sigma	1983	45	65	100
Han Solo Figurine Paint Set	Craftmaster		16	23	35
Han Solo Mug (ceramic)	Sigma		23	35	50
Hoth Premium Poster	Burger King	1980	5	7	10
How the Ewoks Saved the Trees	Random House	1985	6	8	12
Ice Planet Hoth Play-Doh Set			16	23	35
Inflatable Lightsaber	Kenner	1977	45	60	95

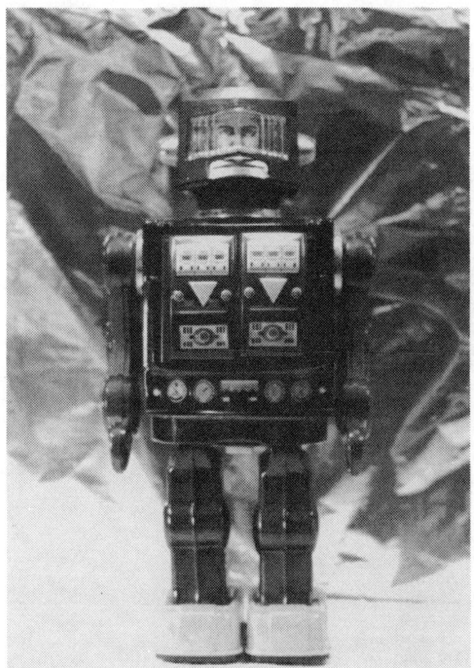

Top to Bottom: Super (Apollo) Space Capsule, 1960s; Attacking Martian, 1950s, (Japan); Super Astronaut Robot, 1981; Star Trek: The Motion Picture Poster Pen Set, 1979, by Aviva.

TOY	MANUFACTURER	YEAR	GOOD	EX	MIB
Interceptor (INT-4) Mini-rig			16	23	35
Introducing Yoda Press Kit		1980	20	30	45
Jabba the Hut Digital Watch	Bradley	1970s	30	45	65
Jabba the Hut Play-Doh Set			11	16	25
Jabba the Hut Puzzle	Craft Master	1983	3	4	6
Jabba the Hutt Bank	Sigma	1983	25	35	55
Jabba's Prison (Sears exclusive)			45	65	100
Jawa Punching Bag (50")	Kenner	1977	45	65	100
Jawas Capture R2-D2 Jigsaw Puzzle (140 pieces)	Kenner		4	6	9
Kneesaa Bank	Adam Joseph	1983	7	10	15
Lando Calrissian Figure (bisque)	Towle/Sigma	1983	30	45	65
Lando Calrissian Mug (ceramic)	Sigma		16	23	35
Lando Fighting Skiff Guard Coloring Book	Kenner	1983	7	10	15
Lando in Falcon Cockpit Coloring Book	Kenner	1983	7	10	15
Learn-to-Read Activity Book	Random House	1985	6	8	12
Leia & Han Solo Glow-in-the-Dark Paint Set			9	13	20
Leia Figurine Paint Set	Craftmaster		11	16	25
Leia Mug (ceramic)	Sigma		20	30	45
Lost Prince, The (book)	Random House	1985	6	8	12
Luke & Leia Leap for their Lives Jigsaw Puzzle (500 pieces)	Kenner		6	8	12
Luke & Tauntaun Figurine Paint Set	Craftmaster		14	20	30
Luke & Tauntaun Teapot Set			25	35	55
Luke Coloring Book	Kenner	1983	7	10	15
Luke Mug (ceramic)	Sigma		20	30	45
Luke Skywalker AM Headset Radio			95	135	210
Luke Skywalker Figure (bisque)	Towle/Sigma	1983	30	45	65
Luke Skywalker Glow-in-the-Dark Paint Set			9	13	20
Luke Skywalker Jigsaw Puzzle (500 pieces)	Kenner		11	16	25
Luke Skywalker Poster	Burger King	1978	5	7	10
Luke Skywalker Poster	Nestea	1980	9	13	20
Luke Skywalker Poster			18	25	40
Luke Skywalker Premium Poster	Proctor & Gamble	1980	4	5	8
Max Rebo Coloring Book	Kenner	1983	7	10	15
May the Force Be with You Ring	W. Berrie	1980	6	8	12
Movie Viewer	Kenner	1978	14	20	30
My Jedi Journal	Ballantine		7	10	15
Notebooks (school supplies, each)			5	7	10
Original Fan Club Kit			20	30	45
Original Press Kit		1977	25	35	55
Pillowcase			4	5	8
Pirates of Tarnoonga, The (book)	Random House	1985	6	8	12
Placemats (complete set)			14	20	30
Portable Clock/Radio	Bradley	1984	11	16	25
Portfolio (school supplies)			5	7	10
Princess Leia's Beauty Bag			14	20	30
R2-D2 & C-3PO Belt Buckles	Leather Shop	1977	14	20	30
R2-D2 & C-3PO Jigsaw Puzzle (140 pieces)			6	8	12
R2-D2 & C-3PO Premium Poster	Proctor & Gamble	1980	4	5	8
R2-D2 Bank	Adam Joseph	1983	7	10	15
R2-D2 Bank (ceramic)	Roman Ceramics	1977	25	35	55
R2-D2 Belt Buckle	Leather Shop	1977	14	20	30
R2-D2 Birthday Candle	Wilton		6	8	12
R2-D2 Coloring Book	Kenner		5	7	10
R2-D2 Cookie Jar	Roman Ceramics	1977	90	130	200
R2-D2 Earrings			7	10	15
R2-D2 Pendant			9	13	20
R2-D2 Picture Frame	Sigma		30	45	65
R2-D2 Poster	Burger King	1978	5	7	10
R2-D2 Punching Bag (50")	Kenner	1977	25	40	60

Star Wars

TOY	MANUFACTURER	YEAR	GOOD	EX	MIB
R2-D2 Ring			10	14	22
R2-D2 Stickpin			6	8	12
R2-D2 String Dispenser with Scissors	Sigma		20	30	45
Read & the Force is with You Poster (Yoda)			14	20	30
Return of the Jedi Activity Book	Happy House	1983	5	7	10
Return of the Jedi Art Portfolio			9	13	20
Return of the Jedi Belt, Illustrated	Leather Shop	1977	5	7	10
Return of the Jedi Candy Container (complete set of eighteen)	Topps	1983	45	65	100
Return of the Jedi Coloring Book		1984	2	3	5
Return of the Jedi Dinnerware Set			14	20	30
Return of the Jedi Maze Book	Happy House	1983	5	7	10
Return of the Jedi Monster Activity Book	Happy House	1983	5	7	10
Return of the Jedi Picture Puzzle Book	Happy House	1983	5	7	10
Return of the Jedi Pop-up Book	Random House	1983	11	16	25
Return of the Jedi Punch-out & Make It Book	Random House		14	20	30
Return of the Jedi Sketchbook	Ballantine	1983	11	16	25
Return of the Jedi Storybook	Random House	1983	9	13	20
Return of the Jedi Word Puzzle Book	Happy House	1983	5	7	10
Selling of Driods Jigsaw Puzzle, The (500 pieces)	Kenner		4	6	9
Sheets			11	16	25
Sleeping Bag			15	21	32
Snow Speeder Toothbrush Holder	Sigma		25	35	55
Space Battle Jigsaw Puzzle (500 pieces)	Kenner		7	10	15
Star Destroyer Poster	General Mills	1978	9	13	20
Star Tours Stamp Set			4	5	8
Star Wars Action Play-Doh Set			20	30	45
Star Wars Adventure (Movie Poster) Jigsaw Puzzle (1000 pieces)			7	10	15
Star Wars Blueprint Set			14	20	30
Star Wars Calendars (1978-1990)			7	10	15
Star Wars Dinnerware Set			20	30	45
Star Wars ESB Coloring Book		1980	2	3	5
Star Wars ESB Story Book (hardcover)		1980	4	5	7
Star Wars Intergalactic Passport & Stickers	Ballantine	1983	7	10	15
Star Wars Luke Skywalker's Activity Book	Random House		2	3	5
Star Wars Pop-up Book	Random House	1978	11	16	25
Star Wars Poster Art Coloring Set	Craftmaster	1978	9	13	20
Star Wars Question & Answer About Space Book	Random House	1979	5	7	10
Star Wars Question & Answer Book About Computers, The			5	7	10
Star Wars Radio Program Poster			23	35	50
Star Wars ROTJ "The Ewoks Join the Fight" Book	Golden		2	3	5
Star Wars Sketchbook	Ballantine	1977	14	20	30
Sticker Book (256 stickers)	Panini	1977	23	35	50
Sticker Set & Album	Burger King		7	10	15
Stickers (set of four stickers)	Trix		3	4	6
Stickers (set of four stickers)	Lucky Charms		3	4	6
Stickers (set of four stickers)	Monster Cereal		3	4	6
Stickers (set of four stickers)	Cocoa Puffs		3	4	6
Stormtrooper Pendant			9	13	20
Stormtroopers Stop the Landspeeder Jigsaw Puzzle (140 pieces)	Kenner		5	7	10
Sy Snootles & Rebo Band	Sigma	1983	25	35	55
The Jedi Master's Quizbook	Random House	1985	6	8	12
TIE Fighter & X-Wing Poster	General Mills	1978	9	13	20
TIE Fighter Rocket Kit	Estes	1978	11	16	25

Star Wars

TOY	MANUFACTURER	YEAR	GOOD	EX	MIB
Trapped in the Trash Compactor Jigsaw Puzzle (140 pieces)	Kenner		5	7	10
Turret Music Box with C-3PO			20	30	45
Victory Celebration Jigsaw Puzzle (500 pieces)	Kenner		6	8	12
Wicket & the Dandelion Warriors (book)	Random House	1985	6	8	12
Wicket 3 in 1 Stamp Set			4	5	8
Wicket Bank	Adam Joseph	1983	7	10	15
Wicket Figurine Paint Set	Craftmaster		9	13	20
Wicket Play Phone			23	35	50
Wicket the Ewok Dinnerware Set			11	16	25
Wicket the Ewok Roller Skates			14	20	30
Wicket the Ewok Watch (stars & planet on face)	Bradley	1970s	30	45	65
Wicket Toothbrush (battery operated)		1984	9	13	20
Wookie Doodle School Pad			5	7	10
Wookie Storybook, The	Random House	1979	7	10	15
World of Star Wars, The	Paradise Press	1981	9	13	20
X-Wing Fighter Rocket Kit	Estes	1978	11	16	25
X-Wing Fighters Prepare to Attack Jigsaw Puzzle (500 pieces)	Kenner		6	8	12
X-Wing Medal	W. Berrie	1980	6	8	12
X-Wing Ring	W. Berrie	1980	6	8	12
X-Wing with Maxi-Brutel Rocket Kit	Estes	1978	18	25	40
Yoda Backpack	Sigma		14	20	30
Yoda Bank	Sigma	1983	25	35	55
Yoda Bank (lithographed tin with combination dials)			11	16	25
Yoda Coloring Book	Kenner		5	7	10
Yoda Figurine Paint Set	Craftmaster		9	13	20
Yoda Glow-in-the-Dark Paint Set			9	13	20
Yoda Hand Puppet			14	20	30
Yoda Jedi Master Fortune Teller Ball			45	65	95
Yoda Sleeping Bag			16	23	35
Yoda Tumbler/Pencil Cup	Sigma		20	30	45
Yoda Watch	Bradley	1970s	30	45	65

Tom Corbett

TOY	MANUFACTURER	YEAR	GOOD	EX	MIB
Flash X-1 Space Gun (5" long)			65	95	145
Model Craft Molding Super Set (six-figure set)	Kay Standley	1950s	115	165	250
Official Space Gun (sparking gun, 21" long)	Marx		100	150	200
Polaris Rocket Ship (wind-up, 12" long, 1952)	Marx		250	375	500
Space Cadet 2 Spaceship (tin wind-up, 12" long, 1930s)	Marx		250	450	575
Tom Corbett Ring (Rocket Scout)			9	13	20
Tom Corbett Space Cadet Belt		1950s	75	105	165
Tom Corbett Space Cadet Binoculars			70	100	150
Tom Corbett Space Cadet View-Master Reels	Sawyer's	1950s	35	50	75
Tom Corbett Space Gun (9 1/2" long light blue & black sparking)		1950s	85	120	185

KENNER STAR WARS TOYS

Die Cast Vehicles

TOY	YEAR	MNP	MIP
Series I			
Darth Vader Tie Fighter	1979	25	50
Land Speeder	1979	25	50
Tie Fighter	1979	25	50
X-Wing	1979	22	55
Series II			
Imperial Cruiser	1979	50	150
Millennium Falcon	1979	50	125
Tie Bomber	1979	275	750
Y-Wing	1979	40	125
Series III			
Slave I	1979	25	75
Snowspeeder	1979	25	85
Twin Pod Cloud Car	1979	25	75

Droids

3 3/4" Figures

TOY	YEAR	MNP	MIP
A-Wing Pilot	1985	20	75
Boba Fett	1985	10	75
C-3PO	1985	20	40
Jann Tosh	1985	5	10
Jord Dusat	1985	5	10
Kea Moll	1985	5	10
Kez-Iban	1985	5	10
R2-D2 with pop-up lightsaber	1985	20	30
Sise Fromm	1985	5	20
Thall Joben	1985	5	10
Tig Fromm	1985	5	20
Uncle Gundy	1985	5	10

Accessories

TOY	YEAR	MNP	MIP
Droids Light Saber	1985	41	150

Vehicles

TOY	YEAR	MNP	MIP
A-Wing Fighter, Droids Box	1983	25	75
ATL Interceptor	1985	20	40
Imperial Side Gunner	1985	10	30

Empire Strikes Back

3 3/4" Figures

TOY	YEAR	MNP	MIP
2-1B	1980	8	25
4-LOM	1981	7	35
AT-AT Commander	1980	8	25
AT-AT Driver	1981	7	20

Empire Strikes Back

TOY	YEAR	MNP	MIP
Bespin Security Guard, black	1980	8	25
Bespin Security Guard, white	1980	6	30
Bossk, bounty hunter	1980	8	25
C-3PO with removable limbs	1982	10	35
Cloud Car Pilot	1982	7	20
Dengar	1980	7	20
FX-7	1980	7	25
Han Solo in Bespin outfit	1981	10	40
Han Solo in Hoth outfit	1980	10	35
IG-88	1980	10	30
Imperial Commander	1981	7	20
Imperial Storm Trooper in Hoth battle gear	1980	10	20
Imperial Tie Fighter Pilot	1982	10	30
Lando Calrissian		5	20
Lobot	1981	5	15
Luke Skywalker in Bespin outfit	1980	10	35
Luke Skywalker in Hoth battle gear	1982	10	30
Princess Leia in Bespin gown	1980	10	30
Princess Leia in Hoth outfit	1981	10	30
R2-D2 with sensorscope		5	30
Rebel Commander	1980	8	25
Rebel Snow Soldier in Hoth battle gear	1980	10	30
Ugnaught	1981	8	25
Yoda with brown snake	1981	8	25
Yoda with orange snake	1981	8	25
Zuckuss	1982	10	35

Accessories

TOY	YEAR	MNP	MIP
3 Position Laser Rifle	1980	41	135
Darth Vader Carring Case	1982	7	20
Display Arena	1980	13	40
Hoth Wompa	1982	5	15
Laser Pistol	1980	15	55
Light Saber, red or green	1980	17	50
Light Saber, yellow	1980	17	75
Mini Figure Case	1980	8	25
Tauntaun, solid belly	1980	8	25
Tauntaun, split belly	1982	10	30

Playsets

TOY	YEAR	MNP	MIP
Cloud City Playset (Sears Exclusive)	1981	100	375
Dagobah	1982	12	35
Darth Vader Star Destroyer		30	100
Hoth Ice Planet	1980	26	100
Imperial Attack Base	1980	20	60
Imperial TIE Fighter	1980	35	100
Rebel Command Center	1980	66	200
Turret and Probot	1980	26	80

Star Wars toys, top to bottom: Boba Fett Action Figure, 1978, by Kenner; 12 inch Princess Leia Organa Action Figure, 1977, by Kenner; Hoth World Playset (Micro Collection), 1982, by Kenner.

Empire Strikes Back

TOY	YEAR	MNP	MIP

Vehicles

TOY	YEAR	MNP	MIP
AT-AT All-Terrain Armored Transport	1980	45	100
Rebel Armored Snowspeeder	1980	17	50
Rebel Transport	1982	21	65
Scout Walker	1982	12	35
Slave I (Bobba Fett's Space Ship)	1980	25	75
Twin-Pod Cloud Car	1980	15	45

Ewoks

3 3/4" Figures

TOY	YEAR	MNP	MIP
Dulok Scout	1985	5	10
Dulok Shaman	1985	5	10
King Gornesh	1985	5	10
Logray (Ewok Medicine Man)	1985	5	12
Urgah Lady Gorneesh	1985	5	10
Wicket W. Warrick	1985	5	12

Vehicles

TOY	YEAR	MNP	MIP
Ewoks Fire Cart	1985	7	20
Ewoks Treehouse	1985	17	50
Ewoks Woodland Wagon	1985	7	20

Large Figures

12" Figures

TOY	YEAR	MNP	MIP
Ben (Obi-Wan) Kenobi	1979	55	185
Boba Fett with Empire Strikes Back box	1979	80	200
Boba Fett with Star Wars box	1979	95	200
C3-PO	1979	40	105
Darth Vader	1978	50	150
Han Solo	1979	125	350
IG-88	1980	175	450
Jawa	1979	50	125
Luke Skywalker		50	160
Princess Leia Organa	1977	50	150
R2-D2	1979	40	100
Storm Trooper	1979	58	200

Mail Away Figures

Bagged Figures

TOY	YEAR	MNP	MIP
AT-AT Commander			10
AT-ST Driver			10
C-3PO, removable limbs			10
Han Solo in Hoth outfit			10

Mail Away Figures

TOY	YEAR	MNP	MIP
Han Solo in trench coat			10
Luke Skywalker in Hoth outfit			10
Pruneface			10
R2-D2 with sensorscope			10

White Box

TOY	YEAR	MNP	MIP
Anakin Skywalker		13	30
Nien Numb		5	10
The Emperor		5	10

Micro Series

TOY	YEAR	MNP	MIP
Bespin Control Room	1982	8	25
Bespin Freeze Chamber	1982	17	50
Bespin Gantry	1982	8	25
Death Star Compactor	1982	8	25
Death Star Escape	1982	8	25
Death Star Escape (Sears white box)	1982	8	25
Death Star World	1982	20	75
Hoth Generator Attack	1982	7	23
Hoth Ion Cannon	1982	7	35
Hoth Turrent Defense	1982	7	20
Hoth Wompa Cave	1982	7	20
Hoth World	1982	17	100
Imperial Tie Fighter	1982	20	50
Millinium Falcon	1982	75	225
Snow Speeder	1982	50	150
X-Wing Fighter	1982	15	45

Mini Rigs

TOY	YEAR	MNP	MIP
AST-5	1983	3	8
CAP-2 Captivator	1982	3	10
Desert Sail Skiff	1984	3	8
Endor Forest Ranger	1984	3	8
INT-4 Interceptor	1982	3	10
ISP-6 Imperial Shuttle Pod	1983	4	12
MLC-3 Mobile Laser Cannon	1981	4	12
MTV-7 Multi-Terrain Vehicle	1981	4	12
PDT-8 Personal Deployment Transport	1981	4	12
Radar Lase Cannon	1982	4	12
Security Scout		19	57
Tatoonie Skiff		50	125
Tatoonie Skiff in Droid Box		50	125
Tri-Pod Laser Cannon	1982	4	12
Vehicle Maintence	1982	4	12

Figures With Coins

TOY	YEAR	MNP	MIP
A-Wing Pilot	1985	15	45
Amanaman	1985	15	45
Anakin Skywalker	1985	26	80
B-Wing Pilot	1985	5	15
Barada	1985	12	40

Star Wars toys, top to bottom: Luke Skywalker AM Headset Radio, by Kenner; Luke Skywalker Action Figure, 1977, by Kenner; Bespin Security Guard Action Figure (ESB), 1980, by Kenner; Ewoks Urgah Lady Gorneesh Action Figure, 1985, by Kenner.

Power of the Force

TOY	YEAR	MNP	MIP
Ben (Obi-Wan) Kenobi	1985	12	35
Biker Scout	1985	7	25
EV-9D9	1985	15	45
Han Solo in Carbonite outfit	1985	33	100
Imperial Dignitary	1985	15	40
Imperial Gunner	1985	15	35
Jawa	1985	13	40
Lando Calrissian General Pilot	1985	12	40
Luke in stormtrooper outfit	1985	40	125
Luke Skywalker X-Wing fighter pilot	1985	10	35
Lumat	1985	10	30
Paploo	1985	10	30
R2-D2 with pop-up light saber	1985	20	40
Romba	1985	10	30
The Emperor	1985	15	40
Warok	1985	10	30
Wicket	1985	7	30
Yak Face	1985	75	175

Vehicles

TOY	YEAR	MNP	MIP
Ewok Battle Wagon	1985	21	70
Imperial Sniper Vehicle	1985	40	120
One-Man Sand Skimmer	1985	25	75
Sand Skimmer		15	45
Security Scout Vehicle	1985	40	120
Tatooine Skiff	1985	60	175

Return of the Jedi

3 3/4" Figures

TOY	YEAR	MNP	MIP
4-LOM		5	15
8D8	1983	5	30
Admiral Ackbar	1983	3	10
AT-ST Commander		4	12
AT-ST Driver		4	12
Biker Scout	1983	3	10
Chief Chirpa	1983	4	12
Emperor's Royal Guard		5	25
Gamorrean Guard	1983	3	8
General Madine	1983	3	10
Han Solo in trench coat	1984	5	15
Klaatu	1983	3	8
Klaatu in Skiff guard outfit	1983	10	25
Lando Calrissian in Skiff outfit	1983	5	15
Logray (Ewok Medicine Man)	1983	4	12
Luke Skywalker in Jedi Knight outfit	1983	8	25
Lumat	1983	10	25
Nein Numb	1983	5	15
Nikto	1984	3	10
Princess Leia in combat poncho	1984	10	20

Return of the Jedi

TOY	YEAR	MNP	MIP
Princess Leia Organa in Boushh outfit	1983	10	20
Prune Face	1984	5	10
Rancor Keeper	1984	5	10
Rebel Commander	1983	5	15
Rebel Commando	1983	5	15
Ree-Yees	1983	4	12
Squid Head	1983	3	10
Sy Snootles and the Reebo Band (boxed set)	1984	13	40
Teebo	1984	4	12
The Emperor	1983	7	20
Warok	1983	10	25
Weequay		3	8
Wicket W. Warrick	1984	5	15
Zuckuss		5	15

Accessories

TOY	YEAR	MNP	MIP
Biker Scout Laser Pistol	1984	20	50
C-3PO Collectors Case	1983	10	40
Chewbacca Bandoiler Strap	1983	5	10
DV Head Carring Case with three figures	1983	10	30
Ewok Assault Catapult	1983	7	20
Jabba the Hutt (regular issue)		10	25
Laser Rifle Carring Case	1984	5	15
Light Saber (red or green plastic)		15	45
Rancor Monster	1983	10	30
Tri-Pod Cannon	1983	3	8
Vehicle Maintenance Energizer	1983	3	8

Playsets

TOY	YEAR	MNP	MIP
Ewok Village	1983	17	50
Jabba the Hutt (loose figure)		10	
Jabba the Hutt Dungeon (Sears Exclusive)	1983	25	125
Jabba the Hutt Dungeon (Sears Exclusive)	1983	25	75

Vehicles

TOY	YEAR	MNP	MIP
B-Wing Fighter	1984	12	35
Ewok Combat Glider	1984	3	10
Imperial Shuttle	1984	45	150
Speeder Bike	1983	7	20
TIE Interceptor	1984	20	35
Y-Wing Fighter	1983	20	35

Star Wars

TOY	YEAR	MNP	MIP
Early Bird figures in mailing box (set of four)	1977	140	340
Early Bird Kit	1977	100	300

Star Wars toys, top to bottom: Radio Controlled R2-D2, by Kenner; Ewoks King Gornesh Action Figure, 1985, by Kenner; Squid Head Action Figure (ROTJ), 1983, by Kenner; Yoda the Jedi Master Fortune Teller, by Kenner; AT-AT Vehicle (ESB), 1980, by Kenner.

Star Wars

3 3/4" Figures

TOY	YEAR	MNP	MIP
Ben (Obi-Wan) Kenobi (original 12)	1977	10	55
Boba Fett	1978	25	125
C-3PO (original 12)	1977	10	60
Chewbacca (original 12)	1977	10	55
Darth Vader (original 12)	1977	10	60
Death Squad Commander (original 12)	1977	10	50
Death Star Droid	1978	15	45
Greedo	1978	13	50
Hammerhead	1978	13	40
Han Solo in vest (original 12)	1977	10	100
Jawa with cloth cape (original 12)	1977	10	60
Jawa with plastic cape (original 12)	1977	100	400
Luke Skywalker (original 12)	1977	10	65
Luke Skywalker X-Wing Pilot	1978	13	55
Power Droid	1978	17	50
Princess Leia Organa (original 12)	1977	10	120
R2-D2 (original 12)	1977	10	60
R5-D4	1978	15	45
Snaggletooth (blue body) Sears Exclusive	1978	100	
Snaggletooth (red body)	1978	10	40
Stormtrooper (original 12)	1977	10	75
Tuskan Raider, sand person (original 12)	1977	10	75
Walrus Man	1978	12	40

Accessories

TOY	YEAR	MNP	MIP
Action Figure Display Stand (Mail-In Premium)	1977	50	125
Han Solo's Laser Pistol		20	75
Inflatible Light Saber	1977	55	75
R2-D2 (radio controlled)	1978	50	125
SW 24 Figure Vinyl Figure Case		10	30

Playsets

TOY	YEAR	MNP	MIP
Cantina Adventure Set (Sears Exclusive)	1977	150	375
Creature Cantina	1977	25	75
Death Star Space Station	1977	75	150
Droid Factory	1977	18	55
Land of the Jawas	1977	30	90
Patrol Dewback	1977	20	60

Vehicles

TOY	YEAR	MNP	MIP
Darth Vader TIE Fighter	1977	25	50
Imperial TIE Fighter	1977	25	75
Jawa Sand Crawler (remote controlled)	1977	125	350
Land Speeder (battery operated)	1977	20	75
Millennium Falcon Spaceship	1977	50	175
Sonic Land Speeder (J.C. Penney Exclusive)	1977	120	400
X-Wing Fighter	1977	25	45

Star Wars toys, top to bottom: R2-D2, Chewbacca Action Figures, 1977, by Kenner; AT-ST Driver Action Figure with Collector Coin (POF), 1985, by Kenner; 12 inch Luke Skywalker Action Figure, 1977, by Kenner.

Toy Guns

By George H. Newcomb

There was a time when my neighborhood was ruled by gangs of kids with guns. Don't panic, no one died, no one called 911; it was a different world over 30 years ago. The words "Fanner 50," "Roy Rogers," "The Rifleman," "The Rebel" and "Mares Laig" were as familiar to us as "Teenage Mutant Ninja Turtles," "Super-Soaker" and "X-Men" are to us today.

Our guns fired roll caps, darts, water or Shootin' Shell bullets (when we had them). The youngest gunslinger was less than six years old; the oldest no more than 12 (the cut-off age varied in relation to the discovery of girls and/or cars). We fought wars (civil and world), robbed stages, robbed banks, fought Indians, fought as Indians, disintegrated aliens and even shot at dinosaurs (you couldn't kill them with anything short of a bazooka.) I thought those days were just a pleasant memory before I started buying and selling toy guns. I was wrong; toy guns are back.

Almost anyone alive today who grew up in the United States remembers the toy guns of their childhood. Baby boomers who grew up watching TV westerns and space operas have been largely responsible for the increased interest in toy gun collecting. This, plus the increasing interest in related western and cowboy hero collectibles, have brought prices and demand into new realms.

Toy guns fall into a number of major categories and production periods. The first cap gun patent dates to about 1860. Most major U.S. toy manufacturers produced a variety of designs throughout their histories. The preferred material of construction until World War II was cast iron (as it was for most toys), though variations of plastic, tin and stamped metal also appear. Most early cap guns, exploders and figural guns were made of cast iron.

The late 1930s was a golden age of cast iron guns. Many guns of this period have realistic revolving cylinders, fine nickel finishes, colorful plastic grips and complicated mechanisms.

Metal toy gun production ceased in about 1940. The companies that survived in the postwar years after 1946 experimented with a variety of materials and methods of production, the most successful of which was die casting. This involved injecting an alloy mixture into a mold, which resulted in good detail, lowered costs and a much lighter gun. Die cast guns dominated the 1950s and 60s marketplace. Television brought little buckaroos daily installments of the thrilling adventures of cowboy heroes such as Roy, Gene and Hoppy. Manufacturers such as the George Schmidt Company, Classy Products, Marx, Hubley, Nichols, Kilgore and Wyandotte Toys all scrambled to arm these cowpokes and compete for a piece of the market. This, by some standards, was the golden age of die cast guns.

Most major manufacturers probably chuckled as they passed the Mattel booth at the 1956 Toy Fair Trade Show in New York. Mattel, a relative newcomer to the business, was taking orders for their first western-style cap gun, due out in 1957, known as the "Fanner 50." Little did anyone know that this shiny, oversized gun would, by its incredible success, drive many manufacturers out of the toy gun market and even some out of business completely.

The bottom line of toy making has always been costs. The less money spent on production, the greater the profit. Mattel produced a line of low-priced plastic and die cast cap guns, rifles and machine guns that arrived on the market at a time when TV western heroes such as Maverick, The Lawman, Sugarfoot, Bronco and Matt Dillon were replacing the older serial cowboys.

Cap guns would never be the same. All of the major producers added plastic to their lines, and the race was on to lower production costs and remain competitive. As far as most collectors are concerned, things went downhill from there. Each year toy guns seemed to decrease in quality and detail.

While cap guns sold in the American market were largely produced by American manufacturers in both the prewar and postwar periods, other styles of toy guns flowed from overseas producers. Tin lithography, the printing of colorful designs directly on metal, became an art form in postwar Japan. The same Japanese companies that produced the robots and tin cars so widely sought by today's collectors also produced space ray guns, cowboy, "G-Men" and military-style tin litho guns for the American market.

While prewar Japanese toy guns are rare, postwar sparking ray guns, pop guns, water and clicker guns abound. These guns were generally cheaper than their American competition and provided a profitable "low end" product for American retailers. Louis Marx even went as far as to begin their own subsidiary production in Japan and later Hong Kong. As the postwar Japanese economy grew and workers demanded more money, toy gun manufacturing moved from Japan to Hong Kong to Taiwan to Korea and eventually to mainland China, currently one of the major producers of toy guns and caps.

By the late 1960s, the majority of TV westerns had been cancelled. Cowboy heroes were forgotten, and toy guns in general were seen in a more ominous light by parents and child psychiatrists. Fads of spy guns and space guns revived the market for a while, but the golden age was over. The eventual end point of this tale can be found in the Toys R Us or Kay-Bee Toys near you today. Go there and visit the toy gun section. You'll see a fair assortment of multi-colored Super-Soakers and noise making space guns, but you won't find a Roy Rogers holster set or even a Fanner 50.

Walking through any toy or collectibles show or picking up any toy publication these days will bring you in contact with collectible toy guns. The prices, conditions and varieties are confusing to say the least. To make sense of toy gun collecting, you must first understand that there are all sorts of toy guns. I refer to the hobby as "toy gun" collecting instead of "cap gun" collecting because all toy guns are not cap guns. There are cap guns, water guns, dart guns, cork guns, clicker guns, BB guns, air guns, pellet guns, guns that shoot peas and even some that can fire four or five types of the aforementioned ammunition.

As in collecting anything, you have to decide some basic questions before you begin. What do you want to collect and why do you want to collect it? Most toy gun collectors are buying back a bit of their childhood. They played with these guns in countless childhood fantasies, and holding them again unlocks a wealth of memories. Some collectors are searching only for the toy guns they had (or wish they had) as children. These folks may actually play with their guns and (heaven forbid!) fire caps in them. They may not be as particular about condition and packaging as collectors on the other side of the spectrum, who collect for the investment. Investment collectors seek only the highest grade, unplayed with, mint-from-the-store-shelves quality pieces that will appreciate in value. They never play with their guns, and the idea of firing caps in a gun gives them shivers. Most collectors fall between these two extremes.

Some collectors amass only guns by a specific manufacturer -- Hubley, Mattel, Nichols, and so on -- while others search for the shootin' irons that bear the names of their cowboy heroes. Some collectors specialize in military-style toy weapons, bullet-firing machine guns, rocket-firing bazookas and cap-firing hand grenades. Recently, space guns have begun to increase in popularity. Toy gun collectors don't even have to be limited to the guns themselves. One collector I know only collects boxes of caps. He doesn't have a single gun to shoot them with but carries photos of the hundreds of different cap boxes that he's found. The photos help him avoid buying duplicates. Another collector buys only cap gun advertising, catalogs and store displays.

Unless you have unlimited funds and storage space, you may want to limit your collection to certain types of guns. You should be happy with what you're collecting.

The condition of a toy gun can be a subjective matter. More than once I've read descriptions or talked to people on the phone about a supposed "New Old Stock In Box" piece that, after a bit of investigation, was found to be non-working, damaged, missing parts and in a water-damaged box. Yes, it is "Old Stock" from somewhere, and, yes, it is "In Box," and it may be "New" to you, but reality has to come into play somewhere along the line. There has to be an agreement as to grading of toy guns.

It may be a Holy Grail type of quest to collect only the most perfect Mint In Box pieces. Many times guns came off the assembly line in less than perfect condition, due to bad batches of metal, lack of quality control or poor design. Toy guns are, after all, just that: toys. They were meant to be played with, used and abused and then discarded. To expect them to exist in pristine condition for decades is, perhaps, wishful thinking. The high acid content of the paper pulp used to make toy gun boxes has damaged the finish of many guns. The Mattel Fanner guns are especially prone to this problem. Some guns have inherent problems that surface with age, such as flaking or lifting of their finish. This occurs because the gun was not properly prepared before being plated or the particular batch of plating wasn't properly mixed. The big Nichols Stallion .45s suffer from this problem. As noted in Talley Nichols book, sometimes a better quality of nickel just wasn't available and the production line had to use what was on hand. Any grading system used should be flexible and take all this into consideration.

As in collecting any toy, the Mint In Box piece will always be the most desirable. Common and lower quality guns may provide the quantity to fill collections, but the quality of any collection will always be measured by the finer and more sought-after pieces.

Variations enhance the quality and expand the depth of a collection, but they can also drive you crazy. Forced by economic considerations, most companies would continue production of a popular gun for years with only minor changes to the molds or packaging. Each of these changes, no matter how minor, is technically a variation.

A good example of variations in production can be found in the Hubley "Texan" series of cap guns. The Texan began life in the golden age of cast iron, the mid-1930s. It was a large, well- designed, sturdy pistol that fired roll caps and had a revolving cylinder and the look of the Old West that young hombres desired. The initial cast iron version was offered in a cap-firing version and a dummy version. Most manufacturers offered dummy versions of guns for states and cities where caps were classified as fireworks and therefore prohibited by law. The dummy version had a different hammer than the standard version; it lacked the inside of the hammer so that it never touched and couldn't fire caps.

For a while, Hubley boosted their sales appeal by obtaining a license to use the famous Colt Firearms rearing horse logo instead of the traditional Hubley star. This variation is a must for any complete Texan collection. After World War II, the Texan reappeared in a nearly identical die cast version that was offered in nickel, gold, gray or blue finishes with both standard or dummy hammers.

Then, to make matters even more complicated, Hubley changed the basic design of the gun and issued that as a "Texan," offering it in nickel, gold and metal finishes. All of these guns had the familiar Hubley longhorn steer head plastic grips. These vary by being either all white or white with a black painted steer. There is a possibility that postwar "swirl" plastic grips of different colors may also exist.

So far, we've only talked about variations in one gun. Hubley also produced a smaller version of the Texan, called the Texan Jr. It was also produced in many variations. All of these guns were sold in different style boxes. The point is, collecting every variation of just this one gun would make a sizeable collection by itself. This is why deciding what you want to collect is so important and also what makes undetailed price guides so dangerously inaccurate.

Reproductions and misrepresentations are common in any collecting field and a hazard for both the novice and experienced collector. Reproductions of highly sought toy guns have yet to appear on the scene, mainly because the production and tooling costs for the potential market demand would be too high. But this has not stopped many small-time entrepreneurs from producing reproduction hammers, plastic grips and laser-copy boxes. I have no problem with toy gun restoration or repair. As certain pieces become more difficult to find it is the logical approach to fill the collecting demand. But restored or repaired pieces should always be presented as such and should be priced accordingly lower than an unrestored version.

Most laser-copy boxes are easy to spot. The inside cardboard is usually whiter than an original and many times flaws, tears and dirt from the original are visible. Remember, copy machines copy everything as it is and producing a mint copy requires a mint original.

Repro hammers are usually easy to spot, especially when placed next to an original. The original usually tends to be cleaner and has better detail. Clues such as a mint hammer and pitted pan or anvil (striking surface) are also dead giveaways.

Misrepresentations are sometimes the most difficult situations to unmask. Many dealers misrepresent pieces simply from lack of knowledge and experience. Many beginning collectors fall victim for the same reasons. Simple mistakes such as giving a gun the wrong date and misidentifying the manufacturer of a gun are common. Beware of the dealer who doesn't know the difference between cast iron and die cast. Experience will show you that an "H" in a diamond or oval on the side of a gun is usually the trademark of either Leslie-Henry (the "Diamond H brand") or the Halco (J. Halpern) Company, not Hubley. Hubley guns are usually marked "Hubley" somewhere on the gun. Knowing trademarks and distinguishing styles is simply learned through experience.

One area of major confusion seems to be centered around the question of "what gun went in what holster?" Holster makers were often not the same companies that made the guns. The cowboy cap gun craze of the 1940s through the 1950s supported the growth of many small production leather holster manufacturers. Companies such as Keyston Bros., Halco, Classy Products and Pilgrim Leather Goods produced holsters for major manufacturers and at the same time produced empty holsters. These empty sets were sold to jobbers who would buy quantities of guns -- whatever there was a surplus of, the cheaper the better -- from different manufacturers to fill them. They would then sell the "married" sets to individual retailers. Remember, large chain stores such as Toys R Us and K-Mart didn't exist at this time. Every local department store, hardware store, hobby shop and sporting goods store was a potential customer. Years later, it's not uncommon to find Leslie

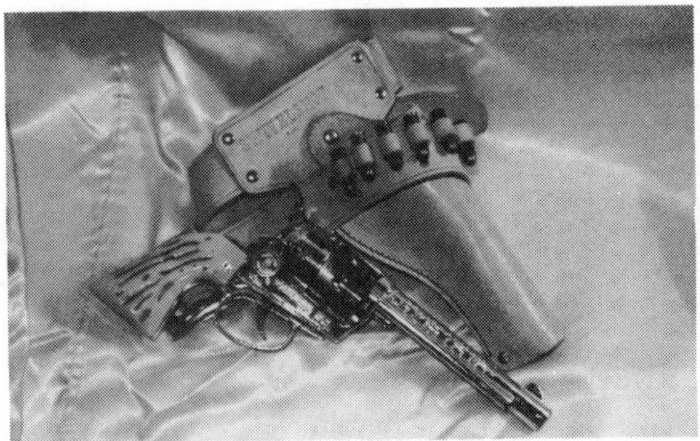

Swivelshot Holster and Fanner 50 by Mattel.

Henry Gene Autry Pistols in a Lasso 'Em Bill Holster set by Keyston Bros. What is this set? It's not really a Gene Autry set, no matter how nice it looks, and it shouldn't be represented as such. I usually solve the problem by "divorcing" the set and selling the guns and the holsters separately.

The majority of character holster sets were produced by major companies that paid rather hefty licensing fees to use cowboy names on both guns and holsters. Though there were a number of exceptions, most of these sets were sold with matching guns and holsters. The "Gunsmoke" set would have "Gunsmoke" or "Marshall Matt Dillon" guns in it, the "Have Gun Will Travel" set would have "Paladin" guns, and so forth. Beware of the Mint In Box character set with a photo of the cowboy star on the box cover, his name on the holsters and common, no-name guns in them. Always ask questions.

There is very little printed information available on toy guns and toy gun companies. Original wholesale and retail sales catalogs are hard to find and are often quite expensive. Many companies simply ceased to exist overnight or were consumed by bigger corporations. Company records, advertising art and production information were lost in the shuffle.

A few interesting books do exist, and more will certainly follow. Charles Best and Sam Logan have authored a rather comprehensive guide to cast iron toy guns called *Cast Iron Toy Guns and Capshooters*, listing over 1250 cast iron guns. Talley Nichols, ex-CEO of Nichols Industries, has written *Brief History of Nichols Industries, Inc. and Its Toy Guns*, a 66-page book with 35 photos. Stuart Schneider's *Collecting The Race Into Space* has a section on space guns, and Leslie *Singers Zap, Ray Gun Classics* book has beautiful pictures but somewhat inaccurate dating. More comprehensive material is needed, especially about postwar toy guns.

Collecting toy guns can be a fascinating and rewarding hobby. The majority of collectors and dealers are friendly and good-natured. After all, we're having fun. When my Fanner 50 is in my hand, I'm eight years old again. This is the magic that will keep us forever young.

George H. Newcomb, born in 1952, began collecting and dealing in antiques over 20 years ago as a college student. He has focused on toy guns for the last five years.

TOY GUNS

Detective

TOY GUN	DESCRIPTION	YEAR	GOOD	EX	MIB
	Hubley				
Dick Cap Pistol	4 1/8" cast iron automatic style, side loading, nickel finish, Dick oval in red paint	1930	75	125	195
	Knickerbocker				
Dragnet Badge 714 Triple Fire Comb. Game	Tin litho stand-up target has four plastic spinners, includes two 6" black plastic guns, one fires darts, the other cork gun, includes 4 plastic darts & 3 corks	1955	90	150	225
Dragnet Water Gun	6" black plastic, .38 Special-style with gold "714" shield on grip	1960s	15	20	35
	Mattel				
Agent Zero M Snap-Shot Camera Pistol	7 1/2" extended, camera turns into pistol at press of a button	1964	35	60	100
Agent Zero W Potshot	3" die cast potshot derringer, gold finish, has brown vinyl armband holster holds 2 Shootin' Shell cartridges, gold buckle with Agent Zero W logo	1965	40	85	125
Official Detective Shootin' Shell Snub-Nose	.38 die cast chrome with brown plastic grips, black vinyl shoulder holster, wallet, badge, ID card, Pistol Range Target & bullets	1959	95	175	275
Official Detective Shootin' Shell Snub-Nose	.38 die cast 7" chrome finish, gold cylinder, brown plastic grips, Private Detective badge & Shootin' Shell bullets	1960	75	125	185
Official Dick Tracy Shootin' Shell Snub-Nose .38	Die cast chrome .38 with brown plastic grips, chrome finish with Shootin' Shell bullets & Stick-m caps	1961	75	125	185
Shootin' Shell Snub-Nose .38	.38 with brown plastic grips & silver finish	1959	65	145	200
	Nichols				
Detective Shell Firing Pistol	5 1/2" snub-nose pistol chambers & fires 6 3-pc. cap cartridges, cut-out badge, bullet cartridges, extra red plastic bullet heads	1950s	100	175	275

Military

TOY GUN	DESCRIPTION	YEAR	GOOD	EX	MIB
	Buddy L				
Spitfire Cap Firing Machine Gun	Biped stand attached to muzzle, black plastic stock & grip with cap or clicker firing	1950	80	130	175
	Daisy				
Model 12 SoftAir Gun	Machine gun style, loads "SoftAir" pellets in plastic cartridge, 10 rounds, spring fired, can be cocked by barrel grip or bolt	1990	35	50	75
SA Automatic Burp Gun	10" with stock, black plastic, burp-gun style, removeable clip, loads & fires white plastic bullets	1970s	20	35	50
	Edison				
Matic 45 Cap Gun	24", plastic gun with stock, fires "Supermatic System" strip caps	1980s	10	15	20

Military

TOY GUN	DESCRIPTION	YEAR	GOOD	EX	MIB
Esquire/Nichols					
7580 UZI Automatic	10 1/2", battery operated, black plastic uses 250 shot roll caps, shoulder strap	1986	20	45	60
Hubley					
Army .45 Cap Pistol	6 1/2" automatic, dark grey finish, white plastic grips, pop-up cap	1950s	45	90	165
Automatic Cap Pistol No. 290	Die cast, 6 1/2", nickel finish, brown checkered grips, magazine pops up when slider is pulled back		85	150	225
Larami					
9mm Z-Matic Uzi Cap Gun	8" replica, removeable cap storage magazine, black finish, small orange plug in barrel	1984	5	10	15
Maco					
Molotov Cocktail Tank Buster Cap Bomb	6" plastic & die cast, insert caps in head & throw	1964	10	15	25
Paratrooper Carbine	24" carbine, removeable magazine, fires plastic bullets, bayonet & target	1950s	75	115	165
USA Machine Gun	12" tripod-mounted gun fires plastic bullets, red & yellow plastic	1950s	125	175	275
Main Machine					
Mustang Toy Machine Gun	25" long chrome and hard plastic paper firing gun	1950s	75	125	175
Marx					
Anti Aircraft Gun	Mechanical, sparks, tin litho, 16 1/2" long, 1941		35	100	195
Army Automatic Pistol	2 1/2" automatic, (ACP style), black with white grips, small leather holster with flaps (Marx Miniature)	1950s	10	15	25
Army Pistol with Revolving Cylinder	Tin litho		35	60	95
Army Sparkling Pop Gun	1940-50		45	75	125
Desert Patrol Machine Pistol	Plastic, 11" long		30	45	75
G-Man Gun Wind-up Machine Gun	23" tin-litho, red, black, orange & grey litho, round drum magazine, wind-up mechanism makes sparks from muzzle, uses cigarette flint, wooden stock	1948	145	200	275
Green Beret Tommy Gun	Sparkles, trigger action, on card	1960s	35	55	95
Mini-M.A.G. Combat Gun	Cap pistol, miniature scale, diecast		20	30	40
Siren Sparkling Airplano Pistol	Heavy-guage enamel steel, 9 1/2" wingspan, 7" long		50	75	100
Sparkling Siren Machine Gun	26" long, 1949		45	75	110
Special Mission Tommy Gun			20	35	45
Tommy Gun	Sparks and makes noise, 1939		65	95	150

Military

TOY GUN	DESCRIPTION	YEAR	GOOD	EX	MIB
Mattel					
Burp Gun	17" plastic with die cast works, perforated roll caps fired by cranking the handle	1957	25	50	75
National					
Automatic Cap Pistol	4 1/4" automatic style, grip swivels to load, black finish	1925	45	75	135
Automatic Cap Pistol	6 1/2" silver finish with simulated walnut grip	1950s	35	65	90
Nichols					
Army 45 Automatic	4 1/4" all metal, side loading automatic, olive	1959	15	20	35
Parris Mfg.					
M-1 Kadet Training Rifle	32" wood/metal M-1 carbine, clicker action, metal barrel, trigger guard, bolt	1960s	20	35	50
Redondo					
Revolver Mauser Cap Pistol	6 1/4", Mauser style automatic pop-up magazine, silver finish, brown plastic grips	1960s	4	7	10
Stevens					
Spitfire Automatic Cap Pistol	4 5/8" cast iron, side loading, silver finish, "flying airplanes" white plastic grips	1940	60	110	165
Topper/Deluxe					
Johnny Seven One Man Army-OMA	36" multi-purpose seven guns in one, removeable pistol fires caps, rifle fires white plastic bullets, bolt spring fired machine gun "tommy gun" sound, rear launcher fires grenades, forward diff. shell	1964	125	225	350
Unknown					
MM Automatic Carbine	24" recoil red slide in muzzle & flashing light, brown & black plastic	1960s	15	30	45

Miscellaneous

TOY GUN	DESCRIPTION	YEAR	GOOD	EX	MIB
Atomic Industries					
Dynamic Automatic Repeating Bubble Gun	8" black plastic pistol projects bubbles		25	40	65
Benton Harbor Novelty					
Dick Cap Pistol	4 3/4", automatic, side loading, black finish	1950s	20	30	45
Buddy L					
Paper Cracker Rifle	26" steel & machined aluminum mechanism, barrel, trigger & operating lever, uses 1000 shot paper roll, brown plastic stock	1940s	95	165	225

Miscellaneous

TOY GUN	DESCRIPTION	YEAR	GOOD	EX	MIB
	Daisy				
Buck Rogers in the 25th Century Pistol Set	Holster is red, yellow & blue leather gun is 9 1/2" pressed steel pop gun	1930s	200	300	425
Buzz Barton Special, No. 195	Blue metal finish, wood stock with ring sight	1930s	85	125	200
Jack Armstrong Shooting Propeller Plane Gun	5 1/2" gun, shoots flying disc, pressed tin	1933	35	60	95
Model No. 25 Pump Action BB Gun	Plastic stock	1960s	35	65	125
Targeteer No. 18 Target Air Pistol	10" gun metal finish, push barrel to cock, Daisy BB tin with special BBs, spinner target	1949	50	85	125
Water Pistol No. 17	5 1/4" tin	1940	25	40	65
Water Pistol No. 8	5 1/4" tin	1930s	25	50	80
	Edison				
Sharkmatic Cap Gun	6" automatic, style pistol, fires "Supermatic System" strip caps	1980s	10	15	20
	EMU Rififi				
Automatic Sparking Pistol	6 1/2", plastic/metal, uses cigarette lighter flints to make sparks, available in green-red, yellow-green, red or white colors	1960s	15	30	45
	Esquire Novelty				
Hideaway Derringer	3 1/2" single shot, loads solid metal bullet, grip is removeable to store two more bullets, gold finish, white plastic grips	1950s	65	90	110
	Hubley				
Dick Cap Pistol	Die cast, 4 1/4" automatic style, side loading with nickel finish	1950s	25	40	65
Midget Cap Pistol	5 1/2" long, diecast, all metal flintlock with silver finish	1950s	20	35	50
Pirate Cap Pistol	9 1/2" side-by-side flintlock style with die cast frame & cast double hammers & trigger, chrome finish, white plastic grips feature Pirate in red oval	1950	50	100	175
Tiger Cap Pistol	6 7/8", single action, mammoth caps, metal finish	1935	35	65	100
Trooper Cap Pistol	6 1/2" all metal, pop up cap magazine, nickel finish, black grips	1950	30	50	85
Winner Cap Pistol	4 3/8" automatic style, pop-up magazine release in front of trigger guard, nickel finish	1940	65	100	165
	Kilgore				
Clip 50 Cap Pistol	4 1/4", unusual automatic style, black Bakelite plastic frame, removeable cap magazine clip	1940	75	110	175
Mountie Automatic Cap Pistol	6", double action, automatic style with pop-up magazine, unusual nickel finish, black plastic grips		20	30	45
Presto Cap Pistol	5 1/8", pop up cap magazine nickel finish brown plastic grips	1940	65	120	185
Rex Automatic Cap Pistol	3 7/8", blue metal finish cast iron, small size automatic style, side loading, white pearlized grips	1939	45	80	125

Miscellaneous

TOY GUN	DESCRIPTION	YEAR	GOOD	EX	MIB
Langson Mfg. Co.					
Nu-Matic Paper Popper Gun	Pressed steel, 7" squeeze grip trigger, mechanism pops roll of paper (reel at top of gun) to make loud noise, black finish	1940s	30	50	75
Leslie-Henry					
Gene Autry Cap Pistol	9" break-to-front, lever release, nickel finish, black plastic horse-head grips	1950s	65	145	250
Marx					
Automatic Repeater Paper Pop Pistol	7 3/4" long		35	65	95
Blastaway Cap Gun	50 shooter repeater		25	35	50
Burp Gun	20" battery operated, green & black plastic	1960s	20	35	50
Click Pistol	Tin litho		20	35	50
Click Pistol	Pressed steel, 7 3/4" long		30	45	60
Famous Firearms Deluxe Edition Collectors Album	Set of 4 rifles, 5 pistols & 4 holsters miniature series, includes: Mare's Laig, Thompson machine gun, Sharps rifle, Winchester saddle rifle, Derringer, .38 snub-nose, Civil War Pistol, 6 shooter/Flink	1959	75	125	175
Marx Miniatures Famous Gun Sets	4 gun set features Tommy Gun, Civil War Revolver, "Mare's Laig" & Western Saddle Rifle	1958	25	45	65
Marxman Target Pistol	Plastic, 5 1/2" long		35	50	70
Popeye Pirate Click Pistol	Tin litho, 10" long, 1930's		100	150	200
Repeating Cap Pistol	Aluminum		20	30	50
Sparkling Pop Gun			25	40	65
Streamline Siren Sparkling Pistol	Tin litho		25	45	65
Mattel					
Burp Gun	23" with folding stock extended, 16 1/2" from rear of breech to muzzle, wind up mechanism fires perforated roll caps, pressed steel gun body & barrel, white metal folding stock, red plastic magazine	1950s	90	150	225
Fanner 50 Cap Pistol	Later version 11" fires perforated roll caps, black finish, white plastic antelope grips	1960s	30	65	95
Mattel-O-Matic Air Cooled Machine Gun	16" machine gun fires perforated roll caps by cranking handle, plastic with die cast, tripod-mounted	1957	45	85	125
Meldon					
P-38 Clicker Pistol	7 1/2" black finish, automatic style	1950s	35	50	75
Midwest					
Long Tom Dart Gun	11" pressed steel	1950s	35	50	75
Nichols					
Model 95 Shell Firing Rifle	35 1/2" rifle uses shell firing cartridges, holds 5 in removeable magazine & one chamber, lever action ejects cartridges, open frame box holds 6 bullets & 12 additional red bullet heads	1961	200	350	550

Miscellaneous

TOY GUN	DESCRIPTION	YEAR	GOOD	EX	MIB
Pinto Cap Pistol	3 1/2", chrome finish, black plastic grips, flip out cylinder, white plastic "Pinto" holster in leather holster clip	1950s	20	35	50
Spitfire with Clip	9" mini rifle, chrome finish, plastic stock, plastic holders with 2 extra cartridges	1950s	20	35	50
Tophand 250 Cap Pistol	9 1/2" break-to-front, lever release, black finish, brown plastic grips with a roll of "Tophand 250" caps	1960	65	110	165

Palmer Plastics

TOY GUN	DESCRIPTION	YEAR	GOOD	EX	MIB
Airplane Clicker Pistol	4 1/2" yellow & black plane, red pilot & guns	1950s	25	45	65
Ray Gun Water Pistols	5 1/2" many color variations green, orange, translucent blue, royal blue, black, yellow & red	1950s	10	15	20

Park Plastics

TOY GUN	DESCRIPTION	YEAR	GOOD	EX	MIB
Atomee Water Pistol	4 1/4" black plastic	1960s	10	20	35

Ronsom

TOY GUN	DESCRIPTION	YEAR	GOOD	EX	MIB
Sparking Pistol	7 1/2" black finish, cock hammer to fire cigarette flint mechanism, "Ronson" on grips	1930s	45	80	115

Rosvi

TOY GUN	DESCRIPTION	YEAR	GOOD	EX	MIB
Revolver Aquila Pop Pistol	10" green finish, pop gun breaks to cock, fires cork from barrel, sparks from mechanism under barrel	1960s	15	20	35

Stevens

TOY GUN	DESCRIPTION	YEAR	GOOD	EX	MIB
25 Jr. Cap Pistol	4 1/8" automatic, side loading, silver finish	1930	25	50	75
6 Shot Cap Pistol	6 3/4", six separate triggers revolve to deliver caps to hammer, metal finish		85	135	175
Model 25-50	4 1/2" nickel finish	1930	35	65	95
Pluck Cap Pistol	3 1/2" cast iron, single shot single action	1930	15	30	45

Unknown

TOY GUN	DESCRIPTION	YEAR	GOOD	EX	MIB
Double Holster Set	Black leather, large size, steer head conches, lots of red jewels, fringe, holsters only, no guns	1950s	65	100	150

Unknown - Hong Kong

TOY GUN	DESCRIPTION	YEAR	GOOD	EX	MIB
Potato Gun	Spud Gun, plàstic, pneumatic action fires potato pellet from muzzle	1991	3	7	10
Ratchet Water Pistol Ray Gun	6 1/2" unusual pull back mechanism loads pistol, ratchet forces water out when trigger is pulled	1960s	30	45	65

US Plastics

TOY GUN	DESCRIPTION	YEAR	GOOD	EX	MIB
Rocket Jet Water Pistols	5" ray gun fills through hole in top, orange or yellow plastic	1960s	6	12	17

Welco

TOY GUN	DESCRIPTION	YEAR	GOOD	EX	MIB
Spud Gun (Tira Papas)	6" all-metal gun	1960s	10	20	35

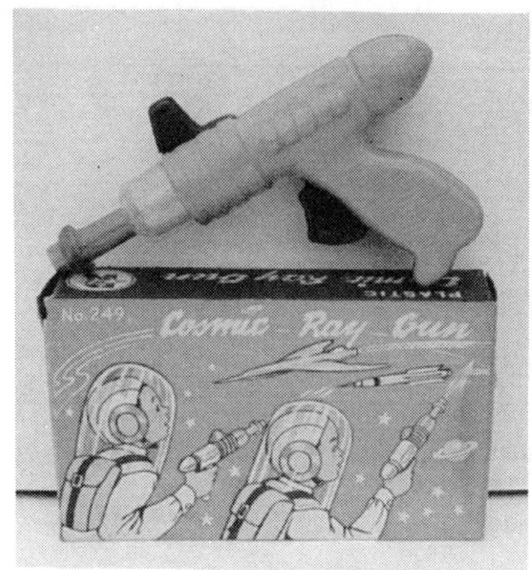

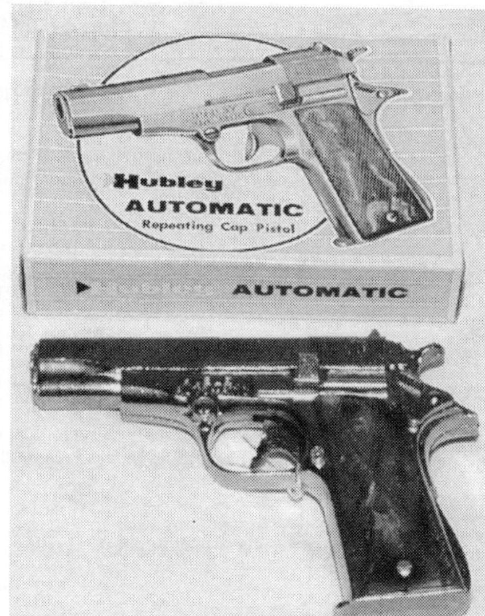

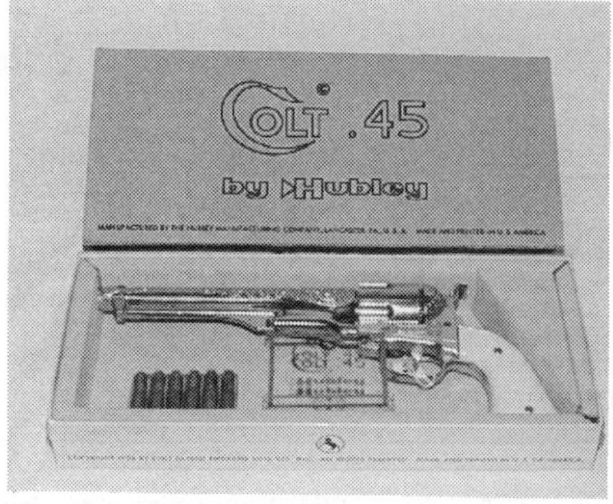

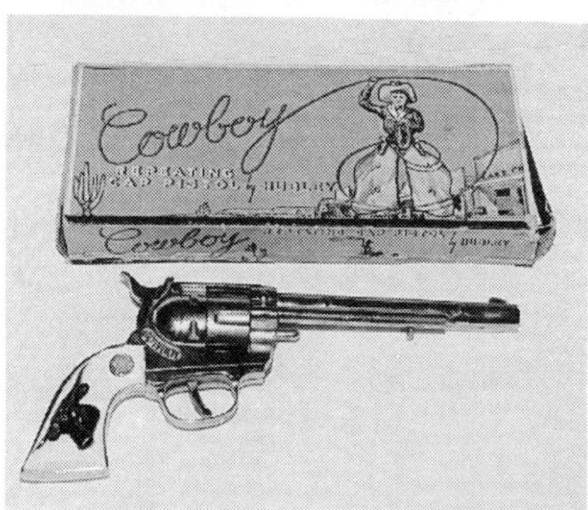

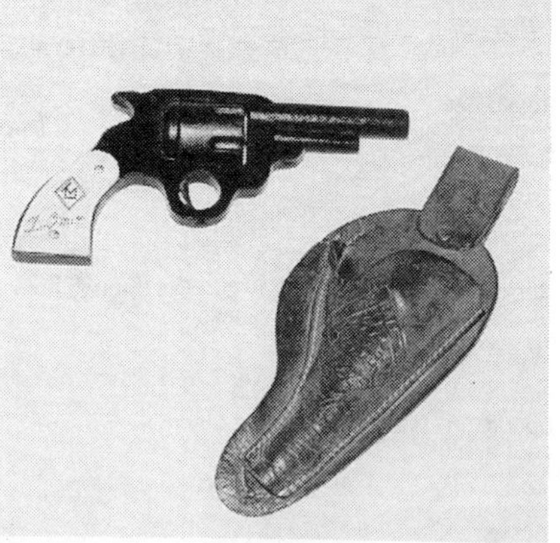

Top to Bottom: Cosmic Ray Gun #249, 1950s, Ranger Steel Products; Automatric Repeating Cap Pistol # 290, 1956, Hubley; Space Rocket Gun, 1950s, M&L; Colt .45 Cap Pistol, 1959, Hubley; Cowboy Cap Pistol, 1950s, Hubley; Tom Mix Wooden Gun, 1938, Ralston Purina premium item.

Police

TOY GUN	DESCRIPTION	YEAR	GOOD	EX	MIB
Acme Novelty					
G-Boy Pistol	7" automatic (ACP) style entire left rear side of gun swings down to load	1950s	15	35	50
Hubley					
Mountie Automatic Cap Pistol	Diecast, 7 1/4" automatic style, pop up lever-release magazine, blue finish	1960s	20	35	55
Kilgore					
Machine Gun Cap Pistol	5 1/8", long cast iron crank-fired gun	1938	100	175	250
Marx					
.38 Cap Pistol	With caps, miniature scale, diecast		35	75	125
Detective Snub-Nose Special	Die cast, 5 3/4" top release break, unusual revolving cylinder, fires Kilgore style disc caps, chrome finish with black plastic grips	1950s	65	100	150
Dick Tracy Click Pistol			35	50	75
Dick Tracy Jr Click Pistol	Aluminum, 1930's		100	150	200
Dick Tracy Siren Pistol	Pressed steel, 8 1/2" long, 1935		40	75	125
Dick Tracy Sparkling Pop Pistol	Tin litho		35	55	95
G-Man Automatic Silent Arm Pistol	Tin		35	55	70
G-Man Automatic Sparkling Pistol	Pressed steel, 4" long, 1930's		45	65	110
G-Man Machine Gun	Tin miniature, windup, 1940's		25	35	65
G-Man Sparkling Sub-Machine Gun			50	75	100
G-Man Tommy Gun	Sparkles when wound, 1936		55	80	110
Gang Buster Crusade Against Crime Sub-Machine Gun	Litho, metal with wooden stock, 23" long, 1938		95	150	225
Marx Miniatures Detective Set	Miniature cap firing brown and gray tommy gun, chrome pistol and holster on card with wood grain frame border	1950s	25	45	65
Official Detective-Type Sub-Machine Gun			35	55	75
Sheriff Signal Pistol	Plastic, 5 1/2" long, 1950		20	30	50
Siren Sparkling Pistol	Tin litho		20	35	45
Mattel					
Official Dick Tracy Tommy Burst Machine Gun	25" Thompson style machine gun fire perforated roll caps, single shot or in full burst when bolt is pulled back, brown plastic stock & black plastic body, lift up rear sight, Dick Tracy decal on stock	1960s	100	175	275

Police

TOY GUN	DESCRIPTION	YEAR	GOOD	EX	MIB
Pilgrim Leather					
Peter Gunn Private Eye Revolver & Holster Set	36" die cast Remington gun with six 2-pc. bullets, badge & wallet, Peter Gunn business cards, black leather shoulder holster	1959	200	325	450

Space

TOY GUN	DESCRIPTION	YEAR	GOOD	EX	MIB
Budson					
Flash Gordon Air Ray Gun	10" unusual air blaster, handle on top cocks mechanism, shoots blast of air, pressed steel	1950s	350	450	550
Chemtoy					
Pop Gun	4 1/2" long red hard plastic gun with space designs on handle	1967	20	35	50
Daisy					
Buck Rogers 25th Century Pop Gun	Pressed steel, ray gun makes loud "pop" noise when fired, handle breaks to cock, flat dark metal finish, chrome trim, embossed side with Buck Rogers figure & logo	1930s	85	200	350
Daiya					
Baby Space Gun	6" friction siren & spark action	1950s	30	65	95
Futuristic Products Inc.					
Strato Gun	Die cast, 9" cap firing space gun, internal hammer, top of gun lifts to load, gray finish	1950s	85	145	200
Strato Gun	Die cast, 9" cap firing space gun, internal hammer, top of gun lifts to load, chrome finish	1950s	125	250	350
Hasbro					
Jet Plane Missile Gun	Jet shaped handgun shoots darts, targets supplied on box back	1968	30	65	95
Ideal					
Star Team Ionization Nebulizer	9" water gun fires water mist, red, white, blue & black plastic, Star Team decal	1969	25	50	75
Irwin					
Space Ship Flashlight Game	7 1/4", blue plastic ray gun has cockpit with orange spaceman, nose unscrews for AAA batteries, pulling trigger lights nose & moves guns & spaceman	1950s	55	100	150
LJN					
Dune Sardaukar Laser Gun	7" black plastic with flashing lights, battery operated	1984	20	35	50
M & L Toy Co.					
Space Rocket Gun	9" grey plastic, spring loaded, rocket projectiles	1950s	35	65	95

Space

TOY GUN	DESCRIPTION	YEAR	GOOD	EX	MIB
Marx					
Flash Gordon Radio Repeater Clicker Pistol	10" long, 1930's		150	225	550
Flash Gordon Signal Pistol	7" siren sound when trigger is pulled, tin/pressed steel, green finish with red trim	1930s	225	375	500
Flash Gordon Water Pistol	Plastic with whistle in handle, 7 1/2" long, 1940's		85	145	200
Rex Mars Planet Patrol 45 Caliber Machine Gun	Tin and plastic, windup, 22" long		75	125	150
Sparkling Atom Buster Pistol	Aluminum		35	50	75
Sparkling Space Gun Rifle			45	85	125
Tom Corbett Space Cadet Offical Space Pistol			35	55	125
Tom Corbett Space Cadet Rifle			50	100	175
Mil Jo Mfg.					
Space Scout Spud Gun	7" black & white plastic	1960s	15	25	45
Norton-Honer					
Buck Rogers Sonic Ray Flashlight Gun	7 1/4" black, green & yellow plastic with code signal screw	1950s	65	135	225
Ohio Art					
Astro Ray Laser Lite Beam Dart Gun	10" red & white plastic flashlight lights target with four darts	1960s	65	125	175
Ranger Steel Prod.					
Cosmic Ray Gun #249	Red blue and yellow hard plastic ray gun	1950s	25	55	100
Ray Line (Grand Toys-Jouets Grand)					
Star Trek Tracer Gun	6 1/2" plastic firing tracer gun	1966	45	70	100
Remco					
Jupiter 4 Color Signal Gun	9" long black, red and yellow plastic gun that lights up in 4 colors, red telescoping sight	1950s	70	110	150
Royal Plastics					
Flash-O-Matic, The Safe Gun	7" long red and yellow plastic battery operated light beam gun	1950s	65	95	150
Stevens					
Jet Jr. Cap Gun	6 1/2" fires roll caps, side loading door, silver finish, rear jet "Blast Off Fins"	1948	95	200	350

Space

TOY GUN	DESCRIPTION	YEAR	GOOD	EX	MIB
Space Police Neutron Blaster Cap Pistol	7 3/4" die cast, cap firing ray gun, lock mechanism pulls out through the top of the gun, silver finish	1949	200	400	600

Unknown

TOY GUN	DESCRIPTION	YEAR	GOOD	EX	MIB
Bicycle Water Cannon Ray Gun	10", red plastic, swivel mount attached to bicycle handles, fired by lever	1950s	25	50	75
Clicker Ray Gun	5" red & yellow and/or red & blue hard plastic, no boxes, sold loose	1950s	10	20	35
Clicker Ray Gun	5" green and/or rose swirl plastic	1950s	15	20	30
Clicker Ray Gun	5" grey plastic	1950s	10	20	35
Radar Gun Clicker Ray Gun	6 1/4" long, rose colored plastic with green spaceman and trigger	1950s	15	25	40
Space Atomic Gun	4" silver, orange & red litho, sparking action, tin-litho	1960s	25	45	75
Visible Sparking Ray Gun	8 1/2" mechanism visible (Hong Kong)		35	50	75
Whistle Clicker Ray Gun	5" plastic, two color variations: blue-green or olive-green swirl plastic, imprinted spacemen & rocket ships, back of gun is a whistle	1950s	10	20	35

Colbel

TOY GUN	DESCRIPTION	YEAR	GOOD	EX	MIB
Official James Bond 007 Thunderball Pistol	4 1/2" Walther PPK style, single shot fires plastic caps, Secret Agent ID	1985	15	25	45

Ideal

TOY GUN	DESCRIPTION	YEAR	GOOD	EX	MIB
Man From U.N.C.L.E. Pistol and Holster	7" long pistol and plastic holster, both with orange ID sticker	1965	45	85	125

GUNS

Western

Actoy

TOY GUN	DESCRIPTION	YEAR	GOOD	EX	MIB
Pony Cap Pistol	Single shot, all-metal, nickel finish with eagle on grip	1950s	25	45	65
Wells Fargo Buntline Cap Pistol	11" long barrel, break-to-front, cream plastic stag grips	1950s	85	135	195
Wyatt Earp Buntline Special	11" barrel, die cast, friction break-to-front, white plastic grips, nickel finish	1950s	95	135	175

Ambrit Industries

TOY GUN	DESCRIPTION	YEAR	GOOD	EX	MIB
Spud Gun	Case aluminum, pneumatic all-metal gun shoots pellets	1950s	30	50	70

Buzz-Henry

TOY GUN	DESCRIPTION	YEAR	GOOD	EX	MIB
Lone Rider Cap Pistol	8" die cast, white plastic inset rearing horse grips	1950s	35	50	90

Carnell

TOY GUN	DESCRIPTION	YEAR	GOOD	EX	MIB
Maverick Cap Pistol	9" break-to-front, lever release, nickel finish, Maverick on sides, cream & brown swirl colored grips features notch bar with extra set of black plastic grips	1960	40	85	135

TOY GUN	DESCRIPTION	YEAR	GOOD	EX	MIB
	Western				
Maverick Two Gun Holster Set	9" break-to-front, lever release, nickel finish, Maverick on sides, cream & brown swirl grips features notch bar, black leather dbl. holster set with silver plates, studs & white trim, 6 loops, buckle	1960	175	250	365
	Classy				
Double Holster Set	Imitation alligator-texture brown leather, steer-head conches on holsters, lots of studs, yellow felt backing, holsters only, no guns	1950s	100	150	225
Roy Rogers Double Gun & Holster Set	Die cast 2-8 1/2" nickel finish pistols with copper figural grips, holster is brown & black leather with raised detail, plastic play bullets & leather tie-downs	1950s	350	475	685
Roy Rogers Double Holster Set	10" guns with plain nickel finish & copper grips, lever release, brown & cream leather set, silver studs, gold fleck jewels, & 4 wooden bullets		165	300	425
Roy Rogers Double Holster Set	Black & white leather set, silver studs & conches, 9" classy Roy Rogers pistols with plain nickel finish & copper figural grips, friction release	1950s	200	350	585
	Classy Mfg.				
Dale Evans Holster Set	Brown & yellow leather, white fringe on holsters, stylized blue butterflies are also "DE" logo, if buckled in front, holsters are backwards; holsters only, no guns		55	100	150
	Daisy				
760 Rapid Fire Shotgun Air Rifle	31" pump shotgun, grey metal one piece frame, brown plastic stock & Slider grip, fires blast of air	1960s	65	95	135
Red Ryder BB Rifle	Carved wooden stock	1980	25	40	60
Spittin Image Peacemaker BB Pistol	10 1/2" die cast, spring fired, single action, BBs load into spring fed magazine under barrel		45	75	120
	Edison Giocattoli				
Susanna 90 12 Shot Cap Pistol	9" uses ring caps, wind out cylinder, black finish, plastic wood grips	1980s	10	15	25
	Esquire				
Johnny Ringo, Adventure of, Gun & Holster	10 3/4" long barrel Actoy, friction break, w/blk. & gld. plastic stag grips, blk. leather two gun holster (cut out flowers over a gld. background), felt backing, loops hold 4 to 6 bullets, silver buckle	1960	200	350	485
	Esquire Novelty				
Authentic Derringer	Die cast, 2" cap firing, copper finish, twin swivel barrel	1960	15	25	45
Authentic Derringer	Classic miniature Series #10, 2" cap firing, copper finish. twin swivel barrel	1960	15	25	45
Pony Boy Double Holster Set	Brown leather double holster with bucking broncs & studs, cuffs, spurs & spur leathers, guns are Actoy "Spltfires", die cast 8 1/2" copper finish, white plastic grips	1950s	100	195	275
	Haig				
Western Buntline Pistol	13", pistol fires single caps and/or BBs, BBs are propelled down barrel sleeve by cap explosion	1963	75	120	165

GUNS

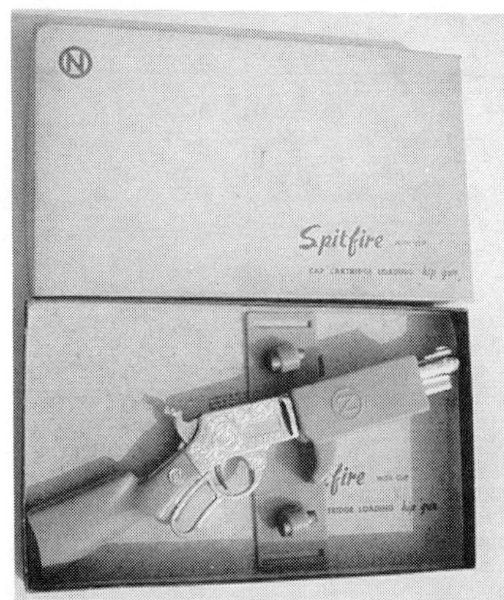

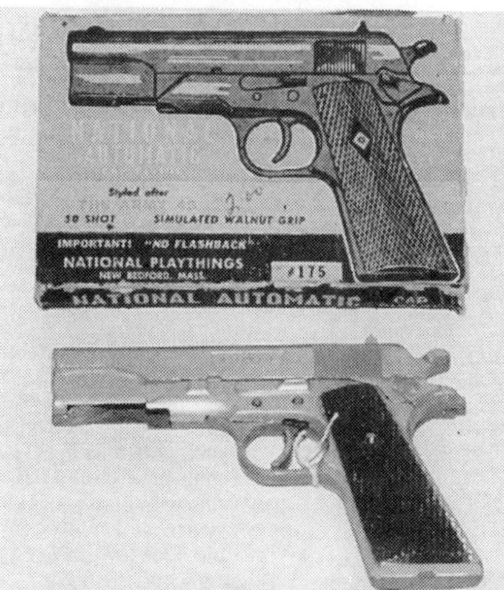

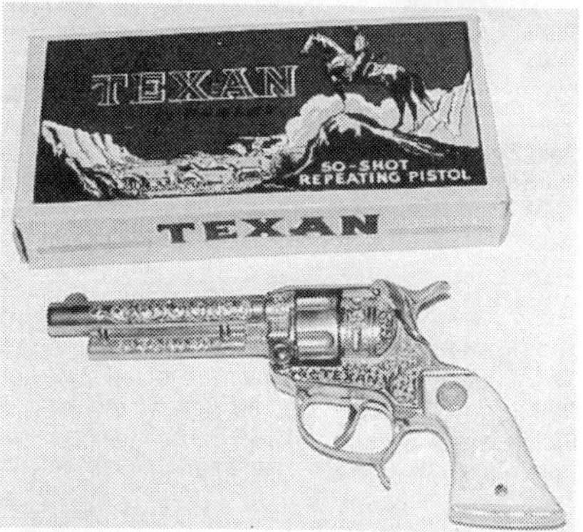

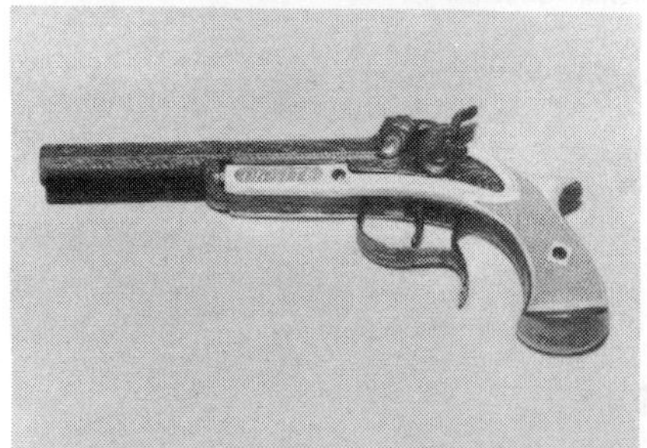

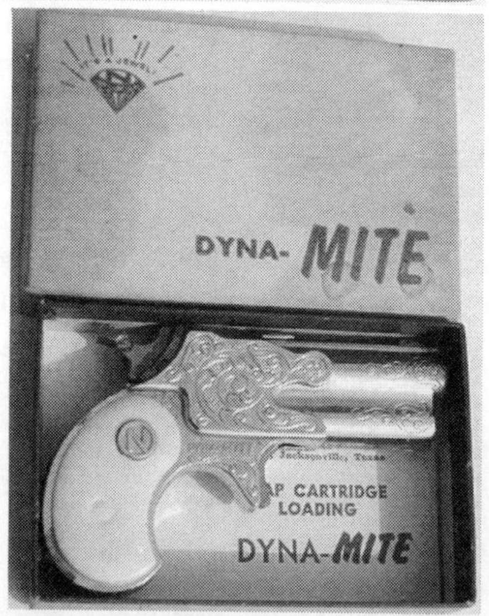

Top to Bottom: Spitfire Hip Gun #100, 1950s, Nichols; Automatic (Army .45) Cap Pistol, 1950s, National; Army .45 Cap Pistol, 1950s, Hubley; Texan Cap Pistol, 1940, Hubley; 2 Guns in 1 Cap Pistol, 1950s, Hubley; Pirate Cap Pistol, 1950, Hubley; Dyna-Mite Derringer, 1955, Nichols.

Harvel-Kilgore

TOY GUN	DESCRIPTION	YEAR	GOOD	EX	MIB
Classy The Rebel Holster & Pistol	12" die cast long barrel pistol, brown plastic grips, black leather single holster left side, Rebel insignia on holster flap,	1960s	175	300	450

Hubley

TOY GUN	DESCRIPTION	YEAR	GOOD	EX	MIB
2 Guns in 1 Cap Pistol	Die cast, 8" with long barrel, twist-off barrels to change from long to short, side loading, white plastic grips	1950s	75	125	200
Colt .38 Detective Special	4 1/2" Colt .38 pistol single shot caps & loads 6 play bullets with suspenders chest holster	1959	35	75	125
Cowboy Cap Gun	Die cast, 12" swing out revolving cyclinder, release on barrel, nickel or aluminum finish, white plastic steer grips with black steer head	1950s	95	165	225
Cowboy Cap Gun	12" swing-out revolving cylinder, release on barrel, gold finish, black plastic steer grips	1950s	100	160	250
Cowboy Cap Pistol	8" friction break-to-front nickel finish cast iron, rose swirl plastic grips w/Colt logo	1940	85	150	200
Cowboy Jr. Cap Pistol No. 225	9" die cast, revolving cylinder, side loading, release on barrel, silver finish, white plastic cow grips, lanyard ring & cord	1950s	65	125	185
Dagger Derringer	7", unusual over & under pistol has hidden red plastic dagger that slides out from between barrels, rotating barrels load & fire 2-pc. bullets	1958	55	100	145
Davy Crockett Buffalo Rifle	25" die cast & plastic, unusual flintlock, style fires single cap under pan cover, brown plastic stock, ammo storage door in stock	1950s	75	145	200
Deputy Cap Pistol	10" die cast, front breaking, release on barrel ornate scroll work, nickel finish	1950s	45	75	115
Flintlock Jr. Cap Pistol	7 1/2" single shot, double action, brown swirl plastic stock	1955	10	20	35
Flintlock Pistol	9 1/4", two shot cap shooting single action double barrel, over & under style, brown swirl plastic stock, nickel finish	1954	50	95	145
Flip Special from the Rifleman Cap Rifle	3' long rifle, resembles classic Winchester with ring lever, brown plastic stock, pop down cap magazine	1959	85	150	275
Frontier Repeating Cap Rifle	35 1/4" rifle nickel finish with brown plastic stock & forestock, blue metal barrel, red plastic choke & front sight, pop down magazine, released by catch in front of trigger, scroll work	1950s	75	165	210
Model 1860 Cal .44 Cap Pistol	13", revolving cylinder with closed chamber ends, 6 2-pc. bullets, flat aluminum finish, white plastic grips, complete with wooden display plaque	1959	125	250	375
Panther Pistol	Die cast, 4" derringer style pistol snaps out from secret spring-loaded wrist holster	1957	85	130	185
Remington .36 Cap Pistol	8" long, nickel finish, black plastic grips, revolving cylinder chambers 2-pc. bullets	1950s	75	145	225
Rex Trailer Two Gun & Holster Set	9 1/2" side loading, nickel finish, stag plastic grips, brown textured tooled leather with white holsters & trim, 6 bullet loops with plastic silver bullets, plain buckle	1960	90	165	250
Rodeo Cap Pistol	7 1/2" single shot, white plastic steer grips	1950s	20	40	60
Texan .38 Cap Pistol	10" long, revolving cylinder gun chambers 6 solid brass bullets (rd. caps go into cylinder first), top release front break automatically ejects shells, plastic steer grips	1950s	100	165	225
Texan Cap Pistol	9 1/4" cast iron revolving cylinder lever release, white plastic steer grips, nickel finish, Colt rearing horse logo on grips	1940	90	175	275

Western

TOY GUN	DESCRIPTION	YEAR	GOOD	EX	MIB
Texan Cap Pistol	Die cast, nickel finish, white plastic steer grips, star logo on grips	1950s	75	145	200
Texan Cap Pistol No. 285	9 1/4", cast iron, revolving cylinder, lever release, white plastic steer grips, nickel finish with star logo in grip	1940	85	185	300
Texan Dummy Cap Pistol	9 1/4", revolving cylinder, lever release, white plastic steer grips, nickel finish, star logo on grip	1950s	90	165	225
Texan Dummy Cap Pistol	9 1/4" revolving cylinder, lever release, white plastic steer grips, nickel finish, Colt rearing horse logo	1940	65	110	165
Texan Jr. Cap Pistol	10", spring button release on side of cylinder, break-to-front, nickel finish white plastic grips with black steers	1950s	65	90	125
Texan Jr. Cap Pistol	Die cast, release under cylinder, nickel finish, white plastic Longhorn grips	1954	50	75	110
Texan Jr. Gold Plated Cap Pistol	9", gold finish with black longhorn steer grips, break-to-front release from cylinder	1950s	85	130	185
Wyatt Earp Double Holster Set	Black & white leather holster with silk screened "Marshal Wyatt Earp" logo, two No. 247 Hubley Wyatt Earp Buntline Specials, 10 3/4" nickel finish, purple swirl grips	1950s	175	275	385

Ideal

TOY GUN	DESCRIPTION	YEAR	GOOD	EX	MIB
Yo Gun	7 1/4" red plastic gun releases yellow plastic ball which snaps back when trigger is pulled, functions like a yo-yo	1960s	30	45	60

Kenton

TOY GUN	DESCRIPTION	YEAR	GOOD	EX	MIB
Gene Autry Dummy Cap Pistol	Cast iron, 8 3/8", long barrel, dark grey gun, metal finish, white plastic grips	1939	70	110	185
Lawmaker Cap Pistol	8 3/8", break-to-front friction break, unusual dark grey gunmetal finish, white plastic raised grips	1941	100	175	250

Kilgore

TOY GUN	DESCRIPTION	YEAR	GOOD	EX	MIB
Big Horn Cap Pistol	7" all metal revolving cylinder, break-to-front, disc caps, silver finish	1950s	85	125	175
Bronco Cap Pistol	8 1/2", revolving swing-out cylinder fires Kilgore disc caps, silver finish, black plastic "Bronco" grips	1950s	50	100	175
Champion Quick Draw Timer Cap Pistol	Silver finish, side loading, wind up mechanism in grip records elapsed time of draw, black plastic grips	1959	65	150	225
Cheyenne Cap Pistol	9 3/4" side loading, "Sure-K" plastic stag grips, silver finish	1974	10	15	25
Fastest Gun Electronic Draw Game	Die cast, wire plug into "Rangers" gun grips, gun that shoots first lights eye of plastic battery operated steer head, red & blue plastic holsters w/matching cowboy gun grips, plastic belts	1958	80	145	250
Grizzly Cap Pistol	10" revolving cylinder fires disc caps, swing out cylinder, black plastic grips with grizzly bear	1950s	95	165	230
Hawkeye Cap Pistol	4 1/4" all metal, automatic style, side loading, silver finish	1950s	20	35	55
Lone Ranger Cap Pistol	8 1/2", large hammer, nickel finish, spring release on side for break, red-brown, Hi-Yo Silver grips	1940	85	135	185
Lone Ranger Cap Pistol	8 1/4", small hammer, nickel finish, friction break, purple plastic "Hi-Yo Silver" grips	1938	95	165	225
Mustang Cap Pistol	9 1/2" chrome finish with "stag" plastic grips	1960s	20	35	55
Ranger Cap Pistol	8 1/2" nickel finish, brown swirl plastic grips, spring release on right side, break-to-front	1940	90	125	165
Roy Rogers Cap Pistol	10" revolving cylinder swings out to load, fires disc caps, white plastic horse-head grips with "RR" logo	1950s	95	165	225

TOY GUN	DESCRIPTION	YEAR	GOOD	EX	MIB
Langson					
Cody Colt Paper Buster Gun	7 3/4", paper popper, nickel finish, white plastic steer grips fires Cody Colt ammunition	1950s	35	65	90
Leslie-Henry					
Gene Autry 44 Cap Pistol	11" lever release, side loading, long barrel, loads solid metal bullets, nickel finish, brown translucent plastic horse-head grips	1950s	85	175	285
Gene Autry 44 Cap Pistol	11" lever release, side loading, long barrel, nickel finish, white plastic horse-head grips	1950s	75	135	275
Gene Autry Cap Pistol	9", break-to-front lever release, nickel finish, white plastic horse-head grips	1950s	90	145	250
Gene Autry Cap Pistol	9" break-to-front lever release, copper finish, white plastic horse-head grips	1950s	65	155	250
Gene Autry Cap Pistol	7 3/4" die cast, small size, lever release, break-to-front, nickel finish with extension scroll work, black plastic horse-head grips	1950s	65	145	250
Marshal Cap Pistol	10" revolving cylinder chambers Nichols-style bullets, white plastic grips with star ovals	1950s	35	75	110
Marshal Matt Dillon "Gunsmoke" Cap Pistol	10" pop-up cap magazine, release in front of trigger guard, scroll work, bronze steer-head grips	1950s	50	80	135
Maverick Derringer	3 1/4" with removeable cap-shooting bullets, tan vinyl holster with two bullets	1958	35	55	85
Ranger Cap Pistol	7 3/4" derringer with removeable cap, shooting bullets, tan vinyl holster with two bullets	1950s	85	110	150
Texas Cap Pistol	9" die cast, break-to-front, lever release, nickel finish, plastic horse-head grips	1950s	65	95	125
Texas Ranger Cap Pistol	8 1/4" die cast, lever release break to front, nickel finish, scroll work, vasoline colored plastic grips		65	95	125
Wagon Train Complete Western Cowboy Outfit	Plastic flip ring lever rifle & wagon train pistol (late model L-H pistol) & leather holster	1960	75	145	200
Wild Bill Hickok 44 Cap Pistol Set	11" nickel finish, swing out side loading action, revolving cylinder chambers 6 metal bullets, amber plastic horse head grips, single holster black & brown leather w/silver studs, diamond conches	1950s	200	325	475
Wild Bill Hickok Cap Pistol	10" pop-up cap magazine, release in front of trigger guard, scroll work, translucent brown plastic grips with oval star inserts	1950s	90	135	190
Young Buffalo Bill Cowboy Outfit	Black & white leather holster set with pistol, white grip, holster bands read Texas Ranger		100	175	225
Lone Star					
Gun Fighter Holster Set	9" Frontier Ace, lever release, break-to-front, silver finish, brown plastic grips, holster white & red leather "Laramie" single holster with separate belt	1960s	55	85	145
Pecos Kid Cap Pistol	9" silver chrome finish, brown plastic grips, lever release	1970s	10	15	30
Pepperbox Derringer Cap Pistol	Die cast, 6 1/4" rotating barrel holds four cap loads, silver finish with black plastic grips	1960	75	110	185
Long Island Die Casting Inc.					
Texas Cap Pistol	Die cast, 8 1/2" friction break, Circle "T" logo, scroll work on barrel	1950s	45	85	110

Western

TOY GUN	DESCRIPTION	YEAR	GOOD	EX	MIB
Maco					
MP Holster Set	Plastic pistol has removeable magazine, loads & ejects bullets, white leather belt & holster	1950s	65	120	175
Marx					
Bonanza Guns Outfit	25" cap firing saddle rifle, magazine pulls down to load, 9 1/2" western pistol fires 2-pc. Marx shooting bullets, wood plastic stocks & gun metal gray plastic body, tan vinyl holster	1960s	75	145	225
Buffalo	50 shooter repeater		70	100	140
Centennial Rifle	With big sound		25	35	65
Cork-Shooting Rifle			25	40	60
Double Holster Set	10" two pistols similar to 1860s Remington, fires roll caps by use of a lanyard that is pulled from the bottom of the grip, internal hammer, white plastic horse & steer grips, silver, brown vinyl holster	1960	70	120	175
Double-Barrel Pop Gun Rifle	22" long, 1935		45	75	100
Double-Barrel Pop Gun Rifle	28" long, 1935		50	85	125
Hi-Yo Silver Lone Ranger Pistol	Tin gun		45	65	90
Historic Guns Derringer	Marx Historic Guns series, Derringer with plastic presentation case, 4 1/2" long, on card	1974	15	25	30
How the West Was Won Gun Rifle	Deep gray winchester model with tan stock, in box		55	85	145
Johnny Ringo Gun & Holster Set	Die cast gun, white plastic head grips, vinyl quick draw holster has rawhide tie, gun is fired by lanyard which passes through grip butt & attaches to belt, when pulled lanyard trips internal hammer	1960	80	130	185
Lone Ranger 45 Flasher Flashlight Pistol			25	50	85
Lone Ranger Carbine	26" grey plastic repeater-style rifle has pull down cap magazine, western trim & Lone Ranger signature on stock	1950s	65	100	165
Lone Ranger Clicker Pistol	8", nickel finish, red jewels, inlaid white plastic grip with the Lone Ranger, Hi-Yo Silver & LR head embossed, brown leather holster	1938	60	100	150
Lone Ranger Double Target Set	9 1/2" square stand up target, tin litho, wire frame holds target upright, backed with bullseye target, 8" metal dart gun fires wooden shaft dart	1939	95	165	245
Lone Ranger Sparkling Pop Pistol	Tin litho		45	65	90
Mare's Laig Rifle Pistol	13 1/2" brown plastic, black plastic body, pull down magazine		60	95	135
Official Wanted Dead or Alive Mare's Laig Rifle	19" bullet loading, cap firing saddle rifle-pistol ejects plastic bullets		50	90	145
Ranch Rifle	Plastic, repeater		30	45	60
Roy Rogers Carbine	26" grey plastic repeater-style rifle has pull down cap magazine, western trim & Roy Rogers signature on stock	1950s	80	120	155
Side-By Double Barrel Pop Gun Rifle	9" long		20	35	45
Thundergun Cap Pistol	12 1/2" single action,"Thundercaps" perforated roll cap system, silver finish, brown plastic grips	1950s	100	175	250

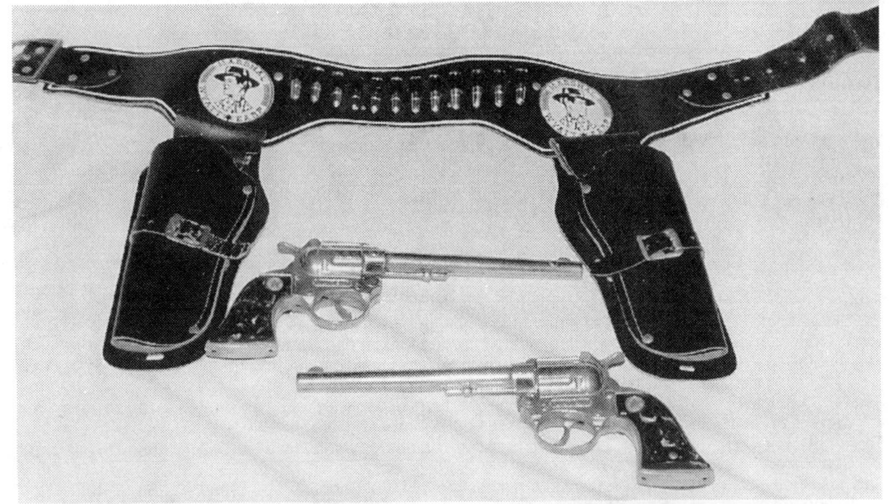

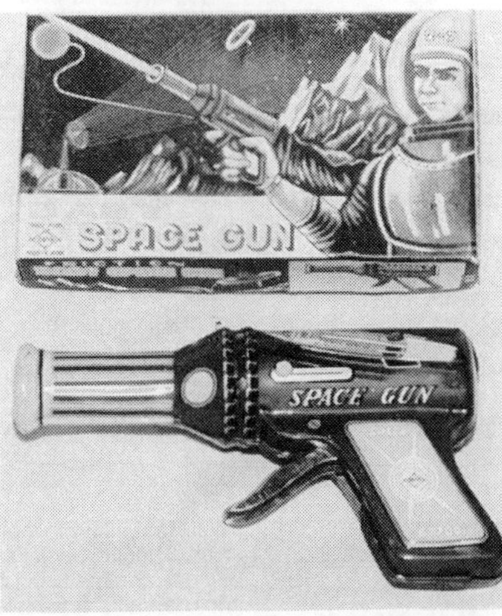

Top to Bottom: Wyatt Earp Double Holster Set, 1959, Hubley; Gene Autry Cap Pistol, Jr. Model, 1940, Kenton; Baby Space Gun, 1950s, Daiya; Texan Jr. Cap Pistol, 1950s, Hubley; Stallion 45, first version in rare lift-off top box, 1950, Nichols.

Western

TOY GUN	DESCRIPTION	YEAR	GOOD	EX	MIB
Wanted Dead or Alive Miniature Mares Laig	Marx Miniatures series miniature cap rifle on "wood frame" card, 1959		20	35	50
Zorro Flintock Pistol			30	45	75
Zorro Rifle			60	90	120

Mattel

TOY GUN	DESCRIPTION	YEAR	GOOD	EX	MIB
Fanner 50 "Swivelshot Trick Holster" Set	Die cast bullet loading Fanner 50, leather swivel style holster, attached to any belt, gun fires in holster when swiveled, string included for last ditch draw	1958	150	275	345
Fanner 50 Cap Pistol	11" fanner non-revolving cylinder, stag plastic grips, nickel finish, black vinyl "Durahyde" holster	1960s	50	75	110
Fanner 50 Smoking Cap Pistol	10 1/2" with revolving cylinder, first version with grapefruit cylinder does not chamber bullets	1957	75	150	250
Fanner 50 Smoking Cap Pistol	10 1/2" with revolving cylinder, chambers 6 metal play bullets, die cast	1958	55	120	200
Shootin' Shell .45 Fanner Cap Pistol	11" revolving cylinder pistol shoots Mattel Shootin' Shell cartridges, shell ejector	1959	250	400	650
Shootin' Shell Buckle Gun	Cap & bullet shooting copy of Remington Derringer pops out from belt buckle, 2 brass cartridges & 6 bullet head	1958	45	80	125
Shootin' Shell Fanner	9" die cast chrome finish, revolving cylinder chambers 6 Shootin' Shell bullets	1958	65	125	225
Shootin' Shell Fanner & Derringer Set	Small size Shooting Shell Fanner w/chrome finish, revolving cylinder, chambers 6 Shootin' Shell bullets, brown leather holster	1958	75	145	250
Shootin' Shell Fanner Single Holster	Cowhide holster takes small size Shootin' Shell Fanner with six brass play bullets & tie-downs	1959	80	145	250
Shootin' Shell Indian Scout Rifle	29 1/2" plastic/metal Sharps rolling block rifle, chambers 2-pc. Shootin' Shell bullets, secret compartment in stock for ammo storage, plastic stock & metal barrel	1958	100	145	250
Shootin' Shell Potshot Remington Derringer	3" derringer, on card	1959	35	60	90
Showdown Set with 3 Shootin' Shell Guns	30" single shot rifle with metal barrel, die cast w/plastic stock, Shootin' Shell Fanner sm. size, revolving cylinder, chrome finish & Imitation stag plastic grips, tan holster w/bullet loops	1958	300	600	950
Winchester Saddle Gun Rifle	33" die cast & plastic, perforated roll caps & chambers 8 play bullets loaded thru side door	1959	45	95	350

Nichols

TOY GUN	DESCRIPTION	YEAR	GOOD	EX	MIB
Dyna-Mite Derringer	3 1/4" die cast, loads single cap cartridge, silver finish, white plastic grips	1955	15	30	45
Dyna-Mite Derringer in Clip	3 1/2" die cast, fires single cap in Nichols cartridge, nickel finish, white plastic grips with small leather holster		25	45	65
Nichols Cap Gun Store Display	24 x 14" wood board, derringer & 2 strips of Nichols bullets	1950s	300	600	950
Silver Pony Cap Pistol	7 1/2" single shot, silver metal grip & one replacement black plastic grip, silver finish	1950s	30	45	70
Spitfire Hip Gun No. 100	9" cap cartridge loading mini rifle, chrome finish, tan plastic stock	1950s	15	20	35
Stallion .22 Cap Pistol	7" revolving cylinder chambers five two piece cartridges, single action, black plastic stag grips	1950s	65	90	145
Stallion .22 Double Action Cap Pistol	7" double action, pull trigger to fire, white plastic grips, nickel finish, cylinder revolves	1950s	85	145	200

Western

TOY GUN	DESCRIPTION	YEAR	GOOD	EX	MIB
Stallion .38 Cap Pistol	9 1/2", chambers 6 2-pc. cap cartridges, nickel finish, white plastic grips	1950s	75	115	175
Stallion .45 MK I Cap Pistol	Die cast, 12" chrome finish, revolving cylinder, chambers 6 2 pc. bullets, shell ejector, white "pearlescent" plastic grips with rearing stallion, red jewels & 6 bullets & Stallion caps	1950	100	250	375
Stallion .45 MK II Cap Pistol	12" pistol, chrome finish, revolving cylinder, chambers 6 2-pc. bullets, shell ejector, extra set of white grips to replace black grips on gun & box of Stallion caps	1956	100	185	275
Stallion 32 Six Shooter	8" revolving cylinder chambers 6 2-pc. cartridges, nickel finish, black plastic grips	1955	75	110	165
Stallion 41-40 Cap Pistol	10 1/2" revolving cylinder chrome finish pistol, swing out cylinder that chambers 6 2-pc. cap cartridges, shell ejector, scroll work on frame, creme-purple swirl colored plastic grips	1950s	150	250	345

Ohio Art Co.

TOY GUN	DESCRIPTION	YEAR	GOOD	EX	MIB
Sheriff's Derringer Pocket Pistol	3 1/4" silver finish derringer chambers 2-pc., Nichols style cartridge, red plastic grips with an "A" logo, on card	1960s	10	20	25

Pilgrim Leather Goods

TOY GUN	DESCRIPTION	YEAR	GOOD	EX	MIB
Ruff Rider Western Holster Set	Brown leather double holster, variety of studs & red jewels, 12 plastic silver bullets, tie-downs		100	150	200

Product Engineering Co.

TOY GUN	DESCRIPTION	YEAR	GOOD	EX	MIB
45 Smoker	10" single cap, shoots talcum-like powder by use of bellows when trigger is pulled, aluminum finish	1950s	45	75	115
Frontier Smoker	9 1/2" cap pistol, die cast, pop up magazine & shoots white powder from internal bellows, all metal, black grips, silver finish, gold magazine, hammer & trigger		85	135	200

Ralston Purina

TOY GUN	DESCRIPTION	YEAR	GOOD	EX	MIB
Tom Mix Wooden Gun	3 all-wood versions with leather holster, came in mailer, each	1930s	125	250	350

Schmidt

TOY GUN	DESCRIPTION	YEAR	GOOD	EX	MIB
Buck 'n Bronc Marshal Cap Pistol	10" long barrel revolver style, lever release, break-to-front, plain silver finish, copper color metal grips	1950s	90	150	225

Smart Style

TOY GUN	DESCRIPTION	YEAR	GOOD	EX	MIB
Real Texan Outfit with Nichols Stallion .22	Brown & white leather double holsters have silver conches with red reflectors, silver horses at top of holster, belt with 3 bullet loops, guns are a pair of double action .22s	1950s	95	175	265

Stevens

TOY GUN	DESCRIPTION	YEAR	GOOD	EX	MIB
49-er Cap Pistol	Cast iron, 9", unusual internal hammer with revolving steel cylinder, nickel finish, white plastic figural grips	1940	100	200	350
Buffalo Bill Cap Pistol	7 3/4", silver nickel finish, side loading magazine door, white "tenite" plastic horse & cowboy grips, red jewels	1940	65	110	175
Colt Cap Pistol	6 1/2", revolver style double action	1935	15	25	50

TOY GUN	DESCRIPTION	YEAR	GOOD	EX	MIB
Western					
Cowboy Cap Pistol	3 1/2" cast iron, single shot single action, sold loose	1935	20	35	50
Cowboy King Cap Pistol	9" break-to-front release, gold finish cast iron, black plastic grips, yellow jewels	1940	85	175	225
Topper/Deluxe Reading					
Johnny Eagle Red River Bullet Firing	Over 12" double action revolving cylinder pistol, die cast hammer, trigger, blue plastic overall with wood plastic grips with gold horse, side loading, shell ejector, fires 2 piece plastic bullets	1965	65	95	150
Unknown					
Davy Crockett Frontier Fighter Cork Gun	21" pop gun shoots cork on string & has cigarette flint mechanism at muzzle that makes sparks when fired, wood stock, leather sling	1950s	65	135	195
Gene Autry Champion Single Holster Set	Leather & cardboard, red, yellow & green "jewels," four white wooden bullets, silver buckle	1940s	125	175	250
Lone Ranger Holster	9" , leather & pressboard, Hi-Yo Silver & Lone Ranger printed, red jewel, belt loop		35	45	60
Tom Mix Gun & Holster Outfit (Box Only)	10 x 5 x 2" box, gun and holster unknown	1930s	55	85	125
Wyatt Earp Double Holster Set	Med. size, reflectors, black leather with brown rawhide fringe, holsters only	1950s	50	70	95
Wyandotte					
Red Ranger Jr. Cap Pistol	7 1/2" lever release, break-to-front, silver finish, white plastic horse grips	1950s	55	85	120
Young Premiums					
Official Wyatt Earp Buntline Clicker Pistol	18 1/2" plastic		35	60	90

Model Kits

Model kits have always been popular toys for boys, and in recent years the kits have found a new following among older collectors... primarily former boys recapturing a part of their youth.

Plastic model kits were first produced shortly before World War II, but it wasn't until after the war that plastic kit building really began to take off. Automobiles, aircraft and ships all became subject matter for the miniature replicas popularized by such companies as Aurora, Revell, Monogram, Frog and Lindberg.

Each type of model kit has its own enthusiastic following, but probably the most collectible kits today are the figure and character kits produced primarily in the 1960s. These kits have seen dramatic increases in collector values over the past 10 years.

The company that did the most to popularize the figure kit was Aurora, with its introduction in the early 1960s of a line of kits representing the monsters from Universal Pictures. Aurora had been producing figure kits prior to that time, but the monster craze of the period was responsible for a highly successful line of kits.

Starting with the Frankenstein monster in 1961, Aurora went on to produce kits of many memorable movie monsters before moving into more general monstrosities, such as its famous working guillotine kit. Such toys offended the sensibilities of some groups, who brought about political pressure that spelled the end of this line of kits. The firm also produced kits based on popular television shows, comic characters and sports celebrities. Some of the kits originally made by Aurora were later reissued by Monogram and Revell. And resin copies of the more hard-to-get Aurora kits are still being produced and sold today by independent garage kit makers.

Other popular monster kits were also a fad in the '60s. These weren't the traditional movie monsters, but rather an assortment of strange characters that often came in wild hot rods. Among the more popular were those based on Ed "Big Daddy" Roth's Rat Fink concept. These kits were produced by Revell. Other firms, most notably Hawk, also produced kits of this new type of monster.

Even popular celebrities of the day became the subject of model kits. Revell, for example, issued figure kits of each of the four Beatles.

Figure kits began to enjoy new popularity in the 1980s as new large-scale kits of rather limited production runs were being made in vinyl and resin. Billiken, a Japanese company, produced vinyl kits of the classic movie monsters, some of which have become highly collectible. Screamin' and Horizon have also produced a line of large-scale vinyl kits of movie and comic book characters. Both firms' kits are still widely available and have not shown price increases. There are also many individuals and small firms producing small-run resin kits of monsters and film characters.

Frankenstein, by Monogram, from original Aurora molds.

Some of the kits we have characterized in the category of collectible figure/character kits don't represent actual figures. However, they are generally considered to fall into this category because they have some relationship to a popular character, personality or historical figure.

The prices indicated are intended to provide general guidelines as to what these kits would sell for today at retail. MIB refers to a kit that is mint in box. It is in like-new condition in the original like-new box, with instructions. The box may not be in the original factory seal, but if the kit pieces were contained in bags inside the box, the bags have not been opened. Kits that remain in pristine condition in factory seals may command a slight premium. NM refers to a near-mint condition kit that is like new, complete and unassembled. The box may show some shelf wear and the interior bags may have been opened. B/U refers to a kit that has been assembled or built up. These price guidelines assume a neatly built, complete kit.

FIGURE/CHARACTER KITS

Addar

NO.	MODEL KIT	YEAR	BU	NM	MINT
106	Caesar, Planet of the Apes	1974	15	40	45
101	Cornelius, Planet of the Apes	1974	12	30	35
216	Cornfield, Planet of the Apes	1975	15	40	45
102	Dr. Zaius, Planet of the Apes	1974	10	25	30
105	Dr. Zira, Planet of the Apes	1974	10	25	30
104	Gen. Aldo, Planet of the Apes		10	25	30
103	Gen. Ursus, Planet of the Apes		12	30	35
217	Jailwagon, Planet of the Apes	1975	15	40	45
270	Jaws diorama		20	50	60
107	Stallion & Soldier, Planet of the Apes	1974	25	70	80
215	Treehouse, Planet of the Apes	1975	15	40	45

Airfix

NO.	MODEL KIT	YEAR	BU	NM	MINT
3542	Anne Boleyn	1974	7	15	20
823	Aston Martin, James Bond	1965	60	200	225
2502	Black Prince	1973	10	25	30
212	Boy Scout	1965	7	15	20
211	Charles I	1965	10	20	25
2501	Henry VIII	1973	4	8	10
2504	Julius Caesar	1973	10	25	30
	Monkeemobile	1967	75	240	275
2508	Napolean	1978	4	8	10
3546	Queen Elizabeth I	1980	7	15	20
3544	Queen Victoria	1976	7	15	20
203	Richard I	1965	10	25	30
2507	Yeoman of the Guard	1978	4	8	10

AMT

NO.	MODEL KIT	YEAR	BU	NM	MINT
7701	Big Foot	1978	20	60	75
	Brute Farce		5	10	15
610	Cliff Hanger		5	10	15
	Dragula, Munsters	1965	40	200	225
497	Flintstones Rock Crusher	1974	20	50	60
495	Flintstones Sports Car	1974	20	55	65
	Girl From U.N.C.L.E. Car	1974	75	200	250
309	Graveyard Ghoul Duo (Munsters cars)	1970		100	125
2501	KISS Custom Chevy Van	1977	20	50	60
462	Laurel & Hardy '27 T Roadster	1976	20	50	60
461	Laurel & Hardy '27 T Touring Car	1976	20	50	60
	Man From U.N.C.L.E. Car	1966	75	175	200
6058	Monkee Mobile (AMT/Ertl)		20	55	65
956	Mr. Spock, large box	1973	20	125	150
	Mr. Spock, small box	1973	20	125	150
901	Munsters Koach	1964	50	150	175
904	My Mother The Car	1965	15	35	40
	Sonny & Cher Mustang		75	250	300
	Threw'd Dude		5	10	15
614	Touchdown?		5	10	15
	UFO Mystery Ship		15	60	75
950	USS Enterprise Bridge, Star Trek	1975	10	25	30
921-200	USS Enterprise w/lights, Star Trek	1967	40	200	250
951-250	USS Enterprise, Star Trek	1966	40	125	150

Aurora

NO.	MODEL KIT	YEAR	BU	NM	MINT
805	Addams Family Haunted House	1964	300	750	800
409	American Astronaut	1967	15	60	75
402	American Buffalo	1964	8	20	25
402	American Buffalo, re-issue	1972	8	12	15
401	Apache Warrior on Horse	1960	175	300	400
K-10	Aramis, Three Musketeers	1958	20	55	75

Figure/Character Kits

NO.	MODEL KIT	YEAR	BU	NM	MINT
582	Archie's Car	1969	25	85	100
819	Aston Martin Super Spy Car		40	125	175
K-8	Athos, Three Musketeers	1958	20	55	75
832	Banana Splits Banana Buggy	1969	150	300	350
811	Batboat	1968	150	400	450
810	Batcycle	1967	125	350	400
467	Batman	1964	15	200	250
187	Batman, Comic Scenes	1974	15	35	40
486	Batmobile	1966	100	275	325
487	Batplane	1967	75	200	250
407	Black Bear and Cubs	1962	15	30	40
407	Black Bear and Cubs, re-issue	1969	15	20	25
400	Black Fury	1958	10	25	30
400	Black Fury, re-issue	1969	10	13	15
K-3	Black Knight	1956	10	30	35
473	Black Knight, re-issue	1963	10	13	15
463	Blackbeard	1965	75	200	225
K-2	Blue Knight	1956	10	35	50
472	Blue Knight, re-issue	1963	10	17	20
414	Bond, James	1966	150	325	600
482	Bride of Frankenstein	1965	300	650	750
863	Brown, Jimmy	1965	75	150	175
409	Canyon, Steve	1958	75	175	200
480	Captain Action	1966	100	275	300
476	Captain America	1966	85	250	300
192	Captain America, Comic Scenes	1974	30	100	125
464	Captain Kidd	1965	25	70	80
738	Cave Bear	1971	15	35	40
416	Chinese Girl	1957	10	20	25
415	Chinese Mandarin	1957	12	25	30
213	Chinese Mandarin & Girl set	1957		175	225
828	Chitty Chitty Bang Bang	1968	30	85	100
402	Confederate Raider	1959	150	300	350
426	Creature From The Black Lagoon	1963	65	325	400
483	Creature From The Black Lagoon, Glow Kit	1969	65	175	200
483	Creature From The Black Lagoon, Glow Kit	1972	65	100	125
653	Creature, Monsters of Movies	1975	50	175	200
730	Cro Magnon Man	1971	10	20	25
731	Cro Magnon Woman	1971	7	17	20
K-7	Crusader	1959	75	150	200
410	D'Artagnan, Three Musketeers	1966	50	150	175
861	Dempsy vs Firpo	1965	20	75	75
631	Dr. Deadly	1971	25	70	80
632	Dr. Deadly's Daughter	1971	25	65	75
460	Dr. Jekyll as Mr. Hyde	1964	45	250	300
482	Dr. Jekyll, Glow Kit	1969	45	85	100
482	Dr. Jekyll, Glow Kit	1972	45	65	80
462	Dr. Jekyll, Monster Scenes	1971	40	100	125
654	Dr. Jekyll, Monsters of Movies	1975	25	60	70
424	Dracula	1962	25	225	300
466	Dracula's Dragster	1966	125	300	350
454	Dracula, Frightning Lightning	1969	20	300	450
454	Dracula, Glow Kit	1969	20	85	100
454	Dracula, Glow Kit	1972	20	60	75
641	Dracula, Monster Scenes	1971	100	150	200
656	Dracula, Monsters of Movies	1975	100	175	225
413	Dutch Boy	1957	10	25	30
209	Dutch Boy & Girl set	1957		175	225
414	Dutch Girl	1957	10	20	25
817	Flying Sub	1968	35	175	200
254	Flying Sub, re-issue	1975	35	85	100

Top to Bottom: Adolph Hitler, Born Losers, Parks, 1965; Wyatt Earp, Pyro; Robin, Aurora, 1966; Aramis, Three Musketeers, Aurora, 1958.

Figure/Character Kits

NO.	MODEL KIT	YEAR	BU	NM	MINT
422	Forgotten Prisoner	1966	65	350	400
453	Forgotten Prisoner, Frightning Lightning	1696	65	325	450
453	Forgotten Prisoner, Glow Kit	1696	65	175	200
453	Forgotten Prisoner, Glow Kit	1972	65	150	175
423	Frankenstein	1961	20	210	250
449	Frankenstein, Frightning Lightning	1969	20	375	400
470	Frankenstein, Gigantic 1/5 scale	1964	400	1000	1200
449	Frankenstein, Glow Kit	1969	20	65	75
449	Frankenstein, Glow Kit	1972	20	50	60
633	Frankenstein, Monster Scenes	1971	50	75	100
651	Frankenstein, Monsters of Movies	1975	90	175	200
465	Frankie's Flivver	1964	150	300	350
451	Frog, Castle Creatures	1966	75	200	250
658	Ghidrah	1975	95	260	300
643	Giant Insect, Monster Scene	1971	95	350	400
469	Godzilla	1964	75	425	500
485	Godzilla's Go-Cart	1966	400	1100	1300
466	Godzilla, Glow Kit	1969	75	200	250
466	Godzilla, Glow Kit	1972	75	150	175
K-5	Gold Knight on Horse	1957	125	250	300
475	Gold Knight on Horse	1965	125	250	275
413	Green Beret	1966	75	150	175
489	Green Hornet 'Black Beauty'	1966	125	300	350
634	Gruesome Goodies	1971	25	80	100
800	Guillotine	1964	100	350	400
637	Hanging Cage	1971	20	80	100
481	Hercules	1965	95	250	275
184	Hulk, Comic Scenes	1974	25	75	85
421	Hulk, original	1966	75	250	300
460	Hunchback of Notre Dame	1964	45	250	300
481	Hunchback of Notre Dame, Glow Kit	1969	45	75	85
481	Hunchback of Notre Dame, Glow Kit	1972	45	65	75
417	Indian Chief	1957	40	90	100
212	Indian Chief & Squaw set	1957		125	150
418	Indian Squaw	1957	15	38	45
411	Infantryman	1957	20	75	100
813	Invaders UFO	1968	35	85	100
256	Invaders UFO	1975	25	65	75
853	Iwo Jima	1966	75	175	200
408	Jesse James	1966	75	175	200
851	Kennedy, John F.	1965	50	100	150
885	King Arthur	1973	100	125	200
825	King Arthur of Camelot	1967	30	65	75
468	King Kong	1964	75	350	400
484	King Kong's Thronester	1966	350	850	1000
468	King Kong, Glow Kit	1969	75	175	200
468	King Kong, Glow Kit	1972	75	150	175
816	Land of the Giants (diorama)	1968	150	360	400
830	Land of the Giants Space Ship	1968	150	300	350
808	Lone Ranger	1967	75	150	175
188	Lone Ranger, Comic Scenes	1974	20	45	50
420	Lost In Space, large kit w/ chariot	1966	450	1100	1300
419	Lost In Space, small kit	1966	300	800	900
418	Lost In Space, The Robot	1968	250	600	700
455	Mad Barber	1972	45	125	150
457	Mad Dentist	1972	45	125	150
456	Mad Doctor	1972	45	125	150
412	Man From U.N.C.L.E., Ilya Kuryakin	1966	75	150	175
411	Man From U.N.C.L.E., Napoleon Solo	1966	75	225	250
412	Marine	1959	20	80	100
860	Mays, Willie	1965	100	250	300

Top to Bottom: Frankenstein, Monogram, 1983; Dragnut, Revell, 1963; Neanderthal Man and Cro-Magnon Man, Aurora Prehistoric Scenes, 1971; Batmobile, Aurura, 1966, Barnabas Vampire Van, MPC; Sweathogs Dream Machine, MPC, 1976.

MODELS

Figure/Character Kits

NO.	MODEL KIT	YEAR	BU	NM	MINT
421	Mexican Caballero	1957	75	90	100
422	Mexican Seniorita	1957	50	90	100
583	Mod Squad Wagon	1970	35	125	150
463	Monster Customizing Kit #1	1964	35	110	125
464	Monster Customizing Kit #2	1964	65	150	175
828	Moon Bus from 2001	1968	100	275	300
655	Mr. Hyde, Monsters of Movies	1975	25	65	75
922	Mr. Spock	1972	25	100	125
427	Mummy	1963	20	275	300
459	Mummy's Chariot	1965	200	400	450
452	Mummy, Frightning Lightning	1969	20	300	350
452	Mummy, Glow Kit	1969	20	65	75
452	Mummy, Glow Kit	1972	20	50	60
804	Munsters	1964	400	800	900
729	Neanderthal Man	1971	15	35	40
802	Neuman, Alfred E.	1965	100	250	300
806	Nutty Nose Nipper	1965	45	175	200
415	Odd Job	1966	100	225	250
635	Pain Parlor	1971	25	100	125
636	Pendulum	1971	25	65	75
416	Penguin	1967	200	450	500
428	Phantom of the Opera	1963	20	275	300
451	Phantom of the Opera, Fright'ng Light'ng	1969	20	300	350
451	Phantom of the Opera, Glow Kit	1969	20	85	100
451	Phantom of the Opera, Glow Kit	1972	20	70	80
409	Pilot USAF	1957	75	150	175
K-9	Porthos, Three Musketeers	1958	25	65	75
814	Pushmi-Pullyu, Dr. Dolittle	1968	30	75	85
340	Rat Patrol	1967	30	75	90
K-4	Red Knight	1957	15	70	75
474	Red Knight	1963	15	20	25
488	Robin	1966	40	70	75
193	Robin, Comic Scenes	1974	20	45	50
657	Rodan	1975	125	300	350
405	Roman Gladiator with sword	1959	75	150	175
406	Roman Gladiator with trident	1964	75	150	175
216	Roman Gladiators set	1959		225	250
862	Ruth, Babe	1965	100	250	300
410	Sailor, U.S.	1957	10	25	30
419	Scotch Lad	1957	10	25	30
214	Scotch Lad & Lassie set	1957		85	100
420	Scotch Lassie	1957	10	20	25
707	Seaview, Voyage to the Bottom of Sea	1966	100	250	300
253	Seaview, Voyage to the Bottom of Sea	1975	100	175	200
K-1	Silver Knight	1956	12	45	50
471	Silver Knight	1963	12	18	20
881	Sir Galahad	1973	15	45	50
826	Sir Galahad of Camelot	1967	25	100	175
882	Sir Kay	1973	20	45	50
883	Sir Lancelot	1973	20	45	50
827	Sir Lancelot of Camelot	1967	25	100	125
884	Sir Percival	1973	20	45	50
405	Spartacus (Gladiator/sword re-issue)	1964	85	200	225
477	Spider-Man	1966	85	250	300
182	Spider-Man, Comic Scenes	1974	50	75	85
923	Star Trek, Klingon Cruiser	1972	20	65	75
921	Star Trek, USS Enterprise	1972	20	85	100
478	Superboy	1964	75	225	250
186	Superboy, Comic Scenes	1974	35	50	60
462	Superman	1963	25	275	300
185	Superman, Comic Scenes	1974	20	45	50

Top to Bottom: Athos, Three Musketeers, Aurora, 1958; Mr. Gasser, Revell, 1963; Dr. Jekyl & Mr. Hyde, Aurora, 1972; Dragula and Munster Koach, AMT, 1965; Daddy the Suburbanite and Huey's Hut Rod, Hawk, 1963.

Figure/Character Kits

NO.	MODEL KIT	YEAR	BU	NM	MINT
735	Tarpit	1972	50	100	125
820	Tarzan	1967	25	175	200
181	Tarzan, Comic Scenes	1974	15	30	35
207	Three Knights Set	1959		150	175
398	Three Musketeers Set	1958		300	350
809	Tonto	1967	10	175	200
183	Tonto, Comic Scenes	1974	10	20	25
818	Tracy, Dick	1968	75	200	250
819	Tracy, Dick, Space Coupe	1968	50	125	150
408	U.S. Marshall	1958	50	90	100
864	Unitas, Johnny	1965	75	150	175
452	Vampire, Castle Creatures	1966	60	200	250
638	Vampirella	1971	75	125	150
632	Victim	1971	20	65	75
K-6	Viking	1959	75	175	200
831	Voyager, Fantastic Voyage	1969	150	400	450
807	Wacky Back Whacker	1965	50	175	200
852	Washington, George	1965	25	65	75
865	West, Jerry	1965	50	125	150
401	White Stallion	1964	10	25	30
401	White Stallion, re-issue	1969	10	17	20
403	White Tail Deer	1962	10	25	30
403	White Tail Deer, re-issue	1969	10	17	20
204	Whoozis, Alfalfa	1966	25	65	75
203	Whoozis, Denty	1966	25	65	75
202	Whoozis, Esmerelda	1966	25	65	75
205	Whoozis, Kitty	1966	25	65	75
206	Whoozis, Snuffy	1966	25	65	75
201	Whoozis, Susie	1966	25	65	75
483	Witch	1965	50	225	250
470	Witch, Glow Kit	1969	75	125	150
470	Witch, Glow Kit	1972	75	100	125
425	Wolfman	1962	20	250	300
458	Wolfman's Wagon	1965	175	350	400
450	Wolfman, Frightening Lightning	1969	20	350	400
450	Wolfman, Glow Kit	1969	20	85	100
450	Wolfman, Glow Kit	1972	20	65	75
652	Wolfman, Monsters of Movies	1975	150	200	225
479	Wonder Woman	1965	150	450	500
801	Zorro	1965	125	275	300

Billiken

NO.	MODEL KIT	YEAR	BU	NM	MINT
	Batman, type A	1989	35	85	90
	Batman, type B	1989	35	90	100
	Bride of Frankenstein		100	200	225
	Colossal Beast	1986	20	35	40
	Creature From Black Lagoon	1991	50	90	100
	Dracula		60	135	150
	Frankenstein		60	100	125
	Joker	1989	35	85	90
	Mummy	1990	60	135	150
	Phantom of the Opera		125	225	250
	Predator		25	60	65
	Saucer Man		20	35	40
	She-Creature		25	45	50
	Syngenor		100	200	225
	The Thing		150	275	300
	Ultraman		20	35	40

Hawk

NO.	MODEL KIT	YEAR	BU	NM	MINT
542	Beach Bunny	1964	25	65	75

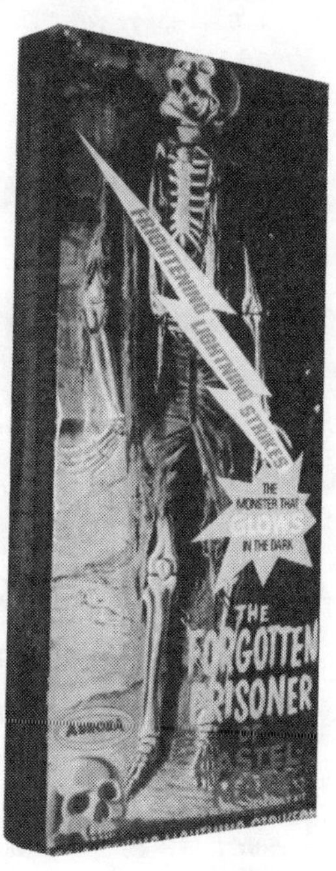

Top to Bottom: Odd Job and James Bond, Aurora, 1966; Wonder Woman, Aurora, 1965; Crusader, Aurora, 1958; Dutch Boy, Aurora, 1957; Forgotten Prisoner, Aurora, 1966.

Figure/Character Kits

NO.	MODEL KIT	YEAR	BU	NM	MINT
532	Daddy the Suburbanite	1963	30	75	85
531	Davy the Way-Out Cyclist	1963	30	75	85
530	Digger and Dragster	1963	30	75	85
	Drag Hag	1963	30	75	85
537	Endsville Eddie	1963	20	50	60
535	Francis The Foul	1963	15	35	40
548	Frantics Banana Skins	1965	20	80	100
550	Frantics Cats	1965	20	70	75
547	Frantics Steel Pluckers	1965	20	70	75
549	Frantics Totally Fab	1965	20	80	100
533	Freddy Flameout	1963	20	65	75
543	Hodad Silly Surfer	1964	20	65	75
541	Hot Dogger Hanging' Ten	1964	20	65	75
538	Huey's Hut Rod	1963	20	45	50
	Killer McBash	1963	40	125	150
534	Leaky Boat Louie	1963	25	80	90
	Riding Tandem		25	65	75
637	Sling Rave Curvette	1964	12	25	30
636	Wade A Minute	1963	12	25	30
	Weird-Oh Customizing Kit	1964	75	250	300
545	Wild Woodie Car		20	50	55
540	Woodie On Safari	1964	25	85	100

Lindberg

NO.	MODEL KIT	YEAR	BU	NM	MINT
6422	Bert's Bucket	1971	30	80	90
	Big Wheeler	1964	30	80	90
6420	Fat Max	1971	30	80	90
276	Road Hog	1964	30	80	90
	Satan's Crate	1964	75	125	150
	Scuttle Bucket	1964	30	80	90
6421	Sick Cycle	1971	30	80	90

Monogram

NO.	MODEL KIT	YEAR	BU	NM	MINT
6028	Battlestar Galactica	1979	15	35	40
6008	Dracula	1983	20	25	30
105	Flip Out	1965	50	150	175
6007	Frankenstein	1983	20	30	35
6300	Godzilla	1978	40	65	75
6010	Mummy	1983	20	30	35
	Snoopy & Motorcycle	1971	15	25	30
6779	Snoopy & Sopwith Camel	1971	20	30	35
MM106	Speed Shift	1965	70	175	200
	Super Fuzz	1965	80	200	225
6301	Superman	1978	20	30	35
6012	UFO, The Invaders	1979	15	35	40
6009	Wolfman	1983	20	30	35

MPC

NO.	MODEL KIT	YEAR	BU	NM	MINT
1-1961	Alien	1979	25	75	100
0303	Ape Man Glow Head	1975	10	20	25
	AT-AT, Empire Strikes Back	1980	12	30	35
	Barnabas Vampire Van		75	200	225
550	Barnabas, Dark Shadows	1968	100	300	350
1702	Batman	1984	20	30	35
612	Beverly Hillbillies Truck	1968	60	150	175
0609	Bionic Bustout, Six Million $ Man	1975	12	25	30
0610	Bionic Repair, Bionic Woman	1976	12	25	30
5003	Condemned to Chains Forever	1974	20	45	50
103	Curls Girl		25	65	75
	Darth Vader bust	1977	20	45	50
	Darth Vader with light saber	1977	15	35	40

Top to Bottom: Sailor, U.S., Aurora, 1957; Hunchback of Notre Dame, Aurora, 1964; Man from U.N.C.L.E., Napoleon Solo, Aurora, 1966; Frankenstein, Monogram, 1983; Bonanza, Revell, 1965; Digger and Dragster, Hawk, 1963.

Figure/Character Kits

NO.	MODEL KIT	YEAR	BU	NM	MINT
5005	Dead Man's Raft	1974	20	90	100
5001	Dead Men Tell No Tales	1974	20	45	50
1983	Encounter With Yoda diorama	1981	15	30	35
5053	Escape From the Crypt	1974	20	45	50
5004	Fate of the Mutineers	1974	20	45	50
0602	Fight for Survival, Six Million $ Man	1975	12	20	25
0635	Fonzie & Dream Rod	1976	12	30	35
0634	Fonzie & Motorcycle		8	15	20
5007	Freed in the Nick of Time	1974	20	70	75
5006	Ghost of the Treasure Guard	1974	20	45	50
5051	Grave Robbers Reward	1974	20	45	50
402	Hogan's Heroes Jeep	1968	25	85	100
5002	Hoist High the Jolly Roger	1974	20	45	50
101	Hot Curl		20	45	50
	Hot Shot		20	45	50
1932	Hulk	1978	20	30	35
	Jabba's Throne Room	1983	20	35	40
1925	Millenium Falcon with light	1977	35	85	100
605	Monkeemobile	1967	70	170	200
1-0702	Muldowny, Shirley, Drag Kit		20	55	65
0304	Mummy Glow Head	1975	10	20	25
	Night Crawler Wolfman Car	1971	45	100	125
622	Paul Revere & The Raiders Coach	1970	40	100	125
5052	Play It Again Sam	1974	35	90	100
1906	Raiders of the Lost Ark Chase Scene	1982	15	35	40
	Road Runner Beep Beep T		20	65	75
1931	Spider-Man	1978	20	30	35
0902	Strange Changing Mummy	1974	15	35	40
0903	Strange Changing Time Machine	1974	20	45	50
0901	Strange Changing Vampire	1974	20	45	50
100	Stroker McGurk & Surf Rod		30	85	100
102	Stroker McGurk Tall T		30	85	100
1701	Superman	1984	15	20	25
641	Sweathog Dream Machine	1976	7	15	20
5050	Vampire's Midnight Madness	1974	20	45	50
	Werewolf, Dark Shadows	1969	75	200	225
2651	Wile E. Coyote		20	55	65
617	Yellow Submarine	1968	70	170	200

Multiple

NO.	MODEL KIT	YEAR	BU	NM	MINT
955	Automatic Baby Feeder	1965	25	65	75
958	Back Scrubber	1965	25	65	75
956	Painless False Tooth Extractor	1965	25	65	75
957	Signal for Shipwrecked Sailors	1965	25	65	75

Parks

NO.	MODEL KIT	YEAR	BU	NM	MINT
803	Castro, Born Losers	1956	25	65	75
802	Hitler, Born Losers	1965	25	65	75
801	Napolean, Born Losers	1965	25	65	75

Precision

NO.	MODEL KIT	YEAR	BU	NM	MINT
402	Captain Kidd		25	65	75
501	Jesus Christ		20	45	50

Pyro

NO.	MODEL KIT	YEAR	BU	NM	MINT
166	Der Baron	1958	80	225	250
278	Earp, Wyatt		20	50	60
175	Gladiator Show Cycle		20	40	50
281	Indian Chief		20	50	60
282	Indian Medicine Man		20	50	60
283	Indian Warrior	1960	20	50	60

Figure/Character Kits

NO.	MODEL KIT	YEAR	BU	NM	MINT
168	Lil Corporal	1970	25	65	75
276	Rawhide, Gil Favor	1958	20	50	60
277	Restless Gun Deputy	1959	20	50	60
176	Surf's Up	1970	15	35	40
286	U.S. Marsahll		20	50	60

Revell

NO.	MODEL KIT	YEAR	BU	NM	MINT
1307	Angel Fink	1965	40	100	125
	Beatles, George Harrison	1965	100	200	250
1352	Beatles, John Lennon	1965	100	200	250
	Beatles, Paul McCartney	1965	100	175	200
1351	Beatles, Ringo Starr	1965	100	150	185
1931	Bonanza	1965	50	125	150
1304	Brother Rat Fink	1963	20	50	55
2000	Cat in the Hat	1960	45	100	130
1397	Charlie's Angels Van	1977	10	20	25
1303	Dragnut	1963	20	50	60
1310	Fink Eliminator	1965	30	175	200
1450	Flash Gordon & Alien	1965	60	125	150
1930	Flipper	1965	75	125	150
	Horton the Elephant	1960	35	85	100
323	McHale's Navy PT-73	1965	25	65	75
1302	Mother's Worry	1963	20	60	75
1301	Mr. Gasser	1963	30	75	90
3181	Mr. Gasser BMR Racer	1964	30	75	90
1451	Phantom & Witch Doctor	1965	50	175	200
1305	Rat Fink	1963	25	60	70
	Rat Fink Lotus Racer	1964	25	65	75
	Robbin' Hood Fink	1965	200	350	400
1309	Scuz Fink	1965	200	300	350
	Super Fink	1964	150	300	350
1306	Surf Fink	1965	35	85	100
1271	Tweedy Pie & Boss Fink	1965	200	350	400

Marx Playsets and Figures

For all practical purposes, the word "playset" could have been invented by Louis Marx... at least as far as boys growing up in the '50s and '60s were concerned.

The words "Marx" and "playset" just went together, and they still go together today for many dedicated collectors.

A typical Marx playset included buildings, figures and lots of realistic accessories that helped bring the miniature world to life. The Fort Apache Stockade, for example, came with a hard plastic log fort, a colorful lithographed tin cabin, and, of course, pioneers and Indians locked in deadly combat. It was no wonder millions of kids had a burning desire for these toys. The play scenarios were almost endless.

This modern version of an age-old toy was a tribute to the marketing/manufacturing talents and whimsical genius of Louis Marx, the modern-day king of toys.

Not only was he responsible for developing the playset, but he popularized the yo-yo and produced some of the most innovative tin wind-ups, guns, dolls, trains, trikes, trucks and other types of toys that were commercially feasible. In 1955, Marx sold more than $50 million worth of toys, easily making him the largest toy manufacturer in the world.

What makes his domination even more impressive was the fact that Louis Marx rose from humble beginnings. He was born in Brooklyn in 1896 and didn't learn to speak English until he started school. At age 16, Marx went to work for Ferdinand Strauss, a toy manufacturer who produced items for Abraham & Strauss Department Stores. By the age of 20, Marx was managing the company's New Jersey factory.

After being fired by Strauss, Marx started contracting with manufacturers to produce toys he designed. By the mid-1920s, Marx had three plants in this country. By 1955 there were more than 5,000 items in the Marx toy line with plants worldwide.

Mass production and mass marketing through chain stores such as Sears and Wards allowed Marx to keep his price levels low and quality high. Marx was also a master at producing new toys from the same basic components. Existing elements could be modified slightly and new lithography would produce a new building from standard stock.

Part of Marx's repackaging genius included using popular TV or movie tie-ins to breathe new life into existing products. The Rifleman Ranch, Roy Rogers Ranch, and Wyatt Earp and Wagon Train playsets were examples of toys produced by Marx where existing parts were repackaged to capture the fad of the day.

Marx enjoyed his recreation as well as his work. He had a table reserved at the "21" nightclub in Manhattan and would hand out toys from oversized

Top: Marx Ben Hur Series 5000 Large Playset; Right: Marx Series 3 Nutty Mad figure, "Now Children."

pockets in his custom-made suits. He also donated truckloads of toys to churches and other charities.

Believing that toy manufacturing was a young man's business, Louis Marx sold his company to the Quaker Oats Company in 1972 for $51 million. Quaker Oats sold the Marx company four years later for $15 million after losing money every year it owned the company.

With the passing of a few short decades, what were once affordable children's toys have become highly prized collectibles. Playsets are among the price leaders in today's market for childhood treasures. And the figures that went with the playsets are also highly desired by collectors because of their quality and detail.

Most of the figures listed in this section are soft plastic in 54mm and 60mm size and were packaged with various playsets. Other Marx plastic figures are also listed here, such as their larger scale figures and the individually sold hand-painted "Warriors of the World."

A playset listed as MIB (Mint In Box) is as originally sold with all pieces in the original box. Excellent (Ex) condition means a complete well-cared for set, but the buildings are assembled and the box may be worn or damaged. Good condition means the playset shows wear and may have a few minor pieces missing.

MARX SETS

Miniature Playsets

NAME	DESCRIPTION	NO.	GOOD	VG	MIP
20 Minutes to Berlin	174 pieces, 1964		100	175	500
8 Miniature Sports Cars		5930	12	20	25
Battleground	170 pieces, 1963	HK-6111	50	75	100
Blue and Grey	101 individual pieces, 1960's	HK-6109	75	100	150
Border Battle	Mexican American War		75	100	300
Charge of the Light Brigade	Sears, 216 pieces, 1964		125	200	250
Charge of the Light Brigade	Photograph of the playset on the box		75	100	150
Charge of the Light Brigade	Red-coated British soldiers/blue uniformed Hussar Russians		75	100	150
Covered Wagon Attack			50	75	200
Custer's Last Stand	181 pieces, 1964		75	100	150
Flintstones			125	200	250
Fort Apache	90 individual pieces, 1963	HK-7526	75	100	200
Guerrilla Warfare	1960's		100	150	400
Invasion Day	304 pieces, 1964		75	100	150
Jungle	Smaller than Jungle Safari		100	150	200
Jungle Safari	Over 260 pieces		75	100	150
Knights & Vikings Play Set	143 pieces, 1964		75	100	150
Knights and Castle	132 pieces, 1963	HK-7563	75	100	150
Knights and Castle	64 pieces, 1964	HK-7562	65	75	125
Knights and Vikings			100	150	200
Nativity Set		3315	35	50	75
Noah's Ark	100 pieces, 1968		25	35	50
Sands of Iwo Jima	296 pieces, 1964		75	100	250
Sands of Iwo Jima	205 pieces, 1963		60	85	125
Sands of Iwo Jima	88 pieces, 1963		50	75	100
Ten Commandments	Montgomery Ward		500	750	800
Troll Town			75	100	150
Western Town		48-24398	25	45	60
Western Town	1960's	48-24398	50	75	100
Western Town	Over 170 pieces	48-24398	125	150	250

Disneykins

NAME	DESCRIPTION	NO.	GOOD	VG	MIP
"The Lost Boys" Play Set	2nd Series, 1961		100	150	200
101 Dalmations	"The Barn Scene", 1961		100	175	225
101 Dalmations	"The Wedding Scene", 1961		100	175	225
Alice in Wonderland Play Set	2nd Series, 1961		100	150	200
Cinderella	Original series		50	75	100
Donald Duck	Original series		50	75	100
Dumbo's Circus Play Set	Original series		50	75	100
Lady and the Tramp Play Set	2nd Series, 1961		50	60	100
Ludwig Von Drake	"A Nearsighted Professor", 1962		50	60	100
Ludwig Von Drake	"The Professor Misses", 1962		50	60	100
Mickey Mouse and Friends Play Set	Original series, display box		50	60	100
Panchito "Western" Play Set	Original series, display box		50	60	100

Miniature Playsets

NAME	DESCRIPTION	NO.	GOOD	VG	MIP
Pinocchio	Original series, display box		50	60	100
Sleeping Beauty Play Set	2nd Series, display box, 1961		50	60	100
Snow White and the Seven Dwarfs	Original series, display box		50	60	100

Fairykins

NAME	DESCRIPTION	NO.	GOOD	VG	MIP
Fairykins '3 in 1' Diorama			75	125	150
Fairykins Diorama			30	35	60

Fantasy Playsets

NAME	DESCRIPTION	NO.	GOOD	VG	MIP
Disney See and Play Castle			75	100	150
Disney See and Play Doll House			75	100	150

TV-Tinykins

NAME	DESCRIPTION	NO.	GOOD	VG	MIP
Hanna-Barbera's Flinstones	Display box		75	95	150
Huckleberry Hound Presents TV Play Set	Display box		75	95	150
Quick Draw McGraw	Display box		75	95	150

Playsets

NAME	DESCRIPTION	NO.	GOOD	VG	MIP
Adventures of Robin Hood	Richard Greene TV Series	4722	400	500	800
Alamo Playset	54mm figures	3534	300	375	600
Alamo Playset		3546	250	325	500
Alaska Frontier Playset	100 pieces, 1959	3708	150	225	300
American Airline Astro Jet Port		4822	225	300	300
American Airlines International Jet Port	98 pieces, 1962	4810	150	225	300
Arctic Explorer	1960	3702	450	675	900
Army Combat Set	Sears, 411 pieces	6019	100	150	500
Army Combat Training Center		2654	45	65	90
Army Combat Training Center		4150	60	95	125
Atomic Cape Canaveral Missile Base		2656	85	100	175
Atomic Cape Canaveral Missle Base Set		2656	150	225	300
Babyland Nursery		3379	125	160	250
Bar-M Ranch		3956	80	120	175
Battle of Iwo Jima	247 pieces, 1964	4147	200	275	400
Battle of Iwo Jima	128 pieces, 1964	6057	75	125	155
Battle of the Blue & Gray	Series 1000, small set, no house	2646	150	200	250
Battle of the Blue & Gray	Series 2000, large set	4658	500	750	900
Battle of the Blue & Gray	Centennial, 1963	4744	300	450	800
Battle of the Blue & Gray	Series 2000, 1959, 54mm	4745	350	450	775
Battle of the Little Big Horn	1972	4679MO	375	500	800
Battleground	Montgomery Ward, 1963	3745	200	300	400
Battleground	U.S. and Nazi troops	4169	75	115	150
Battleground	Montgomery Ward, 1971	4752	100	135	200
Battleground	200 pieces, 1962	4754	90	125	185
Battleground	180 pieces, 1959	4751	90	140	185

Marx playsets, top to bottom: Gunsmoke Dodge City Series 2000, 1960; Yogi Bear at Jellystone National Park, 1962; The Rifleman Ranch, 1959; The Flintstones, 1961.

Playsets

NAME	DESCRIPTION	NO.	GOOD	VG	MIP
Battleground	1958, largest of military sets	4750	325	400	650
Battleground	Sears, 160 pieces, 1963		175	260	350
Battleground	1970's	4756	100	135	200
Beachhead Landing Set	U.S. and Nazi Troops	4939	25	45	55
Ben Hur	217 pieces, 1959	2648	475	550	950
Ben Hur	132 pieces, 1959	4696	425	550	850
Ben Hur	Series 2000, medium set	4702	600	900	1000
Ben Hur	Series 5000, large set	4701	800	950	1800
Big Inch Pipeline	Sears, 201 pieces, 1964, 54mm SP	4445	175	260	400
Big Inch Pipeline	200 pieces, 1963	6008	200	300	400
Big Top Circus		4310	225	335	350
Boot Camp Playset		4645	175	250	350
Boy Scout Playset			35	55	75
Cape Canaveral		4524	85	100	175
Cape Canaveral		4526	50	75	100
Cape Canaveral	Tin litho bldg with plastic parts	5963	85	100	175
Cape Canaveral Missile Center		2686	125	190	250
Cape Canaveral Missile Center		4525	70	115	145
Cape Kennedy Carry All		4625	35	45	75
Captain Gallant of the Foreign Legion	1956	4729	500	650	1000
Captain Gallant of the Foreign Legion	1956	4730	450	650	900
Captain Space Solar Academy		7026	225	300	450
Captain Space Solar Academy		7018	90	140	185
Castle and Moat Set	Sears Exclusive	4734	100	135	200
Castle Fort		4710	75	125	150
Cattle Drive	Mid 1970's	3983	20	35	45
Comanche Pass	1976	3416	150	215	300
Complete Happitime Dairy Farm	Sears	5957	75	95	150
Complete U.S. Army Training Center		4124	45	65	90
Construction Camp	1954, 54mm	4442	125	185	250
Construction Camp	1954	4439	225	200	450
Custer's Last Stand	Series 500, 1963	4779	200	325	600
Custer's Last Stand	Sears, 187 pieces, 1963	4670	200	325	600
D-Day Army Set	U.S. and Nazi troops	6027	250	350	500
D.E.W. Defense Line Arctic Satellite Base	4802		250	350	500
Daktari	110 pieces, 1966	3717	35	55	400
Daktari	140 pieces, 1966	3720	325	500	650
Daniel Boone Frontier Playset	1958	1393	350	475	500
Davy Crockett at the Alamo		3442	300	375	600
Davy Crockett at the Alamo	Official Walt Disney, 100 pieces, 1955	3530	400	500	800
Davy Crockett at the Alamo	Official Walt Disney, 100 pieces, 1955	3544	400	500	800
Desert Fox	244 pieces, 1966	4177	225	300	450
Desert Patrol	U.S., Nazi Troops	4174	45	65	150
Farm Set	100 pieces	3942	55	75	115
Farm Set		3943	25	40	55

Playsets

NAME	DESCRIPTION	NO.	GOOD	VG	MIP
Farm Set		5942	25	35	55
Farm Set		6006	40	65	85
Farm Set		6050	25	35	50
Fighting Knights Carry All	1966	4635	65	100	135
Fire House		3779	125	185	250
Fire House		3780	125	185	250
Fire House		3782	125	185	250
Flintstones Set		2670	238	250	400
Flintstones Set	50 pieces, 1961	4672	110	175	250
Fort Apache		3609	55	75	115
Fort Apache	1952, 60mm	3612	55	85	115
Fort Apache		3616	75	115	150
Fort Apache		3680	100	65	225
Fort Apache	1970's	3681	40	65	85
Fort Apache		3682	40	65	85
Fort Apache	Giant set	3685	375	635	700
Fort Apache	1970's	4202	40	60	80
Fort Apache	Sears	6059	25	40	55
Fort Apache	Sears, 335 pieces, 1965	6063	250	350	525
Fort Apache		6068	80	100	165
Fort Apache	Sears, over 100 pieces, 1972	59093C	75	100	150
Fort Apache	Sears, 147 pieces, 1965		100	145	200
Fort Apache		3681A	125	145	150
Fort Apache Carryall		4685	35	50	75
Fort Apache Rin Tin Tin		3512	238	400	475
Fort Apache Rin Tin Tin		3616	250	375	500
Fort Apache Rin Tin Tin		3627	250	400	500
Fort Apache Rin Tin Tin		3628	250	375	500
Fort Apache Rin Tin Tin		3658	225	375	450
Fort Apache Rin Tin Tin		3957	225	375	450
Fort Apache Stockade	1960, 60mm	3660	100	150	200
Fort Apache Stockade	1953	3612	128	175	255
Fort Apache Stockade	Series 2000, 1960	3660	160	250	325
Fort Apache Stockade	Series 5000, 1961		130	200	275
Fort Apache with Famous Americans		3636	135	190	270
Fort Dearborn	With metal walls	3510	175	250	350
Fort Dearborn		3514	50	75	100
Fort Dearborn	With plastic walls	3688	200	300	400
Fort Mohawk		3751	150	225	300
Fort Pitt	Series 750, 54mm, 1959	3741	100	150	350
Fort Pitt	Series 100, 54mm, 1963	3742	100	175	300
Four Level Allstate Service Station		6004	50	75	200
Four Level Parking Garage		3502	50	75	200
Four Level Parking Garage		3511	50	75	200
Freight Trucking Terminal		5220	75	100	150
Freight Trucking Terminal		5422	75	125	150
Freight Trucking Terminal		5420	45	75	95
Galaxy Command	1976	4206	25	40	50
Gallant Men Army Playset	U.S. Troops	4632	338	475	675
Gallant Men Playset	Official set from TV Series	4634	150	225	300
Gunsmoke Dodge City	Official, series 2000, 80 pieces, 1960	4268	400	625	900

Marx playsets, top to bottom: Lone Ranger Ranch Set Series 500, 1958; Border Battle Miniature Playset, 1964; Ben-Hur Series 2000, 1959.

Playsets

NAME	DESCRIPTION	NO.	GOOD	VG	MIP
Happitime Army and Air Force Training Center	147 pieces, 1954	4159	125	200	250
Happitime Civil War Centennial	Montgomery Wards, 1962	5929	100	150	300
Happitime Farm Set		3480	35	55	75
Happitime Roy Rogers Rodeo Ranch		3990	60	100	125
Heritage Alamo Playset		590906	100	150	200
History in the Pacific		4164	113	125	225
Holiday Turnpike	Battery-operated with HO scale vehicles	5230	20	35	45
I.G.Y Arctic Satellite Base	Series 1000, 1959	4800	250	400	700
Indian Warfare	Series 2000	4748	75	100	150
Irrigated Farm Set	Working pump	6021	20	25	35
Johnny Apollo Moon Launch Center		4630	55	75	115
Johnny Ringo Western Frontier Set	Series 2000, 1959	4784	625	875	1250
Johnny Tremain Revolutionary War	Official Walt Disney, series 1000	3401	500	875	1000
Jungle Jim Playset	Official,series 1000, 1950's	3706	275	475	750
Jungle Playset	Metal trading post, series 500	3705	275	475	550
Jungle Playset	48 pieces, Sears, 1968	3716	125	175	250
Knights and Vikings		4743	100	175	150
Knights and Vikings		4733	135	195	150
Knights and Vikings		4773	125	175	150
Little Red School House		3382	75	100	150
Lone Ranger Ranch	Series 500, 1958	3969	100	150	225
Lone Ranger Ranch		3980	135	205	275
Lone Ranger Rodeo Set	1953	3696	75	115	150
Marx Masterbuilder Kit	The White House and 35 Presidents		25	40	55
Medieval Castle	1964	4704	75	85	150
Medieval Castle	With knights and vikings	4707	90	135	180
Medieval Castle	Sears, series 2000, 1959	4708	225	200	450
Medieval Castle	1954	4709	250	375	500
Medieval Castle	With knights and vikings	4733	45	70	95
Medieval Castle	Sears, with knights and vikings	4734	125	175	250
Medieval Castle	1953	4710	250	375	500
Medieval Castle	1960	4700	85	90	175
Midtown Service Station		3420	40	55	80
Midtown Shopping Center		2644	75	100	150
Military Academy		4718	225	340	455
Modern Farm Set	1960's, 54mm	3931	30	45	60
Navarone Mountain Battleground Set	1976	3412	90	155	185
New Car Sales and Service		3466	55	85	115
Operation Moonbase		4654	60	90	125
Pet Shop		4209	125	185	250
Pet Shop		4210	125	185	250
Prehistoric	1969	3398	85	125	175
Prehistoric	Series 500	3389	75	125	150
Prehistoric Dinosaurs	1978	4208	25	35	55
Prehistoric Times		2650	150	225	300
Prehistoric Times		3388	60	80	125
Prehistoric Times		3390	110	120	225

Playsets

NAME	DESCRIPTION	NO.	GOOD	VG	MIP
Prehistoric Times		3391	45	70	95
Prince Valiant Castle	1955	4705	250	400	500
Prince Valiant Castle	1955, has figures	4706	375	560	600
Project Apollo Cape Kennedy		4523	60	85	125
Project Apollo Moon Landing		4646	125	175	250
Project Mercury Cape Canaveral		4524	40	65	85
Raytheon Missile Test Center	1961	603-A	150	175	300
Real Life Western Wagon		4998	35	50	75
Red River Gang	Mini set with cowboys	4101	90	155	185
Revolutionary War Set	Series 1000	3404	250	325	500
Revolutionary War Set	80 pieces, Sears, 1959	3408	80	125	400
Rex Mars Planet Patrol		7040	250	325	500
Rifleman Ranch, The	1959	3997	160	250	400
Rifleman Ranch, The	1959	3998	225	325	600
Rin Tin Tin at Fort Apache	Series 5000, 1956	3658	225	335	450
Rin Tin Tin at Fort Apache	Series 500, 1956, 60mm	3628	250	400	500
Rin Tin Tin at Fort Apache	Series 1000, 1956, 54mm		150	250	300
Robin Hood Castle Set	60mm	4717	325	500	600
Robin Hood Castle Set	1958, 54mm	4718	75	100	150
Roy Rogers Double R Bar Ranch		3982	125	190	275
Roy Rogers Mineral City	95 pices, 1958	4227	250	400	500
Roy Rogers Ranch		3980	50	75	100
Roy Rogers Rodeo		3689	50	70	100
Roy Rogers Rodeo Ranch		3979	45	65	90
Roy Rogers Rodeo Ranch		3986	45	70	95
Roy Rogers Rodeo Ranch	54mm	3988	160	240	325
Roy Rogers Rodeo Ranch		3996	40	65	85
Roy Rogers Rodeo Ranch	1952, 60mm	3985	110	125	225
Roy Rogers Western Town		4216	60	80	125
Roy Rogers Western Town	Large set	4258	190	285	395
Roy Rogers Western Town	Official, series 5000	4259	190	285	395
Sears Store		5980	65	95	130
Service Station		54595	35	50	75
Service Station		5952	30	50	65
Service Station		3469	75	100	150
Service Station	With parking garage	3485	75	100	150
Service Station	With elevator	3495	75	100	150
Service Station	Deluxe	3501	125	185	250
Shopping Center		3755	100	125	200
Silver City Western Town	Has Custer, Boone, Carson, Buffalo Bill, Sitting Bull	4220	125	185	250
Skyscraper	Working elevator	5449	175	260	375
Skyscraper	Working elevator and light	5450	175	260	375
Sons of Liberty	Sears	4170	125	150	250
Space Patrol Rocket Port Set	Official	7020	150	225	300
Strategic Air Command		6013	75	95	500
Super Circus		4220	150	250	300
Super Circus	Over 70 pieces, 1952	4319	225	335	400
Super Circus		4320	250	375	400
Tales of Wells Fargo		4263	125	150	400
Tales of Wells Fargo	Series 1000	4264	325	300	750

Marx playsets, top to bottom: Battleground, 1971, Montgomery Ward exclusive; Medieval Castle Fort; Davy Crockett at the Alamo, 1955; Battle of the Blue and Grey, Series 2000, 1959.

Playsets

NAME	DESCRIPTION	NO.	GOOD	VG	MIP
Tank Battle	Sear, U.S., Nazi Troops	6056	60	90	200
Tank Battle	U.S., Nazi Troops	6060	63	90	200
Tom Corbett Space Academy	Official, 1952, 45mm	7010	225	325	475
Tom Corbett Space Academy		7012	225	325	475
U.S. Airforce Playset		4807	80	115	160
U.S. Armed Forces		4151	60	75	125
U.S. Armed Forces Training Center	Series 500, 1955	4149	60	75	125
U.S. Armed Forces Training Center	Marines, soldiers, sailors, airmen, tin litho bldg, etc.	4144	95	140	190
U.S. Armed Forces Training Center		4158	175	275	350
U.S. Army Mobile Set	Flat figures, 1956	3655	50	75	100
U.S. Army Training Center		3146	45	65	95
U.S. Army Training Center		3378	45	68	95
U.S. Army Training Center		4122	50	75	100
U.S. Army Training Center		4123	60	75	125
U.S. Army Training Center		4153	40	65	85
Untouchables	90 pieces, 1961	4676	600	900	1200
Vikings and Knights		6053	150	200	300
Wagon Train	Series 1000	4785	325	450	800
Wagon Train	Official, series 5000	4788	225	300	800
Wagon Train	Official, series 2000	4787	225	375	600
Walt Disney Television Playhouse	1953	4350	175	250	500
Walt Disney Television Playhouse	1953	4368	175	250	500
Walt Disney Zorro	Official	3754	350	450	850
Walt Disney Zorro	Official, series 1000, 1962	3758	300	400	800
Western Frontier Set			175	225	450
Western Mining Town	1950's	4266	300	450	675
Western Mining Town	1950's	4265	300	450	675
Western Ranch Set		3954	80	100	175
Western Ranch Set		3980	80	100	175
Western Stagecoach Playset	1965	1395	50	75	100
Western Town	1950's	2652	150	225	300
Western Town		4229	150	225	300
White House	House with 8 figures		35	50	70
White House & Presidents	House & figures, 1/48 scale presidents	3920	35	50	70
White House & Presidents	House & figures	3921	35	50	70
Wild Animal Jungle Play Set	Large animals	3716	25	35	50
World War II Battleground	1970's	4204	75	115	150
World War II European Theatre		5949	125	190	275
World War II Set	U.S., Nazi troops	5938	60	100	125
World War II Set	Sears, British, French, Russian troops	5939	388	525	775
Yogi Bear Jellystone National Park	1962, 60mm	4364	175	300	375

MARX PAINTED FIGURES

Animal Kingdom

NAME	MNP	MIB
Ape	4	8
Eland	4	8
Elephant	4	8
Giraffe	4	8
Gorilla	4	8
Gray Squirrel	4	8
Grizzly Bear	4	8
Ibex	4	8
Jaguar	4	8
Kangaroo Female	4	8
Kangaroo Male	4	8
Leopard	4	8
Lion	4	8
Moose	4	8
Mule Deer	4	8
Panther	4	8
Red Fox	4	8
Rhinoceros	4	8
Striped Skunk	4	8
Tiger	4	8
Wolf	4	8
Zebra	4	8

Warriors of the World

Cadets

NAME	MNP	MIB
James Henry	5	10

Chinese

NAME	MNP	MIB
Chao Yun	5	8
Machao	5	8

Confederate Soldiers

NAME	MNP	MIB
Gatt Random	5	12
General Longstreet	5	12
General Markstone	5	12
Red Miller	5	12
William Morris	5	12

Cowboys

NAME	MNP	MIB
Brown Bart	3	8
Jack Straight	3	8
Jim Ralston	3	8
Mike Nichols	3	8
Mike Riley	3	8
Roger Dawson	3	8
W.B. Foster	3	8

Generals

NAME	MNP	MIB
General Grant	8	15
General Lee	8	15

Indians

NAME	MNP	MIB
Black Kettle	5	12
High Wolf	5	12
Little Crow	5	12
Long Bow	5	12
Slipping Bird	5	12
Strong Eagle	5	12

Mexican Soldiers

NAME	MNP	MIB
Francisco Ruiz	6	12

Pirates

NAME	MNP	MIB
Bonnet	8	18
Caesar	8	18
Captain Cobham	8	18
Captain Flood	8	18
Dixey Bull	8	18
Greaves	8	18
Jack	8	18
Veale	8	18

Revolutionary Soldiers

NAME	MNP	MIB
Ebenezer Bray	5	10
John Reeves	8	10
Johnny Wilson	8	10
Joseph Shipan	8	10
Michael Campbell	8	10
R. Jaynes	5	10
Richard Travis	5	10
Roger Medford	8	10

Revolutionary War British Redcoats

NAME	MNP	MIB
Edward Sharp	8	15
Richard Ellis	8	15

Roman Warriors

NAME	MNP	MIB
Flavius	4	8
Laelius	4	8
Markius	6	8
Maximus	4	8
Septimus	4	8
Stilecho	4	8
Tiverius	4	8

Union Soldiers

NAME	MNP	MIB
Bill Mason	5	10
Harry Dungan	5	10
Herb Tanner	5	10
Joe Bates	5	10
Mike Burns	5	10
Richard Golden	5	10

Vikings

NAME	MNP	MIB
Bjarni	6	8
Eric the Red	6	8
Gustaf	6	8
Haakon	6	8
Ketil	6	8
Leif Ericsson	6	8
Olaf	6	8
Thorfinn	6	8

Marx painted figures, top to bottom: Various Warriors of the World, Union Soldier figures; Cowboy, Roman Warrior and Indian Brave.

Marx painted figures, top to bottom: Warriors of the World, Series III, World War I figures; Warriors of the World, Chinese, Chao Yun and Machao figures; Warriors of the World, Series II, Mexican War figures.

Warriors of the World

NAME	MNP	MIB
WWI French		
Andre Tredier	8	15
Joseph Frantz	8	15
Jules Clemenceau	8	15
Leon Pichon	8	15
WWI German		
Friedrich Baden	8	15
Joseph Schnelling	8	15
WWII Marching Soldier		
Dick Grover	5	15
WWII Sailors		
George Dempsey	5	15
Ken Randolph	5	15
WWII U.S. Combat Soldiers		
Bill James	5	15
Charley Hamilton	5	15
Dan Warner	5	15
Flip Marbles	5	15
Hank Meyers	5	15
Harry Byrd	5	15
Jim Pallozzo	5	15
Joe Dixon	5	15

Wild Animals

NAME	MNP	MIB
Alligator	4	8
Baby Giraffe	4	8
Bear	4	8
Bear Cub	4	8
Buffalo	4	8
Camel	4	8
Eland	4	8
Giraffe	4	8
Gray Squirrel	4	8
Kangaroo Male	4	8
Leopard	4	8
Moose	4	8
Mule Beer	4	8
Striped Skunk	4	8
Tiger	4	8
Wolf	4	8
Zebra	4	8

Marx painted figures, top to bottom: Warriors of the World, Roman Warriors figures Septimus Pius, Flavius Stilecho and Marius; Warriors of the World, Roman Warriors Tiberius, Laelius, Maximus and Marius boxes; Warriors of the World, Revolutionary War Soldier figure boxes.

MARX PLASTIC FIGURES

4" Figures

Firemen

*Four-inch white or cream figures, valued at $7 each.
Firechief with bullhorn
In boots, overcoat, hat, with fire extinguisher
Running, putting on coat
With axe
With axe in boots, tie
With fire extinguisher
With firehose

5" Figures

Spacemen

*Issued in various colors, valued at $10 each.
Advancing with ray pistol
Alien
Crewman turning to fan ray pistol
In uniform, with knife
Kneeling with radio phone
Robot
Running, one foot off ground
Signalman with props
Taking careful aim with ray pistol
Walking carrying geiger counter
Walking with rifle
With flare gun
With geiger counter
With pistol
With radio antenna

6" Figures

Blame-Its

*Blame-Its were impish looking children made of light blue soft plastic. Valued as indicated.
I Didn't Break It, $25
I Didn't Get Dirty, $40

Campus Cuties, Series 1

*Figures of college girls made of flesh-colored soft plastic. Series 1 figures valued at $13 each.
Dinner for Two
Lazy Afternoon
Lodge Party
Nightly Night
On the Beach
On the Town
Shopping Anyone
Stormy Weather

Campus Cuties, Series 2

*Figures of college girls made of flesh-colored soft plastic. Series 2 figures valued at $25 each.

6" Figures

Belle of the Ball
Bermuda Holiday
Day at the Races
Night at the Opera
Our Girl Friday
Saturday Afternoon
Touch of Mink
Twist Party

Cavemen Figures

*From the 1960s, valued at $12 each.
Holding rock in both hands overhead
Running with raised club and knife
Running with raised tomahawk
Standing left hand extended forward
Standing with long spear in right hand
Swinging raised club

Disney Figures

*From the 1960s. Fluorescent blue figures valued at $12; others higher, as indicated.
Bambi, $12
Donald Duck strutting/waddling, $45
Dopey (Snow White), $12
Goofy, $45
Mickey Mouse, left hand waving, $50
Peter Pan, $12
Pinocchio, catch the movie this summer, $40
Pluto, $12
Snow White, $12
Tinker Bell (Peter Pan), $12

Man from U.N.C.L.E. Figures

*Blue, soft plastic figures from 1960s. Valued as indicated.
Agent #1, firing rifle, $15
Agent #2, with kepi, pistol, karate chop, $15
Illya Kuryakin, $30
Inspector Waverly pointing, $20
Napoleon Solo, $30
Officer crouching with pistol, $20

Marvel Super Heroes

*These figures were produced in fluorescent colors. Valued at $12-$25, depending on color.
Captain America
Daredevil
Hulk
Iron Man
Spider-Man
Thor

Nutty Mad Soldiers

*Caricatures of military personnel. Valued at $100 each.
American Sergeant
British Colonel
Cuban Guerilla

6" Figures

German Officer
Japanese Lieutenant
Russian Officer

Nutty Mads, Series 1

*Soft plastic caricatures produced in the 1960s. Series 1 and 2 valued at $10 each (unless indicated); Series 3 at $50.

Dippy the Deep Diver
Donald the Demon
Rocko the Champ
Roddy the Hot Rod
Waldo the Weight Lifter

Nutty Mads, Series 2

All Heart Hogan
Bullpen Boo Boo
Chief Lost Teepee, $15
End Zone, $15
Suburban Sidney
The Thinker

Nutty Mads, Series 3

Mudder
Now Children
Smokey Sam
U.S. Male

Secret Agents

*Brown soft plastic figures from the 1960s. Valued at $10.

Attacking with flashlight and pistol
Bearded with weird pistol
Clubbing with pistol
Firing revolver
Leaving with briefcase in right hand
With pistol and walkie-talkie

African Hunters and Natives

Characters

*Cream colored, valued at $10, except as indicated.

Daktari with stethescope and bag
Jungle Jim with rifle, pointing
Kulu with knife and slung rifle
Missionary with bible
Paula
Tamba, tan colored

Hunters

*Cream colored, valued at $7 each.

Lost hunter, arms at side
Sitting, driving jeep
Standing, shooting rifle
With separate rifle
Woman with rifle

African Hunters & Natives

Natives

*Brown colored, valued at $5 each.

Chief in top hat, with cigar
Crouching, arms at side
Kneeling, beating separate drum
Marching with rifle on shoulder
Throwing separate spear
Throwing separate spear, with tattoos
Witch doctor in leopard head
With bow, drawing arrow
With spear, hand to cheek
With staff, hand to head

Alamo & Zorro Figures

Mexicans with Sombrero Hats

*Figures from both Alamo and Zorro sets. Blue soft plastic valued at $2 each; blue flat finish at $5.

Advancing with bayoneted rifle across waist
Guard, standing with lance
Lunging with sword
Mounted with lance
Mounted with sword
Running with rifle across chest
Standing shooting rifle
Walking with rifle in right hand
With pistol
With sword overhead

Alamo Figures

Mexicans with Shako Hats

*Reported in three finishes: sky blue valued at $5 each, metallic blue at $10 and cream at $15.

Advancing with rifle across waist
Climbing ladder with rifle
Clubbing with rifle
Mounted with sword and rifle
Standing shooting rifle
Walking with rifle in right hand

American Heroes

Cereal Premiums

*Came in cream and white finishes. Valued at $3 each.

Daniel Boone
Davy Crockett
George Washington
J.P. Jones
N. Hale
P. Henry
Robert Lee
U.S. Grant

American Heroes

Generals

*60mm hard white plastic figures from the 1950s. Valued at $10 each unless indicated otherwise.
Admiral Dewey
Admiral Halsey
Admiral Radford
Colonel Roosevelt
Commodore Perry
General Arnold
General Bradley
General Clark
General Clay
General Doolittle
General Eisenhower
General George Patton
General Grant
General Gruenther
General Jackson
General Lee
General Lemay
General MacArthur
General Marshall
General O'Donnell
General Pershing
General Pickett, $15
General Ridgeway
General Sheridan, $15
General Smith
General Snyder
General Spaatz
General Stillwell
General Taylor, $15
General Vandergrift, $30
General Washington

Archies

*Characters from the Archie comic strip, valued at $40.
Archie
Betty
Jughead
Veronica

Astronauts

*In orange and white valued at $1, unless indicated otherwise. Higher valued figures came in white, cream or silver.
Climbing rock, both feet down, $6
Climbing rock, one foot up, $6
In separate bell space suit, $20
On side with camera, $6
Separate tool box
Sitting in separate capsule, $6
Space Walker
Space walking with wrench, $6
Standing pointing, $6
Walking

Astronauts

Walking carrying tool box
Walking with bag
Walking with box
Walking with hand on visor, $6
With camera
With flag
With hammer and stake
With mine sweeper
With scoop and bag
With shovel
With square scoop

Bavarian Figures

*Hand-painted hard plastic figures valued at $25 each.
Baker standing wearing white hat holding spatula
Night watchman holding lantern
Old gentleman with moustache
Old lady hunched over with age
Shoeman standing wearing leather apron
Short man standing
Short woman
Woman standing wearing apron with stains
Young man standing, smiling, hands in pockets
Young peasant happily drunk standing, arms on pole
Young peasant walking holding pipe and umbrella

Ben Hur Figures

*Unless indicated, these figures came in cream, brown and grey soft plastic and are valued at $5 each.
Ben Hur, purple, $45; cream $100
Chained slave
Chariot driver with spear
Chariot driver, no armor, curled whip
Chariot driver, with armor, straight whip
Citizen, thumbs down, yelling
Emperor, purple, $45; cream, $100.
Empress, purple, $45; cream $100.
Gladiator kneeling with sword and shield
Gladiator with long sword, square shield
Gladiator with long sword, round shield
Gladiator with long sword, square shield
Gladiator with net and trident
Gladiator with short sword, round shield
Man sitting
Merchant with money box
Slave master with whip
Slave woman with vase
Stopping horse, brown or black, $3
Trumpeter
Woman sitting bathing

Birds

*60mm in various colors. Valued at $3.
Baltimore Oriole

Birds

Cardinal
Gold Finch
House Sparrow
House Wren
Parakeet
Scarlet Tanager
Tufted Titmouse

Boy Scouts

*54mm blue or tan figures. Valued at $7 each.
Blowing bugle
Kneeling, making fire
On hands and knees, reading map
Playing basketball
Saluting
Scoutmaster with map and compasslight
Scoutmaster with staff and flashlight
Shooting basketball
Shooting bow, with quiver
Sitting, hands on ground
Sitting, hands on knees
Standing with paddle
With axe
With first aid book and stretcher
With rope tying knots
With signal flags

Cavemen

*Came in cream or tan colors. Valued at $2 each.
Crouching with spear
Crouching, skinning rabbit
Walking with club
With club and knife
With rock and flint
With rock overhead

Champion Show Dogs

*1950s soft plastic 60mm scale in brown or white. Valued at $5 each.
Airedale
Basset Hound
Boxer
Cocker Spaniel
Doberman Pinscher
English Bulldog
French Poodle
German Sheperd
Gordon Setter
Pointer

Civil War Figures

Animals

Falling Horse, cream, $35, or grey, $50.

Civil War Figures

Characters

*Cream colored figures valued at $6 each.
Abraham Lincoln
General Robert E. Lee
General U.S. Grant
Jefferson Davis

Confederate Soldiers

*60mm figures from the 1950s valued at $15 each.
Advancing with bayonet and rifle
Cannoneer
Cavalryman riding with sabre
Loading rifle
Marching with rifle and pack
Officer saluting
Standing Officer
Standing shooting rifle

Confederates/Centennial Poses

*54mm figures in light grey generally valued at $5 and dark grey at $3 unless indicated otherwise.
Bayonetting downward
Calling, seated, $25
Clubbing with rifle
Crawling with rifle
Drummer boy running
Falling off horse with sword, $50
Kneeling with binoculars
Lying wounded
Mounted with felt hat and sword
Officer with sword and pistol
Running with ramrod and bucket
Shot, dropping rifle
Sitting with arm in sling
Sitting wounded
Stretcher
Stretcher bearer

Confederates/First Issue Poses

*Issued in light grey, generally valued at $1, but the flat finish issues valued at $3.
Advancing with bayoneted rifle
Calling with rifle overhead
Kneeling, shooting rifle
Marching, shouldered rifle
Mounted with kepi and sword
Running with rifle, brim hat
Shot, dropping pistol
Standing, loading rifle
Standing, shooting rifle
Standing, sword overhead
Waving with flag

Union Soldiers

Bugler
Charging with rifle and bayonet
Dispatch carrier
Kneeling, shooting pistol

MARX

Marx plastic figures, top to bottom: Man From U.N.C.L.E. 6 inch figures, brown villains and grey heroes; American Heroes George Washington and Revolutionary War Soldiers set and box, creme colored; Nutty Mad Series II End Zone Eddie figure, mustard brown.

Civil War Figures

Marching with rifle
Riding holding banner
Riding officer with sword
Standing, shooting rifle

Union/Centennial Poses

*Dark blue finish valued at $7; light blue at $1; flat light blue at $3.
Bayonetting downward
Calling, seated
Clubbing with rifle
Drummer boy running
Kneeling with binoculars
Lying wounded
Mounted with felt hat and sword
Mounted with kepi and sword
Mounted with whip
Officer with sword and pistol
Running with ramrod and bucket
Shot, dropping rifle
Sitting with arm in sling
Sitting wounded
Stretcher
Stretcher bearer

Union/First Issue Poses

*Light blue figures valued at $1 each; flat finish valued at $3.
Advancing, rifle across waist
Lighting cannon with fire stick
Lying, shooting rifle
Marching, shouldered rifle
Officer with pistol, arm out
Running with rifle across waist
Standing shooting rifle
Standing with flag and pistol
Standing with pistol and bugle
Standing with ramrod across waist

Civilian Figures

*54mm cream colored figures valued at $7 each.
Boy with Ping-Pong paddle
Deliveryman with box and paper
Doorman as if holding door
Doorman in overcoat with whistle
Girl with Ping-Pong paddle
Lifeguard with whistle
Man with both arms to front
Man with right hand in pocket, with paper
Newsboy with paper, paper facing downward
Pharmacist with bottle and pen
Policeman
Walking with briefcase and overcoat
With briefcase, hand in pocket
Woman sitting, writing
Woman with child on leash

Construction Workers

*45mm cream colored workmen valued at $2 each.
Barechested, poised with pick
Carrying 3 boards
Digging with shovel
Flagman
Gloved, kneeling with oil can
Jackhammering
Lineman straddling position for pole
Right hand up, directing traffic
Surveying, slouched
Walking with lantern
With folded map
With hammer and chisel

Disneykins

*Disney characters issued in the 1960s. Individual figures generally valued at $15 unless indicated otherwise.
Disneykins TV-scenes store display
Piper Pig
The Disneykin "Gift Box" Set
Toby Tortoise
Willie the Whale

101 Dalmatians

Perdita, $25
Pongo, $25
Sgt. Tibbs (cat), $25

Alice In Wonderland

Alice, $7
Mad Hatter, $7
March Hare, $7
Queen of Hearts, $7
White Rabbit, $7

Babes in Toyland

Soldier with bayonet
Soldier with drum
Soldier with gun
Soldier with trumpet

Bambi

Bambi, $35
Flower the Skunk, $35
Thumper, $35

Donald Duck and Friends

Daisy, $7
Dewey, $7
Donald, $7
Huey, $7
Louie, $7
Uncle Scrooge, $7

Dumbo

Dumbo, $10
Fireman clown, $10
Regular clown, $10
Ringmaster, $10

Disneykins

Timothy, $10

Jungle Book

Baby Elephant "Sonny," $20
Bagheera, $20
Baloo, $20
Colonel Hathi, $20
King Louie, $20
Mowgli, $20
Shere Khan, $20

Lady and the Tramp

Lady and the Tramp Kennel Box Set, 12-figure set, $50
Lady, the dog
Tramp, the dog

Mickey Mouse and Friends

Goofy, $7
Mickey Mouse, $7
Minnie, $7
Monty, $7
Pluto, $7

Panchito Western

Brer Rabbit
Joe Carioca
Panchito
Pecos Bill

Peter Pan

Captain Hook
Lost Boys
Peter Pan
Smee
Tinker Bell
Wendy

Pinocchio

Blue Fairy
Cleo
Figaro
Fowlfellow
Geppetto
Jiminy Cricket
Lampwick
Pinocchio
Stromboli

Sleeping Beauty

Fauna
Flora
Maleficent
Merryweather
Prince Charming
Sleeping Beauty

Snow White and the Seven Dwarfs

Bashful
Doc
Dopey
Grumpy
Happy
Sleepy
Sneezy
Snow White

Doll House Figures

*60mm soft plastic figures from the 1950s, valued at $3 each.
Boy brushing teeth
Boy catching
Boy pitching
Boy with bat
Boy with sand pail
Crawling baby
Girl drying dishes
Girl sitting to play with kitten
Girl standing on toes
Girl to sit at vanity
Governess
Playful kitten
Standing brother
Standing father
Standing mother
Standing sister
Toddling baby in pajamas

English Guards

*60mm silver or cream valued at $8 each.
Marching with sword on shoulder
Standing blowing trumpet
Standing with sword held out

Eskimos, Trappers, Explorers

*Grey colored, valued at $8 each.
Bearded, gun drawn
In buckskins, walking with rifle in crook of arm
Man drawing against another
Man fighting
Wagon driver
Walking with rifle and lantern
With trap, stocking cap

Eskimos

*Issued in blue and yellow; valued at $7.
Dog sled
Kayak
Kneeling with kayak paddle
On skis with poles
Sled dog to dog sled
Spearing with rope
Walking with spear and fish
With dead seal
With pelt
With sling rifle to dog sled
With snowshoes and rifle

Eskimos, Trappers, Explorers

Woman sitting to dog sled
Woman with spear and fish

Explorers

*Issued in grey and blue, valued at $8 each.
Crouching, rope only to hand
Kneeling with pan
Pilot with helmet
Pulling rope, rope separate
With flare gun
With pistol and gold bag

Fairy Tale Figures

*60mm soft plastic figures in various colors, valued at $5 unless otherwise indicated.
Goldilocks
Goldilocks - Baby Bear
Goldilocks - Mama Bear
Goldilocks - Papa Bear
Humpty Dumpty
Jack Be Nimble
Jack of Jack and Jill
Jill of Jack and Jill
Kitten with mittens
Kitten with no mittens, crying
Little Bo Peep
Little Boy Blue
Little Jack Horner
Little Miss Muffet
Little Red Riding Hood
Little Red Riding Hood - Wolf
Mother Cat
Old Mother Hubbard
Old Mother Hubbard's Dog
Simple Simon

Famous Comic Figures

*60mm soft plastic comic characters issued in the 1950s and valued at $8-10 each, unless indicated otherwise.

Blondie Series

Alexander Bumstead
Blondie Bumstead
Cookie Bumstead
Dagwood Bumstead
Daisy

Bringing Up Father Series

Jiggs
Maggie

Dick Tracy Series

B.O. Plenty
Dick Tracy, $12
Gravel Gertie
Junior

Fairy Tale Figures

Sparkle Plenty

Lil Abner Series

Daisy Mae
Li'l Abner
Mammy Yokum
Pappy Yokum
Salomey Pig

Orphan Annie Series

Orphan Annie
Sandy, Annie's dog

Popeye Series

Olive Oyl
Popeye
Swee' Pea
Wimpy

Snuffy Smith Series

Jug Haid
Loweezie
Snuffy Smith, $12
Sut Tattersall

Farm Animals

*Cream colored 60mm figures from the 1950s.
Calf
Draft horse
Grazing colt
Lying down cow
Mule with pack
Pig
Standing cow
Standing horse

Farm People

*60mm figures from the 1950s. Cream colored figures valued at $3 each; white versions at $1.
Barefoot boy with big bucket of pig slop
Farmer boy with pail
Farmer standing with hoe
Farmer working with shovel
Farmer's wife
Hatless, in sun, hoeing, sleeves up
Lugging feed sack
Man sitting to milk cow
Moustached, retrieving chicken
Scarecrow with arms out
Sitting with gear shift
Straw hat, pitchfork
Threatening with wrench and clinched fist

Flintstones

*60mm issued in cream and blue. Values as indicated.
Baby Puss, $7
Barney Rubble, $10
Betty Rubble, $10
Construction worker with board, $3
Cop with whistle, $3
Dino, $8
Fireman with axe, $3
Fred Flintstone, $5
Gas attendant with hose, $3
Waiter with glass and menu, $6
Waitress with pad and pencil, $6
Wilma Flintstone, $6

Foreign Legion

Arabs

*60mm red-brown figures valued at $25; chocolate brown or silver figures at $35.
Kneeling with rifle
Mounted with rifle overhead
Mounted with sword overhead
Standing shooting rifle
Standing with curved sword overhead
Standing with knife in air
Walking with rifle across waist

Characters

Camel, brown, black or tan, $40
Captain Gallant, running with rifle, blue or silver, $15
Cuffy, saluting, blue or silver, $10

Legionaires

*60mm blue or silver figures valued at $7 each.
Guard with rifle on ground
Guard with rifle, saluting
Lying shooting rifle
Marching, shouldered rifle
Mounted with sword overhead
Pointing, with binoculars
Standing shooting rifle
Walking with pistol

Fox Hunt

Animals

*54mm brown or cream colored, valued at $10 each.
Dog chasing fox
Dog sniffing
Fox outwitting chasing dog
Fox outwitting sniffing dog
Horse jumping, cropped mane and tail
Horse standing, cropped mane

Freight Station Figures

*60mm blue, cream or grey, valued at $5 each.
Checker
Man carrying a crate
Man sleeping on carton
Man with broom
Man with crate hook
Sitting on box, arms crossed
With broom
With freight hook, left hand on bibs
With papers, hand on hat

Gas Attendants

*Issued in blue, yellow and grey, valued at $3 each.
Changing tire
Crouching on knee
Sitting on box
With rag, waving
With wrench and rag

Ground Crew Figures

*Issued in blue, cream or tan, valued at $2 each.
Crouching, with wrench
Officer with hands clasped behind back
Running with firehose, in hood
Standing with firehose, in hood
With fire extinguisher, in hood
With gas tank, in hood
With geiger counter
With microphone looking up
With paper, waving gloves
With wrench pointing up

Howdy Doody

*60mm white figures valued at $35 each; mint green versions at $45.
Clarabell
Dilly Dally
Howdy Doody
Mr. Bluster
The Princess

Knights

*54mm silver soft plastic, valued at $2 each.
Horse, running, $3
Horse, stopping, $12
Horse, walking, $3
Mounted with lance
Pointing, with shield
Stabbing with spear
Standing with lance
Swinging ball and chain
With ax overhead
With shield and sword

Marx plastic figures, top to bottom: Famous Americans, Daniel Boone, Buffalo Bill, Sitting Bull and Davy Crockett, flesh colored on bases; Fairy Tale Figures, Simple Simon, Pieman, Mother Hubbard and her dog, 60mm soft plastic in various colors; Indians, flesh colored; Knight figures, 54mm silver soft plastic.

Lassie

*Cream colored, valued at $5 each.
Gramps
Jeff
Lassie

Lone Ranger

*Cream colored, valued at $20 each.
Lone Ranger riding
Lone Ranger standing
Tonto standing

Mexican War Figures

*Metallic blue figures valued at $10 each.
Marching with rifle
Running with rifle across waist
Standing shooting
With paper

Military Figures

Air Force

*50mm in metallic blue, grey or cream colors, valued at $1 each.
Bending over with wrench
Crouching with rocket overhead
Pilot crouching with paper
Pilot walking in high altitude suit and helmet
Pilot walking with left hand at chest
Pilot walking, swinging arms
With air hose in right hand
With ammo belt on shoulders
With gas hose across waist
With signal light

British WWII

*Khaki colored figures valued at $15 each.
Advancing with rifle across waist
British with pistol and ammo can
Officer with pistol
Standing shooting rifle
Throwing grenade
With walkie-talkie

French WWII

*Sky blue figures valued at $8 each.
Advancing with rifle across waist
Kneeling shooting rifle
Officer with pistol
Running with machine gun in left hand
Standing shooting rifle
Walking, slung rifle

Frontier Cavalry

*60mm in light blue, metallic blue or cream, valued at $5, unless indicated otherwise.
Kneeling shooting pistol, $10
Kneeling shooting rifle, $20

Mounted shooting pistol, $15
Mounted with sword, $15
Officer with sword and pistol, $7
Officer with sword and pistol, tan, $10
Officer with sword and pistol, light grey, $20
Standing shooting rifle, $10
With pistol and bugle, $12
With sword, no hat, $7
With sword, no hat, light grey, $20
With sword, no hat, tan, $12

Germans WWII

*Light grey figures valued at $1 each; dark grey versions at $2.
Advancing with rifle across waist
Goose-stepping
Kneeling shooting rifle
Lying dead, machine gun across legs
Motorcycle with separate sidecar
Officer pointing down
Running with machine gun in right hand
Running with pistol
Sitting with right arm out
Standing shooting rifle
Throwing grenade
Walking with bazooka across chest
Walking with machine gun across shoulder
With binoculars
With machine gun across waist

Horses

*54mm in various cream, tan, brown or black, valued at $3 unless indicated otherwise.
Cavalry horse
Dead horse, $10
Wagon horse

Japanese

*Khaki colored, valued at $2 each; flat finish valued at $3.
Advancing with rifle across chest
Bayonetting down
Being shot, dropping machine gun
Crouched with rifle
Firing machine gun from hip
Kneeling with radio and pistol
Running with flag
Running with long knife
Running with pistol and sword
Throwing grenade
With hands behind neck
With machine gun waving

Marching Army Band

*60mm vinyl in olive drab green, valued at $7 each.
Clarinet player
Cymbal player
Drum major with baton
Drummer
Trumpet player
Tuba player

Military Figures

Marines

*60mm green versions valued at $1, olive drab green and khaki at $2, blue and grey at $3, metallic blue at $10.

Advancing with rifle across waist
Guard with rifle across chest
Guard with rifle on ground
Guard with rifle on shoulder
Kneeling with pistol and radio
Kneeling with rifle
Kneeling with rifle and ammo clip
Lying with rifle at right side
Marching with flag
Marching with rifle
Marching with rifle on shoulder
Running with machine gun on shoulder
Running with pistol, waving
Running with slung rifle and ammo can
Sitting with right arm out
Standing at attention
Standing at ease rifle on ground
Standing presenting arms
Throwing grenade with tommy gun
Walking swinging arms
With flamethrower
With pistol, in life jacket
With rifle across chest

Military Cadets

*White figures valued at $10 each.

Blowing bugle
Drummer
Guard with rifle along leg
Guard with rifle out from leg
Guard with rifle to front
Marching with flag
Marching with rifle, dress uniform
Marching with rifle, in overcoat
Marching with sword on shoulder
Saluting
Walking to class with notebook

Russians WWII

*Green figures valued at $5 each.

Being shot, dropping pistol
Butting with rifle
Officer with pistol
Running with machine gun in right hand
Standing shooting rifle
Throwing grenade

Sailors

*60mm in white and various blue finishes, valued at $5.

Heaving on rope
In life vest, with pistol
Marching
Marching with rifle on shoulder
Officer at attention
Officer with binoculars
Pulling rope
Scuba diver with knife
Shore patrol on guard with night stick
Signaling with flags
Slung rifle, with arms crossed
Swabbing the deck with mop and bucket
Walking with duffle bag
With arms crossed, slung rifle
With duffle bag
With duffle bag on shoulder
With pistol, hand on helmet
With signal flags
With signal light
With tommy gun and life vest

Soldiers in Training

*60mm olive drab from 1950s, valued at $5.

At parade rest with rifle
Inspecting officer
Kneeling with field glasses
Kneeling with walkie-talkie
Military policeman standing at parade rest
Sergeant reading orders
Sitting to shoot machine gun
Standing at port arms
With mine detector

U.S. GIs

*60mm in shades of green and khaki. So many produced hard to pinpoint values. Generally from $.25-3 depending on colors.

Advancing with bayonetted rifle
Advancing with rifle across chest, with grenade
Advancing with rifle across chest
Advancing with rifle across waist
Attacking with knife
Being shot, dropping pistol
Blowing bugle
Butting with rifle
Carrying ammunition box
Carrying separate wounded GI
Clubbing rifle
Crawling with rifle
Crawling with tommy gun
Crawling wounded, with hand to chest
Crouching with rifle in right hand
Crouching with tommy gun
Flagbearer
Guard with rifle across chest
Guard with rifle on ground
Kneeling shooting rifle
Kneeling with bazooka
Kneeling with binoculars
Kneeling with m.g. on tripod
Kneeling with mortar shell
Kneeling with radio and pistol
Kneeling with shovel
Kneeling with walkie-talkie
Lying shooting rifle
Lying with rifle on bipod
Lying wounded
M.P. with hands behind back
Marching with flag
Marching with rifle on shoulder
Nurse, kneeling with canteen

Officer marching, swinging arms
Officer with right hand up
Running with pistol and ammo can
Running with rifle across chest
Saluting
Sergeant holding paper up
Sergeant marching
Sergeant marching with side arms
Sitting drinking from cup
Sitting paddle to left
Sitting right wrist on knee
Sitting with hands on knees
Sitting with rifle with telescopic sight
Sitting with scoped rifle
Sitting, paddle to right
Soldier marching with rifle and helmet
Squatting with elbow on knee
Standing shooting rifle
Stretcher
Stretcher bearer
Throwing grenade
Throwing grenade, with tommy gun
Walking swinging arms
Walking with slung rifle
Waving, with pistol in right hand
Waving, with walkie-talkie
With artillery shell across waist
With ax, pouch on belt
With binoculars
With box
With gas mask and bayonetted rifle
With gas mask and slung rifle
With mess kit and cup
With mine sweeper
With pistol in right hand
With pistol, waving
With radio and rifle
With rifle across chest
With rifle overhead
With rings for parachute
With rings, gathering separate parachute
With tommy gun across waist
With two gas cans
With walkie-talkie
Wounded GI being carried

U.S. Medical Corps

*60mm olive drab from 1950s, valued at $7 unless indicated otherwise.
Army nurse administering plasma, $10
Being carried by GI (MX486)
Chaplain with bible, $10
Digging foxhole
Kneeling peeling potatoes
Kneeling with rolled bandages
Kneeling with shovel
Nurse kneeling
Sitting and eating
Stretcher
Stretcher bearer - front, $10
Stretcher bearer - rear
To carry wounded soldier, $10
Wounded for stretcher, $10
Wounded to be carried, $10

WWI Soldiers

*60mm medium brown from 1950s, valued at $15 each.
Charging with rifle and gas mask
Marching officer with sword
Marching with rifle and campaign hat
Marching with rifle and overcoat
Throwing a grenade

Paint Your Own Series

Louis Marx, "The Toy King," $25
Simple Simon and Pieman

English Royalty

*60mm white hard plastic, valued at $12 each.
Duke of Edinburgh
Duke of Windsor
Prince Charles
Princess Anne
Princess Margaret
Queen Elizabeth II
Queen Mother

Military Figures

*60mm white figures, valued at $12 unless indicated otherwise.
Admiral Dewey
Admiral Radford
Commodore Perry
General Arnold
General Clay
General George Pickett, $20
General Gruenther
General John Pershing
General Marshall
General O'Donnell
General Phil Sheridan
General Ridgeway
General Robert E. Lee, $20
General Taylor
General U.S. Grant
Marshal Zhukov

U.S. Presidents

*60mm hard white plastic, valued at $5 each.
Abraham Lincoln
Arthur
B. Harrison
Buchanan
Cleveland
Coolidge
F.D. Roosevelt
Filmore
Garfield
George Washington
Grant
Harding
Harry Truman
Hayes

Paint Your Own Series

Hoover
Ike and Mamie Eisenhower
J.Q. Adams
Jackson
Jefferson
John Adams
Johnson
Madison
Martha and George Washington
Mary Todd and Abraham Lincoln
McKinley
Monroe
Pierce
Polk
Taft
Taylor
Theodore Roosevelt
Tyler
W.H. Harrison
Wilson

Pirates

*60mm cream, blue, yellow and white figures from the 1950s, valued at $12 each; hand-painted versions at $7.
Charging figure with belaying pin and dagger
Dueling figure
Hands on pistol and sword
Lunging with sword
Peg-leg, with sword and crutch
Searching figure holding oar
Standing figure, hands on belt
With club, knife in teeth
With hand on chest, parrot and sword
With pistol, hand on sword hilt
With shovel digging

Prehistoric Creatures

*Issued in brown, tan, green and grey. Valued at $8 unless indicated otherwise.
Allosaurus
Ankylosaurus
Brontosaurus, $12
Cynognaurus
Dimetrodon
Hadrosaurus
Iguanodon
Kronosaurus
Megatherium, $12
Moschops
Parasaurolophus
Plateosaurus
Pteranodon
Smilodon, $12
Sphenagodon
Stegosaurus
Struthiomimus, $12
Styracosaurus
Trachodon
Triceratops

Prehistoric Creatures

Tyrannosaurus, flat belly, $12
Tyrannosaurus, sleek
Wooly Mammoth, $12

Prince Valiant & Knights

Characters

*54mm silver figures, valued at $20 each.
Aleta
Boltar
Prince Valiant
Sir Gawain
The Black Knight

Knights

*54mm silver figures valued at $2 each.
Guard with spear
Guard with sword
Mounted with flag
Mounted with separate lance
Mounted with shield and separate lance
Pointing, with shield
Separate lance
Swinging club
Swinging sword, shield with horse head
With sword and round shield
With sword and tricorner shield

Race Track Figures

*54mm cream or blue figures valued at $7 each.
Crouching with arm out
Holding up sign
Man sitting
Sitting with Coke bottle
Waving flag
With binoculars
With gas can and rags
With stop watch in right hand
Woman sitting

Railroad Figures

*60mm cream or grey figures valued at $2 each.
Boy with newspaper
Conductor with lantern
Engineer with oil can
Hobo
Lady with dog
Little boy with toy locomotive
Man with briefcase
Man with newspaper
Porter
Trainman with signal flag

Marx plastic figures, top to bottom: Detail view of Knight figures, 54mm soft silver plastic; Fairy Tale Figures, Jack be Nimble, Wolf, Red Riding Hood, Mama Bear, Mary and Her little Lamb, Humpty Dumpty and a Lamb, 60mm soft plastic in various colors.

Railroad/Gas Station/ Airport Figures

*OO scale in cream plastic or off-white vinyl, valued at $1 unless indicated otherwise.
1940's paperboy
Abestos suited, extinguishing, $3
Bargain shopper leaving Woolworth's
Clod pushing luggage cart, $2
Crazed body man with chisel, hammer, $2
Executive hurrying into propwash, looking at watch
Fueler dispensing kerosene
Ground crewman parking plane, $2
Hardhat shirking with light load on shoulder, $3
Hiding something in hatbox
Kid in argyle sweater with pencil, "nerd" pose
Mechanic in glasses feeling cowling
Mother and child walking
Mother with child in baby carriage, $2
Motorcycle cop, 40's-50's uniform, Harley, $3
Pilot seated, talking into mike, $4
Pilot walking in high altitude suit, $3
Pilot walking out of lounge
Policeman halting mother with child in carriage
Secretary waiting with paper sack of groceries
Seductive woman in '50's fashion fur stole
Spy in suit with two parcels awaiting metal detector
Stewardess walking away from propwash
Supervisor with pink slip consoling workman
Sweeping with push broom, improperly
Tiny, tiny girl with ice cream cone, $2
Workman in coveralls with wood crate, weeping

Religious Figures

*60mm white or cream colored, valued at $8 each.
Andrew
Bartholomew
James the Greater
James the Less
Jesus, left hand raised in a blessing
John
Judas
Jude
Matthew
Matthias
Paul
Peter
Philip
Simon
Thomas

Revolutionary War

*60mm white or cream valued at $8; hand-painted versions at $5.
Drummer
Fife player
In winter dress
Marching drummer
Marching fifer
Marching soldier with flag

Revolutionary War

Marching soldier with rifle
Marching with rifle on shoulder
Mounted, pointing, in overcoat
Officer with walking stick at side
Standing officer with sword
Standing sentry with rifle
Walking with rifle in right hand
With flag

Characters

James Otis, cream color, $20
Johnny Tremain, cream color, $20
Minute Man with musket, white or cream, $8
Paul Revere riding, white or cream, $20

Continental Soldiers

*Blue figures valued at $2; flat finish at $3.
Bayonetting
Drummer
Kneeling shooting rifle
Marching with rifle on shoulder
Mounted, arms at side
Running with rifle in right hand
Standing shooting rifle
Walking with pistol
With flag
With sword, left arm up

English

*Red figures valued at $2; flat finish at $3.
Kneeling shooting rifle
Marching with rifle on shoulder
Mounted with sword
Officer afoot with sword, right arm up
Running with rifle at waist
Standing shooting rifle

Rex Mars Space Figures

*60mm figures, valued at $3 each.
Crouching with ray pistol with helmet
Kneeling with space phone with helmet
Robot
Running with helmet
Standing, shooting flare gun with helmet
Walking with geiger counter with helmet
Walking with space rifle with helmet
Wiring equipment with helmet

Robin Hood

Characters

*Came in 54mm and 60mm sizes; valued as indicated.
Friar Tuck with scroll, 54mm silver $6, other versions $15
Friar Tuck with staff, 60mm green or brown, $20
Little John with staff across chest, 60mm green or brown $20
Little John with staff, $10

Robin Hood

Maid Marian, 54mm cream or silver $10, 60mm versions $20
Minstrel with harp, 54mm cream $10, other versions $6
Robin Hood shooting bow, 60mm, $20
Robin Hood with bow and sword, 54mm silver $6, cream $10
Robin Hood with bow and sword, 60mm $20
Sheriff of Nottingham with sword, 54mm silver $6, cream $10
Sheriff of Nottingham with sword, 60mm $20
Sheriff of Nottingham with sword and knife, 60mm, $20
Stag, tan, $8

Knights

*60mm silver figures valued at $7.
Mounted with club and shield
Mounted with separate lance
Mounted with shield and separate lance
Running with sword and shield
Standing, shooting crossbow
With axe overhead in both hands
With club and shield
With shield, sword overhead
With spear across waist
With sword and knife
With sword and long axe

Merry Men

*54 and 60mm versions; 54mm valued at $3 each, 60mm at $5 each.
Blowing horn
Blowing horn with axe
Calling, hand on hip
Carrying rock
Jumping down with sword and knife
Lunging with knife
Lunging with sword and knife
Running with chest and bow
Shooting bow
Squatting with bow
Standing with sword
Walking with bow and arrow
With bow and arrow
With bow, drawing arrow
With staff and knife
With staff overhead

Roy Rogers

*60mm cream colored figures from the 1950s, valued at $10 each unless indicated otherwise.
Dale Evans with hat in hand
Lt. Rip Masters with pistol, $20
Pat Brady, hand on hat, $12
Rin Tin Tin and Bullet
Roy Rogers mounted waving
Roy Rogers standing with hands on holsters, $15
Roy Rogers standing with pistols
Rusty with rifle, $25

Royal Canadian Mounted Police

*60mm figures from the 1950s, valued at $10 each.
Mountie riding
Mountie standing
Mountie walking
Mountie with binoculars

Sea

*1950s figures in silver, grey, cream or metallic blue, valued at $7.
Barracuda
Marlin
Porpoise
Sailfish
Sea Horse
Shark
Skin Diver
Swordfish
Tuna

Spacemen, Aliens and Cadets

Aliens

*45mm tan, grey or blue, valued at $3 each.
Lying with pistol
Robot, walking
With arms crossed
With big ears, waving
With face mask and pistol
With pistol
With translator

Cadets

*45mm tan, grey or blue, valued at $3.
Arms in air
Climbing ladder
Crouching with pistol
Fighting
Kneeling with pistol
Looking through sextant
Pushing something
Running wearing cap
Sitting with book in lap
Sitting, hand to head
Sitting, no cap
Sitting, wearing cap
Standing at attention
Standing hands on belt
Throwing punch
With microphone
With paper in right hand
Woman climbing ladder
Woman wearing cap
Woman with hands on hips

Spacemen, Aliens and Cadets

Spacemen

*45mm tan, grey or blue figures valued at $3; cream colored versions at $6.
Arms around wounded
Carrying equipment
Carrying walkie-talkie near head
Floating with light
Helmet for figures, clear plastic
Holding up hoops
Kneeling with left hand to head
Looking through device
Pointing
Putting on helmet
Throwing punch
Walking with geiger counter
Walking with large pistol
Walking with small pistol
With hose
With large pistol
With small pistol left arm out
Woman walking
Wounded, hand at chest

Spanish American War Rough Riders

*Brown 60mm figures, vlaued at $15 each.
Marching with rifle
Mounted, sword overhead
Officer standing
Running with rifle across waist
Running, rifle across waist
Standing, shouldered rifle

Sports Figures

*60mm in cream, white, light blue and yellow, valued at $10.
Baseball batter
Baseball pitcher
Basketball player
Bowler
Boxer, jabbing with left
Boxer, jabbing with right
Figure skater
Football player
Golfer
Hockey player
Polo player
Runner
Skiing
Soccer Player
Swimmer
Tennis player

Football Players

*54mm red figures from 1967, valued at $5 unless indicated otherwise.

Sports Figures

Ball carrier stiff-arming #22
Coach, $12
Defensive end slow getting up #78
Defensive left cornerback, incredulous #40
Defensive left linebacker angered at referee #66
Defensive receiver #42
Defensive right end misreading sweep #73
Defensive right linebacker signaling #61
Defensive tackle in 3-point stance #63
Defensive tackle in 3-point stance #72
Down center, with ball #51
Down guard #60
Down tackle # 70
End going out of bounds #85
Fullback, slow getting up #33
Going out for pass #87
Guard pulling #65
Holding football, #44, $8
Middle linebacker #67
Offensive flanker back yelling #23
Place kicker #27, $7
Punting, jersey #22
Quarterback in shotgun calling signals #16, $7
Quarterback passing, #14, $8
Referee signaling a clipping penalty
Referee signaling a touchdown
Referee with watch and whistle
Referee with whistle and penalty flag, $8
Tackle cross-blocking #62

Super Circus

*Issued in yellow, orange-brown or tan, valued at $4 each.
Acrobat lying on back
Balloon vendor
Barker with cane
Boy carrying bucket
Boy lifting tent
Clown cop
Clown walking, hands on hips
Clown with hole in hat
Clown with umbrella
Elephant trainer with hook
Fat lady
Father with son
Hula dancer
Lion tamer with whip and gun
Man hanging by knees with rope
Man on stilts with cane and hat
Man on trapeze
Mother with daughter
Mr. Tom Thumb with cane
Mrs. Tom Thumb with umbrella
Policeman grabbing boy lifting tent
Popcorn vendor
Ringmaster, holding top hat
Siamese twins
Snake charmer
Strongman with barbells
Sword swallower
Woman hanging by neck

Super Circus

Woman on trapeze
Woman rider for horse
Woman sitting, waving (for elephant howdah)
Woman with arms out
Woman with hands on hips
Woman with stick across waist

Animals

*Issued in grey or green, valued at $4 unless indicated otherwise.
Baby bear
Baby giraffe
Buffalo
Camel
Crocodile
Dog for barrel act
Dressed monkey
Elephant sitting
Elephant walking
Large bear
Large giraffe
Leopard
Lion sitting, right paw out, $8
Monkeys (6 poses), $20 for all
Performing bear, hands up
Performing dog, in clothes, walking
Performing dog, in clothes, sitting
Performing dog, in clothes, sitting with cane
Performing gorilla, hands up, $6
Performing horse, prancing, $8
Performing seal with ball on nose, $8
Tiger
Zebra

Characters

*Off-white figures valued at $10 each.
Cliffy Clown
Juggler
Mary Hartline
Nicky Clown
Ringmaster Kirchner
Scampy Clown

Train Depot Figures

*45mm grey figures, valued at $3 each.
Businessman walking with paper, briefcase
Businessman with paper and pipe
Conductor with lantern, glasses fogged, checking water
Flagman
Newsboy peddling papers
Oiler stopping
Porter, carrying bags
Small boy with toy engine, waving
Tramp, staggering with sack and stick
Woman waving with dog on leash

TV-Tinykins

Boo-Boo Bear, $9

TV-Tinykins

Hokey Wolf, $12
Pixie Mouse, $15
Quick Draw McGraw, $19

Flintstones

Baby Puss, $25
Fire Chief, $25
Traffic Cop, $25

Untouchables

Characters

Al Capone, 54mm cream color, $20
Eliot Ness, 54mm cream color, $20

Cops and Robbers

*54mm flat finish versions valued at $12.
Being shot, dropping hat and pistol
Cop shooting machine gun
Cop shooting pistol
Crouching with pistol
Handcuffed with hands behind back
In shirt with pistol and shoulder holster
In trenchcoat with machine gun
Lady 'flapper' with purse
Lying dead
Pointing pistol, wearing mask
Pulling shotgun from golf bag
Reaching right hand in coat
Running with pistol and axe
Shooting down with pistol
Surrendering, hands in air
With machine gun across waist

Vikings

*Green, valued at $.50 each; flat finish versions at $3.
Axe overhead in both hands
Running with knife and shield
Running with sword and ax
Swinging ax with both hands
Walking with sword on ground
With knife and shield
With spear and shield
With sword and round shield

West Point Cadets

*Issued in white and grey, valued at $5 each.
Marching in full dress with sword
Marching in full dress with banner
Marching in full dress with rifle
Marching with overcoat and rifle
Standing at attention

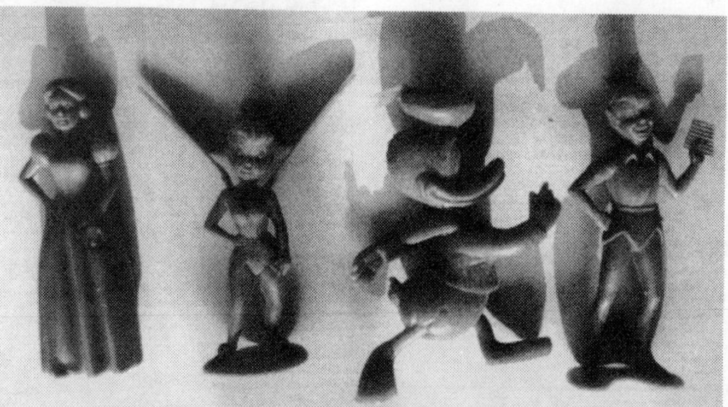

Marx plastic figures, top to bottom: Sea animals in silver, grey, creme or metallic blue, 1950s; Fairy Tale Figures Mother Cat and Her Three Kittens, 60mm, 1950s; Doll House Family on card; Disney six inch figures, Snow White, Tinker Bell, Donald Duck and Peter Pan.

MARX

Western Figures

Boonesborough Pioneers

*54mm caramel color, valued at $15 each.
Clubbing with rifle
Daniel Boone with rifle across chest
Running with rifle, felt hat
Shot with arrow in shoulder
Shouldered rifle with pheasant in right hand
Standing shooting pistol, knife in left hand
Standing shooting rifle
Walking with knife poised and axe
Walking, rifle butt on ground, left hand raised

Cavalry

*Turquoise blue versions valued at $1; silver, tan and yellow at $2.
Butting down with rifle
Clubbing with pistol
Kneeling shooting rifle
Marching, rifle on shoulder
Mounted blowing bugle
Mounted with flag
Mounted with flag and pistol
Mounted with hand on belt
Mounted with sword
Mounted, arms at sides
Running with pistol
Running with rifle in right hand
Running with rifle, hand on hat
Running with sword
Shot, dropping pistol
Sitting with whip, wagon driver
Standing shooting rifle
Standing with rifle
Standing, arms to back
Walking, swinging arms
With pistol and bugle
With pistol, arrow in chest
With rifle across chest
With rifle, blowing bugle
With sword, holding scabbard

Characters

*60mm cream colored figures, valued at $10 unless indicated otherwise.
Bullet
Chester, $50
Custer with pistol, waving, turquoise, $50
Dale Evans waving
Davy Crockett
Doc, $50
Flint McCullough, $25
Jim Hardy, $25
Kitty, $50
Lone Ranger afoot, drawing pistol, $20
Lone Ranger mounted shooting pistol, $15
Lone Ranger mounted with pistol, $15
Major Seth Adams, $25
Mark McCain, $15
Matt Dillon, $50
Pat Brady with hammer
Roy Rogers, mounted with pistol
Tonto with feather
Tonto, no feather
Wyatt Earp, $15

Cowboys

*54mm and 60mm, various colors, valued at $.25-2.50 depending on color.
Arms forward, standing on fence
Arms out, leg up mounting horse
Bad man knocked down
Bad man with hands up
Bandit fanning pistol
Bandit with arms in air
Bandit with pistol and bag
Bandit with pistol and strongbox
Being punched, wearing scarf
Boy on knees, wrestling
Clenched fists, head turned
Drawing pistol
Fighting cowboy
Fighting, no hat
Fighting, with hat
Hands in air
Hands to mouth, calling
Kneeling cowboy with carbine
Kneeling with branding iron
Kneeling with separate rifle
Lady with bonnet and basket
Mounted bandit shooting pistol
Mounted cowgirl waving hat
Mounted falling off horse
Mounted left hand waving
Mounted shooting rifle
Mounted waving hat
Mounted with pistol
Mounted with right arm at side
Mounted with rope
Mounted, right arm out
Mounted, with rope
Pointing pistol, no hat
Riding cowboy for bucking bronco
Riding cowboy shooting to rear
Riding cowboy with lasso
Right hand on belt, left arm out
Running bad man shooting to rear
Running with pistol
Running with rifle
Seated with hat, waving
Sheriff in hat with pistol
Sheriff with gun and money sack
Sheriff with pistol and bag
Sheriff with pistol drawn
Sheriff with two pistols
Sheriff with two pistols drawn
Sitting on box with guitar
Sitting on ground, being punched
Sitting wagon driver
Sitting with arm out, leg up
Sitting with right arm up
Standing cowboy with harness
Standing in lasso
Standing punching
Standing with rope
Standing with whip

Turned, fanning pistol
Turned, shooting pistol
Walking with arms at side
Walking with harness
Walking with rope
Walking with saddle
Walking, swinging arms
With branding iron and rope
With cradled rifle across waist
With rope
With two pistols drawn
Woman with basket
Woman with hands on hips
Woman with right arm out

Early Frontier

Man crouching with pistol, $5
Man kneeling shooting rifle, $5
Man running with musket, $5
Man smashing with rifle butt, $5
Woman loading musket, $5

Indians

*Flesh colored valued at $1; others at $2 unless indicated otherwise.
Advancing with tomahawk overhead
Charging with rifle and tomahawk
Chief dancing with rattles, red or light rust version $5
Chief sitting with pipe
Chief sitting with right hand extended, $5
Chief with knife
Chief with knife and tomahawk
Chief with raised club
Chief with rifle
Climbing wall with club
Climbing wall with tomahawk
Crawling with knife
Crawling with knife and tomahawk
Crawling with tomahawk
Crouched with tomahawk, arrow in side
Dancing with bow and flail
Kneeling beating drum
Kneeling shooting bow
Kneeling shot with arrow
Medicine man with drum and beater
Mounted chief waving
Mounted chief with feathered lance
Mounted with bow, drawing arrow
Mounted with rifle and knife
Mounted with spear
Rider with spear
Running with tomahawk and rifle
Scout rifle in left hand
Shooting arrow, bow on ground
Shooting bow, Mohawk haircut
Squaw crawling with baby
Squaw sitting on knees, $5
Squaw standing with bowl, $5
Squaw walking with papoose on back, $5
Stabbing with knife
Standing chief with bow, lance and shield
Standing shooting bow
Standing shooting rifle
Standing with bow
Throwing spear
Throwing spear with shield
With bow and club
With bow, drawing arrow
With knife in right hand
With spear and shield
With tomahawk
With tomahawk and rifle
With tomahawk and scalp
With tomahawk and shield
With tomahawk overhead
With tomahawk, bow and shield

Long Coat Cavalry

*54mm sky blue, valued at $3 unless indicated otherwise.
Mounted blowing bugle
Mounted turning arms down
Mounted with flag, $6
Mounted with pistol
Mounted with sword in air

Miners and Trappers

*54mm butterscotch color valued at $1 each; tan, brown or grey versions at $2.
Standing with fur
Walking with cradled rifle
Walking with pan on stick
With lantern, carrying separate sack
With pistol and bag
With rifle and lantern
With shovel and jacket

Pioneers

*54mm most colors valued at $1-3; brown, grey, cream at $5; metallic blue at $8.
Butting with rifle
Clubbing with rifle
Kneeling shooting rifle
Mounted bandit with pistol
Mounted with sword overhead
Running with axe and rifle
Running with rifle in buckskins
Running with rifle in left hand
Sitting on ground with pipe
Standing shooting rifle
Walking with rifle and turkey
Walking with rifle in right hand
With pistol and powder horn
With pistol, no base
With rifle across waist
With rifle and powder horn
With rifle, no base
With sword and bugle
Woman loading rifle

Zorro

*Cream colored versions (and black Zorro) valued at $20 each; grey versions at $35.
Bernardo with lantern
Don Alejandro with hat in hand
Don Diego with walking stick
El Commandante with sword
Sergeant Garcia with hands on belt
Zorro, mounted with sword, in cape

Barbie

By Marcie Melillo

The Barbie doll was issued in 1959, and after 34 years it is still one of the most popular toys of all time. Mattel was one of the first toy companies to use television extensively to advertise its merchandise, and the Barbie doll was given a tremendous campaign. In the commercials, the doll was dressed for dating and a variety of careers. Children quickly responded to these television images, and the toy became a phenomenon.

Modern American culture is uniquely chronicled through her beautifully detailed wardrobe. What a range of styles, from the early 1960s Jackie Kennedy suits with pillbox hats to the wild mod fashions! Remember the 1970s peasant dresses and shiny polyester disco attire? The Barbie doll wore all of those styles and currently is wearing Benetton separates -- a wardrobe that would make Imelda Marcos jealous.

Today, the Barbie doll, her friends and accessories, whether new or old, are highly collectible. One reason for the popularity of collecting and selling Barbie dolls is that they were favorite playthings for most baby boomers.

These grown-ups are now attempting to replace their long discarded toys and recapture a part of their childhood. Many are also interested in the investment potential of Barbie paraphernalia.

Of course, not all Barbie dolls increase in value. Predicting which dolls will rise, fall, or remain static in value is work for the Las Vegas odds makers. The 1970s dolls and accessories were of poorer quality than the 1960s dolls and thus, slow to increase in value. The limited edition dolls released in the 1980s and 1990s show mixed results dependent upon the size of the production run.

The 1988 Holiday Barbie doll is a perfect example of the effect that size of release has on price appreciation.

First in a series, the doll has rapidly increased in value because of both its beauty and limited issue. Due to the success of the 1988 doll, the 1989-1992 Holiday Barbie dolls were released in large quantities. While a very popular series, subsequent dolls have not matched the meteoric rise of the 1988 Holiday Barbie.

A couple of years ago, an unexpected problem arose for collectors and dealers alike. Mattel reissued three dolls from the International Barbie series. These dolls were packaged differently, and the boxes were easily identifiable as a reissue, but collectors perceived the originals as less valuable, and prices began to drop for the entire group. Additional dolls from the series have been reissued,and the valuation on the entire group remains depressed. Until the reissue, the International Barbie dolls had increased in value at amazing speed. Whether the reduction is permanent or temporary is anyone's guess.

Before using the pricing guidelines in this section, a few terms should be clarified. The values given are for dolls Mint In Box (MIB), defined as never played with and still in the original boxes with all accessories, and Mint No

The original 1959 Barbie #1.

Package (MNP), defined as mint condition dolls and outfits and missing only the original packaging.

The earliest Barbie dolls were packaged in two-piece boxes and held in place by a cardboard liner. The doll could be taken out of the liner with no difficulty. Thus, the popular Not Removed From Box (NRFB) term that is frequently used with the older Barbie dolls is accurate only for later issue dolls which were sealed in the box. For consistency, the MIB term is used throughout this portion of the price guide, and it indicates a doll in the condition tha' it left the Mattel factory.

Pricing Barbie dolls that are not MIB or MNP is usually left to th' involved. A doll that has been played with may have a myriad green ears, neck splits, missing fingers, hair cut or missing thus pricing is difficult and usually reached by hard-fought Remember that MIB and mint condition dolls and o' price for these toys reflects that scarcity. Played-' plentiful and command a very small percentag'

es
i.e.
etc.,
ement.
and the
ashions are
nint price.

BARBIE

Barbie & Friends

NO.	TOY NAME	YEAR	MNP	MIP
	2+1 Dress Me German Barbie	1988	10	25
3553	All Star Ken	1981	7	20
	All Stars Barbie	1989	5	12
	All Stars Christie	1989	5	12
	All Stars Ken	1989	5	12
	All Stars Midge	1989	5	12
	Allan, bendable leg	1966	125	225
	Allan, straight leg	1964	55	135
4930	American Beauty Mardi Gras Barbie	1987	40	85
1070	American Girl Barbie, all blondes, titian	1965	375	975
1070	American Girl Barbie, brunette	1966	375	1100
	American Girl Side-Part Barbie, brunette, blonde, titian	1965	2225	3500
5640	Angel Face Barbie	1982	8	25
4828	Animal Lovin' Barbie, black version	1988	5	15
1350	Animal Lovin' Barbie, white version	1988	6	12
	Animal Lovin' Ginger Giraffe	1988	7	15
1351	Animal Lovin' Ken	1988	5	12
1352	Animal Lovin' Nikki	1988	7	15
	Animal Lovin' Zizi Zebra	1988	7	15
1207	Astronaut Barbie, black version	1985	30	80
2449	Astronaut Barbie, white version	1985	25	65
9000	Baggy Casey, blonde	1975	30	75
9093	Ballerina Barbie	1978	15	27
9093	Ballerina Barbie	1976	15	40
9613	Ballerina Barbie on Tour, gold	1978	65	155
	Ballerina Cara	1975	15	45
9805	Barbie & Her Fashion Fireworks	1976	17	40
1144	Barbie with Growin' Pretty Hair	1971	55	150
3237	Beach Blast Barbie	1988	3	10
	Beach Blast Christie	1988	4	9
	Beach Blast Ken	1988	4	9
3244	Beach Blast Miko	1988	4	9
	Beach Blast Skipper	1988	4	9
	Beach Blast Steven	1988	5	10
	Beach Blast Teresa	1988	4	9
9907	Beautiful Bride Barbie	1978	75	225
1290	Beauty Secrets Barbie, 1st issue	1979	25	60
1295	Beauty Secrets Christie	1979	25	60
1018	Beauty, Barbie's Dog	1979	12	30
1293	Black Barbie, 1st issue black	1979	15	50
	Brad, bendable leg	1970	50	100
850	Bubblecut Barbie, all blondes	1961	75	175
850	Bubblecut Barbie, black haired	1961	85	250
850	Bubblecut Barbie, brunette	1961	75	180
850	Bubblecut Barbie, titian	1961	75	200
[illegible]	Bubblecut Barbie, white ginger	1961	85	200
3[illegible]	Buffy and Mrs. Beasley	1968	65	150
33[illegible]	[illegible]sy Hand Barbie	1972	95	200
331[illegible]	[illegible] Hand Francie	1972	90	175
1195	[illegible]and Ken	1971	25	75
1196	[illegible]d Steffie	1971	90	175
1186	[illegible] Barbie	1972	175	385
4547	Ca[illegible]en	1972	100	300
4439	Cali[illegible]ie	1972	180	425
4443	Califo[illegible]ating Barbie	1987	25	60
4441	Californ[illegible]ie	1987	5	15
4442	[illegible]	1987	6	13
[illegible]	[illegible]	1987	8	12
[illegible]	[illegible]	1987	3	12

Barbie & Friends

NO.	TOY NAME	YEAR	MNP	MIP
4440	California Dream Skipper	1987	13	50
4403	California Dream Teresa	1987	15	35
7377	Carla	1976	65	125
1180	Casey, brunette, blonde	1967	75	275
3570	Chris, titian, blonde, brunette	1967	35	100
1150	Color Magic Barbie, black haired	1966	655	2000
1150	Color Magic Barbie, brunette, blonde	1966	455	1300
3022	Cool Times Barbie	1988	5	15
3217	Cool Times Christie	1988	5	15
3219	Cool Times Ken	1988	5	10
3216	Cool Times Midge	1988	7	15
3218	Cool Times Teresa	1988	9	17
	Cool Tops Courtney	1989	7	15
	Cool Tops Skipper	1989	7	15
4859	Crystal Barbie, black version	1983	10	35
4598	Crystal Barbie, white version	1983	10	35
	Crystal Ken, black version	1983	15	50
4898	Crystal Ken, white version	1983	8	25
3509	Dance Club Barbie	1989	5	12
3513	Dance Club Devon	1989	5	12
3512	Dance Club Kayla	1989	5	12
3511	Dance Club Ken	1989	5	12
7945	Day-to-Night Barbie, black version	1984	10	30
7944	Day-to-Night Barbie, hispanic version	1984	17	60
7929	Day-to-Night Barbie, white version	1984	10	30
9018	Day-to-Night Ken, black version	1984	8	25
9019	Day-to-Night Ken, white version	1984	8	25
9217	Deluxe Quick Curl Barbie	1973	15	70
9219	Deluxe Quick Curl Cara	1973	15	70
	Deluxe Quick Curl P.J.	1973	25	75
9428	Deluxe Quick Curl Skipper	1973	12	65
	Deluxe Tropical Barbie	1986	10	30
3850	Doctor Barbie	1987	8	25
4118	Doctor Ken	1987	5	20
1116	Dramatic New Living Barbie, all hair colors	1969	45	175
1117	Dramatic New Living Skipper	1969	50	110
9180	Dream Date Barbie	1982	7	30
4077	Dream Date Ken	1982	5	20
5869	Dream Date P.J.	1982	8	40
2242	Dream Glow Barbie, black version	1985	12	40
1647	Dream Glow Barbie, hispanic version	1985	25	65
2248	Dream Glow Barbie, white version	1985	12	40
	Dream Glow Ken, black version	1985	13	20
2250	Dream Glow Ken, white version	1985	13	20
9180	Dream Time Barbie	1985	10	20
9180	Dream Time Barbie, pink	1985	10	20
7093	Fabulous Fur Barbie	1983	20	40
5313	Fashion Jeans Barbie	1981	15	45
5316	Fashion Jeans Ken	1981	12	45
2210	Fashion Photo Barbie	1978	20	80
	Fashion Photo Christie	1978	20	80
2323	Fashion Photo P.J.	1978	35	85
7193	Fashion Play Barbie	1983	10	20
4835	Fashion Play Barbie	1987	10	20
870	Fashion Queen Barbie	1963	100	475
1189	Feelin' Fun Barbie	1987	5	10
3421	Feelin' Groovy Barbie	1985	50	160
	Flight Time Barbie, black version	1989	5	15
	Flight Time Barbie, hispanic version	1989	7	18
	Flight Time Barbie, white version	1989	5	15
	Flight Time Ken	1989	5	15

NO.	TOY NAME	YEAR	MNP	MIP
1143	Fluff	1971	35	85
1122	Francie Hair Happenins'	1970	85	225
1170	Francie Twist and Turn, bendable leg, all hair colors	1967	65	200
	Francie with Growin' Pretty Hair	1971	65	200
1170	Francie, bendable leg, black version	1967	275	650
1130	Francie, bendable leg, white version, blonde, brunette	1966	65	225
1140	Francie, straight leg, brunette, blonde	1966	125	325
	Free Moving Barbie	1974	10	35
	Free Moving Cara	1974	10	35
7280	Free Moving Ken	1974	8	25
7281	Free Moving P.J.	1974	10	40
7668	Fun to Dress Barbie, black version	1987	3	6
1373	Fun to Dress Barbie, black version	1988	3	6
4558	Fun to Dress Barbie, white version	1987	3	6
4372	Fun to Dress Barbie, white version	1988	3	6
4808	Fun to Dress Barbie, white version	1989	3	6
	Funtime Barbie, black version	1986	5	12
	Funtime Barbie, white version	1986	5	12
7194	Funtime Ken	1974	7	15
1953	Garden Party Barbie	1989	8	20
1922	Gift Giving Barbie	1985	5	15
1205	Gift Giving Barbie	1988	5	15
7262	Gold Medal Olympic Barbie Skater	1975	15	75
7264	Gold Medal Olympic Barbie Skier	1975	12	75
7263	Gold Medal Olympic P.J. Gymnast	1974	12	75
7261	Gold Medal Olympic Skier Ken	1974	15	75
7274	Gold Medal Olympic Skipper	1975	15	75
1974	Golden Dreams Barbie	1980	8	35
3533	Golden Dreams Barbie Glamerous Night	1980	25	85
3249	Golden Dreams Christie	1980	10	40
7834	Great Shapes Barbie, black version	1983	5	12
7025	Great Shapes Barbie, white version	1983	5	12
7025	Great Shapes Barbie, with walkman	1983	12	25
7310	Great Shapes Ken	1983	5	12
7417	Great Shapes Skipper	1983	5	12
4253	Groom Todd	1982	15	45
	Growing Up Ginger	1977	35	85
7259	Growing Up Skipper	1977	10	55
	Guardian Goddess Ice Empress	1979	60	200
	Guardian Goddess Lion Queen	1979	85	225
2757	Guardian Goddess Moonmystic	1979	55	145
	Guardian Goddess Soaring Eagle	1979	85	225
2757	Guardian Goddess Sunspell	1979	35	120
	Happy Birthday Barbie	1983	8	30
	Happy Birthday Barbie	1980	8	35
1703	Happy Holidays Barbie, red velvet gown	1988	125	350
3253	Happy Holidays Barbie, white satin gown	1989	25	75
7470	Hawaiian Barbie	1977	25	100
	Hawaiian Barbie	1975	30	125
2960	Hawaiian Ken	1978	7	15
7495	Hawaiian Ken	1983	13	45
3698	High School Chelsie	1989	5	15
3600	High School Dude, Jazzie's boyfriend	1989	5	15
3636	High School Stacie	1989	5	15
1292	Hispanic Barbie	1979	10	45
2390	Homecoming Queen Skipper, black version	1988	8	15
1952	Homecoming Queen Skipper, white version	1988	12	25
1757	Horse Lovin' Barbie	1982	10	45
3600	Horse Lovin' Ken	1982	8	30
5029	Horse Lovin' Skipper	1982	8	30
7927	Hot Stuff Skipper	1984	5	18

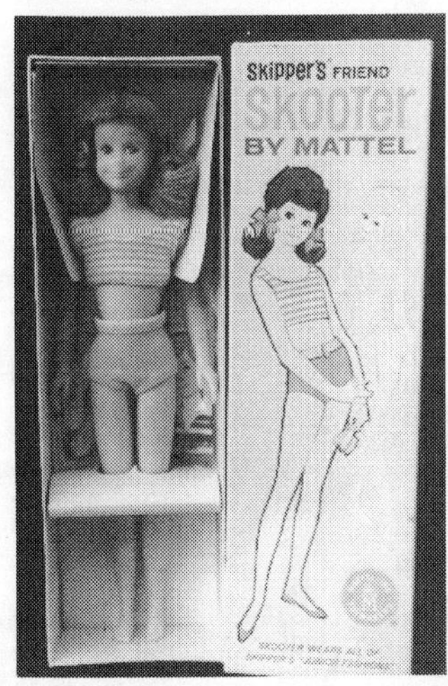

Barbie, top to bottom: Scooter, 1965; close-up of Bubble Cut Barbie, 1961 and American Girl Barbie, 1965; Black Francie, 1965; the rare Ponytail Blonde Barbie #1, 1959.

Barbie & Friends

NO.	TOY NAME	YEAR	MNP	MIP
	Ice Capades Barbie, black version	1989	5	12
	Ice Capades Barbie, white version	1989	5	12
4928	International Barbie Canadian	1988	12	25
3898	International Barbie Eskimo	1982	75	150
3188	International Barbie German	1986	35	75
2997	International Barbie Greek	1986	20	45
3189	International Barbie Iceland	1987	27	60
3897	International Barbie India	1982	30	65
7517	International Barbie Irish	1984	55	125
1601	International Barbie Italian	1980	65	250
9481	International Barbie Japanese	1985	55	125
4929	International Barbie Korean	1988	10	25
1917	International Barbie Mexican	1989	10	25
3262	International Barbie Oriental	1981	65	150
1600	International Barbie Parisienne	1980	75	215
2995	International Barbie Peru	1986	25	55
1602	International Barbie Royal	1980	95	250
1916	International Barbie Russian	1989	12	27
3263	International Barbie Scottish	1981	80	185
4031	International Barbie Spanish	1983	65	140
4032	International Barbie Swedish	1983	40	95
7451	International Barbie Swiss	1984	40	95
4061	Island Fun Barbie	1987	3	10
	Island Fun Christie	1987	3	10
4060	Island Fun Ken	1987	3	10
	Island Fun Skipper	1987	3	10
4093	Island Fun Steven	1987	3	10
4117	Island Fun Teresa	1987	3	10
3633	Jazzie Workout	1989	5	12
1756	Jewel Secrets Barbie, black version	1986	6	18
1737	Jewel Secrets Barbie, white version	1986	6	18
3232	Jewel Secrets Ken, black version	1986	6	18
1719	Jewel Secrets Ken, rooted hair	1986	6	18
3133	Jewel Secrets Skipper	1986	6	18
3179	Jewel Secrets Whitney	1986	8	25
1124	Ken, bendable leg	1970	20	65
750	Ken, bendable leg, brunette, blonde	1965	115	225
750	Ken, flocked hair, brunette, blonde	1961	50	125
750	Ken, painted hair, brunette, blonde	1962	38	110
2597	Kissing Barbie	1978	8	50
2955	Kissing Christie	1978	10	55
	Live Action Barbie Touch n' Go	1971	65	145
1151	Live Action Barbie, blonde	1971	20	55
1116	Live Action Barbie, titian, blonde, brunette	1970		
	Live Action Christie	1971	60	135
1172	Live Action Ken on Stage	1971	30	85
1156	Live Action P.J.	1971	65	145
7072	Lovin' You Barbie	1983	10	55
3989	Magic Curl Barbie, black version	1981	8	20
3856	Magic Curl Barbie, white version	1981	10	30
3137	Magic Moves Barbie, black version	1985	6	20
2126	Magic Moves Barbie, white version	1985	6	20
1067	Malibu Barbie	1975		
	Malibu Barbie	1971	15	55
	Malibu Christie	1975	10	25
7745	Malibu Christie	1977	15	40
1068	Malibu Francie	1971	15	45
1088	Malibu Ken	1976	8	20
	Malibu P.J.	1975	5	10
1069	Malibu Skipper	1977	8	20
1080	Midge, bendable leg, blonde, titian	1965	200	400

NO.	TOY NAME	YEAR	MNP	MIP
1080	Midge, bendable leg, brownette	1965	250	525
860	Midge, straight leg, blonde, titian	1964	50	125
860	Midge, straight leg, brunette	1964	55	135
1080	Midge, with teeth, all hair colors	1965	100	250
1060	Miss Barbie (Sleep-eye)	1964	175	725
1060	Miss Barbie (Sleep-eye), silver-haired	1964	395	975
4224	Mod Hair Ken	1972	45	100
9988	Music Lovin' Barbie	1985	15	45
2388	Music Lovin' Ken	1985	15	45
2854	Music Lovin' Skipper	1985	20	75
1875	My First Barbie, aqua and yellow dress	1980	10	35
1875	My First Barbie, pink checkered dress	1982	5	25
1801	My First Barbie, pink tutu, black version	1986	5	15
1788	My First Barbie, pink tutu, white version	1986	5	15
	My First Barbie, white dress, black version	1984	7	30
1875	My First Barbie, white dress, white version	1984	5	25
1281	My First Barbie, white tutu, black version	1988	6	14
1282	My First Barbie, white tutu, hispanic version	1988	6	20
1280	My First Barbie, white tutu, white version	1988	5	14
	My First Ken, 1st issue	1989	4	10
9342	New Look Ken	1973	23	70
7807	Newport Barbie	1974	25	75
1127	Nurse Julia, 1 piece nurse outfit	1970	70	185
1127	Nurse Julia, 2 piece nurse outfit	1969	75	225
4405	Nurse Whitney	1987	20	45
4885	Party Treats Barbie	1989	8	25
9516	Peaches n' Cream Barbie, black version	1984	8	40
7926	Peaches n' Cream Barbie, white version	1984	8	45
4869	Pepsi Spirit Barbie	1989	10	35
4867	Pepsi Spirit Skipper	1989	10	33
	Perfume Giving Ken, black version	1989	6	20
	Perfume Giving Ken, white version	1989	6	20
4552	Perfume Pretty Barbie, black version	1989	8	25
4551	Perfume Pretty Barbie, white version	1989	8	25
4557	Perfume Pretty Whitney	1987	8	35
	Pink Jubilee Barbie, only 1200 made	1989	1900	
3551	Pink n' Pretty Barbie	1981	13	37
3554	Pink n' Pretty Christie	1981	8	35
5336	Playtime Barbie	1983	15	20
850	Ponytail Barbie #1, blonde	1959	1700	3500
850	Ponytail Barbie #1, brunette	1959	2500	4000
850	Ponytail Barbie #2, blonde	1959	1500	2200
850	Ponytail Barbie #2, brunette	1959	2100	3000
850	Ponytail Barbie #3, blonde	1960	400	650
850	Ponytail Barbie #3, brunette	1960	450	750
850	Ponytail Barbie #4, blonde	1960	175	400
850	Ponytail Barbie #4, brunette	1960	195	450
850	Ponytail Barbie #5, blonde	1961	155	255
850	Ponytail Barbie #5, brunette	1961	175	275
850	Ponytail Barbie #5, titian	1961	175	350
850	Ponytail Barbie #6, blonde	1962	150	250
850	Ponytail Barbie #6, brunette	1962	175	275
850	Ponytail Barbie #6, titian	1962	175	350
850	Ponytail Barbie #7, blonde	1963	150	255
850	Ponytail Barbie #7, brunette	1963	175	275
850	Ponytail Barbie #7, titian	1963	175	350
850	Ponytail Swirl Style Barbie, blonde	1964	195	425
850	Ponytail Swirl Style Barbie, brunette	1964	225	525
850	Ponytail Swirl Style Barbie, platinum	1964	225	775
850	Ponytail Swirl Style Barbie, titian	1964	225	550
1117	Pose n' Play Skipper	1973	75	300

Barbie, top to bottom: Titian Swirl Ponytail Barbie, 1964; Miss Barbie, 1964; Barbie Masquerade Outfit; Titian American Girl Barbie, 1965.

Barbie & Friends

NO.	TOY NAME	YEAR	MNP	MIP
2598	Pretty Changes Barbie	1978	8	40
7194	Pretty Party Barbie	1983	12	30
	Quick Curl Barbie	1973	15	105
7291	Quick Curl Cara	1975	15	60
4222	Quick Curl Francie	1973	15	55
4221	Quick Curl Kelley	1973	15	150
8697	Quick Curl Miss America, blonde	1974	35	75
8697	Quick Curl Miss America, brunette	1973	45	175
4223	Quick Curl Skipper	1973	20	50
1090	Ricky	1965	55	135
1140	Rocker Barbie, 1st issue	1985	7	35
3055	Rocker Barbie, 2nd issue	1986	7	20
1196	Rocker Dana, 1st issue	1985	7	35
3158	Rocker Dana, 2nd issue	1986	7	20
1141	Rocker Dee-Dee, 1st issue	1985	7	20
3160	Rocker Dee-Dee, 2nd issue	1986	7	20
2428	Rocker Derek, 1st issue	1985	7	20
	Rocker Derek, 2nd issue	1986	7	20
2427	Rocker Diva, 1st issue	1985	7	20
3159	Rocker Diva, 2nd issue	1986	7	20
3131	Rocker Ken, 1st issue	1985	7	20
1880	Rollerskating Barbie	1980	8	40
1881	Rollerskating Ken	1980	8	43
4973	Safari Barbie	1983	8	30
1019	Scott	1979	15	50
9109	Sea Lovin' Barbie	1984	8	30
9110	Sea Lovin' Ken	1984	8	35
4931	Sensations Barbie	1987	5	12
4977	Sensations Becky	1987	5	12
4976	Sensations Belinda	1987	5	12
4967	Sensations Bopsy	1987	5	12
4960	Sensations Bopsy Bibops	1987	15	95
7799	Show and Ride Barbie	1988	8	35
1030	Skipper, bendable leg, brunette, blonde, titian	1965	60	155
950	Skipper, straight leg, brunette, blonde, titian	1964	45	100
	Skipper, straight leg, re-issues, brunette, blonde, titian	1970	30	85
	Skooter, bendable leg, brunette, blonde, titian	1965	65	175
1040	Skooter, straight leg, brunette, blonde, titian	1965	55	125
1294	Sport n' Shave Ken	1980	8	40
1190	Standard Barbie, all hair colors	1967	85	280
1281	Starr Kelley	1979	8	35
1283	Starr Shaun	1979	8	40
1280	Starr Starr	1979	8	35
1282	Starr Tracy	1979	8	35
3966	Stars n' Stripes Army Barbie	1989	10	40
1283	Style Magic Barbie	1989	5	15
1288	Style Magic Christie	1989	5	15
1915	Style Magic Skipper	1989	10	30
1290	Style Magic Whitney	1989	5	15
7745	Sun Gold Malibu Barbie, black version	1983	5	18
	Sun Gold Malibu Barbie, hispanic version	1985	3	7
1067	Sun Gold Malibu Barbie, white version	1983	5	15
3849	Sun Gold Malibu Ken, black version	1983	3	18
	Sun Gold Malibu Ken, hispanic version	1985	3	7
1088	Sun Gold Malibu Ken, white version	1983	3	7
1187	Sun Gold Malibu P.J.	1983	5	15
1069	Sun Gold Malibu Skipper	1983	5	15
1067	Sun Lovin' Malibu Barbie	1978	5	15
1088	Sun Lovin' Malibu Ken	1978	5	15
1187	Sun Lovin' Malibu P.J.	1978	5	18
1069	Sun Lovin' Malibu Skipper	1978	5	15

Barbie & Friends

NO.	TOY NAME	YEAR	MNP	MIP
7806	Sun Valley Barbie	1974	15	55
7809	Sun Valley Ken	1974	10	50
4970	Sunsational Hispanic Barbie	1983	20	40
1067	Sunsational Malibu Barbie	1981	6	15
4970	Sunsational Malibu Barbie, hispanic version	1981	8	20
7745	Sunsational Malibu Christie	1981	6	15
	Sunsational Malibu Ken, black version	1981	15	35
1187	Sunsational Malibu P.J.	1981	6	15
1069	Sunsational Malibu Skipper	1981	5	12
7745	Sunset Malibu Christie	1971	20	45
1068	Sunset Malibu Francie	1971	25	55
1088	Sunset Malibu Ken	1971	15	35
1187	Sunset Malibu P.J.	1977	10	25
1069	Sunset Malibu Skipper	1971	20	45
3296	Super Hair Barbie, black version	1986	8	20
3101	Super Hair Barbie, white version	1986	8	20
5839	Super Sport Ken	1982	8	20
2756	Super Teen Skipper	1978	7	15
	Supersize Barbie	1976	45	135
	Supersize Christie	1976	45	135
	Supersize Super Hair Barbie	1978	50	125
4983	Superstar Ballerina Barbie	1983	33	60
9720	Superstar Barbie	1977	33	60
1605	Superstar Barbie 30th Anniversary, black version	1989	6	13
1604	Superstar Barbie 30th Anniversary, white version	1989	8	17
9950	Superstar Christie	1977	25	60
2211	Superstar Ken	1978	17	40
1550	Superstar Ken 30th Anniversary, black version	1989	5	13
1535	Superstar Ken 30th Anniversary, white version	1989	7	17
1067	Superstar Malibu Barbie	1977	10	25
7796	Sweet 16 Barbie	1974	25	65
7635	Sweet Roses Barbie	1989	15	40
7455	Sweet Roses P.J.	1983	15	40
2064	Tahiti, Barbie's Pet Parrot	1985	3	8
1115	Talking Barbie, all hair colors	1968	65	225
	Talking Brad	1970	100	300
	Talking Christie	1968	60	150
	Talking Julia	1968	55	150
1111	Talking Ken	1968	40	125
	Talking P.J.	1968	50	225
1125	Talking Stacey, blonde, titian	1968	60	175
1107	Talking Truely Scrumptious	1969	125	400
3634	Teen Dance Jazzie	1989	7	15
5893	Teen Fun Skipper Cheerleader	1987	5	15
5899	Teen Fun Skipper Party Teen	1987	5	15
5889	Teen Fun Skipper Workout	1987	5	15
3631	Teen Looks Jazzie Cheerleader	1989	4	10
3633	Teen Looks Jazzie Workout	1989	4	10
3634	Teen Scene Jazzie	1989	4	15
4855	Teen Sweetheart Skipper	1987	5	15
1950	Teen Time Courtney	1988	5	10
1951	Teen Time Skipper	1988	5	10
	Tennis Barbie	1986	5	22
	Tennis Ken	1986	5	22
	Todd	1966	50	110
	Tracey Bride	1982	8	40
1022	Tropical Barbie, black version	1985	3	10
1017	Tropical Barbie, white version	1985	3	10
	Tropical Ken, black version	1985	3	10
4060	Tropical Ken, white version	1985	3	10
2056	Tropical Miko	1985	3	10

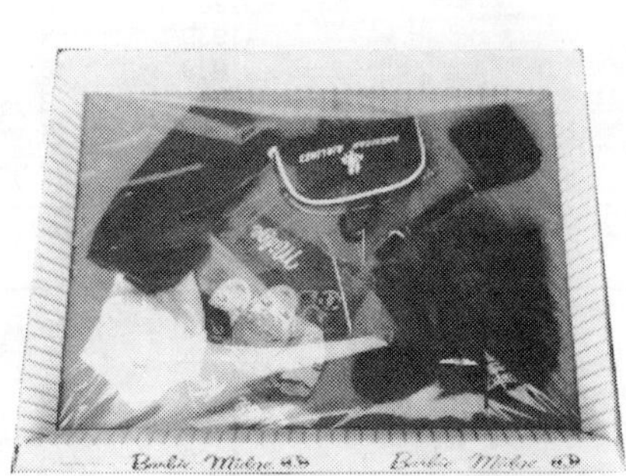

Barbie, top to bottom: Midge, 1963; Fashion Queen Barbie, 1963, and Miss Barbie, 1964; American Airlines Stewardess Set; Ken, 1962.

Barbie & Friends

NO.	TOY NAME	YEAR	MNP	MIP
4064	Tropical Skipper	1985	3	10
	Truly Scrumptious, straight leg	1969	175	300
	Tutti	1976	40	90
	Tutti, all hair colors	1967	45	75
	Tutti, all hair colors	1965	50	110
	Twiggy	1967	125	380
5723	Twirley Curls Barbie, black version	1982	8	25
5724	Twirley Curls Barbie, hispanic version	1982	10	30
5579	Twirley Curls Barbie, white version	1982	8	25
1160	Twist and Turn Barbie, all hair colors	1967	75	300
	Twist and Turn Christie	1969	75	195
	Twist and Turn Flip Barbie, all hair colors	1969	75	325
1118	Twist and Turn P.J., blonde	1970	45	175
1105	Twist and Turn Skipper, all hair colors	1969	50	125
	Twist and Turn Stacey, blonde, titian	1967	75	200
4774	UNICEF Barbie, asian version	1989	17	35
	UNICEF Barbie, black version	1989	7	15
4782	UNICEF Barbie, hispanic version	1989	7	15
1920	UNICEF Barbie, white version	1989	7	15
1675	Vacation Sensation Barbie, pink	1988	12	45
1675	Vacation Sensations Barbie, blue	1986	10	32
1182	Walk Lively Barbie	1972	55	135
1184	Walk Lively Ken	1972	20	70
3200	Walk Lively Miss America Barbie, brunette	1972	55	125
	Walk Lively Steffie	1972	65	145
	Wedding Fantasy Barbie, black version	1989	7	25
	Wedding Fantasy Barbie, white version	1989	7	25
3469	Western Barbie	1980	8	30
3600	Western Ken	1980	7	20
5029	Western Skipper	1980	8	25
	Western Sun Barbie, black version	1989	5	15
	Western Sun Barbie, white version	1989	5	15
	Western Sun Ken	1989	5	15
	Western Sun Nia	1989	5	15
4103	Wet n' Wild Barbie	1989	8	18
4121	Wet n' Wild Christie	1989	3	7
4104	Wet n' Wild Ken	1989	3	7
4120	Wet n' Wild Kira	1989	3	7
4138	Wet n' Wild Skipper	1989	3	7
4137	Wet n' Wild Steven	1989	3	7
4136	Wet n' Wild Teresa	1989	3	7
	Wig Wardrobe Midge	1964	125	350
	Yellowstone Kelley	1974	60	195

Department Store Specials & Gift Sets

NO.	TOY NAME	YEAR	MNP	MIP
	Ballerina on Tour Gift Set	1976	25	85
5531	Barbie and Friends Gift Set	1982	25	55
4431	Barbie and Friends: Ken, Barbie, PJ	1982	25	75
	Barbie and Ken Camping Out	1983	25	95
892	Barbie and Ken Tennis Gift Set	1962	275	750
3303	Barbie Beautiful Blues Gift Set	1967	350	850
1596	Barbie Pink Premier Gift Set		300	600
	Barbie Twinkle Twon Set	1968	250	500
1013	Barbie's Round the Clock Gift Set	1964	275	750
1011	Barbie's Sparkling Pink Gift Sett	1963	250	550
1017	Barbie's Wedding Party Gift Set	1964	450	1000
1702	Beauty Secrets Barbie Pretty Reflections Gift Set	1979	40	85
3304	Casey Goes Casual Gift Set	1967	400	1000
4893	Cool City Blues: Barbie, Ken, Skipper	1989	20	45

Department Store Specials and Gift Sets

NO.	TOY NAME	YEAR	MNP	MIP
4917	Dance Club Barbie Gift Set	1989	25	60
	Dance Magic Gift Set	1985	27	65
9058	Dance Sensation Barbie Gift Set	1984	15	40
7734	FAO Schwarz: Golden Greetings Barbie	1989	65	155
863	Fashion Queen Barbie & Her Friends	1964	250	650
864	Fashion Queen Barbie & Ken Trousseau Gift Set	1964	100	500
1194	Francie Rise n' Shine Gift Set	1971	175	450
1042	Francie Swingin' Separates Gift Set	1966	450	900
9519	Happy Birthday Barbie Gift Set	1984	35	85
	Hawaiian Barbie	1982	25	100
4843	Hills: Party Lace Barbie	1989	15	30
	Julia Simply Wow Gift Set	1976	145	475
4870	K-Mart: Peach Pretty Barbie	1989	10	30
2977	Kissing Barbie Gift Set	1978	25	65
1585	Living Barbie Action Accents Gift Set	1970	250	500
7583	Loving You Barbie Gift Set	1983	45	100
1703	Malibu Barbie "The Beach Party", with case	1979	17	35
1248	Malibu Ken Surf's Up Gift Set	1971	75	250
4983	Mervyns: Ballerina Barbie	1983	30	75
1012	Midge's Ensemble Gift Set	1964	100	700
	Mix n' Match Gift Set	1962	215	895
3210	Montgomery Wards: Barbie	1972	350	600
	Montgomery Wards: Ken	1972	30	85
1979	My First Barbie Gift Set, pink tutu	1986	15	35
5386	My First Barbie Gift Set, pink tutu	1987	18	40
1875	My First Barbie, pink tutu, zayres hispanic	1987	8	45
1014	On Parade Gift Set, Barbie, Ken, Midge	1964	500	1000
5239	Pink & Pretty Barbie Gift Set	1981	35	85
2598	Pretty Changes Barbie Gift Set	1978	35	85
2998	Sears: 100th Celebration Barbie	1986	20	70
3596	Sears: Evening Enchantment Barbie	1989	10	20
7669	Sears: Lilac and Lovely Barbie	1988	10	25
	Sears: Perfectly Plaid Gift Set	1962	125	450
4550	Sears: Star Dream Barbie	1987	10	65
1021	Skipper Party Time Gift Set	1964	100	450
1172	Skipper Swing 'a' Rounder Gym Gift Set	1972	100	250
	Skooter Cut n' Button Gift Set	1967	150	500
	Talking Barbie Perfectly Plaid Gift Set	1971	155	495
7476	Target: Gold and Lace Barbie	1989	10	25
7801	Tennis Star Barbie & Ken	1988	18	40
	Toys-R-Us: Show n' Ride Barbie	1989	10	37
2996	Tropical Barbie Deluxe Gift Set	1985	20	45
3556	Tutti and Todd Sundae Treat Set	1966	120	300
	Tutti Me n' My Dog	1966	40	125
	Tutti Nighty Night Sleep Tight	1965	65	175
4097	Twirley Curls Barbie Gift Set	1982	30	85
4589	Wal-Mart 25th year: Pink Jubilee Barbie	1987	20	60
1374	Wal-Mart: Frills and Fantasy Barbie	1988	7	30
3963	Wal-Mart: Lavender Look Barbie	1989	7	20
	Walking Jamie Strollin' in Style Gift Set	1972	250	550
7637	Winn-Dixie: Party Pink Barbie	1989	7	18
7326	Woolworth: Special Expressions Barbie, black version	1989	5	15
4842	Woolworth: Special Expressions Barbie, white version	1989	5	10

Porcelain Barbies

NO.	TOY NAME	YEAR	MNP	MIP
5475	Benefit Performance Barbie	1988	115	375
1708	Blue Rhapsody Barbie	1986	215	500
3415	Enchanted Evening Barbie	1987	100	300
	First Wedding Barbie	1989	150	550
2641	Wedding Party Barbie	1989	150	550

BARBIE FASHIONS

Barbie Vintage Fashions 1959-1966

NO.	OUTFIT	MNP	MIB
1631	Aboard Ship	125	250
934	After Five	50	125
984	American Airlines Stewardess	60	175
917	Apple Print Sheath	40	125
0874	Arabian Nights	100	200
989	Ballerine	45	150
953	Barbie Baby-Sits	75	175
1605	Barbie in Hawaii	60	125
0823	Barbie in Holland	75	175
0821	Barbie in Japan	200	400
0820	Barbie in Mexico	75	175
0822	Barbie in Switzerland	60	150
1634	Barbie Learns to Book	100	250
1608	Barbie Skin Diver	40	85
962	Barbie-Q Outfit	65	150
1651	Beau Time	45	100
1698	Beautiful Bride	350	600
1667	Benefit Performance	350	600
1609	Black Magic	65	150
947	Bride's Dream	80	175
1628	Brunch Time	90	200
981	Busy Gal	125	250
956	Busy Morning	90	200
1616	Campus Sweetheart	200	350
0889	Candy Striper Volunteer	50	125
954	Career Girl	65	175
1687	Caribbean Cruise	70	175
0876	Cheerleader	75	175
0872	Cinderella	125	250
1672	Club Meeting	125	250
1670	Coffee's On	70	150
916	Commuter Set	350	650
1627	Country Club Dance	80	200
1603	County Fair	40	150
1604	Crisp 'n Cool	75	175
918	Cruise Stripes	50	125
1626	Dancing Doll	100	200
1666	Debutante Ball	250	450
946	Dinner At Eight	50	150
1633	Disc Date	100	200
1613	Dog n' Duds	100	225
1669	Dreamland	60	150
0875	Drum Majorette	75	175
983	Enchanted Evening	100	200
1695	Evening Enchantment	250	450
1660	Evening Gala	115	225
961	Evening Splendor	85	175
1676	Fabulous Fashion	100	250
943	Fancy Free	25	65
1635	Fashion Editor	275	550
1656	Fashion Luncheon	250	500
1691	Fashion Shiner	85	200
971	Faster Parade	875	1500
1696	Floating Gardens	200	375
921	Floral Petticoat	35	100
1697	Formal Occasion	175	375
1638	Fraternity Dance	175	375
979	Friday Night Date	55	150
1624	Fun At The Fair	125	200
1619	Fun n' Games	125	200
931	Garden Party	45	125
1606	Garden Tea Party	60	150
1658	Garden Wedding	100	200
964	Gay Parisienne	500	1000
1647	Gold n' Glamour	350	750
992	Golden Elegance	85	175
1610	Golden Evening	95	175
911	Golden Girl	60	125
1645	Golden Glory	150	300
945	Graduation	35	70
0873	Guinevere	125	250
1665	Here Comes The Bride	375	750
1639	Holiday Dance	150	250
942	Icebreaker	50	125
1653	International Fair	50	300
1632	Invitation To Tea	175	350
0819	It's Cold Outside, brown	45	100
0819	It's Cold Outside, red	70	150
1620	Junior Designer	125	250
1614	Junior Prom	175	350
1621	Knit Hit	75	150
1602	Knit Separates	50	125
957	Knitting Pretty, blue	75	175
957	Knitting Pretty, pink	125	225
978	Let's Dance	50	125
0880	Little Red Riding Hood & The Wolf	200	400
1661	London Tour	135	275
1600	Lunch Date	35	100
1649	Lunch On The Terrace	75	150
1673	Lunchtime	85	175
1646	Magnificience	250	500
944	Masquerade	55	150
1640	Matinee Fashion	275	550
1617	Midnight Blue	175	350
1641	Miss Astronaut	300	600
1625	Modern Art	175	300
940	Mood For Music	75	175
933	Movie Date	253	100
1633	Music Center Matinee	225	450
965	Nightly Negligee	50	125
1644	On The Avenue	300	600
985	Open Road	125	500
987	Orange Blossom	50	150
1650	Outdoor Art Show	175	350
1637	Outdoor Life	100	200
1601	Pajama Party	15	50
1678	Pan American Stewardess	600	1200
958	Party Dance	75	150
1692	Patio Party	125	250
915	Peachy Fleecy	60	t150
1648	Photo Fashion	125	250

BARBIE

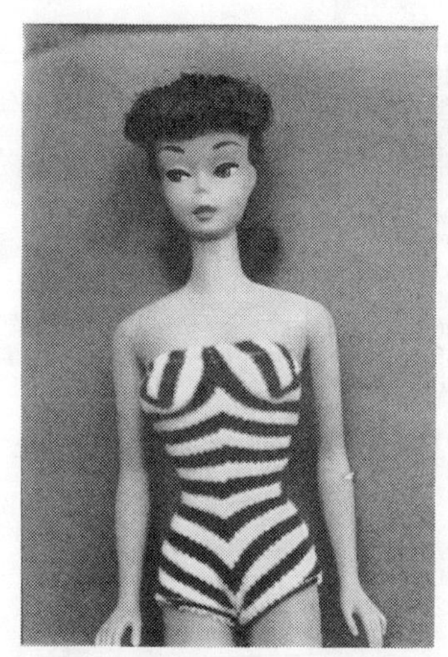

Barbie, top to bottom: PJ and Talking Barbie, 1968; Montgomery Ward Anniversary Barbie, 1972; Swirl Ponytail Barbie, 1964: Bendable Leg Midge, 1965, and American Girl Barbie, 1965.

Barbie Vintage Fashions

NO.	OUTFIT	MNP	MIB
967	Picnic Set	125	225
1694	Pink Moonbeams	100	200
966	Plantation Belle	150	300
1643	Poodle Parade	200	375
1652	Pretty As A Picture	100	200
1686	Print Aplenty	125	250
949	Rain Coat	45	125
1654	Reception Line	175	350
939	Red Flare	70	150
991	Registered Nurse	70	150
963	Resort Set	45	125
1668	Riding In The Park	275	650
968	Roman Holiday	1500	2500
1611	Satin n' Rose	85	175
1615	Saturday Matinee	350	650
951	Senior Prom	50	150
986	Sheath Sensation	50	150
1664	Shimmering Magic	550	950
977	Silken Flame	45	150
988	Singing In The Shower	45	125
1629	Skater's Waltz	125	250
948	Ski Queen	75	150
1636	Sleeping Pretty	90	175
1674	Sleepytime Gal	95	200
1642	Slumber Party	95	200
982	Solo In The Spotlight	35	250
993	Sophisticated Lady	150	275
937	Sorority Meeting	50	150
1671	Sporting Casuals	60	150
0949	Stormy Weather	45	125
1622	Student Teacher	50	300
1690	Studio Tour	100	200
969	Suburban Shopper	65	175
1675	Sunday Visit	250	500
1683	Sunflower	125	225
976	Sweater Girl	50	150
973	Sweet Dreams, pink	150	300
973	Sweet Dreams, yellow	50	150
955	Swingin' Easy	50	150
941	Tennis Anyone	50	150
959	Theatre Date	65	175
1612	Theatre Date	45	175
1688	Travel Togethers	100	200
1655	Under Fashions	65	150
919	Undergarments	35	125
1623	Underprints	50	125
1623	Vacation Time	75	175
972	Wedding Day Set	125	250
1607	White Magic	75	175
975	Winter Holiday	50	150

Ken Vintage Fashions 1961-1966

NO.	OUTFIT	MNP	MIB
0779	American Airlines Captain, two versions	100	200
797	Army and Air Force	60	125
1425	Best Man	150	300
1424	Business Appointment	150	300

Ken Vintage Fashions

NO.	OUTFIT	MNP	MIB
1410	Campus Corduroys	20	40
770	Campus Hero	25	65
0782	Casuals, striped shirt	50	125
782	Casuals, yellow shirt	25	65
1416	College Student	100	200
1400	Country Clubbin'	50	100
793	Dr. Ken	60	125
785	Dreamboat	25	65
0775	Drum Major	75	150
1407	Fountain Boy	75	150
1408	Fraternity Meeting	30	75
791	Fun On Ice	45	100
1403	Going Bowling	25	60
1409	Going Huntin'	50	100
795	Graduation	20	45
1426	Here Comes The Bride	250	500
1412	Hiking Holiday	75	150
1414	Holiday	100	200
780	In Trading	20	60
1420	Jazz Concert	75	150
1423	Ken A Go Go	150	300
0774	Ken Arabian Nights	75	150
1404	Ken In Hawaii	70	125
0777	Ken In Holland	75	150
0778	Ken In Mexico	75	150
0776	Ken In Switzerland	75	150
1406	Ken Skin Diver	25	50
0773	King Arthur	100	200
794	Masquerade (Ken)	55	125
1427	Mountain Hike	125	250
1415	Mr. Astronaut	200	450
1413	Off To Bed	70	150
	Pak Items Various Shirts Slacks, Sweaters		520
792	Play Ball	45	100
788	Rally Day	20	60
1405	Roller Skate Date, with hat	35	70
1405	Roller Skate Date, with slacks	35	70
1417	Rovin' Reporter	80	175
796	Sailor	60	125
786	Saturday Date	25	65
1421	Seein' The Sights	75	150
798	Ski Champion	60	125
0781	Sleeper Set, blue	50	125
781	Sleeper Set, brown	25	65
1401	Special Date	75	150
783	Sport Shorts	20	60
1422	Summer Job	125	250
784	Terry Togs	25	75
0772	The Prince	100	200
789	The Yachtsman, no hat	50	100
0789	The Yachtsman, with hat	75	150
790	Time For Tennis	25	75
1418	Time To Turn In	65	125
799	Touchdown	35	75
787	Tuxedo	50	125
1419	TV's Good Tonight	60	125
1411	Victory Dance	35	100

Francie Fashions 1966

NO.	OUTFIT	MNP	MB
1259	Checkmates	75	150
1258	Clam Diggers	75	150
1256	Concert In The Park	50	125
1257	Dance Party	50	125
1260	First Formal	75	150
1252	First Things First	50	125
1254	Fresh As A Daisy	50	125
1250	Gad-About	50	125
1251	It's A Date	50	125
1255	Polka Dots N' Raindrops	50	125
1261	Shoppin' Spree	75	150
1253	Tuckered Out	50	125

Ricky Fashions 1965-1966

NO.	OUTFIT	MNP	MB
1506	Let's Explore	50	100
1501	Lights Out	35	75
1504	Little Leaguer	35	75
1502	Saturday Show	35	75
1505	Skateboard Set	50	100
1503	Sunday Suit	35	75

Skipper Vintage Fashions 1964-1966

NO.	OUTFIT	MNP	MB
1905	Ballet Class	30	65
1923	Can You Play?	35	75
1926	Chill Chasers	40	100
1912	Cookie Time	50	100
1933	Country Picnic	150	250
1911	Day At The Fair	85	150
1929	Dog Show	65	125
1909	Dreamtime	30	65
1906	Dress Coat	30	65

Skipper Vintage Fashions 1964-1966

NO.	OUTFIT	MNP	MB
1904	Flower Girl	30	65
1920	Fun Time	50	100
1919	Happy Birthday	75	175
1934	Junior Bridesmaid	150	250
1917	Land & Sea	45	100
1935	Learning To Ride	125	250
1932	Let's Play House	75	175
1930	Loungin' Lovelies	30	65
1903	Masquerade (Skipper)	40	75
1913	Me N' My Doll	85	150
1915	Outdoor Casuals	50	100
1914	Platter Party	35	75
1916	Rain Or Shine	30	75
1928	Rainy Day Checkers	50	100
1901	Red Sensation	30	65
1907	School Days	35	75
1921	School Girl	75	150
1918	Ship Ahoy	55	100
1902	Silk N' Fancy	30	65
1908	Skating Fun	35	75
1936	Sledding Fun	60	125
1910	Sunny Pastels	35	75
1924	Tea Party	50	100
1922	Town Togs	65	125
1900	Under-Pretties	25	50
1925	What's New At The Zoo?	50	100

Tutti Fashions 1966

NO.	OUTFIT	MNP	MB
3601	Puddle Jumpers	25	50
3603	Sand Castles	25	50
3602	Ship Shape	25	50
3604	Skippin' Rope	25	50

Character Toys

Character toy collecting is without question the broadest field in the hobby. If time and space would have permitted, we could have filled this book entirely with character toys and still have only sampled the field. Any number of categories in this section could easily sustain complete books, and several of them have. From Batman to Mickey Mouse, Popeye, Little Orphan Annie and a dozen other areas in between, the collecting opportunities in character toys are boggling.

Collectors of character toys are restrained only by their budgets, as the variety of tin wind-ups, bisques, dolls, books, puppets, playsets, sand toys, puzzles and battery-operated toys -- even within single categories such as Mickey Mouse or Popeye -- are vast enough to comprise entire collections and offer decades of the thrill of the hunt. To attempt to collect the entire range and scope of character toys would be akin to counting the stars in the sky, and at this point would cost about as much as buying them.

Beginning collectors are faced with "narrowing" their collecting specialties to within an absurdly wide range of options, and toys outside those broad boundaries prove so frequently tempting that many collections never achieve any specialization at all. Flash Gordon and Mickey Mouse look just fine together. Dick Tracy, Doctor Who and Donald Duck fit perfectly side by side on a toy shelf, and whatever configuration a developing toy collection takes, it will tell a fascinating and logical story of its time and its relationship to the times of those toys around it. Different toys from different periods of our history each have unique tales to tell; it can be argued that "non-specialization" can be one of the most personally satisfying "specializations" in the study and appreciation of toys. Ultimately it comes down to collecting what appeals to us most, of satisfying our particular appetites. Some of us are crazy for ethnic foods, some are meat and potatoes folks, and some just go for the grand buffets and try a bit of everything.

Attempting to organize such a broad spectrum is not easy. This section is organized by primary characters as opposed to being grouped by any other classification system. Rocky and Bullwinkle could logically be placed under a heading of "TV Cartoon Toys," but since most collectors would look for them by name first, we chose to list them that way. Similarly, we could have listed all Disney-related toys together under one massive subhead, but again the name-first approach seemed simpler to use and just as logical. So you will not find Mickey Mouse and Donald Duck under a single Disney category, but rather by name of the character and item. Disney toys with multiple characters present a problem, but we chose to use the item's common name or dominant character as a referent.

As with all general rules, there are exceptions. The overall organization of this book required the separation of toys into various categories, and then by item within each chapter. Buck Rogers and Flash Gordon, while certainly

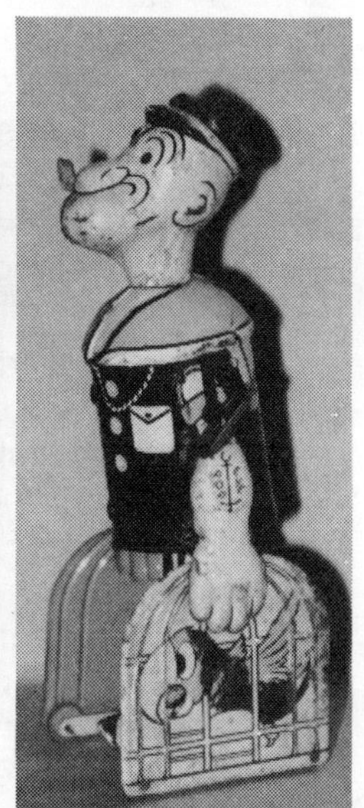

Top: Snow White Paint Book, 1940s; Right: Popeye Express, 1932, Marx.

characters, are most often thought of as space characters, so for this reason they are placed in the Science Fiction and Space Toys section of this book. Certain other character toys will also be found in the Vehicles, Classic Tin, Fast Food, Games and Action Figures sections, and some noteworthy items will be found in duplicate listings in more than one section.

Again, deadline and space considerations restrict this presentation to a sampling of toys available in each category. The editors plan to expand this section in coming editions and welcome reader submissions of unlisted items for inclusion for the next edition.

For those who are already engaged in, or are considering specialization, a few words of introduction to some of the major classes in this section are in order.

If grouped together, Disney-related toys would easily occupy the bulk of this section. The collecting of Disneyana is one of the largest and most vigorously thriving of all areas in the toy hobby and shows no signs of slowing. Walt Disney has often been called the single greatest contributor to American culture and the original "imagineer" of many of our country's greatest cultural icons.

There is also no question that no literary or comic creations have ever been as honored (or as frequently pirated) as have his exceptional stable of characters. From the earliest rat-like long-nosed mouse to the pie-eyed mouse of the late 1930s and 1940s, to the virtually human Mickey of today, the various incarnations of Mickey Mouse adorn more toys and trinkets and clothes and whatnots than any other image in modern history. And thanks to the continuing growth of the Disney empire through Disney Worlds, the Disney Channel and the virtually guaranteed success of each new animated film, the Disney cast of collectible characters grows almost as fast as the mass of people dedicated to collecting it all.

The implication seems clear for the little mouse who first appeared in 1928's "Steamboat Willie" black and white cartoon. The collectibility and probability of appreciation for the classic toys of Mickey Mouse, Donald Duck, Snow White and Pinocchio is secured. We can only wonder what the Disney toys of the 1930s will be worth when they finally turn 100 years old.

But it is also a safe bet that not all toys will endlessly escalate in value. Enduring popularity of a character is a key element in predicting future demand for popular culture collectibles. The number of people familiar with a character during its period of initial release, the degree of its original popularity and the span of that popularity are all factors that will impact future collectibility. As collectibles mature and their active collecting public increases, it is reasonable to expect their prices to rise. But once the collector base begins to erode, whether through attrition or changing cultural tastes, the values of those items will begin to erode as well. When collectors lose interest and go away, for whatever reason, sometimes an entire hobby goes with them. The best insurance against this is the continued popularity of some aspect of their identity, particularly if it is character-based.

Another prime example of enduring popularity is Popeye, who made his first appearance in 1929 in a comic strip called the "Thimble Theatre," created by E.C. Segar. He rapidly became one of the most popular characters of his day, bringing fame to his cartoon companions as well. That fame manifested itself in some of the most beautiful and well-designed toys of the 1930s. Classic toys such as Popeye the Champ and Popeye and Olive Oyl Jiggers (both by Marx) have risen to their respective mint values of $3,200 and $1,500 not only because they are superb examples of the toy maker's art, but also because their characters continue to charm children to this day. Even though they are often over 50 years old, Popeye cartoons are still seen every day by children over their morning cereal, and the average four-year-old is well acquainted with the pipe-smoking sailor man and his string bean girl friend. They may be too young to read, but they know Popeye's theme song by heart.

It is this durability that translates into strength in collectibility, and that draws more new collectors into the field from each maturing generation. The universal and continuing appeal of Mickey and Minnie Mouse, Donald Duck, Snoopy, Popeye, Snow White, and others like Little Orphan Annie and Dick Tracy, are assurances that future generations of collectors will seek out their toys and place them proudly on their shelves, perhaps right next to 50-year-old Teenage Mutant Ninja Turtle figures.

CHARACTER TOYS

101 Dalmatians

TOY	COMPANY	YEAR	DESCRIPTION	GOOD	EX	MIB
101 Dalmatians Snow Dome	Marx	1961	3x5x3 1/2" tall	35	65	100
101 Dalmatians Wind-up Toy	Linemar	1959		60	115	175
Dalmatian Pups Figurine Set of Three	Enesco	1960s	4 1/2" tall	12	23	35
Lucky Figure "101 Dalmatians"	Enesco	1960s	4" tall	35	65	100
Lucky Squeeze Toy	Dell		7" tall, squeakers in the bottom	5	10	15

Addams Family

TOY	COMPANY	YEAR	DESCRIPTION	GOOD	EX	MIB
Addams Family Bank		1964	The Thing mechanical plastic battery operated bank, hand takes money	35	65	95
Addams Family Movie Key Chains				2	4	6
Lurch Figure	Remco	1964		55	105	160

Alice in Wonderland

TOY	COMPANY	YEAR	DESCRIPTION	GOOD	EX	MIB
"Mad Hatter's Tea Party" Story Book	Disney	1951		5	10	15
Alice in Wonderland Card Game	Thos. De LaRue & Co.	1980s		45	80	125
Alice in Wonderland Cookie Jar	Regal		13 1/2" tall	185	345	525
Alice in Wonderland Doll	Whitman	1972	9 1/2" tall, paper doll	25	50	75
Alice in Wonderland Figurine			5" tall, ceramic	9	16	25
Alice in Wonderland Makeup Kit				17	30	50
Alice in Wonderland Puzzle Set	Parker Brothers	1940s	Set of four 7x18" puzzles in illustrated box	20	35	55
Alice in Wonderland Quartz Watch			Blue	9	16	25
Alice in Wonderland Salt, Pepper & Sugar Bowl Set	Disney		6" tall White Rabbit sugar bowl, salt & pepper shakers 5 1/2" tall	35	65	100
Alice in Wonderland Sewing Kit	Hasbro	1951	7" sewing machine and 5" doll all plastic	18	35	50
Alice in Wonderland Snow Dome	Marx	1961	3" tall featuring Alice & the White Rabbit in front of tree	11	20	30
Alice in Wonderland Stand-up Figurines	Whitman	1951	Fifteen figures with plastic stand-up bases, Alice 6" tall	25	50	75
Alice in Wonderland Stationery Set		1951	Set of 18 sheets and 12 envelopes in full color litho folder	16	30	45
Alice in Wonderland Tea Set		1980s	3 piece china tea set with Alice, the White Rabbit, March Hare & the Mad Hatter, cups, creamer, teapot and sugar bowl	11	20	30
Alice in Wonderland Wallet			Plastic	5	10	15

Alice in Wonderland

TOY	COMPANY	YEAR	DESCRIPTION	GOOD	EX	MIB
Alice in Wonderland Watch	Timex	1958	Alice in flower on face, leather band	25	50	75
King of Hearts Pitcher	Regal		5" in diameter & 7" tall	105	195	300
Mad Hatter Marionette	Peter Puppet	1950s	15" tall character in red shoes and shirt, yellow pants, green jacket and top hat, box illustrated with Alice, Hatter and Hare	35	65	100
Mad Hatter Nodder	Marx		1 1/4"X 2"X2 1/2" bobbing head figure	11	20	30

Amos & Andy

TOY	COMPANY	YEAR	DESCRIPTION	GOOD	EX	MIB
Amos & Andy Card Party		1930	6"x8", score pads & tallies	14	25	40
Amos & Andy Fresh Air Taxicab Co.	Marx	1930s	5"x8" long, wind-up, tin	650	875	1400
Amos & Andy Jigsaw Puzzle	Pepsodent	1932	8 1/2"x10", pictured Amos, Andy, Brother Crawford, Lightin! & King Fish	20	35	55
Amos Wind-up	Marx	1930	12" tall, tin, wind-up	315	585	900
Andy Wind-up	Marx	1930	12" tall, tin, wind-up	315	585	900

Andy Gump

TOY	COMPANY	YEAR	DESCRIPTION	GOOD	EX	MIB
Andy Gump Automobile	Arcade		7"x6", cast iron with a large figure	350	650	1000
Andy Gump Brush & Mirror			4" diameter, red on ivory colored surface of brush	18	35	50
Chester Gump Playstone Funnies Mold Set		1940s		50	95	145
Chester Gump/Herby Nodders		1930s	Ceramic 2 1/4" string nodders, each	55	100	150

Archie

TOY	COMPANY	YEAR	DESCRIPTION	GOOD	EX	MIB
Archie Picture Puzzle	Jaymar	1960s	"Swinging Malt Shop" complete	9	16	25
Veronica Figure	Mattel	1977	6 1/2" tall, huggable cloth vinyl head	9	16	25

Atom Ant

TOY	COMPANY	YEAR	DESCRIPTION	GOOD	EX	MIB
Atom Ant Kite	Roalex			11	20	30
Atom Ant Punch-out Set	Whitman	1966		16	30	45
Atom Ant Push Button Puppet	Kohner			14	25	40
Morocco Mole Bubble Club Soap Container	Purex	1960s	7" hard plastic	11	20	30
Squiddley Diddly Bubble Club Soap Container	Purex	1960s	10 1/2" hard plastic	11	20	30
Winsome Witch Bubble Club Soap Container	Purex	1960s	10 1/2" hard plastic	11	20	30

Babes in Toyland

TOY	COMPANY	YEAR	DESCRIPTION	GOOD	EX	MIB
Babes in Toyland Go Mobile Friction Car	Linemar	1961	4"x5"x6"	60	115	175
Babes In Toyland Hand Puppets	Gund		Silly Dilly Clown, Soldier, or Gorgonzo figures, each	35	65	100
Babes in Toyland Puzzle	Jaymar	1961	7 1/2"x8 /12"	7	13	20
Babes in Toyland Twist'n Bend Toy	Marx	1963	4" tall flexible toy with Private Valiant holding a baton	11	20	30
Babes in Toyland Wind-up Toy	Linemar	1950s	Tin wind-up toy 66"	75	135	210
Cadet Doll "Babes in Toyland"	Gund		15 1/2" tall, fabric	11	20	30

Bambi

TOY	COMPANY	YEAR	DESCRIPTION	GOOD	EX	MIB
Bambi & Thumper Lamp			Figural lamp	11	20	30
Bambi & Thumper Throw Rug		1960s	21"x39"	25	50	75
Bambi Book	Grosset & Dunlap	1942	Black & white illustrations	12	23	35
Bambi Prints	New York Graphic Soc	1947	11"x14" framed, 8"x10" matted	25	50	75
Bambi Soakie				6	12	18
Flower Bank		1940s	5"x5"x7" tall, plaster bank	45	90	135
Thumper Ashtray	Goebel	1950s	4" tall	45	85	130
Thumper Ceramic Figural Bank	Leeds	1950s		45	80	125
Thumper Doll			16" tall, plush	12	23	35
Thumper Pull Toy	Fisher-Price	1942	#533, 7 1/2"x12", wood & metal, Thumper's tail rings the bell	18	35	50
Thumper Soakie				9	16	25
Thumper Story Book	Grosset & Dunlap	1942	Color & black & white illustrations	12	23	35

Barbie

TOY	COMPANY	YEAR	DESCRIPTION	GOOD	EX	MIB
Barbie Wristwatch	Mattel	1973	3/4 figure illustration, articulated arms, vinyl band	23	40	65

Barnacle Bill

TOY	COMPANY	YEAR	DESCRIPTION	GOOD	EX	MIB
Barnacle Bill in a Barrel	Chein	1932	7 1/2" tall, tin, wind-up	225	400	550

Barney Google

TOY	COMPANY	YEAR	DESCRIPTION	GOOD	EX	MIB
Barney Google & Spark Plug	Nifty	1920s	7 1/2" tall, wind-up	400	750	1150
Barney Google & Spark Plug Figurines			3"x3", bisque, on white bisuqe pedestal	45	80	125
Barney Google Doll	Schoenhut	1922	8 1/2" tall, wood & wood composition	155	295	450
Spark Plug Doll	Schoenhut	1922	9" long & 6 1/2" tall, jointed wood construction with fabric	155	295	450
Spark Plug Pull Toy			10"x8" tall, wood	80	145	225
Spark Plug Squeaker Toy		1923	5" long, rubber with squeaker in mouth	14	25	40

Barney Google

TOY	COMPANY	YEAR	DESCRIPTION	GOOD	EX	MIB
Spark Plug Toy		1920s	5" tall, wood construction on wheels	45	90	135

Batman

TOY	COMPANY	YEAR	DESCRIPTION	GOOD	EX	MIB
Bat Bomb	Mattel	1966		40	70	110
Bat Cycle	Toy Biz			5	10	15
Batboat	Duncan	1987	12x8" on card	18	35	50
Batboat Pullstring Toy	Eidai (Japan)			60	115	175
Batman & Robin Society Button	Button World	1966	Large size pinback button	11	20	30
Batman Action Figure	Takara	1989	12" tall doll in box	45	80	125
Batman Action Figure	Biken	1989	8" tall on card	11	20	30
Batman Baterang Bagatelle	Marx	1966	Colorful bagatelle game in long, illustrated box showing Batman, Robin, and Batman knocking down a crook in a bright yellow suit	60	110	165
Batman Bendie Action Figure	Bully	1989	7" tall bendie	14	25	40
Batman Bendie Figure	Deline	1960s	On card	45	80	125
Batman Candy Cigarettes	(England)	1960s		25	45	65
Batman Cast and Paint Set		1960s	Plaster casting mold and paint set	25	50	75
Batman Cereal Bank		1989	Figural bank given away with Batman Cereal	4	7	10
Batman Charm Bracelet			On card	25	50	75
Batman Christmas Ornament	Presents	1989		7	13	20
Batman Colorforms		1976		12	23	35
Batman Crazy Foam		1974	Metal car, plastic top, artwork on both	25	50	75
Batman Figure	Applause		12" tall with stand	18	35	50
Batman Give-A-Show Projector Cards	Kenner	1960s	Set of four slide cards in package	45	80	125
Batman Kid's Belt		1960s	Elastic belt with bronze logo buckle	25	45	65
Batman Kite	Hiflyer	1982		4	7	10
Batman Oil Paint By Numbers Set	Hasbro	1966	In 9 1/2x13" box	16	30	45
Batman Pencil Box	Empire Pencil Co.	1966	Gun shaped pencil box with set of Batman pencils, on card	23	40	65
Batman Pinball Game	Marx	1960s	Tin litho with plastic casing	25	50	75
Batman Radio Belt and Buckle		1966		25	50	75
Batman Raygun		1960s	7" long blue and black futuristic space gun with bat sights and bats on handgrip	80	145	225
Batman Road Race Set		1960s	Slot car racing set	90	165	250
Batman Shooting Arcade	AHI	1970s	Graphics of Joker, Catwoman and Penguin against brightly colored Gotham City background	25	50	75
Batman Slot Car	Magicar (England)	1966	5" long Batmobile being driven by Batman and Robin in illustrated display window box	115	210	325
Batman Soakie				23	45	65
Batman Standing Figure on Base	Presents		15 1/2" tall vinyl and cloth figure	9	16	25

Batman

TOY	COMPANY	YEAR	DESCRIPTION	GOOD	EX	MIB
Batman String Puppet	Madison	1977		25	50	75
Batman Stuffed Doll Plush	Commonwealth	1960s		105	195	300
Batman Super Powers Stain & Paint Set		1984		5	10	15
Batman Superfriends Lite Brite Refill Pack		1980		9	16	25
Batman Superhero Stamp Set		1970s		9	16	25
Batman Talking Alarm Clock	Janex	1975	Molded plastic clock with bat logo at center of face and Batman figure running beside Batmobile with Robin driving	20	35	55
Batman Utility Belt	Remco	1979	Includes handcuffs, communicator, decoder glasses, watch, Gotham City decoder map, ID card and secret message	23	45	65
Batman, Robin and Superman Costume Patterns	McCalls	1960s	Complete patterns for making all three costumes in paper envelope	12	23	35
Batmobile	Duncan	1987	12x8" on card	18	35	50
Batmobile	Corgi	1966	5" long in display box	85	130	175
Batmobile	Toy Biz			9	16	25
Batmobile	Simms	1960s	Plastic car on card	18	33	50
Batmobile	AHI	1972	11" long tin litho battery op. mystery action car with blinking light and jet engine noise	90	165	250
Batmobile & Batboat Set	Corgi			200	300	400
Batmobile AM Radio	Bandai			45	80	125
Batmobile, Motorized Kit	Aoshinu (Japan)	1980s		30	55	85
Batmobile, Motorized Kit	Aoshinu (Japan)	1980s	Smaller snap kit	20	40	60
Batmobile, Pullback	Bandai	1980s	Pullback vehicle with machine guns	35	60	95
Batmobile, Radio Controlled	Matsushiro			60	115	175
Batmobile, Radio Controlled	Apollo (Japan)			60	115	175
Batwing	Toy Biz			12	23	35
DC Comics Robin Figure	Palitoy		8" figure on card	25	45	70
Inflatable TV Chair		1982	In box	16	30	45
Joker Cycle	Toy Biz			5	10	15
Joker Figure	Presents		15" vinyl figure	11	20	30
Joker Mobile	Corgi	1975	Model #99, white van with Joker decals, on card	16	30	45
Joker Van	Ertl	1989	Die cast vehicle on card	4	8	12
Joker Watch	Fossil	1980s		25	50	75
Joker Wind-up	Billiken	1989		45	80	125
Joker YoYo		1980s	On card	4	7	10
Penguin Mobile	Corgi	1970s		35	55	75
Riddler Music Box		1978	Ceramic figural music box	25	50	75
Robin Christmas Ornament	Presents	1989		7	13	20
Robin Shuttle	Mego	1979	Sized for British made Mego figures, in box	9	16	25
Robin Soakie				23	45	65

Batman

TOY	COMPANY	YEAR	DESCRIPTION	GOOD	EX	MIB
Robin Standing Figure on Base	Presents		Cloth and vinyl standing figure on base	9	16	25
Super Accelerator Batmobile	AHI	1970s	On card	11	20	30
View-Master Set	View-Master	1960s	Set of three reels in package	7	13	20

Beany & Cecil

TOY	COMPANY	YEAR	DESCRIPTION	GOOD	EX	MIB
Beanie Doll			Closed eyes version	90	165	250
Beany & Cecil & Their Pals Record Player	Vanity Fair	1961		19	35	55
Beany & Cecil Animated Clock			Wood	700	1300	2000
Beany & Cecil Carrying Case			9" diameter with strap, vinyl covered cardboard	9	16	25
Beany & Cecil Play Luggage Set	Mattel	1962		18	35	50
Beany & Cecil Propeller Disks	Mattel	1961		35	65	100
Beany & Cecil Round Travel Case		1960s	8" tall red vinyl case with zipper and strap	25	50	75
Beany & Cecil Skill Ball		1960s	Colorful tin with wood frame	16	30	45
Beany & Cecil Square Travel Case		1960s	4 1/2x3 1/2x3" red vinyl case with carrying strap, illustrated with characters on four sides	35	65	100
Beany Figure	Caltoy	1984	8" tall	5	10	15
Beany Talking Doll	Mattel	1960s	17" tall, stuffed cloth, vinyl head with a pull string voice box	55	105	160
Bob Clampetts' Beany Coloring Book	Whitman	1960s		18	35	50
Captain Huffenpuff Puzzle		1961	Large puzzle	16	30	45
Cecil and His Disguise Kit	Mattel	1962	17" tall plush Cecil with disguise wigs, mustaches, etc.	30	55	85
Cecil in the Music Box	Mattel	1961		45	90	135
Cecil Soakie			8 1/2" tall, plastic	18	35	50
Cecil Talking Doll	Mattel	1965	17" tall, stuffed cloth, vinyl head with a pull string voice box	55	105	160
Leakin' Lena Plastic Boat	Irwin	1962		60	115	175
Leakin' Lena Pound 'n Pull Toy	Pressman	1960s	Wood	50	90	140

Betty Boop

TOY	COMPANY	YEAR	DESCRIPTION	GOOD	EX	MIB
Betty Boop	NJ Croce	1988	Bend-n-flex 9" figure	4	8	12
Betty Boop	M-Toy	1986	Outfits for 12" dolls high fashion boutique, each	4	7	10
Betty Boop 3" Figure			3" collectible PVC figure eight different poses and outfits, each	2	3	5
Betty Boop Delivery Truck	Schylling Assn., Inc.	1990	Tin litho	16	30	45
Betty Boop Doll 12"	M-Toy	1986	Vinyl jointed with six different outfits, fur coat, winter woolens, Mae West-pink gown, Flapper, business suit or ballerina	9	16	25

Blondie & Dagwood

TOY	COMPANY	YEAR	DESCRIPTION	GOOD	EX	MIB
Blondie Featured Funnies Jigsaw Puzzle		1930s	9 1/2"x14" puzzle	23	40	65
Blondie Paint Book	Whitman	1947	8 1/2"x11"	18	35	50
Blondie Paint Set	American Crayon Co.	1946		16	30	45
Blondie Paper Doll Book	Whitman	1944		45	90	135
Blondie Paper Doll Book	Whitman	1955	Paper dolls and clothes	25	50	80
Blondie's Peg Board Set	King Features	1934	9"x15 1/2", multi-colored pegs, hammer, cut-outs of Dagwood, Blondie, etc.	55	100	150
Blondie's Presto Slate	Presto Productions	1944	10"x13" illustration of Blondie & Dagwood and other characters	20	35	55
Dagwood & Kids Figures	K.F.S.	1944	Dagwood 5" tall, included are: Alexander & Cookie	20	35	55
Dagwood Marionette		1945	14"	65	120	185
Dagwood's Solo Flight Airplane	Marx	1935	12" wingspan, plane 9" in length	200	300	400
Lucky Safety Card		1953	2"x4" cards, Dagwood warns you about playing in safe areas	9	16	25
Miniature Blondie Figure		1940s	2 1/2" tall, lead	7	13	20
Miniature Dagwood Figure			2 3/4" tall, lead	7	13	20

Bonanza

TOY	COMPANY	YEAR	DESCRIPTION	GOOD	EX	MIB
Ben Cartwright with Palomino	American Character	1966		50	90	140
Bonanza Figures on Buckboard with Three Horses and Accessories	American Character			80	145	225
Bonanza Jigsaw Puzzle	Milton Bradley	1964	Jigsaw puzzle	12	23	35
Four in One Wagon	American Character			105	195	300
Hoss Cartwright with Stallion	American Character	1966		50	90	140
Little Joe Cartwright with Pinto	American Character	1966		55	100	150
Mustang	American Character		The Outlaw's horse	23	45	65
Outlaw, The	American Character	1966		40	70	110
Palomino	American Character		Ben's horse	23	45	65
Pinto	American Character		Little Joe's horse	23	45	65
Stallion	American Character		Hoss's horse	23	45	65

Bozo

TOY	COMPANY	YEAR	DESCRIPTION	GOOD	EX	MIB
Bozo the Clown			Stuffed doll	9	16	25
Bozo the Clown Figure		1970s	Vinyl figure 5" tall	5	10	15
Bozo the Clown Push Button Marionette	Knickerbocker	1962		35	65	100

Top to Bottom: Green Hornet Movie Viewer, 1966, Greenway Prod.; Mr. Potato Head Ice Pop Molds, Hasbro; Dragnet Badge 714, 1955, Sherry T.V. Inc.; Charlie's Angels Underwater Intrigue Outfit, 1970s, Palitoy.

Bozo

TOY	COMPANY	YEAR	DESCRIPTION	GOOD	EX	MIB
Bozo the Clown Slide Puzzle		1960s	2 1/2"x2 1/2"	16	30	45
Bozo the Clown Soakie	Stephen Riley Co.			11	20	30
Bozo the Clown Towel		1960s	Beach towel 16"x24"	16	30	45
Bozo Trick Trapeze		1960s	Red base	20	35	55

Bringing Up Father

TOY	COMPANY	YEAR	DESCRIPTION	GOOD	EX	MIB
Bringing Up Father Paint Book with Jiggs & Maggie			8 1/2"x11"	15	30	45
Maggie Statue			12" tall	30	55	85

Bugs Bunny

TOY	COMPANY	YEAR	DESCRIPTION	GOOD	EX	MIB
Bugs Bunny			Wearing Uncle Sam outfit	11	20	30
Bugs Bunny	Dakin			7	13	20
Bugs Bunny "Chatter Chum"	Mattel	1982		9	16	25
Bugs Bunny & Tweety Bird Costume	Collegeville	1960s	Thin plastic mask & one piece costume	9	16	25
Bugs Bunny Bank		1940s	5 3/4"x5 1/2", pot metal barrel bank with figure on base	45	80	125
Bugs Bunny Bank	Dakin	1971	On a basket of carrots	16	30	45
Bugs Bunny Bendable Figure	Applause	1980s	4" tall	4	8	12
Bugs Bunny Charm Bracelet		1950s	Brass charms of Bugs Bunny, Tweety, Sniffles, Fudd, etc.	20	35	55
Bugs Bunny Clock	Litech	1972	12"x14"	23	45	65
Bugs Bunny Colorforms		1958	Bugs Bunny, Tweety Bird and Elmer	23	45	65
Bugs Bunny Figure	Warner Bros.	1975	2 3/4" tall, ceramic	12	23	35
Bugs Bunny Figure	Dakin	1971	10" tall	11	20	30
Bugs Bunny Figure	Dakin	1976	Yellow globes in "Cartoon Theater" box	9	16	25
Bugs Bunny Figure Holding Carrot	Warner Bros.	1975	5 1/2" tall, ceramic	12	23	35
Bugs Bunny in Uncle Sam Outfit	Dakin	1976	Distributed through Great America Theme Park, Illinois	23	45	65
Bugs Bunny Mini Snowdome	Applause	1980s		5	10	15
Bugs Bunny Musical Ge-tar	Mattel	1977		9	16	25
Bugs Bunny Nitelite	Applause	1980s		5	10	15
Bugs Bunny Soakie			Soft rubber	9	16	25
Bugs Bunny Talking Alarm Clock				18	35	50
Bugs Bunny Talking Doll	Mattel	1971		25	50	75
Bugs Bunny Wristwatch	Lafayette	1978		14	25	40

Captain America

TOY	COMPANY	YEAR	DESCRIPTION	GOOD	EX	MIB
Captain America Bendie Figure	Lakeside			45	80	125
Captain America Rocket Racer	Buddy-L	1984	Secret Wars remote controlled battery operated car	14	25	40

Captain Midnight

TOY	COMPANY	YEAR	DESCRIPTION	GOOD	EX	MIB
Air Heroes Stamp Album		1930s	Twelve stamps	25	50	75
Captain Midnight Cup			Plastic, 4" tall, "Ovaltine-The Heart of a Hearty Breakfast"	23	45	65
Captain Midnight Medal		1930s	Gold medal pin with centered wings and words "Flight Commander" embossed. Capt. is embossed on top with medal dangling beneath	55	100	150
Captain Midnight Secret Society Decoder		1949	Used to decode messages only known by "Society" members	20	35	55
Membership Manual		1930s	Secret Squadron official code and manual guide	25	50	75

Captain Video

TOY	COMPANY	YEAR	DESCRIPTION	GOOD	EX	MIB
Rocket Launcher	Lido	1952		50	95	145

Cartoon & Comic Characters

TOY	COMPANY	YEAR	DESCRIPTION	GOOD	EX	MIB
Alfred E. Neuman Bust Figurine		1960s	Base says "What Me Worry?"	55	105	165
Andy Panda Bank	Walter Lantz Prod.	1977	7" tall hard plastic bank	14	25	40
Banana Splits Mug		1969	Plastic yellow dog mug	5	10	15
Banana Splits Record	Kelloggs	1969		9	16	25
Banana Splits Stuffed Figure	General Mills	1960s	12" tall Drooper figure	23	45	65
Bloom County Opus Doll		1986	10" tall, plush Christmas Cheer doll Opus wearing a Santa Claus cap	5	10	15
Cadbury the Butler Figure, (Ritchie Rich)	DFC	1981	3 1/2" figure on illustrated card	7	13	20
Casper, Popeye, Chipmunks, Dick Tracy, Bozo, Mr. Ed	Kenner	1965	Easy Show movie projector movies, each	9	16	25
Chilly Willy Figure	Walter Lantz Prod.	1982	Plush	5	10	15
Cool Cat Figure		1969	Vinyl 9" tall	23	45	65
Daffy Dog in "The Morning After" Poster			10"x13"	9	16	25
Dan Dunn Pin Back Button		1930s	1 1/4"	25	50	75
Doggie Daddy Metal Trivet		1960s	Says "You have to work like a dog to live like one"	12	23	35
Dudley Doright Doll	Wham-O	1972	Bendable	7	13	20
Dudley Doright Jigsaw Puzzle	Whitman	1975	Dudley and Snidley	7	13	20
Favorite Funnies Printing Set		1930s	Set no. 4004, Orphan Annie, Herby & Dick Tracy, six stamps, pad, paper and instructions	55	105	165
Geoffrey Jack-In-The-Box	Toys-R-Us	1970s	1/2"x5 1/2"x5 1/2" tin litho	12	23	35
Goober Bank			Vinyl figural bank	20	35	55
Hagar the Horrible Doll		1983	12" tall	9	16	25

Cartoon & Comic Characters

TOY	COMPANY	YEAR	DESCRIPTION	GOOD	EX	MIB
Hair Bear Bunch Square Bear Figural Mug		1978		4	8	12
Hair Bear Bunch Wristwatch		1972	Medium gold tone case, base metal back, articulated hands, red leather snap down band	60	115	175
Harold Teen Playstone Funnies Mold Set		1940s		35	60	95
Henry on Trapeze Toy	G. Borgfeldt Co.		6"x9", celluloid, wind-up, jointed Henry suspended from trapeze	155	295	450
Herman and Katnip Punch Out Kite	Saalfield	1960s	Folds into a kite	14	25	40
Hollie Hobbie Wristwatch	Bradley	1982	Small gold tone case, base metal back, yellow plastic band,	5	10	15
Houndcats Board Game	Milton Bradley	1970s		9	16	25
Incredible Hulk Action Figure	Palitoy		8" figure on card	11	20	30
Jets Photo Album & Cards		1950s	64 cards	23	45	65
Katzenjammer Kids Featured Funnies Jigsaw Puzzle		1930s	9 1/2"x14" puzzle	30	55	85
King Leonardo and his Loyal Subjects Board Game	Milton Bradley	1960		25	50	80
King Leonardo Doll	Holiday Fair	1960s	Cloth stuffed doll dressed in his royal robe	35	60	95
Lil' Abner Mugs		1940s	Four ceramic mugs: Abner, Daisy, Pappy & Mammy Yokum	90	165	250
Little Audrey Dress Designer Kit	Saalfield	1962	Die cut doll and 29 clothing accessories in illustrated box	12	23	35
Little Audrey Shoulder Bag Leathercraft Kit	Jewel	1961		30	55	85
Little Lulu Bank			8" tall hard plastic with black fire hydrant	11	20	30
Little Lulu Dish		1940s	5 1/2" hand painted ceramic dish with pictures of Lulu, Tubby and her friend	50	95	145
Mary Marvel Wristwatch	Marvel Imp.	1948	Small chrome case, face shows profile of Mary flying up toward one o'clock	60	115	175
Merlin Mouse Figure	Dakin			7	13	20
Mush Mouse Pull Toy	Ideal	1960s	Pull toy with vinyl figure	45	80	125
Nancy Music Box	UFS Inc.	1968	Ceramic music box	30	55	85
Peter Potamus Bubbles Soakie			11" tall	12	23	35
Rosie's Beau Featured Funnies Jigsaw Puzzle		1930s	9 1/2"x14" puzzle	20	40	60
Scrappy Bank			3"x3 1/2" metal bank with an embossed illustration of Scrappy and his dog	35	60	95
Smilin' Jack Featured Funnies Jigsaw Puzzle		1930s	9 1/2"x14" puzzle	23	45	65
Smokey the Bear Bank			8" tall, Smokey waves and holds shovel	12	23	35
Smokey the Bear Figure	Dakin		8 1/2" tall plastic figure with cloth parts and shovel	12	23	35
Spider-Man Bend'em Figure	Just Toys	1991	#12056, Marvel Super Heroes Series, on card	2	4	6

Cartoon & Comic Characters

TOY	COMPANY	YEAR	DESCRIPTION	GOOD	EX	MIB
Spider-Man Spider Cycle, Spider Copter, Spider Van Set	Buddy-L	1984	Secret Wars vehicle set	16	30	45
Spider-Man Spider Racer Car	Buddy-L	1984	Secret Wars remote controlled battery operated car	14	25	40
Strawberry Shortcake Wristwatch		1970s		9	16	25
Super Heroes Flashy Flickers Filmstrip Reel		1960s	Filmstrip cartoons with Wonder Woman, Aquaman & Tomahawk	9	16	25
Supercar Moulding Colour Kit	Sculptorcraft	1960s	Set of rubber plaster casting models of vehicle and show characters, including Mike Mercury, Beaker and Popkiss, Jimmy and Mitch, Masterspy	35	60	95
Touche Turtle Soakie				16	30	45
Winnie Winkle Playstone Funnies Mold Set		1940s		45	80	125
Wonder Woman Standing Figure on Base	Presents		14" tall cloth and vinyl figure on base	9	16	25
Yipee Pull Toy	Ideal	1960s	Pull toy with vinyl figure of Yipee, Yapee & Yahoee	50	95	145

Casper the Friendly Ghost

TOY	COMPANY	YEAR	DESCRIPTION	GOOD	EX	MIB
Casper Doll	Sutton & Sons	1972	Rubber squeeze doll with logo	12	23	35
Casper Doll		1960s	15" cloth	25	45	70
Casper Figure Lamp	Archlamp Mfg.	1950	17" tall	25	50	75
Casper Halloween Costume	Collegeville	1960s	Mask and costume	16	30	45
Casper Hand Puppet			8" tall, cloth and plastic head	18	35	50
Casper Light Shade		1960s	Features Casper & his friends	12	23	35
Casper Night Light	Duncan	1975	6 1/2" tall	18	35	50
Casper Puffy Sticker	Chex Cereal (Ralston Purina)	1970s	Glows in the dark	9	16	25
Casper Soakie				12	23	35
Casper Spinning Top		1960s	Blue top with figure of Casper inside	16	30	45
Casper Stand Up		1960s	18"x10"	30	55	85
Casper the Friendly Ghost Vinyl Doll			7 3/4" tall squeeze doll holds black spotted puppy	30	55	85
Casper Wind-up Toy	Linemar	1950s	Tin	70	130	200
Casper, The Friendly Ghost Four Jigsaw Puzzles	Ja-Ru	1988		2	4	6
Casper, The Friendly Ghost Game	Schaper	1974		7	13	20
Casper, The Friendly Ghost Pinball Game	Ja-Ru	1988		2	4	6
I'm Casper the Friendly Ghost Talking Doll	Mattel	1961	15" tall, terrycloth, plastic head with a pull string voice box	45	80	125
Wendy the Good Witch Soakie				9	16	25

Charlie Chaplin

TOY	COMPANY	YEAR	DESCRIPTION	GOOD	EX	MIB
Charlie Chaplin Character			8 1/2" tall, tin with cast iron feet, wind-up	325	600	925
Charlie Chaplin Doll			11 1/2" tall, wind-up	155	295	450
Charlie Chaplin Novelty Toy			4" tall, spring mechanism tips his hat when string is pulled	12	23	35
Charlie Chaplin Pencil Case			8" long	19	35	55
Charlie Chaplin Quartz Watch	Bradley	1985	Oldies series, large black plastic case and band, sweep seconds, shows Chaplin as Little Tramp	16	30	45
Charlie Chaplin Toy			7" tall, plastic	23	45	65
Charlie Chaplin Wristwatch	Bubbles/ Cadeaux	1972	Swiss, large chrome case, black and white dial, articulated sweep cane second hand, black leather band	45	80	125
Miniature Charlie Chaplin			2 1/2" tall, lead	19	35	55

Charlie's Angels

TOY	COMPANY	YEAR	DESCRIPTION	GOOD	EX	MIB
Cheryl Ladd Figure	Mattel	1978	12" tall	16	30	45
Farrah Fawcett-Majors Figure	Remco	1977	In swim suit	16	30	45
Kate Jackson Figure	Mattel	1978	12" tall	16	30	45
Kelly	Hasbro	1977		8	15	22
Kris	Hasbro	1977		8	14	22
River Race Outfits	Palitoy	1977		16	30	45
Sabrina	Hasbro	1977		8	14	22
Sabrina, Kelly and Kris Gift Set	Hasbro	1977		16	30	45
Slalom Caper Outfits	Palitoy			14	25	40
Underwater Intrigue Outfits	Palitoy			14	25	40

Chipmunks

TOY	COMPANY	YEAR	DESCRIPTION	GOOD	EX	MIB
Alvin Plush Doll	Knickerbocker	1963	14" tall plush doll with vinyl head	16	30	45
Alvin Soakie		1960s	8" tall	9	16	25
Chipmunks Toothbrush		1984	Battery operated	7	13	20
Chipmunks Wallet		1959	Vinyl	5	10	15
Soakie, Alvin, Theodore or Simon		1960s	10" tall, plastic & vinyl, each	5	10	15

Cinderella

TOY	COMPANY	YEAR	DESCRIPTION	GOOD	EX	MIB
Cinderella & Prince Wind-up Toy	Irwin		5" tall, plastic	35	65	100
Cinderella Alarm Clock	Westclox		2 1/2"x4 1/2"x4' tall	35	65	100
Cinderella Bank		1950s	Ceramic with Cinderella holding a magic wand	16	30	45
Cinderella Charm Bracelet		1950	Golden brass link with five charms, Cinderella, Fairy Godmother, slipper, pumpkin coach and Prince	25	50	75
Cinderella Doll	Horsman		8" tall classic doll in illustrated box	12	23	35

Cinderella

TOY	COMPANY	YEAR	DESCRIPTION	GOOD	EX	MIB
Cinderella Doll			11" tall, blue stain ballgown with white bridal gown, glass slippers, holding Little Little Golden Book	20	35	55
Cinderella Figurine			5" tall, ceramic	9	16	25
Cinderella Figurine			5" tall, plastic	5	10	15
Cinderella Molding Set	Model Craft	1950s	Set of character molds in illustrated box	45	80	125
Cinderella Musical Jewelry Box			Mahogany musical box which plays "So This Is Love"	20	35	55
Cinderella Paper Dolls	Whitman	1965	Included are: Cinderella, Stepmother, Anastasia, Drizella, Prince plus clothes for each doll	23	45	65
Cinderella Puzzle	Jaymar	1960s	9 1/2"x12 1/2"	12	23	35
Cinderella Soakie		1960s	11" tall blue bubble bath container	11	20	30
Cinderella Story Book	Whitman	1950		5	10	15
Cinderella Wind-up Toy	Irwin	1950	5" tall with Cinderalla & Prince dancing	55	100	150
Cinderella Wristwatch	US Time	1950		45	80	125
Cinderella Wristwatch	Timex	1958	Small chrome case shows Cinderella in foreground with castle at 12 o'clock, pink leather band	45	80	125
Cinderella Wristwatch	Bradley	1970s	Basemetal, small gold bezel, picture and "Cinderella" on face, pink leather band	16	30	45
Fairy Godmother Pitcher			7" tall figural	25	50	75
Gus Doll	Gund	1950s	13" tall, gray doll with dark red shirt & green felt hat	60	115	175
Gus/Jaq Serving Set	Westman	1960s	Creamer, pitcher and sugar bowl	45	80	125
Prince Charming Hand Puppet	Gund	1959	10" tall	25	50	75

Crusader Rabbit

TOY	COMPANY	YEAR	DESCRIPTION	GOOD	EX	MIB
Crusader Rabbit Book	Wonder Book	1958		12	23	35
Crusader Rabbit in Bubble Trouble Book	Whitman	1960		9	16	25
Crusader Rabbit Trace & Color Book	Whitman	1959		18	35	50
Paint Set			13x19"	20	35	55

Daffy Duck

TOY	COMPANY	YEAR	DESCRIPTION	GOOD	EX	MIB
Daffy Duck Bendable Figure	Applause	1980s	4" tall	9	16	25
Daffy Duck Figural Bank	Applause	1980s		9	16	25
Daffy Duck Figure	Dakin	1968	8 1/2" tall	11	20	30
Daffy Duck Mug			Large size plastic	2	5	7

Danger Mouse

TOY	COMPANY	YEAR	DESCRIPTION	GOOD	EX	MIB
Danger Mouse Doll	Russ	1988	15" tall	18	35	50
Danger Mouse I.D. Set	Gordy	1985		7	13	20

Danger Mouse

TOY	COMPANY	YEAR	DESCRIPTION	GOOD	EX	MIB
Danger Mouse Pendant Necklace	Gordy	1986		5	10	15

Davy Crockett

TOY	COMPANY	YEAR	DESCRIPTION	GOOD	EX	MIB
Davy Crockett Figure	Marx	1964	6" tall, vinyl	11	20	30
Davy Crockett Figure	Marx		2" tall, rubber figure, cream color with "Official Davy Crockett As Portrayed by Fess Parker" under base	25	50	75
Davy Crockett Guitar		1955	11x24x1 1/2" varnished plywood guitar shaped like a bell	45	80	125
Davy Crockett Jigsaw Puzzle	Marx		14"x19" titled "Siege on the Fort"	16	30	45
Davy Crockett Official Wallet		1955	Wallet contains calendar card for 1966 and 1956, in box	18	35	50
Davy Crockett Puzzle	Whitman	1955	11 1/4"x15"	11	20	30
Davy Crockett Puzzle	Jaymar		8"x10"x2"	16	30	45
Davy Crockett Travel Bag	Neevel	1950s	6 1/2"x12"x10" heavy cardboard with brass hinges & plastic handle	35	65	100

Dennis the Menace

TOY	COMPANY	YEAR	DESCRIPTION	GOOD	EX	MIB
Dennis the Menace & Ruff Book Ends		1974	Ceramic	18	35	50
Dennis the Menace Colorform Kit	Colorforms	1961		16	30	45
Dennis the Menace Giant Mischief Kit	Hasbro	1950s	Snap gum, spilled ink, floating sugar and etc.	35	60	95
Dennis the Menace Inlay Jigsaw Puzzle	Whitman	1960		12	23	35
Dennis the Menace Paint Set	Pressman	1954	Paints, crayons, brush and trays	35	60	95

Deputy Dawg

TOY	COMPANY	YEAR	DESCRIPTION	GOOD	EX	MIB
Deputy Dawg Figure	Dakin	1977	6" tall, plastic body with vinyl head	25	50	75
Deputy Dawg Soakie Bath Soap Container		1966	9 1/2" tall, plastic	9	16	25
Deputy Dawg Stuffed Doll	Ideal	1960s	14" tall, cloth with plush arms & vinyl head	25	50	75

Dick Tracy

TOY	COMPANY	YEAR	DESCRIPTION	GOOD	EX	MIB
"The Capture of Boris Arson" Story Book	Pleasure Books, Inc.	1935	Pop-up book	95	180	275
2-Way Electronic Wrist Radios	Remco	1960s	5", battery operated set	55	100	150
2-Way Wrist Radio Set	Am. Doll & Toy	1960s	Plastic with power pack, battery operated	45	80	125
Air Detective Badge - Member		1939	Brass, star shape	30	55	85
Air Detective Cap		1938		35	65	100
B.O. Plenty & Sparkle Wind-up Toy	Marx	1940s	8 1/2" tall	190	275	350
Big Boy & Police Car	Playmates	1990		11	20	30

Top to Bottom: Bullwinkle Radio, 1960s, Ward Productions; Secret Squirrel and Magilla Gorilla Push Button Puppets, 1960s, Kohner Brothers; Disneyland Rollercoaster, Chein; Lone Ranger Movie Film Ring, 1950s, General Mills; Dick Tracy Flashlight, 1940s, Bantam Lite.

Dick Tracy

TOY	COMPANY	YEAR	DESCRIPTION	GOOD	EX	MIB
Bonny Braids Stroll Toy	Charmore	1951		55	100	150
Breathless Mahoney Figure	Applause	1990	14" tall	9	16	25
Button with Dick Tracy & Little Orphan Annie	Genung Promo			25	50	75
Chicago Tribune Suspender Set				35	65	100
Click Pistol No. 36	Marx			35	65	100
Convertible Squad Car	Marx	1948	22", friction power with flashing lights	105	195	300
Copmobile	Ideal	1963	24" plastic with sirens, battery operated	80	145	225
Crime Stoppers Set		1961	Handcuffs, nightstick & badge	45	80	125
Deluxe Dick Tracy Set			Suspenders, badge, whistle & magnifying glass	80	145	225
Detective Badge		1930s	Leather "secret" pouch	45	80	125
Detective Button			Celluloid with portrait	14	25	40
Detective Club Badge "Crime Stoppers"	Guild	1937		35	65	100
Detective Club Belt		1937	Leather "secret" pouch	35	65	95
Detective Club Pin		1942	Yellow, tab back	30	50	80
Detective Fingerprint Set		1933		80	145	225
Dick Tracy Air Detective Ring		1938		30	55	85
Dick Tracy Baking Set		1937	8 cookie cutters, bright colored press out pictures of Dick Tracy and his pals	55	100	150
Dick Tracy Bendie	Lakeside			18	35	50
Dick Tracy Black Light Magic Kit	Stroward	1952	Ultra-violet bulb, cloth, invisible pen, brushes & fluorescent dyes	35	60	95
Dick Tracy Braces for Smart Boys & Girls			12"x6", set of matching suspenders with badge, whistle & magnifying glass	25	50	75
Dick Tracy Candid Camera	Seymour Sales Co.		3x3x5 1/4" with 50mm lens, plastic carrying case & 127 film	70	130	200
Dick Tracy Chalk Figure	Professional Art	1940s	7" unpainted detailed white chalk figure	80	145	225
Dick Tracy Christmas Bulb		1930s	Early figure of Dick Tracy	16	30	45
Dick Tracy Colorforms	Colorforms	1962		16	30	45
Dick Tracy Coloring Book	Saalfield	1946	9"x11"	12	23	35
Dick Tracy Detective Set	Pressman	1930s	Color graphics of Junior and Dick Tracy, ink roller, glass plate, and Dick Tracy fingerprint record paper	60	105	165
Dick Tracy Enameled Portrait Ring	Quaker Oats	1937		40	70	110
Dick Tracy Featured Funnies Jigsaw Puzzle		1930s	9 1/2"x14" puzzle	30	55	85
Dick Tracy Hand Puppet	Ideal	1961	10 1/2" tall, fabric & vinyl, with record	55	100	150
Dick Tracy Handcuffs	John Henry	1946		35	65	100
Dick Tracy Hat				35	65	100
Dick Tracy Jigsaw Puzzle	Jaymar	1960s	10"x14"	12	23	35
Dick Tracy Jr. Click Pistol No. 78	Marx		Aluminum	35	65	100

Dick Tracy

TOY	COMPANY	YEAR	DESCRIPTION	GOOD	EX	MIB
Dick Tracy Junior Detective Kit	Golden	1962	Punchout book of Tracy tools, including badges, revolver, wrist radio	45	80	125
Dick Tracy Mask	Philadelphia Inquire	1930s	1 1/2" full color paper mask	45	80	125
Dick Tracy Puzzle	Jaymar		14x22"	12	23	35
Dick Tracy Secret Compartment Ring		1938		45	90	135
Dick Tracy Soakie		1965	9" tall, plastic	25	50	75
Dick Tracy Sparkle Paint Set	Kenner	1960s	Color cartoon graphics	16	30	45
Dick Tracy Sub-machine Gun	Tops Plastics	1948	12" long	35	60	95
Dick Tracy Super Detectice Book	Whitman			7	13	20
Flashlight	Bantam Lite	1940s	Hand size, metal	23	45	65
G-Man Gun			Wind-up	35	65	100
Joe Jitsu Hand Puppet	Ideal	1961	10 1/2" tall, fabric & vinyl	25	50	75
Junior Detective Kit	Sweets Co. of Am.	1945	Certificate, secret code dial, wall chart, file cards & tape measure	60	115	175
Little Honey Moon Doll	Ideal	1965	16" space baby, bubble helmet and outfit with white pigtails, doll sitting on half a moon with stars in the background	60	105	165
Moviescope Viewer		1940s	Two films included	55	100	150
Pocket Watch	Bradley	1959		60	115	175
Private Telephones		1939		55	100	150
Riot Car		1946	7 1/2", friction power	70	130	200
Secret Code Dial		1945		18	35	50
Secret Detector Kit		1938	Secret Formula Q-11 & negatives	55	100	150
Secret Service Patrol Badge - Captain		1938		55	100	150
Secret Service Patrol Badge - Girl's Division		1938	Litho	18	35	50
Secret Service Patrol Badge - Inspector General		1938		80	145	225
Secret Service Patrol Badge - Lieutenant		1938		45	80	125
Secret Service Patrol Badge - Member		1939	2nd yr. Chevron	25	50	75
Secret Service Patrol Badge - Sergeant		1938		30	55	85
Secret Service Patrol Bar Pin - Leader		1938	Litho	16	30	45
Secret Service Patrol Bracelet		1938		30	55	85
Secret Service Patrol Member Button		1938	1 1/4" blue & silver, pinback	16	30	45
Secret Service Patrol Sergeant Badge				19	35	55
Siren Code Pencil		1939		45	80	125
Siren Pistol	Marx	1930s		55	100	150
Siren Police Whistle No. 64	Marx		Tin	35	65	100
Six Shooter Wristwatch	Marx	1948		115	210	325
Sparkle Plenty Doll	Ideal	1947		55	100	150
Sparkle Plenty Savings Bank	Jayess Co.		12" tall, plastic	200	375	575

Dick Tracy

TOY	COMPANY	YEAR	DESCRIPTION	GOOD	EX	MIB
Sparkling Pop Pistol No. 96	Marx			55	100	150
Squad Car	Marx		9" green plastic, remote control with siren	95	180	275
Squad Car	Marx		18", tin, friction power	115	210	325
Squad Car #1			6 1/2", tin, wind-up or battery operated option	95	180	275
Steve the Tramp Figure	Playmates	1990		9	16	25
Sub-machine Gun			12" plastic, Tops	35	65	100
Sub-machine Gun Raider		1946		45	80	125
Suspect Wall Chart		1945		25	50	75
Suspenders & Badge on Card		1940		30	55	85
Tape Measure				14	25	40
Target Game	Marx			125	175	275
Target Play Set	Placo	1982	Dartgun, eight villains & handcuffs	45	80	125
Target with Gould Art		1960s	17" diameter	80	145	225
Wristwatch	New Haven	1937	Oblong face	95	180	275
Wristwatch	New Haven	1937	Round face	60	115	175
Wristwatch	New Haven	1948		90	165	250
Wristwatch with Animated Gun	New Haven	1951		115	210	325

Disney

TOY	COMPANY	YEAR	DESCRIPTION	GOOD	EX	MIB
20,000 Leagues Under the Sea Board Game	Gardner	1950s	8x16x1 1/2"	12	23	35
2nd National Duck Bank	Chein		3 1/2" tallx7" long	85	145	185
Aristocats Thomas O'Malley Figure	Enesco	1967	8" tall ceramic figure	35	65	100
Black Hole Puzzle	Whitman	1979	Jigsaw puzzle 9"x11", V.I.N.C.E.N.T. or Cygnus	4	8	12
Carousel	Linemar		7" tall with 3" figures, wind-up	50	95	145
Casey Jr. Disneyland Express Train	Marx	1950s	12" long, tin, wind-up	175	275	350
Character Molding & Coloring Set		1950s	Red rubber molds of Bambi, Thumper, Dumbo, Goofy, Flower and Joe Carioca to make plaster figures	40	70	110
Chitty Chitty Bang Bang Candy Card Set		1960s	1 1/2"x2 1/2" set of fifty color photos	11	20	30
Disney "Sea Scouts" Puzzle	Williams Ellis & Co.	1930s	5x8x1"	16	30	45
Disney Fantasy Jigsaw Puzzle	Whitman	1981	Large size 22x33" puzzle with many characters shown	4	7	10
Disney Ferris Wheel	Chein		17" tall, wind-up	490	625	850
Disney Figure Golf Balls			Set of twelve	12	23	35
Disney Filmstrips	Craftman's Guild	1940s	Set of thirteen color filmstrips	95	180	275
Disney Metal Tub		1960s	20" in diameter 11" tall pictures of Donald, Mickey and Pluto putting toys into their tub	25	50	75
Disney Rattle	Noma	1930s	4" tall with Mickey & Minnie, Donald & Pluto carrying a Christmas tree	60	115	175

Disney

TOY	COMPANY	YEAR	DESCRIPTION	GOOD	EX	MIB
Disney Shooting Gallery	Welso Toys	1950s	8"x 12"x1 1/2" tin target with molded figures of Mickey, Donald, Goofy and Pluto	60	115	175
Disney Tray	Ohio Art		8"x10", tin, pictures are: Mickey & Minnie Mouse, Goofy, Horace, Pluto, Donald Duck & Clarabelle	23	45	65
Disney Treasure Chest Set	Craftman's Guild	1940s	Red plastic film viewer and filmstrips stored in a blue box designed like a chest	65	125	190
Disney World Globe	Rand McNally	1950s	6 1/2" metal base, 8" diameter with Disney characters	25	50	75
Disney's Bunnies	Fisher-Price	1936	2x3x2 1/2" tall wooden toys titled Wee Bunny, Big Bunny and Little Bunny	60	115	175
Disneyland ashtray		1950s	5" diameter, china ashtray with Tinker Bell & castle	11	20	30
Disneyland Auto Magic Picture Gun & Theater		1950s	Battery operated metal gun with oval filmstrip	45	85	130
Disneyland Bagatelle	Wolverine	1970s	Large size bagatelle game with Disneyland graphics	11	20	30
Disneyland China Ash Tray	Eleanor Welborn Art	1955	3 1/2x4 1/2x1 1/2" light green outer rim, with Tinkerbell in white middle with yellow hair, green suit and wings	11	20	30
Disneyland Electric Light	Econlite Corp.	1950s	Picture of Disney characters leaving a bus on a drum base	45	80	125
Disneyland F.D. Fire Truck	Linemar		18" long, battery operated, moveable, Donald Duck fireman climbs the ladder	70	130	200
Disneyland Felt Banner	Disney	1960s	"The Magic Kingdom" 24 1/2" red/ white/blue coat of arms	25	50	75
Disneyland Give-A-Show Projector Color Slides		1960s	112 color slides	60	115	175
Disneyland Haunted House Bank	(Japan)	1960s		35	65	100
Disneyland Metal Craft Tapping Set	Pressman	1950s		16	30	45
Disneyland Miniature License Plates	Marx	1966	2x4" plates with Mickey, Minnie and Pluto, or Snow White, Donald and Goofy, each	12	23	35
Disneyland Pen		1960s	6" long with a picture of a floating riverboat in liquid	11	20	30
Disneyland Tray Puzzle	Whitman	1956	11 1/2x14 1/2" with Mickey & friends in Fantasyland tea cup ride	14	25	40
Disneyland Tray Puzzle	Whitman	1956	11 1/2x14 1/2" with Mickey & friends riding the stagecoach through Frontierland	14	25	40
Disneyland View-Master Set		1960s	Scenes of Fantasyland	12	23	35
Disneyland Wind-up Rollercoaster	Chein		8"x19"x10", tin	425	650	875
Disneyland Wood Pencil		1970s	11x1/2" thick	5	10	15
Duck Tales Travel Tote		1980s	Travel agency premium	4	7	10
Early Settlers Log Set	Halsam	1960s	Log building set based on Disneyland's Tom Sawyer's Island	25	45	70

Disney

TOY	COMPANY	YEAR	DESCRIPTION	GOOD	EX	MIB
Fantasia Bowl	Vernon Kilns	1940	12" diameter & 2 1/2" tall, pink bowl with a winged nymph from Fantasia	115	210	325
Fantasia Ceramic Unicorn Figure	Vernon Kilns	1940s	Black-winged unicorn	45	80	125
Fantasia Cup & Saucer Set	Vernon Kilns	1940	6 1/4" diameter saucer & 2" tall cup	60	115	175
Fantasia Figure	Vernon Kilns		Half-woman, half-zebra centaur	80	145	225
Fantasia Musical Jewelry Box	Schmid Bros.	1990	Box features Mickey and plays "The Sorcerer's Apprentice"	30	55	85
Fantasyland Tray Puzzle	Whitman	1957	11 1/2x14 1/2" Mickey & Donald on an amusement ride	12	23	35
Figural Light Switch Plates	Monogram		Hand painted switch plates, Goofy, Donald, Mickey, on card, each	5	10	15
Golf Club Guards			Mickey, Minnie, Donald, Pluto and Goofy, each	4	7	10
Grasshopper & the Ants Album	Disney	1949	45 RPM record-reader album	14	25	40
Happy Birthday/Pepsi Placemats	Pepsi Co.	1978	Set of four mats: Goofy, Uncle Scrooge, Mickey at a party and Mickey & Goofy fishing	11	20	30
Hayley Mills Paper Doll Kit	Whitman	1963	9 1/2" tall, "Summer Magic"	25	50	75
Horace Horsecollar Hand Puppet	Gund	1950s		25	50	75
Horace Horsecollar/ Clarabelle Cow Set	Pepsi Co.	1977	Glass "Pepsi Collector/Happy Birthday Mickey" Set	11	20	30
Johnny Tremain Figure & Horse	Marx	1957	Plastic 9 1/2" tall horse and 5 1/2" tall Johnny	60	115	175
Jose Carioca Figure	Marx	1960s	5 1/2" tall plastic figure, wire arms and legs, in box	45	80	125
Jose Carioca Figure	Marx		2" tall, plastic	30	55	85
Jose Carioca Wind-up Toy	France	1940s	3 1/2x5x7 1/2" tall	115	210	325
King Brian Hand Puppet	Gund	1959	10" tall	25	50	75
Lap Trays	Hasko	1960s	Set of four features Donald, Goofy & Pluto, Peter Pan and the Seven Dwarfs	35	65	100
Lil' Hiawatha Charm		1960s	Laminated/sterling silver charm	16	30	45
Merry-Go-Round Lamp			10" tall, metal & plastic, when light heats up it makes cylinder	18	35	50
Mother Goose Hand Puppet	Gund	1950s	11" tall	25	50	75
Nautilis Expanding Periscope	Pressman	1954	Inspired by 20,000 Leagues Under the Sea, 19" long	35	65	100
Nautilis Wind-up Submarine	Sutcliffe/ England	1950s		80	145	225
Official Santa Fe & Disneyland R.R. Scale Model Train	Tyco	1966	Model Ho electric train set 16x19x1 1/2"	155	295	450
Pecos Bill Wind-up Toy	Marx	1950s	10" tall, riding his horse Widowmaker and holding a metal lasso	100	150	200
Peculiar Penguins	Disney	1934	Storybook	25	50	75
Pedro Hand Puppet	Gund			16	30	45
Robin Hood Colorforms	Colorforms	1973		5	10	15
Rocketeer Doll	Applause		9" tall	7	13	20
Sand Pail & Shovel	Ohio Art	1930s	Features pie-eyed Mickey selling cold drinks to Pluto, Minnie & Clarabell	50	95	145

Disney

TOY	COMPANY	YEAR	DESCRIPTION	GOOD	EX	MIB
Shaggy Dog Figures	Enesco	1959	Three versions: blue hat & jacket with a white "S" green/black base; white pajamas with blue stripes, brown base; blue hat holding a red steering wheel, black base, each	25	50	75
Shaggy Dog Hand Puppet	Gund	1959	9" tall, red cloth body with white felt hands, yellow ribbons tied around his neck	16	30	45
Silly Symphony Fan			Wooden handle	25	50	75
Silly Symphony Lights	Noma		8 original lights	55	100	150
Sketchagraph	Ohio Art			14	25	40
Swamp Fox Board Game	Parker Brothers	1960	18 1/2x18 1/2" game board, from the TV series with Leslie Nielson	30	50	80
Swamp Fox Coloring Book	Whitman	1961		7	13	20
Toby Tyler Circus Playbook	Whitman	1959	Punch out character activity book	25	50	75
Walt Disney Movie Viewer & Cartridge	Action Films	1972	Action set #9312 with the cartridge "Lonesome Ghosts"	9	16	25
Walt Disney Paint Book	Whitman	1937	11"x14"	20	35	55
Walt Disney's Character Scramble	Plane Facts Co.	1940s	10 cardboard figures 6" tall	23	40	65
Walt Disney's Clock Cleaners, Picture Book	Whitman	1938	Linen-like illustrated book	40	70	110
Walt Disney's Game/ Parade/Academy Award Winners	American Toy Works		15 games for all ages	60	115	175
Walt Disney's Jimmie Dodd Coloring Book	Whitman	1956		11	20	30
Walt Disney's Realistic Noah's Ark	W.H. Greene Co.	1940s	6"x7"x18" Ark, 101 2" animals, and 4" human figures on cardboard	185	345	525
Walt Disney's Silly Symphony Bells	Noma		Christmas tree bells pictured: Three Little Pigs, Elmer the Elephant, The Tortoise & The Hare, etc.	55	100	150
Walt Disney's Snap-Eeze Set	Marx	1963	12 1/2x15x1" box with 12 flat plastic figures: Peter Pan, Pinocchio, Donald, Jiminy Cricket, Gepetto, Bambi, Dewey, Goofy, Pluto, Mickey, Joe Carioca and Bere Rabbit	60	115	175
Walt Disney's Television Car	Marx		8" long, friction toy lights up a picture on the roof when motor turns	125	200	250

Donald Duck

TOY	COMPANY	YEAR	DESCRIPTION	GOOD	EX	MIB
Carpet Sweeper		1940s	Red wood and metal sweeper shows Donald sweeping while Minnie Watches	35	65	100
Daisy Duck Watch	US Time	1948	Daisy is in black & white, yellow & light blue	105	195	300
Disneyland Frame Tray Puzzle	Whitman	1955	11x15" with Donald & his nephews on a pirate ship	16	30	45
Donald & His Gang Puzzle	Ontex	1940s		25	50	75

Top to Bottom: Dick Tracy Braces, De Luxe Products; Mickey Mouse Mousegetar Jr., 1960s, Mattel; Popeye soakie bottle; Little Audrey's Dress Designer Kit, 1962, Saalfield.

Donald Duck

TOY	COMPANY	YEAR	DESCRIPTION	GOOD	EX	MIB
Donald Drum Major Doll	Knickerbocker	1938	17" tall, red jacket with yellow piping & a black plush hat	175	325	500
Donald Duck & Minnie Mouse Sweeper	Ohio Art	1930s	3" with wooden handle	55	100	150
Donald Duck & Nephews Puzzle	Whitman	1960s	Acrobatics themed illustration	7	13	20
Donald Duck & Pluto Car	Sun Rubber Co.		6 1/2" long, hard rubber	18	35	50
Donald Duck Alarm Clock	Glen Clock/ Scotland	1950s	5 1/2x5 1/2x2", Donald pictured with blue bird on his hand	95	180	275
Donald Duck Alarm Clock	Bayard	1960s	2x4 1/2x5"	80	150	230
Donald Duck and Mickey Mouse Crayon Box	Transogram	1946	Tin illustrated crayon box	25	50	75
Donald Duck Bank	Crown Toy	1938	6" tall, composition, head is moveable	55	100	150
Donald Duck Bank, Ceramic			3 1/2x4x7" tall, Donald in a cowboy outfit	35	65	100
Donald Duck Bank, Ceramic		1940s	4 1/2x4 1/2x6 1/2" tall, Donald holding a rope with a large brown fish by his side	35	65	100
Donald Duck Bank, China		1940s	5 1/2x6x7 1/2" tall, Donald seated holding a coin in one hand	70	130	200
Donald Duck Bank, Plastic			4x4x8 1/2" tall, Donald seated on a treasure chest dressed as a cowboy	9	16	25
Donald Duck Bathtub		1960s		25	50	75
Donald Duck Bubble Bath		1950s	3 1/2" diameter, 7" tall	9	16	25
Donald Duck Camera	Herbert-George Co.	1950s	3x4x3"	25	50	75
Donald Duck Choo Choo Pull Toy	Fisher-Price	1940	#450, Donald in red cap rings bell as toy is pulled	90	165	250
Donald Duck Disney Dipsy Car	Marx	1953	6" tall, wind-up with a spring-necked Donald	425	650	850
Donald Duck Driving Pluto Toy			9" long, wind-up, celluloid	275	500	775
Donald Duck Duet Dancing Toy	Marx	1946	10 1/2" tall, wind-up, Goofy dances & Donald Duck plays drum	325	475	650
Donald Duck Dump Truck	Linemar	1950s	2x5x2" tall	80	145	225
Donald Duck Electric Lamp	Dolly Toy Co.	1970s	Donald on a tug boat	25	50	75
Donald Duck Figure, Celluloid	(Japan)	1930s	Long billed Donald walking	55	100	150
Donald Duck Figurine			3 1/2" tall, celluloid, jointed arms & leg, winking	35	60	95
Donald Duck Framed Picture		1950s	8 1/2x10 1/2", glow-in-the-dark with Donald on a bike	9	16	25
Donald Duck Fun-e-Flex Figure	Fun-E-Flex	1930s	Wooden Donald on red sled with rope	40	80	120
Donald Duck Funnee Movie Set	Transogram	1940	Box features Donald, Mickey, and the nephews	45	90	135
Donald Duck Funnee Movie Set	Irwin	1949	Hand crank movie 'camera' viewer and 4 films in box	80	145	225
Donald Duck Hair Brush	Disney		2x3 1/2x1 1/2"	18	35	50
Donald Duck Jack-In-The-Box			Paper covering on box, figure made of fabric with composition head	45	80	125
Donald Duck Lamp, China		1940s	6x7x9" tall, Donald holding an axe standing next to a tree trunk	55	100	155

Donald Duck

TOY	COMPANY	YEAR	DESCRIPTION	GOOD	EX	MIB
Donald Duck Light Switch Cover	Dolly Toy Co.	1976	Plastic light switch cover, Donald on a boat	4	7	10
Donald Duck Marionette	Peter Puppet	1950s	6 1/2" tall	25	50	75
Donald Duck Moving Eye Clock	Disney	1960s	3x5x9" tall, small brass/plastic pendulum moves back & forth below Donald's feet while his eyes follow it	25	50	75
Donald Duck Music Box	Anri	1971	Donald with guitar, music "My Way"	35	65	100
Donald Duck Nodder		1960s	5 1/2" tall on green base	12	23	35
Donald Duck Paint Box	Transogram	1938	8" long, paint set	16	30	45
Donald Duck Pencil Sharpener			1 1/2" tall, red celluloid	16	30	45
Donald Duck Pitcher, Ceramic		1940s	4x4 1/2x6" tall, shaped like Donald Duck's body with a small handle & spout on top	30	60	90
Donald Duck Plate, Ceramic	Disney	1960s	1 1/4' deep & 9" diameter, light green background with a dark blue hat	14	25	40
Donald Duck Pocket Watch	Ingersoll	1939		60	115	175
Donald Duck Projector	Stephens Prod.	1950s	Projector in box with 4 films	65	120	185
Donald Duck Pull Toy	Fisher-Price	1941	4 1/2x11x10" tall, wood, Donald's arms swing back and forth while in a forward motion	90	165	250
Donald Duck Pull Toy	Fisher-Price	1953	10", wood, baton twirling Donald with a white sailor hat	60	115	175
Donald Duck Puppet	Pelham Puppets	1960s	10" tall, hollow composition	25	50	75
Donald Duck Push Cart			18" plastic, colorful	11	20	30
Donald Duck Push Figure	Kohner	1950s	Wood jointed push toy, Donald is steering a ship dressed as a sailor	45	90	135
Donald Duck Push Toy	Gong Bell	1950s	4 1/2x8x1" thick with an 18" handle	30	55	85
Donald Duck Puzzle	Jaymar	1940s	7x10x2", Donald & his nephews having a picnic	14	25	40
Donald Duck Ramp Walker	Marx	1950s	1 1/4x3 1/2x3" tall, Donald is pulling red wagon with his nephews	100	125	250
Donald Duck Rubber Car	Sun Rubber Co.	1950s	2 1/2x3 1/2x6 1/2" long	35	65	100
Donald Duck Rubber Figure	Seiberling		3x3 1/2x5" tall	45	80	125
Donald Duck Rubber Figure	Dell	1950s	7" tall	35	65	100
Donald Duck Rubber Figure	Seiberling		6" tall, solid rubber with moveable head	40	70	110
Donald Duck Rubber Figure	Seiberling		6" tall, hollow rubber with squeaker in the base	35	65	100
Donald Duck Sand Pail	Ohio Art	1939	4 1/2" tall, Donald at beach playing tug-of-war with his two nephews	55	100	150
Donald Duck Scooter	Marx	1960s	Tin wind-up, 4x4x2" tall	80	140	175
Donald Duck Skating Rink Toy	Mettoy	1950s	4" diameter, Donald is skating while other Disney characters circle the rink	35	65	100
Donald Duck Snow Shovel	Ohio Art		Wood, tin, litho	60	115	175
Donald Duck Soakie			Large size bottle	12	25	35

Donald Duck

TOY	COMPANY	YEAR	DESCRIPTION	GOOD	EX	MIB
Donald Duck Soap Figure	Disney		Castile soap	35	65	100
Donald Duck Squeeze Toy	Dell	1960s	8" tall, rubber	7	13	20
Donald Duck Sweeper	Ohio Art		6" wide base	25	50	75
Donald Duck Talking Figure	Mattel	1976	4x5x6 1/2" tall, Donald says "I'm Donald Duck" and sneezes when string is pulled	25	50	75
Donald Duck Tea Set	Ohio Art		7 1/2" long tray, 2 1/4" diameter cups & 2 1/2" & 4 1/4" diameter sizes of saucers with lithography	40	80	120
Donald Duck Telephone Bank	N.N. Hill Brass Co.	1938	5" tall with cardboard figure of character	70	130	200
Donald Duck the Drummer	Marx	1940s	5x7x10" tall, Donald as a drummer beating on a metal drum	150	250	350
Donald Duck Tin Sand Pail	Ohio Art	1950s	3 1/2" diameter & 3 1/2" tall, Donald in life preserver fighting off seagulls	30	55	85
Donald Duck Toothbrush Holder		1930s	Ceramic 4 1/2" tall, with detail of Donald holding the toothbrush holder, orange base	90	165	250
Donald Duck Toothbrush Holder		1930s	Bisque, two Donald Duck figures stand side by side, with faces in opposite directions, toothbrush hole is behind figures	55	100	150
Donald Duck Toothbrush Holder, Bisque		1935	2x3x5" tall, holds two toothbrushes	90	165	250
Donald Duck Toy	Schuco		5 1/2" tall, wind-up with a bellows quacking sound	300	550	850
Donald Duck Toy Raft	Ideal	1950s	2" tall, blue plastic raft with yellow sail with Donald looking through a telescope	35	65	100
Donald Duck Trapeze Toy	Linemar		5" tall, celluloid, wind-up	55	105	160
Donald Duck Umbrella Handle		1930s	3 1/4" tall	35	60	95
Donald Duck Watch	US Time	1940s		125	225	350
Donald Duck Watering Can	Ohio Art	1938	6" tall, tin, litho	18	35	50
Donald Duck Wind-up	Durham Plastic Co.	1972	6 1/2" tall hard plastic wind-up toy	14	25	40
Donald Duck Wooden Xylophone Pull Toy	Fisher-Price	1938	11x12 1/2" pulltoy has Donald play xylophone, red wheels, dark blue base, Donald in blue cap	105	195	300
Donald Duck WW I Pencil Box	Dixon		5x8 1/2x1 1/4" deep, Donald flying a plane, holding a tomahawk	35	60	95
Donald Duck, Mickey & Minnie Mouse Toothbrush Holder			4 1/2" tall, bisque, Donald Duck hugging Mickey & Minnie Mouse	55	100	150
Donald Tricycle Toy	Linemar	1950s	Tin	235	440	675
Donald's Hockey Bowl	Ontex	1940s	6 1/2x11x2"	18	35	50
Donald's Olympic Try-Out Puzzle	Jaymar	1960s		9	16	25
Frontierland Donald Figure	Arco		Bendable	9	16	25
Huey, Dewey and Louie Stuffed Dolls	Gund	1950s	Set of three 8" tall dolls	105	195	300
Louie Stuffed Doll "Huey, Dewey & Louie"	Gund	1940s	8" tall, body is white & light green plush with yellow felt on the legs, beak & tail	35	65	100

Donald Duck

TOY	COMPANY	YEAR	DESCRIPTION	GOOD	EX	MIB
Louie Wrist Watch	US Time			130	245	375
Ludwig Von Drake Mug		1961	Handle mug with raised face on mug	11	20	30
Ludwig Von Drake Wonderful World of Color Pencil Box	Hasbro	1961	Box shows Ludwig and the nephews	25	50	75
Professor Ludwig Von Drake Figure Toy	Marx	1961	3" tall, from the "Snap-Eeze" Collection	9	16	25
Professor Ludwig Von Drake in Go Cart	Linemar	1960s	Tin and plastic	130	245	375
Professor Ludwig Von Drake Mug		1961	3 1/2" white china	7	13	20
Professor Ludwig Von Drake Squeeze Toy	Dell	1961	8" tall, rubber	11	20	30
Professor Ludwig Von Drake Tiddly Winks	Whitman	1961	10x10x1 1/2"	9	16	25
Uncle Scrooge "Frame Tray Puzzle Funnies"	Whitman	1980s	11 1/2x14 1/2", showing 12 panel Uncle Scrooge and Donald Duck comic	11	20	30
Uncle Scrooge Charm		1960s	Laminated/sterling silver charm	16	30	45
Uncle Scrooge Wallet		1970s	3x4", Uncle Scrooge tossing coins	9	16	25
W.D. Easter Parade #475	Fisher-Price	1936	Donald Duck on wooden wheels	105	195	300
Walt's Disney Easter Parade Push Toy Play Set	Fisher-Price	1930s	On wooden ball wheels, three rabbits, a hen & 4" tall Donald Duck	130	245	375

Dr. Doolittle

TOY	COMPANY	YEAR	DESCRIPTION	GOOD	EX	MIB
Dr. Doolittle Figure	Mattel	1967	7" tall	14	25	40
Dr. Doolittle Figure	Mattel	1967	5" tall with parrot	12	23	35
Dr. Doolittle Giraffe in the Box				11	20	30

Dr. Seuss

TOY	COMPANY	YEAR	DESCRIPTION	GOOD	EX	MIB
Dr. Seuss "Cat in the Hat" Doll	Coleco	1983	Stuffed	20	35	55
Dr. Seuss "Yertle the Turtle" Doll	Coleco	1983	12"	18	35	50

Dumbo

TOY	COMPANY	YEAR	DESCRIPTION	GOOD	EX	MIB
Dumbo 50th Anniversary Christmas Ornament			2" porcelain bisque	5	10	15
Dumbo Figure	Dakin			9	16	25
Dumbo Milk Pitcher		1940s	6" tall	25	50	75
Dumbo Plush Figure			12" tall	9	16	25
Dumbo Roll Over Wind-up Toy	Marx	1941	4" tall, tin with tumbling action	150	225	300
Dumbo Squeak Toy	Dakin			11	20	30
Dumbo Squeeze Toy	Dell	1950s	3x4 1/2x5" tall	18	35	50

Elmer Fudd

TOY	COMPANY	YEAR	DESCRIPTION	GOOD	EX	MIB
Elmer Fudd Figural Mug	Applause	1980s		7	13	20
Elmer Fudd Figure	Dakin	1968	8" tall	14	25	40
Elmer Fudd Figure	Dakin	1971	In a red hunting outfit	23	40	65
Elmer Fudd Figure		1950s	Metal 5" high on a 3X5 1/2" green base with his name embossed, next to him a brown bucket, Elmer dressed in hunting outfit	55	105	160
Elmer Fudd Fun Farm Figure	Dakin	1977		11	20	30
Elmer Fudd Mini Snowdome	Applause	1980s		7	13	20
Elmer Fudd Pull Toy Car	Brice Toys	1940s	Wooden, Elmer in the Fire Chief's car 9" long, pull and he rings the bell	60	105	165

Felix The Cat

TOY	COMPANY	YEAR	DESCRIPTION	GOOD	EX	MIB
Felix Cartoon Lamp Shade			6" tall	25	50	75
Felix Soakie Soap Bottle			10" tall, plastic	16	30	45
Felix Squeaker Toy			6" tall soft rubber	16	30	45
Felix the Cat Doll		1920s	13" tall, jointed arms	135	250	385
Felix the Cat Doll		1920s	8" tall, wood, fully jointed	45	80	125
Felix the Cat Figure	Schoenhut	1920s	4" tall, wood, leather ears, stands on a white wood base	35	60	95
Felix the Cat Flashlight			Contains whistle	9	16	25
Felix the Cat on a Scooter	Nifty	1924	Tin, wind-up	165	310	475
Felix the Cat Pencil Case		1950s		25	50	75
Felix the Cat Pull Toy	Nifty	1920s	5 1/2" tall, 8" long, tin, cat is chasing two red mice on the front of the cart, litho pictures of Felix on side	115	210	325
Felix the Cat Punch Bag		1960s	11" tall inflatable bobber	25	45	65
Felix the Cat Sip-a-Drink Cup			5" tall	14	25	40
Felix Wrist Watch		1960s		45	80	125

Ferdinand the Bull

TOY	COMPANY	YEAR	DESCRIPTION	GOOD	EX	MIB
Ferdinand Card Game	Whitman	1938	5x6 1/2x1" deep, set of black, white & red cards picturing Ferdinand, the matador, picador, trumpeter & banderilleo	25	50	75
Ferdinand Ceramic Figure	Delco	1938	4 1/2" tall, ceramic figure seated with a purple garland around his neck	35	65	100
Ferdinand Figure	Knickerbocker	1938	5x 9x8 1/2" tall, joint composition with cloth tail & flower stapled in his mouth	95	180	275
Ferdinand Hand Puppet	Crown Toy	1938	9 1/2" tall	45	80	125
Ferdinand Plush Doll	Knickerbocker	1930s	10" tall, 14" long, with a flower in mouth	80	145	225
Ferdinand Rubber Figure	Seiberling	1930s	3x5 1/2x4" tall	25	50	75

Ferdinand the Bull

TOY	COMPANY	YEAR	DESCRIPTION	GOOD	EX	MIB
Ferdinand the Bull & the Matador	Marx	1938	5 1/2" high by 8" long, wind-up action between the matador & Ferdinand "bull fight"	225	425	550
Ferdinand the Bull Bisque Figure			3 1/2" bisque	11	20	30
Ferdinand the Bull Book	Whitman	1938	Linen picture book	18	35	50
Ferdinand the Bull Figure	Disney	1940s	Composition figure	70	130	200
Ferdinand the Bull Plastic Figure			9" tall	16	30	45
Ferdinand the Bull Savings Bank	Crown Toy		5" tall, wood composition with silk flower with metal trap door	20	40	60
Ferdinand the Bull Toy	Knickerbocker	1940	Wood composition with jointed head & legs with flower in his mouth	40	75	115
Ferdinand the Bull Wind-up Tail Spinning Toy	Marx	1938	6" long, tin, wind-up, when wounded, the wire tail of the figure spins & causes him to jump around	150	250	350

Flintstones

TOY	COMPANY	YEAR	DESCRIPTION	GOOD	EX	MIB
Baby Pebbles Doll	Ideal	1963	15" tall	45	80	125
Baby Puss Figure	Knickerbocker	1961	10" tall, vinyl	55	100	150
Bamm Bamm Bank			11" tall, hard plastic figure sitting on turtle	16	30	45
Bamm Bamm Bubble Pipe	Transogram	1963	Figural pipe on illustrated card	18	35	50
Bamm Bamm Doll	Ideal	1962	15" tall	45	80	125
Bamm Bamm Figure	Dakin	1970	7" tall	12	25	35
Bamm Bamm Soakie				9	16	25
Barney Figure	Knickerbocker	1961	10" tall, vinyl	45	80	125
Barney Finger Puppet	Knickerbocker	1972		4	8	12
Barney Policeman Action Figure	Flintoys	1986		4	8	12
Barney Rubble Action Figure	Flintoys	1986		4	7	10
Barney Rubble Bank		1973	Solid plastic, Barney holding a bowling ball	9	16	25
Barney Rubble Doll		1962	6" tall, soft vinyl doll, moveable arms & head	18	35	50
Barney Rubble Figural Night Light	Electricord	1979		4	8	12
Barney Rubble Figure	Dakin	1970	7 1/4" tall	18	35	50
Barney Rubble Riding Dino Toy	Marx	1960s	8" long, metal & vinyl, wind-up	175	295	375
Barney Rubble Wind-up	Marx	1960s	3 1/2" tall figure, tin	70	130	200
Barney's Car	Flintoys	1986		7	13	20
Betty Figure	Knickerbocker	1961	10" tall, vinyl	60	115	175
Betty Rubble Action Figure	Flintoys	1986		4	7	10
Dino Action Figure	Flintoys	1986		4	7	10
Dino Bank			Hard vinyl, blue with Pebbles on his back	9	16	25
Dino China Bank			Dino carrying a golf bag	60	115	175
Dino Doll			Moveable head and arms	9	16	25
Dino Figure	Dakin	1970	7 3/4" tall	25	50	75

Top to Bottom: Supercar Moulding & Colour Kit, 1960s, Sculptorcraft; Radio Orphan Annie's Secret Society Manual, 1930s; Rocky & Bullwinkle Movie Viewer, 1960s.

Flintstones

TOY	COMPANY	YEAR	DESCRIPTION	GOOD	EX	MIB
Dino the Dinosaur Toy Bath Puppet Sponge			Bath glove	7	13	20
Dino Wind-up	Marx	1960s	3 1/2" tall figure, tin	90	165	250
Fang Figure	Dakin	1970	7" tall	25	50	75
Flintmobile	Flintoys	1986		9	16	25
Flintmobile with Fred Action Figure	Flintoys	1986		16	30	45
Flintstones 3" Colored Figures	Empire	1976	Solid figures of Fred, Barney, Wilma and Betty	7	13	20
Flintstones Ashtray		1960	Ceramic with Wilma	9	16	25
Flintstones Bank		1971	19" tall with Barney & Bamm Bamm	16	30	45
Flintstones Bank		1961	8" tall	25	50	75
Flintstones Car	Remco	1964	Battery operated car with Barney, Fred, Wilma and Betty	45	80	125
Flintstones Eight Figure Set	Spoontigues	1981		30	55	85
Flintstones Figures	Imperial	1976	Eight acrylic figures, Fred, Barney, Wilma, Betty, Pebbles, Bamm Bamm, Dino and Baby Puss	14	25	40
Flintstones House	Flintoys	1986		12	25	35
Flintstones Lamp			9 1/2" tall, plastic Fred with lampshade picturing characters	60	115	175
Flintstones Party Place Set	Reed	1969		18	35	50
Flintstones Pillowcase		1960		12	25	35
Flintstones Roto Draw	(England)	1969	British	19	35	55
Flintstones Tru-Vue Stereo Film Card	Tru-Vue	1962	Viewer card #T-37, with strips of Fred	16	30	45
Flintstones Tru-Vue Stereo Film Card	Tru-Vue	1962	Viewer card #T-58, with strips of Pebbles and Bamm Bamm	15	25	40
Fred Figure	Knickerbocker	1961	10" tall, vinyl	45	80	125
Fred Flintstone Action Figure	Flintoys	1986		4	8	12
Fred Flintstone Bubble Blowing Bust Pipe			Soft vinyl with curved stem	5	10	15
Fred Flintstone Doll		1960	13" soft vinyl doll with moveable head	45	90	135
Fred Flintstone Doll	Perfection Plastic	1972	11" tall	12	23	35
Fred Flintstone Figural Night Light		1970		9	16	25
Fred Flintstone Figure	Dakin	1970	8 1/4" tall	12	23	35
Fred Flintstone Figure	Knickerbocker	1960	15" tall	50	95	145
Fred Flintstone Gum Ball Machine			In the shape of Fred's head	7	13	20
Fred Flintstone Push Puppet	Kohner			12	23	35
Fred Flintstone Riding Dino	Marx	1962	18 " long battery operated with Fred in Howdah	250	350	550
Fred Flintstone Riding Dino	Marx	1962	8" long, tin & vinyl, wind-up	200	350	450
Fred Flintstone's Bedrock Bank	Alps	1962	9", tin & vinyl battery operated	155	295	450
Fred Flintstone's Lithograph Wind-up	Marx	1960s	3 1/2" tall figure, metal	90	165	250
Fred Loves Wilma Bank			Ceramic	60	115	175

Flintstones

TOY	COMPANY	YEAR	DESCRIPTION	GOOD	EX	MIB
Fred Playing Xylophone	Fisher-Price	1962		60	105	165
Fred Policeman Action Figure	Flintoys	1986		4	8	12
Great Big Punch-out Book	Whitman	1961		14	25	40
Just For Kicks Target Game				85	160	245
Motorbike	Flintoys	1986		5	10	15
Pebbles Bank			9" tall vinyl with Pebbles sitting in chair	9	16	25
Pebbles Figure	Dakin	1970	8" tall with blonde hair and purple velvet shirt	11	20	30
Pebbles Flintstone Doll	Mighty Star	1982	Vinyl head, arms and legs, cloth stuffed body 12" tall	15	30	45
Pebbles Flintstones Cradle	Ideal	1963	For a 14" doll	15	25	40
Pebbles Soakie				9	16	25
Police Car	Flintoys	1986		7	13	20
Wilma Figure	Knickerbocker	1961	10" tall, vinyl	60	115	175
Wilma Flintstone Action Figure	Flintoys	1986		4	7	10
Wilma Friction Car	Marx	1962	Metal	90	165	250

Foghorn Leghorn

TOY	COMPANY	YEAR	DESCRIPTION	GOOD	EX	MIB
Foghorn Leghorn Figure	Dakin	1970	6 1/4" tall	25	45	65
Foghorn Leghorn Hand Puppet		1960s	9" hand puppet, fabric with vinyl head	12	25	35
Foghorn Leghorn PVC Figure	Applause	1980s		3	5	8

Fontaine Fox

TOY	COMPANY	YEAR	DESCRIPTION	GOOD	EX	MIB
Cast Metal Toonerville Trolley			4" tall, red pot metal	75	135	210
Metal Toonerville Trolley			3" tall	70	130	200
Miniature Toonerville Trolley	Nifty		2" tall	130	245	375
Powerful Katrinka Figure		1923	5 1/2" tall, wind-up, pushing a wheel barrow with Jimmy	245	450	700
The Toonerville Trolley		1922	7 1/2" tall, wind-up	265	495	750

Garfield

TOY	COMPANY	YEAR	DESCRIPTION	GOOD	EX	MIB
Garfield 3-D Light Switch Plate	Prestigeline	1978		4	8	12
Garfield Chair Bank	Enesco	1981		12	23	35
Garfield Easter Figure	Enesco	1978		4	7	10
Garfield Figural Music Box/Dancing	Enesco	1981		18	35	50
Garfield Figure Bank	Enesco	1981	4 3/4"	12	23	35
Garfield Graduate Figurine	Enesco	1978		4	7	10
Garfield Large Mug, Soup Mug & Snack Dish				9	16	25

Gasoline Alley

TOY	COMPANY	YEAR	DESCRIPTION	GOOD	EX	MIB
Skeezix Comic Figure		1930s	6" chalk statue	4	7	10
Skeezix Stationery		1926	6"x8 1/2"	9	16	25
Uncle Walt & Skeezix Figure Set			Bisque, Uncle Walt, Skeezix, Herby & Smitty, heights range from 3 1/2" tall to 2 1/4"	70	130	200
Uncle Walt & Skeezix Pencil Holder	F.A.S.		5" tall, bisque	25	50	75

Goofy, Disney

TOY	COMPANY	YEAR	DESCRIPTION	GOOD	EX	MIB
Backwards Goofy Watch	Helbros	1972		265	490	750
Backwards Goofy Watch	Pedre		Silver case 2nd edition	35	65	100
Fantasyland Goofy Figure	Arco		Bendable	9	16	25
Goofy Laughing Doll		1970s	5x6x13" tall, fabric & vinyl doll of Goofy with recording of his laugh	25	50	75
Goofy Lil' Headbobber	Marx			16	30	45
Goofy Nite Lite	Horsman	1973	Green figural nite light	16	30	45
Goofy Safety Scissors	Monogram	1973	On card	4	7	10
Goofy Snap-eeze Figure	Marx		On a white plastic base, background of 3 apples hanging from the sky with green grass along the bottom	18	35	50
Goofy Toothbrush	Pepsodent	1970s		4	7	10
Goofy Walt Disney's Twist'n Bend Flexible Toy	Marx	1963	4" tall	11	20	30
Goofy with Bump 'n Go Action Lawn Mower	Illfelder	1980s	3 1/2x10x11", plastic figure pushing lawn mower with silver handle	35	65	100
Goofy-Rolykins Figures	Marx		1x1x1 1/2" tall, plastic, one of the "Walt Disney Rolykins with ball bearing action set	25	50	75

Green Hornet

TOY	COMPANY	YEAR	DESCRIPTION	GOOD	EX	MIB
Black Beauty Car			12", battery operated	210	390	600
Black Beauty H.O. Scale Race Car	Aurora	1966		70	130	200
Coloring Book, Kato's Revenge				14	25	40
Green Hornet Agent Wall Clock				25	50	75
Green Hornet Bendie Figure	Lakeside	1966	On card	70	130	200
Green Hornet Bendie Figure		1966		30	60	90
Green Hornet Bubble Gum Ring	Frito Lay		Rubber ring, in cello pack	25	50	75
Green Hornet Charm Bracelet	Grenway Prod.	1966	Gold finish chain with five charms, Hornet, Van, Kato, Pistol, Black Beauty, on 3x7 1/2" illustrated card	45	80	125
Green Hornet Colorforms Set	Colorforms			105	195	300
Green Hornet Coloring Book				9	16	25

Green Hornet

TOY	COMPANY	YEAR	DESCRIPTION	GOOD	EX	MIB
Green Hornet Costume Set	Ben Cooper	1960s	Mask, cape, in box	55	100	150
Green Hornet Cutlery Set			Set of fork and spoon	11	20	30
Green Hornet Flasher Ring Store Display	Chemtoy	1960s	On illustrated display card	200	375	575
Green Hornet Flasher Rings	Chemtoy	1960s	Eight designs, Hornet Sting, Kato and GH in action, GH running w/hostage, Hornet logo, Black Beauty/TV logo, Kato running down thief, GH and Miss Case, each	25	45	70
Green Hornet Flasher, Large			7"	30	55	85
Green Hornet Flicker Ring			Plastic	5	10	15
Green Hornet Frame Tray Puzzle		1960s		23	45	65
Green Hornet Frame Tray Puzzles	Whitman	1960s	Set of four puzzles in illustrated box	45	80	125
Green Hornet Milk Mug		1966		23	45	65
Green Hornet Movie Viewer				35	60	95
Green Hornet Squeeze Candy		1960s		175	325	500
Green Hornet Sticker Packs				25	50	75
Green Hornet Strikes!, The	Whitman		Book	7	13	20
Green Hornet Thingmaker Plate	Mattel	1966		25	50	75
Green Hornet View-Master Reels	View-Master		Set of 3 reels in illustrated envelope	35	60	95
Green Hornet Wallet		1966		25	50	75
Green Hornet Wallet Store Display Set		1966	One wallet and header card	125	225	350
Green Hornet Wrist Radios	Remco	1960s	Set of two batt. op plastic wrist radios, send and receive messages by voice or code	130	145	375

Gumby

TOY	COMPANY	YEAR	DESCRIPTION	GOOD	EX	MIB
Adventures of Gumby Electric Drawing Set	Lakeside	1966		12	23	35
Gumby Adventure Costume	Lakeside	1960s	Fireman, cowboy, knight and astronaut, each	23	45	65
Gumby Bendable Figure	Applause	1980s	5 1/2 " tall three different kinds	4	8	12
Gumby Hand Puppet	Lakeside	1965	9" tall with vinyl head	9	16	25
Gumby Modeling Dough	Chemtoy	1960s		23	45	65
Gumby Poseable Figure	Applause	1980s	12" tall	9	16	25
Gumby's Jeep	Lakeside	1960s	Yellow tin litho, Gumby & Pokey's names are printed on seat,	95	175	265
Gumby's Pal Pokey Figure	Lakeside	1960s		23	45	65
Gumby's Pal Pokey Modeling Dough	Chemtoy	1960s		23	45	65

Happy Hooligan

TOY	COMPANY	YEAR	DESCRIPTION	GOOD	EX	MIB
Happy Hooligan Nesting Toy Set	Anri		4" tall, wooden set of four pieces, three being smaller and fit into the larger one	60	105	165
Happy Hooligan Toy	Chein	1932	6" tall, wind-up, walking figure	250	275	350

Hardy Boys

TOY	COMPANY	YEAR	DESCRIPTION	GOOD	EX	MIB
Hardy Boys Figures	Kenner	1979	12" tall Joe Hardy (Shaun Cassidy) or Frank Hardy (Parker Stevenson)	7	13	20

Heathcliff

TOY	COMPANY	YEAR	DESCRIPTION	GOOD	EX	MIB
Heathcliff "Sonja" Friction-Powered Mover	Talbot Toys	1982		4	8	12
Heathcliff Schoolhouse Game	Hourtou	1983	Game with figures	7	13	20

Heckle & Jeckle

TOY	COMPANY	YEAR	DESCRIPTION	GOOD	EX	MIB
Heckle & Jeckle Figures			7" tall soft foam figures	12	23	35
Heckle & Jeckle Storybook	Wonder Book	1957		9	16	25
Little Roquefort Figure		1959	8 1/2" tall,wood	23	45	65

Honey West

TOY	COMPANY	YEAR	DESCRIPTION	GOOD	EX	MIB
Accessory Set	Gilbert	1965	Telephone purse, lipstick, handcuffs and telescope lens necklace	23	45	65
Accessory Set	Gilbert	1965	Cap-firing pistol, binoculars, shoes and glasses	23	45	65
Formal Outfit	Gilbert	1965		25	50	75
Honey West Doll	Gilbert	1965	12" tall with black leotards, belt, shoes, binoculars and gun	105	195	300
Karate Outfit	Gilbert	1965		25	50	75
Pet Set with Ocelot	Gilbert	1965		35	65	100
Secret Agent Outfit	Gilbert	1965		25	50	75

How the West Was Won

TOY	COMPANY	YEAR	DESCRIPTION	GOOD	EX	MIB
Dakota Figure	Mattel	1978		7	13	20
Lone Wolf Figure	Mattel	1978		7	13	20
Zeb Macahan Doll	Mattel	1978		7	13	20
Clarabell Jumping Toy	Linemar	1950s	7" tall tin litho Clarabell, squeeze lever to make figure hop forward and squeak	265	490	750
Flub A Dub Flip A Ring Game		1950s	9" long ring toss game, object is to toss ring over Flub A Dub's nose.	12	23	35

Howdy Doody

TOY	COMPANY	YEAR	DESCRIPTION	GOOD	EX	MIB
Howdy Doody Air-O-Doodle		1950s	Red and yellow plastic combination train, boat and plane toy on card with cut out character passengers	16	30	45
Howdy Doody Alarm Clock		1971	Howdy centered in clock face, pink	45	80	125
Howdy Doody Bubble Pipe	Lido	1950s	4" long silver plastic pipe with bowl shaped like Howdy's face	35	60	95
Howdy Doody Coloring Books	Whitman	1955	Set of six 8"x8" coloring books in box	25	50	75
Howdy Doody Dominos		1950s		45	80	125
Howdy Doody Figure	Stahlwood Co.		5"x7" rubber squeeze figure on airplane	235	440	675
Howdy Doody Fingertronic Puppet Theater	Sutton's	1970s		4	8	12
Howdy Doody Paint Set	Milton Bradley	1950s	11"x16" set in box	45	80	125
Howdy Doody Puppet Show Set	Kagran	1950s	Includes, Howdy, Clarabell, Mr. Bluster, Flub, Dillie Dally	90	165	250
Howdy Doody Ranch House Toolbox	Liberty Steel	1950s	14x6x3" illustrated steel box with handle	45	80	125
Howdy Doody Ukelele	Emenee	1950s	Small plastic guitar labelled with Howdy art	45	80	125
Howdy Doody Ventriloquist's Dummy	Goldberger	1970s	30" tall Howdy dressed in blue pants and red plaid shirt	55	100	150
Howdy Doody Vinyl Doll		1950s	7" tall vinyl squeeze toy of Howdy in blue pants and red shirt	50	90	135
Howdy Doody Wrist Watch	Ingraham	1954	Deep blue band with blue and white dial showing character faces, came with a box showing Howdy holding the watch	175	325	500
Howdy Doody Wristwatch		1987		23	45	65

Huckleberry Hound

TOY	COMPANY	YEAR	DESCRIPTION	GOOD	EX	MIB
Hokey Wolf Figure	Dakin	1970		30	55	85
Hokey Wolf TV-Tinykin Figure	Marx	1961		9	16	25
Huckleberry Hound China Figure		1960s	6" tall, glazed china	18	35	50
Huckleberry Hound Doll	Knickerbocker	1959	18" tall, stuffed plush doll with vinyl hands & face	45	80	125
Huckleberry Hound Figural Bank	Dakin	1980	5" tall figural bank of Huck sitting	19	35	55
Huckleberry Hound Figural Bank	Knickerbocker	1960	10" tall, hard plastic figure bank	9	16	25
Huckleberry Hound Figure	Dakin		8" tall figure	16	30	45
Huckleberry Hound Figure	Dakin		7" tall	35	60	95
Huckleberry Hound Go Cart	Linemar	1960s	6 1/2" tall, in go-cart, friction	90	165	250
Huckleberry Hound Tiddleywinks	Milton Bradley	1959	Small board game, tennis tiddleywinks, Huck and Mr. Jinks on cover	16	30	45
Huckleberry Hound TV Playset	Marx	1961	With five plastic figures	45	80	125

Huckleberry Hound

TOY	COMPANY	YEAR	DESCRIPTION	GOOD	EX	MIB
Huckleberry Hound TV Scenes Miniature Figure Set	Marx	1961		18	35	50
Huckleberry Hound TV-Tinykin Figure	Marx	1961		18	35	50
Huckleberry Hound Wind-up Toy	Linemar	1962	4" tall, tin	70	130	200
Huckleberry Hound Wristwatch	Bradley	1965	Medium size chrome case, wind-up mechanism, grey leather band, face shows Huck in full view	45	90	135
Huckleberry Hound's Huckle Chuck Target Game	Transogram	1961	Target game with plastic rings, beanbags & darts	25	50	75
Mr. Jinks Bubble Soap Container	Purex	1960s	10" tall, Pixie & Dixie hard plastic container	9	16	25
Mr. Jinks Stuffed Doll	Knickerbocker	1959	13" tall, stuffed plush doll with vinyl face	25	50	75
Pixie & Dixie Dolls	Knickerbocker	1960	12" tall, each	25	50	75
Pixie & Dixie Magic Slate		1959		12	23	35

Indiana Jones

TOY	COMPANY	YEAR	DESCRIPTION	GOOD	EX	MIB
3-D Indiana Jones View-Master Gift Set	View-Master		View-Master	16	30	45
Indiana Jones Sticker Sheet			Two sets	12	23	35
Indiana Jones The Legend			Coffee mug	5	10	15
Indy "Pepsi" Backpack				18	35	50
Last Crusade Pepsi Retailer Button				5	10	15
Temple of Doom Calendar				5	10	15
Temple of Doom Storybook			Hardbound	7	13	20

James Bond

TOY	COMPANY	YEAR	DESCRIPTION	GOOD	EX	MIB
Disguise Kit	Gilbert	1965		45	80	125
Disguise Kit #2	Gilbert	1965		45	80	125
James Bond	Gilbert	1965	Large figure	105	195	300
James Bond Aston Martin Car	Gilbert	1965	12", battery operated	225	425	650
James Bond Aston Slot Car	Gilbert	1965		30	60	95
James Bond Hand Puppet	Gilbert	1965		60	115	175
James Bond Harpoon Gun (Thunderball)	Lone Star	1960s	Box is illustrated with undersea fight scene graphics	45	80	125
James Bond Secret Attache Case	MPC	1965		225	400	625
James Bond View-Master Pack, Live & Let Die	View-Master	1973		11	20	30
Jaws Doll	Mego	1979		145	270	415
Moonraker Doll	Gilbert	1979		25	50	75
Odd Job	Gilbert	1965	12" doll in karate outfit, with hat	140	260	400

Top to Bottom: The Flying Nun Oil Paint By Numbers Set, 1960s, Hasbro; Yogi Bear Friction Toy, 1960s; Rocky & Bullwinkle china banks, 1960s; Bugs Bunny and Tweety Chatter Chums, 1982, Mattel.

James Bond

TOY	COMPANY	YEAR	DESCRIPTION	GOOD	EX	MIB
Scuba Outfit #2	Gilbert	1965		45	80	125
Scuba Outfit #3	Gilbert	1965		20	40	60
Scuba Outfit #4	Gilbert	1965		20	40	60
Scuba Outfit Deluxe	Gilbert	1965		45	80	125
Ski Outfit	Gilbert	1965		60	115	175
Thunderball Set	Gilbert	1965		55	100	150
Tuxedo Outfit	Gilbert	1965		60	115	175

Jetsons

TOY	COMPANY	YEAR	DESCRIPTION	GOOD	EX	MIB
Jetsons Colorforms Kit		1963		35	65	100
Jetsons Elroy Toy	Transogram	1963		45	80	125
Jetsons Jigsaw Puzzle	Whitman	1962	70 pieces	12	23	35
Judy Jetson Figure	Applause	1990	10" tall figure	5	10	15
Rosie Doll	Applause	1980s	10" tall	9	16	25
The Jetsons Birthday Surprise	Whitman	1963	Book	12	23	35

Jungle Book

TOY	COMPANY	YEAR	DESCRIPTION	GOOD	EX	MIB
Baghera the Tiger Flasher	Disney	1966		5	10	15
Baloo Doll			12" tall, plush	9	16	25
Jungle Book Carrying Case	Ideal	1966	5x14x8" tall	25	50	75
Jungle Book Dinner Set			Vinyl placemat, 6 1/2" bowl, 8" plate & 8 oz. cup	7	13	20
Jungle Book Fork & Spoon Set			Flatware with melamine handles	4	7	10
Jungle Book Fun-L Tun-L	New York Toy Corp.	1966	108" long by 2 feet wide tunnel	35	65	100
Jungle Book Magic Slate	Watkins-Strathmore	1967	8 1/2x13 1/2"	9	16	25
Jungle Book Sand Pail and Shovel	Chein	1966	Tin litho pail and shovel are illustrated with Jungle Book characters	23	45	65
Jungle Book Tea Set	Chein	1966	Tin litho set of three 5" plates, 4" saucers & 1 1/2" tea cups and a 7x10 1/2" serving tray	25	50	75
Mowgli Figure	Holland Hill	1967	8" vinyl figure	19	35	55
Mowgli's Hut Mobile Toy & Figures	Multiple Toymakers	1968	2x3x3" mobile with Baloo & King Louis figures	35	65	100
Mowgli/Baloo Digital Watch			Clear plastic band	5	10	15
Shere Kahn Figure	Enesco	1965	5" tall, ceramic	12	23	35

Lady & the Tramp

TOY	COMPANY	YEAR	DESCRIPTION	GOOD	EX	MIB
Lady Doll	Woolikin	1955	5x8x8 1/2", light tan with brunt orange accents on face, ears, stomach & tail, plastic eyes, nose & a white silk ribbon around neck	45	80	125
Modeling Clay	Pressman	1955	10 1/2x14 1/2x2"	25	50	75
Perri Plush Doll	Steiff		3x5x6" tall	35	65	100
Plastic Figures	Marx	1955	Lady is 1 1/2" tall & white, Tramp is 2" tall & tan	25	50	75
Plush Dolls	Schuco	1955		60	115	175

Lady & the Tramp

TOY	COMPANY	YEAR	DESCRIPTION	GOOD	EX	MIB
Toy Bus	Modern Toys/ Japan	1966	3 1/2x4x14" long	140	260	400
Tramp Plush Doll	Schuco	1955	4x9x8" tall, brown with a white underside & face, hard plastic eyes & nose	60	115	175
Tray Puzzle	Whitman	1954	11x15"	9	16	25

Laurel & Hardy

TOY	COMPANY	YEAR	DESCRIPTION	GOOD	EX	MIB
Laurel & Hardy Die Cut Puppets	Larry Harmon	1970s	Moveable, each	11	20	30
Laurel & Hardy Squeeze Toy	Dell	1982	Soft vinyl, squeeze and hat pops up on their heads	7	13	20
Oliver Hardy Doll	Dakin		5" tall wind-up dancing/shaking vinyl doll	16	30	45
Oliver Hardy Figure	Dakin	1974	7 1/2" tall	25	50	75
Stan Laurel Figural Bank		1974	8" tall hard plastic bank, brown with green pants	9	16	25
Stan Laurel Figural Bank		1972	15" tall, vinyl	16	30	45
Stan Laurel Figure	Dakin	1974	8" tall	25	50	75

Li'l Abner

TOY	COMPANY	YEAR	DESCRIPTION	GOOD	EX	MIB
Li'l Abner Dogpatch Band	Unique Art Mfg. Co.	1945	9"x9" tall, wind-up, Daisy Mae plays piano, Li'l Abner dances, Pappy Yokum plays drums & Mammy Yokum sits on top of piano smoking her pipe	225	425	650
Li'l Abner Snack Vending Machine			2" vending machine that dispenses nutritious snacks for 10 cents	115	210	325

Lippy the Lion

TOY	COMPANY	YEAR	DESCRIPTION	GOOD	EX	MIB
Lippy the Lion Game	Transogram	1963		25	45	70
Lippy the Lion Soakie	Purex	1960s	11 1/2" tall, hard plastic	12	23	35

Little Mermaid

TOY	COMPANY	YEAR	DESCRIPTION	GOOD	EX	MIB
Ariel Doll			9" tall, in gown	9	16	25
Ariel Musical Jewelry Box			5 3/4x4 1/2"	9	16	25
Ariel PVC Doll				9	16	25
Ariel Toothbrush			7 1/2x10" battery operated with holder	9	16	25
Backpack				7	13	20
Eric Doll			9 1/2" tall in full dress uniform	9	16	25
Flounder & Ariel Faucet Cover			Plastic	5	10	15
Flounder Plush Figure			15" fish figure	9	16	25
Flounder Shaped Pillow			14x24"	7	13	20
Globe			4" water globe	9	16	25
Pencil Box				7	13	20
Purse			6" diameter, vinyl, canteen styles purse	5	10	15

Little Mermaid

TOY	COMPANY	YEAR	DESCRIPTION	GOOD	EX	MIB
PVC Figures	Applause		King Triton, Ariel & Sebastian on rock, Ariel sitting alone, Ariel human in dress, Ariel w/mirror, Ariel leaping from water, Eric, Ariel & Flounder, each	1	3	4
Scuttle Plush Figure			15" seagull	11	20	30
Sebastian Plush Figure			16" crab figure	9	16	25
Under the Sea Muscial Jewelry Box			4" mahogany	18	35	50

Little Orphan Annie

TOY	COMPANY	YEAR	DESCRIPTION	GOOD	EX	MIB
Annie Doll	Knickerbocker	1982	10" tall, complete with two dresses and a removable heart locket	5	10	15
Annie Doll without Locket	Knickerbocker	1982		2	5	7
Annie Miniatures Set of Seven			Annie in a red dress, Daddy Warbucks, Punjab, Grace, Rooster, Sandy and Annie in a white dress and Rooster, each	1	3	4
Annie Set of Six Miniature Figures	Knickerbocker	1982	2" tall, Annie blue dress, Punjab, Grace, Daddy Warbucks, Sandy and Miss Hannigan, each	1	3	4
Beetleware Cup			4" tall, green plastic	14	25	40
Beetleware Mug			3" tall, white	9	16	25
Daddy Warbucks	Knickerbocker	1982		9	16	25
Little Orphan Annie & Chizzler Big Little Book				23	45	65
Little Orphan Annie & Sandy Ash Tray			3" tall, ceramic	55	100	150
Little Orphan Annie & Sandy Dolls	Famous Artists Synd.	1930	9 3/4" tall	45	80	125
Little Orphan Annie & Sandy Toothbrush Holder			Bisque	30	60	90
Little Orphan Annie & the Gooneyville Mystery Book	Whitman	1947		9	16	25
Little Orphan Annie & the Haunted House Book	Cupples & Leon	1928		25	45	70
Little Orphan Annie Bucking the World Book	Cupples & Leon	1929	Hardcover	25	50	75
Little Orphan Annie Clothes Pins	Gold Metal Toys	1938	Clothesline & pulley	23	45	65
Little Orphan Annie Colorforms Kit		1970s		9	16	25
Little Orphan Annie Costume Set			Mask & slip-over paper dress	16	30	45
Little Orphan Annie Cut Out Toys	Miller Toys	1960s	Cut out cook with Sandy-Grunts the Pig-Pee Wee the Elephant	25	50	75
Little Orphan Annie Doll	Well Toy Co.	1973	7" tall	11	20	30
Little Orphan Annie Famous Comics Jigsaw Puzzle	Novelty Dist.			18	35	50
Little Orphan Annie Figural Music Box	N.Y. News Co.	1970		18	35	50

Little Orphan Annie

TOY	COMPANY	YEAR	DESCRIPTION	GOOD	EX	MIB
Little Orphan Annie in the Circus Book	Cupples & Leon	1927	9"x7", 86 pages	25	50	75
Little Orphan Annie Light Up the Candles Game			3 1/2"x5"	16	30	45
Little Orphan Annie Ovaltine Cup	Harold Gray	1930		35	65	100
Little Orphan Annie Punch Outs	King,Larson, McMahon	1944	3-D toys, punch-outs of Annie, Sandy, Punjah & Daddy Warbucks	19	35	55
Little Orphan Annie Rummy Cards	Whitman	1937	5"x6", colored silhouettes of Annie on the back	19	35	55
Little Orphan Annie Shipwrecked Book	Cupples & Leon	1931	9"x7", 86 pages	25	50	75
Little Orphan Annie Stove			Non-electric model, gold-brass lithographed labels of Annie & Sandy, oven doors functional	30	55	85
Little Orphan Annie Stove			Electric version, 8"x9", gold metal, litho plates, functional oven doors & back burner	35	65	95
Little Orphan Annie Toothbrush Holder			3 1/2"x3", bisque	45	80	125
Little Orphan Annie Wind-up Toy	Marx	1930s	5" tall, tin, wind-up	150	275	425
Miniature Orphan Annie Figure		1940s	1 1/2" tall, lead	9	16	25
Miniature Sandy Figure		1940s	3/4" tall, lead	6	12	18
Miss Hannigan	Knickerbocker	1982		4	8	12
Molly	Knickerbocker	1982		4	8	12
Punjab	Knickerbocker	1982		5	10	15
Radio Annie's Secret Decoder Pins		1930s	Used to decode messages	25	45	70
Radio Annie's Secret Society Booklet		1936	6"x9"	35	65	100
Radio Annie's Secret Society Manual		1938	6"x9", 12 pages	25	50	75
Sandy Wind-up Toy	Marx	1930s	4" tall, tin, wind-up	50	75	100

Lone Ranger

TOY	COMPANY	YEAR	DESCRIPTION	GOOD	EX	MIB
Banjo Figure	Gabriel	1979		11	20	30
Buffalo Bill Cody Figure	Gabriel	1980	3 3/4" tall	11	20	30
Butch Cavendish Figure	Gabriel	1980	3 3/4" tall	9	18	27
Dan Reid Figure	Gabriel	1979		9	18	27
Little Bear with Nama the Hawk Figure	Gabriel	1979		9	18	27
Lone Ranger & Silver Figures	Gabriel	1979		14	26	40
Lone Ranger Doll		1987	10" tall, poseable with removeable mask, costume, gun, holster, rifle, hat, shoes and bandana	11	20	30
Lone Ranger Figure	Gabriel	1980	3 3/4" tall	9	16	25
Lone Ranger Hand Puppet		1940s	Cloth body puppet in blue and white polka dot shirt with bells in both hands	55	100	150
Lone Ranger Movie Film Ring	General Mills	1950s	Gold ring holds silver finish viewer with adjustable focus, came with film which slid into slot at end of viewer	80	145	225

Lone Ranger

TOY	COMPANY	YEAR	DESCRIPTION	GOOD	EX	MIB
Lone Ranger Sheriff Jail Keys	Esquire Novelty	1945	5" jail keys on ring, came on 8 1/2x7" card with cut out Sheriff card	60	115	175
Lone Ranger Wooden Record Player	Dekka	1940s	12x10x6" wooden box with burned in illustrations, leather carry strap	140	260	400
Red Sleeves	Gabriel	1979		9	18	27
Silver with 8-Way Action Saddle	Gabriel	1979		11	20	30
Smoke	Gabriel	1979		11	20	30
Tonto and Scout Figures	Gabriel	1979		14	25	40
Tonto Figure	Gabriel	1980	3 3/4" tall	9	16	25

Looney Tunes

TOY	COMPANY	YEAR	DESCRIPTION	GOOD	EX	MIB
Cool Cat	Dakin	1969		23	45	65
Merlin the Magic Mouse "Goofy Gram"	Dakin	1971		18	35	50
Merlin the Magic Mouse Figure	Dakin	1970	7 3/4" tall	16	30	45
Second Banana Figure	Dakin	1970	6" tall	12	23	35

Maggie & Jiggs

TOY	COMPANY	YEAR	DESCRIPTION	GOOD	EX	MIB
Bringing Up Father Figure Set	G. Borgfeldt Co.	1934	4" tall, bisque	70	130	200
Maggie & Jiggs Figure Set		1940s	2 1/2" tall-Maggie, 1" tall Jiggs	16	30	45

Magilla Gorilla

TOY	COMPANY	YEAR	DESCRIPTION	GOOD	EX	MIB
Droop-A-Long Coyote Soakie	Purex	1960s	12", plastic	7	13	20
Magilla Gorilla Big Golden Book	Golden	1964		7	13	20
Magilla Gorilla Cannon	Ideal	1964		14	25	40
Magilla Gorilla Cereal Bowl	MB Inc.			9	16	25
Magilla Gorilla Coloring Book	Whitman	1964		11	20	30
Magilla Gorilla Doll			11" tall, moveable cloth body,hard arms & legs, hard plastic head	23	45	65
Magilla Gorilla Plate			8"	7	13	20
Magilla Gorilla Plush Doll	Ideal	1966	18 1/2" tall with vinyl head	30	55	85
Magilla Gorilla Pull Toy	Ideal	1960s	Pull toy with vinyl figure	45	80	125
Magilla Gorilla Push Puppet	Kohner	1960s	Brown plastic figure in pink shorts and shoes holding a stick on a yellow base with gold label	23	45	65
Punkin' Puss Soakie	Purex	1960s	11 1/2" tall, plastic	14	25	40
Ricochet Rabbit Hand Puppet	Ideal	1960s	11" tall with a vinyl head	35	65	100
Ricochet Rabbit Soakie with a Six Shooter	Purex	1960s	10 1/2" tall, plastic	23	45	65

Man from U.N.C.L.E.

TOY	COMPANY	YEAR	DESCRIPTION	GOOD	EX	MIB
Arsenal Set #1	Gilbert			45	80	125
Arsenal Set #2	Gilbert			25	50	75
Illya Kuraykin Figure	Gilbert		12" figure	65	120	185
Jumpsuit Set	Gilbert			45	80	125
Man from U.N.C.L.E. Wristwatch		1966	Medium chrome case, Napoleon on dial , sweep seconds, black leather band	60	115	175
Napolean Solo Figure	Gilbert		12" figure	80	145	225
Napoleon Solo Costume	Halco		Costume in box see thru mask, Napoleon Solo	60	115	175
Parachute Set	Gilbert		for 12" tall figure	45	80	125
Pistol Conversion Kit	Gilbert			25	50	75
Scuba Set	Gilbert			45	80	125
Target Set	Gilbert			45	80	125

Mary Poppins

TOY	COMPANY	YEAR	DESCRIPTION	GOOD	EX	MIB
Mary Poppins Ceramic Statue			8" tall	14	25	40
Mary Poppins Doll	Gund	1964	11 1/2" tall, bendable	25	50	75
Mary Poppins Manicure Set	Tre-Jur	1964		12	23	35
Mary Poppins Pencil Case		1964	Vinyl with zipper top, shows cartoon graphics of Mary and the kids	9	16	25
Mary Poppins Tea Set	Chein	1964	Creamer, tin plates, large plates, place settings, cups & a serviing tray	30	55	85

Mickey & Minnie Mouse, Disney

TOY	COMPANY	YEAR	DESCRIPTION	GOOD	EX	MIB
Adventureland Frame Tray Puzzle	Whitman	1957	11x15" with Mickey, Minnie, Donald & his nephew in a boat surrounded by jungle beasts & an alligator	16	30	45
Adventures of Mickey Mouse, The	David McKay Co.	1931	Full color illustrations, softcover book	45	80	125
Characters Schmid Bisque Spirit of '76 Music Box	Schmid Bros.		3x6x7 1/2" tall, plays "Yankee Doodle", Mickey, Goofy and Donald are dressed as Revolutionary War Minutemen	60	115	175
Craftmen's Guild Mickey Mouse Viewer	Craftman's Guild	1940s	Film viewer in box with set of 12 films, each individually boxed	65	120	185
Crayons From Your Favorite Funsters Mickey & Donald	Transogram	1946	Crayon set	20	40	60
Hitchhiking Hobo Mickey Squeeze Toy	Dell	1950s	Rubber figure with his belongings tied in a bandana around a stick which he holds over one shoulder	35	60	95
Mickey & Minnie Mouse Sled			Wooden with steering portion "Mickey Mouse" decal	140	260	400
Mickey & Minnie Mouse Tea Set	Ohio Art	1930s	5"x8", pitcher pictures Mickey at piano & cups picture Mickey, Pluto & Minnie	45	80	125
Mickey & Three Pigs Top	Lackawanna Mfg. Co.		9" diameter, tin	35	65	100

Mickey & Minnie Mouse, Disney

TOY	COMPANY	YEAR	DESCRIPTION	GOOD	EX	MIB
Mickey and Minnie Trash Can	Chein	1970s	13" tall tin litho can shows Mickey and Minnie fixing a flat tire on one side, other side shows Mickey feeding Minnie soup	25	50	75
Mickey and Pluto Quartz LCD Wrist Watch	Bradley	1980	5 fuction LCD, base chrome bezel, black vinyl band	19	35	55
Mickey Mouse "50 Years with Mickey" Quartz Wrist Watch	Bradley	1983	Small round chrome case, insription and serial number on back	45	80	125
Mickey Mouse & Donald Duck Alarm Clock	Jerger/ Germany	1960s	2 1/2x5x7" tall with a metal case on a dark brass finish, 3-D plastic figures of Mickey & Donald on either side	55	100	150
Mickey Mouse & Little Mice Sugar Bowl,Salt & Pepper Set			Sugar bowl is 4" tall-Mickey with the little mice on the side of tray as salt & pepper shakers	45	80	125
Mickey Mouse & Minnie Toothbrush Holder			4 1/2" tall, bisque, toothbrush holes are located behind their heads	55	100	150
Mickey Mouse Activity Book	Whitman	1936	40 big pages of stories, coloring, gags & activities	20	35	55
Mickey Mouse Alarm Clock	House Martin	1988	5x7x2"	11	20	30
Mickey Mouse Alarm Clock	Bayard	1960s	2x4 1/2x4 1/2" tall, 1930's style Mickey with moveable head that ticks off the seconds	95	180	275
Mickey Mouse Alarm Clock	Bradley	1970s	2x4 1/2x5" tall	35	65	100
Mickey Mouse Ash Tray			3 1/2" tall, wood composition figure of Mickey	35	65	100
Mickey Mouse Baby Gift Set		1930s	Boxed set of silver plated cup, fork, spoon, cup and napkin holder have inlaid Mickey, box interior shows Mickey, Minnie, and Donald sitting down to eat	90	165	250
Mickey Mouse Band Drum		1936	7" tallx14" diameter, cloth mesh & paper drum heads	50	90	140
Mickey Mouse Band Leader Bank	Knickerbocker		7 1/2" tall, plastic	9	16	25
Mickey Mouse Band Sand Pail	Ohio Art	1938	6" tall, tin, pictures of Mickey Mouse, Minnie, Horace, Pluto, & Clarabelle the cow parading down street	35	60	95
Mickey Mouse Band Top			9" diameter	35	65	95
Mickey Mouse Bank		1930s	2 1/2" diameter by 6" tall, shaped like a mailbox with Mickey holding an envelope	55	100	150
Mickey Mouse Bank	Fricke & Nacke	1978	3x5x7" tall, embossed image of Mickey in front, side panels have Minnie, Goofy, Donald and Pluto	12	23	35
Mickey Mouse Bank	Crown Toy	1938	6" tall, composition, key locked trap door on base, with figure standing next to treasure chest & head is moveable	55	100	150
Mickey Mouse Beanie Hat		1950s	Blue and yellow felt hat with Mickey on front	16	30	45
Mickey Mouse Bicentennial Pocket Watch	Bradley	1976	3 1/2x4 1/2x3/4", Mickey in his Bicentennial outfit	55	100	150

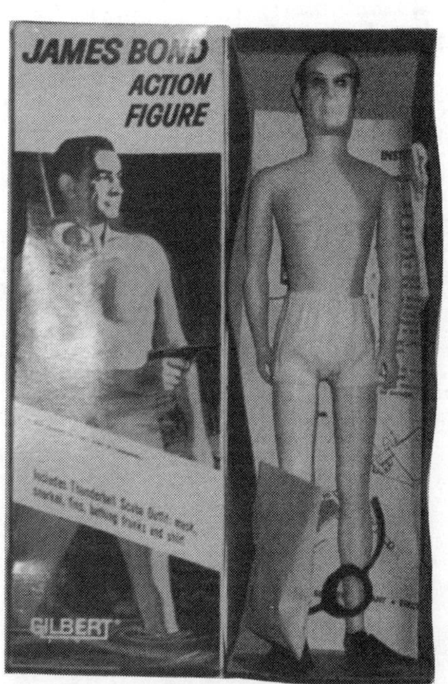

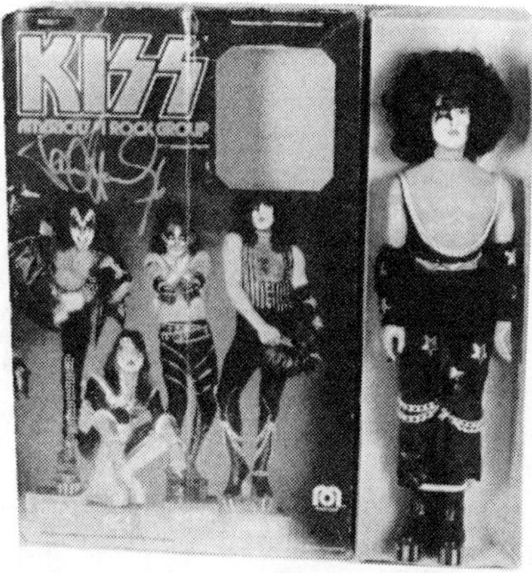

Top to Bottom; Huckleberry Hound Tiddly Winks, 1960s, Chad Valley; James Bond Action Figure, 1965, Gilbert; KISS Paul Stanley Doll, 1979, Mego.

Mickey & Minnie Mouse, Disney

TOY	COMPANY	YEAR	DESCRIPTION	GOOD	EX	MIB
Mickey Mouse Boxed Lantern Slides	Ensign	1930s	5x6x2", cartoons: Traffic Troubles, Gorilla Mystery, Cactus Kid, Castaway, Delivery Boy, Fishin Around, Firefighters, Moose Hunt & Mickey Steps Out	150	275	425
Mickey Mouse Bubble Buster	Kilgore Mfg.	1936	8" long, cork gun	55	100	150
Mickey Mouse Bump & Go Spaceship	Matsudaya	1980s	Battery op. tin litho spaceship with clear dome, has 6 flashing lights, rotating antenna	35	65	100
Mickey Mouse Camera	Ettelson Corp.	1960s	3x3x5"	18	35	50
Mickey Mouse Camera	Child Guidance	1970s	4x7x7"	9	16	25
Mickey Mouse Camera	Helm Toy Corp.	1970s	2x5x4 1/2", Mickey in engineer's uniform riding on top of the train	11	20	30
Mickey Mouse Car	Polistil	1970s	2x4x1 1/2" tall plastic car with rubber figure, Mickey in driver's seat	25	50	75
Mickey Mouse Cardboard House	O.B. Andrews	1930s	14x 12x13" tall	115	210	325
Mickey Mouse Chatty Chums	Mattel	1979		6	12	18
Mickey Mouse China Bank		1950s	5x 5 1/2x6" shaped like Mickey's haead with slot between his ears	25	50	75
Mickey Mouse China Dinner Set	Empresa Electro	1930s	2" creamer, 3-4 1/2" plates and 3-5" plates, 7" long dish, two oval platters, 1-5 1/2" and the other 6 1/2"	130	245	375
Mickey Mouse China Milk Pitcher	(Germany)	1930s	2" tall by 3" diameter, white with green shading around the base, Mickey on each side	60	115	175
Mickey Mouse China Music Box	(Japan)	1970s	4x6" tall, plays "Side by Side", Mickey is brushing a kitten in a washtub	12	23	35
Mickey Mouse Choo Choo Pull Toy	Fisher-Price	1938	#432, blue base, yellow wheels, Mickey in red hat rings bell as toy is pulled	115	210	325
Mickey Mouse Christmas Lights	Noma	1930s	Set of 8 lamps with holiday decals of Mickey, Minnie, Donald, Clarabelle, Pluto & Mickey's nephews	115	210	325
Mickey Mouse Club Bank	Play Pal Plastics	1970s	4 1/2x6x11 1/2" tall, vinyl	16	30	45
Mickey Mouse Club Coffee Tin		1950s	Illustrated lid promotes the club, tin included MM badge	30	55	85
Mickey Mouse Club Fun Box	Whitman	1957	9x11 1/2x1 1/2" deep, includes a stamp book, club scrapbook, 6 coloring books and 4 small gameboards	40	70	110
Mickey Mouse Club Magic Divider	Jacmar	1950s	Arithmetic game	25	50	75
Mickey Mouse Club Magic Kit	Mars Candy	1950s	2- 8x20" punch-out sheets	25	50	75
Mickey Mouse Club Magic Subtractor	Jacmar	1950s	Arithmetic game	11	20	30
Mickey Mouse Club Marionette		1950s	3x6 1/2x13 1/2" tall, composition figure of a girl with a black felt hat & mouse ears	45	80	125
Mickey Mouse Club Mouseketeer Doll	Horsman	1960s	8" tall doll in blue jumpsuit , in box	23	45	65

Mickey & Minnie Mouse, Disney

TOY	COMPANY	YEAR	DESCRIPTION	GOOD	EX	MIB
Mickey Mouse Club Mouseketeer Doll	Horsman	1960s	8" tall doll in red dress , in box	23	45	65
Mickey Mouse Club Mousketeer Ears	Kohner		7x12 1/2"	11	20	30
Mickey Mouse Club Newsreel with Sound	Mattel	1950s	4x4 1/2x9" tall, orange box, plastic projector with 2 short filmstrips, record, cardboard screen, cartoons "Touchdown Mickey" and "No Sail"	90	165	250
Mickey Mouse Club Plastic Plate	Arrowhead	1960s	9" diameter, clubhouse with Goofy, Pluto & Donald wearing mouse ears and sweaters with club emblems	16	30	45
Mickey Mouse Club Puzzle	Jaymar	1960s	Pluto's Wash and Scrub Service	12	23	35
Mickey Mouse Club Toothbrush	Pepsodent	1970s		4	7	10
Mickey Mouse Cowboy Tin Top	Chein	1950s	Tin litho top features Mickey in cowboy outfit, and other characters	55	100	150
Mickey Mouse Cube Travel Alarm Clock	Bradley (Germany)	1975	Large red cube case, shut off button on top, separate alarm wind, in sleeve box	30	55	85
Mickey Mouse Cup	Cavalier	1950s	3" tall, silver-plated cup with a 2 1/2" opening	25	50	75
Mickey Mouse Dart Gun Target	Marks Brothers	1930s	10" target, dart gun & suction darts	30	55	85
Mickey Mouse Disney Dipsy Car	Marx	1953	Tin litho car illustrated with Disney characters, plastic Mickey with head on spring, hand out signaling a turn	425	655	875
Mickey Mouse Doll		1930s	4x7x10 1/2" tall, moveable arms & legs, swivel head, black velveteen body & red felt pants	300	575	875
Mickey Mouse Doll	Schuco	1950s	10" tall	115	210	325
Mickey Mouse Doll	Knickerbocker	1935	11" tall, stuffed, cloth, removeable shoes & jointed head	70	130	200
Mickey Mouse Drum	Ohio Art	1930s	6" diameter	30	55	85
Mickey Mouse Drum	Ohio Art	1938	6" diameter	30	55	85
Mickey Mouse Electric Casting Set	Home Foundary	1930s	9 1/2x16x2"	60	115	175
Mickey Mouse Electric Table Radio	General Electric	1960s	4 1/2x10 1/2x6" tall	25	50	75
Mickey Mouse Electric Wall Clock	Elgin	1970s	10x15x3"	11	20	30
Mickey Mouse Electric Watch	Timex	1958		115	210	325
Mickey Mouse Fabric Doll	Knickerbocker		5x7x12" tall, Mickey in checkered shorts & green jacket with a white felt flower stapled to it	175	340	525
Mickey Mouse Figure	Marx	1970	6" tall, vinyl	9	16	25
Mickey Mouse Figure	Seiberling	1930s	3 1/2" tall, latex figure	55	100	150
Mickey Mouse Figure	Seiberling	1930s	6 1/2" tall, latex figure	80	145	225
Mickey Mouse Figure		1930s	3" tall, bisque, plays saxophone	35	60	95
Mickey Mouse Figure		1930s	3" tall, bisque, holding a parade flag & sword	35	60	95
Mickey Mouse Figure	Seiberling	1930s	3 1/2" tall, black hard rubber	25	50	75
Mickey Mouse Figure			Composition, part of the Lionel Circus Train Set	55	100	150
Mickey Mouse Figurine	Goebel	1930s	3 1/2" tall, in a hunting outfit reading a book	35	65	100
Mickey Mouse Figurine			4" tall, bisque, dressed in a green nightshirt	35	65	100

Mickey & Minnie Mouse, Disney

TOY	COMPANY	YEAR	DESCRIPTION	GOOD	EX	MIB
Mickey Mouse Fire Engine	Sun Rubber Co.		7" long, rubber, push toy	40	80	110
Mickey Mouse Fire Truck with Figure	Sun Rubber Co.		2 1/2x6 1/2x4", Mickey driving & mold-in image of Donald standing on the back holding onto his helmet	45	80	125
Mickey Mouse Fireman Doll	Gund	1960s	12" tall	25	50	75
Mickey Mouse Fork & Spoon Set	Wm. Rogers & Son	1947	6" fork and 5 1/2" spoon	45	80	125
Mickey Mouse Fun-E-Flex Figure	Fun-E-Flex	1930s	7" tall figure with four-finger hands, chest decal says 'Mickey Mouse', in red shorts with orange feet	245	455	700
Mickey Mouse German Tin Bank		1934	2 1/2" diameter by 3" tall, bright yellow bank shaped like a beehive, Mickey approaching door holding a honey jar in one arm & key to open the door in the other	175	340	525
Mickey Mouse Gumball Bank	Hasbro	1968		16	30	45
Mickey Mouse Has a Busy Day Storybook	Whitman	1937	16 pages	25	35	55
Mickey Mouse Imitation Digital Wristwatch	Bradley	1973	Wind-up 'digital' watch, rectangular base, 2 windows show date and minutes on rotating disks, black leather band, face show Mickey to right of windows	35	65	100
Mickey Mouse in Giantland Book	David McKay Co.	1934	45 pages, hardcover	45	80	125
Mickey Mouse in the Music Box		1960s	5x5x6" tall, plays "Pop Goes the Weasel", designed like a Jack-in-the-box, Mickey pops up	30	50	80
Mickey Mouse Jack-In-The-Box		1970s	5 1/2" square tin litho box shows Mickey, Pluto, Donald and Goofy, inside is Mickey	23	45	65
Mickey Mouse Jigsaw Puzzle	Disney	1933	8"x10"	30	55	85
Mickey Mouse Lamp	Soreng-Manegold Co.	1935	10 1/2" tall	70	130	200
Mickey Mouse Lionel Circus Train	Lionel	1935	Train set with 5 cars w/Mickey in #1509 tender, train is 30 inches long, 84 inches of track, circus tent, Sunoco station, truck, tickets, Mickey composition statue	550	1050	1600
Mickey Mouse Lionel Circus Train Handcar	Lionel		9" long with 6" tall figures, metal, figures of Mickey & Minnie are composition & rubber	235	440	675
Mickey Mouse Magic Slate	Watkins-Strathmore	1950s	8 1/2x14" tall	16	30	45
Mickey Mouse Map of the United States	Dixon	1930s	9 1/4x14"	35	65	100
Mickey Mouse Marbles	Monarch		Marbles and Mickey bag , on card	4	7	10
Mickey Mouse Mechanical Pencil		1930s	Head of Mickey on one end and decal of Mickey walking on other side of pencil	35	65	100
Mickey Mouse Mechanical Robot	Gabriel			65	120	185

CHARACTER

Mickey & Minnie Mouse, Disney

TOY	COMPANY	YEAR	DESCRIPTION	GOOD	EX	MIB
Mickey Mouse Mousegetar		1960s	10x30x2 1/2" black plastic	45	80	125
Mickey Mouse Mousegetar	Mattel	1950s	8x23x2" dark red plastic front	35	65	100
Mickey Mouse Movie Projector	Keystone	1934	5 1/2x11 1/2x11" tall for 8mm movies	140	260	400
Mickey Mouse Movie-Fun Shows	Mastercraft Toy Co.	1940s	7 1/2" square by 4" deep, animated action movies	95	180	275
Mickey Mouse Music Box			4 1/2x5x7", plays "It's a Small World", Mickey in conductor's uniform standing on cake	18	35	50
Mickey Mouse Music Box	Anri	1971	5" tall & 3 1/2" diameter, plays "If I Were Rich Man"	45	80	125
Mickey Mouse Music Box	Schmid Bros.	1970s	3 1/2" diameter by 5 1/2" tall, plays "Mickey Mouse Club March," cereamic figure of Mickey in western clothes standing next to a cactus	30	55	85
Mickey Mouse Musical Money Box		1970s	3" diameter by 6" tall, tin box with Mickey, Pluto, Donald and Goofy	30	55	85
Mickey Mouse Nite Light	Disney	1938	4" tall, tin	90	165	250
Mickey Mouse Old Timers Fire Engine	Matsudaya	1980s	Tin and plastic red fire truck with Mickey at the wheel	35	65	100
Mickey Mouse Pencil Box	Dixon	1930s	5 1/2x10 1/2x1 1/4" Mickey illustrated in a gymnasium	35	65	100
Mickey Mouse Pencil Box	Dixon	1930s	Mickey ready to hitch Horace to a carriage in which Minnie is sitting	35	65	100
Mickey Mouse Pencil Box	Dixon	1937	5 1/2x9x3/4", Mickey, Goofy & Pluto riding a rocket	35	65	100
Mickey Mouse Pencil Box	Dixon	1937	5x8 1/2x1 1/4", Mickey is a circus ringmaster & Donald riding a seal	35	65	100
Mickey Mouse Pencil Holder	Dixon	1930s	4 1/2" tall	60	115	175
Mickey Mouse Pencil Sharpener	Hasbro	1960s	Pencil sharpener is the shape of Mickey's head, pencil goes into mouth	12	23	35
Mickey Mouse Pencil Sharpener			3" tall, celluloid, sharpener located on base	55	100	150
Mickey Mouse Pendant Watch	Bradley	1970s	White plastic case, bubble crystal, articulated hands, gold chain	25	50	75
Mickey Mouse Picture Gun	Stephens Prod.	1950s	6 1/2x9 1/2x3", metal picture gun, lights to show filmstrips	55	100	150
Mickey Mouse Plastic Bank	Transogram	1970s	5x7 1/2x19" tall, plastic with Mickey standing on a white chest	12	23	35
Mickey Mouse Plastic Bank	Wolverine	1960s	1 1/2x5 1/2x'1" tall	25	50	75
Mickey Mouse Pocket Watch	Ingersoll	1930s	2" diameter	195	350	550
Mickey Mouse Pocket Watch	Bradley	1970s		35	65	100
Mickey Mouse Presents a Silly Symphony Book	Whitman	1934	Big Little Book	23	45	65
Mickey Mouse Print Shop Set	Fulton Specialty Co.	1930s	6 1/2x6 1/2", ink pad, stamper, metal tweezers & a wooden tray	70	130	200
Mickey Mouse Puddle Jumper	Fisher-Price			17	30	50

TOY	COMPANY	YEAR	DESCRIPTION	GOOD	EX	MIB
Mickey Mouse Pull Toy	Fisher-Price	1936	3x4x1/2" wooden figure of Mickey running with bright color paper labels on side	90	165	250
Mickey Mouse Pull Toy	Toy Kraft		7x22x8" tall, horse cart drawn by wooden horses	300	550	850
Mickey Mouse Pull Toy	N.N. Hill Brass Co.	1935	14" tall, wood & metal	130	245	375
Mickey Mouse Puppet Forms	Colorforms	1960s		9	16	25
Mickey Mouse Push Toy	Fisher-Price	1930s	6" longx4 1/2" tall, wood	95	180	275
Mickey Mouse Quartz Pocket Watch	Lorus	1988	#2202, small gold bezel, gold chain and clip fob, articulated hands	20	40	60
Mickey Mouse Radio	Philgee Int.	1970s		16	30	45
Mickey Mouse Radio	Emerson	1934	Wood composition cabinet with designs of Mickey Mouse playing various musical instruments	335	625	950
Mickey Mouse Record Player	General Electric	1970s	1 12/x14x4 1/2", Mickey in blue & white striped shirt & bow tie, the playing arm is the design of Mickey's arm	55	100	150
Mickey Mouse Registered Commemorative Ed. Wrist Watch	Bradley	1978		60	115	175
Mickey Mouse Riding Toy	Mengel	1930s	6x17x16" tall	385	715	1100
Mickey Mouse Rodeo Rider	Matsudaya	1980s	Plastic wind-up cowboy Mickey rides a bucking bronco	20	40	60
Mickey Mouse Rolykins	Marx		1x1x1 1/2" tall, Walt Disney Rolykins with ball bearing action set	9	16	25
Mickey Mouse Rub'n Play Magic Transfer Set	Colorforms	1978	Rub'n clothing transfers to Mickey, Donald Duck, Pluto, Peg Leg Pete, Big Bad Wolf, Pluto and other characters	14	25	40
Mickey Mouse Rubber Figure	Seiberling	1930s	6 1/2" tall, rubber	65	120	185
Mickey Mouse Safety Blocks	Halsam	1930s	Set of nine blocks	80	145	225
Mickey Mouse Sand Pail	Ohio Art		4 1/2" tall, Mickey, Minnie & Pluto at the beach	45	80	125
Mickey Mouse Sand Pail	Ohio Art	1938	6" tall, Mickey, Donald & Goofy playing golf	45	80	125
Mickey Mouse Sand Pail	Ohio Art	1938	3" tall	40	70	110
Mickey Mouse Sand Shovel	Ohio Art		10" long	25	50	75
Mickey Mouse Saxophone	Harbo	1930s	3" wide at opening, 10" wide, 16" tall	115	210	325
Mickey Mouse Scissors	Disney		3" long, child's scissors with Mickey figure	20	35	55
Mickey Mouse Sewing Cards	Colorforms	1978	7 1/2"x12" cut-out card designs of Mickey, Minnie, Pluto, Clarabelle, Donald Duck and Horace	11	20	30
Mickey Mouse Silk Ornament	Hallmark	1978	4x4x5 1/2" tall, Mickey as Santa riding a stream train	12	23	35
Mickey Mouse Snowdome			Figure with cake	5	10	15

Mickey & Minnie Mouse, Disney

TOY	COMPANY	YEAR	DESCRIPTION	GOOD	EX	MIB
Mickey Mouse Spirit of '76 Colorforms Set	Colorforms	1976	8x 12 1/2x1"	9	16	25
Mickey Mouse Squeeze Toy	Dell	1960s	8" tall	16	30	45
Mickey Mouse Squeeze Toy	Sun Rubber Co.	1950s	10" tall	20	40	60
Mickey Mouse Stamp Pad		1930s	3" long	25	50	75
Mickey Mouse Steamboat	Matsudaya	1988	Wind-up plastic steamboat with Mickey as Steamboat Willie, runs on floor as smokestacks go up and down, box says "60 years With You"	30	55	85
Mickey Mouse Stuffed Doll	Knickerbocker	1935	11" tall, stuffed with removeable shoes & jointed head in red shorts	115	210	325
Mickey Mouse Talking Figure	Hasbro	1970s	4x5 1/2x7 1/2" tall	18	35	50
Mickey Mouse Talking Figure	Horsman	1972	3x10x12" tall, says five different phrases	18	35	50
Mickey Mouse Tea Set	Wolverine		Plastic	55	110	165
Mickey Mouse Tea Set		1930s	3" saucer, 2" pitcher, 2 1/2" sugar bowl each piece shows Mickey & Minnie in a rowboat	25	50	75
Mickey Mouse Telephone Bank	N.N. Hill Brass Co.	1938	5" tall with cardboard figure of character	70	130	200
Mickey Mouse Throw Rug	Alex. Smith Carpet	1935	26x42", Mickey, Donald & a pig are playing musical instruments	125	225	350
Mickey Mouse Tin Bank		1930s	2x3x2 1/4" tall, shaped like a treasure chest with Mickey & Minnie next to a treasure chest on the "Isle of the Thrift"	150	295	450
Mickey Mouse Tin Serving Tray		1960s	11" diameter, tin	11	20	30
Mickey Mouse Top	Fritz Bueschel	1930s	7" diameter, 7" tall, Mickey, Minnie, a nephew, Donald & Horace playing a musical instrument	125	225	350
Mickey Mouse Toy Tractor	Sun Rubber Co.		3x4x4" tall, red body & white rubber tires, Mickey sitting in seat with moveable head	30	55	85
Mickey Mouse Tractor	Sun Rubber Co.		5" long, rubber	25	50	75
Mickey Mouse Transistor Radio	Gabriel	1950s	6 1/2x7x1 1/2"	35	65	100
Mickey Mouse Tricycle Toy	Steiff	1932	8 1/2"x7", wood & metal frame, action movement	420	780	1200
Mickey Mouse Twirling Tail Toy	Marx	1950s	3x5 1/2x5 1/2" tall, with a built in key & his tail is a metal rod that spins around as the toy vibrates	70	100	200
Mickey Mouse Wall Clock	Elgin	1978	9" diameter dial, 15" long vinyl straps for watchband look, giant wrist watch with the "50 Happy Years" logo on dial	25	50	75
Mickey Mouse Washer	Ohio Art		8" tall, tin, litho with Mickey & Minnie Mouse pictured doing their wash	45	80	125
Mickey Mouse Watering Can	Ohio Art	1938	6" tall, tin, litho	65	120	180
Mickey Mouse Wind-up Musical Toy	Illco	1970s	6" tall, plays "Lullaby & Goodnight", 3-D figure of Mickey in dark red pants & yellow shirt	20	35	50

Mickey & Minnie Mouse, Disney

TOY	COMPANY	YEAR	DESCRIPTION	GOOD	EX	MIB
Mickey Mouse Wind-up Toy	Gabriel	1978	Plastic transparent figure of Mickey with visible metal gears	9	15	25
Mickey Mouse Wind-up Trike	(Korea)	1960s	Tin litho trike with plastic Mickey with flag and balloon on handle, bell on back	80	145	225
Mickey Mouse Wooden Bell Pull Toy	N.N. Hill Brass Co.		8 1/2" tall, 13" long, Mickey on roller skates	125	225	350
Mickey Mouse Wooden Sled	Flexible Flyer	1930s	18x30x6" tall	125	210	325
Mickey Mouse Wrist Watch	Bradley	1983	Medium black octagonal case, articulated hands, no numbers on face, in plastic window box	20	35	55
Mickey Mouse Wrist Watch & Figural Stand	Ingersoll	1950s		25	50	75
Mickey Mouse Wrist Watch, Hologram (Woman's)			18K gold, electroplate with black leather band	23	45	65
Mickey Mouse Wrist Watch, Hologram Sorcerer			18K gold, electroplate with black leather band	23	45	65
Mickey Mouse Wristwatch	Bradley	1984	Medium white case, articulated hands, black face, sweep seconds, white vinyl band, in plastic window box	20	35	55
Mickey Mouse Wristwatch	Timex	1960s	Large round case, stainless back, articulated hands, red vinyl band	45	80	125
Mickey Mouse Wristwatch	Ingersoll	1939		115	210	325
Mickey Mouse Wristwatch	Ingersoll	1939	Rectangular with standard second hand between Mickey's legs	200	375	575
Mickey Mouse Xylophone Player Pull Toy	Fisher-Price	1939	#798, 11" tall, wood, pull string and his arms move up & down and he plays the five notes on the xylophone	80	145	225
Mickey Mouse Yarn Sewing Set	Marks Brothers	1930s	9x17x1 1/2"	20	35	50
Mickey's Air Mail Plane	Sun Rubber Co.	1940s	3 1/2x6" long, 5" wingspan, rubber plane	35	65	100
Mickey, Minnie & Donald Throw Rug			26 x41", Mickey & Minnie in an airplane with Donald parachuting	60	115	175
Mickey, Minnie, Pluto & Donald Sand Pail	Ohio Art		5" tall and 5" diameter, Mickey, Minnie, Pluto & Donald in boat looking across water at castle, with swivel handle	45	80	125
Mickey/Donald Crayons & Box Set	Transogram	1946	4 1/2x5 3/4x1/2", tin box, with crayons from your favorite funsters Donald Duck & Mickey Mouse	25	50	75
Mickey/Donald Jack-In-The-Box	Lakeside	1966	3 1/2x3 1/2x4 1/2", Mickey is pictured on one side of the box with a small piece of fabric which says "Pull My Tie", when it is pulled Donald pops out	25	50	75
Mickey/Minnie & Pluto Flashlight	Usalite Co.	1930s	6" long, Mickey leading Minnie through the darkness guided by flashlight & Pluto	35	65	100
Mickey/Minnie Carpet			27x41", Pegleg Pete is lassoed by Mickey; all characters in western outfits	115	210	325

Top to Bottom: Mickey Mouse Club Mouseketeer Dolls, Boy and Girl, Horsman, 1960s; Roy Rogers Composition Nodder from Japan; Bullwinkle Bank.

Mickey & Minnie Mouse, Disney

TOY	COMPANY	YEAR	DESCRIPTION	GOOD	EX	MIB
Mickey/Minnie Dolls	Gund	1940s	13" tall, each	115	210	325
Mickey/Minnie Puzzle	Marks Brothers	1930s	10x12", Mickey polishing the boiler on his "Mickey Mouse R.R." train engine and Minnie waving from the cab	40	70	110
Mickey/Minnie Snow Dome	Monogram	1970s	3x4x3" tall, Mickey & Minnie with a pot of gold at the end of the rainbow	12	23	35
Mickey/Minnie Toothbrush Holder			2 1/2x4x3 1/2", Mickey & Minnie on sofa with Pluto at their feet	70	130	200
Mickey/Pluto Ceramic Ashtray			3x4x3" tall, Mickey & Pluto playing banjos while sitting on the edge of the ashtray	115	210	325
Minnie Mouse Alarm Clock	Bradley (Germany)	1970s	Pink metal electric two-bell clock with articulated hands	23	45	65
Minnie Mouse Car	Matchbox	1979		5	10	15
Minnie Mouse Choo-Choo Train Pull Toy	Linemar	1940s	3x8 1/2x7" tall, green metal base & green wooden wheels	70	125	195
Minnie Mouse Doll	Petz	1940s	3x5x10" tall	115	210	325
Minnie Mouse Doll	Knickerbocker	1935	14" tall, stuffed, cloth, polka-dot skirt & lace pantaloons	105	195	300
Minnie Mouse Figure	Ingersoll	1958	5 1/2" tall, plastic	30	55	85
Minnie Mouse Figure			6" tall, plastic	9	16	25
Minnie Mouse Figurine			4" tall, bisque, dressed in a nightshirt	40	70	110
Minnie Mouse Fun-E-Flex Figure	Fun-E-Flex	1930s	5" Minnie with fingered hands	125	225	350
Minnie Mouse Hand Puppet		1940s	11" tall, white on red polka-dot, fabric hard cover and a pair of black & white felt hands	50	95	145
Minnie Mouse Music Box	Schmid Bros.	1970s	3 1/2" diameter, plays "Love Story"	11	20	30
Minnie Mouse Plastic Clock	Phinney-Walker	1970s	8" diameter by 1 1/2" deep, "Behind Every Great Man, There is A Woman!"	35	65	100
Minnie Mouse Rocker	Marx	1950s	Tin, wind-up, rocker moves back & forth with gravity motion of her head & ears	250	350	500
Minnie Mouse Wristwatch	Timex	1958	Small round chrome case, stainless back, articulated hands, yellow vinylite band	55	100	150
Minnie Mouse Wristwatch	Bradley	1978	Meduim gold case, sweep seconds, red vinyl band, articulated hands	16	30	45
Minnie with Bump-n-Go Action Shopping Cart	Illfelder	1980s	4x9 1/2x11 1/2" tall, plastic, battery operated Minnie pushing cart	25	50	75
Mousegetar Jr.	Mattel	1955	Hand crank play guitar with paper litho label of Mickey's face	35	60	95
Mouseketeer Cut-outs	Whitman	1957	Figures & clothing sheets	23	45	65
Mouseketeer Fan Club Typewriter		1950s	Lithographed tin	45	85	135
Tennis Sport Watch	Bradley	1970s	2 1/2x6x2 1/2" tall with a plastic case, white dial with Mickey playing tennis, the second hand has a tennis ball on the end of it	35	65	100
Tin Tray (Mickey & Minnie in a Rowboat)	Ohio Art	1930s	5 1/2"x7 1/4", tin, lithograph	20	40	60
Two Gun Mickey Mouse Watch			Saddle tan western style band	23	45	65

Mickey & Minnie Mouse, Disney

TOY	COMPANY	YEAR	DESCRIPTION	GOOD	EX	MIB
Walt Disney's Mickey Mouse Play Tiles	Halsam	1964	336 tiles to create Pinocchio, Jiminy Cricket, Goofy, Donald and etc.	12	23	35
Walt Disney's Mickey Mouse Water Globes		1970s	3x4 1/2x5" tall, three dimensional plastic figures of Mickey seated with a plastic water globe between his legs	25	50	75

Mighty Mouse

TOY	COMPANY	YEAR	DESCRIPTION	GOOD	EX	MIB
Mighty Mouse & Heckle & Jeckle Sliding Puzzle	Fleetwood	1979		6	12	18
Mighty Mouse & His TV Pals Puzzle			2 1/2" square, tile	9	16	25
Mighty Mouse Ball Game	Ja-Ru	1981		4	7	10
Mighty Mouse Charm Bracelet		1950s	Brass charms of Gandy Goose, Terry Bear, Mighty Mouse and other Terrytoon characters	25	50	75
Mighty Mouse Cinema Viewer	Fleetwood	1979	Has four strips	7	13	20
Mighty Mouse Dynamite Dasher	Takara	1981		5	10	15
Mighty Mouse Figure		1950s	9" vinyl, squeeze toy	16	30	45
Mighty Mouse Figure	Dakin	1977	Hard & soft vinyl figure	18	35	50
Mighty Mouse Flashlight	Dyno	1979	3.5" figural light	5	10	15
Mighty Mouse Fun Farm Figure	Dakin	1978		23	45	65
Mighty Mouse Make a Face Sheet	Towne	1958	With dials to change face parts	12	23	35
Mighty Mouse Mighty Money	Fleetwood	1979		2	4	6
Mighty Mouse Money Press	Ja-Ru	1981	Stamps, pads and money	2	4	6
Mighty Mouse Movie Viewer	Chemtoy	1980		5	10	15
Mighty Mouse Picture Play Lite	Janex	1983		6	11	17
Mighty Mouse PVC Figures		1988	Hands on hips, taking off, hands clasped at chest, each	2	4	6
Mighty Mouse Sneakers	Randy Co.	1960s	Children sizes 7 1/2 unused, graphics on box, picture on sneakers	35	65	95
Mighty Mouse Squeaker Figure		1950s	9 1/2" rubber	25	50	75
Mighty Mouse Stuffed Doll	Ideal	1950s	14" tall, stuffed, cloth	40	75	115
Mighty Mouse Vinyl Doll			9 1/2" tall	35	65	100
Mighty Mouse Wallet	Larami	1978		5	10	15
Mighty Mouse Wristwatch	Bradley	1979	Medium chrome case,	30	55	85

Miscellaneous Characters

TOY	COMPANY	YEAR	DESCRIPTION	GOOD	EX	MIB
Bewitched Samantha Doll	Ideal	1967	12 1/2" tall	185	340	525
Bonzo Scooter Toy			7" in length & Bonzo 6", wind-up	140	260	400
Bruce Lee Figure	Largo	1986		6	12	18

Miscellaneous Characters

TOY	COMPANY	YEAR	DESCRIPTION	GOOD	EX	MIB
Captain Kangaroo and Bunny Rabbit Presto Slate	Fairchild	1960s	Lift-to-erase drawing slate on card illustrated with pictures of the Captain and Bunny Rabbit	14	25	40
Captain Kangaroo and Mr. Green Jeans Presto Slate	Fairchild	1960s	Lift-to-erase drawing slate on card illustrated with pictures of the Captain and Mr. Green Jeans	14	25	40
Daniel Boone Figure	Remco	1964	5" tall, hard plastic body with large vinyl head, has cloth coonskin cap and longrifle	35	60	95
Debby Boone Doll	Mattel		10" tall	20	40	60
Diamond Jim		1930s	5 1/2" tall	45	80	125
Donny & Marie Country & Rock Rhythm Set		1976		7	13	20
Dr. Kildare Photo Scrapbook		1962	Photo scrapbook	23	45	65
Dragnet Badge 714	Knickerbocker	1955	2 1/2" bronze finish badge in yellow box with illustration of Jack Webb, box bottom has ID card	23	456	65
Flipper Tray Puzzles		1966	Set of four frame tray puzzles	20	40	60
Flying Nun Doll	Kayline Co.	1970		16	30	45
Flying Nun Oil Paint By Numbers	Hasbro	1960s	Boxed set of two scenes and 10 paint vials	11	20	30
Jimmy Carter Radio			Peanut shaped transistor radio with Jimmy	16	30	45
Jimmy Carter Wind-up Walking Peanut			5" tall	9	16	25
Joan Palooka "Stringless Marionette"	Nat'l Mask & Puppet	1952	12 1/2" tall 'daughter of Joe Palooka' doll comes with pink blanket and birth certificate	60	115	175
Joe Penner & His Duck Goo Goo	Marx	1934	Wind-up, "Wanna buy a duck?" lithographed on ths side of Joe's basket of ducks	300	450	650
Komic Kamera Film Viewer Set			5" long, Dick Tracy, Little Orphan Annie, Terry & the Pirates & The Lone Ranger	35	65	105
Little King Lucky Safety Card		1953	2"x4" cards, Little King warns you about crossing the street at night	11	20	30
Lyndon Johnson Figure	Remco	1960s		30	55	85
Mr. & Mrs. Potato Head Set	Hasbro	1960s	Cars, boats, shopping trailer and etc.	30	55	85
Mr. Potato Head Frankie Frank	Hasbro	1966	Companion toy to Mr. P., with accessories	25	45	70
Mr. Potato Head Frenchy Fry	Hasbro	1966	Companion toy to Mr. P., with accessories	25	45	70
Mr. Potato Head Ice Pops	Hasbro	1950s	Plastic head molds for freezing treats in box	16	30	45
Patton Figure	Excel Toy Corp.		Poseable doll with cloth cloths and accessories	16	30	45
Pinky Lee Costume		1950s	Hat, pants and shirt	50	95	145
President Bush Figure			7" tall	11	20	30
Prince Charles of Wales Figure	Goldberger	1982	13" tall, dressed in palace guard uniform	25	50	75
Red Ranger Ride 'em Cowboy	Wyandotte	1930s	Tin wind-up rocker	140	260	400
Ringling Bros & Barnum & Bailey Circus Playset		1970s	Vinyl fold out set with animals, trapeze personnel, clowns and assorted circus equipment	16	30	45
Robin Hood View-Master Pack		1954		7	13	20

Miscellaneous Characters

TOY	COMPANY	YEAR	DESCRIPTION	GOOD	EX	MIB
Sir Reginald Play-N-Save Bank		1960s	7" tall plastic lion & hunter, on a 15" green plastic base, the hunter fires the coin into the lion's mouth	45	80	125
Starsky & Hutch Shoot-Out Target Set	Berwick	1970s		9	16	25
Sylvester Stallone Rambo Figure		1986	18" tall, poseable figure	9	16	25
Uncle Don's "Puzzy & Sizzy" Membership Card		1950s		12	23	35
Willie Whopper Pencil Case		1930s	Green with illustrations of Willie, Pirate and his gal	40	75	120
Winky Dink Magic Crayons		1960s		16	30	45
Winky Dink Secret Message Game	Lowell	1950s		70	125	195

Moon Mullins

TOY	COMPANY	YEAR	DESCRIPTION	GOOD	EX	MIB
Moon Mullins & Kayo Railroad Handcar Toy	Marx	1930s	6" long, wind-up, both figures bendable arms & legs	300	450	600
Moon Mullins & Kayo Toothbrush Holder			4" tall, bisque	35	60	95
Moon Mullins Featured Funnies Jigsaw Puzzle		1930s	9 1/2"x14" puzzle	35	60	95
Moon Mullins Figure Set			Bisque, Uncle Willie, Kayo, Moon Mullins & Emmy, heights range from 2 1/4" tall to 3 1/2"	95	180	275
Moon Mullins Playstone Funnies Mold Set		1940s		35	65	100

Mr. Magoo

TOY	COMPANY	YEAR	DESCRIPTION	GOOD	EX	MIB
Magoo Car	(Japan)		9" battery operated car	80	145	225
Magoo Soakie Soap Container		1960s	10" tall, vinyl & plastic	12	23	35
Mr. Magoo Car	Hubley	1961	7 1/2" tallx9" long, metal, battery operated	90	165	250
Mr. Magoo Doll	Ideal	1962	5" tall, vinyl head with cloth body	30	55	85
Mr. Magoo Doll	Ideal	1970	12" tall	20	35	55
Mr. Magoo Drinking Glass		1962	5 1/2" tall	12	23	35
Mr. Magoo Figure	Dakin		7" tall	25	50	75
Mr. Magoo Hand Puppet		1960s	Vinyl head with cloth body	30	50	80

Munsters, The

TOY	COMPANY	YEAR	DESCRIPTION	GOOD	EX	MIB
Herman Munster	Remco	1964		105	150	230
Lilly Figure	Remco	1964		115	165	250
Lilly Munster Baby Figure	Ideal	1965		30	45	65
Set of Three Munsters (Herman, Lilly and Grandpa)	Remco			225	425	700

Music

TOY	COMPANY	YEAR	DESCRIPTION	GOOD	EX	MIB
Andy Gibb Figure	Ideal	1979	6" tall	9	16	25
Andy Gibb Figure	Ideal	1979	8" tall	15	25	40
Beatles Coloring Book	Saalfield	1964	Thick coloring book	23	45	65
Beatles Toy Watches		1960s	Set of four nonworking play watches, tin w/plastic bands, on card	25	50	75
Boy George Doll	LJN	1980s	12" tall posable in alphabet shirt	35	60	95
Boy George Doll	LJN	1980s	15" Huggard Cute Cuddly version in polka dot shirt	25	50	75
Dolly Parton Doll	Goldberger	1970s	12" tall	25	45	70
Donny Osmond Figure	Mattel	1976	12" tall	14	25	40
Elvis Doll	World Doll	1984	18" tall doll in box	30	60	90
Elvis Doll	World Dolls	1984	21" tall	55	100	150
Elvis Presley Figure			12" tall	25	50	75
Elvis Presley Quartz Wrist Watch	Bradley	1983	White plastic case, stainless back, face shows a young Elvis, white vinyl band	16	30	45
KISS Ace Doll	Mego	1979		40	70	110
KISS Gene Simmons Doll	Mego	1979	12' tall in costume and makeup	35	65	100
KISS Paul Stanley Doll	Mego	1979	12" tall makeup and costume	35	65	100
KISS Peter Criss Doll	Mego	1979		35	65	100
Marie Osmond Figure	Mattel		12" tall	11	20	30
Marie Osmond Modeling Doll			30" tall	35	60	95
Michael Jackson AM Radio	Ertl	1984		9	16	25
Michael Jackson American Music Awards Doll	LJN			18	35	50
Michael Jackson Beat It Doll	LJN			18	35	50
Michael Jackson Cordless Electronic Microphone	LJN	1984		7	13	20
Michael Jackson Grammy Awards Doll	LJN			18	35	50
Michael Jackson Thriller Doll	LJN			18	35	50
Michel Jackson Thriller Gang/Glow Bendy Set of Six				23	45	65
Paul McCartney Doll	Remco	1964		80	150	230
Ringo Starr Doll	Remco	1964		80	150	230
Toni Tennile Figure			12" tall	11	20	30

Mutt & Jeff

TOY	COMPANY	YEAR	DESCRIPTION	GOOD	EX	MIB
Mutt & Jeff Coin Bank			5" tall, cast iron, two piece construction held together by screw in the back	45	80	125
Mutt & Jeff Doll Set		1920s	8" & 6 1/2" tall, composition hands & heads with heavy cast iron feet, moveable arms & legs, fabric clothing	165	310	475
Mutt & Jeff Statue Set	A. Steinhardt & Bros	1911	Ceramic, with a coin inserted into the base of each one	70	125	195
Character Figures		1958	9" tall, vinyl, Charlie Brown, Snoopy and Lucy, each	18	35	50
Charlie Brown Nodder	(Japan)	1960s	5 1/2" tall, bobbing head	18	35	50

Peanuts

TOY	COMPANY	YEAR	DESCRIPTION	GOOD	EX	MIB
Lucy Wristwatch	Timex	1970s	Small chrome case, articulated arms, sweep seconds, white vinyl band	23	45	65
Peanuts Coloring Book	Saalfield	1960s		9	16	25
Peanuts Gang Five Figural Banks	United Features	1970	Set of five	45	80	125
Peanuts Gang Five Figural Music Boxes	Schmid Bros.	1970	Set of five music boxes	35	65	100
Peanuts Music Box	Schmid Bros.	1980		15	25	40
Peanuts Tea Set		1961	One tray, 2 plates, 2 cups, 4 small plates all with Peanuts artwork on all of them	25	50	75
Peppermint Patty Peanuts Gang Rag Doll			14" tall	7	13	20
Snoopy as Astronaut Music Box	Schmid Bros.	1970s		20	35	55
Snoopy Belle Figure	Knickerbocker		Figure	4	8	12
Snoopy Figural Bank	United Features	1968	7"	14	25	40
Snoopy Jack in the Box	Mattel	1970s	Tin box with a plastic Snoopy that pops out after you crank it	16	30	45
Snoopy Nodder	(Japan)	1960s	5 1/2" tall, bobbing head	19	35	55
Snoopy Pop Up Figure Music Box	Mattel	1966	5", steel	16	30	45
Snoopy Snowdome			On top of doghouse	6	12	18
Snoopy Tennis Animated Wristwatch	Timex	1970s	Gold bezel, tennis ball circles Snoopy on clear disk, articulated hands holding racket, denim background and band	25	50	75

Pee Wee Herman

TOY	COMPANY	YEAR	DESCRIPTION	GOOD	EX	MIB
Ball Dart Set				5	10	15
Billy Baloney Figure	Matchbox	1988	18" tall	7	13	20
Chairry Figure	Matchbox	1988	5" tall	3	5	8
Chairry Figure	Matchbox		15" tall	6	12	18
Conky Wacky Wind-up	Matchbox	1988		3	5	8
Cowboy Curtis Figure	Matchbox			5	10	15
Deluxe Colorforms				5	10	15
Globey with Randy	Matchbox	1988		4	7	10
King of Cartoons Figure	Matchbox	1988	5" tall	3	5	8
Magic Screen Figure	Matchbox	1988	5" tall poseable	3	5	8
Magic Screen Wacky Wind-up	Matchbox	1988	6" tall	3	5	8
Miss Yvonne Figure	Matchbox	1988	Poseable 5" tall	3	5	8
Pee Wee Doll			15" tall, non talking	7	13	20
Pee Wee Herman	Matchbox	1988	Poseable 5" tall	4	8	12
Pee Wee Herman Play Set	Matchbox	1989	Deluxe play set 20"x28"x8" for use with all 5" figures, Pee Wee's bike and folds into large carrying case	12	23	35
Pee Wee Herman Ventriloquist Doll				14	25	40
Pee Wee with Scooter and Helmet	Matchbox	1988		4	7	10
Pee Wee Yo Yo				2	3	5
Pterri Doll			13" tall	14	25	40

Pee Wee Herman

TOY	COMPANY	YEAR	DESCRIPTION	GOOD	EX	MIB
Pterri Wacky Wind-ups	Matchbox	1988		3	5	8
Reba Figure	Matchbox	1988	Poseable	3	5	8
Ricardo Figure	Matchbox	1988		3	5	8
Slumber Bag	Matchbox	1988		11	20	30
Vance the Talking Pig	Matchbox	1987		14	25	40
View Master Gift Set				5	10	15

Pepe Le Pew

TOY	COMPANY	YEAR	DESCRIPTION	GOOD	EX	MIB
Pepe Le Pew "Goofy Gram"	Dakin	1971		20	35	55
Pepe Le Pew Figure	Dakin	1971	8" tall	23	45	65

Percy Crosby

TOY	COMPANY	YEAR	DESCRIPTION	GOOD	EX	MIB
Our Beloved Skippy Jigsaw Puzzles				25	50	75
Skippy Doll	Effanbee		Wood composition	55	100	150
Skippy Figurine		1930s	5" tall, bisque	45	80	125
Skippy Jigsaw Puzzle		1933	Framed	15	25	40
Skippy Mug			Silverplate	45	80	125
Skippy Silverware Set			Spoon & fork 4 1/2" long, plate 8" diameter	55	100	150

Peter Pan

TOY	COMPANY	YEAR	DESCRIPTION	GOOD	EX	MIB
Captain Hook Figurine			8" tall, plastic	9	15	25
Captain Hook Hand Puppet	Gund	1950s	9" tall	30	60	90
Peter Pan Baby Figure	Sun Rubber Co.	1950s		45	80	125
Peter Pan Cardboard Statuettes	Whitman	1952	7 1/2x12 1/2x1", set of 11 diecut cardboard figures	35	65	100
Peter Pan Charm Bracelet		1974		11	20	30
Peter Pan Doll	Duchess Doll Corp.	1953	11 1/2" tall, brown trim fabric shoes, green mesh stockings with flocked outfit, hat with a large red feather, shiny silver white metal dagger in belt, eyes, arms & head move	150	275	425
Peter Pan Doll	Ideal	1953	18" tall	95	180	275
Peter Pan Frame Tray Puzzle	Jaymar	1950s	Puzzle show Peter, Wendy, John and Michael flying over Neverland	16	30	45
Peter Pan Hand Puppet	Oak Rubber Co.	1953	Rubber hand puppet	45	80	125
Peter Pan Map of Neverland		1953	18x24", collectors issue, dedicated to the users of Peter Pan Beauty Bar	45	80	125
Peter Pan Nodder		1950s	6" tall	25	50	75
Peter Pan Push Puppet	Kohner	1950s	6" tall, green & flesh colored beads with plastic head & a light green thin plastic hat	30	50	80
Peter Pan Sewing Cards	Whitman	1952		14	25	40

Top to Bottom: Red Ranger Mechanical Ride 'em Cowboy, Wyandotte, 1930s; Popeye Getar, Mattel, 1950s; Dick Tracy Junior Detective Kit, Golden, 1962; Captain Kangaroo and Mr. Green Jeans/Bunny Rabbit Presto Magic Slates, Fairchild, 1960s

Peter Pan

TOY	COMPANY	YEAR	DESCRIPTION	GOOD	EX	MIB
Tinker Bell Doll	Duchess Doll Corp.	1953	8" tall, flocked green outfit with a pair of large white fabric wings with gold trim, eyes open & close, jointed arms & head moves	115	210	325
Tinker Bell Figure	A.D. Sutton & Sons	1960s	7" tall, plastic & rubber figure	25	50	75
Tinker Bell Pincushion with Figure		1960s	Pincushion with 1 1/2" tall Tink figure, in clear plastic display can	25	45	65
Wendy Doll	Duchess Doll Corp.	1953	8" tall, full purple length skirt with purple bow in back of dress, eyes open & close, jointed arms & head moves	115	210	325

Peter Potamus

TOY	COMPANY	YEAR	DESCRIPTION	GOOD	EX	MIB
Breezley Soakie	Purex	1967	9" tall, plastic	25	50	75
Peter Potamus Soakie	Purex	1960s	10 1/2" tall, plastic	12	23	35

Pink Panther

TOY	COMPANY	YEAR	DESCRIPTION	GOOD	EX	MIB
Pink Panther & Inspector Hiking Puzzle	Whitman		100 pieces	4	8	12
Pink Panther & Sons Fun at the Picnic Book	Golden			5	10	15
Pink Panther & Sons Lite	Ja-Ru		Mini flashlight, plastic	4	7	10
Pink Panther & Sons Target Game	Ja-Ru			5	10	15
Pink Panther & The Fancy Party Book	Golden			5	10	15
Pink Panther & The Haunted House Book	Golden			5	10	15
Pink Panther at Castle Kreep Book	Whitman			4	7	10
Pink Panther at The Circus Sticker Book	Golden	1963		5	10	15
Pink Panther Coloring Book	Whitman	1976	Cover shows PP roasting hot dogs	7	13	20
Pink Panther Figure	Dakin	1971	8" tall, with legs closed	16	30	45
Pink Panther Figure	Dakin	1971	8" tall, with legs open	14	25	40
Pink Panther Memo Board			Write on or off memo board	5	10	15
Pink Panther Motorcycle			2 1/2" plastic	4	7	10
Pink Panther One Man Band	Illco	1980	10" tall, battery operated, plush body with vinyl head	25	50	75
Pink Panther Pool Game	Ja-Ru			4	7	10
Pink Panther Putty	Ja-Ru			4	7	10
Pink Panther Puzzle	Whitman		100 pieces "in refrigerator"	4	8	12
Pink Panther Puzzle, "Club Posh"	Whitman		100 pieces	4	8	12
Pink Panther Wind-up			3" tall, plastic, walking wind-up with trench coat & glasses	7	13	20
Xmas Music Box	Royal Orleans	1982	1982 limited edition	25	45	65

Pink Panther

TOY	COMPANY	YEAR	DESCRIPTION	GOOD	EX	MIB
Xmas Music Box	Royal Orleans	1983	1983 limited edition	25	45	65
Xmas Music Box	Royal Orleans	1984	1984 limited edition	25	45	65

Pinocchio & Jiminy Cricket

TOY	COMPANY	YEAR	DESCRIPTION	GOOD	EX	MIB
"Walt Disney Tells the Story of Pinocchio"	Whitman	1939	4 1/4"x6 1/2" paperback, 144 pages	25	50	75
Figaro Figure	Multi-Wood Products	1940	3" tall, hand-carved wood composition	30	55	85
Figaro Roll Over Wind-up Toy	Marx	1940	5" long with ears & tail, tin	65	100	145
Figaro Tin Friction Toy	Linemar	1960s	1 1/2x3x1 1/2" tall	25	50	75
Gepetto Figure	Multi-Wood Products	1940	5 1/2" tall, wood composition	50	95	145
Gideon Figure	Multi-Wood Products		5" tall	35	65	100
Honest John Figure	Multi-Wood Products		2 1/2x3" base with a 7" tall figure	45	80	125
Jiminy Cricket Hand Puppet	Gund	1950s	11" tall	35	60	95
Jiminy Cricket Marionette	Pelham Puppets	1950s	3x6x10" tall, head is a dark green with a reddish/orange mouth and large black & white eyes with yellow accents in a gray felt hat	70	130	200
Jiminy Cricket Pushing Bass Fiddle Ramp Walker	Marx	1960s	1x3x3" tall, pushing a bass fiddle	110	150	220
Jiminy Cricket Snap-eeze Figure	Marx		3 1/2x4 3/4" tall, white plastic base with moveable arms & legs	25	50	75
Jiminy Cricket Soakie			7" tall bottle	9	16	25
Jiminy Cricket Toothbrush Set	Dupont	1950s	Plastic wall hanging Jiminy holds a toothbrush	25	50	75
Jiminy Cricket Wooden Doll	Ideal	1940	Wooden jointed doll	140	260	400
Jiminy Cricket Wristwatch	US Time	1948	"1948 US Time Birthday Series"	60	115	175
Lampwick Figure	Multi-Wood Products	1940	5 1/2" tall, wood composition	40	75	115
Pin the Nose on Pinocchio Game	Parker Brothers	1939	15 1/2"x20"	45	80	125
Pinocchio Bank	Pal Plastics	1970s	7x7x10" tall, vinyl, 3-D molded head of Pinocchio	12	23	35
Pinocchio Bank	Crown Toy	1939	5" tall, wood composition with metal trap door on back	65	120	185
Pinocchio Bell-Ringing Pull Toy	Fisher-Price	1939	7" long by 9" tall, Pinocchio figure rocks back & forth on donkey and rings the bell on top of donkey's head	70	130	200
Pinocchio Big Little Book		1940		23	45	65
Pinocchio Color Box	Transogram		Also known today as paint box	12	23	35
Pinocchio Cut-Out Books	Whitman	1940		40	70	110
Pinocchio Doll	Knickerbocker	1940	3 1/2x4x9 1/2" tall, jointed composition doll with moveable arms & head	185	345	525
Pinocchio Doll	Ideal	1939	12" tall with wire mesh arms & legs	105	195	300
Pinocchio Doll	Ideal	1940	19 1/2" tall, composition doll	225	425	650

Pinocchio & Jiminy Cricket

TOY	COMPANY	YEAR	DESCRIPTION	GOOD	EX	MIB
Pinocchio Doll	Ideal	1940	10" tall, wood composition head & jointed arms & legs attached to body	70	130	200
Pinocchio Doll	Ideal	1940	8" tall, wood composition head, others are jointed wood	55	105	160
Pinocchio Figure	Crown Toy		9 1/2" tall, jointed arms	50	90	140
Pinocchio Figure	Crown Toy		3 1/2x4x9 1/2", joint composition figure	55	100	150
Pinocchio Figure	Multi-Wood Products	1940	5" tall, wood composition figure	45	80	125
Pinocchio Hand Puppet	Knickerbocker	1962		25	45	70
Pinocchio Hand Puppet	Crown Toy		9" tall, composition	25	50	75
Pinocchio Hand Puppet with Squeeker	Gund	1950s	10" tall	30	60	90
Pinocchio Music Box			Plays "Puppet on a String"	12	23	35
Pinocchio Paint Book	Disney	1939	11"x15" heavy paper cover	30	35	55
Pinocchio Paperweight & Thermometer	Plastic Novelties	1940		25	50	75
Pinocchio Picture Book	Grosset & Dunlap	1939	9 1/2"x13", laminated cover	25	50	75
Pinocchio Plastic Bank	Play Pal Plastics	1960s	11 1/2" tall, plastic	12	23	35
Pinocchio Plastic Cup	Safetyware	1939	2 3/4" tall, plastic	35	65	100
Pinocchio Push Puppet	Kohner	1970s	5" tall	9	16	25
Pinocchio Puzzle	Jaymar	1960s	5x7", titled "Pinocchio's Expedition"	11	20	30
Pinocchio Soakie				9	16	25
Pinocchio Story Book	Whitman	1939	8 1/2"x11 1/2", 96 pages	16	30	45
Pinocchio Story Book Set	Whitman	1940	8 1/2"x11 1/2" complete set of six books 24 pages each	95	180	275
Pinocchio Tea Set	Ohio Art	1939	Tin, tray, plates, saucers, serving platter, cups, bowls & smaller plates	45	85	130
Pinocchio the Acrobat Wind-up Toy	Marx	1939	2 1/2x11x17" tall, turning on a trapeze-like frame, titled "Pinocchio the Acrobat"	125	200	250
Pinocchio Tin Crayon Box	Transogram	1940s	4 1/2x5 1/2x1/2" deep	16	30	45
Pinocchio Vinyl Bank	Play Pal Plastics		4 1/2x5x11" tall	12	23	35
Pinocchio Walker	Marx	1938	9" tall, rocking action	200	275	400
Pinocchio Water Dome	Disney	1970s	3x4 1/2x5" tall, Pinocchio is sitting and holding a plastic dome between his hands & feet, plastic small house with snowflakes creating a winter scene when shaken	25	50	75
Pinocchio Wind-Up Toy	Linemar		6" tall, wind-up, arms & legs move	80	145	225
Pinocchio/Cricket Dolls	Knickerbocker	1962	6" tall, vinyl, titled "Knixies", each	25	50	75
Pinocchio/Jiminy Push Puppet	Marx	1960s	2 1/2x5x4" tall, double puppet	25	50	75
Walt Disney's Version of Pinocchio	Random House	1939	8 1/2"x11 1/2" hardcover	20	40	60

Pluto

TOY	COMPANY	YEAR	DESCRIPTION	GOOD	EX	MIB
Miniature Pluto	Linemar		4" long, when pushed friction motor makes his tongue wag	30	55	85

Pluto

TOY	COMPANY	YEAR	DESCRIPTION	GOOD	EX	MIB
Pluto	Linemar		9" friction toy, Pluto pulling red wagon	60	115	175
Pluto "Pop Up Critter" Figure	Fisher-Price	1936	Wooden figure of Pluto standing on base 10 1/2" long	80	145	225
Pluto Bank	Animal Toys Plus Inc.	1970s	9" tall vinyl, Pluto standing in front of a doghouse	15	30	45
Pluto Ceramic Bank	Disney	1940s	4x4 1/2x6 1/2" tall	35	65	100
Pluto Drum Major	Marx	1950s	Tin	225	355	475
Pluto Electric Alarm Clock	Allied Mfg.	1955	4x5 1/2x10" tall, eyes and hands shaped like dog bones and they glow in the dark	80	145	225
Pluto Friction Toy	Linemar		4"	35	60	95
Pluto Fun-E-Flex Figure	Fun-E-Flex	1930s	Wood	35	65	100
Pluto Hand Puppet	Gund	1950s	9" tall	25	50	75
Pluto Lantern Toy	Linemar	1950s		150	275	425
Pluto Pop-A-Part Toy	Multiple Toymakers	1965	9" long, plastic	11	20	30
Pluto Purse	Gund	1940s	9x14x2"	30	55	85
Pluto Push Toy	Fisher-Price	1936	8" long, wood	70	130	200
Pluto Rolykins Figure	Marx		1x1x1 1/2" tall, with ball bearing action set	14	25	40
Pluto Rubber Figure	Seiberling	1930s	3 1/2" long	35	65	100
Pluto Rubber Figure	Seiberling	1930s	7" tall, rubber	35	65	100
Pluto Sports Car	Empire		2" long	9	16	25
Pluto the Acrobat Trapeze Toy	Linemar		10" tall, metal, celluloid, wind-up	70	125	195
Pluto Tricycle Toy	Linemar	1950s	Tin	195	350	550
Pluto Watch Me Roll Over	Marx	1939	8" long, tin, Pluto turns over as his tail passes beneath him	125	180	275

Popeye

TOY	COMPANY	YEAR	DESCRIPTION	GOOD	EX	MIB
Brutus Doll	Presents	1985	Medium size	7	13	20
Brutus Soakie	Colgate	1960s	10" tall, wearing a striped shirt & captain's hat	9	16	25
Funny Fire Fighters	Marx	1930s	Celluloid Popeye & Bluto figures	800	1200	1600
Give-A-Show Projector	Kenner		112 color slides	45	80	125
Official Popeye Pipe "It Lites, It Toots"		1958	5" stem with 2" bowl, battery operated	25	50	75
Olive Oyl Doll	Presents	1985	11 1/2" tall, with black yarn hair	12	23	35
Olive Oyl Doll	Uneeda	1979	Removeable clothing	4	7	10
Olive Oyl Doll	Dakin	1960s	8" tall	7	13	20
Olive Oyl Figural Toy	King Features	1940	8" tall	50	95	145
Olive Oyl Figurine	Ben Cooper	1974	Rubber	7	13	20
Olive Oyl Hand Puppet	Gund	1960s	Olive illustrated with comic strip body	23	45	65
Olive Oyl Miniature Figure			Lead	7	13	20
Olive Oyl Push Puppet	Kohner	1960s		11	20	30
Olive Oyl Squeeze Toy	Rempel	1950s	Vinyl	18	35	50
Olive Oyl TV "Cartoon Theater"		1976		15	30	45
Olive Oyl with Swee' Pea Doll			9" tall vinyl sqeeze doll	6	12	18
Popeye	Dakin			20	40	60
Popeye & Brutus Jump-Up Figures	Imperial	1979	Each	2	5	7
Popeye & His Punching Bag Toy	Chein	1930s	8" tall, tin, wind-up	1000	1250	1400

Popeye

TOY	COMPANY	YEAR	DESCRIPTION	GOOD	EX	MIB
Popeye & Olive Oyl Bendables	Bronco Co.	1978	Each	3	5	8
Popeye & Olive Oyl Figural Music Box	Schmid Bros.		8 /14"	45	80	125
Popeye & Olive Oyl Jiggers	Marx	1936	9 1/2" tall, wind-up Popeye and he dances wildly while Olive rocks as she plays her accordion	850	1200	1500
Popeye Bank	Play Pal Plastics	1972	Shape of Popeye's head, plastic	7	13	20
Popeye Bendable	Jesco	1988		3	5	8
Popeye Bubble Liquid	M. Shimmel Sons Inc.	1970s	Shaped like Popeye with a necktie similar to a sailors knot	4	7	10
Popeye Bubble Set	Transogram	1936	5"x7 1/2", two wooden pipes, tin soap tray & a piece of soap for bubbles	30	60	90
Popeye Chase Set			15" long, wooden push cars, one with Bluto driving showing Olive Oyl screaming in the back seat, the other Popeye on the fender of the Police car with Swee' Pea driving	55	100	150
Popeye Color & Recolor Book	Jack Built	1957	Color, wipe & color again	12	23	35
Popeye Costume & Mask	Collegeville	1950s		18	35	50
Popeye Costume & Mask	Collegeville	1960s		9	16	25
Popeye Costume & Mask	Collegeville	1980s		4	7	10
Popeye Crazy Colorfoam	American Aerosol	1980	Squeeze can & white foam comes out of mouth	4	7	10
Popeye Daily Quarter Bank	Kalin	1950s	4 1/2" tall, metal	60	115	175
Popeye Dime Register Bank		1929	2 1/2"x2 1/2", square, window shows total deposits in bank	45	80	125
Popeye Doll	Gund	1958	20" tall	45	80	125
Popeye Doll	Lakeside	1968	12" tall, sponge-like rubber	14	25	40
Popeye Doll	Stack Mfg.	1936	12" tall, wood jointed with pipe	95	180	275
Popeye Doll	Presents	1985	Large size	16	30	45
Popeye Doll	Presents	1985	Medium size	7	13	20
Popeye Doll	Uneeda	1979	Vinyl	4	7	10
Popeye Doll	Etone International	1983		4	7	10
Popeye Earring Holder		1970s	5 1/2" tall, metal	9	16	25
Popeye Express	Marx	1932	9" tall, wind-up with Popeye carrying a pair of parrot cages	425	600	850
Popeye Figural Head Pipe	Edmonton Pipe Co.	1970		14	25	40
Popeye Figural Puppet	Kohner	1960	4" tall	20	35	55
Popeye Figural Toothbrush Holder	Vandor		5" tall	9	16	25
Popeye Figural Toy	Kohner		4 1/4" tall	11	20	30
Popeye Figure	Dakin		8" tall with spinach can	16	30	45
Popeye Figure	Duncan	1970	8" tall	16	30	45
Popeye Figure			5" tall, wood jointed held together with internal string	35	65	100
Popeye Figurine	Ben Cooper	1974	Rubber	7	13	20
Popeye Figurine	Combex	1960s	Rubber with a can of spinach	12	23	35

Popeye

TOY	COMPANY	YEAR	DESCRIPTION	GOOD	EX	MIB
Popeye Getar	Mattel	1950s	14" long, shaped like Popeye's face, use crank and guitar plays "I'm Popeye the Sailor Man" or remove pipe and strum	25	50	75
Popeye Gumball Machine	Hasbro	1968	6" tall in shape of Popeye's head	9	16	25
Popeye Hammer Game	Holgate		When wooden hammer strikes one of the two wedges, Popeye kicks the weight to the other side	20	35	55
Popeye Hand Puppet	Gund	1960s	Popeye's head on a cloth body with little ships on material	25	50	75
Popeye in the Music Box	Mattel	1957	Metal, crank handle with plastic Popeye pop-up in spinach can	55	100	150
Popeye Jigsaw Puzzle	Jaymar	1945	22"x13 1/2" with frame	12	23	35
Popeye Lantern	Linemar	1960s	7 1/2" tall, metal, battery operated	90	165	250
Popeye Magic Play Around	Amso	1950s	Popeye characters with magnetic bases that slide across playset	35	65	95
Popeye Marionette	Joan	1987	Wood	4	7	10
Popeye Mechanical Pencil	Eagle	1929	10 1/2" long illustrated pencil with box	25	50	75
Popeye Music Box		1980	Plays "I'm Popeye the Sailor Man" with figure dancing the jig	18	35	50
Popeye on Tricycle	Linemar		4 1/2", tin wind-up with celluloid arms & legs, bell rings behind Popeye	70	130	200
Popeye Paints	American Crayon Co.	1933	6", tin	23	45	65
Popeye Pistol	Marx	1935		55	100	150
Popeye Playset	Cribmates, Inc.	1979	Popeye vinyl squeak toy, Olive Oyl and Swee' Pea squeak toy, mirror, rattle and pillow	11	20	30
Popeye Push Puppet	Kohner	1960s	Push button on the base and Popeye's arms & waist move	12	23	35
Popeye Soakie	Colgate	1960s	Shape of Popeye	9	16	25
Popeye Soap Set	Kerk Guild Soap	1930s	Olive Oyl, Swee' Pea & Popeye soap figures	45	80	125
Popeye Spinach Pop-up Toy	Mattel	1957	4 1/2" tall, steel spinach can with plastic figure	40	70	110
Popeye Squeeze Toy	Rempel	1950s	8" tall, vinyl	18	35	50
Popeye Talking Hand Puppet	Mattel	1968	Remove pipe and it can be used to blow bubbles	15	30	45
Popeye Talking View-Master Cartridges		1983		5	10	15
Popeye the Champ	Marx	1936	Tin & celluloid wind-up, with Popeye & Bluto fighting until one is knocked backwards to ring a bell	1500	2500	3200
Popeye the Juggler Bead Game		1929	3 1/2"x5", covered with glass	18	35	50
Popeye the Weatherman Colorforms Kit		1959		15	30	45
Popeye Toothbrush Set	Nasta	1980s	Popeye toothbrush dispenser in a boat holds two toothbrushes	5	10	15
Popeye Tricky Walker	Jaymar	1960s	Plastic	9	16	25
Popeye TV "Cartoon Theater"		1976		15	30	45
Popeye with Swee' Pea Doll			9" tall vinyl sqeeze doll	9	16	25
Popeye Xylophone Pull Toy	Metal Masters		10 1/2"x11 1/2", wood with paper litho labels & metal wheels	45	90	135

Popeye

TOY	COMPANY	YEAR	DESCRIPTION	GOOD	EX	MIB
Sea Hag Doll, The	Presents	1985		12	23	35
Swee' Pea Doll	Presents	1985		7	13	20
Swee' Pea Figural Bank	Vandor	1980	6 1/2" tall	12	23	35
Swee' Pea Hand Puppet	Gund	1960s	Bonnet on head with cloth body decorated with baby lambs	16	30	45
Wimpy Doll	Presents	1985	Holding a hamburger	12	23	35
Wimpy Hand Puppet	Gund	1950s	Fabric hand cover, vinyl squeaker head & voice	20	35	55
Wimpy Hand Puppet	Gund	1960s	Wimpy's head on a cloth body with squares on material	12	23	35
Wimpy Squeeze Toy	Rempel	1950s	Vinyl	18	35	50

Porky Pig

TOY	COMPANY	YEAR	DESCRIPTION	GOOD	EX	MIB
Porky & Petunia Pig Figurines	Warner Bros.	1975	4 1/2" tall	9	16	25
Porky Pig Bank		1930s	Tall bisque bank of Porky, hand painted orange, blue and yellow	55	100	150
Porky Pig Doll	Mattel	1960s	17" tall, cloth doll, vinyl head	15	30	45
Porky Pig Doll	Gund	1950	14" tall	45	80	125
Porky Pig Figure	Marx	1939	8" tall, tin, wind-up, umbrella with whirling action, with hat	195	250	375
Porky Pig Figure	Dakin	1968	7 3/4" tall in black velvet jacket	11	20	30
Porky Pig Soakie				11	20	30
Porky Pig Umbrella		1940s	Hard plastic 3" figure on end, Porky & Bugs printed in red cloth	40	75	115

Quick Draw McGraw

TOY	COMPANY	YEAR	DESCRIPTION	GOOD	EX	MIB
Auggie Doggie Soakie	Purex	1960s	10" tall, plastic	16	30	45
Augie Doggie Plush Doll	Knickerbocker	1959	10" tall, stuffed with vinyl face	16	30	45
Babalooey Bank	Knickerbocker	1960s	9" tall, vinyl bank with plastic head	16	30	45
Babalooey Plush Doll	Knickerbocker	1959	20" tall, with vinyl donkey ears & sombrero	35	65	100
Blabber Plush Toy	Knickerbocker	1959	15" tall, stuffed with vinyl face	25	50	75
Blabber Soakie	Purex	1960s	10 1/2" tall, plastic	16	30	45
Quick Draw McGraw Bank		1960	9 1/2" tall hard plastic figural bank, orange, white & blue	20	35	55
Quick Draw McGraw Playbook	Whitman	1960		15	25	40
Quick Draw McGraw Plush Toy	Knickerbocker	1959	16" tall, stuffed, vinyl face in cowboy hat	45	80	125
Quick Draw Mold & Model Cast Set		1960		25	50	75
Scooper Plush Toy	Knickerbocker	1959	20" tall, vinyl face	30	55	85

Raggedy Ann & Andy

TOY	COMPANY	YEAR	DESCRIPTION	GOOD	EX	MIB
Raggedy Andy Figure		1970s	Rubber/wire figure 4" tall	5	10	15
Raggedy Ann Coloring Book		1968		5	10	15

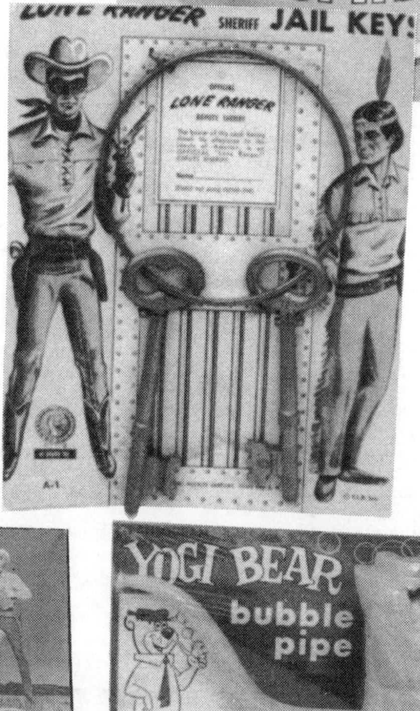

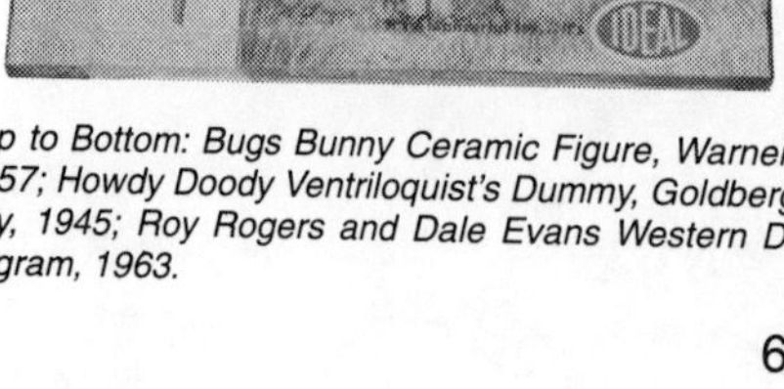

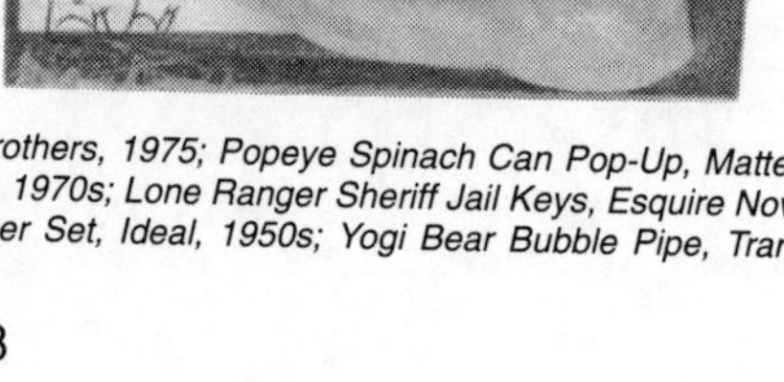

Top to Bottom: Bugs Bunny Ceramic Figure, Warner Brothers, 1975; Popeye Spinach Can Pop-Up, Mattel, 1957; Howdy Doody Ventriloquist's Dummy, Goldberger, 1970s; Lone Ranger Sheriff Jail Keys, Esquire Novelty, 1945; Roy Rogers and Dale Evans Western Dinner Set, Ideal, 1950s; Yogi Bear Bubble Pipe, Transogram, 1963.

Road Runner & Wile E.Coyote

TOY	COMPANY	YEAR	DESCRIPTION	GOOD	EX	MIB
Road Runner "Cartoon Theater" Figure			Plastic	9	16	25
Road Runner "Goofy Gram"	Dakin	1971		14	25	40
Road Runner & Coyote Lamp		1977	12 1/2" tall, with figures standing on base	20	35	55
Road Runner Bank			Standing on base	5	10	15
Road Runner Figure	Dakin	1968	8 3/4" tall	12	23	35
Road Runner Hand Puppet	(Japan)	1970s	10" tall, vinyl head with plastic hand cover	4	7	10
Road Runner Stuffed Doll	Mighty Star	1971	13" tall	9	16	25
Wile E. Coyote "Cartoon Theater"	Dakin	1976		9	16	25
Wile E. Coyote "Goofy Gram"	Dakin	1971	Fused bomb in right hand	14	25	40
Wile E. Coyote & the Road Runner Figurine	Royal Crown	1979	7" tall	11	20	30
Wile E. Coyote Doll	Mighty Star	1971	18" tall, stuffed	9	16	25
Wile E. Coyote Doll	Dakin	1970	On explosive box	15	30	45
Wile E. Coyote Figure	Dakin	1968	10" tall	12	23	35
Wile E. Coyote Hand Puppet	(Japan)	1970s	10" vinyl head, plastic hand cover	4	7	10
Wile E. Coyote Miniature Figure	Dakin		5 1/2" tall	9	16	25
Wile E. Coyote Nitelite	Applause	1980s		12	23	35

Rocky

TOY	COMPANY	YEAR	DESCRIPTION	GOOD	EX	MIB
Apollo Creed Doll	Phoenix Toys	1983	8" tall	3	6	9
Clubber Lang Doll	Phoenix Toys	1983	8" tall	5	10	15
Rocky Doll	Phoenix Toys	1983	8" tall	5	10	15

Rocky & Bullwinkle

TOY	COMPANY	YEAR	DESCRIPTION	GOOD	EX	MIB
Bullwinkle & Rocky Clock Bank	Larami	1969	4 1/2" tall, plastic	25	50	75
Bullwinkle & Rocky Waste Can		1961	11" tall, metal with Jay Ward cast pictured	35	65	100
Bullwinkle Bank		1960s	6" tall, glazed china	60	115	175
Bullwinkle Colorforms Cartoon Kit		1962		35	65	95
Bullwinkle Double Boomerangs	Larami	1969	Two boomerangs on 11x5" card illustrated with Rocky, Bullwinkle and a chicken	12	23	35
Bullwinkle Figure "Cartoon Theater"	Dakin	1976	7 1/2" tall, plastic	25	50	75
Bullwinkle for President Bumper Sticker		1972		9	16	25
Bullwinkle Jewelry Hanger		1960s	5" tall with a suction cup on back of head	12	23	35
Bullwinkle Magic Slate		1963		15	30	45
Bullwinkle Magnetic Travel Game	Larami	1971		15	30	45
Bullwinkle Melmac Dinner Set	Boonton Molding	1960s	Plate and cup illustrated with pictures of Bullwinkle and the Cheerios Kid	25	45	65

Rocky & Bullwinkle

TOY	COMPANY	YEAR	DESCRIPTION	GOOD	EX	MIB
Bullwinkle Moose Figure	Dakin			25	45	65
Bullwinkle Spell & Count Board		1969		9	16	25
Bullwinkle Stamp Set	Larami	1970		11	20	30
Bullwinkle Stickers		1984	3-2 1/2" Bullwinkle, Sherman and Peabody, Snidley Wiplash	5	10	15
Bullwinkle Talking Doll	Mattel	1970		25	50	75
Bullwinkle the Moose Paintless Paint Book	Whitman	1960		15	30	45
Bullwinkle Travel Adventure Board Game	Transogram	1960s		30	55	85
Bullwinkle's Circus Time Toy		1969	Bullwinkle on a elephant	20	35	55
Bullwinkle's Circus Time Toy		1969	Rocky on a circus horse	20	35	55
Dudley Do-Right "Cartoon Theater" Figure	Dakin	1976		15	30	45
Dudley Do-Right Flexible Figure	Wham-O	1972	5" tall	9	16	25
Mr. Peabody Bank		1960s	6" tall, glazed china	80	145	225
Mr. Peabody Flexible Figure	Wham-O	1972	4" tall	9	16	25
Natasha Figure	Wham-O	1972		7	13	20
Rocky & Bullwinkle "Presto Sparkle" Painting Set	Kenner	1962	Six cartoon pictures & two comic strip panels	25	50	75
Rocky & Bullwinkle Bank		1960	5" tall, glazed china	80	145	225
Rocky & Bullwinkle Coloring Book	Watkins-Strathmore	1962		15	30	45
Rocky & Bullwinkle Movie Viewer		1960s	Item #225 on card, red and white plastic viewer with three movies	23	45	65
Rocky & Bullwinkle Toothpaste & Holder		1960s	Glazed china	60	114	175
Rocky & His Friends Little Golden Book	Little Golden Books	1960s	Graphics of Rocky, Bullwinkle, Sherman and Peabody	9	16	25
Rocky Bank		1950s	5" tall, slot in large tail, glazed china	60	115	175
Rocky Figure "Cartoon Theater"	Dakin	1976	6 1/2" tall, plastic	18	35	50
Rocky Soakie			10 1/2" tall, plastic	12	23	35
Rocky the Flying Squirrel Coloring Book	Whitman	1960		15	30	45
Sherman Flexible Figure	Wham-O	1972	4" tall	9	16	25
Snidely Whiplash Flexible Figure	Wham-O	1972	5" tall	9	16	25

Roger Rabbit

TOY	COMPANY	YEAR	DESCRIPTION	GOOD	EX	MIB
Animates		1988	Doom, Roger, Eddie & Smart Guy, each	4	7	10
Baby Herman & Roger Rabbit Mug	Applause			4	7	10

Roger Rabbit

TOY	COMPANY	YEAR	DESCRIPTION	GOOD	EX	MIB
Baby Herman Disney Ceramic Figurine	LJN	1988		7	13	20
Baby Herman Figure	LJN	1987	6" figure on card	9	16	25
Baby Herman Flexie				9	17	25
Benny the Cab	LJN			20	40	60
Benny the Cab Plush	Applause	1988	6" long	5	10	15
Book with Cassette Tape				4	7	10
Boss Weasel Animate	LJN	1988		3	5	8
Boss Weasel Flexie	LJN	1988	4" bendable	3	5	8
Deluxe Color Activity Book	Golden		#5523	4	7	10
Dip Flip Game	LJN			7	13	20
Eddie Valiant Animate	LJN	1988	6" tall poseable	3	5	8
Eddie Valiant Flexie	LJN	1988	4" bendable	3	5	8
Jessica Fashions			Gold tone pendant on Jessica and Roger	11	20	30
Jessica Flexie				11	20	30
Jessica License Plate				5	10	15
Jessica Zipper Pull				5	10	15
Judge Doom Animate	LJN	1988	6" tall poseable	4	7	10
Judge Doom Flexie	LJN	1988	4" bendable	3	5	8
Paint with Water	Golden		#1702	5	10	15
Paint-A-Cel Set			Benny the Cab and Roger pictures	5	10	15
Photo Fantasy	LJN	1988	Roger, Jessica, Baby Herman and two weasels	5	10	15
Read Along Book & Tape				5	10	15
Roger Flexie				4	7	10
Roger Rabbit Animate	LJN	1988	6" poseable	4	7	10
Roger Rabbit Blow-Up Buddy			36" tall	5	10	15
Roger Rabbit Bullet Hole Wristwatch	Shiraka	1987	White case and leather band, in plastic display box	20	35	55
Roger Rabbit Figure	Applause		17" tall	5	10	15
Roger Rabbit Figure	Applause		8 1/2" tall	4	7	10
Roger Rabbit Flexie	LJN	1988	4" bendable	3	5	8
Roger Rabbit Silhouette Wrist Watch	Shiraka	1987	Large gold case, black band	18	35	50
Roger Wacky Head Puppets	Applause		Hand puppets	4	7	10
Roger Wind-up	Matsudaya	1988		18	35	50
Set of Four Animated Figures	LJN	1988	Roger Rabbit, Judge Doom, Eddie Valiant and Weasel	9	16	25
Smart Guy Animate	LJN	1988		3	5	8
Smart Guy Flexie	LJN	1988		3	5	8
Sticker Fun Book				4	7	10
Suction Cup Figure			cloth	5	10	15
Talking Roger in Benny the Cab			17" tall	11	20	30
Trace & Color Book	Golden		#2355	4	7	10
View-Master Gift Set				7	13	20

Rookies, The

TOY	COMPANY	YEAR	DESCRIPTION	GOOD	EX	MIB
Rookie Chris Doll	LJN	1973	8" tall	4	8	12
Rookie Mike Doll	LJN	1973	8" tall	4	8	12
Rookie Terry Doll	LJN	1973	8" tall	4	8	12
Rookie Willy Doll	LJN	1973	8" tall	4	8	12

Rootie Kazootie

TOY	COMPANY	YEAR	DESCRIPTION	GOOD	EX	MIB
Rootie Kazootie Club Button		1950s	1" tin litho	15	30	45
Rootie Kazootie Drum		1950s	8" diameter drum with Rootie on the drum head	23	45	65

Roy Rogers

TOY	COMPANY	YEAR	DESCRIPTION	GOOD	EX	MIB
Dale Evans Wrist Watch	Ingraham	1951	Shows Dale inside upright horseshoe, tan background, chrome case, black leather band	60	105	165
Roy Rogers & Dale Evans Western Dinner Set	Ideal	1950s	Cooking and eating utensils in 14x24" box	35	65	95
Roy Rogers Nodder	(Japan)		Composition Roy stands in blue shirt, white hat and pants and red bandana and boots on green base	90	165	250

Ruff & Reddy

TOY	COMPANY	YEAR	DESCRIPTION	GOOD	EX	MIB
Ruff & Reddy Draw Cartoon Set Color	Wonder Art			45	80	125
Ruff & Reddy Go To A Party Tell-A-Tale Book	Whitman	1958		15	30	45
Ruff & Reddy Magic Rub Off Picture Set	Transogram	1958		45	80	125

Secret Squirrel

TOY	COMPANY	YEAR	DESCRIPTION	GOOD	EX	MIB
Secret Squirrel Bubble Club Soap Container	Purex	1960s		12	23	35
Secret Squirrel Frame Tray Puzzle		1967		14	25	40
Secret Squirrel Push Button Puppet	Kohner			14	25	40
Secret Squirrel Push Button Puppet	Kohner	1960s	Plastic figure in white coat, blue hat holding binoculars on yellow base with gold label	18	35	50
Secret Squirrel Ray Gun				14	25	40

Sleeping Beauty

TOY	COMPANY	YEAR	DESCRIPTION	GOOD	EX	MIB
3 Fairy Godmother Hand Puppets		1958	10 1/2" tall, Flora, Merryweather & Fauna, each	35	65	100
King Huber/King Stefan Hand Puppets	Gund	1956	10" tall, molded rubber heads with fabric hand cover	25	50	75
Sleeping Beauty Alarm Clock	Phinney-Walker	1950s	2 1/2x4x4 1/2" tall, Sleeping Beauty surrounded by 3 birds and petting a rabbit	30	55	85
Sleeping Beauty Doll Crib Mattress		1960s	9x17" mattress with illustration of Sleeping Beauty and the Fairies	12	23	35
Sleeping Beauty Magic Paint Set	Whitman			25	45	65

Sleeping Beauty

TOY	COMPANY	YEAR	DESCRIPTION	GOOD	EX	MIB
Sleeping Beauty Musical Jack-In-The-Box	Enesco	1980s	Princess Aurora on illustrated wooden box , plays "Once Upon A Dream"	35	60	95
Sleeping Beauty Puzzle	Whitman	1958	11 12/x14 1/2", Sleeping Beauty with forest animals	15	30	45
Sleeping Beauty Puzzle	Whitman	1958	11 1/2x14 1/2". Sleeping Beauty with Prince Phillip and Three Good Fairies circling in the air around Sleeping Beauty	15	30	45
Sleeping Beauty Puzzle	Whitman	1958	11 1/2x14 1/2", Three Good Fairies circling around a baby in a crib	15	25	40
Sleeping Beauty Squeeze Toy	Dell	1959	4x4x5" tall, rubber, Sleeping Beauty nestling a rabbit in her arms, dressed in a yellow gown	25	45	65
Sleeping Beauty Sticker Fun	Whitman	1959	Sticker push out activity book	12	25	35

Smokey the Bear

TOY	COMPANY	YEAR	DESCRIPTION	GOOD	EX	MIB
Smokey Bobbing Head Figure		1960s	6 1/4" tall	15	30	45
Smokey Figure Bank			6" tall, china	12	23	35
Smokey Soakie Soap Container		1960s	9" tall, plastic	5	10	15
Smokey the Bear Figure	Dakin	1971	Figure on a tree stump	25	50	75
Smokey the Bear Wrist Watch	Hawthorne	1960s		35	65	100

Snow White & the Seven Dwarfs

TOY	COMPANY	YEAR	DESCRIPTION	GOOD	EX	MIB
Baby Rattle	Krueger	1938	Snow White at piano & the Dwarfs playing instruments	130	245	375
Bashful Doll	Ideal	1930s		55	100	150
Big Little Book	Whitman	1938		15	30	45
Dime Register Bank	Disney	1938	Holds up to five dollars	50	95	145
Doc & Dopey Pull Toy	Fisher-Price	1937	12" long by 9" tall, with a chopping tree stump action when it moves back or forward	80	145	225
Doc Doll	Ideal	1930s		55	100	150
Doc Lamp	LaMode Studios	1938	8" tall, plaster	45	80	125
Dopey Bank	Crown Toy	1938	7 1/2" tall, wood composition	55	100	150
Dopey Dime Register Bank	Disney	1938	Holds up to five dollars	45	80	125
Dopey Doll	Ideal	1930s		55	100	150
Dopey Doll	Chad Valley	1938	All cloth body	50	95	145
Dopey Doll	Krueger		14" tall	90	165	250
Dopey Doll	Knickerbocker	1938	3x6x11" tall composition	90	165	250
Dopey Lamp		1940s	9" tall, ceramic base with Dopey figure	35	65	100
Dopey Rolykin	Marx		2" tall, mounted on a weighted plastic half sphere so he can rock around	25	50	75
Dopey Soakie		1960s	10" tall	11	20	30
Dopey Storage Barrel		1960s	Ceramic figure and barrel	15	30	45
Dopey Ventriloquist Doll	Ideal	1938	5x9 1/2x18" tall	115	210	325
Dopey Walker	Marx	1938	9" tall, tin, rocking walker	150	250	350

Snow White & the Seven Dwarfs

TOY	COMPANY	YEAR	DESCRIPTION	GOOD	EX	MIB
Grumpy Doll	Knickerbocker	1938	3x6x11" tall, composition	90	165	250
Happy Doll		1930s	5 1/2" tall, composition, holding a silver pick with a black handle	35	65	100
Happy the Dwarf Mechanical Toy	YS Toys (Taiwan)		Battery op. Happy fries eggs, picture of Snow White on front	40	75	115
Radio	Emerson	1938	8x8" with characters on cabinet	325	625	950
Seven Dwarfs Figure Set "Snow White"	Seiberling	1938	5 1/2" tall rubber figures	115	210	325
Seven Dwarfs Target Game "Snow White"	Chad Valley	1930s	6 1/2x11 1/2" target, spring locked gun that shoots wood pieces at target	115	210	325
Sneezy Doll	Krueger		14" tall	115	210	325
Snow White & the Seven Dwarfs Picture Puzzles	Whitman	1938	Set of 2 puzzles in box	50	95	145
Snow White & the Seven Dwarfs Safety Blocks	Halsam	1938	7 1/2"x14 1/2"	35	65	100
Snow White & the Seven Dwarfs Sand Pail	Ohio Art	1938	8" tall, tin pictured with Snow White playing hide-n-seek with the Dwarfs	45	80	125
Snow White & the Seven Dwarfs Tea Set	Ohio Art	1937	Tray 7 1/2" long, large plates 4" diameter, small saucers 2 1/2" diameter & cups are 2 1/2" across the top	65	120	185
Snow White Cut-out Dolls & Dresses	Whitman	1938	10x15x1 1/2"	80	145	225
Snow White Doll	Knickerbocker	1940	12" tall, composition	80	145	225
Snow White Doll	Horsman		8" tall classic doll in illustrated box	12	23	35
Snow White Doll	Knickerbocker	1939	3x7x3 1/2" tall, composition with moveable arms and legs	60	115	175
Snow White Doll Set	Deluxe	1940s	22" tall Snow White and 7" tall dwarfs	250	475	725
Snow White Ironing Board	Wolverine		Ironing board cover & iron	14	25	40
Snow White Lamp	LaMode Studios	1938	8 1/2" tall	35	65	100
Snow White Marionette Figure	Tony Sarg/ Alexander	1930s	12 1/2" tall	60	115	175
Snow White Mirror		1940s	9 1/2" long with plastic sculptured looking handle	23	45	65
Snow White Model Making Set	Sculptorcraft	1930s		60	115	175
Snow White Pencil Box	Venus Pencil Co.		3x8x1"	60	115	175
Snow White Puzzle	Jaymar	1960s	11x14"	18	35	50
Snow White Sewing Set	Ontex	1940s	10x14x1 1/4"	25	50	75
Snow White Sink	Wolverine	1960s	6 1/2x11x11" tall	15	25	40
Snow White Soakie				12	23	35
Snow White Stuffed Doll	Ideal	1938	3 1/2x6 1/2x16" tall, fabric face and arms, red/white dress with dwarf and forest animal design	245	450	700
Snow White Table Quoits	Chad Valley	1930s	9 1/2x21x1 1/4" deep	115	210	325
Snow White Tea Set	Wadeheath Co.	1930s	Teapot 3" tall with Snow White & Dopey standing behind her skirt, 2" tall cups, saucers 4" in diameter and 2" tall creamer with a fawn all in white china	115	210	325
Snow White Tea Set	Marx	1960s	Teapot 2x5x3 1/2" tall, 5 saucers, large plates and tea cups	35	65	100

Snow White & the Seven Dwarfs

TOY	COMPANY	YEAR	DESCRIPTION	GOOD	EX	MIB
Snow White Tin Refrigerator	Wolverine	1970s	15" tall single door unit in white and yellow decorated with picture of Snow White	14	25	40

Speedy Gonzales

TOY	COMPANY	YEAR	DESCRIPTION	GOOD	EX	MIB
Speedy Gonzales Figure	Dakin	1970	7 1/2" tall, vinyl	12	25	35
Speedy Gonzalez Doll	Dakin		5" tall, vinyl squeeze doll	9	16	25

Sports

TOY	COMPANY	YEAR	DESCRIPTION	GOOD	EX	MIB
Dorothy Hamil Figure	Ideal	1975	11 1/4" tall	25	50	75
Dr. J. (Julius Erving) Figure		1974		20	40	60
Evel Knievel Figure	Ideal		6" tall	15	30	45
Gretzky, Wayne	Mattel		12" tall	25	50	75
Muhammed Ali Wristwatch	Bradley	1980	Chrome case, sweep seconds, brown leather band, face shows Ali in trunks and gloves, with signature beneath	25	50	75
O.J. Simpson Figure		1974		30	50	80

Steve Canyon

TOY	COMPANY	YEAR	DESCRIPTION	GOOD	EX	MIB
Steve Canyon's Costume	Halco	1959		25	50	75
Steve Canyon's Interceptor Station Punch Out	Golden	1950s		30	55	85
Steve Canyon's Membership Card & Badge			1/2"x4" Milton Caniff membership card for the Airagers, Morse code on back, 3" tin litho color badge with gold feathers with Steve's face centered	70	130	200

Superman

TOY	COMPANY	YEAR	DESCRIPTION	GOOD	EX	MIB
Jor-El Figure		1977	In box	30	55	85
Superman Action Figure	Palitoy		8" figure on card	20	40	60
Superman Bust Bank		1974		12	23	35
Superman Figure on Base	Presents		15" vinyl and cloth figure on base	9	16	25
Superman Jigsaw Puzzle	Whitman	1966	150 piece jigsaw puzzle 14x18	12	23	35
Superman Plush Doll	Knickerbocker		20" tall plush doll in box	12	23	35
Superman Rub Ons	Hasbro	1966	Magic picture transfers in box illustrated with picture of Superman flying	11	20	30
Superman Rubber Figure	Fun Things		6" figure on card	9	16	25
Superman Rubber Figures	Chemtoy		Three different poses, on card, each	5	10	15
Superman Wall Clock	New Haven	1978	Plastic and cardboard battery op. framed wall clock showing Superman fighting alien shaceship	25	45	65

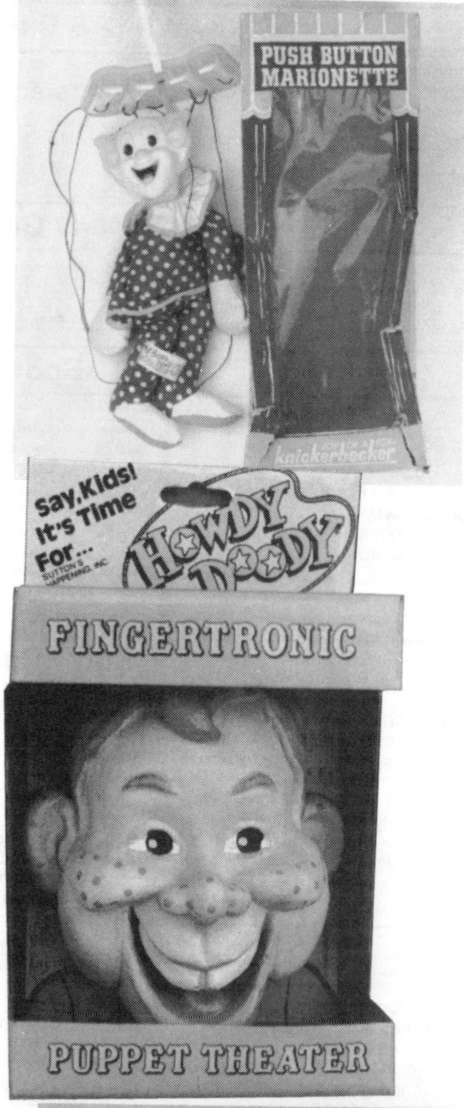

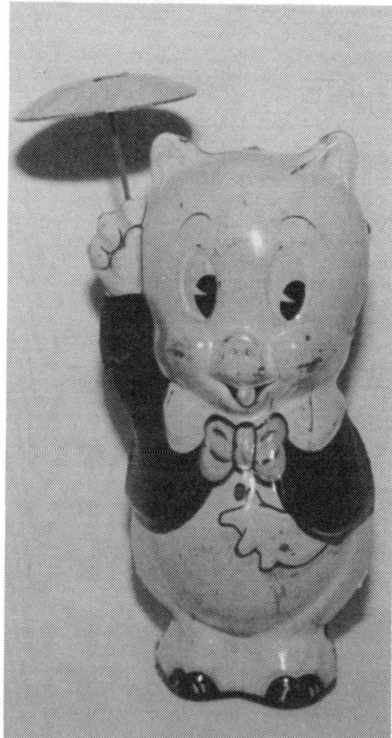

Top to Bottom: Superman Rub Ons, Hasbro, 1966; Bozo the Clown Push Button Marionette, Knickerbocker, 1962; Howdy Doody Fingertronic Puppet Theatre, Sutton, 1970s; Porky Pig Wind-up Figure, Marx, 1939; Mr. Magoo Car, battery operated, Japan.

Superman

TOY	COMPANY	YEAR	DESCRIPTION	GOOD	EX	MIB
Superman Wrist Watch		1977	Gold bezel, stainless back, blue leather band, face shows Superman flying upward from below	35	65	100

Sylvester the Cat & Tweety Bird

TOY	COMPANY	YEAR	DESCRIPTION	GOOD	EX	MIB
Sylvester & Tweety Bank		1972	Vinyl	14	25	40
Sylvester & Tweety Figurines	Warner Bros.	1975	6" tall	9	16	25
Sylvester Figural Toy	Oak Rubber Co.	1950	6" tall	16	30	45
Sylvester Figure	Dakin	1969		11	20	30
Sylvester Figure "Cartoon Theater"	Dakin	1976		9	16	25
Sylvester Figure on Fish Crate	Dakin	1971		15	25	40
Sylvester Soakie				9	16	25
Tweety "Goofy Gram"	Dakin	1971	Holding red heart	15	25	40
Tweety Doll	Dakin	1969	6", moveable head & feet	9	16	25
Tweety Figure	Dakin	1971	On bird cage	14	25	40
Tweety Figure "Cartoon Theater"	Dakin	1976		9	16	25
Tweety Soakie		1960s	8 1/2" tall, plastic	9	16	25

Tarzan

TOY	COMPANY	YEAR	DESCRIPTION	GOOD	EX	MIB
Kala Ape Figure	Dakin	1984	3" tall	4	7	10
Tarzan & Giant Ape Set				80	145	225
Tarzan & Jungle Cat Set				80	145	225
Young Tarzan Figure	Dakin	1984	4" tall and bendable	4	8	12

Tasmanian Devil

TOY	COMPANY	YEAR	DESCRIPTION	GOOD	EX	MIB
Tasmanian Devil Doll	Mighty Star	1971	13" tall, stuffed	9	16	25
Tasmanian Devil Figural Bank	Applause	1980s		5	10	15
Tasmanian Devil Figure	Superior	1989	7" tall, plastic figure on base	3	5	8

Terry & the Pirates

TOY	COMPANY	YEAR	DESCRIPTION	GOOD	EX	MIB
Terry & the Pirates Featured Funnies Jigsaw Puzzle		1930s	9 1/2"x14" puzzle	30	55	85
Terry & the Pirates Playstone Funnies Mold Set		1940s		25	50	75

Three Little Pigs

TOY	COMPANY	YEAR	DESCRIPTION	GOOD	EX	MIB
Big Bad Wolf Pocket Watch	Ingersoll	1934		175	340	525

Three Little Pigs

TOY	COMPANY	YEAR	DESCRIPTION	GOOD	EX	MIB
Three Little Pigs "Tubby Time" Soakie Set	Drew Chemical Corp.	1960s	8" tall each: Three Little Pigs and the Big Bad Wolf	60	115	175
Three Little Pigs Puzzle	Jaymar	1940s	7x10x2"	25	50	75
Three Little Pigs Sand Pail	Ohio Art		3" tall	35	65	100
Three Little Pigs Sand Pail	Ohio Art	1930s	4 1/2" tall, tin, Three Little Pigs pictured in the woods	45	80	125
Three Little Pigs Wind-up Toy	Schuco	1930s	4 1/2" pigs playing fiddle, fife & drum	245	450	700
Three Little Pigs/Big Bad Wolf Bracelet		1930s	1/2" wide by 2 1/4" diameter, the wolf blowing down a house & a little pig running away	55	100	150
Who's Afraid of the Big Bad Wolf, Game of	Marks Brothers	1930s	9x20x1 1/2"	60	115	175
Who's Afraid of the Big Bad Wolf, Game of	Parker Brothers	1930s	13x16x1", Walt Disney's	60	115	175

Tom & Jerry

TOY	COMPANY	YEAR	DESCRIPTION	GOOD	EX	MIB
Jerry Figure	Marx	1973	4" tall	12	23	35
Tom & Jerry & Droopy Walking Figure Set		1975		15	30	45
Tom & Jerry Figural Bank	Gorham	1980	6" tall	18	35	50
Tom & Jerry Go Kart	Marx	1973	Plastic, friction drive	25	50	75
Tom & Jerry on a Scooter	Marx	1971	Plastic friction drive, figures on scooter	12	23	35
Tom & Jerry Quartz Wristwatch	Bradley	1985	Oldies series, small white plastic case and band, sweep seconds, face shows Tom squirting Jerry with hose	9	16	25
Tom & Jerry Tray Puzzles	Whitman		Set of four frame tray puzzles	15	25	40
Tom Figure	Marx	1973	6" tall	12	23	35

Top Cat

TOY	COMPANY	YEAR	DESCRIPTION	GOOD	EX	MIB
Top Cat Soakie		1960s	10" tall, vinyl	11	20	30
Top Cat TV-Tinykins Figure	Marx	1961	Plastic	15	30	45
Top Cat View-Master			With three reels and booklet	12	23	35
Top Cat Viewmarx Micro-Viewer	Marx	1963	Plastic with lens to view cartoon scenes	15	30	45

Underdog

TOY	COMPANY	YEAR	DESCRIPTION	GOOD	EX	MIB
Underdog Bank				12	23	35
Underdog Dot Funnies Kit	Whitman	1974		9	16	25
Underdog Figure "Cartoon Theater"	Dakin	1976	Plastic	25	50	75
Underdog Jigsaw Puzzle	Whitman	1975	100 pieces	9	16	25

Welcome Back Kotter

TOY	COMPANY	YEAR	DESCRIPTION	GOOD	EX	MIB
Barbarino Figure	Mattel	1976	With comb	15	30	45

Welcome Back Kotter

TOY	COMPANY	YEAR	DESCRIPTION	GOOD	EX	MIB
Epstein Figure	Mattel	1976	With bandanna	15	30	45
Horshack Doll	Mattel	1976	9" tall, with lunch box	11	20	30
Mr. Kotter Figure	Mattel	1976	With attache case	12	23	35
Sweathogs School Mechanical Bank	Fleetwood	1975	Wind-up bank features Horshack and Barbarino snatching money	15	30	45
Washington Figure	Mattel	1976	With basketball	15	30	45

Winky Dink & You

TOY	COMPANY	YEAR	DESCRIPTION	GOOD	EX	MIB
Winky Dink & You Super Magic TV Kit	Standard Toy	1968		23	45	65
Winky Dink Little Golden Book	Golden	1956		9	16	25
Winky Dink Winko Magic Kit		1950s		15	30	45

Winnie the Pooh

TOY	COMPANY	YEAR	DESCRIPTION	GOOD	EX	MIB
Kanga and Roo Vinyl Squeek Toy	Holland Hill	1966	Vinyl toy made in shape of stuffed doll	12	23	35
Winnie the Pooh Button		1960s	3 1/2" celluloid button	5	10	15
Winnie the Pooh Doll		1960s	12" tall	12	23	35
Winnie the Pooh Frame Tray Puzzle	Whitman	1964		7	13	20
Winnie the Pooh Jack-In-The-Box	Carnival Toys	1960s		15	30	45
Winnie the Pooh Lamp	Dolly Toy Co.	1964	7" tall	25	50	75
Winnie the Pooh Magic Slate	Western Publishing	1965	8 1/2x13 1/2"	15	30	45
Winnie the Pooh Musical Snow Globe			5 1/2"	15	30	45
Winnie the Pooh Radio	Thilgee Inter'l	1970s	5x6x1 1/2" tall	25	50	75
Winnie the Pooh/ Christopher Robin Dolls	Horsman	1964	Winnie the Pooh 3 1/2" tall and Christopher 11" tall, set	60	115	175

Woody Woodpecker

TOY	COMPANY	YEAR	DESCRIPTION	GOOD	EX	MIB
Woody Woodpecker & Andy Panda Paper Dolls	Saalfield	1968	Punch out and cut	15	30	45
Woody Woodpecker Card Set		1950s	Two decks in a carrying case	30	55	85
Woody Woodpecker Electric Lamp		1971	20" tall, plastic	11	20	30
Woody Woodpecker Talking Hand Puppet	Mattel	1963	Pull-string voice box	30	60	90
Woody Woodpecker's Funorama Punch Out Book		1972		9	16	25
Woody's Cafe Animated Alarm Clock	Columbia Time Prod.	1959		60	115	175

Yogi Bear

TOY	COMPANY	YEAR	DESCRIPTION	GOOD	EX	MIB
Boo Boo Plush Doll	Knickerbocker	1960s	9 1/2" tall, stuffed	35	60	95
Cindy Bear Plush Doll	Knickerbocker	1959	16" tall stuffed Cindy, with vinyl face	35	65	100
Snagglepuss Figure	Dakin	1970		30	55	85
Snagglepuss Soakie	Purex	1960s	9" tall, vinyl/plastic	12	23	35
Snagglepuss Sticker Fun Book	Whitman	1963		11	20	30
Yogi and Boo Boo Coatrack	Wolverine	1979	48" tall red wood coatrack with 8 white wooden hangers, 20" tall Yogi and Boo Boo cut out in front, back of piece is marked for growth chart	35	65	95
Yogi Bear & Boo Boo Hot Water Bottle		1966		25	50	75
Yogi Bear and Pixie & Dixie Game Car	Whitman		7 1/2" pile on game in car	12	23	35
Yogi Bear Bubble Pipe	Transogram	1963	Figural plastic pipe on illustrated card	15	30	45
Yogi Bear Cartoonist Stamp Set	Lido	1961		25	50	75
Yogi Bear Doll		1962	6" tall soft vinyl with moveable arms & head	20	40	60
Yogi Bear Doll	Knickerbocker	1959	10" tall	35	65	100
Yogi Bear Figural Bank	Dakin	1980	7" tall bank	5	10	15
Yogi Bear Figural Bank	Knickerbocker	1960s	22" tall figural bank	15	30	45
Yogi Bear Figure	Knickerbocker	1960s	9" tall, plastic	23	45	65
Yogi Bear Figure	Dakin	1970	7 3/4" tall	15	30	45
Yogi Bear Flashlight	Laurie	1976		4	7	10
Yogi Bear Friction Toy		1960s	Friction toy of Yogi upright in yellow tie and green hat, in illustrated red box	35	65	95
Yogi Bear Hand Puppet	Knickerbocker			15	30	45
Yogi Bear Magic Slate		1963		11	20	30
Yogi Bear Plush Doll	Knickerbocker	1960s	19" tall, stuffed	25	50	75
Yogi Bear Plush Doll	Knickerbocker	1959	16" tall stuffed Yogi, with vinyl face	35	65	100
Yogi Bear Push Puppet				12	23	35
Yogi Bear Safety Scissors	Monogram	1973	On card	4	7	10
Yogi Bear Stuff & Lace Doll	Knickerbocker	1959	Items to make a 13x5" stuffed Yogi, in 16x9" box with pictures of Yogi and Huck Hound	20	40	60
Yogi Bear TV-Tinykins Figure	Marx	1961		15	30	45
Yogi Bear Wrist Watch		1963		35	65	100
Yogi Bear Yo Yo with Sleeper Action		1976		9	16	25
Yogi Bear, Boo Boo & Ranger Smith Figurines		1960	12" tall, each	15	30	45
Yogi Score-A-Matic Ball Toss Game	Transogram	1960		40	75	115
Yogi Vinyl Squeeze Doll	Sanitoy	1979	12" tall Yogi	9	16	25
Yogi Wristwatch	Bradley	1967	Medium base metal case, shows Yogi with hobo sack on stick, black vinyl band	35	65	100

Yosemite Sam

TOY	COMPANY	YEAR	DESCRIPTION	GOOD	EX	MIB
Yosemite Sam "Fun Farm" Figure	Dakin	1978		11	20	30
Yosemite Sam Figure	Dakin	1968	7" tall	12	23	35
Yosemite Sam Figure on Treasure Chest	Dakin	1971		14	25	40
Yosemite Sam Mini Snowdome	Applause	1980s		9	16	25
Yosemite Sam Musical Snowdome	Applause	1980s		15	30	45
Yosemite Sam Nodder		1960s	6 1/4" tall with bobbing head & spring mounted head	35	65	100

Zorro

TOY	COMPANY	YEAR	DESCRIPTION	GOOD	EX	MIB
Amigo Figure	Gabriel	1982		4	7	10
Captain Ramon Figure	Gabriel	1982		3	5	8
Picaro Figure	Gabriel	1982		4	7	10
Sergeant Gonzales Figure	Gabriel	1982		3	5	8
Tempest	Gabriel	1982		4	7	10
Zorro "Bean Bag-Dart" Game		1950s	14x16" target	14	25	40
Zorro & Horse	Lido	1950s	4 1/2" tall black plastic figure of Zorro with gun and sword, black horse has white harness and saddle, included paper mask, on card	35	65	100
Zorro Activity Box	Whitman	1965	9x12x1 1/2"	30	60	90
Zorro Board Game	Parker Brothers	1966	16 12/x16 1/2" board	18	35	50
Zorro Board Game	Whitman	1965	5 1/2x8x1 1/2"	14	25	40
Zorro Oil Painting By Numbers	Hasbro		10x13 1/2" cardboard canvas	35	60	95
Zorro Pencil Holder & Pencil Sharpener		1950s	6" tall	15	30	45
Zorro Pinwheel		1950s	Red and black pinwheel with Zorro logos on petals and black mask in front	15	30	45
Zorro Puzzle "Zorro/ Sgt. Garcia & Don Diego"	Jaymar	1960		15	25	40
Zorro Puzzle "Zorro/ The Dual"	Jaymar	1960	10x14"	15	25	40
Zorro Secret Sight Scarf Mask	Westminster	1960	Black fabric mask with 2 black & silver hard plastic eye pieces, cardboards with 2 pictures of Zorro	25	50	75
Zorro Target & Dart-Shooting Rifle Set	T. Cohn	1960	21" long plastic rifle, black plastic darts and target	60	115	175
Zorro View-Master	Sawyer's Inc.	1958	4 1/2x4 1/2" envelope with 3 reel story & booklet	15	30	45
Zorro Wristwatch	US Time	1957	Chrome case, black leather band	60	115	175

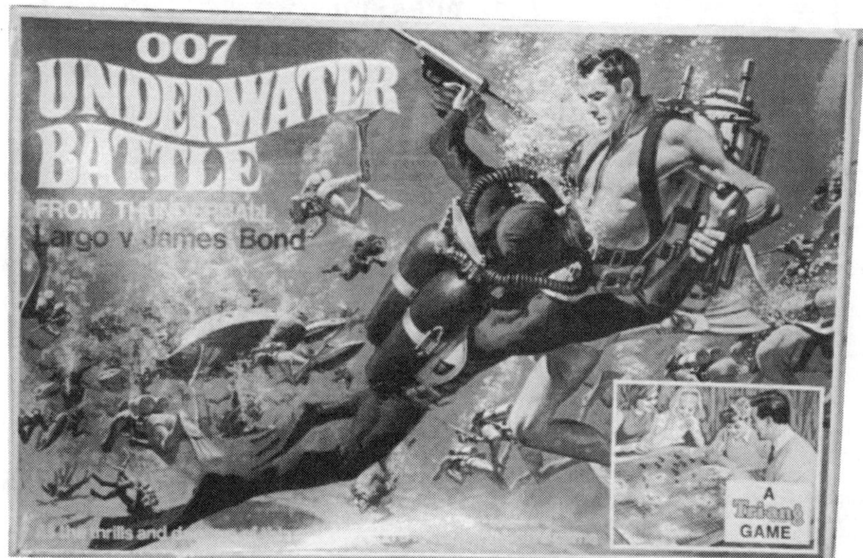

James Bond Thunderball Underwater Battle, Triang; Joan Palooka Stringless Marionette, National Mask & Puppet, 1952; Alice in Wonderland Mad Hatter Marionette, Peter Puppet, 1950s; Howdy Doody Air-O-Doodle, 1950s.

CHARACTER

THE FACTS... THE FIGURES... THE FUN!

You get it all in every bi-monthly issue of TOY COLLECTOR AND PRICE GUIDE. In-depth articles give you the history of your favorite toys, along with present-day values by condition. Plus, you'll enjoy toy show reports, an extensive toy show calendar, and a coast-to-coast classified ad section with hundreds of hot toys for sale and wanted.

ONLY $12.95
1 year, 6 issues

Don't get left behind!

Stay current in the fastest growing hobby, with one of the hobby's fastest growing magazines... **TOY COLLECTOR AND PRICE GUIDE!**

Toy Collector and Price Guide
700 E. State St.,
Iola, WI 54990-0001

- SAVE $4.00 -

NEW SUBSCRIBER SPECIAL!

MasterCard & VISA Cardholders save time by calling toll-free to order:
800-258-0929 Dept. ABAGTD
Mon. - Fri. 6:30 a.m. to 8:00 p.m. • Sat. 8:00 a.m. to 2 p.m., CST.

❑ **YES... Please renew my subscription to TOY COLLECTOR & PRICE GUIDE for 1-year (6-issues) @ $12.95**
(a $4.00 savings off the regular price!)

Name ____________________
Address ____________________
City ____________________ State ________ Zip ________
ABAGTD
( ) Check or money order enclosed for $ ____________________
(Payable to: Toy Collector and Price Guide)
( ) MasterCard ( ) VISA
Credit Card No. ____________________
Expires: Mo. ____________ Yr. ____________
Signature ____________________